ROUTLEDGE HANDBOOK OF LATIN AMERICAN POLITICS

Latin America has been one of the critical areas in the study of comparative politics. The region's experiments with installing and deepening democracy and promoting alternative modes of economic development have generated intriguing and enduring empirical puzzles. In turn, Latin America's challenges continue to spawn original and vital work on central questions in comparative politics: about the origins of democracy; about the relationship between state and society; about the nature of citizenship; about the balance between state and market.

The richness and diversity of the study of Latin American politics makes it hard to stay abreast of the developments in the many sub-literatures of the field. The *Routledge Handbook of Latin American Politics* offers an intellectually rigorous overview of the state of the field and a thoughtful guide to the direction of future scholarship. Kingstone and Yashar bring together the leading figures in the study of Latin America to present extensive empirical coverage, new original research, and a cutting-edge examination of the central areas of inquiry in the region.

Peter Kingstone is Associate Professor of Political Science and Director of the Center for Latin American and Caribbean Studies at the University of Connecticut. He is the author of *Crafting Coalitions for Reform: Business Preferences, Political Institutions, and Neoliberal Reform in Brazil* and co-editor of *Democratic Brazil: Actors, Institutions, and Processes*.

Deborah J. Yashar is Professor of Politics and International Affairs and Co-director of the Project on Democracy and Development at Princeton University. She is the author of *Demanding Democracy: Reform and Reaction in Costa Rica and Guatemala* and *Contesting Citizenship in Latin America: The Rise of Indigenous Movements and the Postliberal Challenge*.

ROUTLEDGE HANDBOOK OF LATIN AMERICAN POLITICS

Edited by Peter Kingstone and Deborah J. Yashar

Routledge
Taylor & Francis Group

NEW YORK AND LONDON

First published in paperback 2016
First published 2012
by Routledge
711 Third Avenue, New York, NY 10017

and by Routledge
2 Park Square, Milton Park, Abingdon, Oxon OX14 4RN

Routledge is an imprint of the Taylor & Francis Group, an informa business

Library of Congress Cataloging in Publication Data
Routledge handbook of Latin American politics / edited by Peter Kingstone and Deborah J. Yashar.
  p. cm.
  Includes bibliographical references.
  1. Latin America—Politics and government—1980– 2. Latin America—Politics and government—1948–1980. 3. Democracy—Latin America. 4. Latin America—Social conditions—1982– 5. Latin America—Economic conditions—1982– 6. Latin America—Economic policy. 7. Latin America—Social policy. 8. Latin America—Foreign relations—1980– I. Kingstone, Peter R., 1964– II. Yashar, Deborah J., 1963–
  JL960.R68 2012
  320.98—dc23
  2011043304

ISBN: 978-0-415-87522-6 (hbk)
ISBN: 978-0-415-87523-3 (pbk)
ISBN: 978-0-203-86026-7 (ebk)

Typeset in Bembo and Minion
by EvS Communication Networx, Inc.

Printed and bound by CPI Group (UK) Ltd, Croydon, CR0 4YY

CONTENTS

List of Figures   *ix*
List of Tables   *xi*
Contributors   *xiii*
Introduction   *xxiii*

PART I
Democratic Governance and Political Institutions   **1**

1   The Origins and Durability of Democracy   3
    Gerardo L. Munck

2   Presidentialism and Legislatures   21
    Mark P. Jones

3   Decentralization and Federalism   33
    Kent Eaton

4   Parties, Party Systems, and Political Representation   48
    Kenneth M. Roberts

5   "A Tale of Two Cities": The Judiciary and the Rule of Law
    in Latin America   61
    Daniel M. Brinks

6   The Latin American Military   76
    David Pion-Berlin

Contents

7 Informal Institutions and Politics in Latin America   88
   Steven Levitsky

8 Accountability and Representation in Latin America   101
   Frances Hagopian

9 Human Rights and Military Abuses   114
   Anthony W. Pereira

PART II
Development   **131**

10 Neoliberalism and Its Alternatives   133
    Javier Corrales

11 Declining Inequality in Latin America: Some Economics,
    Some Politics   158
    Nancy Birdsall, Nora Lustig, and Darryl McLeod

12 Environment and Sustainable Development   181
    Eduardo Silva

13 Social Policies in Latin America: Causes, Characteristics,
    and Consequences   200
    James W. McGuire

14 The Political Economy of Regulatory Policy: Economic Crisis and
    Privatization in the 1990s   224
    Luigi Manzetti and Carlos Rufin

PART III
Actors/Social Groups   **235**

15 Social Movements in Latin America   237
    Kathryn Hochstetler

16 Understanding the Vagaries of Civil Society and Participation
    in Latin America   248
    Philip Oxhorn

Contents

17 Labor   262
    Maria Lorena Cook

18 Business Politics in Latin America: Investigating Structures, Preferences,
    and Influence   273
    Sebastian Karcher and Ben Ross Schneider

19 Indigenous Politics: Between Democracy and Danger   285
    José Antonio Lucero

20 Race, Politics, and Afro-Latin Americans   302
    Ollie A. Johnson III

21 Gender   319
    Lisa Baldez

PART IV
International Concerns   **333**

22 U.S.-Latin American Relations: Power, Politics, and Cooperation   335
    Peter H. Smith

23 Intra-Latin American Relations: The Challenge of Promoting
    Cooperation While Defending Sovereignty   348
    David R. Mares

24 International Economic Relations/International Development
    Institutions   364
    Grigore Pop-Eleches

25 The Politics of Drugs and Illicit Trade in the Americas   380
    Peter Andreas and Angelica Duran Martinez

PART V
Theories/Methods   **393**

26 Institutionalism   395
    Aníbal Pérez-Liñán and Néstor Castañeda Angarita

Contents

27 Culture and/or Postmodernism   407
   Sujatha Fernandes

28 The Integration of Rational Choice into the Study of Politics
   in Latin America   419
   Barbara Geddes

29 The Enduring Influence of Historical-Structural Approaches   433
   Jennifer Cyr and James Mahoney

30 Natural and Field Experiments in the Study of Latin American Politics   447
   Thad Dunning

31 Public Opinion Research in Latin America   467
   Elizabeth J. Zechmeister and Mitchell A. Seligson

PART VI
Critical Reflections on the State of the Field   **483**

32 What's Next? Reflections on the Future of Latin American
   Political Science   485
   Barry Ames, Miguel Carreras, and Cassilde Schwartz

33 The Blessings of Troubles: Scholarly Innovation in Response to Latin
   America's Challenges   512
   Jorge I. Domínguez

34 State of the Field: Political Regimes and the Study of Democratic
   Politics   528
   Robert R. Kaufman

35 Latin American Political Regimes in Comparative Perspective   542
   Adam Przeworski

36 Popular Representation in Contemporary Latin American Politics:
   An Agenda for Research   564
   Ruth Berins Collier and Christopher Chambers-Ju

Index   579

LIST OF FIGURES

5.1   De Jure Autonomy and Scope of Authority of Latin American Courts as of 2009   64
10.1 Diversity of Achievements: Highest Economic Freedom Scores Achieved by
      Latin American Countries and Year of Achievement   145
10.2 Changes in Economic Freedom Index Scores from 2002 to 2011   146
10.3 Economic Freedom Scores in Self-Declared Leftist Governments in Latin
      America in the 2000s   147
11.1 Change in Gini Coefficients for Latin America: 2000–2008   159
11.2 Gini Coefficients for Countries Around the World   160
11.3 Comparison of 90% Gini vs. Total Gini in Latin America   160
11.4 The Education Gap   162
11.5 Inequality in Argentina, Brazil, Chile, and Venezuela (Gini coefficients, rounded)   164
11.6 Annual Income Redistribution by Quintile (cumulative years in office starting
      in year 2)   167
11.7 Latin American Public Spending on Social Programs as Percentage of GDP
      (education, health, and transfers)   168
11.8 Redistributive Impact of Changes in Social Spending Budget Share by Quintile
      (change significant at *5% or **1% level)   168
11.9 Government Effectiveness by Political Regime Types (2000–2007)   169
11.10 Average Terms of Trade (2002–2006)   170
11.11 Change in Middle Class Size (proportion of population) between 1990 and 2005   172
24.1 Trade Balance — Cross-Regional Trends   365
24.2 Trade Volume — Cross-Regional Trends   366
24.3 Composition of Latin American Trade   367
24.4 Debt Composition in Latin America (1970–2008)   368
30.1 A Typology of Research Designs   448
35.1 Periods of Instability or Rule Without Elections   547
35.2 Uncontested Elections   548
35.3 Contested Elections Continuously Won by Incumbents   551
35.4 Alternations by Year   554
35.5 Rule by Force in Latin America and in Europe   557
36.1 Traditional Party Decline   571

LIST OF TABLES

5.1 Homocide Rates by Country (most recent available, as of 2008) and Concerns that Crime Threatens Future Wellbeing (2008) — 70

7.1 A Typology of Informal Institutions — 91

9.1 Lethal Violence by State Forces and Other Indicators of Political Repression, 1964–90 — 119

10.1 Moderate and Radical Lefts in Relation to the Washington Consensus and Second Generation Reforms — 148

10.2 Explanatory Variables and Varieties of Leftist Governments in Latin America in the 2000s — 151

11.1 New Left Political Regimes in Latin America — 165

11.2 Determinants of Latin American Inequality 1990–2008 — 166

11A.1 Key Economic Indicators by Political Regime: 1988–2009 — 178

11A.2 Changes in Quintile Share by Political Regime — 179

11A.3 Change in Quintile Shares, Random Effects Estimates — 180

12.1 Relationship of Conceptualizations of Environment and Development to Analytic Approaches — 184

12.2 Compatibility of Sustainable Development with Competing Conceptualizations of the Problem of Environment and Development — 185

12.3 Environmental Politics: Actors, Interests, and Coalitions, 1980–Present — 186

13.1 Public Spending on Social Insurance, Social Assistance, and Education/Health, circa 2000, Sixteen Latin American Countries — 201

22.1 Profiles for United States and Latin America: Selected Countries, 2009 — 336

22.2 U.S. Shares of Latin American Trade, 2000–2010 — 337

22.3 Soft Power Index, 2010 — 341

23.1 Currently Unresolved Interstate Disputes Within Latin America — 352

23.2 Central America's Institutional Context, c. 1967 — 356

30.1 Natural Experiments in the Study of Latin American Politics — 451

30.2 Field Experiments in the Study of Latin American Politics — 458

35.1 Number of Occupants of Office After Elections — 546

35.2 Long Lasting Regimes with Regular Pluralistic Elections Always Won by Incumbents — 550

35.3	Causes of Termination of Pluralistic Non-Competitive Regimes	552
35.4	Partisan Alternations in Office as a Result of Elections	553
35.5	Proportion of Elections Lost by Incumbents, by Suffrage Qualifications	554
36.1	Union Density Before and After Neoliberal Reform	572
36.2	Salience of Material Interests, 1995–2007	573

CONTRIBUTORS

Barry Ames is the Andrew Mellon Professor of Comparative Politics at the University of Pittsburgh and former chair of the Department of Political Science. He is the author of two major monographs, *Political Survival: Politicians and Public Policy in Latin America* and *The Deadlock of Democracy in Brazil* as well as many articles in political science journals. His early work focused on institutions in Latin America, especially in Brazil; more recent work concentrates on the relationship between social context and political behavior.

Peter Andreas is a professor in the Department of Political Science and at the Watson Institute for International Studies, Brown University. His research focuses on the intersection of security, political economy, and cross-border crime. Published works include *Policing the Globe: Criminalization and Crime Control in International Relations* (co-author, Oxford University Press, 2006), *Border Games: Policing the U.S.-Mexico Divide* (Cornell University Press, 2nd ed. 2009), and *Sex, Drugs, and Body Counts: The Politics of Numbers in Global Crime and Conflict* (co-editor, Cornell University Press, 2010). Andreas is currently completing a book on the politics of smuggling in American History, titled *Smuggler Nation: How Illicit Trade Made America* (forthcoming, Oxford University Press).

Lisa Baldez is Associate Professor of Government and Latin American, Latino and Caribbean Studies at Dartmouth College. She is the author of *Why Women Protest: Women's Movements in Chile* (Cambridge University Press, 2002). Her work on gender and politics in Latin America and in the United States has appeared in numerous journals, including *Comparative Politics, Legislative Studies Quarterly* and *The Journal of Legal Studies*. She is one of the founding editors, with Karen Beckwith, of *Politics & Gender*.

Nancy Birdsall is the Center for Global Development's founding president. She has also served as executive vice president of the Inter-American Development Bank, director of the Policy Research Department at the World Bank, and Senior Associate and Director of the Economic Reform Project at the Carnegie Endowment for International Peace. She is the author, co-author, or editor of more than a dozen books and over 100 articles in scholarly journals and monographs. Shorter pieces of her writing have appeared in dozens of U.S. and

Latin American newspapers and periodicals. Birdsall received her Ph.D. from Yale University and her M.A. from Johns Hopkins School of Advanced International Studies.

Daniel M. Brinks is Associate Professor of Political Science at the University of Texas at Austin, specializing in Comparative Politics and Public Law. His current project explores constitutional and judicial transformations in Latin America since the 1970s. Some of his previous projects address the courts' response to police violence in South America, the use of courts and law to enforce social and economic rights in the developing world, judicial independence, and the role of informal norms in the legal order. Brinks has a Ph.D. in Political Science from the University of Notre Dame, and a J.D. from the University of Michigan Law School.

Miguel Carreras is a Ph.D. candidate at the University of Pittsburgh. He holds a B.A. in History and a B.A. in Political Science from the Sorbonne University and an M.A. in International Studies from the Graduate Institute of International and Development Studies (Geneva). His current research agenda has two main components: the impact of exposure to crime on political behavior; and the rise of outsider presidents in Latin America. His previous research is forthcoming in *Comparative Political Studies* and *Latin American Research Review*.

Néstor Castañeda-Angarita is a Ph.D. candidate in the Department of Political Science at the University of Pittsburgh. He earned a B.A. in Economics from the Universidad Nacional de Colombia and an M.A. in Latin American Studies from the University of Texas at Austin. His research interests include comparative political economics, legislative politics, and formal theory. His doctoral dissertation addresses the influence of special interest groups and legislative coalitions on fiscal politics and deficit reduction in Latin America.

Christopher Chambers-Ju is a Ph.D. candidate in political science at the University of California, Berkeley. His dissertation, "Teachers' Unions, Governing Coalitions, and Education Policy, 1980-2010" explains different patterns of electoral participation and contentious politics by teachers' unions, and the policy consequences of these patterns in Argentina, Colombia, Mexico, and Peru.

Ruth Berins Collier is Heller Professor of the Graduate School at UC Berkeley. Her research has focused on the interplay of regime change and forms of popular participation and has included comparative analyses of Latin America, Africa, and Europe. She is the author of *Regimes in Tropical Africa: Changing Forms of Supremacy, 1945–1975; Shaping the Political Arena: Critical Junctures, the Labor Movement, and Regime Dynamics; The Contradictory Alliance: State-Labor Relations and Regime Change in Mexico; Paths Toward Democracy: The Working Class and Elites in Western Europe and South America;* and *Reorganizing Popular Politics: Participation and the New Interest Regime in Latin America*.

Maria Lorena Cook is a professor in the Department of International and Comparative Labor at the School of Industrial and Labor Relations, Cornell University. She is the author of *The Politics of Labor Reform in Latin America: Between Flexibility and Rights* (Penn State Press, 2007) and *Organizing Dissent: Unions, the State, and the Democratic Teachers' Movement in Mexico* (Penn State Press, 1996); co-editor of *The Politics of Economic Restructuring: State-Society Relations and Regime Change in Mexico* (Center for U.S.-Mexican Studies, 1994) and

Regional Integration and Industrial Relations in North America (ILR, Cornell, 1994); and author of numerous articles and chapters on Latin American labor politics.

Javier Corrales is professor of Political Science at Amherst College in Amherst, Massachusetts. He is the co-author of *Dragon in the Tropics: Hugo Chávez and the Political Economy of Revolution in Venezuela* (Brookings Institution Press, 2011), winner of the *Foreign Affairs'* award for the Best International Relations Book on the Western Hemisphere for 2011. Corrales is also the co-editor of *The Politics of Sexuality in Latin America* (University of Pittsburgh Press 2010), and author of *Presidents without Parties: the Politics of Economic Reform in Argentina and Venezuela in the 1990s* (Penn State Press 2002).

Jennifer Cyr is a Ph.D. candidate in Political Science at Northwestern University and has a Master of Arts in Latin American and Caribbean Studies from Florida International University. Her research centers on political parties, political institutions, and processes of democratization in the Andean region, specifically in Peru, Bolivia, and Venezuela. She has authored or co-authored several publications in the United States, Latin America, and Europe. She is currently completing a dissertation tentatively entitled, "From Collapse to Comeback? The Fates of Political Parties in Latin America."

Jorge I. Domínguez is Antonio Madero Professor for the Study of Mexico at Harvard University, vice provost for international affairs, special advisor for international studies to the dean of the faculty of arts and sciences, and chairman of the Harvard Academy for International and Area Studies. He is the author or co-author of many books and articles on domestic and international politics in Latin America and the Caribbean. His most recent books include *La política exterior de Cuba, 1962–2009*; *Consolidating Mexico's Democracy: The 2006 Presidential Campaign in Comparative Perspective*; *The United States and Mexico: Between Partnership and Conflict, 2nd ed.*; *Constructing Democratic Governance in Latin America, 3rd ed.* A past president of the Latin American Studies Association, he currently serves on many editorial boards.

Thad Dunning is Associate Professor of Political Science and a research fellow at Yale's MacMillan Center for International and Area Studies as well as the Institution for Social and Policy Studies. He studies comparative politics, political economy, and methodology. His first book, *Crude Democracy: Natural Resource Wealth and Political Regimes* (2008, Cambridge University Press), won the Best Book Award from the Comparative Democratization Section of the American Political Science Association. His current research on ethnic and other cleavages draws on field and natural experiments and qualitative fieldwork in Latin America, India, and Africa.

Angelica Duran Martinez is a doctoral candidate in Political Science at Brown University. She obtained a B.A. in Political Science from Universidad Nacional de Colombia and an M.A. in Latin American and Caribbean Studies at New York University thanks to a Fulbright Scholarship. She has been a Fulbright Fellow at the United Nations Secretariat and a consultant for the UNODC, the UNDP, and Global Integrity. Her dissertation analyzes the relationship between drug trafficking and violence in Colombia and Mexico, and has been funded by the United States Institute of Peace, the Social Science Research Council, and the Open Society Foundation.

Kent Eaton is Professor and Chair of Politics at the University of California, Santa Cruz. His articles on decentralization and federalism have appeared in *Comparative Politics, Latin American Politics and Society, Latin American Research Review, Politics and Society, Security Studies*, and *World Politics*. He is also the author/editor of several recent monographs on decentralization, including *Making Decentralization Work: Democracy, Development and Security* (Lynne Rienner Press, 2010), *The Democratic Decentralization Programming Handbook* (USAID, 2009), and *The Political Economy of Decentralization Reforms: Implications for Aid Effectiveness* (The World Bank, 2010).

Sujatha Fernandes is an Associate Professor of Sociology at Queens College and the Graduate Center of the City University of New York. She is the author of *Cuba Represent! Cuban Arts, State Power, and the Making of New Revolutionary Cultures* (Duke University Press, October 2006) and *Who Can Stop the Drums? Urban Social Movements in Chávez's Venezuela* (Duke University Press, April 2010). Her most recent book is *Close to the Edge: In Search of the Global Hip Hop Generation* (Verso, September 2011).

Barbara Geddes, who earned her Ph.D. from UC, Berkeley, has written about autocratic politics, regime transition, bureaucratic reform and corruption, political bargaining over institutional change, and research design. Her current research focuses on institutional choice in dictatorships, supported by an NSF grant for the collection of information about dictatorial politics. Her publications include *Paradigms and Sand Castles: Theory Building and Research Design in Comparative Politic* (2003); *Politician's Dilemma: Building State Capacity in Latin America* (1994); and "What Causes Democratization?" in *The Oxford Handbook of Political Science*. She teaches Latin American politics, authoritarian politics, and research design at UCLA.

Frances Hagopian is Jorge Paulo Lemann Visiting Associate Professor for Brazil Studies in the Department of Government at Harvard University. She specializes in the comparative politics of Latin America, with emphasis on democratization, political representation, political economy, and religion and politics. She is author of *Reorganizing Representation in Latin America* (forthcoming, Cambridge University Press) and *Traditional Politics and Regime Change in Brazil* (Cambridge 1996); editor of *Religious Pluralism, Democracy, and the Catholic Church in Latin America* (University of Notre Dame Press, 2009), co-editor (with Scott Mainwaring) of *The Third Wave of Democratization in Latin America* (Cambridge 2005); and author of numerous journal articles and book chapters.

Kathryn Hochstetler is CIGI Chair of Governance of the Americas in the Balsillie School of International Affairs and Professor of Political Science at the University of Waterloo, in Canada. She has published a number of articles and book chapters on civil society and social movements in Brazil and Argentina, the Mercosur free trade area, and in United Nations conferences and negotiations. Her most recent book is the award-winning *Greening Brazil: Environmental Activism in State and Society* (Duke University Press, 2007, with Margaret Keck).

Ollie A. Johnson III is an Associate Professor in the Department of Africana Studies at Wayne State University. He received his Ph.D. in Political Science from the University of California at Berkeley. His first book, *Brazilian Party Politics and the Coup of 1964*, was published in 2001. He co-edited *Black Political Organizations in the Post-Civil Rights Era* in 2002.

Johnson has conducted extensive research on Black political groups and social movements in the United States and Latin America. His current research focuses on Afro-Brazilian and Afro-Latin American politics.

Mark P. Jones (Ph.D. University of Michigan, B.A. Tulane University) is the Joseph D. Jamail Chair in Latin American Studies, the James A. Baker III Institute for Public Policy's Fellow in Political Science, and Chairman of the Department of Political Science at Rice University in Houston, Texas. He also has been a visiting professor at several universities in Latin America, including the Universidad de San Andrés and Universidad Nacional de San Martín in Argentina and the Universidad de la República in Uruguay. Jones's research focuses on the impact of democratic institutions on elections, elite and mass behavior, governance, and representation.

Sebastian Karcher is a Ph.D. Candidate in political science at Northwestern University. His main research interests are the politics of business and labor markets as well as methodological and conceptual questions in political economy. His work has been published in *Socio-Economic Review, International Studies Quarterly*, as well as several edited volumes. The chapter in this volume was written while he was a guest scholar at the Kellogg Institute for International Studies, University of Notre Dame.

Robert R. Kaufman is Professor of Political Science at Rutgers University. He has written widely on authoritarianism and democratic transitions in Latin America, economic reform, and social welfare policies. His most recent book is *Development, Democracy, and Welfare States: Latin America, East Asia, and Eastern Europe*, 2008), co-authored with Stephan Haggard. He is also co-author (with Stephan Haggard) of *The Political Economy of Democratic Transitions*, winner of the 1995 Luebbert Prize for the best book in comparative politics, awarded by the Comparative Politics Section of the American Political Science Association. He is also co-editor (with Joan M. Nelson) of *Crucial Needs, Weak Incentives: Social Sector Reform, Globalization and Democratization in Latin America*, 2004.

Peter Kingstone (Ph.D. University of California, Berkeley) is Associate Professor of Political Science at the University of Connecticut. He is author of *Crafting Coalitions for Reform: Business Preferences, Political Institutions and Neoliberal Reform in Brazil* (Penn State Press, 1999) and *The Political Economy of Latin America: Reflections on Neoliberalism and Development* (Routledge, 2010), as well as co-editor (with Tim Power) of *Democratic Brazil: Actors, Institutions and Processes* (University of Pittsburgh Press, 2000) and *Democratic Brazil Revisited* (University of Pittsburgh Press, 2008). He has published various articles and book chapters on the subject of democratization and the politics of neoliberal economic reforms.

Steven Levitsky is Professor of Government at Harvard University. His research interests include political parties, authoritarianism and democratization, and weak and informal institutions, with a focus on Latin America. He is author of *Transforming Labor-Based Parties in Latin America: Argentine Peronism in Comparative Perspective*, co-author of *Competitive Authoritarianism: Hybrid Regimes after the Cold War*, and co-editor of *Argentine Democracy: The Politics of Institutional Weakness*; *Informal Institutions and Democracy: Lessons from Latin America*; and *The Resurgence of the Left in Latin America*. He is currently working on projects on the durability of revolutionary regimes, relationship between populism and competitive authoritarianism, and party collapse and democracy in Peru.

José Antonio Lucero is Associate Professor in the Henry M. Jackson School of International Studies at the University of Washington, where he is also Chair of the Latin American and Caribbean Studies Program. Lucero's main research and teaching interests include Indigenous politics, social movements, Latin American politics, and development. His current research examine the cultural politics of conflicts between Indigenous peoples and the agents of extractive industry in Peru, including mining companies, oil companies, and the German filmmaker Werner Herzog.

Nora Lustig is Samuel Z. Stone Professor of Latin American Economics at Tulane University and a nonresident fellow at the Center for Global Development and the Inter-American Dialogue. She co-directed the World Bank's World Development Report 2000/1, *Attacking Poverty* and was the president of LACEA (Latin American and Caribbean Economic Association). She is currently the director of the Commitment to Equity Project and editor of the *Journal of Economic Inequality*'s Forum. She received her doctorate in Economics from the University of California, Berkeley. Her current research focuses on assessing the impact of fiscal policy on inequality and poverty in Latin America.

James W. McGuire is Professor and Chair in the Department of Government at Wesleyan University. He received his B.A. from Swarthmore and his Ph.D. from the University of California, Berkeley. McGuire specializes in comparative politics, with a regional focus on Latin America and East Asia and a topical focus on democracy, social policies, and public health. He is the author of *Peronism without Perón: Unions, Parties, and Democracy in Argentina* (Stanford, 1997) and of *Wealth, Health, and Democracy in East Asia and Latin America* (Cambridge, 2010), which won the 2011 Stein Rokkan Prize for Comparative Social Science Research.

Darryl McLeod is an Associate Professor of Economics at Fordham University specializing in economic development. His research focuses on poverty, inequality, employment and immigration issues. McLeod recently co-directed a survey of Mexican immigrants in New York and Mexico funded by the Packard Foundation, UCLA NAID and Fordham University. In 2006-2008 he worked as a consultant to UNDP's Poverty Group and helped write chapter 4 of UNDP BCPR's 2008 report *Post-conflict economic recovery*. He has also worked as a consultant to the World Bank, the IADB, Lehman Brothers Latin America Group, and the OAS. He has an M.S. and Ph.D. from the University of California at Berkeley.

James Mahoney is a Professor in the Departments of Political Science and Sociology at Northwestern University. His books include *Colonialism and Postcolonial Development: Spanish America in Comparative Perspective* (2010); *Explaining Institutional Change: Ambiguity, Agency, and Power* (co-edited with Kathleen Thelen; 2010); *Comparative-Historical Analysis in the Social Sciences* (coedited with Dietrich Rueschemeyer; 2003); and *The Legacies of Liberalism: Path Dependence and Political Regimes in Central America* (2001). He is a past president of the Section on Qualitative and Multimethod Research of the American Political Science Association and a past chair of the Section on Comparative and Historical Sociology of the American Sociological Association.

Luigi Manzetti is Associate Professor of Political Science at Southern Methodist University. He specializes in issues that include governance, corruption, and market reforms in Latin America. His most recent book is entitled *Neoliberalism, Accountability, and Reform Failures in*

Emerging Markets: Eastern Europe, Russia, Argentina, and Chile in Comparative Perspective (Penn State Press 2010). His journal articles have appeared in *World Politics*, *Comparative Political Studies*, *Comparative Politics*, the *Journal of Latin American Studies*, and the *Latin American Research Review*.

David R. Mares (Ph.D. Harvard 1982) holds the Institute of the Americas Chair for Inter-American Affairs at the University of California, San Diego where he is also Director of the Center for Iberian and Latin American Studies, Professor of Political Science and Adjunct Professor at the Graduate School of International Relations and Pacific Studies. He is also the Baker Institute Scholar for Latin American Energy Studies at the James A. Baker III Institute for Public Policy at Rice University and an elected member of the International Institute for Strategic Studies (London). Mares was previously Professor at El Colegio de México (1980–82), Fulbright Professor at the Universidad de Chile (1990), and Visiting Professor at FLACSO Ecuador (1995).

Gerardo L. Munck, Argentinian by birth, received his Ph.D. in political science from the University of California, San Diego (UCSD) and is Professor in the School of International Relations at the University of Southern California (USC). His research focuses on democracy, methodology, and Latin America. His books include *Measuring Democracy: A Bridge Between Scholarship and Politics* (Johns Hopkins University, 2009); *Regimes and Democracy in Latin America* (Oxford, 2007); *Passion, Craft, and Method in Comparative Politics* (with Richard Snyder; Johns Hopkins, 2007); and *Authoritarianism and Democratization. Soldiers and Workers in Argentina, 1976–83* (Penn State Press, 1998).

Philip Oxhorn is a Professor of Political Science and Editor-in-Chief of the *Latin American Research Review*. He has published extensively on the comparative study of civil society and democracy. This includes *Sustaining Civil Society: Economic Change, Democracy and the Social Construction of Citizenship in Latin America* (Penn State Press, 2011), as well as *Organizing Civil Society: The Popular Sectors and the Struggle for Democracy in Chile* (Penn State Press, 1995). Professor Oxhorn has lectured extensively in North and South America, Western Europe, Asia and Australia. He has a Ph.D. in Political Science from Harvard University.

Anthony W. Pereira is a Professor of Brazilian Studies and Director of the Brazil Institute at King's College London. He obtained his B.A. from Sussex University (U.K.) in 1982 and his M.A. and Ph.D. degrees from Harvard University in 1986 and 1991, respectively. He has held positions at the New School, Tufts, Tulane, and the University of East Anglia. His research interests include the issues of democracy, human rights, and military rule, particularly in Brazil and the southern cone of Latin America. His latest book *Ditadura e Repressão* was published in Brazil by Paz e Terra in 2010. He is currently engaged in research on police and public security reform in Brazil.

Aníbal Pérez-Liñán is Associate Professor of Political Science and member of the core faculty at the Center for Latin American Studies at the University of Pittsburgh. His research focuses on political stability, institutional performance, and the rule of law in new democracies. He has served as chair of the Political Institutions Section of the Latin American Studies Association, and is the author of *Presidential Impeachment and the New Political Instability in Latin America* (Cambridge University Press, 2007). His research has been funded by the

National Science Foundation, the United States Agency for International Development, and the Inter-American Development Bank.

David Pion-Berlin is a Professor of Political Science at the University of California, Riverside. He is a Latin Americanist widely known for his research and writings on civil-military relations, defense, security, political repression and human rights, and is the author of numerous books and articles on these subjects. Recent articles have appeared in *Comparative Politics, Armed Forces & Society, The Latin American Research Review,* and *Latin American Politics and Society.* He has consulted for the Organization of American States and the U.S. Navy. His recent scholarship is on the phenomenon of military disobedience in the face of presidential orders to suppress civilian uprisings.

Grigore Pop-Eleches is Associate Professor of Politics and International Affairs at Princeton University. His main research interests lie at the intersection between political economy and comparative political behavior, with a particular interest in Eastern Europe and Latin America. He has worked on the politics of IMF programs in Eastern Europe and Latin America, the rise of unorthodox parties in East Europe, and on the role of historical legacies in post-communist regime change. His publications include *From Economic Crisis to Reform: IMF Programs in Latin America and Eastern Europe* (Princeton University Press, 2009) and articles in *The Journal of Politics, World Politics, Comparative Political Studies, Comparative Politics,* and *International Studies Quarterly.*

Adam Przeworski is the Carroll and Milton Professor of Politics and (by courtesy) Economics at New York University. Previously he taught at the University of Chicago, where he was the Martin A. Ryerson Distinguished Service Professor, and held visiting appointments in India, Chile, France, Germany, Spain, and Switzerland. A member of the American Academy of Arts and Sciences since 1991, he is the recipient of the 1985 Socialist Review Book Award, the 1998 Gregory M. Luebbert Article Award, the 2001 Woodrow Wilson Prize, the 2010 Lawrence Longley Award, and the 2010 Johan Skytte Prize. He recently published Democracy and the Limits of Self-Government (New York: Cambridge University Press. 2010).

Kenneth M. Roberts is Professor of Government and the Robert S. Harrison Director of the Institute for the Social Sciences at Cornell University. He specializes in the study of Latin American politics and the political economy of inequality. He is the author of *Deepening Democracy? The Modern Left and Social Movements in Chile and Peru* (Stanford University Press) and co-editor of *The Diffusion of Social Movements* (Cambridge University Press) and *The Resurgence of the Latin American Left* (Johns Hopkins University Press). His research on party systems, populism, and political representation in Latin America has been published in a number of scholarly journals. He is currently writing a book on party system transformation in Latin America's neoliberal era.

Carlos Rufin is Associate Professor of International Business at Suffolk University in Boston, with a Ph.D. in Public Policy from the Harvard Kennedy School. His research focuses on access by the urban poor to utility services in developing countries, regulatory reform and governance, political economy, and energy sector development. He has also taught at Babson College, the Harvard Kennedy School, Instituto de Empresa Business School, and PUC-Rio. As an independent consultant, he has worked for Rio Light, the World Bank, the Inter-American Development Bank, USAID, AES Corporation, Gas Natural, and other private and public organizations.

Ben Ross Schneider is Ford International Professor of Political Science at MIT and director of MIT-Brazil and MIT-Chile programs. His books include *Reinventing Leviathan: The Politics of Administrative Reform in Developing Countries*, and *Business Politics and the State in 20th Century Latin America*. He also has written on topics such as economic reform, democratization, the developmental state, industrial policy, and comparative bureaucracy. Schneider's current research focuses on the institutional foundations of capitalist development in Latin America with special attention to business groups, MNCs, labor markets, and skills.

Cassilde Schwartz is a doctoral student at the University of Pittsburgh, where she also earned her B.Phil. in History, Politics and Philosophy and her M.A. in Political Science. Schwartz's fields of specialization include Comparative Politics and Political Behavior, and her current research focuses on the consequences of protest activity in Latin America.

Mitchell A. Seligson is the Centennial Professor of Political Science and Professor of Sociology at Vanderbilt University and Director of the Latin American Public Opinion Project (LAPOP). He has published over 140 articles, 14 books, and more than 35 monographs and occasional papers. His most recent books are *The Legitimacy Puzzle in Latin America: Democracy and Political Support in Eight Nations* (Cambridge University Press, 2009, co-authored with John Booth), and *Development and Underdevelopment, the Political Economy of Global Inequality (Fourth Edition,* Lynne Reinner Publishers, co-edited with John Passé-Smith). He is an elected member of the General Assembly of the Inter-American Institute of Human Rights and a member of the editorial boards of *Comparative Political Studies* and the *European Political Science Review.*

Eduardo Silva is the Lydian Professor of Political Science at Tulane University. He has published extensively on environmental issues, especially the political ecology of development policies supportive of community forestry, in journals—including *Development and Change, Latin American Politics and Society, The Journal of Latin American Studies, European Review of Latin American and Caribbean Studies*, and *Global Environmental Politics*—as well as in edited volumes. His most recent book is *Challenging Neoliberalism in Latin America* (Cambridge University Press, 2009). His current research focuses on popular sector interest intermediation in new left governments in South America.

Peter H. Smith is Distinguished Professor of Political Science and Simón Bolívar Professor of Latin American Studies at the University of California, San Diego. He is a specialist on comparative politics, Latin American politics, and U.S.-Latin American relations. A *magna cum laude* graduate of Harvard College, Smith received the Ph.D. from Columbia University in 1966. His recent publications include *Talons of the Eagle: Latin America, the United States, and the World* (3rd edition, 2008), *Democracy in Latin America: Political Change in Comparative Perspective* (2nd edition, 2012), and the coauthored *Modern Latin America* (7th edition, 2010).

Deborah J. Yashar is Professor of Politics and International Affairs at Princeton University, former director of Princeton's Program in Latin American Studies, co-editor of the Cambridge University series on Contentious Politics, and a member of the editorial committee of *World Politics*. Her books include *Demanding Democracy: Reform and Reaction in Costa Rica* *and Guatemala* (Stanford University Press, 1997) and *Contesting Citizenship in Latin America: The Rise of Indigenous Movements and the Postliberal Challenge* (Cambridge University Press, 2005)—which received the 2006 Best Book Prize, awarded by the New England Council on Latin American Studies and the 2006 Mattei Dogan Honorable Mention, awarded by the Society for Comparative Research. She is currently writing a book about violence in Latin America.

Elizabeth J. Zechmeister is Associate Professor of Political Science and Associate Director of the Latin American Public Opinion Project (LAPOP) at Vanderbilt University. She received her Ph.D. from Duke University in 2003. Her research focuses on comparative political behavior, in particular in Latin America. Her work includes studies of voting, ideology, representation, charisma, and crisis. She has published articles in the *Journal of Politics*, *Electoral Studies*, *Comparative Political Studies*, and *Political Behavior,* among others. She is coauthor of *Democracy at Risk: How Terrorist Threats Affect the Public* (University of Chicago Press, 2009) and *Latin American Party Systems* (Cambridge University Press, 2010).

INTRODUCTION

Peter Kingstone and Deborah J. Yashar

The study of comparative politics has been defined in critical ways by research on Latin America. Latin America's experiments with problems such as democratization, good governance, social movement politics, or socioeconomic development have generated intriguing and enduring empirical puzzles about core social science questions. In turn, those puzzles have fostered conceptual, theoretical, and methodological innovations that have significantly shaped the larger field of comparative politics. In this sense, Latin Americanists have played a critical role in shaping the field of comparative politics as a whole.

Latin America continues to be a laboratory of developmental and democratic struggles with concomitant theoretical exploration. With the third wave of democracy, the region has largely transitioned away from military rule—marking a nearly region-wide regime change that foreshadowed what would follow in other developing regions. Most of these third wave democracies have endured despite the numerous obstacles in place. Yet, if the region is mostly democratic, democratic politics in the region suffers from a host of deficiencies, including weak institutions, uneven patterns of accountability, weak rule of law, and inequality of access—making it hard to sustain and deepen democratic experiences in the region. Moreover, Latin America's third wave democracies have struggled to redefine state-society relationships—including constitutional and legal debates about how to incorporate social actors—including labor, women, indigenous peoples, and Afro-Latin Americans. Similarly, Latin America has become a critical battleground between market-oriented visions of economic development and a variety of leftist and/or nationalist state-led visions. These contemporary empirical challenges continue to spawn original and vital work on central questions in comparative politics: about regime change and democratic governance; changing state-society relations; the terms of citizenship; and the balance between states and market. As such, there are fundamental social science issues at play in Latin America and some of the most interesting contemporary comparative politics scholarship is taking place in studies of Latin America.

Given the richness and diversity of scholarship on Latin American politics, it is hard to stay abreast of the developments in the many sub-literatures of the field. Scholars have produced many fine edited volumes that explore a single aspect or dimension of Latin American politics, such as informal institutions, electoral authoritarianism, democratic quality or the resurgence of left wing governments. Yet, there is no single volume that provides a broad survey of the literature and identifies the cutting edge of research across the field. The *Routledge Handbook of Latin American Politics* addresses that intellectual gap by bringing together a comprehensive collection of essays that define the field and where it is going.

The handbook speaks to three different audiences. First and perhaps foremost, the volume is intended for scholars who are interested in an intellectually rigorous overview of the state of the field and a thoughtful (at times provocative) guide to the direction of future scholarship. Each chapter reviews the existing literature in its topic area, identifies the research and theoretical trends, and offers reflections on the most promising and important puzzles for future research. Second, the volume is an invaluable guide to graduate and advanced undergraduate students seeking a comprehensive history of the field, assistance in identifying key questions for future research, and access to leading scholar's insights on where the field should be going. Thus, the handbook is a vital tool for students looking to begin their own investigations. Third, the handbook should be of interest to policy makers seeking insight into the core issues defining the field.

Compiling leading scholarship on the core issues facing the field posed a real challenge as there are more important topics than any single volume can include. With such a large, disparate, and theoretically rich area of study, it is impossible to cover every issue. We respectfully accept that some may disagree with our choices of what to include, what to exclude, and how to organize the work. Ultimately, we chose topics that we believed were both critical to the theoretical debates in Latin America and comparative politics and/or germane to an understanding of the region of Latin America (and how it fits into the world and/or social science debates). The volume is thus divided into six sections: democratic governance; economic development; social actors and collective action; international relations; methodological debates; and critical reflections by leading senior scholars.

Themes and Contributions

Part One examines crucial topics in the contemporary study of democracy. Latin America used to be defined by political instability—with regime swings between authoritarian and democratic regime. However, since 1979, the region has largely transitioned away from military rule and instantiated enduring democracy in most countries of the region. As such, Part I of the volume focuses on a range of issues associated with the origins of democracy and democratic practices. These questions are all the more important in the region given that democratic governance, while enduring, has remained troubled, conflicted, and uncertain in the third wave of democratization. As a consequence, it has been a vital source of theorizing as well. Thirty odd years of this current wave of democracy have demonstrated the difficulty of defining and measuring democratic "quality" and has revealed the importance of examining a variety of dimensions of democratic rule beyond elections.

In Chapter 1, Gerardo Munck argues forcefully that the origins and durability of democracy is far from a settled matter. Disagreements *about* the rules of democracy remain relevant and regularly flare up into overt conflict. As Munck states it, "the history of democracy continues to unfold." Part of that history includes the study of institutions. Beginning with Juan Linz' seminal work, which called into question the suitability of presidentialism for democracy, scholars have been engaged in an extensive inquiry into the causes and effects of institutional design and its relation to democratic rule. In Chapter 2, Mark Jones addresses this large literature, reviewing the cumulative learning about the presidential form of government, the relationship between presidents and legislatures, and their consequences for democratic governance. Kent Eaton's Chapter 3 explores federalism and decentralization, issues that require us to think about levels of government, where power is lodged, and how it is exercised strategically by different actors. Decentralization has been widely promoted by international agencies as a solution to development and a mechanism of democratic deepening. As a result, it has become a global trend. As Eaton notes, Latin America has been a leading laboratory for innovative and influential experiments in decentralization. As such, he argues that understanding decentralization as a global trend requires a focus on Latin America, and in turn understanding Latin American politics today requires understanding the myriad ways that subnational actors influence politics. In Chapter 4, Kenneth Roberts turns our gaze to political parties and highlights that while some have experienced a crisis of representation, others have endured with a contrasting resilience in the face of economic crisis. This flux and endurance calls out for attention to the changing social bases of parties that have had to confront both the dual transitions of democratization and economic globalization. The challenge of the rule of law is the subject of Chapter 5. Daniel Brinks observes that a kind of dualism has appeared in Latin American democracies. On the one hand, the judiciary has become more active and courts are increasingly contributing to the creation of more accountable regimes. On the other hand, at the same time that the courts are helping to deepen democracy, pervasive public insecurity undermines the rule of law and the legitimacy of law enforcement and the judiciary. Chapter 6 explores the domestic role of the military. David Pion-Berlin observes that the Honduran military's ouster of President Manuel Zelaya reminds us that while civilians largely govern, the retreat of the military to the barracks is not a given. As polls show widespread dissatisfaction with the performance of democracy, we lack good answers to vital questions, empirically and theoretically, about what motivates the military.

Both Brinks and Pion-Berlin's chapters raise questions about the gap between the written "rules of the game" and actual behavior. Steve Levitsky further considers the issue of "informal institutions" in Chapter 7. As Levitsky states: "[a]n exclusive focus on formal rules thus risks missing many of the real incentives driving political behavior in Latin America, which can limit our understanding of how politics works." In his chapter, Levitsky surveys the state of our knowledge of informal institutions and notes that the tendency is to focus on the way they subvert formal rules, yet such rules often support formal goals as well (supportive functions that have been subject to much less scrutiny). Frances Hagopian's Chapter 8 also goes beyond simple specification of the rules and considers the myriad mechanisms and processes that have strengthened or weakened accountability and representation since the spread of democracy in the region. Hagopian observes that economic development strategies and broad regime tendencies have moved in a common direction, but the paths that citizens and leaders have followed and the outcomes (in terms of accountability and representation) have varied widely. The result is a patchwork pattern of both old and new forms of exclusion as well as both old and new forms of mobilization, organization and representation. Finally, in Chapter 9, Anthony Pereira explores the legacy of military rule and the efforts to address the human rights abuses of the past. In particular, Pereira considers the problem of transitional justice and whether and how a commitment to social justice and human rights is enshrined in society. He notes, however, the disturbing fact that everyday violence in places like Brazil and El Salvador has produced more casualties than dictatorship or civil war ever did, a disturbing reminder of the need to understand better what produces a just society.

Part II turns to the challenges of development, a central concern of comparative inquiry. The field has long debated why some regions and countries are more successful in pursuing industrialization, economic growth, poverty alleviation, and/or equity. Latin America and

Latin American scholarship has been central to these debates, as the essays in this volume highlight. Latin American intellectuals and policy makers have sought to close the developmental gap since independence. Long standing concerns with growth, poverty and inequality have been joined with relatively newer discussions of social policy, human capital, and environmental sustainability. The essays in Part II thus address these classic and new questions from a variety of angles.

In Chapter 10, Javier Corrales reviews the controversy over neoliberal economic development policies and the apparent rise of the left in the region. He contends that the issue cannot be understood in binary terms—i.e., as if neoliberal reforms are right or wrong. Corrales argues that neoliberal reforms have demonstrated important benefits, particularly that macro-economic discipline can be good for growth and can be progressive. However, market reforms do not have good answers for a range of development challenges including social justice issues leftist critics often emphasize. As a result, neoliberal hegemony has weakened as the left has re-emerged. But, as Corrales states, "As long as there exist advocates for state involvement, there will be neoliberals ready to assert the dangers of statist excesses." Nancy Birdsall, Nora Lustig, and Darryl McLeod tackle one of the central issues of contention in debates about development: poverty and inequality. Chapter 11 relies on recent data to show that both inequality and poverty are in decline in most of the region. For most of Latin America's history, high levels of both contributed to low growth rates and a host of perverse social and political outcomes. The expansion of basic education, introduction of innovative social policies, and declining relative returns to skilled labor have all contributed to an ongoing and potentially sustainable trend of improvement. The authors note that the improvement has been strongest in the moderate left regimes in the region, i.e., those that have moderated neoliberalism, but not abandoned its emphasis on macro-economic restraint. An additional concern with neoliberalism has been the danger of unfettered markets for the environment. In Chapter 12, Eduardo Silva examines the difficult problem of sustainable development. As Silva notes: in "Latin America, environmental politics inescapably involve conflicts over land, democracy, and civil rights." How these problems are understood depends on distinct approaches to the environment. Finally, Chapter 13 reviews the dramatic shifts in social policy in the region and their impact on equitable development. James McGuire's examination reveals the wide array of social and political forces that led to the emergence of innovative and surprisingly effective policies over time. One important conclusion McGuire reaches is that democracy was critical for the expansion of social policy, although not in unidirectional or automatic ways. The weakness of the state is a central element in the analysis of privatization and regulation by Luigi Manzetti and Carlos Rufin. In Chapter 14, the authors warn that the technical nature of the subject has led to little scrutiny by political science. Yet, the wave of privatizations of public utilities in the 1990s represented an important turning point in the region's development with important consequences for public welfare. Privatization and regulation has produced a surprising record. On the one hand, the weakness of the state in much of the region has led to serious failings such as regulatory capture, clientelism, and corruption. On the other hand, it has also created new opportunities for citizens to hold government accountable and make demands as citizens and consumers. As the authors note, the "implications for democratic governance in Latin America remain to be explored by scholars."

Part III turns to focus on the social actors that have defined Latin American politics. Studies of class and labor politics, in particular, were crucial to early experiments in democracy and state-society relations, such as in studies of corporatism. More recently, the focus on labor has tended to recede. Nonetheless, there has been a sustained interest in social movements and civil society—even though the cleavages, forms of organization, and targets of policy have changed over time and across the region. In particular, there has been a rising scholarship about ethnic, racial, and gender politics, including an expanding attention to indigenous peoples, Afro-Latin Americans, and women—all of whom have mobilized in significant ways around demands for greater inclusion and social justice.

In Chapter 15, Kathryn Hochstetler considers the long and vivid history of social movements in the region. The dramatic and transformative power of social movements has generated a considerable literature on the causes and consequences of social mobilization. The issue has become more salient in the neoliberal age as debates over the impact of market reforms have raised questions about the conditions under which social mobilization occurs and when it is effective. As Hochstetler notes, the empirical record of mobilization across Latin America and its relation with democracy and market reforms varies widely. The question of state-society relations is the subject as well of Chapter 16. Phillip Oxhorn considers the character of political participation and the tension between alternative conceptions of citizenship: "a normative vision of democracy emphasizing its unique capacity to resolve conflict nonviolently with more instrumentalist perspectives on democracy that focus on the material quality of life and the conflicts of interests this inevitably entails given the region's high level of socio-economic inequality." Many observers connect claims about the weakness of social movements and/or civil society with the weakness of labor. In Chapter 17, Maria Cook acknowledges the decline of unions, yet notes that both work and workers remain critical to understanding the politics of the region. Cook's review points to significant cross-regional variation in the power of workers and unions, the under-studied role of the informal sector, as well as gaps in our understanding of how employees and employers interact and the extent to which this arena has democratized. Cook's discussion calls attention to a tendency to focus on organized and elite actors. However, in Chapter 18, Sebastian Karcher and Ben Ross Schneider argue that research on business has come in waves, but "despite these waves, research on business politics is first characterized by how little there is." The authors' review highlights the need to understand Latin America's distinctive business profile as well as the need to engage in cross-regional work to better understand business preferences and power.

Labor, business, and social movements are long-standing subjects of interest. In Chapter 19, José Antonio Lucero turns his attention to a newly mobilized actor in the region. Citing Ecuadorian Kichwa leader Luis Macas, Lucero observes that "the 1980s was not a "lost decade" for Indigenous people in Latin America but a *"década ganada,"* a decade in which Indigenous people won." The new mobilization challenged the established political, economic, and social order. But, as of the 2000s, indigenous mobilization has led to a more varied mix of gains and setbacks. Like Lucero, Ollie Johnson considers people with a long history of exclusion in the region that is only recently changing. Chapter 20 considers the issue of race and the politics of Afro-Latin Americans. Johnson explores the intersection of race, marginalization and discrimination and the important role of Afro-Latin Americans as citizens, activists, and politicians. In order to better understand the centrality of race, especially in certain key countries in the region, Johnson navigates the contested conceptions of race and racism in a region that has tended to hide behind powerful myths of racial harmony and democracy. Finally, in Chapter 21, Lisa Baldez considers the politics of gender. As with both indigenous and Afro-Latin Americans, women have made notable strides in the region. Women have been elected to office, including a number of presidencies, and have successfully advanced an array of women's rights. As Baldez states, "[t]hese successes challenge assumptions about the prevalence of traditional gender stereotypes that portray

Latin American women as submissive, subordinated by men and relegated to the private sphere." Yet, at the same time, women continue to face important obstacles and gender discrimination persists.

Part IV turns to the international arena. The "war on terror" as well as actual wars in Afghanistan, Iraq and now Libya, the global financial crisis, and the rapid rise of China have tended to obscure the importance of Latin America on the international stage. Yet, crucial issues remain, both in U.S.-Latin American relations and inter-American relations. Furthermore, the link between the United States and Latin America manifests in distinct areas including the role of international financial institutions, the presence of large foreign multinationals in key areas of resource extraction and utilities, and through illicit trade.

In Chapter 22, Peter Smith points out that relationships between the United States and Latin America receive less attention than they merit, primarily because of the absence of major wars or crises. Yet, Latin America is part of a global process of changing power relations and spreading democratization. Some Latin American countries, such as Brazil and Mexico, are playing leading roles in the global transformation and the United States' place in the world is very much affected by its connection to the region. Thus, examining the connection between the United States and Latin America is part and parcel of understanding a changing world. David Mares turns his attention to intra-regional relations. Chapter 23 explores the long history of both cooperation and competition in the region. Latin America has a rich and varied history of both. Unfortunately, like inter-American relations, scholars have paid less attention than the issues warrant. As with inter-American relations, however, the complex pattern across space and over time provides scholars with a rich empirical tableau for conceptual and theoretical innovation. By contrast, international political economy of the region has received considerably more attention. In Chapter 24, Grigore Pop-Eleches continues the argument for putting Latin America in a broader global context by focusing on the links to the global economy. The economic history of Latin America is a continuing shifting between good periods based on capital inflows and commodity booms and painful downturns marked by capital flight and acrimonious relations with international creditors and financial institutions. Finally, Chapter 25 tackles another under-studied topic—drugs and other illicit trade in the region. Peter Andreas and Angelica Duran Martinez point out that the topic suffers from a lack of adequate data and insufficient comparative analysis. As with privatization and regulation, however, the lack of political science attention "is unfortunate, given that some of the field's central preoccupations, ranging from democracy to development to violence, are intimately intertwined with illicit trade and the domestic and international politics of policing such trade. Nowhere is this more evident than in the Americas." Andreas and Duran Martinez' review points to the intimate connections between illicit trade and democracy as well as violence and neoliberal economic reforms.

A range of methodological discussions feature in Part V of the volume. Latin American politics has been a key context for debates and disagreements about the benefits and costs of different methodological approaches. This section offers a review of the key strengths of diverse modes of inquiry.

In Chapter 26, Aníbal Pérez-Liñán and Néstor Castañeda-Angarita review the burgeoning literature on political institutions. As they note, the transition to democracy brought increased attention to "the rules of the game" with the accompanying desire to understand how they shaped preferences for key actors in ways that were conducive (or not) to democracy. Institutionalism "yielded promising answers and has become one of the dominant perspectives for the study of Latin American politics." Yet, Pérez-Liñán and Castañeda-Angarita warn that specifying the institutions is not sufficient and lay out an agenda for understanding "when (and not just how) particular rules become relevant. Perhaps the most important lesson of the institutional approach is that institutions matter most when they matter the least—that is, when they are potentially crucial and yet not respected." In Chapter 27, Sujatha Fernandes considers the cultural turn and postmodern approaches in Latin American politics. Postmodern and cultural theorists challenge the broad explanatory frameworks of modernism and positivism—highlighting not only multiple realities but also alternative ways of assessing the meaning and experiences of social actors. Scholars in these traditions contend that the exercise of power needs to be understood in a decentered fashion that privileges culture and cultural identity. This insight has informed studies of political organizing, governance, subject formation, among other topics. Within cultural studies and postmodernist studies of Latin America, however, a lively debate continues, including the ways in which class and culture interact. By contrast, in Chapter 28, Barbara Geddes examines the value of a positivistic approach in her exploration of rational choice in the study of Latin American politics. As she notes, those who study values may find it less useful, but "[r]ational choice has become a part of the standard toolkit for many Latin Americanists, as it is for many other social scientists, because it helps us to understand some aspects of the political world." Among other areas of importance, the logic of collective action is routinely brought into accounts of mass behavior and rational choice is particularly valuable in understanding both elite decision-making as well as the individual behavior operating in political machines and clientelist networks. Rational choice's focus on individuals' cost-benefit calculus has shaped much contemporary scholarship on the workings of democracy. She observes that this is so even among those who do not consciously identify with it. In Chapter 29, Jennifer Cyr and James Mahoney review the enduring contributions of historical-structural approaches and their concern with mid-level theorizing and explaining specific cases. Like rational choice, historical-structural approaches are widespread in the field, both explicitly and implicitly. Cyr and Mahoney explore the contributions of the approach to a host of issues and contemporary problems showing its significant contributions to knowledge forty years after the publication of classics such as Henrique Cardoso and Enzo Faletto's *Dependency and Development in Latin America*. Cyr and Mahoney argue that historical structural approaches have been dynamic—evolving over time as scholars have increasingly introduced a greater attention to agency and incorporated mixed-methods. As a result, it "continues to offer a powerful basis for addressing both longstanding questions and the most pressing contemporary issues." In contrast to the long tradition of historical-structural approaches in the field, Chapter 30 turns to the emergence of new methods of inquiry in recent years. Thad Dunning notes that confounding poses a vexing problem in the social sciences that neither qualitative nor conventional quantitative methods adequately solve. As a result, a sharp increase in the use of natural and field experiments has occurred, with Latin America producing some of the most interesting exemplars. Dunning provides both a review of some of the powerful contributions of experiments as well as a discussion of the kinds of questions they can answer and the limits/challenges to doing so. The various types of experiments have yielded powerful insights on a range of issues such as the impact of social policy and the effects of electoral institutions. As Dunning argues, combining strong research design with contextual knowledge holds out great promise for bolstering causal inference and informing a host of broad debates in the field. Finally, Chapter 31 considers the state of public opinion research in Latin America. Elizabeth Zeckmeister and Mitchell Seligson point out that public opinion research began with *The Civic Culture*, but then largely disappeared from the field. In recent years, renewed interest, improved data and methods, and vital questions related to the link between citizens and state/regime have led to a boom in public opinion research. Scholars are asking crucial questions about attitudes towards issues like hyperpresidentialism, partisan attachments, and satisfaction with regime performance, but that the surface has barely been scratched in our efforts to understand how citizens' views affect contemporary democracies.

Finally, Part VI offers a unique opportunity to learn what some of the leading senior scholars in the field identify as the critical issues in the field—past and present. We gave these scholars an open slate, asking them to write about where they see the field going and what they would advocate. In this section, each author offers their unique view of central contributions or puzzles facing the field—engaging with some of the core theoretical issues identified in earlier sections of the volume.

In Chapter 32, Barry Ames, Miguel Carreras, and Cassilde Schwartz observe that the study of Latin American politics has been very productive, benefiting in particular from the way democracy has facilitated research and the large increase in sophisticated Latin American researchers. Nevertheless, important gaps remain. In particular, the authors point to bureaucracy and business lobbying as two areas critical to understanding contemporary politics and political economy, but about which we have little knowledge and on which there is little active scholarship. Furthermore, they note that we have focused extensively on the workings of institutions, but not on their formation or transformation. They conclude by advocating *analytic narratives* as a promising tool for understanding the process of institutional change. Jorge Domínguez also argues that political science research on and from Latin America has been very productive. In Chapter 33, he focuses his attention on several problems (including the political economy of globalization, political regime transitions, presidentialist institutions, and voting behavior) that have led to considerable theoretical innovation that "contributed insights of value not just to those focused on Latin America but also more generally to scholars in comparative politics." As such, he calls our attention to the synergy and two-way flows between Latin America as a field of inquiry and comparative politics. In Chapter 34, Robert Kaufman points out that research on Latin America has responded to a history of tumultuous events and profound social problems. One consequence is that our efforts aim at a moving target and sometimes overreach or are premature in our efforts to explain. Nevertheless, Kaufman argues that earlier research, despite the prevalence of descriptive monographs, built a lasting foundation of knowledge that informs contemporary debates and is the base for more sophisticated research designs. In his chapter, Kaufman makes the case that the endurance of democratic regimes and the deepening of markets make conceptual and methodological tools developed for analyzing the United States appropriate. But, a fuller understanding of politics continues to benefit from its integration with rich, contextual approaches that "may require us to "think smaller and deeper"—to focus on critical cases, small-N comparisons, or intensive examinations and comparisons of sub-national regions." Adam Przeworski's Chapter 35 considers the problem of understanding the dynamics of political regimes. In his discussion, he notes that Latin American cases, contemporary and historically, challenge conceptions of democracy. Since the independence of the region, Latin America has featured a host of regimes that defy simple classification as either democracy or dictatorship. They have featured regimes in which at least some portion of the citizenry could vote and the opposition was permitted to compete, but not win. It also includes a host of regimes in which no leader was able to remain in office, regardless of selection process—in effect regimes characterized by turmoil. For Przeworski, this variation on two dimensions—suffrage and competition—calls into question many stereotyped or conventional notions of democracy and democratic quality, both within the region and in comparative perspective. Finally,

Ruth Berins Collier and Christopher Chambers-Ju close the volume with a reflection on popular representation in Latin America. The authors note the pervasiveness of the problem of popular representation and that the struggle of the lower classes for inclusion has gone on for over a century. The contemporary period of democratization and market reform has raised the issues anew across a host of issues. But, for Collier and Chambers-Ju, "these studies have generally remained ahistorical and fragmented, usefully focusing on discrete components or aspects of structures of popular representation and frequently limited to a restricted set of comparisons." In this concluding chapter, the authors lay out an agenda for analyzing popular sector representation at a macro level over time and across cases.

Drawing Lessons for Future Research

In a volume as comprehensive as this one, it is difficult to point to a single unifying lesson or theme. Indeed, the prior discussion highlights how rich and diverse the individual essays are. As such, we strongly encourage readers to engage with these readings and wrestle with the agenda-setting suggestions made at the end of each chapter. At the risk of overgeneralizing, however, we conclude this preface by highlighting three themes that strongly resonate throughout the volume.

First, while this volume focuses on Latin America, the theoretical issues raised in the following chapters strike at the core of comparative politics, a point emphasized especially in the chapter by Jorge Domínguez. Theorizing about the third wave of democratization has many of its strongest roots in studies of and about the region—including discussions of regime change, institutional design, informal institutions, emerging party systems, and the like. Moreover, Latin American has provided fertile ground for theorizing about economic growth and redistribution, policy reforms, and international financial institutions. Social movement and civil society theorizing has, moreover, learned a great deal from studies of labor, ethnicity, gender, and race. In this regard, Latin American politics and comparative politics have long been engaged in a healthy cross-fertilization—with the former informing debates in the latter; and with theories and techniques in the latter reinvigorating debates in the former. Reading this volume's chapters together highlights how central Latin America has been to theory building in the discipline as a whole. In this regard, we are thankful to the contributing authors for identifying areas for future research—areas that we think will continue to invigorate the field of Latin American politics but which will certainly reverberate in studies of comparative politics as a whole.

The key to this research, as *all* authors highlight, is attention to assessing the *comparative scope* of the questions at hand. Lisa Baldez, for example, argues for greater comparative research: "My vision for future work in this field is to make it more comparative and more gendered. Political scientists who conduct research on Latin America are also comparativists, and most of us are by now familiar with debates about the comparative method (for example, Brady and Collier 2010; King, Keohane, and Verba 1994)." Pop-Eleches, moreover, argues: "This does not obviously mean that Latin America cannot be productively be analyzed on its own terms or that it invariably needs to be imbedded in a global sample of countries but that our understanding of the region's insertion into the world economy can benefit from more explicit comparisons to the experiences of other region." As other authors highlight, the challenge is not simply to expand the cases and regional scope of our research, but it is also to pay attention to variation (including keeping track of, and paying attention to, themes that wax and wane in political salience; or that vary across cases). In this light, Hochstetler cautions against overprivileging studies of "positive" cases in the study of social movements and contentious politics.

Second, a related concern that emerges in the volume is the need to sustain a focus on core political issues, even when intellectual winds seem to shift. Theoretical debates on core issues are rarely resolved quickly. Thus, we should remain focused on these issues, even when their political salience seems to decline over time—raising the critical question of why change occurs. Otherwise stated, original research means that we need to pursue research that not only responds to the intellectual market (where the spotlight is shining at this moment) but also brings attention to issues where the spotlight might be less bright. This is not just to give a comprehensive picture of politics but, more importantly, to gain insight into change and variation. Yet, a cursory overview of the field highlights that intellectual foci has been more episodic—dependency, bureaucratic authoritarianism and corporatism in the 1970s; democratization and neoliberal reforms in the 1980s and 1990s; institutions and globalization in the 2000s; etc. These were all powerful and innovative debates and yet their salience has waxed and waned in ways that can hinder the accumulation of knowledge and the pushing of intellectual boundaries. As such, future scholarship should resist the bandwagon temptation to pursue only the most "topical" subjects of the day—a dynamic that can short circuit debates that remain unresolved or overshadow dynamics that remain salient. As both Munck and Przeworski highlight in their chapters, the study of democratization and regime change is not closed; there are new ways to pursue these questions that can shed light on unresolved debates about how we identify regimes, why and how regime change occurs, as well as why and how regimes function. So too, if attention to democratization has declined, attention to labor has dwindled, although both Maria Cook and Ruth Collier and Chris Chambers-Ju raise concerns about abandoning it since the dynamic field of work and labor continues to pose challenging research questions that merit the attention of political scientists." Indeed, Roberts highlights how our understanding of labor is critical to understanding the contemporary shape and trajectory of political parties in the region. Otherwise stated, labor movements might have declined, but class analytics are still essential to our understanding of politics the region. In a similar vein, Smith, Mares, and Andreas and Duran Martinez call on us to refocus attention on international relations of America, where there has been an apparent decline in focus. Yet, the issues facing Latin American relations are very much part of the process of global change and the lack of attention undermines empirical understanding and theoretical elaboration of critical global trends. If studies of international relations have lost momentum in recent years, scholarship on ethnicity and race has gained it. After many years of intellectual oversight, race and ethnicity has become an important field of political science inquiry in Latin America, with significant theoretical and political implications. Indeed, Lucero and Johnson highlight how much we have learned but also how much more there is to do. In light of these advances, both scholars encourage ongoing research on these critical and pressing issues.

Third, the various chapters make clear the value of *methodological pluralism*. We would go so far as to say that methodological pluralism is an imperative for the field as a whole. Different ways of seeing and different ways of knowing yield distinct and important insights about politics and political processes. No method or approach can claim to reveal the fullness of the political world. The generation of diverse insights not only enriches our analytical understanding of the world around us; but it also keeps us intellectually "honest"—forcing us to consider and evaluate the power of alternative insights and arguments—arguments that can have quite powerful and consequential policy consequences. From this perspective, no one method or approach should *a priori* dominate our intellectual horizon. Otherwise, we are likely to fall victim to the narrowness generated by the proverbial blind men who seek to understand one part of the elephant—or to recreate a version of Kurosawa's *Rashomon*. To the contrary, we need open, rigorous, and ongoing debate rather than sacred cows. As Geddes notes, while the field at one point hotly debated the salience of rational choice approaches, it is now seen as part of our intellectual toolkit, with many scholars combining insights from this approach, but not necessarily limited by it. As she states: "Currently, few studies ignore the insights provided by rational choice completely, and fewer still limit themselves to ideas from rational choice alone." Yet she also concludes that no study should presume that rational choice is necessarily the right tool to deploy in all situations. This kind of methodological pluralism is key to ongoing innovation and rigorous debate in the field.

Accordingly, a wide array of methods and approaches are self-consciously included in this volume: qualitative approaches (comparative historical, analytic narratives, interviews, ethnography, among others); quantitative analysis; original surveys; and experiments. Similarly, distinct theoretical approaches (including Marxist, Weberian, rational choice, and/or interpretivist, to name but a few) are vital to ongoing debate. These contributions however are not only interesting in their juxtaposition, but more strikingly where scholars seek to attack problems from multiple perspectives. Many authors conclude by calling on future scholarship to combine methods in ongoing comparative research. This is because the world improves through openness to employing and combining alternative ways of seeing, knowing, and evaluating—a point forcefully made by many authors, including Ames, Carreras and Schwartz; Dunning; Kaufman; Cyr and Mahoney; among others. Some of the authors in the handbook state the need for this diversity of approaches—with a special call for sustained empirical research in the field; they remind us that more sophisticated methods provide the best insight where they are combined with a deep and original knowledge of the cases. Thus, Barry Ames, Miguel Carreras, and Cassilde Schwartz make the case that insight must rest on "soaking and poking" or risk "not so much *incorrect* findings as simply *limited* findings." They express concern that narrow empiricist or excessively economic thinking have led to less research based on time and labor intensive field work—even though deep "soaking and poking" actually constituted the basis for much more rigorous quantitative work on the U.S. Congress that many young scholars emulate today. Ames et al. exemplify this call for intellectual pluralism as they make a strong argument for the explanatory power of analytic narratives built on deep knowledge of the case. Similarly, Robert Kaufman welcomes the introduction of sophisticated methods and the treatment of Latin American politics through "normal science" approaches. But, he goes on to argue that these methods "should be accompanied by a sustained skepticism about whether they can account fully for the continuities and changes we can see in Latin America's complex political landscape." Thad Dunning's chapter reviews the impressive explanatory advantages of experiments and argues that here again sophisticated methods depend on rich, textured knowledge of cases. Finally, Pop-Eleches's own research fruitfully highlights how qualitative, quantitative, and formal methods can work together to evaluate different aspects of international political economy, among other issues.

★★★★★

This handbook can be read in many ways—telescopically or panoramically. For those interested in a single theme, they can readily read individual chapters according to interest; chapters can easily be read as stand-alone essays and provide a comprehensive analysis of individual issue areas. That said, we hope that readers will take advantage of the thematic organization of the volume and the conversations that take place across them. For this volume is more than a compendium of individual essays. It provides a rich opportunity to reflect on focused debates within issue areas as well as to reflect on conversations that might readily take place across them. In this sense, this volume hopes to enhance our Hirschmanian understanding of the theoretical ground on which we all stand as well as to stimulate cutting-edge research that *trespasses* across thematic boundaries (taking insight from theoretical debates, methodological innovations, and agenda-setting comments made across the chapters). Lastly, we thank all our contributors for their incredible insight and commitment to this project. These conversations would not have been possible without the remarkable work of our colleagues, excellent research assistance of Steven Williamson, and the intellectual vision and support of our editor, Michael Kerns.

PART I

Democratic Governance and Political Institutions

1

THE ORIGINS AND DURABILITY OF DEMOCRACY[1]

Gerardo L. Munck

The option between democracy and its alternatives has been a central axis of political conflicts in Latin America since the early twentieth century. A prelude to these conflicts was the process of state formation, which occupied the center stage of political life in the wake of the attainment of independence by Latin American countries roughly 200 years ago. But, inasmuch as the process of state formation resulted in a recognized center of political power and hence a semblance of political order, the struggle between forces in favor and opposed to subjecting political power to democratic control moved to the fore.

The history of the struggle over democracy in Latin America is relatively long and varied. The most vivid manifestations of this struggle were the waves of democratization and de-democratization, that is, fluctuations toward and away from democracy, that swept the region after World War II, and that involved a long period of harsh authoritarian rule in the 1960s and 1970s and the transitions to democracy of the 1980s and 1990s. Thereafter, a new, extremely positive phase was opened. Fears of a return to authoritarianism proved to be unwarranted and democracy gradually assumed the status of a regional norm. Indeed, an unequivocal fact of Latin American political life in the twenty-first century is that never before have so many countries in the region been democratic for so long.

It would be a mistake, nonetheless, to assume that the struggle over democracy can be taken as a settled matter. Analyses of Latin American politics in the twenty-first century can legitimately address the functioning of democracy, as has been standard in the study of the established democracies in wealthy countries. But current politics in Latin America cannot be reduced to conflicts that occur entirely *within* the institutional rules of democracy, as though conflicts *about* such rules had ceased to be relevant. Rather, as keen observers of current Latin American politics insist, the struggle over democracy continues to simmer beneath the surface and occasionally erupts into overt political conflict. In other words, the history of democracy continues to unfold.

This chapter offers an overview of the scholarship that has addressed the struggle over democracy in Latin America. The first section locates the study of Latin American politics within the broader disciplinary field of comparative politics, traces the origins of a research agenda centrally concerned with political regimes and democracy in Latin America, and identifies the key characteristics of this agenda. The second and the longest section focuses on the main explanatory theories and debates about the origins and demise of democracy

3

understood as a type of political regime, discusses theoretical ideas and critiques, and summarizes the findings of empirical research. Finally, the third section turns to the frontiers of
current research on democracy in Latin America and identifies some challenges concerning
old questions tied to a minimalist definition of democracy and new questions that address
other aspects of democracy.

1. A Research Agenda on Regimes and Democracy in Latin America

Latin American politics was rarely studied in comparative politics, the academic field within
political science dedicated to the study of politics around the world, during the foundational
period of this field in the early part of the twentieth century.[2] This can be seen clearly in the
classic works on comparative politics of the 1920s and 1930s, such as James Bryce's *Modern
Democracies* (1921), Herman Finer's *Theory and Practice of Modern Government* (1932) and Carl
Friedrich's *Constitutional Government and Politics* (1937). These texts invariably focused on
the United States, the United Kingdom, France and Germany, in some cases with side-
glances to Canada and Australasia and an occasional reference to Russia. In contrast, even
in the work of Bryce, one of the few established authors who had actually traveled to South
America, the twenty countries of Latin America entered into the analysis briefly—receiving attention for twenty-one pages of a massive 1,117 page work (Bryce 1921: Vol. 1, Ch.
17)—and essentially as contrast cases, that is, as cases where the conditions for democracy
found in the better known cases were lacking (Bryce 1921: Vol. 1, 188). Before World War
II, comparative politics was a relatively parochial affair.

The status of the study of Latin American politics, and the empirical scope of comparative politics, changed considerably as a result of the new literature on modernization
and dependency in the 1950s and 1960s. The modernization literature brought in Latin
America, as well as Asia and Africa, to mainstream debates in comparative politics. And, in
an even more significant break with prior patterns, thinking about Latin America during
this period began to be shaped by authors who were based in the region—these authors
were mainly sociologists, as political science was practically nonexistent in Latin America
at the time[3]—who had a closer knowledge about Latin American politics than their U.S.
counterparts, and who offered an alternative to the perspective on Latin American politics
offered by the modernization literature.

The differences between modernization theory and its alternatives were quite notable.[4]
Much of the modernization literature on Latin America consisted of applications of the
structural-functional framework developed by Gabriel Almond (Almond and Coleman
1960) with no prior knowledge of Latin America, or analyses that uncritically assumed,
along with Seymour Lipset (1959a), a scholar who was knowledgeable about Latin America,
that economic modernization unfolded in the same way, and had the same political consequences, around the world. In contrast, Gino Germani (1962) offered a conceptualization
that drew attention to the specific model of politics that was associated with the process of
economic development undergone by Latin American societies. And dependency theorists such as Fernando Cardoso and Enzo Faletto (1969) stressed how the different location
within the international economic system of Latin American countries, compared to the
United States and Western Europe, led to a different pattern of development in Latin America and how this different pattern of development was associated with a different politics.
In short, during the 1950s and 1960s an interesting debate took place, as Latin American
authors challenged the orthodoxy of modernization theory and offered their own conceptualizations and theorizations. And this debate did much both to transform comparative

politics in the United States from a parochial affair to an enterprise of global scope and to boost the study of Latin American politics.

The real takeoff in the study of Latin American politics, which firmly established it as part of comparative politics, occurred in the 1970s however, in large part spurred by the work of the Argentine and Yale-trained political scientist Guillermo O'Donnell (1973) on the breakdown of democracy in South America. O'Donnell's work triggered a lively exchange between U.S. authors who studied Latin America and Latin American authors (Collier 1979),[5] setting an example of scholarly collaboration between North and South that transformed the way knowledge about Latin American politics was produced. Moreover, O'Donnell's work and the discussion about it was seminal in that it gave impetus to a new research agenda focused on Latin American political regimes and democracy that has been sustained over the past four decades.

This agenda of research has been wide ranging and has been fueled by the contributions of a large number of scholars. Thus, it is hard to characterize. But, as a point of entry into this research agenda, three features deserve highlighting.[6] First, this research agenda has been firmly driven by a concern with understanding Latin American politics in its own terms and has been driven in large part by the desire to make sense of the evolving turns of Latin American politics. In broad strokes, this agenda has centered on the problem of the breakdown of democracy during the 1970s, the transition to democracy in the 1980s, the consolidation of democracy in the 1990s, and the quality of democracy in the 2000s. In other words, the central motivation for this research agenda has been the desire to understand Latin American political realities and the main forms that the democratic question has assumed in the past decades.

Second, even though scholars working on this agenda have shown an ongoing concern with matters of conceptualization and engaged in conceptual debates—these matters are particularly salient in current research on the quality of democracy—they have also managed to develop considerable agreement on many basic conceptual issues. Specifically, rather than take the macro dimensions of politics as a constant and focusing only on variations within a given political regime or within democracies, as in common in much research in the field of comparative politics, these scholars share an interest in variations at a macro level related to the political regimes and the democraticness of Latin American countries. Moreover, they have largely converged on a conceptualization of political regimes in terms of the procedures regulating access to the highest political offices in a country and of democracy as, at the very least, a type of regime characterized by mass suffrage and electoral contestation (Dahl 1971; Mazzuca 2007).

Third, this agenda has placed a heavy emphasis on explanatory theories and has sought to develop theory in an avowedly cosmopolitan fashion, that is, through a dialogue with existing theories on other regions of the world, especially the United States and Europe. Indeed, in this regard, it is important to recall that the community of scholars who have contributed to this agenda have been Latin Americanists from Latin America, the United States and Europe; but also broad comparativists who have worked more on other countries (e.g., the United States in the case of Lipset; European countries in the case of Alain Touraine, Juan Linz, and Philippe Schmitter) or who have addressed Latin America within the context of broad cross-national studies (e.g., Adam Przeworski). This has been a distinctive and very positive characteristic of this literature.

In sum, important steps have been taken in the study of Latin American politics over the past forty years. A real agenda of research on political regimes and democracy, shared by a distinguished set of scholars, has taken shape. The political realities of Latin America, or at least some aspects of politics of great normative concern, have been studied in a systematic manner. And, as discussed next, a rich debate has flourished regarding how to explain the varied experience of Latin American countries with democracy and other political regimes.

2. Explanatory Theories and Debates

The main explanatory theories and debates in the literature on regimes and democracy in Latin America have focused on the two closely related yet distinct questions: (1) What are the conditions for a transition from some form of authoritarianism to democracy? and (2) What are the factors that account for the durability or endurance of democracy? And, it is important to note that real debates about these two questions have been enabled by the widely shared view that, even though the definition of democracy remains the subject of much discussion, democracy is at least a type of regime in which access to the highest political offices in a country is characterized by mass suffrage and electoral contestation. Indeed, the consensus developed about the basic concept of democracy has served the key purpose of providing the conceptual anchor for fertile debates about explanatory theories among a diverse range of authors.

It is no simple matter to offer a comprehensive evaluation of explanatory debates about democracy. Explanations vary in terms of their goal, some purporting to offer an answer to both the question of the origins and the endurance of democracy, others focusing on only one of these questions. Explanations vary in terms of their parsimony, some highlighting the impact of a single variable, while others invoke multiple variables; and in terms of their clarity, that is, whether hypotheses are specified with precision. Finally, the explanations vary in terms of extent to which they have been subject to rigorous testing. Nonetheless, this fairly wide ranging and somewhat disparate body of literature has advanced discernable lines of research and generated fruitful debates that can be summarized under five headings: (1) the economic modernization thesis, (2) the civic culture thesis, (3) theories of capitalist development and class, (4) critical juncture models, and (5) political-institutional theories.[7]

2.1. The Economic Modernization Thesis

A standard point of reference in research on regimes and democracy in Latin America has been the modernization thesis that economic development, understood as practically synonymous with an increase in a country's level of income, enhances both (1) the prospects of a transition to democracy and (2) the endurance of democracy (Lipset 1959a). Different reasons have been posited regarding why economic development was expected to have a positive effect on democracy (e.g., its impact on culture, class structure, etc.). And these reasons have been the subject of different debates, which are addressed later. To begin, however, the debate about the core claim of modernization theory—the Lipset thesis—is reviewed.

The initial discussion of the Lipset (1959a) thesis occurred in the context of the wave of breakdowns of democracy in Latin America during the 1960s and 1970s and centered on O'Donnell's (1973) direct challenge of the second part of the modernization thesis, concerning the prospects of democracy's durability. Drawing on ideas about Latin American economic development elaborated by Albert Hirschman (1968), O'Donnell posited that in settings such as South America the process of economic development had not replicated the process of the advanced economies and had led to an increased level of social conflict, and that these conflicts had been resolved in ways that undermined democracy. This modernization thesis was also questioned, in a different way, by Linz (1975: 182), who emphasized the need to understand the political dynamics of different types of political regimes and drew attention to the political process itself and the choices of political actors within institutional settings (Linz 1978; see also Valenzuela 1978). That is, while O'Donnell did not dispute the emphasis on economic determinants in modernization theory but questioned the link between economic and political development posited by modernization theory, Linz questioned the more basic premise that economic factors should be highlighted at the expense of political factors.

The first part of the modernization thesis, concerning the prospects of transitions to democracy, was the focus of discussion in the context of research on the transitions to democracy in Latin America during the 1980s and 1990s. And, again, even as some modernization theorists began to refer to a resurgence of modernization, the literature on Latin America was largely critical of the modernization thesis. Most notably, O'Donnell and Schmitter (1986: 3–5, 18–19) suggested that, even if the endurance of democracy might be strongly influenced by structural economic factors, democratic transitions are more open and contingent processes. Thus, they argued, in a way that was reminiscent of Linz's (1978) analysis of the breakdown of democracy, that the strategic choices of political and social actors can override structural pre-requisites, including those identified in the Lipset thesis (see also Przeworski 1991: Ch. 2).

In addition to being a standard point of reference in debates about regimes and democracy in Latin America, the modernization thesis has probably been the most tested hypothesis in the quantitative literature. These tests have important limitations. They have used simple economic measures as GDP per capita, which neither captures the thicker sense of economic development conveyed by some of the literature nor distinguishes among various phases of development. They are further constrained due to the limited availability of data on other variables, altogether ignoring arguments about the strategic choices made by actors and the interaction between structure and agency. Nonetheless, it is noteworthy that such tests offer some support for the critiques of the modernization thesis elaborated in studies on Latin America.

Research by Przeworski (Przeworski and Limongi 1997; Przeworski et al. 2000: Ch. 2; Przeworski 2009), which has included Latin American cases along with the rest of the world, has supported the view that higher levels of economic development are associated with a reduced risk of democratic breakdown (counter to O'Donnell 1973) but not with a greater propensity to a transition to democracy (in line with O'Donnell and Schmitter 1986, and Przeworski 1991). And research by Scott Mainwaring and Aníbal Pérez-Liñán (2003, 2005: 25–38), focused exclusively on Latin America, goes even further in undermining the modernization thesis. Indeed, Mainwaring and Pérez-Liñán's research reinforces Przeworski's finding concerning the lack of a link between economic development and democratic transitions. But they also find (in line with O'Donnell 1973) that, at least in Latin America, higher levels of economic development are associated with greater prospects of a breakdown of democracy and hence posit the possibility of Latin American exceptionalism (for a similar conclusion, see Landman 1999). The statistical research on the topic is ongoing.[8] Nonetheless, over the past four decades Lipset's thesis about the political consequences of economic modernization has been weakened by research on Latin America.[9]

2.2. The Civic Culture Thesis

Another argument about the origins and endurance of democracy that can trace its pedigree to modernization theory and, more specifically, to the civic culture literature (Almond and

Verba 1963), holds that a country is likely to become and remain a democracy inasmuch as its inhabitants display democratic attitudes, that is, support a set of values that are seen as consistent with the workings of democracy, and hence see democratic regimes as legitimate and undemocratic regimes as illegitimate. This standard cultural argument, known as the civic culture thesis, is usually linked quite explicitly to the economic modernization thesis in that modernization theorists frequently posit that cultural change is an intervening micro level variable between economic modernization and democracy. Moreover, it is similar to the economic modernization thesis in that it identifies a factor outside of the political sphere to account for both the origins and endurance of democracy. At the same time, the civic culture thesis should be distinguished from other cultural arguments in that it focuses on the attitudes of the mass public as opposed to the attitudes of social classes (a line of inquiry addressed below), the attitudes of elites, or the interactive and constructed sense of meaning and identity.

Students of regimes and democracy in Latin America are quite divided about the civic culture thesis. Many are quite skeptical about such explanations and have criticized them largely on grounds laid out by Brian Barry (1978: 48–52). Some of these skeptical scholars have placed cultural arguments in the same bag as the economic modernization thesis and seen them as overlooking the key role played by elite interactions and political institutions (O'Donnell and Schmitter 1986). In contrast, they hold that it is possible to have "democracy without democrats," and that a civic culture is "better thought of as a *product* and not a producer of democracy" (Schmitter and Karl 1991: 83; Schmitter 2009: 18).[10]

In turn, other authors have questioned the civic culture thesis as part of a broader rejection of an individual level concept of legitimacy, which is seen as failing to take note that regime change comes about only through the actions of organized political forces (Przeworski 1986: 50–53; 1991: 28, 54). Diverging from this culturalist explanation, they argue that, at least with regard to the durability of democracy, an explanation can be offered based on economic and institutional factors, and on interests in particular, and that there is no need to turn to culture (Przeworski, Cheibub and Limongi 2004; see also Przeworski 2006: 324–26).

But many scholars find the civic culture thesis theoretically appealing. Though focusing initially on Europe, Ronald Inglehart (1990) launched a defense of the civic culture thesis. And, relatedly, other highly regarded scholars and theorists of democracy declared the "centrality of political culture" and that "democracy requires a supportive culture" (Lipset 1994: 3); that democratization and the endurance of democracies hinges "largely on two factors," one of them being culture (Huntington 1997: 4–5); and that "political culture—particularly beliefs about democratic legitimacy—[is] a central factor in the consolidation of democracy" (Diamond 1999: 162).[11]

Rigorous tests of the civic culture thesis rely largely on survey data. And, both because the collection of survey data is a relatively recent development in the social sciences and because survey data is inherently suspect when collected in non-democratic contexts, cultural arguments about transitions to democracy have only been addressed indirectly. Nonetheless, this research has yielded interesting results. Part of the focus of this research has been on identifying the components of a civic culture, that is, the attitudes that are relevant to a civic culture. And, as that research has advanced, the link between civic culture and democracy has been addressed and some answers have been gaining increased credibility.

A few authors, most prominently Inglehart, have held steadfast to the view that democratization and the stability of democracy can be explained in terms of the attitudes of the mass public.[12] But a key study by Edward Muller and Mitchell Seligson (1994: 646–47), that broke with the Euro-centric nature of survey research at the time by including six Central American countries, rejected "the thesis that civic culture attitudes are the principal or even a major cause of democracy" and held instead that key civic culture attitudes, such as interpersonal trust, are "a product of democracy rather than a cause of it." Moreover, the results of Inglehart's ongoing research have been increasingly questioned.[13] Thus, even if some authors continue to argue for some sort of an updated version of the civic culture thesis, in the face of weak results other scholars who analyze culture have moved on. Indeed, the analysis by John Booth and Seligson (2009), using survey data on eight Latin American countries, takes the lack of effect of a civic culture—and hence of legitimacy—on the endurance of democracy as the starting point of research and, in a notable change of focus, sets out to "account for the puzzling absence of a legitimacy effect upon regimes" (Booth and Seligson 2009: 1, 237).

In short, even though survey researchers in particular have not given up in looking for the effects of a civic culture and searching for possible links with the stability of democracy,[14] the empirical evidence has been mainly on the side of the critics of the civic culture thesis.[15] The beliefs of the population at large about the legitimacy of democracy are not, in themselves, a key factor either in transitions to democracy or in the endurance of democracy.

2.3. Theories of Capitalist Development and Social Class

A third strand in the literature on regimes and democracy in Latin America, which has some links with the two previous lines of research, focuses on the nature of the process of economic development, traces the impact of economic development on the social structure, and then connects differences in the social structure to the prospects of attaining and retaining democracy. The core thesis in this literature, about which there is a large degree of agreement, is that a specific class of economic development, capitalist development, is associated with democracy because it fosters the strengthening of social classes that can offer a counterweight to the state and are likely to strive for political representation. In brief, capitalism is widely held to be a necessary, though not sufficient, condition of democracy. Nonetheless, there has been a debate about precisely what class configuration is more conducive to democracy.

Succinctly, regarding the class origin of democracy, the standard view of modernization theorists, advanced both in cross-regional analyses (Lipset 1959a: 83, 85) and work on Latin America (Johnson 1958), is that capitalist development fosters democracy because it creates a middle class, and the middle class is a key promoter of democracy. Moreover, modernization theorists have held that the working class is the class with the most extremist and authoritarian attitudes;[16] thus, the modernization view is that democracy requires a strong middle class and a weak working class. But other arguments have also been proposed. Though Barrington Moore (1966: Ch. 7) did not include Latin America in his analysis, his argument that capitalist development leads to democracy inasmuch as it brings about a shift in power from the landed upper class to an urban bourgeoisie became a point of discussion in the literature on the social origins of democracy in Latin America. And Dietrich Rueschemeyer, John Stephens and Evelyne Huber Stephens (1992: 40–63; see also Therborn 1977) added a new perspective to the debate with their argument that democracy depends on a shift in power from the bourgeoisie to the working class.

Theories of capitalist development and social class have not been subjected to the same degree of scrutiny through quantitative analyses as the modernization thesis about the level of economic development or the modernization argument about culture. But empirical research on Latin America does shed some light on the validity of these theories. The general thesis about the link between capitalism and democracy has received support in Touraine's (1989) study of Latin America during the 1930–80 years. Indeed, drawing on a line of analysis that can be traced to a classic of dependency theory (Cardoso and Faletto 1969), Touraine shows that even though economic development was capitalist in nature in the dependent societies of Latin America, it was not led by a domestic bourgeoisie. And, as would be expected, social classes were less independent of the state, the push to democracy was weaker, and the democracies that did emerge were better characterized as mass democracies than as representative democracies.[17]

With regard to the more specific arguments about social classes, the current picture has not yielded any overall generalization. As Peter Smith (2005: 55–62; see also Drake 2009: 10–13) summarizes a broad literature,[18] during "1900–39, democratization was adopted by traditional elites," that is, the land owning oligarchy; during "1940–77, middle classes made effective demands for democratic change"; and during 1978–2000, organized labor and the middle classes were key forces in the move toward democracy. Complicating matters further, there is evidence that the landed upper class as well as the urban bourgeoisie both supported authoritarian regimes and backed military coups regularly, that the middle class supported military coups as well, and that the working class supported authoritarian regimes.[19] Indeed, it is fair to say that none of the theories that see a single class as the key carrier of democracy or the key obstacle to democracy receives strong empirical support.

One reason for the lack of support for class theories of democracy is, as Samuel Valenzuela (2001) argues, a basic theoretical shortcoming of class analysis (see also Valenzuela and Valenzuela 1983: 27–29, 36). As Samuel Valenzuela shows, the historical record of Chile not only runs counter to Moore's claim about the anti-democratic stance of the landed elites, in that the reforms that put Chile on a democratic path early in the late nineteenth century were driven by conservative elites linked with the traditional landed interests. More importantly, as Valenzuela points out, the impetus behind these reforms was the desire of the conservative political elites to gain an advantage over liberal elites. In short, though research on Latin America supports the broad argument that capitalism is a necessary but not sufficient condition for democracy, it has not supported any generalization about specific classes and has yielded an important theoretical critique of class analyses: their failure to address the role of political elites and the possible divisions and competition among these elites.

In sum, the research on Latin America supports the general argument that capitalism is a necessary but not sufficient condition of democracy. But it has not validated the multiple hypotheses about specific classes. And it has generated an important critique of class analysis, the lack of attention to the role of political elites.

2.4. Critical Juncture Models

A fourth body of literature that theorized regimes and democracy in Latin America has relied on a critical juncture model and has presented a family of arguments that rely on a critical juncture model. One distinctive feature of these models is that they explain political developments in terms of the legacies of events that occurred many decades in the past as opposed to positing causes and effects that are close in time, as is more standard in the theories discussed previously. Another key feature is that critical juncture models, though invoking economic and social variables, usually incorporate political variables as explanatory factors quite centrally and thus propose theories of regimes and democracy that systematically recognize the autonomy of politics. Thus, though the literature on critical junctures is quite diverse, it introduces a significant break with the previous three lines of research and offers alternatives to the societal theories discussed thus far through its emphasis on historical and political explanations.

The first analysis of critical junctures in Latin America was Ruth Berins Collier and David Collier's (1991) *Shaping the Political Arena*.[20] This book argued that the breakdown of democracies in the 1960s and 1970s could be attributed to the dynamics of the party systems that was shaped by events roughly in the 1920s and 1930s, when political decisions—determined in turn by the power of the oligarchy relative to middle-class reformers—were made regarding the incorporation of labor into the national political arena. This book remains, twenty years after its publication, the best and most carefully argued analysis of critical junctures in Latin America. But this book also opened a discussion that is ongoing.

The debate within the critical juncture literature largely hinges on what key event shaped Latin America's regimes during the second half of the twentieth century and how far back one must go to find the roots of these regimes.[21] Indeed, while many authors place an emphasis on the incorporation of labor or more broadly the political response to the social question roughly during the second quarter of the twentieth century,[22] as do Collier and Collier (1991), others point to a range of earlier landmark events. For example, some authors suggest that the origins of regimes in Latin America during the twentieth century are to be found in the liberal reforms carried out in the late nineteenth century (Mahoney 2001). But others see the process of state formation during the nineteenth century as the key formative events (López-Alves 2000). And yet others posit that the prospects of democracy in twentieth century Latin America were largely shaped by the colonial experience and in particular by the Iberian culture Spain and Portugal brought to the Americas and transferred to Latin American elites (Lipset and Lakin 2004: Chs. 10 and 11).[23]

This is a rich, broad ranging and suggestive literature. But its conclusions remain unclear. On the one hand, the various arguments that have been advanced in this literature have not always been clearly linked to regime outcomes, that is, the origins and durability of democracy. On the other hand, these arguments have not been subjected to systematic empirical tests. Indeed, arguments about critical junctures have typically been developed inductively and have not been tested on new cases. Moreover, we lack tests of different arguments that rely on a critical juncture model and of critical juncture models in comparison with other standard arguments in the literature on regimes and democracy. Thus, it is important to recognize that we still cannot adjudicate among the various competing arguments and assess the validity of the theoretical challenge introduced by critical juncture models.

2.5. *Political-Institutional Theories*

The fifth and final line of research on regimes and democracy in Latin America considered here places attention squarely on the actual agents of politics, that is, the actors that engage in political activity and make political decisions, and the political institutions that are crafted by political actors and that, in turn, enable and constrain routinized political actions. This research, like the critical juncture literature, breaks with theories that see the roots of regimes and democracy solely in societal factors—a common thread in the modernization hypotheses about economic development, civic culture and class—and acknowledges the autonomy of politics. But political-institutional theories usually go further than the critical juncture literature in putting an accent on features of the political elites and the dynamics of the political sphere proper.

This line of research initially focused on the impact on democratic transition of non-democratic rulers and institutions. The most ambitious theorizing was carried out by Linz (1975; Linz and Stepan 1996: Chs. 3–4, 66–71), who developed a typology of all twentieth century regimes and hypothesized that the political dynamics of each regime affect the prospects of a transition to democracy. Relatedly, the political process models of democratic transitions developed by O'Donnell and Schmitter (1986) emphasizes that, given a certain type of non-democratic regime, democratic transitions were likely to occur only if actors made certain strategic choices, such as agreeing to a pact on some fundamental political issues. And developing this line of analysis, more focused research theorized about the prospects of democratization in the broad range of non-democratic regimes found in Latin America during the twentieth century, regimes characterized as bureaucratic authoritarian (O'Donnell 1979, 1988; Rouquié 1987: Chs. 8–9; Munck 1998), sultanistic (Chehabi and Linz 1998; Snyder 1998), dominant party (Magaloni 2006; Greene 2007) and mobilization authoritarian (Pérez-Stable 1998).

A second line of research has addressed the prospects of endurance of democracies. One hypothesis that was the subject of discussion as countries in Latin America moved to democracy in the 1980s and 1990s was that the mode of transition from authoritarian rule affected the prospects of the consolidation of democracy and that negotiated transitions were the most propitious mode of transition (Karl 1990: 8–17; Munck and Leff 1997). But more attention was given to the political institutions chosen in the course of a transition to democracy. Once more, Linz framed much of the discussion. Expanding on a point introduced in the political process model of democratic breakdowns he had formulated in the 1970s (Linz 1978: 71–74), Linz developed the thesis that presidential democracies were less likely to endure than parliamentary democracies (Linz 1994; Linz and Valenzuela 1994). And supplementing this thesis, others argued that the choice of presidentialism was especially problematic when presidentialism was associated with a fragmented, multiparty system (Mainwaring 1993; Hartlyn and Valenzuela 1994: 114).

The hypotheses in the political-institutional literature have received different degrees of support. Various tests have addressed the durability of different types of non-democratic regimes. Barbara Geddes (2003: 69–85) has shown that single-party regimes are the most durable, military regimes the least durable, with personalist regimes constituting an intermediary type. A study of the survival of individual leaders as opposed to regime durability shows that non-democratic rulers endure longer when they succeed in incorporating somewhat autonomous parties within a legislature (Gandhi and Przeworski 2007: 1290–91; Gandhi 2008: Ch. 6). And tests have also shown that the reason why single-party dominant systems endure as much as they do is because of resource asymmetry, that is, the incumbents use of public resources for partisan purposes (Greene 2010: 817–20). Thus, the overarching hypothesis that non-democratic rulers and institutions affect the prospects of democratic transitions has received some backing.

Turning to the hypotheses about the endurance of democracy, an admittedly preliminary test, using data on Europe and Latin America during the 1974–2000 period, does not offer strong support for the argument that modes of transition, and especially pacted transitions, have an impact on the consolidation of democracy (Schneider 2009: Ch. 7). But a more extensive empirical analysis, encompassing all democratic transitions in roughly 150 countries since 1900, does buttress the view that transitions through cooperative pacts are associated with the greater durability of democracy (Stradiotto 2009). In turn, as José Antonio Cheibub (2007: 2) shows, the record of all democratic regimes in the world between 1946 and 2002 confirms that presidential democracies have not lasted as long as parliamentary democracies. But, as Cheibub (2007: Ch. 6) goes on to argue, an analysis of the data also shows that this is so not because of the institutional features of presidentialism but rather because presidential democracies have emerged in countries with a higher propensity toward military intervention, a particularly Latin American phenomenon. Moreover, though minority presidents are frequent in presidential democracies, as feared by those who see presidentialism and fragmented multipartism as a particularly pernicious combination, the occurrence of minority governments has been shown to have no impact whatsoever on the survival of presidential democracies (Cheibub 2002: 294–302; 2007: 95–98).

In brief, the distinctive perspective on regimes and democracy in Latin America offered by political-institutional theories has been elaborated in a large literature. And this literature has the indisputable merit of focusing on the political sphere proper and of searching for political determinants of political outcomes. However, though the thoroughness of the empirical tests has varied considerably, these tests reveal mixed support for political-institutional theories.

3. Research Frontiers

Research on regimes and democracy in Latin America has addressed a key political issue and made important strides. It has contributed to theoretical debates, sometimes through critiques of theories developed outside the region, other times by proposing new theories. And it has contributed to the empirical testing of theories, sometimes through the study of Latin American countries by themselves, other times through the analysis of Latin American countries along with countries from other regions. Indeed, since the 1970s the research agenda on regimes and democracy in Latin America has offered a Latin American perspective—as opposed to a mere point of contrast for ideas spelled out in the context of rich societies—on mainstream discussions within comparative politics and has helped to make comparative politics a genuinely global enterprise.

At the same time, some big challenges remain to be tackled in the study of regimes and democracy in Latin America. It is critical to explicitly formulate and directly tackle these challenges. After all, a research agenda makes progress only inasmuch as it addresses the new challenges that emerge in the course of research. Thus, by way of conclusion, I present my vision about the frontiers of current research on democracy in Latin America.

A first set of challenges pertains to the old questions of the origins and the endurance of democracy, defined in minimalist terms, which have been addressed in this chapter. With regard to theorizing, further work is needed to formulate theories more clearly, both in the sense of specifying whether they seek to account for the origins and/or the endurance of democracy, and of specifying whether theories are complementary or competing. Relatedly, further work is needed to develop theories that are formulated not simply in terms of this or that variable, an approach to theorizing that is leading to the positing of an increasingly large number of potential hypotheses,[24] but that instead explicitly address how different variables form causal chains and interact.

The organization of the literature under five headings that this chapter proposes offers a point of departure for a discussion about the similarities and differences among multiple explanations that have been advanced. But, as the reader has surely noted, the theoretical status of the arguments presented under these five headings are somewhat uncertain, because they are in part alternative arguments and in part complementary arguments. Therefore, the development of clearer and stronger theories requires more work both of disaggregation and analysis as well as theoretical integration and synthesis.[25]

In turn, with regard to empirical testing, it is important to overcome several basic weaknesses of existing tests. The most rigorous tests, conducted with statistical techniques, have mirrored theories somewhat loosely, both inasmuch as they rely on data that are poor measures of the concepts used in theories and inasmuch as they have followed the convention of testing the impact of one variable at a time even when theories suggest they operate otherwise. Even more seriously, though tests have focused largely on hypotheses related to modernization theory, and increasingly on institutional arguments, we lack tests of some central hypotheses—for example, we do not have a rigorous empirical study of the class base of democracy—and we do not have tests that compare the full range of current theories—for example, no one has carried out a study comparing arguments based on the critical juncture model to the various arguments derived from modernization theory. Thus, it is important to recognize that in general terms the literature on regimes and democracy in Latin America has put greater emphasis on constructing new theories than in testing these theories and, given that theory building and theory testing are two sides of the same coin, that it is necessary to dedicate more attention to the testing of theories about the origins and durability of democracy.

A second set of challenges pertain to the study of aspects of democracy that go beyond the features used in minimalist definitions of democracy, that is, the selection of national leaders in free and fair elections. Research on democracy broadly understood, or what has been frequently referred to as the quality of democracy (O'Donnell, Vargas Cullell, and Iazzetta 2004; O'Donnell 2010), was not addressed in this chapter due to space constraints. But it is pertinent to conclude this chapter with some brief comments on the matter.

The reason for addressing issues relevant to the quality of democracy in a research agenda on democracy is that democracy is not just a matter of how high-level government offices are accessed (Munck 2007c). Politics is, at its core, a struggle over the direction of society, and democracy is thus a system in which the people have a say, through political institutions, in the decisions about who should occupy high-level government offices but also about where their societies are headed. Thus, though it is always important to highlight the value of democracy understood in minimalist terms—which, to avoid confusion, should be called electoral democracy—it is also imperative not to reduce the study of democracy to electoral democracy.

Another reason to think about democracy in broad terms is that the current political debate in Latin America has placed the issue on the agenda (Munck 2010). As mentioned previously, even though some of the most dramatic struggles in the process of democratization in Latin America occurred during the twentieth century, it would be a mistake to assume that the struggle over democracy can be taken as a settled matter. Indeed, the transformation of the democracies Latin Americans currently have into fuller democracies, that is, democracies in which political power matters and in which political power is subjected to democratic control, is emerging as the next big political challenge in the region.

Thus, along with a revisiting of old questions, anchored in a minimalist conception of democracy, research on regimes and democracy in Latin America should also address other aspects of democracy, which open up a whole set of new questions that call for conceptual, theoretical and empirical work. In other words, continuing a tradition that has come to characterize research on Latin American politics, researchers interested in current Latin American politics should seek to understand the democratic question in the twenty-first century and to produce knowledge that in some measure contributes to the new challenge of democratizing democracy.

Notes

1 I thank Mariano Bertucci, Sebastián Mazzuca, Richard Snyder and Deborah Yashar for many useful suggestions.

2 For overviews of the field of comparative politics, see Eckstein (1963) and Munck (2007a); on the study of Latin American politics, see Valenzuela (1988) and Drake and Hilbink (2003).

3 On the late institutionalization of political science in Latin America, see Altman (2006) and Huneeus (2006).

4 For an overview of the modernization and dependency literature on Latin America, see Valenzuela and Valenzuela (1978).

5 On the importance of this book by O'Donnell and the decisive character of the debate it generated, see Touraine (1987: 4–12).

6 For a more detailed characterization of this research agenda, see Munck (2007b: 1–14).

7 These lines of research are not unrelated to each other, and scholars working on one line of research frequently borrow from other lines of research. However, as the following discussion seeks to show, it is useful to organize a review of the literature under these five headings.

8 See, especially, Boix and Stokes (2003) and Acemoglu et al. (2008).

9 Another strand of this debate has been the discussion about resource curses in Latin America, which is relevant to the modernization thesis because it focuses not just on an aggregate level of economic development but on the composition of economic activities and the sectors of the economy that gain prominence (Karl 1997; Dunning 2008). This literature articulates the political consequence of economic factors in a more direct fashion than is standard in modernization theory and offers a bridge with the literature on capitalist development discussed below.

10 This line of analysis is similar to Lijphart's (1968), who argued, against Almond (1956), that democracy was possible in culturally divided societies, like the Netherlands, if political elites could agree on certain political institutions.

11 Linz and Stepan (1996: 6) take a step further and argue that, by definition, a democracy is not consolidated unless "a strong majority of public opinion holds the belief that democratic procedures and institutions are the most appropriate way to govern collective life in a society."

12 Indeed, Inglehart (1990) argued early on that civic culture attitudes increase the likelihood that democracy will endure and has continued to subscribe to a strong culturalist explanation of both the origins and endurance of democracy (Inglehart and Welzel 2005: 9, Ch. 8).

13 For critiques of Inglehart's recent work, see Hadenius and Teorell (2005), Teorell and Hadenius (2006), Booth and Seligson (2009: 11), and Fails and Pierce (2010).

14 After carefully disentangling what they mean by legitimacy and proposing a multidimensional measure of legitimacy, Booth and Seligson (2009) consider the impact of legitimacy on citizen attitudes and behaviors. Though they do not focus on actual events directly associated with the breakdown of democracy, they make a case that a lack of legitimacy could provide fertile ground for elites to undermine democracy and, interestingly, suggest that, on the basis of the analysis of the eight countries they studied using 2004 data, they are most concerned about the prospects of democracy surviving in Honduras—Guatemala is also singled out (Booth and Seligson 2009: 150, 220, 241–57). Given that Booth and Seligson's book was published in February 2009 and that the elected President Zelaya of Honduras was displaced from power in June 2009, there may well be something to their argument about the importance of the beliefs of the mass public.

15 A related literature has focused on religion. For example, Lipset (1959a: 65, 92–93) argued that while Protestantism is conducive to the development of democratic values, Catholicism does not have a similar effect. However, an admittedly preliminary test, based on a simple distinction between Protestant, Catholic and Muslim countries, finds no impact of the culture thus understood on either the likelihood of a transition to democracy or the endurance of democracy (Przeworski, Cheibub and Limongi 2004). For further empirical evidence against cultural theories, see Valenzuela and Valenzuela (1983: 15–22).

16 Much of the modernization literature on the class basis of democracy is linked with a culturalist theory. For example, Lipset (1959a: 83, 89, 1959b: 482) held that the strengthening of a middle class was conducive to democracy because members of the middle class held a moderate political outlook that counteracted the extremist and authoritarian values of the working class.

17 For an updating of this line of analysis, see Garretón et al. (2003).

18 See Therborn (1979), Rueschemeyer, Stephens and Stephens (1992), Huber and Safford (1995), Drake (1996), and Collier (1999).
19 See Nun (1967), O'Donnell (1978), Baloyra-Herp (1983), Bartell and Payne (1995), Paige (1997), Middlebrook (2000), and Levitsky and Mainwaring (2006).
20 Though the broader literature on critical juncture in comparative politics was largely initiated by Lipset and Rokkan (1967), Collier and Collier's (1991: Ch. 1) explicit formalization of this kind of explanation also helped spur a larger discussion about the critical juncture model.
21 Another question that has been discussed recently is whether the neoliberal reforms implemented in Latin America during the 1980s and 1990s constitute a new critical juncture See, among others, Collier and Handlin (2009) and Tanaka (2009).
22 Mouzelis (1986), Waisman (1987), Scully (1992), Yashar (1997), Munck (2002).
23 See also Morse (1964), Véliz (1980), and Wiarda (2001).
24 The problem of theorizing that leads to a quite unwieldy list of independent variables and hypotheses is illustrated by Diamond, Hartlyn and Linz (1999).
25 For attempts at synthesis, see Mahoney and Snyder (1999) and Mazzuca (2010).

Bibliography

Acemoglu, Daron, Simon Johnson, James A. Robinson and Pierre Yared. 2008. "Income and Democracy," *American Economic Review* Vol. 98, No. 3: 808–42.
Almond, Gabriel A. 1956. "Comparative Political Systems," *Journal of Politics* Vol. 18, No. 3: 391–409.
Almond, Gabriel and James Coleman (eds.). 1960. *The Politics of the Developing Areas* (Princeton, N.J.: Princeton University Press).
Almond, Gabriel and Sidney Verba (eds.). 1963. *The Civic Culture: Political Attitudes and Democracy in Five Nations* (Princeton, N.J.: Princeton University Press).
Altman, David. 2006. "From Fukuoka to Santiago: Institutionalization of Political Science in Latin America," *PS: Political Science & Politics* Vol. 39, No. 1: 196–203.
Baloyra-Herp, Enrique A. 1983. "Reactionary Despotism in Central America," *Journal of Latin American Studies* Vol. 15, No. 2: 295–319.
Barry, Brian. 1978. *Sociologists, Economists and Democracy* (Chicago: University of Chicago Press).
Bartell, Ernest and Leigh A. Payne (eds.). 1995. *Business and Democracy in Latin America* (Pittsburgh, Pa.: University of Pittsburgh Press).
Boix, Carles and Susan C. Stokes. 2003. "Endogenous Democratization," *World Politics* Vol. 55, No. 4: 517–49.
Booth, John A. and Mitchell A. Seligson. 2009. *The Legitimacy Puzzle in Latin America: Democracy and Political Support in Eight Nations* (New York: Cambridge University Press).
Bryce, James. 1921. *Modern Democracies* 2 Volumes (New York: The Macmillan Company).
Cardoso, Fernando H. and Enzo Faletto. 1969. *Dependencia y desarrollo en América Latina* (México: Siglo XXI). [An English version was published as: *Dependency and Development in Latin America* (Berkeley: University of California Press, 1979).]
Chehabi, H. E. and Juan L. Linz (eds.). 1998. *Sultanistic Regimes* (Baltimore, Md.: The Johns Hopkins University Press).
Cheibub, José Antonio. 2002. "Minority Governments, Deadlock Situations, and the Survival of Presidential Democracies," *Comparative Political Studies* Vol. 35, No. 3: 284–312.
Cheibub, José Antonio. 2007. *Presidentialism, Parliamentarism, and Democracy* (New York: Cambridge University Press).
Collier, David (ed.). 1979. *The New Authoritarianism in Latin America* (Princeton, N.J.: Princeton University Press).
Collier, Ruth Berins. 1999. *Paths Toward Democracy: Working Class and Elites in Western Europe and South America* (New York: Cambridge University Press).
Collier, Ruth Berins and David Collier. 1991. *Shaping the Political Arena: Critical Junctures, the Labor Movement, and the Regime Dynamics in Latin America* (Princeton: N.J.: Princeton University Press).
Collier, Ruth Berins and Samuel Handlin (eds.). 2009. *Reorganizing Popular Politics: Participation and the New Interest Regime in Latin America* (University Park, Pa.: Pennsylvania State University Press).
Dahl, Robert A. 1971. *Polyarchy* (New Haven, Conn.: Yale University Press).
Diamond, Larry. 1999. *Developing Democracy: Toward Consolidation* (Baltimore, Md.: Johns Hopkins University Press).

Diamond, Larry, Jonathan Hartlyn, and Juan J. Linz. 1999. "Introduction: Politics, Society, and Democracy in Latin America," pp. 1–70, in Larry Diamond, Jonathan Hartlyn, Juan J. Linz, and Seymour Martin Lipset (eds.), *Democracy in Developing Countries: Latin America* (Boulder, Colo.: Lynne Rienner, 2nd edition).

Drake, Paul W. 1996. *Labor Movements and Dictatorships: The Southern Cone in Comparative Perspective* (Baltimore, Md.: John Hopkins University Press).

Drake, Paul. 2009. *Between Tyranny and Anarchy: A History of Democracy in Latin America, 1800–2006* (Stanford, Calif.: Stanford University Press).

Drake, Paul and Lisa Hilbink. 2003. "Latin American Studies: Theory and Practice," in David L. Szanton (ed.), *The Politics of Knowledge: Area Studies and the Disciplines.* University of California Press/University of California International and Area Studies Digital Collection, Edited Volume #3, 2003. http://repositories.cdlib.org/uciaspubs/editedvolumes/3/2

Dunning, Thad. 2008. *Crude Democracy: Natural Resource Wealth and Political Regimes* (New York: Cambridge University Press).

Eckstein, Harry. 1963. "A Perspective on Comparative Politics, Past and Present," pp. 3–32, in Harry Eckstein and David Apter (eds.), *Comparative Politics* (New York: Free Press).

Fails, Matthew D. and Heather Nicole Pierce. 2010. "Changing Mass Attitudes and Democratic Deepening," *Political Research Quarterly* Vol. 63, No. 1: 174–87.

Finer, Herman. 1932. *The Theory and Practice of Modern Government* 2 Volumes (London: Methuen).

Friedrich, Carl J. 1937. *Constitutional Government and Politics: Nature and Development* (New York: Harper).

Gandhi, Jennifer. 2008. *Political Institutions under Dictatorship* (New York: Cambridge University Press).

Gandhi, Jennifer and Adam Przeworski. 2007. "Authoritarian Institutions and the Survival of Autocrats," *Comparative Political Studies* Vol. 40, No. 11: 1279–1301.

Geddes, Barbara. 2003. *Paradigms and Sand Castles: Theory Building and Research Design in Comparative Politics* (Ann Arbor, Mich: University of Michigan Press).

Garretón, Manuel Antonio, Marcelo Cavarozzi, Peter S. Cleaves, Gary Gereffi and Jonathan Hartlyn. 2003. *Latin America in the Twenty-First Century: Toward a New Sociopolitical Matrix* (Boulder, Colo.: Lynne Rienner).

Germani, Gino. 1962. *Política y sociedad en una epoca de transición* (Buenos Aires: Paidós).

Greene, Kenneth F. 2007. *Why Dominant Parties Lose: Mexico's Democratization in Comparative Perspective* (New York: Cambridge University Press).

Greene, Kenneth F. 2010. "The Political Economy of Authoritarian Single-Party Dominance," *Comparative Political Studies* Vol. 43, No. 7: 807–34.

Hadenius, Axel and Jan Teorell. 2005. "Cultural and Economic Prerequisites of Democracy: Reassessing Recent Evidence," *Studies in Comparative International Development* Vol. 39, No. 4: 87–106.

Hartlyn, Jonathan and Arturo Valenzuela. 1994. "Democracy in Latin America since 1930," pp. 99–162, 610–622, in Leslie Bethell (ed.), *The Cambridge History of Latin America* Vol. VI. *Latin America since 1930* Part 2. *Politics and Society* (New York: Cambridge University Press).

Hirschman, Albert O. 1968. "The Political Economy of Import-Substituting Industrialization in Latin America," *Quarterly Journal of Economics* Vol. 82, No. 1: 1–32.

Huber, Evelyne and Frank Safford (eds.). 1995. *Agrarian Structure and Political Power. Landlord and Peasant in the Making of Latin America* (Pittsburgh, Pa.: University of Pittsburgh Press).

Huneeus, Carlos. 2006. "El lento y tardío desarrollo de la ciencia política en América Latina, 1966–2006," *Estudios Internacionales* No. 155: 137–56.

Huntington, Samuel P. 1997. "After Twenty Years: The Future of the Third Wave," *Journal of Democracy* Vol. 8, No. 4: 3–12.

Inglehart, Ronald. 1990. *Culture Shift in Advanced Industrial Society* (Princeton, N.J.: Princeton University Press).

Inglehart, Ronald and Christian Welzel. 2005. *Modernization, Cultural Change, and Democracy* (New York: Cambridge University Press).

Inglehart, Ronald F. and Christian Welzel. 2007. "Modernization," pp. 3071–78, in George Ritzer (ed.), *Blackwell Encyclopedia of Sociology* (New York: Blackwell).

Johnson, John J. 1958. *Political Change in Latin America: The Emergence of the Middle Sectors* (Stanford, Calif.: Stanford University Press).

Karl, Terry Lynn. 1990. "Dilemmas of Democratization in Latin America," *Comparative Politics* Vol. 23, No. 1: 1–21.

Karl, Terry Lynn. 1997. *The Paradox of Plenty: Oil Booms and Petro-States* (Berkeley, Calif.: University of California Press).

Landman, Todd. 1999. "Economic Development and Democracy: The View from Latin America," *Political Studies* Vol. 47, No. 1: 607–26.

Levitsky, Steven and Scott Mainwaring. 2006. "Organized Labor and Democracy in Latin America," *Comparative Politics* Vol. 39, No. 1 (October): 21–42.

Lijphart, Arend. 1968. *The Politics of Accommodation: Pluralism and Democracy in the Netherlands* (Berkeley, Calif.: University of California Press).

Linz, Juan J. 1975. "Totalitarianism and Authoritarian Regimes," pp. 175–411, in Fred Greenstein and Nelson Polsby (eds.), *Handbook of Political Science* Vol. 3, *Macropolitical Theory* (Reading, Mass.: Addison-Wesley Press).

Linz, Juan J. 1978. *The Breakdown of Democratic Regimes. Crisis, Breakdown, and Reequilibriation* (Baltimore, Md.: The Johns Hopkins University Press).

Linz, Juan J. 1994. "Presidential or Parliamentary Democracy: Does it Make a Difference?" pp. 3–87, in Juan J. Linz and Arturo Valenzuela (eds.), *The Failure of Presidential Democracy*. Volume 1. *Comparative Perspectives* (Baltimore, Md.: The Johns Hopkins University Press).

Linz, Juan J. and Alfred Stepan. 1996. *Problems of Democratic Transition and Consolidation: Southern Europe, South America and Post-Communist Europe* (Baltimore, Md.: The Johns Hopkins University Press).

Linz, Juan J. and Arturo Valenzuela (eds.). 1994. *The Failure of Presidential Democracy Volume 2. The Case of Latin America* (Baltimore, Md.: The Johns Hopkins University Press).

Lipset, Seymour Martin. 1959a. "Some Social Requisites of Democracy: Economic Development and Political Legitimacy," *American Political Science Review* Vol. 53, No. 1: 69–105.

Lipset, Seymour Martin. 1959b. "Democracy and Working-Class Authoritarianism," *American Sociological Review* Vol. 24, No. 4: 482–501.

Lipset, Seymour Martin. 1994. "The Social Requisites of Democracy Revisited," *American Sociological Review* Vol. 59, No. 1: 1–22.

Lipset, Seymour Martin and Jason M. Lakin. 2004. *The Democratic Century* (Norman, Okla.: University of Oklahoma Press).

Lipset, Seymour Martin and Stein Rokkan. 1967. "Cleavage Structures, Party Systems, and Voter Alignments: An Introduction," pp. 1–64, in Seymour M. Lipset and Stein Rokkan (eds.), *Party Systems and Voter Alignments: Cross-National Perspectives* (New York: Free Press).

López-Alves, Fernando. 2000. *State Formation and Democracy in Latin America, 1810-1900* (Durham, N.C.: Duke University Press).

Magaloni, Beatriz. 2006. *Voting for Autocracy: Hegemonic Party Survival and its Demise in Mexico* (New York: Cambridge University Press).

Mahoney, James. 2001. *The Legacies of Liberalism: Path Dependence and Political Regimes in Central America* (Baltimore, Md.: The Johns Hopkins University Press).

Mahoney, James and Richard Snyder. 1999. "Rethinking Agency and Structure in the Study of Regime Change," *Studies in Comparative International Development* Vol. 34, No. 2: 3–32.

Mainwaring, Scott. 1993. "Presidentialism, Multipartism, and Democracy: The Difficult Combination," *Comparative Political Studies* Vol. 26, No. 2: 198–228.

Mainwaring, Scott and Aníbal Pérez-Liñán. 2003. "Level of Development and Democracy: Latin American Exceptionalism, 1945–1996," *Comparative Political Studies* Vol. 36, No. 9: 1031–67.

Mainwaring, Scott and Aníbal Pérez-Liñán. 2005. "Latin American Democratization since 1978: Democratic Transitions, Breakdowns, and Erosions," pp. 14–59, in Frances Hagopian and Scott P. Mainwaring (eds.), *The Third Wave of Democratization in Latin America. Advances and Setbacks* (New York: Cambridge University Press).

Mazzuca, Sebastián L. 2007. "Reconceptualizing Democratization: Access to Power versus Exercise of Power," pp. 39–49, in Gerardo L. Munck (ed.), *Regimes and Democracy in Latin America. Theories and Methods* (Oxford: Oxford University Press).

Mazzuca, Sebastián L. 2010. "Macro-foundations of Regime Change: Democracy, State Formation, and Capitalist Development," *Comparative Politics* Vol. 43, No. 1: 1–19.

Middlebrook, Kevin J. (ed.). 2000. *Conservative Parties, the Right, and Democracy in Latin America* (Baltimore, Md.: Johns Hopkins University Press).

Moore, Jr., Barrington. 1966. *Social Origins of Dictatorship and Democracy. Lord and Peasant in the Making of the Modern World* (Boston: Beacon Press).

Morse, Richard M. 1964. "The Heritage of Latin America," pp. 123–77, in Louis Hartz (ed.), *The Founding of New Societies* (New York: Harcourt, Brace & World).

Mouzelis, Nicos P. 1986. *Politics in the Semi-periphery: Early Parliamentarism and Late Industrialization in the Balkans and Latin America* (London: Macmillan).

Muller, Edward N. and Mitchell Seligson. 1994. "Civic Culture and Democracy: The Question of the Causal Relationships," *American Political Science Review* Vol. 88, No. 3: 635–52.

Munck, Gerardo L. 1998. *Authoritarianism and Democratization. Soldiers and Workers in Argentina, 1976–83* (University Park, Pa.: Pennsylvania State University Press).

Munck, Gerardo L. 2002. "La transición a la política de masas en América Latina," *Araucaria. Revista Iberoamericana de Filosofía, Política y Humanidades* Vol. 3, No. 7: 95–132.

Munck, Gerardo L. 2007a. "The Past and Present of Comparative Politics," pp. 32–59, in Gerardo L. Munck and Richard Snyder, *Passion, Craft, and Method in Comparative Politics* (Baltimore, Md.: The Johns Hopkins University Press).

Munck, Gerardo L. 2007b. "Introduction: Research Agendas and Strategies in the Study of Latin American Politics," pp. 1–21, in Gerardo L. Munck (ed.), *Regimes and Democracy in Latin America. Theories and Methods* (Oxford: Oxford University Press).

Munck, Gerardo L. 2007c. "The Study of Politics and Democracy: Touchstones of a Research Agenda," pp. 25–37, in Gerardo L. Munck (ed.), *Regimes and Democracy in Latin America. Theories and Methods* (Oxford: Oxford University Press).

Munck, Gerardo L. 2010. "Repensando la cuestión democrática: La región Andina en el nuevo siglo," *Revista de Ciencia Política* Vol. 30, No. 1: 149–61.

Munck, Gerardo L. and Carol Leff. 1997. "Modes of Transition and Democratization. South America and Eastern Europe in Comparative Perspective," *Comparative Politics* Vol. 29, No. 3: 343–62.

Nun, José. 1967. "The Middle-Class Military Coup," pp. 66–118, in Claudio Véliz (ed.), *The Politics of Conformity in Latin America* (London: Oxford University Press).

O'Donnell, Guillermo. 1973. *Modernization and Bureaucratic-Authoritarianism: Studies in South American Politics* (Berkeley, Calif.: Institute of International Studies/University of California).

O'Donnell, Guillermo. 1978. "State and Alliances in Argentina, 1956–1976," *Journal of Development Studies* Vol. 15, No. 1: 3–33.

O'Donnell, Guillermo. 1979. "Tensions in the Bureaucratic-Authoritarian State and the Question of Democracy," pp. 285–318, in David Collier (ed.), *The New Authoritarianism in Latin America* (Princeton, N.J.: Princeton University Press).

O'Donnell, Guillermo. 1988. *Bureaucratic Authoritarianism. Argentina, 1966–1973, in Comparative Perspective* (Berkeley, Calif.: University of California Press).

O'Donnell, Guillermo. 2010. *Democracy, Agency, and the State: Theory with Comparative Intent* (Oxford: Oxford University Press).

O'Donnell, Guillermo and Philippe Schmitter. 1986. *Transitions From Authoritarian Rule. Tentative Conclusions about Uncertain Democracies* (Baltimore, Md.: The Johns Hopkins University Press).

O'Donnell, Guillermo, Jorge Vargas Cullell and Osvaldo Iazzetta (eds.). 2004. *The Quality of Democracy. Theory and Applications* (Notre Dame, Ind.: University of Notre Dame Press).

Paige, Jeffery M. 1997. *Coffee and Power: Revolution and the Rise of Democracy in Central America* (Cambridge, Mass.: Harvard University Press).

Pérez-Stable, Marifeli. 1998. *The Cuban Revolution: Origins, Course, and Legacy* (Oxford: Oxford University Press, 2nd edition).

Przeworski, Adam. 1986. "Some Problems in the Study of the Transition to Democracy," pp. 47–63, in Guillermo O'Donnell, Philippe Schmitter and Laurence Whitehead (eds.), *Transitions from Authoritarian Rule. Comparative Perspectives* (Baltimore, Md.: The Johns Hopkins University Press).

Przeworski, Adam. 1991. *Democracy and the Market. Political and Economic Reforms in Eastern Europe and Latin America* (New York: Cambridge University Press).

Przeworski, Adam. 2006. "Self-enforcing Democracy," pp. 312–28, in Barry R. Weingast and Donald Wittman (eds.), *Oxford Handbook of Political Economy* (New York: Oxford University Press).

Przeworski, Adam. 2009. "The Mechanics of Regime Instability in Latin America," *Journal of Politics in Latin America* Vol. 1: 5–36.

Przeworski, Adam, Michael E. Alvarez, José Antonio Cheibub and Fernando Limongi. 2000. *Democracy and Development: Political Institutions and Well-Being in the World, 1950–1990* (New York: Cambridge University Press).

Przeworski, Adam, José Antônio Cheibub and Fernando Limongi. 2004. "Democracia y Cultura Política," *Metapolítica*, Vol. 8, No. 33: 52–69.

Przeworski, Adam and Fernando Limongi. 1997. "Modernization: Theories and Facts," *World Politics* Vol. 49, No. 2: 155–83.

Rouquié, Alain. 1987. *The Military and the State in Latin America* (Berkeley, Calif.: University of California Press).

Rueschemeyer, Dietrich, John D. Stephens and Evelyne Huber Stephens. 1992. *Capitalist Development and Democracy* (Chicago: University of Chicago Press).

Schmitter, Philippe C. 2009. "Twenty-five Years, Fifteen Findings," *Journal of Democracy* Vol. 21, No. 1: 17–28.

Schmitter, Philippe and Terry Karl. 1991. "What Democracy is ... and What it is Not," *Journal of Democracy* Vol. 2, No. 3: 75–88.

Schneider, Carsten Q. 2009. *The Consolidation of Democracy: Comparing Europe and Latin America* (London: Routledge).

Scully, Timothy R. 1992. *Rethinking the Center. Party Politics in Nineteenth- and Twentieth-Century Chile* (Stanford, Calif.: Stanford University Press).

Smith, Peter H. 2005. *Democracy in Latin America: Political Change in Comparative Perspective* (New York: Oxford University Press).

Snyder, Richard. 1998. "Paths out of Sultanistic Regimes: Combining Structural and Voluntarist Perspectives," pp. 49-81, 244-55, in H. E. Chehabi and Juan J. Linz (eds.), *Sultanistic Regimes* (Baltimore, Md.: Johns Hopkins University Press).

Stradiotto, Gary A. 2009. "The Democratic Revolution," unpublished Ph.D. dissertation, Department of Political Science, University of California, Davis.

Tanaka, Martin (ed.). 2009. *La nueva conyuntura crítica en los países andinos* (Lima: IEP and International IDEA).

Teorell, Jan and Axel Hadenius. 2006. "Democracy without Democratic Values: A Rejoinder to Welzel and Inglehart," *Studies in Comparative International Development* Vol. 41, No. 3: 96-111.

Therborn, Göran. 1977. "The Rule of Capital and the Rise of Democracy," *New Left Review* No. 103: 3–41.

Therborn, Göran. 1979. "The Travails of Latin American Democracy," *New Left Review* No. 113/114: 71–109.

Touraine, Alain. 1987. *Actores sociales y sistemas políticos en América Latina* (Santiago de Chile: PREALC/OIT).

Touraine, Alain. 1989. *América Latina: Política y sociedad* (Madrid: Espasa-Calpe).

Valenzuela, Arturo. 1978. *The Breakdown of Democratic Regimes: Chile* (Baltimore, Md.: The Johns Hopkins University Press).

Valenzuela, Arturo. 1988. "Political Science and the Study of Latin America," pp. 63–86, in Christopher Mitchell (ed.), *Changing Perspectives in Latin American Studies* (Stanford, Calif.: Stanford University Press).

Valenzuela, Arturo and Samuel Valenzuela. 1983. "Los orígenes de la democracia: Reflexiones teóricas sobre el caso de Chile," *Estudios Públicos* No. 12: 3–39.

Valenzuela, J. Samuel. 2001. "Class Relations and Democratization: A Reassessment of Barrington Moore's Model," pp. 240–86, in Miguel Angel Centeno and Fernando López-Alves (eds.), *The Other Mirror: Grand Theory Through the Lens of Latin America* (Princeton, N.J.: Princeton University Press).

Valenzuela, J. Samuel and Arturo Valenzuela. 1978. "Modernization and Dependency: Alternative Perspectives in the Study of Latin American Development," *Comparative Politics* Vol. 10, No. 4: 535–52.

Véliz, Claudio. 1980. *The Centralist Tradition of Latin America* (Princeton, N.J.: Princeton University Press).

Waisman, Carlos H. 1987. *Reversal of Development in Argentina. Postwar Counterrevolutionary Policies and Their Structural Consequences* (Princeton, N.J.: Princeton University Press).

Wiarda, Howard J. 2001. *The Soul of Latin America: The Cultural and Political Tradition* (New Haven, Conn.: Yale University Press).

Yashar, Deborah. 1997. *Demanding Democracy: Reform and Reaction in Costa Rica and Guatemala, 1870s–1950s* (Stanford, Calif.: Stanford University Press).

2

PRESIDENTIALISM AND LEGISLATURES

Mark P. Jones

One of the defining characteristics of Latin American politics is the prevalence of the presidential form of government in the region. This chapter provides an overview of the functioning of presidentialism and of the legislatures in Latin America. First, it identifies those countries where the presidential regime type is present. Second, it discusses the relationship between presidentialism and democracy in the region. Third, it explores the basic dynamics of the presidential election process. Fourth, it details the basic dynamics of the legislative election process within these presidential systems. Fifth, it examines executive-legislative relations in Latin America's presidential democracies from both a constitutional and partisan perspective.

Presidentialism in Latin America

In his seminal work on democracy, Arend Lijphart provides a simple yet effective set of criteria for distinguishing between the world's two most common democratic regime types (presidential and parliamentary) based on whether or not the executive is dependent upon the confidence of the legislature, and whether or not the executive is collegial or unipersonal.[1] Based on these criteria, we can identify 18 pure presidential democracies in the region: Argentina, Bolivia, Brazil, Chile, Colombia, Costa Rica, Dominican Republic, Ecuador, El Salvador, Guatemala, Honduras, Mexico, Nicaragua, Panama, Paraguay, Peru, Uruguay, and Venezuela. Following Lijphart's binary coding of the French case, the Haitian semi-presidential regime type can also be included in this presidential category. It is upon these nineteen presidential democracies that this chapter will focus.

With two exceptions, all of the remaining democracies in the region employ a parliamentary form of government: Jamaica, Trinidad & Tobago, and a host (nine total) of microstates with populations ranging from 40,000 to 308,000. The two exceptions are Guyana and Suriname, which represent hybrid regime types that in form and practice do not fall as neatly into either the category of presidential or of parliamentary. Cuba, the Western Hemisphere's sole remaining dictatorship, remains outside the scope of this analysis.

As will be discussed in greater detail below, there exists considerable variance in the constitutional and electoral rules which shape politics in the nineteen presidential democracies. There also, however, is a wide range of variance in which the country's constitutional and statutory environment constrain and influence the behavior of political actors, with *de jure* factors notably more relevant for understanding politics in Latin America's most consolidated and successful democracies (e.g., Chile, Costa Rica, Uruguay, Panama, Brazil) than in its least consolidated and more flawed democracies (e.g., Guatemala, Honduras, Nicaragua, Haiti, Venezuela).[2]

Presidentialism and Democracy in Latin America

At the dawn of the third wave of democratization in the early-1980s, with a majority of Latin America's historically presidential systems transitioning from a dictatorial to democratic regime, scholars concerned with the future of democracy in Latin America began to place the region's presidential regime type under scrutiny, questioning if perhaps presidentialism was at least in part responsible for the region's rather dismal democratic track record. It is important to recall that during the 1960s and 1970s numerous democratic regimes (e.g., Argentina, Brazil, Chile, Peru, Uruguay) were replaced by authoritarian dictatorships, reaching the nadir of only three (out of the nineteen countries discussed here) democracies in the region in 1977 (Colombia, Costa Rica, Venezuela).

This scrutiny resulted in a seminal edited volume by Juan Linz and Arturo Valenzuela, anchored by a chapter by Linz (which had been circulating in different forms for a decade).[3] Based on a well-crafted argument grounded both in theory and empirical evidence, Linz concluded that while Latin America's democracies had in the past failed for many reasons, it was reasonable to conclude that the region's use of the presidential form of government had very likely been a contributing factor to democratic breakdown in a notable number of instances.[4]

The most authoritative response to the position of Linz and Valenzuela that presidentialism was in part responsible for Latin America's spotty democratic history, and to the implicit assumption that a parliamentary regime type would have been better for the health of Latin American democracy, came from Scott Mainwaring and Matthew Shugart.[5] After a thorough theoretical discussion and review of the empirical evidence, Mainwaring and Shugart concluded by agreeing with Linz and Valenzuela that Latin American democracies have performed poorly, but disagreeing with the conclusion that presidentialism (as opposed to parliamentarism) was a major contributing factor to the downfall of the region's democracies. At the same time however, Mainwaring and Shugart made the extremely important point that the presidential regime type is not a homogenous one, and that factors such as a president's constitutional and partisan powers could have a profound effect on the functioning of a presidential democracy, concurring with Linz that some facets of presidentialism were detrimental to the well-being of a country's democracy.[6]

By the early 2000s, all nineteen Latin American presidential democracies (with the exception, depending on the year, of Haiti) were considered to meet the minimal criteria needed to be classified as electoral democracies, with Chile (1989), Mexico (1991/1994), and Paraguay (1993) being the last to join the ranks of the electoral democracies in the region. Furthermore, the 1990s and 2000s witnessed no democratic governments overthrown by military or military-supported coups with the sole exception of the case of Peru in 1992 when democratically elected president Alberto Fujimori staged a self-coup (*autogolpe*).[7] In sum, Linz's fear that the third wave Latin American democracies would fail due to their use of presidentialism appears today to have been unfounded.

However, while Latin America's democratic regimes did not break down during the past twenty years, over one dozen democratically elected presidents were forced from office during this period of regime stability. Often the vehicle by which presidents were removed from office was through the route of impeachment or through a credible threat of impeachment resulting in an anticipated resignation by the president. Aníbal Pérez-Liñán has aptly referred to this dynamic as "stable presidentialism with unstable presidents."[8] While Pérez-Liñán highlights the positive role of the impeachment process in avoiding the types of conflicts which in the past often resulted in military intervention, he at the same time underscores the traumatic and extraordinary nature of impeachment as a tool for the removal of an unpopular and/or ineffective president from power.[9]

Central to the new focus of scholars concerned with presidential democracy in Latin America over the past dozen years have been those factors which affect presidential-legislative relations, in particular those which result in gridlock and conflict between the two branches as well as in simply inefficient/sub-optimal policymaking.[10] Present concerns with the presidential regime type thus now lie much less with its relationship to democratic breakdown than with the greater possibility (compared to parliamentarism) of serious executive-legislative conflict that either results in the anticipated departure of the president from office[11] or deficient policymaking.[12]

Presidential Elections

All Latin American presidents are directly elected, with Argentina (in 1989) being the last county to indirectly elect its president via an electoral college. The most popular method of presidential election in Latin America is the majority runoff/two-round method under which if no candidate receives at least 50% + 1 of the vote in the first round, a second round runoff election is held between the top-two candidates from the first-round. Brazil, Chile, Colombia, the Dominican Republic, El Salvador, Guatemala, Haiti, Peru, and Uruguay utilize this method. Costa Rica uses an identical approach, except that instead of a threshold of 50% + 1, a 40% threshold is employed. The second most popular method is the plurality formula, under which the candidate garnering the most votes in a single round is elected president. Honduras, Mexico, Panama, Paraguay, and Venezuela utilize this method.

Advantages of the majority runoff method of presidential election are linked primarily to its ability to insure that no candidate is elected without the support of a majority of the country's voters, something that can and does happen quite frequently in countries that utilize the plurality method of presidential election.[13] For instance, it is less likely that an extremist candidate would emerge victorious in a presidential contest held under the majority runoff framework than using the plurality rule.[14] Disadvantages of the majority runoff method include its tendency to encourage the fragmentation a country's party system by providing incentives for several viable candidates/parties to compete in the presidential contest as well as by creating incentives for the establishment of a national party system with more than two major political parties.[15] This fragmentation of the party system in turn increases the probability that a president's party will not possess a majority of the seats in the legislature, potentially undermining the president's ability to implement his/her policy agenda or even to effectively govern the country. Finally, critics of the majority runoff system also point out that the legitimacy provided to a candidate who wins a second round runoff (i.e., a "majority) is at times tarnished by the reality that in this runoff voters are restricted to only two choices, and thus to varying degrees forced to opt merely between the lesser of two evils.[16]

Another group of countries each employ a distinct variant of the double-complement rule to elect their president. First adopted by Argentina in 1994,[17] in this version a runoff is held between the two top finishers from the first round unless either: (1) a candidate receives at least 45% + 1 of the vote, or (2) a candidate wins at least 40% of the vote and at the same time garners at least 10% more of the vote than the first runner-up. Bolivia, Ecuador, and Nicaragua also employ variations of this methodology.

The two most important trends over the past twenty years in the rules governing presidential elections have been the replacement of the plurality rule by the majority runoff method (Colombia, Dominican Republic, Uruguay) and the replacement of a variety of other methods of presidential election (Argentina, Bolivia, Nicaragua) by the modified versions of the double complement rule.[18] The latter method is considered to provide many of the benefits of the majority runoff rule (e.g., avoiding the legitimacy problems resulting from a president being elected with a small share of the vote and/or the election of an extremist candidate) while attenuating many of the problems associated with the majority runoff formula (e.g., problems of governance stemming from its tendency to fragment the party system and thereby reduce the size of the president's legislative contingent).

The constitutions which guided the Latin American presidential democracies during the early days of the third wave of democratization almost uniformly (the Dominican Republic and Nicaragua represent two partial exceptions) prohibited the immediate re-election of presidents.[19] The underlying fear in most countries was that unfettered by constraints on re-election, incumbent presidents might abuse their control of the state and in doing so undermine the country's democratic system.[20] However, starting with Peruvian President Alberto Fujimori in 1993 and Argentine President Carlos Menem in 1994, popular and ambitious Latin American presidents began to actively work to throw off the shackles of term-limits via constitutional reforms to allow for the immediate re-election of the president (normally for one term). Since that time, several other presidents have successfully pushed through similar reforms to allow them to run for immediate re-election, including Fernando Henrique Cardoso in Brazil (1997), Hugo Chávez in Venezuela (1999), Álvaro Uribe in Colombia (2001), Hipólito Mejía in the Dominican Republic (2002), Rafael Correa in Ecuador (2008), and Evo Morales in Bolivia (2009). Of these eight presidents, all but Mejía were re-elected. However, not all reform efforts by sitting presidents during this period were successful, with the failed 2009 attempt of Manuel "Mel" Zelaya in Honduras, which resulted in his forced removal from power, the most dramatic example.

At present, seven of the region's democracies (all but one located in South America) allow for the immediate re-election of the president, while a majority of the remaining countries allow for presidential re-election, but only after the president has been out of office for one or two terms. Guatemala, Honduras, Mexico, and Paraguay alone retain the absolute prohibition on any form of presidential re-election.

Historically, the presidential candidates of the major political parties in Latin America were selected by small groups of elites or by party conventions.[21] Over the past twenty years however the selection process for choosing a party's presidential candidate has moved increasingly from the smoked-filled back rooms of yore to the ballot box via the implementation of direct primary elections.[22] However, the adoption of democratic primaries for the selection of presidential candidates has not been uniform across the region nor has the use of primaries been found to have improved the level of intra-party democracy.[23] In some countries mandatory primaries are now in force for the selection of presidential candidates, with Honduras, Paraguay, and Uruguay the prime examples of this model. In other countries primaries are not mandated, yet their use is relatively common within at least one of the principal parties or alliances (e.g., Chile, Dominican Republic, Panama). Lastly, there are many countries where the use of primaries to select the leading presidential candidates has never occurred or is extremely rare (e.g., Bolivia, Brazil, Guatemala).

The overall impact of the use of direct primaries to choose a party's candidate on general election performance (compared to selection by elites) is unclear. There exists some evidence that primaries produce candidates who are more popular among the electorate at large as well as better enable parties to resolve internal conflicts, but other evidence which suggests primaries can have a negative impact on general election performance if they are especially divisive, poorly run, or restricted to a relatively limited selectorate (e.g., party members only).[24]

In an overwhelming majority of the Latin American presidential democracies, presidential and legislative elections are held at the same time (concurrently). The advantages for governability provided by concurrent elections are widely acknowledged by scholars and policymakers, with two countries (Chile, Dominican Republic) that previously held their presidential and legislative elections at separate times reforming their respective constitutions over the past decade to adopt concurrent elections. To date, El Salvador, Haiti, and Venezuela remain as the region's sole examples of nonconcurrent systems, along with Colombia which though does always hold its elections in the same year, with legislative elections in March and presidential elections in May.[25] In addition, Argentina and Mexico employ a mixed electoral cycle with elections held at the midpoint of a president's term in office. In Argentina one-half of the Chamber of Deputies and one-third of the Senate is elected in the midterm elections while in Mexico the entire Chamber is renewed. Finally, in the case of the Argentine (one-third every two years), Brazilian (one-third or two-thirds every four years), and Chilean (one-half every four years) senates, the terms of the senators are longer than that of the president, with the senate renewed via partial renovation.

Legislative Elections

Within the checks-and-balances framework of presidentialism, the legislative branch (and the individual legislators who comprise its membership) plays a much more active and prominent role in governance than is generally the case in parliamentary systems. The number of legislative chambers, the geographic distribution of legislative seats, and the rules governing the election of legislators therefore have far more direct consequences for the nature of executive-legislative relations and public policy in presidential democracies than is the case in most parliamentary systems.

Within the Latin American presidential systems there exist both bicameral and unicameral legislative branches. In contrast to the case in bicameral parliamentary systems, the two legislative chambers in the Latin American presidential bicameral systems are essentially equal (symmetric) in terms of their constitutional powers.[26] The region is roughly divided equally between those countries with bicameral legislatures (Argentina, Bolivia, Brazil, Chile, Dominican Republic, Haiti, Mexico, Paraguay, Uruguay) and those with unicameral legislatures. During the third wave of democratization, two countries have eliminated their senate (Peru, Venezuela), while no country has moved from a unicameral to bicameral structure.

The nine senates vary considerably in terms of the allocation of seats across the national territory. At one extreme are countries which have an equal number of senators elected from each of their principal sub-national units (Argentina, Bolivia, Brazil, the Dominican Republic, Haiti). The next most common mode of senate election is from a nation-wide district (Colombia, Paraguay, and Uruguay). Mexico represents a mixture of these two models as does Chile to some extent, albeit in a more complex manner.

All of the single/lower houses allocate their seats across the national territory based principally on the population of the subnational territorial units. However, in all countries there is at least some overrepresentation of the most rural/least populated districts, which varies from noteworthy (Argentina, Bolivia, Brazil) to minimal (Costa Rica, Honduras, Uruguay).[27]

Four general families of electoral systems are utilized to elect legislators in Latin America. At the majoritarian extreme are a handful of systems (one lower house and three senates) that select all legislators from single-member or two-member districts using either the plurality or majority runoff formula.

At the other extreme is the large number of systems (fifteen lower/single houses and five senates) where legislators are electing entirely utilizing proportional representation (PR). These systems can be subdivided based on the type of electoral districting utilized (multi-member or national, with the former by far the most common) and whether citizens cast a vote for a closed list of candidates presented by a party or are able to cast a preferential vote for specific legislators.

Three countries utilize a mixed-member system (Bolivia–Chamber, Mexico–Chamber, Venezuela) where a portion of the legislators are elected from single-member districts using the plurality rule and a portion from multi-member districts via PR. Finally, the members of entire Argentine Senate and three-fourths of the Mexican Senate are elected from three-member districts (the province/state), with two seats allocated to the party which receives the most votes and one seat to the first runner-up (the remaining quarter in Mexico is elected from a nation-wide PR district).

In districts where more than one legislator is being elected, two general types of party lists are utilized. Most common in Latin America are closed lists, where the party presents a rank-ordered list of candidates that cannot be altered by the voter. For instance, in a district electing five members, a party will present a list of candidates ranked from one to five. Voters cast a single vote for a party list, and, if, for example, the party is allocated three seats based on its vote total, then the first three individuals on the rank-ordered list are elected.

An alternative to closed lists are lists which allow a voter to cast a preference vote for one or more candidates. In contrast to closed list systems, where the seats are awarded based on the order of the list presented by the party, in open list systems the seats are awarded to the party's candidates based on the number of preference votes they garnered in the election. Under the most common form of preference voting in Latin America (Brazil–Chamber, Chile–Chamber and Senate, Colombia–Chamber and Senate [most parties], Dominican Republic–Chamber, Panama, Peru–unicameral), voters may only cast a preference vote(s) for the candidates of a single party or alliance. In Ecuador and Honduras, voters are allowed to cast preference votes across multiple parties or alliances.

Other factors held constant, the utilization of preference voting tends to result in legislators who are less beholden to their parties, and more responsive to voters, than is the case with legislators who are elected from closed lists. These latter legislators generally follow the instructions of the party leaders who were responsible for placing them on the ballot in an electable position.[28]

Over the past twenty years, the Latin American legislatures have been in the global vanguard of efforts to increase the proportion of women legislators via the use of positive action. In 1993 Argentina was the first country in the world to implement gender quota legislation for the election of national legislators. The impact on the election of women to the country's Chamber was profound. Between 1983 and 1991, an average of only 5% of deputies elected were women (ranging from 3% to 6%). Following the adoption of quotas, the proportion of women elected increased to 21% in 1993, 28% in 1995, and since 2001 has not dropped below 31% (averaging 34%). As a result of the use of effective quota legislation, the percentage of women in the Argentine Chamber and Senate today is 39% and 35%, respectively.

In all, two-thirds of the Latin American presidential democracies have adopted some form of gender quota legislation for the election of national legislators over the past twenty years.[29] However, not all of this legislation has been well-designed, resulting in many cases (e.g., the Brazilian Chamber, Panamanian Assembly, and Paraguayan Chamber) in which the implementation of quota legislation has failed to substantially improve the presence of women in the legislature. Legislatures elected using well-designed quota legislation on average have a comparatively large proportion of female members, with all of the Latin American legislatures whose composition is 25% or more female employing well-designed quota legislation to elect either all or some of their legislators (Bolivia–Senate 47%, Argentina–Chamber 39%, Costa Rica 39%, Argentina–Senate 35%, Ecuador 32%, Peru 28%, Mexico 26%, Bolivia–Chamber 25%).[30]

In contrast to the case for presidents, virtually all Latin American legislators are allowed to run for unlimited re-election. The noteworthy exceptions are Costa Rica and Mexico, where legislators must sit out for one term prior to running for re-election, and Venezuela where legislators may only be re-elected twice.[31]

Executive-Legislative Relations

The relationship between the executive and legislative branches in Latin America's presidential democracies is powerfully shaped by the constitutional powers granted to each body as well as the partisan powers of the president vis-à-vis the legislature and the level of polarization in the country's political party system.[32] The combination of these factors (along with others related to legislative careers and legislative capacities) has a prominent impact on the extent to which the legislature is a mere rubber-stamp of executive initiatives versus an effective and active participant in the policymaking process.[33]

The president's constitutional powers can be divided into two general categories: legislative powers and non-legislative powers.[34] Principal legislative powers include veto, decree, and agenda-setting powers. There is little variance in non-legislative constitutional powers in Latin America.[35]

Two aspects of the veto process are most relevant for understanding presidential power in this area.[36] The first is whether or not the president can only veto an entire bill approved by congress (package veto) or if the president has the power to strike-down specific articles/sections of a bill (line-item veto). Given the greater latitude allowed to the president, the line-item veto enhances presidential power in relation to the legislature to a greater extent than the package veto alone. A majority of the Latin American constitutions provide the president with both package and line-item veto powers, with the exception of Costa Rica, El Salvador, Guatemala, Haiti, Honduras, and Mexico where the president only has the option of vetoing the entire bill.

The second aspect is the proportion of the members of the legislature who must vote to override a veto. At one extreme are systems where a veto can only be overridden by a two-thirds vote of the full membership of the legislature (Dominican Republic, Ecuador, El Salvador, Guatemala, Panama) followed by those where a two-thirds vote is required, but the denominator is the number of legislators present at the session, not the full member-ship (Argentina, Chile, Mexico). At the other extreme are the remaining systems where a veto may be overridden by simple majority of legislators (in some cases the denominator is the full membership and in others the legislators present). Uruguay, with a 60% threshold, occupies an intermediate position.

Legislative decree power allows the president to legislate without going through Con-gress.[37] The degree of this power to bypass Congress in the legislative process varies across the presidential democracies considerably. Roughly half of the presidents in the region have no decree powers, while many of those who enjoy this prerogative do so in a constrained manner as the use of legislative decrees is limited to specific policy areas, emergency situa-tions, or can be in force only for a limited period of time.

In addition to veto and decree powers, presidents are advantaged in their interaction with the legislative branch via the possession of a series of agenda-setting powers. First, is the conditional agenda-setting power under which a president can amend vetoed bills returned to Congress.[38] Second, is the exclusive right of a president alone to introduce legislative bills in specific thematic areas. Third, is the power of the president in the budget process, with particular focus on the ability of the congress to modify the budget bill sub-mitted by the president and the reversion point in the event congress fails to pass a budget.[39] In the former case some legislatures can modify all aspects of the budget bill, in others the legislature is unable to increase spending in specific budget lines nor overall. In the latter case, the most common reversion point in Latin America is the prior year's budget, although in one-third of the countries if no budget is passed, the budget bill originally submitted by the executive is automatically adopted.[40]

The Latin American presidential democracies can be divided into three rough groups in terms of the constitutional power of their president vis-à-vis the legislature: Strong (Brazil, Chile, Colombia), Moderate (Argentina, Ecuador, Panama, Uruguay, Bolivia, Peru, El Sal-vador, Honduras, Venezuela), and Weak (Costa Rica, Dominican Republic, Guatemala, Haiti, Nicaragua, Mexico, Paraguay).[41]

Three party system related factors are crucial for understanding executive-legislative relations in a country: the size of the presidential legislative contingent, the level of polar-ization existing among the political parties in the legislature, and the extent to which the members of the presidential legislative contingent are responsive to the party leadership and/or president. These factors combined have a prominent impact on the degree of a presi-dent's partisan powers vis-à-vis the legislature as well as affect the level of difficulty experi-enced by president in forming either long-term of short-term alliances to pass legislation in particular and to govern more generally.[42]

At present in several countries (e.g., Brazil, Chile, Guatemala Paraguay), the president's party holds only a modest (e.g., less than 40%) of the legislative seats while in other coun-tries the president's party occupies an absolute majority of the seats (e.g., Bolivia, Domini-can Republic, Honduras, Uruguay, Venezuela). There is considerable debate regarding the consequences of presidential legislative contingents that are below majority status, particu-larly those that drop below one-third or one-quarter of the legislative body.[43] While some consider small presidential contingents (especially those that are around 33% and below) to be problematic for governance, others do not. However, there is substantial agreement that in instances where the president's party lacks a majority of the seats in the legislature (or does not at least approach a majority, with, for instance, at least 40% or 45% of the seats), that in order to be able to govern effectively the president must form some type of legisla-tive coalition.[44] Where these coalitions are not formed, governance problems are likely to emerge.[45] The formation of coalitions is most feasible when there are low levels of ideological polarization in the party system.[46] Where high levels of ideological polarization exist, the barriers to forming coalitions are much greater, and the costs (in terms of payoffs/side-payments) much greater.

To summarize, where there is a large presidential legislative contingent, presidents should be able to effectively implement their policy agenda regardless of the level of ideological polarization. While low levels of polarization may have some positive attributes, they are not necessary for effective and efficient governance in these situations. When the president lacks a legislative majority or near-majority, the level of ideological polarization becomes more important. Where ideological polarization is low, presidents should on average be more likely to be able to form, and then successfully maintain, legislative coalitions. Where polarization is high, coalition formation and maintenance is likely to be much more difficult, as well as much more costly in terms of payoffs (e.g., inefficient pork expenditures, bribes, excess patronage positions).

The size of a president's legislative contingent is only one side of the partisan powers coin. Also of great relevance to a president is the degree of responsiveness or discipline of his/her party's/alliance's legislative contingent. This level of responsiveness can vary significantly across countries (as well as across parties within countries), thereby influencing the extent to which a president can count on the support of his or her co-partisans in the legislature. This level of responsiveness to the president (and to the central party leadership) can also influence the nature of legislative coalitions, particularly the individuals with whom a president negotiates the formation and maintenance of the legislative coalitions (e.g., the national party leadership vs. intra-party faction/regional leaders vs. individual legislators).

The level of responsiveness of legislators to the president is influenced by a host of factors, with four of particular importance. First, is the locus of nomination authority for the selection of legislative candidates, with legislators more responsive when this authority is completely centralized in the hands of the presidential candidate/party leadership and legislators less responsive when nomination authority resides with district-level party leaders or primary-voters.[47] Second, is election timing, with legislators likely to be more responsive to the president when elections are concurrent than when they are either nonconcurrent or mixed.[48] Third, is the ballot format for legislative elections, with systems which provide incentives to cultivate a personal vote for legislators (e.g., multi-member districts, PR, and preference voting; single-member districts) producing legislators who are less responsive to the president/party leadership than those systems that do not provide such incentives.[49] Fourth, is the value of the party label/access to the ballot under the party label, with systems in which the party label is a valuable commodity engendering greater responsiveness than those where the label and/or the ballot access it provides has little value for legislators.

Conclusion

Contrary to the case twenty years ago, presidentialism in Latin America is no longer associated with democratic breakdown. The structure of a country's presidential system is however extremely relevant for the functioning of its democratic system and its ability to effectively adopt and implement optimal public policies. As the above review underscores, while a total of nineteen Latin American democracies employ a presidential form of government, these nineteen presidential systems are extremely diverse in structure and functioning. This chapter has served to underscore the considerable variance in several key features related to the executive, the legislature, and the interaction between these two branches of government, variance which is extremely relevant for the quality of these countries' democracies and the public policies they produce. Whereas in some countries the design of the political institutions helps to foster the crafting, passage, and implementation of public policies which work to advance economic and social development in the country, in others suboptimal institutional arrangements often undermine development efforts. It is for this reason that the world's most prominent multi-lateral institutions whose mission centers on development such as the Inter-American Development Bank (in particular), the United Nations Development Programme, and the World Bank have in recent years made tremendous investments in improving scholarly understanding of the design and functioning of democratic political institutions in Latin America, with particular focus on the consequences of institutional design and functioning for the policymaking process.

Notes

1 Arend Lijphart, *Patterns of Democracy: Government Forms and Performance in Thirty-Six Countries* (New Haven, CT: Yale University Press, 1999); Jorge Lanzaro, "Tipos de Presidencialismo y Modos de Gobierno en América Latina," in Jorge Lanzaro (ed.), *Tipos de Presidencialismo y Coaliciones Políticas en América Latina* [Types of Presidentialism and Political Coaltions in Latin America] (Buenos Aires: CLACSO, 2001), pp. 15–40.
2 Freedom House, *Freedom in the World 2011*. www.freedomhouse.org.
3 Juan J. Linz and Arturo Valenzuela (eds.), *The Failure of Presidential Democracy* (Baltimore: Johns Hopkins University Press, 1994).
4 Juan J. Linz, "Presidential or Parliamentary Democracy: Does It Make a Difference?", in Juan J. Linz and Arturo Valenzuela (eds.), *The Failure of Presidential Democracy*, pp. 3–87.
5 Matthew Soberg Shugart and Scott Mainwaring, "Presidentialism and Democracy in Latin America: Rethinking the Terms of the Debate," in Scott Mainwaring and Matthew Soberg Shugart (eds.), *Presidentialism and Democracy in Latin America* (New York: Cambridge University Press, 1997), pp. 12–54.
6 Shugart and Mainwaring, "Presidentialism and Democracy in Latin America"; Scott Mainwaring and Matthew Soberg Shugart, "Conclusion: Presidentialism and the Party System," in Scott Mainwaring and Matthew Soberg Shugart (eds.), *Presidentialism and Democracy in Latin America* (New York: Cambridge University Press, 1997), pp. 394–437. Also relevant to this initial concern with presidential regime-type heterogeneity are: Matthew S. Shugart and John M. Carey, *Presidents and Assemblies: Constitutional Design and Electoral Dynamics* (New York: Cambridge University Press, 1992); Scott Mainwaring "Presidentialism, Multipartism, and Democracy: The Difficult Combination," *Comparative Political Studies* 26 (1993): 198–228; Mark P. Jones, *Electoral Laws and the Survival of Presidential Democracy* (Notre Dame, IN: University of Notre Dame Press, 1995).
7 Charles D. Kenney, *Fujimori's Coup and the Breakdown of Democracy in Latin America* (Notre Dame, IN: University of Notre Dame Press, 2004).
8 Aníbal Pérez-Liñán, *Presidential Impeachment and the New Political Instability in Latin America* (New York: Cambridge University Press, 2007), p. 204.
9 Pérez-Liñán, *Presidential Impeachment*.
10 Barry Ames, *The Deadlock of Democracy in Brazil* (Ann Arbor: University of Michigan Press, 2001); Ernesto Stein and Mariano Tommasi (with Pablo Spiller and Carlos Scartascini), *Policymaking in Latin America: How Politics Shapes Policies* (Washington D.C.: Inter-American Development Bank, 2008); Eduardo Alemán and Ernesto Calvo, "Unified Government, Bill Approval, and the Legislative Weight of the President," *Comparative Political Studies* 43 (2010): 511–34.
11 Arturo Valenzuela, "Latin American Presidencies Interrupted," *Journal of Democracy* 15:4 (2004): 5–19.
12 Stein and Tommasi, *Policymaking in Latin America*; Carlos Scartascini, Ernesto Stein, and Mariano Tommasi (eds.), *How Democracy Works: Political Institutions, Actors, and Arenas in Latin American Policymaking* (Washington D.C.: Inter-American Development Bank, 2010).
13 Shugart and Mainwaring, "Conclusion."

14 Giovanni Sartori, *Comparative Constitutional Engineering* (New York: New York University Press, 1994).

15 Jones, *Electoral Laws*; David J. Samuels, "Presidentialized Parties: The Separation of Powers and Party Organization and Behavior," *Comparative Political Studies* 35 (2002): 461–83.

16 Linz, "Presidential or Parliamentary Democracy."

17 Matthew S. Shugart and Rein Taagepera, "Majority Versus Plurality Election: A Proposal for a Double Complement Rule," *Comparative Political Studies* 27 (1994): 323–48.

18 Karen Remmer, "The Politics of Institutional Change: Electoral Reform in Latin America, 1978–2002," *Party Politics* 14 (2008): 5–30.

19 Presidential term lengths in Latin America range from four to six years, with all countries having four or five year terms with the exception of Mexico and Venezuela.

20 John M. Carey, "The Reelection Debate in Latin America," *Latin American Politics and Society* 45 (2003): 119–33.

21 Manuel Alcántara Sáez and Flavia Freidenberg (eds.), *Partidos Políticos de América Latina* [Political Parties of Latin America]: Volumes 1, 2, and 3 (Salamanca: Ediciones Universidad de Salamanca, 2001); John M. Carey and John Polga-Hecimovich, "Primary Elections and Candidate Strength in Latin America," *The Journal of Politics* 68 (2006): 530–43; Bonnie N. Field and Peter M. Siavelis, "Candidate Selection Procedures in Transitional Polities," *Party Politics* 12 (2008): 620–39.

22 Flavia Freidenberg and Manuel Alcántara Sáez, "Selección de Candidatos, Política Partidista y Rendimiento Democrático: Una Introducción" [Candidate Selection, Party Politics and Democratic Performance: An Introduction], in Flavia Freidenberg and Manuel Alcántara Sáez (eds.), *Selección de Candidatos, Política Partidista y Rendimiento Democrático* [Selection of Candidates, Democratic Party Politics and Performance] (Mexico City: Tribunal Electoral del Distrito Federal, 2009), pp. 13–34.

23 Freidenberg and Alcántara Sáez, "Selección de Candidatos."

24 Carey and Polga-Hecimovich, "Primary Elections"; Miguel De Luca, Mark P. Jones, and María Inés Tula, "Revisando las Consecuencias Políticas de las Primarias. Un Estudio Sobre las Elecciones de Gobernador en la Argentina" [Reviewing the Political Consequences of the Primaries. A Study of Governor Elections in Argentina], *POSTData* 13 (2008): 81–102; Ozge Kemahlioglu, Rebecca Weitz-Shapiro, and Shigeo Hirano, "Why Primaries in Latin American Presidential Elections?", *The Journal of Politics* 71 (2009): 339–52; Gilles Serra, "Why Primaries? The Party's Tradeoff Between Policy and Valence," *Journal of Theoretical Politics* 23 (2011): 21–51.

25 In El Salvador the executive and legislature are respectively elected for five and three year terms, resulting in every fifth legislative election and every third presidential election being held in the same year (though in 2009 legislative elections were held in January and the presidential elections in March).

26 Lijphart, *Patterns of Democracy*.

27 David Samuels and Richard Snyder, "The Value of a Vote: Malapportionment in Comparative Perspective," *British Journal of Political Science* 31 (2001): 651–71.

28 John M. Carey and Matthew S. Shugart, "Incentives to Cultivate a Personal Vote: A Rank-Ordering of Electoral Formulas," *Electoral Studies* 14 (1995): 417–39; Brian F. Crisp, Maria C. Escobar-Lemmon, Bradford S. Jones, Mark P. Jones, and Michelle Taylor-Robinson, "Electoral Incentives and Legislative Representation in Six Presidential Democracies," *The Journal of Politics* 66 (2004): 823–46; J. Mark Payne, Daniel Zovatto G., and Mercedes Mateo Díaz, *Democracies in Development: Politics and Reform in Latin America* (Washington D.C.: Inter-American Development Bank, 2007).

29 Mark P. Jones, "Gender Quotas, Electoral Laws, and the Election of Women: Evidence from the Latin American Vanguard," *Comparative Political Studies* 42 (2009): 56–81.

30 Inter-Parliamentary Union, "Women in National Parliaments," www.ipu.org.

31 Michelle M. Taylor, "Formal Versus Informal Incentive Structures and Legislator Behavior: Evidence from Costa Rica," *The Journal of Politics* 54 (1992): 1053–71; Joy Langston, "Legislative Recruitment in Mexico," in Peter M. Siavelis and Scott Morgenstern (eds.), *Pathways to Power: Political Recruitment and Candidate Selection in Latin America* (University Park: Pennsylvania State University Press, 2008), pp. 143–63.

32 Sebastián Saiegh, "Active Players or Rubber Stamps? An Evaluation of the Policymaking Role of Latin American Legislatures," in Carlos Scartascini, Ernesto Stein, and Mariano Tommasi (eds.), *How Democracy Works: Political Institutions, Actors, and Arenas in Latin American Policymaking*

(Washington D.C.: Inter-American Development Bank, 2010); Shugart and Mainwaring, "Presidentialism and Democracy"; Payne, Zovatto G. and Mateo Díaz, *Democracies in Development*.

33 Gary W. Cox and Scott Morgenstern, "Latin America's Reactive Assemblies and Proactive Presidents," *Comparative Politics* 33 (2001): 171–89; Saiegh, "Active Players or Rubber Stamps?".

34 Payne, Zovatto G., and Mateo Díaz, *Democracies in Development*.

35 Payne, Zovatto G., and Mateo Díaz, *Democracies in Development*. Haiti represents a noteworthy exception due to its semi-presidential system.

36 Payne, Zovatto G., and Mateo Díaz, *Democracies in Development*.

37 Carey and Shugart, "Incentives to Cultivate."

38 George Tsebelis and Eduardo Alemán, "Presidential Conditional Agenda Setting in Latin America," *World Politics* 57 (2005): 396–420.

39 Payne, Zovatto G., and Mateo Díaz, *Democracies in Development*.

40 Payne, Zovatto G., and Mateo Díaz, *Democracies in Development*; Stein and Tommasi *Policymaking in Latin America*; Scartascini, Stein, and Tommasi, *How Democracy Works*.

41 Payne, Zovatto G., and Mateo Díaz, *Democracies in Development*.

42 Daniel Chasquetti, "Democracia, Multipartidismo y Coaliciones en América Latina: Evaluando la Difícil Combinación" [Democracy, Multipartism and Coalitions in Latin America: Assessing the Difficult Combination], in Jorge Lanzaro (ed.), *Tipos de Presidencialismo en América Latina*, pp. 319–59; Andrés Mejía Acosta and Carlos Pereira, "Policymaking in Multiparty Presidential Democracies: A Comparison Between Brazil and Ecuador," *Governance* 23 (2010): 641–66; Mainwaring and Shugart, "Conclusion".

43 Joe Foweraker, "Review Article: Institutional Design, Party Systems and Governability-Differentiating the Presidential Regimes of Latin America," *British Journal of Political Science* 28 (1998): 651–76; Payne and Díaz, *Democracies in Development*.

44 Cecilia Martínez-Gallardo, "Inside the Cabinet: The Influence of Ministers in the Policymaking Process," in Carlos Scartascini, Ernesto Stein, and Mariano Tommasi (eds.), *How Democracy Works: Political Institutions, Actors, and Arenas in Latin American Policymaking* (Washington D.C. and Cambridge MA: Inter-American Development Bank, 2010).

45 Gabriel L. Negretto, "Minority Presidents and Democratic Performance in Latin America," *Latin American Politics and Society* 48 (2006): 63–92; Chasquetti, "Democracia, Multipartidismo y Coaliciones."

46 David Altman, "The Politics of Coalition Formation and Survival in Multiparty Presidential Regimes," Ph.D. Dissertation, University of Notre Dame (2001); Octavio Amorim Neto "The Presidential Calculus: Executive Policy Making and Government Formation in the Americas," *Comparative Political Studies* 39 (2006) 415–40; Foweraker, "Review Article"; Hebert Kitschelt, Kirk A. Hawkins, Juan Pablo Luna, Guillermo Rosas, and Elizabeth J. Zechmeister, *Latin American Party Systems* (New York: Cambridge University Press, 2010).

47 Peter M. Siavelis and Scott Morgenstern (eds.), *Pathways to Power: Political Recruitment and Candidate Selection in Latin America* (University Park: Pennsylvania State University Press, 2008); Brian F. Crisp and Juan Carlos Rey, "The Sources of Electoral Reform in Venezuela," in Matthew Soberg Shugart and Martin P. Wattenberg (eds.), *Mixed-Member Electoral Systems: The Best of Both Worlds?* (New York, Oxford University Press, 2001), pp. 173–93.

48 Samuels, "Presidentialized Parties"; David J. Samuels and Matthew S. Shugart, *Presidents, Parties, and Prime Ministers: How the Separation of Powers Affects Party Organization and Behavior* (New York: Cambridge University Press, 2010).

49 Carey and Shugart "Incentives to Cultivate"; Samuels and Shugart, *Presidents, Parties, and Prime Ministers*.

3

DECENTRALIZATION AND FEDERALISM

Kent Eaton

Latin America is home to some of most innovative, radical and influential experiments with decentralization in the world, a governance trend that by now has affected all regions—developing and developed alike.[1] Just as any attempt to understand the significance of this global trend requires considerable attention to Latin America, making sense of Latin American politics today is unthinkable without sustained attention to decentralization and federalism. Decentralization is having a direct impact on the challenges that generations of Latin Americanists have emphasized as the most critical facing the region, including the struggle to deepen democratic practices, the search for broad-based and sustainable economic development, and the effort to push forward processes of state formation that are still very much ongoing.

Conflicts between national and subnational actors over which level of government gets to do what—and with whose revenues—have a long history in Latin America. From the territorial fracturing of power that occurred in the early post-colonial period to the export-led consolidation of central state power toward the end of the 19th century, the region has experienced multiple periods of both decentralizing and re-centralizing change.[2] Decentralization is nothing new, and yet the last three decades have indeed witnessed historic changes in the relationship between levels of government and in the significance of what can now happen beyond national capitals. This chapter first describes what these most recent decentralizing changes have looked like in Latin America, followed by a discussion of the chief causes and consequences of this latest move toward more decentralized patterns of governance. The chapter closes with an analysis of the relationship between decentralization and federalism, and a discussion of possible future research directions.

What Has Decentralization Looked Like in Latin America?

While decentralization has taken a number of forms in Latin America, changes that devolve authority along three main dimensions—political, fiscal and administrative—have been particularly critical.[3] One of the distinctive features of political decentralization in Latin America is that it reflects the logic of both representative and direct models of democracy. For example, in a region where mayors were mostly appointed by higher-level political authorities as late as 1980, the widespread introduction of elections for municipal authorities represents a significant extension of the principle of representative democracy into local spheres.[4] At the same time, reformers have sought to do other than merely extend representative democracy downward by introducing changes that attempt to create more direct forms of local democracy, such as new participatory spaces and stakeholder councils that broaden the range of decision making to include non-governmental actors.[5] Beyond mayoral elections, decentralization in Latin America has involved the incorporation of plebiscites and referenda, the strengthening of indigenous oversight mechanisms, and the expansion of citizen participation in budgeting, the governance of watersheds and the use of local natural resources.[6] In addition to these institutional changes, ongoing developments within political parties—including the collapse of traditional party systems in several cases—have also affected the ability of subnational officials to assert their independence from national politicians, which is the essence of political decentralization.[7] Changes within parties, including the increasingly common use of party primaries to select candidates for subnational races, have also helped to decrease upward accountability to national party leaders and to enhance downward accountability to local constituents.

If many more subnational officials are elected today in Latin America than in the past, it is also the case that they have access to far more significant fiscal revenues.[8] When national politicians decide to decentralize fiscal resources, they generally either transfer the authority to collect certain taxes to subnational governments (giving them "own source" revenues), or keep collection centralized but increase the sharing of the proceeds with these governments. In Latin America, the second option has dominated, in part due to significant problems of inequality between subnational regions that would disadvantage poorer regions if expected to raise their own revenue, and in part due to subnational disinterest in paying the administrative and political costs of collecting taxes.[9] As a result, fiscal decentralization in Latin America has mostly taken shape as the introduction of revenue sharing systems that transfer resources to subnational governments, but not control over significant tax bases. The decision to rely on revenue transfer systems has elevated the importance of the rules according to which these transfers are released by the center. In many countries, revenue sharing is truly automatic and unearmarked, meaning that subnational officials have significant freedom in the assignment of these revenues. In other countries, subnational officials complain that transfers are heavily earmarked and issued at the discretion of national politicians, who condition their release on subnational support for national policy proposals. Rather than plead for their own tax bases, subnational officials in Latin America spend most of their time and political capital demanding greater transparency, automaticity, and generosity in the transfer systems that have been established.

Thanks to administrative decentralization, which refers to the transfer of expenditure responsibilities, mayors in Latin America are now responsible for far more than beautifying their cities and collecting the trash. Not only have subnational officials been given real resources, but they have also been given significant functions to perform, reversing in some cases centuries of practice according to which local service provision required the intervention of central actors—typically national legislators.[10] In a period marked by a much deeper understanding of the role that human capital plays in promoting or hindering economic development, Latin American countries opted to decentralize authority over precisely those investments most likely to enhance human capital: education and health care. Transferring built schools and hospitals to local governments is an obvious and increasingly widespread form of decentralization, but just as significant are the less visible changes in civil service codes that relax centralized control over the employees who work in these schools and hospitals—changes that public sector unions in Latin America have often resisted.[11] Now that so many government-provided goods and services have been decentralized, the frontier of conflict over administrative decentralization has moved toward intra-bureaucratic struggles over who can hire and fire whom. Bureaucrats themselves often prefer to report to national line agencies rather than (newly elected) subnational officials or, alternately, try to take advantage of ambiguity in these dual lines of authority in ways that strengthen their autonomy from politicians at both levels.

Almost all countries in Latin America have contemplated decentralizing changes along the three dimensions described above, and yet significant cross-national differences characterize the scope, depth, sequencing and content of the changes they have adopted. For example, while the scope of decentralization in Argentina, Brazil and Mexico has included all three dimensions, others such as Chile have introduced elections and transferred key responsibilities while keeping subnational officials on a tight fiscal leash and eschewing automatic revenue sharing. In greater contrast still, Peru has witnessed political decentralization at the regional level, but still no meaningful devolution of administrative or fiscal authority.

Countries likewise differ in the depth of the changes they have introduced in any one dimension. Compare, for example, the Brazilian case where municipal governments are automatically entitled to significant revenue sharing from both federal and state governments, with the Bolivian and Colombian cases where municipalities receive substantial automatic transfers only from the national government. With respect to the political dimension, one can say that decentralization has gone deeper in Bolivia and Peru than in Chile: whereas chief executives and representatives in regional governments are now directly elected in Bolivia as of 2005 and Peru as of 2002, in Chile regional councilors are still only indirectly elected by municipal councils and regional executives are still appointed by the president.

A range of sequencing decisions can also be identified. If, as Tulia Falleti argues, national politicians prefer administrative to fiscal and political decentralization, and subnational politicians prefer the opposite ordering, then the relative balance of power between each set of actors influences the sequence according to which decentralizing changes have been adopted in Latin America.[12] For example, whereas the process in Argentina began with the decentralization of schools due to the weakness of subnational actors under military rule, Brazil led with political decentralization due to the greater political leverage enjoyed by its governors. In other cases, like Peru, explicit attempts to sequence decentralization reforms ran aground when the introduction of elections generated opposition victories that then cooled the president's interest in further fiscal or administrative changes.

Finally, a critical design difference among Latin American countries can be seen in the decision about which level of subnational government to privilege via decentralization: either local governments (e.g., municipalities, cantons) or intermediate-level governments (e.g., departments, provinces, states).[13] In Bolivia and Brazil, national politicians from Gonzalo Sánchez de Losada to Getúlio Vargas have favored municipal governments in their attempts to keep in check officials at the more threatening intermediate-level of government. In other countries, such as Mexico and Argentina, municipalities were disadvantaged by decentralization relative to the provincial and state governments that have become, in effect, the new center.[14]

Why Did Latin America Decentralize?

Decentralization occurred in Latin America because powerful actors understood that it could advance their interests as they participated in the larger struggles that have dominated politics in recent decades, including conflicts over economic liberalization, democratization and public security. On balance, normative commitments to decentralized governance as a good in and of itself were far less significant than the belief that decentralization could be a useful tool in other important battles. Nowhere was this more critical than in the shift from statist to market-oriented economics, during which neoliberal reformers came to embrace certain types of decentralization as a mechanism that would help them disempower advocates of statism and shrink the central state. In Chile, for example, decentralization appealed to dictator Augusto Pinochet because the transfer of schools and hospitals to municipal governments promised to permanently weaken the negotiating strength and relevance of national public sector unions. These unions were an important component of the coalition that brought Socialist President Salvador Allende to power in 1970, and in the wake of his overthrow decentralization in the late 1970s and 80s can be understood as a political strategy to disarticulate Chile's statist coalition and to lay the long-term bases for a more liberal approach to economic policy. Other neoliberal reformers followed Pinochet's lead, including Carlos Menem in Argentina who passed on costly education expenditures to provincial governments without additional revenues in the early 1990s as a way to balance his budget, lower inflation, and restore macroeconomic stability. Thus, in addition to the normative commitment to decentralization as a market-friendly reform that would trigger more efficient behaviors by encouraging competition between subnational governments, decentralization also generated very concrete political benefits for neoliberal reformers.

While liberalization has been an important driver of decentralization in many Latin American countries, the two phenomena should not be conflated. Critics of neoliberal economics have perhaps been too quick to dismiss all decentralization as merely a sub-variety of liberalization. Just because neoliberals like Pinochet and Menem have endorsed certain forms of decentralization does not mean that it only appeals to those who have advocated liberalization or that it cannot be used in the service of other, often radically distinct, economic policy paradigms.[15] Brazil is a case in point. In its authoritarian period, Brazil's military rulers pursued a statist model of development in the 1960s and 70s by expanding the governing authority of subnational governments and by enabling the steady expansion of subnationally-owned banks and enterprises (e.g., *estatais estaduais*).[16] More recently, furthering municipal decentralization in Brazil has appealed to those who wish to deepen state capacity and generate more efficacious forms of state intervention—hardly a neoliberal project.[17] Indeed, one of the most intriguing aspects of decentralization in Latin America is the appeal it generates among actors who hold quite different beliefs about the appropriate role of the state in the economy.

In the form of national transitions to liberal representative democracy, democratization has been a second major driver of decentralization in Latin America.[18] Democratic reformers across the region equated centralism with authoritarianism and saw in decentralization an opportunity to push democratic transitions forward and to make authoritarian reversals in the future less likely. Democratization can trigger decentralization in a number of ways. In Mexico, the declining legitimacy of the governing party in the 1980s led it to accept state-level electoral victories for the National Action Party (PAN), a democratizing reform that then enabled opposition governors to demand fiscal decentralization "from below."[19] Subsequent to the transition to competitive party politics at the national level in 2000, Mexican governors have secured greater autonomy in a range of critical dimensions. Brazil is another important case, where the lengthy process of political liberalization and then democratization in the 1980s opened up new decision-making spaces that were dominated by governors, whose preferences for fiscal decentralization were then directly written into revenue sharing arrangements and inserted into the country's new 1988 constitution.[20] Democratization also generated decentralizing outcomes in Chile. When that country's 1990 transition to democracy only occurred at the national level and not in municipalities, democratization enabled the new Concertation government to re-introduce elections for municipal governments in 1992, having correctly calculated that it would win the great majority of these elections.[21]

Beyond its occurrence during and in the close aftermath of transitions to democracy, decentralization has also taken place due to the regular holding of elections subsequent to democratization. Once democracy was (re)established in Latin America, ambitious politicians have viewed decentralization through the lens of its likely impact on their own electoral futures. More specifically, according to Kathleen O'Neill, when national parties calculate that their electoral fortunes are more promising at the subnational level than at the national level, and consequently that holding subnational offices will be important to them in the future, they are more likely to support decentralization in order to make these offices more powerful.[22] Consider the Bolivian case, where the combination of a fragmented party system and constitutional rules that let Congress pick the president from among the top three vote winners encouraged the party that was victorious in the 1993 elections (*Movimiento Nacionalista Revolucionario* or MNR) to believe that it would be unlikely to hold onto national power in the future. Because the MNR had a more developed organizational apparatus than other parties at the municipal level, along with a more stable base of support there, the MNR leadership endorsed a quite bold approach to decentralization, as reflected in the 1994 Law of Popular Participation. The fear of likely electoral results also produced a pre-emptive approach to decentralization in Peru, where President Alan García introduced regional elections in the late 1980s when it looked certain that his APRA party would fare poorly in the 1990 national elections.

In addition to economic liberalization and democratization, a less widespread but still significant cause of decentralization in Latin America can be located in the search for political settlements to armed conflicts. Latin America has suffered from fewer internal ethnic conflicts than other regions, and yet many of the same decentralizing reforms adopted in the course of post-conflict settlements elsewhere have also been attempted here. Peace negotiators have looked to decentralization as a reform that can lower the stakes associated with winning control of the central government (militarily) while simultaneously heightening the desirability of winning control of municipal governments (via local elections). According to the logic of "pacification via decentralization," the possibility of participating in or influencing the behavior of subnational governments with real resources and real spending authority may be sufficient to encourage combatants to lay down their arms and/or to prevent them from taking up arms again in the future.

The adoption of decentralization as a pacification measure occurred in the most important and deadliest of Latin America's internal armed conflicts. For example, decentralization was an important component of the internationally mediated peace accords that ended devastating civil wars in El Salvador and Guatemala in the early to mid-1990s. In both cases, strengthening municipal governments appealed to former insurgents who correctly feared that their opponents would continue to control the resources of the center. While progressive parties failed to win presidential elections in either country until very recently, they successfully competed in municipal elections, and in this limited sense decentralization succeeded in giving political voice to formerly armed groups. The search for an end to armed conflicts also generated decentralizing reforms in Colombia. In 1982, after the election of a president who believed that the country's overly closed political system had encouraged violent, anti-system behavior, the national government agreed to introduce elections for mayors and to alter the constitution to allow the direct election of governors as well.[23] Like Guatemala and El Salvador, the strategy worked in that candidates associated with Colombia's various guerrilla movements successfully contested municipal offices. Unlike these other cases, however, guerrilla candidates competed in elections (and/or coerced sitting mayors) without laying down their arms, and used decentralized resources to continue their war on the Colombian state.

What Has Decentralization Changed in Latin America?

Adopted as a strategy that its sponsors thought would enable them to implement market reforms, secure transitions to democracy and/or preserve the peace in post-conflict environments, decentralization has altered political life in Latin America in ways that these sponsors could scarcely have imagined. Advocates of decentralization have often been pleased with the performance of the more decentralized institutions that they created, and can point with satisfaction to the emergence of new political parties, participatory experiments and exciting policy innovations that decentralization has made possible. But the story of how decentralization has unfolded is also rife with examples of the perils of institutional engineering and the law of unintended consequences.

One of the most striking and perhaps easily anticipated results of decentralization is the growing salience of mayors in the region. Reflecting the traditional norm of concentrating power in the executive branch—one of the defining features of politics in Latin America—decentralization has disproportionately benefited mayoral offices. Decentralization has certainly challenged the vertical concentration of power in the national government, but it has mostly replicated at the municipal level the horizontal concentration of power in executive rather than legislative bodies. In most cases mayors have become by far the most important protagonists within municipal political society, dominating with relative ease their counterparts in representative bodies (e.g.. municipal councilors). For example, when fiscal decentralization has taken the form of revenue sharing from higher levels of government or the devolution of property tax bases to municipalities, mayors tend to decide how the associated funds are spent. As administrative decentralization has shifted the authority to appoint local governmental employees to the municipal level, mayors are the individuals who typically wield these new appointment powers (and can and do exchange these appointments for a variety of benefits). Relative to the past when mayors were appointed, political decentralization in the form of local elections has obviously enhanced their independence relative to higher levels of government, but it has also strengthened the mayoral office locally since mayors can defend their actions by invoking the local mandate that they have received.

Mayoral dominance has generated both positive and negative consequences for governance. On the positive side, according to one of the most salient findings in the new literature on decentralization in Latin America, mayoral leadership has played a key role in whatever improvements have occurred in municipal governance.[24] Behind most municipal success stories one can find a talented and entrepreneurial mayor committed to changing the status quo.[25] Opposition to changes proposed by reformist mayors is often concentrated in municipal councils, a dynamic that replays at the local level the national deadlock that took place in the 1950s and 60s over land reform and other issues between reformist presidents and national legislatures dominated by land-owning elites. Mayoral dominance, however, is also cause for growing concern. In the municipalities that have made effective use of decentralization, reforms are closely associated with individual mayors and therefore tend not to outlast them. The dependence of municipal reforms on talented mayors tends to make these reforms highly vulnerable either to their subsequent reversal or to benign neglect from the mayor's successors in office. Furthermore, where mayors pursue their reforms by sidelining municipal councilors, what we are seeing is the "decentralization of hyper-presidentialism" and the repetition of a debate that took place at the national level in the 1990s when the concentration of power in the presidency raised questions not only about the sustainability of (market and other) reforms, but about the quality and transparency of democracy as well.

The introduction of subnational elections has also altered party systems in Latin America, where the national transition to representative democracy in the 1980s exposed the basic inability of many parties to reflect societal preferences. The experience of the last fifteen years partially—though not wholly—validates the expectation that decentralization could create opportunities for "subnational party building." In Bolivia, for instance, decentralization facilitated the emergence in the 1990s of two new indigenous parties: the Movement toward Socialism (*Movimiento al Socialismo* or MAS) and the Pachakutik Indigenous Movement (*Movimiento Indígena Pachakutik* or MIP).[26] Fueled by a decade of successes in mostly rural municipalities, the MAS launched a successful bid for the presidency in 2005, and in the process transformed the national party system. Though perhaps less dramatically, the Colombian case reveals a similar dynamic, but in highly urban municipalities. After the introduction of mayoral elections two decades ago, mayors like Antanas Mockus and Enrique Peñalosa in Bogotá have sought to use their successful mayoralties to aid in the construction of new national parties, including the Alternative Democratic Pole and the Green Party. In El Salvador, the experience of governing in over half of the country's municipalities helped the Farabundo Martí National Liberation (FMLN) party appeal to centrist voters and to elect Mauricio Funes as the country's first FMLN president in 2009.

In addition to new parties, the introduction and/or strengthening of subnational elections has also proved to be critical for established parties that were previously unable to win national electoral contests. The Brazilian and Mexican cases are instructive here. In Brazil, subsequent to its establishment in 1971, the Worker's Party (*Partido dos Trabalhadores* or PT) had a difficult time convincing substantial numbers of Brazilians to vote for it in congressional and presidential elections subsequent to re-democratization in the late 1980s and 1990s. Meanwhile, the PT did win municipal offices—particularly in Brazil's more industrialized south—and the record that it accumulated running municipalities helps explain the party's victory in national elections in 2002.[27] Turning from Brazil to Mexico and from left to right, the subnational sphere also played a critical role in the rise to power nationally of the right-of-center PAN.[28] Founded in the 1920s as a socially conservative alternative to the governing party, the PAN's performance in the municipalities and states shifted the party in a more pragmatic and less intolerant direction and increased its appeal among many voters. Mexican analysts underscore the PAN's subnational record in explaining how it convinced so many Mexicans to vote for the party in the critical presidential elections that it won in 2000.[29] For new as well as for more established parties, then, subnational executive experience has delivered important national benefits.

In addition to changing the landscape for political parties, decentralization in many cases has opened up new spaces for the direct participation of local community organizations. At first glance, the establishment of new participatory mechanisms across post-decentralization Latin America may be hard to reconcile with the pattern of mayoral dominance discussed above. If mayors have captured most of the political authority that has been devolved to the local level in Latin America, then why would they allow the creation of new participatory spaces? According to Donna Van Cott, the two phenomena are not unconnected: charismatic mayors in Bolivia and Ecuador have enlisted participatory councils and the unelected civil society organizations that populate them in their policy struggles against elected municipal councilors. Mayors are able to more easily circumvent municipal councilors if they can credibly claim that their reforms are supported by legitimate and mobilized civil society organizations. According to other common patterns, powerful mayors have agreed to the constitution of participatory bodies whose powers are merely advisory rather than binding, or bodies whose powers are indeed binding but that are dominated by organizations with political ties to the mayor or his/her family.

Despite cross-national variation in the form that new participatory councils have taken, it is now clear that many municipalities in the region have sought to repeat the participatory budgeting (PB) model that was first developed in Porto Alegre, Brazil and that has been extensively documented in the literature.[30] The Porto Alegre experience has been credited with the redistribution of funds toward areas prioritized by the city's lower-income residents, leading to a doubling in the number of schools, an increase in sewerage from less than 50% to 95% of residents, and an increase in access to the municipal water system from 75% to 98% of residents.[31] As an innovation that radically decentralizes control over the budget among a city's residents, participatory budgeting has now gone viral—both in municipalities across Latin America and also at higher levels of government. But whether these reforms are really enhancing meaningful participation in Latin America depends in large part on whether fiscal revenues have been simultaneously decentralized. For example, Benjamin Goldfrank's comparison of participatory budgeting in Caracas, Montevideo and Porto Alegre leads him to identify the level of fiscal decentralization as a necessary (but not sufficient) condition for its success.[32] Likewise, according to Merilee Grindle, Mexico's Municipal Development Committees have succeeded in eliciting participation by civil society organizations only when mayors have been successful in lobbying for resources from state and federal sources. In a similar vein, Allison Rowland argues that automatic fiscal transfers to municipal governments help explain why decentralization has produced greater participation and accountability in small municipalities in Bolivia relative to Mexico (where discretionary grants still dwarf automatic transfers).[33] This argument also finds echo in work by Tim Campbell, who argues that what others criticize as the "premature" transfer of funds to local governments in Latin America has been a boon for democracy because it has given people real reasons to participate.

In addition to fiscal revenues, political parties and party systems are also critical in determining whether decentralized budgeting has succeeded so far in Latin America. Attempts to create participatory spaces that displace elites and empower poor people in practice require the political cover provided by "left-of-center political parties that were born of popular struggles."[34] In Brazil, for example, it would be impossible to understand Porto Alegre's experience with PB without references to the PT, which cultivated and protected participatory councils due to its own electoral interests.[35] In addition to the incentives that lead a party in power at the municipal level to open up its budgetary process to civil society (e.g., Brazil's PT), the nature of the opposition party is just as critical to the success of participatory budgeting. According to Goldfrank, weakly institutionalized opposition parties were powerless to prevent the adoption of participatory budgeting in Brazil (and the significant electoral benefits it generated for the PT), but much more institutionalized opposition parties were indeed able to kill similar attempts to expand participation by governing parties (at the municipal level) in Uruguay and Venezuela.[36]

Decentralization has thus generated positive and negative consequences for a host of political phenomena, from local forms of hyper-presidentialism to subnational party building and new opportunities for civil society participation. It has also generated a mixed record vis-à-vis economic development. On the one hand, decentralization in the form of automatic revenue sharing has encouraged subnational profligacy, financed a rapid expansion in public sector payrolls, and introduced much greater rigidity into the inter-governmental system.[37] In Argentina, generous fixed transfers forced the government of Carlos Menem to overadjust at the national level in the late 1990s and to adopt fiscal austerity measures that pushed the country into a devastating economic collapse.[38] In Brazil, electoral competition at the municipal level led to a sharp increase in patronage and public sector payrolls at the expense of collective goods, which encouraged the federal government under President Cardoso to mandate additional transfers from states to municipalities and to earmark these transfers for education and health investments.[39] In response to these problems, many countries have experienced re-centralizing episodes designed to trim the size of revenue transfers to subnational governments.

On the other hand, while decentralization has yet to bring online previously untapped fiscal resources at the local level, it has facilitated the re-emergence of often very traditional forms of in-kind contributions, which in some cases resurrect the communal labor obligations that were so important in the colonial and republican eras (though now apparently on a voluntary rather than coercive basis). Relative to national governments, mayors appear to be in a better position to leverage in-kind contributions, typically from neighborhoods that are asked to provide labor for projects that will be financed by municipal revenues. For example, communities throughout the state of Oaxaca have used the *tequio* (collective and reciprocal labor service) to lower the overall cost to the municipality of a given project, thereby making municipal funding of that project more likely.[40] In Ecuador, the election of indigenous mayors in municipalities that were governed by non–indigenous individuals before the 1990s has led to the return of the *minga*, according to which members of a community are expected to volunteer a day's labor on collective projects. Whereas charges of racism made it increasingly difficult for *mestizo* (e.g., mixed-race) mayors to use *minga* labor in the 20th century, indigenous mayors have been able to more successfully exact these non–fiscal contributions.[41]

Finally, understanding the consequences of decentralization requires looking beyond the transfer of political, fiscal and administrative authority to *existing* subnational governments. One of the most important results of decentralization in Latin America is that it has produced the proliferation of *new* subnational governments, chiefly through the subdivision of existing subnational units. In Brazil, for example, generous constitutional reforms in 1988 that mandated federal-municipal and state-municipal revenue sharing help account for a sharp increase in the number of municipalities over the last two decades. In countries with sizable indigenous populations, fiscal decentralization to municipalities has encouraged the organization of rural and indigenous communities who have been marginalized historically, but who are now demanding their fair share of municipal resources relative to the more urbanized town centers that have dominated municipal spending decisions.[42] In some cases, indigenous communities are demanding that submunicipal units be separated out of existing municipalities as the only way to ensure that *mestizo* authorities do not continue to benefit disproportionately from public revenues. The fragmentation of subnational units into ever greater numbers has raised concerns about the viability of many municipalities and regions, and pushed the amalgamation of existing subnational governments onto the policy agenda. These projects face huge challenges, however, as in Peru where voters in a

2005 plebiscite defeated the proposed fusion of the country's 25 regional governments into a smaller set of larger units. In the meantime, additional provinces and districts continue to be created in Peru despite the fact that many of them do not meet minimum population requirements established by law.

Is Latin America Becoming More Federal?

In contrast to decentralization, which can be defined without much controversy as the transferring of political, fiscal and administrative authority to subnational actors, the concept of federalism has generated sharp definitional disagreements. Scholars dispute whether or not federalism requires the representation of subnational governments in national institutions (typically upper chambers and senates), the election of subnational chief executives or subnational legislatures, and the assignment of administrative or fiscal authority.[43] Notwithstanding the absence of scholarly consensus about federalism, since the late 19th century four countries in Latin America have consistently identified themselves as federations: Argentina, Brazil, Mexico and Venezuela. Remarkably for a period that has witnessed such incessant struggles over the terms of decentralization, the set of Latin American countries that consider themselves to be federations in their constitutions has been quite stable. Some unitary countries have introduced changes that would qualify them as federations according to certain definitions of federalism, but all have eschewed the federal label. However, while no countries have formally crossed the line between federal and unitary, decentralization in the last three decades has undoubtedly made federal countries more federal, and it has blurred significantly the distinction between federal and unitary countries—even if no new federations have formally emerged in the region.

The decision to endorse federalism in 19th-century Argentina, Brazil, Mexico and Venezuela was the outcome of important institutional bargains and inter-regional conflicts in each country.[44] Despite the significance of its adoption, the 20th century was nevertheless unkind to federalism in these four cases, even if it remained formally intact. Federal designs intended to protect subnational prerogatives from the center fell victim to military-led authoritarianism in Argentina, Brazil and Venezuela, and to a lengthy period of civilian authoritarianism in Mexico. In addition to illiberal regime types, the emergence of disciplined and mostly centralized political parties also served to hollow out federalism in Argentina, Mexico and Venezuela, generating arrangements that Riker would call "centralized federalism." During significant periods in the 20th century when subnational elections were regularly held in these countries, if the loyalty of subnational officials to their national party leaders conflicted with the interests of their subnational constituents, the former tended to trump the latter.

Against this backdrop, decentralization has breathed new life into long-established federal institutions. In Argentina, the steady expansion in fiscal resources under the control of provinces since the 1970s has made it easier for governors to stand up to presidents and national party leaders—even when they happen to belong to the Peronist party. In Brazil, decentralization in the course of democratization yielded one of the most "robust" forms of federalism anywhere in the developing world.[45] At the lowest level of government, municipal revenue sharing has infused real meaning into the elevation of municipalities to separate federal status in Brazil's 1988 constitution. In Mexico, whose single party hegemonic system made a mockery of federalism after the revolution, genuine political decentralization has thrown into relief the importance of the country's three-tiered governmental structure. Venezuela is perhaps the most complex of the four cases. Support for decentralizing measures on the part of traditional parties in the late 1980s and early 1990s, including the introduction of direct elections for mayors and governors, reinvigorated Venezuela's federal status for a short period before the collapse of the party system. Under Hugo Chavez, re-centralizing changes have once again enervated Venezuelan federalism.[46]

Turning from federal to unitary systems, decentralization has yet to produce the formal federalization of a single unitary country in Latin America. In Colombia, which experienced turbulent periods of federalism in the 19th century before adopting a highly centralist and unitary constitution in 1886, concerted movement in a decentralizing direction in the 1980s and 1990s stopped short of federalism. Instead, the 1991 constitution identifies the country as a "decentralized unitary republic." As in Bolivia, which fought a deadly "federal war" between the regions at the end of the 19th century, the association between federalism and inter-regional conflict in Colombia has probably limited its rhetorical appeal. Instead, many advocates of what would be called "federalism" elsewhere have championed the ideal of a unitary state that recognizes subnational autonomy. Territorial autonomy—and not federalism—is likewise the demand articulated by indigenous communities in unitarian Bolivia, Ecuador and Peru. This stands in stark contrast to other world regions where "peace-preserving federalism" has been an important institutional response to accommodate ethnic diversity and ethnic conflict.

The cumulative effects of decentralizing changes may not convert unitary systems into federations anytime soon in Latin America, but decentralization has nonetheless pushed many unitary countries in a federal direction in ways that have complicated the distinction between federal and unitary. Most significantly, decentralization has involved the creation and/or strengthening of intermediate-level governments. Traditionally in Latin America, unitary countries only had two tiers of government and intermediate governments were considered the preserve of federal systems. Four cases are particularly important here: Chile, Colombia, Peru, and Bolivia. In Chile, where Pinochet introduced regional administrations in his attempt to shrink the central state, the political right demanded the transformation of these administrative units into actual governments as the price of their support for municipal decentralization in 1992. In Colombia, the strengthening of department governments through the introduction of elections and revenue sharing was a critical piece of the proposed political settlement through which national officials hoped to end that country's protracted armed conflict. In Peru, where Alberto Fujimori's *auto golpe* closed regional governments (and not just the national congress), Alejandro Toledo sought to distinguish himself in his campaign for the presidency in 2000 and 2001 by promising to re-introduce elections for regional presidents, which he did in 2002. Finally, the 2005 introduction of elections for regional prefects in Bolivia operated as a key mechanism through which national officials sought to forestall the growth of an increasingly radical movement for regional autonomy in the east.

In each case, far from representing merely formal changes in the architecture of government that had little bearing on substantive politics, reforms at the intermediate level of government have been part and parcel of highly contentious struggles in all four "unitary" countries. Here and elsewhere, decentralization and federalism can only fully be understood as contested responses to some of the most significant political challenges that Latin America continues to face as a region.

Looking forward as the decentralization trend ages, scholars should continue to broaden their frame of analysis beyond the questions of causation that initially dominated the literature. We now have compelling theories about what causes decentralization, but know less about the conditions under which decentralization produces or not its intended effects.

Studying the consequences of decentralization holds out real promise, but also faces considerable challenges. On the one hand, the adoption of mostly symmetric reforms in Latin America will make it easier for scholars to heed Richard Snyder's call for the use of the subnational comparative method.[47] If asymmetric reforms had been adopted—devolving education to some provinces but not to others or holding elections in some municipalities but not all—then examining the effects of these changes across large numbers of subnational governments would have been far more difficult. Instead, scholars are mostly able to hold constant the content of the changes that were adopted in far-flung subnational jurisdictions, a research design option that naturally directs our attention to the host of factors (partisan? demographic? societal? economic?) that might explain why common changes have generated disparate outcomes in different cases. On the other hand, shifting from the study of causes to consequences is a tall order precisely because it requires extensive field research and data collection in multiple research sites, many of which are far more demanding and data poor than the national capitals where the initial decisions to decentralize took place.

The study of decentralization's consequences will dominate—as it should—the literature in the years to come, but scholars should also focus on the politics of re-centralization, about which we still know very little. In most cases, decisions to decentralize in Latin America have not been reversed—hence the urgency of studying the consequences of those decisions. But in other cases, decentralization proved short-lived and resulted in counter moves in a re-centralizing direction.[48] For example, after the adoption of generous, unearmarked revenue sharing measures in Argentina and Brazil in the mid-1980s and Colombia in the early 1990s, national governments in each case secured the passage of changes that by the mid-1990s had either cut transfers or forced subnational officials to spend them on centrally-defined priorities. More recently, "21st century socialists" in Bolivia, Ecuador and Venezuela have all succeeded in re-centralizing fiscal resources that had been decentralized by earlier, neoliberal governments, thereby threatening the independence of opposition-controlled subnational jurisdictions. When does decentralization stick, and when is it vulnerable to efforts by opponents to re-centralize? Are grassroots actors and subnational officials better able to resist re-centralization when it was they who took the lead in demanding decentralization in the first place? Or should we resist the temptation to approach the politics of re-centralization as merely the mirror image of the politics of decentralization? Why is it that we seem to be seeing examples of fiscal and administrative re-centralization (i.e., reducing transfers, taking back authority over highways and ports) but little in the way of political re-centralization (i.e., canceling local elections)?

In addition to uncovering the conditions under which the center is able to claw back resources and authority from subnational governments, scholars should also focus on relationships among subnational governments that are no longer as directly mediated by the center as they were in the past. Decentralization means that the "bilateral" relationship between the national government and individual subnational governments should become less significant, and that competition, conflict and collaboration between subnational governments will become more interesting subjects for research. For example, after decentralization are subnational governments using their expanded set of policy tools to woo (foreign or domestic) capital away from neighboring jurisdictions, and if so to what effect? If decentralization in an era of liberalization seems to be worsening regional inequality in Latin America, are growing tensions between "have" and "have not" subnational regions producing conflicts that go beyond recriminations? Are subnational governments coming together horizontally to provide decentralized goods and services, and if so what new governance structures are they building to share the costs and benefits of their collective action? Given material incentives for the continued proliferation of subnational units, and deep political obstacles that have prevented their amalgamation into units of more viable size, the number of subnational governments is likely to continue to grow in the future, which will further complicate the important relationships between them that are unfolding in post-decentralization Latin America.

Notes

1 For a cross-regional study, see Philip Oxhorn, Joseph Tulchin and Andrew Selee, eds., *Decentralization, Democratic Governance and Civil Society in Comparative Perspective* (Washington, D.C.: Woodrow Wilson Center Press, 2004).
2 Kent Eaton, *Politics beyond the Capital: The Design of Subnational Institutions in South America* (Stanford University Press, 2004).
3 One other dimension—contractual authority for subnational governments—is beginning to receive attention. See J. Tyler Dickovick, *Decentralization and Recentralization in the Developing World* (Penn State University Press, 2010). See also Aaron Schneider, "Decentralization: Conceptualization and Measurement," *Studies in Comparative International Development* 38 (3) 2003: 32–56.
4 Tim Campbell, *The Quiet Revolution* (University of Pittsburgh Press, 2003).
5 Rebecca Abers, *Inventing Local Democracy: Grassroots Politics in Brazil* (Boulder: Lynne Rienner, 2000).
6 See Jonathan Hiskey and Mitchell Seligson, "Pitfalls of Power to the People: Decentralization, Local Government Performance, and System Support in Bolivia," *Studies in Comparative International Development* 37 (4): 64–88; Donna Van Cott, *Radical Democracy in the Andes* (New York: Cambridge University Press, 2008); and Margaret Keck and Rebecca Abers, "Mobilizing the State: The Erratic Partner in Brazil's Participatory Water Policy," *Politics & Society* 37 (2) 2007: 289–314.
7 Christopher Sabatini, "Decentralization and Political Parties." *Journal of Democracy* 14 (2) 2003: 138–150.
8 Maria Escobar-Lemmon, "Fiscal Decentralization and Federalism in Latin America," *Publius* 31 (4) 2001: 23–41.
9 Carlos Gervasoni, "A Rentier Theory of Subnational Regimes," *World Politics* 62 (2) 2010: 302–340.
10 Claudio Véliz, *The Centralist Tradition in Latin America* (Princeton University Press, 1980).
11 M. Victoria Murillo, "Recovering Political Dynamics: Teachers' Unions and the Decentralization of Education in Argentina and Mexico," *Journal of Inter-American Studies* 41 (1) 1999: 31–57.
12 Tulia Faletti, *Decentralization and Subnational Politics in Latin America* (New York: Cambridge University Press, 2010).
13 J. Tyler Dickovick, "Municipalization as Central Government Strategy: Center-Regional-Local Politics in Peru, Brazil and South Africa," *Publius* 37 (1) 2007: 1–25.
14 Merilee Grindle, *Going Local: Decentralization, Democratization and the Promise of Good Governance* (Princeton University Press, 2009).
15 For an important study that examines variation in subnational responses to liberalization and decentralization, see Richard Snyder, *Politics after Neoliberalism: Reregulation in Mexico* (Cambridge University Press, 2001).
16 Kent Eaton, "Decentralization's Non-democratic Roots: Authoritarianism and Subnational Reform in South America," *Latin American Politics and Society* 48 (1) 2006: 1–26.
17 Benjamin Goldfrank and Andrew Schrank, "Municipal Liberalism and Municipal Socialism: Urban Political Economy in Latin America," *International Journal of Urban and Regional Research* 33 (2) 2009: 443–462.
18 Alfred Montero and David Samuels, eds., *Decentralization and Democracy in Latin America* (University of Notre Dame Press, 2004).
19 Caroline Beer, *Electoral Competition and Institutional Change in Mexico* (University of Notre Dame Press, 2003).
20 David Samuels and Fernando Abrucio, "The 'New' Politics of the Governors: Federalism and the Brazilian Transition to Democracy," *Publius: the Journal of Federalism* 30 (2) 2001: 43–61.

21 Gary Bland, "Enclaves and Elections: The Decision to Decentralize in Chile," in Montero and Samuels, *Decentralization and Democracy*.

22 Kathleen O'Neill, *Decentralizing the State: Elections, Parties and Local Power in the Andes* (Cambridge University Press, 2005).

23 Kent Eaton, "The Downside of Decentralization: Armed Clientelism in Colombia," *Security Studies* 15 (4) 2006: 1–30.

24 See, for examples, Grindle, *Going Local*, Van Cott, *Radical Democracy*, and Brian Wampler, *Participatory Budgeting in Brazil: Contestation, Cooperation, Accountability* (University Park: Penn State University Press, 2007).

25 For a similar finding that the leadership of regional presidents explains the success or failure of the participatory mechanisms that were adopted in Peruvian regions in 2003, see Stephanie McNulty, *Voice and Vote: Decentralization, Participation, and the Crisis of Representative Democracy in Peru* (Stanford University Press, 2011).

26 Bert Gustafson, "Paradoxes of Liberal Indigenism," in David Marbury Lewis, ed., *The Politics of Ethnicity: Indigenous Peoples in Latin American States* (Cambridge: Harvard University Press, 2002); Donna Van Cott, *From Movements to Parties* (Cambridge University Press, 2005).

27 David Samuels, "From Socialism to Social Democracy: The Evolution of the Workers' Party in Brazil," *Comparative Political Studies* 37 (9) 2004: 999–1024.

28 Yemile Mizrahi, "*From Martyrdom to Power: The Partido Acción Nacional in Mexico* (University of Notre Dame Press, 2003).

29 Note, however, that Grindle's *Going Local* partially refutes this argument in that she finds that PAN-governed municipalities did not tend to outperform other municipalities.

30 Gianpaolo Baiocchi, *Militants and Citizens* (Stanford University Press, 2005); Benjamin Goldfrank, *Participation, Decentralization and the Left: Deepening Local Democracy in Latin America* (Penn State University Press, 2011); and Wampler, *Participatory Budgeting*.

31 Peter Evans, "Government Action, Social Capital and Development: Reviewing the Evidence on Synergy," *World Development* 24 (6) 1996: 1119–1132. Notwithstanding these gains, it is important to note that the PB model has largely been neglected subsequent to the electoral defeat of its sponsors in 2004, an indicator of the sustainability problems discussed in the previous section.

32 Benjamin Goldfrank, "The Politics of Deepening Local Democracy," *Comparative Politics*, January 2007: 147–168.

33 Allison Rowland, "Population as a Determinant of Local Outcomes in Decentralization: Illustrations from Small Municipalities in Bolivia and Mexico," *World Development* 29 (8) 2001: 1373–1389.

34 Patrick Heller, "Moving the State: The Politics of Democratic Decentralization in Kerala, South Africa and Porto Alegre," *Politics & Society* 29 (1) 2001: 133. That parties in the last ten years have proved to be so critical in the success of these expanded forms of participation is significant given the long-standing concerns that advocates of social movements have had about building alliances with leftist parties.

35 Sybil Rhodes, "Progressive Pragmatism as a Governance Model," in Susan Eckstein and Timothy Wickham-Crowley, eds., *What Justice? Whose Justice? Fighting for Fairness in Latin America* (University of California Press, 2003).

36 Goldfrank, *Participation*.

37 Erik Wibbels, *Federalism and the Market* (Cambridge University Press, 2005).

38 Karen Remmer and Erik Wibbels, "The Subnational Politics of Economic Adjustment: Provincial Politics and Fiscal Performance in Argentina," *Comparative Political Studies* 33 (2000): 419–451.

39 David Brown, "Democracy, Authoritarianism, and Education Finance in Brazil," *Journal of Latin American Studies* 34 (1) 2002: 115–141.

40 Grindle, *Going Local*, p. 131.

41 Van Cott, *Radical Democracy*.

42 See John Cameron, *Struggles for Local Democracy in the Andes* (Lynne Rienner Press, 2009); and Jonathan Fox, "Rural Democratization and Decentralization at the State/Society Interface: What Counts as 'Local' Government in the Mexican Countryside," *Journal of Peasant Studies* 34 (3/4) 2007: 527–559.

43 For different approaches, see Alberto Diaz Cayeros, *Federalism, Fiscal Authority and Centralization in Latin America* (New York: Cambridge University Press, 2006) and Wibbels, *Federalism and the Market*.

44 Edward Gibson, ed., *Federalism and Democracy in Latin America* (Johns Hopkins University Press, 2004).

45 Scott Mainwaring, "Multipartism, Robust Federalism and Presidentialism in Latin America," in Mainwaring and Shugart, eds., *Presidentialism and Democracy in Latin America* (New York: Cambridge University Press, 1997).

46 Javier Corrales and Michael Penfold, "Venezuela: Crowding Out the Opposition," *Journal of Democracy* 18 (2) 2007: 99–113.

47 Richard Snyder, "Scaling Down: The Subnational Comparative Method," *Studies in Comparative International Development* 36 (1) 2001: 93–110.

48 Dickovick, *Decentralization and Recentralization*.

4

PARTIES, PARTY SYSTEMS, AND POLITICAL REPRESENTATION

Kenneth M. Roberts

A basic paradox lies at the heart of the wave of democratization that swept across Latin America in the waning decades of the 20th century. On one hand, new democratic regimes have proven to be more stable and resilient than virtually any observer anticipated when the wave began. This stability made it possible to hope that democratic consolidation would finally put an end to the historic pattern of pendular swings between authoritarian and democratic governance.[1] On the other hand, the core representative institutions of liberal democracy—party systems in particular—proved to be remarkably fragile in many countries, and they generally inspired little in the way of public confidence or support. Paradoxically, then, democratic consolidation appeared to coincide with a "crisis of representation" and a generalized disillusionment with—or even the wholesale rejection of—the political establishment in much of the region.[2] This crisis was manifested in widespread electoral volatility, the breakdown of party systems in a number of countries, and the rise of new protest movements and/or populist "outsiders" who frontally challenged the political establishment.

Clearly, this crisis of representation afflicted some party systems much more than others. Over the course of the 1990s and early 2000s, established party systems largely collapsed in Peru, Venezuela, Colombia, Ecuador, and Bolivia, while partial breakdowns occurred in Argentina and Costa Rica. Party systems proved more resilient in Uruguay, Chile, and the Dominican Republic, however, and they even became more institutionalized or competitive in countries like Brazil, Mexico, and El Salvador. This mixed record makes it difficult to render a generalized assessment of the status of party systems and democratic representation in the region. Indeed, it places a premium on efforts to develop mid-range theories that are capable of explaining variation in forms and patterns of partisan representation, both spatially (i.e., across cases) and temporally (i.e., over time within individual cases).

Such explanations should be grounded in a historical understanding of the formative experiences that shaped and differentiated party systems in the region, especially following the onset of mass politics in the first half of the 20th century. More fundamentally, however, they need to be based on a systematic analysis of the party system effects of the "dual transitions" towards political democracy and globalized market liberalism in the waning decades of that century. These dual transitions institutionalized electoral competition in a context of tumultuous social and economic change—a context that included the demise of state-led development in the debt crisis of the 1980s, the wrenching adoption of neoliberal stabilization and structural adjustment policies, and the social dislocation and re-articulation of popular subjects who resisted market liberalization and ultimately helped revive left-of-center political alternatives at the turn of the century.[3] Although some party systems weathered this storm of socioeconomic and political transformation, few, if any, were left unscathed, as even the survivors were forced to adapt to new policy landscapes, cleavage patterns, and competitive alignments.

Recent scholarship has greatly advanced our understanding of these challenges, and in the process it has shed new light on the properties of both individual parties and national party systems in Latin America. As this chapter suggests, however, formidable questions remain unanswered, especially regarding the dynamic properties of parties and party systems and their sources of change over time. Exploring these dynamic properties, in turn, suggests that Latin America's crisis of representation is not simply a function of weak, corrupt, or unresponsive parties and party systems, prevalent as these may be in much of the region. Parties are, ultimately, intermediary institutions that link states and societies through a competitive struggle to aggregate societal interests, articulate their preferences through public policy platforms, and advance these platforms within decision-making arenas. A crisis of representation, therefore, may not only be rooted in parties as intermediary institutions, but also, more fundamentally, in fragmented civil societies that impede the aggregation and articulation of popular sector interests, and debilitated states that cannot respond to societal claims, enforce citizenship rights, or translate policy platforms into meaningful programmatic alternatives. A full understanding of Latin America's crisis of representation thus requires that parties be analyzed in the larger state and societal contexts that they seek to link.

Explaining Variation in Latin American Party Systems

Anyone who studies Latin American politics quickly encounters a set of generalized impressions about parties and party systems. Although these impressions are not always based on systematic measurement or comparative analyses—Western Europe, the source of most theorizing about party politics, generally serves as an implicit point of reference—they are widely assumed to reflect modal patterns or traits in the region. Latin American parties, it is thought, are organizationally weak and undisciplined. They are organized around dominant personalities and their clientele networks rather than strong local branches; they are ideologically diffuse and ill-defined; they have shallow roots in society and weak partisan identities; and they appeal to heterogeneous, "catch-all" constituencies that are often sociologically indistinguishable from those of their competitors. Given these organizational traits, it is hardly surprising that party systems are likewise presumed to be fluid and unstable, with competitive alignments that are not well-anchored by social cleavages or programmatic distinctions.

Whether or not these impressions are descriptively accurate portrayals of modal tendencies, they suffer from two primary limitations. First, until recently, these modal tendencies have not only been under-measured, but also dramatically under-theorized. That Latin American parties differed from those in Western Europe was plain to see; the reasons for their divergence, however, were far from clear, and they certainly were not systematically explained. Second, the modal tendencies clearly masked substantial variation around the mean. Indeed, it was difficult to locate some prominent "outliers" within the modal patterns at all, making the explanation of variation at least as important as the identification of central tendencies. These challenges, and efforts to address them, are elaborated on below.

With respect to the problems of under-measurement and under-theorization, recent scholarship has taken great strides towards conceptualizing, measuring, and explaining some of the distinctive features of parties and party systems in Latin America. Flavia Freidenberg and Steven Levitsky, for example, introduced the concept of informal institutions to the study of party organizations in Latin America, arguing that "the weakness of formal party structures ... should not obscure the vast *informal* organizations that often lie behind them," producing a "vast gap" between how parties "are organized on paper and how they function in practice."[4] The authors proceed to identify a series of indicators of formal and informal party structures, in areas as diverse as finance, membership, decision-making, internal rules, and bureaucratic organization. Advances have also been made in measuring party system attributes in the region; especially noteworthy is the ambitious survey of national legislators overseen by Manuel Alcántara and other researchers at the Universidad de Salamanca. The Salamanca survey provided a treasure trove of information on the political attitudes of party elites and the ideological structuring of partisan competition.[5] At the grass-roots level, survey research by Ruth Berins Collier and Samuel Handlin and their collaborators has broken new ground for understanding popular participation in partisan networks and its relationship to other forms of civic activism.[6] Similarly, Mark Jones has made a systematic effort to operationalize and measure many of the traits that are often incorporated in empirical studies of Latin American party systems.[7]

In a recent pathbreaking study, David Samuels and Matthew Shugart advance toward a more generalized explanation of the distinctive features of parties in Latin America and other countries with presidential democracies.[8] In contrast to parties in Western Europe, which have been shaped historically by the institutional incentives of parliamentarism, parties in Latin America are "presidentialized"—that is, they are heavily conditioned by the separation of powers between executive and legislative branches and the implications of this separation for party organization and leadership. Since executive and legislative branches have separate origins and survival in office, not to mention different electoral constituencies, parties are required to operate in two different arenas with distinct incentive structures. Leaders seeking executive office may thus act with relative independence and undermine partisan accountability. Presidential regimes, therefore, spawn party organizations characterized by relatively weak central authority, internal conflict and indiscipline, ambiguous or incoherent programmatic stands, and diffuse electoral constituencies.

The Samuels and Shugart volume offers a compelling, institutionally-grounded explanation of central tendencies among Latin American parties. But what, however, accounts for the second major challenge identified above—the reality of widespread variation across parties and party systems in the region? Anomalies such as the bureaucratic organization and hierarchical discipline of Venezuela's historic parties,[9] or the ideological structuring and class-based constituencies of Chile's, do not fit neatly within overarching generalizations. Indeed, Latin America provides a wealth of information for scholars who seek to analyze variation in the attributes of parties and party systems. At the level of individual party organizations, the region has possessed both mass parties and elite or cadre-based parties; parties that are disciplined and undisciplined; parties that are bureaucratic as well as personalistic; parties with catch-all and class-based constituencies; and parties that cultivate programmatic as well as clientelistic linkages to voters. Likewise, all the main dimensions or properties of party systems that preoccupy scholars exhibit substantial cross-national variation in the region—from the number of parties to the nature of their cleavage structures and competitive alignments, not to mention their levels of stability, institutionalization, ideological polarization, and programmatic structuring.

In part, this variation reflects the diverse developmental experiences of party systems in Latin America. In contrast to Western Europe—where class cleavages, left-right programmatic structuration, and partisan institutionalization in the 20th century provided a shared analytical "core" that was conducive to comparative analysis[10]—party systems in Latin America sharply diverged in their development trajectories following the onset of mass politics during the early stages of industrialization. In Colombia, Uruguay, Honduras, and Paraguay, parties with roots in the 19th century period of oligarchic competition and restricted suffrage remained electorally dominant following the rise of mass politics in the 20th century, relying primarily on patron-client linkages to broaden their bases of support among the working and lower classes (or, where that failed, authoritarian interludes to short-circuit the rise of populist and leftist competitors). In other countries, however, such as Argentina, Brazil, Chile, Mexico, Peru, and Venezuela, electoral competition was reconfigured by the rise of a mass-based labor-mobilizing populist or leftist party during the middle of the 20th century.[11] In still others, including Costa Rica, Ecuador, Panama, and the Dominican Republic, traditional oligarchic parties were eclipsed by new multi-class or personality-based parties that provided little impetus for labor mobilization.

Scholarship on the region has long struggled to make sense of this variation, often resorting to case-specific interpretations or descriptive overviews of national patterns that fall well short of generalizable explanation. Early cross-national research, for example, tended to focus on simple "format" features such as the number of parties comprising a given party system[12]—a useful starting point, to be sure, but nevertheless one that provided little insight into the types of party organizations, societal linkages, or cleavage patterns that existed in different national party systems. As the "third wave" of democratization institutionalized electoral competition across the region, however, scholars increasingly explored the complex inner workings and social embeddedness of party systems, such as their cleavage structures and degrees of institutionalization.[13] In so doing, they shed new light on cross-national variation among party systems in the region, as well as the patterns that differentiated Latin American party systems from those in Western Europe.

One strand of research, for example, sought to identify and explain variation in the stability and institutionalization of party systems, an area in which Latin American party systems are strikingly more diverse than those in Western Europe. In a seminal contribution, Mainwaring and Scully not only distinguished between institutionalized and inchoate party systems, but also provided a set of criteria to assess degrees of institutionalization—namely, the stability of electoral competition, the depth of party roots in society, the legitimacy of parties and elections for determining who governs, and the strength of internal party organizations.[14] Subsequent research built on this foundation to explore the correlates of electoral stability and volatility, finding the latter to be associated with economic crises, ethnic cleavages, and unstable institutional rules.[15]

By definition, where electoral contests are volatile and unpredictable, parties' roots in society must be fluid, fragile, contingent, or shallow. A related line of research has thus focused attention on the linkages between parties and society, a natural concern for anyone seeking to understand a crisis of representation. In this area as well, Latin American parties differ from those in Europe; although clientelistic linkages are ubiquitous in party systems around the world, many Latin American parties appear to be inordinately dependent on them, whereas policy-based or programmatic linkages are unevenly developed in the region. The centrality of patron-clientelism has inspired a number of works—including sophisticated ethnographic, game-theoretic, and survey-based studies—that break new ground in explaining how clientelist exchanges work, and how they shape party organizations, social constituencies, and electoral behavior. Historically, clientelism enabled oligarchic parties to sink roots in popular constituencies following the expansion of the suffrage, and it helped hegemonic parties reproduce authoritarian rule in countries like Mexico and Paraguay.[16] More recently, it provided a lifeline for some parties—in particular, the Peronist party in Argentina—to maintain partisan loyalties among low income voters in the midst of market liberalization, despite dramatic changes in their policy orientations and the erosion of traditional corporatist ties to labor union constituencies.[17]

Programmatic linkages between parties and voters may be less consistently established, but they are far from absent, as the landmark study by Kitschelt et al. demonstrates.[18] This study is the first systematic attempt to measure and compare the programmatic structuring of partisan competition in Latin America, and—perhaps more importantly—to explain variation across countries. Kitschelt et al. marshal a wealth of legislative and public opinion survey data to show that some national party systems offer voters reasonably coherent and differentiated programmatic alternatives—structured primarily but not exclusively by rival preferences toward economic and redistributive policies—whereas others do not. This variation, they argue, is deeply rooted in historical patterns of political and economic development: programmatic competition in the late 20th century existed in countries that were relatively "early" in their economic and industrial development, that experienced extended periods of democratic competition, and that adopted relatively encompassing social welfare or protection policies during the era of import-substitution industrialization (ISI). Countries that lacked these favorable historical conditions were more likely to structure partisan competition around non-programmatic, clientelistic linkages, or to lack coherent structuring of partisan competition altogether.

In short, recent scholarship has greatly enhanced our understanding of cross-national variation in core party system attributes like levels of institutionalization and programmatic competition. It is important to note, however, that these systemic features are dynamic rather than static properties. Explaining their variation over time in any individual country is as daunting as explaining their variation across cases. Venezuela, for example, surely boasted one of the most institutionalized party systems in the region in the 1970s and 1980s, as Coppedge's work persuasively showed.[19] The collapse of this "partyarchy" in the 1990s, and its subsequent displacement by a populist outsider, remains one of the enduring enigmas of recent Latin American political development. Conversely, a Brazilian party system long noted for being volatile, inchoate, and undisciplined became increasingly institutionalized and programmatic over the course of the 1990s and 2000s.[20] Given such dynamic processes of institutionalization and de-institutionalization, essentialist characterizations or single-shot measurements of individual party systems can easily become dated, placing a premium on efforts to understand longitudinal patterns of political development.

Similar challenges beset efforts to explain the programmatic structuring (or non-structuring) of party systems in Latin America. Given the importance of historical conditioning factors in the study by Kitschelt et al., the level of programmatic structuring in any given party system is presumed to be durable and at least partially path dependent. That is, development experiences in the early part of the 20th century spawned political and institutional trajectories that weighed heavily on party system dynamics at the end of the century; more recent regime changes, economic crises, and policy shifts were generally incapable of dislodging countries from these trajectories. But while Kitschelt et al. should be applauded for demonstrating that history matters and that economic structures condition political competition, their empirical analysis—based on a cross-sectional snapshot of programmatic competition at the end of the 20th century—does not allow us to assess longitudinal variation in programmatic structuration within or across countries. Such variation, in fact, clearly exists; the collapse of import substitution industrialization and the spread of market liberalization across the region at the end of the 20th century, for example, undermined programmatic competition in countries like Peru and Costa Rica, while enhancing it in Brazil and Uruguay. While this longitudinal variation hardly denies the significance of the long-term inducements to structuration identified by Kitschelt et al., it does suggest that scholars should also be sensitive to more short-term and conjunctural factors that encourage or inhibit programmatic forms of partisan competition.

Indeed, there are reasons to believe that both the institutionalization and the programmatic structuring of party systems in contemporary Latin America have been heavily conditioned by their experiences during the period of transition from ISI to neoliberalism in the waning decades of the 20th century. This transition posed significant challenges to forms of political representation—deeply embedded in the state-centric logic of the ISI development model—that emerged following the onset of mass politics earlier in the century. To understand Latin America's crisis of representation, it is essential to explore the fate of party systems during this transition.

Change and Continuity in Contemporary Party Systems

Historically, one of the major factors impeding the institutionalization of party systems in Latin America was the frequent interruption of electoral competition by military coups, authoritarian regimes, and the proscription or repression of individual parties (especially those with strong popular sector support).[21] Although established party systems are sometimes "frozen" into place during authoritarian interludes, over the long haul, party systems need routinized electoral contestation to consolidate. Partisan identities, after all, are not constructed overnight, and neither are the competitive alignments that structure party systems; they only congeal over time as rival parties develop reputations or "brand names" based on their performance in office, their pursuit of distinct policy goals, or their distribution of benefits to favored constituencies (the bases, respectively, for valence, programmatic, and clientelist appeals or societal linkages). Where parties are banned or electoral competition interrupted, these societal linkages may wither or fail to congeal, and the processes of voter socialization and habituation that foster durable partisan identities may get short-circuited.

If that is the case, the wave of democratization underway in Latin America since the late 1970s might appear to offer unusually favorable conditions for consolidating some of the region's notoriously inchoate party systems. With remarkably few regime breakdowns or interruptions of democracy, this wave of democratization has offered party organizations throughout the region an unprecedented period of time in which to mobilize voters, build partisan identities, and align (or re-align) electoral competition. Arguably, elements of such institutionalization have occurred in countries like Brazil, Chile, El Salvador, Mexico, and Uruguay. In much of the region, however, the opposite has occurred; established parties have weakened, collapsed, or been displaced by new parties or movements with uncertain staying power, often little more than registration labels for dominant personalities. In some cases, these personalities are recognized members of the political establishment who have abandoned traditional parties to chart a more independent path to the presidency; that was the case, for example, with Rafael Caldera in Venezuela and Álvaro Uribe in Colombia. In other cases, however, they have arisen outside the party system to challenge the political establishment, as seen in Peru with Alberto Fujimori and Alejandro Toledo, Venezuela with Hugo Chávez, Ecuador with Lucio Gutiérrez and Rafael Correa, Paraguay with Fernando

Lugo, and Bolivia with Evo Morales. Why, then, has the institutionalization of electoral competition coincided not with a consolidation of party systems in so much of the region, but rather with their *de*-institutionalization—and thus an informalization and personalization of political representation?

De-institutionalization could simply be a regional variant of the widely-recognized international trend toward the decline of mass party organizations. As Philippe Schmitter succinctly puts it, "Parties are not what they once were,"[22] even in their historic West European bastions, in part because many of their traditional roles in socializing citizens, mobilizing voters, and shaping the political agenda have been taken over by a plethora of more specialized interest groups and media outlets.[23] If that is the case—if near-universal patterns of social diversification and modernization are weakening the centrality of parties to democratic political representation—then more party systems are likely to break down in Latin America, and there is little reason to expect new ones to emerge from the ruins of the old. Alternatively, as Martín Tanaka suggests,[24] party system de-institutionalization may be a function of perverse political agency, when opportunistic leaders exacerbate factionalism or abandon established parties in pursuit of narrow and short-term political self-interests.

However insightful, neither of these approaches is fully satisfactory. Universalistic interpretations are too deterministic to explain variation in timing or outcomes, while the particularism of voluntaristic accounts gives inadequate attention to common challenges that may shape the strategic behavior of political elites. In between universalism and particularism, however, lie middle-range explanations that adopt a comparative perspective on the historical juncture under which electoral competition spread across Latin America in the 1980s and 1990s. Democratic transitions in the region coincided with a collapse of the ISI model of development and a transition to market liberalism that posed formidable challenges to traditional party systems. As briefly explained below, these dual transitions left an indelible mark on both the institutionalization of party systems and their patterns of programmatic structuring.

Electoral competition in a context of economic crisis can be highly destabilizing for party systems, and this was certainly the case for those in Latin America in the 1980s and much of the 1990s. The debt crisis, fiscal deficits, and acute foreign exchange constraints that accompanied the demise of the ISI model forced Latin American governments to impose politically costly austerity and stabilization packages, which typically produced painful economic recessions; governments that postponed or failed to adjust often paid an even steeper price down the road in the form of hyperinflation. The most direct impact of these economic crises on party systems was widespread anti-incumbent vote shifts that weakened governing parties[25]—in some cases, successive governing parties saddled with the costs of chronic and inconclusive crisis management.

These performance costs were unevenly borne within and across party systems, depending on the depth and duration of economic crises and the dynamics of the reform process. Where crises were relatively mild and short-lived, their political costs were sometimes contained within a particular governing party or coalition, and parties that successfully stabilized their economies were sometimes able to reap performance dividends. Where crises were more severe or prolonged, however, performance costs were higher, and broader systemic effects became more likely. This was especially the case in party systems that had been reconfigured by the rise of major labor-based populist or leftist parties during the ISI era—what I elsewhere call labor-mobilizing party systems.[26] Countries with these party systems—namely Argentina, Bolivia, Brazil, Chile, Mexico, Nicaragua, Peru, and Venezuela—had powerful union movements that had been spawned by some combination of deep import-substituting industrialization, state-dominated extractive industries, or short-lived socialist experiments. They subsequently suffered the most severe economic crises during the transition to neoliberalism—including all the cases of hyperinflation in the region—as well as steep declines in trade unionization, which eroded the social and organizational bases of the leading mass parties. Given these disruptions, countries with labor-mobilizing party systems, on average, experienced greater electoral volatility during the 1980s and 90s (with the exception of Chile, where military dictatorship shielded the party system from the electoral costs of economic adjustment).

Clearly, the decline of traditional labor and peasant movements, combined with the fragmentation and informalization of the work force that accompanied economic crisis and market restructuring, posed unique challenges to populist and leftist parties that historically specialized in the corporatist representation of organized working and lower class constituencies. It also seriously impaired the ability of these popular sectors to defend their interests through collective action and articulate their demands in the political arena.[27] This fragmented social landscape was thus far from conducive to the aggregation of interests by parties—the "bottom-up" dimension of the crisis of representation in the region. The erosion of societal linkages, however, was not restricted to populist and leftist parties with corporatist ties to popular sectors; in countries like Uruguay, more conservative parties that relied on clientelist linkages to the unorganized poor were also affected by austerity measures and market reforms that limited the resources and interventionist tools available to incumbents to reproduce voter loyalties.[28]

As Jana Morgan persuasively demonstrates in her work on Venezuela's party system collapse,[29] programmatic linkages between parties and voters could also be damaged during the transition to market liberalism. For strong programmatic linkages to exist, three basic conditions need to be met. First, parties must adopt relatively coherent stands on salient issues that divide the body politic. Programmatic stands are diffused when different sub-units or factions of a party adopt highly disparate positions on major issues, or when parties compete on the basis of clientelist rewards, personalistic appeals, or their ability to achieve "valence" goals about which everyone agrees (such as "clean" government or economic growth). Second, meaningful differences must exist in the policy alternatives offered by major competing parties. Where all the major parties adopt similar policy platforms, voters have no rational basis to prefer one party over another on programmatic grounds. Finally, the policies adopted by a party in public office must have some meaningful resemblance to the platform on which it ran. Few governing parties ever fully implement their campaign platforms, given the emergence of unforeseen circumstances and the inevitable compromises and modifications that arise during legislative and policymaking processes. Nevertheless, for programmatic linkages to be sustained, voters need to be confident that platforms provide at least a basic policy or philosophical orientation to guide a party's response to changing conditions.

Along all three of these dimensions, the collapse of both ISI and socialist development models in the 1980s and the emerging technocratic consensus for neoliberal reform were programmatically de-aligning for party systems. Whatever their policy preferences, governing parties found their policy options severely limited by fiscal deficits, balance of payments crises, and acute inflationary pressures, while financial relief from the IMF and international creditors was made conditional on the adoption of orthodox structural adjustment policies. To be sure, grass-roots opposition to neoliberal orthodoxy was widespread (if highly fragmented and, in most cases, politically ineffectual), and tightening global market constraints did not entirely dissolve partisan differences in policymaking; as María Victoria Murillo convincingly shows, historic populist parties with core labor constituencies liberalized differently than conservative parties backed by business elites.[30] Nevertheless, the range of viable policy options clearly narrowed by the end of the 1980s, when the heterodox stabilization experiments in Argentina, Brazil, and Peru were thoroughly discredited by hyperinflationary crises. Over the next decade, even governing parties and political leaders who did not embrace neoliberal orthodoxy in the normative sense accepted one or another variant of market liberalism as "the only game in town."

This technocratic consensus may have dampened ideological conflict in the region, but it also made it difficult for parties to appeal to voters on the basis of recognizable programmatic distinctions. Indeed, policy switching was widespread, as a diverse range of populist, labor-based, and center-left parties often played a leading or collaborative role in the process of market liberalization, usually after campaigning against it.[31] Such policy switches produced internal dissent and factionalism that undermined the programmatic coherence of governing parties. They also blurred the historic differences between conservative and populist or center-left parties, and eroded the significance of the electoral process for signaling collective policy preferences. As Noam Lupu argues in a compelling micro-analytic account, when major parties converge programmatically, their "brands" become diluted, and voters are more prone to abandon them when performance in office falters.[32] To the extent that policy switches were driven not by political opportunism, but rather by tightening global market constraints on state behavior, they were indicative of the top-down dimension of Latin America's crisis of representation—the diminished capacity of states to respond to societal demands that departed from orthodox conceptions of market efficiency, even where these demands were clearly transmitted via the electoral process to governing institutions.

These policy switches highlight a central paradox of Latin America's transition to neoliberalism: business-allied, pro-market conservative parties were generally unable to lead the process of market reform, especially in countries with a strong labor-based populist or leftist challenger. Since conservative parties were sure to encounter well-organized opposition to neoliberal reforms in these countries, parties with historic ties to organized labor had a comparative advantage in the reform process; they could offer inducements for cooperation, coopt union leaders, and draw upon reservoirs of political capital and trust to contain popular mobilization (at least in the short term).[33] Consequently, historic populist or labor-based parties (such as the Peronists in Argentina, the PRI in Mexico, AD in Venezuela, and the MNR in Bolivia) assumed political responsibility for initiating structural adjustment policies in the midst of economic crises, even though these policies clashed dramatically with their historic commitments. Conservative parties played major roles in the reform process primarily in countries with weak labor movements and recent experiences with authoritarian rule or military repression that had constrained the political mobilization of popular sectors.

These different alignments of partisan actors in the process of market liberalization had important implications for party systems in the post-adjustment era—that is, after the mid-1990s—when mass social protests against the neoliberal model erupted in a number of countries,[34] and a generalized reconstruction of leftist political alternatives occurred. The adoption of market reforms by major populist or labor-based parties may have enhanced the political viability of liberalization policies in the short term, but it left programmatically de-aligned party systems vulnerable to a range of destabilizing tendencies in the post-adjustment period, including the rise of mass protest movements, new leftist parties, or anti-system populist figures. All of these actors challenged party systems that failed to provide institutionalized channels for the articulation of dissent from neoliberal orthodoxy. Similar "outsider" challenges were faced by party systems that lacked an institutionalized leftist challenger to reforms led by more conservative parties.

By contrast, where pro-business conservative or centrist political actors led the process of market liberalization and faced an institutionalized leftist challenger, the programmatic alignment of party systems tended to be maintained or even strengthened. The competitive alignments produced by this latter pattern of reform tended to be quite stable in the post-adjustment period, in part because they channeled societal resistance to market liberalism into institutionalized partisan and electoral arenas. Variants of this latter pattern can be found in Brazil, Chile, El Salvador, Mexico, and Uruguay, all of which maintained relatively stable patterns of electoral competition between established conservative and leftist parties in the aftermath to market liberalization.

Crafting a Research Agenda

These challenges to party systems during Latin America's neoliberal era have left a number of puzzles and questions on the agenda for future research. The proliferation of studies on the region's post-adjustment "left turn," for example, has an obvious, but largely unexplored, counterpart: the electoral demise of the partisan right in a surprising number of countries. The partisan right not only played a modest role in the two-decade long process of neoliberal restructuring in the region, but it also reaped remarkably few political rewards from the dramatic shift in public policies towards its ideological positions and the structural empowerment of its business and financial allies, both domestically and internationally. Studies by Gibson and Middlebrook provide a strong foundation on which to build,[35] but much work remains to be done to explain why some conservative parties continue to fare well, while so many others have entered into decline. Clearly, this is a topic where comparative historical research and micro-analytic accounts of strategic behavior and voter choice can complement each other.

Second, scholarly understanding of the resurgence of populist and leftist alternatives is far from complete. It is not clear, for example, to what extent the "left turn" is a product of simple anti-incumbent vote shifts that produce democratic alternations in office, as opposed to potentially more durable shifts in public opinion, political identities, and programmatic preferences. Likewise, the social bases and cleavage structures that undergird the "left turn" remain poorly understood, both at the micro-level of vote choice and the meso-level of organized social constituencies and activist networks. As the volume by Collier and Handlin emphasizes,[36] the "party-union hubs" that dominated popular political representation during the ISI era have largely broken down, and the reconstruction of populist and leftist alternatives since the late 1990s has been grounded in quite different, and highly varied, organizational bases and activist networks. Latin America's political landscape has been indelibly marked by the mobilization of new popular subjects—most prominently, indigenous movements in the Andean region—which have frontally challenged traditional parties and at least partially reconfigured party systems, at least in the Bolivian case. The relationships between these new popular subjects and populist or leftist parties are remarkably varied, however, and they are inevitably transformed as movements travel along the continuum from social protest to institutionalized participation to governing responsibilities. These relationships cry out for more systematic comparative research.

Third, and related to the above, scholarship on the region has barely begun to tackle the thorny question of how—or whether—party systems will be reconstituted in the aftermath of their breakdown. Democratic theorists typically emphasize the centrality, if not indispensability, of parties for democratic representation, but to date the region's track record of rebuilding competitive party systems following their demise is woeful. Indeed, the track record amply demonstrates that in an era of mass media and cybernetic communications, traditional forms of partisan organization are hardly prerequisites for winning elections, though they may well be essential to institutionalize competitive politics and uphold democratic accountability. Analyses of the strategic behavior of political entrepreneurs and voters who choose or eschew party-mediated forms of representation should occupy a central place on the region's research agenda.

Finally, much work remains to be done on the programmatic realignment of party systems in the aftermath of market liberalization. The "left turn" clearly embodies varied national attempts to break with the technocratic consensus around the neoliberal model and expand the range of development alternatives. In that sense, it has "repoliticized" development policies and reinvigorated programmatic competition in party systems. It is far from clear, however, how much latitude states have, whatever their partisan makeup, to experiment with macroeconomic and social policies that break with market orthodoxy. The relative caution and pragmatism of most new leftist governments outside oil-rich Venezuela suggests that programmatic competition may remain fairly tightly bounded by global market constraints. Perceptions of these constraints—which are likely to vary across national conditions—will undoubtedly influence how polarized or consensual party systems are, and whether their competitive dynamics exert centrifugal or centripetal effects.

Conclusion

The restoration of democratic rule in Latin America in the 1980s occurred in a context of economic crisis and social dislocation. These conditions undermined the ability of popular sectors to organize political alternatives, and they narrowed the range of developmental and social welfare policies that states could adopt in response to societal claims. The crisis of political representation was rooted as much in these state and societal constraints—above and below parties, respectively—as it was in parties as intermediary institutions.

By the late 1990s and 2000s—that is, in the post-adjustment period—both of these constraints began to loosen. Populist and leftist political alternatives re-emerged, the technocratic consensus around the neoliberal model began to unravel, and a commodity export boom provided governments greater policy latitude. As a result, political competition was re-aligned along programmatic lines—in some countries, for the first time in their history. This programmatic restructuring, however, varies widely in its level of partisan institutionalization; established parties of the left and right exist in a number of countries, but in many others one or both are engaged in a process of organizational reconstruction. As yet, it is unclear whether these new partisan alternatives will congeal organizationally and construct durable linkages to voters. Neither is it clear, in some cases—especially Venezuela—whether these new alternatives will contribute to the institutionalization of political pluralism and democratic contestation, or become institutionalized hegemonies that limit competition. As such, Latin America's political shift to the Left since the late 1990s—which brought a leftist alternative into power in eleven different Latin American countries, and strengthened others that remained in opposition—may have altered the character of the region's crisis of representation, but it hardly resolved it.

Notes

1 For an overview of democratic stabilization in the region, see Scott Mainwaring and Aníbal Pérez Liñán, "Latin American Democratization since 1978: Democratic Transitions, Break-

downs, and Erosions," in Frances Hagopian and Scott P. Mainwaring, eds. *The Third Wave of Democratization in Latin America: Advances and Setbacks* (Cambridge: Cambridge University Press, 2005), pp. 14–59.

2 On the crisis of representation in the region, see Frances Hagopian, "Democracy and Political Representation in Latin America in the 1980s: Pause, Reorganization, or Decline?", in Felipe Agüero and Jeffrey Stark, eds. *Fault Lines of Democracy in Post-Transitional Latin America* (Miami: North-South Center Press, 1998), pp. 85–120; Scott Mainwaring, Ana María Bejarano, and Eduardo Pizarro Leongómez, eds. *The Crisis of Democratic Representation in the Andes* (Stanford, CA: Stanford University Press, 2006); and Marcelo Cavarozzi and Esperanza Casullo, "Los Partidos Políticos en América Latina Hoy: ¿Consolidación o Crísis?", in Marcelo Cavarozzi and Juan Abal Medina, eds. *El Asedio a la Política: Los Partidos Latinoamericanos en la Era Neoliberal* (Buenos Aires: Homo Sapiens Ediciones, 2002), pp. 9–30.

3 See Eduardo Silva, *Challenging Neoliberalism in Latin America* (Cambridge: Cambridge University Press, 2009); Kurt Weyland, Raúl L. Madrid, and Wendy Hunter, eds. *Leftist Governments in Latin America: Successes and Failures* (Cambridge: Cambridge University Press, 2010); and Steven Levitsky and Kenneth M. Roberts, eds. *The Resurgence of the Left in Latin America* (Baltimore: Johns Hopkins University Press, 2011).

4 Flavia Freidenberg and Steven Levitsky, "Informal Institutions and Party Organization in Latin America," in Gretchen Helmke and Steven Levitsky, eds. *Informal Institutions and Democracy: Lessons from Latin America* (Baltimore: Johns Hopkins University Press, 2006), pp. 178–179.

5 See Manuel Alcántara Sáez, ed. *Politicians and Politics in Latin America* (Boulder, CO: Lynne Rienner Publishers, 2007).

6   Ruth Berins Collier and Samuel Handlin, eds. *Reorganizing Popular Politics: Participation and the New Interest Regime in Latin America* (University Park: Pennsylvania State University Press, 2009).

7 Mark P. Jones, "Beyond the Electoral Connection: The Effect of Political Parties on the Policy-making Process," in Carlos Scartascini, Ernesto Stein, and Mariano Tommasi, eds. *How Democracy Works: Political Institutions, Actors, and Arenas in Latin American Policymaking* (Washington, D.C.: Inter-American Development Bank and David Rockefeller Center for Latin American Studies, Harvard University, 2010), pp. 19–46.

8 David J. Samuels and Matthew S. Shugart, *Presidents, Parties, and Prime Ministers: How the Separation of Powers Affects Party Organization and Behavior* (Cambridge: Cambridge University Press, 2010).

9 See Michael Coppedge, *Strong Parties and Lame Ducks: Presidential Partyarchy and Factionalism in Venezuela* (Stanford, CA: Stanford University Press, 1994).

10 See, for example, Seymour Martin Lipset and Stein Rokkan, eds. *Party Systems and Voter Alignments: Cross-National Perspectives* (New York: Free Press, 1967), and Stefano Bartolini and Peter Mair, *Identity, Competition, and Electoral Availability: The Stabilisation of European Electorates 1885–1985* (Cambridge: Cambridge University Press, 1990).

11 Ruth Berins Collier and David Collier, *Shaping the Political Arena: Critical Junctures, the Labor Movement, and Regime Dynamics in Latin America* (Princeton: Princeton University Press, 1991).

12 Ronald H. McDonald and J. Mark Ruhl, *Party Politics and Elections in Latin America* (Boulder, CO: Westview Press, 1989).

13 See, for example, Robert H. Dix, "Cleavage Structures and Party Systems in Latin America," *Comparative Politics* 22, 1 (October 1989): 23–37, and Robert H. Dix, "Democratization and the Institutionalization of Latin American Political Parties," *Comparative Political Studies* 24, 4 (January 1992): 488–511.

14 Scott Mainwaring and Timothy Scully, eds. *Building Democratic Institutions: Party Systems in Latin America* (Stanford, CA: Stanford University Press, 1995).

15 Kenneth M. Roberts and Erik Wibbels, "Party Systems and Electoral Volatility in Latin America: A Test of Economic, Institutional, and Structural Explanations," *American Political Science Review* 93, 3 (September 1999): 475–590, and Raúl Madrid, "Ethnic Cleavages and Electoral Volatility in Latin America," *Comparative Politics* 38, 1 (October 2005): 1–20.

16 See the excellent studies by Beatriz Magaloni, *Voting for Autocracy: Hegemonic Party Survival and Its Demise in Mexico* (Cambridge: Cambridge University Press, 2006), and Kenneth F. Greene, *Why Dominant Parties Lose: Mexico's Democratization in Comparative Perspective* (Cambridge: Cambridge University Press, 2007).

17 See, in particular, Steven Levitsky, *Transforming Labor-Based Parties in Latin America: Argentine Peronism in Comparative Perspective* (Cambridge: Cambridge University Press, 2003); Javier Auyero, *Poor People's Politics: Peronist Survival Networks and the Legacy of Evita* (Durham, NC: Duke University Press, 2000); Susan C. Stokes, "Perverse Accountability: A Formal Model of Machine Politics with Evidence from Argentina," *American Political Science Review* 99, 3 (August 2005): 315–325; and Ernesto Calvo and María Victoria Murillo, "Who Delivers? Partisan Clients in the Argentine Electoral Market," *American Journal of Political Science* 48, 4 (October 2004): 742–757.

18 Herbert Kitschelt, Kirk A. Hawkins, Juan Pablo Luna, Guillermo Rosas, and Elizabeth J. Zechmeister, *Latin American Party Systems* (Cambridge: Cambridge University Press, 2010).

19 Coppedge, *Strong Parties and Lame Ducks.*

20 See the shift in scholarly assessments from Scott Mainwaring, *Rethinking Party Systems in the Third Wave of Democratization: The Case of Brazil* (Stanford, CA: Stanford University Press, 1999), and Barry Ames, *The Deadlock of Democracy in Brazil: Interests, Identities, and Institutions in Comparative Politics* (Ann Arbor: University of Michigan Press, 2001), to Frances Hagopian, Carlos Gervasoni, and Juan Andrés Moraes, "From Patronage to Program: The Emergence of Party-Oriented Legislators in Brazil," *Comparative Political Studies* 42, 3 (March 2009): 360–391.

21 See Noam Lupu and Susan Stokes, "Democracy, Interrupted: Regime Change and Partisanship in Twentieth-Century Argentina," *Electoral Studies* 29 (2010): 91–104.

22 Philippe C. Schmitter, "Parties Are Not What They Once Were," in Larry Diamond and Richard Gunther, eds. *Political Parties and Democracy* (Baltimore: Johns Hopkins University Press, 2001), pp. 67–89.

23 See, for example, Russell J. Dalton and Martin P. Wattenberg, eds. *Parties Without Partisans: Political Change in Advanced Industrial Democracies* (New York: Oxford University Press). On the impact of television on election campaigns and the personalization of political competition in Latin America, see Taylor Boas, "Television and Neopopulism in Latin America: Media Effects in Brazil and Peru," *Latin American Research Review* 40, 2 (June 2005): 27–49.

24 Martín Tanaka, "From Crisis to Collapse of the Party Systems and Dilemmas of Democratic Representation: Peru and Venezuela," in Mainwaring, Bejarano, and Pizarro Leongómez, eds. *The Crisis of Democratic Representation in the Andes*, pp. 47–77.

25 Karen L. Remmer, "The Political Impact of Economic Crisis in Latin America in the the 1980s," *American Political Science Review* 85, 3 (September 1991): 777–800.

26 Kenneth M. Roberts, *Changing Course: Parties, Populism, and Political Representation in Latin America's Neoliberal Era* (Cambridge: Cambridge University Press, forthcoming).

27 See, for example, Marcus Kurtz, *Free Market Democracy and the Chilean and Mexican Countryside* (Cambridge: Cambridge University Press, 2004).

28 Juan Pablo Luna, "Frente Amplio and the Crafting of a Social Democratic Alternative in Uruguay," *Latin American Politics and Society* 49, 4 (Winter 2007): 1–30.

29 Jana Morgan, *Bankrupt Representation and Party System Collapse* (University Park: Pennsylvania State University Press, 2011).

30 María Victoria Murillo, *Political Competition, Partisanship, and Policy Making in Latin American Public Utilities* (Cambridge: Cambridge University Press, 2009).

31 Susan Stokes, *Mandates and Democracy: Neoliberalism by Surprise in Latin America* (Cambridge: Cambridge University Press, 2001).

32 Noam Lupu, "Partisanship, Brand Dilution, and the Breakdown of Political Parties in Latin America," Ph.D. dissertation in progress, Princeton University.

33 See María Victoria Murillo, *Labor Unions, Partisan Coalitions, and Market Reforms in Latin America* (Cambridge: Cambridge University Press, 2001), and Katrina Burgess, *Parties and Unions in the New Global Economy* (Pittsburgh: University of Pittsburgh Press, 2004).

34 Deborah Yashar, *Contesting Citizenship in Latin America: The Rise of Indigenous Movements and the Postliberal Challenge* (Cambridge: Cambridge University Press, 2005), and Silva, *Challenging Neoliberalism in Latin America.*

35 See Edward Gibson, *Class and Conservative Parties: Argentina in Comparative Perspective* (Baltimore: Johns Hopkins University Press, 1996) and Kevin J. Middlebrook, ed. *Conservative Parties, the Right, and Democracy in Latin America* (Baltimore: Johns Hopkins University Press, 2000).

36 Collier and Handlin, *Reorganizing Popular Politics.*

5

"A TALE OF TWO CITIES"

The Judiciary and the Rule
of Law in Latin America

Daniel M. Brinks

The Latin American legal landscape has undergone a paradoxical shift in the last thirty years. On the one hand, formerly supine courts have become more efficient, more effective, and far more consequential in both the region's politics and the daily lives of its people. Quite simply, laws matter more now. Long gone—in many though not all countries—are the days when authoritarian and democratic leaders alike could safely ignore their apex courts, trampling on rights and transgressing the constitutional separation of powers. Social interactions, especially for the middle class, are no longer a pure power game, if they ever were, but are now more structured by a matrix of rights and responsibilities. Courts are striking down some ambitious government policies and imposing others, in the name of constitutional rights. Observers speak of a new kind of court and possibly a new, rights-conscious, way of understanding constitutions and democratic citizenship. Students of Latin American politics will have to come to grips with the origins and consequences of this new legal order, as well as the causes of its absence in certain countries.

On the other hand, public security has deteriorated in many countries, and has become one of the overriding concerns of publics and observers alike. Crime, and violent crime in particular, seems to threaten the very foundations of the state and the regime. The fear of violence and sensation of insecurity leads to public support for draconian public policies, increased state violence against a perceived criminal class, and vigilante justice. Increasingly well-armed, well-funded, and well-organized criminal networks infiltrate democratic governments and threaten the state itself. In the most extreme cases, as in the border region between the United States and Mexico, certain areas of Rio de Janeiro, and some cities in Central America, the situation is reminiscent of a civil war with the state fighting multiple combatants who are also fighting each other. From the assassination of gubernatorial candidates in Mexico to the drug money financing of campaigns, crime increasingly infiltrates politics, while ordinary politics are increasingly tinted by demands for an effective public safety response.

The rule of law and the judiciaries in Latin America are marked by this dualism. Courts are now contributing to the creation of more accountable regimes and a more robust, more inclusive democracy. At the same time, however, there are growing concerns about unaccountable judiciaries meddling in important public policy issues, and about their failure to respond to crime and corruption in the region. Crime and violence erode the legitimacy of the courts precisely when the latter are taking on a more visible role in politics. In this chapter I explore this disjointed legal reality, setting out what we have learned and what remains unknown. In the first section I describe the largely positive changes that have taken place in the area of judicial politics, but that may now be leading to some excesses. In the second I address some of the shortcomings of the rule of law more broadly. I conclude with a very brief reflection on the possible relationship between these two contradictory trends. As in Dickens' *A Tale of Two Cities*, then, "it [is] the best of times, it [is] the worst of times" for courts and the rule of law in Latin America, and we have yet to understand how these disparate realities can coexist, let alone how they are related.

Judicial Politics in Latin America

The last twenty-five years have seen an explosion of work on Latin American judiciaries. Until the mid-1990s, political scientists largely left the study of law and courts in Latin America to lawyers and law and society/law and development scholars. Beginning in about 1995, however, courts started to draw the attention of comparativists, and by now we have a relatively well-developed literature on the emergence, behavior and impact of courts in the region. Taking the central research concerns in more or less logical progression, we have at least begun to study (a) the political origins of more (and less) powerful courts; (b) why judges behave the way they do; (c) how courts interact with the regime transitions of the 1980s, especially in relation to transitional justice issues; and (d) how judicial interventions affect political dynamics and public policies. I will deal with each of these issues, in that order.

First, however, a very brief definitional note. Although many scholars use terms like judicial *independence, power, authority, autonomy,* and *judicialization* as if their meaning were self-evident, these are widely contested terms. My own preferences in the use of these terms and some brief references to the debates can be found elsewhere.[1] In this chapter, I will simply adopt what I think is a fairly commonsensical usage, even if it elides difficult conceptual issues. I use autonomy as a synonym for a standard notion of independence—judges' freedom to make decisions according to their own vision of what the law requires, without *undue* interference; I will use authority to refer to a court's legal scope of action—the kinds of cases and claims a court can decide; I will refer to judicial power as the capacity to make consequential decisions—that is, important decisions that diverge from the preferences of dominant political actors and that generate the desired real world effects (power, thus, requires both autonomy and authority); and judicialization or legalization, interchangeably, to describe the extent to which courts become relevant actors, and legal categories become relevant considerations, in the design and implementation of public policy.

One of the crucial substantive concerns of the literature on courts and the rule of law in Latin America is to establish the political origins of powerful courts. Perhaps one of the most striking developments in Latin American politics, after the transition to democracy, is the emergence of many powerful courts. The constitutional chamber of the Costa Rican Supreme Court has transformed the way majority and minority parties conduct legislative negotiations and has intervened on important substantive issues, including the adequacy of health care and the rights of gay and lesbian Costa Ricans.[2] In February of 2010, the Colombian Constitutional Court invalidated a constitutional amendment allowing the reelection of President Uribe, at a moment when Uribe's popularity was as high as it had ever been. Among other major interventions, this court has also mandated free primary education (outlawing the existing tuition scheme), re-shaped the entire public health system, and directed the government's attempts to address the situation of about 4 million displaced persons. The Argentine Supreme Court has been, for most of the successive Kirchner administrations, nearly the only effective opposition actor in the Argentine political arena. The Brazilian Supremo Tribunal Federal, the highest constitutional court in the country, has occasionally vetoed crucial policy initiatives, under both Cardoso and da Silva. It seems clear that courts in Latin America are asserting themselves in unprecedented ways.

There are, of course, marked exceptions. Most observers agree that the Venezuelan Supreme Court has become far less autonomous under President Hugo Chávez. This is the result both of intentional design features built into the 1999 Constitution, and of ongoing interference with the operation of the courts in Venezuela, including the naming of unconditionally adherent judges, the firing of judges who hold the government to account, the use of temporary appointees without constitutional protection to fill vacancies, and similar measures. One of the more egregious examples of the nakedly political use of courts occurred in October, 2009, when the Nicaraguan Constitutional Chamber allowed sitting president Daniel Ortega to run for reelection, despite a constitutional prohibition. To cobble together a majority for that decision, the Sandinista block of judges called for an unexpected hearing, slipped notices under the doors of non-Sandinista judges at a time when they could not reasonably be discovered, then brought in (friendly) replacement judges to fill the empty seats. The decision stood, even though the opposition judges cried foul. These courts are victims—sometimes willing ones—of intentional, far-reaching politicization.

Other courts act in a passive, non-confrontational way out of conviction rather than coercion or nakedly political allegiance. For many years after democratization, at least until 2006 or so, the Chilean Constitutional Court was essentially invisible, while the Chilean Supreme Court acted as one of the last defenders of Pinochet's legal order, standing in the way of an effective investigation into the excesses of the prior regime. The Mexican Supreme Court was largely quiescent under the dominance of the PRI, and even today prefers to focus on arbitrating separation of powers disputes than on the vigorous protection or expansion of constitutional rights. The Costa Rican Supreme Court had, until 1989, largely abdicated its constitutional oversight role. Clearly, there are strong courts and weak courts in Latin America; in spite of the clear examples of the latter, however, the trend has been largely in the direction of more powerful courts.

A purely institutional analysis backs up this observation. Coding no more than their formal constitutionally protected features and creating an index for each court's de jure scope of authority and level of autonomy, we can array the courts in terms of their expected autonomy and authority, as in Figure 5.1.[3] Note, of course, that this is a coding of formal institutional features, and thus at best a candidate for an independent variable in any analysis of the actual behavior of these courts.

There is not, to date, a reliable, systematic, behavior-based measure of judicial power or autonomy for the region, but the results of this institutional analysis more or less track non-systematic observations of court behavior. Many observers would agree that Chile has very autonomous courts with relatively limited scope of action; that the constitutional courts in Colombia and Brazil, and the Mexican Supreme Court, are at the high end of both autonomy and authority for the region. They would also agree that Venezuela and (at least historically) the Dominican Republic deserve to be on the low end, though the latter has recently behaved far better than its institutional score would suggest. Honduras, Panama, and Argentina also appear well placed. Uruguay's court has a deserved reputation for autonomy, but is not exceptionally active, as the index predicts. Whether because institutional design is an intervening variable, produced by deeper political causes, or because it

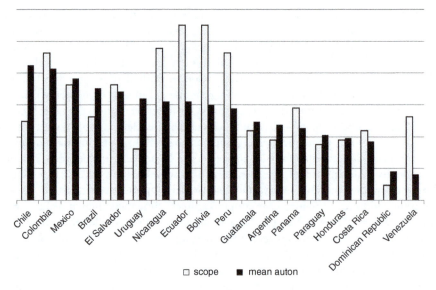

Figure 5.1 De Jure Autonomy and Scope of Authority of Latin American Courts as of 2009.

has independent causal effects, then, institutional measures of formal autonomy and authority seem to track some of the variation in judicial power.

The behavior of some courts, however, does not reflect their institutional DNA. Again drawing on impressionistic personal observations and individual case studies, most would agree that Costa Rica in particular has, since shortly after the 1989 constitutional reforms, one of the more activist constitutional bodies in the region. El Salvador should be nearer the low end, and certainly below Uruguay on any measure, and Nicaragua should also be further down the scale. Either our measure misses some crucial institutional variables, therefore, or some courts exercise far more or far less power than their institutional design would suggest. If the latter is true, then the discrepancies highlight the need to further develop our explanations for the appearance of more powerful courts in the region.

The dominant paradigm applied so far to explain the emergence of powerful courts holds that the primary cause of stronger courts is the increasing level of political fragmentation in the region. The theory, advanced in the Latin American context by Finkel and Bill Chavez[4] among others, addresses both the creation of stronger courts through constitutional design or judicial reform, and the actual operation of courts, once created. As to the former, the basic notion is that political actors who are certain they will be in control will not want to be constrained by a powerful court. On the other hand, politicians who are uncertain whether they will be in charge in the future will delegate substantial power to autonomous courts in order to reduce the risk of greater losses while they are out of power. Political uncertainty, in this view, creates a demand for the low cost political insurance that courts can provide: courts are created as arbiters of the political contest, to ensure that the losers in any given round will be able to contest power effectively in the next round, and to police constitutional boundaries.[5] An alternative logic suggests that a higher number of veto players in the design process prevents dominant actors from creating courts that will respond exclusively to their interests, thus producing courts that are more autonomous of top power holders. Either way, a more pluralistic political environment is thought to breed stronger courts.

Once courts are created, political fragmentation also creates the space for them to act decisively. Under the veto player logic, it is more difficult to punish or reward courts for their behavior when there are more players in the political arena; moreover, a more fragmented legislature should have greater difficulty enacting policy, thus creating a governance vacuum that courts can fill. And under the insurance logic, dominant political actors are more likely to protect courts if they anticipate that they might need judicial protection in the future, when they are less dominant. Both of these accounts seem to explain when courts might escape punishment for decisions that defy either the executive or the legislature—they explain the *opportunity* for judicial activism. They do not, however, do much to explain when courts might want to challenge a majoritarian viewpoint—they do not provide a *motive* for judicial activism.

This basic theory has found considerable empirical support in other regions, and seems to have some empirical basis in Latin America. Surely the emergence of a stronger court in Mexico owes much to the PRI's loss of its hegemonic status; the Colombian court benefited from the fragmentation of the political arena there after the collapse of the Frente Nacional pact and appeared to be losing ground as Uribe consolidated control; Costa Rica's and Uruguay's courts are as strong as they are in part because they operate in a reliably pluralistic political environment. But there are other cases that fit the paradigm less well. The Argentine Supreme Court began acting in a much more autonomous way after a change in personnel starting in 2002, despite the Justicialist (Peronist) Party's continued hegemony. The Chilean Constitutional Court appears to have awoken to its mission in the last five years or so, without any marked contemporaneous changes in the number of players in that political arena (although it is true that the Concertación has been weakening in this period). The Brazilian court should be more activist than it is, given its highly fragmented political environment. And the Colombian Constitutional Court ultimately surprised everyone with its anti-reelection decision at a time of heightened dominance by an extremely popular president. There is plenty of variation left unexplained by this dominant paradigm.

Recently, other theories have emerged to explain these anomalies, without denying that a pluralistic political environment is important. One possibility is that institutional variables are more important than we have recognized so far. There have been a number of country studies, but we have yet to see a well-crafted comparative look at Latin American judiciaries that explores the consequences of institutional variables for court behavior. In any event, it is surely true that political context variables interact with institutional design. With more robust institutional insulation, it seems likely that courts could tolerate lower levels of political fragmentation. The ability of outside actors to exercise institutional levers of control should be a function of the veto points defined by formal and informal rules, the thresholds required for their action, and the level of fragmentation in the political arena. Any explanation grounded in the capacity of political actors to appoint or to punish judges must pay attention both to the political context and to the formal and informal institutional mechanisms that specify how judges can be appointed and punished.

If these explanations deal primarily with opportunity, an alternative set of explanations is emerging that addresses judicial motivations more frontally. These theories focus less on political pragmatism, and more on the nature of the law and current ideas about courts. One argument that has gained considerable attention in Latin America is that there has been a large-scale cultural change in the region—in terms of "legal culture" if nothing else. The essence of this change is the appearance of a new generation of jurists and legal scholars who "take rights seriously" in the Dworkinian sense.[6] In some cases, the argument goes, these neo-constitutionalist scholars come to occupy courts, pushing out the earlier generation of formalistic, deferential judges. Clearly, there is a struggle, especially visible within the judicial ranks of Brazil, Chile, and Colombia, between the old traditionalist formalistic judges and the new more consequentialist, socially conscious and self-consciously progressive judges.[7] The sources and effects of this ideational change are certainly worth exploring further.

This brings us to the second of the research questions identified in the introduction, the individual level complement to the institutional question addressed above—the political origins of judicial behavior. In the United States, much of the literature revolves around a debate between those who argue that judges, once appointed, follow their policy preferences,[8] those who emphasize judges' strategic anticipation of outside actors' reaction to their rulings,[9] and those who give more credence to role orientations and the importance of the law to the judicial enterprise.[10] In Latin America, most of the work focusing on judicial behavior has adopted the strategic approach,[11] although there are exceptions that focus more on institutional legacies and judicial role conceptions.[12]

Because the literature evolved largely in the context of the U.S. Supreme Court, with little or no institutional and political variation, it tends to essentialize these attributes of courts, as if all judges at all times act the same way for the same reasons. In the comparative context, by contrast, we need to be open to the possibility that individual judicial behavior on different courts might be better explained by different theories. It seems clear, for instance, that both institutional variables—the degree of political insulation and hierarchical control built into judicial systems, for example—and contextual variables—the history of judicial autonomy, the ideological strands present in the political arena, or the level of political fragmentation—affect the pressures brought to bear on judges. Different constellations of factors might require them to be more or less strategic, allow them to follow their policy preferences to a greater or lesser degree, or change the extent to which they must adhere to dominant judicial role conceptions. Our task in comparative judicial politics is to identify the conditions under which different variables matter, and to better specify the relationships among the different variables.

Once courts are in place and judges have begun to decide cases, of course, we come to the third question: how do these decisions affect the politics of the region? There is one area in which courts have naturally played a starring role, remarkable either for their failures or their successes. In the aftermath of grievous human rights abuses, the question arose in nearly all the countries of the region: what should be done with the violations from prior regimes? In nearly all the countries there were some demands to place human rights violators on trial. In nearly all the countries, for the first period after the transition, these demands went unheeded. Early exceptions were Argentina, although the first set of convictions was followed by an amnesty law and a series of pardons for those already convicted; and Bolivia, where a thoroughly discredited set of leaders was convicted and imprisoned in the wake of a corrupt and crime-tainted dictatorship. More recently, however, there has been remarkable progress in the prosecution of human rights violations in Peru (against Fujimori and several of his military officials), in Argentina (with a revival of largely dormant prosecutions of participants in the 1970s Dirty War), in Uruguay (where two former presidents have been imprisoned), and in Chile (once the Supreme Court stopped punishing trial judges who dared look into the record of the Pinochet regime). There have been isolated cases against military personnel in other countries as well, such as El Salvador and Guatemala, with mixed success.

The conventional explanation is that transitional justice becomes possible as the members of the previous regime (and their political allies) weaken. This explanation probably accounts for the courts' increased activism on this issue in Chile after the discovery of

Pinochet's foreign bank accounts, and the successful prosecution of a weak and discredited military regime in Bolivia. It explains why the first set of prosecutions in Argentina ended in amnesties and pardons, after a series of military rebellions in the 1980s. It does not seem complete, however, as it cannot account for the great delays in Argentina or Uruguay, the continuing inaction in Mexico long after the PRI lost its dominance, or the timing of many of the prosecutions in other places. It seems likely that the political and military strength of backers of the previous regime is sufficient to prevent effective investigations and prosecutions, but their mere weakness does not explain when these will be initiated or where they will be successful. We are still, therefore, looking for the causes of the active and effective prosecution of human rights violations in the aftermath of a transition to democracy. Moreover, we still have little or no research on the effect of these prosecutions on reconciliation, the establishment of the rule of law, and the other goals they are claimed to advance.

Despite the importance of this issue, however, much more attention has been focused on the fourth question advanced above: exploring the courts' actions with respect to the workings of democracy and the protection of substantive rights. Although these categories will blend in some instances, we can conceptualize the court's role in this regard as either procedural—safeguarding the rules of the game, policing boundaries between branches or levels of government and the like—or substantive—protecting substantive rights, vetoing or requiring particular policies and otherwise changing the content of public policy. Courts clearly play an important procedural role in many of today's Latin American democracies, and they are increasingly playing a significant substantive role.

The discussion of the courts' procedural role has largely centered on their capacity to improve accountability. They are a crucial component of what Peruzzotti and Smulovitz have called societal accountability, and have begun to perform what Gloppen et al. call their accountability function.[13] The Colombian and Costa Rican courts stand out in this regard. The Argentine court, after a period of extreme politicization, has begun to enforce some accountability since its reconstitution under former president Néstor Kirchner. The Brazilian court has done so as well, although in a relatively non-confrontational way.[14] The Mexican court has focused its attention largely on policing the constitutional separation of powers and federal allocation of responsibilities, although it is starting to attend to questions of substantive rights as well. In short, many courts have brought a measure of accountability to public officials and changed the bargaining dynamics of majority and minority parties in the legislature.

As the earlier discussion of judicial power anticipates, however, not all courts have excelled at this task. Until very recently, and despite a national history of strong respect for the rule of law, the Chilean courts had been generally disappointing in this regard, rarely challenging the executive or legislature. The Central American courts (with the exception of Costa Rica) and the courts of Venezuela and Ecuador are even more passive. The court in Ecuador has a long history of being shaped and reshaped to suit those in power, and that has largely not changed. The Bolivian court is currently undergoing a dramatic reconfiguration, and it is unclear what sort of court will emerge. The Venezuelan court has been singled out by Human Rights Watch (in 2004 and 2008) and the Interamerican Commission on Human Rights (in December 2009) for its lack of independence and failure to restrain the executive. Still, despite these notable exceptions, there appears to be an upward trend in the willingness of courts to hold political actors to the rules of the game.

High courts across the region have also intervened in more substantive ways, on behalf of economic, social and cultural rights, including health rights, indigenous rights to land and culture, the right to a clean environment, the right to basic subsistence, land rights, and more. Costa Rica and Colombia are two of the most prominent examples of courts that have demonstrated their willingness and capacity to inject substantive rights into policy debates. In one of the more dramatic examples, the Colombian Constitutional Court's decision T-760 (July 31, 2008) requires the legislature to reconfigure the design of the entire public health system, merging the contributory with the non-contributory systems, so that everyone has access to a similar standard of care. In Costa Rica, Argentina, Venezuela, and to a lesser extent elsewhere, a more limited number of cases requires the government to treat patients with HIV/AIDS, produce "orphan" vaccines, and otherwise address the needs of particular excluded populations.[15] The Argentine courts have required the state to care for and feed children when their parents cannot. Even putting aside large scale structural cases, tens of thousands of individual cases are transforming public health in Brazil, Costa Rica, and Colombia.[16]

Courts have occasionally singled out traditionally marginalized communities and unpopular issues for their protection. Indigenous rights in particular have received a favorable hearing. Indigenous communities claiming rights to land or self-governance have had some success in domestic courts in Colombia and elsewhere. They have won significant legal victories in the Interamerican Court of Human Rights (see, for example, the famous case brought by the Awas Tingni community of Nicaragua in the Interamerican Court of Human Rights).[17] Courts in Argentina have required the government to set up an adequate health care system for marginalized indigenous communities in the northern Chaco region. Gays and lesbians in Costa Rica and Argentina have found considerable judicial protection. In Argentina, a lower court decision allowing a gay couple to marry has triggered a legislative debate that at the time of this writing seems poised to produce legislative authorization for same sex marriage. Courts from Mexico, through Nicaragua, to Chile and Argentina have weighed in on longstanding contentious social issues—abortion and birth control, same sex marriage, divorce, and the rights of children born out of wedlock.

In spite of their fairly robust interventions on behalf of many economic, social and cultural rights, however, Latin American courts have not been uniformly progressive. Most of the region's courts continue to fail to defend core rights of physical integrity for the poor and marginalized, especially against police violence.[18] In some cases, well meaning judges are stymied by all-too-powerful police forces, but in most cases the politics of crime (explored in more detail below) create a strong disincentive for judges, prosecutors and police investigators, virtually guaranteeing impunity. The courts are at the forefront of significant attempts at social transformation in some cases (Costa Rica, Colombia), but fighting a rearguard action in others (Nicaragua, Chile). In Chile, for instance, the apex courts have been exceptionally hostile to Mapuche environmental activists; in Nicaragua the court has for three years refused to rule on a law prohibiting abortion in all cases, even if the life of the mother is at risk. In Brazil, indigenous and afro-descendant land rights continue to struggle to get a hearing in court. Moreover, implementation of and compliance with the boldest of these decisions is far from assured in any case. Both the ideological orientation of decisions and compliance with them are issues that cry out for further research.[19]

The initial criticism of some of these decisions was precisely this question of effectiveness—whether all this judicial intervention ever produces any change on the ground. It now appears that it can,[20] but the question has become, to what end? Research is beginning to appear that questions whether the judicialization or legalization of politics might have a regressive effect and whether it is somehow anti-democratic. In Brazil there are tens of thousands of cases claiming the right to one medication or another. These cases raise the question whether the middle class is using the court system to capture or even bypass the public health system, to the detriment of the poor, who have less access to courts and lawyers. Others question whether judges should be the ones to make such important decisions, with obvious distributive and budgetary implications, or whether this is better left to the executive and the legislature. We have only tentative answers to the question whether the introduction of courts into the policy-making and implementation process promotes greater equity and distributive justice in an unequal continent (possibly not), improves outcomes for the poor (occasionally), improves the accountability of public officials (more often), and generally improves the condition of anyone at all (occasionally). Theorizing and evaluating the implications of the surge in judicial power and activism for particular groups in particular countries remains one of the crucial questions in the study of judicial politics everywhere, but especially in Latin America, given the region's activist courts.

In short, there is considerable variation to explore, and many questions left open, but it seems clear that courts have become important players in Latin American politics. We are seeing the emergence of more powerful courts, and our theories only partially account for them. The impact of political fragmentation on judicial power seems fairly well established, but only tells part of the story. To fill in the gaps, new theories are exploring the impact of institutional and ideational factors as well. Judges across the region continue to behave in ways that challenge US-originated theories of judicial behavior. But new work is beginning to specify more clearly the conditions under which judges will challenge political actors, and when they will act more submissively. At the same time, it is still unclear what all this judicial activism adds up to, whether—or more precisely, under what conditions—it improves or detracts from democracy, equality and justice.

The Rule of Law

The literature on the rule of law, while always stating clearly that one of the prerequisites is an independent judiciary, carries on a conversation that is almost completely innocent of everything we have been discussing so far. Moreover, while the recent work on judiciaries in Latin America tends to focus on a more or less positive story, the outlook in the rule of law literature is almost universally bleak. The focus here tends to be on crime, corruption, the failure to enforce laws, or the sheer presence of illegal behavior. And it is clear that Latin America is facing a dramatic challenge in this regard. This section will present a necessarily abbreviated overview of the topic, meant more to introduce themes than to deal with them in any detail.

As with judicial politics, the rule of law literature is plagued with a fundamental debate concerning this basic term. Here I use rule of law in a minimalist sense, to mean simply compliance with existing law. Others call this "rule by law" or advocate so-called "thicker" definitions. Clearly, this is a far cry from a *democratic* rule of law, which would require the introduction of some substantive elements in the definition. Even in this minimalist sense, the rule of law serves two purposes—regulating relationships among citizens (horizontal), and regulating the relationship between citizens and the state (vertical)—and has the virtue of improving predictability, if nothing else. On the vertical dimension, with some prominent exceptions, courts are performing increasingly well, as we saw in the previous section, certainly compared to earlier more authoritarian periods. On its horizontal dimension, however, the rule of law seems to be falling apart. In this section I focus most of the discussion on the citizen-to-citizen dimension.

There is no question that crime and violence have become crucial issues for Latin American democracies. Homicide rates have gone up dramatically in many countries, especially

Honduras, El Salvador, Guatemala, Venezuela; they have decreased in some countries, most notably Colombia and somewhat in Brazil, although they remain high there still. In almost every country, however, crime is seen as a crucial problem, threatening the future of the country. In Table 5.1, the first two columns present the most recent homicide rates available, from highest to lowest. The last two show the answers to the question "And speaking of the country in general, how much do you think that the level of crime that we have now represents a threat to our future well-being?" from the Latin American Public Opinion Project's 2008 Americas Barometer survey. The figure in column 4 is the percentage of people who answered "very much" or "somewhat," again ranked from highest to lowest.

At least three things are notable about Table 5.1. The first is the exceptionally high level of homicides in some countries. For comparison, homicide rates in Western Europe average less than 3 per hundred thousand. The United States, the industrialized country with the highest homicide rate, reports 5.2 homicides per hundred thousand. Seventeen of the top twenty homicide rates in the world belong to Latin American or Caribbean countries (the other three are Russia, South Africa, and Lesotho). Six of the region's countries have homicide rates that are between ten and twenty times that of most advanced industrial democracies. Central America especially is suffering from a dramatic increase in violence.

Table 5.1 Homicide Rates by Country (most recent available, as of 2008)[1] and Concern that Crime Threatens Future Wellbeing (2008)[2]

Country	Homicide Rate per 100,000	Country	Very Much + Somewhat
Honduras	60.9	Paraguay	96.6
Venezuela	52	Venezuela	95.4
El Salvador	51.8	El Salvador	93.4
Guatemala	45.2	Argentina	92.7
Colombia	38.8	Nicaragua	91.9
Belize	34.3	Costa Rica	91.7
Brazil	22	Panama	91.2
Guyana	20.7	Brazil	90.4
Ecuador	18.1	Guatemala	89.2
Panama	13.3	Bolivia	89.1
Nicaragua	13	Ecuador	88.9
Paraguay	12.2	Uruguay	88.6
Mexico	11.6	Colombia	87.8
Bolivia	10.6	Mexico	85.8
Costa Rica	8.3	Chile	85.7
Chile	8.1	Peru	85.3
Uruguay	5.8	Honduras	77.5
Argentina	5.2	Guyana	77.1
Peru	3.2	Belize	75.3

1 Source: International Homicide Statistics report by the United Nations Office on Drugs and Crime, available at http://www.unodc.org/unodc/en/data-and-analysis/homicide.html (last visited June 3, 2010). The table presents the most recent data available for each country, as of 2008.
2 Available at http://lapop.ccp.ucr.ac.cr/Lapop_English.html. Table generated June 3, 2010.

And if we look at particular areas within each country, the picture is even more grim. Ciudad Juarez, on the border between Mexico and the United States, had a murder rate of approximately 22 per hundred thousand in 2007. The rate climbed to 113 the very next year, then to 189, and by 2010 it was ten times higher than it had been just three years earlier—222 killings per hundred thousand or more than 3,100 homocides in a single year. The cities of Escuintla, Guatemala, and San Salvador have reported homicide rates as high as 165 and 150 per hundred thousand, respectively. In Brazil, the cities of Recife and Vitória, and particular neighborhoods within large cities, have homicide rates around 90 per hundred thousand—even though the average rate for the country is "only" 22 per hundred thousand, and homicide rates as a national average have gone down slightly since the early 2000s. Clearly, violent crime is a real and growing phenomenon in Latin America.

The second notable thing about Table 5.1 is, of course, the very high level of citizen concern about crime. In every country, at least 75% of all citizens express concern that current levels of crime threaten their future well-being. The final remarkable feature, however, creates interesting questions for the political relevance of crime: there is no statistical relationship between actual rates of violent crime and the level of citizen preoccupation with it. Indeed, the correlation coefficient between the two is negative (–.18) although not significant. Honduras has the highest homicide rate and the third lowest level of concern. Argentina has the second lowest homicide rates, but the fourth highest levels of concern. These high rates of violence and public concern raise important questions that comparativists have barely begun to address: what is the relationship between politics—or the state—and violence? What is the relationship between violence and the state's response? Do high levels of crime threaten democracy itself? Do they threaten the state, or at least its presumed near-monopoly on the use of force?

Some answers have begun to emerge, but much more research is needed around these issues. There have been numerous individual reports of the influence of drug cartels on politics, the effect of violent threats on the operation of the judiciary, and other possible ill effects of crime. On June 29, 2010, for example, members of the drug cartels gunned down the leading candidate for governor of the state of Tamaulipas in Mexico. On the same day, the president of the Supreme Judicial Council in Colombia reported that illegal groups had threatened seven hundred judges in the previous four years.[21] Is this a systemic problem or simply an occasional one? It is clear that crime, along with other state failures, threatens the legitimacy of representative institutions.[22] But why are policymakers not responding more effectively? It is also clear that crime, the perception of crime, and the fear they produce, erodes support for core democratic principles like due process and human rights.[23] In response to an online article about an alleged police death squad in Peru, for example, outraged readers responded (80% of them, as of May 2010) with unconditional *support* for the extermination of any and all alleged criminals. Some of the respondents called criminal suspects a plague of rats, others clamored in addition for the death squad to take care of the author of the article, members of human rights commissions, and others who were seen to be on the side of the criminals.[24] Is this a significant problem for democracy, as seems likely, or just a way to express justified anger? Vigilantism has become common in Guatemala,[25] as well as in Andean Peru, rural Mexico, urban Brazil, and elsewhere. What are the political roots of this epidemic of lynching? Clearly, these are difficult issues to research, with a host of attendant conceptual, methodological, and practical data collection issues. But they cannot be ignored.

Other shortcomings in the rule of law have a longer history in Latin America. Many court systems, regardless of the performance of their apex courts, suffer from inefficiency, corruption, and sheer incompetence, denying ordinary citizens the opportunity to effectively enforce legal obligations. There is very little research on the operation and politics of lower courts, even though it is clear that politics affects them just as much as it affects high courts,[26] and they are crucial to the construction of the day-to-day experience of democracy. Traditionally marginalized groups still find it difficult to enforce their rights. In particular, women, indigenous groups (and afro-descendants even more so), homosexuals, and the poor find very often that the improvement in formal laws is not matched by an improvement in actual practices. Poor urban males, often tarred as a criminal class, find little protection from arbitrary police violence, as the previous paragraphs would suggest. Corruption continues to be endemic, even in countries that have otherwise lower levels of crime. Much of the research on these issues has been left to lawyers and human rights NGOs, while comparativists have done less work on them.

Some of the answers to these puzzles are surely to be found in a familiar list of variables for Latin Americanists. Inequality consistently appears as a significant predictor in cross-national studies of crime rates; and Latin America continues to show high levels of inequality. Continued marginalization and prejudice hamper attempts by indigenous groups and afro-descendants to achieve real social gains; and Latin America is far from immune to prejudice. Any state response to powerful actors like the well-funded drug cartels will require a strong and effective state; and Latin America continues to have weak states. Still, much more research needs to be done around these basic issues of the rule of law.

Conclusion

Most would agree that an effective judicial system is one of the key ingredients of a successful rule of law regime. And yet, in Latin America, high courts are becoming stronger at the same time that sheer lawlessness appears to be spreading to more and more cities. Some politicians have argued that the advent of democracy—and presumably the more robust intervention of its apex courts on behalf of rights is a part of this—made states less effective at repression, opening up space for crime. This would suggest, somewhat counterintuitively, an inverse relationship between the horizontal (citizen-citizen) dimension of the rule of law and its vertical (citizen-state) dimension. Human rights and due process protections, in this view, weaken the state and shield criminals from effective policing—in Brazil and many other places, people often equate "human rights" with "criminal's rights." The answer to crime would then be to craft a more repressive, less rights-oriented democracy.

It seems unlikely, however, that a sudden respect for due process and the rights of criminal suspects is truly at the root of the crime epidemic. One of the places where these democracies are most deficient is precisely in controlling state violence against suspected criminals. The police in many countries continue to exercise their own brand of parallel justice, with extrajudicial executions and torture part of their ordinary repertoire.[27] Moreover, there is little evidence that more arbitrary, less controlled state/police action is an *effective* response to crime. In many cases, an under-supervised police is active in controlling and managing low-level criminality, such as car theft, prostitution, gambling and the like. And more police discretion, in a continent riddled with violent and corrupt police forces, has yet to be proven an effective crime-fighting tool. If anything, an emphasis on due process, proper procedure, and more police accountability might improve the police's propensity to effectively investigate and prevent crime. As a result, the question whether these two contrary trends are related, and if so, how, remains open.

We are left, therefore, with the simple observation that advances in the functioning of apex courts are matched by setbacks in crucial aspects of the rule of law. We have a robust and growing literature in many of these areas, although it has as yet given us only partial and incomplete answers to the most important questions. The region has moved toward greater democracy, with a consequent increase in pluralistic political representation and the apparent spread of new notions of citizenship and rights. This new model of democracy includes rights that were previously rare in Latin America, such as consumer rights, rights to a clean environment, or equality rights for women. One set of key actors advancing those rights—constitutional and other high courts—is increasingly taking center stage, after a long history of either being passive, or serving as a tool of powerful political actors. Paradoxically, however, a lack of implementation of criminal and ordinary laws, constitutional provisions and judicial decisions continues to plague the region. Formal laws and formal legal institutions have improved dramatically over the last thirty years in Latin America. Fully implementing these formal advances may well be the crucial challenge for Latin American democracy and the rule of law in the twenty-first century.

Research to address this central challenge will need to take up a host of questions about the politics of law and courts. This may reflect my own biases and predispositions, but it seems likely that research on these issues will require us to integrate our understanding of how courts and law operate with other, more contextual factors. We will need to incorporate into our theories a clearer understanding of the potential and limitations imposed by citizen capabilities—especially in the unequal context of Latin America. We will have to produce additional theoretically informed research on the relationship between law and courts, on the one hand, and other state institutions, on the other. We will need better insight into the social and political origins of the rule of law. All of this calls for an ambitious research agenda, in a literature that already shows considerable promise, but that is still far short of answering many of the most interesting questions about judicial politics and the rule of law in Latin America.

Notes

1 See Daniel M. Brinks, "Judicial Reform and Independence in Brazil and Argentina: The Beginning of a New Millennium?," *Texas International Law Journal* 40, no. 3 (Spring) (2005) on judicial independence; Daniel M. Brinks and Abby Blass, "The Role of Diffusion and Domestic Politics in Judicial Design: A Theoretical Framework and Preliminary Results" (paper presented at the Annual Meeting of the American Political Science Association, 3–6 September, 2009, Toronto, Canada, 2009), and Daniel M. Brinks, "'Faithful Servants of the Regime': The Brazilian Constitutional Court's Role under the 1988 Constitution," in *Courts in Latin America*, Julio Rios-Figueroa and Gretchen Helmke, eds. (New York: Cambridge University Press, 2011) on power, authority, and autonomy; Varun Gauri and Daniel M. Brinks, eds., *Courting Social Justice: Judicial Enforcement of Social and Economic Rights in the Developing World* (New York: Cambridge University Press, 2008): 4–5 on judicialization vs. legalization.
2 Bruce M. Wilson, "Claiming Individual Rights through a Constitutional Court: The Example of Gays in Costa Rica," *International Journal of Constitutional Law* 5, no. 2 (2007).
3 The coding scheme is set forth in more detail in Brinks and Blass, "The Conceptualization and Measurement of Formal Judicial Power," paper presented at APSA 2011. We use an additive index, based on constitutional provisions, to code courts from 0 to 1 on three dimensions: scope of authority, which measures the kinds of disputes that fall within the court's jurisdiction, ease of access to the court, and the number and types of actors who can access the court; ex ante autonomy, which measures the ease with which any one outside actor can control nominations to the court; and ex post autonomy, which measures how easy it is for any one actor to punish or reward sitting judges, based on their behavior on the bench. For the Figure 5.1 graph, I averaged the two autonomy dimensions.

4 J. Finkel, "Judicial Reform as Insurance Policy: Mexico in the 1990s," *Latin American Politics and Society* 47, no. 1 (2005); J. Finkel, "Judicial Reform in Argentina in the 1990s: How Electoral Incentives Shape Institutional Change," *Latin American Research Review* 39, no. 3 (2004); Rebecca Bill Chavez, *The Rule of Law in Nascent Democracies: Judicial Politics in Argentina* (Stanford: Stanford University Press, 2004).

5 Tom Ginsburg, *Judicial Review in New Democracies: Constitutional Courts in Asian Cases* (Cambridge: Cambridge University Press, 2003).

6 Ronald Dworkin is one of the more prominent defenders of judicial activism on behalf of rights. His 1977 book, *Taking Rights Seriously*, is well known to and often cited by jurists and judges in Latin America.

7 Rodrigo Nunes, "Ideational Origins of Progressive Judicial Activism: The Colombian Constitutional Court and the Right to Health," *Latin American Politics and Society* 52, no. 3 (2010).

8 Jeffrey Segal and Harold Spaeth, *The Supreme Court and the Attitudinal Model Revisited* (Cambridge: Cambridge University Press, 2002).

9 Lee Epstein and Jack Knight, *The Choices Justices Make* (Washington, D.C.: Congressional Quarterly Press, 1998).

10 See, e.g., Lawrence Baum, *Judges and Their Audiences: A Perspective on Judicial Behavior* (Princeton, N.J.: Princeton University Press, 2006); Howard Gillman, "What's Law Got to Do with It? Judicial Behavioralists Test the 'Legal Model' Of Judicial Decision Making," *Law & Social Inquiry* 26, no. 2 (2001).

11 See, e.g., Gretchen Helmke, *Courts under Constraints: Judges, Generals and Presidents in Argentina* (New York: Cambridge University Press, 2005); Juan Carlos Rodriguez-Raga, "Strategic Deference in the Colombian Constitutional Court, 1992–2006," in *Courts in Latin America*, Julio Rios-Figueroa and Gretchen Helmke, eds. (New York: Cambridge University Press, 2011).

12 Lisa Hilbink, *Judges Beyond Politics in Democracy and Dictatorship : Lessons from Chile*, Cambridge Studies in Law and Society (New York: Cambridge University Press, 2007), Javier Couso and Elisabeth C. Hilbink, "From Quietism to Incipient Activism: The Institutional and Ideational Roots of Rights Adjudication in Chile," in *Courts in Latin America*, Julio Rios-Figueroa and Gretchen Helmke, eds. (New York: Cambridge University Press, 2011).

13 Enrique Peruzzotti and Catalina Smulovitz, eds., *Enforcing the Rule of Law: Social Accountability in New Latin American Democracies* (Pittsburgh: University of Pittsburgh Press, 2006); Siri Gloppen, Roberto Gargarella, and Elin Skaar, eds., *Democratization and the Judiciary: The Accountability Function of Courts in New Democracies* (London: Taylor and Francis Group, 2004); Siri Gloppen et al., *Courts and Power in Latin America and Africa* (New York: Palgrave Macmillan, 2010).

14 Diana Kapiszewski, "Tactical Balancing and Prioritizing Pragmatism: High Court Decision-Making on Economic Policy Cases in Brazil" (paper presented at the Judicial Politics in Latin America Conference, CIDE, Mexico, D.F., March 4–8 2009), Brinks, "'Faithful Servants of the Regime'."

15 Alicia Ely Yamin and Siri Gloppen, eds., *Health Rights in Comparative Perspective* (Cambridge, Mass.: Harvard University Press, 2011).

16 Florian F. Hoffmann and Fernando R.N.M. Bentes, "Accountability for Social and Economic Rights in Brazil," in *Courting Social Justice: Judicial Enforcement of Social and Economic Rights in the Developing World*, Varun Gauri and Daniel M. Brinks, eds. (New York: Cambridge University Press, 2008); Bruce M. Wilson, "Litigating Health Rights in Costa Rica," in *Health Rights in Comparative Perspective*, Alicia Ely Yamin and Siri Gloppen, eds. (Cambridge, Mass.: Harvard University Press, 2011); Nunes, "Ideational Origins of Progressive Judicial Activism: The Colombian Constitutional Court and the Right to Health."

17 Judgment of August 31, 2001, Inter-Am. Ct. H.R., (Ser. C) No. 79 (2001).

18 Daniel M. Brinks, *The Judicial Response to Police Killings in Latin America: Inequality and the Rule of Law* (New York: Cambridge University Press, 2008).

19 See, e.g., Jeffrey K. Staton, *Judicial Power and Strategic Communication in Mexico* (Cambridge: Cambridge University Press, 2010) for an analysis of compliance in Mexico.

20 See, e.g., César Rodríguez Garavito and Diana Rodríguez Franco, *Cortes Y Cambio Social: Cómo La Corte Constitucional Transformó El Desplazamiento Forzado En Colombia* (Bogotá, Colombia: Dejusticia, 2010); Gauri and Brinks, eds., *Courting Social Justice*.

21 See Pandora Pugsley. "700 Colombian Judges Threatened in 4 Years," *Colombia Reports* (June 29, 2010), available at http://colombiareports.com/colombia-news/news/10538-700-colombian-judges-threatened-in-4-years.html (last visited July 15, 2010).

22 Mainwaring, Scott. "The Crisis of Democratic Representation in the Andes." *Journal of Democracy* 17, no. 3 (2006): 13–27.

23 Daniel M. Brinks, "Violencia De Estado a Treinta Años De Democracia En América Latina," *Journal of Democracy en Español* 2 (2011): 10–27.

24 One can view the article and accompanying reader comments at http://www.poder360.com/article_detail.php?id_article=3011&pag=1.

25 Angelina Snodgrass Godoy, *Popular Injustice: Violence, Community and Law in Latin America* (Stanford: Stanford University Press, 2006).

26 Brinks, *The Judicial Response to Police Killings in Latin America*.

27 Ibid.; Brinks, "Violencia De Estado a Treinta Años De Democracia En América Latina."

6

THE LATIN AMERICAN MILITARY

David Pion-Berlin

The removal and forced exile of Honduran President Manuel Zelaya, on June 28, 2009, reminds us all that the Latin American military cannot be written off as a potentially powerful, political agent. Democracies with weak institutions, battered economies and dissatisfied publics are vulnerable to the predation of praetorian actors, whether they be military or civilian in nature. And yet, the region has also made considerable progress from the dark days of de facto regimes and dirty wars. Coups are a rarity, and most militaries stay confined to the barracks unless ordered out by the political authorities. Interactions between governments and soldiers are generally more stable and respectful then they were a generation ago. This chapter will peer into those relations by way of assessing the scholarship that has built up around *la cuestión militar* [the military issue] over the years. Because of the enormity of the field, the chapter will also largely restrict itself to domestic contexts, omitting regional, inter-state dimensions to military politics.

Each generation's research interests are powerfully conditioned by the realities of the time. The turbulence of the 1960s obliged scholars to first study the forces of modernization and then the forces of unrest, turning their attention to political violence, praetorianism, and coup d'etat as the decade neared its end. Once the military had seized power throughout the region, researchers set their sights on understanding the origins of and institutional nature of authoritarian rule during the 1970s. With either the phased withdrawal or complete breakdown of these regimes by the early 1980s, attention shifted toward the causes of military extrication and the transition toward democracy. By the late 1980s and into the final decade of the twentieth century, civilian control issues came to the fore. In the first decade of this new century, priorities have again shifted to concerns about defense and security.

Research trends also reflect theoretical developments in the field of civil-military affairs. Theories are varied, but have tended to revolve around four principal axes: structural, rational, institutional, and subjective.[1] Structural theorists examine large, often remote forces that indirectly shape military behavior. These may be economic, social and political in nature and located either within or outside of national borders. What unites structuralism is an attention to macro units of analysis: social classes, economic systems, political systems, and security environments. By contrast, rationalists perform close up examinations, using the individual as the unit of analysis (or treating groups as unitary actors). They identify the underlying interests, intentions and strategic goals that motivate and enable politicians and soldiers. Politicians must weigh their electoral fortunes (surviving in office, serving constituents) with their need to subordinate the military and provide for defense. Depending on context, these may or may not be compatible goals. The military, on the other hand, is concerned first and foremost with its institutional well-being, including material interests, career aspirations and organizational cohesion.

Many rationalists would agree with institutionalists that the strategic options of either side are limited by opportunity structures which arise from particular historical circumstances. In addition institutionalists put their stock in the enduring influence of organizational rules, patterns and procedures. Whether it be new constitutions, formal pacts, or informal agreements between civil and military elites, once these institutional arrangements are forged they have a tendency to persist. Thus while institutions are susceptible to change, change is difficult or path dependent. Finally, subjective analysts are united by their concerns about the ideational underpinnings of behavior. While ideas may serve an objective interest, subjectivist would claim that ideas help interpret that interest or even generate their own. Thus military views matter. Whether they be held by an entire institution or a few, their content must be unveiled so we can understand how soldiers "size up" events around them. Much of the scholarship that follows reflects or borrows from these four theoretical approaches.

The Causes of Military Intervention

The earliest debates revolved around modernization theory: could the armed forces serve a useful developmental function for societies? Latin American military scholars have always had a healthy skepticism about the utility of military immersion in political, social and economic life. When modernization theorists of the early 1960s praised the virtues of military civic action projects, civil-military specialists were not so sanguine. They cautioned that militaries which purported to be working on behalf of the nation were actually looking out for themselves, and that this could lead to harmful, predatory behavior. They also took issue with Samuel Huntington's view that as armies professionalized they would become politically inert, reluctant to interfere with the work of politicians, and ultimately subordinate to civilian control.

The waves of military coups in the mid to late 1960s and again in the 1970s seemed to bear the skeptics out. Military interveners would, of course, rationalize their conduct by framing it in selfless terms; that they had no choice but to rescue the nation from the grip of inept, venal, corrupt politicians who had left the economy in tatters and the nation divided and defenseless in the face of grave threats; that all constitutional means had been exhausted, thus leaving military intervention as regrettably the only option. But Latin Americanists quickly pierced below the veneer to reveal the underlying causes of the coup d'etat. Turning Huntington's formulation on its head, scholars such as Guillermo O'Donnell, Alfred Stepan, J. Samuel Fitch and Frederick Nunn argued that it was because of their professionalism, not in spite of it, that the armed forces sought power.[2] More precisely, it was the Latin American military's own version of professionalism which was the source of praetorian conduct. Relying on historical, institutional and ideational arguments, scholars peered deep inside the military to reveal the origins of its mindset, its interpretations and beliefs.

There were two debates here. The first was whether Latin American military professionalism was old or new. Historians discovered its origins in the late nineteenth century and the influence of Prussian and French military missions who fashioned an elitist contempt for "failed" democratic institutions and actors that seemed to resonate well with Latin American officers. Others, notably political scientists contended that there was a new professionalism that had emerged from Latin American and U.S. War Colleges in the 1950s and 1960s that promoted a belief in the legitimacy of military internal security missions and role expansion.

The second was a debate about the relative weight to place on professionally self-generated ideas vs. socially rooted interests. While some scholars could acknowledge the importance of professional belief transformations, these would not have occurred without fundamental change in the larger socio-economic system of which the military was a part. As a structuralist, but one who also incorporated organizational theories of behavior, Guillermo O'Donnell observed that the military became more cohesive, ideologically committed and coup prone in response to threats from its environment. As the larger social and political system descended into mass praetorianism—replete with economic crises, social polarization, union militancy and escalating violence—the military became convinced it had to seize power in order to permanently transform the system to ensure stability and its own survival. Others located the source of military praetorianism squarely in social classes. According to José Nun and others, the Latin American middle class was both threatened by the advancing tide of a militant working class and unable to defend itself. Thus it built a pro-coup alliance with the armed forces whose own ranks were filled with middle class soldiers.[3]

Not until most of the armed forces had left power in the 1980s did scholars begin to seriously investigate the nature of authoritarian rule. These studies focused either on the strategic acumen of military leaders or more commonly on the organization of power within their regimes.[4] It became evident that regimes with concentrated authority—often in the hands of a single general—could outlive regimes where power was more dispersed between service branches, or between government and the military institution itself. Others followed by examining some of the built-in limitations to military rule endurance, noting either how officers were generally ill-equipped to govern (as opposed to administering) or how the structure of incentives—especially the drive to preserve institutional unity—pushed generals back to the barracks.[5]

A decade later and well into the twenty-first century, a wave of studies emerged on authoritarian regimes of the past and the specific roles played by the military. Most of these were centered on the Southern Cone and Central America.[6] Autocratic regimes have long been thought to be unrestrained and unaffected by law. Interestingly, some of the Southern Cone studies suggest otherwise, arguing that legal frameworks mattered to the conduct of autocratic rule. In some regimes, military rulers exploited court proceedings to legitimize their repressive policies. In others juntas found it useful to bind themselves to the laws they created in order to resolve elite-level conflicts and preserve a certain distribution of power.[7]

There have been a handful of scholars who have dug even deeper into the past, probing the development of Latin American armies in the nineteenth century. These are fascinating studies that for the first time in Latin American scholarship treat the military and civil-military relations as central to understandings about state formation, national development and democratization. Miguel Centeno argues that wars were limited in nature: they did not modify national borders and accordingly, placed fewer demands on state leaders to create powerful war-waging armies by generating tax-based revenues. As a result, Latin America failed to develop into strong West-European styled states. Fernando López-Alves traces the evolution of weaker or stronger democratic tendencies to the nature and location of nineteenth century wars. The difference hinges on whether battles raged in cities or the country side and whether the rural poor were mobilized to fight by political parties or by central armies. João Resende-Santos demonstrates why Brazil, Argentina and Chile all strove to emulate the same military system—Germany's—despite considerable differences between them. They were driven by turn of the century inter-state power rivalries, and in their emulation of the best fighting force in the world at that time succeeded not only at building the physical capacity of their armies, but at strengthening their states as well.[8]

The Military, Authoritarian Legacies, and the Democratic Transition

The impact of different military dictatorships on the democratic transitions that followed depended upon what analytical point of view scholars embraced. There are several discernible positions here. The first tended to downplay the legacy impact altogether. For these scholars, what decisions were made had less to do with the past and more to do with the future. Hard-line and soft-line officers, and moderate and radical civilians alike would strategically jockey for position, exchange offers, issue threats, make bluffs, and finally negotiate, all with the objective of working out arrangements for the eventual transfer of power to democrats.[9]

Military authoritarian legacies mattered more to those who adopted historical-institutionalist, path dependent analyses to transition. According to the common version of path dependency, once a course of action is plotted—be it the result of practices, pacts, or power imbalances—it is very difficult for a society to veer off course. Early choices become institutionalized in the form of organizations, power-sharing agreements, prerogatives, and, in the economist's lingo, increasing returns and sunken costs.

But here there are two variants in the Latin American literature. The first recognizes that the legacy effect has differed considerably between Latin American cases because institutional arrangements within the military regimes were quite different. Those regimes which were better able to suppress or accommodate disputes, forge unity, and develop a strategic plan for the future, could exert a more powerful influence on the mode of transition, and the democracies that followed. Those that could not, never seized control over the transitions, and had negligible influence over the re-emerging democracies.[10] The process yielded democratic progenies with more limited options (Chile, Brazil) and ones with considerably more (Argentina).

A second variant of path dependence is less discriminating between the cases. It looks at the broad sweep of military history and how the replication and reinforcement of rituals, myths and values became embedded as a political culture of militarism. Others move the discussion forward to the centrality of military figures in de facto regimes of the second half of the twentieth century, and their success in setting down conditions and altering balances of power which helped them shape the transition to democracy to their liking.[11] Both cohorts agree that the armed forces were able to institutionalize lasting, negative legacies throughout the region: the retention of informal power enclaves, constitutional prerogatives, and limits on presidential, judicial and legislative influence and oversight on the armed forces.

Scholars of the military have paid less explicit attention to another version of path dependence, one with contrasting implications. This is the version where legacies produce intense, countervailing reactions that can increase the determination of democratic societies to free themselves from the shackles of the past.[12] A harshly repressive dictatorship could, rather than instilling fearful memories that invite caution and retreat, trigger a greater resolve to inoculate democratic practices, alter the balance of civil-military power and strengthen the prospects for civilian control. This perspective might give us leads into why repressive military regimes can induce robust civilian counter-reactions in Argentina and Chile—ones that have helped to reduce military power—but not in Guatemala.[13]

Civil-Military Relations and Civilian Control

The completed transition in Latin America naturally shifted the center of attention again, this time to the patterns of civilian-military relations developing under democratic auspices. Researchers appraised the degree to which respective civilian and military spheres of influence had narrowed or widened since the inauguration of democratic rule. To what degree, if any, were militaries subordinate to civilian rule? And what exactly were the ingredients to civilian control? Was it an alteration in the balance of power, a reduction in military prerogatives and autonomy, a competent management of military affairs, an internalization of new norms, or strengthened defense-related institutions?

At the dawn of the new century, civil-military relations in Latin America were more stable than they were a decade or two prior. Scholars could generally agree with the proposition that the Latin American military was less oriented toward regime overthrow and more preoccupied with guarding its own corporate well-being within the democratic order. The coup d'etat was no longer the defining theme of this new era. But researchers diverged over how much progress, if any, had been made. Perhaps the majority of researchers at the time would agree with Rut Diamint's sobering critique that from the vantage point of both state and society, there remained serious deficits. Civil society and non-governmental organizations (NGOs) in particular, were noticeably silent when it came to military themes. They chose to keep a low profile due to lingering fears about military retaliation as well as a lack of encouragement from legislators, political parties and especially executives who were blamed for not making defense a more accessible topic to an unknowing public. Governments, meanwhile, had practiced avoidance. Rather than challenge military autonomy by building stronger civilian-led defense ministries, they deferred to the armed forces hoping somehow that the services would transform themselves. Of course, they never did, but rather clung to prerogatives which the civilian leaders refused to strip away from them.[14]

An alternative set of views were more sanguine about the prospects for improved civil-military relations even while acknowledging that full civilian control still proved elusive. Once democracies are up and running, the logic of democratic institutions and rational political action take hold, producing outcomes that are often beneficial if not unexpected. Institutions of state can mediate between soldiers and civilians and in doing so often blunt military pressure. They create barriers of entry, directions of influence, and bureaucratic distance between soldiers and those who make policy. The more institutionally insulated and autonomous policymakers are from soldiers, the more able they are to craft their own policies unperturbed by disgruntled officers. Electoral competition meanwhile creates new incentives for politicians who must mind what their own parties and constituents want. To earn votes, and retain political office, it is in their interest to contest the military over budget shares and more broadly over a whole host of policies. For example, politicians on the political right find themselves compelled to win over the median voter who favors prosecution for human rights abusers, or more money spent on prioritized programs, not defense.[15]

What would it take to achieve civilian control? There was agreement that a first order of business for democracies still moving through transitional periods was to roll back military perks and privileges. Alfred Stepan provided a useful though long list of prerogatives which would have to be annulled if civilians were to make headway. These were areas where the military had a self-proclaimed right to exercise effective control or influence, and ranged from occupying cabinet positions to coordinating the defense sector to dominating intelligence gathering, judiciaries, and the police. To strip the military of all these "rights" at once would no doubt be daunting to any new democratic government, which raised the issue of strategic priorities: couldn't some battles over privileges be waged now, while others be deferred to later, and *mustn't* it be that way, to avert demand overloads that could trigger military animosity? One scholar has proposed a phasing in of military reforms, with early measures invoked during democratic transitional process aimed at curtailing military inter-vention in politics, while others are installed during consolidation where politicians assume real leadership on defense.[16]

Most researchers use the terms "prerogatives" and "autonomy" interchangeably. While close in meaning, autonomy refers more specifically to an institution's decision-making independence. The prevailing wisdom has been that military autonomy is harmful to civil-ian control and must be curbed. In fact, no obstacle has so perturbed civil-military scholars as has military autonomy. I have argued there are actually two kinds of autonomy, the first less injurious to civilians than the second. Institutional autonomy refers to the military's effort to guard its *core* professional functions from excessive political meddling which it believes may interfere with the goals of professionalization and modernization. Military guardianship over its educational system and training programs might be two examples. Political autonomy on the other hand refers to the military's move beyond core professional boundaries to challenge the government's control over non-defense policies (i.e., economy, foreign policy) or the selection of policy-makers themselves. If we can visualize a spectrum of professional and political functions, then military influence varies across that continuum. The military may have full authority over some decisions, shared authority over others, and little or no authority over still others. As Harold Trinkunas points out, civilian control efforts are most threatened when the military asserts dominance in the political areas of public policy or leadership selection. They are least threatened by military participation in the core professional area of national defense. It is both the sphere of influence and the degree of military authority within each sphere, that should define for scholars whether military autonomy poses a risk or not.[17]

The military may, of course, contest any civilian attempt to reduce its autonomy or prerogatives. While most scholars agree with Stepan that a maturing civil-military relation is one that finally overcomes contestation, it is also true that conflicts have been decisive turning points in the power struggle between governments and soldiers. When and where civilians have prevailed in conflicts, they have dramatically shifted the balance in their favor. This phenomenon was displayed in showdowns between rebel soldiers and loyalists in the suppressed coup attempt in Spain in February 1981, and in the failed military uprising in Argentina in December 1990. But confrontation needn't be physical. If political leaders, for example, prevail upon the military to submit to objectionable policy decisions, then having assumed the risk of confrontation and having won, they alter the equation between them-selves and their commanders, enhancing their credibility as authority figures and earning greater respect from the public. A majority of Latin American scholars have yet to acknowl-edge the benefits of civil-military conflict, but a few have.[18]

Even if civilians reduce military prerogatives and prevail in conflicts, these are but pre-liminary steps in the struggle to achieve long lasting democratic civilian control. Latin Americanists generally agree that there is a distinction between gaining some short term leverage over the military vs. institutionalizing a longer term advantage.

Building a lasting edifice of control is more difficult, and multidimensional. The first dimension is legal. Governments must legislate restrictions on military missions and the use of force, as well as establish the legal basis for defense-relevant state bureaucracies. The second facet is institutional. Democracies need to actually build or refurbish a set of well-staffed, civilian-led organizations, including National Defense and Security Councils,

Ministries of Defense, and Congressional Defense Commissions. And they need to insure that the design of defense organizations in the executive branch facilitate asymmetric power relations, so that directives flow from politically appointed civilians through ministerial staffs and down through the chain of command, not the other way around.

The third is educational. If civilians are to direct and staff defense organizations, they need to get up to speed on defense-related issues. That means devising university career tracks that equip civilians to enter the civil service with an eye toward the defense ministry and relevant congressional committees. The fourth is informational. Scholars agree there must be greater transparency about military and defense affairs. Topics once thought too remote for the average citizen must be availed to him. For that to occur, government officials and the public alike must have more data at their disposal to generate a national conversation about defense. More than that, citizens must become involved in the actual work: networks of specialists are needed-a defense establishment if you will—that can be welcomed to the table by military and government figures to advise on if not participate in the construction of defense policies for the nation.

There are some but not many purely academic works on these subjects.[19] The rest of the work is widely scattered across numerous national think tanks and networks, and is informational, descriptive, and policy-oriented in nature, not theoretical. For example, RES-DAL—The Red de Seguridad de America Latina—has proved to be an invaluable source of information. They have, among other many items, published a methodology handbook for analyzing defense ministries, guidelines for strengthening the role of parliaments in defense and analyzing budgets, and a bi-annual Atlas that is the most comprehensive, informational research tool available. And the Facultad Latinoamericana de Ciencias Sociales (FLACSO) has produced an exhaustive study of the security sector for each of eighteen Latin American Republics and the region as a whole, part of which relates to defense ministries and civilian capacity to manage defense affairs.[20]

If there is a debate about democratic civilian control, it is less normative than analytical. While scholars agree that institutionalized, democratic civilian control is a worthy goal, they disagree about whether all of its elements can be realized, and if not, how politically costly is that? If, for example, control hinges on political leaders and civilian staffers accumulating defense wisdom, how likely is that to happen? And must it? Thomas Bruneau has argued that civilians need to comprehend enough about defense topics to assign the armed forces proper missions, and to ensure that they fulfill them and do so effectively and efficiently. Trinkunas and Pion-Berlin argue that the defense wisdom deficit is unlikely to be vanquished any time soon, because civilians lack the incentives to become defense savvy. In the Latin American corner of the globe, existential threats to territorial sovereignty are rare, publics and parties are disinterested in defense, and defense contracting delivers few jobs to home districts.[21] If that is the reality, then some would say that so long as the armed forces are adroitly managed politically, civilian control can survive without defense wisdom. Others are not so sure.

Defense and Security Studies

Civilian control remains relevant though in many respects, the intellectual conversation has shifted in the last decade towards the subjects of defense and security. Defense refers to the development of plans and processes designed to provide for the oversight, organization, training, deployment and funding of the armed forces. Security is a broader term referring to the harnessing of *any and all* assets necessary to protect regional, national and individual well-being. For some specialists, defense must become a matter of prioritized public policy, and if not, complete civilian control will never be attained.[22] For them, civilians can only exercise their power properly when they make defense policy theirs, ending the military's long held monopoly on the topic. To do that, they must not only own the issue, but elevate it to a stature equal to that of other public policies.

For these scholars, defense has taken on precedence because it some sense it reflects the maturation of their democracies. Having largely met the earlier phase challenges of reducing military contestation and autonomy, and having stabilized civil-military relations, states have now focused on the later phase challenges of defense preparedness, including ministerial and force modernization, improved education and training, logistics, sophistication of hardware, and joint military action. Trends in the direction of greater civilian defense attentiveness include the convocation of hemispheric defense ministerial meetings since 1995; the release of *White Books* on defense; the emphasis on strengthening defense ministries; and the 2009 creation of a South American Defense Council aimed at achieving common positions on defense matters.

At the same time, experts would also caution that these efforts are incipient; there remain noticeable gaps to fill, on the military and civilian side.[23] On the military side, improvements need to be made in defense preparedness, in scientific R&D, and in the updating of antiquated doctrines that warn about enemy neighbors at a time when subregional peace and cooperation is the name of the game. And on the civilian side, educational deficits in defense are rampant, ministries are still understaffed with able non-uniformed personnel, and governments have not fully harnessed military power to advance foreign policy objectives.

It is in one respect immensely surprising that there has been such interest in defense. After all, Latin America continues to be a region largely free of inter-state wars, and with one exception, guerrilla insurgencies. The region lies at the periphery of the international system, and so states are rarely subject to the security dilemmas found elsewhere. Where are the existential threats to national security that would demand attention to defense capability? There are hardly any. It seems therefore, that defense awareness and activity is largely prophylactic: to protect the region from reversions to the geopolitical rivalries of the past; to assure that the region remains a zone of peace; to build on the cooperative security ventures already forged; and to support the diplomatic efforts that have settled border disputes and reduced tensions between neighbors.

In another respect, the interest in defense is ironic, since it comes at the same time that Latin America *is* faced with real security threats but ones which do not lend themselves to a military response. The region is ravaged by violent, well-organized criminal syndicates, gangs and drug traffickers who operate with near-impunity. And although Latin America is not traditionally thought of as a hotbed of terrorism, in recent years, the number of organizations using terrorist tactics, particularly in urban areas, is notable. These groups make it unsafe for citizens to conduct their normal lives and may even make certain areas ungovernable, calling into question the legitimacy of leaders.

Thus, it is not surprising at all to see a surge in security studies.[24] But the new threats to the region have little or nothing to do with defense, and ought not and usually do not, invite the armed forces in as primary responders. In fact, it is mostly *public* security that is at risk, not *national* security. Public security is about making public spaces, buildings, institutions and individuals safe from the violence of criminal elements. Naturally, the main burden of protection falls on the police and other internal security forces. Thus, the bulk of scholarship on internal security has gravitated toward the study of citizen (in)security, (un)rule of law, police conduct, misconduct, and the requisites for police reform.

While the military is not at the center of this stage, it has not been completely thrown off stage either. Reluctantly, some states have introduced the armed forces in anti-crime and anti-narcotic missions, given the inadequate response of police forces to these threats. Law enforcement is widely condemned for being ill-trained if not incompetent, and highly corrupt. Polls indicate the public has greater trust in the military as an institution than the police, and in Central America citizens support the use of soldiers to patrol city streets.[25]

These facts draw scholarly attention to the role of the military in combating crime, though there are differences in perspective. Probably the majority of scholars posit that it is never advisable to involve the military in public security functions. They contend that soldiers are trained to destroy an enemy, not protect and defend citizens. They are hard-wired to use maximal force, not show restraint, and thus their use is inappropriate if not dangerous within densely populated centers. Moreover, a dependence on the military to fight crime will only lessen incentives to reform the police so that they can perform their professional obligations more effectively.[26]

A second cohort of scholars lament the use of the military for public security but also agree there may be no choice.[27] With crime and violence out of control and police ineffectual, some military immersion may be necessary. Besides, they argue, many countries have legal, even constitutional safeguards that restrict the nature, length and scope of military public security operations. That means there is less danger of mission creep or military usurpation of powers. Others agree, and add there cannot be a strict separation of military and police functions, since the line between external and internal threats has been blurred by the transnational character of organized crime. A smaller cohort actually advocates military use. They contend that the security threat is multidimensional and demands a multifaceted response, one that makes use of all the state's assets—the military included.[28] And finally, a fourth position maintains that neither military nor police forces can or should respond to these threats and that it may take hybrid organizations (i.e., gendarmes or national guard) to fill the gap.[29]

The Future

There are a number of potentially fruitful research avenues worth traversing in the future. The first returns us to the Honduran question: just what would it take for the military to overthrow other governments in the region? It would be unwise to generalize from a single case, as many of the circumstances surrounding the Zelaya overthrow are unique to that country. But scholars nonetheless fret over regional polls indicating declines in citizen diffuse support for democracy, particular dissatisfaction with performance, and an increased willingness to tolerate non-democratic solutions under dire economic circumstances. Could these trends portend civil-military trouble? Not necessarily. As many "subjectivists" would argue, it depends on the views of officers themselves. Are they prepared to arbitrate when politicians cannot resolve their own difficulties? Do they see intervention as consistent with their own institutional interests? What costs are they willing to bear? We simply do not know, for lack of new military interview data that would shed light on attitudes of recently retired officers. Conducting military interviews is never easy, but may be necessary if we are to fully evaluate the risks to troubled democracies in the region.

What we do know, what we have observed in recent years is a trend toward military shirking of responsibilities, when confronted with civilian commands perceived to be institutionally harmful. On occasion, the armed forces have confined themselves to barracks rather than suppress civilian protesters. This occurred in Argentina in 2001, and Bolivia and Ecuador in 2005. At other times, they have refused to conduct certain operations unless judicial immunity is granted, clear rules of engagement are written or a bargain is struck for side payments. Because military shirking is almost always a calculated response to protect institutional interests in a context of uncertainty, then rational choice theories should prove useful in assessing the underlying motivations for defiance, what the full slate of strategic options are, along with the risks and opportunities associated with each.

Military shirkers are not coup plotters; they are not interested in acquiring political power. They accept the democratic order and the civilian leader's *right* to make decisions. They are principally out to protect their professional well-being. It would be worthwhile knowing more about this phenomenon. What other forms of shirking can be observed? Do certain kinds of missions and operations trigger greater military apprehension than others? If so, why? When does military apprehension finally cross over into disobedience? And have politicians learned anything from these episodes?

Military shirking also leads us to consider the issue of military adaptability. It is well known that throughout the world, soldiers are often asked to perform those duties no one else can or will carry out. Witness the range of tasks that Latin American peacekeepers undertake in Haiti and in other trouble spots around the globe. To what extent does that flexibility transfer back home? Apparently not very easily, or at all. Notwithstanding peacekeeping experiences, Latin American militaries fail to perform police-like security functions very well. In fact they would rather not, since these functions are viewed as demeaning, and detrimental to maintaining combat effectiveness. Why then can soldiers help keep the peace abroad, but not at home? Can soldiers ever be transformed into police surrogates, or must that role be reserved for others? And if new threats demand new security responses, what will become of a military unable or unwilling to transform itself? Will it be relegated to more numerous, non-lethal, development-oriented missions, or simply confined to its barracks? Or has the military outlived its usefulness altogether? Hopefully, these and other provocative questions will keep scholars motivated to pursue research into the Latin American military for years to come.

Notes

1   For an elaboration on these theoretical approaches and their practitioners, see David Pion-Berlin, "Introduction," in David Pion-Berlin (ed.), *Civil-Military Relations in Latin America: New Analytical Perspectives*, pp. 1–35 (Chapel Hill: University of North Carolina Press, 2001).
2   Guillermo O'Donnell, *Modernization and Bureaucratic-Authoritarianism: Studies in South American Politics* (Berkeley: Institute of International Studies, 1973); J. Samuel Fitch, *The Military Coup d'Etat as a Political Process: Ecuador 1948–1966* (Baltimore: Johns Hopkins Press, 1977); Alfred Stepan, "The New Professionalism of Internal Warfare and Military Role Expansion," in Abraham F. Lowenthal and J. Samuel Fitch (eds.), *Armies and Politics in Latin America*, pp. 134–150 (New York: Holmes & Meier, 1986); Frederick Nunn. *Yesterday's Soldiers: European Military Professionalism in South America, 1890–1940* (Lincoln: University of Nebraska Press, 1983).
3   Guillermo O'Donnell, *Modernization and Bureaucratic-Authoritarianism*; José Nun, "The Middle Class Military Coup," in Lowenthal and Fitch (eds.), *Armies and Politics in Latin America*. Martin Needler argued that the coup had become a conservative weapon in defense of the "possessing classes" seeking to maintain their position in the face of mobilized, classes of lower status. See Martin Needler, "Political Development and Military Intervention in Latin America," *The American Political Science Review*, 60, 3 (September 1966): 616–626.
4   Genaro Arriagada Herrera, *Pinochet: The Politics of Power*, trans. Nancy Morris (Boston: Unwin Hyman, 1988); Karen L. Remmer, *Military Rule in Latin America* (Boston: Unwin Hyman, 1989).
5   María Susana Ricci and J. Samuel Fitch, "Ending Military Regimes in Argentina, 1966–1973 and 1976–1983," in Louis W. Goodman, Johanna S. R. Mendelson, and Juan Rial (eds.), *The*

Military and Democracy: The Future of Civil-Military Relations in Latin America, pp. 55–74 (Lexington, MA: Lexington Books, 1990); Barbara Geddes, "What Do We Know about Democratization after Twenty Years?" *Annual Review of Political Science* II (1999): 115–144.

6 On the Southern Cone see Glen Biglaiser, *Guardians of the Nation? Economists, Generals, and Economic Reform in Latin America* (Notre Dame: University of Notre Dame Press, 2002); on Chile, see Carlos Huneeus, *The Pinochet Regime*, trans. Lake Sagaris (Boulder: Lynne Rienner, 2007); on El Salvador see William Stanley, *The Protection Racket: Elite Politics, Military Extortion, and Civil War in El Salvador* (Philadelphia: Temple University Press, 1996); also see Philip J. Williams and Knut Walter *Militarization and Demilitarization in El Salvador's Transition to Democracy* (Pittsburgh: University of Pittsburgh Press, 1997); on Guatemala, see Jennifer Schirmer, *The Guatemalan Military Project: A Violence Called Democracy* (Philadelphia: University of Pennsylvania Press, 1998).

7 Anthony W. Pereira, *Political (In)justice: Authoritarianism and the Rule of Law in Brazil, Chile, and Argentina* (Pittsburgh: University of Pittsburgh Press, 2005); Robert Barros, *Constitutionalism and Dictatorship: Pinochet, the Junta, and the 1980 Constitution* (Cambridge University Press, 2002).

8 Miguel Centeno, *Blood and Debt: War and Nation-State in Latin America* (University Park: Pennsylvania State University Press, 2002); Fernando Lopez-Alves, *State Formation and Democracy in Latin America, 1810–1900* (Durham, NC: Duke University Press, 2000); João Resende-Santos, *Neorealism, States, and the Modern Mass Army* (Cambridge: Cambridge University Press, 2007).

9 Guillermo O'Donnell and Philippe C. Schmitter, *Transitions from Authoritarian Rule: Tentative Conclusions About Uncertain Democracies* (Baltimore: Johns Hopkins Press, 1986) best typifies this approach to civil-military affairs in a transitional setting, while Adam Przeworski's *Democracy and the Market: Political and Economic Reforms in Eastern Europe and Latin America* (Cambridge: Cambridge University Press, 1991) formalized this approach through the use of game theory.

10 The chief proponent of this view is Craig Arceneaux. See his *Bounded Missions: Military Regimes and Democratization in the Southern Cone and Brazil* (University Park: Pennsylvania State University Press, 2001).

11 See Brian Loveman, *For la Patria: Politics and the Armed Forces in Latin America* (Wilmington, DE: Scholarly Resources, 1999); Frederick M. Nunn, *The Time of the Generals: Latin American Professional Militarism in World Perspective* (Lincoln: University of Nebraska Press, 1992.); Felipe Agüero, *Soldiers, Civilians and Democracy: Spain in Comparative Perspective* (Baltimore: Johns Hopkins University Press, 1995).

12 Paul Pierson, "Not Just What But When: Timing and Sequence in Political Processes," *Studies in American Political Development* 14 (Spring 2000): 84.

13 One study places emphasis on the military's own recounting of its past deeds, and its impact on Southern Cone democracies. See Eric Hershberg and Felipe Agüero (eds.), *Memorias militares sobre al represión en el Cono Sur: visiones en disputa en dictadura y democracia* (Madrid: SigloXXI editores, 2005).

14 Rut Diamint, "Estado y Sociedad Civil Ante la Cuestión Cívico-Militar en los '90," in Rut Diamint (ed.), *Control civil y fuerzas armadas en las nuevas democracias latinoamericanas* (Buenos Aires: Nuevo Hacer, 1999), pp. 35–68.

15 David Pion-Berlin, *Through Corridors of Power: Institutions and Civil-Military Relations in Argentina* (University Park: Pennsylvania State University Press, 1997); Wendy Hunter, *Eroding Military Influence in Brazil: Politicians Against Soldiers* (Chapel Hill: University of North Carolina Press, 1997). Chilean scholars in particular have recognized that the logic of electoral competition has caused political parties of the right to distance themselves from the Pinochet legacy.

16 Narcís Serra, *The Military Transition: Democratic Reform of the Armed Forces* (Cambridge University Press, 2010), pp. 66–89.

17 David Pion-Berlin, "Military Autonomy and Emerging Democracies in South America," *Comparative Politics*, 25 (October, 1992): 83–102; Harold Trinkunas, *Crafting Civilian Control of the Military in Venezuela: A Comparative Perspective* (Chapel Hill: University of North Carolina Press, 2005).

18 See Agüero *Soldiers, Civilians, and Democracy*, pp. 21–22; David Pion-Berlin, "Strong Tests of Civilian and Military Power in Latin America," unpublished manuscript, January, 2000.

19 On defense and security legislation, see José Manuel Ugarte, *Los conceptos jurídicos y políticos de la seguridad y la defensa* (Buenos Aires: Editorial Plus Ultra, 2003); On the difference between leverage and institutionalizing civilian control, see Harold Trinkunas, *Crafting Civilian Control*;

On defense organizational designs, see David Pion-Berlin, "Defense Organization and Civil-Military Relations in Latin America," *Armed Forces & Society*, 35, 3 (April 2009): 562–586; And on the need to transform defense into a matter of public policy and debate, see Rut Diamint, *Democracia y Seguridad en America Latina* (Buenos Aires: Nuevo Hacer, 2001), and Lourdes Hurtado et al., eds. *Los nudos de la defensa: enredos y desenredos para una política pública en democracia* (Lima: Instituto de Defensa Legal, 2005).

20 Elsa Llenderrozas y Guillermo Pacheco Gaitán, Metodología para el análisis de los ministerios de defensa (Buenos Aires: RESDAL, 2007); Proyecto RESDAL Transparencia, Una guía para el control de la transparencia de los presupuestos de defensa (Buenos Aires: RESDAL); and Roberto Cajina, Gustavo Fabian Castro, and Luis Tibiletti (eds.), *Control civil de las fuerzas armadas: fortaleciendo el papel de la asesoria parlamentaria* (Buenos Aires: RESDAL, 2008); RESDAL Atlas, biannual, 2005–2009 (Buenos Aires: RESDAL, 2010), accessed August 23, 2010, http://www.resdal.org/; Lucía Dammert (ed.), *Reporte del sector seguridad de América Latina y Caribe* (Santiago, Chile: Facultad Latinoamericana de Ciencias Sociales, 2007).

21 Thomas Bruneau, "Civil-Military Relations in Latin America: The Hedgehog and the Fox Revisited," *Fuerzas Armadas y Sociedad*, 19, 1 (2005): 111–131; David Pion-Berlin and Harold Trinkunas, "Attention Deficits: Why Politicians Ignore Defense Policy in Latin America," *Latin American Research Review*, 42, 4 (2007): 76–100.

22 The leading proponent of this view is Rut Diamint. See her Democracia y Seguridad en America Latina.

23 Hector Saint Pierre, "Algunas consideraciones sobre la profesionalización del personal de la defensa," delivered at Modernización de Ministerios de Defensa Seminar, Consejo de Defensa Suramericano de UNASUR, November 19–20, 2009.

24 For example, see Joseph Tulchin, Raúl Benitez, and Rut Diamint (eds.), El Rompecabezas: conformando la Seguridad Hemisferica en el Siglo XXI. Buenos Aires: Prometeo Libros, 2006; Claudio Fuentes, *Contesting the Iron Fist: Advocacy Networks and Police Violence in Democratic Argentina and Chile* (Oxon, UK: Routledge, 2005); Fruhling and Tulchin (eds.) *Crime and Violence in Latin America: Citizen Security, Democracy and the State* (Baltimore, MD: Johns Hopkins University Press, 2003); Niels Uildriks (ed.), *Policing Insecurity. Police reform, Security, and Human Rights in Latin Americ* (Lanham, MD: Lexington Books, 2009).

25 According to a poll conducted by El Salvador's *El Diario de Hoy*, in November of 2009, 93 percent of respondents said they favor the use of soldiers to fight crime. Inter Press Service, "Salvadoran President Deploys Troops to Fight Crime," November 14, 2009. On public confidence in the military vs. police, see Latino Barómetro, Informe 2009, p. 36. http://www.latinobarometro.org/latino/, accessed on September 28, 2010.

26 See Oscar Bonilla, "Las reformas al sector seguridad en America Latina," and Lilian Bobea, "Encarando al jano bifronte: reforma o militarización policial?" in José Raúl Perales (ed.), *Reforma de las fuerzas armadas en América Latina: y el impacto de las amenazas irregulares,* pp. 5–14 (Washington, D.C.: Woodrow Wilson Center Series, 2008).

27 See Gabriel Aguilera Peralta, "Las amenazas irregulares en la agenda de seguridad de Centroamérica," and Guillermo Pacheco, "Comentarios: Guatemala, El Salvador, República Dominicana," in José Raúl Perales (ed.), *Reforma de las fuerzas armadas,* pp. 25–27.

28 Max Manwaring is a principle exponent of this view. See "A Contemporary Challenge to State Sovereignty," *Strategic Studies Institute*, U.S. Army War College, December 2007.

29 David Pion-Berlin and Harold Trinkunas, "Latin America's Growing Security Gap," *Journal of Democracy* 22, 1 (January, 2011): 39–53.

7

INFORMAL INSTITUTIONS AND POLITICS IN LATIN AMERICA

Steven Levitsky

The 1990s and 2000s witnessed a resurgence of institutionalism in the study of Latin American politics. It is easy to understand why. The region experienced an extraordinary degree of formal institutional change, as widespread democratization was accompanied by a wave of constitutional, electoral, judicial, and other reforms. These reforms triggered renewed interest—among both scholars and practitioners alike—in the consequences of institutional design.

Nevertheless, the new institutionalism in Latin America faced important limitations. Much of the early literature was based on the assumption that formal institutions are stable and effective—that parchment rules actually shape politicians' expectations and behavior in practice. Although such assumptions hold up relatively well in the advanced industrialized democracies, they travel less well to Latin America. As a growing body of research has demonstrated, the strength of formal rules varies widely in Latin America.[1] Whereas some formal rules are stable and effective, many others are routinely circumvented, manipulated, or changed. Moreover, many of the "rules of the game" that structure politics diverge from—and even contradict—the parchment rules: these are *informal institutions*.[2] An exclusive focus on formal rules thus risks missing many of the real incentives driving political behavior in Latin America, which can limit our understanding of how politics works.

Informal institutions have long coexisted—and competed—with formal institutions in Latin America. A classic example is authoritarian Mexico. Although Mexico's post-revolutionary regime was formally democratic, many of the rights granted by the 1917 constitution were ignored. The PRI ruled, in large part, through informal institutions. Thus, notwithstanding regular elections, presidential succession was governed by the *dedazo*, an elaborate but unwritten system in which sitting presidents chose their successor from a select pool of candidates (cabinet members) who followed a set of clear rules (e.g., abstain from campaigning, mobilizing supporters, or attacking rivals; publicly support the eventual nominee).[3] PRI hegemony was reinforced by a range of other informal practices, including clientelism, ballot stuffing (e.g., "flying brigades," in which voters were bussed from precinct to precinct to cast multiple ballots),[4] and mechanisms of media manipulation such as planted newspaper stories (*gacetillas*), and monthly bribes to journalists (*chayotes*).[5]

Informal institutions are pervasive in contemporary Latin American democracies. For example, voting in much of the region is mediated by clientelism, an informal system of exchange that is often embedded in shared rules, procedures, and expectations that guide both politicians and voters.[6] In multiparty presidential systems, executives rely on informal institutions such as "ghost coalitions" (Ecuador), the *cuoteo* and *democracia de los acuerdos* (Chile), and coalitional presidentialism (Brazil) to build and sustain legislative majorities.[7] In civil-military relations, many important interactions "do not occur within the chain of command, are not mandated by law, and do not conform to official rules and procedures;" rather, civilian and military officials often turn to "off script" practices, such as informal "conferences," to resolve conflicts.[8] Finally, informal institutions have been shown to both undermine the rule of law (e.g., norms enabling police violence in Brazil) and enhance access to justice where the rule of law is weak (e.g., *rondas campesinas* in Peru).[9]

The pervasiveness of informal rules has forced students of Latin America to incorporate them more systematically into analyses of political institutions. Initial scholarship focused primarily on the dysfunctional effects of informal institutions—for example, on how persistent patterns of patrimonialism, clientelism, and corruption undermined the performance of formal institutions (and consequently, the quality of democracy).[10] Increasingly, however, scholars have highlighted how informal institutions help strengthen—and improve the performance of—formal institutions, which, as will be argued below, can be critical to democratic governability.

This chapter offers an introduction to informal institutions in Latin America. After making the case for why they matter, the chapter compares different types of informal institution and asks why they emerge. It then examines the impact of informal rules, arguing that they play an important—and heretofore under-studied—role in making democratic institutions work.

Why Informal Institutions Matter

Informal institutions may be defined as "socially shared rules, usually unwritten, that are created, communicated, and enforced outside officially sanctioned channels."[11] They are unwritten rules of the game, rooted in shared expectations, the violation of which triggers some kind of social sanction (ranging from mild disapproval to outright violence).

For students of comparative politics, informal institutions matter to the extent that they shape political outcomes. In other words, they are considered important if they alter politicians' incentives, generating behavior that diverges from that prescribed by (or expected from) the formal rules. Recent research has shown that such is frequently the case. Consider, for example, presidentialism in Chile and Mexico. Chile's 1980 constitution—imposed by dictator Augusto Pinochet—created an "exaggerated presidential system," with a powerful executive and a weak legislature.[12] Given this constitutional design, Chilean presidents might have been expected to strong-arm or circumvent Congress, as occurred in Argentina, Brazil, and other delegative democracies in the 1990s.[13] Yet Chilean presidents did not govern in a delegative democratic manner; rather, they routinely negotiated legislation with congressional and party leaders. As Peter Siavelis shows, this pattern of "consensus democracy" was rooted in informal power sharing norms (the *cuoteo*, *partido transversal*, *democracia de los acuerdos*) that emerged within the governing Democratic Concertation.[14] By contrast, even though Mexico's 1917 constitution prescribed one of the weakest executives in Latin America, Mexican presidents were virtually unchecked by Congress through the mid-1990s. This outcome was rooted in a set of "metaconstitutional" powers that enabled presidents to dominate the legislature.[15] Thus, whereas a reading of the Chilean and Mexican constitutions would lead us to expect hyper-presidentialism in Chile but not Mexico, the reality in the 1990s was just the opposite.

Informal institutions also shape outcomes in judicial politics. For example, Argentina's constitution has long granted U.S.-style tenure security, via lifetime appointment, to Supreme Court justices. Yet as Gretchen Helmke shows, an established pattern of court packing, dating back to the 1940s, generated a distinct set of expectations and behavior: rather than acting independently of the executive, as might be expected given the formal rules, justices follow a logic of "strategic defection," in which they rule with sitting governments while they are politically strong but defect—toward the most likely successor—once it is clear that the government's days are numbered.[16]

Informal institutions also mediate the effects of electoral rules. For example, Costa Rica's proportional representation electoral system and ban on legislative re-election create no incentive for legislators to perform constituency service. Yet, as Michelle Taylor has shown, Costa Rican legislators routinely engage in such activities. This outcome is explained by the existence of informal mechanisms created by parties—such as the creation of informal districts and the blacklisting of uncooperative politicians—to encourage legislators to attend to local needs.[17]

Finally, informal institutions mediate the effects of candidate selection rules. Research on congressional elections in the United States suggests that closed party primaries are likely to produce ideologically polarizing candidates, because more ideologically extreme activists are more likely to vote in primary elections.[18] In patronage-based systems, however, the dynamics are quite different. Where activists are linked to parties via patronage and voters are mobilized via clientelism, primary elections are determined by the size of the competing candidates' patronage machines.[19] Rather than producing ideological candidates, then, primaries in patronage-based parties produce machine candidates.

Not all informal institutions distort formal institutional outcomes. Indeed, many of them underlie and reinforce formal rules.[20] Effective formal institutions are frequently embedded in informal norms. These underlying norms create incentives for institutional compliance that might otherwise not exist. Parchment rules are thus reinforced by shared expectations generated by the underling informal norms. Take presidential term limits. In the United States, term limits were formally established—via the Twenty-second Amendment—in the mid-twentieth century, but an informal norm limiting presidents to two terms existed since the early days of the republic.[21] Likewise, Mexico's constitutional ban on presidential re-election is embedded in a widely shared "no re-election principal" that served as a rallying cry during the 1917 Revolution and later formed part of the country's revolutionary mythology.[22]

Varieties of Informal Institution

The concept of informal institution is broad, encompassing everything from bureaucratic routines and legislative norms to patterns of clientelism and corruption. In an effort to map out this variation, Helmke and Levitsky develop a four-fold typology, based on two dimensions: (1) the strength or effectiveness of the relevant formal institution, or whether or not the formal rules are actually enforced in practice; and (2) whether the informal institution generates outcomes that converge with or diverge from those expected from the formal rules (see Table 7.1).[23]

Two types of informal institution exist where formal rules are stable and effective. First, those which generate convergent outcomes may be characterized as *complementary*. Comple-

Table 7.1 A Typology of Informal Institutions[1]

Outcomes	Strong Formal Institutions	Weak Formal Institutions
Convergent	Complementary	Substitutive
Divergent	Accommodating	Competing

1 Taken from Helmke and Levitsky, "Informal Institutions and Comparative Politics," p. 728.

mentary informal institutions "complete" or "fill in the gaps" within formal institutional arrangements, addressing contingencies not dealt with in the formal rules or helping actors pursue their goals more effectively within the given institutional framework. Many of the norms and procedures found within established legislatures, judiciaries, state bureaucracies, armies, and political parties fall into this category. An example of a complementary informal institution is the "election insurance" developed by Chile's Democratic Concertation.[24] As Carey and Siavelis have shown, Chile's binomial electoral system generates considerable risk for candidates. Because two legislators are elected per district, parties or coalitions must double the vote of their rivals to capture both seats—an outcome that requires two strong candidates. Yet because such "doubling" outcomes are rare, strong politicians are reluctant to share a ticket with another high quality candidate. To deal with this problem, the Concertacion developed the practice of compensating strong but unsuccessful candidates with government appointments, which, by reducing the individual risk associated with joining a strong ticket, enhanced the coalition's overall competitiveness.[25]

Informal institutions that generate divergent outcomes within a framework of effective formal rules may be characterized as *accommodating*. Accommodating informal institutions enable actors to pursue goals within formal institutional frameworks that they dislike but cannot change or openly violate. By modifying actors' incentives and behavior, they alter the substantive outcomes generated by formal rules—but without directly violating the rules themselves. In effect, they violate the spirit, but not the letter, of the rules. Again, an example may be drawn from post-authoritarian Chile. Chile's 1989 democratic transition left intact numerous Pinochet-era institutions, including the hyper-presidentialist 1980 constitution. The center-left Democratic Concertation, which took office in 1990, opposed many of these institutions but lacked the political power to replace them. Unable to reform the majoritarian presidentialist system they inherited, Concertation politicians developed a set of informal norms of consultation and power sharing—including the *cuoteo*, the *partido transversal*, and *democracia de los acuerdos*—aimed at counteracting its effects.[26] According to Siavelis, these informal institutions helped to "mitigate the most negative characteristics of exaggerated presidentialism" and multiparty politics.[27]

Two types of informal institution exist where formal institutions are *ineffective*. The first is competing informal institutions, or those which encourage the subversion of formal rules. Competing informal institutions structure actors' incentives in ways that are incompatible with the formal rules: to follow one rule, actors must violate the other. Because parchment rules are not effectively enforced, they are trumped by informal ones, generating outcomes that diverge markedly from those prescribed by the formal rules. Patterns of patrimonialism, corruption, and patronage distribution fall into this category.[28] In such cases, it is widely known and expected that politicians will use public office to engage in particularistic behavior that violates bureaucratic procedure. An example is what Daniel Gingerich calls "party-directed corruption."[29] Governing parties in Argentina, Bolivia, Venezuela, and elsewhere place activists in key positions in the public bureaucracy with the understanding that patronage appointees will channel a specified percentage of their income into party coffers and use state resources to campaign for the party—in violation of bureaucratic rules and campaign finance laws. Competing informal institutions also underlie police violence in Brazil. Although Brazilian law prohibits the extra-judicial killing of suspected violent criminals, a set of informal norms and procedures within the security forces and the judicial system permits—and even rewards—such killing.[30]

Finally, substitutive informal institutions enable actors to achieve goals that formal institutions were designed, but fail, to achieve. For example, in northern Peru, citizens responded to problems of insecurity and lawlessness in the 1970s by creating informal *rondas campesinas* to defend their communities and *ronda* assemblies (informal courts) to resolve local disputes.[31] These informal structures effectively substituted for the state, dispensing community-level justice where the state had virtually disappeared.[32] Another example is *concertacesiones* ("gentleman's agreements") in Mexico during the 1990s. Through *concerta-cesiones*, government and opposition officials bypassed the country's judicial and electoral authorities, which lacked credibility, and negotiated solutions to conflicts that emerged in the wake of flawed elections.[33] According to Todd Eisenstadt, *concertacesiones* served as a "way station" for government and opposition elites until formal institutions of electoral dispute resolution strengthened in the late 1990s.[34]

Informal institutions thus interact with state structures in diverse ways. Where state and other formal institutions are effective, informal institutions are predominantly complementary and accommodating. Where formal institutions are weak and ineffective, informal institutions are more likely to be competing or substitutive.

Why Informal Institutions?

Informal institutions emerge for diverse reasons. As noted above, many are created to address gaps or ambiguities in the formal rules. No set of parchment rules covers all possible contingencies or provides clear guidelines for behavior under all circumstances. Thus, in stable formal institutional contexts, actors frequently develop norms, routines, and operating procedures to address contingencies that are not covered by the formal rules.

Other informal institutions emerge as a "second best" solution, in that they are created by actors who find it too costly to pursue their goals through formal structures.[35] In many instances, actors would prefer a parchment solution but lack the political power to change the formal rules. This was the case with Chile's Democratic Concertation in the 1990s: unable to radically overhaul the majoritarian constitutional and electoral framework imposed by Pinochet, Concertation politicians constructed informal rules that enabled them to maintain their coalition and a "consensus democracy."[36] Likewise, Costa Rican party leaders' use of informal devices to encourage constituency service may have been easier than overturning the ban on legislative re-election.[37]

Informal institutions may also be a second best strategy where formal institutions exist on paper but are ineffective in practice. This was clearly the case with substitutive informal institutions such as *concertacesiones* in Mexico and *rondas campesinas* in Peru. It is also true of clientelist "problem-solving networks."[38] As Javier Auyero has shown, poor people in the shantytowns of Greater Buenos Aires participate in clientelist networks in order to solve problems generated by the absence of basic public services.[39] In effect, clientelism substitutes for the state.

Third, informal institutions may be created by actors who engage in activities that are not viewed as publicly legitimate.[40] Examples include patrimonialism, corruption, and vote buying. Even where these practices are widely known and accepted, they cannot be legalized due to prevailing norms of universalism. Another example is what the Dutch call *gedogen*: the lax enforcement of laws that prohibit behavior that is publicly viewed as morally inappropriate but nevertheless widely tolerated in private. In many Latin American countries, activities such as prostitution, abortion, euthanasia, and soft drug use cannot be legalized, but it is widely known that laws banning these activities will not be strictly enforced. For example, although punitive anti-abortion laws were on the books in Argentina, Brazil, and Chile throughout most of the twentieth century, they were designed largely for symbolic purposes and were "hardly ever enforced."[41]

Informal institutions may also be created to pursue ends that are deemed *internationally* inappropriate. Many of the informal mechanisms of competitive authoritarian rule emerged in this manner. During the post-Cold War period, the international cost of openly violating or dismantling formal democratic institutions rose sharply, inducing many authoritarian governments to turn to informal mechanisms to skew the playing field against opponents. These included the mobilization of thug or gang violence, organized corruption and blackmail, tactics of "legal" repression (e.g., tax audits, defamation lawsuits), co-optation of independent media, and organized ballot stuffing and/or vote buying.[42]

Informal Institutions and Democratic Governability in Latin America

Analyses of informal institutions in Latin America have focused largely on their negative effects. Scholars have drawn attention to informal norms and practices that subvert legal and democratic institutions, often generating normatively undesirable outcomes.[43] For example, Guillermo O'Donnell, Jonathan Hartlyn, and others have shown how norms of patrimonialism undermine constitutional checks and balances and the rule of law;[44] Brinks shows how informal police rules regarding extra-judicial killing undermine basic constitutional and legal rights;[45] Gingerich's innovative study of patronage and party corruption links these phenomena to bureaucratic inefficiency, distortions in public policy-making, and low public confidence in political institutions;[46] and scholars such as Jonathan Fox and Susan Stokes argue that clientelism inhibits political participation and undermines electoral accountability.[47] Such subversive informal institutions are indeed widespread in Latin America, and they often *do* undermine democratic rights, representation, and accountability, and public goods provision.

Nevertheless, scholars have paid insufficient attention to how informal institutions *contribute to* democratic governability in Latin America. Recent research suggests that informal norms are often critical to making formal democratic institutions work. Take presidentialism. During the 1990s, scholars such as Juan Linz and Arturo Valenzuela argued that presidentialism undermined democratic stability in Latin America.[48] Scott Mainwaring refined this argument, arguing that multiparty presidentialism was a particularly difficult combination for new democracies, due to the high likelihood of divided government.[49] In the early 1990s, Brazil was viewed as a clear case of the perils of multiparty presidentialism. Brazilian presidentialism coexisted with a fragmented party system composed of weak, undisciplined parties, which, together with federalism, created an "excess of veto players."[50] Brazil experienced serious problems of governability in the early 1990s, and these problems were widely expected to persist.[51] Yet they did not. Notwithstanding the persistence of multiparty presidentialism, Brazilian democracy stabilized and even thrived in the late 1990s and 2000, generating a wave of more optimistic scholarship regarding the prospects for democratic governability in that country.[52]

Although many factors contributed to Brazil's surprising democratic success, one factor seems to be the emergence of a set of informal norms and procedures known as coalitional presidentialism (*presidencialismo de coalizão*).[53] As the name suggests, coalitional presidentialism is based on the construction and maintenance of multiparty coalitions through which executive power is shared—via the distribution of cabinet positions—and presidents enjoy stable legislative majorities. Unlike parliamentarism, presidential systems do not require the construction of legislative majorities, and indeed, scholars have argued that presidents lack incentives to build or sustain multiparty coalitions.[54] Nevertheless, coalition-building became the "'best practice' of executive-legislative coordination" under Presidents Fernando Henrique Cardoso and Luiz Inácio (Lula) da Silva.[55] An informal presidential "user's manual" emerged, the central guideline of which was that minority presidents must forge multiparty coalitions.[56] This informal rule was complemented by several ancillary norms and procedures, including: (1) executive power must be shared; thus, coalitions are constructed via the distribution of cabinet posts; (2) cabinet appointments are supplemented by pork, budgetary clientelism, and other discretionary side payments; (3) coalitions should be oversized.[57]

Brazil is not the only Latin American democracy to develop informal institutions of coalitional presidentialism. As noted above, the Chilean Democratic Concertation developed a set of informal norms and practices that helped sustain their multiparty presidential coalition for two decades.[58] Norms of coalition building also emerged in Ecuador. Like Brazil, Ecuador was a case of extreme multiparty presidentialism in which the prospects for democratic governability were considered poor.[59] Presidents lacked legislative majorities and opposition parties had few incentives to join a governing coalition.[60] Between 1979 and 1996, however, Ecuadorian presidents achieved considerable legislative success through what Mejía Acosta labels "ghost coalitions."[61] Unlike presidential coalitions in Brazil, ghost coalitions were clandestine: opposition parties did not join the government (indeed, they often continued to criticize it in public). Nevertheless, they routinely voted for key elements of the president's legislative agenda in exchange for access to pork and other discretionary resources.[62] Secrecy was a central rule in the maintenance of ghost coalitions: politicians were only willing to trade their legislative support for government largess if they could remain publicly in opposition.[63] Although ghost coalitions were hardly a model of good governance, they clearly enhanced democratic governability in Ecuador between 1979 and 1996.[64]

Where informal norms of coalition-building were absent, multiparty presidential democracies were more prone to governability crises. Thus, in Argentina, which has little tradition of multiparty alliances, a brief experiment with coalition rule under Fernando De la Rua (1999–2001) failed miserably.[65] President De la Rua "disregarded the coalition while managing the business of government and relied only on an inner circle of close advisors."[66] The governing *Alianza* collapsed within a year, contributing to the early demise of De la Rua's presidency. Coalition-building norms were also weak in Peru, where Alberto Fujimori's reluctance to forge a working relationship with the parties that dominated Congress was a major factor behind the democratic breakdown of 1992.[67] (According to one of his aides, Fujimori "couldn't stand the idea of inviting the President of the Senate to lunch in the Presidential Palace every time he wanted to pass a law."[68]) Finally, in Ecuador, the collapse of ghost coalitions in the mid-1990s contributed to severe problems of governability. In 1995, a violation of the secrecy rule underpinning ghost coalitions generated a major corruption scandal, which led to political reforms that reduced presidents' control over discretionary funds.[69] Although eliminating these funds may have enhanced "good governance," it limited presidents' ability to build ghost coalitions, which, according to Mejía

Acosta and Polga-Hecimovich, undermined governability.[70] In the decade that followed, three consecutive elected presidents (Abdalá Bucaram, Jamil Mahuad, and Lucio Gutierrez) were toppled before the end of their mandate.[71]

Another area in which informal institutions may contribute to democratic governability is in civil-military relations. Because military coups have historically been the primary cause of democratic breakdown in Latin America, the institutionalization of effective channels of civil-military communication is critical to democratic stability in the region. As David Pion-Berlin has argued, these channels are often informal.[72] Despite the "huge premium … placed on strict observation of formal commands, channels, and practices" within most Latin American armed forces,[73] civilian and military officials routinely turn to "off script" practices such as informal civil-military "conferences" to settle conflicts before they escalate and become public. In Chile, for example, when judicial efforts to prosecute military officers for human rights violations threatened to trigger a civil-military crisis in 1999, the Defense Ministry spearheaded a series of Roundtable Talks that "operated outside of official channels, outside of the chain of command, and free from any governmental regulation."[74] The talks produced an agreement—"inconceivable within a formal, hierarchical setting"—in which the military officially condemned Pinochet era human rights abuses and divulged information on the whereabouts of hundreds of disappeared prisoners.[75]

Finally, informal institutions may contribute to long-term democratic governability by strengthening formal institutions. Institutional weakness is widespread in Latin America.[76] In much of the region, constitutional and other formal rules have consistently failed to take root; rather, they are routinely circumvented, manipulated, and/or changed. Such institutional fluidity narrows actors' time horizons, undermines cooperation, and has contributed to repeated political crises.

Part of the explanation for this weakness may lie in the origins of formal institutions. In older democracies, many core political institutions rules emerged *endogenously*, in the sense that they were designed in accordance with the preferences of domestic actors with the power to enforce them. Endogenous institutions are also more likely to be embedded in supportive informal norms. In the case of the U.S. Constitution, for example, it "seems clear that the founders had a set of understandings that underpinned the written text."[77] Such informal understandings give force to formal institutions by creating incentives for compliance that are not necessarily inherent in the formal rules, *per* se. They also increase the likelihood that formal rules will endure. Indeed, the durability of the U.S. Constitution has been attributed to its embeddedness in broader societal norms and "paraconstitutional" rules.[78]

In Latin America, by contrast, many formal institutions are *exogenous* in origin. Rather than being designed by domestic actors with the power to enforce and sustain them, institutional arrangements are often borrowed from abroad.[79] Consequently, they are less likely to conform closely to pre-existing norms or the preferences of domestic actors. Such a disjuncture may undermine institutional effectiveness: incentives for compliance tend to be weaker, and domestic actors may seek to overturn the rules as soon as the opportunity arises.

Although weak formal institutions provide fertile ground for competing informal institutions (as noted above), other types of informal institution can be critical to *strengthening* them and enabling them to take root. For example, informal rules often help actors adapt to—and improve the functioning of—formal institutional arrangements, as in the case of coalition presidentialism in Brazil, ghost coalitions in Ecuador, and civil-military conferences in Chile. They may also enable "losers" under particular formal institutional arrangements to better achieve their goals, thereby dampening their opposition to (and perhaps even giving them a stake in) the formal rules of the game. In Chile, for example, "election insurance" and informal rules of consensus democracy helped to reconcile Democratic Concertation leaders' goals with the constitutional and electoral arrangements they inherited from Pinochet, which enhanced the durability of those institutions.

There is a tension here, however. Adaptive informal institutions take time to develop. They are a product of collective learning, through repeated interaction over multiple rounds—a process that can take years and even decades. In many Latin American democracies, particularly in the Andes, formal rules have rarely had such time. Rather, formal institutional weakness—often manifested by the persistence of competing informal institutions—generates a near-constant pressure for reform. Thus, the formal rules change before adaptive informal institutions can emerge. The process can be self-reinforcing: repeated institutional redesign reinforces institutional weakness, which in turn generates further pressure for reform.[80] This suggests that the kind of perpetual institutional reform processes seen in many Andean polities since the 1980s can be costly: if constitutions, electoral systems, and other institutional arrangements are repeatedly re-written, even with the best intentions, the kinds of supportive informal rules that help such arrangements take root may never emerge. How to break this vicious cycle—to move from Ecuador to Brazil—is an important question for future research.

Conclusion

Informal institutions are pervasive in politics. Although they are no more widespread in Latin America than in the advanced industrialized democracies, they appear to have a more visibly negative impact. Due to the weakness of state institutions in much of the region, informal rules often trump formal rules, subverting democratic institutions and generating normatively undesirable outcomes. Equally important, however, are the less visible norms that underlie effective formal institutions. This chapter has suggested that the failure of many formal institutions in Latin America may be rooted less in the parchment rules themselves than in the absence of supportive informal rules.

Informal institutions are notoriously difficult to study. Because they are unwritten, they are not easily identified or measured. Nevertheless, scholars made significant advances in identifying and measuring the effects of informal institutions during the 2000s.[81] These studies focused mainly on informal institutions that subvert the formal rules. We continue to know little about the (even less visible) informal institutions that reinforce and strengthen formal rules.[82] This is a critical area for future research.

Notes

1 See Guillermo O'Donnell, "Delegative Democracy," *Journal of Democracy* 5, No. 1 (January 1994): 55–69 and "Illusions about Consolidation," *Journal of Democracy* 7, No. 2 (April 1996): 34–51; Gretchen Helmke and Steven Levitsky (eds.), *Informal Institutions and Democracy: Lessons from Latin America* (Baltimore: Johns Hopkins University Press, 2006); and Steven Levitsky and María Victoria Murillo, "Variation in Institutional Strength," *Annual Review of Political Science* 12 (2009): 115–133.
2 See O'Donnell, "Illusions about Consolidation;" Hans-Joachim Lauth, "Informal Institutions and Democracy," *Democratization* 7, No. 4 (2000): 21–50; Levitsky and Helmke, *Informal Institutions and Democracy*.

3 Joy Langston, "The Birth and Transformation of the Dedazo in Mexico," in Helmke and Levitsky (eds.), *Informal Institutions and Democracy.*

4 Wayne A. Cornelius, *Mexican Politics in Transition: The Breakdown of a One-Party Dominant Regime* (San Diego: Center for U.S.-Mexican Studies, 1996), p. 60.

5 Chappell Lawson, "Building the Fourth Estate: Media Opening and Democratization in Mexico." In Kevin J. Middlebrook (ed.), *Dilemmas of Political Change in Mexico* (London: Institute of Latin American Studies, 2004), pp. 378–380.

6 Robert Gay, "The Broker and the Thief; A Parable (Reflections on Popular Politics in Brazil)." *Luso-Brazilian Review* 36, No. 1 (Summer 1999), 49–70 and Javier Auyero, *Poor Peoples Politics* (Durham, NC: Duke University Press, 2001).

7 See Andrés Mejía Acosta, "Crafting Legislative Ghost Coalitions in Ecuador: Informal Institutions and Economic Reform in an Unlikely Case;" Peter Siavelis, "Accommodating Informal Institutions and Chilean Democracy" in Helmke and Levitsky (eds.), *Informal Institutions and Democracy*; and Timothy J. Power, "Optimism, Pessimism, and Coalitional Presidentialism: Debating the Institutional Design of Brazilian Democracy," *Bulletin of Latin American Research* 29, No. 1 (January): 18–33.

8 David Pion-Berlin, "Informal Civil-Military Relations in Latin America: Why Politicians and Soldiers Choose Unofficial Venues," *Armed Forces and Society* 36, No. 3 (2009), pp. 527, 533–535.

9 On norms underlying police violence in Brazil, see Daniel Brinks, "The Rule of (Non)Law: Prosecuting Police Killings in Brazil and Argentina," in Helmke and Levitsky (eds.), *Informal Institutions and Democracy;* and Brinks, *The Judicial Response to Police Killings in Latin America: Inequality and the Rule of Law* (New York: Cambridge University Press, 2007). On informal community justice institutions in the Andes, see Donna Lee Van Cott, "Dispensing Justice at the Margins of Formality: The Informal Rule of Law in Latin America," in Helmke and Levitsky (eds.), *Informal Institutions* page numbers for the chapter you cite.

10 See O'Donnell, "Illusions about Consolidation" and Lauth, "Informal Institutions and Democracy."

11 Gretchen Helmke and Steven Levitsky, "Introduction," in Helmke and Levitsky (eds.), *Informal Institutions and Democracy*, p. 5.

12 Siavelis, "Accommodating Informal Institutions and Chilean Democracy," p. 33.

13 O'Donnell, "Delegative Democracy."

14 Siavelis, "Accommodating Informal Institutions and Chilean Democracy."

15 Jeffrey Weldon, "Political Sources of Presidentialism in Mexico," in Scott Mainwaring and Matthew Soberg Shugart (eds.), *Presidentialism and Democracy in Latin America* (New York: Cambridge University Press, 1997).

16 Gretchen Helmke, *Courts under Constraints: Judges, Generals, and Presidents in Argentina* (New York: Cambridge University Press, 2004).

17 Michelle Taylor, "Formal versus Informal Incentive Structures and Legislative Behavior: Evidence From Costa Rica," *Journal of Politics* 54, No. 4 (1992): 1053–1071.

18 Barry C. Burden, "The Polarizing Effects of Congressional Primaries," in Peter F. Galderisi, Michael Lyons, and Marni Ezra (eds.), *Congressional Primaries in the Politics of Representation* (Lanham, MD: Rowman and Littlefield, 2001).

19 Mark P. Jones, "The Recruitment and Selection of Legislative Candidates in Argentina," in Peter M. Siavelis and Scott Morgenstern (eds.), *Pathways to Power: Political Recruitment and Candidate Selection in Latin America* (University Park, PA: Pennsylvania State University Press, 2008), pp. 50–51.

20 Susan C. Stokes, "Do Informal Rules Make Democracy Work? Accounting for Accountability in Argentina," in Helmke and Levitsky (eds.), *Informal Institutions and Democracy.*

21 Prior to Franklin Roosevelt's four-term presidency during World War II, real or perceived efforts to run for a third term met with "popular outcry" (Grant), intra-party rejection (Cleveland), and an assassination attempt and electoral defeat (Theodore Roosevelt). See Zachary Elkins, Tom Ginsburg, and James Melton, *The Endurance of National Constitutions* (New York: Cambridge University Press, 2009), pp. 46–47.

22 Jorge Carpizo, "The No Re-Election Principle in Mexico, *The Mexican Forum* 3, No. 4 (1983): 9–13. The only serious effort to break this norm, that of former President Alvaro Obregón, ended with Obregón's assasination.

23 Gretchen Helmke and Steven Levitsky, "Informal Institutions and Comparative Politics: A Research Agenda," *Perspectives on Politics* 2, No. 4 (2004): 725–740. The following section draws on this article.

24 John M. Carey and Peter Siavelis, "Election Insurance and Coalition Survival: Formal and Informal Institutions in Chile," in Helmke and Levitsky (eds.), *Informal Institutions and Democracy.*

25 Carey and Siavelis, "Election Insurance and Coalition Survival."

26 Siavelis, "Accommodating Informal Institutions and Chilean Democracy."

27 Siavelis, "Accommodating Informal Institutions and Chilean Democracy," p. 37.

28 O'Donnell, "Illusions about Consolidation" and Hans-Joachim Lauth, "Informal Institutions and Democracy," *Democratization* 7, No. 4 (2000): 21–50.

29 Daniel W. Gingerich, "Corruption and Political Decay: Evidence from Bolivia," *Quarterly Journal of Political Science* 4 (1) (2009): 1–34; and "Bolivia: Traditional Parties, the State, and the Toll of Corruption," in Charles Blake and Steven Morris (eds.), *Corruption and Politics in Latin America: National and Regional Dynamics* (Boulder: Lynne Rienner, 2010).

30 Brinks, "The Rule of (Non)-Law."

31 Orin Starn, *Nightwatch: The Politics of Protest in the Andes* (Durham, NC: Duke University Press 1999).

32 Van Cott, "Dispensing Justice at the Margins of Formality."

33 Todd Eisenstadt, "Mexico's Postelectoral *Concertacesiones*: The Rise and Demise of a Substitutive Informal Institution," in Helmke and Levitsky (eds.), *Informal Institutions and Democracy.*

34 Eisenstadt, "Mexico's Postelectoral *Concertacesiones*."

35 Carol A. Mershon, "Expectations and Informal Rules in Coalition Formation," *Comparative Political Studies* 27, No. 1 (1994): 40–79 and Helmke and Levitsky, "Informal Institutions and Comparative Politics," p. 730.

36 Carey and Siavelis, "Election Insurance and Coalition Survival;" and Siavelis, "Accommodating Informal Institutions and Chilean Democracy."

37 Taylor, "Formal versus Informal Incentive Structures and Legislative Behavior."

38 Auyero, *Poor People's Politics.*

39 Auyero, *Poor People's Politics.*

40 Informal institutions of this type are a second best solution in the sense that formal rules permitting such activities might be preferable in theory but cannot be enacted in practice.

41 Mala Htun, *Sex and the State: Abortion, Divorce, and Family under Latin American Dictatorships and Democracies* (Cambridge University Press, 2003), pp. 153–154.

42 Steven Levitsky and Lucan A. Way, *Competitive Authoritarianism: Hybrid Regimes after the Cold War* (New York: Cambridge University Press).

43 See, for example, O'Donnell, "Illusions about Consolidation;" Lauth, "Informal Institutions and Democracy.

44 Guillermo O'Donnell, "On the State, Democratization, and Some Conceptual Problems: A Latin American View with Some Postcommunist Countries," *World Development* 21, No. 8 (1993): 1355–1369; Jonathan Hartlyn, *The Struggle for Democratic Politics in the Dominican Republic* (Chapel Hill: University of North Carolina Press, 1998).

45 Brinks, *The Judicial Response to Police Killings in Latin America.*

46 Gingerich, "Corruption and Political Decay" and "Bolivia: Traditional Parties, the State, and the Toll of Corruption."

47 Jonathan Fox, "The Difficult Transition from Clientelism to Citizenship: Lessons from Mexico," *World Politics* Vol. 46, No. 2 (January 1994): 151–184 and Susan C. Stokes, "Perverse Accountability: A formal Model of Machine Politics with Evidence from Argentina," *American Political Science Review* 99 (2005): 315–326.

48 See Juan J. Linz 1990, "The Perils of Presidentialism," Journal of Democracy 1, No. 1 (January 1990): 51–69; and Juan J. Linz and Arturo Valenzuela (eds.), *The Failure of Presidential Democracy* (Baltimore: The Johns Hopkins University Press, 1994).

49 Scott Mainwaring, "Presidentialism, Multipartism, and Democracy: the Difficult Combination," *Comparative Political Studies* 26, No. 2 (1993): 198–228.

50 Barry Ames, *The Deadlock of Democracy in Brazil* (Ann Arbor: University of Michigan Press, 2002); also Scott Mainwaring, *Rethinking Party Systems in the Third Wave of Democratization: The Case of Brazil* (New York: Cambridge University Press, 1999).

51 Ames, *The Deadlock of Democracy in Brazil and Mainwaring, Rethinking Party Systems in the Third Wave of Democratization.*

52 See Argelina Figueiredo and Fernando Limongi, *Executivo e Legislativo na Nova Ordem Constitucional* (Rio de Janeiro: Editora FGV, 1999); Argelina Figueiredo and Fernando Limongi "Presidential Power, Legislative Organization, and Party Behavior in the Brazilian Legislature," *Comparative Politics* 32, No. 2 (2000): 151–170; Power, "Optimism, Pessimism, and Coalitional Presidentialism."

53 Power, "Optimism, Pessimism, and Coalitional Presidentialism."

54 Linz, "The Perils of Presidentialism" and Mainwaring, "Presidentialism, Multipartism, and Democracy: the Difficult Combination."

55 Power, "Optimism, Pessimism, and Coalitional Presidentialism," p. 26.

56 Power, "Optimism, Pessimism, and Coalitional Presidentialism," p. 29.

57 Power, "Optimism, Pessimism, and Coalitional Presidentialism."

58 Carey and Siavelis, "Election Insurance and Coalition Survival" and Siavelis, "Accommodating Informal Institutions and Chilean Democracy."

59 Catherine Conaghan, "Politicians against Parties: Discord and Disconnection in Ecuador's Party System," in Scott Mainwaring and Timothy R. Scully (eds.), *Building Democratic Institutions: Party Systems in Latin America* (Stanford: Stanford University Press, 1995).

60 Mejía Acosta, "Crafting Legislative Ghost Coalitions in Ecuador."

61 Mejía Acosta, "Crafting Legislative Ghost Coalitions in Ecuador."

62 Mejía Acosta, "Crafting Legislative Ghost Coalitions in Ecuador"; and Andrés Mejía Acosta and John Polga-Hecimovich, "Parliamentary Solutions to Presidential Crises in Ecuador," in Mariana Llanos and Leiv Marsteintredet (eds.), *Presidential Breakdowns in Latin America: Causes and Outcomes of Eexecutive Stability in Developing Democracies* (New York: Palgrave Macmillan, 2010), pp. 77–78.

63 Mejía Acosta, "Crafting Legislative Ghost Coalitions in Ecuador," pp. 75–76.

64 Mejía Acosta, "Crafting Legislative Ghost Coalitions in Ecuador."

65 Mariana Llanos and Ana Marghertis, "Why Do Presidents Fail? Political Leadership and the Argentine Crisis (1999–2001)," *Studies in Comparative international Development* 40, No. 4 (Winter 2006): 77–103; and Mariana Llanos, "Presidential Breakdowns in Argentina," In Mariana Llanos and Leiv Marsteintredet (eds.), *Presidential Breakdowns in Latin America: Causes and Outcomes of Eexecutive Stability in Developing Democracies* (New York: Palgrave Macmillan, 2010).

66 Llanos, "Presidential Breakdowns in Argentina," p. 63.

67 Cynthia McClintock, "La voluntad política presidencial y la rupture constitucional de 1992 en el Perú. In Fernando Tuesta Soldevilla, ed., *Los Enigmas del Poder: Fujimori 1990–1996* (Lima: Friedrich Ebert Foundation, 1996); Charles D. Kenney. *Fujimori's Coup and the Breakdown of Democracy in Latin America* (Notre Dame: University of Notre Dame Press, 2003).

68 Quoted in McClintock, "La voluntad política presidencial y la rupture constitucional de 1992 en el Perú," p. 65.

69 Mejía Acosta and Polga-Hecimovich, "Parliamentary Solutions to Presidential Crises in Ecuador," p. 78.

70 Mejía Acosta and Polga-Hecimovich, "Parliamentary Solutions to Presidential Crises in Ecuador."

71 Mejía Acosta and Polga-Hecimovich, "Parliamentary Solutions to Presidential Crises in Ecuador," pp. 80–87.

72 Pion-Berlin, "Informal Civil-Military Relations in Latin America."

73 Pion-Berlin, "Informal Civil-Military Relations in Latin America," p. 530.

74 Pion-Berlin, "Informal Civil-Military Relations in Latin America," p. 535.

75 Pion-Berlin, "Informal Civil-Military Relations in Latin America," p. 535.

76 See O'Donnell, "Delegative Democracy;" Levitsky and Murillo, "Variation in Institutional Strength."

77 Elkins, Ginsburg, and Melton, *The Endurance of National Constitutions*, p. 46. Also Douglass North, William Summerhill, and Barry Weingast, "Order, Disorder, and Economic Change: Latin America versus North America," in Bruce Bueno de Mesquita and Hilton Root (eds.), *Governing for Prosperity* (New Haven: Yale University Press, 2000).

78 Fred W. Riggs, "The Survival of Presidentialism in America: Para-constitutional Practices," *International Political Science Review* 9, No. 4 (1988): 247–278; and North, Summerhill, and Weingast, "Order, Disorder, and Economic Change."

79 Kurt Weyland, "Toward a New Theory of Institutional Change," *World Politics* 60 (January 2008): 281–314.

80 Levitsky and Murillo, "Variation in Institutional Strength." An example is Ecuador, which had three different constitutions in the 1990s and 2000s, and where "not a single election has been carried out under the same rules as the previous election." See Simón Pachano, "Gobernabilidad Democrática y Reformas Instituciones y Políticas en Ecuador," in Martín Tanaka and Francine Jácome (eds.), *Desafíos de la Gobernabilidad Democrática: Reformas Político-Institucionales y Movimientos Sociales en la Región Andina* (Lima: Instituto de Estudios Peruanos, 2010), p. 80.

81 See Helmke, *Courts under Constraints*; Brinks, "The Rule of (Non)Law"; and Daniel Gingerich, "Corruption in General Equilibrium: Political Institutions and Bureaucratic Performance in South America" (unpublished Ph.D Dissertation, Department of Government, Harvard University, 2006)

82 One effort in this direction is Stokes, "Do Informal Rules Make Democracy Work?"

8

ACCOUNTABILITY AND REPRESENTATION IN LATIN AMERICA

Frances Hagopian

Whether citizen interests and preferences are represented in government, and whether or not citizens can hold their governments accountable, is a critical defining feature of modern mass democracies. In Latin America, institutions of representation and accountability were historically weak. In what have been called "elitist democracies," large segments of the population were excluded from political and economic life, popular interests went under-represented, and mechanisms of accountability were nonexistent. In the past three decades as democratization has broadened access to national and local political life, loosened restrictions on association, and leveled the playing field for old and new parties to compete for constituents that in earlier periods did not enjoy the full rights of citizenship, the challenges to tried-and-true forms of political representation and accountability to deepen their reach and the opportunities for new ones to take root have multiplied. Whether these opportunities have always been realized, in what ways, and why, is the subject of this chapter.

Political representation and accountability can assume different forms. Citizens can be connected to government along multiple, sometimes parallel and sometimes intersecting, avenues and they can hold their representatives accountable in a variety of vertical and horizontal institutions or some combination of the two at different levels of the political system. Thus in order to accurately chart the landscape of political representation past and present, we must extend our scope of inquiry beyond national political elections, and to identify the processes and mechanisms by which political representation and accountability may have grown stronger or weaker, we need to recognize that the factors shaping political representation may exercise different impacts at different levels of national territory or in different institutional settings. The chapter focuses on two processes that stand out as critical in altering the terrain on which citizens either individually or in movements, associations, or parties, meet the institutions of accountability and representation: the decentralization of government and politics, and the liberalization of states and markets. Both prompted citizens to mobilize, old forms of representation to adapt or wither, and innovative experiments to flourish.

A recurring theme of the chapter is that if economic development strategies and even broad regime tendencies have moved in a common direction in recent decades, the paths that various citizen groups, constituents, and political leaders have pursued, and their destinations, have markedly varied across borders. In some party monopolies have crumbled and party systems have realigned to more closely express citizen policy preferences whereas in others, parties more closely resemble political machines and vote-buying is as pervasive as ever, subverting the possibility of accountability and representation. Moreover, the weakening of class organizations that were the bedrock of representation have brought different and at times diametrically opposite results. In some countries, they have been replaced by a patchwork of new associations whose members are mobilized politically where they live or along ethnic lines; the most successful of these serve as transmission belts to articulate citizen interests, pry open government books, and broaden considerably the venues of accountability beyond periodic elections. Elsewhere, the collapse of old institutions of representation, however restricted, has left a void in public associational life and a new generation of populist leaders has flourished in an institutional vacuum. Finally, sweeping away national authoritarian regimes has not guaranteed democratic representation and accountability for all. To the contrary, too frequent manifestations of subnational authoritarianism make a mockery of accountability and representation beyond the capital. The challenge is to explain this pattern of variation, especially when it is not easily predictable from the past. I argue that how economic liberalization took place affected the opportunities for reorganizing representation and creating new venues for accountability, trumping the otherwise powerful effects of socioeconomic modernization and the design of electoral institutions on forms of political representation.

The chapter proceeds as follows. First, I define political accountability and representation. Next, I review the evolution of political representation in Latin America and identify some early weaknesses. The third section examines the effects of neoliberalism, decentralization, and the organizing initiatives of civil society on the formal institutions of political representation. The fourth evaluates competing perspectives on why the forms of political representation and accountability vary, and briefly advances an alternative approach. The final section concludes with an agenda for future research.

What Is Political Accountability and Representation?

Citizens in modern, mass democracies are not self-governing but delegate to political agents the task of representing their interests and preferences in government. Since the beginning of the era of modern, mass democracy, political theorists have debated whether the best outcomes are produced when superior men of wisdom and ability, a "natural aristocracy," govern not according to popular wishes but to what they believe is in the best interests of the national good, as famously argued by Edmund Burke; when men and women are selected for office who are "like" the people they represent and act spontaneously as the people would have acted, the view championed by John Adams; or when elected officials do as their constituents direct them and are held accountable for their actions in government if they do not, the essence of what we understand today as mandate representation. Although accountability is superfluous to both Burke's "trustee" representation and to "descriptive" or identity-based representation,[1] "mandate" representation requires that representatives must be *responsive* and held *accountable* to the ordinary citizens who elected them. As *principals,* citizens hold even remote officeholders, or *agents,* accountable for their actions in government through retrospective judgments in elections; they reward representatives who were faithful to the diverse political ideas, programs, and policy proposals they put forward during election cycles as a basis for government action, and punish the violators for not keeping up their end of the electoral bargain.

As we see next, for much of Latin American history a restricted franchise, state-imposed representational monopolies, and pervasive patron–client relations robbed the concepts of representation and accountability of much of their meaning. But since the "third wave" of democratization reestablished democratic procedures in the past three decades, institutions of representation and accountability have come under closer scrutiny as scholars have debated whether democracies are truly representative and officeholders accountable for the policies they have pursued in office, as well as which institutions hold the greatest promise for democratic representation.

The Tentative Emergence of Political Representation in Latin America

During the days when politics consisted of what Alexander Wilde has called "conversations among gentlemen," scholars took for granted that Latin American political parties were unrepresentative and exclusionary.[2] The lucky few workers in urban industrial employment gained representation along with the middle and lower-middle classes, but the urban and rural poor were not so fortunate. Illiterates could not vote, and indigenous peoples were either made objects of attempted assimilation or excluded altogether.[3] In Brazil and many other countries, a work card registering one in the formal economy—which half the population did not hold—was a passport to health care, title to one's home, the right to a fair hearing before a judge, and in every meaningful sense of the term, citizenship.[4] Accountability, it was often said in scholarly circles in the 1990s, could not be translated into Spanish (since then, "rendición de cuentas" has come into wider usage).

Political representation based on clientelism, the proffering of pork, state patronage jobs, or cash assistance in exchange for votes, was pervasive. Clientelistic networks that crisscrossed the Latin American countryside for much of its history and the urban periphery in the twentieth century were sustained in mass democracies by state employment, funding for construction and infrastructural projects, and discretion in the delivery of social services. Patrons in state and party offices channeled public employment and cash assistance as well as their own personal resources to mobilize votes for themselves and their parties. Traditional and labor parties alike divided, monopolized, and competed, respectively, for the spoils of state.

During the era of import-substituting industrialization from roughly the Second World War until the 1970s, without displacing these networks, states organized interests and regulated representation for those in the urban, formal economy along functional lines, and the intellectual development of the topic largely mimicked that reality. Philippe Schmitter's 1971 landmark, *Interest Conflict and Political Change in Brazil,* introduced students of Latin American politics to the concept of corporatism, the philosophy that underpinned interwar fascism in Europe and was embraced by politicians in Brazil, Argentina, and elsewhere in the 1930s and 1940s.[5] Schmitter contended that in order to preempt labor radicalism, bind workers to the state, and ensure the smooth functioning of critical industries, states strictly regulated labor markets, created and conferred upon noncompetitive labor unions monopoly status, established avenues of representation leading directly from these unions to state institutions, and reserved the right to remove leaders that stepped out of line.[6] Labor leaders accepted the incursions on union autonomy and the bargain that was offered to them in exchange for more generous wages and benefits than they could gain in collective bargaining with employers, and for the prerogative to dispense them.[7] Schmitter's thesis for why pluralist interest representation had not taken root became the received wisdom, triumphing over accounts that stressed the particular features of Iberian culture.[8]

Eventually, as more aspiring entrants beat on the doors of the polity, pressures for land

and other forms of redistribution multiplied, and radical competitors to entrenched populist parties gained footholds among the poor, political systems were slammed shut by military coups. With democracies in recess, the study of political representation, along with other facets of democratic governance and institutions, fell out of vogue for many years. Even the literature on regime transitions and democratization, which was largely focused on the bargaining between authoritarian regime elites and the democratic opposition, did not pay much explicit attention to the study of representation, except to suggest overrepresenting conservative forces for the sake of stability.[9] Yet even once democracies seemed safe from authoritarian regressions, a question lurking beneath the surface was what the cost might be of making officeholders more accountable to the median voter who might reject short-term policies necessary to produce good macroeconomic outcomes. In an important volume on the crisis of representation in the Andes, Scott Mainwaring did not dodge the hard question of whether institutional reforms that enhanced representation and accountability carried a tradeoff with governance, and he suggested not only that they had but that the resulting deficits in state capacity and performance, in turn, may have eroded citizen trust in representative political institutions.[10]

Political scientists returned to studying political representation and accountability because of a broader concern with the quality of democracy. One stream of research focused on the proliferation of new social movements, civil society organizations, and nongovernmental organizations, some of which were embedded in transnational networks,[11] through which citizens sought the means to defend their living standards, human and cultural rights, and communities. Although many of their champions valued them as *alternative* avenues of representation that could substitute for unrepresentative political parties, paradoxically some compelling studies showed that local institutions of participatory democracy worked best as sites of deliberation as well as representation and accountability when they had the support of incumbent political parties.[12] By supplying political parties and state actors with crucial information about citizen preferences, they effectively *supplemented* political representation, and when awarded power sharing and veto privileges, they also served as instruments of citizen accountability.

A second body of research has examined the representation of historically underrepresented interests in Latin America through the prism of the potential for descriptive political representation. Of particular interest have been policies that reserve slots on party ballots for women and representatives of ethnic and racial minority groups. Political science research suggests that quotas are more likely to be adopted for women than for Indians, and are significantly more effective when they carry placement mandates with provisions for strict compliance and are applied in closed-list proportional representation systems such as Argentina and Costa Rica, where roughly two in five members of the national legislatures today are women, than in open-list and especially district systems.[13]

A third steam of research broadly addresses the relationship between parties and voters within the tradition of mandate representation. In one important volume on the quality of democracy Bingham Powell usefully defined democratic responsiveness as a causal chain that begins with the party preferences held by citizens, then moves "link by causal link through such stages as voting, election outcomes, the formation of policy-making coalitions, the process of policymaking between elections, and public policies themselves."[14] Specifically, governments are responsive when their composition reflects the outcome of elections, fulfilling the requirements of *procedural representation,* and when they implement policies that match citizen preferences, the essence of *substantive representation.*

By these measures, many Latin American democracies fell short in the first decade of democracy, and still do. Legislatures in Brazil and Argentina are marred by significant malapportionment of seats in their lower *and* upper chambers,[15] and in Chile, administrative regions are governed by appointed intendants and non-elected councils. Substantively, in the mid-1990s political representation via ideological voting was weak throughout Latin America except in Uruguay and Chile, and "extraordinarily weak" in Ecuador, Bolivia, and Peru. Some of the highest "representation gaps" between the mean ideological positions of voters and their parties were seen in Venezuela and Guatemala.[16] Legislators also most closely shared the positions of their voters across "issue baskets" in Chile and Uruguay, as well as Argentina, and on economic issues—typically the most salient—in Colombia and Costa Rica, but the match was much weaker in nearly all countries on law and order issues.[17] Complicating the lines of accountability was the fact that so many party systems were unstable, so many political parties did not have roots in the electorate, and so many politicians had the habit of changing parties after their election and the freedom to do so.

The match between voter preferences and policies in Powell's "chain of responsiveness" was even more deeply problematic in the first decade of democracy. Susan Stokes' influential work showed that from 1982 to 1995 "dramatic changes of policy took place after 12 of 42 elections," and in three others, "campaigns were too vague for voters to infer much of anything about the future course of policy." In each of the dozen cases of blatant violations of mandate, presidential candidates switched from a campaign message promising economic security to policies that promoted economic efficiency.[18] Voters forgave policy switches that produced good outcomes in Argentina and Peru, but harshly judged the Acción Democrática government in Venezuela which did not. Citizen disaffection with incumbents across much of Latin America in the 1990s was reflected in high rates of electoral volatility, and the success of several presidential candidates who positioned themselves as political outsiders riding to the rescue to stabilize prices and create jobs. This new breed of politicians—widely referred to as the neopopulists—had success in the Andes as well as, at least temporarily, Brazil and Argentina.

When political parties and politicians compete by proffering public goods and services in exchange for friendship, loyalty, or votes, as is so often true in Latin America, it is even harder for ordinary citizens to hold representatives to account. They also cannot hold parties collectively accountable for policy outcomes if candidates for legislative office do not commit to a *national* party program, leadership, and decisions; parties do not cohere, or if they vanish from one election to the next. At best, such representation can be effective when "clientelist politics establishes very tight bonds of accountability and responsiveness" given the direct exchange relation between patrons and clients that makes "very clear" what politicians and constituencies have to bring to the table to make deals work.[19] But more often, it is in fact inherently difficult for voters to "throw out the bums" that fail to deliver the goods but show up at every election cycle promising anew that they will. Incumbents have the advantage of being able to offer access to resources not available to their opponents, and voters who vote against the patron run a great risk. As scholars have aptly noted, a voter can elect or vote out a given politician only if many other voters in a district act in the same way.[20] But herein lies the problem: "the voter who votes against him when a majority of others does not risks suffering the patron's retaliation. Each voter minimizes her risk and maximizes her payoffs when she votes for the unpopular patron but all other voters (or at least a majority) vote against him. Yet because all voters face this same incentive, the unpopular patron remains in power."[21] Moreover, accountability can be worse than weak: as Susan Stokes contends, when parties buy votes, they know, or can make inferences about, what individual voters have done in the voting booth and reward or punish them conditional on these actions, making a "mockery" of democratic accountability and engendering *perverse accountability.*[22]

Of course, the accountability that citizens exercise at the ballot box at election time is only one manifestation of the sort of accountability that is critical for democracy. Gravely concerned about the power-aggrandizing strategies of the neopopulist presidents elected in Latin America in the 1990s, Guillermo O'Donnell highlighted the need for "horizontal accountability," or the sorts of checks and balances that other branches of government and a free press could exercise on the presidency.[23] At best, the newly created Office of the Ombudsman in Peru, Ministério Público in Brazil and similar institutions elsewhere, could serve as agents of accountability to investigate abuses of power by state actors on behalf of ordinary citizens and society at large.[24] But more generally, Latin American legislatures can only react to the initiatives of far more powerful executives,[25] and courts lack the requisite independence to make accountability work.

In a particularly influential article, Catalina Smulovitz and Enrique Peruzzotti introduced the concept of "societal" accountability to describe the ways in which popular mobilization could trigger the mechanisms of horizontal accountability that could investigate abuses and prosecute them. They illustrated their important argument with the poignant case of the Argentine teenager, Maria Soledad, who was raped and murdered in 1990 by a son of a provincial congressman in her home province of Catamarca, long the dominion of the powerful Saadi family. Local "marches of silence" organized by her family and nuns to press for an investigation and trial in the face of an obvious cover-up grew in number, size, and stature over the course of six years, and provoked other civil society actions including strikes by professional associations. Eventually, the attention of the provincial and national press forced an investigation, a nationally televised trial, the appointment of new judges, and ultimately a conviction in 1998.[26] More dramatically, elsewhere popular mobilizations resulted in the resignations of sitting presidents in Ecuador and Bolivia, though whether or not such mobilizations are evidence of a *democratic accountability* is questionable.

The Next Decade and Beyond: Reshaping Representation and Accountability

Political representation and accountability from the 1990s onward were profoundly shaped by two processes—decentralization and economic liberalization. The decentralization of power and resources raised the stakes of winning local office and created possibilities of new forms of citizen participation and institutions of accountability. Economic liberalization that deregulated markets emptied corporatist associations of their representative function, and made organizing to influence political parties and legislatures all the more important. The received wisdom is that decentralization had a salutary impact on political representation and accountability, while neoliberal reform endangered fragile institutions of democratic representation and accountability and disorganized society, snuffing out promising civil society associations. Yet, decentralization also strengthened less-than-democratic subnational elites, and neoliberal reforms also created the possibility of better political representation by restricting politicians' access to state patronage, creating new forms of citizenship, and opening new avenues for programmatic contention. In fact, the impact of these economic and political processes was uneven. In some cases, they transformed existing parties, interest groups, and institutions in ways that allowed representation takes shape; in others, they resulted in their substitution in favor of new and even traditional forms of representation and accountability.

Democratization and Decentralization

A motley set of political forces in Latin America converged to push decentralization in the 1980s and 1990s. Democratic forces demanded the decentralization of power and elections for previously appointed mayors and governors, and were backed by regional elites who thought they would have a better chance of defending their policy interests—such as stopping land reform—in the polities they dominated. Governors and mayors sought ever more resources to distribute, while international financial institutions and local economists favored the decentralization of resources and responsibilities to local governments as a means to improve the efficiency of resource allocation on the logic that citizens could better restrain government officials if they were closer to those spending their tax dollars and could threaten credibly to take their business elsewhere. Parties about to lose power in national elections but who retained some regional strength embraced decentralization schemes as political insurance against electoral oblivion,[27] and central government officials who had to cut payroll to make ends meet were all too content to offload their commitments to provincial governments. Between 1985 and 1996, decentralizing reforms instituted the direct election of mayors in Brazil's state capitals, Colombia, Chile, Buenos Aires, and Mexico City and of governors in Colombia and Venezuela; municipal autonomy in Argentina, Brazil, and Mexico and the Law of Popular Participation (LPP) in Bolivia (1994); fiscal decentralization in the four federal countries—Argentina, Brazil, Colombia, and Mexico; and the transfer of administrative responsibilities for education and health services throughout the region. In all, the devolution of revenues and expenditures in Latin America doubled between 1980 and 2000.[28]

Decentralization did not always produce unambiguously good economic or political outcomes. In Brazil and Argentina, profligate state and provincial governments drove up public sector deficits to alarming levels. The effects of decentralization on political representation were also not uniformly positive. Rene Mayorga has suggested that the Bolivian Law of Popular Participation that invested power in local communities enhanced local democracy and indigenous participation also undermined the connections between those communities and national political parties.[29] Kathleen O'Neill concluded that at best, the crisis of democratic representation in Bolivia and four other Andean countries "seems to have occurred despite decentralization, rather than because of it."[30] In Argentina, the same process of decentralization that produced gaping public sector budget deficits also lined the pockets of patronage-seeking politicians, thus undermining the model of representation based on programmatic mandates. In recent work, Carlos Gervasoni even raises the specter that federal fiscal transfers and a high percentage of public employees dependent upon political patrons has led to "subnational authoritarianism" in several, electorally noncompetitive Argentine provinces.[31]

At the same time, some of the most promising new institutions of accountability in the region have arisen in decentralized settings. An important forthcoming work contends that decentralization in Mexico laid the groundwork for the metamorphosis of Mexico's poverty assistance programs.[32] The world famous participatory budgeting institutions of Brazil that allow local communities to arrive at a set of priorities for public funding and examine the books to hold officeholders to account took shape as a local alliance of civil society organizations and the local Workers' Party administration of the city of Porto Alegre in the state of Rio Grande do Sul. Although participatory budgeting does not work nearly as well across Brazil, citizens' health councils and other local assemblies with the right to veto city master plans have clearly enhanced the accountability of local administrations to citizens across a wide range of policy areas,[33] and national conferences have put new issues on the agenda, extended rights, and made them meaningful.

Neoliberalism and Political Representation and Accountability

The economic crisis of the 1980s delivered a shock to systems of political representation in Latin America. Debt service and fiscal insolvency prompted neoliberal reformers to sell off state enterprises, liberalize trade, court foreign investment, and loosen the restrictions on labor markets, thus making state corporatism anachronistic. Moreover, the deindustrialization that accompanied trade liberalization jettisoned workers to the informal sector, thereby loosening their attachments to those vehicles of representation to which they had been bonded for decades—unions and labor parties—and made them available for new options.

The effects of this transformation on political representation were uneven and subject to change over time. Initially, political representation appeared to scatter. Parties linked to unions saw their electoral bases erode, and rates of electoral volatility spiked upward in Venezuela, Peru, Argentina, Bolivia, and elsewhere as voters abandoned established parties for political newcomers and outsiders.[34] In Chile, Uruguay, and Costa Rica, existing parties were able to ride out the storm, but in Bolivia, Ecuador, and Colombia, new political forces effectively challenged the old and redrew the electoral maps, and in Peru and Venezuela, once proud parties collapsed altogether in favor of radical partisan alternatives.

Many held the view in the 1990s that neoliberalism was destroying whatever political representation there was. At the level of institutions, Adam Przeworski famously warned that neoliberalism by stealth devalued representative institutions by instructing citizens and political actors alike that they did not matter.[35] Neoliberalism indeed bred a new generation of "neopopulist" leaders,[36] who claimed to rule on behalf of the majority. Particularly vulnerable to what amounted to the abrogation of republican principles of separation of powers, a model which Guillermo O'Donnell famously branded "delegative" democracies," were countries that did not have prior histories of strong democratic institutions.[37] At the level of society, scholars contended that neoliberalism destroyed union, class, and community solidarities along with the impetus to and capability for collective action to defend living standards, a claim initially supported by data showing that strikes and protests declined in the 1990s.[38] It was also claimed that impoverished and dislocated workers who were no longer encapsulated by unions and other social organizations and who lost protection from unemployment, ill health, and old age, and drove up the demand for clientelism.[39] During their presidencies, Carlos Salinas (Mexico) and Alberto Fujimori (Peru) introduced funds (PRONASOL and FONCONDES) to compensate victims of neoliberal policies with public projects targeted for political gain, with strong results in the 1991 midterm elections in Mexico and the 1995 presidential elections in Peru.[40] The Peronists in Argentina degenerated from a party with a platform of distributive justice to a political machine.[41] Voter dealignment coupled with individualistic material and political exchanges thus became the new way of doing business in neoliberal times.

But almost as soon as a consensus emerged that neoliberalism had deleterious effects on political representation, deeply unpopular economic reform gave birth to new left parties and sparked vibrant public protests, suggesting that the decline in representation may have been temporary, or a prelude to a more fundamental reorganization.[42] Neopopulism disappeared quickly in Brazil, evolved in Argentina, and although the quintessential populist Hugo Chávez did best Venezuela's political parties, in Peru a viable center-right alternative coalesced at least temporarily to stem the populist tide. In Bolivia and Ecuador, existing parties were arguably supplanted not by neopopulism but by parties that mobilized voters on the basis of ethnic identities. Paradoxically, indigenous mobilization was sparked, Deborah Yashar explains, by neoliberal reforms that dismantled the corporatist citizenship regimes under which indigenous communities had gained rights to communally held land and social services.[43]

Contending Perspectives on the Organization of Political Representation

Because describing how representation takes place is neither straightforward nor obvious, and so much of the debate has focused on characterizing what is (and what should be), less attention has been paid to explaining variation in the emergent patterns of representation and accountability, as well as to why representation is sometimes "successful"—supported by citizens' beliefs and behaviors—and sometimes not.

Scholars are divided over the relative importance of incentives generated by the rules under which politicians gain office and the poverty and isolation of their constituents in explaining the lines of representation, but most seem to agree about the particular institutional features and socioeconomic conditions that engender parties of clientelism or program. They expect candidate-centered electoral systems, those in which party leaders do not control ballot access, to engender an "electoral connection" by giving politicians incentives to serve their constituents, not their party leaders, which makes programmatic politics next to impossible and clientelistic politics most probable. They also expect that where voters are poor, live in rural isolation, and are preoccupied with survival and heavily discount the future, they are more likely to demand such immediate, tangible benefits as a free lunch, a job, or a paved road for themselves, their families, and their communities (clientelism) over potentially better, but slower to be delivered global policy outcomes (program). Both explanations expect that since the socioeconomic foundations of social cleavages change slowly and political institutions are rarely reformed, systems of representation should be fairly stable. Indeed, in an important new work, Herbert Kitschelt and others contend that parties structure programmatic representation today only in those countries where electoral cleavages formed over socio-economic divisions, such as those between workers and employers, that emerged from import-substituting industrialization decades ago. Where these linkages either broke down or did not previously exist, new ones have not been formed. In other words, where programmatic representation was historically weak, it had little chance of emerging.[44]

Yet from the late-1990s forward some indications of new programmatic cleavages taking root, most notably in Brazil but also in Uruguay and perhaps in Mexico, belied this interpretation. We have also seen dramatic collapses and hopeful signs of new constructions of local and national institutions of accountability and representation in Latin America. In short, scholars underestimated the effect of successful neoliberal reform on the possibilities of representation.

Why this is so may be attributed to two salutary developments accompanying state and market reform under democratic auspices. First, consistent with a quintessentially liberal view that extols the possibilities for democracy of scaling back the tentacles of a parasitic state—a view more popular among economists and policy makers than among political scientists[45]—state reforms that trimmed public payrolls, removed discretionary resources for pork-barrel spending, and depoliticized access to public services threatened patronage politics to the point of extinction. Of course, where politicians effectively protected these besieged assets and state reform sprang leaks, as in Argentina, the impact of state reform was obviously attenuated. Second, the need to debate weighty economic reforms in the public eye and on the floor of the Congress prompted partisan delegations to cohere and provided parties such as the Brazilian Party of Social Democracy, the Uruguayan Colorado and National Parties, and the Mexican National Action Party the opportunity to develop new brands in the electorate, allowing programmatic competition to crystallize. Whether this monumental a transformation could have taken place without grassroots organizing and sharper competition with electorally viable parties of the left (the Workers' Party [PT], Broad Front [FA], and Democratic Revolutionary Party [PRD], respectively) is an open question.

Conclusions: New Opportunities and New Directions in the Study of Accountability and Representation

Keeping pace with the multiple venues in which political representation and accountability have been organized across Latin America in the past two decades requires ways of studying accountability and representation that can bridge different institutional and associational forms of accountability and representation. We need to know not just the mechanisms by which leaders are chosen and deselected in parties, but whether citizens' associations plead their cases to agencies of local, provincial, or national states, or to local councils, provincial assemblies, or national legislatures, and with what effect.

As I write, scholars of Latin American politics have become more sophisticated in their treatment of representation and accountability in national political institutions, especially the legislative branch of government, than ever before. They have also creatively reached beyond the legislature to research policy making and accountability in other branches of government. The judiciary, for example, can in addition to its constitutional purpose to check the executive and legislative branches of government, also provide ordinary citizens a venue for challenging policy and holding government accountable. The judicialization of politics, however, can cut both ways as the powerful can take cases to court to vacate the decisions taken by political majorities. There is clear evidence, at least in Brazil where the judiciary is less conservative and more independent than in most Latin American countries, that the cases that are taken up by higher courts cater to the privileged, while the only recourse of the poor is the lower courts, where the dockets are hopelessly backlogged. [46]

Also beyond the legislature at the level of parties and voters, some truly excellent work has focused on clientelism. Thanks to careful empirical research and innovative field experiments, we know more about who buys votes and who sells them than ever before. We know not only that voters that are poor and lack political information are more susceptible to such appeals, but also when parties and politicians are likely to invest in buying votes, which voters they are likely to target, and with what type and size of payoff. We are also learning when voters can be persuaded through civic education campaigns not to sell their votes. As programmatic politics becomes possible, it now seems particularly important to explore more deeply the gap between voter preferences and party offers. Although some fine work (referenced in this chapter) has been done on matching the preferences of parliamentarians to public opinion, the study of matching policy *outputs* to public preferences is in its infancy.

Finally, a new generation of research is focused on local experiments in participatory budgeting, popular participation, and citizens' councils, of which there are more than ever before. On the surface, it appears these sites of deliberation can serve many important functions: they can engage the citizenry in public life and deepen their attachment to democracy; inform public policy in such a way that improves its design and outputs; and serve as a way to build consensual solutions to pressing problems. What we know less about is whether or not these experiments are "scalable," and can become templates for national policies and policy processes.

In short, though we have learned much about accountability and representation in Latin America, there is much still to be discovered. Fortunately, the diversity of approaches and creativity of political science research examined here signals a bright future ahead.

Notes

1   As Adams expressed it, the members of a "true" representative legislature, one that is "an exact portrait, in miniature, of the people at large," will "think, feel, reason, and act" like the people, understand the issues of concern to them, and elevate those concerns once in office, thus rendering accountability at once inherent and superfluous (quoted in Hannah Pitkin, *The Concept of Representation* (Berkeley: University of California Press, 1967, p. 60).

2   Alexander Wilde, "Conversations among Gentlemen: Oligarchical Democracy in Colombia, in Juan J. Linz and Alfred Stepan, eds. *The Breakdown of Democratic Regimes: Latin America* (Baltimore, MD: Johns Hopkins University Press, 1978), pp. 28–81.

3   Deborah Yashar, "Indigenous Politics in the Andes: Changing Patterns of Recognition, Reform, and Representation," in Scott Mainwaring, Ana María Bejarano, and Eduardo Pizarro Longómez, eds., *The Crisis of Democratic Representation in the Andes* (Stanford, CA: Stanford University Press, 2006), pp. 259–260.

4   Brodwyn Fischer, *A Poverty of Rights: Citizenship and Inequality in Twentieth Century Rio de Janeiro* (Stanford, CA: Stanford University Press, 2008).

5   Philippe C. Schmitter, *Interest Conflict and Political Change in Brazil* (Stanford, CA: Stanford University Press, 1971).

6   Philippe C. Schmitter, "Still the Century of Corporatism" in Frederick B. Pike and Thomas Stritch, eds., *The New Corporatism: Social-Political Structures in the Iberian World* (Notre Dame, IN: University of Notre Dame Press, 1974), pp. 85–131.

7   See also Ruth Berins Collier and David Collier, "Inducements versus Constraints: Disaggregating 'Corporatism," *American Political Science Review* 73, 4 (1979): 967–986.

8   Howard Wiarda, "Corporatism and Development in the Iberic-Latin World: Persistent Strains and New Variations," *The Review of Politics* 36 (January, 1974): 3–33.

9   Guillermo O'Donnell and Philippe C. Schmitter, *Transitions from Authoritarian Rule: Tentative Conclusions about Uncertain Democracies* (Baltimore, MD: Johns Hopkins University Press, 1986), pp. 61–64.

10 Scott Mainwaring, "State Deficiencies, Party Competition, and Confidence in Democratic Representation in the Andes," in Mainwaring et al., *The Crisis of Democratic Representation,* p. 26.

11 Margaret E. Keck and Kathryn Sikkink, *Activists Beyond Borders: Advocacy Networks in International Politics* (Ithaca, NY: Cornell University Press, 1998).

12 Leonardo Avritzer, *Participatory Institutions in Democratic Brazil* (Washington, DC/Baltimore, MD: Woodrow Wilson Center Press/Johns Hopkins University Press, 2009).

13 Mala Htun, "Is Gender like Ethnicity? The Political Representation of Identity Groups." *Perspectives on Politics* 2, 3 (2004), p. 439; Mark Jones, "Gender Quotas, Electoral Laws, and the Election of Women: Evidence from the Latin American Vanguard," *Comparative Political Studies* 42, 1 (January 2009): 57–58, 68, 76.

14 Bingham Powell, "The Chain of Responsiveness," in Larry Diamond and Leonardo Morlino, *The Quality of Democracy: Improvement or Subversion?* (Baltimore: Johns Hopkins University Press, 2005), p. 62.

15 Richard Synder and David J. Samuels,"Legislative Malapportionment in Latin America: Historical and Comparative Perspectives," in Edward L. Gibson, ed., *Federalism and Democracy in Latin America* (Baltimore, MD: Johns Hopkins University Press, 2004), pp. 131–172.

16 Scott Mainwaring, Ana María Bejarano, and Eduardo Pizarro Leongómez, "The Crisis of Democratic Representation in the Andes: An Overview," in Mainwaring et al., *The Crisis of Democratic Representation,* pp. 26–28.

17 Elizabeth Zechmeister and Juan Pablo Luna, "Political Representation in Latin America," in Herbert Kitschelt, Kirk Hawkins, Juan Pablo Luna, Guillermo Rosas, and Elizabeth J. Zechmeister, *Latin American Party Systems* (Cambridge: Cambridge University Press, 2010), pp. 131–138.

18 Susan Stokes, *Mandates and Democracy: Neoliberalism by Surprise in Latin America* (Cambridge: Cambridge University Press, 2001), pp. 12–13, 14–15.

19 Herbert Kitschelt, "Linkages between Citizens and Politicians in Democratic Polities," *Comparative Political Studies* 33 (2000): 851–852.

20 Mona Lyne, "Rethinking economics and institutions: the voter's dilemma and democratic accountability," in Herbert Kitschelt and Steven I. Wilkinson, eds., *Patrons, Clients, and Policies: Patterns of Democratic Accountability and Political Competition* (Cambridge: Cambridge University Press, 2007), p. 162.

21 Susan C. Stokes, "Political Clientelism," in Carles Boix and Susan Stokes, eds., *Oxford Handbook of Comparative Politics* (Oxford: Oxford University Press, 2007), p. 607.

22 Susan C. Stokes, "Perverse Accountability: A Formal Model of Machine Politics with Evidence from Argentina," *American Political Science Review* 99, 3 (August 2005): 316.

23 Guillermo O'Donnell,"Horizontal Accountability: The Legal Institutionalization of Mistrust," in Scott Mainwaring and Christopher Welna, eds., *Democratic Accountability in Latin America* (Oxford: Oxford University Press, 2003), pp. 34–54.

24 The Ministério Público in Brazil with broad powers and 1,300 federal and state-level members with life-tenure, for example, has charged and convicted hundreds of mayors and ex-mayors for misuse of public funds and even investigated members of Congress. Maria Tereza Sadek and Rosângela Batista Cavalcanti, "The New Brazilian Public Prosecution: An Agent of Accountability," in Mainwaring and Welna, eds., *Democratic Accountability in Latin America,"* pp. 209, 210–211, 213–215, 225.

25 Gary W. Cox and Scott Morgenstern, "Epilogue: Latin America's Reactive Assemblies and Proactive Presidents," in Scott Morgenstern and Benito Nacif, eds., *Legislative Politics in Latin America* (Cambridge: Cambridge University Press, 2002), pp. 446–468.

26 Catalina Smulovitz and Enrique Peruzzotti, "Societal and Horizontal Controls: Two Cases of a Fruitful Relationship," in Mainwaring and Welna, eds., *Democratic Accountability in Latin America*, pp. 309–331.

27 Kathleen O'Neill, *Decentralizing the State: Elections, Parties, and Local Power in the Andes* (Cambridge: Cambridge University Press, 2005).

28 Tulia Faletti, *Decentralization and Subnational Politics in Latin America* (Cambridge: Cambridge University Press, 2010), pp. 6–11.

29 Rene Mayorga, "Bolivia's Democracy at the Crossroads," in Frances Hagopian and Scott Mainwaring, eds., *The Third Wave of Democratization in Latin America: Advances and Setbacks* (Cambridge: Cambridge University Press, 2005), pp. 168–170.

30 Kathleen O'Neill, "Decentralized Politics and Political Outcomes in the Andes," in Mainwaring et al., *The Crisis of Democratic Representation*, p. 197.

31 Carlos Gervasoni, "A Rentier Theory of Subnational Regimes: Fiscal Federalism, Democracy, and Authoritarianism in the Argentine Provinces," *World Politics,* 62, 2 (April 2010): 302–340.

32 Alberto Díaz-Cayeros, Federico Estévez, and Beatriz Magaloni, *Strategies of Vote Buying: Social Transfers, Democracy, and Poverty Reduction in Mexico* (unpublished manuscript).

33 Avritzer, *Participatory Institutions.*

34 Kenneth M. Roberts and Erik Wibbels. "Party Systems and Electoral Volatility in Latin America: A Test of Economic, Institutional, and Structural Explanations." *American Political Science Review* 93, 3 (1999): 575–590.

35 Adam Przeworski, *Sustainable Democracy* (Cambridge: Cambridge University Press, 1995).

36 Kurt Weyland, "Neopopulism and Neoliberalism in Latin America: Unexpected Affinities." *Studies in Comparative International Development,* 31, 3 (1996): 3–31, and Kenneth M. Roberts, "Neoliberalism and the Transformation of Populism in Latin America: The Peruvian Case," *World Politics* 48, 1 (1996): 82–116.

37 Guillermo O'Donnell, "Delegative Democracy," *Journal of Democracy* 5, 1 (January 1994): 55–69.

38 Marcus Kurtz, The Dilemmas of Democracy in the Open Economy: Lessons for Latin America," *World Politics* 56 (January 2004): 262–302.

39 Kenneth Roberts, "Social Inequalities without Class Cleavages in Latin America's Neoliberal Era," *Studies in Comparative International Development* 36 (2002) 4: 3–33.

40 Beatriz Magaloni, *Voting for Autocracy: Hegemonic Party Survival and its Demise in Mexico* (Cambridge: Cambridge University Press, 2006).

41 Steven Levitsky, *Transforming Labor-based Parties in Latin America* (Cambridge: Cambridge University Press, 2003).

42 Moises Arce and Paul T. Bellinger, Jr., "Low-Intensity Democracy Revisited: The Effects of Economic Liberalization on Political Activity in Latin America," *World Politics* 60, 1 (October 2007): 97–121, and Kathryn Hochstetler and Albert Palma, "Globalization, Social Mobilization, and Partisan Politics in Latin America," paper presented at the Annual Meeting of the Midwest Political Science Association, Chicago, IL, April 2–5, 2009.

43 Deborah Yashar, *Contesting Citizenship in Latin America* (Cambridge: Cambridge University Press, 2005).

44 *Latin American Party Systems*, pp. 47–52.

45 An important exception was Joan Nelson, ed. *Intricate Links: Democratization and Market Reforms in Latin America and Eastern Europe* (New Brunswick, NJ: Transaction Publishers, 1994), pp. 150–51.

46 Matthew M. Taylor, *Judging Policy: Courts and Policy Reform in Democratic Brazil* (Stanford, CA: Stanford University Press, 2008), p. 160.

9

HUMAN RIGHTS AND MILITARY ABUSES

Anthony W. Pereira

Military regimes, authoritarian regimes in which the military as an organization holds a preponderance of power, were ubiquitous in Latin America in the post-World War II period. The region became associated with the military *junta*, a group of commanders of each of the branches of the armed forces ruling either collectively or in the service of a preeminent personality. The 1970s was the high water mark of military rule, when generals controlled most Latin American countries, with the exception of Colombia, Costa Rica, Cuba, Mexico, Venezuela, and the English and French-speaking Caribbean.

The trend of military rule began to decline in the 1980s.[1] While militaries remain powerful actors behind the scenes in many countries today, they no longer rule directly anywhere in the region. Understanding the origins and decline of military rule is important, because these regimes committed more human rights abuses, in the aggregate, than did their civilian counterparts.[2] (This is not to say that human rights abuses do not occur under civilian rule.) Furthermore, different patterns of repression under military rule engendered different forms of resistance, and these multiple resistances shaped Latin America's new democracies in significant ways. In particular, new democracies engaged in very different forms of transitional justice, or mechanisms taken after the end of an authoritarian regime to address the human rights violations that occurred. This variation in transitional justice has affected the quality of Latin America's new democracies.[3]

This chapter traces the emergence and decline of military rule in Latin America in the post-World War II period, exploring debates about how and why these regimes rose and fell, and the legacies they left for their successors. It focuses selectively on a few countries to highlight larger trends in the region. After discussing the creation of military regimes, the chapter discusses variation and changes in military regimes' repressive practices, focusing on the institutional dimension of human rights abuses. The third section analyzes the link between repression and resistance, while the fourth part compares and contrasts transitional justice measures taken in different countries. The conclusion argues that Latin America's truth commissions had an international impact, in that they influenced many other governments and multilateral institutions in the realm of transitional justice.

Military Rule

The end of World War II generated a surge of optimism about the prospects for democracy and economic development in Latin America. The political defeat of the Axis powers created the impression that democracy was on the march, and many Latin American leaders hoped that the United States would reward its Latin American allies with some sort of Marshall Plan for the region.[4] A wave of democratization, marked by labor militancy and the rise of leftist parties, including the Communist Party, took place in Latin America in the 1944–46 period.[5] Reformist governments responding to the demands of the urban middle and working class were elected in several countries. In Brazil, for example, the *Estado Novo* (New State) dictatorship (1937–45) came to an end, and was replaced by a democratic regime.[6] In Guatemala an anti-authoritarian movement was ascendant for ten years, overthrowing the dictatorship of Jorge Ubico (1931–44) and installing reformist governments led by President Juan José Arévalo (1945–51) and President Jacobo Arbenz (1951–54).[7] In Argentina, the nationalist-populist government of Juan Domingo Perón was elected in 1946, helped by the backing of much of the organized working class, elements of the middle class, and domestically-oriented industrialists.[8]

By the late 1940s, this democratic moment began to wane throughout Latin America, replaced by the pressures of the Cold War. Trade unions were brought under greater state control; Communist parties were banned almost everywhere, and many governments moved to the right. As Bethell and Roxborough write, "An opportunity, however, limited, for significant political and social change was lost."[9] U.S. military assistance to Latin America increased, and U.S. policymakers looked to the military to protect U.S. interests in the region in many countries.

The overthrow of the Arbenz government in Guatemala in 1954 was significant in signalling the limits of democratic reformism in Latin America during this period. The Arbenz government had engaged in agrarian reform that expropriated land belonging to the U.S.-based United Fruit Company. The Eisenhower administration in the United States responded with a CIA-orchestrated invasion, launched from Honduras, that toppled Arbenz and installed President Castillo Armas in his place.[10] In subsequent years the Guatemalan military grew in importance within the state apparatus, and military governments remained in power until 1986.[11] The Guatemalan intervention had a demonstration effect in Latin America. For example, Che Guevara, who was in Guatemala at the time and witnessed the invasion, claimed that it influenced his subsequent decision to join the Cuban revolution.[12]

1954 was also the year that saw the rise to power of General Alfredo Stroessner Matiauda in Paraguay. Stroessner, an artillery officer who had fought in the Chaco War against Bolivia (1932–35), overthrew President Frederico Chávez in a coup d'état on May 4, 1954. His regime relied on the power of the military and the Colorado Party, the latter winning rigged elections. The regime endured until 1989, when Stroessner was removed in a coup d'état led by a regime insider, General Andrés Rodríguez. The Stroessner regime's human rights record was notorious and in the 1970s it participated in a system of regional cooperation in the area of political repression, linking the military regimes of Argentina, Chile, Brazil, Paraguay, and Uruguay known as "Operation Condor."[13]

While Paraguay remained a backwater in Latin America during the Stroessner years, the Cuban revolution of 1959 was far more significant in contributing to the political polarization, and eventual militarization, of the region. The Batista regime (1952–59), overthrown in the revolution, had been supported by the United States. The eventual consolidation in Cuba of a Communist regime, backed by the Soviet Union, led the United States to create the Alliance for Progress, a program of aid designed to keep Latin American governments on a reformist, capitalist path that was formally inaugurated at an inter-American conference in Punte del Este, Uruguay in August 1961. It also led the United States to reorient its hemispheric security policy towards counter-insurgency. Counter-insurgency tactics were underpinned by a doctrine of national security that saw the principal enemy to friendly regimes in the region as internal. The doctrine accorded the military a preeminent place in preserving order and determining which parties and groups represented subversive threats to the nation, and which did not. In such a climate, increasing military intervention in politics became commonplace.

In March 1964 the then-Undersecretary of State for Inter-American Affairs Thomas Mann enunciated what became known as the Mann Doctrine, or the principle that the United States would not automatically refuse to diplomatically recognize a political regime that came to power through a coup d'etat. The enunciation of the Mann Doctrine came only days before the coup that overthrew the elected government of João Goulart in Brazil, on March 31 1964. Later that same year, in November, the Bolivian military came to power in a coup. And in the spring of 1965 the United States sent 20,000 troops to the Dominican Republic to prevent the return of the democratically elected government of Juan Bosch. Subsequent years saw a series of coups in the region, including Argentina in 1966, Peru in 1968, Chile and Uruguay in 1973, and Argentina again in 1976. The era of military rule had arrived.

The violence of the era of military rule in Latin America had certain common characteristics. It usually involved a coalition of traditional, conservative political forces (often including the upper echelons of the Catholic Church and the military, large landowners, industrialists, and members of the middle class) supported by the United States against a left made up of Communist and Socialist parties, some members of the middle class, especially university youth, urban trade unionists, lower echelons of the Catholic Church, members of peasant organisations and, in some countries, guerrilla movements.[14] While many on the left were inspired by revolutions such as those that had taken place in Cuba in 1959, China in 1949, and Russia in 1917, conservative forces wanted to defend existing institutions, the system of property, and what they saw as "national security." Military intervention in politics in defense of "national security" usually led to the militarization of domestic security, the polarization of politics, and an acceleration of cycles of violence. In almost all countries, the left, unable to count on significant support from the Soviet Union, was defeated. The confrontation between these forces was different in the more industrialised, urbanised southern cone (Argentina, Brazil, Chile, and Uruguay) than it was in the more agrarian and ethnically divided Andean and Central American regions, but the broad lines of the conflict were similar throughout Latin America.

Explanations of the rise of military rule in Latin America vary. Some scholars attribute the phenomenon to political economy, and specifically Latin America's dependent capitalist development and inegalitarian class structure. In this view there was an affinity between an economy oriented to the export of primary products, with an unequal distribution of wealth and income and relatively small domestic market, and authoritarian regimes that repressed civil society. Guillermo O'Donnell, for example, ascribes the military coups in Brazil in 1964 and Argentina in 1966 to the "exhaustion" of a particular phase of industrialization in those countries. A period of expansion of the domestic market and labor mobilization was followed by bottlenecks in the importation of capital goods, foreign exchange crises, and inflation. This led to an alliance of military officers and civilian technocrats who "demobilized" labor after the coups and inaugurated a new phase of industrialization based on reducing the wages of industrial workers and opening up to foreign capital. These "bureaucratic-authoritarian" regimes combined a high degree of technical capacity with military-police repression involving purges of the legislature and public sector, torture, and disappearance.[15]

Not all political economy explanations of military rule in Latin America focus on the requirements of industrialization. For some scholars, the lack of industrialization, and the strength of "labor-repressive" landlords, is the foundation of military rule. For example, Rueschemeyer, Stephens, and Stephens base their analysis on Barrington Moore's claim that without a powerful urban and industrial capitalist class democracy is impossible, because large landowners dependent on cheap labor oppose the extension of democratic rights to their employees, tenants, and dependents. Because of the political power of reactionary landed interests in Latin America (especially in the Central American countries of El Salvador, Honduras, Nicaragua, and Guatemala, but also in South America), the region suffered numerous coups and military dictatorships. It was only with the expansion of the working class and—crucially for Rueschemeyer and colleagues, the middle class—that democracy was possible in the 1980s and 1990s.[16]

The applicability of these kinds of political economy arguments to the origins of military regimes in Latin America is disputed. An alternative perspective rejects what it sees as the structuralist and deterministic rigidity of such approaches in favor of more conjunctural, interactive, and institutionalist explanations focused on the level of domestic politics. Youssef Cohen, for example, claims that the 1964 coup in Brazil and the 1973 coup in Chile can be explained by game theory. Moderates on both the left and right feared cooperating with each other more than they did allying with radicals on their own side, leading to political polarization that culminated in deadlock and crisis, a crisis resolved by the intervention of the military. Rather than being the inevitable outcome of economic forces, these military regimes were produced by the strategic choices of political actors who could have behaved differently.[17] Yashar takes a complementary approach in accounting for the many years of military rule in Guatemala between 1954 and 1985, and the absence of a military regime in Costa Rica during the same period. Arguing that the political economy of Costa Rica and Guatemala were more similar than many people believed, she points to coalitional politics (and specifically the inability of ruling coalitions in Guatemala to redistribute land and establish control in the countryside) as the key difference between the two countries. While the focus of her analysis is groups rather than individuals, like Cohen she rejects an exclusive reliance on political-economic structures to explain military rule.[18] Similarly Linz and Stepan claim that O'Donnell's "exhaustion" thesis does not explain the 1973 coup in Chile, and identify the "centrifugal" tendencies of the party system as the most important mechanism leading to the coup.[19]

Yet another approach to military rule in Latin America focuses on geopolitical dynamics, including the hemispheric alliance between military regimes and the United States during the Cold War. Grandin's important work, for example, emphasizes how U.S. anti-Communism led to support for military regimes in Latin America, thus reducing the scope for social democratic reformism in the region.[20] Similarly, for Loveman and Davies, U.S. military aid focused on enhancing the "professionalism" of Latin American militaries reinforced the tendency of those militaries to intervene in politics.[21]

A fourth perspective ascribes military rule to specific national and regional cultures. Wiarda represents this perspective when he describes military rule as part of a traditional, hierarchical, centralizing, "corporatist" mentality that distinguished Spain and Portugal, and their colonies in the New World, from their northern European and North American counterparts.[22] In a slightly different culturalist vein, Robert Holden argues that state violence in Central America arises from a specific regional culture that arose after the collapse of the Spanish Empire in the early 19th century. In this culture, subaltern groups followed local strongmen or caudillos. When U.S. military power was projected into the region after the end of World War II, the result was military regimes in many countries.[23]

In summary, there are a variety of competing approaches to explaining the phenomenon of military regimes in Latin American politics. While culturalist and political economy explanations are probably outnumbered in the contemporary literature by studies that emphasize either geopolitical or domestic institutional factors, they remain influential and could become resurgent again, should Latin American militarism be reborn.

Patterns of Repression

Military regimes are usually marked by one or more of the following characteristics: key political leadership held by military officers; the lack of central, civilian political control over the armed forces; the application of military law to civilians; and the threat or use of extrajudicial repression (such as torture, disappearances, and killings) by the state's security forces. This last factor is important and has only been seriously studied after the demise of military rule.

Data on military regimes' repression in Latin America are not and probably never will be definitive. They vary depending on the source, usually represent some degree of guesswork (even in official government reports), and are subject to revision as new evidence comes to light. Nevertheless, variation in the estimated numbers of victims at different times and places are large, and can show us where and when some of the peaks in violence occurred. Victims of military regime repression suffered kidnapping, detention, torture (physical and psychological), execution, and forced "disappearance" (a term that originated in Latin America), as well as other punishments such as loss of employment, loss of political rights, internal and external exile, the loss of property, and the kidnapping of young children.

Some observers have argued that focusing on numbers in cases of mass violence is inappropriate because it turns human beings into statistics, and is thereby part of the same mentality that produced the violence in the first place. A better way to capture the violence, they assert, is simply to allow long-silenced individuals to tell their stories. Statistics and story-telling are not mutually exclusive, however.[24] Numbers are part of the process of human reasoning and are not in and of themselves dehumanizing. Attempting to calculate the numbers of victims gives us a sense of proportion and the depth of the moral problems involved, in the same way that knowing the number of victims of the Holocaust helps us to understand the enormity of that particular crime. Therefore quantitative estimates such as those in Table 9.1, showing some aspects of the repression in six countries in Central and South America (Argentina, Brazil, Chile, El Salvador, Guatemala, and Uruguay) should not be ignored.

Table 9.1 shows that of the six countries featured, Guatemala's repression took place on the largest scale in both absolute and per capita terms. This repression came closest to genocide, in that entire indigenous communities were wiped out at the height of the repression under President Efraín Ríos Montt (1982–83) in the early 1980s.[25] This brings us to one important difference in the pattern of violence under military rule in Latin America. Military repression in ethnically divided societies with large indigenous populations, such

Table 9.1 LethalViolence by State Forces and Other Indicators of Political Repression, 1964–90

Country	Period	Deaths and Disappearances (approximate)	Political Prisoners (approximate)	Exiles (approximate)	Population in 1988 (millions)
Argentina	1976–83	20,000–30,000	30,000	500,000	32
Brazil	1964–85	400	25,000	10,000	144
Chile	1973–90	3,000–5,000	60,000	40,000	13
El Salvador	1978–83	40,000–50,000	n.a.	n.a.	5
Guatemala	1978–85	75,000–150,000	n.a.	200,000	10
Uruguay	1973–84	300	60,000	50,000	3

Sources: Argentine National Commission on the Disappeared, *Nunca Más* (New York: Farrar Straus Giroux, 1986); Servicio Paz e Justicia, *Uruguay Nunca Más* (Philadelphia: Temple University Press, 1989); National Commission on Truth and Reconciliation, *Report of the Chilean National Commission on Truth and Reconciliation* (South Bend: Univerisity of Notre Dame Press, 1993); Paul Drake, *Labor Movements and Dictatorships: The Southern Cone in Comparative Perspective* (Baltimore: Johns Hopkins University Press, 1996) pp. 29-30; Nilmário Miranda and Carlos Tibúrcio, *Dos Filhos Deste Solo: Mortos e Desaparecidos Políticos Durante a Ditadura Militar: A Responsibilidade do Estado* (São Paulo: Editora Fundação Perseu Abramo/Boitempo Editorial, 1999), pp. 15-16; William Stanley, *The Protection Racket State: Elite Politics, Military Extortion, and Civil War in El Salvador* (Philadelphia: Temple University Press, 1996), p. 3; Susanne Jonas and Thomas Walker, "Guatemala: Intervention, Repression, Revolt, and Negotiated Transition" in Thomas Walker and Ariel Armony, eds. *Repression, Resistance, and Democratic Transition in Central America* (Wilmington, DE: SR Books, 2000), p. 10.

as Guatemala and Bolivia (and Peru under civilian President Fujimori in the 1990s) tended to be more indiscriminate than the more selective repression that took place in the 1970s in more homogenous societies such as Argentina, Chile, and Uruguay.

Another important difference between these regimes is between "roll-back" coups and those that arose from "pre-emptive" coups.[26] The former occurred after extensive popular incorporation and mobilization, such as that which took place under President Salvador Allende (1970–73) in Chile, when Allende's Popular Unity government engaged in extensive land reform and nationalizations of businesses. The latter took place before this kind of mobilization, as in Brazil in 1964. Violence was usually greater after "roll-back" than after "pre-emptive" coups, because militaries were involved in reconstructing societies that had undergone extensive reform, rather than simply preventing reform from occurring.

State capacity also mattered to the scope and style of repression. The relatively sophisticated "bureaucratic-authoritarian" regimes of the more urbanized and industrialized southern cone countries such as Chile, Argentina, and Uruguay, as well as Brazil, relied upon centralized intelligence agencies to monitor individual political opponents and groups. These intelligence agencies shared information and coordinated their activities with myriad civilian and military security organizations. In these regimes, the bureaucratic machinery of the modern state was deployed, often secretly, in a process of ideological "cleansing" of selected individuals and groups. States in Andean and Central American countries, on the other hand, generally had lower levels of state capacity and less refined systems of intelligence gathering. This resulted in Army control of broad swathes of territory and more broad-brush approaches to political repression. The latter approach was harder for regime leaders to keep secret and often triggered migrations, for example when indigenous people in the Guatemalan highlands escaped to Mexico to avoid the massacres of the early 1980s.

The degree of legalization of repression also varied across countries. Under Brazilian military rule from 1964 until the late 1970s, for example, a large proportion of dissidents and opponents were prosecuted in military courts. Many prosecutions resulted in acquittals, while those convicted served relatively short sentences (the average was about four years). While many of those treated in this way were tortured, their treatment was ultimately "judicialized" in proceedings controlled by judges aligned with the military regime. In Argentina after the 1976 coup, on the other hand, most victims of repression were "disappeared," executed in clandestine camps controlled by the military. Their deaths were not officially recognized under a system of repression that was neither judicialized nor even officially acknowledged. This variation can be at least partly explained by the different relationship between the military and the judiciary in the two countries, and the greater cooperation between the two in Brazil.[27]

This brings us to another difference in repressive styles, between the clandestine and the public. The Argentine repression after 1976 is perhaps the most notorious example of clandestine repression whose responsibility was denied by regime leaders, especially in the first two years of the regime.[28] The tactic of denying knowledge of disappearances was devised, in part, to avoid the costs incurred by the Pinochet regime in Chile in its first few years of rule, when the killing of presumed opponents conducted openly in Santiago's National Stadium and other places had led to United Nations sanctions and other indications of disapproval from the international community.

Inter-service rivalry was another variable in patterns of repression under military rule in Latin America. While the Army tended to be the leading branch of the armed forces in all military regimes, and the supplier of most military presidents, the Navy and the Air Force lent varying degrees of support to these regimes. In Argentina from 1976–83, for example, the military junta went to great pains to avoid the inter-service rivalries and conflicts that had marked the 1966–73 military regime. This was done by strictly dividing up ministries and territorial jurisdictions among the three main service branches.[29] Inter-service conflict was also a feature of the Chilean military regime of 1973–90. One explanation for the junta's promulgation of a constitution (ratified by the Chilean public in 1980 under controversial circumstances) was that it was a mechanism to ensure harmony between the branches and prevent the rivalry that had flared up between Chile's President General Pinochet Ugarte and the head of the Air Force, General Leigh, in the late 1970s.[30]

Another facet of military regime repression is the power that it gave to certain security units within and outside of the armed forces. A notorious example of this occurred after the 1973 coup in Chile. President Pinochet Ugarte sent what later came to be called a "caravan of death" around the northern part of the country to review the sentences of, and in many instances execute, defendants who had been convicted in military courts. A careful study of the caravan of death suggested that it might have been put into operation by Pinochet to instill fear within the military itself, and to make it clear that the coup plotters were determined to secure power and brook no opposition.[31] Members of the security forces under military rule could also use their power to enrich themselves. One analyst of what he calls the "protection racket state" in El Salvador in the 1970s argues that security forces were able to use the perceived threat of leftist guerrillas to obtain resources from landowners.[32] Extortion from the family members of the kidnapped and disappeared was also common under other military regimes. In addition, a desire to rein in the security forces might have been a factor in transitions to democracy in some countries. Stepan argues that in Brazil in the mid-1970s, military President Geisel reached out to moderate civil society opponents of the regime in order to restrain his own security forces and enact a process of liberalization that eventually ended with the indirect election of a civilian president in 1985.[33]

While military regime repression was largely a domestic phenomenon, it sometimes spread beyond national borders. The most aggressively international military regime, when it came to repression, was probably the Chilean. For example, Chilean security forces were behind the assassination of Chilean General Carlos Prats González in Buenos Aires, Argentina in 1974 (Prats had been loyal to President Allende prior to the coup). They also attempted to kill Christian Democratic politician and critic of the regime Bernardo Leighton in Rome a year later. Most notoriously, the Chilean DINA (*Dirección de Inteligencia Nacional*) was behind the assassination of the former Minister of Foreign Affairs Orlando Letelier, and his assistant, in Washington DC in 1976. Evidence also suggests that the Chilean military government was a major actor in the creation and maintenance of Operation Condor, mentioned previously, which served as a network among the security forces of Argentina, Paraguay, Uruguay, Chile and Brazil in the 1970s.[34]

In summary, while broad patterns of military repression in Latin America can be identified, variations in the intensity, breadth, and character of that repression were significant and were shaped by institutional factors including state capacity, inter-service rivalries, the degree of autonomy within the state of the security forces, and the relationship between the military and the judiciary.[35] Perhaps equally important, resistance to military rule and authoritarian repression took several different forms. It is to patterns of resistance that we now turn.

Resistance

Repression did not always "work," in the sense of securing power for military regime leaders, but it usually had similar psychological and social effects. In those regimes that used selective repression, the arrest, torture, detention (or execution), and (sometimes) trial of dissidents criminalized, and individualized collective protest against military rule. This created fear and drove oppositional groups underground, leading to the latter's fragmentation and atomization. Some groups on the left also militarized their operations (if they had not already done so) in the face of repression. For those who witnessed or heard about repression, state violence often led to suspicion of others, isolation, depoliticization, and feelings of shame and guilt. Those picked up by security forces would sometimes be ostracized and considered guilty by those who were not. The question of "What had the victim done?" to deserve being arrested was often met with the answer, "He or she must have done something."[36]

Resistance to military rule took many forms and the most violently repressive regimes that closed down public space for dissent and discussion were often those most vulnerable to simple acts of defiance and criticism. In many places the Catholic Church and/or Protestant churches were some of the few organizations whose expressions of dissent were tolerated by military regime leaders. In Central America and the southern cone of South America (with the exception of Argentina) parts of the Church served as an umbrella organization for lawyers representing victims of repression and their family members. By recording the names and fates of those targeted, these Church-sponsored organizations preserved the memories of those tortured and killed under military rule, even if they had little room to contest the repression in legal or political terms. The Vicaría de la Solidariedade in Chile, the Servicio de Justicia y Paz in Uruguay, the Archdiocese of São Paulo and Comissões de Justiça e Paz in Brazil, and similar entities in El Salvador and Guatemala are examples of organizations that engaged in this kind of resistance. Such organizations served as a witness and a conscience in the face of fear and violence, and offered some small measure of consolation and solidarity to family members of the victims of repression.

In each country certain well-known victims became emblematic of the resistance of thousands of others, and their deaths sometimes sparked renewed efforts at resistance. Archbishop of San Salvador Óscar Romero, gunned down in his church by a death squad in El Salvador in 1980, and six Jesuit priests, as well as their housekeeper and her daughter killed by a death squad in the same country in 1989, are examples of this. Folk singer Victor Jara, killed in the National Stadium in Santiago, Chile in the aftermath of the 1973 coup, and journalist Vladimir Herzog, called in for questioning and found hanging in his cell in São Paulo in 1975, are examples of these well-known and much-mourned victims of repression. In other instances the eloquence of a political prisoner drew attention to the plight of many others, as in the case of Jacobo Timmerman, an Argentina journalist arrested in 1977 whose torture and imprisonment resulted in his publication of a well-known book highlighting the arbitrary nature and violent repression of the military junta.[37]

Direct, armed resistance to military repression failed almost everywhere in Latin America.[38] The Cuban revolution, successful in 1959, was only emulated by the Nicaraguan Sandinista movement (FSLN, or *Frente Sandinista de Liberación Nacional*) in 1979. The El Salvadoran and Guatemalan guerrilla movements of the FMLN (*Frente Farabundo Martí para la Liberación Nacional*) and URNG (*Unidad Revolucionária Nacional Guatemalteca*) respectively, could be considered partially successful in that they avoided military defeat and negotiated peace settlements with governments that later allowed them to become legal political parties. But everywhere else non-state armed actors under military rule were either crushed by the repressive apparatus or allowed to become political parties under terms largely dictated by the government of the day.

Far more transformative for the region was the broader non-violent resistance to military rule that relied on civil society organizations and transnational networks. In the 1970s the latter become increasingly influential. Organizations such as Amnesty International, Human Rights Watch, the Washington Office on Latin America and the Lawyers' Committee for Human Rights protested human rights abuses from a non-partisan perspective and coordinated their actions with domestic human rights organizations in campaigns that were often effective in isolating military regimes and publicizing their abuses. These human rights organizations formed what have been called "principled issue networks" that gave sustenance to grass-roots resistance in each country.[39] By the late 1970s parts of the U.S. foreign policy establishment under President Jimmy Carter, most notably the Office of Human Rights in the State Department, added their voices to these criticisms, creating friction between the U.S. government and the military governments of Argentina and Brazil.

Women played a particularly prominent role in this non-violent resistance to military rule in many countries. The Mothers of the Plaza de Mayo in Argentina (*Madres de la Plaza de Mayo*), who protested the disappearance of their children in a peaceful and public way, were the best-known example of this, but women's groups played a similarly important role in other countries. The Madres were able to use their status as mothers to gain some measure of immunity from the highly repressive Argentine junta, and to ask for the right to information about their loved ones. After the transition to democracy their political role became more complicated, but under military rule they could symbolize the disapproval and hope of an entire segment of the population.[40]

Campaigns for amnesty for political prisoners and against human rights abuses can be thought of as a sort of "civil society in embryo" under military rule, democratic enclaves created within the confines of authoritarian regimes. Participants in these campaigns included mothers of the disappeared, religious leaders from the Catholic Church and Protestant churches, lawyers, journalists, artists, intellectuals, students, trade unionists, indigenous leaders, and neighborhood activists. They were part of the movements that successfully brought military regimes to an end throughout Latin America. Given Latin America's history of political violence, it is extraordinary that these regimes came to an end in an almost entirely peaceful process.

There were three main modes of transition from military to civilian rule: the collapse of the military regime; a series of elections leading to the eventual replacement of generals by elected civilian politicians; and a negotiated agreement between political forces within and outside the military regime.[41] In some countries, all three mechanisms were part of the transition to formally democratic, civilian regimes. The regime that came closest to collapse was the Argentine military regime of 1976–83, which lost power after a debilitating recession and humiliating military defeat to U.K. forces in the Malvinas War. Pacts were the form by which the military regimes of Brazil, Chile, and Uruguay negotiated their way out of power, while in El Salvador and Guatemala, insurrectionary guerrilla armies eventually engaged in negotiations with interlocutors in the government.

In summary, even the most violent military regimes did not succeed in fully subduing society in Latin America. Resistance, ranging from collective armed actions to solitary protests by individuals, laid the foundation for the transitions to democracy that occurred in the 1980s and 1990s. After the military retreated to the barracks and formal democracy was achieved, however, serious questions about what to do next remained. The violence of military rule left important legacies that Latin America is still struggling with today.

Transitional Justice

Since the early 1980s, Latin America has witnessed new and important attempts to achieve transitional justice. Transitional justice refers to those measures taken after the end of an authoritarian regime or war to address past human rights abuses. These measures can include investigation of those abuses; reparations for the victims and/or their families; the construction of memorials to the victims; amnesty for and/or punishment of the perpetrators of violence; the production of new histories that are critical of the authoritarian past; and reforms, including purges of authoritarian-era public sector personnel, that push the new regime closer to the ideals of the rule of law. One or more of these measures have been adopted in Argentina, Bolivia, Brazil, Chile, Ecuador, El Salvador, Guatemala, Peru, and Uruguay. Transitional justice efforts have been global as well as national, involving the assertion of norms of human rights by a wide array of transnational advocacy groups, and including unprecedented actions such as a Spanish judge's attempted extradition of former Chilean dictator Augusto Pinochet Ugarte in 1998–2000 and the establishment of the International Criminal Court in the Hague in 2002.

Transitional justice in Latin America began with the end of military rule and the asking of several basic questions in each country. The first question was whether to do anything at all about the past human rights abuses. When an affirmative answer was given several related questions were then raised: When should something be done, and covering which historical period? Who should decide what to do? Who should be affected by the proposed transitional justice measures? How should those measures be enacted?[42]

In several countries general amnesties were passed, either before or after the democratic transition, that prevented the investigation and prosecution of political crimes, both by the state and its opponents. An amnesty of this type, promulgated in 1979, has endured in Brazil, for example. However, in other countries, three different mechanisms of transitional justice have been enacted, piecemeal or all together. These are trials, truth commissions, and reparations.[43]

Perhaps the best-known trials of perpetrators of human rights abuses under military rule took place in Argentina. In 1983 the Argentina Congress annulled the military regime's self amnesty, paving the way for the prosecution of military officers deemed responsible for human rights abuses in the so-called "dirty war". The most visible of these trials was the 1985 "Big Trial" involving the prosecution of leaders of the military junta. Five of those prosecuted were convicted and sentenced to prison. While those convicted were subsequently pardoned by President Menem in 1990, the trial itself was unprecedented and amounted to a judicial repudiation of military rule.[44]

A more common approach to transitional justice in Latin America was to limit or prohibit prosecutions while creating a truth commission to investigate the human rights abuses of the past. This was done in, among other countries, Argentina, Chile, El Salvador, Guatemala, and Peru. The idea behind this approach was that by detailing human rights abuses (sometimes naming alleged perpetrators, more usually not), the state could officially take responsibility for the crimes of its agents and, in the process of recording the testimony of victims and their families, help ensure that such crimes would not occur again. Although the first truth commission is believed to have been created in Uganda in the 1970s, the institution came to international prominence in the 1980s and 1990s and was strongly associated with Latin America.[45]

Latin America's experience with truth commissions had an international impact. In 1994 after the first democratic election in South Africa after 46 years of apartheid, the new ANC government studied ways to address the violence of the apartheid era. It invited a delegation from Chile to present information on the Chilean government's truth and reconciliation commission led by Senator Rettig, which produced its findings in 1991.[46] Partly as a result of its understanding of the Chilean experience, the South African government produced its own truth and reconciliation commission to hear testimony from victims of violence by both the National Party government of the apartheid era and the ANC.[47] The truth commission has subsequently been used as a mechanism of transitional justice in other countries in Sub-Saharan Africa as well as in Cambodia.

Attempts to address past human rights abuses continue in Latin America but they are no longer, strictly speaking, efforts at transitional justice, as the transitions to democracy are generally considered to have been completed. (The term "late justice" has been suggested as an alternative to describe these post-transitional efforts.) Perhaps surprisingly, many of the early settlements in this area have proved not to be definitive, and new developments have continued to take place. In Chile, for example, judges ruled that the military regime's 1978 self-amnesty did not apply to cases of kidnapping and disappearance, because the absence of a body made it an ongoing crime. This paved the way for the trial of hundreds of accused perpetrators. As of 2010, 483 people had been charged with human rights abuses under military rule in Chile, resulting in 309 convictions.[48] Similarly in Argentina under the Kirchner governments, the laws ending prosecutions were deemed to be unconstitutional, and new trials have taken place there. As of 2010, 755 people had been charged in Argentina for crimes that occurred under the 1976–83 military dictatorship.[49] Meanwhile in Brazil, where no trials of perpetrators had taken place and the Supreme Court upheld the 1979 amnesty in 2010, the federal government's Amnesty Commission, part of the Ministry of Justice, spent $2.6 billion reais (roughly US$1.5 billion) between 2000 and 2009 compensating more than 24,000 victims of the military regime's repression.[50] This makes the Brazilian reparations program one of the biggest in the world. It is not yet over. In 2011 a bill to create an official truth commission in Brazil was signed into law by President Dilma Rousseff, despite the fact that the military regime's repression had ended almost three decades earlier. In the words of the human rights scholar Paulo Sergio Pinheiro, "the past is not yet the past" in Latin America, and the legacies of the region's large-scale violence under military rule are likely to be a feature of the political landscape for several more years to come.

An important debate about transitional justice in Latin America concerns the efficacy of these measures, and specifically, their impact on human rights enforcement and the quality of the new democracies in the region. Some scholars argue that trials of perpetrators and truth commissions destabilize democracy, exacerbate conflict, and make continued human rights violations more likely. Sikkink and Walling constructed a data set involving 91 transitional countries (not all of which are in Latin America) in the period 1974–2006 to examine these claims. (Their source was U.S. State Department Country Reports on Human Rights Practices.) They found that the skepticism described above was unjustified, and that countries that had created a truth commission on its own, conducted trials on their own, or combined a truth commission with trials had stronger human rights protections and more robust democracies than those that had not.[51] One problem with Sikkink and Walling's analysis, however, is that their correlations are not necessarily causal relationships. Are democracies that have established truth commissions and staged trials more solid and respectful of human rights because they have enacted these measures, or for other, unrelated reasons, or even in spite of transitional justice? Furthermore, there is some disagreement in this literature about how best to measure the strength of human rights protections and the quality of democracy.

A different empirical study has produced slightly different conclusions from those of Sikkink and Walling. Olsen, Payne, and Reiter compiled a data base from 161 countries in the period 1970–2007, using Keesings World News Archives as a source. They found that truth commissions on their own had a negative impact on human rights and democracy. However, transitional justice had a positive impact when it combined two sets of mechanisms: amnesties and trials, or amnesties, trials, and truth commissions. Labelling their insights a "justice balance approach", the authors of this study challenge the findings of Sikkink and Walling.[52] The two teams of researchers are engaged in a joint venture that will produce new findings in 2012.[53] At present, this debate is unresolved.

An interesting example of a strong disagreement over this issue can be found in the debate between Carlos Santiago Nino and Jaime Malamud-Goti, Argentines who were both involved in transitional justice policies under President Alfonsín. For Nino, the Sabato commission that produced the truth commission report Nunca Más and the "Big Trial" of military regime commanders were part of an experience of transitional justice that "created a social awareness of the risks of authoritarianism and inclination to reject the very model of organic society that led to the violation of human rights in the first place. It minimized the possibility that a social consensus will ever come to favor military intervention in the future."[54] Reflecting further on the "Big Trial" and accompanying trials of other, lower-level military officers in Argentina in the mid-1980s, Nino concludes that they "are great occasions for social deliberation and for collective examination of the moral values underlying public institutions …"[55] In this perspective, transitional justice was an essential concomitant to the rebirth of Argentine democracy. It helped citizens to understand the evils of authoritarianism, to reject the violence of the past, to see that perpetrators were not above the law, and to re-commit themselves to a polity based on the rule of law.

Malamud-Goti, like Nino, was a protagonist in Argentina's transitional justice policies, but he draws very different conclusions about those policies' legitimacy and efficacy. For Malamud-Goti, the truth commission and trials scapegoated the military (while leaving civilian participants in the Argentine dirty war, such as the police, untouched), produced new sources of conflict, and set the stage for further instances of state violence. In this view, the trials over-simplified reality, creating individuals who were unequivocally either guilty or innocent, and thus reproducing the authoritarian, bipolar world view of "friends and enemies" that had spawned the military regime's repression. Furthermore, transitional justice was not a deterrent to state violence, as witnessed by the four revolts of junior officers that occurred under the presidency of Raul Alfonsín (1983–1989). Nor did the trials improve the image of the judiciary, which was seen by many Argentines as having merely adjusted, once again, to the demands of the executive branch. For Malamud-Goti, it was naive to think that transitional justice could revitalize Argentine democracy in the absence of more far-reaching, structural reforms, and "the trial of the generals in 1985 failed to teach the Argentine citizenry the value of their own worth as individuals."[56] In this assessment, the critics and defenders of Argentina's last military regime are locked in a bitter "game without end." Transitional justice has not led to reconciliation, nor the creation of a re-energized democracy based on a broadly-shared understanding of the importance of human rights, constitutionalism, and the rule of law

As this example shows, disagreement about the appropriateness and usefulness of transitional justice for Latin American democracies is intense and at least partly interpretive rather than purely empirical. It is therefore unlikely that further research alone will change people's minds in this debate. However, as more archival work is done and as each new generation comes to terms with the authoritarian past, new understandings will emerge, and fresh debates will occur.

Conclusion

The tide of military rule in Latin America has been rolled back in recent decades. Internally, economic development and the growth of civil society have created a stronger sense of citizenship and more support for civilian, democratic rule. Externally, pressures to civilianize military regimes and to avert or roll back military coups have grown. The end of the Cold War, economic globalization, and the creation of regional trade blocs have created an environment in Latin America in which overt military rule is less accepted than it was in the past and in which military interventions are more likely to falter or fade than they were previously. Failed coup attempts in Guatemala in 1993, Paraguay in 1996, Ecuador in 2000 and again in 2010, and Venezuela in 2002 are cases in point (although the degree of their failure is open to interpretation as in some instances, such as Ecuador in 2000, coup participants did succeed in ousting an elected president). Nevertheless, the coup that ousted President Zelaya in Honduras in 2009 shows that the military can still engage successfully in an extra-constitutional change of government. This interpretation can be contested, but the fact that the military's actions did not lead to a military regime does not, in and of itself, contradict the assertion that a coup took place. Furthermore, the subsequent government was eventually accepted by the regional and international community. This is a worrying development that tells us that it is too early to write the obituary for military intervention in Latin America. The military's control over the means of coercion still gives it significant power, and this power tends to become more useful, and more overt, in moments of crisis.

It is helpful for democracy in Latin America that most military regimes are now regarded as failures by popular majorities in their respective countries. Political leaders who opposed military rule are in power in Argentina, Brazil, Bolivia, Ecuador, El Salvador, Nicaragua, Paraguay, Peru, and Uruguay. Furthermore, the seeds of many of Latin America's new democracies were planted by social movements working under the constraints of military rule. Campaigns in favor of human rights, amnesty for political prisoners, and information about the disappeared were reactions to authoritarian repression, and precursors to broader movements of democratic renewal and the revival of civil society that led to the return of the generals to the barracks. Transitional justice mechanisms were established in an attempt to restore the rule of law and build a solid foundation for democracy. Latin American truth commissions were created throughout the region in the 1980s and 1990s and had world-wide impact.

The literatures on human rights and the military in Latin America reflect these developments. Once closely linked, they have becoming increasingly divergent and confront very different sets of research questions. With regard to human rights, scholars are questioning for how long, and where, the phenomenon of "late" or transitional justice will occur, especially since the generation that had direct experience of authoritarian rule is now quite old in many countries. Perhaps more importantly, scholars are struggling to explain why human rights abuses are still worryingly prevalent in Latin American democracies, despite the firm guarantee of political rights that exist in most countries.[57] In several countries such as Brazil and El Salvador, everyday violence practiced by both state and non-state actors claims more lives than the authoritarian repression (or in El Salvador's case, civil war) that preceded democracy. Police violence is an especially intractable problem. This is a reminder that the widespread enforcement of political rights does not guarantee civil rights, and that more research on how human rights have been and can be protected in the region needs to be done.

When it comes to militaries, a literature on post-transition civil-military relations and military missions arose. Some specialists insisted that the best protection of democracy was to limit the military to a narrow role of protecting the nation from external threats, despite the fact that such threats have rarely been less salient in Latin America's history than they are now, in the post-Cold War world. Limiting the military to such a role, argued these scholars, would make the establishment of civilian control over the military easier. Other scholars responded that militaries entrusted with a variety of roles, such as counter-narcotics, rural health, and infrastructural development would acquire greater legitimacy with the population and have less time for interfering in civilian politics.[58] This debate was gradually superceded by a newer focus on the need for "security sector reform" in new democracies. In other words, reformers had to go beyond civil-military relations in order to restructure and improve the police, the judiciary, and the prison system. Those scholars who continue to focus on the military are increasingly looking at the transformation of the strategy, tactics, weaponry, and personnel of Latin American militaries in the twenty-first century, at a time when the trend is towards smaller, more flexible, better-trained and equipped armed forces.

The decline of military rule in Latin America, a decline seen elsewhere in the developing world, has been a significant and welcome development, but it has not ended research into new aspects of Latin American militaries and the challenge of protecting human rights in democratic successor regimes. It is to be hoped that the last wave of democratization will not be reversed, but instead strengthened and enlarged, so that the research program on Latin American military rule, now entirely an historical enterprise, will not become a contemporary subfield once again.

Notes

1 See Anthony Pereira, "Military Rule" in Bertrand Badie, Dirk Berg-Schlosser, and Leonardo Morlino, eds., *International Encyclopedia of Political Science* (Beverly Hills: Sage, 2011).

2 Charles Tilly cites a study by the think tank World Priorities that shows that in developing countries (including Latin America), half of all military regimes "frequently" engaged in violence against their citizens, while only one fifth of non-military regimes did so. As Tilly puts it, "military control and state violence against citizens go hand in hand." From Charles Tilly, *Coercion, Capital and European States, AD 990–1992* (Cambridge, MA: Blackwell, 1992).

3 For more on the quality of democracy, see Guillermo O'Donnell, Jorge Vargas Cullel, and Osvaldo Iazzetta, *The Quality of Democracy: Theory and Applications* (South Bend: University of Notre Dame Press, 2004) and Larry Diamond and Leonardo Morlino, eds. *Assessing the Quality of Democracy* (Baltimore: Johns Hopkins University Press, 2005).

4 See the comments, for example, of Brazilian diplomat Roberto Campos in *A Lanterna na Popa* (Rio de Janeiro: Topbooks, 1994), pp. 112–115.

5 See Leslie Bethell and Ian Roxborough, eds., *Latin American Between the Second World War and the Cold War 1944–1948* (Cambridge University Press, 1992) and John Markoff, *Waves of Democracy: Social Movements and Political Change* (Newbury Park: Pine Forge Press, 1996).

6 See John French, *The Brazilian Workers' ABC: Class Conflict and Alliances in Modern São Paulo* (Chapel Hill: University of North Carolina Press, 1988).

7 See James Dunkerley, "Guatemala" in Leslie Bethell and Ian Roxborough, eds., *Latin American Between the Second World War and the Cold War 1944–1948* (Cambridge University Press, 1992), p. 300, and Deborah Yashar, *Demanding Democracy: Reform and Reaction in Costa Rica and Guatemala, 1870s–1950s* (Palo Alto: Stanford University Press, 1997).

8 See Daniel James, *Resistance and Integration: Peronism and the Argentine Working Class, 1946–1976.* New York: Cambridge University Press, 1988.

9 Bethell and Roxborough, *Latin American Between the Second World War and the Cold War 1944–1948*, p. 2.

10 Stephen Schlesinger and Stephen Kinzer, *Bitter Fruit: The Story of the American Coup in Guatemala* (Cambridge: Harvard University Press, expanded edition, 1999).

11 Andrew James Schlewitz, *The Rise of the Military State in Guatemala, 1931–1966* (New York: New School University Department of Political Science, unpublished dissertation, 1999).

12 For more on Che Guevara's experiences in Guatemala, see Jorge Castañeda, *Compañero: The Life and Death of Che Guevara* (New York: Alfred A. Knopf, 1998), pp. 63–75.

13 For more on the Stroessner regime, see Paul Lewis, *Paraguay Under Stroessner* (Chapel Hill: University of North Carolina Press, 1980). For information on Operation Condor, see J. Patrice McSherry, *Predatory States: Operation Condor and Covert War in Latin America* (Boulder: Rowman and Littlefield, 2005).

14 The Peruvian military regime under Velasco is an important exception to the generalizations made here, in that it was left-wing and engaged in a land reform that dispossessed many large landowners. See Alfred Stepan, *The State and Society: Peru in Comparative Perspective* (Princeton: Princeton University Press, 1978).

15 See Guillermo O'Donnell, *Modernization and Bureaucratic-Authoritarianism: Studies in South American Politics* (Berkeley: Institute of International Studies, University of California, 1973).

16 For the Moore thesis, which he summed up as "no bourgeoisie, no democracy" see Barrington Moore, *The Social Origins of Dictatorship and Democracy: Lord and Peasant in the Making of the Modern World* (Boston: Beacon Press, 1967). The Moore thesis is used by Deitrich Rueschemeyer, Evelyne Huber Stephens, and John Stephens, *Capitalist Development and Democracy* (Chicago: University of Chicago Press, 1992).

17 See Youssef Cohen, *Radicals, Reformers, and Reactionaries: Prisoner's Dilemma and the Collapse of Democracy in Latin America* (Chicago: University of Chicago Press, 1994).

18 Unlike Cohen, Yashar integrates both historical political and economic structures with agency. In her words, her book "assumes neither that historical outcomes dictate future political outcomes nor that political actors forge political regimes on the basis of will alone." From Deborah Yashar, op. cit. (1997), p. 3.

19 Juan Linz and Alfred Stepan, eds., *The Breakdown of Democratic Regimes: Chile* (Baltimore: Johns Hopkins University Press, 1978.

20 Greg Grandin, *The Last Colonial Massacre: Latin America in the Cold War* (Chicago: University of Chicago Press, 2011, updated edition). For an edited volume with many chapters that describe the U.S. government's abandonment of democratic reformers when their reforms did not coincide with U.S. strategic and economic interests, see Abraham Lowenthal, ed. *Exporting Democracy: The United States and Latin America: Themes and Issues* (Baltimore: Johns Hopkins University Press, 1991).

21 Brian Loveman and Thomas Davies, *The Politics of Antipolitics: The Military in Latin America* (Oxford: Scholarly Resources, 1997)

22 See Howard Wiarda, "Historical Determinants of the Latin American State" in Howard Wiarda and Margaret MacLeish Mott, *Politics and Social Change in Latin America: Still a Distinct Tradition?* (Westport: Greenwood 2003, fourth edition), pp. 129–150.

23 Robert Holden, "Constructing the Limits of State Violence in Central America: Towards a New Research Agenda" in *Journal of Latin American Studies* Volume 28, Number 2, 1996, pp. 435–459.

24 For a discussion of quantitative and qualitative approaches to past human rights abuses, see Phong Pham and Patrick Vinck, "Empirical Research and the Development of Transitional Justice Mechanisms" in *The International Journal of Transitional Justice*, Volume 1, Issue 2, 2007, pp. 231–248. Another useful source on the dilemmas of measuring human rights violations is Alison Brysk, "The Politics of Measurement: The Contested Count of the Disappeared in Argentina" in *Human Rights Quarterly*, Volume 16, Number 4, 1994, pp. 676–692.

25 For insights into Guatemalan military repression, see Jennifer Schirmer, *The Guatemalan Military Project: A Violence Called Democracy* (Philadelphia: University of Pennsylvania Press, 1998).

26 Paul Drake, *Labor Movements and Dictatorships: The Southern Cone in Comparative Perspective.* Baltimore: Johns Hopkins University Press, 1996.

27 From Anthony W. Pereira, *Political (In)justice: Authoritarianism and the Rule of Law in Argentina, Brazil, and Chile* (Pittsburgh: University of Pittsburgh Press, 2005).

28 For a fascinating account of the Argentine military junta's use of language to disguise its actions and terrorize the population, see Marguerite Feitlowitz, *A Lexicon of Terror: Argentina and the Legacies of Torture* (Oxford: Oxford University Press, 1998).

29 See Craig Arcenaux, *Bounded Missions: Military Rule and Democratization in the Southern Cone and Brazil* (University Park: Pennsylvania State University Press, 2001).

30 See Robert Barros, *Constitutionalism and Dictatorship: Pinochet, the Junta, and the 1980 Constitution* (New York: Cambridge University Press, 2002).

31 From Patricia Verdugo, *Chile, Pinochet, and the Caravan of Death* (Boulder: Lynne Rienner, 2001).

32 William Stanley, *The Protection Racket State: Elite Politics, Military Extortion, and Civil War in El Salvador* (Philadelphia: Temple University Press, 1996).

33 See Alfred Stepan, *Rethinking Military Politics* (Princeton: Princeton University Press, 1988).

34 See John Dinges, *The Condor Years: How Pinochet and his Allies Brought Terrorism to Three Continents* (New York: The New Press, 2004).

35 For some useful insights into some of these institutional factors, see Brian Loveman and Thomas Davies, eds., *The Politics of Antipolitics: The Military in Latin America* (Lincoln: University of Nebraska Press, 1989, second edition); and Brian Loveman, *For la Patria: Politics and the Armed Forces in Latin America* (Wilmington: Scholarly Resources, 1999).

36 For more analysis of the psychological and social impacts of state repression, see Juan Corradi, *Fear at the Edge: State Terror and Resistance in Latin America* (Berkeley: University of California Press, 1992).

37 Jacobo Timmerman, *Prisoner Without a Name, Cell Without a Number* (Madison: University of Wisconsin Press, 2002).

38 For more on guerrilla movements in Latin America, see Jorge Castañeda, *Utopia Unarmed: The Latin American Left After the Cold War* (New York: Vintage Books, 1994); Richard Gott, *Guerrilla Movements in Latin America* (London: Nelson, 1970); and Timothy Wickham-Crowley, *Guerrillas and Revolution in Latin America* (Princeton: Princeton University Press, 1992).

39 For more on "principled issue networks," see Margaret Keck and Kathryn Sikkink, *Activists Beyond Borders: Advocacy Networks in International Politics* (Ithaca: Cornell University Press, 1998).

40 See Alyson Brysk, *The Politics of Human Rights in Argentina: Protest, Change, and Democratization* (Stanford: Stanford University Press, 1994).

41 For more on the transitions, see Juan Linz and Alfred Stepan, *Problems of Democratic Transition and Consolidation* (Baltimore: Johns Hopkins University Press, 1996).

42 Timothy Garton Ash, "The Truth About Dictatorship" in *The New York Review of Books*, January 19, 1998, pp. 35–40.

43 Martha Minow, *Between Vengeance and Forgiveness: Facing History After Genocide and Mass Violence* (Boston: Beacon Press, 1988).

44 For more on the Argentine process of transitional justice under President Alfonsín, see Carlos Santiago Nino, *Radical Evil on Trial* (New Haven: Yale University Press, 1996) and Jaime Malamud-Goti, *Game Without End: State Terror and the Politics of Justice* (Norman: University of Oklahoma Press, 2008).

45 For a discussion of truth commissions that includes many examples from Latin America, see Patricia Hayner, *Unspeakable Truths: Confronting State Terror and Atrocity* (New York: Routledge, 2001).

46 An English-language version of the Rettig report is Chilean National Commission for Truth and Reconciliation, *Report of the Chilean National Commission for Truth and Reconciliation* (South Bend: University of Notre Dame Press, 1993), 2 volumes.

47 See the moving and lucid account of the South African TRC in Alex Boraine, *A Nation Unmasked: Inside South Africa's Truth and Reconciliation Commission* (Oxford: Oxford University Press, 2001).

48 From presentation by Catherine Collins entitled "The Chile Database: Introduction and Overview" presented at the conference "Late Justice in Latin America", Institute for the Study of the Americas, University of London, October 21, 2010.

49 From presentation by Lorena Balardini entitled "The Argentine Database: Constructing Comparability with Chile" presented at the conference "Late Justice in Latin America", Institute for the Study of the Americas, University of London, October 21, 2010.

50 For a critical analysis of the Supreme Court's decision upholding the amnesty, see Marcelo Torelly, *Justiça Transicional e Estado Constitucional de Direito: Perspectiva Teórico-Comparativa e Análise do Caso Brasileiro* (Brasília: Master's thesis, Law School of the University of Brasília, 2010). The data on reparations to victims of human rights abuses under military rule in Brazil is from Paulo Abrão and Marcelo D. Torelly, "O sistem brasileiro de reparação aos anistiados politicos: contextualização histórica, conformação normative e aplicação crítica" in Revista OABRJ, Volume 25, Number 2, June-December 2009, pp. 165–203. The figure can be found on page 197.

51 Kathryn Sikkink and Carrie Booth Walling, "The Impact of Human Rights Trials in Latin America" in *Journal of Peace Research*, Volume 44, Number 4, July 2007, pp. 427–445.

52 From Tricia Olsen, Leigh Payne, and Andrew Reiter, "The Justice Balance: When Transitional Justice Improves Human Rights and Democracy" in *Human Rights Quarterly*, Volume 32, Number 4, November 2010, pp. 980–1007.

53 See "The Impact of Transitional Justice on Human Rights and Democracy" at the web site of the School of Interdisciplinary and Area Studies at the University of Oxford, www.area-studies.ox.ac.uk/research/research_programmes_and_projects accessed on February 16, 2011.

54 Carlos Santiago Nino, *Radical Evil on Trial* (New Haven: Yale University Press, 1996), p. 117.

55 Carlos Santiago Nino, op. cit., 1996, p. 131. Nino, who had been an assistant to President Alfonsín, died in 1993.

56 Jaime Malamud-Goti, *Game Without End: State Terror and the Politics of Justice* (Norman: University of Oklahoma Press, 1996), p. 17. Malamud-Goti is a former Solicitor General of Argentina who managed the "big trial" of military regime leaders in 1985.

57 See, for example, Desmond Arias and Daniel Goldstein, eds., *Violent Democracies in Latin America (The Cultures and Practice of Violence)* (Durham: Duke University Press, 2010) and James Holston, *Insurgent Citizenship: Disjunctions of Democracy and Modernity in Brazil* (Princeton: Princeton University Press, 2009).

58 See, for example, David Pion-Berlin, ed. *Civil-Military Relations in Latin America: New Analytical Perspectives* (Chapel Hill: University of North Carolina Press, 2001).

PART II

Development

10

NEOLIBERALISM AND ITS ALTERNATIVES

Javier Corrales

In political economy, neoliberalism is the school of thought that advocates privileging market forces over state intervention in most areas of economic activity. Neoliberals believe that Adam Smith's classic economic dictum—that the "invisible hand" of supply and demand forces are better left unencumbered—can be fruitfully adapted to address the worst economic problems of our time.

Neoliberalism became the predominant thinking in policy circles in Latin America in the late 1980s and through the 1990s. In the 2000s, neoliberalism lost ground, although it is unclear that its intellectual rivals have displaced it entirely.

Since the heyday of neoliberalism in Latin America, countries have veered in three directions. Some governments became interested in finding "alternatives" to neoliberalism; other governments focused on introducing "supplementary" policies, and a third group of governments stayed on some sort of automatic pilot, opting not to alter policy significantly. None except perhaps Colombia has deepened neoliberalism, but none except a few (Venezuela, Ecuador, Argentina, Bolivia) has actually reversed the most important neoliberal reforms of the 1990s. By the early 2010s, neoliberalism does not appear triumphant in the region, but it is not dead either.

I. What Neoliberalism Is … And Is Not

Like the classical liberals of the 19th century, neoliberals share a strong suspicion of any form of concentrated and collective power, and they see the state precisely as the epitome of such power.[1] Without rigorous checks, state interventions in the economy cause harm because they curtail economic inventiveness, distort incentives, expand or protect inefficiencies, and tamper with individual freedoms. Yet, unlike classical liberals, neoliberals do not advocate necessarily reducing state power to the bare minimum of simply upholding the law and adjudicating between quarreling parties. Today's neoliberals believe that state power must be deployed (to raise human capital, provide forms of social insurance, mitigate the volatility of markets)[2] so long as state power is held at bay, and always in the direction of bolstering rather than hampering market forces.[3]

More than a blind faith in markets, neoliberals share a profound distrust of *economic* intervention by the state. For them, state failures are more frequent and insidious than market failures. Neoliberals regard state involvement as neither omniscient nor free of political bias. These flaws make states ill-suited to decide the proper allocation of resources in a society. Letting supply and demand forces determine this allocation is less error-prone than relying on politicians and bureaucrats.[4] For neoliberals, the most serious economic problems of our time—inflation and unsustainable macroeconomic environments, lack of competitiveness, clientelistic and inefficient public spending, financial crises, poverty, and corruption—result from state interventions that distort incentives and induce unsustainable economic activities. If, according to Berman, the three main ideologies of the 20th century—social democracy, fascism, and Marxism—share the same mantra, namely that it is "the state's right and duty to control capitalism," then it can be said that neoliberalism is decidedly a school that challenges all three ideologies.[5]

Neoliberalism in political economy should not be confused with liberalism in U.S. politics, an ideology in favor of using state regulation to advance socially progressive agendas and lessen inequalities. In economics, neoliberalism stands instead for disbanding or easing policies such as price controls, trade restrictions, and state subsidies to economic activities, especially unprofitable ones. Neoliberalism should not be confused either with conservatism in U.S. politics. While many conservatives in the United States appreciate market forces, they often call for various forms of state intervention (in deciding moral questions, offering protection to national industries, expanding military spending) that neoliberals would not condone. Furthermore, conservatives in the United States have come to develop a dislike for taxes that neoliberals do not necessarily share. More than taxes, neoliberals dislike deficits, inflation, and debt, and thus, they often recommend raising taxes or easing tax loopholes. Finally, neoliberalism should not be assumed to be the economic preference of business firms. More likely, neoliberalism splits the business sector. Firms that are able to compete at home and abroad tend to welcome neoliberalism; those that are uncompetitive and depend on protectionism tend to oppose neoliberalism. Neoliberals believe that in most statist economies,[6] the latter type of firms is the norm, so it makes little sense to suggest that firms in developing countries welcome market forces as a majority.

Neoliberals like to use the term "state failures," to counter the more popular term "market failure" used in economics to describe problems with market forces. For neoliberals, state failures are numerous and serious. First, neoliberals argue that the state can never become a truly public-minded regulator because it is always captured by preeminent, self-serving political forces, such as biased ruling parties, trade unions, rent-seeking lobbyists, and hard-to-fire bureaucrats. Because the state is always under the control of powerful political groups (a given majority in a democracy, a tiny elite group in autocracies, or powerful economic lobbies under any regime), the state can never be trusted to ever be truly impartial.[7] And because state leaders safeguard their stranglehold in power above any other goal, they will subvert economic efficiency to political considerations. Policy is evaluated for its capacity not so much to enhance welfare, but to ensure continuity in office of those in power. This inherent political priority renders the state unreliable as a promoter of "impersonal" economic decisions, to borrow from Friedman. For neoliberals, it is neither the state nor the bureaucracy that is ever impersonal, but only competitive markets.

Second, neoliberals believe that states, precisely for their inherent political bias, cannot be trusted to hold themselves fully accountable. Top state leaders will reward top bureaucrats for the political service they fulfill or the political problems that they solve, rather than the public goods such as efficiency that they deliver. In a business firm, managers work with funds that belong to the company's owners, share-holders, and creditors, and thus, are always operating under constant scrutiny by these actors who have a high stake in seeing their assets not get squandered. And if consumers and investors dislike a firm's products, profits collapse and the firm disappears, which is a welcomed form of power check on firms that states hardly face with equal severity.[8] Furthermore, state bureaucrats work with resources that belong to tax payers, and tax payers are never in a strong enough position to monitor the activities of the state, especially state-owned enterprises.[9] In other words, the information asymmetry between the state and voters is more acute than between private-owned firms and consumers/owners. For these reasons, states suffer from an accountability problem that renders them flawed purveyors of the public good.

Finally, neoliberals argue that state interventions typically distort price mechanisms, which for neoliberals, is a huge loss to society due to the informational and incentive-generating power of prices. For neoliberals, prices determined by supply-side and demand-side forces generate invaluable information about what an economy can produce and what millions of consumers actually desire (willingness to pay) to a degree that few other information gathering instruments can match. Furthermore, the price mechanism—or the opportunity to make a profit by finding the right price that a given market can afford—creates a powerful incentive for suppliers to take the risk of making large investments, adopt cost-cutting measures, incorporate new technologies, and develop new products and services. Likewise, the price mechanism allows consumers to figure out their priorities (if consumers truly want something, they will invest in what is necessary to afford that price). Because state interventions typically block the free interaction of supply-side and demand-side forces in setting prices, neoliberals have enormous concerns about state intervention.

For neoliberals, the solution to state failures is to maximize competitiveness among private firms. States (or alternatively, an economy comprised of mostly self-employed people) can never match the ability of competing firms to reduce "transaction costs."[10] Thus, neoliberals strongly advocate for economies based on competitive firms rather than bazaar economies dominated by self-employment, or statist economies dominated by regulation.

II. Critics

Neoliberal ideas themselves are hardly immune from criticisms. Even when market forces function optimally, i.e., when they wipe out inefficiencies and revolutionize modes of production, they can end up "dissolving traditional social relations and institutions."[11] Markets create new practices *and* destroy old practices, what Schumpeter called "creative destruction."[12] Because these disruptions can be so acute, no state, however liberal, permits markets to remain unregulated.[13]

Furthermore, critics argue that markets seldom operate optimally. Supply-side forces can end up being governed by self-serving interests that have little to do with community values or even efficiency. Producers, for instance, can form cartels that distort prices and quantity; investors can become too risk averse and thus under- or mal-invest (e.g., in low-income areas or in capital-intensive sectors) or too risk-taking and thus too eager to overinvest (or over-produce assets such as excess homes or excess credit), leading to asset bubbles that are prone to burst unexpectedly (the so-called "momentum" and "reversal" effects);[14] or be oblivious to the costs of production and what they entail for third parties (negative externalities). Suppliers can also engage in discrimination (refusing to offer services to some groups, or discriminating in the hiring and firing of personnel). Finally, development scholars, especially in Latin America, focus on the negative (or unimpressive) effects of market forces on income inequality. They also contend that market reformers themselves pursue questionable (and covert) political goals, such as weakening labor unions (more on this later).

135

Neoliberals retort that for most of the 20th century, the economic and policy world, especially in Latin America, focused too much on market failures to the neglect of state failures. And in a way, they are correct. Neoliberalism remained unimportant in the region until the late 1970s, and reigned supreme for less than two decades. The rest of the time, non-neoliberal ideas have dominated.

III. The Ascendance of Neoliberalism

Between the 1930s and 1970s, neoliberals were considered extreme and irrelevant, and their influence in policy circles in Latin America was secondary to that of rival ideologies such as Keynesianism, protectionism, populism, socialism, and even Marxism. During this time, policy in Latin America's largest economies (Mexico and most of South America) was characterized by inward-oriented statism or import-substitution industrialization (ISI). Based on *dependency theory,* which posited that there is a long-term decline in the value of commodity exports relative to manufactures, and the *structuralist theory*, which posited that local demand was insufficient to boost manufacturing,[15] ISI was predicated on the idea that by restricting trade, offering subsidies to local manufacturers, and protecting labor, states could promote home-grown industries. Typical ISI policies included: high tariffs, expansion in the number and scope of state-owned enterprises, especially in utilities, subsidized credits to local industry, buy-national laws, price controls, labor codes that protected labor from firing, regulation of competition to protect nascent industries.[16] In multiple ways, these ISI policies contravened market economics.

A series of developments at the level of ideas and world politics coalesced in the 1970s and 1980s to propel neoliberal ideas to gain ground in Latin America. First, the field of development was revolutionized in the 1970s by advances in theories of state capturing and bargaining. Scholars were able to prove empirically that states become captured easily by producers' groups, organized constituencies, or both. For either electoral or self-serving reasons, states were shown to use regulation to cater to pressure groups, ultimately converting them into the main drivers of policy. Anne Krueger in particular showed how rent-granting, once it starts, becomes hard to contain, encouraging most other groups to jockey for influence and eventually overwhelming states with pressures. Once a state embarks on the path of protectionism, it induces non-winners to seek equal forms of protection, leading to a rising spiral of rent-seeking and rent-granting.[17] In 1974 and 1976, respectively, two leading proponents of neoliberalism, Friedrich von Hayek and Milton Friedman, won Nobel prizes in economics, further boosting the renaissance of neoliberal ideas.[18] In Latin America, the 1980s also saw the rise of technopols—a new class of U.S.-trained Latin American economists who became disenchanted with statism, often after having been strong statists themselves. These technopols returned home to pursue careers within parties, state agencies, or think-tanks, from which they became national advocates for pro-market ideas.[19]

At the level of world events, the changes were equally significant. The inability of traditional Keynesianism to solve the problem of stagflation in advanced economies created a thirst for new answers, and some governments turned to neoliberal ideas. One of the first governments in the world to explicitly borrow from neoliberal ideas was the military government of General Augusto Pinochet in Chile, who went as far as inviting Friedman and his disciples to visit the country to offer advice. The Chicago Boys, as these advisers came to be known, focused their attention on battling inflation, regulation, and protectionism.[20] Subsequently, the United Kingdom, and to a lesser extent, the United States, turned to neoliberal ideas to end inflation (through strict monetarism) and stimulate growth (through deregulation).

Neoliberalism was further boosted by the collapse of most Latin American economies following the onset of the debt crisis in 1982.[21] Latin America entered a process of contraction, high inflation or hyperinflation, capital flight, exchange rate instability, and underinvestment that lasted the entire decade and in some cases into the early 1990s. Because Latin America was the region of the world to have implemented ISI the deepest, the collapse of its economy proved to many that the model was misguided to begin with. For neoliberals, these outcomes (statism and economic collapse in the 1980s) were causally connected. Furthermore, the command economies of communist nations were also collapsing (the Soviet bloc) or changing in the direction of market reforms with positive results (China), further boosting the global trend away from statist economics.

More important, a series of successful cases, or "victorious globalizers," to paraphrase Jeffrey Frieden,[22] made it onto the radar screen, and the initial interpretation of these cases seemed to validate key tenets of neoliberalism. For instance, the spectacular rise of Asian economies (Korea, Taiwan, Singapore, Hong Kong, China) was explained by neoliberals as a result of less statism and more openness to market forces, stable macroeconomics, and trade opening.[23] And in Latin America, the divergent experiences of Chile and Peru in the 1980s proved decisive. Each nation attempted to deal with the debt crisis using different approaches—Chile was borrowing explicitly from neoliberals while Peru was implementing a more statist approach.[24] By the late 1980s, the Chilean model seemed buoyant while Peru plunged deeper into a crisis. Many scholars concluded that neoliberal reforms could turn things around, if implemented to the fullest as in Chile (rather than haphazardly as the military juntas of Brazil and Argentina did).

Thus, by the late 1980s, neoliberal ideas and scholars seemed unstoppable. Considered the "dissenting school" during most of the 20th century, neoliberalism became the "new orthodoxy" in the late 1980s.[25] The World Bank, which up until the 1970s felt comfortable with ISI policies, together with the IMF, started to advocate large-scale privatizations, together with handsome loans to help economies adjust.[26] A famous economist, John Williamson, attempted to summarize these then-in-vogue ideas in a small report for a conference at the Institute for International Economics: tight fiscal discipline (through expenditure and debt reduction) and tax simplification, avoidance of currency overvaluation, privatization, trade and capital account liberalization, and deregulation. In the early 1990s, this paper adopted the label of the Washington Consensus.

For Williamson, this list of policies represented a sort of "opinion survey" recapping the areas of major agreement among policy gurus. However, Williamson also explained that his paper was a political document, deliberately designed to exclude certain policy prescription so as not to offend certain constituencies. To please conservatives, for instance, Williamson's list hardly discussed social policies, and to please progressives, hardly discussed spending on infrastructure. Williamson's papers became the blueprint for most neoliberal reform models in the early 1990s, and these reforms, in line with Williamson's paper, downplayed the need for spending and reified instead the value of fiscal austerity.

Yet, the neoliberal impetus, however formidable in the late 1980s, still confronted two challenges. One was intellectual; the other, political. The intellectual challenge came from two opposing schools of thought. One was "neostructuralism," which argued, *a grosso modo*, that the Washington Consensus's emphasis on macroeconomics and trade opening leads to de-industrialization and insufficient aggregate demand stimulus, with grave consequences for employment, wages and thus inequality. The other was the "developmental state" school, which argued that the economic success of Asia was not the result of free-markets, as neo-liberals contended, but of peculiar forms of "state-business" collaboration and coordination. These scholars argued that state associations with business was indispensable for firms to develop new export products, secure new export markets, reduce redundant investments, and guarantee sufficient investments in human capital needed for business competitiveness. The neostructuralist approach was associated with economists mostly at the United Nations Economic Commission for Latin America and the Caribbean (ECLAC), while the developmental state argument was associated with scholars working on Southeast Asia. While these schools, which one scholar labeled as the "Southern Consensus,"[27] took a back seat in the 1990s, they would make a major comeback in Latin America in the 2000s, when politicians and citizens started to question, often in large numbers, the merits of neoliberal reforms in the 1990s.

The second challenge was political. Outside of Chile, it proved politically difficult for neoliberal policies, however in vogue, to become policy in Latin America. Instituting them entailed enormous political costs, and Latin American governments hesitated to rock the boat too much in fear that they would destabilize the newly democratic regimes recently inaugurated across the region. Thus, excepting Chile, the 1980s were considered a period of "muddling through" rather than fully embracing of neoliberal reforms.[28]

Two major economic changes in the late 1980s ended this hesitancy. First, high inflation turned into hyperinflation (in Bolivia, Brazil, Argentina, Peru, Nicaragua) and low inflation turned into high inflation (in Mexico, Ecuador, and Venezuela). These augmented levels of inflation lasted several years, setting world historic records, devastating economies, shrinking the middle classes, and multiplying poverty in a matter of months. High inflation made nations enter into what Weyland describes as "the domain of losses," which according to prospect theory, is the precondition for actors to take risks, and this meant a greater appetite for risky market-oriented reforms.[29] The other economic change was the emergence of the Brady Plan, an effort on the part of the U.S. government to work with the IMF to reduce debt obligations in exchange for economic reform. Unlike the previous debt relief programs of the 1980s, the Brady Plan offered governments a clear incentive to enact reform: debt reduction rather than just more lending.[30]

As a result of these price pressures and creditor incentives, most governments in the region found themselves announcing neoliberal reforms by the late 1980s, in some cases such as Mexico (with drastic trade opening to the United States, NAFTA), Argentina (with its strict monetary policy and the convertibility law), Peru (with its massive privatization program), Colombia (with its sweeping banking liberalization), Ecuador (with its strict dollarization), and Venezuela (with its profound decentralization reforms) going further than the World Bank and the IMF were advocating.

In short, neoliberalism gained ascendance as a result of multiple factors, all coalescing at the end of 1980s: theoretical refinement, Nobel prizes, comparative studies, economic crises, model cases, rising technopols, smart packaging, and plenty of international sticks and carrots. By the early 1990s, neoliberal policies and minds dominated policy circles not just in Latin America, but essentially anywhere government authorities were interested in economic reform.

IV. The Heyday of Neoliberalism, Late 1980s–Early 2000s

The high-implementation period spanned from the mid-1980s to early 2000s. During this period, no region in the world matched Latin America in terms of at least three pillars of neoliberal reforms: (1) inflation–abatement (through fiscal, monetary, and exchange rate adjustments), (2) trade liberalization, and (3) privatizations (which were especially extensive in Argentina and Mexico in the early 1990s, followed by Brazil and to some extent Colombia in the late 1990s).

The high-implementation period prompted two major debates in political science. One was the question of reform sustainability, in essence a discussion on the factors that allow states to manage, respond, and prevail over societal pressures. Market reforms pose at least three serious governance problems.[31] First, market reforms create the classic problem of "diffused benefits" (more efficiency, less inflation, resumed growth) and "concentrated costs" (higher taxes, job losses for many, discontinued services), which scholars have long known to be a recipe for political resistance by cost-bearers and a lack of enthusiasm by everyone else. Another problem has to do with credibility: the reforms require societal groups to cooperate with the state (bear costs, pay taxes, accept deregulated prices) in return for a future reward to be delivered by states that in turn were deemed chronically incapable of upholding promises. The third problem is that the costs of reforms fall heavily either on the states' closest political allies—members of the ruling party and state-dependent business firms—or on the state's strongest enemies—labor unions. The former expect their electoral victories to translate into control of state activities, and thus, they do not exactly welcome the reforms. The latter group feels intensely threatened by the reforms and in many cases launches political wars against them (in the forms of strikes, refusals to cooperate, street protests, etc.).

Because of these challenges, political scientists discovered that studying the conduct of neoliberal reforms offered a rare chance to test theories of the conditions for "effective governance" by "new democracies" in "hard times." Research during this period was abundant and innovative, with scholars offering unexpected findings and answers to long-standing questions of political economy.

For instance, on the question of whether authoritarian regimes are better able to implement market reforms than democracies, scholars argued not exactly; some democracies implemented deep reforms.[32] Although many democracies did develop some autocratic practices[33] and non-transparent reform coalitions to advance reforms,[34] the overall survival of democracies while moving forward with market reforms provided evidence on behalf of Mancur Olson's argument, late in his career, that markets and democracy share a mutual affinity: both rely on trust (and independent courts), and both can thrive jointly.[35] Do right-wing parties have an advantage (the partisan hypothesis)? Again, not exactly: at least in terms of major aspects of reforms (reduce inflation, open trade, privatize), parties with a statist past made huge strides (the "Nixon-in-China" hypothesis),[36] although, in terms of the second stage of reforms (e.g., post-privatization re-regulation), party ideology was found to matter a bit more, with left-wing parties placing more restrictions on competition than right-wing parties.[37] Does exposure to the IMF/World Bank/USAID explain reforms? Partly. On the one hand, these institutions offered strong incentives (or punishments) for countries to privatize and move away from universalistic social spending (in Spain and Portugal, where these institutions played a lesser role during the reforms, social spending was not compromised as much as in Latin America, which could be seen as evidence of the special imprint of external actors in Latin America).[38] On other hand, many countries that worked closely with these external organizations floundered (Ecuador, Venezuela), and other countries actually implemented reforms that went further than what the IMF/World Bank supported (Argentina's convertibility law, Mexico's NAFTA, Brazil's Petroleum Law permitting private ownership of the state-owned company). Were trade unions able to derail the process? Again, not exactly. Reforms proceeded in countries with strong unions (e.g., Mexico and Argentina), although unions did extract important concessions, manage to stop some privatizations, and essentially blocked reform of labor markets.[39] Do fragmented party systems impede reform implementation? To a large extent, yes,[40] but countries found democratic ways around this institutional handicap, with Brazil in the late 1990s becoming a good example of reform implementation in the context of party fragmentation.[41] Does crisis explain the depth of reform? Yes, but it explains mostly the decision of presidents to finally adopt extreme reform packages ("shock policies") and not necessarily whether citizens accepted them, at least initially. Did presidents get voted out of office for introducing harsh medicines? It depends. Presidents who managed to stabilize the economy and restore growth tended to be reelected once,[42] but second reelections never went that smoothly, in part because constitutions banned them or the electorate thought that in carrying out a post-reform agenda, the existing ruling parties were no longer apt for the new tasks at hand.

The reforms were also studied for their outcomes, and this has been a polemical debate in multiple disciplines, not just political science. Critics contended that neoliberal reforms deprived vulnerable economic sectors, social groups, and even the environment of protection against the negative effects of globalization, while failing to deliver sufficient economic growth to reduce poverty and inequality.[43] For critics, the neoliberal penchant for de-funding universalistic public programs in favor of "targeted" social programs might have helped financial stability, but it also increased inequality, in part because cutbacks were severe and means-testing to qualify for targeted programs was imperfectly implemented.

Neoliberals retort that economic growth in the 1990s, while not as spectacular as in the 1950s–1960s, was qualitatively superior because it was more sustainable (i.e., less dependent on state spending and debt) and generated fewer distortions (e.g., inflation, red-tape, resource misallocation) that disproportionately harm the poor. They insist that most observed shortcomings were due to spotty policy implementation, rather than to flaws in the prescriptions themselves. They also emphasize that inequality and poverty actually exploded when the region was under the heavy influence of statist schemes, not under neoliberalism.

Another set of critics fault the reforms for failing to unleash the promised "productivity revolution." Except in Central America, the region's export base did not diversify away from land-based products (although manufacturing exports did expand); except for Mexico, Costa Rica, and perhaps Brazil, the export base did not become high skill-oriented; and except for Chile, productivity actually declined significantly in the service sectors, which is the largest sector in most countries.[44]

Finally, critics also argue that rather than embracing neoliberalism, the region actually suffered an imposition of neoliberalism—from abroad or, more important, from above: it was too forcefully imposed by the state.[45] The debt crisis, they argue, produced an uneven distribution of power: creditors, donor nations, and multilaterals, which advocated reforms, saw a rise in their bargaining power when their "clients" (borrowing governments) plunged into serious recessions.[46] This negotiation was thus intrinsically biased against domestic actors relative to external ones.

A persistent problem during reform implementation was the absence or weakness of an organized constituency in favor of reform. Latin American countries except Chile, Mexico, and perhaps Colombia and El Salvador have never had electorally strong political parties advocating less rather than more statism, austerity rather than profligacy. Furthermore, while trade liberalization was popular (because it lowered prices of consumer goods), privatizations stayed relatively unpopular (because in many cases they raised prices, reduced services, or acquired the reputation of occurring through corruption).[47] Thus, presidents interested in reforms faced the predicament that economies needed medicine, while the electorate, in most cases, remained unwilling to swallow the bitter pill of reforms.[48] This meant that neoliberal reforms were often introduced "by surprise,"[48] too hastily,[50] or in coalition with non-transparent actors.[51] Presidential candidates would campaign advocating more statist responses only to announce IMF-supported market reforms once in office and align themselves with extra-partisan constituencies. This policy "switch," or "electoral betrayal," was traumatizing for many voters and ruling parties. Only when presidents managed to turn things around and generate growth would voters turn favorable toward voting for reforming presidents and even re-elect them or their parties (in Brazil, Argentina, Peru, Mexico). But when presidents failed to deliver growth and stability, the electorate reacted angrily.

In either case—whether the reforms worked or failed—this type of governance "by surprise" contributed to the so-called "representational crisis" that swept through Latin American democracies in the late 1990s. This crisis refers to the idea that Latin American institutions, though more democratic than ever in terms of degrees of contestation and civic and political freedoms, left many citizens and interest groups feeling unrepresented, betrayed, and even economically at a loss.[52]

By the late 1990s, neoliberalism had become one of the most polarizing forces in development, not just in Latin America. Even the use of the term "neoliberal" became controversial, with critics preferring the term "neoliberalism," while more sympathetic analysts preferred instead the term "market-oriented" to describe the reforms.

The controversy surrounding the merits of neoliberalism had political and intellectual repercussions. Politically, anti-neoliberal/anti-globalization movements expanded worldwide, and made headlines, especially when they forced the cancellation of the opening ceremonies of the Ministerial Conference of the World Trade Organization in Seattle, Washington, in 1999. The IMF, seen by many as the primary global advocate of neoliberalism, was being criticized like never before, recriminated by the left for its glorification of the market and by the right for its laxity with non-compliant debtors.

Intellectually, polarization led to a boom in scholarship on the outcomes of neoliberalism. However, at least two methodological problems associated with studying the outcome of reforms made assessments difficult. First, there is a wide variety of degrees of implementation. Some countries implemented reforms more profoundly than others, and even among the deep reformers there are gaps in implementation. Thus, it is difficult to establish an agreeable ranking of levels of implementation. Second, it is hard to isolate the effect of reforms from other factors at play (e.g., the effect of lingering policies and institutions from the past, other non-economic reforms occurring simultaneously such as decentralization, external shocks). Thus, after observing the outcomes of reforms during 15 years of implementation, few analysts ultimately changed their normative views on neoliberalism. The outcomes were often too mixed or too overspecified to attribute performance, whether positive or negative, to one factor. Both neoliberals and their critics found plenty of evidence to bolster each of their claims.[53]

For instance, the IMF established in 2000 the first internal unit charged with evaluating operations and outcomes, the Independent Evaluation Office. One of its principal outputs was a study on its role in the Argentine 1999–2002 crisis, one of the deepest at the time in the world. Rather than condemn the economic model that predated the crisis, the report essentially blamed the government's deviation from IMF prescriptions, the government's failure to implement correctives, and the IMF's lax monitoring of these deviations.[54] If anything, the report toned down the criticism of the IMF: the final version of the report was found to be less critical of the IMF than the earlier draft, before it was approved by the IMF's authorities.[55] By the same token, critics of neoliberalism—neostructuralist and development state scholars in particular—treated the economic crisis of 1995 and again in 1998–2002 in emerging markets worldwide, not just in Latin America, as evidence of the noxious impact of rolling the state back too much, even though some deep-reforming countries achieved impressive results (Chile, Peru, Brazil, Uruguay, El Salvador, the Dominican Republic).

Likewise, the region's performance during the global financial crisis of 2008–2010 did not help settle disputes either. For instance, in trying to explain why this time around Latin America weathered the crisis better than so many other economies, and far better than in previous crises, each camp offered its own take. Neoliberals attributed the better performance to the region's overall respect of key pillars of neoliberalism: adherence to fiscal discipline, especially low deficits and low debts, strengthened financial sectors, higher levels of reserves, and openness to trade. Neostructuralists and neodevelopmentalists, in contrast, emphasized the ways in which orthodoxy was eased in the 2000s: heavy demand stimulus in the pre-crisis years, post-2002 commitment to poverty alleviation programs, use of government credit to finance exports, and new government-supported industrial policies.[56] In short, neither the dismal performance during the 1998–2002 crisis nor the decent performance during the 2008–2010 crisis persuaded neoliberals—or their critics—to reconsider their views significantly.

V. Second-Generation Reforms: Bringing Institutions and Equity Back In

Nevertheless, one area where thinking among mainstream market-oriented economists did shift, starting in the mid-1990s, was on questions of *institutions* and *equity*. On the former, economists sympathetic to market-oriented reforms began to accept the notion, long established by economic historian Douglass North and many political scientists,[57] that without appropriate institutions of governance, markets cannot function properly.[58] On the latter, neoliberals came to accept the neostructuralist critique that market reforms, at least as encapsulated by the Washington Consensus, paid insufficient attention to poverty, inequality, and access to social services.[59] And so, regional and multilateral lending and donor institutions, both unsympathetic[60] and sympathetic to neoliberalism,[61] began calling for more attention to "growth with equity," a slogan made famous by the center-left government that in the 1990s succeeded Pinochet in Chile.

This call on behalf of institutional reform *and* equity-oriented social policies led to a series of amendments to the Washington Consensus that came to be known as "second-generation reforms."[62] In a nutshell, this new call for reform combined "monetary and fiscal orthodoxies with progressive social policies."[63] To some extent, the new mantra of the early 2000s implied a departure from hard-core neoliberal thinking: markets and (streamlined) states necessitate, rather than repel, each other. Politically and cognitively, this new thinking appealed to voters and politicians in the center and center-left, less so to hard-core neoliberals, and even less, to the immoderate left.

Judged in terms of this new mantra, there is no question that Latin America made impressive inroads by the late 2000s. For instance, in terms of equity concerns, there was a general increase in social spending per inhabitant across most countries, increasing by 50 percent even during the heyday of neoliberalism between 1990/91 and 2000/01 and by an additional 30 percent between 2000/01 and 07.[64] Also regarding equity, there was progress not just in spending levels, but also on institutional innovation. Latin American countries became famous worldwide for so-called "conditional cash transfers." These are poverty-alleviation programs in which governments offer cash to households that make investments in the health and education of their younger generations. By mid-2000s, more than 26 million households in 19 countries were benefitting from conditional cash transfer programs across the region.

Remarkably, this renewed investment in social programs was accomplished without compromising fiscal stability in most countries. This was an unprecedented economic triumph for a region that during most of the 20th century was well known for macroeconomic disarray. To explain this triumph, scholars have invoked innovations at the level of institutions, the other side of the mantra of the 2000s.

According to the chief economist of the Inter-American Development bank, there were two sets of institutional reforms in the region that had a bearing on fiscal outcomes. Some reforms increased pressures for fiscal outlays (e.g., changes in electoral systems that encouraged party system fragmentation, expansion of participation to new groups, constitutional changes requiring greater fiscal spending). But these pressures for fiscal indiscipline were successfully counteracted by other institutional changes that permitted the state to preserve fiscal balance. The first of these changes had to do with reforms in electoral processes that made presidents come to office with greater legitimacy (the introduction of runoffs, which diminished minority presidents; strengthening of checks and balance). The other was the adoption of strict fiscal laws: 12 of 18 countries in the region adopted some version of a "fiscal responsibility" law. These laws typically mandate limits on spending, deficits, or debts. In addition, 10 countries imposed limits on the ability of various branches of government and subnational governments to spend without approval of the minister of finance. For Lora, these institutional innovations constitute nothing less than a silent revolution. They explain Latin America's better fiscal performance since 1990.[65] They meant that when presidents were serious about fiscal balance, they enjoyed the authority and the rules to accomplish those goals.

Clearly, not all countries scored high on these political and institutional innovations, but Lora argues that those that did obtained better macroeconomic performance. One way or another, Latin America in the 2000s offered evidence that concerns with equity and institutional reform can be compatible, perhaps even necessary, for the survival and well functioning of key tenets of neoliberalism.

VI. Supplements, Alternatives, and Automatic Pilots in the 2000s

The main criticisms levied against neoliberalism can be grouped into three categories of arguments: that it was insufficiently implemented; that it was fundamentally flawed; that it was sound but lacked vital elements.[66] By the same token, the response in Latin America in the 2000s also varied, both at the level of voters (electoral behavior), and at the level of states (policy).

A. Electoral Trends

While few analysts changed their minds significantly about the merits of neoliberalism, at least based exclusively on the region's performance between 1989 and 2010, the Latin American electorate did seem to have undergone a change, at least in the 2000s. In the mid-1990s most electorates rewarded market-oriented governments that restored growth and eased inflation. But by the end of the 1990s, except in Chile and El Salvador, electoral behavior turned heavily anti-incumbent. Parties, movements, and candidates campaigning against neoliberalism, or against governments with a neoliberal record, gained the upper hand. Even successful reformers in the 1990s were voted out of office.

Except in Mexico and Colombia, this anti-incumbent wave produced governments that self-identified as, or aligned themselves with, "the left." By the mid-2000s, the self-defined left was "stronger than ever everywhere in Latin America," whether it was in power or in opposition.[67] At least five different explanations for this turn to the left have been offered: (1) latitude in reform implementation, which produced incomplete/uneven results; (2) the effects of the global economic crisis of 1998–2002 (which hit especially hard in Argentina, Uruguay, Ecuador, Bolivia, Venezuela); (3) discontent with microeconomic problems: some privatized sectors, for instance, yielded rising prices, discontinued services, weak job growth, or little compliance with anti-trust policies; (4) in many countries neoliberalism was accompanied by political decentralization, which permitted new political parties and movements to dislodge traditional parties, thereby opening opportunities for the non-traditional left to make electoral inroads; (5) issue-shifting: once the neoliberal administrations addressed the ailments of the early 1990s (recession, debt, inflation, bloated SOEs, capital outflows), the electorate focused on a host of new "non-economic" issues such as greater transparency, democratic participation, gender equity, crime, social policy, for which the neoliberal tool-kit was deemed ill-suited; (6) new forms of protest groups that produced innovative ways to build new networks across different social groups, each disaffected by different issues; and (7) a change in discourse by leftist leaders to appeal to a broader audience, rather than the traditional left constituency (as Morales says, rather than the electorate becoming more leftist, it was the leftist politicians that became more "Latin American").[68]

Much scholarship in the 2000s turned attention to assessing which of these explanations fared better. Unsurprisingly, the answer not only varied from country to country, but also included elements of each explanation, however mutually exclusive they might seem, sometimes even in the same country.[69]

B. Policy Trends

At the policy level, there were some commonalities as well as some major variations across cases in the 2000s. In terms of commonalities, two areas of policy convergence were already discussed: greater investments in social policy and vigilance against fiscal deficits and debt. Another was a major reliance on agro-exports, mostly in South America, and continued openness to imports.

But on a number of areas, there was enormous variation. One way to gauge this variation is to look at the Heritage Foundation Index of Economic Freedoms, which since 1995 has been ranking countries according to many policies cherished by neoliberals.

This data set reveals not just that implementation varied during the heyday of neoliberalism (Figure 10.1), but also that three conflicting trends emerged since then (Figure 10.2).

The first trend consisted of countries that improved their standing in this index, suggesting that they reinforced their commitment to a market-oriented economy. Curiously, a few of these governments were formed by parties that campaigned on the left (e.g., the Socialists in Chile, the Frente Amplio in Uruguay, the APRA in Peru). Also, it is noteworthy that within this group there were no major neoliberal leaps, but rather, modest movement. A second trend consisted of governments that stayed on some sort of automatic pilot. A third and larger category of countries moved away from market-economics, as evidenced by the number of cases moving downwards in the Economic Freedom Index.

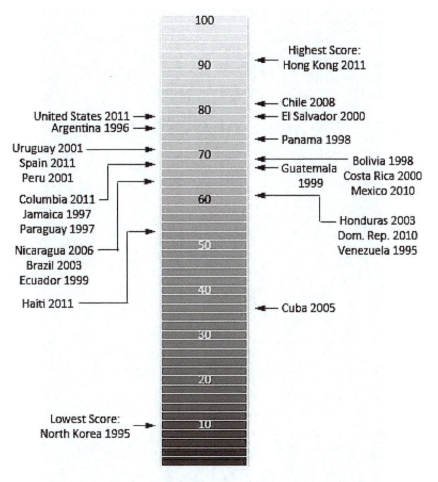

Figure 10.1 Diversity of Achievements: Highest Economic Freedom Scores Achieved by Latin American Countries and Year of Achievement. *Source:* The Heritage Foundation.

Most of these reversals came by way of leftist governments. Scholars divide this category of leftist governments into at least two groups: the moderate or pragmatic left and the radical or populist left, with the latter departing from the Washington Consensus to a greater degree.[70] When measured in terms of percentage change in the index of economic freedom between 2002 and 2011 (see Figures 10.2 and 10.3), it is clear that this latter group of radical populists introduced some of the largest reversals in economic freedom recorded on earth in the 2000s. Whereas Latin America was a world champion of neoliberal reforms in the 1990s, in the 2000s, it was the radical left that became world champions, but this time, in the direction of reversing economic freedoms.

To illustrate the difference between the moderate and the radical lefts, it might be useful to focus on two specific cases, rather than to offer generalizations or to rely on one numerical index. There is no question that two of the most "illustrative" cases of each tendency respectively are Brazil under Lula (2003–2011) and Venezuela under Hugo Chávez (1999–present). Table 10.1 compares how each administration fared regarding both the original Washington Consensus *and* second-generation reforms. Lula, emblematic of the moderate

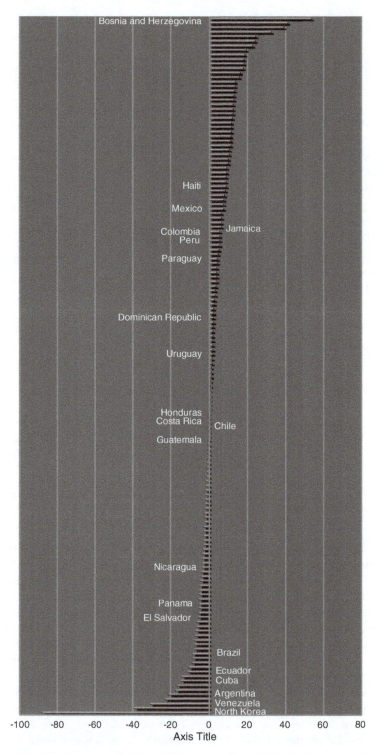

Figure 10.2 Changes in Economic Freedom Index Scores from 2002 to 2011 (in percentage).
Source: The Heritage Foundation.

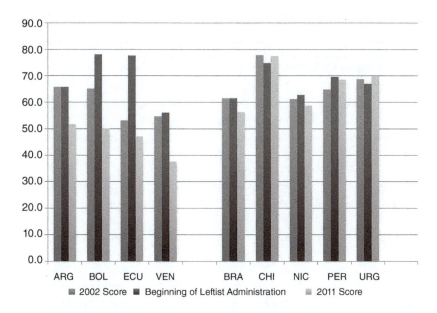

Figure 10.3 Economic Freedom Scores in Self-Declared Leftist Governments in Latin America in the 2000s. Beginning of self-declared leftist administrations: Argentina 2002 (Duhalde), Bolivia 2006 (Morales), Ecuador 2007 (Correa), Venezuela 1999 (Chávez), Brazil 2002 (Lula), Chile 2000 (Lagos, Bachelet), Nicaragua 2007 (Ortega), Perú 2001 (Toledo, García), Uruguay 2005 (Tabaré Vázque). *Source:* Economic Freedom Index Scores.

left, preserved many aspects of the Washington Consensus (fiscal discipline, streamlined budgets, enhanced tax collections, competitive exchange rates, openness to FDI, protection of property rights) and moved forward on some key aspects of second-generation reforms, though not all. Kurtz and Brooks have called this economic openness combined with state-centric investments in human capital and industrial policies "embedded neoliberalism."[71]

Chávez, in contrast, preserved far fewer Washington Consensus policies, even reversing key tenets (e.g., by expanding state ownership of utilities, banks, lands, shipping, food, and energy sectors), and showed less interest than Lula in most second-generation reforms (e.g., independent central banks, efficiency in social spending, savings during boom times, checks and balances on the Executive branch). In fact, Chávez introduced policies that are at odds with both lists: enhancing the power of the executive branch, financing cooperatives rather than privately owned business, fiscal profligacy, restrictions on businesses, price and exchange rate controls, overreliance on commodity exports.

In short, it could be said that the moderate left preserved some though not all aspects of the Washington Consensus and adopted some though not all elements of second-generation reforms, whereas the radical left adopted even fewer items from either list. Having said that, there remains enough variation within each group (in terms of approaches to monetary policy, exchange rates, debt, deficits, and trade) to suggest that even this dichotomous classification of the left is not always useful.[72]

And while it might be too soon to offer judgments, the evidence thus far seems to be that the moderate left achieved faster poverty- and inequality-alleviation outcomes than the non-left, and possibly even the radical left (after controlling for the effects of the commodity boom).[73] The reason for the superior performance of the moderate left relative to the

Table 10.1 Moderate and Radical Lefts in Relation to the Washington Consensus and Second Generation Reforms

Policy Recommendation★	Moderate Left★★ (Brazil)	Radical Left★★ (Venezuela)
Original Washington Consensus		
Fiscal discipline	Yes	Lax
Reorientation of public expenditures	Yes: less emphasis on subsidizing the inefficient private sector	Pro-cyclical spending
Positive, moderate, and market-determined real interest rate	Somewhat	Negative real interest rates
Tax reforms	Enhance collection	Raise taxes on business
Unified and competitive exchange rate	Yes	No
Trade Liberalization	Yes	Yes, but with exchange rate controls
Openness to DFI	Yes	Modest (mostly for state-owned multinationals)
Privatization	Some	Some reversals
De-regulation	Minimal	Increased regulations
Secure property rights	Yes	Not a priority; discussion of "social property;" confiscations increasingly common
Second Generation or "Enhanced" Reforms (selected items)★		
Institutions of governance and representation	Modest enhancements	Lessen checks and balances on the executive branch
Anti-corruption (strengthening autonomy of courts and watchdog institutions)	Modest	Low priority; undermine the autonomy of courts; antagonize the free press
Flexible labor markets	Not a priority	Protections for government-friendly unions
Adherence to WTO discipline	Yes	Not a priority
Prudent capital account opening	Yes	Yes
Independent central banks/ inflation targeting	Yes	Not a priority
Increase investments in human capital (education, health, social security)	Yes	Yes
Increase efficiency of investments in human capital	Modest	Not a priority
Targeted poverty reduction programs	Reliance on conditional-cash transfers	Reliance on traditional redistributive policies
Investments in infrastructure	Significant	Not a priority

Policy Recommendation*	Moderate Left** (Brazil)	Radical Left** (Venezuela)
Export diversification	Modest, with some successes (Embraer, Vale)	Not a priority
Support small and medium-size firms	Modest forms of microcredit	Cooperatives (with participation of state or state-sponsored NGOs)

* List of policies drawn from: Nancy Birdsall, Augusto de la Torre, and Rachel Menezes, "Washington Contentious: Economic Policies for Social Equity in Latin America"(Washington, DC: Carnegie Endowment for International Peace and Inter-American Dialogue, 2001); Nancy Birdsall, Augusto de la Torre, and Rachel Menezes, *Fair Growth: Economic Policies for Latin America's Poor and Middle-Income Majority* (Washington, DC: Center for Global Development and Inter-American Foundation, 2008); Moisés Naím, "Latin America: The Second Stage of Reform," *Journal of Democracy* 5, 4 (1994); Manuel Pastor and Carol Wise, "The Politics of Second-Generation Reform," *Journal of Democracy* 10, 3 (1999); Dani Rodrik, *One Economics, Many Recipes: Globalization, Institutions, and Economic Growth* (Princeton, NJ: Princeton University Press, 2007); The Center for Global Development Task Force, "Helping Reforms Deliver Growth in Latin America: A Framework for Analysis," in *Growing Pains in Latin America,* ed. Liliana Rojas-Suárez (Washington, DC: Center for Global Development, 2009); Javier Santiso, Jean Grugel, and Pía Riggirorzzi, "The End of the Embrace? Neoliberalism and Alternatives to Neoliberalism in Latin America, in *Governance After Neoliberalism in Latin America,* eds. Jean Grugel and Pía Riggirozzi (New York: Palgrave/Macmillan, 2009); Philip Oxhorn and Graciela Ducantenzeiler, "Economic Reform and Democratization in Latin America," in *What Kind of Democracy? What Kind of Market? Latin America in the Age of Neoliberalism,* eds. Peter Oxhorn and Graciela Ducatenzeiler (University Park: The Pennsylvania State Univeristy Press, 1998); John Williamson (2003).

**Country experience drawn from Peter R. Kingstone and Aldo F. Ponce, "From Cardoso to Lula: The Triumph of Pragmatism," and Javier Corrales, "The Repeating Revolution: Chávez's New Politics and Old Economics," in *Leftist Governments in Latin America, Successes and Shortcomings* eds. Kurt Weyland, Raúl L. Madrid, and Wendy Hunter (New York: Cambridge University Press, 2010).

non-left and the radical left has to do with differences in social spending. Relative to the non-left, the moderate left invested more in social spending, and, relative to the radical left, it targeted spending more effectively to groups in need, offered a more optimal combination of conditional cash transfers plus education and health spending, and is more transparent in how it spends.[74] This may explain why, by the late 2000s, the electoral appeal of radical leftist candidates relative to moderate candidates began to dwindle.[75]

Regardless of the political category—market-oriented, moderate left, or radical left—Latin American governments in the 2000s hardly advanced neoliberalism, certainly compared to the 1990s. Revenues from privatization, for instance, dropped sharply across the region after 1999, a consequence of a major slow-down in privatizations (in contrast to other regions such as Asia and Africa, where privatizations actually accelerated in the 2000s). In fact, privatizations were no longer a central component of IMF programs in Latin America, which is remarkable considering how central they were in most IMF programs of the 1980s and 1990s.[76] Even ruling parties that were sympathetic to neoliberalism on the campaign trail introduced only modest neoliberal reforms.

Why this slowdown? Two main explanations can be offered. One applies to all countries in the region, the other, to just a few but important cases. The explanation that applies to the region as a whole focuses on the United States and, more important, China. After 9/11 and the return of economic growth in the world by 2002, the United States became focused on the war of terror. This focus came with an opportunity cost: less concern with advancing the Washington Consensus.[77] In terms of economic policy, the only issue that was a major concern for the United States was negotiating bilateral free-trade agreements. Other than that, the United States cared less about microeconomic conditions in the region.

But it was China's new economic relationship with the region, more so than U.S. declining interest, that proved more decisive in slowing down the advance of neoliberalism. In the 2000s, China developed a huge appetite for Latin American imports, giving a major boost to economies everywhere, but concentrated mostly on agricultural and primary commodity export sectors.[78] From a growth and fiscal perspective, this booming trade with China was enormously positive, leading to record-level growth rates, spending rates, and debt reduction across the region.[79] However, from a market-oriented reform perspective, this trade had a negative impact: by easing fiscal pressures on governments, trade with China eliminated incentives for microeconomic reforms. To use Kurt Weyland's terminology,[80] trade with China took Latin American governments away from the "domain of losses," and thus from a position of needing to reform. Why bother with politically difficult productivity-enhancing reforms in stagnant sectors when the productivity growth in the agricultural sector was generating so much economic dynamism and fiscal income? Thus, Latin America in the 2000s experienced the paradox of impressive growth rates *with* unimpressive productivity gains across all but the primary commodity sectors.[81] This is reflected in export figures. For the region as a whole, exports of primary commodities grew on average by a spectacular 11.4 percent annually in 2000–2009, compared to 2.6 percent in the neoliberal era of 1990–1999. Manufacturing exports moved in the exact opposition direction: they grew by 5.3 percent in the 2000–2009 period, a major drop from 14.7 percent in the neoliberal era.[82] As insufficient as neoliberalism might have been in diversifying South America's economy, the post-neoliberal era seems to have been more dependency-generating.

The explanation for the neoliberal slowdown that applies to some cases has to do with "ISI legacies." Countries that had better experiences with state-led industrial policies prior to the 1980s never totally dismantled such policies in the 1990s, and thus found it easy to reinforce state-based industrial policies in the 2000s.[83] The export boom of the 2000s gave the state enough revenues, and it seems that prior ISI-related sectors were able to appropriate much of it. This argument best applies to Brazil, and to some extent, Colombia and Uruguay.

Another key question is what explains the moderation of leftist governments, where they acted with moderation. For instance, why did Lula, who campaigned prior to 2002 on a platform that was not that different from Chávez's in 1998, retain so many aspects of the Washington Consensus?[84] Various answers have been offered: Latin American countries are more dependent on foreign capital, or foreign markets for the creation of jobs, and this creates pressure to comply with market demands.[85] Also, in Corrales (2008) I argued that countries that experienced greater macro-/micro-economic troubles and greater party-dealignment/fragmentation during the implementation stage tended to have more radical governments, facing fewer checks and balances, and this trio of calamities doesn't apply to all countries.[86] Weyland suggests that a more important variable was whether the country was highly dependent on land-based resource exports, oil and gas.[87] Table 10.2 shows how these arguments apply to the various cases of leftism in Latin American in the 2000s.

Table 10.2 also shows key exceptions. Nicaragua, for instance, saw the rise of a radical-leftist government without natural resource dependence; Peru had moderate-left government even with one of the region's most significant episodes of party system collapse; and Uruguay had displayed one of the region's greatest dependencies on agro-exports.

Table 11.2 Explanatory Variables and Varieties of Leftist Governments in Latin America in the 2000s

	Macro and Micro Problems Prior to 2002	Party Fragmentation and Party Dealignment	Natural Resource Dependence (for fiscal revenues)
Radical Cases (Ven, Bol, Ecu) Exception: Nic	Severe	High	High
Semi-Radical Cases (Arg)	Severe	Medium	Medium
Semi-Moderate Case (Bra)	Medium	Low	Low
Moderate Case (Chi) Exceptions: Per and Uru	Low	Low	Low

In short, the field has not been able to offer a unified, one size-fits-all theory to explain the origins and actual policies of self-declared leftist governments in the region, although it is coming closer to a consensus that moderation—on both the left and the right—offers better prospects for institutional development and equity.

VII. Conclusion

Today, neoliberalism is neither triumphant nor dead. While the neoliberal reforms of the 1990s missed many promised outcomes, at least universally, neoliberalism did not emerge from this period mortally wounded. During its heyday, neoliberalism was able to demonstrate the validity of some of its tenets: fiscal discipline and low inflation can be pro-growth and progressive; intra-firm competition and secured property rights generate efficiencies that liberate resources as well as trust-based institutions (independent Central Banks, stronger contract regimes) that help build communities; trade openness introduces competitive forces and price reductions that please consumers; and the price system is an unrivaled mechanism for discerning what consumers demand, and this information-generation feature endemic to market economies is both an economic and a democratic asset. Furthermore, recent historical research boosts some basic neoliberal claims. For instance, there is evidence that during periods of intense protectionism, not just in the 1960s and 1970s, but also between 1860 and 1914, when Latin America had some of the highest tariffs in the world, economic performance was suboptimal relative to other regions, and the higher the tariff rate, the worse the performance.[88] When looking at Latin America, therefore, neoliberals have an arsenal of data and historical evidence to support their claims.

However, it is not clear that neoliberalism, in its most fundamentalist version, offers today the best answers to some of the new more serious developmental challenges that Latin America confronts. In addition to the well-known and discussed problem of income inequality, these challenges include:

1. the middle-income trap—the fact that labor costs in the region are too high to compete globally with low-cost manufacturers (e.g., China), but skill levels are not high enough to compete with the more advanced capitalist countries;[89]
2. the commodity-dependence curse—the fact that the region, especially South America, has become too dependent on commodity exports, due to natural comparative advantages and the rise of trade with China, which discourages export diversification;[90]
3. the propensity toward asset bubbles, especially now that the region is experiencing an avalanche of foreign exchange, which might require more sophisticated and

complex forms of Central Bank interventions in the economy beyond traditional inflation-targeting;[91]

4. the productivity gap—the idea that the largest components of the economy—manufacturing, services, small business firms, and informal sectors—display low levels of productivity and demand for high-skill labor, which causes a drag on growth;[92]

5. uneven levels of state presence within any given country, which precludes nations from mobilizing resources, solving coordination problems, consolidating the rule of law, and addressing negative externalities;[93]

6. the institution-structure trap—the idea that institutions do not easily change reality, but instead end up reflecting and thus reinforcing the very same reality that they seek to change.

Today, mainstream scholars seem to argue that solutions to these region-specific and general development challenges cannot rely exclusively on laissez-faire principles, free trade policies, and cookie-cutter/one-size-fits-all prescriptions, as neoliberals tended to suggest in the late 1980s. The new thinking is that some form of state involvement is necessary, and that underperforming cases and sectors require their own tailor-made approaches.[94]

Thus, given the nature of the challenges in the region and the trends in political economy, neoliberalism may never reign supreme again. Yet neoliberalism will never whither entirely. Neoliberalism will remain relevant if for no other reason than for its power as a critical theory. Like few other schools, neoliberals offer some of the most forceful arguments about the frequency, causes, and impacts of state failures. Unfettered, unrestrained, unregulated states lead to unwelcome abuses. Protectionism leads to diversion of talent and assets into unproductive activities. State-business associations carry a high risk of collusion, and thus, of subverting the public good. Political competition continuously impels states to stray from impartiality unless autonomous and independent institutions are strong enough to watch over politicians. And democracies with high inflation and weak firms are prone to authoritarian reversals.[95]

As long as there exist advocates for state involvement, there will also exist neoliberals ready to assert the dangers of statist excesses and the virtues of competitive firms. Neoliberals will continue to play a role in development thinking, even if they never dominate policy-making again.

Notes

1 Friedrich von Hayek, *The Road to Serfdom* (Chicago: University of Chicago Press, 1944).

2 See Jagadeesh Gokhale, "Globalization: Curse or Cure?" *Policy Analysis* 659 (Washington, DC: Cato Institute, 2010).

3 See Center for Global Development Task Force, "Helping Reforms Deliver Growth in Latin America: A Framework for Analysis," in *Growing Pains in Latin America: An Economic Growth Framework as Applied to Brazil, Colombia, Costa Rica, Mexico, and Peru,* Liliana Rojas-Suarez, ed., (Washington, DC, Center for Global Development, 2009).

4 Milton Friedman with the assistance of Rose D. Friedman, *Capitalism and Freedom* (Chicago: University of Chicago Press, 1962).

5 Sheri Berman, "The Primacy of Economics versus the Primacy of Politics," *Perspectives on Politics* 7, 3 (September 2009): 572.

6 On firms and developmental states, see Peter Evans and Dietrich Rueschmeyer, "The State and Economic Transformation: Toward an Analysis of the Conditions Underlying Effective Intervention," in *Bringing the State Back In,* eds. Peter Evans, Dietrich Rueschemeyer, and Theda Skocpol (Cambridge: Cambridge University Press, 1985).

7   For a theory on the importance of impartiality in governance, see Bo Rothstein and Jan Teorell, "What Is Quality of Government? A Theory of Impartial Government Institutions," *Governance* 21, 2 (April 2008).

8   Ludwig von Mises, *Bureaucracy* (Yale University Press, 1944).

9   Yair Aharoni, "State-Owned Enterprise: An Agent Without a Principal," in *Public Enterprises in Less Developed Countries*, ed. L.P. Jones (Cambridge, UK: Cambridge University Press, 1981); Ravi Ramamurti, "Controlling State-Owned Enterprises" in *Privatization and Control of State-Owned Enterprises*, eds. Ravi Ramamurti and Raymond Vernon (Washington, DC: The World Bank, 1991).

10   Ronald Coase, "The Nature of the Firm," *Economica* 4, 16 (1937); and "The Problem of Social Cost," *Journal of Law and Economics* (1960).

11   Robert Gilpin with the assistance of Jean M. Gilpin, *The Political Economy of International Relations* (Princeton, NJ: Princeton University Press, 1987), 22.

12   Joseph Schumpeter, *Capitalism, Socialism and Democracy* (New York: Harper & Row 1975, c1950).

13   Gilpin, *International Relations*, 23.

14   Dimitri Vayanos and Paul Woolley, "An Institutional Theory of Momentum and Reversal," London School of Economics, The Paul Woolley Centre Working Paper Series No. 17, FMG Discussion Paper 666 (January 2011).

15   Raúl Prebisch, *The Economic Development of Latin America and its Principal Problems* (New York: United Nations, 1950).

16   For the intellectual history of this model of development, see Joseph L. Love, "The Rise and Decline of Economic Structuralism in Latin America: New Dimensions," *Latin American Research Review* 40, 3 (October 2005).

17   Anne O. Krueger, "The Political Economy of the Rent-Seeking Society," *American Economic Review* 64 (1974): 291–303.

18   Another boost was the awarding of a Nobel Prize in 1991 to Ronald Coase.

19   Jorge I. Domínguez, ed., *Technopols: Freeing Politics and Markets in Latin America in the 1990s* (University Park: Pennsylvania State University, 1997). Examples include Pedro Aspe in Mexico, Hernando de Soto in Peru, Guillermo Perry in Colombia, Domingo Cavallo in Argentina, Ricardo Hausmann in Venezuela. It also included intellectuals who used to be on the left (e.g., Alejandro Foxley in Chile, Fernando Henrique Cardoso in Brazil, Mario Vargas Llosa in Peru).

20   Anil Hira, *Ideas and Economic Policy in Latin America: Regional, National, and Organizational Case Studies* (Westport, CT: Praeger, 1998).

21   The collapse of African economies, though less severe than the Latin American collapse, also played a role, with economists and non-economists blaming domestic policies, especially state interventions, for the continent's crisis. See World Bank (IBRD), *Accelerated Development in Sub-Saharan Africa: An Agenda for Action* ("The Berg Report"), Report No. 3358 (Washington, DC: IBRD, 1981); also, Robert Bates, *Markets and States in Tropical Africa* (Berkeley: University of California Press, 1981).

22   Jeffry A. Frieden, *Global Capitalism: Its Fall and Rise in the Twentieth Century* (New York: W.W. Norton, 2006), 392.

23   World Bank, *The East Asian Miracle: Economic Growth and Public Policy* (Washington, DC: The World Bank, 1993).

24   Barbara Stallings, "Politics and Economic Crisis: A Comparative Study of Chile, Peru and Colombia," in *Economic Crisis and Policy Choice*, ed. Joan Nelson (Princeton: Princeton University Press, 1991), 113–169.

25   John Rapley, *Understanding Development: Theory and Practice in the Third World* (Boulder: Lynne Rienner, 1990).

26   Thomas J. Biersteker, "Reducing the Role of the State in the Economy: A Conceptual Exploration of IMF and World Bank Prescriptions," *International Studies Quarterly* 34, 4 (1990): 477–492.

27   Charles Gore, "The Rise and Fall of the Washington Consensus as a Paradigm for Developing Countries," *World Development* 28, 3 (2000): 789–804.

28   Sebastian Edwards, *Crisis and Reform in Latin America: From Despair to Hope* (Washington, DC and New York: World Bank and Oxford University Press, 1995), Chapter 2.

29   Kurt Weyland, *The Politics of Market Reforms in Fragile Democracies: Argentina, Brazil, Peru, and Venezuela* (Princeton: Princeton University Press, 2002).

30 Judith A. Teichman, *The Politics of Freeing Markets in Latin America: Chile, Argentina, and Mexico* (Chapel Hill: University of North Carolina Press, 2001).

31 Joan Nelson, *Fragile Coalitions: The Politics of Economic Adjustment* (New Brunswick, NJ: Transaction Press, 1989); Stephan Haggard and Steven B. Webb, eds., *Voting for Reform: Democracy, Political Liberalization, and Economic Adjustment* (New York: Oxford University Press, 1994).

32 Barbara Geddes, "The Politics of Economic Liberalization," *Latin American Research Review* 30, 2 (1995): 195–214.

33 Guillermo O'Donnell, "Delegative Democracy," *Journal of Democracy* 5, 1 (1994): 55–69.

34 Alfred P. Montero, "From Democracy to Development: The Political Economy of Post-Neoliberal Reform in Latin America," *Latin American Research Review* 40, 2 (June 2005).

35 Mancur Olson, *Power and Prosperity: Outgrowing Communist and Capitalist Dictatorships* (Oxford University Press, 2000); Jorge I. Domínguez, "Free Politics and Free Markets in Latin America," *Journal of Democracy* 9, 4 (October 1998): 70–84; Kurt Weyland, "Neoliberalism and Democracy in Latin America: A Mixed Record," *Latin American Politics and Society* 46, 1 (2004): 135–157.

36 Alex Cukierman and Mariano Tommasi, "When Does it Take a Nixon to Go to China?" *The American Economic Review* 88, 1 (March 2009): 180–197.

37 María Victoria Murillo, *Political Competition, Partisanship, and Policy Making in Latin American Public Utilities* (New York: Cambridge University Press, 2009).

38 See Witold J. Henisz, Bennet A. Zelner, and Mauro F. Guillén, "The Worldwide Diffusion of Market-Oriented Infrastructure Reform, 1977–1999," *American Sociological Review* 70, 871 (2005). I am grateful to Evelyne Huber for suggesting this comparison with Europe.

39 Katrina Burgess, *Parties and Unions in the New Global Economy* (Pittsburgh: University of Pittsburgh Press, 2004); María Victoria Murillo, *Labor Unions, Partisan Coalitions, and Market Reforms in Latin America* (New York: Cambridge University Press, 2001).

40 Stephan Haggard and Robert R. Kaufman, *The Political Economy of Democratic Transitions* (Princeton: Princeton University Press, 1995); Javier Corrales, *Presidents Without Parties* (University Park: Pennsylvania State University Press, 2002).

41 Peter R. Kingstone, *Crafting Coalitions for Reform: Business Preferences, Political Institutions, and Neoliberal Reform in Brazil* (University Park: Pennsylvania State University Press, 1999).

42 Karen L. Remmer, "Elections and Economics in Contemporary Latin America," in *Post-Stabilization Policies in Latin America: Competition, Transition, Collapse*, eds. Carol Wise and Riordan Roett (Washington, DC: Brookings Institution Press, 2003).

43 For a summary of these critiques, see Alastair Greig, David Hulme, and Mark Turner, *Challenging Global Inequality: Development Theory and Practice in the 21st Century* (New York: Palgrave/Macmillan 2007).

44 Carmen Pagés, ed., *The Age of Productivity: Transforming Economies from the Bottom Up* (Washington, DC: Inter-American Development Bank, 2010); Eva Paus, "Productivity Growth in Latin America: The Limits of Neoliberal Reforms," *World Development* 32, 3 (2004): 427–445.

45 William Easterly, *The White Man's Burden: Why the West's Efforts to Aid the Rest Have Done So Much Ill and So Little Good* (New York: Penguin Press, 2006); Judith A. Teichman, *The Politics of Freeing Markets in Latin America: Chile, Argentina, and Mexico* (Chapel Hill: University of Carolina Press, 2001).

46 For summaries of these debates, see Javier Corrales, "Market Reforms," in *Constructing Democratic Governance in Latin America*, 2nd edition, eds. Jorge I. Domínguez and Michael Shifter (Baltimore: The Johns Hopkins University Press, 2003); Javier Corrales, "The Backlash against Market Reforms in Latin America," in *Constructing Democratic Governance in Latin America*, 3rd Edition, eds. Jorge I. Domínguez and Michael Shifter (Baltimore: Johns Hopkins University Press, 2008).

47 Andy Baker, *The Market and the Masses in Latin America: Policy Reform and Consumption in Liberalizing Economies* (New York: Cambridge University Press, 2009).

48 Kurt Weyland, "Swallowing the Bitter Pill: Sources of Popular Support for Neoliberal Reform in Latin America," *Comparative Political Studies* 31, 5 (October 1998): 539–568.

49 Susan Stokes, *Mandates and Democracy: Neoliberalism by Surprise* (New York: Cambridge University Press, 2001).

50 Evelyne Huber and Frederick Solt, "Successes and Failures of Neoliberalism," *Latin American Research Review* 39, 3 (2004): 150–164.

51 Montero, "From Democracy to Development."

52 Frances Hagopian, "Conclusions: Government Performance, Political Representation, and Public Perceptions of Contemporary Democracy in Latin America," in *The Third Wave of Democratization in Latin America: Advances and Setbacks*, eds. Frances Hagopian and Scott P. Mainwaring (New York: Cambridge University Press, 2005).

53 For a review of these arguments, see Jeromin Zettelmeyer, "Growth and Reforms in Latin America: A Survey of Facts and Arguments" (Washington, DC: International Monetary Fund, 2006).

54 Independent Evaluation Office, "Report on the Evaluation of the Role of the IMF in Argentina, 1991–2001" (Washington, DC: International Monetary Fund, 2004).

55 Independent Evaluation Office, "Report of the External Evaluation of the Independent Evaluation Office" (Washington, DC: International Monetary Fund, 2006).

56 For the debate on whether Latin Americas's better performance was the result of "strong fundamentals" or to pre-crisis spending, see José Antonio Ocampo, "Latin America and the Global Financial Crisis," *Cambridge Journal of Economics* 33, 4 (2009): 703–724. For the region's performance in reducing poverty and inequality, see Luis F. López-Calva and Nora Lustig, *Declining Inequality in Latin America: A Decade of Progress?* (Washington, DC: Brookings Institution Press, 2010); Evelyne Huber, Thomas Mustillo, and John D. Stephens, "Politics of Social Spending in Latin America," *The Journal of Politics* 70, 2 (2008).

57 Douglass North, *Institutions, Institutional Change, and Economic Performance* (New York: Cambridge University Press, 1990).

58 World Bank, *World Development Report 2002: Building Institutions for Markets* (Washington, DC: The World Bank, 2001); Inter-American Development Bank, *The Politics of Policies: Economic and Social Progress in Latin America 2006 Report* (Cambridge, MA and Washington, DC: Harvard University David Rockefeller Center for Latin American Studies and the Inter-American Development Bank, 2005).

59 John Williamson, "Overview: An Agenda for Restarting Growth and Reform," in *After the Washington Consensus: Restarting Growth and Reform in Latin America*, eds. Pedro-Pablo Kuczynski and John Williamson (Washington DC: Institute for International Economics, 2003).

60 Economic Commission for Latin America and the Caribbean, *Economic Growth with Equity: Challenges for Latin America and the Caribbean* (Santiago: United Nations, 2007); United Nations Development Program, *Human Development Report 2003: Millenium Development Goals: A Compact Among Nations to End Human Poverty* (New York: Oxford University Press, 2003).

61 Inter-American Development Bank, *Facing Up to Inequality in Latin America, Economic and Social Progress Report, 1998–99 Report* (Washington, DC: IADB, 1999). World Bank, *World Development Report 2006: Equity and Development* (Washington, DC: World Bank, 2005).

62 Moisés Naím, "The Second Stage of Reform," *Journal of Democracy* 5, 4 (October 1994): 32–48; Manuel Pastor and Carol Wise, "The Politics of Second-Generation Reform," *Journal of Democracy* 10, 3 (July 1999): 34–48.

63 Javier Santiso, *Latin America's Political Economy of the Possible: Beyond Good Revolutionaries and Free-Marketeers* (Cambridge, MA: The MIT Press, 2006).

64 United Nations Development Program, *Regional Human Development Report for Latin America and the Caribbean 2010* (New York: UNDP, 2010).

65 Eduardo Lora, "La Revolución Silenciosa de las Instituciones y la Estabilidad Macroeconómica," Working Paper Number 649 (Washington, DC: Inter-American Development Bank, November 2008); Eduardo Lora, ed., *The State of State Reform in Latin America* (Washington, DC: Inter-American Development Bank, 2006).

66 Nancy Birdsall, Augusto de la Torre, and Felipe Valencia Caicedo, "The Washington Consensus: Assessing a Damaged Brand," Policy Research Working Paper 5316 (Washington, DC: World Bank and Center for Global Development, May 2010). See also Zettelmeyer 2006.

67 Jorge G. Castañeda, "Where Do We Go from Here?" in *Leftovers: Tales of the Latin American Left*, eds. Jorge G. Castañeda and Marco A. Morales (New York: Routledge, 2008).

68 For an overview of these factors, see Eduardo Silva, *Challenging Neoliberalism in Latin America* (New York: Cambridge University Press, 2009). On the change in the discourse of politicians, see Marco A. Morales, "Have Latin American Americans Turned Left?" in Jorge G. Castañeda and Marco A. Morales, *Leftovers*.

69 For an example of scholarship offering competing and overlapping explanations, for the same country (in this case Bolivia), cf. Håvard Haarstad and Vibeke Andersson, "Backlash

Reconsidered: Neoliberalism and Popular Mobilization in Bolivia," *Latin American Politics and Society* 51, 4 (2009): 1–28 and Moisés Arce and Roberta Rice, "Societal Protest in Post-Stabilization Bolivia," *Latin American Research Review* 44, 1 (2009): 88–101.

70 Many scholars are uncomfortable with this over-dichotomization of the Latin American left in the 2000s, arguing that each case has its unique (set of) salient features, as well as overlapping features with other cases, rather than just one of two labels. Thus, the proliferation of labels for leftist governments in the 2000s has been inevitable: "old," "new," "renewed," "autocratic,""hybrid," "radical," "moderate," "pragmatic," "militaristic," "contestatory," "participatory," "carnivorous," "social-democratic," "globalizing," "globalophobic," "anti-American," "movement-oriented," "ethno-mobilized," "Castro-philiac," "caudillo-dependent," or "caudillo-free," etc.

71 Marcus J. Kurtz and Sarah M. Brooks, "Embedding Neoliberal Reform in Latin America," *World Politics* 60, 2 (January 2008).

72 Diana Tussie and Pablo Heidrich, "A Tale of Ecumenism and Diversity: Economic and Trade Policies of the New Left," in *Leftovers: A Tale of the Latin American Left*, ed. Jorge G. Castañeda and Marco A. Morales (New York: Routledge, 2008).

73 Nora Lustig, "Poverty, Inequality and the New Left in Latin America," Report No. 5 from the Democratic Governance and the "New Left" Project (Washington, DC: Woodrow Wilson Center, Latin America Program, October 2009).

74 Nancy Birdsall, Nora Lustig, and Darryl McLeod, "Declining Inequality in Latin America: Some Economics, Some Politics," Washington, D.C., Center for Global Development Working Paper 251 (May 2011).

75 Michael Shifter, "A Surge to the Center," *Journal of Democracy* 22, 1 (January 2011): 107–121.

76 This is taken from the anonymous paper "Privatization in the Developing World" (International Transactions).

77 For a related argument, see Laurence Whitehead, "Navigating in a Fog: Metanarrative in the Americas Today," in *Which Way Latin America? Hemispheric Politics Meets Globalization*, eds. Andrew F. Cooper and Jorge Heine (New York: United Nations University Press, 2009).

78 Chinese imports from Latin America in 2006 were concentrated on ten different sectors all of which are primary products or natural resources. See Kevin Gallagher and Roberto Porzecanski, *The Dragon in the Room: China and the Future of Latin American Industrialization* (Stanford University Press, 2010), 17–18. See also Alex E. Fernández Jilberto and Barbara Hogenboom, eds., *Latin America Facing China: South-South Relations beyond the Washington Consensus*, CEDLA Latin American Studies (Berghahn Books, 2010).

79 The most important exception was Mexico, for which China represented a serious competitor in terms of exports of manufactures into the United States.

80 Kurt Weyland, *The Politics of Market Reform in Fragile Democracies: Argentina, Brazil, Peru, and Venezuela* (Princeton: Princeton University Press, 2002).

81 Carmen Pagés, ed., *The Age of Productivity*.

82 The exception to this trend was the Central American Common Market, where manufacturing exports grew at a faster rate than primary product exports in the 2000–09 period. See ECLAC, *Latin American and the Caribbean in the World Economy, 2009–2010* (Santiago: ECLAC, 2010), Chapter 2.

83 Marcus J. Kurtz and Sarah M. Brooks, "Embedding Neoliberal Reform in Latin America," *World Politics* 60, 2 (January 2008).

84 Although Lula moderated his discourse in the last months of his campaign, he built his political career in the 1990s by being the most vociferous critic of the economic reforms of the 1990s.

85 Francisco Panizza, *Contemporary Latin America: Development and Democracy beyond the Washington Consensus* (Zed Books, 2009): 226.

86 See Gustavo A. Flores-Macías, "Statist v. Pro-Market: Explaining Leftist Governments' Economic Policies in Latin America," *Comparative Politics* 42, 4 (July 2010); Javier Corrales, "The Backlash against Market Reforms," in *Constructing Democratic Governance in Latin America*, 3rd edition, eds. Jorge I. Domínguez and Michael Shifter (Baltimore, Johns Hopkins University Press, 2008).

87 Kurt Weyland, "The Rise of Latin America's Two Lefts," *Comparative Politics* 41, 2 (January 2009).

88 John H. Coatsworth and Jeffrey G. Williamson, "The Roots of Latin American Protectionism," in *Integrating the Americas: FTAA and Beyond*, eds. Antoni Estevadeordal, Dani Rodrik, Alan M. Taylor, and Andres Velasco (Cambridge, MA: David Rockefeller Center for Latin American Studies and Harvard University Press, 2004).

89 Eva Paus, "Latin America's Middle Income Trap," *Americas Quarterly* (Winter 2011).

90 ECLAC, *Latin America and the Caribbean in the World Economy* (Santiago: ECLAC, 2010), Chapter 2; David R. Mares, "Resource Nationalism and Energy Security in Latin America: Implications for Global Oil Supplies," *Energy Forum Working Paper* (Houston: James A. Baker III Institute for Public Policy, Rice University, January 2010).

91 Mauricio Cárdenas and Eduardo Levy-Yeyati, "Latin America Economic Perspectives: Shifting Gears in an Age of Heightened Expectations," (Washington, DC: Brookings Institution: Latin America Initiative, 2011).

92 Carmen Pagés, ed., *The Age of Productivity.*

93 Javier Corrales, "Markets, States, and Neighbors," *Americas Quarterly* (Spring 2009).

94 See Matthew M. Taylor, "Development Economics in the Wake of the Washington Consensus: From Smith to Smithereens?" *International Political Science Review* 29, 5 (2008).

95 See Morton H. Halperin, Joseph T. Siegle, Michael M. Weinstein, *The Democracy Advantage: How Democracies Promote Prosperity and Peace,* Revised Edition (New York: Routledge, 2010).

11

DECLINING INEQUALITY IN LATIN AMERICA

Some Economics, Some Politics

Nancy Birdsall, Nora Lustig, and Darryl McLeod[1]

Latin America is known to be the region of the world where income inequality is among the highest. Its high inequality has been invoked by economists as an explanation for its low rates of growth compared to East Asia, for its poor record on education given its per capita income, and for the volatility of its macroeconomic policies—the best-known example being its governments' periodic recourse to inflationary policies to cope with political demands for greater social justice (Inter-American Development Bank, 1999; Birdsall and Jaspersen, 1997; Sachs, 1989; Dornbusch and Edwards, 1991). High inequality has also been linked to its long history of political instability, authoritarian regimes and civil strife. Historians attribute its high, persistent and region-wide inequality (in virtually all countries of the region) to its unfortunate past—in which colonial victors exploited indigenous labor or imported slaves to enrich themselves via exploitation of the region's natural resource wealth—its gold, silver, tin, and copper—and its comparative advantage in plantation crops such as sugar (Engerman and Sokoloff, 1997). In a typical tale of the curse of natural resources, the result is a high concentration of income of a tiny ruling elite that had no interest in delivering such basic services as education and health to the poor majority, or in creating institutions of government accountable to the great majority of people.

Thus the prevailing view of economists has been that in much of Latin America the economics of initial comparative advantage generated a political dynamic that in turn undermined the region's long-run economic potential and probably slowed the emergence of accountable and responsive democracies as well. Or put another way, economics explains the politics which explains the economics.

But now new research by economists suggests a change. In the last decade, inequality (and the poverty that has accompanied it) has been declining in 13 of the region's countries (out of 17 for which comparable data are available), including all the larger ones (see Figure 11.1).[2]

In this chapter we discuss the possible causes—economic and political—of these inequality declines, and their implications for whether the trend will be sustained. We first summarize findings on the decline of inequality and its causes. We then present and discuss an assessment of how the type of political regime matters and why. The latter is followed by a brief discussion of the relationship between changes in inequality and changes in the size of the middle class in the region. We conclude with some questions about whether and how changes in income distribution and in middle-class economic power will affect the politics

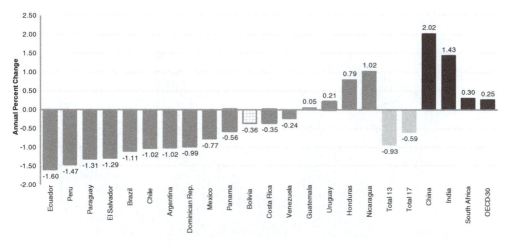

Figure 11.1 Change in Gini Coefficients for Latin America: 2000–2008. *Source:* Updated from Lopez-Calva, Lustig and Ortiz (2011). Based on SEDLAC (CEDLAS and The World Bank), August 2010 (http://sedlac.eco....unlp.edu.ar/eng/) *Note:* The bars in grey mean that the change was not statistically significant.

of distribution in the future: Will political changes help lock in recent advances against Latin America's long-standing pathology of high and stubborn inequality?

High Inequality Finally Declining: Economic and Political Causes

Almost all countries in Latin America have high income inequality compared to countries in other regions (with the possible exception of some countries in sub-Saharan Africa, where only a few countries have relatively good data) and higher than predicted inequality given their income per capita (Figure 11.2).

The region's high inequality is due in large part to the very high concentration of income at the top of the distribution. Dropping the top 10 percent of households in income per capita from the distributions in many countries of the region would make their Gini coefficients similar to that in the United States (Figure 11.3).[3] Moreover, inequality in the region and its concentration at the top is likely to be even higher than that measured in household surveys, both because of underreporting of income especially at the top (Székely and Hilgert, 1999; Alvaredo and Piketty, 2010) and because most household surveys collect primarily labor income, not property income or income from financial assets.[4]

Inequality did decline in some countries of the region during the good years of the 1970s, prior to the debt crisis and lost decade of the 1980s. But inequality rose in the tough years of the 1980s; Lustig (1995) reports that in most countries the share of income of not only the bottom but of the middle as well fell, while the share of the top ten percent grew. And inequality continued to rise in the 1990s as most economies recovered (Gasparini and Lustig, 2010).

Regarding the impact of market-oriented reforms on inequality, a detailed review of this vast literature goes beyond the scope of this chapter. Morley (2001) does such a review and concludes "... that work shows that the recent[5] reforms have had a negative but small regressive impact on inequality mainly because many of the individual reforms had offsetting effects. Trade and tax reform have been unambiguously regressive, but opening up the

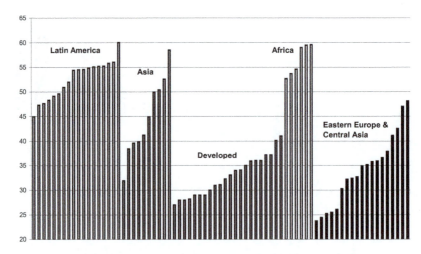

Figure 11.2 Gini Coefficients for Countries Around the World. *Source:* Gasparini and Lustig (2010). *Note:* Each bar represents the Gini coefficient for the distribution of household per capita income in a given country (last available observation in period 1995–2005).

capital account is progressive" (Abstract). Better management of macroeconomic policies—fiscal, monetary and exchange rate—was a good thing for growth and for reducing poverty, the latter since the poor were badly hurt by earlier bouts of inflation and frequent economic crises.[6] But this consensus is about the benefit of ending inflation for the poor; on the effects of the Washington Consensus policies on inequality there is less agreement.

The decline in inequality across most countries since the early 2000s thus has the markings of a breakthrough. The decline has been measurable and substantial in economic terms

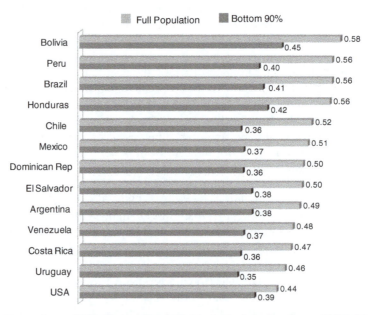

Figure 11.3 Comparison of 90% Gini vs. Total Gini in Latin America. *Source:* SEDLAC (CEDLAS and the World Bank) and U.S. Census Bureau, Income Inequality, Historical Table F-7, see also Inter-American D. *Note:* From IDB calculations based on household surveys.

in at least ten countries with different political systems and styles and approaches to social policy—including Argentina, Bolivia, Brazil, Chile, El Salvador, Mexico, Peru and Venezuela. Inequality declined in countries that enjoyed high growth thanks to a benign external environment (with higher commodity prices and lower interest rates) such as Argentina, Chile and Peru and in countries where economic growth was lackluster such as Brazil and Mexico.[7]

As shown in the country studies for Argentina, Brazil, Mexico and Peru included in Lopez-Calva and Lustig (2010), two key factors have mattered: the decline in the premium to skills (in effect to higher education)[8] and more active and progressive social policies including targeted spending in the four countries (in particular, in Argentina, Brazil and Mexico) benefiting a large proportion (as high as two thirds in Mexico; see Lustig, Pessino and Scott, 2011) of households at the bottom of the income distribution (households with income per capita below US$2.50 a day).[9] The decline in the premium to skills seems to be mainly the result of the expansion of basic education during the last couple of decades;[10] it might also be a consequence of the petering out of the one-time unequalizing effect of skill-biased technical change in the 1990s associated with the opening up of trade and investment. In any case, in the race between skill-biased technical change and educational upgrading, in the past ten years the latter has taken the lead.[11]

In some ways those are proximate causes of the decline; noneconomists might justifiably ask about the political dynamics underlying the greater access to higher levels of education and the progressive social policies.

Consider first education. Acemoglu and Robinson (2010) note that in the mature Western economies, the expansion of education in the 19th century followed democratization and its consolidation (Lindert and Williamson, 2001, and Lindert, 2004, make that case for the United States). Of course, democratization in currently advanced economies can also be associated with other changes that have not historically been associated with inequality decline in Latin America, such as increases in the share of wages in national income (which Rodrik, 1997, shows tend to follow democratization), and the creation of labor market institutions including unions that are associated with that rise in wage share.[12] In contrast, in the cases of Mexico and Peru, the decline in inequality has coincided with a period of weakening labor market institutions.

At the same time, it may be that what political scientists refer to as "consolidated democracy" is still far off in much of Latin America—including Peru, Bolivia, and certainly Guatemala. Instead, increasing access to education, at least at the primary and secondary level, could be viewed as a long-term trend common throughout the region and indeed throughout the developing world. That would suggest that it is not primarily democratization that increased education (indeed the increasing trend persisted during the 1980s military period in Brazil, Chile and Argentina) but the participation of Latin America in a worldwide trend reflecting changing global norms in the post-World War II period (Figure 11.4). In terms of increasing access to schooling, Latin America has not been, over the past 50 years, exceptional; until 1995, schooling increased faster and schooling inequality declined faster in less democratic Asia and even in Africa's weak democracies, schooling access has increased remarkably in the post-war era (Clemens, 2004). In Brazil and Mexico, there was a push for basic education especially in the second half of the 1990s, and in Mexico, between 1992 and 2002 spending per primary school student rose by 63 percent (Esquivel, Lustig and Scott, 2010).[13] In addition to "enlightened leadership," this big push for education was possible because of the demographic transition—fewer and fewer children have been entering into primary school because of how the age pyramid has been shifting. However, those who

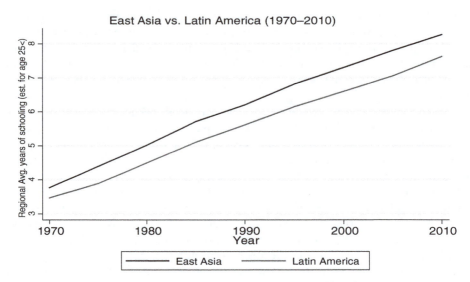

Figure 11.4 The Education Gap. *Source:* Barro and Lee (2010) available at http://www.barrolee. com/. The East Asia group excludes small island economies, Laos, and Myanmar.

benefited from the new priority on education are, of course, only now becoming adults and entering the labor force, so any effect on wage inequality of resulting shifts in returns to skills is in the future.

What about the political dynamics behind the targeted transfer programs? The first large-scale of these began in Mexico in the late 1990s with PROGRESA (later called *Oportunidades*) and spread to other countries later in that decade and especially in the 2000s. Robinson (2010, citing Scott 2008) asserts that the "spread of programs such as PRO-GRESA in Mexico is clearly related to the democratization that took place in the 1990s, which shifted political power away from corporatist groups like labor unions toward rural voters" (p. 53). He also suggests this and other redistribution programs are more likely where the poor beneficiaries for one reason or another become politically organized—so that even where clientelism still dominates (i.e., democracy is still not fully institutionalized), politics begins to benefit them directly. He contrasts the situation after the year 2000 in Brazil and Bolivia to that in Guatemala. The redistribution program Bolsa Familia in Brazil was instituted nationwide when a political party reliant on votes by the rural as much as urban poor, the PT (party of workers) under the leadership of Luis Ignacio "Lula" da Silva won the 2000 presidential election. (It was a PT governor who started such a program in the federal district of Brasilia in the 1990s.) In Bolivia, policies of redistribution took hold in 2005 when the rural party movement (the MAP) led to the election of Evo Morales. Political parties are, in short, critical in allowing the poor to solve the collective action problem they face in being adequately represented; otherwise even where they are a clear majority of citizens and voters, they will not influence policies that affect the distribution of income.

In short, a long-run increase in access to education, which finally, as the supply of educated workers began to catch up with demand, brought down what had been high returns to those most skilled; growth in some of the countries (even though still heavily commodity-based), and more progressive government spending came together after the year 2000 to reduce longstanding inequality (see Barros et al., 2010; Esquivel et al., 2010; Gasparini and Cruces, 2010a,b; Gray-Molina and Yañez, 2009; Jaramillo and Saavedra, 2010).[14] In a number of countries (but not in all) the new influence of political parties representing the poor may be what explains this shift in government spending—these came together after the year 2000 to reduce longstanding inequality in most countries of the region.

But we also want to suggest there is more to the story.

Declining Inequality and Leftist Regimes: What Really Matters?

Inequality declines in the region coincided with the election of leftist regimes starting with the 1999 election of Hugo Chavez in Venezuela and the 2000 victory of Ricardo Lagos in Chile. These elections were followed by 2003 victories of Néstor Kirchner in Argentina and Luiz Inácio "Lula" da Silva in Brazil. This swing to the left was repeated in Uruguay, Bolivia, Ecuador and Nicaragua where candidates promising a radical break with past neoliberal policies won elections in 2006 and 2007. And it continued in Paraguay (2008) and El Salvador (2009). This section reviews the criteria political scientists and economists have used to distinguish populist from non populist new Latin left regimes and provides some evidence of the efficacy and sustainability of redistributive policies.

The regimes classified as "new left" have accumulated some 34 effective policy years across eight countries, governing at one point about two-thirds of the region's population. Using the consistent survey based inequality estimates prepared by SEDLAC for 18 countries in the region covering the period from 1988 to 2008, we evaluate inequality changes for three political regime groups: left populist, social democratic and non-left governments,[15] focusing mainly on public social spending on transfers, education and health[16] as both a measure of political will and as a key redistributive mechanism.[17] Our analysis builds on Lustig and McLeod (2009) and McLeod and Lustig (2010), who show that both types of left regimes boosted social spending and reduced inequality during the decade ending in 2009, especially compared to the non-left regimes. However, the left populist group led by Argentina and Venezuela has largely just managed to bring inequality down to pre-crisis levels. Brazil and Chile on the other hand lowered inequality to historic lows during this period, lowering their respective Gini coefficients by a full six and three percentage points, respectively (see Figure 11.5). In addition, though macroeconomic indicators of external and internal balance of all the Latin America's new left regimes are benign by historical standards, since 2007 inflation in Argentina and Venezuela has risen into double digits fueled by a rapid expansion of domestic credit, perhaps an early indication of unsustainable redistributive policies.

Table 11.1 classifies the various "new left" regimes that have come to power in Latin America since the turn of the century. Though a common denominator in the rhetoric of these regimes was rejection of previous "neoliberal" or market oriented policy regimes, over time differences emerged in the methods and economic policies of these regimes. Kaufman (2007) distinguishes between "… parties that combine distributive goals with market oriented policies and those advocating a return to more traditional forms of state control and economic nationalism" (p. 24). Dornbusch and Edwards (1991) famously characterize "economic populism' as "… an approach to economics that emphasizes growth and income distribution and deemphasizes the risks of inflation and deficit finance, external constraints, and the reaction of economic agents to aggressive nonmarket policies" (p. 9). Similarly, Edwards (2009) argues that left governments in Brazil, Chile and Uruguay have found a way to marry laudable redistributive policies with sustainable market oriented economic policies, while the "left populist" regimes listed in Table 11.1 have not. Over time,

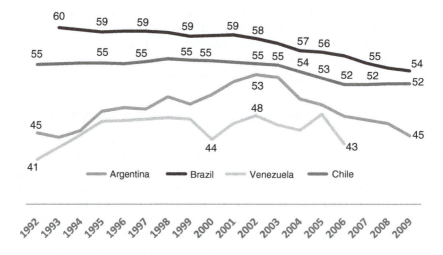

Figure 11.5 Inequality in Argentina, Brazil, Chile, and Venezuela (Gini coefficients, rounded). *Source:* McLeod and Lustig (2010). SEDLAC (CEDLAS and the World Bank) as downloaded December 2010.

Edwards argues, this difference will be manifested in slower growth and ultimately ineffective redistributive policies.[18]

From a political point of view, the fear is that the left populist regimes have become too sustainable, tampering with institutions and electoral systems in ways that work to extend their hold on power indefinitely. Arnson and Perales (2007), for example, note that in Brazil, Chile and Uruguay "left parties have moderated over time and participate fully in stable, competitive electoral systems," (p. 4) while under populist regimes in Argentina, Bolivia, Ecuador, Nicaragua and Venezuela the "political system is 'refounded' via new constitutions that strengthen the executive at the expense of checks and balances" and where the political discourse is highly polarizing between "the people" and an oligarchic elite (Cynthia Arnson email correspondence, November 15th, 2010). And where "new forms of political participation are created outside traditional institutions, such as parties, and are linked to the president in corporatist fashion, the state intervenes in the economy in ways that are hostile to private capital, etc." (Cynthia Arnson email correspondence, November 15th, 2010). Similarly, Roberts, Bethell and Mayorga (2007) see the social democratic regimes of Brazil, Chile and Uruguay as "the maturation of democracy" but see recent political developments in Venezuela and Bolivia as "not the maturation of democracy, but rather its crisis: namely, the failure of representative democratic institutions to respond effectively to social needs and demands" (p. 13). In "Argentina, Peru, Venezuela and Bolivia populist or leftist leaders operate in political systems where opposition parties have virtually evaporated, and representative institutions are struggling to rebuild" (Roberts, Bethell and Mayorga, 2007, p. 13-14). Similarly, Acemoglu, Ergorov and Sonin (2010) see the rise of left populist governments with charismatic leaders and "left of median voter" policies as a response of electorates that are convinced that corruption and existing checks and balances allow elites to capture governments thereby preventing promised redistribution toward the middle class: voters choose radical populist leaders precisely because they promise to dismantle traditional checks and balances.

Table 11.1 New Left Political Regimes in Latin America

Country	Leader	Took Office	Effective year★	Classification[1]	Cumulative years regime is in power★		
					2000–2002	2003–2005	2006–2008
Argentina	The Kirchners	May-03	2004	Left Populist	0	2	5
Bolivia	Evo Morales	Jan-06	2007	Left Populist	0	0	2
Brazil	Lula da Silva	Jan-03	2004	Social Democratic	0	2	5
Chile	Ricardo Lagos	Mar-00	2001	Social Democratic	2	5	8
Ecuador	Rafael Correa	Jan-07	2008	Left Populist	0	0	1
Nicaragua	Daniel Ortega	Jan-07	2008	Left Populist	0	0	1
Uruguay	Tabaré Vázquez	Mar-05	2006	Social Democratic	0	0	3
Venezuela	Hugo Chavez	Feb-99	2000	Left Populist	3	6	9
Total effective years					5	15	34

Source: McLeod and Lustig (2010).

★ Effective year" is one year after the government takes office, as new policies take time to implement. Both Nicaragua and Ecuador elected left populist governments in 2008, outside the window of the present analysis.

1 This table begins with the political regime classification discussed in Arnson and Perales (2007). After 2007 left populist governments took office in Ecuador (Rafael Correa) and Nicaragua (Daniel Ortega). As Acemoglu et al. (2010, p. 1) notes the "resurgence of populist politicians in many developing countries, especially in Latin America. Hugo Chavez in Venezuela, the Kirchners in Argentina, Evo Morales in Bolivia, Alan Garcia in Peru, and Rafael Correa in Ecuador are examples of politicians that "use the rhetoric of aggressively defending the interests of the common man against the privileged elite." Unfortunately, Nicaragua could not be included among the left populist countries in the regression analysis because its data end in 2006.

There is some evidence that the new century's left regimes (both types) have reduced inequality in Latin America more than non-left regimes (see Lustig and McLeod, 2009; Cornia, 2010; McLeod and Lustig, 2010), and that within the left regimes, that it is the social democratic regimes that have done better. Table 11. 2 presents estimates from Lustig and McLeod (2009) using the cumulative years in power index for each regime presented in Table 11.1. The key result is that though both regimes reduced inequality and poverty during the past decade, once one controls for unobserved factors (fixed effects) or initial levels of inequality, only the social democratic regimes appear to break with the past, reducing inequality to historic lows.

What made the difference between the two types of leftist regimes? An obvious possibility is their macroeconomic policies. Columns 2 and 3 of Table 11.2 suggest that underlying factors associated with left populist regimes, including higher inflation, may underlie their lesser success in policy terms in reducing inequality. But the differences in key macroeconomic indicators between the two types of leftist regimes have not been all that great in the last decade. Inflation though higher since 2000 in the populist regimes, has been far below rates in the 1980s (see Appendix Table 11A.1). (Inflation in the social democratic regimes has been even lower than in the non-leftist regimes; the social democratic left has been

Table 11.2 Determinants of Latin American Inequality 1990–2008 (as measured by the Gini coefficient, including fixed effects)

3 year panel	with fixed effects[1]		
Dependent Varaiable:	Gini Coefficient		
(t-statistics in parentheses)	I	II	IIi
Social Democratic Regime (years)[3]		−1.31	−1.42
or cumulative years in office	−0.40	−(3.2)	−(4.1)
	−(2.7)		
Left-Populist Regime (years in office)		0.47	0.11
or cumulative years in office	−0.14	(0.8)	(0.2)
	−(0.7)		
Government Cibso (log % GDP)	6.2		5.0
	(3.7)		(2.4)
Public Social Spending (log % GDP)	−2.4		−3.2
	−(1.7)		−(2.2)
Per capita income $ppp 2005 (log)	1.0	−3.6	−1.8
	(0.3)	−(1.1)	−(0.6)
Inflation rate (average CPI change)	0.23		
	(2.9)		
Net barter terms of trade (log)		−4.6	−3.0
		−(2.4)	−(1.4)
Remitances/GDP		−0.19	−0.18
		−(3.0)	−(2.8)
Merchandise Exports % of GDP		−3.5	−3.1
		−(1.8)	−(2.1)
Fuel exports % of merchandise exports		0.60	0.63
		(3.5)	(3.4)
Constant	34	119	88
	(1.2)	(4.2)	(2.7)
Number of Observations 85	80	80	
Number of Countries[2]	17	17	17
Adjusted R^2	0.80	0.78	0.80
Std Error of Regression	2.1	2.2	2.1
Cross-section/period fixed effects redundancy F test	6.7	7.9	5.7
prob value for fixed effects F-test (joint period/cross section)	(0.0)	(0.0)	(0.0)

1 Includes both period and country fixed effects, t-statistics based on white diagonal rogust errors.
2 Gini coefficients are actual survey values from CEDLAS, selected to represent each three year interval.
 If available the last year in the three year interval is used, otherwise the first or last year are used.
3 Includes Uruguay.
Source: Lustig and McLeod (2009)

conservative not only relative to the past but relative to the right.) The populist left regimes enjoyed better terms of trade and also had higher fuel exports as a percent of merchandise trade. But as with inflation the differences are not dramatic—except possibly for Argentina and Venezuela in just the last couple of years. For much of the decade, left populist regimes ran healthy primary surpluses (though lower than in social democratic regimes) and they managed to reduce their external debt to GDP ratios to below 20 percent (see Appendix Table 11A.1). As a result it is hard to attribute the differences in the success of the two types of leftist regimes in reducing inequality primarily to differences in their macroeconomic policies—at least up to now. (Of course, to the extent these favorable conditions constitute an ongoing boom the question is whether the growth and inequality reduction (and poverty reduction) the populist regimes have enjoyed can be sustained if and when those conditions change).[19]

More important than macroeconomic indicators to explain the difference between the two types of leftist regimes are two other factors. First have been changes in social policy, including social spending. Cornia (2010) suggests that a wide range of social and redistributive policies, ranging from social spending to minimum wage increases, have reduced inequality in all countries. Have the two different types of left regimes been different in their social and other redistributive programs and policies? Figure 11.6 portrays estimates by the two types of left regimes of the annual redistribution of household income across quintiles in the last two decades (see also Appendix Table 11A-2). These estimates show much greater redistribution from richer to poorer in the social democratic regimes. Social democratic regimes basically ignore the fourth quintile, whose income share is remarkably constant, but redistribute about 0.4 percent of GDP each year in office from the top quintile to the bottom three quintiles. For the left populist regimes there has not been much change in the quintile shares from the early 1990s (though there is certainly improvement compared to the crisis years of the late 1990s and 2001 in Argentina). This result is not consistent with the usual characterization (e.g., Acemoglu et al., 2010) of populist political movements as "left of the median voter" policy regimes, implying the poorest groups may benefit most (and this is certainly the rhetoric of left regimes).

What was the role of social policy in the social democratic regimes in effecting this greater redistribution? There is considerable evidence from household surveys that education expenditures and conditional cash transfer programs have reduced inequality and poverty. Is that what mattered at the national level, and more so in the social democratic regimes? As Table 11.2 indicates, public social spending had an equalizing effect in the region overall (and total government spending a disequalizing effect).[20] But our sample by regime type is too small to directly estimate differential effects of social and other spending. To address the question, we first plot changes in social spending (as a share of GDP) for the three types of regimes,

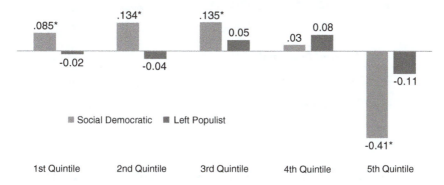

Figure 11.6 Annual Income Redistribution by Quintile (cumulative years in office starting in year 2). ★Significant at 5% level, random effects estimates, see Appendix A, Table A-2 and McLeod and Lustig (2011).

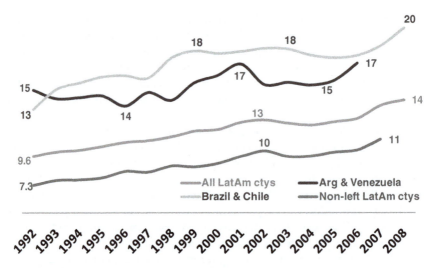

Figure 11.7 Latin American Public Spending on Social Programs as Percentage of GDP (education, health, and transfers). *Source:* Unweighted average for each group. CEPAL - CEPALSTAT, Estadisticas E Indicadores Sociales, Gasto Publico social, downloaded December, 2010 websie.eclasc.cl/infest/ajax/cepalstate.asp?carpeta=estadisticas. *Source:* McLeod and Lustig (2011).

focusing on the early and largest social democratic and left populist regimes in Figure 11.7. Both Chile and Brazil (mainly the latter) increased public spending on transfers, education and health[2] during this period, according to CEPAL. Though data for Venezuela are not available after 2006, the left populist regimes also allocated considerably more than non-left governments to social spending but less than the social democratic regimes.

We present random estimates of changes in the share of social spending in total government spending across quintiles for the period 1990–2008, this time by type of regime in Figure 11.8 (the regression on which the figure is based is shown in Table 11A.2). Social

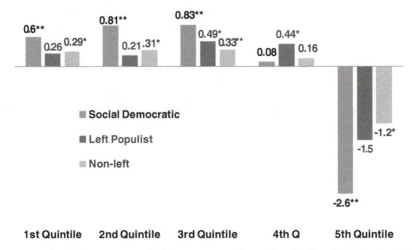

Figure 11.8 Redistributive Impact of Changes in Social Spending Budget Share by Quintile (change significant at *5% or **1% level). *Source:* Appendix A, Table A-3 and McLeod and Lustig (2011).

spending is progressive across all regime types, but is most progressive in the social democratic regimes, with redistribution again (as with overall income) from the top to the bottom three quintiles. This result is consistent with both spending on cash transfers targeted
to the poor in the bottom quintile, but also with greater increases in spending on health and
education that reach the lower and middle quintiles (probably in most countries compared
to changes in the proportion spent on pensions), and within those sectors, probably greater
increases on basic services—in education with greater increases in spending on primary and
secondary schooling than on public universities.

The second factor by which the two types of leftist regimes differ sharply is in indicators
of transparency and government effectiveness (including as viewed by outside investors).
One example is the understatement of Argentina's inflation by its official agency (INDEC).
In 2007 several staff members of INDEC were fired, and for the next three years Argentina's
official inflation rate stabilized at about 8 percent, while other estimates (e.g., the independent FIEL) put inflation over 20 percent in 2008–2010 (see below).[21] And of the five left
populist regimes, only Venezuela reports its primary deficit to the IMF.

Differences in transparency are not well measured across countries. However there are
various measures of government effectiveness. Figure 11.9 reflects the scores of countries
in the region by regime type reported by Kaufman, Kraay and Mastruzzi (2008)—in turn
based on views expressed within countries by measuring perceptions of the quality of public
services, the quality of the civil service and the degree of its independence from political
pressures, the quality of policy formulation and implementation, and the credibility of
the government's commitment to such policies through surveys of a range of stakeholders
(firms, individuals, NGOs, commercial risk rating agencies, multilateral aid agencies, and
other public sector organizations). The left populist regimes are rated considerably below
the non-left regimes, and the social democratic regimes are rated well above.[22] Brazil, Chile
and Uruguay are considered more effective governments overall.

Finally, we ask whether the reductions in inequality in the new left regimes of Latin
America are permanent or transitory? Historically, populist policies have been financed by

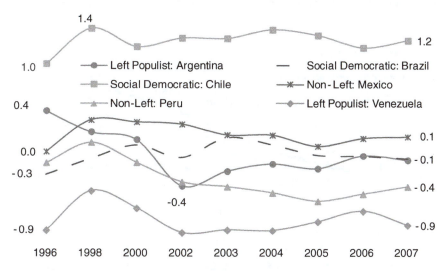

Figure 11.9 Government Effectiveness by Political Regime Types (2000–2007). *Source:* Kaufmann
and Kraay (2008)

favorable terms of trade shifts that provide the public revenues needed to finance redistributive programs (until the commodity price boom ends).[23] The current era is no exception. As shown in Figure 11.10, terms of trade have treated both the populist and social democratic regimes well, especially compared to other non-left Latin countries (Table 11A.1). Chile and Venezuela experienced the most dramatic improvements in their terms of trade, as high petroleum and copper prices added directly to government revenues. The improvements in Brazil's terms of trade have been more modest, as shown with the population-weighted terms of trade index, dominated by Brazil (Argentina and Venezuela are similar in size so the population-weighted terms of trade index is not much different than the simple average shown in Figure 11.10 and Appendix Table 11A.1). Improvements in the terms of trade have had a progressive impact at least in the short term, but cannot explain much of Brazil's reduction in equality; as shown in Table 11.2, when controlling for the terms of trade, it is the political regime that made a difference.

Apart from transient commodity price booms, what can make redistribution unsustainable are macroeconomic imbalances, particularly the accumulation of internal public sector or external debt. In this regard both types of left regimes have been relatively conservative, paying down external debt (see Table 11A.1) and avoiding large fiscal deficits (in fact, by most measures, the social democratic regimes have been more conservative that non-left regimes, perhaps as a way to boost their credibility with the private sector). A worrisome trend, however, is the recent expansion of domestic credit and the recent double digit rates of inflation in Argentina and Venezuela. In the short term, inflation can undermine efforts to redistribute income as the inflation tax is regressive (we present some evidence of this below). Over the longer term, high inflation fueled by domestic credit growth can lead to exchange rate appreciation and capital flight, though at the moment both countries are running current account surpluses (due in part to high commodity prices).

In short, during the first decade of the 21st century, our econometric evidence suggests that though inequality fell in most leftist regimes, those with left populist governments were more likely to benefit from good luck than good policy, including increases in the prices of oil and other commodities, while those with social democratic regimes reduced inequality more than they would have otherwise because of good policy—including effec-

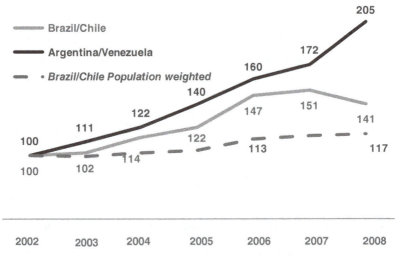

Figure 11.10 Average Terms of Trade (2002–2006). *Source:* CEPAL Database, December 2010.

tive redistribution programs. The difference does not appear to have been dramatically better macroeconomic management, at least as reflected in traditional indicators. We do not have enough data over enough periods to estimate directly the impact of inflation, government spending and other variables on inequality for each of the three regime types. But the descriptive data suggest the differences between the two leftist regime types as measured by traditional macro indicators have until very recently been small—perhaps because the external environment has made reasonably "good macro" relatively easy.

Instead, the difference between the two types of regimes appears to have more to do with the elusive quality of "government effectiveness" as seen by observers, including in the type of and management (not the amount) of social spending. On that score it could be that observers (particularly private investors) are noting the success of Chile in adhering to its fiscal rules and the political support for Lula's inflation fighting in Brazil; but it also could be that the social democratic governments are seen as more efficient and effective as managers of social and other expenditure programs.

It would be ironic if governments in Latin America were more successful in reducing inequality because they are more effective at managing such social programs as conditional cash transfers and are simultaneously viewed as more reliable and business-friendly. At the same time, insofar as private investors also view macroeconomic stability as a key indicator of government effectiveness, it appears that the inequality declines in the social democratic regimes are more likely to be sustained in the future than the declines in the populist regimes.

Declining Inequality, the Middle Class and Politics

How might changes in the size and economic command of the middle class change the politics of distribution in Latin America? Might the history of political power being controlled by a landed elite and industrialists with little interest in expanding economic opportunity change where the middle class is growing, at least in democratic regimes? Where clientelist politics have led to populist economic programs, consistent with median voter theory, might a larger middle class encourage more fiscally sustainable while still stable and progressive policies?

Birdsall (2010) defines a global middle class in income terms across both advanced and developing countries as those households with income per capita of at least $10 (2005 PPP terms) who are not among the richest 5 percent in their own country. This "indispensable" middle class is likely to demand capable and accountable government and economic policies conducive to market-led growth.

The relatively high $10 floor means that in developing countries the global middle class tends to be concentrated in the top quintiles of the income distribution. In the lowest-income countries, for example in Africa, by this definition there was no middle class at all in 2005—all households enjoying per capita income of at least $10 were in the excluded top 5 percent of the income distribution.

In Latin America, the middle class so defined consists entirely of households in the top quintile in all countries studied, except Mexico, urban Argentina and Chile (Figure 11.11).

By this definition, the size of the middle class as a proportion of the population in 2005 ranged from 7 percent in Honduras to 33 percent in Chile; the proportion of total income commanded by the middle class ranged from 14 to 42 percent (in 2005, middle-class size in the United States and Sweden were 91 and 95 percent, respectively, and their shares of income were 81 and 88 percent, respectively).

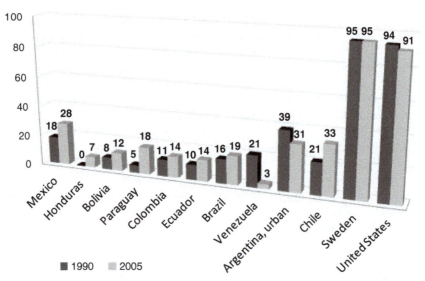

Figure 11.11 Change in Middle Class Size (proportion of population) between 1990 and 2005.
Source: Birdsall (2011).

Three countries in the region showed the largest increases in the global middle class by the two measures between 1990 and 2005: Brazil, Chile and Mexico—two social demo-cratic regimes and one non-left regime, consistent with the inequality declines in those countries noted above. Our analysis of changes in quintile share per capita growth elastici-ties by political regime in almost the same period (see Table 11A.3) indicates that in the social democratic regimes where the middle class grew, it grew despite the fourth and fifth quintiles capturing much less of the benefits of growth (indeed, the fifth or richest quintile's elasticity of per capita growth to overall growth is negative) than did the lower three quin-tiles. Incomes at the top of the distribution (which are absolutely higher to start with) grew far less than incomes at the bottom in these social democratic regimes and more so than in the populist left regimes. But they did grow, so that more people crossed beyond the $10 per day line and entered the middle class, as overall incomes rose in those countries.[24]

Meanwhile two left populist countries by 2005 had suffered absolute declines in the size of their middle classes by 2005: Venezuela (where the middle class fell from 21 to 3 percent of the population, and its proportion of income from 35 to 8 percent) and urban Argentina where the middle class fell from 39 to 31 percent and its proportion of income from 53 to 46 percent). The declines in inequality reported for those countries by 2008 are associated with declines in income overall, and relatively greater declines in the incomes of households in the top two "middle-income" quintiles, where the middle class (by the $10 per day defini-tion) is concentrated.[25]

Might the growing middle classes in countries like Chile and Brazil help lock in leftist social democratic political regimes (whether because or in spite of its concentration in the top quintile of households)? There is no evidence that a large middle class is necessary, let alone sufficient, to these regimes. But a growing global middle class does seem likely to reinforce effective government that manages moderate redistribution while retaining inves-tor confidence in the likelihood of continuing growth and price stability.

Put another way, when is the middle class large enough to become politically salient in supporting or at least tolerating the kind of social and other distributive policies that are good for them but turn out to be good for the poor—for example, universal public education? When is middle class status potentially attainable to the median voter so that he or she votes for the regime type that represents "middle-class" interests? The numbers above, which say nothing about the causal effect of a large middle-class size on the type of political regime, suggest the answer in Latin America is not yet but getting close in Chile and Mexico, and possibly in Brazil as well. At the same time, considering causality in the other direction, it does appear that social democratic regimes are good for growing the middle class—as growth itself increases household income in the third and fourth quintiles—and politics permits that relatively more of the benefits of that growth are shared at the bottom of the distribution.

Conclusion: Some Politics, Some Economics

Countries of all political stripes in Latin America enjoyed a reduction in inequality in the 2000s. Nonetheless, the region continues to be the most unequal one in the world, and while in the last decade social policy became more pro-poor, in most countries public spending continues to be neutral or regressive.

In this chapter we show that there is more to the story, however. In some countries the politics of redistributive policy appears to be changing in a fundamental way, suggesting that in those countries at least the recent declines in inequality are likely to stick.

On the basis of our econometric analysis and our comparison of governance and other characteristics, we conclude that in the social democratic regimes at least (but not in the populist regimes), the inequality decline is the outcome of what might be called a structural change. In contrast, in the populist regimes our evidence indicates that the declines in inequality have been due more to good luck than to good policy; that in Argentina and Venezuela inequality levels fell from levels higher than they had been historically is consistent with the good luck explanation.

Our conclusion rests primarily on the evidence that the economic policies and programs of social democratic regimes have been clearly redistributive—perhaps because they have some political logic in open and growing economies reliant on and benefiting a growing middle class. In terms of broadly defined economic conditions in the 2000s, the difference between the two types of leftist regimes were not all that great. Over the period 1990–2008, both types of leftist regimes had, not surprisingly, higher government expenditures (as a percent of GDP) than non-leftist regimes (and the social democratic regimes actually had higher overall government expenditures than the populist regimes). They also had lower inflation and higher social spending as a percent of GDP (than populist and non-left regimes), though not markedly so.

At the same time, controlling for differences in economic policies and characteristics, the social democratic regimes were more effective in designing and managing social policies that were more redistributive to the poorest groups, while maintaining good—indeed, somewhat better—macroeconomic programs than the populist left regimes and indeed than the non-left regimes. They delivered the right combination of healthy growth, macroeconomic stability and social policies (including increased social spending and higher minimum wages as well as cash transfer programs for the poor), building on a foundation of increased education. In those countries, growth benefited most the bottom three quintiles, partly because high social spending was highly redistributive. At the same time, with rapid economic growth overall, the incomes of the top quintiles continued to grow in absolute terms, increasing the size and share of income of households in the middle class, i.e., enjoying income of at least $10 a day. In the social democratic regimes, it appears to have been more attractive politically to deliver a combination of low inflation and social programs and spending targeted to the poor.

In short, what might be called a new redistributive *politics* in Brazil and Chile compared to Argentina and Venezuela is what distinguishes the two types of leftist regimes.

In those settings, if those "politics" continue,[26] inequality declines are likely to be sustained in the future—a good thing given that their levels of inequality are still high. For the more populist political regimes, we are less confident. Whether because of or independent of their political characteristics, their macroeconomic policies are beginning to deteriorate, and their institutions are viewed as delivering government that is less "effective" than are the social democratic governments.

Notes

1 The authors thank without implicating Jorge Mariscal for help with data, Amanda Glassman for excellent comments, and Pronita Saxena for excellent research assistance.
2 For a comprehensive analysis of the factors behind this change, see Lopez-Calva and Lustig (2010).
3 According to the Inter-American Development Bank (1999), the Gini for 90 percent of the population in Latin America would be, on average, only 0.36 instead of 0.52, and in six countries income inequality would be less than that of the United States. The Gini coefficient takes values between zero (no inequality at all) and one (maximum inequality). Measured at the country level, Ginis tend to be between .25 (Sweden) and .60 (Brazil and South Africa). The Gini coefficient in the United States was about 0.34 in 1996.
4 Household data on wealth are rare for countries in Latin America and other developing countries. The distribution of wealth is everywhere more unequal than the distribution of income (Davies et al., 2006).
5 Recent here refers to the 1980s and 1990s, depending on the country.
6 On effects of macroeconomic policies on the poor via crises, see Lustig (2000).
7 Brazil and Mexico's per capita GDP growth rate until 2007 were below 3 percent.
8 On the extraordinary rise in the wage premium to higher education in Latin America in the 1990s, see Behrman, Birdsall and Szekely (2007).
9 For more on economic causes, see Lopez-Calva and Lustig (2010).
10 Basic education includes grades 1–9 in Argentina and Mexico; 1–8 in Brazil; and 1–11 in Peru. The number of grades includes what countries call basic primary and secondary education.
11 Tinbergen (1975) was among the first to use this expression and, more recently, it was the central theme of Goldin and Katz's illuminating analysis of the United States (2008).
12 Latin America has had active unions, especially in the public sector, but these have tended to increase the dual structure of the labor market, leaving those in the informal sector farther behind and increasing wage inequality overall. In the cases of Mexico and Peru, the decline in inequality coincided with a period of weakening labor market institutions. However, the decline in inequality in Argentina may well be the result of a pro-union/pro-disenfranchised government stance at least in part (Pages, Pierre and Scarpetta, 2008).
13 Spending for tertiary education also rose, but for the first time in the 1990s, it rose less than spending for basic (primary and secondary) education.
14 The populist left regimes include Argentina, Bolivia, Ecuador, Nicaragua and Venezuela; the social democratic left include Brazil, Chile and Uruguay; the non-left countries include Colombia, Costa Rica, Dominican Republic, El Salvador, Guatemala, Honduras, Mexico, Panama, Paraguay and Peru. The classification by regime type is based on Arnson and Perales (2007; see also Table 11.1.) We are not political scientists and make no explicit claims ourselves about the classifications. In the regression analysis, the populist left is comprised of Argentina, Bolivia, Ecuador, and Venezuela. Note that in the econometric analysis, Nicaragua is included among the non-left regimes because the available data end in 2006, before the leftist government took power. The same applies to El Salvador and Paraguay where the available data do not correspond to when the left took power.
15 As estimated and assembled by CEPAL (Gasto Público Social).

16 We rely on the excellent standardized survey based inequality estimates assembled by SEDLAC (Socio-economic Database for Latin American and the Caribbean, CEDLAS and the World Bank) 1989 to 2008.

17 Edwards (2009) also classifies Alan Garcia's regime in Peru as social democratic; others might reasonably classify Fernandez' regime in Dominican Republic as social democratic.

18 The classic populist response to favorable terms of trade is external borrowing and capital inflows which make a boom unsustainable. In early 2010 there is little evidence of excessive external borrowing or capital inflows.

19 Social spending was greater in social democratic than populist left regimes throughout the past decades (and greater than in non-left regimes), but so was overall government spending—with presumably offsetting effects on inequality in each regime (see Appendix Table 11A.1).

20 As estimated and assembled by CEPAL (Gasto Público Social) available at http://www.eclac.org/.

21 The IMF prints Argentina's official inflation with a footnote saying private estimates put inflation considerably higher, and recently Argentina asked for and is getting technical assistance from the IMF at INDEC.

22 A Moody's credit rating's tell a similar story. As of 2011: Leftist: Argentina (rate B3); Venezuela (rate B2); Bolivia (rate B1) vs. Non-Leftist: Chile (rate AA3); Brazil (Baa2)) Source: http://www.moodys.com accessed October 26 2011. Moody's is not, of course, an unbiased observer of Latin regimes but whatever its bias there are real consequences in terms of lower credit ratings.

23, The classic example is first Peron regime in the early 1950s (Dornbusch and Edwards, 1991).

24 In a country like Brazil, by this definition (a minimum of $10 per day per capita), all members of the middle class were in the top quintile. With overall growth, households in the fourth quintile moved over the $10 day line into the middle class.

25 Because the middle class defined in Birdsall (2010) is not the middle stratum, it is possible to have a growing middle class and increasing inequality—the case for Bolivia, Colombia, and Ecuador between 1990 and 2005—and similarly to have a declining middle class and declining inequality.

26 How political factors affect the economic policies that ultimately matter for inequality constitutes in itself a rich future research agenda. Lustig et al. (2011) set out in detail the analytic underpinnings of economic analysis of various individual redistributive programs and policies—a first step in political analysis of how those economic policies are shaped.

Bibliography

Acemoglu, D., G. Ergorov and K. Sonin (2010). "A Political Theory of Populism" [mimeo], August, Cambridge, MA: MIT.

Acemoglu, Daron and James A. Robinson (2001). "A Theory of Political Transitions," *The American Economic Review*, Vol. 91, No. 4 (Sep.,), 938–963.

Alvaredo, Facundo and Thomas Piketty (2010). "The Dynamics of Income Concentration in Developed and Developing Countries: A View from the Top," in *Declining Inequality in Latin America: A Decade of Progress?*, eds. Luis F. Lopez-Calva and Nora Lustig, Washington, DC: Brookings Institution Press and UNDP.

Arnson, Cynthia with José Raúl Perales. (2007). *The 'New Left' and Democratic Governance in Latin America*. Washington, DC: Woodrow Wilson International Center for Latin American Studies. http://www.wilsoncenter.org/topics/pubs/NewLeftDemocraticGovernance.pdf

Barros, Ricardo,Mirela de Carvalho, Samuel Franco and Rosane Mendonca (2010). "Markets, the State, and the Dynamics of Inequality in Brazil," *in Declining Inequality in Latin America: A Decade of Progress?*, eds. Luis F. Lopez-Calva and Nora Lustig, Washington DC: Brookings Insitution Press and UNDP.

Behrman, Jere R., Nancy Birdsall and Miguel Székely (2007). "Economic Policy Changes and Wage Differentials in Latin America," in *Economic Development and Cultural Change*, Vol. 56, pages 57–97, Chicago: University of Chicago Press.

Birdsall, Nancy (2010). "The (Indispensable) Middle Class in Developing Countries; or The Rich and the Rest, Not the Poor and the Rest," CGD Working Paper No. 207, Washington DC: Center for Global Development.

Birdsall, Nancy, Augusto de la Torre and Felipe Valencia Caicedo (2010). "The Washington Consensus: Assessing a Damaged Brand," CGD Working Paper 213. Washington DC: Center for Global Development. http://www.cgdev.org/content/publications/detail/1424155.

Birdsall, Nancy and Frederick Jaspersen (1997). *Pathways to Growth: Comparing East Asia and Latin America*. Washington DC: Inter-American Development Bank.

Clemens, Michael A. (2004). "The Long Walk to School: International education goals in historical perspective," CGD Working Paper No. 37, Washington DC: Center for Global Development.

Cornia, Giovanni Andrea (2010). "Income Distribution under Latin America's New Left Regimes," *Journal of Human Development and Capabilities*, Vol. 11, No. 1, (Feb.), 85-114.

Davies, James, Susanna Sandstrom, Anthony Shorrocks and Edward N. Wolff (2006). "The World Distribution of Household Wealth," World Institute for Development Economics Research of the United Nations University (UNU WIDER), Helsinki, Finland: UNU WIDER.

Dornbusch, R. and S. Edwards (1991). *The Macroeconomics of populism in Latin America*, Chicago: University of Chicago Press.

Edwards, Sebastian (2009). "Latin America's Decline: A Long Historical View," NBER Working Paper 15171, Cambridge: National Bureau of Economic Research.

Engerman, Stanley L. and Kenneth L. Sokoloff (1997). "Factor Endowments, Institutions, and Differential Paths of Growth Among New World Economies: A View from Economic Historians of the United States," in *How Latin America Fell Behind*, ed. Stephen Haber, Stanford: Stanford University Press.

Esquivel, Gerardo, Nora Lustig and John Scott (2010). "Mexico: A Decade of Falling Inequality: Market Forces or State Action," in *Declining Inequality in Latin America: A Decade of Progress?*, eds. Luis F. Lopez-Calva and Nora Lustig, Washington DC: Brookings Institution Press and UNDP.

Gasparini, Leonardo and Guillermo Cruces (2010a). "A Distribution in Motion: The Case of Argentina," in *Declining Inequality in Latin America: A Decade of Progress?*, eds. Luis F. Lopez-Calva and Nora Lustig, Washington, DC: Brookings Institution Press and UNDP.

Gasparini, Leonardo and Guillermo Cruces (2010b). "Las Asignaciones Universales po Hijo: Impacto, Discusion u Alternativas," CEDLAS Working Paper No. 102, La Plata: Center for Distributive, Labor, and Social Studies, Universidad Nacional de La Plata.

Gasparini, Leonardo, Walter Sosa Escudero, Mariana Marchionni and Sergio Olivieri (2010). "Multidimensional poverty in Latin America and the Caribbean: New evidence from the Gallup World Poll," CEDLAS, Working Papers 0100, CEDLAS, Universidad Nacional de La Plata.

Gasparini, Leonardo and Nora Lustig (2011). "The Rise and Fall of Income Inequality in Latin America" Chapter 28 in *Oxford Handbook of Latin American Economics*, eds. Jose Antonio Ocampo and Jaime Ros, Oxford, U.K.: Oxford University Press.

Gasparini, Leonardo, Guillermo Cruces and Leopoldo Tornarolli (2009). "Recent trends in income inequality in Latin America," Working Papers 132, ECINEQ, Society for the Study of Economic Inequality.

Goldin, Claudia and Lawrence F. Katz (2008). *The Race Between Education and Technology*, Cambridge: Harvard University Press.

Gray Molina, Georg and Ernesto Yañez (2009). "The Dynamics of Inequality in the Best and Worst Times, Bolivia 1997–2007." Paper prepared at the UNDP Project Markets, the State and the Dynamics of Inequality: How to Advance Inclusive Growth, coordinated by Luis Felipe Lopez-Calva and Nora Lustig. (http://www.beta.undp.org/content/dam/aplaws/publication/en/publications/poverty-reduction/poverty-website/inequality/inequality-bolivia/UNDP_Bolivia.pdf)

Inter-American Development Bank (1999). "Facing Up to Inequality in Latin America," *Economic and Social Progress in Latin America: 1998–1999 Report*, Washington DC: Johns Hopkins University Press.

Jaramillo, Miguel and Jaime Saavedra (2010). "Inequality in Post-Structural Reform Peru: The Role of Market Forces in Public Policy," *in Declining Inequality in Latin America: A Decade of Progress?*, eds. Luis F. Lopez-Calva and Nora Lustig, Washington DC: Brookings Institution Press and UNDP.

Kauffman, Daniel, Aart Kray and Massimo Mastruzzi (2008). "Governance Matters VII: Aggregate and Individual Governance Indicators 1996–2007," Policy Research Working Paper 4654, Washington DC: World Bank.

Kauffman, Robert (2007). "Political Economy and the 'New Left'" in *The 'New Left' and Democratic*

Governance in Latin America eds. Cynthia J. Arnson and Jose Raul Perales, Washington DC: Woodrow Wilson International Center for Scholars.

Lindert, Peter H. (2004). *Growing Public: Social Spending and Economic Growth Since the Eighteenth Century*, New York: Cambridge University Press.

Lindert, Peter H. and Jeffrey G. Williamson (2001). "Does Globalization Make the World More Unequal?," NBER Working Paper 8228, Cambridge: National Bureau of Economics Research.

Lopez-Calva, Luis F., Nora Lustig and Eduardo Ortiz (2011). "The Decline in Inequality in Latin America: How Much, Since When and Why," drawn from UNDP-sponsored project "Markets, the State, and the Dynamics of Inequality in Latin America" coordinated by Luis Felipe López-Calva and Nora Lustig, Tulane University Economics Working Paper 118, New Orleans: Tulane University.

Lopez-Calva, Louis F. and Nora Lustig (2010). *Declining Inequality in Latin America: a Decade of Progress?*, Washington, DC: Brookings Institution Press and UNDP.

Lustig, Nora, Coordinator (2011). "Fiscal Policy and Income Redistribution in Latin America: Challenging the Conventional Wisdom. Argentina (Carola Pessino), Bolivia (George Gray-Molina, Wilson Jimenez, Veronica Paz and Ernesto Yañez), Brazil (Claudiney Pereira and Sean Higgins), Mexico (John Scott), and Peru (Miguel Jaramillo)," background paper for Corporacion Andina de Fomento (CAF) *Fiscal Policy for Development: Improving the Nexus between Revenues and Spending/ Política Fiscal para el Desarrollo: Mejorando la Conexión entre Ingresos y Gastos*. This paper is an output of *Commitment to Equity*, a joint initiative of the Inter-American Dialogue and Tulane University's CIPR and Department of Economics Working Paper 1124, New Orleans: Tulane University.

Lustig, Nora and Darryl McLeod (2009). "Are Latin America's New Left Regimes Reducing Inequality Faster? Addendum to Nora Lustig, 'Poverty, Inequality, and the New Left in Latin America," Washington, DC: Woodrow Wilson International Center for Scholars, Latin American Program (July). Available online: http://www.wilsoncenter.org/sites/default/files/ LUSTIG%2526MCLEOD_INEQ%2526LEFT_JUL%2027_09.pdf

Lustig, Nora (2000). "Crises and the Poor: Socially Responsible Macroeconomics," *Economia, A Journal of the Latin American and Caribbean Economic Association (LACEA),* No. 1, Washington DC: Brookings Institution.

Lustig, Nora (1995). *Coping with Austerity: Poverty and Inequality in Latin America,* Washington DC: Brookings Institution.

McLeod, Darryl and Nora Lustig (2010). "Poverty and Inequality under Latin America's New Left Regimes," Paper prepared for the 15th Annual LACEA Meeting, Medellin, Colombia: Universidad de Antioquia and Universidad Eafit.

McLeod, Darryl and Nora Lustig (2011) "Inequality and Poverty under Latin America's New Left Regimes" Tulane University Economics Working Paper 1117, New Orleans: Tulane University (March).

Morley, Samuel A. (2001). "Distribution and Growth in Latin America in an Era of Structural Reform," Trade and Macroeconomics Division (TMD) Discussion Paper No. 66. Washington, DC: International Food Policy Research Institute (Jan). Available online: http://www.ifpri.org/ sites/default/files/publications/tmdp66.pdf.

Pages, Carmen, Gaelle Pierre and Stefano Scarpetta (2008). *Job Creation in Latin America and the Caribbean: Recent Trends and Policy Challenges,* Washington DC: World Bank Publications.

Roberts, Kenneth, Leslie Bethell and Rene Antonio Mayorga (2007). "Conceptual and Historical Perspectives" in The 'New Left' and Democratic Governance in Latin America eds. Cynthia J. Arnson and Jose Raul Perales, Washington DC: Woodrow Wilson International Center for Scholars.

Robinson, James A. (2010). "The Political Economy of Redistributive Policies" in *Declining Inequality in Latin America: A Decade of Progess?,* eds. Luis F. Lopez-Calva and Nora Lustig (pp. 39–71), Washington DC: Brookings Institution Press and UNDP.

Rodrik, Dani (1997). "Democracy and Economic Performance," unpublished paper, Harvard University.

Sachs, Jeffrey D. (1989). "Social Conflict and Populist Policies in Latin America," NBER Working Paper No. 2897, Cambridge: National Bureau of Economics Research.

Székely, Miguel and Marianne Hilgert (1999). "What's Behind the Inequality We Measure: An Investigation Using Latin American Data," Research Department Working Paper #409, Washington DC: Inter-American Development Bank.

Tinbergen, Jan (1975). *Income Differences: Recent Research.* Amsterdam: North Holland.

Appendix

Table 11A.1 Key Economic Indicators by Political Regime: 1988–2009 (3 year averages)

	1988–90	1991–93	1994–96	1997–99	2000–02	2003–05	2006–08	2009
Inflation (% change in CPI)[2]								
Social Democratic	580	581	22	5.4	8.5	5.0	5.8	4.5
Left Populist	1100	25	23	20	12	8.4	14	11
Other Latam	447	456	14	3.6	4.7	4.4	5.7	4.2
Average per capita GDP Growth								
Social Democratic	0.7	4.5	3.5	0.2	-0.2	4.0	3.2	-0.5
Left Populist	3.1	1.8	1.4	-1.4	-1.4	5.6	2.0	-1.5
Other Latam	2.0	3.4	2.8	0.9	0.4	3.5	3.1	-2.7
Terms of Trade (2000=100, WDI)								
Social Democratic	109	101	113	110	99	106	126	124
Left Populist	99	86	88	90	97	108	143	133
Other Latam	97	92	103	103	98	97	103	100
Government Consumption spending as a share of GDP (WDI)								
Social Democratic	15	16	18	18	19	19	20	
Left Populist	12	12	12	13	14	14	15	
Other Latam	6	7	8	9	10	10	11	
Social Spending as a Share of GDP (CEPAL)[1]								
Social Democratic	13	13	14	14	15	14	14	
Left Populist	7	9	11	13	13	13	12	
Other Latam	10	9	10	11	12	12	11	
Domestic Credit Growth % change Dec/Dec								
Social Democratic					18	2.0	21	-0.6
Left Populist					12	12	17	17
Other Latam					9.5	11	18	7.9
Addendum: Domestic Credit Growth % change Dec/Dec								
Brazil & Chile					9	10	17	9.0
Argentina & Venezuela					27	20	32	31
Inflation (% change in CPI, IMF WEO)								
Brazil & Chile	1105	580	364	4.9	5.4	5.9	5.0	7.4
Argentina & Venezuela	1380	53	38	18	13	16	18	27
Average per capita GDP Growth								
Brazil & Chile	0.4	4.2	4.2	0.6	1.1	3.5	1.9	
Argentina & Venezuela	4.0	2.5	1.8	-1.9	-4.5	9.2	2.8	

1 Social spending is not available for Bolivia, Venezuela or Ecuador in 2007 or 2008 so the 2006 value is used for the 2006–08 period. Most other CEPAL social spending estimates end in 2008.

2 Changes in CPI are as reported by the IMF, WEO October 2010 database, except for 2007 to 2009 Argentina inflation for which are based on higher FIEL (not official INDEC) estimates.

Table 12A.2 Changes in Quintile Share by Political Regime

Dependent Variable: Quintile Share and Gini	Cumultive Political Regimes Years						
	Quintile Shares						
	Q1	Q2	Q3	Q4	Q5	Q4*	Gini
	A-2.1	A-2.2	A-2.3	A-2.4	A-2.5	A-2.4a	A-2.6
Left–Populist Regime	−0.02	−0.04	0.05	0.08	−0.11	0.04	−0.05
Cumulative years in power	−(0.3)	−(1.6)	(1.2)	(1.9)	−(0.7)	(1.1)	−(0.2)
Social Democratic Regime	0.09	1.13	0.14	0.03	−0.41	0.10	−0.42
cumulative years in power	(7.6)	(2.9)	(3.8)	(0.7)	−(4.4)	(2.8)	−(4.3)
Initial income share or Gini	0.61	0.76	0.68	0.70	0.67		0.70
	(4.2)	(6.1)	(7.9)	(9.1)	(7.1)		(7.4)
Constant	1.25	1.7	3.8	6.0	19	20	16
(t-statistics in parentheses)	(2.4)	(1.7)	(3.7)	(3.9)	(3.4)	(2.7)	(3.3)
Estimation Method	RE	RE	RE	RE	RE	FR	RE
Number of Observations	96	96	96	96	96	96	96
Number of Countries[1]	17	17	17	17	17	17	18
Weighted adjusted R^2	0.18	0.29	0.40	0.55	0.49	0.49	0.35
Unweighted R^2	0.45	0.62	0.65	0.64	0.64		0.33
Std Error of Regression	0.50	0.56	0.61	0.61	0.72	0.72	2.31
Mean dependent variable	3.4	7.2	12	20	57	20	52
Hausman test prob value	0.92	0.33	0.36	0.02	0.49		0.87

* The null of unbiased random effects estimates is rejected for quintile 4 at the 2% significance level, equation A-2.4a provides unbiased fixed effects estimates.

1 The quintile regressions exclude Uruguay. but the Gini equation A-2.6 inclues Uruguay. Including Uruguay does not substantially alter the quintile results.

Table 12A.3 Change in Quintile Shares, Random Effects Estimate

	Social spending as a share of total government consumption						
	Quintile Shares					Gini	Gini
	Q1	Q2	Q3	Q4	Q5	Gini	Gini
	A-3.1	A-3.2	A-3.3	A-3.4	A-3.5	A-3.6	A-3.7
Left–Populist Regime	0.26	0.21	0.49	0.44	−1.5	−1.7	−2.2
	(1.1)	(0.8)	(2.0)	(1.9)	−(1.8)	−(1.7)	−(2.3)
Social Democratic Regime	0.59	0.81	0.83	0.08	−2.6	−3.1	−3.1
	(3.7)	(4.2)	(3.7)	(0.4)	−(3.5)	−(3.6)	−(4.3)
Non-Left Regimes	0.29	0.31	0.33	0.16	−1.2	−1.5	−2.2
	(1.9)	(2.1)	(2.7)	(1.7)	−(2.4)	−(2.3)	−(3.9)
Initial income share/Gini	0.56	0.72	0.64	0.67	0.63	0.60	0.57
	(3.5)	(5.4)	(6.8)	(8.7)	(6.1)	(5.1)	(4.5)
Inflation							1.2
							(3.2)
Constant	1.2	1.7	4.0	6.4	22	23	25
(t-statistics in parentheses)	(2.1)	(1.7)	(3.6)	(4.2)	(3.7)	(3.6)	(3.6)
Estimation Method	RE	RE	RE	RE	RE	FE	RE
Number of Observations	96	96	96	96	96	96	96
Number of Countries	17	17	17	17	17	17	17
Weighted adjusted R^2	0.19	0.29	0.39	0.52	0.34	0.28	0.28
Unweighted R^2	0.47	0.61	0.65	0.65	0.62	0.59	0.60
Std Error of Regression	0.49	0.55	0.60	0.73	2.06	2.30	2.26
Mean dependent variable	3.4	7.2	12.2	19.8	57	52	52

12

ENVIRONMENT AND SUSTAINABLE DEVELOPMENT

Eduardo Silva

The comparatively young literature on environmental politics in Latin America casts a wide net in terms of scope, approaches, and geographic scale. Its scope spans natural resource use, biodiversity conservation, climate change policy, and urban environmental problems. Major approaches include environmental economics, political economy, political ecology, and conservation biology. The scale ranges from the sub-national level to the national, regional, and the global. Many of these studies are highly policy oriented, concentrating on the diagnosis of problems and prescribing solutions.

Over the past 25 years or so, this literature has significantly advanced our knowledge on key questions. Studies have specified the concepts of sustainable development, nature conservation, and related environmental issues. They have operationalized conditions, prescribed policy instruments, and evaluated implementation. Research has covered the gamut of scales, from global, to regional, national, and local. Meanwhile, the literature on the politics of the environment leaves little doubt that the core tenets of sustainable development—and their uneasy relationship to nature conservation—are contested terrain. In Latin America, environmental politics inescapably involve conflicts over land, democracy, and civil rights. In a region characterized by high levels of socio-economic inequality, tensions over the social equity component of sustainable development cut through every aspect of Latin American environmental politics.

This chapter surveys how diverse approaches to the problem of environment and development shape our understanding of environmental politics in four critical issue areas: natural resource use, biodiversity conservation, climate change policy, and urban landscapes. It begins with an examination of how competing conceptualizations of sustainable development broadly writ, and their uneasy coexistence with a conservation paradigm, shape the diagnosis of environmental problems and policy prescriptions. We also trace the affinity of three major analytic approaches—environmental economics, political economy, and political ecology—to those competing conceptualizations of sustainable development. Second, we review how analysts have specified the major factors that influence the politics of sustainable development—actors, interests, and power—including political institution-building. Third, we examine each of the four issue areas mentioned above individually. For each issue area, we summarize key characteristics, how major analytic approaches define problems and solutions, who supports them, and how they have fared in the policy process over time. The concluding section reflects on directions for future research.

Environment and Sustainable Development

Although the concept of sustainable development remains controversial because of its broad scope, aspirations, and trade-offs pose problems for implementation, in practice it has become the dominant environmental discourse in policy circles and has gained widespread currency in civil society. This makes the concept a good point of departure for a discussion of environmental politics in Latin America. The concept is broad enough to fit a wide range of approaches under its umbrella. However, it is not always a comfortable fit, and some conceptualizations of the problem of environment and development fall outside of its parameters.

Sustainable development emerged in the 1980s as a concept to bridge incompatibilities between environmental integrity and economic development. In the 1960s and 1970s, environment and development were on a collision course. Environmental activists advocated reining in consumption and development because of its destructive effects on the environment. Developing countries expressed concern over this trend. They saw it as a brake on economic growth, which they argued was necessary to overcome poverty and to improve general living standards. By contrast, sustainable development posited a strong relationship between economic development, poverty, and environmental quality. In 1987, the Brundtland Commission report emphasized the effects of poverty on environmental degradation.[1] Poor economic performance increases poverty which accelerates environmental degradation. The report, which popularized the concept of sustainable development, stressed the need for a style of development capable of meeting the basic needs of a country's population while maintaining its stock of natural resources so as not rob future generations of their use.

A consensus formed in policy circles that sustainable development rests on four principles. These were sustaining a healthy economy, a commitment to social equity or sustaining livelihoods, sustaining environmental integrity upon which life depends, and sustaining citizen participation in decision-making. There are, however, sharp differences over how to define these values and the relationship between them.

Although there are many models of sustainable development, for heuristic purposes they cluster around two general types. One is a market-friendly type, with strong influences from the environmental economics field.[2] Drawing on neoclassical economics, this conceptualization focuses on rapid free market-based economic growth to reduce poverty, a major cause of environmental degradation. It offers the best possibilities for raising living standards sufficiently for people to develop environmental awareness (an environmental Kuznets curve, as it were). The market-friendly interpretation of sustainable development promotes the expansion of private property rights on the assumption that they are more conducive to environmentally friendly behavior than collective property rights, as famously argued in the "tragedy of the commons."[3] It favors the replacement of state centered "command and control" policy instruments (regulation) with private governance arrangements. In this schema private interests regulate themselves based on properly designed economic incentives by national government agencies and international organizations.

Since large-scale urban and agricultural enterprises are critical to rapid economic development, environmental impact reporting for new ventures has become a standard policy instrument for prevention. These reports, in theory, involve rigorous evaluations of the environmental effects of a project by independent consultants. If a project does not live up to environmental standards, again in theory, it could be rejected. Input from civil society organizations is also part of the process.

Additional policy instruments include markets in tradable pollution certificates. These certify that the bearer has undertaken measures that abate environmental degradation beyond a certain minimal threshold. They acquire value as others who are above the threshold buy them to offset their excess emissions. Similar certificates and markets exist for the environmental services of natural habitat—for example by placing a value on forests for the amount of carbon dioxide they are estimated to sequester or their watershed protection function. Further market instruments include tax breaks for end-of-pipe treatment (i.e., scrubbers for smoke stack industries) or employing sustained yield harvests, which involves limiting extraction of trees from forest stands to an amount that does not threaten their regenerative capacity.

Another key characteristic of market-friendly sustainable development is its highly technocratic approach to policy formulation and implementation. Technical experts tend to prescribe one-size-fits all textbook solutions to problems based on the cannons of their respective professions in a top down manner. They rarely take into account whether the specific context and conditions in the field might pose problems for policy implementation and effectiveness and may thus require modifications to their institutional and policy prescriptions. Nor do they seek genuine input from affected populations.

An alternative livelihoods-centered perspective to sustainable development, which is supported by the critical political economy and political ecology analytical approaches, argues that market-friendly sustainable development blames the victims of economic development for ecological problems.[4] The livelihoods perspective recognizes that economic growth is necessary for development, but it questions whether market-led growth alone is the best path for economic, social, and environmental sustainability. Its proponents favor more ecologically-centered concepts and have a keen sensibility for the socioeconomic distributive effects of development models. Development efforts should be more decentralized, emphasize alternative technologies and techniques, promote smaller scale over large enterprises, and take citizen participation seriously. Above all, environmental problems are inextricably linked to impoverished, vulnerable rural and urban populations. The livelihoods of these people are better served through community organization and small-scale enterprise. Ecological integrity is best achieved by technologies that mimic or harness natural processes and projects that promote local self-reliance and local control over resource planning and distribution to achieve greater social equity.[5]

The livelihoods conceptualization of sustainable development is most often associated with natural resource utilization in rural and frontier settings. However, as we shall see, studies in the new field of environmental justice apply many of these principles to urban settings in their struggle to protect themselves from the disproportionate location of polluting industries and services in poor communities. The same holds true for the nascent field of environmental citizenship with its emphasis on rights for popular sectors to, for example, water, sanitation, and transportation.

Of course, some important approaches to the politics of environment and development lie outside of this general schema, although with significant overlaps in some areas. For example, in urban areas although the growing field of ecological modernization is sometimes classified as a variant of sustainable development, it does not fit neatly into a market or livelihoods dichotomy. It focuses on industry, pollution reduction, and civil society input but does not advocate that market mechanisms best solve problems or that the livelihood of local peoples are of paramount importance. Ecological modernization emerged as a field of study in northern Europe. Thus, the relationship between state and society in promoting industrial transformation take on strong societal corporatist characteristics.

More significantly for the study of the relationship between environment and development in Latin America, the biodiversity conservation paradigm starts from a nature-centered focused conceptualization of environmental problems, which stands in sharp contrast to the anthropocentric discourse of sustainable development. Biodiversity conservation focuses on the preservation of wilderness and ecosystems rich in biodiversity. Some conservationists reject development, sustainable or otherwise, outright and draw mainly from the field of conservation biology for their analyses. They advocate stricter government regulation to enforce conservation and land use, expanded policing of protected areas, and promotion of private parks. Others, however, attempt to incorporate core tenets of sustainable development into conservation practices around the vital environmental services that nature offers to people. Here too we can identify conservationists that lean towards market-friendly or livelihoods oriented approaches. The first group prefers market-based mechanisms to encourage carbon sequestration, genetic prospecting, eco-tourism, and private management of protected areas. Livelihoods-oriented conservations seek to ensure that communities benefit from conservation (see Table 12.1 and Table 12.2).

Table 12.1 Relationship of Conceptualizations of Environment and Development to Analytic Approaches

Analytic Approach	Sustainable Development				Competing Concepts
	Market Friendly		Livelihood		
	In Paradigm[a]	*Affinity*[b]	*In Paradigm*	*Affinity*	*Affinity*
Environmental Economics	Yes	—	No	—	Variants of Conservation
Political Economy	No	—	Yes	—	Some affinity with Environmental Justice and Environmental Citizenship
Political Ecology	No	—	Yes	—	Variants of Conservation Strong affinity to Environmental Justice and Environmental Citizenship

Source: Own elaboration

a In Paradigm means that the assumptions, problem specifications, and policy prescriptions of an analytic framework are wholly congruent with the sustainable development discourse, one of its sub-types, or some other conceptualization of the problem of environment and development.

b Affinity means that these are only partially congruent; hence they only address some specific issues or problems within the sustainable development paradigm or some other conceptualization of the problem of environment and development.

Table 12.2 Compatibility of Sustainable Development with Competing Conceptualizations of the Problem of Environment and Development

Competing Concept	Sustainable Development		
	Market Friendly Compatible	*Livelihood Compatible*	*Other*
Biodiversity Conservation	Yes – some variants	Yes – Some variants	—
Environmental Justice	No	Yes	—
Environmental Citizenship	No	Yes	—
Ecological Modernization	No	No	Industrial transformation in context of societal corporatism

Source: Own elaboration

The Politics of Environment and Development: Actors, Interests, and Power

These different approaches to environment and development generate distinctive diagnoses of the problem and competing policy prescriptions, and much has been written about them. What do we know about why and when they become actual policies? This is where politics takes center stage.

Politics is about the use of power, authority, and influence for resolving societal conflicts and for organizing cooperation to solve public problems. For routine, institutionalized politics this occurs in the policymaking process. Explaining policy outcomes requires knowing the actors involved, their interests, and their power; which are involved depends on the issue area. In the most general terms, these involve international and domestic state and societal sources. Multilateral organizations, foreign governments (generally through their aid programs), transnational corporations, and international NGOs are among the most significant external sources of influence. The domestic side includes national government executive and legislative institutions, political parties, environmental NGOs, and all manner of social groups from business to the subaltern in rural and urban areas.

Unpacking actors, interests, and power resources provides a starting point for analyzing the politics of environmental policymaking (see Table 12.3). However, explaining outcomes depends on the interaction between them; and especially on the dynamics of coalition formation among international actors, state institutions, social groups and NGOs. These alliances aggregate power resources in support or opposition to environmental policy proposals. In this sense, power is considered to be relational, meaning that the capabilities of each side are not fixed, they depend on the power of the other, which can be a shifting quantity. Finding or adding the right partners can be a significant source of leverage. In this respect, it is useful to think about enabling coalitions that support a particular environmental policy proposal and blocking coalitions that oppose it.[6]

The environment is generally not a high salience policy issue in Latin America, meaning it is not high on a national government's priorities, unless intensely pressured by coalitions of external and internal actors.[7] Economic growth, the consolidation of political institutions, the judiciary, security from drugs, crime and terrorism, usually take precedence. Most Latin American governments claim they do not have the funds to address environmental issues to

Table 12.3 Environmental Politics: Actors, Interests, and Coalitions, 1980s–Present

Actors	Sustainable Development		Other Discourses
	Market Friendly	Livelihood	Conservation
World Bank	1990s to present – leader	1980s – weak support	1990s to present – strong support
USAID	1990s to present – leader	1980s – weak support	1990s to present strong support
United Nations Environment Commission	1990s to present – strong support	1980s – leader	1990s to present/low priority
ECLAC	1990s to present – strong support	1980s – leader	
FAO	1990s – weak support	1980s – leader	
Dutch/Scandinavian Government Aid Agencies	1990s to present – weak	1980s to present – leaders	1990s to present/low priority
Latin American Governments	1990s – high priority	1980s – some led 2000s – left governments? (future research topic perhaps)	1990s to present – high priority
INGO/NGOs★	Some have always supported	Some have always supported	Some have always supported
Latin American Social Movements		1980s to present – strong support	1990s to present – some support
Business	1990s to present – some support		1990s to present – some support
Coalitions (Understand as both analytic constructs and real coalitions)	**1990s to present** World Bank; USAID; Business; United Nations; L.A. governments; some INGOs; some NGOs	**1990s to present** Dutch and Scandinavian aid agencies; some INGOs; some NGOs; L.A. social movements; weak L.A. government agencies; some L.A. political parties **1980s only** UN agencies included in the coalition (some weak support from FAO into the present). **2000s?** Need research on coalitional shifts in left governments	**1990s to present** *Core supporters:* World Bank; USAID; some INGOs; some NGOs; some L.A. government agencies *Secondary Support:* European aid agencies, UN, and some business groups

Source: Own elaboration

★INGO – International Nongovernmental Organization; NGOs refer to national nongovernmental organizations the extent needed or demanded by international organizations, advanced industrial country governments, and powerful international environmental NGOs. Some deeply resent insistent international calls to revert environmental degradation, going so far as to claim they are deliberate attempts to keep their countries from using their natural resources to develop—the way economically advanced countries once did. They point to deep global north/south inequities and demand that the economically advanced countries do more to pay for sustainable development and conservation in the global south.

The low saliency of the environmental issue area and the concomitantly low level of state resources devoted to them means that international actors play a significant role in environmental policymaking in Latin America. Foremost among them are the World Bank, the United Nations, and the United States Agency for International Development (USAID). European aid agencies are not insignificant, but do not play as large a role. These agents, along with international environmental NGOs, have over the past 40 years contributed to building international environmental regimes to which most Latin American states are signatories. These institutions have three valuable resources, technical expertise, organizational know-how, and funds.

Although environmental and conservationist concerns have had expression in Latin American state institutions, especially in health, sanitation, and parks, one can trace the emergence of the environmental issue area proper and its institutions to the evolution of international environmental regimes.[8] It was not that national actors were absent from the process, but they needed the leverage international organizations and treaties provided to push their cause. The first push came with the UN 1972 Stockholm conference, which gave an impulse to the creation of the first ministries of the environment, environmental protection agencies, and environmental coordinating commissions.[9] The Brundtland Committee (1987) and the UN Earth Summit in Rio (1992) placed the concept of sustainable development squarely on the policy agenda of Latin American states. At the regional level this manifested itself in the creation of an environmental section in the UN Economic Commission for Latin America and the Caribbean (ECLAC). Initially, UN system agencies supported the livelihoods approach in research and agricultural development and, together with the World Bank, ensured that policy circles adopted sustainable development as the principal framework for analyzing environmental problems in the early to mid 1990s.

However, because the World Bank was a leading architect of the Washington Consensus it favored a market-friendly approach to sustainable development, amplified by its regional branch, the Inter-American Development Bank. This trend penetrated the UN system, which had (and still has) significant pockets that support livelihoods approaches.[10] Generally speaking, the lack of financing for environmental projects and programs encouraged partnership with international business, which added an environmental component to its operations.[11]

The Politics of Environmental Institutional Development

The increased salience of environmental issues and regimes encouraged the development of specialized environmental government agencies to tackle environmental problems that in the past had been addressed by ministries such as health and agriculture, among others. By 2010, with the belated addition of Chile, virtually every major country in Latin America had a ministry of the environment. Unfortunately, the politics of environmental institutional capacity-building has not received much attention in the literature, with the partial exception of Brazil, Mexico, and Costa Rica and, to a lesser extent, Argentina and Chile. Yet, the subject is critical.

How can effective state institutions be built around issues that have low political salience (priority) in national governments? The conditions seem to be similar across the few cases that have been studied. In Brazil, Mexico, and Costa Rica they center on networks of highly knowledgeable activists turned public servants who leverage every opportunity to strengthen the small institutions they head. The key, lies in the network of connections that these public servant/activists cultivate with multilateral development institutions, international and domestic NGOs, and political parties. This facilitates coalition-building to generate political support and for attracting resources to design and implement policy.[12]

Two characteristics stand out. Environmental policy is not an external imposition and governments do provide critical opportunities for institution-building. Environmental policymaking in Brazil and Costa Rica involved an interplay of international and domestic conditions. The governments of these countries were responding to both external and internal pressures to address environmental problems. They appointed nationals who had experience and connections in the issue area. The directors of the fledgling institutions benefitted from the fact that the issue area was gaining saliency from expanding international regimes with resources to disburse and their countries (for different reasons) were in the spotlight. Brazil had been thrust in the limelight due to Amazonian deforestation and Costa Rica promoted its unique biodiversity and willingness to be the first Latin American country to embrace sustainable development.[13] In both countries the directors and key staff of these ministries then developed programs that mobilized external and internal resources for their implementation. The ascent of key political figures, patrons, or political parties from time to time presented additional opportunities for institutional expansion and capacity-building.

Given the importance of state institution-building for effective governance and the paucity of research, more studies into leadership and the political conditions conducive to the task would be welcome. Currently, policy studies dominate the field with work on the failures of policy implementation, the shortcomings of weak state institutions, and their substitution for program design and implementation by international NGOs or their domestic branches. But neither international organizations nor NGOs have the resources to develop and fund national policy and programs. They leverage the resources they have to push governments into certain directions and then offer isolated demonstration projects, many of which are not successful either. In the final analysis, national policy and effective environmental programs with a national reach will require government institutional capacity.[14]

So far in this chapter we have seen how different approaches to the issue of environment and development shape our general understanding of environmental politics in Latin America. We also surveyed the state of the literature on how politics affects both which policy prescriptions become policy and the course of institutional development. How these insights influenced interpretations of Latin American environmental politics in three key issue areas is the subject of the next sections. Where ever possible we will also look at the impact of combinations of actors, interests, and power on policy outcomes.

Environment, Development, and Natural Resources

Latin American development models stress commodity-led economic growth, which puts renewable and non-renewable natural resources under tremendous pressure. To a much greater extent than economically advanced countries, on average, Latin America relies on agro-mineral exports to supply the savings and investment necessary for economic development. The drive for economic expansion generally causes natural resource extraction to intensify in order to sell more on international markets.

The consequences for the environment of this development model are generally clear enough. Land clearing for agro-exports accelerates, forests are cut down, people are displaced, pesticide and chemical fertilizer use increases exponentially, toxic waste run-off accumulates, ill health effects mount, and arable land exhaustion and desertification threaten. Fisheries come under stress and the livelihood of artisan fishers vanishes. Mineral resources are extracted at great environmental cost to water resources, air pollution, and land contamination. More recently, energy production from nonrenewable mineral sources (especially hydrocarbons, but also coal and hydroelectric) has been linked to similar effects.

Given this economic development strategy and its consequences, scholarly and policy debates over the environment and sustainable development in Latin America overwhelmingly focus on natural resource use. A great deal of research concentrates on policy analysis. Studies seek to identify the causes of environmental degradation and then propose solutions. These studies, with their focus on diagnosis and policy prescription generally bypass politics, except perhaps as attempts to influence the agenda of the policy debate. They become political when international and domestic political, economic, and social actors begin to debate their utility, whether or not to adopt their recommendations, and in disputes over their implementation.

Market-Friendly Conceptualizations

Much of the policy analysis from the Multilateral Development Banks, government development aid agencies, and international NGOs has significant political consequences. The World Bank, for example, provides governments with policy recommendations and hires consultants and specialists to work with host government agencies in crafting national policy. Indeed, the World Bank is a political actor in its own right.[15] As of the 1990s, with the fall of Communism and the intensification of free-market globalization, their policy recommendations emphasized a market-friendly approach to sustainable development.[16] This trend is evident in forest policy debates.

Forests have arguably been the most studied natural renewable resource in Latin America. Concern over the rapid rate of deforestation in Amazonia beginning in the mid-1980s sparked intense policy and political debates. In the early 1990s, and with growing intensity, the policy prescriptions from the market-friendly perspective were clear, as evidenced by the cases of Mexico and Costa Rica. Environmental economists and their supporters prescribed privatization of the commons (state or communally-held land) and/or strengthening of private property rights to promote resource conservation because of the self-interest of owners in perpetuating an income stream. Deregulation and encouragement of private sector oversight of forest harvests, transportation, and commercialization to reduce costs was assumed to encourage sustained-yield forestry practices because more profit could be extracted per tree.[17]

Mexico and Costa Rica adopted much of this policy agenda in the 1990s. The politics of the policy process center on the receptivity of national governments to the international consultants and their policy recommendations. Receptivity to market-friendly proposals depended on several factors. In both cases national governments had appointed technocratic teams that supported the market solutions advocated by international agencies and worked directly with their consultants. This occurred because the Mexican and Costa

Rican governments were shifting towards a free-market development model. But that was not the only reason. Environment is a low priority issue compared to economic growth and the international sector offered critical resources in short supply at the domestic level: technical expertise, funds, and organizational know-how. Mexico's signature policy in this area was the abolition of a constitutional clause dating back to the Mexican revolution that established the inalienability of communal land rights. The restoration of private property rights on communally-held land had a significant impact on the forestry sector. Costa Rica, as did Mexico, deregulated most forestry activity.

Livelihood-Based Conceptualizations

Political analyses of market-friendly environmental policies emphasize technocratic politics involving international organizations and agents, national governments, and large international and domestic corporations. When appropriate, legislative politics are included. Critiques of the market-friendly approach focus on their shortcomings in three areas.[18] First, market-friendly environmental policies do not improve the livelihoods of the poor, indeed, markets exacerbate inequalities. Second, security of private property rights and deregulation do not necessarily improve environmental conditions. To the contrary, they usually continue to deteriorate. For example, between 1990 and 2000, Mexico lost an additional 631,000 hectares or 1.1 percent of its forest cover. During the same period Costa Rica lost 16,000 hectares or 0.8 percent of forest cover.[19] Third, politics are conceived as a top-down, technocratic exercise in heavy-handed elite-centered rule guided by the priorities of dominant international actors.

Livelihood-centered studies of the politics of sustainable development predominantly draw on political economy and political ecology analytical frameworks. They generally focus on how and when ideas, state structure, social forces, and international actors influence the adoption or exclusion of policies that address community organization, participation, and control of small-scale production that utilize low impact technologies that mimic natural processes. At its irreducible core, effective participation requires strengthening organized communities as the vehicle for the self-determination of subaltern class and ethnic-based groups.

Political economists stress how political and economic factors such as national policies, commodity prices, and international politics have led to unsustainable resource practices by powerful actors such as local elites, states, and transnational corporations.[20] From this perspective, reversing these trends requires connecting local processes such as adaptive practices, informal institutions, and social capital to large-scale political and economic developments such as national and international economic processes and politics, state institutions, and social conflicts.[21]

Political ecology distinguishes itself from political economy in that environmental concerns stand at the front and center of the discipline. Its analysis focuses tightly on the environmental sources of cleavages, conflict, and cooperation; for example water. Firmly anchored in the ecological dimensions of the problem under study, political ecology investigates with much greater precision than political economy the linkages between local and non-local processes. Also to a much greater extent than political economy it analyzes the articulation between formal and informal networks and institutions in environmental politics and how these affect processes and outcomes. In short, it examines how the dialectics between the environment and social systems at temporal, spatial and institutional scales affect collaborative and conflictive behavior among stakeholders in a given environmental issue and the resulting socio-environmental outcomes. This approach has been applied to the analysis of a large range of socio-environmental systems in Latin America.[22] These include land use, forests, water, fisheries, and mineral extraction.[23]

A great deal of scholarship draws on political economy and political ecology to analyze environmental problems. However, these approaches have had less success in translating their policy prescriptions into actual policy. This is principally due to the fact that the market paradigm predominates in the multilateral institutions, international organizations (even in the United Nations), U.S. agencies for development, and national governments; and these are the actors that primarily shape international environmental regimes and national policy frameworks.

Political fortunes for livelihoods-inspired sustainable development policies were not always so unfavorable. Before the intensification of neoliberal globalization in the 1990s, they had some notable successes in policy circles. For example, both Mexico and Costa Rican national policy significantly supported community forestry in the 1980s. That was a time when the United Nations and national governments aligned more closely with the Brundtland Commission's more social democratic orientation. It was also a time when the World Bank had not yet become the leading multilateral institution in environmental politics, nor was it one of the architects of neoliberal globalization.

Since the mid-1990s, the greatest contributions to policy of the political economy and political ecology schools of thought lie in two areas. First, they help mold the thinking and projects of a few mostly northern European international aid agencies and international NGOs that support the livelihood model of sustainable development and its principles. Second, scholar-activists in the political economy and political ecology schools participate in social movement and NGO networks that advocate and demand livelihoods approach solutions to environmental concerns. Their ideas and connections strengthen pressure from below on policy makers to consider—and at times to halfheartedly adopt—their proposals, albeit always in a subordinate position. Some left of center political parties also support policies inspired by political economy and political ecology thinking.

Biodiversity Conservation

Next to natural resource use, biodiversity conservation and global climate change are among the top policy issues in Latin American environmental politics. Indeed, they have become inextricably linked. Biodiversity conservation gained traction in reaction to rapidly disappearing habitat due to environmentally unsustainable development and the threat it posed to the survival of species (including humans). The destruction of tropical rainforests—the "lungs" of the earth and repository of rich biodiversity (much of it unclassified)—topped the list of concerns. Their disappearance and fragmentation was driven by road building, the slash-and-burn agriculture of a migrant population that poured into erstwhile pristine landscapes that followed, the clearing of forest for cattle and agribusiness, large-scale mining, placer miners polluting rivers and streams, and mega-dam construction.

Policy debates concentrated on conservation versus preservation. Conservation studies focus on habitat protection taking prevailing land use practices into account. They borrow from the political ecology approach to sustainable development recognizing that local peoples rely on the land to provide for their livelihood.[24] A key objective is the preservation of as much of the remaining habitat as possible by researching and supporting small-scale community-centered projects that respect the environment. The goal is for those activities to provide sufficient income to keep people from encroaching on relatively undisturbed land. Ideally, the community becomes a guardian of the commons, rather than its destroyer. The overriding objective is to protect biodiversity rich core habitat areas, usually in protected areas such as parks and nature reserves. Thus, socially and economically sustainable human activities in buffer zones secure the ecological sustainability (integrity) of vital core areas. A number of studies concentrated on the economic worth of traditional and non-traditional marketable crops in local, regional, and export markets. Others focused on community organization for production, distribution, and marketing. Small-scale eco-tourism (and adventure tourism) offered attractive possibilities as well.

Preservation, by contrast, focuses on the protection of parks and nature reserves from human economic activity. The literature tends to be skeptical about the feasibility of sustainable development due to its tradeoffs, conflicting objectives, and difficulties with implementation. From this perspective, the integrity of habits and their biodiversity depend on the capacity of civil society, international organization and cooperation, and, in a few instances perhaps the state, to secure them effectively from humans. Deep ecologists and disenchanted conservationists regarded the money, expertise, and time spent on unworkable sustainable community development projects to be wasted resources. Swelling human encroachment on and depredation in "paper parks" despite concerted efforts to generate economically and socially viable buffer zones signaled a clear policy failure. Better to devote those resources directly to habit protection: policing, land demarcation, zoning enforcement, and strict environmental impact reporting and protective rules and regulations for large-scale extractive projects that could not be stopped.[25]

As noted previously, there is some literature on the politics of the institutional development of parks and protected areas, especially for Costa Rica, Mexico, Brazil, and, to a lesser extent, Argentina and Chile. International organizations and actors (especially NGOs) played an important part in the turn toward strengthening institutions for habitat protection. Over the 1990s and the first decade of the 2000s, international actors and global developments increased the political leverage of political forces seeking to expand conservation, and especially, habitat preservation.

The bulk of new policy initiatives focus on market-based instruments for project design and financing; as well as market incentives for individuals to support those efforts. This trend began with the creation of the World Bank's Global Environmental Facility following the 1992 Rio Conference on Environment and Development, which emphasized biodiversity conservation in its project funding. It has been strengthened in the post-Kyoto Convention (1997) period with the creation of policy instruments for carbon offsets, such as the Clean Development Mechanism (see below). In general, carbon offset projects come under land use, land-use change, and forestry category (LULUCF) of the UN Climate Change Secretariat. These focus on reducing greenhouse gas emissions by protecting natural carbon sinks, principally forests and soil. The basic mechanism is simple. Developed nations pay for the protection of forests in developing countries. In the language of environmental economics, the forests and soil of developing nations supply environmental services (carbon sequestration) that developed nations purchase.[26]

Global Climate Change

For most of the 2000s, climate change policy has dominated debates about sustainable development, eclipsing all other environmental policy issues. The United Nations has spearheaded diplomacy and research to craft an international regime to reduce carbon emissions and other pollutants associated with anthropogenic causes of global climate change.

Following the Kyoto Protocol of 1997, the latest effort was the disappointing December 2009 United Nations Climate Change Conference in Copenhagen and a follow-up conference in Cancun, Mexico in the waning months of 2010. In recent years, the World Bank has devoted significant attention to the issue as well. In Latin America, ECLAC has given global climate change the highest priority by far among environmental policy issues.[27]

Their main policy recommendations emphasize flexible market economic mechanisms to control and reduce greenhouse gas emissions. The principal instruments include cap and trade (a cap on overall emissions and the trading emission certificates), joint implementation, and the clean development mechanism. All have in common that a higher reduction in one place makes up for a lower reduction in another place. Compensatory mechanisms for developing countries are also prescribed in the form of an adaptation fund for developing countries, most likely to be administered by the World Bank's Global Environmental Facility.

Joint Implementation (JI) and the Clean Development Mechanism (CDM) are the most relevant instruments for our purposes. They are similar in that they are project-oriented. A greenhouse gas emission sequestration or reduction project in one country is credited to a diminution in an advanced country's obligation to decrease emissions. The country receiving the credits must pay for the environmental service provided by the greenhouse gas sequestration or reduction project. The difference lies in countries eligible for projects: CDMs are for developing countries and JIs are for former eastern bloc (communist) countries. The CDM admits over 200 types of projects for generating carbon offsets grouped into the following broad categories: renewable energy, methane abatement, energy efficiency, reforestation and fuel switching.

This policy trend supports market-oriented approaches to sustainable development that benefit corporations in the refuse, agribusiness, forestry, and energy industries. They have the expertise and organizational capability to meet project eligibility requirements. It is less clear how "local communities" (a more livelihood-centered approach to sustainable development) can access CDMs. Some studies by NGOS have made important policy recommendations to address this issue. The World Bank itself, with its focus on poverty alleviation has also begun to analyze how to make CDMs more accessible to "vulnerable" populations.[28] Overall, however, the politics of how rules of access to these benefits are decided and their distributive effects merits more research.

Urban Landscapes

The politics of sustainable development in Latin American urban settings is an understudied but growing subject. Three emerging schools of thought offer promising avenues of research: ecological modernization, environmental justice, and environmental citizenship. Although they do not fit neatly with either of the conceptualizations of sustainable development or with any of the analytic frameworks discussed thus far, they do bear a family resemblance to some of them (see Table 12.2). Because they are so new in the Latin American context, here we focus on their principal tenets and potential for future investigation. We also consider the potential contributions of the more established political economy and political ecology frameworks.

Ecological modernization examines the political conditions and institutions that foment policies to generate clean industrial production processes. One reason for the paucity of research may be that those conditions are weak in Latin America. Ecological modernization requires stable, solid political institutions, both of the state and political parties, as well as those that represent industry groups and organized civil society. It also requires institutional linkages among them upon which to build. Nevertheless, some pioneering studies have emerged making innovative adaptations to the framework. [29] One promising line of research would be to identify specific industries and regulatory institutions sufficiently advanced to consider innovation in "pockets of ecological modernization." This could be initially modeled on the "pockets of excellence" research on industrial policy in Latin America—areas with sufficient state capacity interacting with well-established private sector and civil society organizations.

A lively debate exists regarding whether ecological modernization contributes to the sustainable development paradigm. Some of its proponents claim that its transformative potential for industrial society warrants a separate categorization. Moreover, even when considered part of the sustainable development paradigm it does not fit in either the market or livelihoods variants. It advocates neither markets nor grassroots development. It fits best with a social democratic and corporatist conceptualization of the relationship between the state, society, industrial transformation, and the environment.

The environmental justice school has had a better reception in Latin America, although it too has just begun to be applied there. It analyzes the distribution of environmental costs and benefits, the empowerment of marginalized groups cutting across race, ethnicity and class, and poverty reduction.[30] Research focuses on community efforts to fight the concentration of polluting industries, utilities, waste disposal, and poor environmental health conditions in underprivileged neighborhoods. It also examines how people in low income communities cooperate to construct green areas, community gardens, and waste systems conducive to environmentally (and psychologically) healthier communities. One could argue that environmental justice bears a strong affinity to the livelihoods approach to sustainable development and political ecology analysis.

Studies on the intersection of democracy, justice, citizen rights, and their relationship to environmental concerns have proliferated in the last decade. Democratic regimes are clearly a significant beneficial factor shaping environmental politics. They permit fuller debate, contestation, and environmental protection than authoritarian regimes.[31] The revival of democracy renewed interest in citizenship, which has given rise to the concept of environmental citizenship. Environmental citizenship refers to the dynamic interaction between democratic rights and responsibilities and the environment along two distinct dimensions. Policy-oriented studies that focus on environmental rights and obligations is one.[32] The other concentrates on empirical studies of bottom up socio-political struggles to reshape them.[33] Citizenship and the institutions that give it concrete form are contested territory for two reasons. On the one hand, there is Latin America's history of rigid unequal social relations rooted in conquest, imperialism, ethnic conflict, and resource-based economic development. On the other hand, a great variety of political cultures—European, Latin American, and indigenous—with distinctive conceptualizations of socio-ecological relations vie for dominance. The study of environmental citizenship as contested terrain opens space for explicitly political analyses of the concept and its integration into the field of environmental politics.[34]

Framed this way, environmental citizenship opens rich opportunities for research on urban environmental politics and environmental justice. Sharp inequalities in Latin American urban habitats generate conflicts over political rights and institutions and the control of space. In environmental politics, popular sector struggles turn on claims "for more inclusionary urban habitats, where all citizens have rights to space in which to dwell, seek their livelihood, and build healthy communities."[35] For example, one study analyzed control over water rights and institutions in Mexico. Another researched how social movements in Belem, Brazil, fought entrenched elitism and exclusion for rights to space, sanitation, and transportation.[36] However, studies of environmental citizenship and justice in Latin America are not limited to urban landscapes. They include struggles for more inclusionary rights in rural areas where tensions over political community intertwine with rights to land, water, and efforts to conserve resource commons such as forests or pastures.[37] Like environmental justice, the environmental citizenship school bears an affinity with livelihoods approaches to sustainable development and draws from political ecology theorizing.

Of course, the more established political economy and political ecology schools of thought proper potentially also have a lot to contribute to the study of urban environmental politics in Latin America. Political economy can help us clarify our understanding of the structural conditions that explain policy choices regarding urban land use planning, the distribution of services, and opportunity. Such studies can be useful for uncovering institutional bottlenecks and the sources of institutional innovation.[38] Political ecology can shed significant light on the political conditions that support or inhibit poor people's struggles for environmental health and quality, as well as their inclusion in the political processes that decide such issues.

Future Research

Where to go from here? The preceding sections suggested directions for future research in a number of specific issue areas. Here I would like to step back and suggest more general lines of investigation. From the stand point of theory-building, the field of environmental politics could benefit from a more cumulative research effort. So far we have a wealth of studies on individual experiences, topics, and geographical areas. What research strategies will lead us to new concepts and tools applicable to a broader range of those experiences and places? Theoretically focused, empirically grounded work—mid-range theorizing—could be useful for discovering those linkages. Here, the development of comparative environmental politics—with an explicit recognition of international factors—could be very fruitful.[39]

The tension between market and livelihood-centered approaches to sustainable development offers a valuable point of entry to this enterprise. The two "approaches" are a heuristic devise to highlight essential cleavages and conflicts. In most cases the characteristics of these two ideal types intertwine; or the characteristics of an issue area and approaches to studying them may bear only some affinity to them. A cumulative research effort could be built around sorting mixtures, their meaning, and effects. Critical questions include: What are the structural and political conditions that shape opportunities for advancing one or the other agenda? How does the interaction between the imposition of elite-driven, technocratic programs from above and resistance and proactive initiatives from below affect outcomes? What constitutes power in that interaction? Is it possible to transcend the dichotomy in a meaningful way? If so, how?

Current debates over environmental governance and environmental citizenship illustrate how these questions could drive cumulative research. Environmental governance is about building institutions for managing the tension between market and livelihood-centered environmental politics in an equitable and legitimated manner. In the last quarter of a century free-market capitalism dominated, and with it the political conditions for market-friendly policy to sustainable development predominated. Those efforts were resisted by subaltern social groups for material, ideational, and cultural reasons. Does the left-ward political trend in Latin American politics that those social movements helped to usher in offer an opening for a greater inclusion of livelihoods-based approaches to sustainable development? Does the decline in confidence in markets and self-regulation brought on by the Great Recession in 2008 have a similar effect? Do these developments signify a new opportunity for the construction of institutions for environmental governance that do a better job of resolving the tensions of sustainable development?[40]

In a similar vein, are the concepts of environmental citizenship, environmental justice, and ecological modernization innovative means to reframe sharp divisions among people in a language and symbolism capable of inducing more cooperation? Are new national and international realities an opportunity to infuse largely market-based climate change policy initiatives with livelihood concerns in more substantive ways—to embed markets in security from want and in solidarity with nature? If so, under what conditions?

Asking these types of questions can lead to cumulative knowledge because they invite conversations across specialized topics, approaches, and cases. They advance our knowledge of the politics of environmental issues and policy. A clearer understanding of politics is necessary for environmental policy because politics is about cooperation as much as it is about conflict. We need to recognize political opportunities for cooperation and innovation in the principles, norms, processes, and instruments by which societies contain conflict and cooperate to resolve problems.[41]

Notes

1 Brundtland Commission, *Our Common Future* (Oxford: Oxford University Press, 1987).
2 The World Bank coined the concept in World Bank, *World Development Report, 1992: Development and the Environment* (Oxford: Oxford University Press, 1992).
3 Garrett Hardin, "The Tragedy of the Commons," *Science* 162 (1968): 1243.
4 Michael Redclift, *Sustainable Development: Exploring the Contradictions* (London: Methuen, 1987); Michael Redclift and David Goodman, eds., *Environment and Development in Latin America: The Politics of Sustainability* (Manchester: Manchester University Press, 1991).
5 For an introduction to these themes see, D. Ghai and J.M. Vivian, eds., *Grassroots Environmental Action: People's Participation in Sustainable Development* (London: Routledge, 1992); J. Friedmann and H. Rangan, eds., *In Defense of Livelihood: Comparative Studies in Environmental Action* (West Hartford: Kumarian Press, 1993).
6 For first rate studies, see Katheryn Hochstetler and Margaret Keck, *Greening Brazil: Environmental Activism in State and Society* (Durham, NC: Duke University Press, 2007); Heleen van den Hombergh, *No Stone Unturned: Building Blocks of Environmentalist Power versus Transnational Industrial Forestry in Costa Rica* (Amsterdam: Dutch University Press, 2004); Barbara Hogenboom, *Mexico and the NAFTA Environmental Debate: The Transnational Politics of Economic Integration* (Utrecht: International Books, 1998).
7 The Campaign against Amazonian deforestation in Brazil in the 1980s and early 1990s was such an exception, see Stephen Schwartzman, "Deforestation and Popular Resistance in Acre: From Local Social Movement to Global Network," *The Centennial Review* 35 (1991): 422.
8 For an introduction to environmental regimes see, Gareth Porter, Janet W. Brown, and Pamela S. Chasek, *Global Environmental Politics* (Boulder: Westview Press, 2000, third edition).
9 Rodrigo Brañes, *Institutional and Legal Aspects of the Environment in Latin America* (Washington, D.C.: Inter-American Development Bank, 1991).
10 Herweg Cleuren, *Paving the Way for Forest Destruction: Key Actors and Driving Forces of Tropical Deforestation in Brazil, Ecuador, and Cameroon* (Leiden: Leiden University Press, 2001); Ans Kolk, *Forests in International Environmental Politics: International Organizations, NGOs, and the Brazilian Amazon* (Utrecht: International Books, 1996).
11 Ans Kolk and Jonathan Pinske, *International Business and Global Climate Change* (London: Routledge, 2009); Mirjam A.F. Ros-Tonen, Heleen van den Hombergh, and Annelies Zoomers, *Partnerships in Sustainable Forest Resource Management: Learning from Latin America* (Boston: Brill, 2007).

12 For Brazil see, Hochstetler and Keck, *Greening Brazil*; Leslie K. McAllister, *Making Law Matter: Environmental and Legal Institutions in Brazil* (Palo Alto: Stanford University Press, 2008); Roberto F. Guimaraes, *The Ecopolitics of Development in the Third World: Politics and Environment in Brazil* (Boulder: Lynne Rienner Publishers, 1991). For Mexico see, Lane Simonian, *Defending the Land of the Jaguar: A History of Conservation in Mexico* (Austin: University of Texas Press, 1995); For Costa Rica as well as Argentina and Chile see, Jack Hopkins, *Policymaking for Conservation in Latin American National Parks, Reserves, and the Environment* (Westport, CT: Praeger, 1995). For Chile see, Eduardo Silva, "Democracy, Market Economics, and Environmental Policy in Chile," *Journal of Interamerican Studies and World Affairs* 38, 4 (1997).

13 Schwartzman, "Deforestation and Popular Resistance in Acre"; Hopkins, *Policymaking for Conservation.*

14 Martin Jänicke, Helmut Weidner, and Helge Jörgens, eds., *Capacity Building in National Environmental Policy: A Comparative Study of 27 Countries* (Berlin: Springer, 2002).

15 Eduardo Silva, David Kaimowitz, Alan Bojanic, Francois Ekoko, Togu Maurung, Iciar Pavez, "Making the Law of the Jungle: The Reform of Forestry Legislation in Bolivia, Cameroon, Costa Rica, and Indonesia," *Global Environmental Politics* 2, 3 (2002): 63.

16 Ngaire Woods, *The Globalizers: The IMF, the World Bank, and their Borrowers* (Ithaca: The Cornell University Press, 2006); World Bank, *Sustainable Development in a Dynamic World: Transforming Institutions, Growth, and Quality of Life* (Oxford: Oxford University Press, 2003).

17 Oscar Segura, David Kaimowitz, and Jorge Rodríguez, *Política Forestal en Centro América: Análisis de las restricciones para el desarrollo del sector forestal* [Forest Policy in Central America: Analysis of Restrictions for Forest Sector Development] (San Salvador: IICA, 1997); Nalin M. Kishor and Luis F. Constantino, "Forest Management and Competing Land Uses: An Economic Analysis for Costa Rica," The World Bank Latin America Technical Department Environmental Division, Note no. 7, 1993. For Mexico see, World Bank, "Estudio del Subsector Forestal," (Draft, February 1994).

18 Michael Painter and William H. Durham, eds., *The Social Causes of Environmental Destruction in Latin America.* (Ann Arbor: The University of Michigan Press, 1995).

19 United Nations Food and Agriculture Organization, *The State of the World's Forests, 2003.* (Rome: UN Food and Agriculture Organization).

20 Marianne Schmink and Charles Wood, *Contested Frontiers in Amazonia.* (New York: Columbia University Press, 1992); Hogenboom, *Mexico and the NAFTA Environment Debate*; Miriam Cohen Alfie and Luis H. Mendez B., *Maquila y movimientos ambientalistas: Examen de un riesgo compartido* [Maquila and environmental movements: Consideration of a venture] (Mexico: Grupo Editorial Eon, 2000).

21 Joan Martínez-Alier, *The Environmentalism of the Poor: A Study of Ecological Conflicts and Valuation* (Cheltenham: Edward Elgar, 2002); Edward F. Fischer and Peter Benson, *Broccoli and Desire: Global Connections and Maya Struggles in Postwar Guatemala.* (Stanford, CA: Stanford University Press, 2006).

22 Arturo Escobar, *Pacífico, desarrollo o diversidad? Estado, capital y movimientos sociales en el Pacífico colombiano* [Pacific, development or diversity? State, capital and social movements in the Colombian Pacific]. (Bogotá: Serie ecológica. Ecofondo, 1996); Arturo Escobar, *Territories of Difference. Place, Movements, Life, Redes* (Durham: Duke University Press, 2008); Enrique Leff, "La ecología política en América Latina: Un campo en construcción" [Political ecology in Latin America: a field under construction], *Sociedad y Estado* 18 (2003): 17; Víctor M. Toledo, *La Paz en Chiapas: ecología, luchas indígenas y modernidad alternativa* [Peace in Chiapas: ecology, indigenous struggles and alternative modernity] (México City: Quinta Sol, 2000); Anthony Bebbington, "Contesting Environmental Transformation. Political Ecologies and Environmentalisms in Latin America and the Caribbean," *Latin American Research Review*, 44 (2009): 177.

23 For land use see, Lawrence S. Grossman, *The Political Ecology of Bananas: Contract Farming, Peasants, and Agrarian Change in the Eastern Caribbean* (Chapel Hill: University of North Carolina Press, 1998). For forests see, Phillip M. Fearnside (2008) "The roles and movements of actors in the deforestation of Brazilian Amazonia," *Ecology and Society* 13 (2008): 23; for water see, Karl S. Zimmerer, "Rescaling irrigation in Latin America: The cultural images and political ecology of water resources," *Cultural Geographies* 7 (2000): 150. For fisheries see, Silvia Salas, Ratana Chuenpagdee, Juan Carlos Seijo, and Anthony Charles, "Challenges in the assessment and management of small-scale fisheries in Latin America and the Caribbean," *Fisheries Research*

Vol. 87(2007): 5. For mineral extraction see Anthony Bebbington, *Minería, movimientos sociales y respuestas campesinas: una ecología política de transformaciones territoriales* [Mining, social movements and peasant responses: a political ecology of territorial transformations] (Lima: Instituto de Estudios Peruanos, 2007).

24 For an excellent introduction see, R. Edward Grumbie, ed., *Environmental Policy and Biodiversity* (Washington. D.C.: Island Press, 1994).

25 For a comprehensive analysis see, Katrina Brandon, Kent Redford, and Steven Sanderson, *Parks in Peril: People, Politics, and Protected Areas* (Washington, D.C.: Island Press, 1998).

26 For an overview of these and other policy instruments see, Oliver Deke, *Environmental Policy Instruments for Conserving Global Biodiversity* (Berlin: Springer, 2010).

27 For useful overviews of the Kyoto Protocol framework and the policy instruments discussed below see, W.Th. Douma, L. Massai, and M. Montini, eds., *The Kyoto Protocol and Beyond: Legal and Policy Challenges of Climate Change* (The Hague: T.M.C. Asser Press, 2007); Joseph E. Aldy, and Robert N. Stavins, eds., *Architectures for Agreement: Addressing Global Climate Change in the Post-Kyoto World* (Cambridge: Cambridge University Press, 2007); Margie Orford, Margie, *The Kyoto Protocol's Clean Development Mechanism.* (London: ITDG, 2004).

28 For the World Bank see, World Bank, *World Development Report 2010: Development and Climate Change* (Oxford: Oxford University Press, 2010); For carbon offsets and equity issues see, Joyotee Smith and Sara J. Scherr, "Forest Carbon Livelihoods: Assessment of Opportunities and Policy Recommendations," Center for International Forestry Research, Occasional Paper No. 37, 2002; Katrina Brown and Esteve Corbera, "Exploring Equity and Sustainable Development in the New Carbon Economy," *Climate Policy* 3 (2002): 41.

29 Arthur P.J. Mol, David A. Sonnenfeld, and Gert Spaargaren, eds., *The Ecological Modernization Reader: Environmental Reform in Theory and Practice* (London: Routledge, 2010); Jänicke, Weidner, Jörgens, eds., *Capacity Building in National Environmental Policy: A Comparative Study of 27 Countries.*

30 David V. Carruthers, ed., *Environmental Justice in Latin America: Problems, Promise, and Practice.* (Cambridge: MIT Press, 2008); Juanita Sundberg, "Placing race in environmental justice research in Latin America," *Society and Natural Resources* 21 (2008): 569.

31 For an excellent study see, Kathryn Hochstetler, "Comparative Environmental Politics and Democracy: Latin American and Eastern Europe Compared," in *The Comparative Politics of the Environment*, eds., Paul Steinberg and Stacy VanDeveer (Cambridge, MA: MIT Press, forthcoming).

32 Eduardo Gudynas, "Ciudadanía ambiental y meta-ciudadanías ecológicas: Revisión y alternativas en América Latina," in *Urgencia y utopía frente a la crisis de la civilización* [Urgency, Utopia, and the crisis of civilization,], eds. J. Reyes, Ruiz and E. Castro Rosales (Guadalajara: Universidad de Guadalajara, 2009); Derek R. Bell, "Liberal Environmental Citizenship," *Environmental Politics* 14 (2005): 179; Simon Hailwood, "Environmental Citizenship as Reasonable Citizenship," *Environmental Politics* 14 (2005): 195.

33 Alex Latta, "Between Political Worlds: Indigenous Citizenship in Chile's Alto Bío-Bío," *Latin American and Caribbean Ethnic Studies* 4 (2009): 47; Rualdo Menegar, "Participatory Democracy and Sustainable Development: Integrated Urban Environmental Management in Porto Alegre, Brazil," *Environment and Urbanization* 14 (2002): 181; José Esteban Castro, *Water, Power and Citizenship: Social Struggle in the Basin of Mexico* (New York: Palgrave Macmillan, 2006).

34 For a first rate review see, Alex Latta and Hannah Wittman, "Environment and Citizenship in Latin America: A New Paradigm for Theory and Practice," *European Review of Latin American and Caribbean Stuides* 89 (2010): 107.

35 Latta and Wittman, "Environment and Citizenship in Latin America," p. 112.

36 For water rights see Castro, *Water, Power and Citizenship.* For environment and citizenship in urban Brazil see, John Guidry, "Trial by Space: The Spatial Politics of Citizenship and Social Movements in Urban Brazil," *Mobilization: An International Quarterly* 8 (2003): 189.

37 Hannah Wittman, "Agrarian Reform and the Environment: Fostering Ecological Citizenship in Mato Grosso, Brazil," *Canadian Journal of Development Studies* 29 (2010): 281; Carruthers, *Environmental Justice in Latin America.*

38 Kathryn Hochstetler, "The Politics of Environmental Licensing: Energy Projects of the Past and Future in Brazil," unpublished paper, is an excellent example.

39 Paul F. Steinberg, "Comparative Environmental Politics: Beyond an Enclave Approach," *Review of Policy Research* 27 (2010): 95; Paul F. Steinberg and Stacy D. VanDeveer, *Comparative Environmental Politics* (Cambridge, MA: MIT Press, forthcoming).

40 The Center for Latin American Study and Documentation (CEDLA) and the University of Amsterdam (UvA) are coordinating a study on environmental governance. CEDLA and UvA, "Environmental Governance in Latin America and the Caribbean: Developing Frameworks for Sustainable and Equitable Natural Resource Use," European Commission, Socio-economic Sciences and the Humanities, FP7-SSH-2010-3. Michiel Baud, Fabio de Castro, and Barbara Hogenboom, "Environmental Governance in Latin America: Toward an Integrative Research Agenda," *European Review of Latin American and Caribbean Studies*, 90 (April) 2011.

41 Elinor Ostrom, *The Governing of the Commons: The Evolution of Institutions for Collective Action. Political Economy of Institutions and Decisions* (Cambridge: Cambridge University Press, 1990).

13

SOCIAL POLICIES IN LATIN AMERICA

Causes, Characteristics, and Consequences[1]

James W. McGuire

This chapter classifies the main social policies enacted in Latin America from 1920 to 2010, explores the effects of those policies on the well-being of the poor, and outlines some of the forces and circumstances that led to the policies. The study's main findings are that social assistance and the public provision of many basic social services improved in Latin America after about 1990, even as the coverage of social insurance programs fell; that democracy and authoritarianism played an important and multifaceted role in shaping and constraining social policy-making in the region; and that a full explanation for why Latin American social policies evolved in the way that they did requires taking into account a wider range of factors than are usually invoked to explain the origins and evolution of welfare states in advanced industrial countries.

Latin American countries since about 1920 have produced three main types of social policies: *contributory social insurance* (against the "four basic risks" of old age, disability, illness, and unemployment); *social assistance* (general revenue-funded cash or other types of transfers to needy individuals, households, or communities); and the *public provision of general revenue-funded basic social services* (such as health care, nutrition, education, family planning, water, and sanitation).

Most political science research on Latin American social policies has focused on contributory social insurance. If the goal of such research is to find out "who gets what, when, and how," then social insurance is a suitable topic. In 12 of the 16 Latin American countries for which data are available, social insurance around the year 2000 absorbed more than 50 percent of public social spending. In each of the four most populous countries (Brazil, Mexico, Colombia, and Argentina), it absorbed more than 70 percent (Table 13.1). Social insurance is a less appropriate focus, however, if the outcome of interest is the well-being of the Latin American poor. In 2002–2003, discounting the contributions made by employers and workers, public spending on social insurance benefited the richest 20 percent of the population, as compared to the poorest 20 percent, in a ratio of 4:1 in Mexico, 7:1 in Brazil, and 12:1 in Argentina.[2] It thus imposed a huge burden on economic output (more than 10 percent of GDP in Argentina, Brazil, and Uruguay, as Table 13.1 shows) while having a highly regressive benefit incidence. In contrast to social insurance, most types of social assistance and public provision of basic social services had a more progressive benefit incidence, but were funded more frugally and suffered for many years from

Table 13.1 Public Spending on Social Insurance, Social Assistance, and Education/Health, circa 2000, Sixteen Latin American Countries[1]

Country	Col. 1 Public spending on social insurance as a share of GDP, various years 1998-2005	Col. 2 Public spending on social assistance as a share of GDP, various years 1998-2005	Col. 3 Public spending on education and health care as a share of GDP, 2000	Col. 4 "Total" social spending as a share of GDP (sum of Cols. 1, 2, and 3)	Col. 5 Social insurance spending as share of "total" social spending, circa 2000
Costa Rica	8.8	1.5	0.5	10.8	81%
Argentina	10.7	1.5	2.0	14.2	75%
Colombia	8.3	0.6	2.2	11.1	75%
Brazil	11.7	1.4	2.9	16.0	73%
Bolivia	8.6	2.0	1.4	12.0	72%
Mexico	4.2	1.0	0.8	6.0	70%
Uruguay	11.3	0.5	4.4	16.2	70%
Peru	4.5	0.7	1.4	6.6	68%
Chile	7.4	0.7	2.9	11.0	67%
Nicaragua	5.4	1.1	2.6	9.1	59%
El Salvador	4.2	1.0	2.0	7.2	58%
Panama	5.0	1.7	2.7	9.4	53%
Venezuela	1.9	0.6	1.5	4.1	46%
Paraguay	1.8	0.4	1.7	3.9	46%
Dominican Republic	1.1	1.7	1.8	4.6	24%
Guatemala	0.7	1.1	4.2	6.0	12%

1 Cols. 1 and 2: Margaret Grosh et al., "Spending on Social Safety Nets: Comparative Data Compiled From World Bank Analytic Work" (Washington, DC: World Bank, 2008), database accessed February 21, 2011, at http://www.worldbank.org. The "descriptive" tab of this database reveals that only in El Salvador, Guatemala, Nicaragua, Panama, and Paraguay does "social insurance" include public spending on health insurance (net of employer and employee contributions). Accordingly, except in these five countries, the figure in Col. 1 has been raised, and the figure in Col. 3 reduced, by the amount of public spending specifically on health *insurance* as a share of GDP, which is calculated as the product of (a) "Social security expenditure on health as percentage of general government expenditure on health, 2000" times (b) "General government expenditure on health as a share of GDP, 2000" (data from World Health Organization, *World Health Statistics 2010*. Geneva: WHO, 2010, pp. 130-137). Colombia and Mexico require special attention. In Colombia, Grosh et al. (2008) include under social insurance the cost of the Subsidized Health Insurance Regime (0.9 percent of GDP), but not the cost of any other public spending on health insurance. To avoid double-counting, accordingly, 0.9 percent has been subtracted from the resulting Colombia figure in Col. 1 (cost estimate is from Tarsicio Castañeda, "Targeting Social Spending to the Poor With Proxy Means-Testing: Colombia's SISBEN System," World Bank Social Protection Discussion Paper 0529. Washington, DC: World Bank, 2005, p. 23). In Mexico, Grosh et al. (2008) include under social insurance the cost of health insurance for state workers in the ISSSTE scheme. No estimate of that cost was available, however, so the Mexico entry in Col. 1 unavoidably double-counts public expenditure on health insurance for workers in the ISSSTE plan.

Col. 3: Education spending ("Public expenditure on education, 2000") is from UNESCO Institute for Statistics Data Centre, accessed March 3, 2011, at http://stats.uis.unesco.org (the Venezuela figure is from 2006 rather than 2000). Health care spending ("General government expenditure on health as a share of GDP, 2000") is from World Health Organization, *World Health Statistics 2010*, pp. 130-137. Before being added to public spending on education, public spending on health care was reduced by the cost of public spending on health insurance, which was calculated as described in the note to Col. 1.

design and implementation problems. Family planning and primary health care began to improve in some countries in the 1960s and 1970s, but it was not until the 1990s that widespread gains were made in social assistance and in the public provisioning of a range of basic social services.

During the first era of Latin American social policy (1920 to 1980), governments extended social insurance to white-collar and blue-collar formal-sector workers, but not to poor people living in rural areas or urban slums, who relied on usually inadequate social assistance and public social services. During the second era (1980 to 1990), economic hard times led to reduced social insurance coverage and, eventually, to efforts by policy makers to rethink the provision of social assistance and basic public services. These changes inaugurated the third era (1990 to 2010), in which contributory social insurance coverage fell but social assistance and the public provision of basic social services to the poor improved significantly in many countries. Democracy, it will be argued, had a significant, multifaceted, and largely beneficial impact on these changes.

It is useful for the purposes of analysis to distinguish (a) the impact of social policies on well-being from (b) the (causally prior) impact of various political forces and circumstances on social policies. It also bears mention that the ultimate concern of the analysis will be primarily, although not exclusively, with the well-being of the poor and very poor. The sequence of causality (causes, then characteristics, then consequences) differs from the sequence of exposition (characteristics and consequences, then causes) because it makes sense to characterize social policies, and to explore their consequences for the well-being of the poor, before trying to unravel their causes.

Accordingly, starting with characteristics and consequences, the first section of the chapter will inventory and classify the main social policies in Latin America during each of the three eras from 1920 to 2010, and will outline the impact of these policies on the well-being of the poor. Moving on to causes, the second section will identify some of the forces and circumstances that influenced contributory heath and retirement insurance (from the 1920s), primary health care (from the 1970s), and conditional cash transfers (from the 2000s). The third section will draw some conclusions about the impact of political forces and circumstances on social policies, and about the impact of social policies on well-being, in Latin America during the past century.

Characteristics and Consequences of Latin American Social Policies

Mesa-Lago distinguishes three sets of countries in terms of the dates when each first introduced contributory health and retirement insurance: pioneer (pre-1940; Argentina, Brazil, Chile, Costa Rica, Cuba, and Uruguay); intermediate (1940–1960, Mexico, Panama, and the five Andean nations); and latecomer (1960–1980; the rest of Central America, the Dominican Republic, Haiti, and Paraguay).[3] Pension and health insurance programs are funded partly by worker and employer contributions, but are "state" programs to the extent that they are legally mandated or regulated, and that the state itself contributes to the funds either directly (for public employees) or indirectly (by way of subsidies and bailouts to funds covering private-sector workers).

Haggard and Kaufman identify a Latin American regional welfare model, distinct from those of East Asia and Eastern Europe, involving defined benefit social insurance for formal-sector workers; top-heavy, inequitable, and low-quality educational systems; and unequal and incomplete coverage of basic health services.[4] De Ferranti et al. call this model a "truncated" welfare state, which provides health and retirement insurance to many people who receive a paycheck (and sometimes to members of their families), but much less, even next-to-nothing, to the rural poor or to urban informal-sector workers.[5]

During the truncated welfare state era (1920–1980) social assistance took various forms, including family allowances (payments to workers according to number of family dependents), non-contributory pensions for certain groups, university tuition subsidies, hospital fee waivers, emergency public employment, and nutrition programs including food subsidies, food vouchers, free food, milk handouts, and school meals. In 1906, the first public school in Argentina began to distribute milk to students. In 1936, doctors associated with Chile's Mandatory Insurance Fund (CSO), which administered health insurance for blue-collar workers, introduced a milk distribution program. In 1963, Brazil launched the non-contributory FUNRURAL rural health insurance program.[6] Except for generalized food subsidies and university tuition waivers, social assistance programs had a progressive benefit incidence in Latin America before 1990.[7] Their main defects were poor design and implementation, capture by clientelistic elites, and unambitious scale. In 13 Latin American countries from 1972 to 1982 social assistance spending on average absorbed 17 percent of total public social spending, vs. 83 percent for social insurance.[8]

From the 1920s to the 1980s most Latin American countries evolved education and health care sectors that primarily served the interests of the rich, the middle classes, and some sectors of organized labor, while doing much less for the rest of the population. Health and education systems were remarkably top-heavy in some countries. In the mid-1980s Argentina had 69,000 doctors but only 16,000 nurses, giving it the second-highest doctor-to-nurse ratio among 87 countries for which data are available. Not least because of the political clout of students, professors, and university employees, 36 percent of public education spending in Costa Rica in the late 1980s went to universities.[9] By the early 1970s family planning programs had emerged in Chile, Costa Rica, Colombia, the Dominican Republic, El Salvador, and Panama. At the other end of the spectrum was Argentina, which was officially pro-natalist through the 1970s; as well as Bolivia, Brazil, and Nicaragua.[10] Between 1960 and 1980 the share of the Latin American population with access to an improved water source rose from 33 to 70 percent, while the share with access to sewerage rose from 14 to 30 percent. In poorer countries the situation was grimmer. In 1980 the share of the population with access to an improved water source hovered around 20 percent in Haiti and Paraguay, 35–40 percent in Bolivia and Nicaragua, and 50 percent in Ecuador, El Salvador, Guatemala, and Peru.[11]

As time went on the number of contributors to social insurance programs fell, while the number of beneficiaries rose. This maturation process began to affect Uruguay, a very early adopter, in the 1950s, but by the late 1970s population aging, low-yield investments, over-staffing, and often poor administration had reduced the solvency of social insurance funds in the other pioneer countries. The resulting tax-funded bailouts of insurance funds combined with the costs of the single-minded pursuit of premature heavy import substitution, loan pushing by petrodollar-laden international banks, a spike in U.S. interest rates, and a plunge in commodity prices to produce the debt crisis of the early 1980s. To tame inflation and reduce budget and trade deficits most governments enacted economic austerity policies, often accompanied by free-market reforms. These policies led in many Latin American countries to civil service layoffs, privatizations of state corporations, liberalization of trade and capital flows, deregulation of domestic markets, reduced subsidies to industry and agriculture, and cuts in social spending.

These changes shattered lives, but the previous economic model was no longer viable, so some dislocation was inevitable. Moreover, the negative side effects of some of the free-market reforms were not as bad as some critics of "neoliberalism" have claimed, not least because the previous model had done little to help the poor. Privatization was often poorly executed, but many of the privatized state firms had run huge deficits while providing substandard goods and services. Job security was protected inefficiently at the firm level by restricting hiring and firing, not at the market level through economic dynamism and an active labor market policy. Cutbacks in social spending during the 1980s mostly affected social insurance for the urban formal sector (that's where most of the money was), not the underfunded basic social services and social assistance programs that mainly benefited the poor. Lower inflation resulting both from economic austerity and free-market reforms helped the poor, who carried money around, more than the not-so-poor and the rich, who could often shield themselves from inflation using negotiated cost-of-living increases, foreign bank accounts, or other strategies or resources.

The debt crisis and the shift from nationalist and statist to free-market economic policies contributed to profound social policy changes in most Latin American countries. Many governments introduced market mechanisms into health and retirement insurance programs, which were facing demographic as well as economic challenges in the pioneer countries. In so doing they followed the military government in Chile, which as of 1980 had required new entrants to the labor force to enroll in defined contribution, fully-funded individual retirement accounts managed by private companies (AFPs), rather than in the old defined benefit, pay-as-you go public pension system. Current workers could choose whether to keep their own contributions (those of employers were abolished) in the public system or to move them to an AFP. From 1997 to 2001 Bolivia, the Dominican Republic, El Salvador, Mexico, and Nicaragua likewise phased out public defined benefit in favor of private defined contribution pensions. Colombia and Peru created parallel systems, where workers could choose either to stay with the public defined benefit system or to leave it for a private defined contribution account. Argentina, Costa Rica, and Uruguay introduced mixed systems, in which workers had the option of contributing to a private defined contribution plan in addition to the public defined benefit system. (In November 2008, however, the Argentine congress passed a law nationalizing the country's ten private pension fund companies, ending the private option.) Brazil, Cuba, Guatemala, Honduras, Panama, Paraguay, and Venezuela opted not to reform the existing public defined benefit pay-as-you-go systems. In every country except Bolivia, the military and police kept their generous public defined benefit pensions.[12]

Chile pioneered health insurance reform as well as pension reform. A 1981 decree gave workers the option of making their health insurance contributions not to the public health insurance fund (FONASA), but to new private Instituciones de Salud Previsional (ISAPREs), which worked like health maintenance organizations in the United States. From 1983 to 1997 ISAPRE enrollment rose from 2 to 27 percent of Chileans. The ISAPREs attracted the rich, young, and healthy; FONASA retained the poor, old, and ill. In addition, many ISAPRE members used the public system for expensive procedures.[13] Over the years the ISAPREs came to be criticized for fraud, lack of coverage for catastrophic illnesses, and enrollment and premium discrimination against women, the elderly, and people with pre-existing conditions. Between 1997 and 2006 the share of Chileans enrolled in an ISAPRE fell from 27 to 16 percent.[14]

In Argentina, health insurance contributions continued to go to hundreds of union- or government-controlled *obras sociales* that were notorious for corruption and mismanagement. Reforms were attempted, but few were sustained. In Peru, a 1997 law allowed health insurance contributions flowing into the state social security fund (ESSALUD) to be paid to private providers as well as to the fund's own health care personnel and facilities.[15] In both Argentina and Peru, however, a sharp distinction remained between the contributory and general revenue-funded public health care sectors. Mexico in 2003 launched a Popular Health Insurance scheme under which the 50 million or so Mexicans who lacked health insurance became eligible for state-subsidized coverage. Except for those in the poorest 20 percent of the population, Popular Health Insurance beneficiaries were expected to pay a premium. Only about 3 percent wound up doing so, however, so the program cannot really be called contributory.[16]

In Brazil (1993), Colombia (1993), and Uruguay (2005) governments unified public and contributory health care financing. Henceforth a single stream of revenue, fed by both pay-roll deductions and general revenues, funded preventive and curative services alike, ending the distinction between those eligible for higher-quality care funded by social insurance and those eligible only for lower-quality care financed by general revenues.[17] A different type of unification took place in Costa Rica, where the Costa Rican Social Security Fund (CCSS), which insured almost all Costa Ricans, replaced the health ministry as the direct provider of public primary health care.[18]

Employment was protected in Latin America mostly by laws that imposed severance payments on employers who laid off workers. As of 2010 only Brazil (1986), Argentina (1992), and Chile (2002) had adopted pay-as-you-go, state-administered unemployment insurance. In 1997 unemployment insurance covered about 12 percent of the Brazilian unemployed, and in 1999 it covered about 6 percent of the Argentine unemployed—in each case, with meager and ephemeral benefits. Some countries had unemployment insurance security accounts, which operated like individual retirement accounts but were funded entirely by employers. The costs of employment termination were high in Latin America, making employers reluctant to hire new workers.[19]

Across the ten countries that introduced defined contribution, fully-funded, privately-administered individual retirement accounts, average pension coverage fell from 38 percent before the reform to 24 percent afterward. Compared to the preceding (or alternative) defined benefit, pay-as-you-go, publicly-administered pensions, privately-run retirement accounts tended to pay lower benefits for shorter time periods with higher administrative costs and greater disadvantages for women. Meanwhile, health insurance coverage across all Latin American countries with data fell from an average of 52 percent in 1990 to 41 percent 2004.[20]

Beginning with Bolivia in 1987, many countries introduced Social Emergency Funds and (later) Social Investment Funds, which gave cash transfers to community leaders who submitted successful proposals to build or improve public facilities like health clinics, water and sewer lines, roads, and recreation centers. Locals were usually required to contribute labor or other resources. The funds, it was hoped, would help the newly unemployed to stay in the labor force and prepare themselves to graduate to higher-skilled work, while building human capital (through education and training programs) and social capital (through participation in the proposals and projects). Chile's Fund for Solidarity and Social Investment (FOSIS) reduced poverty and improved welfare, but Mexico's National Solidarity Program (PRONASOL) seems to have been operated primarily to win votes. Social investment funds rarely reached the poorest of the poor, who tended to live in communities lacking the social capital needed to propose a project. Also, social investment funds were poorly integrated with other government policies, and few had much success in raising income or employment among the poor.[21]

Microfinance—the provision of small loans, usually to impoverished women, for the startup or expansion of tiny businesses—was a second form of social assistance to expand after 1990. Microfinance in Latin America had varying combinations of state and non-state origins, administration, and financing. Loans were usually provided at above-market rates of interest (partly to cover the cost of handling thousands of tiny accounts), but did not require collateral. Instead, borrowers were often required to form groups designed to increase peer pressure (and support) for repayment. By 2008 there were at least 635 micro-finance institutions in Latin America and the Caribbean; every Latin American country except Cuba had at least one. Microfinance programs in Latin America in 2008 provided loans averaging US$1,149 to a total of 9.5 million borrowers. Penetration (borrowers as a share of business owners and self-employed) was highest in Nicaragua (59 percent), Ecuador (48 percent), and Bolivia (45 percent), and lowest in Argentina and Venezuela (just over 1 percent each). The total loan portfolio of microfinance institutions rose nearly five-fold from 2002 to 2007, before slowing in 2008 because of the financial crisis. Impact studies in Bolivia and Peru suggest that microfinance raised the incomes of borrowers but failed to reach the poorest of the poor, who often feared that they wouldn't be able to repay.[22] Such perceptions may have been well-founded. Recently, programs such as Mexico's Comparta-mos, the region's largest microfinance initiative, have been criticized for charging very high interest rates that have mired borrowers in a debt spiral.

Conditional cash transfers were a third set of social assistance policies to appear in the 1990s. Such programs involve the periodic transfer of cash from the public treasury to cer-tifiably poor households provided that the households meet certain conditions, typically that children go to school and to health clinics and that expectant mothers get prenatal care. Early conditional cash transfer programs included Mexico's Niños en Solidaridad, which was introduced in 1989 in the context of PRONASOL, and Chile's Subsidio Único Famil-iar, which dates from 1990.[23] In 2008 the largest conditional cash transfer programs in Latin America were Bolsa Família in Brazil, which served about 52 million people (84 percent of the Brazilian poor), and Oportunidades (formerly Progresa) in Mexico, which served about 24 million (72 percent of the Mexican poor). By 2008 every Latin American country except for Cuba, Haiti, and Venezuela had a conditional cash transfer program covering from 12 percent (El Salvador's Red Solidaria) to 100 percent (Ecuador's Bono de Desarrollo Humano) of its poor population. Around 2000 the cash transferred to each household, usu-ally monthly, amounted to between 8 and 30 percent of household consumption, depending on the program and the country. Around 2005 most such programs cost between 0.1 and 0.6 percent of GDP, depending on the share of the population participating and on the size of the cash transfer.[24]

Impact evaluations of Mexico's Oportunidades and of Brazil's Bolsa Família generally find that they had beneficial effects on income poverty, school attendance and enrollment, nutrition, height for age, child labor, and the utilization of basic health services.[25] In Brazil, the need to sign up for the Universal Registry in order to receive benefits from Bolsa Famí-lia also encouraged many poor people to acquire state-issued identity cards, without which it is hard to get benefits from state agencies or buy things on installment (a common practice in Brazil).[26] Partly because conditional cash transfer programs do not require beneficiaries to propose projects or borrow money, they reached the poor more successfully than social funds or microfinance initiatives.

Conditional cash transfer programs have been criticized on administrative grounds for excluding poor households while including non-poor ones; for poor monitoring and enforcement of the stipulated conditions; and for saddling beneficiaries with duties that are paternalistic, time-consuming, costly to enforce, and no more effective than unconditional transfers at promoting schooling and health visits. On economic grounds, the programs have been charged with giving recipients an incentive to stay out of the formal-sector labor force in order to qualify as "poor." Critics who focus on gender issues have pointed out that already overtaxed mothers are usually the ones taking children to schools and health clinics, and that the schemes reinforce gender stereotypes by engaging women mainly as mothers. On the political front, conditional cash transfer programs have been denounced for being susceptible to corruption, patronage, and political manipulation; for being politically unsustainable because their beneficiaries are poor and powerless; and for sidelining broader redistributive policies such as a universalistic, unconditional minimum income funded by progressive taxation.

Some of these criticisms may be overstated. A worldwide comparison of 120 social assistance programs found that Bolsa Família and Oportunidades ranked in the top 10 percent for targeting accuracy.[27] Research has found that both of these programs reduced child labor but that neither deterred adults from seeking work.[28] Some studies have found that cash transfer programs without conditions have improved health and education outcomes, but quasi-experiments suggest that conditions—even awareness of conditions that are poorly monitored or enforced—elicit behavioral changes that would probably not otherwise have occurred.[29] Conditional cash transfer programs impose added burdens on mothers, but interviews with participants indicate that some mothers think that these burdens are worth bearing.[30] Also, most cash payments go to women, raising their bargaining power within the household.

As for criticisms on political grounds, it has been argued that Brazil's conditional cash transfer programs have "crowded out investments in the improvement of basic services such as sanitation and health."[31] In Bolsa Família's first six years of operation, however (2003–2009), per capita public health care spending rose 70 percent and primary health care spending more than doubled.[32] In Brazil, Lula's government appears to have expanded eligibility for Bolsa Família, and claimed credit for expanding it, with the explicit aim of winning votes in the 2006 presidential election.[33] That might qualify as a "political" use of a conditional cash transfer program, but it also amounts to electoral incentives having their hypothesized effect of promoting a policy beneficial to the poor. Like all means-tested social policies, conditional cash transfer programs serve people with limited political power, jeopardizing their sustainability.[34] In the eyes of non-participants, however, the conditions that beneficiaries are statutorily required to meet may give conditional cash transfers more legitimacy than they would otherwise enjoy.[35]

In Bolsa Família municipal officials are responsible for certifying the incomes of beneficiaries and for aggregating information about compliance with conditionalities, so the program is potentially vulnerable to local clientelism. In practice, however, the federal government makes available so many spaces in the program that mayors find it hard to exclude any income-eligible household, reducing their leeway for discretion.[36] Also, the penalty for not attending school or for failing to show up for health care visits is that the government sends a social worker to the household to see whether it might need additional support. These low stakes make shenanigans at the compliance monitoring stage less rewarding for patrons seeking to capture new clients or to retain existing ones. In 2009, interviews with focus groups in northeastern cities and towns found little evidence that Bolsa Família was permeated by clientelistic practices of any kind.[37]

Unconditional cash transfer programs including subsidies to poor households, child and family allowances, and non-contributory pensions were a fourth class of social assistance interventions to gain prominence after 1990. At least 11 such programs operated in Latin

America in 2010; most paid beneficiaries US$30–$150 per month. Brazil's Previdência Rural (1991), which absorbed the FUNRURAL program (1963; revamped in 1971), was the earliest and in 2008 the largest unconditional cash transfer program in Latin America, with about 7,500,000 recipients. Bolivia's Bono Dignidad, which was funded by privatization proceeds and by a tax on natural gas exports, was Latin America's only truly universal social pension. In 2008 it paid about US$30 per month to each of the 676,000 Bolivians aged 60 or older, rich and poor alike.[38] A "social pension impact index," which takes into account the share of elderly covered and the size of the benefit relative to GDP per capita, ranked Bolivia highest in Latin America, with Brazil second and the other countries far behind. Bolivia's Bono Dignidad and Brazil's Previdência Rural have been linked to rises in school enrollment, partly by increasing the number of children living with pensioner grandparents.[39] Taken together, social pensions in Brazil have been associated with declines in the severity and incidence of poverty; with greater household investment in human, physical, and social capital; and with other improvements in the well-being of members of vulnerable groups.[40]

Integrated anti-poverty programs comprise a fifth category of recent social assistance initiatives. The Uruguayan PANES program, which originated in 2005 and merged in 2008 with an older family allowances program, included conditional cash transfers, a food debit card, workfare, and training.[41] Chile Solidario, which rolled out in four waves between 2002 and 2005, involved teams of social workers helping members of poor households to improve their employment status, housing, health, education, legal documentation, and intra-household relations. It provided small unconditional cash transfers (US$5–$20 per month) but phased them out over five years. Beneficiaries agreed to collaborate with social workers to lift themselves out of poverty, while the government agreed to tailor its programs more effectively to the needs of specific households. In 2009 Chile Solidario served Chile's 333,000 poorest households, about 8 percent of all households. Research suggests that the program raised school enrollment, adult literacy, housing quality, and health service utilization. Beneficiaries also enrolled in more employment, social pension, family allowance, and water subsidy programs, were more aware of such programs, and were more optimistic about their economic future.[42]

Several Latin American countries improved public primary health care services after 1990, notably Brazil with its 1994 Family Health Program and Costa Rica with its 1995 Comprehensive Basic Health Care Teams (EBAIS). Under each program, teams of health professionals were assigned to provide primary health care services to specific households, partly through home visits. The EBAIS included a doctor, a nursing aide, and a health worker. The Brazilian teams had more personnel and served more households. In each country the health teams came to serve as a gateway to the entire (unified) health system. Statistical analyses find that each program was associated with lower child mortality than would be expected from control variables.[43] El Salvador and Peru, which also implemented effective rural health care programs in the early and mid-1990s, achieved the steepest infant mortality declines in the region from 1990 to 2009.[44]

As with pensions and health insurance, Chile was the first Latin American country to apply market reforms to schooling. In 1980 the military government began to subsidize tuition-free private schools at the same rate as state-run municipal schools. Parents could choose to place their children in either type of school, and each school's subsidy depended on the number of students it enrolled. The subsidy thus worked like a voucher.[45] Beginning about 1990, other Latin American countries began to decentralize authority to municipalities and schools, to raise pre-school and secondary enrollment, to shift resources to under-funded schools, to introduce achievement tests, and to encourage parental involvement. Some of these changes were resisted, particularly by teachers unions. Efforts to impose fees on university students, who tended to come from wealthy families, met ferocious resistance and were dropped. Decentralization altered a core feature of the educational system, but progress was slow on test scores, dropout rates, and teacher training. In Latin American educational systems, improving quality turned out to be harder than improving access.[46] A 2003 study of 15-year-olds' math, language, and science skills showed disappointing proficiency in Argentina, Brazil, Chile, Mexico, and Peru.[47] Primary and secondary school students scored higher in Cuba, partly because of good teacher training and orderly class-room environments.[48]

In 12 of the 18 Latin American countries for which data are available, expert ratings of family planning effort fell between 1989 and 2004, most steeply in Mexico, Central America, and the Andean countries. Only Argentina and Brazil raised their family planning effort scores by double digits (on a 120-point scale) between 1989 and 2004, and each started out from a low baseline.[49] Fertility by 1989 had already fallen to near the replacement rate in many Latin American countries (including the most populous ones), so a generalized decline in family planning effort was not unexpected. In the area of reproductive rights, Chile in 1989, El Salvador in 1998, and Nicaragua in 2006 outlawed abortion even to save the life of the mother. On the other hand, the Colombian congress in 2006 relaxed some restrictions on abortion, and Mexico City in 2007 legalized the procedure in the first trimester. The Uruguayan senate followed suit in 2008, but President Tabaré Vázquez vetoed the bill.[50] Cuba, which in 1996 had the world's second-highest abortion rate after Vietnam, kept its permissive regulations.[51]

In 1990 some 31 percent of Latin America's population lacked access to basic sanitation, and 15 percent lacked access to safe water. By 2008, to be on track to meet the Millennium Development Goal of halving these shares by 2015, the share without access to adequate sanitation should have fallen to 20 percent, and the share without access to safe water to 10 percent. The actual figures, at 20 percent and 7 percent, respectively, matched or exceeded the required pace. Ecuador, in part through well-run municipal provision, and Paraguay, where informal *aguateros* running small-scale water supply systems operated widely, were the most successful Latin American countries from 1990 to 2008 at raising access to safe water and basic sanitation.[52] In Argentina, the privatization of water and sewerage systems in several provinces expanded connections among the poor and contributed to a significant decline in the mortality of children under age 5, almost all of it attributable to a reduction in deaths by water-borne diseases.[53]

To summarize, market reforms to social insurance hurt the not-so-poor, many of whom lost coverage or benefits, without helping the very poor. Some of the new forms of social assistance, especially conditional cash transfers, noncontributory pensions, and integrated anti-poverty programs, helped the very poor; others, like social investment funds and microfinance, bypassed some of the most impoverished. Improvement in the public provision of basic health care, and in access to safe water and adequate sanitation, was beneficial both to the very poor and to the not-so-poor. Education reforms had more modest effects, increasing access to schooling but doing less to meet the more difficult challenge of improving the quality of education. Sexual health and reproductive rights policies advanced these goals in some countries but not in others. On the whole, the very poor in Latin America benefited more from social policies after 1990 than before 1980.

Determinants of Social Policies in Latin America

Research on the origins and evolution welfare states in wealthy countries has highlighted patterns of economic development, legacies of previous institutions, and social class mobilization and class alliances.[54] These factors mattered in Latin America as well, but a full account of the origins and evolution of Latin American social policies needs to include at least three other factors: bureaucratic initiative, international influences, and political regime form (democratic vs. authoritarian). Operationalizing social class mobilization and alliances as the activities of civil society groups and political parties, the determinants of social policies in Latin America may be classified into seven categories:

1. Bureaucratic initiative, whereby officials in state agencies, acting with relative autonomy from forces and constraints in their environments, propose, design, approve, implement, sustain, expand, or repeal particular social policies.
2. Economic forces such as international economic shocks; the dependence of social policies on the prevailing economic model; or the popularity of market-oriented policies.
3. Inherited social policy arrangements, which impose legal, institutional, and political constraints on contemporary and future arrangements.
4. International influences not fully captured under economic forces, such as war, ideological conflict, global norms, national prestige, bilateral foreign aid, international organizations, and foreign models.
5. Political regime form. Democracy can influence social policy through electoral incentives, freedom of expression, freedom to associate, or (in the long run) by fostering a perception of entitlement to social services that encourages the utilization as well as the public provision and financing of such services.
6. Civil society organizations (interest groups, social movements, or issue networks) can influence social policy. Some freedom to organize is a prerequisite for such activities, but civil society groups can influence social policies even under an authoritarian regime.
7. Partisanship. In a democratic regime, certain groups of people, including—but not limited to—those in common economic circumstances, support certain political parties with particular stances on social policies.

Which of these sources of influence had the biggest effect on social policies in Latin America? No general answer to this question can be given, because the importance of each source varied by country, time period, policy type, and policy process stage. The focus here will be on political regime (factor 5), which creates the context in which civil society groups and political parties (factors 6 and 7) operate.[55] Bureaucratic initiative (factor 1) will be considered, but its impact resists generalization.[56] Economic forces, inherited social policy arrangements, and international influences (factors 2, 3, and 4) will be treated analogously to control variables in a statistical analysis—as factors whose omission could bias estimates of the direction or size of the impact of the variable of interest, political regime form. To keep the analysis manageable, the focus will be on three types of social policies: contributory pensions and health insurance (1920s–), primary health care initiatives (1970s–), and conditional cash transfer programs (2000s–).

Contributory Social Insurance

Insulated bureaucratic elites introduced contributory social insurance in Brazil in the 1920s, partly to deter potential labor unrest; and in Costa Rica in the 1940s, where reportedly "the decisive leadership in social security was undertaken as if in an authoritarian system, with little mass participation."[57] Explanations that stress bureaucratic initiative or political will beg the questions, however, of where the will originated and what determined whether and how it influenced policy.[58] Government policy makers always have some freedom of choice, but political will is shaped and constrained by the context in which it is exercised.

One feature of this context is the economy. In the larger Latin American countries, tariffs and subsidies associated with import substitution allowed industrialists producing for the domestic market to pass along to consumers the costs of health and retirement insurance for their employees. The resulting high labor costs reduced work opportunities for the rural poor and for urban informal-sector workers.[59] As the beneficiary-to-contributor ratio rose, and as free-market reforms eliminated tariffs and subsidies, governments were forced to use general tax revenues to keep the funds solvent.

Previous welfare state institutions shaped the evolution of social insurance in Latin America, showing that "policies produce politics."[60] Social insurance initially privileged the military, the police, public employees, private formal-sector workers, and businesses and health professionals dependent on insurance payments. Some of these groups became tenacious opponents of later equity-enhancing reform efforts. In Argentina, union leaders in the 1940s, 1970s, and 1980s blocked efforts by health ministers to use both payroll deductions and general tax revenues to fund a unified public health care system.[61] In Brazil, associations of doctors, hospitals, drug manufacturers, and health insurers delayed until 1993 the debut of the Unified Health System.[62]

The international diffusion of policy models shaped the origins of social insurance in Latin America, as well as in Europe.[63] Chile's 1924 Workers' Insurance Fund law served as a model for Costa Rica's 1941 Social Insurance Law.[64] In some developing countries governments established social insurance "to prove that they [could] give their populations the same protection other nations give to theirs," or "out of a wish to acquire for their nations all of the most visible signs of national modernity."[65] In Costa Rica, worries about the spread of the Cuban Revolution led some legislators to vote in 1961 for a constitutional amendment to extend health insurance to the whole population.[66] The International Labor Office helped to spread contributory social insurance across Europe and later to Latin America.[67] After the debt crisis of the 1980s, the World Bank leaned on Latin American governments to privatize pensions and to introduce market mechanisms into health insurance and health care provision.[68]

Competitive politics and freedom of association contributed during the first part of the 20th century to the appearance of social insurance in many Latin American countries, not so much through electoral incentives as by allowing urban workers, professionals, and others to organize themselves to demand coverage.[69] The greater a beneficiary group's political clout, the earlier and better its insurance. The military, police, and top civil servants got the first, widest-ranging, most highly subsidized, and best-quality benefits.[70] Social insurance was introduced, as in Europe, under leaders from the left (Calderón in Costa Rica), center (Perón in Argentina), and right (Ibáñez in Chile). Pressure groups, accordingly, did more than partisanship (the control of the executive and/or legislative branches by a political party with a specific ideological stance) to influence the timing and content of social insurance in 20th-century Latin America.

Primary Health Care

Bureaucratic initiative contributed to primary health care programs as well as to social insurance. In Costa Rica, the Rural Health and Community Health plans of the 1970s were, one writer concluded, "a bureaucratic achievement. There was no popular crusade."[71] The EBAIS primary health care scheme was designed by a small team of experts commissioned by Guido Miranda, Costa Rica's health minister in 1984.[72] In Chile in the 1970s Miguel Kast and his staff in the National Planning Office, to whom General Pinochet had given significant policy autonomy, expanded maternal and infant health care and nutrition services in poor communities.[73] Primary health care programs in Argentina and Peru in the 1990s were designed and advocated by small groups of technocrats in Argentina's finance ministry and Peru's health ministry.[74]

Primary health care tends to be cheap, making it compatible with difficult as well as benign economic circumstances. In 1977 Costa Rica's Rural Health and Community Health plans together cost about US$8 (in then-current dollars) per beneficiary per year. In June 2000 the annual cost per beneficiary of Brazil's Family Health Program was between US$34 and $53, depending on region and team composition. In Chile from 1974 to 1983 and in Argentina from 1977 to 1982, the improved public provision of basic nutrition and health care helped to reduce infant mortality sharply despite falling GDP per capita and skyrocketing income inequality and income poverty.[75]

Existing social policy arrangements influenced basic health service provision throughout Latin America. Contributory health insurance revenues financed health personnel and facilities that often (but not reliably) treated the uninsured. In countries such as Argentina and Brazil, however, such revenues also supported a powerful private health care industry, which tended to work against the improvement of public health services. "Once private sector entities have become important providers of health and education, they turn into interest groups that fight politically for their and their clients' interests and against financing for the public sector."[76]

In decentralized countries, basic health service provision was also shaped by subnational initiatives. Brazil's Community Health Agents Program (1991), a precursor to the Family Health Program, was modeled on state programs in Ceará, Paraná, and Mato Grosso. Argentina's Plan Nacer (2004) was launched in nine impoverished provinces before expanding to the whole country. Elsewhere, major primary health care initiatives have piggybacked on previous nationwide programs. Costa Rica's Rural Health Plan (1973) started out by using personnel from a successful malaria eradication campaign.[77]

International factors have shaped basic health service provision in Latin America since early in the 20th century. In Costa Rica in the 1910s and 1920s, the Rockefeller Foundation financed hookworm control and health posts. In Brazil in 1942, U.S. government officials helped to establish the Serviço Especial de Saúde Público in order to keep rubber and minerals flowing to the Allies. In Argentina in 2004, the World Bank provided technical advice and funding for the Plan Nacer.[78] The WHO/UNICEF conference in Alma Ata, USSR, in 1978 "boosted the legitimacy of 'health for all' ... after this famous meeting, the universalization goal was on the minds of [Latin American] health officials, that is, cognitively available."[79] In the late 1970s military governments in Argentina and Chile expanded maternal and child health services partly in an effort to win support (or reduce hostility) abroad.[80] Rural health posts in Costa Rica in the 1920s and 1930s were modeled on those the rural United States, and Brazil's Family Health Program was modeled on initiatives in Cuba, Britain, Quebec, and Switzerland.[81]

Of all of the ways in which democracy can affect social policies, electoral incentives have drawn the most attention. In Chile in 1970, in Costa Rica in 1970 and 1974, in Argentina in 1973, and in Brazil in 2002 and 2006, candidates courted votes by expanding or promising to expand primary health care, water supply, or basic nutrition programs.[82] Sometimes, however, electoral incentives have worked against the improvement of basic health services for the poor. In Costa Rica in 1994 legislators advocated placing the EBAIS initially in densely populated areas, where most of the votes were. Health sector technocrats resisted, insisting that the EBAIS commence in impoverished, sparsely populated rural areas. With the backing of President Figueres the technocrats won out, and the EBAIS appeared first in peripheral regions.[83]

The fewer the impediments to the free flow of information, the easier it is to publicize social problems. In Chile in the 1950s, the publication of studies revealing high infant mortality encouraged policy makers to try to do something about the problem. In Brazil in the early 1990s, highly publicized cholera epidemics in the Amazon and the Northeast prompted health ministry officials to introduce a national Community Health Agents program. In Costa Rica in 1992, news coverage of a measles epidemic added urgency to the launch of the EBAIS program.[84]

Democracy also opened the way for left-of-center political parties to capture the presidency and implement pro-poor primary health care policies, as with the Partido Liberación Nacional in Costa Rica in the 1970s and 1990s; Cardoso's Social Democratic Party (1995–2002) and Lula's Workers' Party (2002–2010) in Brazil; and Chile's Socialists in 1970–1973 and 2000–2010. The election of left-of-center presidents is, however, only a supportive condition for such policies. Authoritarian regimes from Castro's to Pinochet's have implemented pro-poor primary health care programs. Conversely, the programs of Hugo Chávez in Venezuela, an elected leftist, are widely touted as pro-poor, but their overall impact has been disappointing. In mid-2003 Chávez started the Misión Barrio Adentro program to expand basic health services in poor areas. By the end of 2004 an influx of Cuban doctors had raised the number of primary care physicians in Venezuela from 1,500 to 13,000 and increased the number of medical consultations from 3.5 to 17 million. From 2003 to 2010, however, Venezuela's infant mortality rate fell only from 18.6 to 16.0 per 1000. This 2.1 percent average annual rate of infant mortality decline placed Venezuela 19th out of 20 Latin American countries, despite oil-fueled GDP per capita growth averaging 6.0 percent per year from 2003 to 2009 (more than double the 2.8 percent rate for Latin America and the Caribbean as a whole). Similarly, the "Misión Robinson" adult literacy program appears to have had little or no effect on literacy.[85]

Freedom of association permits civil society groups to influence health policy. Some such groups, like Brazil's Pastorate of the Children, even deliver primary health care services on a large scale. In Costa Rica, community organizations pressured the Coalición Unidad government (1978–1982) to preserve primary health care policies begun by the PLN in the 1970s, and lobbied the Social Christian government of Miguel Rodríguez (1998–2002) to preserve the EBAIS program started by the preceding PLN administration.[86] Brazil's Sanitarian and Primary Care movements, which emerged in the 1970s and 1980s during the transition from authoritarian rule, helped to persuade the Collor and Franco governments (1990–1994) to scale up to the national level municipal and state experiments with Community Health Agents and Family Health teams.[87] Not all demand-making by civil society groups is good for the poor, however. For doctors, shifting resources to primary health care often means "lower salaries, less sophisticated equipment, pressures to serve where living conditions and career prospects are unattractive, and the substitution of less highly trained health workers (nurses, public health workers, midwives) for doctors in performing certain services."[88] Accordingly, physicians' associations have resisted the expansion of health services in several Latin American countries, including Argentina, Chile, and Costa Rica in the early 1970s.[89]

Democracy is based on the principle that citizens have equal rights. Over time, this principle tends to produce a perception that the state is obliged to provide social services that enable every citizen to live with dignity.[90] The diffusion throughout society of an expectation that the state will attend to basic needs encourages the provision of basic health services to the poor. In Chile, democracy contributed to the emergence of expectations, expertise, and infrastructure that made the military's maternal and infant health care and nutrition initiatives possible, and increased the propensity of impoverished households to respond to them.[91] Cross-national quantitative studies have found that a country's "stock" of long-term democratic experience, above and beyond its current political regime form, is closely associated with the more widespread provision of basic health services and with the reduction of premature mortality.[92]

Conditional Cash Transfer Programs

This section will highlight some of the factors that shaped Mexico's Progresa, which was inaugurated in 1995 and evolved into Oportunidades in 2002, and Brazil's Bolsa Família (2003–), which grew out of Bolsa Escola (2001–2003) and its subnational precursors (1995–). Progresa was mainly a top-down initiative, whereas Bolsa Escola emerged from the activities of civil society groups. Determinants of some other conditional cash transfer programs will also be assessed, but the main focus will be on the Brazilian and Mexican programs, the region's largest.

Progresa was designed and advocated by Santiago Levy, an undersecretary in the Mexican finance ministry, and José Gómez de León, the director of Mexico's National Commission on Population. Levy cites as his main inspirations a 1994 economic crisis, whose severity persuaded him that existing social assistance schemes could not protect the poor, and research underscoring the interdependence of education, nutrition, and health.[93] To ameliorate the impact of the crisis on the poor, Levy and Gómez de León devised a program to replace food subsidies and handouts with cash transfers conditional on regular medical checkups and implemented it in the southern state of Campeche. When an impact assessment revealed that his pilot project had improved nutritional status and increased the utilization of health services, Levy and Gómez de León proposed to scale it up to the whole country. This proposal was resisted by officials in other ministries and by members of congress, including from the governing PRI. Crucial to overcoming such opposition was the backing of president Zedillo, as well as the resources and prestige on which Levy could draw as a top official in the ministry of finance.[94]

Brazil's Bolsa Escola (2001) and Bolsa Família (2003) had two subnational precursors, the Bolsa Escola program in the Federal District of Brasília and the Programa de Garantia de Renda Familiar Mínima in the city of Campinas. Each of these programs was introduced in January 1995. The main policy entrepreneur for the Brasília program was Cristovam Buarque, who was the governor of the Federal District from 1995 to 1998 and at this time belonged to the Workers' Party (PT). His counterpart in Campinas was Eduardo Suplicy, a national senator from the state of São Paulo from Cardoso's Brazilian Social Democratic Party (PSDB). Brasília's Bolsa Escola program was conceptualized in 1986 in seminars involving Buarque and others at a research center at the University of Brasília. The ideas behind the minimum income program in Campinas date back to 1975, when a scholar at the Fundação Getúlio Vargas published an article in a prominent Brazilian economics journal proposing a negative income tax resulting in a guaranteed minimum income. After losing the 1989 presidential election, Lula invited both Buarque and Suplicy to join a "shadow cabinet" to prepare for his next presidential run in 1994.[95]

Economic factors influenced conditional cash transfer programs in several ways. In a climate of economic austerity, such programs appeared to be cost-effective. In 2005 Mexico's Oportunidades had a budget of $5.06 billion, $210 annually for each of 24 million beneficiaries. In 2006 Brazil's Bolsa Família had a budget of $6.76 billion, $153 annually for each of 44 million beneficiaries.[96] In Brazil in 2003 conditional cash transfers took 2 percent of federal spending on social insurance and social assistance; pensions took 87 percent. In Mexico in 2002 the figures were 8 and 73 percent, respectively.[97] The popularity of free-market reform enhanced the appeal of conditional cash transfers, which were said to be consistent with the "logic of the market" and likely to avoid "distortions of relative prices."[98] Also, many Latin American policy makers saw cash handouts contingent on school attendance and medical checkups as a way to improve human capital, and thus international competitiveness.[99]

Existing social policy arrangements shaped the design of both Progresa and Bolsa Família. Each program was initiated in part to compensate for the shrinking coverage of social insurance. Progresa was administered by Mexico's Social Development Ministry, the agency that had run the PRONASOL social investment fund (1989–1994). Progresa built on PRONASOL's Niños en Solidaridad, which in 1994 had given about 650,000 families cash transfers conditional on class attendance by elementary school-aged children.[100] Brazil's Bolsa Família, in late 2003, combined four previous cash transfer programs, two of which, Bolsa Escola and Bolsa Alimentação, were conditional on school attendance. Bolsa Escola, which dated back to the last year of the Cardoso administration (2001), was inspired by Brasília's Bolsa Escola (1995–), by Campinas's Guaranteed Minimum Income program (1995–), and by the national Program to Eradicate Child Labor (1996–), which made cash transfers to households contingent on school attendance for children (this component was folded into Bolsa Família in 2005).[101] The 1988 Brazilian Constitution and the 1999 Statute of the Child and Adolescent provided a legal basis for public policies to promote school attendance. Also crucial to the operation of the demand-side Bolsa Família program was the supply-side FUNDEF initiative, which guaranteed that the equivalent of US$300 would be made available annually for the education of each public school student up to the eighth grade.[102]

International organizations have contributed to Latin America's conditional cash transfer programs. The Inter-American Development Bank (IDB) in 2001 approved a $500 million loan for Bolsa Escola and a $1 billion loan for Progresa, which at the time was the largest loan that the IDB had ever made. It also made loans to support conditional cash transfer programs in Argentina, Colombia, the Dominican Republic, Honduras, and Nicaragua.[103] The World Bank in 2004 lent US$572 million to support Bolsa Família.[104] Multilateral financing has been particularly important in poorer countries like Honduras, Nicaragua, and Paraguay.[105] In 1996 UNICEF gave Brasília's Bolsa Escola its "Children and Peace" award, and several international agencies helped to evaluate the performance of the national Bolsa Escola program.[106]

Brazil's Bolsa Escola influenced Mexico's Progresa, and Progresa's successor, Oportunidades, influenced Bolsa Escola's successor, Bolsa Família. The Mexican government in 1996 sent a delegation to Brazil to visit some of the municipal Bolsa Escola programs.[107] Several years later Mexico's Santiago Levy encouraged the Brazilian government to combine Bolsa Escola with the three other programs into Bolsa Família. The Chile Solidario program inspired Brazilian officials to change case management practices in Bolsa Família.[108] Conditional cash transfer programs in Brazil, Colombia, Honduras, and Mexico influenced Nicaragua's Red de Protección Social, which in turn influenced such programs in the Dominican Republic, El Salvador, and Paraguay.[109]

Electoral incentives shaped various aspects of Brazil's Bolsa Escola and Bolsa Família. In his 1994 campaign for governor of Brasília, Cristovam Buarque touted his Bolsa Escola proposal. When Bolsa Escola was scaled up in 2001, observers opined that the government had shrunk the stipend in order to maximize the number of beneficiaries capable of casting a vote. The rapid growth of the national Bolsa Escola from May to December 2001 (when nearly 5 million families enrolled) has been linked to the presidential hopes of Paulo Renato Souza, the education minister at the time.[110] A 20 percent rise in the income cap for eligibility led to a spike in Bolsa Família coverage in June 2006, when one million Brazilians enrolled before a three-month electoral quarantine closed the program to new entrants. In one town, "the mayor sent a letter to all *Bolsa Família* recipients explaining that [raising the income cap] was a personal initiative of the president himself."[111] In the 2006 race for governor of Piauí, the candidate of the conservative Liberal Front Party made a notarized pledge to maintain the Bolsa Família program that his opponent had introduced.[112] From 1999 to 2003 Bolsa Escola reduced dropout rates 36 percent more in municipalities where the mayor was legally eligible to be re-elected than in municipalities where term limits precluded another run.[113]

Publicity in the mass media, which presupposes some freedom of expression, was another democracy-related factor that affected Bolsa Escola. Reports of the death of a child from malnutrition in Campinas, one of the country's wealthiest large cities, helped to galvanize public opinion in support of the city's 1995 minimum income program. Gilberto Dimenstein, a journalist for *Folha de São Paulo*, called attention to Brasília's local Bolsa Escola program in ways that helped it get on to the national agenda. The Cardoso government, midway through its second term (1998–2002), was taking criticism in the mass media for neglecting social policy; such criticism is said to have contributed to the rapid rollout of the national Bolsa Escola scheme in 2001.[114]

In Chile and Uruguay Socialist governments introduced conditional cash transfer schemes, non-contributory social assistance, and integrated anti-poverty programs.[115] The impact of partisanship on Latin America's conditional cash transfer programs should not be overstated, however. In Brazil Cardoso's center-left PSDB government modeled Bolsa Escola on local PT programs, while Lula's PT government expanded it as Bolsa Família. In Mexico the centrist PRI government of Ernesto Zedillo (1994–2000) initiated Progresa, and the conservative PAN government of Vicente Fox (2000–2006) enlarged it as Oportunidades. Interest groups, whose activities are facilitated by democracy, were not heavily involved in Brazil either in promoting or resisting conditional cash transfer programs. Bolsa Escola raised school enrollment and attendance, creating extra work for teachers, but teachers' unions did not oppose the program. Business organizations were also absent from the conditional cash transfer policy-making process. Issue networks advocating a guaranteed a minimum income, however, along with others lobbying for greater access to schooling, were heavily involved in the local conditional cash transfer programs in Brasília and Campinas respectively. Cristovam Buarque, after losing the gubernatorial election in Brasília in 1998, founded an organization called Missão Criança (Child Mission) to promote conditional cash transfer programs both within Brazil and abroad. Missão Criança reportedly helped to initiate such programs in Recife, Mato Grosso do Sul, Acre, and Goiás, as well as in Argentina and Bolivia.[116]

Conclusion

Bureaucratic initiative influenced social insurance, primary health care, and conditional cash transfers alike. That was to be expected, however, because policies always originate, in an immediate sense, from some sort of bureaucratic initiative. Economic factors were closely intertwined with social policies. During the import-substitution era, tariff protection and industrial subsidies gave employers the resources they needed to provide social insurance for their employees. After the debt crisis of the 1980s this model was exhausted, or at least discredited. The expansion and improvement of social assistance programs and of publicly-provided health care, nutrition, water, and sanitation services in the 1990s and 2000s was facilitated by the relatively low cost of these initiatives at a time when economic difficulties and the prevailing free-market ideology made funds scarce. Previous social policy arrangements created new interests and political actors that shaped and constrained social policies in later years. International factors, notably foreign models and the activities of international organizations, shaped and constrained all three major categories of social policies in Latin America.

Democracy exercised influence on social policies in the context of these other factors. Electoral competition and electoral incentives do not seem to have played a major role in generating social insurance in the "pioneer" countries in the first part of the 20th century, but they were important in producing primary health care programs in the 1970s and conditional cash transfer schemes in the 2000s. Freedom of expression helped to put social problems on the political agenda; facilitated debate and the spread of information that influenced the design, approval, and effectiveness of social policies; and encouraged the uptake of public transfers and services. Freedom to organize (which was granted under certain authoritarian regimes as well as under democratic ones) allowed labor unions in many countries to extract subsidized contributory insurance from employers and the state; or to benefit from such insurance after governments introduced it to deter labor militancy. It also gave rise to medical business and doctors' associations, which in some countries resisted the extension of primary health care to the poor. In Brazil issue networks, as opposed to pressure groups, gave critical support to primary health care programs and conditional cash transfers. Partisanship, however, which requires a democratic regime in order to operate, does not seem to have played a major role in policy making. Social insurance, primary health care programs, and conditional cash transfer schemes were each designed, approved, implemented, and expanded under governments at varying points on the ideological spectrum. Democracy's impact on social policies was neither unique, unidirectional, automatic, nor massive in every case, but no full account of the origins of such policies can ignore it.

Turning from the effects of politics on social policies to the effects of social policies on well-being among the poor, social assistance programs and improvements in the public provision of health, nutrition, water, and sanitation services led after 1990, despite a drop in social insurance coverage, to more rapid gains in the welfare of the poor than had been made during the truncated welfare state era. The improvements in public provision merit special attention. Prior to 1980 the literature on Latin American social policies focused on social insurance; since 1990 it has focused on social assistance. Social insurance and social assistance raise the amount of income that recipients command, but income is only a means to well-being. The public provision of basic health, nutrition, education, family planning, water, and sanitation services often contributes more directly to improving capabilities among the poor.

Notes

1 Earlier versions of this chapter were much improved by the comments of James E. Mahon, Peter Kingstone, Alessandra Stachowski, and Deborah Yashar, as well by those of participants in colloquia in the Public Affairs Center, Wesleyan University (October 2010); Latin America Research Seminar, Department of Political Science, University of California, Berkeley (November 2010); and David Rockefeller Center for Latin American Studies, Harvard University (February 2011). Any errors are my responsibility.

2 Emmanuel Skoufias, Kathy Lindert, and Joseph Shapiro, "Globalization and the Role of Public Transfers in Redistributing Income in Latin America and the Caribbean," UNU-WIDER Research Paper No. 2009/02, p. 20, accessed September 27, 2010, at http://www.wider.unu.edu/publications/working-papers/research-papers/2009/en_GB/rp2009-02

3 Carmelo Mesa-Lago, "Social Security in Latin America and the Caribbean: A Comparative Assessment," in Ehtisham Ahmad et al., eds., *Social Security in Developing Countries* (Oxford: Clarendon Press, 1991), pp. 358–362.

4 Stephan Haggard and Robert R. Kaufman, *Development, Democracy, and Welfare States* (Princeton, NJ: Princeton University Press, 2008), p. 5.

5 David de Ferranti et al., *Inequality in Latin America: Breaking with History?* (Washington, DC: World Bank, 2004), p. 14.

6 James W. McGuire, *Wealth, Health, and Democracy in East Asia and Latin America* (New York: Cambridge University Press, 2010), pp. 105, 129, 159–160.

7 Margaret E. Grosh, *Administering Targeted Social Programs in Latin America* (Washington, DC: World Bank, 2004), pp. 3–5, 39, 153.

8 Evelyne Huber, Thomas Mustillo, and John D. Stephens. "Politics and Social Spending in Latin America," *Journal of Politics*, Vol. 70, No. 2 (April 2008), p. 431.

9 McGuire, *Wealth, Health, and Democracy*, pp. 70, 135.

10 John A. Ross and W. Parker Mauldin, "Family Planning Programs: Efforts and Results, 1972–94," *Studies in Family Planning*, Vol. 27, No. 3 (May/June 1996), p. 146.

11 Pan American Health Organization, *Regional Report on the Evaluation 2000 in the Region of the Americas: Water Supply and Sanitation* (Washington, DC: PAHO, 2001), p. 24; Peter Gleick et al., *The World's Water, 2008–2009* (Washington, DC: Island Press, 2009), pp. 216–217, 225–226.

12 Raúl Madrid, *Retiring the State* (Stanford: Stanford University Press, 2003), pp. 14–15; Carmelo Mesa-Lago and Gustavo Márquez, "Reform of Pension and Social Assistance Systems," in Eduardo Lora, ed., *The State of State Reform in Latin America* (Stanford: Stanford University Press, 2007), pp. 358–359.

13 McGuire, *Wealth, Health, and Democracy*, pp. 109–110.

14 1997: Armando Barrientos, "Health Policy in Chile: The Return of the Public Sector?," *Bulletin of Latin American Research*, Vol. 21, No. 3 (July 2002), p. 447; 2006: Carmelo Mesa-Lago, "Social Protection in Chile: Reforms to Improve Equity," *International Labour Review*, Vol. 147, No. 4 (2008), p. 379.

15 Christina Ewig, "Piecemeal But Innovative: Health Sector Reform in Peru," pp. 238–241; Peter Lloyd-Sherlock, "Ambitious Plans, Modest Outcomes: The Politics of Health Care Reform in Argentina," pp. 102–108, both in Robert R. Kaufman and Joan M. Nelson, eds., *Crucial Needs, Weak Incentives* (Baltimore: Johns Hopkins University Press, 2004).

16 Jason M. Laikin, "The End of Insurance? Mexico's Seguro Popular, 2001–2007," *Journal of Health Politics, Policy and Law*, Vol. 35, No. 3 (June 2010), p. 321.

17 Brazil: McGuire, *Wealth, Health, and Democracy*, pp. 162–163; Uruguay: Fernando Borgia, "Health in Uruguay: Progress and Challenges in the Right to Health Care Three Years After the First Progressive Government," *Social Medicine*, Vol. 3, No. 2 (2008), pp. 110–112. Colombia: Thomas C. Tsai, "Second Chance for Health Reform in Colombia," *Lancet*, Vol. 375, No. 9709 (January 9, 2010), pp. 109–110.

18 Mary A. Clark, "Reinforcing a Public System: Health Sector Reform in Costa Rica," in Kaufman and Nelson, *Crucial Needs, Weak Incentives*.

19 Miguel Jaramillo and Jaime Saavedra, "Severance Payment Programs in Latin America," *Empirica*, Vol. 32, No. 3-4 (September 2005), p. 295; Jacqueline Mazza, "Unemployment Insurance: Case Studies and Lessons for Latin America and the Caribbean," Working Paper 411 (Washington, DC: Inter-American Development Bank, 2000).

20 Mesa-Lago and Márquez, "Reform of Pension and Social Assistance Systems," pp. 361–372; Carmelo Mesa-Lago, "Informal Employment and Pension and Healthcare Coverage By Social Insurance in Latin America," *IDS Bulletin*, Vol. 39, No. 2 (May 2008), p. 7.

21 FOSIS: Judith Tendler, "Why Are Social Funds So Popular?," in Shahid Yusuf, Weiping Wu, and Simon Evenett, eds., *Local Dynamics in an Era of Globalization* (Washington, DC: World Bank, 2000); PRONASOL: Alberto Diaz-Cayeros and Beatriz Magaloni, "The Politics of Public Spending – Part II. The Programa Nacional de Solidaridad (PRONASOL) in Mexico," Background Paper for the *World Development Report 2004* (Washington, DC: World Bank, 2004). Social funds impact: Giovanni Andrea Cornia, "Social Funds in Stabilization and Adjustment Programs," UNU-WIDER Research for Action Paper 48 (1999), accessed September 23, 2010, at http://website1.wider.unu.edu/publications/rfa48.pdf

22 Figures from Paola A. Pedrozas and Sergio Navajas, "Microfinanzas en América Latina y el Caribe: Actualización de datos" (Washington, DC: Inter-American Development Bank, March 2010), accessed September 25, 2010, at http://idbdocs.iadb.org/wsdocs/getdocument. aspx?docnum=3515779, except for total loan portfolio, from MicroRate, "Cautious Resilience: The Impact of the Global Financial Crisis on Latin American & Caribbean Microfinance Institutions," March 2009, p. 7, accessed September 25, 2010, at http://microrate.com/wp-content/ uploads/2009/08/Cautious_Resilience.pdf. Impact studies are discussed in John Weiss and Heather Montgomery, "Great Expectations: Microfinance and Poverty Reduction in Asia and Latin America," Asian Development Bank Institute Discussion Paper 15 (2004), pp. 20–24, accessed September 25, 2010, at http://ssrn.com/abstract=1396122

23 Judith Teichman, "Redistributive Conflict and Social Policy in Latin America," *World Development*, Vol. 36, No. 3 (March 2007), p. 452.

24 Program coverage: Julia Johannsen, Luis Tejerina, and Amanda Glassman, "Conditional Cash Transfers in Latin America: Problems and Opportunities," Inter-American Development Bank, 2009, pp. 6, 32, accessed September 25, 2010, at http://idbdocs.iadb.org/wsdocs/getdocument. aspx?docnum=2103970. Transfer size: Ariel Fiszbein and Norbert Schady, *Conditional Cash Transfers: Reducing Present and Future Poverty*, World Bank Policy Research Report (Washington, DC: World Bank, 2009), p. 105. Program cost: Enrique Valencia Lomelí, "Conditional Cash Transfers as Social Policy in Latin America: An Assessment of their Contributions and Limitations," *Annual Review of Sociology*, Vol. 34 (2008), p. 476; UN Economic Commission for Latin America and the Caribbean, *Shaping the Future of Social Protection: Access, Financing, and Solidarity* (Santiago, Chile: UN ECLAC, 2006), pp. 155–156.

25 Fiszbein and Schady, *Conditional Cash Transfers*, pp. 103–164; Joseph Hanlon, Armando Barrientos, and David Hulme, *Just Give Money to the Poor* (Sterling, VA: Kumarian Press, 2010), pp. 53–69; Johannsen, Tejerina, and Glassman, "Conditional Cash Transfers," pp. 33–34; Akemi Yonemura, "The Changing Social Agenda in Brazil: An Analysis of the Policy Making Process in the Case of Bolsa Escola," EdD Diss., Columbia University, 2005, pp. 63–69.

26 Wendy Hunter and Natasha Borges Sugiyama, "Building Citizenship or Reinforcing Clientelism?: Contributions of the *Bolsa Família* in Brazil," paper prepared for the annual meeting of the American Political Science Association, Toronto, ON, September 3–6, 2009, pp. 10–11.

27 Fábio Veras Soares, Rafael Perez Ribas, and Rafael Guerreiro Osório, "Evaluating the Impact of Brazil's Bolsa Família," *Latin American Research Review*, Vol. 45, No. 2 (2010), p. 178; see also Valencia Lomelí, "Conditional Cash Transfers," pp. 486–487.

28 Kathy Lindert, Emmanuel Skoufias, and Joseph Shapiro, "Redistributing Income to the Poor and the Rich: Public Transfers in Latin America and the Caribbean," Social Protection Paper 0605, August (Washington, DC: World Bank, 2006), pp. 41–42.

29 Francesca Bastagli, "Conditionality in Public Policy Targeted to the Poor. Promoting Resilience?," *Social Policy & Society*, Vol. 8, No. 1 (2008), pp. 130, 135–136.

30 Maxine Molyneaux and Constanza Tabbush, "Conditional Cash Transfers and Women's Empowerment: Annotated Bibliography," Institute for the Study of the Americas, School of Advanced Study, University of London, http://americas.sas.ac.uk/about/docs/CCTANNotatedBibDFID.pdf; Hanlon, Barrientos, and Hulme, *Just Give Money to the Poor*, pp. 59–60; Valencia Lomelí, "Conditional Cash Transfers," pp. 489–490.

31 Anthony Hall, "Brazil's Bolsa Família: A Double-Edged Sword?" *Development and Change*, Vol. 39, No. 5 (September 2008), pp. 816–817; and Marcus André Melo, "Unexpected Successes, Unanticipated Failures: Social Policy from Cardoso to Lula," in Peter R. Kingstone and

Timothy J. Power, eds., *Democratic Brazil Revisited* (Pittsburgh, PA: University of Pittsburgh Press), p. 172 (quotation).

32 Brasil. Ministerio da Saúde. "Avanços na Saúde 2003-2010," p. 71, accessed March 2, 2011, at http://portal.saude.gov.br/portal/arquivos/pdf/Apresentacaov10_161010.pdf

33 Renee Gardner Sewall, "Conditional Cash Transfer Programs in Latin America," *SAIS Review*, Vol. 28, No. 2 (Summer-Fall 2008), p. 183; Melo, "Unexpected Successes," p. 183; Hunter and Sugiyama, "Building Citizenship or Reinforcing Clientelism?," p. 14.

34 Amartya Sen, "The Political Economy of Targeting," in Dominique Van de Walle and Kimberly Nead, eds., *Public Spending and the Poor* (Baltimore: Johns Hopkins University Press, 1994), p. 14.

35 Bastagli, "Conditionality in Public Policy," pp. 131–132; Fiszbein and Schady, "Conditional Cash Transfers," pp. 59–64; Teichman, "Redistributive Conflict," p. 456.

36 Aaron Ansell and Ken Mitchell, "Models of Clientelsm and Policy Change: The Case of Conditional Cash Transfer Programmes in Mexico and Brazil," *Bulletin of Latin American Research*, 2011. DOI:10.1111/j.1470-9856.2010.00497.x

37 Hunter and Sugiyama, "Building Citizenship or Reinforcing Clientelism?"

38 Armando Barrientos, Miguel Niño-Zarazúa, and Mathilde Maitrot, "Social Assistance in Developing Countries Database," Version 5.0 (July 2010), Brooks World Poverty Institute, The University of Manchester, accessed August 17, 2010, at http://www.chronicpoverty.org/publications/details/social-assistance-in-developing-countries-database/ss

39 Robert Palacios and Oleksiy Sluchynsky, "Social Pensions Part I: Their Role in the Overall Pension System," World Bank Social Protection Paper 0601, May (Washington, DC: World Bank, 2006), pp. 11–12, 21–22.

40 Armando Barrientos, "Cash Transfers for Older People Reduce Poverty and Inequality," Background Paper for the *World Development Report 2006* (Washington, DC: World Bank, 2006). Gini decline and number of program beneficiaries: Fabio Veras Soares et al., "Cash Transfer Programmes in Brazil," United Nations Development Programme International Poverty Centre Working Paper 21 (June 2006), p. 26.

41 Verónica Amarante and Andrea Vigorito, "CCTs, Social Capital, and Empowerment: Evidence from the Uruguayan PANES," paper prepared for the PEGNet Conference 2009, Institute of Social Studies, The Hague, September 3–4, 2009, accessed October 29, 2010, at http://www.pegnet.ifw-kiel.de/activities/events/program-papers-2009

42 Armando Barrientos and Claudio Santibáñez, "New Forms of Social Assistance and the Evolution of Social Protection in Latin America," *Journal of Latin American Studies*, Vol. 41, No. 1 (2009), pp. 13–14; Barrientos, Niño-Zarazúa, and Maitrot, "Social Assistance in Developing Countries Database," pp. 23, 47; Fiszbein and Schady, *Conditional Cash Transfers*, pp. 38–39; Emanuela Galasso, "'With Their Effort and One Opportunity': Alleviating Extreme Poverty in Chile," Development Research Group, World Bank, accessed October 31, 2010, at http://www.iadb.org/res/publications/pubfiles/pubS-001.pdf

43 Luis Rosero-Bixby, "Evaluación del impacto de la reforma del sector de la salud en Costa Rica mediante un estudio cuasiexperimental" [Assessing the impact of the reform of the health sector in Costa Rica through a quasi-experimental study], *Revista Panamericana de Salud Pública*, Vol. 15, No. 2 (February 2004), pp. 94–103; James Macinko, Frederico C. Guanais, and Maria de Fátima Marinho de Souza, "Evaluation of the Impact of the Family Health Program on Infant Mortality in Brazil, 1990–2002," *Journal of Epidemiology and Community Health*, Vol. 60, No. 1 (January 2006), pp. 13–19.

44 El Salvador: Maureen Lewis, Gunnar S. Eskeland, and Ximena Traa-Valerezo, "Challenging El Salvador's Rural Health Care Strategy," World Bank Policy Research Working Paper 2164 (Washington, DC: World Bank, 1999); Jill Murphy, "Impact of the Basic Integrated Health System (SIBASI) Program in El Salvador," IDRC Research Results 2006 (Ottawa, ON: International Development Research Center, 2006). Peru: Christina Ewig, "Piecemeal But Innovative," 231–238; Kurt Weyland, *Bounded Rationality and Policy Diffusion* (Princeton, NJ: Princeton University Press, 2006), pp. 158–163. Infant mortality decline from 1990 to 2009 in 20 Latin American countries calculated from World Bank, World Development Indicators online, accessed October 1, 2010.

45 Varun Gauri, *School Choice in Chile* (Pittsburgh: University of Pittsburgh Press, 1998), pp. 1–2, 23–25, 76–78.

46 Merilee Grindle, *Despite the Odds* (Princeton, NJ: Princeton University Press, 2004); Robert R. Kaufman and Joan M. Nelson, "The Politics of Education Sector Reform: Cross-National Comparisons," in Kaufman and Nelson, eds., *Crucial Needs, Weak Incentives*.

47 Emiliana Vegas and Jenny Petrow, *Raising Student Learning in Latin America* (Washington, DC: World Bank, 2008), pp. 18–19.

48 Martin Carnoy, *Cuba's Academic Advantage* (Stanford: Stanford University Press, 2007).

49 Ross and Mauldin, "Family Planning Programs," p. 146; John Ross, "Family Planning Program Effort Scores for 2004," spreadsheet sent to James McGuire, February 24, 2008.

50 Lynn M. Morgan and Elizabeth F. S. Roberts, "Rights and Reproduction in Latin America," *Anthropology News*, March 2009, pp. 12, 16.

51 James W. McGuire and Laura B. Frankel, "Mortality Decline in Cuba, 1900–1959: Patterns, Comparisons, and Causes," *Latin American Research Review*, Vol. 40, No. 2 (June 2005), pp. 93–94.

52 Access figures calculated from data in WHO/UNICEF Joint Monitoring Programme for Water Supply and Sanitation, *Progress on Sanitation and Drinking Water: 2010 Update* (Geneva: WHO and UNICEF 2010), pp. 38–52. Ecuador: Ricardo Buitrón, "Derecho humano al agua en el Ecuador," in Programa Andino del Derechos Humanos, comp., *Estado constitucional de derechos?* (Quito: Edicones Abya-Lala, 2009), pp. 141–142. Paraguay: Franz Drees, Jordan Schwartz, and Alexander Bakalian, "Output-Based Aid in Water: Lessons in Implementation from a Pilot in Paraguay," World Bank Private Sector Development Vice Presidency Note 270 (Washington, DC: World Bank, 2004).

53 Sebastián Galiani, Paul Gertler, and Ernesto Schargrodsky, "Water for Life," *Journal of Political Economy*, Vol. 113, No. 1 (February 2005), pp. 83–120.

54 Gøsta Esping-Anderson, *The Three Worlds of Welfare Capitalism* (Princeton, NJ: Princeton University Press, 1990), p. 29.

55 Huber, Mustillo, and Stephens, "Politics and Social Spending," pp. 421–422.

56 Carmelo Mesa-Lago, *Social Security in Latin America* (Pittsburgh: University of Pittsburgh Press, 1997), p. 6.

57 James M. Malloy, *The Politics of Social Security in Brazil* (Pittsburgh: University of Pittsburgh Press, 1979); Marc B. Rosenberg, *Las luchas por el seguro social en Costa Rica* (San José, CR: Editorial Costa Rica, 1983), p. 184.

58 Michael R. Reich, "The Political Economy of Health Transitions in the Third World," in Lincoln C. Chen et al., eds., *Health and Social Change in International Perspective* (Boston: Harvard School of Public Health, 1994).

59 Evelyne Huber and Juan Bogliaccini, "Latin America," in Francis G. Castles et al., eds., *The Oxford Handbook of the Welfare State* (New York: Oxford University Press, 2010), p. 646; Huber, Mustillo, and Stephens, "Politics and Social Spending," p. 423.

60 Paul Pierson, "When Effect Becomes Cause: Policy Feedback and Political Change," *World Politics*, Vol. 45, No. 4 (July), p. 597.

61 McGuire, *Wealth, Health, and Democracy*, p. 145.

62 Kurt Weyland, "Social Movements and the State: The Politics of Health Reform in Brazil," *World Development*, Vol. 23, No. 10 (October 1995), pp. 1700, 1704–1708.

63 David Collier and Richard E. Messick, "Prerequisites Versus Diffusion: Testing Alternative Explanations of Social Security Adoption," *American Political Science Review*, Vol. 69, No. 4 (December 1975), pp. 1299–1315; Kurt Weyland, ed., *Learning from Foreign Models in Latin American Policy Reform* (Washington, DC: Woodrow Wilson Center Press, 2004); Weyland, *Bounded Rationality*.

64 Marc B. Rosenberg, "Social Reform in Costa Rica: Social Security and the Presidency of Rafael Angel Calderón," *Hispanic American Historical Review*, Vol. 61, No. 2 (May 1981), pp. 284–285.

65 Collier and Messick, "Prerequisites Versus Diffusion," p. 1308.

66 Marc B. Rosenberg, "Social Security Policymaking in Costa Rica: A Research Report," *Latin American Research Review*, Vol. 14, No. 1 (1979), pp. 122, 125.

67 Collier and Messick, "Prerequisites Versus Diffusion," p. 1305; Huber, Mustillo, and Stephens, "Politics and Social Spending," p. 423.

68 Evelyne Huber, "Including the Middle Classes? Latin American Social Policies after the Washington Consensus," in Monique Kremer, Peter van Lieshout, and Robert Went, eds., *Doing*

Good or Doing Better: Development Policies in a Globalizing World (Amsterdam: Amsterdam University Press, 2009), p. 141.

69 McGuire, *Wealth, Health, and Democracy*, pp. 84, 105, 112.
70 Mesa-Lago, *Social Security in Latin America*, pp. 258–297.
71 John C. Caldwell, "Routes to Low Mortality in Poor Countries," *Population and Development Review*, Vol. 12, No. 2 (June 1986), p. 200.
72 Personal interviews with Dr. Guido Miranda and Dr. Fernando Marín, San José, Costa Rica, January 29 and February 5, 2007.
73 McGuire, *Wealth, Health, and Democracy*, pp. 116–117.
74 Argentina: Lloyd-Sherlock, "Ambitious Plans, Modest Outcomes"; Peru: Ewig, "Piecemeal But Innovative."
75 McGuire, *Wealth, Health, and Democracy*, pp. 108–109, 137–138 (cost estimates pp. 79, 169).
76 Huber, "Including the Middle Classes?," p. 150.
77 McGuire, *Wealth, Health, and Democracy*, pp. 76, 142, 173.
78 McGuire, *Wealth, Health, and Democracy*.
79 Weyland, *Bounded Rationality*, p. 172.
80 Susana Belmartino, "Politicas de salud en Argentina: Perspectiva histórica," *Cuadernos Médico Sociales*, No. 55 (1991), p. 23; Joseph Collins and John Lear, *Chile's Free-Market Miracle: A Second Look* (Oakland, CA: Institute for Food and Development Policy, 1995), p. 93.
81 McGuire, *Wealth, Health, and Democracy*, pp. 89, 174.
82 McGuire, *Wealth, Health, and Democracy*, pp. 90, 296.
83 Weyland, *Bounded Rationality*, p. 174.
84 McGuire, *Wealth, Health, and Democracy*, pp. 80, 106, 168.
85 Number of physicians and medical consultations: W.W. Westhoff et al., "Cuban Healthcare Providers in Venezuela: A Case Study," *Public Health*, Vol. 124, No. 9 (2010), p. 522. Infant mortality rate: Pan American Health Organization Table Generator (estimated rate; the reported rate is similar), accessed February 15, 2011. GDP per capita growth: calculated from World Bank, World Development Indicators (GDP per capita, PPP, constant 2005 international $), accessed February 15, 2011. Literacy: Daniel Ortega and Francisco Rodríguez, "Freed from Illiteracy? A Closer Look at Venezuela's Misión Robinson Literacy Campaign," *Economic Development and Cultural Change*, Vol. 57, No. 1 (October 2008), pp. 1–30.
86 McGuire, *Wealth, Health, and Democracy*, pp. 87, 90, 166.
87 Weyland, *Bounded Rationality*, pp. 174–175, 207–209.
88 Joan M. Nelson, "The Politics of Health Sector Reform: Cross-National Comparisons," in Nelson and Kaufman, eds., *Crucial Needs, Weak Incentives*, p. 33.
89 McGuire, *Wealth, Health, and Democracy*, pp. 88, 108, 138, 147.
90 T. H. Marshall, "Citizenship and Social Class," in T. H. Marshall, *Citizenship and Social Class and Other Essays* (Cambridge, UK: Cambridge University Press, 1950), esp. pp. 53, 77, 82.
91 McGuire, *Wealth, Health, and Democracy*, pp. 118–119.
92 Timothy Besley and Masayuki Kudamatsu, "Health and Democracy," *The American Economic Review*, Vol. 96, No. 2 (May 2006), pp. 313–318; John Gerring, Strom C. Thacker, and Carola Moreno, "Centripetal Democratic Governance: A Theory and Global Inquiry," *American Political Science Review*, Vol. 99, No. 4 (November 2005), pp. 567–581; McGuire, *Wealth, Health, and Democracy*, Chapter 2.
93 Santiago Levy, *Progress Against Poverty: Sustaining Mexico's Progresa-Oportunidades Program* (Washington, DC: Brookings Institution Press, 2006), pp. 10–16.
94 Peter Bate, "The Story Behind Oportunidades," *IDBAmérica* (October 2004); Teichman, "Redistributive Conflict," pp. 453–454.
95 Yonemura, "The Changing Social Agenda," pp. 114–116, 129, 140.
96 Calculated from figures for program budget as a share of GDP and for program coverage in Valencia Lomelí, "Conditional Cash Transfers," p. 476; and for total GDP (in constant 2005 international dollars at PPP) in World Bank, World Development Indicators online, accessed February 17, 2011.
97 Calculated from Lindert, Skoufias, and Shapiro, "Redistributing Income," pp. 93, 109.
98 Valencia Lomelí, "Conditional Cash Transfers," p. 478; Santiago Levy and Evelyne Rodríguez, *Sin herencia de pobreza: El programa Progresa-Oportunidades de México* (México, DF: Banco Interamericano de Desarrollo/Planeta, 2005), p. 10.

 99 Huber, "Including the Middle Classes?," p. 141.
100 Joan B. Anderson, "The Effectiveness of Special Interventions in Latin American Public Primary Schools," North-South Center Working Paper No. 5 (May 2002), University of Miami, p. 4; Michelle Dion, "Globalization, Democracy, and Mexican Welfare, 1988–2006," *Comparative Politics*, Vol. 42, No. 1 (October 2009), p. 74; Levy and Rodríguez, *Sin herencia de pobreza*, pp. 47, 125; Sylvia Schmelkes, "Policies Against School Failure in Mexico: An Overview," in Laura Randall and Joan Anderson, eds., *Schooling for Success* (Armonk, NY: M.E. Sharpe, 1999), p. 167.
101 Kathy Lindert et al., "The Nuts and Bolts of Brazil's Bolsa Família Program: Implementing Conditional Cash Transfers in a Decentralized Context," Social Protection Discussion Paper 0709, May (Washington, DC: World Bank, 2007), p. 15 n. 30.
102 Yonemura, "The Changing Social Agenda," pp. 148–149. FUNDEF: McGuire, *Wealth, Health, and Democracy*, p. 155.
103 Inter-American Development Bank, "The End of Inherited Poverty," September 2, 2009, accessed February 16, 2011, at http://www.iadb.org/en/news/webstories/2009-09-02/the-end-of-inherited-poverty,5557.html
104 Hall, "Brazil's *Bolsa Família*," p. 806.
105 Armando Barrientos and Claudio Santibáñez, "Social Policy for Poverty Reduction in Lower-income Countries in Latin America: Lessons and Challenges," *Social Policy & Administration*, Vol. 43, No. 4 (August 2009), pp. 409–424.
106 Yonemura, "The Changing Social Agenda," pp. 90–91, 138; Michelle Morais de Sá e Silva, "Conditional Cash Transfers and Education: United in Theory, Divorced in Policy," EdD Diss., Columbia University, 2010, pp. 121, 157.
107 Lindert et al., "The Nuts and Bolts of Brazil's Bolsa Família," p. 12.
108 Morais de Sá e Silva, "Conditional Cash Transfers and Education," pp. 156, 160.
109 Valencia Lomelí, "Conditional Cash Transfers," p. 478.
110 Yonemura, "The Changing Social Agenda," pp. 110, 116, 124, 162.
111 Hall, "Brazil's *Bolsa Família*," p. 813 n. 27 (quotation); Sewall, "Conditional Cash Transfer Programs," p. 183.
112 Melo, "Unexpected Successes," p. 183.
113 Alain de Janvry, Frederico Finan, and Elisabeth Sadoulet, "Local Electoral Incentives and Decentralized Program Performance," unpublished paper, University of California at Berkeley, December 2010, p. 26. Accessed February 23, 2011, at www.econ.berkeley.edu/~ffinan/Finan_Bolsa.pdf
114 Yonemura, "The Changing Social Agenda," pp. 91, 117, 142–143, 155–156.
115 Huber, "Including the Middle Classes?," p. 138.
116 Yonemura, "The Changing Social Agenda," pp. 91–92, 141, 156–157, 204–205.

14

THE POLITICAL ECONOMY OF REGULATORY POLICY

Economic Crisis and Privatization in the 1990s

Luigi Manzetti and Carlos Rufin

Historically, Latin American governments have often come under intense criticisms for over-regulating their economies, thus discouraging investment, while providing politicians with plenty of opportunities for the manipulation of market rules to favor their own constituencies and/or clientelistic networks. In this chapter, we will focus only on government regulation affecting public utilities that that were privatized in the 1990s. The reason for such a choice is that the wave of public utility privatization that took place in the 1990s represented a turning point in the development of Latin America. First, by its very nature, it marked the reversal of import substitution industrialization policies and of the establishment of vast industrial sectors (either through nationalization or the creation of brand new companies), which many countries in the region adopted from the 1940s until the late 1980s. Second, given the sheer size of state owned enterprises (SOEs) in public utilities like electricity, telecommunications, transportation, water and sanitation, and their sale had profound repercussions for price-setting, investment, technology transfer, market competition, and customer service for the whole economy. Third, because large segments of the population used public utilities, their privatization had multiple repercussions (possibly better service but also higher tariffs), and generated political controversy. Fourth, public utility privatization meant that the government had to build from scratch regulatory policy in these sectors as, prior to state divestiture, SOEs were monopolies that were left to regulate themselves or be supervised by ministries.

The Background of Privatization vs. Regulation in Public Utilities

By 1989, when the so-called "Washington Consensus" emerged with its economic recipe to revitalize the ailing economies of Latin America, there was widespread agreement among the academic and policy community that when markets are characterized by natural monopolies (e.g., water, ground and rail transportation) or where competition is hard to achieve, regulation was necessary to avoid rent-seeking behavior by the firms' new owners.[1] In this regard, analysts underscored the importance of establishing good regulatory mechanisms—and strong institutions to enforce such mechanisms—as prerequisites that must be in place *prior* to the privatization of public utilities. The reason is that regulation can allow a government to formalize and institutionalize its commitments to protecting consumers and investors. Seen in this way, regulation works as a sort of insurance policy. On the one hand, it assures that consumers receive goods and services from the private company at a reasonable price. On the other hand, it protects investors from sudden changes in the rules of the game, by obligating the government to respect the terms of the contract stipulated when the public utility is privatized. At the time, this was a paramount concern to private investors in Latin America, since most countries in the region had a long history of reneging on contracts and expropriating private companies. In short, it was already clear then that privatization per se was only the first step if governments were truly committed to the creation of competition in the marketplace. This was particularly true when state divestiture affected public utilities where little or no competition existed. Thus, regulation was deemed necessary to strike a balance between the need of the private companies to generate good profits and the public's expectation of benefitting from low-cost, high-quality service. Unfortunately, striking the right balance is both critical and politically challenging.

Not surprisingly, the challenge often proved to be too much to handle. In fact, despite much rhetoric about the virtues of competitive markets and the need of regulation in the absence of competition, both international financial institutions (IFIs), which funded and advised public utility privatization (World Bank, Inter-American Development Bank, and the International Monetary Fund), and Latin American governments paid lip service to all these issues. This is because, on the one hand, by selling vertically integrated SOEs to the private sector (particularly in lucrative industries such as telecommunications and electricity), governments could demand higher prices for these companies. On the other hand, IFIs could get their loans repaid quickly at a time when their financial resources were stretched out thin due to the large amounts of countries asking for assistance after the collapse of the Soviet bloc in 1991/92. The most emblematic examples of this quick and dirty approach were the privatizations of the telecommunication companies in Mexico, Argentina, and Peru, and the electricity privatization in Chile.

Obviously, the transfer of monopolies from the state to the private sector made the establishment of a regulatory framework even more compelling, but in most cases such a framework failed to materialize. Latin American governments often looked at the experience of the United Kingdom, Canada, and the United States in crafting their regulatory agencies as a way to appease critics, but the end result was that in most cases such institutions remained purposely weak. In fact, the executive branch continued to retain a substantial amount of control over key regulatory issues such as tariffs, subsidies for the provision of universal services, investment requirements, and anti-competitive behavior. The irony of it all was that one of the arguments behind the adoption of privatization in the late 1980s was to "de-politicize" economic decisions by getting government out of the direct management of crucial economic sectors. However, by the early 2000s it was clear that post-privatization regulatory policy, within a very weak institutional environment, had created many new opportunities for governments and businesses alike to act in autocratic and collusive manners that defied the very notion of market competition and government transparency.

The Politics of Regulatory Policy: What We Know

Notwithstanding the clear impact of politics in crafting post-privatization regulation, the academic literature in the Latin American case continues to be dominated by economic and public administration analyses. In general, these works focus on the cost-effectiveness of regulation and the pros and cons of government intervention. Some see regulation as a means to protect consumers from the abuse of private monopolies. Others emphasize

225

the importance of institutional factors like the establishment of "independent" regulatory agencies and anti-trust legislation to prevent private firms from gaining undue influence on the regulator (regulatory capture) and prevent price gouging and other non-competitive practices. A third line of research sees regulation as the best method to enforce contracts that safeguard the interests of both customers and producers.

Why then only a handful of political science analyses on regulatory policy in public utilities exist to date, as opposed to the large number of studies devoted to privatization in the 1990s? Part of the answer rests on the complexity of regulation, both from a technical and economic standpoint, which makes it difficult for political scientists to master. Moreover, different economic sectors require different types of regulation, thus complicating cross national and industry analyses. For instance, since the 1990s, rapid advances in telecommunications and electricity technology allowed unprecedented levels of competition, thus lessening the need for regulation. Conversely, technological change remained very limited in water supply, making it the purest form of natural monopoly and thus demanding a high degree of regulatory supervision when privatized.

Over the years, the topics related to regulatory policy have also changed. In the early days of privatization, some studies looked at the impact of financial pressure from IFIs and policy diffusion in shaping regulatory policy. More specifically, during the mid-1990s the few studies that analyzed utility regulation concentrated on the role of the World Bank, the IMF, and Inter-American Development Bank in creating strong incentives to speed up privatization in return for financial assistance. Likewise, some works stressed the importance of these institutions in inducing Latin American countries to adopt regulatory frameworks based upon the United States and the United Kingdom experiences through the hiring of international consultants from North America and Europe who were attuned to the IFI's policy goals. Others looked at the influence within many reforming administrations of domestic "technopols," or economists and other highly trained professionals coming often from the private sector and mostly trained in the United States, who served the purpose of carrying out "sound" market reforms and shelter them from public contestation. Since these early works were grounded on the assumption that privatization had to de-politicize utility regulation, much scholarly attention focused on normative issues. That is, how to best craft regulatory institutions that not only were technically competent, but also sheltered from political interference once the state divestiture euphoria was over.

However, as time went on, it became apparent that the "best practice" approach in creating regulatory institutions had often failed. In many instances, government-designed state divestiture policies left governments themselves with the authority to undermine the role of what were supposed to be "independent" regulatory agencies. Another factor that compounded the problem was that the "best practice" approach in regulatory institution building can only work well if supported by pro-competition policies and a legal system that protects property rights and restrains government encroachment. Unfortunately, by the early 2000s both conditions were still sorely missing in most countries in the region. Indeed, as the Latin American economies suffered a downturn in the late 1990s and early 2000s, public opinion became increasingly disillusioned with the way public utilities delivered their service. These resulted on occasions in conflicts pitting private utilities against new administrations that had no commitment to the market reform agenda. In several cases, these heated disputes led to either international arbitration or ended in outright renationalization (Argentina, Bolivia).

This point brings us to the political science contribution to the study of utility regulation. Research on institutions in both economics and politics has long pointed out how political actors (parties, interest groups, and grassroots organizations) and government institutions may impose significant transaction costs on business activity by affecting the willingness of governments to uphold laws and contracts. Likewise, it is clear that best practice models that may work in advanced industrial societies face entirely different constraints in developing countries, which must be understood and addressed for the successful application of such models. There are several transaction costs of a political nature that can significantly alter regulatory policy, which we will group into (1) government and company opportunism, and (2) electoral cycles.

Government opportunism is based on strategic calculations, which figured prominently in the way elected officials privatized public utilities and designed regulatory frameworks. Those political executives that privatized on pragmatic grounds did so in order to boost their domestic support with key political actors. Consequently, the concession contracts benefited friendly domestic companies and the vested interests of the affected unions. Using various excuses, including retaining national control over strategic sectors, ensuring universal service coverage for poor consumers, and protecting jobs, governments that privatized this way usually created artificial monopolies under private control (telecoms in Argentina and Mexico; electricity in Chile), or severely limited competition. This pattern also coincided, not surprisingly, with the establishment of weak regulatory frameworks. In return, companies often bankrolled the electoral campaigns of the political parties that enacted privatization. In several cases, this pattern coincided with collusion and corruption, which undermined the credibility of utility privatization over time, particularly in situations where high tariffs did not correspond to steady service improvement and customer service.

Time Inconsistency and Regulatory Policy

Time inconsistency refers to the lack of coherence in public policies across time, and in particular the pursuit of policies that are directly contradictory with previous policies. For instance, a government decides to balance the budget. It decides to do so by a mix of policies cutting expenditures and raising taxes at the national level. However, it leaves the state and local government to pursue independent policies that create deficits which must be covered by the national government. As a result of this contradictory government behavior, the budget ultimately cannot be balanced. In the case of utility regulation, we can distinguish two broad categories of time inconsistency problems resulting in opportunistic behavior.

The first type is what experts label *company opportunism*. This becomes a possibility because, as just noted, future governments might find it expedient to hold utility rates down knowing that they could do so with impunity (as was the case). For this reason, some private public utilities demanded high tariffs as a condition for acquiring the capitalized companies (high tariffs could shorten the payback period for the investment or increase returns commensurately with the risks involved) and displayed a preference for direct negotiations with the government, bypassing the formal channel of the electricity regulator (the government being the key decision maker). Unfortunately, these strategies increased the likelihood of time inconsistency by creating more backlash (against high rates) and by undermining regulatory agencies' credibility, leading to a vicious cycle of opportunism. When companies opt to strike direct bargains with the executive power in the initial stage of the privatization process, as a way to ensure government commitment, they may gain in the short run but not in the long term. As governments change, chances are that a company may not have the same kind of rapport with the new administration, leaving the private operator with no recourse mechanism. Having ignored regulatory institutions from the beginning, these are unlikely to be sympathetic to the private company when the political climate turns for the worse.

The second type is *political opportunism*. Within this category, electoral cycles are a major source of time inconsistency problems.[2] Indeed, their consequences on regulatory policy cannot be understated. Even those administrations that were most committed to pro-market reforms were susceptible to disaffected constituents before and after privatization. As the economic crisis reached its peak in the late 1990s, it became increasingly difficult to mute the misgivings of powerful electoral allies. A good rule of thumb is that the more precarious the economic situation became, the more privatized utilities became an easy political target. If a government was committed to concession contracts, changes to appease critics from within and outside the government coalition were likely to penalize utility companies. However, the worst case scenario was the election of an anti-privatization candidate. As noted earlier, the weak regulatory and legal environment in many countries provided an opportunity for such candidates to turn the table against private utility companies in the 2000s. Typical examples of these patterns were Argentina, Bolivia, Ecuador, and Venezuela, where "populist left-wing" politicians made public utilities, particularly foreign-owned ones, major targets of their nationalistic campaigns.

The common denominator that has allowed the development of these different patterns is the weak regulatory institutional environment that has emerged in the post reform era. It has turned out to be a double-edged sword by providing the opportunity to governments to either act collusively with utility companies (mostly at the outset of the privatization process) or opportunistically by penalizing private operators when macroeconomic conditions and the public mood turned sour between the late 1990s and the early 2000s.

The Evolution of Reforms

So far we have introduced a conceptual map to understand the major problems plaguing Latin American utilities after privatization. However, to have a comprehensive understanding of regulatory policy, it is important to examine the fate of utility reforms over time and across the region. In this way, we can better comprehend how politics have affected Latin American utilities after the reforms. If the extent of pro-market reforms in public utilities showed significant differences across the region (with few reforms in Ecuador, for instance, contrasting with comprehensive reform in Argentina, and much more privatization in telecoms than in water supply), the evolution of the reformed sectors has also displayed an increasing divergence over time. In fact, the observed divergence goes beyond Murillo's (2009) "market controlling" and "market conforming" typologies. It is fair to say that reform came to a halt throughout the region by 2000. Over the last decade, no major privatizations have taken place in the energy sector, and no country has undertaken any significant deregulation or deepening of the role of market forces. To a large extent, this was due to the completion of reforms through the enactment of deregulation and the privatization of state-owned companies. Yet the stabilization of reforms in some countries contrasts with the reversal of reforms in others. On one hand, Chile and, to varying degrees, Brazil, Colombia, El Salvador, Guatemala, Mexico, Panama, and Peru (in no particular order), have retained the changes introduced by pro-market reforms.[3] In these countries, private ownership is still in place, as is independent regulation and use of market mechanisms for resource allocation. On the other hand, Argentina, Bolivia, Dominican Republic, Nicaragua, and Venezuela, have experienced significant retrenchment from pro-market reforms, with extensive government intervention—particularly in the form of price controls or price freezes for utilities—and, in many cases, renationalization of assets or at least significant impairment of the value of privately-owned assets as a result of government intervention.

In all cases of reversal but the Dominican Republic's, the retrenchment from pro-market reform in the energy and utilities sectors has of course been part of a much more ample process related to the rise of political forces hostile to market forces or of reactions against the perceived failings of those forces. Nevertheless, the divergent paths invite explanation, particularly as they involve fundamental economic policy issues that have a major impact on Latin America's economic development. It is interesting to note that, while the analysis of pro-market reforms has attracted considerable scholarly attention, there is as yet a very limited amount of published research focusing on the post-reform period. The edited volume by Millán and von der Fehr (2003) explicitly considers political responses to pro-market reforms in several Latin American countries. The volume offers a sobering assessment of the aftermath of reform. Finding a balance between the mobilization of private investment, which requires high rates of return and hence high energy prices, and political survival, which calls for low prices and moderate or no price increases, turned out to be a major challenge for Latin American governments. The result has been the alternation between attempts at keeping energy prices low or steady, and supply crises that lead to sharp price rises as governments try to restart private investment in energy supply. Murillo and LeFoulon (2006) analyze one such crisis that severely threatened the post-reform model in the region's pioneer reformer, Chile. Although the crisis exposed a left-of-center government to the limitations of policy decisions made under Pinochet's dictatorship, the reform model emerged largely unscathed from the crisis. Lastly, Millán (2007) reflects on the region's experience with pro-market reforms, noting that the obstacles encountered in the reform process turned out to be greater than expected, and that the reforms came to be viewed negatively in many places. Nevertheless, Millán backs Murillo and LeFoulon's conclusions by arguing that, despite all the problems, the public monopolies do not represent convincing alternatives for many policymakers in the region, so that left-oriented governments in countries like Chile or Brazil have not sought to reverse the reforms even after these countries confronted major crises in the reformed sectors.

Still, other left-leaning governments have carried out major reversals of the reforms in public utilities. Why, then, did reforms survive crises in some countries, such as Brazil (2001–2002) or Chile (1998–1999), but not in others, such as the Dominican Republic (2004)? The standard explanation, in the context of the renewed emphasis on institutions of the last two decades, focuses on the congruence between the requirements posed for the state by privatization and pro-market reform, and the capacity of domestic institutions to meet those requirements (Millán, 2007). One can point, in fact, to the structure of political institutions in the region, and more specifically the absence of veto points or checks and balances in the region's "hyperpresidentialist" political systems. Such an institutionalist explanation certainly has much to offer. With weak judiciaries and with legislatures beholden to patronage dispensed from the presidential palace, presidents have been able to overturn reforms where political expediency or ideological hostility made it desirable. Thus the fate of reforms can be said to depend on the political will of the executive. As the reformist administrations have been replaced by new ones not bound by previous commitments, the newcomers have been able to renege on the promises made by their predecessors without incurring in any major costs, at least in the short term. Thus the Peronist administrations that followed de la Rúa's fall from power in the midst of Argentina's economic and political crisis in 2002–2003, were able to invoke emergency conditions to impose price freezes for all energy products. In conjunction with the severe devaluation of the Argentine currency, such price freezes represented a substantial expropriation of the assets of foreign investors in the energy sector. International arbitration and guarantees turned out to offer little redress for the investors, most of which have exited Argentina after writing off their investments there.

The standard explanation begs, however, for an answer about the apparent lack of checks and balances in some countries but not others in the region. Surely part of the political calculus of a government hostile to the market, or besieged by angry voters, must be its assessment of the feasibility of major policy changes. Brazil's PT, in power since 2003, was historically much more hostile to markets and private property than Argentina's Peronists, and took over from the previous government in the aftermath of a major electricity supply crisis; yet it left the electricity reforms largely untouched, and preserved Petrobrás' ability to operate as a de facto private corporation. What explains these differences?

If hyperpresidentialism and political will do not provide a full explanation for the observed differences, we must consider two possibilities: the consolidation of democratic institutions, making it harder for new governments to alter the policies and institutions created by previous governments; and the development of a consensus among major social forces, particularly political parties and voters, favorable to market forces as mechanisms for the allocation of societal resources even in sectors as sensitive for economic development and for societal welfare as energy and utilities.

Recent research on political transaction costs (Dixit, 2003; Ardanaz, Scartascini, & Tomassi, 2010) suggests that consolidated democracies are characterized by the ability of policy makers to undertake inter-temporal transactions, i.e., to commit credibly to future policies in exchange for specific actions by the transaction counterparts at the present time. Such an ability allows governments to pursue more complex or innovative policies involving non-contemporaneous exchanges or distributions of costs and benefits. Credible commitment depends, in turn, on the existence of veto players that can block attempts at reneging on past agreements. The question, then, is to explain the emergence of such players in the countries that have not abandoned pro-market reforms. We leave this question for others, as it amply exceeds the scope of this chapter.

The other explanation for the divergent paths observed in Latin America's energy and utilities sectors is the presence or absence of a consensus about the role of market forces, private ownership, and foreign investment in these sectors. Where such a consensus has arisen, it is probably the result of practical considerations as much as political interest or even ideological preference. Of course, the demise of the Soviet bloc and the traditional left has also facilitated the emergence of a consensus, but as the cases of Bolivia, Venezuela, and other countries in the region show, there is still plenty of fire left in the opponents of capitalism in the region. What is thus of equal interest is the fact that in other countries, the electoral appeal of statist policies has not made much headway. This would suggest that even where anti-capitalist forces are prominent, as in Peru, the skepticism about market forces among voters and policy makers is tempered by even stronger skepticism about the ability of governments to improve upon market outcomes. The heavy investments required by the energy and utilities sectors to build additional infrastructure, find new sources of supply, and maintain technological capacity, would place heavy demands on governments under the pre-reform public ownership structures. After the heavy costs of fiscal profligacy borne in the "lost decade" of the 1980s, most Latin American governments have been loath to take on heavy spending burdens again, particularly when democracy has meant renewed pressures to attend to social demands for redistribution, leaving limited funds for the capital account of government budgets. Thus, even governments ideologically committed to public-sector primacy, such as Brazil's PT government under Lula, have continued to rely heavily on private investment to ensure that energy supply keeps up with demand. Even in countries where the initial wave of private investment in the energy sector foundered on the imposition of price freezes by governments, such as the Dominican Republic and Argentina, it is striking to observe that those governments have not necessarily pinned their hopes on renationalization, as in Venezuela or Bolivia. Instead, governments have either placed the originally privatized companies in the hands of their cronies (Argentina), or have made it very clear that they regard renationalization as a temporary expedient and have sought to compensate the previous owners fairly (Dominican Republic).

Privatization and Democratization

Where the privatizations of the 1990s have not been reversed, the regulatory institutions and the privatized companies that emerged from the reforms have had unexpectedly positive impacts on the region's young democracies, although this link has received scant scholarly attention in the case of the energy sector. It would not have been unreasonable to expect that utility reforms, like those in other sectors of the economy, could work at cross purposes with democratic principles. Most scholars who have examined the relationship between democratization and reform in Latin America during the 1990s have concluded that this was an unhappy coincidence for the region (Weyland, 2002). In a region of profound social inequality, especially with regard to access to basic education and control over natural resources, the pro-market reforms embodied in the Washington Consensus were bound to increase inequality by rewarding those in control of the region's sources of comparative advantage—natural resources and, to a lesser extent, education—and punishing low-skill labor in the face of competition from Asia. Not surprisingly, growing economic and social inequality has hardly been compatible with the very notion of democracy, built as it is around the idea of political equality of a country's citizens. In some Latin American countries like Venezuela, Bolivia, or Argentina, the tensions provoked in part by this incompatibility have eroded the quality of democratic institutions and even led, arguably, to the breakdown of democracy in the most extreme cases. But even where democracy is not under threat, growing inequality has fostered an extraordinary and unprecedented rise in criminal violence that has also impacted democratic institutions negatively. Growing crime and violence has been met by gross abuses of human rights by the police, and by the loss of public space as people have retreated behind guarded compounds and heavily policed shopping malls to protect themselves from crime.

Surprisingly, however, the record of utility privatization offers a more nuanced picture and even some grounds for hope about the compatibility of markets and democracy in the region. The positive impacts stem from two specific aspects of reform: regulation and access to energy. For all the problems of regulatory capture by politicians and companies pointed out elsewhere in this chapter, as agencies and stakeholders have gained greater knowledge about economic regulation and a greater understanding of the impact of regulatory decisions, they have been increasingly able to monitor the work of agencies, demand participation in regulatory processes, and effectively respond to the demands of the regulated companies, which would otherwise be the privileged "insiders" by virtue of their technical capacity and access to information. Economic regulation may thus be fostering throughout the region the democratic governance of a key sector like energy, offering in the process a model that could be implemented across a wide range of other policy-making processes, from land use and development to environmental regulation, to the management of river basins. Unfortunately, there is as yet little data, especially of a cross-national nature, to ascertain the development of participation in utility regulation, with the exception of Rhodes' (2006) comparative work on consumer movements in the aftermath of telecoms privatization. This important question deserves additional research by political scientists.

The other remarkable consequence of privatization for democracy has been increased access to critical products like energy and utilities for a larger share of the population. Access to these products has profound effects on the quality of life of families and the productivity of economic activities, and is thus rightly regarded as a key element of social inclusion. Electricity, for example, not only provides access to entertainment and information, but also to education—through lighting that allows study after dark, and more recently by facilitating access to the Internet—and it can have dramatic impacts for women and girls through the mechanization of physically demanding tasks like laundry. Utility bills also often provide proof of residence, and with it the ability to demand other basic services provided by the state, such as enrollment in local public schools, which has often been denied to the inhabitants of informal urban settlements.

In this regard, the risk of privatization was that it would make access to utilities harder for the poor. Historically, foreign-owned utilities in Latin America had cared little for increasing access by the poor to their services, as limited capacity to pay meant limited profits from this segment of the population. In fact, the historical record shows this to have been a major reason for the nationalization of utilities throughout the region after 1945. In addition, utility privatization entailed bringing energy prices in line with costs of supply, which were in all cases much higher than prices under public ownership, when utilities could charge low prices at taxpayers' expense. The low profitability of serving low-income consumers, and an international context of rising energy prices, did not bode well for making energy and utilities more available to the poor.

These fears, however, have not materialized as expected. The fact that pro-market reforms have taken place, in most cases (Chile being an exception), in democratic settings has encouraged regulators and governments to worry about access, and spurred privately-owned utilities to search for viable business models to provide affordable services to the masses, creating a virtuous cycle of mutual reinforcement between democracy and privatization. Throughout the region, reform has led to significant increases in the coverage and availability of electricity networks, much as in the case of telecommunications but more remarkably so, since electricity supply has not experienced the dramatic decrease in costs associated with wireless telephony. In Buenos Aires and Lima after 1994, and Bogotá after 1997, to cite only three examples, a combination of government subsidies, regulatory incentives, and company initiatives led to the extension of electricity distribution networks to the large informal settlements (*favelas, villas miseria, pueblos jóvenes*, and so forth) in these metropolitan areas, and the replacement of informal connections by formal ones; more recently, pilot programs and city-wide efforts have been undertaken in some of Brazil's largest cities, including Salvador, Belo Horizonte, and São Paulo. Privately owned utilities have responded well to government programs, subsidies, and regulatory incentives to expand the coverage of utility networks among poorer segments of the population, leading to significant rural electrification increases throughout the region (see Millán, 2007, and the case studies in Márquez, Reficco, & Berger, 2010, and in Márquez & Rufín, 2011).

What is remarkable about these experiences is the range of solutions and approaches followed by governments and companies. Brazilian utilities have used subsidies for energy efficiency to actually help low-income electricity consumers *decrease* their energy use, since this reduces their expenditure on energy and thus increases their ability to pay for electricity. This has been achieved by relatively simple procedures such as the replacement of light bulbs and appliances, or improvements in internal wiring inside homes, which actually make them safer and enhance consumers' quality of life. Buenos Aires utilities have taken a page from South Africa, installing prepayment meters that allow consumers to manage their spending on electricity in the same way that they manage their cellular telephone airtime. In the Dominican Republic, a new program is adding a subsidy for basic electricity consumption to the country's successful conditional cash transfer (CCT) program. Since eligibility for the program is carefully targeted at poor households, this avoids the inefficiencies of traditional energy subsidies, which have tended to benefit middle-class consumers too and thus increase their cost to governments.

Although the energy prices paid by poor households may be higher than before reform in real terms, particularly for those who obtained electricity through informal connections, the high willingness to pay encountered by practically all utility companies that provide good-quality service shows that poor households throughout Latin America find it in their interest to pay for formal connections. The reason is that formal connections provide many benefits, while subsidy schemes often lower the average effective price faced by poor consumers. Many governments in the region offer a basic subsidy covering a volume of energy consumption for essential family needs, particularly lighting. In addition, field research has revealed that in fact, informal connections are costly for poor households, because they are often carried out by local "electricians" who charge a monthly amount for keeping the connection in place. And for many poor households, the price of electricity prior to reform was effectively infinite, since cash-strapped utilities lacked the financial resources to provide service to all comers and connections were instead provided on a clientelistic basis or to the highest bribe payers, as happened with other utilities and telephone service. Informal connections have other costs, too, particularly the increased danger of electrocution and fire associated with shoddy equipment, and the damage to appliances caused by the poor quality of informal supply. A formal connection, by contrast, not only gives consumers the right to demand good service, but is often also a proof of residence which can open the door to a variety of citizenship rights, such as local school registration and even legalization of informal property rights, under the land titling programs enacted in response to Hernando de Soto's hugely popular proposals. In Bogotá, the local utility offers credit for appliance purchases based on electricity consumers' record of payment of their electricity bills on time; lacking other sources of formal (and hence much cheaper) credit, poor households in Bogotá have made the company, CODENSA, the second largest retailer of household appliances in the city (see the chapter by Francisco Mejía in Márquez and Rufín, 2011).

In short, the extension of formal access to energy is rapidly bringing inclusion and extending citizenship to poor households throughout the region. Moreover, this is being carried out largely by private utilities operating under commercial criteria, in contrast to the clientelistic and corrupt criteria that often prevailed prior to reform. This is an important difference as regards social and political inclusion of the poor, for access to a basic necessity like electricity is no longer the result of a political bargain, but the result of a commercial transaction universally available to all households and organizations within a utility's service area. The implications for democratic governance in Latin America remain to be explored by scholars.

Notes

1 A rent is defined as the part of the payment to an owner of resources over and above what those resources could command in any alternative use. In other words, rent is receipt in excess of opportunity cost. In one sense, it is an unnecessary payment required to attract resources to that employment.
2 Murillo (2009) showed how electoral cycles were instrumental in shaping the pace and content of regulatory reform prior and after utility regulation.
3 We omit here Costa Rica, Ecuador, Honduras, Paraguay, and Uruguay, as energy and utility privatizations were very limited in these countries.

Bibliography

Ardanaz, Martín, Scartascini, Carlos, and Tommasi, Mariano. 2010. *Political Institutions, Policymaking, and Economic Policy in Latin America.* Washington, D.C.: Inter-American Development Bank Working Paper 158.
Dixit, Avinash. 2003. Some lessons from transaction-cost politics for less-developed countries. *Economics and Politics* 15(2): 107–133.
Márquez, Patricia, Reficco, Ezequiel, and Berger, Gabriel. 2010. *Socially Inclusive Business: Engaging the Poor Through Market Initiatives in Iberoamerica.* Cambridge, MA: Harvard University Press.
Márquez, Patricia, and Rufín, Carlos, eds. 2011. *Private Utilities and Poverty Alleviation: Market Initiatives at the Base of the Pyramid.* Cheltenham, England: Edward Elgar.
Millán, Jaime. 2007. *Market or State? Three Decades of Reforms in the Latin American Electric Power Industry.* Washington, D.C.: Inter-American Development Bank.
Millán, Jaime, and von der Fehr, Nils, eds. 2003. *Keeping the Lights On: Power Sector Reform in Latin America.* Washington, D.C.: Inter-American Development Bank.
Murillo, María Victoria, 2009. *Political Competition, Partisanship, and Policy Making in Latin American Public Utilities.* Cambridge, England: Cambridge University Press.
Murillo, María Victoria, and Le Foulon, Carmen. 2006. Crisis and Policymaking in Latin America: The Case of Chile's 1998–99 Electricity Crisis. *World Development* 34(9): 1580–1596.
Rhodes, Sybil. 2006. *Social Movements and Free Market Capitalism in Latin America: Telecommunications Privatization and the Rise of Consumer Protest.* Albany: State University of New York Press.
Weyland, Kurt. 2002. *The Politics of Market Reform in Fragile Democracies: Argentina, Brazil, Peru, and Venezuela.* Princeton, NJ: Princeton University Press.

PART III

Actors/Social Groups

15

SOCIAL MOVEMENTS IN LATIN AMERICA

Kathryn Hochstetler

Latin American social movements provide some of the most vivid political images in a region that does not lack for color. To give just a few examples, over a million Brazilians painted their faces black and marched to encourage their National Congress to impeach then-President Collor; Bolivian indigenous peoples gathered behind their own multi-colored flag to successively demand a change in gas policy, two presidents' resignations, and a new constitution; and the Zapatistas transformed global understandings of what was possible in the neoliberal age with their 1994 uprising in Mexico. As these examples show, social movements have been not just present in Latin American countries, but often successful in changing the direction of political systems.

This chapter's conceptual and empirical focus is on social movements as manifestations of contentious politics, meaning "episodic, public, collective" attempts to make claims on key decision-makers.[1] Compared to other actors, social movements are among the most likely to introduce novel demands, new collective actors, and innovative modes of action to the political world, although their collective struggles can also become routine parts of political life. The association of social movements with originality has led to a great deal of analytical focus on the conditions of emergence of new movements and strategies, with secondary attention to questions about the development of social movements over time and whether they achieve their aims. Social movements also generate broader interest as indicators of the quality of more conventional political institutions and mechanisms of representation.

Historical and Intellectual Development of the Study of Latin American Social Movements

Social movements have been part of Latin American political history since the pre-independence period. Early movements of resistance to colonialism and the independence movements themselves are not generally called social movements, but share a familial resemblance to them and fall on the more contestatory end of the spectrum of contentious politics. This section will sketch two partially overlapping generations of more direct study of social movements in Latin America, showing the close relationship between analytical perspectives and historical developments. Scholars in an initial period (roughly 1960–1990s) used class-based analyses to explain emerging working class and revolutionary movements, while their overlapping successors (approximately 1975–present) turned to social movements theories developed in Northern countries in order to explain the proliferation of new movements that took up "smaller" topics from human rights to the environment.

In the first generation of studies, scholars documented the emergence of working-class and revolutionary movements during the first eight decades of the 20th century.[2] As a group, they drew on structural theories inspired by Marxian and related macrosociological perspectives. These explained that such new movements emerged through the working out of class-based conflicts generated by economic production processes. They defined the movements' levels of success in terms of large-scale transformations of economies, states, and societies, and saw success as depending on structural conditions that made existing elites and institutions vulnerable to the movements' challenges. While revolutionary movements fought in half a dozen countries and labor movements hotly contested the rise of neoliberal economic policies in the 1980s in Latin America,[3] that decade also ushered in a whole array of sociopolitical transitions—of democratization, to more market-oriented economies, the end of the Cold War—that made both kinds of movements less prominent afterwards.[4] The predominant academic approaches in political science followed suit.

The next generation of research on social movements reflected changes in the forms of political contention that had been developing since the 1970s. The comparatively low and informal organizational requirements of the social movement form of engagement in politics introduced an astonishing array of actors, interests, and ideas to national political agendas over the next decades, and many eventually made their way into the formal political system. Small-scale movements of neighborhoods and other kinds of communities began to organize themselves to address the needs—day care, soup kitchens, solidarity, credit—that the military governments of the day were not meeting. New social movements including indigenous, environmental, and gender groups also posed demands that seemed small to the previous generation of scholars because they focused on identity and lifestyle concerns that were not seen to require remaking all of state and society.[5] Yet collectively these movements represented real change in a region where the hierarchies of landownership and formal industrial production had largely organized political life. In addition, indigenous and women's movements made demands that turned out to pose significant challenges to traditional ways of doing politics, while the whole shifting array of movements could take on very big agenda items when they managed to form cross-sectoral coalitions.[6]

In general, these social movements chose less-contentious tactics than earlier movements. They certainly did not routinely make the revolutionary movements' explicit commitment to violent strategies, but collectively resolved problems for themselves or made claims for respect and inclusion. Many of their choices were not easily traceable to structural factors, and research approaches changed in turn. Researchers drew on the social movements' theories of scholars of U.S. and European movements, which tended to highlight the agency of activists who mobilized resources, actively networked, and made their choices in the context of fluid circumstances. Theoretical debates centered on questions like whether movements were more responsive to changing political openings ("political opportunity structure") or broader cultural practices of identity and framing.[7] These debates were borrowed from the north, and the answers looked somewhat different in the Latin American context of extreme economic and social inequality and a state that was unusually (but unevenly) strong and just newly democratic.[8] Much of the subsequent empirical debate has asked what those differences mean for social movements practices in the region.

Recent Research on Regional Social Movements:
Major Claims and Developments

The last couple of decades have seen remarkably rapid changes in Latin America. One of the most important for social movements has been the region's economic shift to greater market control over national economies and the corresponding drop in the scope and power of states. After early consensus that this neoliberal turn was demobilizing for social movements, scholars have more recently concluded that the effects were in fact varied, and they have documented a return to the streets in a number of countries in the region. The effects of neoliberalism were mediated by a second important change, the near simultaneous transition to liberal democratic forms of government. Although the resulting regimes have often proved disappointing, they are undoubtedly more inclusive than preceding military and civilian governments. In particular, some of the sectors which arose in social movements— indigenous populations, women, leftists—have even been elected to national presidencies and are newly routine participants in the political process, creating novel opportunities and challenges for social movements. Finally, Latin Americans of many kinds are increasingly crossing national boundaries to trade products and ideas, make political coalitions, and engage in a complex web of transnational interactions. All of these developments carry important implications for social movements, and I use them here to organize a summary of some of the recent empirical debates and discoveries about Latin American social movements.

Neoliberalism and Social Movements in Latin America

By the early 1990s, most Latin American countries had taken steps to significantly reduce the state's role in their national economies, privatizing state-owned enterprises, reducing subsidies and other government spending, and removing barriers to free trade and market transactions. In political science, an initial generation of scholarship saw these changes as profoundly demobilizing for social movements. These "atomization" theorists[9] concluded that neoliberalism was especially destructive of social movements' *capacity* to mobilize, even while economic opening created painful motivations for them to protest. More recently, however, their empirical conclusions have been challenged by a set of scholars, here called "mobilization" theorists, who point out the undeniable presence of anti-neoliberal contention in at least some countries of the region. Here I compare the evidence for their empirical conclusions, and discuss the causal mechanisms each sees at work.

The pessimism of the atomization theorists began with the effects of neoliberal policies on organized labor, which suffered a double hit. On the one hand, the economic policies themselves directly reduced formal workplace employment, leaving workers economically devastated and in a defensive position vis-à-vis employers that discouraged activism.[10] In addition, the economic changes came through repression (as in military Chile) or by the desertion of one-time party allies (in historically labor-mobilizing countries), both of which politically weakened labor as well. Since working-class actors have traditionally led lower-class movements and protests in Latin America, their decline meant that collective action to challenge neoliberal policies and other grievances became much more difficult to organize.[11]

Political developments reinforced the economic mechanisms of demobilization, in this view. The same economic policies left a diminished state that no longer controlled the resources and decision-making power that had made it a long-time target of activists.[12]

Citizens sought individualized solutions from the state, e.g., through new highly targeted social assistance programs, or were simply stymied by their inability to locate someone who might be able to authoritatively address their demands. The fact that essentially all political parties and presidents, even historically leftist ones, presented neoliberal proposals only deepened the sense of exclusion. In combination, these factors contributed to widespread disillusionment with democracy and a general disengagement from politics and mobilization.

In contrast, mobilization theorists have argued that neoliberal reforms *did* generate the kind of resistance mobilizations in Latin America that even atomization theorists say should be the result of widespread economically painful changes. They point to food riots, broad mobilizations for economic policy change, and even mass efforts to overthrow neoliberal presidents as evidence.[13] For the most part, mobilization theorists explain these outcomes through a grievance model that suggests that the failure of neoliberal policies to improve economic life eventually leads citizens to challenge those policies in any way they can. When politicians are non-responsive and the state is both weak and exclusive, the street is an obvious location to make political demands. At the same time, most of these authors also stress the ways that institutional democracy provides a backdrop that allows citizens to stake political rights claims and is generally less repressive than previous military regimes.

With more than two decades of study of the relationship between neoliberalism and contestation, it is clear that there is no simple link between the two. Sorting among the evidence presented, temporal, spatial and issue dimensions all help to explain why scholars have come to such different conclusions about whether neoliberal economic policies stimulate or dampen social movements' activity. The temporal dimension can be seen in part by examining publication dates—as a group, the mobilization theorists largely chronicled a surge of protest and other activism that marked the 2000s, while atomization arguments are grounded in the less-contentious 1990s. Spatially, the largest and most-persistent recent social movements are concentrated in just a few countries of Latin America, especially Argentina, Bolivia, and Venezuela. While social movements also exist in a number of other countries, these have seen thousands of protests, street blockades, and other acts of political contention; as each elected leftist presidents, protest spread across the political spectrum.[14] Many of the case studies of particular movements focus on these most-contentious countries. Finally, the atomization theorists do appear to accurately track a decline in the traditional ways that labor has mobilized. All data report sharp drops in workplace strikes since the 1980s, although labor has continued to mobilize alongside other sectors, sometimes in a leading role. On the other hand, they appear to have missed the rise of contention in other social groupings.[15] Understanding why these patterns have emerged requires further analysis.

Democratization and Social Movements in Latin America

The influence of neoliberalism on social movements is certainly affected by the simultaneous transition in much of the region to institutional democracy. Like liberalization, democratization has also garnered surprisingly opposed assessments of its likely effect on social movements. I briefly address the early expectation that liberal democratic institutions would simply replace social movements as modes of political participation, but spend most of this section discussing the ways that democratization changed both the forms and content of Latin American social movements. Democratic institutions generally allow more institutionalized forms of participation for citizens that have contributed to greater formalization of some parts of the social movement sector, like the rise of regular consultative forums and more formal citizen institutions like the non-governmental organization (NGO). To varying degrees, such opportunities for participation are associated with the more-leftist parties that have begun to flourish in recent Latin American party systems. At the same time, these developments have raised expectations among citizens that they do not necessarily meet. Democracy's disappointments have been especially important for changing some of the content of social movements' demands, with the absence of true citizenship becoming a common phrase for articulating what is still missing after formal political transition.

Many academic stories of the transition from military to civilian rule in Latin America focus on the elite negotiations and interests that accompanied the return to constitutional liberal democracy.[16] While such bargaining undoubtedly was central in the process, others have noted that social movements—from initial small groups of mothers demanding news about their children to hundreds of thousands demanding "direct elections *now!*"—played an important role in communicating that military regimes had lost popular legitimacy and raising the perceived cost of repression and regime continuity.[17] Elite-focused analysts did not deny social movements' role in catalyzing transition, but their standard conclusion was well-summarized in one of the most influential studies of transition: "this popular upsurge is always ephemeral."[18]

The idea that social movements would be simply displaced by institutional actors became a blindspot in a great deal of the subsequent study of Latin American politics, which simply assumes that that is true and moves on to studies of congresses and the like.[19] Theoretically, this is implausible, as virtually the entire body of research on social movements is based on the experiences of social movements in the much-more-institutionalized democracies of Western Europe and North America. The evidence of social movement mobilization in Latin America presented in the last section shows that it is not empirically true in Latin America either. Thus the more relevant question is not *whether* social movements were able to continue in Latin America after political transition, but *how* democratization changed their modes of operation.

For social movements, some of the most important effects of democratic institutions derive from this regime type's generally more favorable disposition toward organized collective action and participation on the part of ordinary citizens. Beyond the opportunity to vote that characterizes the regime type, democracies are more inclined to offer other opportunities for consultation with groups or individuals, seek the cooperation of citizens in providing government services, and are (in principle) more inclusive. These tendencies mean there is more potential for cooperation between state and society; citizens may choose confrontational strategies like protest anyway, and when they do, states are less likely to violently repress them.

To the extent that these general observations are true in Latin America (below, I discuss the governments' frequent failures to live up to the expectations expressed here), perhaps the most novel response was the institutionalization of a part of the social movements sector in many Latin American countries, starting in the mid-1980s. Organizationally, it meant the rise of the NGO, a permanent organization with specialized staff and bureaucratic infrastructure.[20] The NGO form directly contradicts many definitions of social movements, including the one that opens this chapter and includes the word "episodic." Its very permanence and professionalism makes the NGO a preferred interlocutor for democratic governments and international actors who are looking for societal actors who can perform as cooperative partners over time, carrying out contracts and presenting accounts. These same qualities make them less openly contentious. For these reasons, both academics and activists initially saw NGOs as a threat or opposite to social movements, and some continue to do so.[21] Over time, however, these debates have become less fractious, not least because the boundaries have proven to be more porous than once thought. The same individuals may show up on both sides of the divide, and classically episodic explosions of social movements often turn out to be at least partially grounded in permanent organizations, like Ecuador's indigenous CONAIE, Argentina's Mothers of the Plaza de Mayo, or Brazil's IBASE.[22]

Recent liberal democracy in Latin America has offered social movements other opportunities to have more sustained input into national politics, although these vary quite a bit among countries. The rise of political parties with close ties to social movements is one of these, noteworthy as a counter-point to the loosening of party-labor movement ties. The earliest prominent example, the Workers' Party (PT, *Partido dos Trabalhadores*) in Brazil, was created in 1980 on a base of independent unions and religious, human rights, and other social movements.[23] Indigenous movements embraced the partisan strategy in their new democracies, with comparative success in Bolivia, Colombia, Ecuador, and Venezuela and less impact in Argentina, Guyana, Mexico, Nicaragua, and Peru.[24] These and other newer leftist parties like Mexico's Party of the Democratic Revolution (PRD, *Partido de la Revolución Democrática*) and Uruguay's Broad Front (*Frente Amplio*) considered social movements part of their social base as well as electoral constituencies.[25]

As a group, these movement-based parties initiated many of the region's experiments with participatory mechanisms that allow for regular consultation with citizens, not least because their social movements constituents demanded them. Some, such as the PT's participatory budgeting process, became global exemplars.[26] In other cases, the results are less impressive, such as Fox's conclusion that the PRD did not qualitatively change rural state-society relations in Mexico, as "parties across the spectrum continue to block the democratic representation of peasants and indigenous peoples."[27] It is impossible to give a full accounting of the effect of the new parties on social movements in this chapter. On balance, they almost certainly raised or at least maintained the level of political inclusion of the actors and issues that have driven recent Latin American social movements.[28] On the other hand, social movements' expectations for their associated parties are often very high, and the compromises of both electioneering and governing rarely satisfy them. Partisan competition also entered into relations among activists.[29] Ironically, the rise of leftist administrations had its most directly galvanizing effect on social movements in the diffusion of the protest tactic to the right; shut out from their historic routes into politics, landowners and traditional elites also have taken to the streets in Argentina, Bolivia, Venezuela, and elsewhere.[30]

Democratization had its final impact on social movements through the many failures of Latin American democracies to live up to the regime type's promises. For a social movements sector that largely had its origins in the struggle against military dictatorship, these failures were dispiriting, but ultimately provoked both renewed mobilization and efforts to rethink democracy's meaning. Throughout the region, protest continues to be the strategy of last resort for citizens who find their governments behaving unacceptably. The many elected South American presidents pushed from office early—9 of 41 between 1978 and 2003, and more afterwards—all faced mass movements insisting they go, usually for corruption and unpopular economic policies.[31]

Social movements' efforts to redefine and deepen democracy have garnered fewer headlines, but are politically resonant. A number of diverse movements (and scholars of them) settled on the word "citizenship" to capture what institutional democracy still lacked.[32] Citizenship meant redress for the basic inequalities and deficiencies that kept some in society from being able to be full participants in national life. Some citizenship barriers (landlessness, racism, sexism) are grounded in society and must be addressed there, but social movements directed their demands for citizenship primarily at the state. Citizenship demands essentially ask to renegotiate the terms of state-society relations, and are correspondingly contentious. Political elites have rarely responded generously, and one response among movements is to give up on the state and demand autonomy and direct control of collective decisions.[33] To summarize this section, then, democratization has produced quite opposite effects, from the cooperative professional NGO to the ever-more-challenging demands for full citizenship.

The Transnational Context of Latin American Social Movements

The national developments discussed so far are embedded in global contexts that are increasingly important for understanding the resources, choices, and outcomes of Latin American social movements. The international level provides them with potential allies (and threats), norms to embrace or resist, and important examples of new strategies and targets for action. This may happen episodically, or take the form of tightly linked networks and coalitions that may engage in collective action across national boundaries. While not wholly new— labor joined in international networks throughout the 20th century, and many revolutionary movements found international inspiration, support, and resistance—the density of transnational relations and the extent of their reach into Latin American societies have greatly expanded. These developments find their roots in both broad socio-demographic phenomena like urbanization and the increased ease of international communications, as well as in deliberate efforts to create networks and exchange ideas.

One important role of transnational actors has been in supporting Latin American social movements that have a hard time mobilizing at home because of political or general societal rejection of their demands. Keck and Sikkink's book on transnational activist networks laid out a highly influential model of a boomerang pattern, where activists who are stymied at home share information in hopes of finding international allies who can persuade their own governments or international organizations to target the original recalcitrant state.[34] They used Latin American cases to develop their model, discussing the way transnational networks helped Argentine human rights activists and Brazilian rubber tappers to confront their own governments in the 1970s and 1980s, while Mexican human rights activists initially failed because they could not generate international allies. Similar dynamics have improved outcomes for indigenous movements and labor.[35] In these examples, Latin American social movements are generally receiving help from abroad for specific campaigns.

Over time, social movements based in Latin American countries have also become protagonists in global politics in their own right. This development grew in part out of international negotiation processes, where non-state actors from around the world began to demand a more prominent role as early as the Stockholm Conference on the Human Environment in 1972 and the Mexico City Conference on Women in 1975. NGOs and social movements gathered to both lobby their governments and to network with each other. Latin American participants were especially committed to the latter strategy, and even formed more permanent associations with each other and like-minded organizations from the Global South.[36] Such international conference participation has proved important for Latin American social movements, both for taking part in discussions that shape emerging international norms and for making concrete contacts that can lead to strategic coordination and/or new resources. For Brazilian environment and development activists, for example, the personal contacts associated with the 1992 Rio Conference on Environment

Development were instrumental for both pushing and funding the transition among some of them from social movements to more-professionalized NGO forms of organization.[37] International participation can also present more negative effects, introducing new kinds of competition as well as conflicts over the balance between national priorities and international agendas; Brysk uses the word "collision" to describe the impact.[38]

Some of the most sustained international networking has taken place on a topic where national and international activist agendas largely coincide. Social movements have built networks across the hemisphere to take on governmental integration efforts such as the Free Trade Agreement of the Americas and the North American Free Trade Agreement (NAFTA), as well as taking part in global movements against neoliberalism.[39] In these networks, labor, environmentalist, human rights, and other movements have joined forces, recognizing a common aim of blocking free trade agreements. They have challenged their governments' positions on trade at home, and showed up *en masse* to governmental negotiation sessions. Such networks directly forced governments to add labor and environmental protection side agreements to NAFTA and have worked together since to make those agreements more effective.[40] Participants have recognized the generally "anti-" quality of many of these networks—they are against governmental and private initiatives without necessarily presenting clear alternatives—and recent initiatives have tried to set a positive agenda. Among the most influential of these is the World Social Forum, created and first hosted in Porto Alegre, Brazil, in 2001, whose purpose has been to bring together activists from around the world to share experiences and craft a democratic alternative to neoliberal policies.[41]

Criticisms of Recent Research and Proposals for Future Research

Recent research on social movements in Latin America shows many strengths. Many of the weaknesses are closely related to the strengths, however, indicating that more balanced research strategies are needed for the area of research as a whole to advance. Here I highlight several of the dominant tendencies and new research agendas that might be developed in response. I conclude with two sets of questions that push further into what democracy means for social movements in the region.

Several of the strengths/weaknesses derive from what may be the core flaw in the study of social movements, which is that the body of work is heavily skewed toward reporting positive cases. By far the most common approach is case study research of a particular movement in a particular country, with some use of comparative studies of a few movements in the same country or cross-national study of the same movement in a few countries. Within these studies, the focus is often again the close study of several key campaigns—usually campaigns where movements either succeed in their aims or lose in ways that make a political impact. These tendencies mean that the social movements' literature is replete with rich and detailed data about successful and important mobilizations, especially by iconic movements like the 1980s Amazonian rubber-tappers, the Zapatistas in Mexico in the 1990s, or Argentina's *piqueteros* who blocked roads through the 2000s. Failed and disappointing movements that have missed opportunities to mobilize rarely generate studies.[42] Yet standard research design principles suggest a need to look at a fuller range of outcomes in order to understand a phenomenon. Rather than focusing so much attention on the eye-catching examples, whether movements or countries, social movements scholars might better approach their subject as, say, judiciaries are studied—present at some level in virtually every country, with the variations in strength and independence being of interest.

In a related development, many studies of social movements hew closely to the point of view of the activists. This results in part from the fact that concrete research strategies usually include extensive interviewing and observation of activists, while other data sources are less systematically used. In addition, this area of research often attracts scholars with normative commitments to the agenda of the movements they study.[43] From the standpoint of studying Latin American politics as a whole, the typical approach probably overstates the importance of social movements in the phenomenon studied. Activists are excellent sources on their own presence and intentions, but evaluating *impact* requires more careful attention to other actors and institutions to judge their relative weight.[44] The tendency for scholars to study movements with which they are sympathetic also has meant a disproportionate focus on progressive actors. In the 2000s, however, the traditional tools of social movements such as the protest march, the road blockade, and the like are being used across the political spectrum. Once again, understanding the phenomenon requires a broader view of what constitutes it.

Finally, several decades into Latin America's most stable period of liberal democracy, we have the opportunity to rethink the relationship between social movements and democracy in more theoretical and conceptual terms. One set of questions begins with the depiction of social movements as contentious actors, whose mobilizations and tactics convey intensity of preferences—often in unorthodox ways—in a regime type that is supposed to embody (potentially conflicting) principles like representative decision-making by leaders selected by populations in elections that weight all of them equally. In this context, what are the theoretical and conceptual limits of *democratic* protests, and how would we recognize those empirically? Conversely, what are the theoretical and conceptual limits of the kinds of policing of protests compatible with democracy? How can political leaders balance electoral mandates with subsequent demands from the street, especially if there are mobilized counter-movements? These are questions that have received some attention in the social movements' literature, but that have not shaped many studies of Latin American social movements so far.[45]

A second set of questions that deserves further research takes the opposite tack, normalizing the study of social movements (and other contentious forms of politics) as one choice on a menu of options that citizens have to influence and participate in democratic politics. This menu has expanded quite dramatically over recent decades in Latin America. It includes the traditional organizational options for interest intermediation—the social movement, the interest group, partisan options, the union.[46] But citizens can also bring court cases to the region's newly vital judicial systems, participate in a consultative process of some kind, or use international networks to set up fair trade markets. They can also just stay home. These are not exclusive strategies and citizens can choose more than one, but there are practical limits. Social movements will continue to be important in the region only if and when collective, contentious (but not too contentious) strategies make sense to potential participants in the context of these other possibilities. We know far too little about when they will.

Notes

1 Doug McAdam, Sidney Tarrow, and Charles Tilly, *Dynamics of Contention* (Cambridge: Cambridge University Press, 2001), 5.
2 A few representative works on movements of labor and other subordinate classes are Ruth Berins Collier and David Collier, *Shaping the Political Arena* (Princeton, NJ: Princeton University Press,

1992) and Dietrich Rueschemeyer, Evelyne Huber Stephens, and John D. Stephens, *Capitalist Development and Democracy* (Chicago: University of Chicago Press, 1992). On revolutionary movements, see Cynthia McClintock, *Revolutionary Movements in Latin America: El Salvador's FMLN and Peru's Shining Path* (Washington, DC: US Institute of Peace, 1998); Jeffrey Paige, *Agrarian Revolution: Social Movements and Export Agriculture in the Under-Developed World* (New York: Free Press, 1975); Timothy Wickham-Crowley, *Guerrillas and Revolution in Latin America* (Princeton, NJ: Princeton University Press, 1992), Eric R. Wolf, *Peasant Wars of the Twentieth Century* (New York: Harper and Row, 1969).

3 Susan Eckstein, ed., *Power and Popular Protest: Latin American Social Movements* (Berkeley and Los Angeles: University of California Press, 1989).

4 The post-1990 labor movement is discussed in more detail below and in Chapter 18. No revolutionary movements of the classic type have formed since 1990, and while there may conceivably be some in the future, they "may not be our parents' or grandparents' revolutions ..." Eric Selbin, "Resistance, Rebellion, and Revolution in Latin America and the Caribbean at the Millennium (Review Essay)," *Latin American Research Review* 36 (2001): 172. See also John Foran, ed., *The Future of Revolutions: Rethinking Radical Change in the Age of Globalization* (London: Zed Press, 2003).

5 Douglas Chalmers, et al., eds., *The New Politics of Inequality in Latin America: Rethinking Participation and Representation* (Oxford: Oxford University Press, 1997); Eckstein, *Power and Popular Protest*; Arturo Escobar and Sonia E. Alvarez, eds., *The Making of Social Movements in Latin America: Identity, Strategy, and Democracy* (Boulder, CO: Westview Press, 1992); Elizabeth Jelin, ed., *Women and Social Change in Latin America* (London: Zed and Geneva: UNRISD, 1990).

6 Sonia E. Alvarez, *EnGendering Democracy in Brazil: Women's Movements in Transition Politics*; Jane S. Jaquette, ed., *The Women's Movement in Latin America: Feminism and the Transition to Democracy* (Boston: Unwin Hyman, 1989); Eduardo Silva, *Challenging Neoliberalism in Latin America* (Cambridge: Cambridge University Press, 2009); Deborah J. Yashar, *Contesting Citizenship: The Rise of Indigenous Movements and the Postliberal Challenge* (Cambridge: Cambridge University Press, 2005).

7 Jean Cohen, "Strategy or Identity: New Theoretical Paradigms and Contemporary Social Movements," *Social Research* 52 (1985): 663–716; Doug McAdam, John D. McCarthy, and Mayer N. Zald, eds., *Comparative Perspectives on Social Movements: Political Opportunities, Mobilizing Structures, and Cultural Framings* (Cambridge: Cambridge University Press, 1996).

8 Sonia E. Alvarez, Evelina Dagnino, and Arturo Escobar, eds., *Cultures of Politics Politics of Cultures: Re-Visioning Latin American Social Movements* (Boulder, CO: Westview Press, 1996); Diane Davis, "The Power of Distance: Re-theorizing Social Movements in Latin America," *Theory and Society* 28 (1999): 585–639; Joe Foweraker, *Theorizing Social Movements* (London: Pluto Press, 1995).

9 The atomization label comes from Moisés Arce and Paul T. Bellinger, "Low-Intensity Democracy Revisited: The Effects of Economic Liberalization on Political Activity in Latin America," *World Politics* 60 (2007): 97–121.

10 Alejandro Portés and Kelly Hoffman, "Latin American Class Structures: Their Composition and Change During the Neoliberal Era," *Latin American Research Review* 38 (2003): 41–82; Kenneth M. Roberts, "Party-Society Linkages and the Transformation of Political Representation in Latin America," *Canadian Journal of Latin American and Caribbean Studies* 27 (2002): 9–34.

11 Marcus J. Kurtz, "The Dilemmas of Democracy in the Open Economy: Lessons from Latin America," *World Politics* 56 (2004): 262–302; Philip D. Oxhorn, "Is the Century of Corporatism Over? Neoliberalism and the Rise of Neopluralism," in *What Kind of Democracy? What Kind of Market? Latin America in the Age of Neoliberalism*, ed. Philip D. Oxhorn and Graciela Ducatenzeiler (University Park: Pennsylvania State University Press, 1998); Roberts, "Party-Society Linkages and the Transformation of Political Representation in Latin America."

12 Davis, "The Power of Distance"; Kurtz, "The Dilemmas of Democracy"; Oxhorn, "Is the Century of Corporatism Over?"

13 Hank Johnston and Paul Almeida, eds., *Latin American Social Movements: Globalization, Democratization, and Transnational Networks* (Lanham, MD: Rowman and Littlefield, 2006); Moisés Arce and Roberta Rice, "Societal Protest in Post-Stabilization Bolivia," *Latin American Research Review* 44 (2009): 88–101; Arce and Bellinger, "Low-Intensity Democracy Revisited"; Kathryn Hochstetler and Elisabeth Jay Friedman, "Can Civil Society Organizations Solve the Crisis of

Partisan Representation in Latin America?," *Latin American Politics and Society* 50 (2008): 1–32; Silva, *Challenging Neoliberalism in Latin America;* Yashar, *Contesting Citizenship.*

14 Kent Eaton, "Backlash in Bolivia: Regional Autonomy as a Reaction against Indigenous Mobilization," *Politics and Society* 35 (2007): 71–102; Hochstetler and Friedman, "Can Civil Society Organizations Solve the Crisis of Partisan Representation in Latin America?"; Margarita López Maya and Luis Lander, "Popular Protest in Venezuela: Novelties and Continuities," in *Latin American Social Movements.*

15 On labor, see Kathryn Hochstetler, "Rethinking Presidentialism: Challenges and Presidential Falls in Latin America," *Comparative Politics* 38 (2006): 406; Kurtz, "The Dilemmas of Democracy"; Roberts, "Party-Society Linkages and the Transformation of Political Representation in Latin America"; Silva, *Challenging Neoliberalism in Latin America.* On newly mobilized sectors, see the previous footnote as well as Gabriel Ondetti, *Land, Protest, and Politics: The Landless Movement and the Struggle for Agrarian Reform in Brazil* (University Park: Pennsylvania State University Press, 2008); Yashar, *Contesting Citizenship.*

16 Terry Lynn Karl, "Dilemmas of Democratization in Latin America," *Comparative Politics* 23 (1990): 1–21; Guillermo O'Donnell, Philippe C. Schmitter, and Laurence Whitehead, eds., *Transitions from Authoritarian Rule (4 volumes)* (Baltimore: Johns Hopkins University Press, 1986); Dankwart A. Rustow, "Transitions to Democracy: Toward a Dynamic Model," *Comparative Politics* 2 (1970): 337–363.

17 Alvarez, *EnGendering Democracy in Brazil*; Stephan Haggard and Robert R. Kaufman, "The Political Economy of Democratic Transitions," *Comparative Politics* 29 (1997): 263–283; Jaquette, *The Women's Movement in Latin America*; Enrique Peruzzotti, "Towards a New Politics: Citizenship and Rights in Contemporary Argentina," *Citizenship Studies* 6 (2002): 77–93.

18 Guillermo O'Donnell and Philippe Schmitter, *Transitions from Authoritarian Rule: Tentative Conclusions about Uncertain Democracies* (Baltimore: Johns Hopkins University Press, 1986), 55.

19 Hochstetler, "Rethinking Presidentialism"; Deborah Yashar, "Democracy, Indigenous Movements, and the Postliberal Challenge in Latin America," *World Politics* 52 (1999): 76–105.

20 A number of the chapters in Chalmers et al., *The New Politics of Inequality in Latin America,* discuss the rise of NGOs.

21 See Kathryn Hochstetler and Margaret Keck, *Greening Brazil: Environmental Activism in State and Society* (Durham, NC: Duke University Press, 2007) for a discussion of the ways this organizational form could disrupt the field of collective action, in this case among Brazilian environmentalists.

22 Hochstetler, "Rethinking Presidentialism"; Silva, *Challenging Neoliberalism in Latin America.*

23 Margaret Keck, *The Workers' Party and Democratization in Brazil* (New Haven, CT: Yale University Press, 1992).

24 Donna Lee Van Cott, *From Movements to Parties in Latin America: The Evolution of Ethnic Politics* (Cambridge: Cambridge University Press, 2005).

25 Kathleen Bruhn, *Taking on Goliath: The Emergence of a New Left Party and the Struggle for Democracy in Mexico* (University Park: Pennsylvania State University Press); Steve Ellner and Daniel Hellinger, ed., *Venezuelan Politics in the Chávez Era: Class, Polarization and Conflict* (Boulder, CO: Lynne Rienner 2003); Benjamin Goldfrank, "Decentralization, Party Institutionalization, and Participation," *Comparative Politics* 39 (2007): 147–168.

26 Rebecca Neara Abers, *Inventing Local Democracy: Grassroots Politics in Brazil* (Boulder, CO: Lynne Rienner, 2000); Leonardo Avritzer, *Democracy and the Public Space in Latin America* (Baltimore: Johns Hopkins University Press, 2002); Gianpaolo Baiocchi ed., *Radicals in Power: The Workers' Party (PT) and Experiments in Urban Democracy in Brazil* (London: Zed Books, 2003); Goldfrank.

27 Jonathan A. Fox, *Accountability Politics: Power and Voice in rural Mexico* (Oxford: Oxford University Press, 2007).

28 This point is probably most contested in Chávez's Venezuela (Ellner and Hellinger, *Venezuelan Politics in the Chávez Era*).

29 Alvarez, *EnGendering Democracy in Brazil*; Hochstetler and Friedman, "Can Civil Society Organizations Solve the Crisis of Partisan Representation in Latin America?"; Van Cott, *From Movements to Parties in Latin America.*

30 Eaton, "Backlash in Bolivia"; Hochstetler and Friedman, "Can Civil Society Organizations Solve the Crisis of Partisan Representation in Latin America?"; López Maya and Lander; Silva, *Challenging Neoliberalism in Latin America.*

31 Hochstetler, "Rethinking Presidentialism," 404; Silva, *Challenging Neoliberalism in Latin America*.

32 Alvarez et al., *Cultures of Politics Politics of Cultures*; Hochstetler and Friedman, "Can Civil Society Organizations Solve the Crisis of Partisan Representation in Latin America?"; Peruzzotti, "Towards a New Politics"; Yashar, "Democracy, Indigenous Movements, and the Postliberal Challenge in Latin America."

33 Hochstetler and Friedman, "Can Civil Society Organizations Solve the Crisis of Partisan Representation in Latin America?"; Johnston and Almeida, *Latin American Social Movements*; Yashar, "Democracy, Indigenous Movements, and the Postliberal Challenge in Latin America."

34 Margaret Keck and Kathryn Sikkink, *Activists Beyond Borders: Advocacy Networks in International Politics* (Ithaca, NY: Cornell University Press, 1998): 13.

35 Alison Brysk, *From Tribal Village to Global Village: Indian Rights and International Relations in Latin America* (Stanford, CA: Stanford University Press, 2000); Maria Victoria Murillo and Andrew Schrank, "With a Little Help from my Friends: Partisan Politics, Transnational Alliances, and Labor Rights in Latin America, *Comparative Political Studies* 38 (2005): 971–999.

36 Elisabeth Jay Friedman, Kathryn Hochstetler, and Ann Marie Clark, "Sovereign Limits and Regional Opportunities for Global Civil Society in Latin America," *Latin American Research Review* 36(2001): 7–35.

37 Hochstetler and Keck, *Greening Brazil*.

38 Brysk, *From Tribal Village to Global Village*; see also Elisabeth J. Friedman, "The Effects of 'Transnationalism Reversed' in Venezuela: Assessing the Impact of UN Global Conferences on the Women's Movement," *International Feminist Journal of Politics* 1 (1999): 357–381; Laura MacDonald, "Globalising Civil Society: Interpreting International NGOs in Central America," *Millennium – Journal of International Studies* 23 (1994): 267–285.

39 Joe Bandy and Jackie Smith, ed., *Coalitions Across Borders: Transnational Protest and the Neoliberal Order* (Lanham, MD: Rowman and Littlefield, 2005); Roberto Patricio Korzeniewicz and William C. Smith, "Transnational Civil Society Actors and Regional Governance in the Americas: Elite Projects and Collective Action from Below," in *Regionalism and Governance in the Americas: Continental Drift* (Basingstoke: Palgrave, 2005).

40 David Brooks and Jonathan Fox, eds., *Cross-Border Dialogues: U.S.-Mexico Social Movement Networking* (Boulder, CO: Lynne Rienner Publishers and the Center for US–Mexican Studies, University of California, San Diego, 2002).

41 Jackie Smith, *Social Movements for Global Democracy* (Baltimore: The Johns Hopkins University Press, 2008).

42 Silva's book, *Challenging Neoliberalism in Latin America,* is a positive exception and excellent model in this regard. The atomization theorists also studied the lack of mobilization but, as discussed above, saw an excessively uniform lack of mobilization. What is needed are studies of both presence and absence.

43 Whether this is seen as an inherent problem depends on the research tradition, with positivist traditions rejecting the bias in such studies while critical and interpretive traditions argue scholars need this closeness to the research subject.

44 Marco Giugni, Doug McAdam, and Charles Tilly, eds., *How Social Movements Matter* (Minneapolis: University of Minnesota Press, 1999). Other research areas, such as the study of formal institutions, show a similar tendency to assume rather than demonstrate the causal centrality of their object of study.

45 Donatella Della Porta and Herbert Reiter, eds., *Policing Protest: The Control of Mass Demonstrations in Western Democracies* (Minneapolis: University of Minnesota Press, 1998); McAdam et al., *Dynamics of Contention*; Charles Tilly, *The Politics of Collective Violence* (Cambridge: Cambridge University Press, 2003.

46 Jack Goldstone, "More Social Movements or Fewer? Beyond Political Opportunity Structures to Relational Fields," *Theory and Society* 33 (2004): 333–365; Herbert Kitschelt, "Landscapes of Political Interest Intermediation: Social Movements, Interest Groups, and Parties in the Early Twenty-First Century," in *Social Movements and Democracy*, ed. Pedro Ibarra (Houndmills: Palgrave Macmillan, 2003).

16

UNDERSTANDING THE VAGARIES OF CIVIL SOCIETY AND PARTICIPATION IN LATIN AMERICA

Philip Oxhorn

Latin America is undoubtedly more democratic today than at any time in its modern history. As a result, we often take for granted the importance of citizen participation and civil society for politics. Yet the current interest in both is relatively recent. Civil society was only (re)discovered in the 1980s, while interest in participation more generally has been sporadic—like political democracy in the region—and has been understood from a variety of perspectives that often diverged fundamentally from the liberal democratic paradigm that predominates today. These competing perspectives on civil society and participation reflect more than passing intellectual fads; they reflect various attempts to understand the observed ebbs and flows in how Latin Americans actually related to their societies and states.

The changing levels and types of participation, not to mention how we understand them, are particularly relevant to understanding current debates about the quality of democratic governance in Latin America. While there is a greater consensus than ever before among ordinary Latin Americans that democracy is the preferred form of government, there is also growing awareness that people are not satisfied with the governments that are being elected (PNUD 2004). This gap in people's newfound normative preference for democracy and the actual outcomes of democratic political processes raises the danger that political democracy will be seen as, at best, irrelevant to addressing the everyday priorities of Latin Americans (e.g., finding stable employment and with sufficient wages to escape poverty, protection against criminal violence, a good education for their children, a decent place to live, healthcare, and so on), or, at worst, as part of the problem (Oxhorn 2006). How politicians seek to address—or take advantage—of this popular frustration with actually existing democracies has been at the heart of political trends in the region at least since the turn of the 21st century.

In this chapter, I will argue that Latin America is at a crossroads reflected in the choice of creating more robust democratic regimes understood as responsive and accountable governments achieved through autonomous citizen participation or the consolidation of hybrid democratic regimes characterized by greater or less degrees of accountability, responsiveness and autonomous participation. At its core, this alternative juxtaposes a normative vision of democracy emphasizing its unique capacity to resolve conflict nonviolently with more instrumentalist perspectives on democracy that focus on the material quality of life and the conflicts of interests this inevitably entails given the region's high level of socio-economic inequality. As will be discussed in what follows, this juxtaposition is not new and is reflected in the historic debates and patterns of participation. The most important change in this regard is the current strength of the democratic alternative, creating an unprecedented opportunity for creating more inclusionary democratic societies.

The chapter is divided into four sections. After discussing the context of participation in the post-WWII period, I then examine the paradoxical opportunities created for participation and civil society by the imposition of violent authoritarian regimes in the 1960s and 1970s, and the subsequent transitions to democracy. The third section then looks at the challenges of participation and civil society after the return to democracy, with a concluding section discussing possible future paths for research.

Modernization and Latin America's "Exceptionalism"

The driving dynamic behind political participation in Latin America—and much of the world—after WWII was increasingly viewed as being determined by economic structure. For better or worse, participation in the first instance was understood in socio-economic terms, which in turn conditioned the nature of subsequent political participation. The impetus behind this view began with *modernization theory* and its attempt to demonstrate an intrinsic relationship between capitalist development and the emergence of secular, urban liberal democracies (Deutsch 1961).

While capitalist development did lead to rapid urbanization, few of modernization theory's other predictions seemed to hold true for Latin America. The region as a whole stood out for lack of conformity with observed patterns from Western Europe and the United States even in modernization theory's seminal work (Lipset 1959). The empirical reality of high levels of poverty, democratic instability and socio-economic inequality that modernization theory predicted would disappear seemed beyond doubt, generating sometimes heated debates as to why (Hirschman 1981).

Accepting the basic premises of modernization theory (the desirability of capitalist economic development and concomitant inevitability of political democracy), a number of perspectives emerged to explain the region's exceptionalism in terms of the region's society and culture. For some, the problem was the inability of market relations to actually penetrate—and modernize—large segments of Latin America. Based on the work of Belgian priest Roger Vekemans and the DESEAL research institute in Chile which he headed, a *theory of marginality* offered socio-economic policy prescriptions to foster such penetration and promote popular sector participation in the economy and politics (Vekemans et al. 1968). Alternatively, the speed with which market relations penetrated society was seen as the root cause of Latin American populism (Germani 1978). This is because the forces of modernization destroyed traditional normative structures before they could be replaced by more modern ones, leaving the masses in a virtual state of anomie that opportunistic elites could take advantage of. People were mobilized by populist elites, but without the necessary autonomy to ensure a significant level of accountability and under the terms set by the self-interested populist leadership (Oxhorn 1998). Conversely, others suggested it was the resilience of the region's fundamentally non-Western political culture or Iberian heritage that explained why the predictions of modernization theory were inapplicable in the region (Wiarda 1982). Given this allegedly authoritarian, holistic conception of society in which conflict was absent and there is a natural hierarchy, participation essentially consisted of each person fulfilling his or her preordained role. Democratic rule was seen as being neither necessary nor desired by elites and average people alike, regardless of its implications for the penetration of capitalist markets.

In sharp contrast, other perspectives rejected modernization theory's basic premises and argued that capitalist penetration was responsible for low levels of participation, high levels of inequality and democratic instability. For example, marginality theory was challenged by empirical studies that demonstrated how the so-called marginal segments of society—the poor, those working in the informal sector—were in fact intimately intertwined with the modern economy (Castells 1983; Perlman 1976). Rather than being excluded from participating in the modern sectors of the economy, these studies showed how the modern sectors of the economy were dependent on the socio-economic exclusion of the popular sectors as a source of labor that could keep production costs down and the power of organized labor in check, at the same time that this provided less expensive goods and services for workers in formal sector of the economy. More generally, *dependency theory* argued capitalist development undermined any possibility for meaningful participation and democracy. This was a consequence of how markets, particularly international capital, penetrated Latin American societies and economies (Cardoso and Faletto 1970; Dos Santos 1970). The only solution was therefore socialist revolution through working class and peasant mobilization.

Regardless of the theoretical debates arguing about Latin America's exceptionalism compared to modernization theory's portrayal of West European and U.S. development, during the postwar period participation in Latin America was severely constrained by processes of controlled inclusion (Oxhorn 1995a, 2003b). Varying and often significant levels of lower class social mobilization took place, often resulting in important popular sector gains (Collier and Collier 2002; Rueschemeyer, Stephens, and Stephens 1992). But basic rights of citizenship were segmented, social rights were often granted in lieu of political rights of citizenship, and mobilization that threatened to undermine the structural pillars of the status quo was repressed with increasingly high levels of violence. Belying any alleged Iberian cultural consensus, conflict was increasingly rife throughout the region as the constraints of controlled inclusion were pushed to their limits. For the Right, Left and Center, political democracy at best was viewed in instrumental terms—a means to achieve other ends, including political power, wealth or access to state resources, and social revolution (Garretón 1989). As part of the political constraints imposed on participation, clientelism was rife in many countries as a way to restrict political participation by ensuring political loyalty in exchange for limited access to state resources (Cornelius 1975; Eckstein 1988). Populism also played a similar role, dividing societies through the top-down mobilization of the lower classes, particularly workers, in order to allow emergent elites access to political power while severely constraining the autonomous participation of the lower classes (Oxhorn 1998; Conniff 1982).

Authoritarian Rule and Transitions to Democracy: The Civil Society Moment

Beginning with the 1964 military coup in Brazil, the region experienced an unprecedented wave of political violence as controlled inclusion gave way to more extreme forms of political and economic exclusion—particularly for class-based associations. Freed from the shackles of controlled inclusion in the face of extreme levels of political violence and economic instability, an autonomous civil society paradoxically began to grow throughout the region as people organized in order to cope. Not surprisingly, the first organizations were often human rights groups. Costa Rica, Mexico, and Venezuela were exceptions in that the institutions of controlled inclusion proved far more resilient and they were able to avoid the severe military backlash prevalent elsewhere in the region. While the Mexican and Venezuelan regimes would experience important, albeit markedly distinct, transformations beginning in the 1990s as controlled inclusion gave way to alternative forms of interest intermediation, growth of their civil societies remained comparatively stinted.

To understand this paradox, it is necessary to clarify what "civil society" actually is. Civil society is generally defined descriptively as the organizational space outside the state, market and family. While obviously useful, this approach to understanding civil society does not address the important issue of what it actually *does* or *why* people would enter into it. It provides no criteria for understanding the kinds of groups or behaviors that are compatible with civil society, which means other criteria (a belief in a liberal civic culture is the most typical) that become controversial when applied in specific contexts outside of Western Europe and the US, including Latin America where, for example, collective rights are an important part of indigenous culture (Oxhorn 2003a). An alternative definition, while certainly not incompatible with more descriptive definitions, attempts to avoid these problems by focusing on what civil society actually *does*. It conceptualizes civil society as : "the social fabric formed by a multiplicity of self-constituted territorially- and functionally-based units which peacefully coexist and collectively resist subordination to the state, at the same time that they demand inclusion into national political structures" (Oxhorn 1995a, 251–52). Obviously this dual dynamic is particularly relevant under authoritarian regimes, but as will be discussed in the next section, it also highlights the challenges faced by civil society now that the region's transitions to democracy are generally long passed.

It is important to note that the descriptive definition of civil society tends to create a false dichotomy between the state and civil society by implying that each has its own sphere of activity independent of the other. This problem is particularly acute in Latin America, where controlled inclusion meant that civil society was generally subordinated by the state in order to control social mobilization. The dual dynamic stressed here avoids this by highlighting how civil society cannot be understood apart from its relationship to the state. Under authoritarian regimes, as well as democratic regimes associated with controlled inclusion, that relationship was antagonistic. More generally, a complete separation between civil society and the state—something that in practice does not exist in Western Europe or even the more liberal United States—would mean political marginalization. In contrast, the ideal adopted here is one in which both the state and civil society work together to realize a public priorities as determined by democratic processes, what Peter Evans (1997) refers to as "state-society synergy." Rather than shun relations with the state, civil society's relationship with it needs to be understood in terms of the autonomy of civil society organizations to define and defend their interests in competition with other actors, including the state. It was this autonomy that controlled inclusion deliberately attempted to undermine.

The timing for this resurgence of civil society under authoritarian regimes was particularly propitious as a result of important changes in the Catholic Church. Following the important Vatican II reforms of the mid-1960s intended to reverse declining Church membership resulting from the growing secularization of "modern" West European societies, progressive elements within the Latin American national church structures began to assert a new social activism through the practice of liberation theology (Levine and Mainwaring 1989; Levine 1986). Among other things, liberation theology stressed the structural causes of poverty and the role that everyone, particularly the poor, had to play through collective organization in promoting social change. Its primary instrument, Christian Base Communities (CEBs or *Comunidades Eclesiales de Base*) were, despite their religious foundations and direct ties to the Church, pioneers in the development of an autonomous civil society. Not only were the CEBs concerned with directly addressing the needs of their communities, the skills many learned through participation in CEBs were often translated into a variety of other organizational experiences that helped enrich the social fabric in many cities throughout the region.

It is important to emphasize, however, that the Church's contribution to the strengthening of civil society during this period was not limited to the practitioners of liberation theology. Given the unprecedented levels of repression in a number of countries, including Brazil, Chile, El Salvador, and Uruguay, even moderate elements within the traditional church began to assume a new role as "social critic" by publically opposing government repression and other policies (the Catholic Church in Argentina is the most notable exception). Often somewhat reluctantly, especially after the elevation of John Paul II to the papacy, the Church frequently assumed an increasingly political role by seeking to mediate conflict, defend human rights and generally shelter a variety of civil society organizations other than CEBs from state repression.

This unique confluence of a fundamentally repressive environment, the spread of liberation theology and the enabling role for civil society that the Church began to play led to an extraordinary growth in autonomous civil society organizational activity throughout Latin America (Alvarez, Dagnino, and Escobar 1998; Eckstein 1989). Such organizations covered a wide gambit, including human rights groups, organizations of the victims of repression, community self-help organizations of various kinds, women's organizations and, to a lesser extent compared to the late 1990s and later, indigenous groups and environmental organizations, to name but a few. While the extent of such mobilization is impossible to quantify and should not be exaggerated, its importance lies in the impact it had on the communities in which it emerged and subsequent struggles for democracy and respect for basic human rights.

This growth in civil society organizational activity was intrinsically intertwined with a new respect for the importance of democracy as an end in itself rather than a means toward other ends. If democracy is seen only as a means to achieve other ends, participation in civil society organizations also lacks any intrinsic value. Indeed, traditional political parties, particularly those on the Left, viewed such organizations with suspicion, and frequently attempted to co-opt them in order to increase their political power. The relevance of political participation in this sense is directly related to how people view political democracy; the importance of participation per se increases as does the perception of democracy as a good, or even the best, form of government.

Various factors accounted for this change, including the unparalleled harshness of repression in the 1960s and 1970s and the influence of a reformed Catholic Church. For the Left, in particular, there was a new appreciation of the benefits of the basic rights associated with political democracy, even before the end of the Cold War. At the grassroots level, this implied involvement in collective organizations that addressed an array of pressing needs. Looking at national politics, it meant a commitment to replacing dictatorships with political democracy. If anything, for many people political democracy became almost a panacea as key issues concerning the fundamental contours of the post-authoritarian democracies were left unresolved in deference to holding free and competitive elections. This belief that democracy was the best form of government was essential for creating the perception that participating in civil society organizations, and particularly in mobilizations demanding a democratic transition, was essential for resolving people's most pressing needs, despite the closed nature of the state and the often great personal risks that such participation entailed.

Did the growth of civil society organizations actually make a difference? For respect for basic human rights in general, and the status of women in particular, there is little doubt that social movement organizational activity contributed positively to important changes in Latin American attitudes affecting society and politics, even if much remains to be accomplished. Their impact on actual transitions to democracy, however, remains more ambiguous.

As O'Donnell and Schmitter (1986) emphasize in their influential comparative study of recent democratic transitions, elites played a central role in negotiating the democratic "rules of the game" that would usher in elections and a new democratic regime. More controversially, they concluded that the demobilization of civil society and the channeling of participation exclusively into elections was necessary in order to prevent an rightwing backlash, even if the result reinforced the tendency to leave basic issues relating to the post-authoritarian democratic regime unresolved. As the elections approached, non-electoral mobilizations were discouraged by increasingly ascendant political parties and community organizers were instructed to limit their activities to getting out the vote, reinforcing the notion that political participation would be limited to regularly held elections. Surprisingly, O'Donnell and Schmitter's conclusion was harshly criticized both from a more conservative democratic perspective that stressed the inherently democratic legitimacy of the elites who were involved in the bargaining (Levine 1988), and the more radical Left because of O'Donnell and Schmitter's alleged support for the consolidation of an intrinsically authoritarian form of "democracy" that deliberately excluded the popular sectors from any meaningful participation (MacEwan 1988).

Regardless of who is "right" on a normative level, there seems little doubt that recent democratic transitions have been characterized by their conservative, very limited nature apart from the institution of relatively free and fair elections. A more relevant criticism from the perspective of civil society and participation is that O'Donnell and Schmitter downplayed the importance of civil society for achieving any meaningful transition (Oxhorn 1995b; Waylen 1994). This is because O'Donnell and Schmitter focused on elite bargaining. For them, the transition process began with elite divisions and ended with elite agreement. At best, civil society reacted to prior elite decisions and, in particular, divisions, at the same time that their demobilization leading up to the actual elections was seen as unproblematic. Yet the actual dynamic of civil society organizational activity has more to do with the dislocations caused by the very imposition of authoritarian rule—long before people could even imagine any kind of regime change—and other factors unrelated to elite interactions, such as the new role assumed by the Catholic Church. The possibility that social mobilization demanding a democratic transition emerged independently of elite divisions and in at least some cases actually was a cause of such divisions when elites disagreed on an appropriate response is discarded a priori because their analysis begins with the emergence of such elite fissures. Perhaps even more importantly, O'Donnell and Schmitter's focus on elite interactions implied that the demobilization of civil society was unproblematic, both for the transition and subsequent democratic regime.

Civil Society and Participation in Democratic Latin America

With the actual transitions to freely elected governments now complete in every country in the region, with the exception of Cuba, the region continues to confront the flipside of the paradox of civil society under authoritarian regimes: the challenge of effectively reengaging citizens after successful transitions to political democracy (Oxhorn 2006). There may be literally tens of thousands of civil society organizations in the region, yet civil society remains fragmented, with organizations often competing with one another for available resources. Popular sector organizations, in particular, often remain small, atomized and dependent on external (state and/or non-governmental agencies) largesse. It is often unclear who such organizations actually represent, especially given the exponential growth of NGOs since the early 1990s. Organized labor, traditionally a primary representative of the popular sectors, has seen its political influence wane. This reflects the fact that labor movements generally are more fragmented and represent smaller fractions of the economically active population than in earlier periods, due to large informal sectors, changes in industrial structures following the implementation of market-oriented or neoliberal reforms, and changes in national labor laws. At the same time, these changes in organized labor have created new problems of representation as labor leaders often seek to preserve their own positions and prerogatives, increasing the distance between them and their rank and file members at that same time that organized labor increasingly competes with other civil society organizations for access to political power and resources.

There are a number of reasons for this lack of citizenship engagement, including the loss of an unambiguous "enemy" to mobilize against, the longer term consequences of the demobilization of civil society during the transition as people adopted a view that political participation was limited to voting in periodic elections, lingering fears of destabilizing the democratic regime and the Church's withdrawal from politics in favor of elected civilian officials. There also was an inevitable level of exhaustion after the arduous task of mobilizing in a repressive environment. Yet the region's democracies are no longer really "new" (Mexico was the last country to experience a democratic transition in 2000), suggesting that other factors not directly linked to the transition process are at play. In particular, a new mode of interest intermediation has replaced controlled inclusion: *neopluralism* (Oxhorn 2006).

Neopluralism is closely associated with neoliberal or market-oriented economic policies, yet it is not reducible to any specific set of economic policies or correlated with any particular level of economic liberalization. The latter form part of the temporal context within which neopluralism emerges. Economic criteria for political and social inclusion replace the political criteria of social control and loyalty intrinsic to controlled inclusion. It is "pluralist" because through democratic elections, neopluralism reaffirms the normative belief that the best balance of interests and values within a given polity is produced by some form (however limited) of free competition among individuals in the rational pursuit of their self interest. Ultimate political authority is essentially decided upon through a free political market of votes. Individual freedom is valued above all, and this requires respect for private property and (ideally, at least) the rule of law.

The marked authoritarianism of neopluralism distinguishes it from the more traditional pluralist model associated with democracy in the United States. It is this close association of authoritarianism with a normative belief in the value of competitive elections that is unique to the current period and defines neopluralism. While it is important that the people who govern are elected, once elected, they have few checks on their power. Elected leaders frequently bypass and deliberately undermine representative democratic institutions, and in this sense neopluralism has become the structural foundation for what O'Donnell (1994) characterizes as *delegative democracy*. Dominant economic interests, as well as unelected power holders such as the military, exercise control over key state decisions.

More generally, the logic of neopluralism permeates entire political systems in a variety of ways. Market-based incentives come to play a defining role in collective action. An individual's personal economic resources largely determine the extent and nature of her political and social inclusion. For example, one's economic resources directly affect the quality of education and health care a person enjoys. A de facto *marketization of the rule of law* means that even the legal protections a person has access to are determined by economic resources (Brinks 2008). The poor (who are the primary victims of crime) lack access to basic legal structures, yet that they are targeted by repressive police practices designed to deal with rising levels of criminal violence in many countries. People with greater economic resources can escape both the consequences of such crime by purchasing various forms of private security, at the same time that the crimes they commit enjoy high levels of impunity. Greater reliance on markets also has created greater economic insecurity as well. In the large informal sector employment rights are virtually nonexistent, while economic security is further compounded as the distinction between formal sector and informal sector employment blurs through the establishment of free trade zones and other changes in labor legislation.

The negative impact that neopluralism has on the ability of civil society to organize itself is compounded by state reforms. Just as the state is assigned a minimal role in ensuring the smooth functioning of the market in the economic realm, the state largely abdicates its role in providing incentives for collective action. The public and private goods formally available at the state level to those mobilized in earlier periods, as well as the coercive incentives for the hierarchical organization of economic interests under state corporatism, no longer exist or have been significantly reduced. Group identities and collective interests lose any intrinsic value for mobilizing civil society under neopluralism, yet these are a primary potential source of power for subaltern groups. State-civil society synergy becomes all but impossible as the state is generally unwilling and unable to work with civil society, and because neopluralism privileges the economic resources less privileged groups lack.

In this context, a kind of vicious cycle can set in regarding participation, especially among the popular sectors. If the principal dynamics affecting one's socio-economic status are determined outside of democratic processes, the opportunity costs of devoting time and energy to civil society organizations only increase. Just as many people did not participate in civil society during authoritarian rule, even more may abstain from participating after the return of some semblance of normalcy under democratic governments. In other words, why bother participating after political repression is largely curtailed given the pressing day-to-day demands of trying to make ends meet and the limited potential that such participation will result in any meaningful change?

Despite a general problem of a regional lack of citizen participation, there are also important exceptions. As already noted, human rights and women's movements that emerged under periods of authoritarian rule continue to influence state policies in positive ways, even if much remains to be done and the actual movements themselves have often waned. Although civil society in general may have been weakened, there are numerous specific examples of how civil society organizations have attempted to address people's most pressing needs, with varying levels of success (Dagnino, Rivera, and Panfichi. 2006; Avritzer 2002). Indigenous movements, in particular, have gained an unprecedented level of political influence since the 1990s, often in reaction to neoliberal state reforms, in part because of the way such reforms have negatively affected their previous collective entitlements (Yashar 2005). Indeed, there have been a variety of civil society reactions to neoliberal reforms, although their ultimate impact remains ambiguous (Burdick, Osborn, and Roberts 2009). To a certain extent, women and indigenous people have been more successful given high levels of international solidarity and a clearer sense of the specific alternatives they propose, although this is often clearer in the case of gender equality than for indigenous movements which frequently face challenges posed by the existence of multiple indigenous communities within the same country.

These exceptions highlight the importance of neopluralism's association with political democracy. It opens up possibilities for participation that offer the promise of transforming neopluralism into more democratic modes of interest intermediation. Unlike the historical alternatives, political democracy retains its normative valuation, which means that political participation at least retains its potential relevance for addressing the challenges people face in their everyday lives.

More fundamentally, neopluralism's association with political democracy also reflects the co-existence of two contradictory ideals of citizenship, one based on participatory practices aimed at achieving state-society synergy, and another associated with neopluralism's economic criteria for social and political inclusion. This is what Dagnino (2005) cogently refers to as a "perverse confluence." Although both citizenship ideals are based on the same concepts, including participation and civil society, they offer radically different visions of what those concepts entail. Like a pendulum, the quality, if not continued existence, of political democracy in the region will be determined by how this contradiction is resolved.

State decentralization and the various participatory institutions associated with it epitomize this "perverse confluence" better than any other recent trend in state reform. From the perspective of neopluralism, decentralization is an effective mechanism for shrinking the central state by hiving off important functions, particularly basic service delivery, including education and healthcare. Local and, to a lesser extent, regional governments typically assume these responsibilities, although international financial institutions like the World Bank and many national reformers often consider privatization of services like the provision of water, electricity and telecommunications as part of decentralizing state reform packages. The latter point underscores the market principles that guide the kind of decentralization of associated with neopluralism. The recipients of services are viewed as consumers, who chose between the alternatives available to them (supply). "Responsiveness" reflects market-based efficiency criteria, including competition, and proximity to those who make use of the services is viewed as superior to centralized administration. There is little concern for non-market considerations, absolute price levels of the services being provided, or competing priorities. Consumer participation is seen as an important source of information to make these de facto local markets function, but it is generally limited to the implementation of policies made by experts and/or politicians.

This contrasts sharply with an alternative that is compatible with achieving state-society synergy. While market criteria and technical expertise can play an important role, any such role is conditioned by negotiations between civil society actors and local state officials. The institutions associated with this alternative therefore provide non-market participatory mechanisms for priority-setting and service delivery. Responsiveness is directly to the citizenry and not indirectly to consumers through the market, with civil society playing a crucial role in holding officials accountable for their actions (Smulovitz and Peruzotti 2000).

The experience of participatory budgeting offers a good illustration of the potential and limits of participation under neopluralism. Participatory budgeting was first implemented in 1989 in Porto Alegre, Brazil, and has since been replicated in various forms and with the support of international financial institutions throughout the world. Porto Alegre was one of the most, if not the most, successful examples of how the process of participatory budgeting can approach an ideal of state-society synergy. After nearly failing in its early years due to low and declining levels of participation, the process and institutions of civil society were reformed through negotiations between the local government and civil society representatives. The result was a marked growth in participation and the organization of civil society over a number of years (Baiocchi 2002; Wampler and Avritzer 2004). Participation was seen as relevant to meeting pressing needs, even though the level of funds administered amounted to just over $200 per capita and was limited largely to municipal capital expenditures. Other experiments were often far less successful, due to a lack of political will, the inability of local civil society to assume the challenge, and/or poor institutional design that limited the actual power delegated to civil society actors. Even in Porto Alegre, participation began to decline when the Workers Party, which had instituted the reforms, was voted out of office 2005 and the new administration reduced its scope.

Latin America at a Crossroads

Confronting the Challenge of Making Democracy Relevant (Again)

Democracy is more robust than it has ever been in Latin America. Democratic regimes have survived crises that, in the past, would have likely led to their overthrow, such as the literal collapse of the Argentine economy in 2001. Most recently, the 2009 *Latinobarómetro* regional public opinion survey showed significant increases in both respondents' preferences for democratic governance and their satisfaction with their actual governments, in the midst of the global economic downturn. While this is unambiguously positive, it should not lead to an intellectual or political sense of complacence. The frustrations associated with neopluralism's authoritarian and exclusionary qualities could lead to popular support for new leaders attempting to capitalize on such frustrations, or rightwing backlashes to popular mobilization that appears to threaten their fundamental interests. Latin American societies remain the most unequal in the world and, as the 2009 coup in Honduras reminds us, social polarization and political crisis can resurge with dramatic consequences. Economic and political crises in the region are still too frequent, and the region's history suggests numerous threats to democracy can emerge in such contexts. The still sizeable minority who, according to *Latinobarómetro* opinion surveys, say they could opt for authoritarian regimes if circumstances seem to warrant it should not be forgotten.

While the kinds of democracy associated with neopluralism are far from perfect, there are also regime alternatives that fall short of the explicit suspension of democratic rule, yet sharply constrain the potential for self-transformation that exists under neopluralism today. Historically, populism in its various variants has been the most prominent alternative (Oxhorn 1998; Roberts 1994; Weyland 2001). Yet populism's plebiscitarian nature, with the direct relationship it seeks to establish between populist leaders and their followers, is antithetical to both an autonomous civil society and state-society synergy. In societies like those found in most of Latin America, material interests and concerns can quickly displace the normative preference for democracy among the region's people, undermining the perceived importance of participation in the process as democracy again takes on an instrumental connotation. This is the crossroads confronting civil society in Latin America.

To understand which path Latin America is likely to take at this particular crossroads, research should be carried out in several related areas. First, research needs to be carried out to better understand the potential role that civil society can play in working with the state to address the most pressing concerns of Latin Americans. Opinion surveys consistently suggest that these concerns include curtailing the threat of crime and criminal violence, economic insecurity and low-paying employment, as well as the quality of education for children, among others. If civil society can make a meaningful contribution to addressing these issues, participation in civil society becomes directly relevant to citizens, particularly the poor. More generally, research should focus, both comparatively and historically, on the more general factors that influence the decision by Latin Americans to participate in civil society organizations, building on the work found in studies like that by Collier and Handlin (2009). This research begins to examine why and how people participate politically in the current period, as well as the nature this participation's links to the state. It also finds that the middle classes tend to make the most of the opportunities for participation in civil society democratic regimes potentially open up. More research is needed in order to understand why the poor tend to participate less and what kind of institutional structures are needed to increase their participation. We also need to better understand how such participation can retain its autonomy from the state, avoiding the pitfalls of cooptation that were so prevalent in the not too distant past. Historical research that seeks to directly compare today's levels and forms of participation among the poor with earlier experiences might also provide useful insights for making participation more effective today and for avoiding its pitfalls in previous periods.

But to ensure that such participation is effective—and therefore that it remains relevant—more research needs to be carried out in terms of the kinds of participatory institutions that are most likely to realize state-society synergy. As the Porto Alegre experience demonstrates, political will is essential, but institutions need also need to be designed to be more robust and permanent, so that the scope and nature of participation does not fall victim to more short term political cycles. Given the myriad of decentralization programs and the wide variety of participatory experiments they have entailed, researchers are only beginning to systematically investigate which ones work over time and why.

Related to this, more work needs to be done on the kinds of decision-making authority that should be decentralized to local and regional governments. Conversely, we really do not know how to manage the tension between local authority and the need for national policies that ensure that some regions do not benefit more from decentralization than others, due to their greater resources or other factors. Lastly, little if any work has been done in Latin America that examines how civil society can play a more effective role in the decision-making processes that remain at the central level.

Finally, what can be done if civil society itself is not up to the task of engaging with the state in the pursuit of public goals? During the period of authoritarian rule, the Catholic Church often played a vital role in helping civil society assume greater levels of agency. What other actors might fill this role and how? In the more established democracies of Western Europe, Canada, and even the United States, states have played this role (Skocpol 1996). While the history of state-society relations would imply a real danger in trying to implement such policies given the state's tendency to try to co-opt civil society, the same was largely true of the Latin American Catholic Church until a variety of factors converged in the 1960s and led to an often dramatic change. Research should be conducted that tries to understand the factors that allow states to nurture civil society while respecting its autonomy, both comparatively with more established democracies and historically.

Ultimately, Latin America's current political crossroads represents a challenge as well as an opportunity. The unparalleled space for political innovations that go beyond that relatively free and fair elections provide needs to be taken advantage of to broaden the inclusive qualities of democracy in order to help alleviate the region's high level of inequality. Research can play a vital role in helping political actors make the most of today's crossroads and avoid the pitfalls of the past.

Bibliography

Alvarez, Sonia E., Evelina Dagnino, and Arturo Escobar, eds. 1998. *Cultures of Politics, Politics of Cultures: Re-visioning Latin American Social Movements*. Boulder, Colo.: Westview Press.

Avritzer, Leonardo. 2002. *Democracy and the Public Space in Latin America*. Princeton, N.J.: Princeton University Press.

Baiocchi, Gianpaolo. 2002. "Synergizing Civil Society: State-Civil Society Regimes in Porto Alegre, Brazil." *Political Power and Social Theory* 15: 3–52.

Brinks, Daniel M. 2008. *The Judicial Response to Police Killings in Latin America: Inequality and the Rule of Law*. Cambridge: Cambridge University Press.

Burdick, John, Philip Oxhorn, and Kenneth M. Roberts. 2009. *Beyond Neoliberalism in Latin America?: Societies and Politics at the Crossroads*. New York: Palgrave Macmillan.

Cardoso, Fernando Enrique, and Enzo Faletto. 1970. *Dependency and Development in Latin America*. Berkeley: University of California Press.

Castells, Manuel. 1983. *The City and the Grassroots*. Berkeley: University of California.

Collier, Ruth Berins, and David Collier. 2002. *Shaping the Political Arena: Critical Junctures, the Labor Movement, and Regime Dynamics in Latin America*. South Bend, Ind.: University of Notre Dame Press.

Collier, Ruth Berins, and Samuel Handlin, eds. 2009. *Participation and the New Interest Regime in Latin America*. University Park: Pennsylvania State University Press.

Conniff, Michael, ed. 1982. *Latin American Populism in Comparative Perspective*. Albuquerque: University of New Mexico Press.

Cornelius, Wayne A. 1975. *Politics and the migrant poor in Mexico City*. Stanford, Calif.: Stanford University Press.

Dagnino, Evelina. 2005. "We all have rights but...": Contesting Conceptions of Citizenship in Brazil." In *Inclusive Citizenship: Meanings and Expressions of Citizenship*, ed. N. Kabeer. London: Zed Books, 147–63.

Dagnino, Evelina, Alberto Olvera Rivera, and Aldo Panfichi. 2006. *La disputa por la construcción democrática en América Latina*. [The Dispute over the Construction of Democracy in Latin America]. México City, Mexico: Fondo de Cultura Económica.

Deutsch, Karl Wolfgang. 1961. "Social Mobilization and Political Development." *American Political Science Review* 55 (September): 493–514.

Dos Santos, Theotonio. 1970. "The Structure of Dependence." *The American Economic Review* 60 (May): 231–36.

Eckstein, Susan. 1988. *The Poverty of Revolution: The State and Urban Poor in Mexico*. Princeton, N.J.: Princeton University Press.

———, ed. 1989. *Power and Popular Protest: Latin American Social Movements*. Berkeley: University of California Press.

Evans, Peter B., ed. 1997. *State-Society Synergy: Government and Social Capital in Development*. Berkeley: International Area Studies, University of California, Berkeley.

Garretón, Manuel Antonio. 1989. *The Chilean Political Process*. Boston: Unwin Hyman.

Germani, Gino. 1978. *Authoritarianism, Facism, and National Populism*. New Brunswick, N.J.: Transaction Books.

Hirschman, Albert. 1981. "The Rise and Decline of Development Economics." In *Essay in Trespassing: Economics to Politics and Beyond*, ed. A. Hirschman. Cambridge: Cambridge University Press,

Levine, Daniel. 1988. "Paradigm Lost: Dependence To Democracy." *World Politics* XL (April): 377–94.

Levine, Daniel H. 1986. *Religion and Political Conflict in Latin America*. Chapel Hill: University of North Carolina Press.

Levine, Daniel, and Scott Mainwaring. 1989. "Religion and Popular Protest in Latin America: Contrasting Experiences." In *Power and Popular Protest: Latin American Social Movements*, ed. S. Eckstein. Berkeley: University of California Press.

Lipset, Seymour Martin. 1959. "Some Social Requisites of Democracy: Economic Development and Political Legitimacy." *American Political Science Review* 53 (March): 69–105.

MacEwan, Arthur. 1988. "Transitions from Authoritarian Rule." *Latin American Perspectives* 15 (Summer): 115–30.

O'Donnell, Guillermo. 1994. "Delegative Democracy." *Journal of Democracy* 5 (1): 56–69.

O'Donnell, Guillermo, and Philippe C. Schmitter. 1986. *Transitions from Authoritarian Rule: Tentative Conclusions about Uncertain Democracies*. Baltimore: Johns Hopkins University Press.

Oxhorn, Philip. 1995a. "From Controlled Inclusion to Coerced Marginalization: The Struggle for Civil Society in Latin America." In *Civil Society: Theory, History and Comparison*, ed. J. Hall. Cambridge: Polity Press, 250–77.

———. 1995b. *Organizing Civil Society: The Popular Sectors and the Struggle for Democracy in Chile*. University Park: Pennsylvania State University Press.

———. 1998. "The Social Foundations of Latin America's Recurrent Populism: Problems of Class Formation and Collective Action." *Journal of Historical Sociology* 11 (June): 212–46.

———. 2003a. Conceptualizing Civil Society from the Bottom Up: A Political Economy Perspective. Paper presented at Structural Change, Political Institutions, and Civil Society in Latin America, April 24–25, at University of California, San Diego.

———. 2003b. "Social Inequality, Civil Society and the Limits of Citizenship in Latin America." In *What Justice? Whose Justice? Fighting for Fairness in Latin America*, ed. S. Eckstein and T. Wickham-Crawley. Berkeley: University of California, 35–63.

———. 2006. "Neopluralism and the Challenges for Citizenship in Latin America." In *Citizenship in Latin America*, ed. J. S. Tulchin and M. Ruthenberg. Boulder, Colo.: Lynne Rienner Publishers, 123–47.

Perlman, Janice. 1976. *The Myth of Marginality: Urban Poverty and Politics in Rio de Janeiro*. Berkeley: University of California Press.

PNUD. 2004. *Democracia en América Latina: Hacia una democracia de ciudadanas y ciudadanos* [Democracy in Latin America: Towards a Citizens' Democracy]. New York: Programa de las Naciones Unidas Para el Desarrollo.

Roberts, Kenneth.,1994. Neoliberalism and the Transformation of Populism in Latin America: The Peruvian Case. Paper presented at Annual Meeting of the American Political Science Association, at New York, September.

Rueschemeyer, Dietrich, Evelyne Stephens, and John D. Stephens. 1992. *Capitalist Development and Democracy*. Chicago: University of Chicago Press.

Skocpol, Theda. 1996. "Unravelling from Above." *American Prospect* (25).

Smulovitz, Catalina, and Enrique Peruzotti. 2000. "Societal Accountability in Latin America." *Journal of Democracy* 11 (4): 147–58.

Vekemans, Roger, Ismael Silva Fuenzalida, and Centro para el Desarrollo Económico y Social de América Latina (Santiago Chile). 1968. *Integración latinoamericana y solidaridad internacional* [Latin American Integration and International Solidarity]. Santiago, Chile: Centro para el Desarrollo Económico y Social de América Latina.

Wampler, Brian, and Leonardo Avritzer. 2004. "Participatory Publics: Civil Society and New Institutions in Democratic Brazil." *Comparative Politics* 36 (3): 291–312.

Waylen, Georgina. 1994. "Women and Democratization: Conceptualizing Gender Relations in Transition Politics." *World Politics* 46 (April): 327–54.

Weyland, Kurt. 2001. "Clarifying a Contested Concept: Populism in the Study of Latin American Politics." *Comparative Politics* 34 (1): 1–22.

Wiarda, Howard. 1982. *Politics and Social Change in Latin American: The Distinct Tradition*. 2nd ed. Boston: University of Massachusetts.

Yashar, Deborah J. 2005. *Contesting Citizenship in Latin America: The Rise of Indigenous Movements and the Postliberal Challenge*. New York: Cambridge University Press.

17

LABOR

Maria Lorena Cook

Introduction

Political science scholarship on labor in Latin America has generally focused on organized labor—that segment of the workforce that is organized into unions and that typically represents a small and declining proportion of workers in Latin American countries. This is because during much of the twentieth century, Latin American trade unions have had an almost disproportionate impact on issues of central concern to political scientists—parties and elections, democracy and authoritarianism, market reform and institutional change—taking place within the space of national politics.

Recent labor research within political science has maintained this preference for organized labor over studies of workers or the working class. Yet while national politics remains important, globalization pressures and marketization processes have shifted the focus of labor studies in two directions: downward toward the firm or industry-level, and outward toward transnational spaces and beyond the nation-state. In part these shifts reflect the declining presence of unions in traditional political arenas. Unfortunately this has also meant that labor has come to occupy an increasingly marginalized place within political science. However, developments such as the resurgence of unions under left governments; the persistence of authoritarian legacies in labor institutions, laws, and policies; and the largely unexplored politics of the informal sector all pose challenging research questions that merit the attention of political scientists.

This chapter reviews developments in political science studies of labor. It is organized in three parts. I begin with a historical overview of how labor studies have been situated within the major intellectual developments in political science scholarship on Latin America. The second part looks at differences between recent North American scholarship and scholarly production in Latin America. The final section identifies gaps in the field and points to future directions for research on labor in Latin America.

I. Labor and Politics in Latin America: Historical and Intellectual Developments

Corporatism, Populism, and Labor Incorporation

Political science studies of labor early on focused on organized labor's relations with political parties and the state. Concepts such as populism and corporatism were used to define ways of structuring labor participation in politics, with important implications for worker mobilization, political parties, and economic development.

Corporatism emerged as an especially important theme in studies of labor politics. The focus on corporatism was linked to what in the 1960s and 1970s was the dominant framework for interpreting Latin American politics and for distinguishing Latin American state-society relations from those in Western Europe.[1] Studies looked at organized labor's role in national politics, particularly its relations with the state and its associations with authoritarianism or democratization. Although such studies emphasized state control over labor, they also acknowledged labor's capacity for autonomous action. Some paid attention to the internal tensions that close relations with the state produced between union leaders and rank-and-file members.

Corporatist features were present in many countries, but especially in those where organized labor emerged as a powerful social and political actor, such as Argentina, Mexico, and Brazil. These features included state structuring and subsidy of labor organizations and state-imposed constraints on their demands, leadership, and internal governance. Corporatist features were also visible in the labor legislation of countries with weaker labor movements, such as Chile.

In their influential early work on corporatism, Ruth Berins Collier and David Collier tried to bring clarity to the concept by disaggregating corporatism as a set of state inducements to and constraints on labor's political participation.[2] Eventually the focus on corporatism waned, becoming more of "a familiar topic, not … a subject of special analytical interest."[3] More recently variants of the concept have returned to studies of labor in Latin America as "meso-corporatism" and "neo-corporatism," in discussions that draw in part on European debates.[4]

In their landmark volume, *Shaping the Political Arena*, the Colliers built upon the broader concept of labor incorporation, arguing that the way in which labor was brought into national politics constituted a critical juncture in a country's history and shaped subsequent regime dynamics in fundamental ways. *Shaping the Political Arena* was notable among other things for its sophisticated use of comparative methodology, including unusual pairings of countries, and its impressive marshalling of historical detail. Another influential study, *Capitalist Development and Democracy,* used cross-regional comparison to argue that working-class mobilization was essential to democratization in Latin America.[5]

Authoritarianism and Transitions to Democracy

The breakdown of authoritarian regimes and transitions to democracy in the 1980s led to a new strand of research that privileged elites and downplayed the role of non-elite social actors. Organized labor and workers in general were lumped into the broad category of "civil society," in which unions were seen as important primarily for their role in maintaining political stability—by restraining their demands and withholding protest—during the critical stage of negotiations between civilian political elites and the military regime. For some time political scientists generally accepted that a restrained labor movement, largely subordinate to the priorities set by political parties, was central to a successful transition out of authoritarianism. But soon labor scholars began to question the assumptions of this earlier framework. Work by experts on labor in Argentina and Brazil showed that labor was not so quiescent after all.[6] These studies suggested that labor demands could play an important role in shaping the quality of democracy, especially during its early years. This point was later reinforced by political scientists focusing on labor in Chile, where labor's alliance with the coalition of political parties known as the *Concertación* resulted in strong limits on collective labor rights throughout the years of democratic consolidation.[7]

A related argument was that the sequencing of democratic and economic transitions made a difference for labor influence, law, and policy. Elite commitments to market economic reforms that were consolidated prior to democratic transitions placed labor at a disadvantage and limited the prospects for restoration of labor rights under democracy. Conversely, democratic transitions that began prior to the consolidation of market reforms produced environments that were generally more amenable to labor regardless of the orientation of the party in power.[8]

Social Movements

A wave of scholarship also focused on the popular and social movements emerging throughout the region during democratic transitions, both under authoritarianism and in the early years of re-democratization. While many of these movements did not come out of the formal labor sector, several studies looked at the role of worker movements and at alliances that included labor along with other groups in civil society.[9] This scholarship was a response to the almost exclusive focus on the role of elites during transitions and represented an effort to more clearly identify the contributions of popular movements (or civil society) during this period. Some of this research addressed the question of how collective identities formed, drawing largely from the European social movement literature, while other scholars drew upon North American social movement theory in their employment of such concepts as resource mobilization and political opportunity structure.[10]

Neo-Liberalism and Globalization

A third important wave of studies emerged to analyze the transitions to market economies taking place in the 1980s and 1990s throughout the region. Studies of globalization and the transition to neo-liberalism were not the exclusive domain of political scientists. Scholars in other disciplines also studied the impact of these shifts on a range of social and political phenomena. The centrality of economics to this discussion also expanded the central focus of political scientists in the region from comparative politics to political economy. Labor came to be studied not only in relation to political parties and the state, although this remained a central concern, but also in relation to firms, capital, and industrial restructuring.[11] In this way the interests of political scientists, sociologists, and industrial relations scholars started to converge.

Unlike the transitions frame so identified with the arguments of O'Donnell et al, the neo-liberalism/globalization framework lacks a single central work. Instead it is more useful to view scholarship on these developments in terms of three main subject areas.

Labor and Market Reforms

Several studies of labor and market reforms looked at those factors that enabled elites to successfully implement market-oriented reforms such as privatization or labor market flexibility. This included studies of how elites overcome labor unions' resistance to such reforms by marginalizing, dividing, or repressing unions.[12] Some of these studies exhibited a clear normative bias in favor of policymaking elites and drew uncritically upon their characterizations of organized labor as obstacle, insider, aristocracy, and rent-seeker. Ironically, these labels were most prevalent at a point when union density levels in most countries in the region were at an historic low and labor's political influence was weak. The assumption was that organized labor blocked policies that aimed to improve the welfare of a majority of citizens who were not in unions, especially individuals in the informal sector, women and youth. These ideas were also consistent with international financial institution assessments of the period.

In most of these studies that focused on successful implementation of market reforms, labor was an incidental actor. Other studies with a more central focus on labor produced scholarship that examined how market reforms affected labor. Here were studies that analyzed not only how policies such as privatization, industrial restructuring, and labor market de-regulation weakened labor, but also how labor managed to negotiate and resist such changes. For instance, although union density declined in most of the region during the 1990s and the political influence of organized labor has waned, this did not mean that unions were incapable of effective resistance or of shaping reform outcomes. Studies examined such factors as partisan orientation of governments, power resources of organized labor, the sequencing of democratic and economic transitions, social pacts, and international influences in explaining the range of policy outcomes in the face of market pressures.[13] Although much of the comparative research here was cross-national within Latin America, more recent work has used cross-regional comparison to investigate conditions under which labor helped to shape reform outcomes.[14]

Party-Labor Relations

Neo-liberalism and its impact on organized labor also produced consequences for longstanding labor-party alliances. Studies focused on the tensions that market-oriented reforms produced in the relations between labor-based parties and unions. To what extent did parties' pursuit of reforms alienate their labor base? Some examined the conditions under which labor parties were more or less restrained by their alliance with labor, while others analyzed these issues from the vantage point of labor's strategic interests—did unions exit the relationship with the party, use their voice to influence change, or remain loyal and endure a diminished role within the party?[15]

Studies also examined the implications of these party-labor tensions for electoral strategies and outcomes. As labor's role diminished within political parties, parties often appealed to new constituencies. To what extent did parties seek a different or broader base of support among unorganized workers, the urban poor, and the informal sector? Some studies held out social movements and community-based organizations as more important for political parties and elections than unions, whose influence was seen to be declining with democracy and neo-liberalism.[16] Longstanding labor-based parties, such as Mexico's PRI and Argentina's Peronist party, also underwent a process of "de-unionization," in which union leaders' presence in party electoral posts diminished significantly.[17]

Trade and Labor

Trade liberalization and the ensuing debates gave rise to a number of studies that looked not only at trade policy's impact on industrial restructuring and labor, but at labor's resistance to trade policy. This resistance came through relatively novel responses such as the forging of transnational alliances and claims centering on international labor rights. Scholars looking at these issues tended to identify more with a search for working class strategies of resistance under globalization. These studies also tended to place labor outside of a strictly national framework, focusing instead on transnational and cross-border relationships, appeals to international law, and the role of foreign governments and non-governmental actors. In these ways studies of trade and labor often asked questions more central to international political economy and international relations than comparative politics.

An influential reference here was Margaret Keck and Kathryn Sikkink's *Activists Beyond Borders*.[18] Although the book looked at environmental and human rights activism rather than labor, the authors' discussion of the "boomerang pattern" to describe the way that domestic actors and their international allies brought pressure to bear on the state provided the theoretical armature for examining labor's transnational alliances as well. These ideas about transnational activism influenced the scholarship of many younger, U.S.-based scholars interested in Latin American labor.

Beginning in the 1980s and continuing into the early 2000s, the appearance of trade agreements and related instruments such as the Generalized System of Preferences (GSP), the North American Free Trade Agreement (NAFTA), the NAFTA Labor Side Agreement, the Free Trade Area of the Americas (FTAA), the Hemispheric Social Alliance and other cross-border collaborations all gave rise to a wave of studies by scholars exploring issues such as global civil society, transnational labor strategies and alliances, and the role of regional institutions and trade policies in facilitating such alliances.[19] Related interests include monitoring labor conditions in developing country sweatshops, corporate codes of conduct, fair trade campaigns, and other means for enforcing labor rights.[20] This remains an area of considerable productivity and engaging new research.

Labor in the Post-Neoliberal and Post-Authoritarian Era

In the 2000s two key developments signal the need to examine how labor organizations are faring in new economic and political contexts: the election of left governments in much of Latin America in the early to mid-2000s; and an economic crisis early in the decade that called into question neoliberal policies in much of the region, followed by a period of robust economic growth. This improved economic performance was due largely to a commodity boom and to governments' sound management of macro-economic policy. Indeed, in the "global" financial crisis of the late 2000s in the U.S. and Europe, most Latin American countries, with the exception of Mexico, continued to outperform the North.

These are recent developments, and while research on the Left in power is now starting to emerge, relatively few of these studies so far focus on the more surprising tale—given the previous decade's policies– of organized labor's resurgence. In Argentina under Néstor and Cristina Fernández de Kirchner, in Uruguay under the *Frente Amplio*, and in Brazil under Lula, labor's resurgence demonstrated its continued importance in electoral and party politics. This lack of attention might be due to scholars' investment in the earlier claim during the 1990s that forecast labor's secular decline. Or it may be that those who study left regimes in Latin America are instead focusing on the regimes' social re-distribution policies and their impact on largely unorganized groups.

However, the fact that left governments and stable economies have coincided in several countries in the region is especially significant for labor studies because it calls into question many earlier assumptions: about how growth and distribution required weak labor unions; about unions' disappearing influence; and about their zero-sum impact on social policies targeting the poor, in which unions' gains were automatically seen as a burden on unorganized workers and the poor in general. Instead, the still limited number of studies of unions and labor policy under the Left point to increased levels of unionization, rising wages, and greater influence in policy debates in the 2000s as evidence of labor's resurgence. [21]

A second observation has to do with the persistence of authoritarian legacies in shaping labor institutions, laws, and policies in new democracies, in some instances hampering workers and unions and in others enabling organized labor to (re)-appear as a central political actor. This area of analysis uses the study of labor as a way to assess democratic deficits and institutional, legal, and policy constraints for labor under democratic regimes. For instance, countries such as Mexico and Chile continue to experience restrictions on labor rights and on legal and institutional reform of labor markets and industrial relations despite transitions to democracy. In other cases, such as Argentina, authoritarian legacies co-exist with favorable wage policies and with efforts to bolster collective rights, expand social dialogue, and include formerly marginalized actors such as the Central de los Trabajadores Argentinos (CTA).[22]

II. North and Latin American Labor Scholarship: Divergent Theories, Themes, and Methods

North American Scholarship

While research on Latin American labor has typically sought to analyze the empirical developments outlined above, political-ideological preferences and disciplinary trends have also defined subjects and driven methods. Research on labor and social movements tends to be conducted by those with sympathies for the subject matter. Labor studies in particular reflect this predisposition, since labor as a topic has become increasingly marginalized within the discipline of political science, at least as evidenced by articles in mainstream political science journals.

Nonetheless, production of dissertations and monographs indicate continued interest in studies that explore how workers and unions devise new strategies to improve their conditions. The studies of national labor movements in the 1960s, 1970s, and 1980s, which revealed an interest in studying working class formation and conflict, have given way to research on labor responses to globalization, with a focus on transnational alliances, cross-border organizing, trade and labor rights, as well as on innovative worker strategies, as exemplified by the worker-occupied factories and workplaces during the 2001–02 economic crisis in Argentina.[23]

On the other hand, labor scholarship also reflects methodological trends within the discipline. More research by younger scholars is comparative. Such work increasingly relies on a range of methodologies, from case studies to quantitative analysis. Quantitative methods were less common in earlier scholarship, in part because of the absence of good data. Not only have data sources improved, but political science departments have become more focused on training their graduate students in quantitative methods and political science journals continue to attract and publish these studies. Still, in many countries quantitative data on unions, in particular, remain fraught with problems, raising questions about the reliability of analyses that draw heavily on such data.

Although scholars who use these diverse methods are producing sophisticated studies, we may be seeing less of the close, sustained case-study analysis that relies on extensive fieldwork and which typically produces valuable inductive work that helps to generate new theories. This raises a question about political science scholarship on Latin American labor that comes out of North American universities. Are scholars and graduate students, in particular, pursuing as their research topics empirical puzzles that need explaining? Or are they instead seeking out "problems" that provide good tests of their use of quantitative and macro-comparative analysis? These two approaches are not necessarily mutually exclusive. But absent prolonged fieldwork, and given the disciplinary strictures and funding constraints of many graduate programs, younger scholars may find themselves increasingly channeled toward problems of the discipline rather than problems of the field. Full immersion in another country's culture and politics, an experience which for many academics happens only during dissertation field work, can provide scholars with the critical baseline they need throughout their careers to distinguish the important questions and to discern whether a study's assumptions make sense.

Latin American Scholarship

In Latin America scholarship on work and labor has expanded greatly in the last two decades.[24] This has been reflected in the founding in 1993 of the continental *Asociación Latinoamericana de Sociología del Trabajo* (ALAST) and its journal, *Revista Latinoamericana de Estudios del Trabajo*.[25] Regional congresses of ALAST have been punctuated in interim years with meetings of national labor studies groups, culminating in a high level of scholarly production. Indeed, labor studies in Latin America seemed to be on the rise just as the subject started to lose traction in Europe and North America.[26]

Latin American labor scholarship began to expand in the 1970s and 1980s with studies of labor conflicts, workers' struggles and strikes. It then moved into empirical research on workplace changes as a result of industrial restructuring in the wake of the crisis of the ISI model of development. Part of this perspective included a growing focus on the role of employers and firms and a shift away from state-labor relations as the central object of study. Overall, studies of unions and labor politics gave way to a focus on productive, organizational, and workplace restructuring and its impact on workers.

In contrast to the U.S., where Latin American labor studies featured research by historians and political scientists, in Latin America sociologists fueled the upsurge in labor research.[27] The predominance of sociology may account for the greater number of firm, workplace, and industry studies, in contrast with national studies traditionally favored by North American political scientists. This difference may also reflect practical realities. Latin Americans studying developments in their own countries are physically closer to the research subjects and may well be able to engage in the methods a closer view demands: long-term fieldwork and/or participant observation based on a relationship of trust built over time.

Latin American scholarship also tends to be more team-based than North American scholarship. This collaborative work is partly a result of the fewer resources available to Latin American scholars and partly due to the existence of a different reward and incentive structure than the one that prevails in the U.S. academy. North American scholarship, in contrast, is more individualistic, and tends to focus on macro and comparative studies with a heavy reliance on the secondary literature and on theoretical work within the discipline of political science.

In addition, Latin American scholarship tends to draw from European (especially French and Italian) theoretical perspectives and empirical concerns rather than from North American ones. These perspectives are anchored in sociological theories rather than political science or industrial relations, although Latin American researchers also tend to be more interdisciplinary in their approach to labor studies than their North American counterparts. Subjects range beyond formal labor and industrial firms to include non-wage and self-employed workers as well as salaried employees and managers; culture and identity; and more critical and holistic analyses of work processes and environments.

In general, there has been little cross-fertilization between North American and Latin American scholarship. For instance, union revitalization, a topic of recent interest in the U.S., has had limited resonance in Latin American scholarship, where research on unions has declined. These limitations go both ways: North Americans rarely reference major works on labor written by Latin American scholars.[28]

III. Gaps and Directions for Future Research

Future political science research on labor will likely continue to take a back seat to the more privileged attention granted to parties and elite policymaking. In this way we may see more research come from other disciplines, such as sociology or history, and from Latin American rather than North American scholars. One exception is the area of labor transnationalism and labor rights monitoring, which continues to draw U.S. political scientists and remains a dynamic subject. In addition to this, several recent and emerging empirical developments signal the need to continue to consider labor.

The first is the striking resurgence of organized labor as an important actor in national politics in several countries, such as Argentina, Uruguay, and Brazil, as noted earlier. In general there is still insufficient understanding of the circumstances in which this occurs and the implications for party systems and policies. Likewise, the persistence of authoritarian enclaves and institutional legacies in recent democracies—especially in the areas of labor market institutions, labor law, and labor organizations, is little explored. Why in some countries does the labor arena remain out of reach of the democratic changes, transparency, and rule of law that emerge in other areas? What implications do these authoritarian residues in labor have for the broader processes of democratization? One response might lead scholars to look more at the role of employers and other economic actors, domestic and foreign, in institutional and legislative reform and policymaking. Another could have researchers evaluate how restrictions on voice, participation, and representation in non-electoral settings shape political attitudes, actions, and identities. Greater attention to these questions could produce a richer understanding of the segmented and partial nature of democratic "consolidation" and also highlight the political, and not just economic, implications of changes in the labor arena.

Second, many subjects, while not new, continue to remain off the radar of political scientists who study labor. Such topics as the politics of labor relations within firms remain understudied.[29] In general, studies of business-labor relations as opposed to state-labor or party-labor relations are still rare, as are studies that look at workers rather than unions or at workers in relation to unions. National political analyses of labor also still tend to present unions as more homogenous than they really are and overlook the tensions and internal dynamics that can shed light on union leadership, strategic decision-making, and relations with other political actors.

Especially lacking are studies that look at workers in the informal sector, even though nearly half or more of the economically active population in most countries of the region labor under informal conditions. For this reason alone, political scientists should study the organizations, policies, and actors that constitute the vast and varied informal sector(s). Serious research on informal work in Latin America stands to revolutionize the way we think about work processes and relationships and their links to politics. Latin American scholars are beginning to mine this area in creative ways.[30] U.S. scholarship so far remains limited to a small if important selection of works in sociology, political economy, and political science.[31] Research on the politics of informal work is also likely to encompass a greater focus on gender, given the predominance of women outside of the formal workforce. The political science field's traditional focus on national and industry studies and on organized labor has limited, until recently, the use of gender analysis in labor studies.[32]

Similarly, research on the politics of labor migration as distinct from immigration remains limited. The many studies of Latin American immigrants in the United States tend to focus on immigrant settlement and incorporation, whereas studies of the politics of labor migration might look at international migration practices or at state policies and their impact on migrant workers.[33]

Finally, our understanding of these and other labor developments in Latin America would most certainly improve if there were more of a dialogue between Latin American and North American labor scholars. Despite the high quality of labor scholarship in Latin American universities and research centers, there is still little cross-fertilization of ideas, limited collaboration, and scarce awareness of theoretical developments occurring in the other camp. More engagement with the work produced by Latin American scholars *in* Latin America may mean bucking disciplinary trends in the U.S., but it can also create enhanced opportunities to address emerging developments in a dynamic field.

Notes

1 See Philippe Schmitter's widely cited distinction between state and societal corporatism, in Philippe C. Schmitter, "Still the Century of Corporatism?" *The Review of Politics* 36 (1974): 85–131; James M. Malloy, ed. *Authoritarianism and Corporatism in Latin America* (Pittsburgh: University of Pittsburgh Press, 1977).

2 Ruth Berins Collier and David Collier, "Inducements Versus Constraints: Disaggregating 'Corporatism'," *American Political Science* Review 73 (1979): 967–86.

3 David Collier, "Trajectory of a Concept: 'Corporatism' in the Study of Latin American Politics," in Peter H. Smith, ed., *Latin America in Comparative Perspective: New Approaches to Methods and Analysis* (Boulder, CO: Westview, 1995), p. 153.

4 For example, Sebastián Etchemendy and Ruth Berins Collier, "Down But Not Out: Union Resurgence and Segmented Neocorporatism in Argentina (2003–2007)," *Politics and Society* 35 (2007): 363–401.

5 Ruth Berins Collier and David Collier, *Shaping the Political Arena: Critical Junctures, the Labor Movement, and Regime Dynamics in Latin America* (Princeton, NJ: Princeton University Press, 1991); Dietrich Reuschmeyer, Evelyne Huber Stephens and John D. Stephens, *Capitalist Development and Democracy* (Chicago: University of Chicago Press, 1992).

6 James W. McGuire, *Peronism Without Perón: Unions, Parties, and Democracy in Argentina* (Stanford: Stanford University Press, 1997); Gerardo L. Munck, *Authoritarianism and Democratization: Soldiers and Workers in Argentina, 1976–1983* (University Park: Pennsylvania State University Press, 1998); Margaret E. Keck, "The New Unionism in the Brazilian Transition," in Alfred Stepan,

ed., *Democratizing Brazil: Problems of Transition and Consolidation* (Oxford: Oxford University Press, 1989): 252–296.

7 Volker Frank, "Politics Without Policy: The Failure of Social Concertation in Democratic Chile, 1990–2000" in Peter Winn, ed., *Victims of the Chilean Miracle: Workers and Neoliberalism in the Pinochet Era, 1973–2002* (Durham, NC: Duke University Press, 2004), 71–124.

8 Maria Lorena Cook, *The Politics of Labor Reform in Latin America: Between Flexibility and Rights* (University Park: Pennsylvania State University Press, 2007).

9 Margaret E. Keck, *The Workers' Party and Democratization in Brazil* (New Haven: Yale University Press, 1992); Philip Oxhorn, *Organizing Civil Society: The Popular Sectors and the Struggle for Democracy in Chile* (University Park: Pennsylvania State University Press, 1995); Maria Lorena Cook, *Organizing Dissent: Unions, the State, and the Democratic Teachers' Movement in Mexico* (University Park: Pennsylvania State University Presss, 1996).

10 Arturo Escobar and Sonia E. Alvarez, eds., *The Making of Social Movements in Latin America: Identity, Strategy, and Democracy* (Boulder, CO: Westview Press, 1992); Cook 1996; see also Hochstetler, this volume.

11 Maria Victoria Murillo, *Labor Unions, Partisan Coalitions, and Market Reforms in Latin America* (Cambridge, UK: Cambridge University Press, 2001); Katrina Burgess, *Parties and Unions in the New Global Economy* (Pittsburgh, PA: Pittsburgh University Press, 2004).

12 Mark Eric Williams, *Market Reforms in Mexico: Coalitions, Institutions, and the Politics of Policy Change* (Lanham, MD: Rowman and Littlefield, 2001); Sebastian Edwards and Nora Claudia Lustig, eds. *Labor Markets in Latin America: Combining Social Protection with Market Flexibility* (Washington, DC: Brookings Institution, 1997).

13 Murillo; Cook 2007; Maria Victoria Murillo and Andrew Schrank. "With a Little Help from My Friends: Partisan Politics, Transnational Alliances, and Labor Rights in Latin America," *Comparative Political Studies* 38(2005): 971–99; Michelle L. Dion, *Workers and Welfare: Comparative Institutional Change in Twentieth-Century Mexico* (Pittsburgh, PA: University of Pittsburgh, 2010).

14 Agnieszka Paczynska, *State, Labor, and the Transition to a Market Economy: Egypt, Poland, Mexico, and the Czech Republic* (University Park: Pennsylvania State University Press, 2009); José A. Alemán, *Labor Relations in New Democracies: East Asia, Latin America, and Europe* (New York: Palgrave Macmillan, 2010).

15 Murillo; Burgess.

16 Kenneth Roberts, "Social Inequalities without Class Cleavages: Party Systems and Labor Movements in Latin America's Neoliberal Era," *Studies in Comparative International Development* 36(2002): 3–33; Salvador A.M. Sandoval, "Alternative Forms of Working-Class Organization and the Mobilization of Informal-Sector Workers in Brazil in the Era of Neoliberalism" *International Labor and Working Class History* 72 (2007).

17 Steven Levitsky, *Transforming Labor-Based Parties in Latin America: Argentine Peronism in Comparative Perspective* (Cambridge: Cambridge University Press, 2003).

18 Margaret E. Keck and Kathryn Sikkink, *Activists Beyond Borders: Advocacy Networks in International Politics* (Ithaca, NY: Cornell University Press, 1998).

19 See, for example, Mark Anner, *Solidarity Transformed: Labor Responses to Globalization and Crisis in Latin America* (Ithaca, NY: ILR/Cornell University Press, 2011); and Marisa von Bulow, *Building Transnational Networks: Civil Society and the Politics of Trade in the Americas* (Cambridge University Press, 2010).

20 See Shareen Hertel, *Unexpected Power: Conflict and Change among Transnational Activists* (Ithaca, NY: ILR/Cornell University Press, 2006); and Gay W. Seidman, *Beyond the Boycott: Labor Rights, Human Rights, and Transnational Activism* (New York: Russell Sage Foundation, 2007).

21 Cecilia Senén González, "Dinámica y resultados de la revitalización sindical en Argentina," forthcoming in *Revista Trabajo*; Etchemendy and Collier.

22 Paul G. Buchanan, "Preauthoritarian Institutions and Postauthoritarian Outcomes: Labor Politics in Chile and Uruguay" *Latin American Politics and Society* 50(2008): 59–89; Graciela Bensusán and María Lorena Cook, "Political Transition and Labor Revitalization in Mexico," in Daniel B. Cornfield and Holly J. McCammon, eds., *Labor Revitalization: Global Perspectives and New Initiatives,* Vol. 11 Research in the Sociology of Work (Oxford, UK.: Elsevier JAI, 2003), 229–67.

23 Peter Ranis, "Factories without Bosses: Argentina's Experience with Worker-Run Enterprises," *Labor: Studies in Working-Class History of the Americas* 3 (2006): 11–23; Edward C. Epstein, "The

Piquetero Movement of Greater Buenos Aires: Working Class Protest During the Current Argentine Crisis," *Canadian Journal of Latin American and Caribbean Studies* (January–July 2003).

24 For a review of these developments, see Enrique de la Garza and Ludger Pries, "Work, Workers and Social Change in Latin America," *Current Sociology* 45 (1997): 91–107.

25 See Laís Abramo et al, "The Institutionalization of the Sociology of Work in Latin America," *Work and Occupations,* 24 (1997): 348–363.

26 Bruce E. Kaufman, *The Global Evolution of Industrial Relations: Events, Ideas and the IIRA* (Geneva: International Labour Organization, 2004).

27 John D. French, "The Latin American Labor Studies Boom," *International Review of Social History* 45 (2000): 279–310.

28 See Graciela Bensusán, ed. *Diseño legal y desempeño real: instituciones laborales en América Latina* (Mexico: Universidad Autónoma Metropolitana and Miguel Angel Porrúa, 2006); Enrique de la Garza Toledo, ed., *Tratado Latinoameriano de Sociología del Trabajo* (México: El Colegio de México/FLACSO/UAM/Fondo de Cultura Económica, 2000).

29 But see Carolina Bank Muñoz, *Transnational Tortillas: Race, Gender, and Shop-Floor Politics in Mexico and the United States* (Ithaca, NY: ILR/Cornell University Press, 2008); and Scott B. Martin, "Network Ties and Labor Flexibility in Brazil and Mexico: A Tale of Two Automobile Factories," in Christopher Candland and Rudra Sil, eds. *The Politics of Labor in a Global Age: Continuity and Change in Late-industrializing and Post-socialist Economies* (Oxford University Press, 2001): 95–131.

30 Enrique de la Garza, ed., *Trabajo no clasico, organizacion, y accion colectiva* (Mexico, D.F.: Plaza y Valdes and UAM-Iztapalapa, 2011).

31 Jose Itzigsohn, *Developing Poverty: The State, Labor Market Deregulation, and the Informal Economy in Costa Rica and the Dominican Republic* (University Park: Pennsylvania State University Press, 2000); Patricia Fernandez-Kelly and Jon Shefner, eds. *Out of the Shadows: Political Action and the Informal Economy in Latin America* (University Park: Pennsylvania State University Press, 2006); and John C. Cross, *Informal Politics: Street Vendors and the State in Mexico City* (Stanford, CA: Stanford University Press, 1998).

32 For some important exceptions see Teresa Healy, *Gendered Struggles Against Globalisation in Mexico: Gender in a Global/Local World,* (Burlington, VT: Ashgate, 2008), which focuses on male unionized workers in the Mexican auto industry; and Bank Muñoz, 2008.

33 For recent work in this area, see Natasha Iskander, *Creative State: Forty Years of Migration and Development Policy in Morocco and Mexico* (Ithaca, NY: ILR/Cornell University Press, 2010).

18

BUSINESS POLITICS IN LATIN AMERICA

Investigating Structures, Preferences, and Influence[1]

Sebastian Karcher and Ben Ross Schneider

At a dinner party in 1994 with 30 of Mexico's wealthiest businessmen, outgoing President Carlos Salinas asked each of them to contribute $25 million to electing his handpicked successor. Some attendees were shocked, others thought the sum too low, considering how much money they had made during Salinas' tenure, but they collectively committed hundreds of millions of dollars.[2] Almost two decades later, many of these diners were still enjoying and extending favorable regulations. A monopoly on fixed line telephony for Telmex, for example, helped its owner Carlos Slim expand abroad and rise to the top of the Forbes list of the world's richest people. In television, Televisa sought to shore up its privileged position in media markets. In 2006 Congress passed, with little debate, what became known as the Televisa law, restricting entry by potential competitors.[3] Although the sums and protections may be less egregious, similar stories are commonplace throughout Latin America. Business invests heavily in politics and merits a commensurate research effort to understand the impacts of that investment.

The study of business politics in Latin America, especially by U.S.-based scholars, has often come in waves. Some waves corresponded to the emergence of general theories where business was central, starting with the pluralist paradigm of the 1960s. Another wave followed the flourishing of theories of corporatism and dependency in the 1970s.[4] Mancur Olson's theories of collective action and rentseeking inspired a series of studies after the 1990s.[5] However, these theory-inspired waves slowed in the 2000s, and new debates on power resource theory, cross-class alliances, and varieties of capitalism in developed countries reverberated little in research on business politics in Latin America. Other waves of research followed on seismic shifts in regimes or development strategies in the 1980s and 1990s.[6]

Despite these waves, research on business politics is first characterized by how little there is. Beyond scarcity, research on business politics suffers from some biases and blind spots. Overcoming these shortcomings requires several shifts in focus. For one, the political consequences of the distinctive economic structure of business in the region—the ubiquity of diversified business groups, the large informal sectors, as well as the strategic positions of multinational corporations (MNCs)—merit closer attention. In light of this heterogeneity, research should also problematize and examine empirically the sources of business preferences rather than assuming or deducing them. Lastly, research could benefit from more comparative analysis both within Latin America and with countries outside the region, both developed and developing, to specify better what is distinctive about business politics in Latin America.

This overview is structured in three parts that—loosely following Laswell's famous dictum—provide answers to the questions *who* is business in Latin America (section I), *what* does it want (section II), and *how* does it get what it wants (section III).

I. Business Structure

A first step in analyzing business in Latin America is to recognize how different it is from standard, specialized, professionally managed, publicly owned corporations common in the United States and other developed countries. These differences are consequential, as we analyze later, for understanding business preferences and how business engages in politics. Five distinctive features stand out: the small size of firms, the organization of large firms into diversified business groups, the prevalence of family control, foreign ownership by multinational corporations (MNCs), and recently outward expansion by emerging multinational corporations (EMNCs).

The share of small firms in Latin America is higher, and the largest firms are significantly smaller than their counterparts in other regions. The majority of businesses in Latin America are tiny. Whereas in the United States about 30 percent of the private sector workforce is employed in firms with less than ten employees in all Latin American economies except Chile more than 50 percent of the private workforce is in firms with less than five workers, which are often informal.[7] Not only are there more smaller firms, the largest Latin American firms are smaller than elsewhere: the average large firm in Latin America "is about half the size of the average large firm in the rest of the world, either developing or developed."[8] Although small by international standards, the largest businesses are still giants in their domestic economies.

Most large domestic firms belong to a small number of diversified business groups—large, hierarchically organized and usually family-owned holdings of subsidiaries in multiple, often unrelated fields. Contrary to conventional theories of the firm, subsidiaries of diversified business groups—also known as *grupos económicos* or simply as *grupos*—are frequently not vertically or horizontally integrated, but rather spread across multiple sectors, often with few market nor technological synergies.[9]

Family ownership and management is prevalent, even in the largest domestic firms, in a pattern common in developing countries but distinct from most developed countries.[10] Most domestic private firms are owned and controlled by families, few are publicly listed on local stock exchanges, and ownership customarily passes from generation to generation. Even if large business groups list some of their subsidiaries, they maintain ultimate control through majority voting shares, holding companies, and pyramidal corporate structures. Beyond these hierarchical links of ownership, networks interlace huge business groups through corporate boards, where members of some groups sit on boards of one or several other business groups.[11] Sergio Lazzarini has the richest analysis of what he calls relational capitalism in Brazil.[12] In addition to networks across corporate boards (and government agencies), Lazzarini also documents a novel trend in Brazil where business groups engage in joint ventures and join shareholding blocs to control other groups. This sort of inter-group collaboration is rarer in other economies dominated by business groups.

MNCs play a crucial role in Latin American economies though their type and scale varies across countries with more efficiency seeking MNCs in countries closer to the United States and more market and resource seeking MNCs further south. As opposed to much of Asia, where developmental states restricted entry, MNCs played a crucial role in Latin America's development in the 20th century and increased their presence after the 1990s.[13] MNCs in Latin America are dominant players in core sectors of the economy such as finance, telecommunications, higher technology manufacturing, and natural resources.[14] In most countries, a third to a half of the largest firms are foreign. The accumulated stock of inward FDI ranges from 12 percent of GDP for Venezuela to 75 percent of GDP for Chile, with most countries bunched around 30 percent, much higher than in most Asian countries.[15] Moreover, Asian developmental states have been more successful in steering FDI into desired sectors and in negotiating more technology transfer.

EMNCs and outward foreign investment are the main new features of business in Latin America. Many large domestic firms began investing abroad in the 2000s, especially in other countries of Latin America (hence the initial labels of multilatinas or translatinas). The largest such EMNCs—and the only ones to make it into the Fortune 500 list of the world's largest corporations—come from the largest economies, Brazil and Mexico. The majority of the 50 most globalized Latin American companies are from Mexico (12) and Brazil (19), followed by Chile (8) and Argentina (5).[16] The investment strategies of these EMNCs have usually been market seeking, first expanding to other Latin American countries and then beyond.[17] Multilatinas are active in a range of sectors such as mining (Vale, Brazil), food (JBS, Brazil), steel (Techint, Argentina), cement (Cemex, Mexico), telecommunications (America Móvil [Grupo Carso], Mexico), or services like LAN airlines (Chile) and Banco Itaú (Brazil). However, in contrast to EMNCs from other developing countries, multilatinas are heavily concentrated in commodities and regulated services. In comparative terms, this internationalization is still new and relatively limited. The outward FDI stock is around or below ten percent of GDP in most Latin American countries (25 percent for Chile) compared to 40–60 percent for most developed countries. However, both economically and politically, multilatinas are likely to increase in importance.

Despite the conventional view that a country's development trajectory and prospects depend heavily on its leading firms, little research has been done on business-led development in Latin America.[18] Some evidence suggests that the distinctive features of business contribute to problems of lagging productivity and low investment in Latin America. Small, informal firms, for example, lack scale, finance, and technology to play a role as a motor of employment and growth like they do in many developed countries. Larger firms do not realize their potential in size and productivity due to limitations in capital markets and infrastructure.[19] Business groups and MNCs, representing many of the largest players in the business sector, invest little in research and development (with the partial exception of Brazil).[20] While these issues are crucial for Latin America's economic prospects, the focus of this chapter is on the political implications of the structure of business in the region, which we take up in the next sections.

II. Business Preferences

A large literature derives business interests directly from their asset specificity and product markets. This view is most clearly elaborated in Frieden's work and is the dominant approach in quantitative studies.[21] In this sectoral approach, more capital intensive firms with greater asset specificity in more competitive international markets will have strong preferences for tariffs, favorable exchange rates, and other supportive policies. The biggest draw of the sectoral approach is its parsimony in specifying hypotheses deductively and in measuring the distribution of business interests across countries.

Its biggest drawback is that the hypotheses are sometimes wrong. In particular, the process of market-oriented reform in the 1990s dealt this simple sectoral view a severe blow. Many scholars and reform advocates initially expected entrenched protected businesses to mobilize to block reforms. Firms in tradable sectors should have opposed the reforms that would expose them to international competition. In the event, significant opposition did not mobilize (prompting Moisés Naim, a former minister in charge of trade reform, to title his book *Paper Tigers*), and many businesses actively allied with liberalizing reformers.[22] Clearly, business preferences were more complex and more heterogeneous along a number of cleavages. This section delves into the most important sources of this complexity.

Decades ago, Peter Evans and others drew attention to the distinctive preferences of MNCs, which sometimes align with local business but may also conflict. The reasons MNCs invest in Latin America are diverse, as consequently are their preferences. We can distinguish among three main types of FDI in Latin America: resource-seeking, efficiency-seeking, or market-seeking investment.[23] Resource-seeking MNCs, mostly mining and oil companies, value secure property rights and harmonious labor relations but care less about labor costs or skills and many overall macro policies (such as fiscal, monetary, and exchange rate policies). Efficiency-seeking MNCs invest because the destination country offers attractive conditions for manufacturing, especially lower labor costs. As their investment decisions depend on a number of factors, they are more concerned with local politics, as a far wider range of structural factors (infrastructure and education) and policies (labor regulation, taxes, exchange rates, trade restrictions) are crucial to the effective incorporation of local manufacturing operations into global production networks. Market seeking MNCs invest in order to gain access to new markets and are less sensitive to trade and exchange rate policies and other issues in production, but more interested in policies that affect local demand (expansionary monetary and fiscal policy, for example) and regulations in their sector.

The preferences of the large business groups are rooted in the competitive advantages they derive from their size, their diversification, as well as the sectors in which they are active. Diversified business groups may simultaneously import, export, and produce for protected domestic markets, which complicates their preferences on trade protection and exchange rates. Although they are active in a range of sectors, they usually hold core assets where they have inherent advantages in international markets (natural resources) or where they are shielded from international competition (as in non-tradables). Business groups often have some subsidiaries in oligopolistic or favorably regulated sectors that provide them with a reliable cash flow (cement is a common example). Very few groups have most of their assets in highly competitive manufacturing activities. Another source of competitive advantage stems from the ability of business groups to mobilize capital both from their many subsidiaries and from domestic and, more recently, international financial markets.

A final advantage of business groups lies in their flexibility and speed. Business groups are flexible externally in their ability quickly to buy and sell subsidiaries because they have access to sufficient cash and because managerial control is so highly centralized.[24] They have internal flexibility because skill levels are on average low and workers are easily replaceable. This set of competitive advantages helps to explain the surprising lack of opposition to trade liberalization, and market oriented reform overall, in the 1990s. If anything, business groups are well suited to adapting to abrupt changes in overall development strategy. In addition, privatization programs opened up precisely the sorts of opportunities business groups needed as they exited manufacturing.[25]

Business groups have strong interests in maintaining the regulatory environment that gives them competitive advantages over local startups and potential MNC entrants. Business groups share an abiding interest in weak and passive anti-trust regulators, largely because many of them have market power in some segments of their operations that allows them to generate the steady cash flow needed to expand and sustain other firms in the group. Telmex is the most visible, and notorious, example. Its monopoly on fixed line telephony in Mexico charges some of the highest rates in Latin America.[26] In essence Mexican consumers helped finance Grupo Carso's aggressive expansion into telecommunications markets throughout Latin America. Another regulatory example in stock markets are non-voting shares which allow business groups to control large corporate assets with relatively small amounts of equity investment. As business groups rely on such exclusionary mechanisms for their governance, they oppose many reforms of local stock market regulations.

Understanding firm preferences can benefit from a closer examination of production processes. The varieties of capitalism literature argues that business in the coordinated market economies of continental Europe views social policy and employment protection legislation favorably, because they help to insure firm and industry specific skills on which core firms depend.[27] In contrast, few Latin American firms rely on highly skilled labor. At the same time, general education levels in the region are low. The consequence is a low-skill trap, where firms do not create high-skill jobs because they cannot find skilled workers, and workers do not invest in skill acquisition because they cannot find high skill jobs.[28] Moreover, as specific skills play a smaller role in the production strategies, firms show little interest in fostering stable employment patterns or co-operative relationships with labor on the shop-floor. As an additional twist, and distinguishing Latin America from advanced industrialized countries, business pressure for reform of the region's strict labor codes has been muted, in part because firms, especially when they are small, can use informal employment to circumvent regulations.[29] This micro perspective helps explain the absence of strong preferences and mobilization by business to reform education and labor regulation.

Small firms in Latin America have little in terms of formal organizations and little voice in policy debates. Yet, given their sheer number and importance for aggregate employment, it is worthwhile to consider their preferences and how they differ from those of larger firms. Like their counterparts in developed countries, they complain about their lack of access to finance. But in contrast to advanced industrialized countries, small firms are less concerned with regulation, including labor regulation, than larger firms: where regulations are weakly enforced, they provide smaller firms with a comparative advantage because they do not pay the regulatory costs borne by their larger competitors.[30]

In sum, business preferences are divided along multiple cleavages of size, ownership (MNCs versus business groups versus stand alone firms), sector, linkages to the international economy, and strategies. With this heterogeneity it is not surprising that it is hard to find coherent national bourgeoisies or what Kohli calls "cohesive-capitalist states."[31] However, sprawling business groups and networks, or relational capitalism, knit together some of these dispersed firms and provide some means for re-aggregating and reconciling divergent preferences. The next section analyses how these preferences get articulated in politics.

III. Business Power

This section examines four principal, and partly overlapping channels of business power: (1) institutionalized consultation in policy-making, often through business associations; (2) lobbying Congress and the executive; (3) campaign finance; and (4) structural power resulting from international mobility of investment and capital.

Governments throughout Latin America have created thousands of consultative councils or forums designed to bring together policy makers and representatives of business to discuss everything from narrow sectoral issues to broad development strategies.[32] Many councils have little impact, but some decisively shape business input into policy, especially where business organizations are strong. In negotiating NAFTA, for example, the Mexican government created forums that incorporated associations of big business but effectively excluded smaller firms.[33] More recently, Tasha Fairfield shows how Chilean business, with a strong, national organization and institutionalized mechanisms of consultation, provided unified and effective opposition to increases in corporate taxation, while its less organized counterpart in Argentina was less able to block tax increases.[34]

Large businesses usually also have direct contacts to lobby top government officials. With the transition to democracy, business contacts with legislators became more frequent in what Eli Diniz and Renato Boschi call an "Americanization" of business politics in Brazil, though lobbying practices are still evolving and largely unregulated.[35] Several features of Latin American political systems open up lobbying access, especially for big business. Bureaucracies in Latin America are porous and staffed at the top by political appointees. Appointees in top economic positions are sometimes suggested or vetted by business groups (and sometimes are ex-employees) and most consult regularly with business groups.[36] In many cases, presidents appoint business people directly to the cabinet (as is common in the United States but rare in other developed countries). Even countries where business appointees in cabinets are historically uncommon such as Chile and Mexico have seen a significant presence of business people in recent governments. About 15 percent of ministers in the government of Felipe Calderón (2006–) in Mexico and half of the ministers of the government of Sebastián Piñera in Chile (2010–) had backgrounds in business.

The particular combination of majoritarian presidential systems with legislatures elected through proportional representation (PR), common in Latin America but rare elsewhere, creates institutional incentives for parties and legislators to respond to lobbying by organized groups, at the same time it weakens the presidency by generating fragmented party systems in which presidents' parties rarely have legislative majorities. Since parties in a PR-multiparty system are less focused on the median voter than the president, they can be targeted and swayed by lobbying more easily.[37] Put differently, some parties in a fragmented party system will have incentives to be attentive to business lobbying. Moreover, candidate centered electoral systems, as with open-list PR, further fragment the legislature, and provide opportunities for individual firms or small groups of firms to forge close ties, in part through targeted campaign contributions, with individual legislators. While these electoral and party dynamics make legislatures more open to pressures from business, presidential negotiations to get government proposals through the legislature makes the executive more responsive to legislators and parties, either through ad hoc bargains or on an ongoing basis when presidents appoint representatives of congressional coalitions to positions in the cabinet or executive. Although the incentive structures in these presidential cum PR legislature systems are fairly straightforward, empirical documentation of the inner workings are scant, in part because openly pro-business parties have not fared well (outside Mexico and Chile), so politicians and parties have reasons to downplay their ties to business.

The region's systems of campaign and party finance provides business with another important channel to influence policies. Reporting requirements, even where they exist, are weakly enforced, resulting in a scarcity of quality data. This is somewhat paradoxical, for electoral campaigns in Latin America are very expensive and sometimes more expensive in per capita terms than in the United States. Most governments try to limit the extent of private financing by providing public funding, granting free access to the media, and restricting some kinds of contributions (such as from contractors, foreigners, and/or corporations). Yet, in their extensive overview of campaign finance in the region, Griner and Zovatto find that private funding is the dominant source of campaign funds in Latin American countries and fundraising takes place "among a very small group of major entrepreneurs."[38] Research is scarce, but mostly suggests that contributions are consequential both for getting elected and in influencing policy. In Brazil, for example, campaign contributions are crucial for the electoral prospects of candidates, who in turn allocate earmarks ("pork")—largely projects that directly benefit construction and other businesses—so as to maximize contributions.[39]

On a less direct, more diffuse structural dimension, increased capital mobility since the 1970s made exit threats more credible and bolstered the power of business. Several comparative works argue that capital mobility enhances the likelihood of a transition to stable democracy, especially in more unequal societies.[40] Given the credible exit option, the argument goes, the threat of heavily redistributive politics from the left is reduced, and democracy becomes acceptable for business and the wealthy. The effect of structural power may be best appreciated in its absence. Governments less constrained by international credit markets—due to default (Argentina) or commodity rents (Venezuela, Bolivia, and Ecuador)—have abrogated a range of property rights.

Overall, though, this structural power is the least visible and most difficult to document. Understanding this power requires close attention to investor and creditor preferences, often quite variable across different types of investors, and empirical investigation of how policy makers narrow the range of acceptable policy options in an effort to anticipate investor reactions.[41] The recent expansion of domestic business groups abroad vastly increased the size of some firms, and hence their total investment budgets, both of which augment their political leverage and the interests of politicians and government officials in hearing their views and plans. Beyond sheer size, the internationalization of the investment budgets of new EMNCs gives business groups (like traditional MNCs) a new, even more credible threat of exit.

A final factor in analyzing the exercise of business power is the impact of families on business politics. A major, as yet unresearched, question is what difference it makes when the lobbyist or campaign contributor is a member of a family that controls a business group versus a salaried manager from a large firm. At a minimum, politicians and policy makers know families have greater capacity for longer term relationships (reiterated games) and extensive networks for monitoring politicians' behavior. And, family preferences on policies are likely to be more intense since family fortunes are inextricably linked to the family business (whereas salaried managers can move on to other firms). Although many large family firms are expanding abroad, exit options are generally less attractive, so family businesses are likely to invest more in political voice.

When a small number of business actors essentially control, or have veto power over, parts of the government, state capture is an appropriate term. In recent decades instances of capture have been documented in Chile in the 1970s, Argentina in the early 1990s, and most recently Mexico in the 2000s.[42] The discussion of capture in Mexico is revealing on several counts. For one, research has been spearheaded ironically by the World Bank, where economists have been puzzling over Mexico's poor economic performance despite its strong record of market reforms in the 1990s. In addition, Mexico's experience provides a window on capture in a democratic setting, whereas earlier episodes of capture were usually associated with more authoritarian or highly centralized governments. In work focusing on earlier periods in Argentina, Schvarzer and more recently Castellani describe how the close relationship between governments and large companies in Argentina created a "state-business economic complex" with a set of large companies that derived quasi rents from their close relationship with the state.[43] Castellani traces the persistence of this complex through several regime changes and shifts in economic policy in Argentina between 1966 and 1989 and emphasizes the importance of history for understanding business and state relations in Latin America. Yet little contemporary work on business in Latin America addresses the pre–democratization period.[44]

Capture is sometimes followed by backlash. Previously favored business groups were largely excluded from policy making in Chile in the 1980s and to a lesser extent in Argentina in the late 1990s with the consequence that many of the leading business groups collapsed, sold out, or moved. Such abrupt shifts in the political fortunes of business show that state capture can be fleeting and argue against a stricter entrenchment or crony capitalism view where dominant businesses maintain their economic fortunes through continuous political influence. The generally high turnover among top business groups in Latin America also belies an entrenchment argument.

Overall though, with the partial exception of some of the populist left governments, the political systems of Latin America have evolved into congenial and accommodating environments for big business with multiple avenues for effective input. Some features, such as the appointment of business people to cabinet positions, can change dramatically from one government to the next, but most other dimensions—from structural power, through PR legislatures, to increasing demand for campaign resources—are more enduring and favorable to big business.

Conclusions

Why is the study of the political economy of business so underdeveloped? There are a number of institutional and disciplinary impediments ranging from a tendency among social scientists to favor research on more disadvantaged groups, to the relative lack of interest among economists (and consequently among multilateral lending agencies) in studying firms, to the relatively weak research tradition in business schools in the region. Overall, too, we have noted at several points the lack of reliable data. The study of business in Latin America may also suffer from a bias in political science for quantitative methods. Most of the areas of business influence lack easily measurable indicators and so do not attract much attention from quantitatively oriented scholars. Campaign finance is a partial exception and has attracted some work despite the unreliability that usually afflicts these data. And, where quantitative analyses have turned up revealing relationships—as, for example, with the tendency for larger firms to win favorable judgments from Mexican courts—a good deal more qualitative work is necessary to establish how the relationship works.[45]

Looking ahead, the study of business will have to deal with a moving target. Policy makers, judges, regulators, and politicians are likely to be dealing years hence with business groups and MNCs that are larger, more concentrated, more oligopolistic, more international, more interconnected, more concentrated in commodities, and more sophisticated politically. The size asymmetries will likely be the most striking as domestic firms leverage market power and commodity rents to grow by leaps and bounds through foreign acquisitions. The political sophistication, already at a high level in some business groups, is likely to develop further through expanding operations in multiple jurisdictions and through increasing dependence of big business on regulatory and competition agencies.

At the same time, other factors will contribute to continuity on some dimensions. The various competitive advantages business groups derive from the status quo give few reasons to expect an imminent convergence towards U.S.-style corporate governance. Two features of business groups especially show few signs of disappearing in the near term: diversification and family control. Even more specialized business groups, as they grow, often decide to diversify, which gives them greater agility and less fixed and narrow preferences. While families in many traditional business groups have professionalized management by moving to corporate boards, hiring more outside managers, and sending heirs to get MBAs abroad, it is almost impossible to find cases of families relinquishing ownership control. This family control continues to give business groups a longer term perspective, and hence greater credibility, in politics.

Despite the resurgence in state intervention following the financial crisis of 2008–09, the development prospects of most countries in Latin America, especially the non petro-states, depend heavily on the character of each country's leading firms—both national and foreign—and more so than in much of the 20th century. As development theorists have increasingly moved to the consensus that development strategies need to be tailored to the individual characteristics of each country, the trajectory and capacities of its large firms become central to designing these strategies. Overall, this means more comparative research, across firms, across countries, and across regions. Given the increasing concentration of the largest firms in commodity sectors, policy makers will need to know a lot more about what makes some commodity firms more innovative and dynamic than others.

The increasing size and power of the regions' largest firms, however, is not necessarily a blessing for its development process. Several of the studies we have reviewed point to instances in which business influence has not been benign. The concentration of political power among a small number of large firms can have social costs due to various forms rent-seeking. Longer term, it poses a potential threat to both equitable development and democratic legitimacy. More research into the ways in which business influences the political process is thus crucial—for academics seeking to understand the politics of the region as well as for policy makers and civil society activists striving to further Latin America's recent advances in development, equality, and democracy.

Notes

1 We are grateful to Diego Finchelstein and David Steinberg for comments on previous versions and to Joyce Lawrence for research assistance.

2 Andrés Oppenheimer, *Bordering on Chaos: Mexico's Roller-Coaster Journey Toward Prosperity* (Boston, MA: Little, Brown, 1998), pp. 83–87.

3 Carlos Elizondo, "Perverse Equilibria: Unsuitable but Durable Institutions," in *No Growth Without Equity?: Inequality, Interests, and Competition in Mexico*, eds. Michael Walton and Santiago Levy (Washington D.C: World Bank, 2009).

4 For example James Malloy, *Authoritarianism and Corporatism in Latin America* (Pittsburgh, PA: Pittsburgh University Press, 1977); Peter Evans, *Dependent Development* (Princeton, NJ: Princeton University Press, 1979).

5 Jeffry A Frieden, "Invested Interest: The Politics of National Economic Policies in a World of Global Finance," *International Organization* 45, no. 4 (1991): 425–451; Hector E Schamis, "Distributional coalitions and the politics of economic reform in Latin America," *World Politics* 51, no. 2 (1999): 236–268.

6 See, for example, Ernest Bartell and Leigh Payne, eds., *Business and Democracy in Latin America* (Pittsburgh, PA: Pittsburgh University Press, 1995). Peter R. Kingstone, *Crafting Coalitions for Reform: Business Preferences, Political Institutions, and Neoliberal Reform in Brazil* (University Park: Pennsylvania State University Press, 1999); Sebastián Etchemendy, *Models of Economic Liberalization: Regime, Power and Compensation in Latin American* (New York: Cambridge University Press, 2011); Eduardo Silva, *The State and Capital in Chile: Business Elites, Technocrats, and Market Economics* (Boulder, CO: Westview Press, 1996).

7 CEDLAS and World Bank, "SEDLAC — Socio-Economic Database for Latin America and the Caribbean," Online Database, 2010, http://www.depeco.econo.unlp.edu.ar/sedlac/eng/index.php.

8 Ana María Herrera and Eduardo Lora, "Why so small? Explaining the size of firms in Latin America," *The World Economy* 28, no. 7 (2005): 1012.

9 Wilson Peres, ed., *Grandes empresas y grupos industriales latinoamericanos* (Mexico City, Mexico: Siglo XXI, 1998); Asli Colpan, Takahashi Hikino, and James Lincoln, eds., *Oxford Handbook on Business Groups* (New York: Oxford University Press, 2010). Ben Ross Schneider, "Hierarchical Market Economies and Varieties of Capitalism in Latin America," *Journal of Latin American Studies* 41, no. 3 (2009): 558.

10 Rafael La Porta, López-de-Silanes, and Andrei Shleifer, "Corporate Ownership Around the World," *Journal of Finance* 54, no. 2 (1999): 471–517. Francisco Durand, *Incertidumbre y Soledad: Reflexiones Sobre los Grandes Empresarios de América Latina* (Lima, Peru: Friedrich Ebert, 1996).

11 Francisco Valdés, *Autonomia e legitimidad: los empresarios, la política y el Estado en México* (Mexico City, Mexico: Siglo XXI, 1998).

12 Sergio Lazzarini, *Capitalismo de laços: os donos do Brasil e suas conexões* (São Paulo, Brazil: Elsevier, 2010).

13 Jorge Schvarzer, *La industria que supimos conseguir* (Buenos Aires, Argentina: Planeta, 1996); Alice Amsden, "Nationality of Ownership in Developing Countries: Who Should 'Crowd Out' Whom in Imperfect Markets?," in Industrial Policy and Development, ed. Joseph Stiglitz, Giovanni Dosi, and Mario Cimoli (New York: Oxford University Press, 2009).

14 ECLAC, *Foreign Investment in Latin America and the Caribbean* (Santiago, Chile: ECLAC, 2008), 74.

15 Other Southeast Asian countries have comparable levels of FDI to Latin America and FDI stocks in East Europe are significantly higher cf. UNCTAD, UNCTADStat data base. Foreign Direct Investment, 2010, http://unctadstat.unctad.org/

16 Lourdes Casanova, *Global Latinas: Latin America's Emerging Multinationals* (Basingstoke, UK: Palgrave Macmillan, 2009), 165f.

17 Daniel Chudnovsky, Bernardo Kosacoff, and Andrés López, eds., *Las multinacionales latinoamericana: sus estrategias en un mundo globalizado* (Buenos Aires, Argentina: Fondo de Cultura Económica, 1999), 356.

18 Alfred Chandler, Franco Amatori, and Takahashi Hikino, eds., Big Business and the Wealth of Nations (New York: Cambridge University Press, 1997); Amsden, "Nationality of Ownership."

19 Carmen Pagés, *The Age of Productivity* (Washington D.C: IDB, 2010).

20 Schneider, "Hierarchical Market Economies"; ECLAC, *Foreign Investment in Latin America and the Caribbean*, 17.

21 Frieden, "Invested Interest."

22 Moisés Naim, *Paper Tigers and Minotaurs: The Politics of Venezuela's Economic Reforms* (Washington, D.C.: Carnegie Endowment, 1993). Kingstone, *Crafting Coalitions for Reform*.

23 John Dunning, *Multinational Enterprises and the Global Economy* (Reading, MA: Addison Wesley, 1993); Patrick J. W. Egan, "Hard Bargains: The Impact of Multinational Corporations on Economic Reform in Latin America," *Latin American Politics and Society* 52, no. 1 (2010): 1–32. A fourth type of FDI is strategic-asset seeking. This often means establishing or acquiring R&D

facilities which has been quite rare in Latin America, save for the recent establishment of R&D operations in Brazil by firms like IBM, Monsanto, and GE (cf. João Alberto de Negri et al., "Liderança Tecnológica e Liderança de Mercado" unpublished manuscript (Rio de Janeiro, Brazil, 2009). Core interests for these MNCs would be in large pools of engineers and scientists as well as low restrictions on international movement of experts and equipment.

24 Andrea Goldstein, *Multinational Companies from Emerging Economies* (New York: Palgrave Macmillan, 2007).

25 Etchemendy, *Models of Economic Liberalization*.

26 Word Bank, *Democratic Governance in Mexico: Beyond State Capture and Social Polarization* (Washington D.C.: World Bank, 2007).

27 Peter A Hall and David Soskice, "An Introduction to Varieties of Capitalism," in *Varieties of Capitalism. The Institutional Foundations of Comparative Advantage*, eds. Peter A Hall and David Soskice (New York: Oxford University Press, 2001), 1–68.

28 Ben Ross Schneider and David Soskice, "Inequality in developed countries and Latin America: coordinated, liberal and hierarchical systems," *Economy and Society* 38, no. 1 (2009): 17–52.

29 As Friel points out, individual firms such as Argentina's Arcor do pursue high-skill strategies and internalize the necessary institutional structures: Daniel Friel, "Forging a Comparative Institutional Advantage in Argentina," *Human Relations* (forthcoming). Brambilla et al. show that the skill profile of Latin American firms differ drastically depending on its sector: I. Brambilla et al., "Skills, Exports, and the Wages of Five Million Latin American Workers," *NBER Working Paper* No. 15996 (2010). Both findings would suggest the potential for more complex political alignments based on demands for skills.

30 Carmen Pagés, Gaëlle Pierre, and Stefano Scarpetta, *Job Creation in Latin America and the Caribbean: Recent Trends and Policy Challenges* (Washington D.C.: World Bank Publications, 2009).

31 Atul Kohli, *State-Directed Development* (New York: Cambridge University Press, 2004).

32 The CES in the Lula government is a good example of the latter. Mahrukh Doctor, "Lula's Development Council: Neo-Corporatism and Policy Reform in Brazil," *Latin American Perspectives* 34, no. 6 (2007): 131–148. See Lydia Fraile, ed., *Blunting Neo-Liberalism: Tripartism and Economic Reforms in the Developing World* (Geneva, Switzerland: ILO, 2010) for a more comparative analysis of the benefits of tripartite negotiation in smoothing the path of market oriented reform.

33 Strom C. Thacker, *Big Business, the State, and Free Trade: Constructing Coalitions in Mexico* (Cambridge University Press, 2000); Kenneth Shadlen, *Democratization Without Representation: The Politics of Small Industry in Mexico* (University Park: Pennsylvania State University Press, 2004).

34 Tasha Fairfield, "Business Power and Tax Reform: Taxing Income and Profits in Chile and Argentina," *Latin American Politics and Society* 52, no. 2 (2010): 37–71.

35 Eli Diniz and Renato Boschi, *Empresarios, Intereses e Mercado* (Belo Horizonte, Brazil: Editora UFMG, 2004).

36 Ben Ross Schneider, *Business politics and the state in 20th century Latin America* (New York: Cambridge University Press, 2004).

37 For an analysis of this logic in European PR systems, see Torben Iversen and David Soskice, "Distribution and Redistribution: The Shadow of the Nineteenth Century," *World Politics* 61, no. 3 (2009): 438–486.

38 Steven Griner and Daniel Zovatto, *Funding of Political Parties and Election Campaigns in the Americas* (San José: IDEA and OAS, 2005), 46.

39 David J. Samuels, "Pork Barreling Is Not Credit Claiming or Advertising: Campaign Finance and the Sources of the Personal Vote in Brazil," *The Journal of Politics* 64, no. 3 (2002): 845–863. The PT has been generous in rewarding contributors, Boas, Taylor, F. Daniel Hidalgo, and Neal Richardson. 2011. "The Spoils of Victory: Campaign Donations and Government Contracts in Brazil." Unpublished paper.

40 See, for example, Carles Boix, *Democracy and Redistribution* (New York: Cambridge University Press, 2003).

41 Layna Mosley, *Global Capital and National Governments* (New York: Cambridge University Press, 2004); Fairfield, "Business Power and Tax Reform."

42 Silva, *The State and Capital in Chile: Business Elites, Technocrats, and Market Economics*; Schamis, "Distributional coalitions" and Etchemendy, *Models of Economic Liberalization*; Michael Walton and Santiago Levy, eds., *The Inequality Trap and Its Links to Low Growth in Mexico* (Washington

D.C.: World Bank, 2009); Elizondo Mayer-Serra, Carlos, *Por Eso Estamos Como Estamos: La Economic Política de un Crecimiento Mediocre* (México City, Mexico: Debates, 2011).

43 Schvarzer, *La industria que supimos conseguir;* Ana Castellani, *Estado, empresas y empresarios: la construcción de ámbitos privilegiados de acumulación entre 1966 y 1989* (Buenos Aires, Argentina: Prometeo, 2009).

44 This blind spot is not limited to political scientists. Historians lament the virtual absence of business history from the historiography of Latin America: cf. Carlos Dávila and Rory Miller, eds., *Business History in Latin America* (Liverpool, UK: Liverpool University Press, 1999); James P. Brennan and Marcelo Rougier, *The politics of national capitalism: Peronism and the Argentine bourgeoisie, 1946–1976* (University Park: Pennsylvania State University Press, 2009).

45 Isabel Guerrero, Luis López-Calva, and Michael Walton, "The Inequality Trap and Its Links to Low Growth in Mexico," in *No Growth Without Equity*, ed. Michael Walton and Santiago Levy (Washington D.C.: World Bank, 2009).

19

INDIGENOUS POLITICS

Between Democracy and Danger

José Antonio Lucero

In the last decades of the twentieth century, Indigenous peoples in Latin America experienced a remarkable political resurgence. Through large-scale mobilizations, political party formation, and transnational networking, Indigenous actors forged powerful challenges to political and economic orders that had often worked to marginalize them. In the memorable phrase of Ecuadorian Kichwa leader Luis Macas, the 1980s was not a "lost decade" for Indigenous people, but a *"década ganada,"* a decade in which Indigenous people won. They won in challenging orthodox economic reforms, creating pressure for constitutional reforms, and in winning political office at local and national levels. The first decade of the twenty-first century, however, prompted new questions about those gains and debates over their consequences. This chapter examines the evolving scholarly approaches to Latin American Indigenous politics, major developments in the field, and recent debates about the contributions of Indigenous movements to democracy and development. The goal of this chapter is to demonstrate how the study of Indigenous politics has enriched the interdisciplinary study of Latin American politics by challenging our assumptions about the state, citizenship regimes, and social movements.

Approaches to the Study of "The Indian Problem"

The late twentieth century political resurgence of Indigenous peoples and identities caught many observers flat-footed. Reviewing the history of the study of Indigenous politics, one of the more conspicuous problems was that scholars seemed unaware that there was any problem at all. Among many political scientists, there was a long-standing assumption that racial or ethnic cleavages were less important in Latin America than in other regions of the world.[1] This non-finding was influenced in part by modernization theories from both Left and Right that predicted that "primordial" identification would yield to large categories of class or nation. Scholars also seemed to accept too willingly the official ideologies of many Latin American states with large Indigenous and Afro-Latino populations that "racial democracy" and racial mixing (*mestizaje*) had "saved" Latin America from the rigid racial hierarchies of states like the United States. Ironically, rather than celebrate difference, these nation-building discourse of racial democracy continued to rely on notions of national homogeneity ("we are all mestizo") and thus became, in Stutzman's apt formulation, "an all-inclusive ideology of exclusion."[2]

Within Latin America, there was a more complicated reading of what was often called "the Indian Problem," which translated into a view of Indigenous people as obstacles to modernity. In post-revolutionary Mexico, Lazaro Cárdenas declared that the task of the state was to "Mexicanize" the Indian (rather than Indianize Mexico). In mid-twentieth century Peru, one "solution" to the Indian problem was proposed by philosophers like José Carlos Mariátegui and political leaders like General Juan Velasco Alvarado who, in Mariátegui's formulation, saw the problem of the Indian as a problem of land. Land reforms and education programs were part of Velasco's revolutionary emancipation in the 1960s. General Velasco sought to banish the very word Indian from the political lexicon when he declared that the "Day of the Indian" would become the "Day of the Campesino." Despite these disavowals from national leaders, long and deep traditions of *indigenismo,* those artistic and political practices about Indigenous people created by non-Indigenous people, continued to celebrate the Indigenous past and folklorize the Indigenous present. Indigenous symbolism, so powerfully conveyed in the murals of Diego Rivera and Oswaldo Guayasamín, and even recognition of Indigenous languages, in the case of Velasco's failed experiment to officialize Quechua during his revolutionary government in Peru, served largely decorative functions for plans of modernization, agrarian reform, and national integration.

Nahuatl-speakers, Quechua-speakers, and other Indigenous peoples did not cease to become "Indians"—as this remained an all too available category to separate the rural *campo* from the modernizing city—but they formed part of the nation and state to the extent that they approached the state not as Nahua or Quechua peoples but as Mexican, Peruvian, or Bolivian campesinos. In the 1970s, Ecuadorian military dictator Guillermo Rodríguez Lara made the astounding declaration that there was no more "Indian problem" as "we all become white when we accept the goals of the national culture."[3]

Nevertheless, "Indian" communities did not disappear. As Xavier Albó and Deborah Yashar persuasively argue, the persistence of local associational networks is in part due to the unintended consequences of state policies during years of corporatist and populist attempts to, as Albó says, "rebaptize Indians as peasants." As states created local spaces for peasants to organize in legally recognized rural unions, cooperatives, and communities, it was possible for rural people to employ a "Janus-faced" posture in which they showed a productive "peasant" face to a modernizing state, but inwardly cultivated local Quechua, Aymara and other Indigenous identities and practices.[4]

Indigenous communities then were hardly isolated from national political and economic currents. Indeed, many scholars suggested Indigenous politics offered insights into the ways in which colonial legacies and enduring inequalities continued into republican and even democratic times. Mexican sociologist Pablo González Casanova was among the early analysts of the politics of "internal colonialism" who put in relief just how misleading promises of inclusionary orders had been.[5] Building on this insight, Yashar provided an especially clear view of how the changing place of Indigenous peoples in national political orders reveals much about the shifts in what she called "citizenship regimes" in Latin America, or the ways in which political subjects could make claims on civil, political and social rights within the context of distinct political-economic moments. In corporatist citizenship regimes, states or ruling parties provided social and political rights to those that identified with officially sanctioned associations, like peasant and worker federations, that were explicitly tied to the state. These corporatist mediating structures were the product of interventionist, nationalist and developmental states, and required a significant amount of resources in providing subsidies to the country side and pushing through agrarian reform in the face of elite opposition. That state model encountered significant problems during the crisis-prone decade the 1980s.

The economic shocks of oil and debt crisis wreaked havoc on Latin America during the 1980s and set the stage for structural adjustment policies that effectively dismantled the old corporatist state and led the way to the rise of "neoliberal citizenship regimes" throughout the region. The subsidies and credits that agrarian reform had made available were drastically diminished and life in the rural countryside became much harder. This economic transition coincided with democratic transitions of the 1980s. While political and civil rights were arguably enhanced by transitions away from authoritarian rule, social rights were scarce in the countryside during times of austerity and reform. In the language of social movement theorists, the *political opportunity structures* became more permissive at the very moment that economic pressures were getting more oppressive. No longer part of corporatist mediating structures, Indigenous people were able to move beyond what Andres Guerrero calls "ventriloquist" forms of representation (subordinate to peasant unions, political parties, or the state) and find their own national political voice, with the help of transnational allies like progressive churches and non-governmental organizations. These changes in the structures of interest mediation and the models of economic development allow us to understand the dramatic eruption of Indigenous politics during the 1990s.[6]

The "Return" of Indigenous Politics to Latin America

More than a few observers and activists noted that Indigenous movements were hardly part of the "new social movements" that were being celebrated in the post-industrial North Atlantic. Indeed, reaching back centuries, Indigenous leaders and scholars alike noted that there have been multiple moments of Indigenous insurgency since colonial times, including the remarkable waves of Andean rebellions in 1780–81 led by Túpak Amaru and Micaela Bastides (in what is now Peru) and Túpaj Katari and Bartolina Sisa (in what is now Bolivia). Though those massive mobilizations were put down by Spanish colonial authorities, their example entered the imaginary and pantheon of popular sectors like late twentieth-century Kataristas in Bolivia who mobilized around the (possibly apocryphal) dying words of Túpaj Katari who, according to Aymara oral traditions, as he was being literally drawn and quartered declared that he would return "made into millions."[7]

In another example of the multiple time-scales invoked by contemporary Indigenous movements, on January 1, 1994, the day that the North American Free Trade Agreement went into effect, ending Mexico's period of agrarian reform, an army of mostly Maya Indigenous people took the name of Emiliano Zapata who had mobilized for agrarian reform and collective rights during the Mexican revolution of 1910. The Zapatista Army of National Liberation (EZLN, in Spanish) became probably the best known Indigenous social movement in the view of some observers; it was also a "post-modern" revolutionary force in that most of its battles were waged on the new terrain of the Internet and global media rather than the jungle of Chiapas.

Though the Zapatistas were more familiar to international audiences, they burst on to the international scene several years *after* Andean and Amazonian Indigenous organizations had begun to mobilize and organize. In June 1990, the Confederation of Indigenous Nationalities of Ecuador (CONAIE) stunned political elites with their call for a peaceful nationwide *levantamiento* (the term used during the colonial period to refer to Indigenous uprisings), which forced a halt to a series of economic reforms and began a decade-long series of confrontations and negotiations with the national state which created unprecedented political openings for Indigenous people. CONAIE negotiated with the Ecuadorian government and the World Bank the creation of new agencies for Indigenous development and intercultural bilingual education, agencies which were controlled by leaders from CONAIE. Additionally, Indigenous movements in Ecuador also pushed for the inclusion of a set of collective rights that would form part of the constitutional reforms of 1998. With such mobilization strength to change the political landscape, Ecuador was hailed by many as a model to be followed by other Indigenous peoples.[8]

Electorally, Indigenous peoples also became important new actors in party systems that were notorious for their failure to adequately represent the interests or aggregate the demands of Indigenous people. The Andes were again the site of the most notable achievements. CONAIE, in collaboration with other popular organizations, founded the Plurinational Pachakutik Movement which registered respectable gains in its debut election in 1996, winning 10 percent of seats in the Congress and coming in third place in the presidential elections with 17 percent of the votes. Across the national and local races, Pachakutik candidates won a total of 76 positions. Though Pachakutik's electoral fortunes would decline in subsequent elections and its presidential candidate Luis Macas registered a humbling two percent of the vote in a defeat to Rafael Correa in the 2006 presidential elections, it continued to be competitive in several local races.[9]

While Ecuador's Indigenous electoral strength peaked in the mid 1990s, the most extraordinary experience for Indigenous electoral politics in Latin America took place in 2005 in Bolivia, as Evo Morales and his Movement toward Socialism Party won an unprecedented 54 percent of the vote, becoming the first self-identified Indigenous person to become president. Morales won an even more resounding victory in the election of 2010, winning 64 percent of the vote and further consolidating the electoral hegemony of the MAS in Bolivia.[10] In a particularly dramatic example of what James Holston calls "insurgent citizenship," Indigenous people in Latin America have been able achieve remarkable results with the political tools of barricades and ballot boxes. Those achievements have certainly varied across the region, but a consensus has emerged around the resources and opportunities that have enabled this Indigenous political (re-)emergence. These reflect changes on both global and national levels.

First, it is important to underline, following Alyson Brysk, that the Indigenous movement in Latin America was "born transnational." In every case of successful Indigenous mobilization, Indigenous organizations have become part of transnational networks that include non-governmental organizations that advance a variety of environmental or development agendas. Another ally has included that early transnational actor, the Church (both Catholic and Protestant) whose missionary and educational work often provided the early organizational materials that were used as Indigenous protest "scaled up" from community to national and even transnational levels. Moreover, several international organizations helped change the international recognition of Indigenous peoples and Indigenous rights. The most significant was undoubtedly the International Labor Organization Convention No.169 on Indigenous and Tribal Peoples, which, in various important provisions, provides for the participation of and consultation with Indigenous peoples in all issues that affect Indigenous communities and livelihoods. Significantly, ILO 169 also recognizes the rights of Indigenous peoples to collective forms of land tenure, alternative forms of justice, and access to employment and education (ILO 1999). ILO 169 came into effect in 1991 and has been ratified by most Latin American governments, though this does not mean that governments have honored its various provisions especially when dealing with extractive industrial activity in Indigenous territories.[11]

Other important international developments have included the United Nations Decade of Indigenous Peoples and the creation of a special unit within the World Bank to address issues concerning Indigenous people. These international changes have been part of a large shift in development thinking which some have called "development with identity" or "ethnodevelopment." As international multilateral organizations and NGOs began to channel resources to ethnodevelopment projects, new incentives were created for Indigenous recognition. It is also worth pointing out that the world historical moment in which these developments emerged (the early 1990s) coincided with the global crisis of the international Left, a collapse symbolically represented by the fall of the Berlin Wall. Now that traditional leftist causes were seemingly entering the "dustbin of history," Indigenous peoples seemed to emerge from their own histories of oppression and neglect and found new allies in transnational activist networks.[12]

Second, on the national level, a series of changes in the political environment provided new opportunities for Indigenous protest. At the broadest level, changing "citizenship regimes" discussed above, that took the region from corporatist and often authoritarian arrangements to neoliberal and democratic ones, offered a new mix of pressures and organizing spaces became available in many countries in Latin America. At the level of the party systems, weak and inchoate systems suffered dramatic periods of de- and re-alignment as a consequence of declining legitimacy, economic crisis, and even the brute biological fact of death of historic party leaders. In Bolivia, for instance, the deaths of Max Fernández, Carlos Palenque, and Hugo Bánzer generated fatal crises for their respective parties, of both Left and Right. Additionally, new decentralization schemes, often supported by national elites as ways to undermine regional rivals, created a new set of electoral arenas and resources which Indigenous people could now utilize for the construction of their own political projects.[13]

The rise of Indigenous politics, then, can be best understood as a response to a changing constellation of factors. Economically, neoliberal economic reforms change the state-society arrangement that once constrained Indigenous political energies within the confines of top-down corporatist structures and class identities. Politically, new transnational resources and networks allowed Indigenous people to enhance their organizational capacities and take advantage of new openings in changing political opportunity structures. There is a good deal of consensus around these points which are broadly structural and multi-scalar. Nevertheless, there have emerged a set of debates in the field of Indigenous politics over the coding of movement emergence, the confluence of neoliberal and multicultural politics, and the implications for democratic governance of the rise of Indigenous movements.

Debating Indigenous Politics

Movement Success and Failure

The interdisciplinary study of Indigenous politics, like all fields of study, is characterized by diverse perspectives and disagreements. Without pretending to offer an exhaustive survey, briefly I explore three instructive debates that can help clarify the methodological, theoretical, and normative assumptions that guide and perhaps divide the field.

The first debate centers on the seemingly straightforward question regarding where Indigenous movements have emerged and where they have not. As should be evident from the discussion above, there are a series of rather high profile cases of Indigenous movements. There is no doubt that Indigenous movements in Bolivia, Ecuador, and Mexico served to change the direction of national politics. Large scale mobilizations in these countries resulted in the removal of several presidents in the Andean cases and contributed to the demise of single-party rule in the Mexican case. Where controversy arises is over the case of Peru, the seemingly curious exception to the region-wide "return of the Indian" in the very heart of what was once the Inca Empire.[14]

Indigenous political actors in Peru, according to Albó, Yashar, and many others, are characterized by "weakness." At first blush, it is not surprising that Peru does look different from the other cases mentioned. Unlike Bolivia, Ecuador, or Mexico, the decade of the 1980s was not characterized by the largely peaceful organizing of communal and regional association networks, but by the brutal violence of an internal war between the state and leftist insurgents, most notably the Shining Path or Sendero Luminoso. Thus, the political opening and associational capacity that Yashar identifies as crucial for the development of Indigenous movements were notably absent in Peru. While pockets of politicized Indigenous identity exist in Peru, Albó argues that "ethnic identity and Indigenous organizations remained largely restricted to the smaller groups of the Amazonian region, scarce among the more numerous highland Quechua and Aymara, whose organizations continue to emphasize their 'campesino' identity over ethnicity." Compounding this weakness, several scholars note that Indigenous symbolic capital in Peru, and particularly highland Inca legacies, has been appropriated by elites, not popular sectors, in such a way that Indianness is emptied of its subversive potential. Even the election of the Andean-born Alejandro Toledo as president of Peru was hardly seen as an advance for "ethnically minded grassroots" but rather another elitist reformulation of the idea captured by Cecilia Méndez: "Incas yes, Indians no."[15]

Even with this brief account of contrasts between Peru and more clear-cut cases of Indigenous mobilization, it is possible to identify three criteria that scholars have used to distinguish strong from weak movements: identity, scale, and tactics. In terms of identity, new Indigenous movements reject imposed "class" identities and re-assert ostensibly more authentically "ethnic" self-representation. Indigenous identity, then, is a prerequisite for Indigenous mobilization. In terms of scale, strong Indigenous movements articulate local and regional organizations into a nationally cohesive political force. As Mariátegui noted long ago in Peru, without national linkages, Indigenous people would not realize their full political potential. Finally, regarding tactics, successful movements mobilize significant protests, marches, and blockades that resist state projects and influence changes in state policies. Indeed, some scholars have gone so far as to suggest that protest is not only an Indigenous tactic but has become "the primary characteristic of Indian ethnicity."[16] If these define success, they necessarily also lead us to the traits of failure. A movement is in trouble if it remains regional and fragmented, if it cannot forge an independent Indian identity, and if it is unable to mobilize visible political protest.

The need for strong and clear negative cases is a hallmark of positive political science, as having variation in outcomes makes possible the construction of falsifiable causal arguments. Thus Yashar makes effective use of the Peruvian exception to craft a very influential structuralist explanation of movement emergence. Nevertheless, scholars working with more interpretivist orientations suggest that the clarity of causal arguments obscure some salient points about Indigenous identities and contention.

First, it is important to be aware of the danger of teleological discussions in which social and cultural change moves in one particular direction, and thus, some are more advanced, while others must catch up. As Carlos Iván Degregori has noted, "perhaps it is not a matter of being behind or ahead, but rather of the distinct forms through which ethnicity is expressed in different countries."[17] Thus, it is worth exploring the possibility that rather than mutually exclusive, class and ethnic identities can and do co-exist.

Several scholars have made the case that the rise of class-based rural contention throughout the 1960s and 1970s was not a move against Indigenous identity. Rather, "Indigenous utilization of class based rhetoric was a political option that did not represent the loss of Indigenous culture, but was a strategy toward its empowerment."[18] While political struggle means that some identities and discourses are privileged over others, it is important to note that the politics of recognition remains dynamic and full of surprises. For instance, few would have expected former CONAIE president, Antonio Vargas, after leaving CONAIE to run for the presidency of the country with an Evangelical Indigenous political party. He lost badly in 2002, but two years later when President Lucio Gutierrez had his own falling out with CONAIE, he named Vargas to his government along with a representative of the indigenous Evangelical federation (FEINE). With Amazonian (Vargas is from the eastern lowlands) and Evangelical support, Indigenous movements have become fractured. CONAIE leaders speak of crisis and division, while FEINE itself struggles to maintain relations with the government but also keep from being co-opted by the state. Attention to alternative identities can help one understand how Ecuadorian unity has apparently come undone (at least for the moment.) Religion is an important and understudied axis of Indigenous identity.

Second, Indigenous people in Peru have been active politically on local, regional, national and transnational levels.[19] This is important clearly for empirical reasons, but also for conceptual ones. Looking for "national" scale activity has been a bias of much social movement theory that needs to be critically examined.[20] As Orin Starn argues, "the label 'grassroots movement' holds an assumption about the likelihood of growing taller and stronger." However, we should not automatically assume that this kind of community politics will always tend to move toward greater scales of political activity. As Starn notes for the case of the rondas campesinas, local community politics

> force us to recognize that there is nothing natural at all about a movement going regional, national, or global. A collection of tribes in the Amazon in Peru a neighborhood association in the United States or any other movement may join together as a force for change, or they may not, depending on many factors, as occurred with the rondas ... The failure of the rondas to grow into strong federations offers confirmation that even mobilizations for change can proceed in many ways besides up.[21]

By privileging national social movement organizations, scholars often tend to minimize the importance of local or regional actors that do impact national and transnational Indigenous politics.

Finally, there are various local and regional forms of contention that may not resemble "mainstream" tactics of protest and political campaigns. For instance, García's work on the politics of intercultural bilingual education, we find a surprising and unexpected example of Peruvian ethnic mobilization in the tensions between Indigenous Peruvians and Indigenous rights activists. Indigenous parents saw the implementation of bilingual education (designed by outsiders) as a way to keep their children from gaining access to Spanish and thus to greater economic opportunities. Using the same spaces activists developed to gain support from Indigenous peoples, Quechua parents devised strategies to challenge the imposition of education reform in their communities. For instance, the establishment of "parent schools" (*escuelas de padres*), designed by activists to explain the goals of bilingual education policies, quickly became a forum allowing parents to debate concepts such as citizenship, and to contest education reform. Another important strategy of Indigenous leaders was to promote the establishment of community-controlled schools that are *not* managed by the state, nor by NGOs. Discussion among Quechua community leaders about their *own* control of education implies a move toward their own self-determination, even if it does not come in the form of massive protests and marches. Other scholars have documented additional ways in which local peoples have engaged in important forms of contention such as challenging transnational development agendas in struggles over water management.[22] Such examples bear a family resemblance with other movements like the Pan-Mayan movement in Guatemala, where that movement has privileged education and alternative forms of knowledge and cultural production over mass demonstrations.[23]

What does this suggest then about how we think about the tactics of social movements? Perhaps one lesson is that high profile tactics may not always be the most "successful." A particularly glaring example of this, and one to which we will return, was provided on January 21, 2000, when Ecuadorian Indigenous leaders, if for only a few hours, had achieved what no other Indigenous movement in the region had achieved: it had removed an unpopular neoliberal president *and* formed part of a new government with elements from the military, a "Junta of National Salvation."[24] The Junta unraveled before the dawn of the next day. Immediately, many within and without the movement questioned the wisdom of this "rebellion." Critics attacked the secretive and non-democratic character of the coup, which marked a departure from the kind of social movement tactics CONAIE had used for over a decade. On the other hand, defenders noted that CONAIE retained its political power, as demonstrated by recent elections. In the 2002 elections, Pachakutik helped former colonel and leader of the January 21 "coup," Lucio Gutiérrez to win the presidential election. This too would be a pyrrhic victory as the alliance with the new president would last less than a year. Additionally, Gutierrez has managed to split CONAIE in unprecedented ways, a problem that would haunt the organization for years to come.

In Gramscian terms, Peru and Ecuador provide examples of wars of position (the slow going through many trenches of civil society) and wars of maneuver (the storming of government palaces). After decades of the Shining Path's bloody and destructive war of maneuver, Indigenous people have pursued social change in the various spaces and interstices of national, regional, and local civil society. Ecuador's CONAIE moved from a decade of the tactics of the war of position (in the streets and in the halls of government), only to turn to a momentary resort to the maneuver of a coup, which has unleashed a set of dynamics that have served to fragment and weaken CONAIE's place in national society. In the span of less than a decade, Ecuador's Indigenous movement went from being the "model" movement in the region to a cautionary tale about the dangers of success.

Neoliberal Multiculturalism

One of the more devastating rhetorical strategies against reform, Albert Hirschman reminds us, is the claim that any "purposive action to improve some feature of the political, social, or economic order only serves to exacerbate the condition one wished to remedy." In debates over multiculturalism the most powerful version of this "perversity thesis" has come in the form of an argument advanced by Charles Hale under the title, "the menace of multiculturalism:" rather than creating more egalitarian and inclusionary political orders, multiculturalism conspires with neoliberal market reforms to weaken, divide, and ultimately thwart challenges for radical reform. In an argument that owes much to Gramsci and Foucault, Hale argues that neoliberal multiculturalism operates through a cultural logic that divides "radical" and moderate forms of indigeneity, excluding the former and co-opting the later. We find similar sentiments in the work of Bret Gustafson, Peter Wade, and Andean scholars like Silvia Rivera and Luis Tapia. For all these authors "recognition" is hardly an innocent or innocuous act.[25]

Yet, as Van Cott suggested in the most comprehensive empirical review of the neoliberal multicultural thesis, no matter how cunning governing elites have been, official multicultural policies have in several cases been the paths toward more radicalized politics, while in other cases have led to the more limited reforms described by Hale and others. In her examination of several Latin American cases, Van Cott suggests a range of outcomes:

> On one end of the spectrum are states like Chile, Argentina, Peru, and Guatemala, in which neoliberal reforms were undertaken vigorously and now coexist with a modest set of MCPs, the latter limited primarily to language, education, and limited collective land rights. We can call this "neoliberal multiculturalism," borrowing from Hale and Gustafson. On the other end of the spectrum are countries like Ecuador and Venezuela with more expansive sets of multicultural policies that include considerable political representation and autonomy rights. In these countries popular, as well as elite, resistance has delayed the imposition of neoliberal reforms, and been accompanied by political and economic instability, party system fragmentation and decomposition, and widespread social protest. We can call this "populist multiculturalism" to convey the political context in which multicultural reforms were adopted in those countries.[26]

The location of different states between these neoliberal and populist poles, Van Cott argues, depends on the relative balance in the political arena between neoliberal elites, leftists, and Indigenous organizations. A closer examination of the recent history of Bolivia and Ecuador, two states coded by Van Cott as strong examples of multicultural implementation and currently part of South America's turn toward leftist populism, confirms and perhaps even further complicates this complex view of multiculturalism in Latin America.

Bolivia offers a particularly important test case for the neoliberal multicultural thesis. There is no question that multiculturalism and neoliberalism came together in the mid-1990s embodied by the administration of President Gonzalo Sánchez de Lozada, a University of Chicago-educated neoliberal technocrat, and Vice-President Victor Hugo Cárdenas, an Aymara social movement leader and educator. In the mid-1990s, sweeping decentralization, bilingual education, and agrarian legislation accompanied privatization in what Goni called the "Plan for All" (Plan de Todos). The articulation of official multicultural and neoliberal Bolivia had the effect of opening opportunities for Indigenous actors like the lowland confederation (CIDOB, Confederation of Indigenous Peoples of Bolivia) that accepted the terms of the new laws and did not challenge the new economic agenda of the government. At the same time, the new regime of the *pluri-multi* disadvantaged (at least initially) the more radical element of Indigenous actors like cocalero leader Evo Morales and highland Aymara nationalist Felipe Quispe whose anti-imperial and anti-neoliberal stance made his confederation, the CSUTCB an unlikely partner for the government. The effect of these official multicultural policies, as many scholars argue, has been to divide Indigenous actors into pragmatic and radical categories, and thus co-opt and further divide movements.

Beginning in 2000, however, a series of "wars"—over the privatization of water in Cochabamba, over taxes, over escalating militarization in the coca-growing tropics, and finally over the exportation of natural gas—have changed the dynamics in Bolivia. The cycle of protests began with the ill-considered privatization plan that resulted, in some cases, in a 400 percent increase in the cost of water in local communities.[27] Subsequent protests occurred in the valleys by the cocaleros led by Evo Morales, in the altiplano led by the radical Aymara Indianista leader of the highland confederation of rural workers (CSUTCB) Felipe Quispe, and subsequently by the Quechua leader of another faction of the CSTUCB, Román Loayza.[28] The waves of protest continued as Sánchez de Lozada returned to the presidency in 2002 and pursued unpopular tax hikes and an even less popular plan to export gas through the historic national enemy (Chile) to the contemporary imperial center (the United States). Hundreds of thousands of protesters took to the streets and demanded Sánchez de Lozada's resignation, and another round of mobilization forced, Carlos Mesa, the new chief executive, also out of office. Meanwhile, cocalero leader Morales, positioning himself as a pragmatic presidential contender, initially gave Mesa time and remained open to dialogue over how to deal with multinational natural gas corporations. Meanwhile, Quispe escalated his rhetorical assaults by calling for an independent Aymara state. After Mesa was unable to bring calm to the country, a caretaker government paved the way for the historic 2005 elections in which Evo Morales won a resounding, becoming the first Indigenous president to rule in this Indigenous-majority country. Though there are certainly questions about whether the Morales government has lived up to its promise of "decolonizing" Bolivia (the Guarani whose protest of the increased state participation in extractive industry on their lands have expressed their doubts), there is no question that the "neoliberal multiculturalism" of the 1990s was hardly an obstacle to the rise of Morales and a plausible case can be made that he could not have come to power without it.

Ecuador presents a perhaps more puzzling case about the consequences of multiculturalism. On the one hand, Ecuador was one of the strongest examples of not only Indigenous movement activity in the 1990s but also Indigenous-controlled policy making. With agencies for Indigenous development (CODENPE) and intercultural bilingual education (DIN-EIB) in the hands of activists from the main Indigenous confederation, CONAIE, Ecuador was hailed by many as a model. CONAIE and other Indigenous organizations proved to be powerful challengers to neoliberal policymakers including Jamil Mahuad, a Harvard-educated technocratic president, whose controversial handling of a financial crisis (which included the dollarization of the Ecuadorian economy), provoked massive discontent.

This crisis led to what was clearly a pivotal moment in the history of Indigenous politics, the dramatic events mentioned above, of January 21, 2000, in which CONAIE and sectors of the military led by Colonel Lucio Gutiérrez overthrew Mahuad and, for a few hours held power as a "Junta of National Salvation." The high command of the military, under U.S. pressure, abandoned the Junta and returned power to Gustavo Noboa, Mahuad's vice-president. Over the following months, all those involved in the coup were granted amnesty and the negotiations with the IMF were effectively stalled. Aside from dollarization, all the measures Mahuad had sought to implement were abandoned during the remainder of the Noboa administration. Gutiérrez, in alliance with CONAIE again, ran for president in 2002 and won, seemingly opening the doors to a renewed military-Indigenous alliance. However, Gutiérrez quickly disappointed his Indigenous partners. He signed a letter of intent with the IMF which signaled his intention to pursue austerity measures which again would be felt most sharply in the poorest sectors of society. In effect, "the economic policy of the [Gutiérrez] regime is hardly new, to the contrary, it is a more orthodox expression of the dominant thinking in Latin America over the past two decades" (Correa quoted in Acosta 2003–04). The Indigenous members of Gutiérrez's cabinet, Luis Macas and Nina Pacari, left the government in 2003. After less than a year in government, CONAIE returned to its role of opposition.

This time, however, the constellation of forces seems less favorable to the kind of leadership that CONAIE had exercised in the 1990s. First, Gutiérrez was more capable of dividing the Indigenous movement by reaching out to former CONIAE president Antonio Vargas who became Gutiérrez's Minister of Social Welfare (and was denounced as a traitor by CONAIE) as well as to other Indigenous actors including the national Evangelical Indigenous federation, (FEINE) and sectors of the Amazon still loyal to fellow Amazonian Antonio Vargas. Within the office of CONAIE and throughout Ecuador, which I visited in the summer of 2004, one heard worries about a severe organizational crisis. The decline in mobilizing capacity of CONAIE was all too obvious in the noticeably small "uprising" that CONAIE convoked to protest Gutiérrez's policies, only to be called off for lack of participation. Such a thing would have been unthinkable in the 1990s.

In 2005, Gutiérrez faced huge protests against his closing of the Supreme Court which forced him out of office. While Indigenous people were far from the main actors in this case of popular insurrection, which included students, unions and other popular sectors, in many ways Indigenous people paved the way for a broader expression of citizen outrage that took to the streets in defense of democracy. Still, there is no question that the Indigenous movement has lost some of the power that it had in the 1990s. In this last spike of social mobilization in the 1990s, Indigenous organizations were notably absent.

Similarly, Luis Macas' decision to run for president and avoid an alliance with leftist economist Rafael Correa (the ultimate winner in the 2006 elections) has been questioned by many. Macas won just over 2 percent of the vote and fell well short of reproducing the kind of victory that Evo Morales claimed in Bolivia. He also was far behind the party of Lucio Gutiérrez who even without Gutiérrez as a candidate placed third in the national election.

After Correa's election (and subsequent re-election) Indigenous organizations have been divided over how much to support Correa's progressive economic initiatives. As with Evo Morales, Correa's commitment to extractive mineral activities (oil and mining especially) have been the source of serious disagreement with many Indigenous organizations. Correa's declared intention to close the CODENPE development agency and remove the autonomy of the body that coordinate intercultural bilingual education, DINEIB, was seen by some as a reaction to the criticisms of Indigenous organizations and as further evidence of an Indigenous movement that is much weaker than in was only a few years ago. While the picture is complicated, it is clear that the Indigenous movement, which was weakened by its disastrous alliance with Lucio Gutiérrez, has yet to recover the cohesion and influence that it enjoyed during the 1990s. Ironically, as with the rise of Evo Morales, the decline of CONAIE also owes a debt to Ecuador's long moment of multiculturalism. The lesson about the "menace" of multiculturalism seems to be that it can contribute to breakthrough moments and disappointing retrenchment.

Indigenous Movements and Democracy

Finally, let us consider all too briefly, the controversy that has emerged over the contribution Indigenous politics have made to democracy. Much of the literature has made a strong case that the peaceful grassroots mobilization of a largely excluded population can only lead to a broadening and deepening of what in many cases were very thin versions of electoral democracy. Yashar's work in particular has demonstrated that by examining the development of Indigenous movements one could get a clear sense not only of the place where formal democracy did not reach, but also the large swath of the Amazon and Andes where the state, for all intents and purposes, had very little presence. In her analysis of the uneven states that had both excluded Indigenous people but yet allowed them some kind of de facto autonomy, Yashar made a powerful case for just how much the celebratory transitions-to and consolidation-of democracy literatures had missed. Indigenous movements have worked peacefully through civil society, through the creation of new political parties, and through coalitions with non-Indigenous people. As Yashar suggests, Indigenous social movements have been part of the democratic politics of the region. They respond to various sources of authoritarianism in society and state. Haciendas, mining and oil companies, and other economic actors continued colonial patterns of repressive labor practices that functioned to keep Indigenous people marginalized. The state also offered limited protection. It is important to recall that it was not until very 1979 that literacy requirements in Ecuador and Peru (which had effectively excluded many Indigenous people from voting) were finally eliminated.[29]

That said, Yashar and many others have signaled their concern with the potentially illiberal effect of Indigenous politics, especially for women as women continue to be less prevalent than men in leadership positions, though many Indigenous organizations insist that occidental definitions of gender are out of place. Andean organizations, for example, suggest that their communities are characterized by gender complementarity in ways that are different from Western gender relations. In local communities, it is very common for authority to be exercised as a couple, or *chachawarmi* as it is known in Bolivia. Even if men seem to be doing more of the talking, the argument goes, it is often said that women are the "real" decision makers. This discourse, like all discourses, is itself a kind of performance and should be interrogated and investigated empirically, as many scholars have been doing throughout the region.

In Chiapas, Mexico, for example, women Zapatista leaders like Comandantes Ramona and Esther have become important figures in regional and national politics. In Ecuador, there are many high profile women leaders in the Indigenous movement and there is a celebrated tradition of strong women leaders that goes back to the 1930s with historic figures like Dolores Cacuango. Yet, for many scholars these women are the exceptions that prove the rule about the enduring marginalization of women. In many communities in Mexico, for example, women have less of a voice in community meetings because many do not own land. In the community of Nicolas Ruís, Speed reports, community consensus still means the consensus of the men. As Comandante Esther explains "we have to struggle more because we are triply looked down on: because we are Indigenous, because we are women, because we are poor."[30]

Yet, as Speed again reminds us, it is important to question some of the assumptions that are behind this notion. First, the critique of multiculturalism as "bad for women" relies on a binary and oppositional scheme that pits "culture" against "gender." Indigenous women themselves have been among the most vocal in rejecting this false choice. In local, national and transnational spaces, many Indigenous women have carved out the room in which to forge spaces for the elaboration of projects at the intersection of indigeneity, gender, and class. In this task, they have often been aided by NGO agendas that increasingly institutionalize gender as a "transversal" component of their development work. While these spaces and collaborations are not without their own tensions and limitations, Indigenous women are not without the agency to work toward more equitable gender orders within the context of Indigenous projects of autonomy and self-governance. Additionally, it is worth pointing out that liberalism has also had a long history of being "bad for women." The liberal distinctions between private and public spaces have allowed many forms of home-grown authoritarianisms to go unquestioned for much of western history. One is reminded of Gandhi's famous response to a question about what he thought about Western civilization: "it would be a good idea." Similarly, the liberal promise of equal citizenship would also be a good idea, and remains one honored in the breach in too many places.

There have been increasingly vocal claims that Indigenous people are not only potential sources of illiberalism, but that they are on their way to become full blown security threats. Two recent voices of alarm come from writers affiliated with some of the policy-oriented worlds of think tanks and security studies. Consider one particularly loud version of this argument, put forth by Michael Radu of the Foreign Policy Research Institute:

> What is new, however, is the radicalization of Amerindians in the Andean region of South America and their adoption of anti-modern, anti-democratic, reactionary and strikingly fascistic attitudes. This trend is increasingly powerful in Bolivia, Ecuador, and Peru, and if not dealt with quickly, will lead to the region's collapsing into a political, economic, and social Stone Age—and it's becoming a danger to everyone, including the United States.[31]

Another writer, affiliated with the National Defense University, Martin Edwin Andersen has written about the twin dangers of Indigenous movements: they may enable radical populists like Evo Morales or be radicalized by even more dangerous forces, like those of radical Islam. He writes: "It is an open question whether some Chiapas and other Indians may seek alternative means of violent protest, ones that might parallel their disenchantment with Christianity and a subsequent embrace of militant Islam."[32] What evidence is there for such a claim? According to the source Andersen cites, Chris Zambelis writing in the *Jamestown Terrorism Monitor,* "no concrete evidence has surfaced to date substantiating such claims" about these possible terrorist links. Rather, Zambelis suggests "any potential inroads by al-Qaeda into Mexico is not likely to come through ties with Mexico's Muslim community—and this includes local converts or otherwise."[33] The more pressing security concerns, the report accurately suggests, are related to increasing drug violence (fueled by U.S. consumption, I might add) and weak political institutions, not Indigenous people.

Both writers yield more heat than light on the dangers of indigeneity and produce very little if any original research to support their claims. Usually based on long-distance readings of Indigenous critics, they are not the most compelling of critics. Yet, harder to dismiss is a leading Peruvian social scientist like Julio Cotler. Consider the following answer he gave to a reporter's question about the "danger" of Indigenous movements in Bolivia, Ecuador, and Peru:

> Let us begin by saying that in the Andean region, Indigenous people are the poorest of the poor, and Indigenous regions are the most poor and the most forgotten … Second, for a while now, interest groups around coca, to begin with, or related to the problem of mining, have begun to take form. They have people whom they can attack and from whom they can demand things. Increasingly, these ethnic groups or the leaders of these groups begin to make demands based on ethnic or

racial problems. Now, what is the danger that this can lead to? We already know the dangers; it can end in divided countries, in civil wars, in massacres. The Balkans is a good example. There are Bolivian leaders who want to eliminate all the whites ... This is no joke.[34]

In a subsequent interview in his Lima office, I asked Cotler about his views, and he explained that he, as a long-time critic of internal colonialism, was not against Indigenous movements ("that would be absurd," he said). Instead, he suggested that he was against a few extreme voices that spoke of expelling non-Indigenous people, voices affiliated with the campaign of Peruvian presidential candidate Ollanta Humala and some of the more radical parts of the Bolivian Indigenous movement. Moreover, one can respond to Cotler's worry about national fragmentation by wondering if Latin American states are "unified" to begin with. As Cotler's own pioneering work has demonstrated, they were (and continue to be) already "Balkanized" by internal colonialism as many Amazonian and Andean communities are literally at the margins of the nation state. Moreover, what Indigenous movements are asking for is not separation (Felipe Quispe, the one Bolivian leader Cotler probably had in mind, is an exception); they are asking for a new way to imagine nations and states, or more exactly, that many nations can exist within one state. Even thinking about the names of Indigenous organizations like the Army of National Liberation of Emiliano Zapata, EZLN, where the Z stands for Zapata—perhaps the greatest symbol of Mexican nationalism, or Confederation of Indigenous Nationalities of Ecuador, CONAIE (where E stands for Ecuador) , there is no doubt that these are very "national actors." Indeed, it is the claim of many movements that neoliberal elites are *anti*-national given that they are more worried about foreign investors than poor citizens. It is significant that in every negotiation with national government Indigenous peoples make claims not only about "ethnic" or "cultural" matters that are particular to them, but about broad economic issues that affect Indigenous and non-Indigenous peoples alike.

Conclusion: Future Directions

As researchers of indigenous politics examine the challenges that Indigenous peoples pose to existing models of development, democracy, and scholarship, several broad ideas unite the field. First, indigeneity is no longer (if it ever was) a concept associated with primitive, romantic, pre-modern, or pre-political rural worlds; Indigenous people are as modern (or post-modern) as anyone else. Second, Indigenous politics is and has always been transnational and multi-scalar. Third, the stakes of Indigenous politics are high, involving vexing issues such as resource conflicts, development models, and constitutional transformations. Finally, Indigenous people are hardly waiting for "outside" scholars to theorize their worlds for them. Across the Americas, Native intellectuals, in communities, universities, and movements, are challenging scholars to decolonize their own research methods and enter into collaborative and participatory modes of research to explore very difficult issues.

Indeed, the kind of political engagements taken up by Indigenous people are among the more urgent issues in contemporary politics. These include both *material* conflicts over land and natural resources and *cultural* negotiations between the symbolic universe of Native "rites" and a transnational vocabulary of Indigenous rights. Such a sharp distinction between material and cultural concerns has been questioned by scholars who interrogate regimes of recognition (like official multiculturalism) that carry double-edged possibilities of empowerment and co-optation, and the place of indigeneity in broader discussions about race. Additionally, the new legal landscape of Indigenous rights has generated a host of research questions regarding the new meanings of self-determination and rights to consultation in contexts where extractive industries often drill first and ask questions later. The field of Indigenous intercultural education also raises pressing questions about the competing understandings of decolonization and Native knowledge. Additionally, Indigenous feminisms and various understandings of gender relations offer important opportunities for the study of intersectionality.

These themes are necessarily general, but they suggest specific and pressing questions that inform the research agendas of scholars of Indigenous politics. How do Native forms of knowledge production provide alternative sources and strategies for organizing social struggles, theorizing politics, and narrating histories? How do Indigenous people organize and represent themselves in debates over citizenship, resource management, and participation? What consequences do tensions *within* Indigenous communities have on Indigenous politics? How have regimes of recognition affected struggles for greater equity and social inclusion? Why have these struggles resulted in a variety of outcomes? These questions are being explored in local community studies, in cross-national comparison, and through multi-sited ethnographies. In asking these questions and developing such skills, scholars are also forging new forms of collaborative research and dialogues that force a reconsideration of the intersections of ethics and epistemologies in the crafting of research projects.

Notes

1 Donald L. Horowitz, *Ethnic Groups in Conflict* (Berkeley: University of California Press, 1985).
2 Ronald Stutzman, "El Mestizaje: An All Inclusive Ideology of Exclusion," in Norman Whitten, ed., *Cultural Transformations and Ethnicity in Modern Ecuador*, pp. 45–94 (Urbana: University of Illinois Press, 1981); Peter Wade, *Race and Ethnicity in Latin America* (London: Pluto Press, 1997).
3 Stutzman, "El Mestizaje," p. 46.
4 Xavier Albó, "El retorno del indio" *Revista Andina* 9 (2) 1991: 299–357; Deborah J. Yashar, *Contesting Citizenship: Indigenous Movements and the Postliberal Challenge in Latin America* (New York: Cambridge University Press, 2005).
5 Pablo González Casanova, *Democracy in Mexico* (Oxford: Oxford University Press, 1972).
6 Yashar, *Contesting Citizenship*.
7 Thomson provides a different account of the last moments of Túpaj Katari's life, but also a remarkable portrait of Andean insurrections in the 1780s. Sinclair Thomson, *We Alone Will Rule: Native Andean Politics in the Age of Insurgence* (Madison: University of Wisconsin Press, 2002).
8 Yashar, *Contesting Citizenship;* José Antonio Lucero, *Struggles of Voice: The Politics of Indigenous Representation in the Andes* (Pittsburgh: University of Pittsburgh Press, 2008).
9 Donna Lee Van Cott, *From Movements to Parties: The Evolution of Ethnic Politics* (Cambridge: Cambridge University Press, 2005).
10 Van Cott, *From Parties to Movements;* Pablo Stefanoni, "Bolivia despues de las elecciones: ¿Hacia dónde va el evismo?" *Nueva Sociedad,* 225 (Jan./Feb. 2010), pp. 4–17.
11 Alyson Brysk, *From Tribal Village to Global Village: Indian Rights and International Relation in Latin America* (Stanford: Stanford University Press, 2000); A. Bebbington et al., "Mining and social movements: struggles over livelihood and rural territorial development in the Andes," *World Development* 36 (12) 2008, pp. 2888–2905.
12 Brysk, From Tribal Village to Global Village; Robert Andolina, Nina Laurie, and Sarah A. Radcliffe, *Indigenous Development in the Andes: Culture, Power, and Transnationalism* (Durham: Duke University Press, 2009).
13 Van Cott, From Parties to Movements; Kathleen O'Neill, "Decentralization as an Electoral Strategy," *Comparative Political Studies*, 36 (9) 2003, pp. 1068–1091.
14 More extensive and detailed explorations of the Peruvian case can be found in María Elena García, *Making Indigenous Citizens: Identity, Development, and Multicultural Activism in Peru* (Stanford:

Stanford University Press, 2005); María Elena García and José Antonio Lucero, "'Un País Sin Indígenas'? Re-thinking Indigenous Politics in Peru, in Nancy Grey Postero and Leon Zamosc, *Indigenous Struggles in Latin* America (Brighton, UK: Sussex, 2004), 158–188; José Antonio Lucero and María Elena García, "In the Shadows of Success: Indigenous Politics in Peru and Ecuador," in Marc Becker and Kim Clark, eds., *Highland Indians and the State in Modern Ecuador* (Pittsburgh: University of Pittsburgh Press. 2007); Maria Elena García and José Antonio Lucero, "Authenticating Indians and Movements: Interrogating Indigenous Authenticity, Social Movements, and Fieldwork in Contemporary Peru," in Laura Gotkowitz, ed., *Histories of Race and Racism: The Andes and Mesoamerica from Colonial Times to the Present* (Durham: Duke University Press, 2011). The current chapter draws significantly from these works.

15 Yashar, *Contesting Citizenship*; Xavier Albó, "Ethnic Identity and Politics in the Central Andes: The Cases of Ecuador, Bolivia, and Peru," in Jo-Marie Burt and Philip Mauceri, eds., *Politics in the Andes: Identity, Conflict, Reform* (Pittsburgh: University of Pittsburgh Press, 2004), pp. 32–33, Cecilia Méndez, *Incas si, Indios no: Apuntes para el estudio del nacionalism criollo en el Perú* (Lima: Instituto de Estudios Peruanos). For more on Toledo's (in)action in the area of Indigenous politics see García and Lucero, "'Un País Sin Indígenas'?"

16 Les Field, "Who are the Indians? Re-conceptualizing Indigenous Identity, Resistance, and the Role of Social Science in Latin America."*Latin American Research Review* 29 (3) (1994): 239; for a more detailed critique of these criteria see Lucero and García, "In the Shadows of Success."

17 Carlos Iván Degregori, "Identidad étnica: movimientos socials y participación política en el Perú," in Alberto Adrianzén et al., *Democracia, Etnicidad, y Violencia Política en los Países Andinos* (Lima: IEP/IFEA, 1993), 128.

18 Marisol De la Cadena, "Reconstructing Race: Racism, Culture, and Mestizaje in Latin America," *NACLA, Report on the Americas* 34:6 (2001), 20.

19 García and Lucero, "'Un País Sin Indígenas'?"

20 Part of the bias stems from the genealogy of "social movement" that leading scholars like Charles Tilly have popularized. Tilly's historical sociological work in Europe, and especially in Britain, argues that the social movement as a particular form of contention emerged in reaction to the rise of national state structures. The emergence of the social movement marked a shift from local and direct (18th century) forms to national and indirect (19th century) forms. Charles Tilly, *Social Movements, 1768–2004* (New York: Paradigm Press, 2004).

21 Orin Starn, *Nightwatch* (Durham: Duke University Press, 1999), 256.

22 Paul Gelles, "Andean Culture, Indigenous Identity, and the State in Peru," in *The Politics of Ethnicity: Indigenous Peoples in Latin American States*, ed. David Maybury-Lewis (Cambrdige: Harvard University Press, 2002).

23 Kay Warren, "Indigenous Movements as a Challenge to the Unified Social Movement Paradigm for Guatemala," in *Cultures of Politics, Politics of Cultures: Re-visioning Latin American Social Movements*, eds. Sonia Alvarez, Evelina Dagnino, and Arturo Escobar (Boulder: Westview Press, 1998), 165–195; see also Carol Smith's chapter in this volume.

24 Some might say that Bolivia also shares this distinction. Indigenous protests in Bolivia forced President Gonzalo Sánchez de Lozada out of office in 2002. It is also true that an Aymara political leader, Victor Hugo Cárdenas, had been in an earlier Sánchez de Lozada administration as Vice President. Unlike Ecuador, Bolivian Indigenous presence in the Executive is more the result of elite electoral consideration than social movement pressure. The near victory of cocalero leader Evo Morales almost succeeded in translating social movement power into electoral victory. In congressional and local elections, Morales and his MAS parties have done much better.

25 Hale, Charles. 2002, "Does Multicularalism Menace? Governance, Cultural Rights, and the Politics of Identity in Guatemala," *Journal of Latin American Studies* 34: 485–524; Albert Hirschman, *The Rhetoric of Reaction: Perversity, Futility, Jeopardy* (Cambridge: Harvard University Press, 1991), 7.

26 Donna Lee Van Cott, "Multiculturalism against Neoliberalism in Latin America," in *Multiculturalism and the Welfare State*, eds. Keith Banting and Will Kymlicka (Oxford: Oxford University Press, 2006), pp. 272–296, quotation at p. 295.

27 Even officials from the World Bank called the privatization scheme a "fiasco" in terms of design and implementation, and formally withdrew support for the plan. See Michael Walton, "Neo-

liberalism in Latin America: Good, Bad, or Incomplete?" *Latin American Research Review*, 39:3, (2004) 165–183.

28 In 2003, the CSUTCB splintered into two groups: one led by Quispe, the other by Loayza. Quispe was the main figure in the Aymara altiplano while Loyaza commands a greater following in the Quechua valleys. The Confederación Unica was anything but "unica" (Lucero 2008). The subsequent CSUTCB leader, Isaac Avalos, continued to encounter internal divisions in the organization.

29 Yashar, *Contesting Citizenship.*

30 Shannon Speed, "Rights at the Intersection: Gender and Ethnicity in Neoliberal Mexico," in *Dissident Women: Gender and Cultural Politics in Chiapas,* eds. Shannon Speed, R. Aida Hernández Castillo, and Lynn M. Stephen (Austin: University of Texas Press), 2006, p. 206.

31 Michael Radu, "Andean Stormtroopers" Foreign Policy Research Institute, www.frontpagemagazine.com, February 9, 2005.

32 Martin Edwin Andersen, *Peoples of the Earth: Ethnonationalism, Democracy, and the Indigenous Challenge in "Latin" America* (Lanham, MD: Lexington Books, 2010), p. 78.

33 Chris Zambelis, "Islamic Radicalism in Mexico: The Threat from South of the Border," *Jamestown Terrorism Monitor,* 4 (11) June 2, 2006, www.jamestown.org/single/?no_cache=1&tx_ ttnews[tt_news]=790. Accessed June 5, 2010.

34 Julio Cotler, "Existen grupos de interés muy fuertes alrededor del tema minero," Interview conducted by Cecilia Valenzuela, July 4, 2005, http://agenciaperu.com/entrevistas/2005/jul/ cotler.htm.

20

RACE, POLITICS, AND AFRO-LATIN AMERICANS

Ollie A. Johnson III

This chapter explores race and politics in Latin America. Research has confirmed pervasive racial stratification throughout the region. Latin Americans of lighter skin complexions and more European features tend to be in better economic and political positions than Latin Americans of primarily indigenous and African ancestry. Widespread racial discrimination has sparked political organizing and activism which have resulted in legislation to combat racism and create more opportunities for social mobility among Latin America's most vulnerable citizens. While indigenous social movements and political activism have received abundant attention (see chapter 19, this volume), African-descendant activism has been neglected by political scientists as well as news media. This chapter will highlight some of the most important activist, policy, and legislative initiatives relative to Afro-Latin Americans.[1]

The chapter has two key points. First, although contested by scholars, race is an indispensably relevant concept for understanding Latin politics. Second, Afro-Latin Americans represent a large population and, though distributed unevenly throughout the region and within specific countries, play central roles as citizens, activists, and politicians. The main argument is that racial prejudice and discrimination contribute to racial inequality and the marginalization of the black populations. Racial oppression of Afro-Latin Americans is partially disguised by myths of racial democracy and harmony. These myths powerfully influence how Latin Americans see themselves racially and in relation to the United States.

In order to focus on outstanding scholarly contributions and dynamic aspects of racial politics, this chapter is divided into five sections. The first section examines how scholars have defined race and debated its meaning. The second section highlights racial ideologies and racism. The history of Latin American slavery and racial oppression has contributed greatly to contemporary racism and racial inequality. The third section briefly outlines racial inequality and gives a sense of the size of the Afro-Latin American population. The next section emphasizes the explicitly racial dimensions of politics in Latin America by describing social movements and activities of black Latin Americans. The fifth section examines government initiatives and public policies addressing black community issues and promoting racial equality. The conclusion highlights the need for additional research. Throughout the chapter, most of the examples and illustrations come from countries with larger black populations. However, it should be noted that the urgent need for research on race and politics applies to all countries and sub-regions of Latin America.

Race: Identities and Categories

Race is a contested concept. Some scholars believe that the term is inherently unscientific and as a result should not be used. Kwame Anthony Appiah and Naomi Zack have reviewed the problematic definitions and uses of the concept over the nineteenth and twentieth centuries. They conclude that the concept itself is racist because it divides humanity into groups based on alleged corresponding essences which in fact do not exist. They maintain that the concept cannot and should not be salvaged.[2] Other scholars argue that despite past racist uses of the concept, race can be used to understand politics and society. Michael Omi and Howard Winant define race as a social, cultural and political concept that is used to distinguish certain groups of human beings based in part on physical appearance. Omi and Winant emphasize that the social, cultural, and political struggles involved in how racial groups are identified vary by and within countries thereby allowing scholars to use race without anchoring the term in biology or genetics. They also offer the concept of racial formation as a way to focus on how race is created, recreated, and experienced by human beings. According to their perspective, race is central to the human experience and not reducible to class or other "more important" variables.[3]

In Latin America, six racial groups are most prominent. Whites, blacks, and indians (indigenous people) are the groups which came into contact and interaction during the early period of European colonialism and slavery in the Americas. Mestizos (whites and indians), zambos (indians and blacks), and mulattos (blacks and whites) are the groups classified as the products of racial mixing or miscegenation of these base groups. Large scale immigration from Asia, the Middle East, and other regions has also contributed to Latin America's racial and ethnic diversity. The above categories represent a basic overview and simplification of the social construction of race. Race, ethnic, and color identities are complicated by the political, social, and cultural diversity of the Latin America. Finally, race is best understood if approached by multiple levels of analysis.[4]

Officially, few countries in Latin America have consistently conducted racial censuses. As a result, governmental information on racial composition is incomplete. Scholars have conducted surveys and studies which complement official data and form the basis for estimates for different racial or color groups. In addition, political actors often give their estimates and commentary. For example, blacks and indigenous activists regularly charge government officials with undercounting their groups in official studies.[5] In her study of race and national censuses, Melissa Nobles shows how the Brazilian national census, carried out regularly since 1872, exemplified dramatic changes regarding race. In some censuses, race or color was not included. In the others, the terms were changed. Prior to the 1991 census, black activists campaigned to encourage Brazilians to identify themselves accurately given fear that respondents were describing themselves in terms that indicated lighter skin tones. Nobles concludes that census-taking and race-counting are not neutral, objective, and scientific inquiries, but rather political processes that respond to and help explain the interests, values, and conflicts of different political actors and constituencies.[6]

Mixture

Mestizaje or *mestiçagem* refers to racial and cultural mixture and distinguishes Latin America from the United States regarding key aspects of race, politics, and culture. The public recognition of this mixing, combining, or blending of people of different racial lineages is widespread. Popular terms like "mestizo," "zambo," "mulatto," "moreno," and others

303

signify and represent mixture. The legitimacy of mixture also was the basis for cross-racial alliances in social movements, political activities, and electoral campaigns. Most important, these synthetic identities became intertwined with nationalist movements that promoted aspects of indigenous and black culture. Music, dance, food, religion, and other cultural markers associated with oppressed groups are often used as symbols of national identity. Alejandro de la Fuente and Livio Sansone note that racial experiences in Cuba, Brazil, and other Latin American countries made very difficult the emergence of the strict, rigid, and explicit system of racial segregation which characterized the southern United States.[7]

Peter Wade agrees that mestizaje is central to the Latin American experience. He argues that mestizaje should be seen as both ideology and lived experience. While the concept implies hybridity, sameness, and homogeneity, in a recent comparative analysis of popular music in Colombia, religious practice in Venezuela, and family relations in Colombia and Brazil, the concept is seen to have inclusive and exclusive dimensions. At the same time that the ideology and lived experience can bring people together, they can also reproduce racial-cultural difference within individuals, families, and communities. Consequently, along with mestizaje, related concepts such as blackness, indigenousness, and whiteness are constantly recreated.[8]

Although mestizaje is popular in much of Latin America, not enough studies have been done to fully understand accepted notions of identity. In Peru, Tanya Golash-Boza conducted an ethnograhic case study in the Afro-Peruvian community of Ingenio and the capital of Lima. She concluded that among her Afro-Peruvian interviewees, there was no effective buffer category between blacks and whites. She found that the key distinction was between racial categories and color labels. The former tended to be mutually exclusive group classifications (black, white, or cholo) and the latter individual descriptors that represent a continuum (from lighter to darker) and referred primarily to complexion and hair texture. According to Golash-Boza, despite the lack of an effective mulatto category, in Peru there is a societal preference for lighter skin and straighter hair.[9]

In contrast to Peru and other Latin American countries, Brazil has more census and government data available by skin color. Approximately one half of the population is white and the other Afro-Brazilian (i.e., brown and black). The other census categories of yellow and indigenous are each less than 1 percent. Edward Telles, following Livio Sansone, notes that there are at least three major ways to understand Brazilian racial classification as color classification. The official census uses five terms: white, brown (pardo), black, yellow, and indigenous. The popular or mass way of classifying by appearance leads to many colors, terms, or labels. The third way is a biracial approach: black (combined brown and black census categories) and white. This approach is used by academics and black movement activists who see more similarities than differences between brown and black. Telles emphasizes that Brazilians think of race in color terms. When asked in an open-ended question about which color they are, Brazilians give many answers. For example, in a widely-cited survey from 1976, 135 colors were given. However, then and now, more than 90 percent of Brazilians use one of seven color terms to identify themselves. Racial identity (self-classified and interviewer-classified) in Brazil is also influenced by and generally weaker than, though not reducible to, other identities like class, gender, education, and region.[10]

Other countries in Latin America often have less reliable information regarding racial identity. Colombia has a large population of Afro-descendants but exactly how large is unclear. The highest populations of black Colombians are in the Pacific and Atlantic coastal regions (as a percentage of the population) and in the major cities (in absolute numbers).

There is no consensus on the number of Afro-Colombians. The low range of 10 percent stated by the government census bureau is challenged by estimates of 25 percent or more according to academic and activist research. Despite uncertainty regarding their population figures, African descendants have played major roles in Colombian history even if they have not been identified, or identified themselves, in racial terms.[11]

Racial Ideologies and Racism

The ideology or myth of racial democracy lives on in Latin America. This view holds that widespread racial mixture should be a source of pride and that race relations are more harmonious and characterized by less conflict and hostility than race relations in segregated societies such as the United States and South Africa. Furthermore, the myth perpetuates the falsehood that in Latin America racial prejudice and discrimination are minimal. The evident subordinate positions of indians and African descendants are explained as economic divisions attributable to exploitative capitalism and widespread poverty. The paradigm of racial democracy and related notions were initially popularized by Latin American intellectuals such as Gilberto Freyre, José Vasconcelos, José Martí, and Andrés Eloy Blanco. They were critical of the notions of genetic or biological inferiority of blacks and indigenous groups which implied dim prospects for national progress and advancement in the late 1800s and early 1900s.[12]

The staying power of the myth of racial democracy is due to the fact that it represents different things for different sectors of society; a positive reality for national elites, a goal to be achieved by disenfranchised and marginalized citizens, and a source of national and regional pride for all. Though projecting the racially mixed individual, i.e., mestizo, mulatto, or moreno, as the prototypical citizen, racial democracy did not break completely with the reality and ideal of whitening or whiteness. For many Latin Americans, the ideology of racial democracy became an effective tool for criticizing and delegitimizing black political organizing and advancement efforts as examples of black racism and inappropriate efforts to mirror activities of black Americans in the United States.[13]

As a response and an alternative to racial democracy, the black nationalist or pan-Africanist perspective highlights that the experience of Spanish and Portuguese colonialism, slavery, and racial oppression created a structure of white supremacy in the Americas. For three centuries (1500s–1800s), blacks and indians individually and collectively were directly and explicitly marginalized and exploited. Resistance to slavery and abuse was constant as Africans and their descendants fought against, fled, escaped, survived, and adapted to a brutal reality. The abolition of slavery in the 1800s did not automatically improve the living conditions of formerly enslaved people. By 1900, many political and economic elites had embraced the concept of whitening, believing that European immigration would help them overcome the negative implications of large African-descendant populations. These implications were based on racist notions of white superiority and black inferiority.[14]

After slavery, European immigration whitened the populations of some countries in Latin America such as Argentina, Brazil, Cuba, and Uruguay. Countries such as Panama, Costa Rica, and the Dominican Republic experienced growth of their black populations because of immigration from English-speaking Caribbean islands. By the 1930s, white Latin American leaders began to reject the explicit whitening ideals, but not necessarily the negative black images and stereotypes behind them. While African-derived culture, especially religion, music, and dance, became more accepted and sometimes celebrated, black people were denied equal employment and educational opportunities. In countries like Mexico, Cuba, Brazil, and Venezuela, the celebration of cultural and racial mixture as central to national unity and identity became prominent.[15]

Recent studies show that racial prejudice and discrimination continue against browns and blacks. In several national surveys of racial attitudes, Brazilians have consistently more negative attitudes toward browns and blacks than whites.[16] In terms of personal attributes such as intelligence, honesty, education, and manners, whites are ranked higher. In terms of professions, whites rank higher. Even when experiments are done to remove possible effects of class, Brazilians are racially prejudiced against browns and blacks. When Brazilians are asked who they want their daughter to marry, they consistently chose a white male over a brown and black male regardless of occupation; thereby establishing in this instance that race or color is more determinative than class. Stanley Bailey highlights that most Brazilians believe that racial prejudice and discrimination exist in Brazilian society.[17]

Elisa Larkin Nascimento defines racism as "a complex system of psycho-social, cultural, economic and political destitution, depriving a people of their history, identity, dignity, and basic humanity."[18] Telles notes that racial discrimination in Brazil involves formal and informal acts with major negative consequences for Afro-Brazilians. Because negative stereotypes against blacks and browns are pervasive, preferential treatment within the family, school system, labor market, and law enforcement combine to give advantages to whites and disadvantages to Afro-Brazilians. The myth of racial democracy often disguises racial discrimination and makes it more difficult for victims to organize against it.[19]

Racism manifests itself regularly in Latin America. There are many more qualitative case studies of racism in Latin America than national or sub-national public opinion surveys. However, the specific acts, institutions, and structures vary by country. In the Dominican Republic, Ernesto Sagás and David Howard highlight that anti-Haitianism has been a dominant racist ideology in the Dominican Republic since the mid-1800s and remains a vital force in contemporary Dominican society. The ideology has been used politically by Dominican elites to discriminate against Haitians, Haitian-Dominicans, and dark-skinned Dominicans. This nationalist ideology is so powerful that many Afro-Dominicans subscribe to it. A scandalous example of the ideology at work involved the racist attacks against popular Afro-Dominican politician and presidential candidate Jose F. Peña Gomez during his presidential campaigns in the 1990s. Peña Gomez and other Dominican leaders have been hesitant to strongly and directly denounce the racism of anti-Haitianism.[20]

Mark Sawyer, Yesilernis Peña, and Jim Sidanius recently conducted innovative research in Cuba, Puerto Rico, and the Dominican Republic and similarly concluded that racial prejudice against blacks was extensive. Despite distinct national political regimes, civil societies, and government relations with the United States among the three islands, survey research indicated that whites have the highest and blacks the lowest social status. These scholars state that despite widespread interracial marriage and miscegenation, the islands clearly represent Caribbean versions of Latin American color hierarchy or pigmentocracy. Accordingly, they find little evidence for the notion that they have less racial prejudice than the United States.[21]

Venezuela has a reputation of being one of the most racially blended countries in Latin America. Many Venezuelans consider their country a "racial democracy" where miscegenation and mixing over time have created harmonious race relations. That image is incomplete. In Venezuela, as in other Latin American "racial democracies," the ideology of mestizaje rests on the historical reality of racial violence, i.e., European colonialism, slavery, and forced racial mixing by rape. Scholars have documented a series of negative stereotypes associated with indigenous and African descendants in Venezuela. President Hugo Chavez Frias and some of his Afro-Venezuelan political appointees have been attacked regularly in strong racist terms by the opposition. Their brown complexions, facial features, hair textures, and humble origins have all been ridiculed by critics as markers of unfitness for office.[22]

Ariel E. Dulitzky argues that most Latin American governments have been in complete denial regarding the widespread racial discrimination and racism in their countries. He emphasizes that concepts such as racial democracy, racial melting pot, racial harmony, and mestizaje to describe race relations have misrepresented reality and enabled leaders to compare their societies favorably to the United States where brutal, violent, and legal segregation held sway for most of the twentieth century. Dulitzky and other scholars suggest that Latin American elites have resisted thorough research and data collection because they know that the results would reflect poorly on their countries and the region.[23]

Silvio Torres-Saillant believes that racial and ethnic prejudice remains severe in Latin America and the Caribbean. This prejudice results in policies and practices that devastate indigenous and African-descended people. Given the enormity of the problem, his view emphasizes that scholars should feel a moral urgency in their investigations.

> White supremacy has been the conceptual glue that holds together the cultural logic of spoliation, discrimination, compulsory invisibility, and genocide in the hemisphere. Whether by preserving the exclusionary discourse of monoethnicity in the face of observable ethnic diversity or by paying lip service to pluralism while promoting a homogenous picture of the visage of the nation, Eurocentric formulations of national culture and the seduction of the Caucasian ideal have given currency to schemes of thought that endanger the mental and physical well-being of distinct groups among the peoples of Latin America and the Caribbean.[24]

Several scholars have noted the similarities between Cuba, the Dominican Republic, and Puerto Rico regarding race and politics. Despite dramatic differences in regime type, the three societies, as Ernesto Sagás puts it, "are ruled by white or light-skinned elites."[25] In their major qualitative studies, Sagás and Howard also note that the Dominican Republic and the Caribbean demonstrate that Latin American societies with large racially mixed populations can also have significant racial prejudice, stereotyping, and discrimination against darker citizens of their countries. Leaders of these Caribbean and Latin American societies often celebrate racial harmony and a lack of racial segregation despite centuries of racial slavery, racist Spanish colonial rule, and contemporary negative attitudes about blacks.[26]

Racial Inequality

Given the reality of substantial racial discrimination and racial inequality in Latin America, many countries in the region should be described as color hierarchies and pigmentocracies. White and lighter-skinned Latin Americans are over-represented among the region's political, economic, and cultural elites. Indigenous and black people are over-represented among the region's poor and marginalized classes. Black Latin Americans have enjoyed great success as athletes and musicians. On the other hand, it is rare to see dark-skinned Afro-descendants as core members of a national government's economic policy-making team or as prominent members of a country's leading corporations or business associations. Despite long-term and widespread miscegenation and interracial marriage, blackness is still stigmatized as negative, ugly, and unworthy while whiteness connotes beauty, intelligence, and trustworthiness.[27]

Although Latin American governments do not uniformly collect comprehensive census data disaggregated by race, ethnicity, or color, the available information confirms that poverty and inequality remain significant problems. In 2010, nearly one third of Latin Americans were poor and 13 percent were extremely poor. In addition, the poorest sectors of Latin American society represented a small fraction of overall income and wealth. Latin America remains one of the most unequal regions in the world. Latin American governments are still not investing enough resources in quality education for young people and other areas of social spending to decisively reduce the levels of poverty and inequality. This statement does not deny the recent attention that some countries have given to the theme of social inclusion and progress with equity. Some national governments have collaborated with the World Bank, Inter-American Development Bank, and other institutions to understand how social and economic stratification affect the group that has received the least study: Latin Americans of African ancestry.[28]

African descendants represent approximately 30 percent of the region's population. Brazil, Colombia, Venezuela, Cuba, and the Dominican Republic have the largest African-descendant populations. Afro-descendants are also estimated to be at least 5 percent of the population in Panama, Ecuador, Puerto Rico, Nicaragua, Peru, and Uruguay. Overall, Afro-Latin Americans are poorer and less educated. They also have more difficulty accessing decent housing, employment, and health care. Recent statistical studies confirm that racial inequality is extensive and that blacks and indigenous groups are poorer than whites and mestizos. The countries with more accessible racial and ethnic census data are Brazil, Ecuador, Costa Rica, Honduras, and Guatemala. Over the past three decades, case studies of the black experience in Latin America have confirmed that poverty, inequality, and major community and personal difficulties are common features of life. Despite the tremendous demographic, geographic, political, and social diversity of the region, African descendants share the experiences of racial discrimination, economic marginalization, cultural exploitation, and political under-representation.[29]

Edward Telles has demonstrated that Brazil remains deeply racially unequal because of hyperinequality, a discriminatory glass ceiling, and a racist culture. These three factors have intertwined and conspired since the abolition of slavery in 1888 to recreate racial hierarchy. Telles shows how racial discrimination against browns and blacks coexists with class discrimination against working class and poor Brazilians to limit educational, employment, and other opportunities for social mobility. Simultaneously, Telles affirms that Brazilians have high degrees of interracial socio-cultural sociability. These visible measures of horizontal relations do not invalidate the compelling evidence that racism, racial discrimination, and racial inequality remain major features of Brazilian race relations.[30]

Cuba is unique in Latin America because the country made substantial progress toward creating a more racially egalitarian society. The first three decades of the Cuban Revolution witnessed the elimination of racial segregation, the making of racial discrimination illegal, and the provision of unprecedented education and employment opportunities and health care access to the entire population. To some degree, these Cuban advances were reversed with the collapse of the Soviet Union and the interruption of international trade, aid, and subsidies to the Cuban economy. The special period of economic crisis confirmed that the revolution did not defeat racial hierarchy. In fact, explicit racial discrimination returned in many forms.[31] Mark Sawyer's concept of "inclusionary discrimination" and ethnographic and survey research in Cuba highlight the complex Cuban reality where "blacks had formal and symbolic inclusion in the state at the same time that a significant racial gap remained between blacks and whites."[32]

Social Movement and Political Activity

In the last 30 years, Afro-Latin Americans have achieved impressive gains in social movement activism, political organization, and mobilization. Black leaders and groups have publicly criticized racial prejudice, discrimination, and inequality in strong terms. This reality contrasts with the period of the early 1970s for which Anani Dzidzienyo observed minimal black group political activity. Many blacks suffered under and fought against authoritarianism in the 1960s, 1970s, and 1980s. However, black activism has not been limited to exclusively black or majority black efforts. African descendants have taken their concerns into labor unions, community associations, civic organizations, churches, political parties, and social movements where they have been a distinct numerical minority.[33]

Black social movement organizations exist in every sub-region (Caribbean, Central America, Andean, and Southern Cone) and practically every country of Latin America. According to Marta Rangel, these organizations have been successful to varying degrees in denouncing racism and racial inequality and demanding more educational and economic opportunities. In addition, these groups have organized at the local, state, national, and international levels and lobbied governments for resources, specific legislation, and public policy. As a result of their efforts, Afro-descendants are no longer invisible in Latin America. At the same time, many of these groups are not well organized and structured. Some have serious disconnections between leaders and members and between the organizations and their respective broader communities. The positive impact of recent black activity has varied greatly by region and country.[34]

The government of Cuba provides an example of hostility to independent black political activity. From independence to the Cuban revolution, Afro-Cubans had created their own social, cultural, and political organizations to advance their cause. While most blacks supported the advances of the revolution, some black leaders wanted to engage in a broader discussion and effort to root out white racism. They reasoned that blacks must be allowed to organize among themselves to protect and defend their collective interests in addition to the government's anti-racist and pro-equality measures. Carlos Moore became an advocate for this view when he launched his public, and later scholarly, critique of the Cuban Revolution. Moore maintained that despite Fidel Castro's revolutionary rhetoric and policies, the Cuban leadership was unwilling to engage in racial power-sharing.[35]

Cuba is experiencing increasing internal and external pressure to open its one-party system and allow independent voices and organizations to publicly criticize the government and offer alternatives. Afro-Cubans are especially active in these efforts in the area of race and culture. In recent years, rappers, visual artists, writers, intellectuals, and activists have been critical of resurgence racism and racial inequality. Rap lyrics, paintings, writings, and other efforts have challenged the negative stereotypes of black men and women that have become part of the racist explanation for why blacks are not doing well. Cuban authorities are aware of this new racism and allowing more media coverage of Afro-Cuban events and concerns.[36] Despite publicly recognizing racial discrimination as a problem, Cuba's communist party and government are not prepared to engage proposals by Afro-Cubans or other sectors that challenge their monopoly on political power.

There is growing research on how Afro-Brazilians have struggled for racial and social change in their country. Gaining more visibility than other Afro-Latin American activists, black leaders and organizations have worked to persuade Brazilian political leaders and the society at large to recognize the urgency of fighting against racial inequality and affirming the legitimacy of Afro-Brazilian demands for social, economic, and political inclusion.

Since the 1970s, Afro-Brazilian activists have participated in the transition to democracy, creation of new political parties, reemergence of the labor movement, and revitalization of civil society. In each of the last three decades, blacks have protested, lobbied, and succeeded in gaining more space in the political arena.[37]

In recent decades Afro-Colombian activists have become increasingly critical of their position in Colombian society. In the last three decades, leaders have organized activist groups such as Cimarron, a primarily urban group dedicated to struggle against racial discrimination and inequality. Other groups such as the Proceso de Comunidades Negras (PCN), based in Pacific coast black communities, have fought to defend their traditional homes, communities, and lands from government or business takeover. Both groups have framed their activism as part of a national and transnational human rights struggle. The effect of these organizing efforts has been to bring together Afro-Colombians from different regions to determine how they can work together.[38]

Since the transition to civilian rule in 1979, Afro-Ecuadorian leaders have been active in creating social, cultural, and political groups to organize and mobilize blacks for social change. These groups are especially present in Quito, the capital of the country, and the other areas with the strongest concentrations of African descendants: Esmeraldas, the Chota Valley, and Guayaquil. Despite a growing number of groups, there has been less success in maintaining active memberships and programs. There has also been great difficulty in creating strong national organizations. This challenge in organizing reflects the bleak Afro-Ecuadorian socio-economic situation. Many blacks live in poverty and extremely difficult conditions.[39] The Catholic Church, through its Comboni missionaries, has been active in working with black communities and cultivating black leadership. The Afro-Ecuadorian Cultural Center and the Afro-Ecuadorian Pastoral Department, created in the early 1980s, have served black communities by promoting educational opportunities and becoming meeting places for black organizers. Since 1982, the cultural center has published *Palenque*, a quarterly newsletter that provides one of the rare media sources in the country for news and views on Afro-Ecuadorians.

Regional Focus

Afro-Central Americans have intensified their organizing efforts within their countries and on a region-wide basis. In Costa Rica, Epsy Campbell and Edwin Patterson have combined activism and electoral politics. Both served in the Costa Rican legislature as representatives from the Citizens Action Party. Patterson has worked as a business leader on the Atlantic coast and organized a chamber of tourism. Blacks organized to promote economic development and defend their community lands against government and business projects that did not take them into consideration. In Nicaragua, the revolutionary Sandinista government and the post-Sandinista governments have struggled in their attempts to incorporate the Atlantic region with large indigenous and black communities into the national community. These struggles resulted primarily from the national elite's lack of familiarity with and respect for these communities. Juliet Hooker has argued that the elite's emphasis on mestizo nationalism has not fully acknowledged the demands for regional autonomy by indigenous and black communities of the Atlantic coast. In Honduras, Roy Guevara and Celeo Alvarez have led organizing efforts among the black communities. As president of ODECO, Alvarez has been a highly visible Garifuna leader working to organize African descendants on a national, regional, and continental basis.[40]

Celeo Alvarez is president of the Central American Black Organization (ONECA), which is based in Honduras. The group has representatives from all Central American countries and advocates greater funding for education, health care, economic development and other issues affecting black populations. ONECA has been successful in lobbying international organizations such as the World Bank, Inter-American Development Bank, and Organization of American States, to support the group's policy agenda.[41]

Black leaders from the Caribbean, Central America, and South America have begun to meet more frequently and attempted to institutionalize communication and collaboration. Romero Rodriguez, the President of Mundo Afro, a leading black group based in Montevideo, Uruguay, has played a central role in organizing blacks in Latin America. For the last 20 years, Rodriguez has traveled throughout South America, Central America, the Caribbean, and the United States building bridges between black groups, attending conferences, and making the case for international black Latin American cooperation and organization. He is also leader of the Strategic Alliance of Afrodescendants from Latin America and the Caribbean. These efforts were energized by the Latin American meetings in 2000 and 2001 in preparation for the World Conference against Racism, Racial Discrimination, Xenophobia, and Related Forms of Intolerance, held during September 2001 in Durban, South Africa. Afro-Latin American leaders realized that in addition to lobbying their own governments to participate effectively in the conference and embrace formally and enthusiastically an anti-racist political agenda, they had to work together to share information, experiences, and resources to strengthen their work within and across their individual countries.[42]

Electoral Politics

Few blacks have been elected to national political office or appointed to high-level government positions. In this regard, the rise of black women in Latin America politics represents an important development. Although they are still under-represented among black politicians and leaders, Afro-Latinas are increasingly making their voices heard throughout the region. Benedita da Silva represents the State of Rio de Janeiro in the Chamber of Deputies of the Brazilian Congress. She is the most visible black woman politician in Brazilian history and remains a tireless fighter for class, race, and gender reform. In Colombia, Senator Piedad Córdoba Ruíz is likely the most high profile Afro-Colombian politician. Her fight for peace, social justice, and an end to the violence in her country has led to her kidnapping and other traumas.[43]

Epsy Campbell Barr is a former member of the Costa Rican parliament and a leader of the Citizens Action Party. Involved in numerous progressive struggles within Costa Rica, Campbell is also the leader of the Network of Afro-Caribbean and Afro-Latin American women. In this capacity, she travels throughout the region speaking out against racism and sexism. Alexandra Ocles, a leading Afro-Ecuadorian activist served in the national assembly from 2007 to 2009 and recently (2010–2011) was a member of President Rafael Correa's cabinet as minister of the Secretariat of Peoples, Social Movements, and Citizen Participation. These four black activists and politicians, along with black women groups throughout Latin America, have worked in recent decades to place the issues directly affecting Afro-Latinas on the political agenda.[44]

Ethno-Racial Government Initiatives, Legislation and Public Policy

In their historic and contemporary struggles against racism and racial inequality, Afro-Latin Americans have petitioned their national governments for protections and respect for their rights as citizens and human beings. Such support was rarely forthcoming. Furthermore, existing legal protections against racial discrimination were often ignored. Recent efforts to achieve collective group rights within a multicultural citizenship framework have not been as successful for blacks as they have been for indigenous groups. Juliet Hooker explains this difference by arguing that national elites have conceptualized indigenous people as representing a distinct cultural group. Markers of this distinctiveness included indigenous language, long-term occupation of rural lands, and maintenance of traditional customs and authority. Blacks, on the other hand, were seen in more racial than ethnic terms. Thus, to the extent that blacks resembled indigenous groups, the greater their chances of achieving collective group rights. Such was the case in Honduras, Guatemala, and Nicaragua where blacks achieved the same rights as indians. In Colombia, Brazil, and Ecuador, blacks gained limited collective rights compared to indigenous groups. Hooker concludes that explanatory factors such as black population size, degree of black movement organization, and level of black identity consciousness were less relevant.[45]

Overall, blacks in Brazil may have been more successful than other Afro-Latin Americans in persuading government at the local, state, and national levels to embrace initiatives, adopt legislation, and implement public policies of a pro-black nature. As a result of black demands and activism, Brazil has a 25-year history of important experiments in race, politics, and government. Numerous race-specific initiatives have been undertaken in recent decades. Four major race-specific public policies have been passed by government bodies and deserve special attention.

First, in cities and states around the country, Afro-Brazilian leaders were able to persuade mayors, governors, and other elected officials to create black councils or government agencies to focus specific attention on the concerns of black citizens and communities. In the 1980s and 1990s, municipal and state governments of São Paulo, Rio de Janeiro, and other regions created institutions to call attention to racial discrimination, racial inequality, and other specific concerns of Afro-Brazilians. These pro-black government initiatives raised the profile of black government appointees and the issues they raised. However, these spaces were routinely under-funded and under-staffed in relation to overall government budgets and the enormity of the problems facing Afro-Brazilians. Still, most importantly, black leaders gained political, governmental, and public experience in exploring how government resources could be brought to bear on improving black living conditions.[46]

The second successful race-specific policy is affirmative action in higher education and government employment. Since 2001, at least 80 public universities, colleges, and technical institutes have created admissions policies (including racial quotas) to encourage increased enrollment of Afro-Brazilian students. This development has created tremendous controversy among political and academic elites. Brazil's public institutions of higher learning are the country's most prestigious and well-funded. They have also represented government higher education subsidies for largely white, middle- and upper-class families. Graduates of these institutions usually go on to occupy the most prestigious and powerful positions in the national government. According to some scholars and activists, race-specific affirmative action represents a threat to the unequal distribution of power and privilege in the country.[47]

The most controversial element of the new Brazilian affirmative action policies can be identified as racial quotas. These quotas identify specific numbers or percentages to be reserved for black and brown applicants. There is less hostility directed toward quotas for public high school, indigenous, disabled and other allegedly more deserving and disadvantaged students, graduates and job applicants. Critics offer several key reasons why racial quotas are not the best means of promoting social mobility for Afro-Brazilians. It is argued that racial quotas are inappropriate in Brazil because the country does not have strong racial cleavages and identities. Another critique holds that racial quotas are illegal under the country's constitution in that they treat Brazilians differently based on race. A third critique is that they will ultimately be ineffective.[48] So far, racial quotas have been successful in placing more Afro-Brazilian students in higher education and expanding the national debate over racial inequality.

The third major initiative related to race and politics comes from the national government. In 2003, President Luiz Inácio Lula da Silva created the Special Office for the Promotion of Racial Equality [Secretaria Especial de Políticas de Promoção da Igualdade Racial-SEPPIR] by decree. The small office has a large mission, i.e., the coordination of the government's efforts to promote racial equality in the government itself and the larger society. To increase the visibility of this mission, the office was given ministerial status by President Lula. Thus, the presidents of SEPPIR are cabinet ministers. The first three presidents have been Afro-Brazilian members of the Workers Party: Matilde Ribeiro (2003–2007), Edson Santos (2008–2010), and Luiza Bairros (2011–present). SEPPIR is in many ways similar to the black councils founded in the 1980s and 1990s. SEPPIR has the ability to highlight the theme of racial inequality and other black community concerns but it has a small budget and has to persuade other government officials and bureaucrats to take action.[49]

The fourth major initiative also occurred in 2003, the first year of President Lula's administration. In that year, the national congress passed Law 10,639 making the teaching of African and Afro-Brazilian history and culture obligatory in elementary and secondary education throughout the country. The passage of this law represented the achievement of black activists' demand that the black experience be integrated into the school curriculum in a meaningful way. These activists had argued that the myth of racial democracy with its emphasis on racial mixing, harmonious race relations, and inter-racial cordiality had historically minimized racial oppression and black resistance. Law 10,639 was a shock to the Brazilian educational bureaucracy. Supporters of the law within and outside the government have been leading efforts to produce teaching materials, train teachers, explain the law to skeptics, and build support for the law at the local, state, and national levels of the country's educational system. Proponents have conceptualized the law as a public policy emphasizing ethnic and racial diversity. In this way, they see the law as a new public initiative recognizing diversity and promoting racial equality similar to SEPPIR and affirmation action.[50]

Conclusion

Scholars have gained a much better understanding of racial politics in Latin America during the last three decades. Afro-Latin American struggles against racism and racial inequality have been documented. Survey research is beginning to show how racial attitudes manifest, support, or challenge racial prejudice. Ethnographic studies remain central to illuminating how racial identities and ideologies influence individual behavior. Nonetheless, most black political participation has been neglected by researchers. This neglect contributes to an incomplete understanding of Latin American politics. New political demands for laws, policies, and practices promoting racial equality should lead scholars to expand and intensify their investigations into Latin America's complex political reality.

Venezuela and Colombia are countries that should spur scholars to do more case studies, comparative analysis, and theoretical reflection on race and politics. Because even when politic activity is not explicitly about race, political developments usually have racial consequences; suggesting, of course, that race is relevant. The 1998 Venezuelan presidential election of Hugo Chavez Frias has led to major political, class, and racial polarization. The Bolivarian Revolution led by Chavez has challenged the traditional political parties and ruling elites. The Chavez administration has attacked poverty, inequality, and is committed to a radical redistribution of wealth and resources. In power for more than a decade, President Chavez has pursued egalitarian social policies and opened up new opportunities for mass political participation. Many black groups have supported Chavez as Afro-Venezuelans are over-represented among the poor and as victims of racial discrimination. Black leaders argue that President Chavez has affirmed his indigenous and African heritage and been receptive to their demands that the Revolution recognize the specificity of the Afro-Venezuelan situation. At the same time, black leaders believe that government officials should do more to support pro-racial equality policies.[51]

Colombia is the second largest country in South America with a population of more than 40 million. The country has suffered from an internal armed conflict for more than four decades. The violence by repressive government forces, leftist guerilas, and conservative paramilitary groups has killed thousands and displaced as many as three to four million Colombians. Afro-Colombians, generally believed to represent the second largest number of Afro-descendants in a Latin American nation, have historically and increasingly been victims of this violence and displacement. Scholars and activists emphasize that the violence usually involves powerful forces seeking access to and control of resources and land occupied by Afro-Colombians. Colombian and international business elites have been actively displacing Afro-Colombians to develop mining, agriculture, and development projects.[52]

In 1991, a new Colombian constitution was approved that recognized Colombia as pluriethnic and multicultural. Throughout the 1990s to the present, Afro-Colombians have worked for implementation of their constitutional rights and Transitory Article 55 and Law 70. This unprecedented ethno-racial legislation grants collective land rights to rural Afro-Colombian communities on the Pacific Coast, development aid, and education assistance. The new legislation also grants Afro-Colombians two seats in parliament and affirmative action in education. These achievements have coincided with a proliferation of black activism and a continuation of black suffering. Internally displaced Afro-Colombians remain traumatized by the ongoing violence and lack of adequate relief and support efforts.[53]

Most analysts of Venezuelan and Colombian politics do not address the question of race or the role of Afro-descendants. Such a perspective limits understanding of topics central to political analysis: violence, conflict, distribution of power and resources, identities of elites and masses, political representation, among others. A non-racial perspective reinforces the myths of racial democracy and harmony and camouflages the disproportionate suffering of Afro-Venezuelans and Afro-Colombians. As a further result, racism and racial inequality are seen as ambiguous. Colombia and Venezuela, like most countries in the region, do not have reliable demographic information on their national populations disaggregated by race, ethnicity, or color. Basic questions involved in understanding racial politics cannot be answered with full confidence.

Recognizing important similarities in the living conditions of their people throughout the region, Afro-Latin American leaders have met regularly since the 1970s to discuss issues that unite them and formulate strategies and tactics for region-wide collective action. In the late 1970s and early 1980s, these leaders met in Colombia, Brazil, Panama, and Ecuador.

Twenty years later black legislators met in Brazil, Colombia, and Costa Rica and formed a symbolic black parliament to begin a process of uniting black political leaders throughout the hemisphere. These transnational congresses, meetings, and gatherings were historic efforts to internationalize the struggle against racism, inequality, poverty, and ideologies and practices plaguing Afro-descendant communities.[54]

The comparisons between racial politics in the United States and Latin America and between indigenous and black experiences are worth pursuing in the spirit of ascertaining and understanding the living conditions of different racial and ethnic groups. Is the United States becoming more like Latin America? Is Latin America becoming more like the United States? These are serious questions given the growing public acceptance of multiracial identities in the United States and affirmation action policies in Brazil. Although the challenges related to studying race and politics in Latin America are substantial, there remains a need to collect and analyze socio-economic and political data by race, ethnicity, and color to improve understanding of politics in Latin America.

Notes

1 "Afro-Latin Americans" will be used interchangeably with African descendants, Afro-descendants, Latin Americans of African ancestry, and blacks unless otherwise noted. "Blacks" refers to blacks and browns or blacks and mulattos unless otherwise noted. For an alternative formulation in the case of Brazil, see Stanley R. Bailey, *Legacies of Race: Identities, Attitudes, and Politics in Brazil* (Stanford, CA: Stanford University Press, 2009) and Stanley R. Bailey, "Public Opinion on Nonwhite Underrepresentation and Racial Identity Politics in Brazil," *Latin American Politics and Society* 51:4 (2009): 69–99.

2 Kwame Anthony Appiah, *In My Father's House: Africa in the Philosophy of Culture* (New York: Oxford University Press, 1992); Naomi Zack, *Race and Mixed Race* (Philadelphia: Temple University Press, 1993).

3 Michael Omi and Howard Winant, *Racial Formation in the United States: From the 1960s to the 1990s*, 2nd ed. (New York: Routledge, 1994); Howard Winant, *The World is a Ghetto: Race and Democracy since World War II* (New York: Basic Books, 2001).

4 Norman Whitten, Jr., "Los paradigmas mentales de la conquista y el nacionalismo: La formación de los conceptos de las "razas" y las transformaciones del racismo", in *Ecuador racista: Imagenes e identidades*, eds. Emma Cervone and Fredy Rivera (Quito, Ecuador: FLACSO, 1999); Peter Wade, *Race and Ethnicity in Latin America* (London: Pluto Press, 1997); George Reid Andrews, *Afro-Latin America, 1800–2000* (New York: Oxford University Press, 2004).

5 Andrews; Jhon Anton, Alvaro Bello, Fabiana Del Popolo, Marcelo Paixão, and Marta Rangel, *Afrodescendientes en América Latina y el Caribe: del reconocimiento estadístico a la realización de derechos* (Santiago, Chile: United Nations Publications, 2009).

6 Melissa Nobles, *Shades of Citizenship: Race and the Census in Modern Politics* (Stanford, CA: Stanford University Press, 2000).

7 Alejandro de la Fuente, "Myths of Racial Democracy: Cuba, 1900–1912," *Latin American Research Review*, Vol. 34, No. 3 (1999): 39–73; Livio Sansone, *Blackness with Ethnicity: Constructing Race in Brazil* (New York: Palgrave Macmillan, 2003).

8 Peter Wade, "Rethinking Mestizaje: Ideology and Lived Experience," *Journal of Latin American Studies*, 37(2005): 239–257; Peter Wade, "Afro-Latin Studies: Reflections on the field," *Latin American and Caribbean Ethnic Studies*, Vol. 1, No. 1 (April 2006): 105–124.

9 Tanya Golash-Boza, "Does Whitening Happen? Distinguishing between Race and Color Labels in an African-Descended Community in Peru," *Social Problems*, Vol. 57, No. 1 (2010): 138–156.

10 Edward E. Telles, *Race in Another America: The Significance of Skin Color in Brazil* (Princeton: Princeton University Press, 2004); Sansone, 2003.

11 Peter Wade, *Blackness and Race Mixture: The Dynamics of Racial Identity in Colombia* (Baltimore: Johns Hopkins University Press, 1993); Fernando Urrea-Giraldo, "La población afrodescendiente en Colombia," *Pueblos indígenas y afrodescendientes de América Latina y el Caribe: información*

sociodemgráfica para políticas y programas (Santiago, Chile: United Nations Publications, 2006), 219–245.

12 De la Fuente; Michael George Hanchard, *Orpheus and Power: The Movimento Negro of Rio de Janeiro and São Paulo, Brazil, 1945–1988* (Princeton, NJ: Princeton University Press, 1994).

13 Hanchard, 1994; Elisa Larkin Nascimento, O *Sortilégio da Cor: Identidade, raça e gênero no Brasil* (São Paulo, Brazil: Summus, 2003).

14 Leslie B. Rout Jr., *The African Experience in Spanish America: 1502 to the Present Day* (Cambridge: Cambridge University Press, 1976); George Reid Andrews, *Afro-Latin America, 1800–2000* (New York: Oxford University Press, 2004); Kathryn Joy McKnight and Leo J. Garofalo, eds., *Afro-Latino Voices: Narratives from the Early Modern Ibero-Atlantic World, 1550–1812* (Indianapolis, IN: Hackett Publishing, 2009).

15 Andrews; Elisa Larkin Nascimento, O *Sortilégio da Cor: Identidade, raça e gênero no Brasil* (São Paulo, Brazil: Summus, 2003).

16 Alberto Carlos Almeida, *A Cabeça do Brasileiro* (Rio de Janeiro: Record, 2007); Alberto Carlos Almeida, "Core Values, Education, and Democracy: An Empirical Tour of DaMatta's Brazil," in *Democratic Brazil Revisited*, eds. Peter R. Kingstone and Timothy J. Power (Pittsburgh, PA: University of Pittsburgh Press, 2008), 232–256; Cleusa Turra and Gustavo Venturi, eds., *Racismo Cordial: A mais completa análise sobre o preconceito de cor no Brasil* (São Paulo, Brazil: Editora Ática, 1995).

17 Bailey, 2009.

18 Elisa Larkin Nascimento, *Pan-Africanism and South America: Emergence of a Black Rebellion* (Buffalo, NY: Afrodiaspora, 1980), 8.

19 Telles, 2004; Hanchard, 1994; France Winddance Twine, *Racism in a Racial Democracy: The Maintenance of White Supremacy in Brazil* (New Brunswick, NJ: Rutgers University Press, 1998); Minority Rights Group, *No Longer Invisible: Afro-Latin Americans Today* (London: Minority Rights Publications, 1995).

20 Ernesto Sagás, *Race and Politics in the Dominican Republic* (Gainesville: University Press of Florida, 2000); David Howard, *Coloring the Nation: Race and Ethnicity in the Dominican Republic* (Boulder, CO: Lynne Rienner, 2001).

21 Mark Q. Sawyer, Yesilernis Peña, and Jim Sidanius, "Cuba Exceptionalism: Group-based Hierarchy and the Dynamics of Patriotism in Puerto Rico, the Dominican Republic, and Cuba" *Du Bois Review*, 1: 1 (2004): 93–113; Yesilernis Peña, Jim Sidanius, and Mark Sawyer, "Racial Democracy in the Americas: A Latin and U.S. Comparison," *Journal of Cross-Cultural Psychology*, Vol. 35, No. 6 (2004): 749–762; Jim Sidanius, Yesilernis Peña,, and Mark Sawyer, "Inclusionary Discrimination: Pigmentocracy and Patriotism in the Dominican Republic," *Political Psychology*, Vol. 22, No. 4 (2001): 827–851.

22 Jesús María Herrara Salas, "Ethnicity and Revolution: The Political Economy of Racism in Venezuela," *Latin American Perspectives*, 141, Vol. 32, No. 2 (March 2005): 72–91.

23 Ariel E. Dulitzky, "A Region in Denial: Racial Discrimination and Racism in Latin America," in *Neither Enemies Nor Friends: Latinos, Blacks, Afro-Latinos*, eds. Suzanne Oboler and Anani Dzidzienyo (New York: Palgrave Macmillan, 2005), 39–59; Jesús Chucho Garcia and Nirva Rosa Camacho, eds., *Comunidades Afrodescendientes en Venezuela y America Latina* (Caracas, Venezuela: Alcaldía de Caracas, 2002).

24 Silvio Torres-Saillant, "Racism in the Americas and the Latino Scholar," in *Neither Enemies Nor Friends: Latinos, Blacks, Afro-Latinos*, eds. Suzanne Oboler and Anani Dzidzienyo (New York: Palgrave Macmillan, 2005), 281–304.

25 Sagás, 2000, 128.

26 Sagás, 2000; Howard, 2001.

27 Carlos Moore, Tanya R. Sanders, and Shawna Moore, eds., *African Presence in the Americas* (Trenton, NJ: Africa World Press, 1995); Minority Rights Group.

28 ECLAC, *Social Panorama of Latin America* (New York: United Nations Publications, 2010).

29 Alvaro Bello and Marta Rangel, "La equidad y la exculsion de los pueblos indigenas y afrodescendientes en America Latina y el Caribe," *Revista de la CEPAL* 76 (April 2002), 39–53; Marta Rangel, "La población afrodescendiente en América Latina y los Objetivos de Desarrollo del Milenio. Un examen exploratorio en países selecionados utilizando información censal," in *Pueblos indígenous y afrodescendientes de América Latina y el Caribe: información sociodemográfico para políticas y programas* (Santiago, Chile: United Nations Publications, 2006); Jhon Anton, Alvaro

Bello, Fabiana Del Popolo, Marcelo Paixão, and Marta Rangel, *Afrodescendientes en América Latina y el Caribe: del reconocimiento estadístico a la realización de derechos* (Santiago, Chile: United Nations Publications, 2009); Andrews, 2004; Margarita Sanchez and Maurice Bryan, with MRG partners, *Afro-descendants, Discrimination and Economic Exclusion in Latin America* (London: Minority Rights Group, 2003).

30 Telles, 2004; Robin E. Sheriff, *Dreaming Equality: Color, Race, Racism in Urban Brazil* (New Brunswick, NJ: Rutgers University Press, 2001).

31 Alejandro de la Fuente, *A Nation for All: Race, Inequality, and Politics in Twentieth-Century Cuba* (Chapel Hill: The University of North Carolina Press, 2001).

32 Mark Q. Sawyer, *Racial Politics in Post-Revolutionary Cuba* (New York: Cambridge University Press, 2006), 176.

33 Anani Dzidzienyo, "Activity and Inactivity in the Politics of Afro-Latin America," *SECOLAS Annals* (1978): 48–61; Suzanne Oboler and Anani Dzidzienyo, eds., *Neither Enemies Nor Friends: Latinos, Blacks, Afro-Latinos* (New York: Palgrave Macmillan, 2005).

34 Marta Rangel, "Una panorámica de las articulaciones y organizaciones de los afrodescendientes en América Latina y el Caribe," *Afrodescendientes en América Latina y el Caribe: del reconocimiento estadistoc a la realización de derechos* (Santiago, Chile: United Nations Publications, 2009)

35 Sawyer; Carlos Moore, *Castro, the Blacks and Africa* (Los Angeles: CAAS/UCLA, 1989); Carlos Moore, *Pichón: Revolution and Racism in Castro's Cuba: a memoir* (Chicago: Lawrence Hill Press, 2008); Abdias do Nascimento and Elisa Nascimento, *Africans in Brazil* (Trenton, NJ: Africa World Press, 1994); Abdias do Nascimento, *Brazil Mixture or Massacre? Essays in the Genocide of a Black People* 2nd ed. (Dover, MA: The Majority Press, 1989).

36 Alejandro de la Fuente, "The New Afro-Cuban Cultural Movement and the Debate on Race in Contemporary Cuba," *Journal of Latin American Studies*, 40 (2008): 697–720.

37 Hanchard, 1994; Pierre Michel Fontaine, ed., *Race, Class, Power in Brazil* (Los Angeles: Center for Afro-American Studies, University of California, 1985).

38 Kwame Dixon, "Transnational Black Social Movements in Latin America: Afro-Colombians and the Struggle for Human Rights," in *Latin American Social Movements in the Twenty-First Century: Resistance, Power, and Democracy*, eds. Richard Stahler-Sholk, Harry E. Vanden, and Glen David Kuecker (Lanham, MD: Rowman & Littlefield, 2008); Peter Wade, "The Cultural Politics of Blackness in Colombia," *American Ethnologist* 22(2) (1995): 341–357; Juan de Dios Mosquera Mosquera, *Racismo y Discriminación Racial en Colombia* (Bogota: Docentes Editores, 2003); Chomsky, 2007.

39 Henry MediaVallejo and Mary Castro Torres, *Afroecuatorianos: Un movimento social emergente* (Quito: Ediciones Afroamérica/CCA, 2006); Jhon Anton Sanchez, "El Proceso Organizativo Afroecuatoriano: 1979–2009" (Ph.D. Diss., FLACSO-Ecuador, 2009).

40 *Forum Proceedings on Poverty Alleviation for Minority Communities in Latin America: Communities of African Ancestry* (Washington, DC: Inter-American Development Bank, 1996); Juliet Hooker, "'Beloved Enemies': Race and Official Mestizo Nationalism in Nicaragua," *Latin American Research Review*, Vol. 40, No. 3 (2005): 14–39.

41 Tianna S. Paschel and Mark Q. Sawyer, "Contesting Politics as Usual: Black Social Movements, Globalization, and Race Policy in Latin America," *Souls* 10:3 (2008): 197–214.

42 Jhon Anton Sanchez, 2009; *Alianza estrategica Afrolatinoamerica y Caribena 1a 2a Etapa*. Montevideo, Uruguay: Organizaciones Mundo Afro; Romero Jorge Rodriguez, "Entramos Negros; salimos afrodescendientes," *Revista Futuros* No. 5 2004, Vol. II. Accessed December 19, 2010, http://www.revistafuturos.info/futuros_5/afro_1.htm

43 Benedita da Silva, Medea Benjamin and Maisa Mendonça, *Benedita da Silva: An Afro-Brazilian Woman's Story of Politics and Love* (Oakland, CA: Institute for Food and Development Policy, 1997); Piedad Córdoba Ruiz, "Development, Conflict, and Territory," in *Race and Poverty: Interagency Consultation on Afro-Latin Americans* (preliminary ed.) (Washington, DC: Inter-American Dialogue, Inter-American Development Bank, World Bank, 2000), 39–41.

44 Epsy Campbell Barr and Gloria Careaga Perez, eds., *Poderes Cuestionados: Sexismo y Racismo en América Latina* (San José: Diseno Editorial, 2002); Carlos de la Torre, *Afroquiteños: Ciudadanía y Racismo* (Quito: Centro Andino de Accion Popular-CAAP, 2002; Ollie A. Johnson III, "Black Activism in Ecuador, 1979–2009," in *Comparative Perspectives on Afro-Latin America*, ed. Kwame Dixon and John Burdick (Gainesville: University Press of Florida, forthcoming).

45 Juliet Hooker, "Indigenous Inclusion/Black Exclusion: Race, Ethnicity and Multicultural Citizenship in Latin America," *Journal of Latin American Studies*, Vol. 37 (2005): 285–310.

46 Ivair Augusto Alves dos Santos, *O movimento negro e o estado (1983–1987): O caso do conselho de participação e desenvolvimento da comunidade negra no governo de São Paulo* (São Paulo: Coordenadoriados Assuntos da População Negra/Prefeitura da Cidade de São Paulo, 2006); Ollie A. Johnson III, "Locating Blacks in Brazilian Politics: Afro-Brazilian Activism, New Political Parties, and Pro-Black Public Policies," *International Journal of Africana Studies*, Vol. 12, No. 2 (2006): 170–193; George Reid Andrews, *Blacks and Whites in São Paulo, Brazil, 1888–1988* (Madison: University of Wisconsin Press, 1991).

47 Sales Augusto dos Santos, "Universidades Públicas, Sistema de Cotas para os Estudantes Negros e Disputas Acadêmico-Políticas no Brasil Contemporâneo," *Política & Trabalho: Revista de Ciências Sociais*, 22, (2010): 49–73; Marilene de Paula and Rosana Heringer, eds., *Caminhos convergentes: Estado e Sociedade na superação das desigualdades raciais no Brasil* (Rio de Janeiro, Brazil: Fundação Heinrich Boll, ActionAid, 2009); Sales Augusto dos Santos, "Movimento negros, educação, e açoes afirmativas." (Ph.D. diss., Universidade de Brasilia, 2007); Ollie A. Johnson III, "Afro-Brazilian Politics: White Supremacy, Black Struggle, and Affirmative Action," in *Democratic Brazil Revisited*, eds. Peter R. Kingstone and Timothy J. Power (Pittsburgh, PA: University of Pittsburgh Press, 2008), 209–230; Bernd Reiter and Gladys L. Mitchell, eds., *Brazil's New Racial Politics* (Boulder, CO: Lynne Rienner Publishers, 2010).

48 Johnson, 2008; Seth Racusen, "Affirmative and Action and Identity" and Mónica Treviño González, "Opportunities and Challenges for the Afro-Brazilian Movement" in Bernd Reiter and Gladys L. Mitchell, eds., *Brazil's New Racial Politics* (Boulder, CO: Lynne Rienner Publishers, 2010), 89–122, 123–138; Peter Fry, Yvonne Maggie, Marcos Chor Maio, Simone Monteiro, and Ricardo Ventura Santos, eds., *Divisões perigosas: Políticas raciais no Brasil contemporaneo* (Rio de Janeiro, Brazil: Civilização Brasileira, 2007); Bailey, 2009.

49 Johnson, 2006; Paixão and Carvano, 2008.

50 Nilma Lino Gomes, "Limites e Possibilidades da Implementação da Lei 10.639/03 no contexto das politicias publicas em educação" in *Caminhos convergentes: Estado e Sociedade na superação das desigualdades raciais no Brasil*, eds. Marilene de Paula and Rosana Heringer (Rio de Janeiro, Brazil: Fundação Heinrich Boll, ActionAid, 2009), 39–74; *Educação anti-racista: caminhos abertos pela Lei Federal no. 10.639/03* (Brasília, Brazil: Ministerio da Educação, Secretaria de Educação Continuada, Alfabetização e Diversidade, 2005).

51 Colectivo Red Afrovenezolana, *Somos La Red de Organizaciones Afrovenezolanas* (Caracas, Venezuela: Ministerio de la Cultura, 2005).

52 Peter Wade, *Blackness and Race Mixture: The Dynamics of Racial Identity in Colombia* (Baltimore: Johns Hopkins University Press, 1993); Aviva Chomsky, "The Logic of Displacement: Afro-Colombians and the War in Colombia," in Darién J. Davis, ed., *Beyond Slavery: The Multilayered Legacy of Africans in Latin America and the Caribbean* (Lanham, MD: Rowman & Littlefield, 2007), 171–198.

53 Chomsky, 2007; *I Conferencia Nacional Afrocolombiana: Una Minga por la Vida: Memorias y Documentos* (Bogotá: 3 Mundos Editores Ltda, 2003); Tianna S. Paschel, "Explaining Colombia's Shift from Color Blindness to the Law of Black Communities," *The American Journal of Sociology*, Vol. 116, No. 3, (November 2010): 729–769.

54 Ollie A. Johnson III, "Black Politics in Latin America: An Analysis of National and Transnational Politics," in *African American Perspectives on Political Science*, ed. Wilbur C. Rich (Philadelphia: Temple University Press, 2007).

21

GENDER

Lisa Baldez

In the past, Latin America was not known as a global leader in terms of the status of women, but that is no longer the case. In the past two decades, women have been elected to the highest political office in seven countries in the region. Nicaraguans voted for Violeta Chamorro in 1990, Guyanans elected Janet Jagan in 1997, and Panamanians chose Mireya Moscoso as president in 1999. In 2006, Chile elected Michelle Bachelet, and, in 2007, Argentines voted in Cristina Fernández de Kirchner. In 2010, Laura Chinchilla was elected president of Costa Rica, and Dilma Rousseff became president of Brazil. In Jamaica, Portia Simpson-Miller held the post of Prime Minister from 2006 to 2007. These women have achieved what is widely considered to be the most important marker of political power and of gender equality, two goals that remain beyond women's grasp in most of the countries of the world. Women's accomplishments stand out even more when we consider the strength of the executive in Latin America; throughout the region, presidents are not mere figureheads but wield considerable constitutional power, legislative initiative, and budgetary authority.

The large number of women presidents is but one indicator of the considerable advances that Latin American women have made in attaining political power and strengthening women's rights. Dramatic changes in the status of women have occurred throughout the region. Expansion of women's rights is a priority among political parties and political officials at every level of government. Dense networks of women have mobilized to protest against gender inequality and to demand policy change. International institutions have forced domestic governments to make stronger commitments to women's rights. Latin America as a whole has emerged as a world leader in the fight against domestic violence with the Inter-American Convention on the Prevention, Punishment and Eradication of Violence Against Women, also known as the Convention of Belém Do Pará (Inter-American Commission on Human Rights 1994). These successes challenge assumptions about the prevalence of traditional gender stereotypes that portray Latin American women as submissive, subordinated by men, and relegated to the private sphere. At the same time, advances in women's rights are unevenly distributed and we do not yet know how enduring they will prove to be over time. Electing women to political office has not yet brought about the end of gender discrimination. Many women continue to face significant obstacles to living safe and productive lives.

This chapter examines some of the changes that have led Latin America to become a global leader in the status of women and evaluates the scope of those changes for women outside the presidential palace. It begins with an overview of broad demographic trends that have affected men and women. The expansion of women's rights makes sense when we see that women are approaching men in terms of their share of the labor force, and surpassing men in education. It then explores the rise of feminism in the region in the late twentieth century, a phenomenon caused largely by women's rejection of two hyper-masculine forms of political engagement: leftist revolutionary movements and military authoritarian governments. The next section looks at efforts to promote women's rights policy in the context of democracy and the strategic challenges that women's movements face. The chapter then shifts focus to the institutional arena to examine how women and women's rights have fared in legislatures, the executive branch, and the courts.

Each of these areas, particularly public policy, gender-based movements, and political institutions, has generated a wealth of research within political science. My vision for future work in this field is to make it more comparative and more gendered. Political scientists who conduct research on Latin America are also comparativists, and most of us are by now familiar with debates about the comparative method (for example Brady and Collier 2010; King, Keohane, and Verba 1994). In the conclusion to this chapter, I identify some of the ways in which gender research might engage in more expansive and more frequent comparisons. I would also like to see more research that attends more closely to gender than solely to women. Most of the existing research in this subfield presumes that "women" is a meaningful category of analysis that rests on characteristics shared by all women. As this chapter reflects, much of the research in this subfield evaluates women's political activity in terms of its support for women's rights and gender equality. Research that acknowledges the myriad differences among women and that addresses the significance of masculinity is less well developed in political science. Research that acknowledges the *matices* in terms of how gender is defined will provide a more comprehensive view of the ways in which gender is relevant to Latin American politics.

Demographic Trends

Recent changes in women's rights have occurred against a backdrop of long-term improvements in women's access to education and employment in the formal labor force. Theories of modernization predict that gender equality will come about with economic and political development. Demographic data show that the status of women in Latin America generally conforms to these expectations in terms of childbearing and labor force participation; as the region has developed, women are having fewer children and more women are working. About half of working-age women are employed, which represents a 3 percentage point increase since 2000. By comparison, 83% of working-age men are employed, and this figure has remained steady since 2000. The fertility rate for women has declined since the middle of the twentieth century and has continued to drop in the twenty-first century, from an already low median of 2.7 children per woman in 2000 to 2.4 in 2008. The rate of teen pregnancy has also declined, registering a drop of more than 10% since 2000, from a median of 85 live births per 1000 teen-aged women, to 71.5 per 1000 in 2008. Women have achieved parity with men in basic literacy region-wide, with only small differences in the rates of literacy for men and women in most countries (all data from World Bank 2010).

The data on gender ratios in education tell a different story from what modernization theory would predict, however; in Latin America as in other regions of the world, women have surpassed men at higher levels of educational attainment. The higher the level of schooling, the more women outnumber men. At the level of primary education, gender parity has been nearly achieved: the ratio of girls to boys is 97:100. At the secondary and tertiary levels, girls achieved parity with boys some time ago and then began to outnumber boys. Region-wide, the median female to male ratio for secondary enrollment is 104.1. At the university level, gender inequities have become very pronounced: the median ratio of female to male university enrollments is 141.9. The ratio is close to 2:1 in a handful of countries; in Belize, Jamaica, St. Lucia, and Uruguay, close to two women attend university for every man (World Bank 2010). Gender inequality persists in education—but at the expense of boys, not girls.

One explanation for higher levels of education for women in Latin America points to the Catholic Church's historical commitment to educating women. This hypothesis became evident to me once I thought about the region comparatively, relative to other developing areas. Spanish colonial rulers cared deeply about education and built universities in the colonies beginning in the 1500s. The Catholic Church sought to educate women for many reasons: to prepare them for their future roles as wives, nuns, mothers, and servants to the poor; to train them to be good mothers; to espouse strong moral, aesthetic, and religious values; and to steel them for the hardships of colonial life. In the post-independence era, conflicts between clerical forces defending the Catholic Church and secular, liberal forces opposing the Church led to the expansion of education for women. Liberal reforms in the mid-1800s created public schools and *normales* that trained women as teachers. In other regions of the world, by contrast, conflicts between secular and clerical forces often *reduced* women's access to education. Conservative political parties supported women's suffrage early on, consistent with their belief that women supported the Catholic Church and would vote for Catholic candidates. The Catholic Church is usually considered to exert a conservative force when it comes to women, but it has been at least somewhat progressive when it comes to women's education.

Political scientists tend to use demographic data as independent or explanatory variables to explain political outcomes, such as changes in public policy. The data presented here reveal intriguing patterns that warrant investigation in their own right. Teen pregnancy rates vary by country, for example, from a high of 112 in Nicaragua and 108 in the Dominican Republic, to lows of 45 in Cuba and Haiti. What explains the variation across countries? Despite a pattern of overall parity, the educational data reveal some alarming declines; girls' enrollments have dropped an average of 2 points relative to boys' enrollments in 13 countries over the past ten years. What accounts for declines in women's status where they have occurred? These research puzzles have yet to be explored within political science.

Gender-based Movements

Women have mobilized along gender lines in a number of contexts. Following the lead established by Maxine Molyneux (1985), scholars frequently categorize women's movements according to two groups, one that reflects the interests that flow from women's traditional or conventional gender roles and the other than challenges gender hierarchy. Molyneux coined these two categories "practical" and "strategic"; others have used the terms "feminine" and "feminist" (Alvarez 1990). The initial idea behind conceiving of women's interests according to these two types was to challenge the idea that all women share interests in feminism and explicit challenges to the gender status quo. Prior to Molyneux, feminists often resorted to the Marxist concept of false consciousness to understand and explain the actions of women who did not explicitly espouse feminist interests; from this perspective, women who did not support feminism did not properly understand their own gender interests. Molyneux sought to explain the actions of politically active women who do not support women's rights *per se*, as well as those who do (for a critique of this perspective, see Baldez 2011).

Participation in leftist revolutionary movements in the 1960s and 1970s led many women to develop feminist consciousness. Leftist ideology privileged socio-economic class over all other forms of identity, which theoretically made gender differences invisible and politically irrelevant. This afforded women unprecedented opportunities to participate in public life. Women joined parties and movements of all kinds, and made up as much as 40% of the armed combatants who waged guerrilla warfare in Cuba, Nicaragua, El Salvador, Guatemala, and Chiapas (Kampwirth 2002).

Despite the prominent role of women in revolutionary movements and the prevalence of ideologies focused on liberation and radical equality, male leaders remained ambivalent at best about women's status. Revolutionary policies challenged the subordinate role of women within Catholic-dominated culture, but did not transform it. Few women assumed positions of power within the revolutionary leadership. Government efforts to legislate gender equality met with limited success. In Cuba, the Family Code of 1975, which required men to share equally in housework, was widely flouted and proved unenforceable. In Nicaragua, the Sandinistas explicitly supported gender equality in their original platform, but weak commitment on the part of the Sandinista leadership once in power, and the civil war of the 1980s meant that very few of its provisions were ever implemented. Both governments created mass organizations for women (the Federation of Cuban Women and AMNLAE in Nicaragua), but they served more to mobilize women on behalf of the revolution, rather than to represent women's interests. Women's participation often led them to question contradictions between their own experiences and radical ideals; this questioning in turn sparked the creation of feminist consciousness.

The status of women also became a battleground between revolutionaries and reactionaries. Literacy campaigns in Cuba and Nicaragua sent hundreds of young people into the countryside to teach peasants how to read, but many families opposed sending young women unescorted into the countryside. Shutting down Catholic schools constituted a particularly keen threat to daughters in protective middle- and upper-class families. Right-wing women mobilized against leftist regimes in Chile and elsewhere (Baldez 2002; Power 2002).

When authoritarian rulers seized power in coups across the region during the late 1960s to the 1980s, women began to mobilize on the basis of their gender identity to oppose military governments and support of women's rights. The emergence of progressive women's movements reflected not only opposition to authoritarianism, but a response to the limitations of the left that had led to its violent demise. Authoritarian governments thus had the unanticipated consequence of precipitating the emergence of women's movements, particularly in the Southern Cone countries of Argentina, Brazil, Chile, and Uruguay. The overblown *machismo* exemplified by military rule made feminism more appealing than it otherwise may have been, for men and women alike. Widespread human rights violations and economic crisis prompted women to take a public stand too dangerous for men, who were detained, tortured, killed or disappeared at higher rates than women. The Mothers of the Plaza de Mayo in Argentina are perhaps the most well-known example, but women organized everywhere to protest against the military's violation of the private spaces of the home and family. Feminists coined the slogan "democracy in the country and in the home" to highlight the link between military rule and patriarchal culture. The emergence of women's movements amidst authoritarian regimes beginning in the 1970s defied the idea that feminism was a privilege of white, middle-class women in the developed world.

Activism at the regional level has long been central to feminism in Latin America. In the first half of the twentieth century, Latin American women organized the world's strongest networks of suffrage organizations. Starting in 1983, feminist groups have held regional *encuentros* every three years. The *encuentros* have provided a forum to share ideas, debate, network, air their grievances, and recharge the batteries drained by working in often-hostile domestic environments. From a scholarly perspective, the feminist *encuentros* serve as a barometer by which to assess the status of feminism at particular points of time. Teams of scholars have written two insightful essays that provide detailed accounts of these gatherings (Alvarez et al. 2002; Sternbach et al. 1992). I hope future scholars will continue to publish birds-eye descriptions of future *encuentros* as well as other instances of gender-based mobilization. Articles like these are undervalued relative to more abstract, theoretically-motivated research, but they serve the important purpose of documenting events for the historical record and constitute valuable primary sources.

At the transnational level, the United Nations World Conferences on Women (WCW) legitimized incipient feminist movements and forced women's rights policy onto domestic political agendas. The first WCW, held in Mexico City in 1975, increased awareness of feminism in the region and introduced Latin American feminism to the world. Participation at the subsequent conferences—in Copenhagen in 1980, Nairobi in 1985, and Beijing in 1995—provided leverage for domestic activists in their efforts to advance women's rights. Many countries had never previously gathered data on gender inequality and presumed, incorrectly in many cases, that "their" women had already achieved equality. This deceptively simple step of data collection, a prerequisite for attending the conferences, proved sufficiently embarrassing to governments to prompt them to take action to improve women's status relative to men. Interaction between government officials and activists at the parallel NGO forums further strengthened the struggle for women's rights. Government officials found they needed advocates in civil society to provide information about women's status, and advocates in NGOs and grassroots organizations learned more about the constraints under which state officials operate.

In the fifteen years since Beijing, Latin American feminists have moved away from the UN as a crucible of resistance. Virginia Vargas, one of the region's founding feminists, recently critiqued the UN as being captured by forces of "neoliberalism, militarization and fundamentalisms of various kinds" (Vargas 2009, 150). The struggle for women's rights has shifted ground, to alternative venues such as the World Social Forum that allow activists in a wide range of struggles to debate issues and to develop new ways to mobilize against global political oppression and economic crisis.

Democratization gave women's rights advocates opportunities to create a "space in the state" to promote policy change, but also introduced fissures into feminist movements. Embrace of policy development and lobbying required organizations to become more professionalized and to rely more heavily on external financing, in a pattern has been called the "NGO-ization" of feminism. Relatively low levels of GDP per capita make reliance on member donations unfeasible for most organizations, and tax laws do not provide incentives for philanthropic giving among those who might afford it. NGOs that opt to navigate the transnational arena and conduct contract work for domestic governments do so at the expense of mobilizing individual supporters and engaging in strategies that might strengthen a movement at the grassroots level. The NGOs that thrive in this context are those whose staff have the skills to navigate the transnational arena: advanced degrees, fluency in English, and connections to political officials and bureaucrats who have the power to dispense often limited funds for contract work.

Feminist groups that identify themselves as "autonomous," on the other hand, tend to reject engagement with the state altogether. In the contemporary political context, in which many governments embrace neoliberal economic policy, to be autonomous means to be independent from the state and from political parties that have a stake in sustaining the neoliberal system. Autonomous feminists have criticized gender activists who work within the state as necessarily promoting policies that benefit middle-class women at the expense of poor and working class women.

Conflicts between "institutionalized" and "autonomous" feminists may reflect a discrete phase of democratic consolidation. Over time in Chile, for example, women's organizations have learned how to lobby and press for their demands more effectively than they did in the first few years after the democratic transition. Research conducted at various points of time can provide snapshots of the learning curve that feminist activists face and depict how they learn to navigate democratic institutions (see, for example, Haas 2010).

What would it mean for research on movements to become more comparative and more gendered? More comparative work might seek to understand the conditions under which women or men will mobilize on the basis of shared gender identity, or sexuality, as exemplified by new work on GLBT movements in Latin America (Corrales and Pecheny 2010; de la Dehesa 2010). What specific constituencies decide to frame collective action in gendered terms, and why? Framing demands in certain ways and not others may facilitate success. Women were able to assert themselves as leaders and work effectively in a drug- and crime-ridden area of Rio when they framed their activities in terms of their status as mothers, which de Mello e Souza (2008) suggests did not reinforce traditional gender norms, but rather transformed the meaning of motherhood. Why do groups of women decide to mobilize as women rather than along other bases of shared identity, and what are the consequences of doing so (and vice-versa)? Whom do women's movements represent, and whom do they exclude?

What kinds of strategies prove most effective for organizations that promote women's rights? Scholars disagree about the conditions that will best allow women to succeed in pursuing their agendas. Avenues of feminist activism have multiplied in the wake of transitions to democracy around the region. Some applaud this as a positive development while others are less sanguine about the fragmentation of feminist activity and insist that unity is essential to influence policy. Those who work within political institutions find themselves in a weak position when it comes to pressing for policy change if they cannot mobilize grassroots support.

Public Policy

With transitions to democracy across the region in the 1980s and 1990s, feminist activists continued the effort to bring private issues into the public sphere by demanding the adoption and implementation of government policy on a range of issues, including violence against women, reproductive health, poverty reduction, women's participation in public life, and marriage and family law. Democratization shifted the attention of scholars and activists from movement-based politics to the formal policy arena. The bulk of current research on women in Latin America in political science addresses the degree to which governments have adopted and implemented legislation that promotes women's rights and evaluates policy in terms of progress and limitations. Scholars have identified a number of concrete indicators of government commitment to women's rights, including rhetorical commitment to women's issues; the introduction, adoption and implementation of legislation; budgetary allocations for gender-related programs; the degree of women's involvement in the policy process; and the allocation of resources to ensure equitable access to policy benefits. Descriptive research tends to juxtapose accomplishments and limitations and employs the language of a "track record." More theoretically motivated research aims to explain variation across countries, among issues and over time.

Criminalization of violence against women is one of the great successes of policy toward women in Latin America, and yet remains one of the most significant challenges. The murders of hundreds of women in Ciudad Juarez, Mexico, illustrates this horrible dilemma: the cases of hundreds of women brutally murdered and left for dead remain unsolved to this day, but they have garnered world attention and awareness of impunity in cases of violence against women. The Juarez murders have also given rise to the term *femicidio*, which is now used widely throughout the Spanish-speaking world to denounce the murder of women through domestic and other forms of sexualized violence.

The issue of violence against women has seen dramatic changes by virtue of framing it in terms of human rights. Recognition of sexual violence as a human rights violation has given female victims the space to denounce publicly crimes they would not have acknowledged in the past, thus promoting healing and reconciliation for women (Falcón 2009). In some cases, Brazil and Chile, for example, legislators have gradually strengthened existing domestic violence laws by increasing penalties for perpetrators and addressing the needs of victims. At the same time, rates of domestic violence remain high, government funding for shelters to house victims of domestic violence is extremely limited, and prosecutions are rare.

Abortion remains a central issue for feminists in Latin America, who "tend to see the right to have an abortion as the strongest expression of the struggle to broaden the margins of choice women have in their lives" (Vargas 2009, 162). Abortion is illegal almost everywhere in the region, yet criminal penalties for women and their doctors have failed to prevent nearly 4 million abortions a year from being performed. Abortion is legal only in Cuba and in Mexico City. Democracy and more competitive political systems have increased conflicts over reproductive rights. When the Mexico City legislature legalized abortion for all women in the first trimester in 2007, the ruling prompted 17 states in Mexico to adopt constitutional amendments declaring that life begins at conception. Being on the left is no guarantee of support for reproductive rights. Former revolutionary leaders have swerved in their views on abortion: in Nicaragua, President Daniel Ortega outlawed therapeutic abortion and, in Uruguay, President Tabaré Vasquez threatened to overturn legislation liberalizing abortion (Gago 2007).

Support for women's rights and equality has not necessarily translated into, or led to, equal levels of support for rights for gays and lesbians, despite the presence of often well-organized coalitions of gay and lesbian activists (Friedman 2009a). Nonetheless, dramatic advances have rocked the region (Corrales and Pecheny 2010). In 2010, for example, Argentina passed same-sex marriage legislation that extends to gay couples the same rights and legal protections that heterosexual couples enjoy.

Most current research on public policy assumes a democratic institutional context, but regime type can affect the prospects for expansion of women's rights. Despite women's opposition, authoritarian rule had mixed effects on the status of women. Adoption of market-based economic policies fueled demand for female workers, but those same policies eliminated welfare programs and government jobs in healthcare and education, sectors traditionally dominated by women. Massive unemployment thrust many families into poverty and forced women into the informal sector. At the same time, as Mala Htun (2003) demonstrates, an ideological commitment to modernization led some authoritarian leaders to update marriage and family law. Military governments in Argentina, Brazil, and Chile thus brought about some limited advances in women's rights policies.

Scholars disagree about the extent to which populist regimes in Venezuela, Bolivia, and Ecuador have affected the progress of women's rights agendas. Venezuela passed a "gender inclusive" constitution in 1999 and Article 15 of the Bolivia's new constitution guarantees equal rights for women, but these promises of constitutional equality have yet to be borne out in terms of educating citizens about those rights or creating programs to implement them (Monasterios 2007) Critics maintain that political polarization has forced feminist concerns off the agenda: under Hugo Chávez, the three-time president of Venezuela, the gender quota law was suspended, progress on GLBT issues has stalled, and women's issues in general have taken a back seat to more immediate political concerns (Espina 2009). At the same time, the overall focus on poverty alleviation of these and other leftist governments benefits women, even if it does not challenge gender inequality explicitly.

Shifts in economic policy have also affected policy outcomes for women. Economic changes that occurred over the course of the twentieth century, specifically the transition from policies that emphasize state-led growth to those that foster market-based, export-led growth, led to transformations in the nature of political representation and the status of women. Authoritarian and populist regimes sought to develop domestic industry and to reduce reliance on foreign markets; to do so, they fostered strong ties with organized economic sectors (such as workers, business, and government). Political parties relied heavily on male-dominated labor unions as a source of popular support. When statist models of development failed to generate economic growth, governments imposed neoliberal models that promoted exports and reduced government spending. This shift led political parties to seek out new bases of political representation. Economic transition led to the decline of the working class and organized labor as the primary constituents of the left. As governments have done away with protectionist policy, men's share of the labor force has declined and the percentage of women in the workforce has increased. Gendered shifts in the economy contributed to the rise of feminism and lent support to women's demands for greater inclusion in public life. Political parties have responded to these demands by mobilizing female voters, nominating women to candidate spots, and espousing support for women's rights policy.

Legislative Politics

As the result of these efforts, Latin American women have made significant gains in legislative politics. At this writing, four Latin American countries rank among the top 20 countries with highest percentages of women in congress. Women are over one-third of legislators in Argentina (38.5%), Cuba (43.2%), and Costa Rica (38.6%), and Ecuador comes close with 32.3%. The regional average for the Americas has risen 8 percentage points in the last 10 years alone. By contrast, the percentage of women in the U.S. Congress is an anemic 16.9%. The United States ranks #72 on the list of women in legislative office, falling between Greece and Turkmenistan (Inter-Parliamentary Union 2010).

Research on gender and legislative politics in Latin America addresses two basic questions: (1) what factors determine the percentage of women vs. men elected to legislative office, and (2) what difference does gender make in explaining legislator behavior? The main factor contributing to the election of more women to Congress in Latin America is a reform to electoral laws requiring gender equity in the selection of legislative candidates, known as gender quotas. Twelve countries in Latin America have adopted gender quota laws: Argentina, Bolivia, Brazil, Costa Rica, Dominican Republic, Ecuador, Guyana, Honduras, Mexico, Panama, Paraguay, Peru, and Uruguay (for specific details, see International IDEA 2006). These laws require either that women constitute a minimum percentage of candidates, or that neither sex may surpass a determined ceiling for candidate slots. Unlike gender quotas in other regions of the world, quotas in Latin America tend to be legislative or statutory quotas that apply to all political parties operating within the political system. They differ in this regard from voluntary quotas that political parties adopt on their own initiative, and from reserved seats, in which countries set aside a certain number of legislative seats (rather than candidate spots) for women.

According to Argentina's *Ley de Cupos*, adopted in 1991, women must occupy at least 30% of candidate slots for all parties and there must be at most a 2:1 ratio of men to women in the first 10 spots of each list. Party lists that fail to comply with this law will be not be approved by the electoral tribunal. The Argentine law is arguably one of the most effective: prior to the adoption of the *Ley de Cupos*, women seldom won more than 3–4% of legislative seats; now women consistently win more than a third of seats in the Argentine Chamber of Deputies.

The effectiveness of gender quotas hinges on the way they interact with a country's electoral system. Quotas tend to be most effective in closed-list proportional representation systems with medium- to large-sized electoral districts. The logic behind district size is obvious: if a district has more seats, women are more likely to get some of them. This is especially true if the law has a placement mandate that prevents all the members of one sex from being clustered in unwinnable seats at the bottom of a list. The advantage of a closed-list system is that it puts the onus on party leaders to achieve gender balance on a list. An open-list system allows voters to select candidates from a list, so the potential advantage for women depends on a more woman-friendly electorate. Quotas can be effective in open-list systems, especially if advocates mobilize voters to select female candidates. In Peru, activists encouraged people to give one of their two votes to a woman, with the slogan "*dale uno a la mujer*" (Schmidt and Saunders 2004). Finally, the effectiveness of a quota depends on the strength of enforcement mechanisms written into the law itself, and on the willingness of courts to enforce them. If these conditions hold, the percentage of women elected can increase as much as 20% over systems with no quotas or where enforcement of quotas is weak (Jones 2004).

Once in office, to what extent do female legislators differ from men, in terms of their backgrounds, policy agendas, and ability to represent their constituencies? Research conducted by political scientist Elsa Chaney in Chile and Peru in the 1970s characterized female legislators as *supermadres*, who extended their identities as mothers into the political arena and prioritized issues relevant to children and families (Chaney 1979). This characterization is no longer as apt as it once was. On the one hand, female legislators continue to place a higher priority on issues that pertain to women, children and families than do men, while men prioritize agriculture and employment. But on the other hand, male and female legislators do not differ significantly in their views on education, health or economic policy, despite the perception of these issues as typically feminine (Schwindt-Bayer 2006). Women introduce more women's rights bills than do men, but institutional rules hamper legislators' ability to translate their preferences into legislative outcomes (Htun and Power 2006; Schwindt-Bayer 2006). The more women who serve as legislators, the more responsive legislatures are to policy on women's rights and the more confidence people (men and women alike) have in the legislature as an institution (Schwindt-Bayer and Mishler 2005).

Research is mixed about the degree to which gender quotas have an impact beyond the legislative arena. Teresa Sacchet (2008) argues that debates surrounding the introduction of gender quotas increased the visibility and political salience of all women's rights issues, fostering opportunities for collective action that did not exist before. Pär Zetterberg (2009) suggests the impact of quotas has been more limited. In a quantitative study that compares data from 17 countries, Zetterberg finds no evidence that quotas "foster women's political engagement."

One limitation within existing work on gender and legislative behavior centers on a disproportionate amount of research on legislatures relative to research on the executive branch. This limitation is not unique to work on gender, or even to work on legislatures in Latin America, but it does reflect a research agenda that has sought to export scholarship on the U.S. Congress into the comparative arena. The effort to test claims about the U.S. Congress and state legislatures against data from other countries has advanced our understanding of how legislatures operate, but it makes sense to consider the impact of various branches of government in relation to one another. Theoretically, given the predominance of presidential systems with strong executive powers in Latin America, progress on women's rights should rest on the willingness of the president to exert political capital to prioritize women's demands and to implement existing policies. This theoretical expectation has not always been borne out; strong presidents often have a difficult time getting their legislative agenda passed by congress. The discrepancy between theory and reality offers another rich vein for future research.

The Executive Branch

Women's election to the presidency raises many interesting questions, but as a relatively new phenomenon, few scholars have written about it. Let me pose just two of the most obvious ones from a gender politics perspective: first, what explains women's success, and second, to what extent have female presidents used their power to advance women's rights more generally? Chilean President Michelle Bachelet invoked her status as a woman often and self-consciously throughout her campaign and her entire term in office. She effected tremendous changes in reproductive rights policy, passing legislation that legalized the morning-after pill by framing sex education and contraception as public health issues and by emphasizing her role as a medical doctor (Borzutzky and Weeks 2010; Ríos Tobar 2009). The number of women elected opens up the prospects for new research on female executives.

The pool of women leaders is deep and wide. Female candidates have come close to winning the presidency in several countries in the region. Both Bachelet and Fernandez triumphed over female competitors. Soledad Alvear was Bachelet's main competitor until she pulled out of a primary race in 2005. Elisa Carrió came in second to Argentina's Fernandez, garnering 22% of the vote in the 2007 election. In Peru, Lourdes Flores Nano won 24% of the vote in 2001 and 2006. In the 2008 presidential election in Paraguay, Blanca Ovelar finished second with 31% of the vote against little more than 40% for the male winner. Balbina Herrera won 38% of the vote for president of Panama in 2009. Research on gender and cabinet appointments also reveals promising patterns of gender recruitment in the executive branch more broadly, with women holding more positions in non-traditional portfolios (Escobar-Lemmon and Taylor-Robinson 2005, 2009; Friedman 2009a).

Does the election of women represent an enduring shift in the status of women, or does it reflect a temporary electoral mood? In part, political parties have nominated women candidates in an effort to appeal to voters disenchanted by traditional political parties and traditional (male) politicians: women's long-time exclusion from politics allows voters to continue to see women as political outsiders, giving them an advantage over corrupt and mostly male political insiders.

We do not yet know to what extent high numbers of candidates who have come close to winning mean that women are likely to repeat these successes again in future elections. One clue lies in the background of female candidates. How do women's career paths differ from those of male political leaders? Many of the women political leaders today, like many of the men, got their start in politics at the height of power for the revolutionary left. Chilean President Michelle Bachelet was a member of a radical wing of the Socialist Party, Argentine President Cristina Fernandez belonged to the Peronist Youth, and Brazilian Presidential hopeful Dilma Roussef was a guerrilla in a revolutionary movement. Many of them are traditional politicians whose gender allows them to be perceived by voters as something new.

Most of the research on the executive branch has focused on state agencies for women. State machinery for women, such as Brazil's Special Secretariat on Policy for Women and Chile's National Women's Service (SERNAM), seek to mainstream gender policy and to coordinate efforts to address women's rights across various government agencies and ministries. Most governments have created a special agency for women or gender, but these agencies remain weak and underfunded. Their ability to incorporate gender perspectives into mainstream public policy depends on strong relations with civil society organizations (Franceschet 2003).

The Courts

Research on gender and courts is a growth area, reflecting recent changes in the strength of the judiciary throughout the region. As courts in the region have undergone reforms to strengthen and rationalize them, social conflict has become increasingly "judicialized." Feminist advocates in Latin America are turning to the courts to promote the struggle for gender equality. The judicial path represents a potentially effective way to circumvent other political arenas that may be clogged by corruption. Nonetheless, using the courts requires a level of legal capacity that only a tiny minority of women's organizations possesses. Women must know what their rights are and what laws protect them, they need access to affordable and competent lawyers, and they need the resources to file cases. As courts get stronger and more autonomous as the result of judicial reform, it is reasonable to predict that they should uphold claims to defend, protect, and expand women's rights. The extent to which this prediction holds true will foster interesting and important new research.

Domestic political institutions operate in a global arena in which international institutions have come to play critical roles in shaping feminism and public policy. Unable to effect change at home, either because of weak institutions or discrimination, activists have turned to international institutions in the hopes of exerting external pressure (Friedman 2009b). A wide array of international instruments aim to protect women's rights, including UN treaties (especially the Convention to End All Forms of Discrimination Against Women, or CEDAW), regional treaties, resolutions taken by the UN General Assembly, and statements agreed upon by UN members at international conferences, such as the 1995 Beijing Platform for Action. The most important of these are CEDAW and the Treaty of Belém do Pará, which are binding treaties that obligate governments to take action to protect women's rights. The Belém do Pará Treaty has been influential in part because it focuses specifically (and solely) on the relatively noncontroversial issue of violence against women; it protects women from violence in public and private spaces and allows women to file petitions with the Inter-American Commission on Human Rights (IACHR) in cases of rights violations. The first Belém case heard by the IAHCR in 1998 involved a woman who had been given the death penalty for murdering her husband, despite years of prolonged violence she had suffered at his hands. The IACHR succeeded in reducing her sentence (Meyersfield 2010).

Directions for Future Research

I would like to see future research on gender in Latin America embrace two things: first, more expansive and more frequent comparisons, and second, greater attention to masculinity and gendered perspectives on the role of men (for a similar argument, see Baldez 2010). Single-country case studies and cross-national comparisons are central to research on gender in Latin America. We can increase the scope of comparison within this literature by doing more comparisons across localities, regions, movements and issue areas. Research on policy adoption and implementation at the local level can tell us more about the impact of policy on women's lives as well as shed light on our understanding of the development of state capacity. To what extent can states guarantee the protection of rights of women evenly throughout the entire territory? To what extent do sub-national variations in policy delivery affect women from various identity-based groups, such as Afro-Latin women and indigenous women? Research that compares Latin America to other regions can help us understand variation in the meaning and salience of specific issues. While feminists in Latin America care deeply about abortion, the terrain of reproductive rights is different for women in other regions of the world. Cross-regional comparisons may illuminate innovative ways of framing issues to facilitate consensus and coalition building. Comparing instances of gender-based mobilization may also prove fruitful. Scholarship continues to over-represent feminist movements to the exclusion of conservative or right-wing women's movements that may or may not support women's rights (but see Baldez 2002).

One of the most important insights from research on gender-oriented public policy in Latin America is that not all gender issues are alike (Htun 2003). The factors that lead to improvements in women's health may differ from those that result in publicly-funded childcare. More research that compares across issues, such as Franceschet and Krook's (2006) comparison of progress on gender quotas and state feminist agencies, will strengthen the effort to explain policy outcomes. Research that compares gender-based policy to non-gender public policy would test feminist assumptions that limited gains in women's rights policy inevitably reflect gender discrimination or sexist cultural patterns. Much of the research on policy implementation tends to describe the pros and cons of policy changes for women's status. Descriptive studies play an essential role in the construction of knowledge about public policy, but theory-driven research can facilitate more rigorous explanations.

Men are largely missing from research on gender and Latin American politics. Theoretically, research on gender looks at the ways in which conceptions of masculinity and femininity frame and shape political events. Gender analysis looks at the implications that conceptions of women's roles have for men, and vice versa. It examines the extent to which certain assumptions about men and women underpin politics, often with regard to issues that do not center on women's rights. Despite a culture in which machismo is a constant topic of conversation, male behavior in the political arena continues to be considered gender neutral, and expressions of masculinity continue to be seen as politically normal and unproblematic. Research on gender could devote more explicit attention to the significance of masculinity in the Latin American political arena.

Bibliography

Alvarez, Sonia E. 1990. *Engendering Democracy in Brazil: Women's Movements in Transition Politics.* Princeton, NJ: Princeton University Press.

Alvarez, Sonia E., Elisabeth J. Friedman, Ericka Beckman, and Maylei Blackwell. 2002. "Encountering Latin American and Caribbean Feminisms." *Signs* 28 (2): 537–579.

Baldez, Lisa. 2002. *Why Women Protest: Women's Movements in Chile.* New York: Cambridge University Press.

———. 2010. "The Gender Lacuna in Comparative Politics." *Perspectives on Politics* 8 (1): 199–205.

———. 2011. "The UN Convention to Eliminate All Forms of Discrimination Against Women (CEDAW): A New Way to Measure Women's Interests." *Politics & Gender* 7: 1–6..

Borzutzky, Silvia, and Gregory B. Weeks, eds. 2010. *The Bachelet Government: Conflict and Consensus in Post-Pinochet Chile.* Gainesville: University Press of Florida.

Brady, Henry E., and David Collier. 2010. *Rethinking Social Inquiry: Diverse Tools, Shared Standards.* Lanham, MD: Rowman & Littlefield.

Chaney, Elsa. 1979. *Supermadre: Women in Politics in Latin America.* Austin: Institute of Latin American Studies by University of Texas Press.

Corrales, Javier, and Mario Pecheny. 2010. *The Politics of Sexuality in Latin America: A Reader on Lesbian, Gay, Bisexual, and Transgender Rights.* Pittsburgh, PA: University of Pittsburgh Press.

de la Dehesa, Rafael. 2010. *Queering the Public Sphere in Mexico and Brazil: Sexual Rights Movements in Emerging Democracies.* Durham, NC: Duke University Press.

de Mello e Souza, Cecilia. 2008. "Grassroots Leadership in the Network of Healthy Communities in Rio de Janeiro, Brazil: A Gender Perspective." *Gender & Development* 16 (3): 481–494.

Escobar-Lemmon, Maria, and Michelle M. Taylor-Robinson. 2005. "Women Ministers in Latin American Government: When, Where, and Why?" *American Journal of Political Science* 49 (4): 829–844.

———. 2009. "Getting to the Top." *Political Research Quarterly* 62 (4): 685–699.

Espina, Gioconda. 2009. "Feminist Activism in a Changing Political Context." In *Feminist Agendas and Democracy in Latin America*, ed. Jane S. Jaquette. Durham, NC: Duke University Press. 65–82.

Falcón, Julissa Mantilla. 2009. "Gender and Human Rights: Lessons from the Peruvian Truth and Reconciliation Commission." In *Feminist Agendas and Democracy in Latin America*, ed. Jane S. Jaquette. Durham, NC: Duke University Press. 129–144.

Franceschet, Susan. 2003. "'State Feminism' and Women's Movements: The Impact of Chile's Servicio Nacional de la Mujer on Women's Activism." *Latin American Research Review* 38 (1): 9–40.

Franceschet, Susan, and Krook, Mona Lena. 2006. "State Feminism and Gender Quotas in the 'North' and 'South': Comparative Lessons from Western Europe and Latin America." Paper presented at the annual meeting of the International Studies Association, Town & Country Resort and Convention Center, San Diego, California, March 14, 2011. Available at http://www.allacademic.com/meta/p100195_index.html

Friedman, Elisabeth J. 2009a. "Gender, Sexuality and the Latin American Left: Testing the Transformation." *Third World Quarterly* 30 (2): 415–433.

———. 2009b. "Re(gion)alizing Women's Human Rights in Latin America." *Politics & Gender* 5: 349–375.

Gago, Veronica. 2007. "Dangerous Liaisons: Latin American Feminists and the Left." *NACLA Report on the Americas* 40 (2): 17–19.

Haas, Liesl. 2010. *Feminist Policymaking in Chile.* University Park: Pennsylvania State University Press.

Htun, Mala. 2003. *Sex and the State: Abortion, Divorce, and the Family under Latin American Dictatorships and Democracies.* New York: Cambridge University Press.

Htun, Mala, and Timothy J. Power. 2006. "Gender, Parties and Support for Equal Rights in the Brazilian Congress." *Latin American Politics and Society* 48 (4): 83–104.

Inter-American Commission on Human Rights. 1994. *Inter-American Convention on the Prevention, Punishment and Eradication of Violence Against Women.*

Inter-Parliamentary Union. 2010. "Women in National Parliaments." http://www.ipu.org/wmn-e/classif.htm (January 2, 2011).

International IDEA. 2006. "Global Database of Quotas for Women." www.quotaproject.org (April 26, 2006).

Jones, Mark P. 2004. "Quota Legislation and the Election of Women: Learning from the Costa Rican Experience." *Journal of Politics* 66 (4): 1203–1223.

Kampwirth, Karen. 2002. *Women & Guerrilla Movements: Nicaragua, El Salvador, Chiapas, Cuba.* University Park: Pennsylvania State University Press.

King, Gary, Robert O. Keohane, and Sidney Verba. 1994. *Designing Social Inquiry.* Princeton, NJ: Princeton University Press.

Meyersfield, Bonita. 2010. *Domestic Violence and International Law.* Oxford: Hart Publishing.

Molyneux, Maxine. 1985. "Mobilization Without Emancipation? Women's Interests, the State, and Revolution in Nicaragua." *Feminist Studies* 11 (2): 227–254.

Monasterios, Karin. 2007. "Bolivian Women's Organizations in the MAS Era." *NACLA Report on the Americas* 40 (2): 33–37.

Power, Margaret. 2002. *Right-Wing Women in Chile: Feminine Power and the Struggle Against Allende, 1964–1973.* University Park: Pennsylvania State University Press.

Ríos Tobar, Marcela. 2009. "Feminist Policymaking in Contemporary Chile: From the Democratic Transition to Bachelet." In *Feminist Agendas and Democracy in Latin America*, ed. Jane S. Jaquette. Durham, NC: Duke University Press. 21–44.

Sacchet, Teresa. 2008. "Beyond Numbers." *International Feminist Journal of Politics* 10 (3): 369–386.

Schmidt, Gregory D., and Kyle L. Saunders. 2004. "Effective Quotas, Relative Party Magnitude, and the Success of Female Candidates: Peruvian Municipal Elections in Comparative Perspective." *Comparative Political Studies* 37 (6): 704–734.

Schwindt-Bayer, Leslie A. 2006. "Still Supermadres? Gender and the Policy Priorities of Latin American Legislators." *American Journal of Political Science* 50 (3): 570–585.

Schwindt-Bayer, Leslie A., and William Mishler. 2005. "An Integrated Model of Women's Representation." *The Journal of Politics* 67 (2): 407–428.

Sternbach, Nancy Saporta, Marysa Navarro-Aranguren, Patricia Chuchryk, and Sonia E. Alvarez. 1992. "Feminisms in Latin America: From Bogota to Taxco." *Signs* 17 (2): 393–434.

Vargas, Virginia. 2009. "International Feminisms: The World Social Forum." In *Feminist Agendas and Democracy in Latin America*, ed. Jane S. Jaquette. Durham, NC: Duke University Press. 145–164.

World Bank. 2010. "GenderStats." http://go.worldbank.org/YMPEGXASH0 (accesed January 2, 2011).

Zetterberg, Pär. 2009. "Do Gender Quotas Foster Women's Political Engagement?: Lessons from Latin America." *Political Research Quarterly* 62 (4): 715–730.

PART IV

International Concerns

22

U.S.-LATIN AMERICAN RELATIONS

Power, Politics, and Cooperation

Peter H. Smith

Relationships between the United States and Latin America deserve more attention than they get. The subject might seem boring at first glance. There have recently been no major crises, wars, or revolutions. Developments within the region have little impact on global geopolitics. American presidents and leaders pay scant attention to the region, even as they possess the power to exert their will whenever they want. Consequently, interactions between Latin America and the United States appear to lack theoretical and practical importance.

Wrong on all counts. The purpose of this chapter is to identify conceptual and methodological issues in the study of U.S.-Latin American relations, to present some queries and concerns, and to suggest potential avenues for further research. This is neither a full-blown literature review nor an empirical narrative. It deals with politics and political science (and the subfield of international relations) rather than with history or economics.[1] It purports to be a "think-piece," however presumptuous that label seems.

More to the point, I explore three sets of central questions:

1. Has the United States been losing power in Latin America? To what extent? At what cost?
2. What are the impacts of Latin America's democratization on the conduct of inter-American relations? How has it affected policy-making processes?
3. What are the prospects for hemispheric cooperation? Under what circumstances can the United States and Latin America work together to address common problems?

I conclude with broad assessments about the theoretical and practical importance of U.S.-Latin American relations and opportunities for scholarly collaboration.

Power in Perspective

The world is undergoing rapid change. The Cold War has come to an end, globalization has accelerated processes of interdependence, the attacks of 9/11 and the war on terror have unleashed bitter conflicts, and the rise of China and other emerging powers has begun reshaping geopolitical arrangements. Within the Western Hemisphere, the United States has been conducting itself with aloof detachment and uncertainty. Indeed, one leading expert has documented the "gradual decline of U.S. dominance" in the region over the past half-century.[2] In colloquial form, the question thus arises: Has the United States lost control of its backyard?

The answer depends, of course, on the meaning of power. We might begin with the still-classic formulation of Robert Dahl, who defined power as a relationship: "*A* has power over *B* to the extent that he can get *B* to do something that *B* would not otherwise do." It involves not only the use or threat of force but rational calculation of self-interest. As Leslie Gelb has written,

> Power is mental arm wrestling. It derives from establishing psychological and political leverage or advantage by employing resources (wealth, military capability, commodities, etc.), position (such as a geographic regional balancer, or a political protector), as well as maintaining resolve and unity at home. These are embodied in a process whereby *A* convinces *B* that *A* can and will help or harm him, give him pleasure or pain, relieve his difficulties or increase them—whatever the costs to *A* himself. Power thus varies with each and every relationship and changes with each and every situation. It has to be developed and shaped in almost each and every situation, and will vary over time and place. And critically, the wielder of power must take great care to be credible, to be taken seriously, both at home and abroad.[3]

Power is in this sense relational, situational, and changeable. Classic resources include demographic size, economic wealth, military prowess, and technological achievement.

By conventional standards, the United States continues to dominate the Americas. As shown in Table 22.1, the U.S. GDP is nearly 10 times that of Brazil, close to 20 times that of Mexico, about 40 times that of Venezuela, and almost 50 times that of Argentina (not to mention Chile). Its population is much larger than that of any Latin country. GDP per capita is almost 5 times those of Chile and Venezuela, the most prosperous countries in the region. (And in passing, we might note that America's GDP is larger than the combined output of the world's next three largest economies, and almost 3 times that of China.)

The implication is clear: The United States continues to wield enormous power over its hemispheric neighbors. Bilateral relations remain highly asymmetrical. In terms of power resources, no one in the Americas comes close to matching the United States.[4]

Yet it is also apparent that the United States has been losing geopolitical leverage. Symptomatic of this trend are commercial relations. As shown by Table 22.2, Latin America's economic dependence on the United States has declined substantially over the past decade

Table 22.1 Profiles for United States and Latin America: Selected Countries, 2009

	GDP (billions)	Population (millions)	GDP/capita
Argentina	307.1	40.3	7,550
Brazil	1,594.5	193.7	8,070
Chile	163.7	17.0	9,470
Mexico	874.8	107.4	8,960
Venezuela	326.1	28.3	10,090
United States	14,119.0	307.0	46,360

Source: World Bank at <www.worldbank.org>

Table 22.2 U.S. Shares of Latin American Trade, 2000–2010

	Exports		Imports	
	2000	*2010*	*2000*	*2010*
Middle America & Caribbean:				
Costa Rica	55.0	33.6	23.6	40.0
Dominican Republic	87.3	52.0	60.6	44.0
El Salvador	65.4	43.5	50.0	32.1
Guatemala	36.1	36.9	40.1	34.6
Honduras	53.8	65.0	47.6	50.7
Mexico	88.7	73.5	72.0	60.6
Nicaragua	39.7	58.2	25.0	23.4
Panama	45.4	5.3	32.9	10.0
South America:				
Argentina	12.0	5.4	19.1	13.8
Bolivia	24.0	12.3	22.5	11.9
Brazil	22.4	9.6	23.1	15.0
Chile	16.8	10.4	17.8	17.0
Colombia	50.4	37.4	35.5	32.4
Ecuador	38.0	37.3	25.0	29.6
Paraguay	3.9	1.3	7.2	16.6
Peru	28.1	16.1	24.7	24.7
Uruguay	8.4	2.9	9.8	8.8
Venezuela	51.9	38.7	33.5	26.6

Source: IMF, Direction of Trade Statistics accessed at <www2.imfstatistics/org/DOT/>

or so. The U.S. share of exports has declined sharply, especially in South America—from 24 percent to 12 percent in Bolivia, from 22 percent to less than 10 percent in Brazil, from 28 percent to 16 percent in Peru. Overall percentages are higher in Middle America and the Caribbean, but changes are apparent even there: U.S. export shares dropped from 55 percent to 34 percent in Costa Rica, from 87 to 52 percent in the Dominican Republic, and from 89 percent to 74 percent in Mexico (notwithstanding its membership in NAFTA). Some countries send hardly any exports directly to the U.S. market.[5]

U.S. shares of Latin America's imports reveal a similar pattern. In Mexico the proportion slipped from 72 percent to 61 percent, in Argentina it dropped from 19 to 14 percent, and for Brazil it faded from 23 to 15 percent. Data are ambiguous for quite a few other cases, but an indelible impression nonetheless emerges: Diversification in Latin America's commercial relations means less economic leverage for the United States.

Such developments have prompted considerable anxiety in conservative circles, where the loss of U.S. power is exaggerated and lamented. The emergence of China as the largest single trading partner for both Chile and Brazil has prompted especially widespread concern. In contrast, progressive analysts have applauded the resulting surge in economic growth as well as autonomy for Latin America. And predictably enough, centrist observers have embraced contradictions: it's good for Latin America to acquire more independence, but bad for the United States to have less influence. (You really can't have it both ways.)

In retrospect, it is not clear whether or how the United States could have prevented these commercial rearrangements. They respond to underlying economic realities—the process of globalization, the entry of China into the international market, and, not least, the revamping of the American economy. (Less emphasis on manufacturing means less need for raw materials.) And even from a U.S. point of view, this structural shift might have positive results: While promoting growth in Latin America, it has absolved the United States of responsibility for the region's economic destiny.

Theoretically, at least, the United States might have worked harder to forge a Free Trade Area of the Americas with stringent rules of origin and elevated tariffs against non-members, actually a customs union. Alternatively, it might have forged a dense, extensive, and exclusive network of FTAs throughout the hemisphere. Such policies might well have precipitated global trade wars, however, and, fortunately, they never received serious consideration.

The analysis of changing power relationships requires careful distinctions. It is one thing to assess the *direction* of change (from more to less); it is another to measure the *degree* of change (from one level to another); and it is still another to detect critical *thresholds* of change (where incremental changes can make important differences).

It is abundantly clear that the United States has not given high priority to Latin America since the end of the Cold War. Under Bill Clinton, George W. Bush, and Barack Obama, Washington has paid scant attention to the region. Why might this have been the case? Several explanations come to mind:

- Involvement in other parts of the world—i.e., Iraq and Afghanistan—leading to a situation that Paul Kennedy has called "imperial overstretch";[6]
- A calculation that the benefits of greater U.S. attention to the region would not be worth the costs (since, paradoxically, power entails responsibility);
- A related view that conditions within the hemisphere do not require more attention (since U.S. predominance was assured, especially in the absence of a serious extra-hemispheric rival).

The superpower has been inattentive. This poses a conceptual challenge: How to analyze power resources that are not put to visible use?

One approach might consider hard-headed national interests. Has the apparent decline in U.S. power in the Americas led to serious harm? Has it endangered the national interest?

Not in self-evident ways. Take the question of economic integration. Latin America has diversified its trade relationships, as shown in Table 22.2, and managed to defeat a U.S.-backed proposal for a Free Trade Area of the Americas. But this was not a disastrous setback for the United States. The Bush administration had ambivalent views about FTAA and was unwilling to negotiate key terms, especially with regard to agriculture. Moreover, the demise of the FTAA left Washington free to pursue a more selective series of bilateral FTAs. The resulting hub-and-spoke strategy entailed asymmetrical bargaining, served U.S. political purposes, and divided the region into two camps (those with and without FTAs). At the end of the day, the national interest was fully intact.

A second major issue is the war on drugs. For decades, the United States has enlisted Latin American governments in violent campaigns against drug trafficking. Notwithstanding widespread (and increasing) doubts about the efficacy of efforts to curtail the supply of illicit drugs, rather than demand, successive administrations have encouraged

Latin Americans to continue the fight. The Clinton team supported Plan Colombia, the Bush administration approved the Mérida Initiative, and the Obama group has stayed the course. The result has been extensive violence, most recently (and spectacularly) in Mexico. To put it in crass terms, the United States has successfully managed to export its drug war to Latin America.

A third major issue has involved the "global war on terror." Citizens and governments of Latin America have criticized U.S. actions in Iraq and, more recently, in Afghanistan. There has been widespread grumbling about the "securitization" of inter-American relations and, in particular, about efforts to tighten control of the U.S.-Mexican border. At the same time, no Latin American government has challenged the underlying logic of the fight against Al Qaeda.[7] Despite increasing ties with Iran, no one has endorsed the use of terror or the extremist Islamic cause. In this regard the region has provided unstinting support to the United States.

To put it in a nutshell, there has been little need for the United States to devote huge resources to inter-American affairs. The region presents no serious challenge to U.S. national interests. Disagreements occur within the boundaries of diplomacy. Generally speaking, Latin America is a pretty safe place. And this, in turn, has led to my own speculation that

> relative tranquility throughout the Western Hemisphere has proven to be a major benefit to the United States. It has enabled Washington to project its military and economic power around the globe without fear of deadly retaliation on the southern flank. Imagine otherwise: What if we had Lebanon or Iraq as a near neighbor instead of Mexico? What if Venezuela were Iran?... What if Latin America were Africa or central Asia? By being as peaceful and quiet as it has been, Latin America has provided a very substantial (and largely invisible) subsidy for America's foreign policy in other parts of the world.[8]

Silence can be as important as cacophony.

Whatever the merits of my argument, it raises a significant methodological point. The conduct of U.S.-Latin American affairs should be analyzed and understood within the context of the global arena, not as a separate phenomenon. All too often it is interpreted in isolation, with little if any attention to developments in other areas. As a superpower, the United States views the world as a vast checkerboard; what happens in one region might well have an impact on other regions. As scholars and analysts, we therefore need to broaden our horizons.

Chronological perspective raises additional concerns. The assessment of a "decline" (or increase) in U.S. power between t_1 and t_2 depends, very largely, on the selection of the starting point t_1. If the analysis begins at the peak of U.S. power, say the 1950s, the perception of decline is necessarily going to be very acute. But if the starting point is different—say, the decade 1900–1910—the resulting picture would be very different. We might see instead a steady increase in U.S. power as a consequence of World War I, the Great Depression, and World War II. The Cold War tempted the United States to impose its will throughout the hemisphere; the end of that struggle removed the sense of urgency. In this light, the diversification of economic and political interests in contemporary Latin America presents no major cause for concern. Over the course of a century, the historic arc of U.S. power might take the shape of an inverted U. Indeed, the emerging distribution of power within the hemisphere bears a provocative resemblance to the situation of 100 years ago.

Soft Power and Hegemony

The study of power has produced a proliferation of undefined terms. What are the precise meanings of such concepts as unipolarity, predominance, primacy, and—that most-over-used notion of all—hegemony?

Hegemony means different things to different people. It has been used to indicate a virtual monopoly of power. Somewhat differently, it can mean the ability to exert one's will without significant challenge.[9] It can refer to a self-appointed right to rule.[10] And borrowing from the work of Antonio Gramsci, it can mean acceptance by actor B of the right to rule by actor A. In this sense, A's power over B is seen as right and proper, as a suitable expression of values and realities. Domination and subordination thus become legitimate. (All of which raises an empirical question: Who speaks for actor B?)

For the record, I see only two periods when the United States enjoyed Gramsci-style hegemony over Latin America—the 1930s-50s and the 1990s. From FDR's declaration of the "Good Neighbor" policy through the aftermath of World War II, the United States was generally admired as an efficient and effective democratic superpower. Similarly, the collapse of the Soviet Union and of the international communist movement temporarily affirmed the legitimacy and acceptability of U.S. preeminence. The 1990s formed an unusual time of economic, military, political, and ideological supremacy for the United States. It ended with 9/11 and the unleashing of the global war on terror, especially the invasion of Iraq.

These observations lead directly to the notion of "soft power." As framed by Joseph Nye, soft power represents the ability to achieve objectives not through threats, payments, or force, but through co-optation and attraction. Attraction, in turn, can lead to acquiescence. "When you can get others to admire your ideals and to want what you want, you do not have to spend as much on sticks and carrots to move them in your direction."[11] Or in Dahlian terms, if you are A and you can narrow the gap between your objectives and what B "would otherwise do," then you don't have to work so hard.

Such benefits come from appreciation and admiration for the society as a whole—for its culture ("from Harvard to Hollywood" plus Michael Jordan), its political values (if it lives up to them), and its foreign policy (if seen as legitimate).[12] The underlying proposition seems self-evident: The more positive the evaluation of a society, the more effective are its claims to leadership.

Soft power is controversial. High-minded idealists have embraced the concept since it brings normative and ethical dimensions into the analytical equation. Hard-headed realists have dismissed the notion as wishful and fanciful. Methodologists have worried about operationalization. It has supporters and detractors.

My personal view is that the notion of "soft power" substantially enriches our sense of power and politics. It improves understanding of, let us say, the paramount role of the United States in the 1950s and the 1990s. It is especially helpful in the conceptualization of day-to-day influence in the absence of military force.

Only the hardiest of souls would attempt to quantify such an inherently mushy notion. Efforts have nonetheless been made. Table 22.3, for example, presents a slightly Eurocentric "soft power index" based on measurements for 26 countries around the world. France and the United Kingdom come out on top, with the United States close behind in third place (and Brazil and Mexico farther down the list). As the author observes, "The last decade has been a challenging one for ... the USA. The fallout of the Iraq and Afghanistan wars continues to stain America's image in much of the world. But its election of President Obama

Table 22.3 Soft Power Index, 2010

1. France	1.64
2. UK	1.64
3. USA	1.57
4. Germany	1.44
5. Switzerland	1.39
...	
20. Brazil	0.69
22. Mexico	0.61

Source: Jonathan McClory, "The New Persuaders: An International Ranking of Soft Power" (London: Institute for Government, 2010)

in 2008 went far in restoring America's reputation abroad.... And even when American soft power is dented by perceptions of its conduct abroad, the immense reach and appeal of its cultural outputs ensure the American brand remains a strong one."[13]

Soft power exists in the eye of the beholder, however, not in the existential realities of the society in question. France and the UK and the United States might possess all sorts of admirable qualities, but how do we know how they are perceived? As stated above, all dimensions of power—including soft power—are relational and situational. Why would Brazilians and Mexicans share identical views of the United States? It can also vary sharply over time. The soft power of the United States was much less apparent under George W. Bush than under Bill Clinton or Barack Obama.[14]

Variation across place and time raises serious methodological issues. How to analyze long-term fluctuations in soft power? This is an especially acute problem in Latin America, where public opinion surveys are a relatively recent phenomenon. (The World Values survey started only in the 1980s, and the Latin American Barometer—Barómetro Latinoamericano—came on stream in the 1990s.) Potential indicators might include the popularity of Hollywood films, translations and sales of U.S.-produced books, attendance at American universities, levels of tourism and migration, adoptions of American clothing styles, consumption of American cuisine. One of the most fascinating aspects of soft power is its changeability; this is also one of its most vexing features.

Regime Change and Policy-Making

The most remarkable trend in Latin American politics over the past several decades has been democratization. In country after country, mantles of power have passed from self-appointed military chieftains to freely elected civilian politicians. How has this affected the conduct of inter-American relations?

One might imagine that the onset of democracy would subject foreign policy to intense public scrutiny. Citizens would feel entitled to express their view on international affairs. A free press could stimulate discussion, awareness, and debate. Representative officials—deputies, senators, governors—could take part in setting agendas, forging policies, and overseeing implementation. Foreign affairs would no longer be the province of exclusive elites.

Soft power would come to play a significant role. *Ceteris paribus*, in fact, the concept requires the existence of democracy, or, at least, of an active and participant public. Soft power is an expression of popular will. Authoritarians do not have to heed the opinions or voice of the people; democratic leaders do. (In autocratic settings, of course, soft power can inspire and encourage opposition movements.)

All of which brings up a key question: How has Latin America's democratization affected the making of foreign policy? This requires careful study of decision-making processes. More precisely, we need to compare processes and policies under authoritarian regimes with those that take place under democracy. This is a broad and ambitious agenda for future research.

Within democratic frameworks, we need to explore:

- The content of popular opinion on international affairs,
- The salience in political campaigns of foreign-policy questions (including relations with neighboring countries, as well as with the United States),[15] and
- The extent to which foreign policy is seen as a prerogative of the executive branch (including specific cabinet ministries and/or bureaucracies, such as Itamaraty in Brazil).

The more open the process, the greater the relevance of soft power. The more closed the process, the less important are popular views.

Whether democratic processes yield differential policy outputs remains an open question. In some instances, there might be very little room for maneuver with regard to the United States; in other cases or there might exist a widespread and historical consensus on "grand strategy." To resolve such doubts we need detailed studies of policy-making in Latin America as well as in the United States.[16]

The New Left

A crucial dimension of Latin America's democratization has been the rise of a so-called "New Left." Beginning with Venezuela in 1998, the region has witnessed a surge of leftist electoral triumphs—in Brazil, Argentina, Bolivia, Ecuador, Nicaragua, and Uruguay. In 2008 voters in Paraguay threw their support to Fernando Lugo, a former Catholic bishop and advocate of "liberation theology" whose victory ended the 62-year reign of the Colorado Party, his country's equivalent of the Mexican PRI. In 2009 the citizens of El Salvador threw their support in 2009 to Mauricio Funes, a candidate of the once-revolutionary FMLN, while Uruguayans voted for José Mujica, a former member of their country's Tupamaro guerrilla movement. In 2010 Brazilians cast decisive votes in favor of the PT's Dilma Rousseff, and in 2011 Peruvians gave their backing to Ollanta Humala.

What has been the meaning of this trend? First and foremost, the pink tide was a protest movement. It was a protest against conditions of poverty, inequality, and corruption. It was a protest against the inability (or unwillingness) of governments to promote effective social justice. It was a series of spontaneous outbursts, not an organized or orchestrated effort.

In ideological terms, the pink tide represented a broad cluster of values rather than a clear-cut formulation. It was far from doctrinaire—inspiration came from such diverse sources as nationalism, populism, indigenous tradition, Catholicism, and, not surprisingly, diluted forms of Marxism. In contrast to the "radical" movements of the 1960s and 70s, it did not seek "revolutionary" change.[17] Instead, it expressed a general commitment to social justice, support for the poor, and a compassionate world system. More specifically, the movement amounted to a rejection of the neoliberal policies propounded by the Washington Consensus—free-market policies designed to promote free trade, foreign investment, and the reduction of state power. Such critiques helped give the movement an anti-American flavor, augmented by deep-seated resentment of the George W. Bush administration's unilateralist style and, more particularly, from opposition to the U.S.-led war in Iraq. (America's "soft power" plummeted sharply as a result.) This sentiment changed substantially after the 2008 election of Barack Obama, despite subsequent disappointment over his apparent lack of interest in the region.

What have been the consequences for U.S.-Latin American relations? First, the rise of the new Left made it abundantly clear that democratically elected leaders would not necessarily become allies of the United States. It thus demolished one of the most cherished myths of American policy making: the idea that democratization would produce automatic support for U.S. policies. On the contrary, the emergence of the new Left meant that the United States would have to face vigorous criticism—opposition to the war in Iraq, resentment of Washington's arrogance, rejection of pro-U.S. economic policies—from democratic leaders representing popular opinion. This revealed to a profound irony: The more the Latin American policy process resembled that of the United States, the more contentious would be the region's dealings with the United States.[18]

Second, the fact that new Left leaders came to power through elections tied the hands of Washington. U.S. officials and publicists could no longer appeal to the need for "regime change" in order to improve the welfare of the hemisphere and/or the world. This removed a longstanding justification for threats, pressure, or hostility. (During the Cold War the United States had shown little hesitation in displacing "inconvenient democracies" and may well have encouraged an attempted coup against Hugo Chávez as late as 2002, but such episodes look like remnants of an increasingly distant past.)[19] Ultimately, free and fair elections provided left-of-center leaders in Latin America with a protective political shield.

Third, the ubiquity of electoral democracy established a basis for regional cooperation. To be sure, political dynamics have led to partisan divisions—between governments of the Left, Center, and Right. The historic notion of the "Bolivarian dream" of Latin American unity has in the meantime been derided and dismissed, partly because of its contemporary association with the sometimes-outlandish claims of Venezuela's Hugo Chávez.

Equally compelling has been the search for strength in numbers, particularly through organizations that exclude the United States. Leaving aside economic integration schemes (such as MERCOSUR), political efforts include: Ibero-American Summits (initiated 1991), the *chavista* ALBA (2004), UNASUR (initiated 2005), and, perhaps most important, the Comunidad de Estados Latinoamericanos y Caribeños (CELAC, initiated 2010). With more than 30 members, CELAC has been formed as a successor to the Rio Group (1986). But in marked contrast to the Rio forum, essentially an informal gathering of 23 member states, CELAC proposes to become a permanent and official institution. Its ultimate and unstated goal is to establish a capacity for balancing against the still-preeminent United States. Successful or not, it is a remarkable sign of autonomy and coordination.[20]

Even within the Organization of American States (OAS), Latin American nations have sometimes managed to assert their will against the United States. In the case of Honduras, where an elected president was in 2009 removed from office (and the country) by a pre-dawn coup, it was the Latin Americans who resisted recognition of the unconstitutional government that followed. Here was the ultimate irony: Latin American representatives were upholding the spirit of democracy, while the United States (under Barack Obama) was willing to capitulate and compromise.

Inter-American Collaboration

Recent developments throughout the Western Hemisphere add considerable complexity to prospects for inter-American collaboration. Gone are the hegemonic eras when the United States could credibly (and unilaterally) launch a hemisphere-wide initiative and assume that all countries would contentedly consent. That happened at the founding meeting of the OAS in 1948, when John Foster Dulles insisted on an anti-communist declaration, and in 1961, when John Fitzgerald Kennedy proclaimed the Alliance for Progress. It nearly happened at Miami in 1994, when the United States proposed formation of a Free Trade Area of the Americas, although that initiative eventually foundered on the rocks of U.S. intransigence and left-of-center resistance from Latin America.

Does this herald the twilight of inter-American cooperation? Does the fading of American hegemony mean the end of region-wide diplomacy? Not necessarily. It depends upon the convergence (or divergence) of national interests, the pool of stakeholders, the substance of the issue at hand, the relevance of collective action, and the calculation of costs and benefits.[21]

To be sure, some matters might be more effectively managed in bilateral or minilateral settings, where the number of participants is relatively small and bystanders are not so directly affected. Take the question of energy. In principle it would be extremely difficult to forge a regional consensus around oil-related policies, since some nations export petroleum while others have to import.

But some issues have hemispheric scope. And where all actors have stake in the outcome, and the distribution of benefits is acceptable, there might be room for multilateral action. Examples might include:

- Environmental protection—to avoid the "tragedy of the commons," in light of global warming and the degradation of resources. Exactly what is the commons, what are its boundaries, and who are the commoners? Does the Amazon forest belong to everyone or only to Brazil?

- Transnational crime—underground international elements not only operate outside the boundaries of the law, they challenge the reach of the law and pose serious threats to democratic governance. Building upon sophisticated networks, they tend to be mobile, elusive, and strong. One of the most profitable activities has been smuggling—of people, weapons, money, drugs, anything that moved. They sometimes establish de facto rule over geographic territories, carving out semi-sovereign "republics" under their primitive control. They frequently overwhelm public security forces, outgunning local police and even military units. Often operating with impunity, transnational criminal organizations have undermined the capacity, will, and legitimacy of constitutional states. Globalization has its darker side.

- Drug trafficking—which has become the most conspicuous (and lucrative) form of international crime. This is a preeminently transnational activity. Except for pharmaceuticals, drugs are typically produced in one part of the world, transported through another, and consumed in still another. As just one example, coca leaf has historically been harvested in the high Andes (Bolivia, Peru, Colombia), processed in lowland Colombia, and transmitted to northern Mexico or to Caribbean islands for eventual distribution in the United States, where consumption remains at high levels. Where there is demand, there will be supply.

With U.S. urging, Latin American governments have sought to contain the drug trade and re-establish political authority by unleashing "wars" against the traffickers, usually by enlisting the armed forces as well as the police. Colombia endured a decade of all-out violence from the 1990s into the early years of this century. Now a transit route for cocaine, Central America has witnessed a growth of criminality and violence. But the hardest hit area, as of this writing, has been Mexico. Upon taking office in December 2006, President Felipe Calderón declared an open war on the top half-dozen drug trafficking organizations, which responded with lethal force. The carnage took a terrible toll on the nation as a whole—its economy, its democracy, and the fabric of its society.

As numerous policy experts and leading authorities have said, the challenges posed by drug trafficking require a change of focus—and multilateral cooperation. One approach might entail a hemispheric effort to reduce demand—not only in Latin America, where it has been steadily growing, but also (and especially) within the United States. This would redirect energy and resources, complement current efforts, and, by its explicit acknowledgment of responsibility, enhance America's soft power.[22]

Beyond the identification of specific issues, the analytical task is to define the conditions that enable (or preclude) inter-American cooperation. What are the most propitious circumstances? How are these prospects affected by pervasive and long-lasting asymmetries of power?

Such broad questions invite creative exploration of rigorous methodological tools. Statistical measures can help provide quantitative assessments of levels, degrees, and dimensions of asymmetry. Game theory can specify the terms, conditions, and extent of compliance with (or defection from) multilateral schemes. Under what circumstances do weaker countries join with stronger partners in a common enterprise? As "bandwagoning" free riders, or only in return for material side payments? In addition, Bayesian algebra could help identify the conditions—or combinations of conditions—that promote cooperation or defection. What is most notable about such methods is their relative absence from the current literature on U.S.-Latin American relations.[23]

Who Cares?

The inter-American panorama poses fundamental challenges to the study of international relations. One is to appreciate the sheer importance of Latin America to the United States. This derives not only from geographic proximity. It stems also from the connection between the welfare of the region and the welfare of the United States. The current appearance of smooth sailing does not justify inattention and lack of concern. Events in Latin America have threatened U.S. national interests in the past and could do so again. And besides, what happens within hemisphere might have real impacts on U.S. capabilities in other parts of the world.

Latin America offers a fascinating laboratory for the testing of key hypotheses in the field of international relations. It contains a broad diversity of countries, large and small, from high middle-income to poverty-stricken. Once stereotyped as a sleepy backyard, the region has undergone a notable process of democratization. The ideological consequence has been to divide the region into differing camps—socialist, center-left, center-right, and right—all in the shadow of a formerly hegemonic superpower. What conditions could have produced such a counterintuitive result? What has been the interplay of hard and soft power? What gives rise to asymmetric alliances? And in the present environment, what constitute the most effective weapons of the weak?

We need more research on basic questions. We need to enrich our understanding of policy-making processes—in the United States and, especially, within Latin America. Only then will we be able to evaluate the long-term impacts of democratization throughout the region and resulting relationships with the United States, the dynamic processes of give-and-take. One way to promote these objectives would be through collaborative research projects involving American and Latin American scholars and, importantly, area specialists and theorists in international relations.[24]

An especially grand challenge concerns Latin America's changing position within the world order. That will depend, of course, on the nature of the world order—unipolar, multipolar, flat—or some kind of combination. Leslie Gelb has recently argued the contemporary world takes the shape of a "pyramid"—"The United States stands alone at the pinnacle, with formidable and unique global powers of leadership, but not the power to dominate. Stacked below are many tiers of states...." A second level includes China, Japan, India, Russia, the United Kingdom, France, Germany, and "just barely" Brazil. These states together comprise "the Eight Principals, or simply The Eight. If Washington is the sole leader, they are the principals or managing directors of the global realm.... "[25] The key to effective world governance is cooperation between the United States and the Eight.

A third layer includes leading oil and gas producing states (from Saudi Arabia to Venezuela and Nigeria). A fourth stratum consists of mid-level states "with mostly localized potential as Regional Players" including Mexico along with Nigeria, South Africa, Pakistan, South Korea, and Taiwan. Still lower are the "Responsibles," such as Chile, and beneath them are "the Bottom Dwellers or Problem States," nation-states in various conditions of political and/or economic disarray. A final category includes non-state actors such as NGOs, international media, and international business.

It is unclear which scenario will actually come into play. But as Latin America—or individual nations of Latin America—jockey for position, they will have distinctive roles to play. Most attention has focused on the two most prominent states, Mexico and Brazil.[26]

Generally speaking, the geopolitical vocation of Latin America involves the developing world. It can wield considerable clout through a variety of mechanisms:

- Concerted action in regional organizations, including CELAC and the OAS
- Representing developing-world interests in multilateral organizations, such as the UN and the WTO
- Forging ad hoc clubs or alliances with other countries at similar stages of development and empowerment, such as BRIC (which includes Brazil, Russia, India, and China).

In such ways Latin America can aspire to provide firm leadership for the developing world. And, in addition to being a leader, the region might also serve as a model. What would happen if other nations and areas—Africa, the Middle East, Central Asia—were to follow the path of Latin America? How might the "LatinAmericanization" of the developing world affect the global order? Thus can the study of U.S.-Latin American relations fire the geopolitical imagination.

Notes

1 Historians have produced especially creative work on the intersection of high politics and socio-cultural dynamics at the local level. See Gilbert M. Joseph, Catherine C. LeGrand, and Ricardo D. Salvatore, eds., *Close Encounters of Empire: Writing the Cultural History of U.S.-Latin American Relations* (Durham NC: Duke University Press, 1998), and Gilbert M. Joseph and Daniela

Spenser, eds., *In from the Cold: Latin America's New Encounter with the Cold War* (Durham NC: Duke University Press, 2008).

2 Abraham F. Lowenthal, "The United States and Latin America, 1960–2010: From Hegemonic Presumption to Complex Interdependence," published as "Estados Unidos y América Latina, 1960–2010: de la pretensión hegemónica a las relaciones diversas y complejas," *Foro Internacional* 50, nos. 3-4 (julio-diciembre 2010): 552–627.

3 Leslie H. Gelb, *Power Rules: How Common Sense Can Rescue American Foreign Policy* (New York: HarperCollins, 2009), 32–33.

4 Stephen G. Brooks and William C. Wohlforth, "American Primacy in Perspective," *Foreign Affairs* 82, 4 (July/August 2002): 20–33.

5 Uruguay and Paraguay trade mainly with their partners in MERCOSUR, Argentina and Brazil, while Panama functions as an emporium and clearing house for international trade.

6 Paul Kennedy, *The Rise and Fall of the Great Powers: Economic Change and Military Conflict from 1500 to 2000* (New York: Random House, 1987).

7 Hugo Chávez of Venezuela has criticized the military involvements in Afghanistan and Iraq, but not (to my knowledge) the campaign against Al Qaeda.

8 Peter H. Smith, *Talons of the Eagle: Latin America, the United States, and the World,* 3rd edition (New York: Oxford University Press, 2008), 377.

9 Smith, *Talons of the Eagle,* 6.

10 Abraham F. Lowenthal, "The United States and Latin America: Ending the Hegemonic Presumption," *Foreign Affairs* 55, 1 (October 1976): 199–213.

11 Joseph S. Nye, *Soft Power: The Means to Success in World Politics* (New York: Public Affairs, 2004), x. Nye first coined the term in 1990. See also Inderjeet Parmar and Micahel Cox, eds., *Soft Power and U.S. Foreign Policy: Theoretical, Historical, and Contemporary Perspectives* (London: Routledge, 2010).

12 Nye, *Soft Power,* 11.

13 Jonathan McClory, *The New Persuaders: An International Ranking of Soft Power* (London: Institute for Government, 2010), 6.

14 Julia E. Sweig, *Friendly Fire: Losing Friends and Making Enemies in the Anti-American Century* (New York: Public Affairs, 2006).

15 See David Mares, "Intra-Latin American Relations: The Challenge of Promoting Cooperation While Defending Sovereignty," in this volume.

16 Outstanding examples are William L. LeoGrande, *Our Own Backyard: The United States in Central America, 1977–1992* (Chapel Hill: University of North Carolina Press, 1998), and Lars Schoultz, *That Infernal Little Cuban Republic: The United States and the Cuban Revolution* (Chapel Hill: University of North Carolina Press, 2009).

17 See Kurt Weyland, Raúl L. Madrid, and Wendy Hunter, eds., *Leftist Governments in Latin America: Successes and Shortcomings* (New York: Cambridge University Press, 2010).

18 Peter H. Smith, *Democracy in Latin America: Political Change in Comparative Perspective*, 2nd edition (New York: Oxford University Press, 2012), 331.

19 Ibid., ch. 4.

20 See Russell Crandall, "The Post-American Hemisphere: Power and Politics in an Autonomous Latin America," *Foreign Affairs* 90, 3 (May/June 2011): 83–95. In some quarters the emphasis on autonomy and agency has led to retroactive (and controversial) reinterpretations of historical realities, as in the case of Hal Brands, *Latin America's Cold War* (Cambridge MA: Harvard University Press, 2010).

21 Robert O. Keohane, *After Hegemony: Cooperation and Discord in the World Political Economy* (Princeton: Princeton University Press, 1984, 2005).

22 In mid–2009 I actually made this suggestion at a policy seminar organized by the U.S. State Department. It sparked some interest but essentially fell upon deaf ears.

23 Mariano Bertucci, "Towards a Theoretical and Explanatory Turn: A Critical Assessment of Research on U.S.–Latin American Relations" (University of Southern California, 2011).

24 A multivolume series co–edited by Jorge Domínguez and Rafael Fernández de Castro made a promising start in this direction, but it was only a start.

25 Gelb, *Power Rules,* 76.

26 Robert Chase, Emily Hill, and Paul Kennedy, eds., *The Pivotal States: A New Framework for U.S. Policy in the Developing World* (New York: W. W. Norton, 1999).

23

INTRA-LATIN AMERICAN RELATIONS

The Challenge of Promoting Cooperation While Defending Sovereignty

David R. Mares

Intra-Latin American relations provide a rich historical, geostrategic, ideological and even domestic political set of puzzles for scholars and policymakers who seek to understand central theoretical questions or regional empirical challenges. Yet, although Latin American nations have interacted with each other since their founding, most international relations analysts focus on their relations with the United States. Intra-Latin American relations should also draw the attention of analysts with a U.S. focus, however, because they affect bilateral and regional relations with the United States and extra-regional states and institutions.

This chapter proceeds from the perspective that relations among Latin American nations themselves, though inevitably influenced by the world around them, are important objects of study in their own right. As an organizing framework for conceptualizing these relations, I suggest that there has been and continues to be a fundamental tension in intra-Latin American relations: the promotion and defense of national sovereignty on the one hand, and the recognition that the region would be better able to promote and defend its interests in an anarchic world by cooperating with each other.

Historically, competition has consistently won out. Yet, Latin American history is filled with bilateral and multilateral efforts to accommodate the defense of sovereignty with the promotion of cooperation within Latin American as a whole, or within varying subsets of Latin American nations. The research questions that those historical experiences and contemporary labors generate can be grouped into (1) why pursue cooperative relations; (2) where (geographically and by issue area) has progress been achieved and where not; (3) what limitations on cooperation were explicitly set, why and with what consequences; (4) when (time period) did cooperation predominate or make progress; (5) what do these past successes and failures suggest are the key variables that can be affected to promote greater and deeper cooperation; and (6) what can we expect to be the balance between defending sovereignty and promoting intra-Latin American cooperation in the future?

These key questions need to be addressed in intra-regional and bilateral comparative perspectives across time through the rigorous combining of theory and evidence. Unfortunately, too often the work in the field is propelled by the desire for cooperation to reign rather than from an appropriately critical scholarly perspective. The result is the misuse of general theories on cooperation, a reliance on the development of formal agreements, and a selective presentation of data to assert that a new cooperative era is at hand.

These errors are more prevalent when discussing political cooperation and security issues than economic concerns because there are no commonly accepted metrics to evaluate progress on political and security issues. It is common, therefore, for analysts to use the number of diplomatic agreements signed as evidence of increasing cooperation without analyzing their actual impact on behavior over time or when considered with other variables (e.g., impact of geography as a deterrent). In addition, indicators of behavior are often poorly defined (e.g., what constitute confidence building measures), and some variables are used whose alleged impact is theoretically weak (e.g., democracy when governments reject Liberal values and institutional constraints). The problem is less pronounced, though still present, for the study of economic cooperation and integration because empirical economists can identify actual rates of progress using definitions and categories that enjoy widespread, though not universal, agreement. Nevertheless, even here there are debates about whether economic integration is progressing, stagnating or diminishing. Research designs are also often inappropriate for measuring the true impact of causal variables on outcomes (e.g., selecting on the dependent variable, for example when only successful cases of border resolutions are discussed).

The chapter opens with brief discussion of the key concepts of sovereignty and cooperation. A historical overview of intra-Latin American relations illustrates the fact that nations have long desired to cooperate in the promotion of security and development. Just as often, however, those efforts were undermined by competitive pressures. A subsequent section examines contemporary challenges to the promotion of cooperative intra-Latin American relations in the political, military and economic arenas. I end the essay by proposing a research agenda for the study of intra-Latin American relations.

Defining Key Terms

In practice, intra-Latin American relations are characterized by the use of key analytic terms as political rhetoric by governments, NGOs, social groups and others involved in the making of those relations. For example, the creation of a regional organization that denounces militarization of disputes without addressing the sources of tension or the types of arms being purchased is hailed as a great advance in building regional security (the South American Defense Council). As analysts we need to distinguish between the loose use of key concepts for political purpose and their utility as elements in an argument about why and how those interstate relations develop. Our goal should not be simply to describe political battles, but to understand the coordinates of political debate and why that debate is fruitful or not. Clarity in analysis is key to that task.

"Sovereignty" as an analytical concept is most usefully defined as the ability of a government to decide how it will respond to international challenges and opportunities.[1] It is not the ability to decide to do whatever one wants or to be impermeable to transnational flows of goods, ideas and people. No state in the international system can choose to ignore potential costs of their behavior in all arenas at all times, nor can any state that seeks to develop its economy be cut off from all flows except those approved by the government. Every actor on the international stage is constantly making choices in terms of what they want to do and how much they believe they would need to "pay" (not just in monetary terms, but also in terms of reputational and opportunity costs) for the options that they are considering.

The concept of sovereignty, therefore, applies to process (choosing a policy) rather than outcomes. Whether a policy chosen produces the expected outcome depends not only on what that government chooses to do but also on what the other relevant governments choose, i.e., international relations takes place in a context of strategic interaction. There are also variables that could affect the outcome and over which the relevant governments may have little influence: global markets, powerful states from outside the region, etc. For example, the price Bolivia demands of Argentina and Brazil for its natural gas is now going to be significantly affected by the technological breakthroughs in shale gas exploitation and the resulting increase in supply and fall in price of liquefied natural gas (LNG).

Analysts need to be aware of the difference between the way in which the concept sovereignty is used popularly (e.g., "the sovereignty of our borders is violated by illegal activities across them" or "the price we get for our natural resources is not just") and its value as an analytic concept to understand relations among states.

"Cooperation" entails the mutual adjustment of policy, rather than a natural agreement to work together (which is better classified as "harmony" and is exceedingly rare).[2] It represents a policy choice because "adjustment" implies moving away from one's ideal point on any of the three major components that are affected by cooperation: definition of policy goals, strategies for the implementation of a policy, and the distribution of the costs and benefits of that policy. Cooperation does not require that the parties agree to spread the costs of adjustment equally among themselves; rather that distribution will instead reflect the relative bargaining influence of the parties on those issues on which cooperation is being pursued. Cooperation also does not mean that parties agree on all three components: definitions and strategies could be distinct, but complementary, and the distribution of costs in one area could be part of one government's broader foreign or domestic policy agenda, thus making acceptable a less favorable distribution than otherwise. Analysts need to be aware of these possibilities because they make more comprehensible why cooperation happens in some areas (e.g., regional non-proliferation), but not others (international sources of money and arms for groups rebelling against their national governments) or is not lasting (the defense of democracy as defined in the 1991 OAS Declaration of Santiago).

Consequently, a view of sovereignty that emphasizes not ceding on issues that historically defined the nation (territorial boundaries, types of economic activity) or helped define a nation's view of itself (as a producer of certain products) will be a significant obstacle to cooperation, especially that which seeks to promote actual political or economic integration.

Although a policy choice, cooperation could be market or politically driven and its characteristics will reflect that particular logic. Markets can be useful as a relatively impartial (compared to national governments) arbiter among competing interests, but for them to function politics has to permit it, and we'll often see governments complementing economic logic with policies that protect some important interests from the full brunt of market forces. Similarly, politically driven cooperation or integration is also affected by markets. Markets for some products might permit the subsidization of politically driven cooperation or integration, as in the case of Venezuela's petroleum exports to the world market and the promotion of the Bolivarian Alliance for the Americas (ALBA) trade scheme. Too often scholars of Latin America are led by politicians' rhetoric (e.g., "Free" trade or "Bolivarian" integration) rather than by the need to understand the logics and dynamics of different schemes. The challenge for analysts is to distinguish between the two, show the relative influence of each and the implications for cooperation and integration of different combinations.

Competition and Cooperation Throughout History

Latin American countries have historical roots dating back before the birth of the United States that provide constants that influence important issues today (e.g., physical boundaries between communities, movement of peoples, rivalries for influence). This rich colonial and national history needs to be remembered and understood. Ignorance or myth making means some unforeseen obstacles can derail progress though they might have been avoided, mitigated or even resolved if actors had been aware of them. History can provide lessons from what didn't work in the past or how one made progress before something derailed it. One might learn, for example, that the "nation state" in whose defense of sovereignty prior cooperation has been undermined, is itself a construction of the community whose borders have shifted and whose identity is itself a product of internal domination (hence the move towards an ill-defined but fervently pursued "plurinationalism"). In more concrete terms, will the development of "plurinational" states in Bolivia and Guatemala make resolution of the 100+ year-old border disputes with Chile and Belize more likely?

Creating National States Out of Colonial America

At Independence (1810–1823 for most countries), the map of Latin America looked distinctly different than it does today, reflecting the reality that the process of national consolidation created losers and winners within the community of Latin American states. Haiti was the first Latin American country to achieve Independence (in 1804 from France). It was an early powerhouse, conquering the rest of the island of Hispaniola from the Spanish in 1820 until the Spanish-speaking part broke away in 1844 to form the Dominican Republic. But then internal strife rent the nation, and it fell into the economic and political collapse from which it has yet to recover. Haitians fled the chaos in droves, causing problems with recipient countries, including in 1937 a massacre by Dominican Republic police of thousands of Haitians in the country illegally.

Brazil has always been distinct, and always had significant potential to be the leading nation in South America—or a state that would look outside the region for its identity and standing. Not only is the country Portuguese speaking, but decolonization turned it into an Empire, not a Republic as happened in Spanish America (Mexico was a short lived Empire in 1822–1823). Independent Brazil was slave owning until 1888, though most Spanish American nations freed slaves at Independence (slaves were not freed in Cuba until 1886, but the island was still a Spanish colony). Brazil perceived it carried an unfair cost of the fight against Paraguay in the War of Triple Alliance (1864–1870 when Argentina, Uruguay and Brazil decimated Paraguay) and thereafter tried to stay out of intra-Spanish American rivalries. Under the doctrine of *uti possedetis* and the guidance of Baron Río Branco, Brazil gained through international negotiations and arbitrations territory the size of France from its Spanish American neighbors. Throughout most of the 20th century, Brazil engaged in a military rivalry with Argentina that included purchasing dreadnought battleships prior to WWI, a military alliance with the United States during WWII which allowed Brazil to beef up security on its border with Argentina and a competitive race to develop nuclear weapons that lasted into the 1990s. (Given its own rivalry with Argentina, Chile did not sign the Treaty of Tlatelolco banning nuclear weapons in Latin America either, but it had no active nuclear weapons program.) In many ways, Brazil's relationship with the United States (often perceived as a special one by Brazilians) was based on the idea that it was a stable outsider itself having to deal with unruly Spanish American neighbors.

In short, the transition from colony to sovereignty was very contentious within Latin America. Some larger political units lost significant territory (e.g., the Mexican Empire 1822–1823 claimed all of Central America; Mexico lost what is now the U.S. southwest and its claim on Guatemala; Guatemala lost territory to British Honduras, now Belize; Venezuela lost territory to Guyana; Bolivia lost its littoral province to Chile; and Peru also lost territory to Chile and Colombia, while Ecuador lost territory to Peru); others ceased to exist (i.e., the United Provinces of Central America, Gran Colombia, the Peru-Bolivia Confederation); and still others gained significant territory at the expense of their Latin American neighbors' claims (e.g., Brazil from Bolivia and Argentina from Chile through diplomacy backed by the threat of military force; Chile from Bolivia and Peru, and Peru from Ecuador through military force sanctioned by diplomacy). What is now Uruguay was initially part of Portuguese Brazil (1816–1822), then of the Brazilian Empire from 1822–1828; it was only created as a separate nation at the end of the Argentine-Brazil War (1825–1828).

The contemporary result of these territorial disagreements and forced political settlements is that many land and sea borders remain unclear and unresolved (see Table 23.1)

Table 23.1 Currently Unresolved Interstate Disputes within* Latin America

Countries	Disputed Issue
Boundary Related Disputes	
Honduras-El Salvador-Nicaragua	Golfo de Fonseca delimitation
Honduras-Nicaragua	Maritime delimitation in Caribbean; migration
Nicaragua-Colombia	Maritime delimitation
Nicaragua-Costa Rica	Impact of river dredging on boundary
Honduras-El Salvador	Territorial Isla de Conejo
Colombia-Venezuela	34 points on border in dispute; migration; guerrillas; contraband, including but not limited to drugs;
Brazil-Uruguay	Arroio Invernada (Arroyo de la Invernada) area of Rio Quarai (Rio Cuareim) and islands at confluence of Rio Quarai and Uruguay River
Bolivia-Chile	Territorial dispute: outlet to the Pacific
Ecuador-Peru	Maritime delimitation
Chile-Peru	Maritime delimitation
Other Disputes	
Panama-Colombia	Guerrilla incursions into Panama
Ecuador-Colombia	Guerrilla and drug trafficker incursions and environmental impact of Plan Colombia drug war on Ecuador
Argentina/Uruguay	Environmental impacts on the River Uruguay
Haiti-Dominican Republic	Migration

* Latin American nations are involved in inter-state disputes with non-Latin American states as well (e.g., Argentina- Great Britain, Guatemala-Belize, Venezuela-Guyana, and multiple sea-based claims with the U.S.)

Sources: CIA, *The World Factbook 2009,* Department of Defense, *Maritime Claims Reference Manual 2005*; *International Boundary Research Unit* http://www.dur.ac.uk/ibru/resources/ accessed February 17, 2010; ICJ press releases http://www.icj-cij.org/presscom/index.php?p1=6&p2=1 accessed February 17, 2010

Constructing Identities and Politics

The repudiation of colonialism and military struggle for independence stimulated the need for a new identity. Cultural, ideological and political ties have promoted cooperation among the like-minded, but fueled existing tensions or generated new ones. The region has always been internationalized, with regional ties helping those international influences accommodate themselves to Latin America's context.

The reality of cultural diversity across Indigenous, African and European populations created numerous regional and subregional identities and thereby influenced relations among Latin American nations. The first attempts emphasized the distinct nature of life and politics in the New World and ranged from a search for "the western hemisphere Ideal," oriented towards relations with the world (and which fit well within a Monroe Doctrine perspective), to the internal battle of "Civilization v. Barbarism" a la Domingo F. Sarmiento. By the end of the 19th century, writers and thinkers helped construct a sense of cultural commonality among those with Latin roots, with such beacons as Cuban Jose Martí, Mexican Jose Vasconcelos, Nicaraguan Ruben Darío, Chilean Pablo Neruda, Argentine Jorge Luís Borges, and Colombian Gabriel García Márquez, among many others read and identified with across national borders. Mexican *boleros,* Argentine tangos, Brazilian sambas and Cuban *trovas* combine with Mexican, Colombian and Venezuelan *telenovelas* as well as Mexican and Argentine cinema to create a cultural dialogue across the region. Paintings and sculpture by the Ecuadorian Oswaldo Guayasamín, Costa Rican Francisco Zúñiga and Colombian Fernando Botero assumed and encouraged a common regional identity.

Culture can clash with ideology, however. In the latter half of the 19th century and into the early 20th, a Positivist-influenced Liberalism propelled Mexicans to support their counterparts' revolts against Conservative governments in Central America. Anarchists were also active and internationally oriented, particularly across incipient Latin American union movements. Progressive and nationalist movements reached across borders, but were not beyond discriminating among adherents, as when the Nicaraguan Augusto César Sandino expelled the Salvadoran Farabundo Martí from his international army because Martí was a Communist. Marxists followed their class ideology in proselytizing and organizing adherents, and with the establishment of the Cuban Revolution, arming them for revolt across the region. The populist Juan Perón tried to extend his influence across the region by creating a hemispheric labor movement, while the Peruvian non-Communist leader on the left Victor Raúl Haya de la Torre saw his Alianza Popular Revolucionaria Americana (APRA) reproducing itself around the region to promote anti-imperialism and "Indo-Americanism."

Even in retreat, many Latin American leaders internationalized their specific struggles by seeking exile in sympathetic Latin American countries where they could work on creating a political movement back home to return to office. Political leaders in exile, including those involved in conspiracies during the 1940s–1950s to overthrow dictatorships in Central America, Venezuela and the Caribbean[3] remained involved in home country politics. In addition there were large movements of persecuted workers, peasants and middle-class intellectuals from the El Salvador massacre in 1932; in the 1970s refugees from Central & South America's national security focused military dictatorships fled to Mexico, Venezuela, Costa Rica and Cuba to continue their opposition to governments back home.

Security Relations

Efforts to create institutional mechanisms to promote security, peace and cooperation among Latin American nations have been pursued since Independence. In 1826 Simón Bolívar convened the Congress of Panama, attended by Mexico, Central America, Colombia, and Peru, which produced a Treaty of Union, League, and Perpetual Confederation. These leaders believed that the structure of national government fundamentally influenced international behavior, and in a harbinger of the region's contemporary views of the security implications of democracy (see below), called for the suspension from the group of any state that significantly altered its structure as a republic.[4] The Charter of the Organization of American States (OAS) in 1948 banned aggression against another member as well as intervention in the domestic affairs of member states.

Cooperation efforts have historically encompassed security concerns and developed mechanisms to limit arms. For example, Argentina provoked an arms race by attempting to equal Chilean naval strength in 1898; war scares continued until 1902. British mediation successfully brokered the most famous arms control treaty in South American history. The *Pactos de Mayo* of 1902 resulted in both countries selling warships they had under construction in Europe, as well as the disarmament of some ships already in service. Of longer lasting importance, the pacts resolved the power projection rivalry by assigning each its sphere of influence, Chile in the Pacific, Argentina in the Atlantic.[5] The Treaty of Tlatelolco (1967 and still in force) proscribing nuclear weapons in Latin America is probably the most well-known regional effort.

Economic Relations

There have long been efforts to stimulate economic relations among Latin American nations. Brazil was interested in accessing Bolivian energy supplies in the 1930s (oil) and again in the 1970s (natural gas). There was much collaboration among governments and intellectuals throughout the early 20th century as they developed nationalist energy legislation to deal with the private international oil companies. But there was also competition in economics, which produced spectacular events like Chile's seizure of Bolivian and Peruvian nitrate-rich territory in the War of the Pacific. Even less stunning efforts carried serious consequences for the loser, as when Argentina ended Bolivia's dreams of exporting oil in the 1920s by refusing to permit building of an oil pipeline linking Bolivia to the Parana River and placing a high tariff on Bolivian crude passing through its territory in order to keep Argentine oil attractive to the private international oil companies.[6]

After WWII Latin American nations, with the West European example and prodded by the UN Economic Commission on Latin America, promoted regional economic integration as a means of fueling economic development. Most Latin American countries, including Argentina and Chile, signed multiple bilateral trade agreements.[7] In 1953 the democratic governments of General Carlos Ibáñez del Campo (1952–1958) and General Juan Domingo Perón (1948–1955) signed a treaty to create an economic union, with a gradual elimination of tariffs. The Union was to be open to all countries of South America. It was followed by another agreement on trade and financial cooperation.[8]

In 1960 the Latin American Free Trade Association (LAFTA) was created by Argentina, Brazil, Chile, Mexico, Paraguay, Peru and Uruguay to promote the establishment of a common market; Bolivia, Colombia, Ecuador and Venezuela joined in 1970. But little progress was made, and in 1980 it was reorganized as the Latin American Integration Association

(ALADI), with more flexible policies designed to promote greater membership and even bilateral integration agreements. In 1969 Bolivia, Chile, Colombia, Ecuador and Peru created the Andean Pact to promote their economic integration within an import-substitution industrialization paradigm; Venezuela joined in 1973. But Chile withdrew in 1976 as it embarked on an incompatible neo-liberal development strategy and Venezuela left it in 2006, claiming that the Colombian and Peruvian Free Trade Agreements with the United States undermined the organization. In 1987 the organization was significantly modified to emphasize the primacy of market mechanisms, export oriented industrialization and a greater role for foreign investment, to be achieved via tariff reductions, the adoption of a common external tariff and limited policy harmonization across member countries. One of the major objectives of the modifications was to improve the Andean Group's integration with the rest of the world. The Andean Community, as it is now called, developed other integration efforts with a court of justice, parliament and council of foreign ministers in 1979. A development bank created to support the Andean Pact, the Corporación Andino de Fomento (CAF), now has members from outside the Andes as well as fifteen private Latin American banks and funds projects in Brazil, Uruguay, Argentina, Venezuela, the Dominican Republic, and Panama.

The following five Central American countries have the longest current continuous history of integration efforts in the region and these span the economic, political and social realms. A series of bilateral free trade agreements in the 1950s among Guatemala, Honduras, El Salvador, Nicaragua and Costa Rica were the precursors for the General Treaty of Central American Economic Integration ratified in 1961–1962. A number of ancillary organizations were created to promote integration, including a Permanent Secretariat, development bank, monetary clearing house and monetary council (see Table 23.2). Trade among members as a percentage of their total trade expanded rapidly, from 7% in 1960 to 26% in 1970.

But the 1969 war between El Salvador and Honduras began the significant weakening of integration efforts. The two countries had no official commercial or diplomatic relations for a decade afterward. Honduras withdrew from the Common Market in 1970 when the group failed to enact reforms it favored. Although the value of intraregional trade continued to rise in the 1970s, its relative share stagnated, then collapsed when the civil wars and debt crises of the 1980s hit. The integration effort recovered in 1991, when the Central American Integration System agreements were developed. The Dominican Republic became an associate state in 2004, and Mexico, Chile and Brazil joined as regional observers.

The movements of people across Latin American borders looking for work, that is, economic refugees, have generated transnational communities as they have become integrated into a neighboring state's society, e.g., Bolivians into Argentina, Brazilians into Uruguay, Peruvians into Chile, Colombians into Venezuela, and Central Americans into Mexico. That movement has also created tensions and the need for bilateral policies to deal with the social, economic and political externalities generated, particularly by Haitians in the Dominican Republic, Guatemalans in Mexico, and Nicaraguans in Costa Rica. A specter holding continuing threat to neighbors is Brazilians' migration into disputed territory with its neighbors in the early 20th century which resulted in a successful challenge to sovereignty. Currently, on the Paraguayan side of the border with Brazil, there are towns using Brazilian currency, speaking Portuguese in schools and flying the Brazilian flag. In addition, tempers run high at Brazilian soybean farmers' massive land purchase and rentals for mechanized soybean production which throws Paraguayan peasants off the land.

Table 23.2 Central America's Institutional Context, c. 1967

Central American, Official:
>
> Permanent Secretariat of the General Treaty
>
> Executive Council of the General Treaty

Central American Economic Council
>
> Central American Bank for Economic Integration
>
> Central American Institute of Research & Industrial Technology
>
> Central American School of Public Administration
>
> Central American Monetary Council
>
> Central American Clearing House
>
> Superior Council for Central American Universities
>
> Institute of Nutrition of Central American & Panama
>
> Regional Plant & Animal Sanitation Organization
>
> Council of Labor and Social Welfare
>
> Central American Tourism Secretariat

Central American, Private Sector
>
> Central American Air Navigation Service Corporation
>
> Central American Institute of Business Management
>
> Federation of Central American Associations & Chambers of Industries
>
> Central American Institute of Labor Union Studies
>
> Central American Federation of Chambers of Commerce

International
>
> UN Economic Commission on Latin America
>
> U.S. Agency for International Development
>
> Organization of American States
>
> Inter-American Development Bank

Source: Central American Bank for Economic Integration, Investment Development Department, *Investment Opportunities in the Central American Common Market* Tegucigalpa, Honduras, 1967, pp. 62–63

Contemporary Challenges for Studying Intra-Latin American Relations

As the historical review clearly indicates, in evaluating progress on cooperation in the region, or its broader economic, security and political implications, analysts must not get lost in the proliferation of agreements signed and promises made—many of these never come to fruition, or are undermined when governments are replaced or economic conditions change. In this section I propose some avenues for investigation that will further our theoretical understanding of intra-Latin American relations.

Indigenous Rights and the Redefinition of the Nation State

Ethno-nationalism or the assertion of *indigenismo* is a new issue with no historical parallel since heretofore indigenous peoples were to be conquered and excluded or annihilated, or assimilated into *mestizaje*. (The alleged *indigenismo* of the early 20th century was in reality premised on the desirability of assimilation into the *mestizo* world.) Until the last few years integration has been thought of in terms of Western-defined nation states, and though many scholars and activists welcome this assertion of *indigenismo*, we have not systematically and rigorously incorporated this new variable into our studies. If those of us who study Latin America's international relations are to do so, we need to rely on our comparative politics colleagues and their interdisciplinary work with sociologists, anthropologists and philosophers to define and measure the analytic coordinates of these new forms of identity in the region. Assuming that we can distinguish theses categories, a number of important questions arise for the study of intra-Latin American relations.

If we're now dealing with plurinational states, how does an Indigenous America nation that extends from the Yaqui in northern Mexico to the Mapuche in southern Chile, or a pan-Maya or pan-Quechua nation that extends beyond the Western-recognized boundaries of a nation affect relations among plurinational states? And how will the process of finding the basis for cooperation be affected if indigenous peoples truly reject the Western view of dominating nature and the pursuit of material well-being? How will this different world view impact relations with countries where the vast majority want development, including natural resource exploitation, to bring lower prices for fuel, food and recreation? The African heritage in the Caribbean basin has been a factor in its evolution since Independence, but Brazil, Peru and Colombia have been latecomers to thinking about how Afro-Latin America fits into the national identity. Brazil has developed significant relations with African countries as a result. Will an Afro-nationalism become part of Latin America's plurinationalism? In short, how does ethnonationalism or the assertion of indigenismo fit with the efforts to bring Latin American countries and societies closer together?

Cooperation for the Promotion and Defense of Democracy

Although the United States and Latin America gave lip service to the goal of promoting and defending democracy in the Charter of the Organization of American States that called for democracy in the region, it was not until the third wave of democracy had resulted in the 1990s in elected governments in all Latin American countries except Cuba, that Latin American governments took on the defense of democracy as a practical goal to be pursued. While there are moral and human rights arguments for democratic politics, what concerns us here is the use of the "democratic peace" theoretical argument to justify this change.

Within the field of international relations, scholars uncovered an empirical fact: nations with democratic governments have never engaged in war between or among themselves. Explanations were developed that emphasized the determining influence of norms or institutions for explaining that peace. In search of promoting a zone of peace in Latin America, virtually all of the analysts working on security issues in the region concluded that defending democracy was important to peace in the region.

These analysts ignored, however, the conditions under which virtually all of these theories were postulated to hold. The definition of peace meant that no conflict exceeded the technical definition of war: a conflict in which at least one-thousand deaths were battlefield related.[9] While democratic peace theorists in the international relations field have raised the need to explain why democratic nations do engage in militarized conflicts that can result in up to 999 battlefield related deaths, Latin Americanists have tended to equate democratic peace with no militarized conflict at all: military force to resolve interstate disputes is not just illegitimate, but inconceivable. Ignoring the presence of militarized interstate disputes, explaining the 1982 Malvinas/Falklands War between Argentina and Great Britain as an anomaly of military government, and often forgetting about the 1969 war between Honduras and El Salvador, security analysts working on Latin America simply proclaim the region the most peaceful in the world, then move on to assert that democracy is fundamental to the continuation of this state of affairs.

Outside the region, democratic peace theorists have been very concerned to discover the logic of how democratic norms or institutions restrain the use of military force in interstate conflict. For the normative analysts, it is the Liberal principle that dissenting views are considered inherently legitimate. For institutional analysts, it is the dispersal of policymaking power that develops via constraints on the Executive. In fact, some democratic peace theorists have argued that the period of democratization is a particularly dangerous time for war because leaders can use nationalist appeals and the democratic process to raise fear of neighboring states and peoples among the citizenry in order to silence critics and consolidate power at home.[10]

Yet, applications of the democratic peace argument in Latin America refuse to engage in the requisite discrimination among governments to distinguish among which nations a democratic peace can be constructed and which governments in fact represent a threat to peace in the region. The very notion of a participatory rather than Liberal democracy needs to be analyzed for its normative and institutional logics to determine whether the democratic peace outcome can still be expected to result. But in the name of sovereignty and regional peace itself, governments refuse to engage in this discussion and the academic community ignores the issue in their analyses.

For example, the Rio Group developed a democratic clause and expelled Panama when that country held fraudulent elections in 1988 (but Cuba was incorporated in 2008). Other intra-Latin American institutions (e.g., Mercosur and the Central American Integration System) continue to require democracy, but all insist on respecting the principle of non-intervention. This stipulation means that no external definition of democracy or evaluation of whether a country has slipped out of democratic politics is permitted; de facto, what is meant by democracy is that presidents and legislators are selected via some electoral process and that the military not terminate elected officials' tenures early. It is acceptable, however, for a small segment of the civilian electorate to riot in the street and terminate a president's term early. Compare the responses of most Latin American countries to the civil-military coup in Honduras in 2009 with that in Ecuador in 2001, Bolivia in 2003 and Ecuador again in 2005; the Latin American consensus was that the ousted Honduran president had to return to office for subsequent elections to be legitimate, but these conditions were not applied in cases where violent street demonstrations forced presidents out. Although comparative politics analysts do work on the debate about whether democracy exists or not in a number of Latin American countries, regional relations analyses undertaken by Latin Americanists do not incorporate those debates.

The continued agony of a number of Latin American countries with marginally democratic politics is a reality in the region; the events taking place in Haiti, Bolivia, Ecuador, Venezuela and Nicaragua do not suggest a process of democratic consolidation. Consequently, if the new inter-American security institutions seek to promote peace and security via democracies they would need to not only support electoral democracies, but promote the quick movement out of this dangerous transition phase. Unfortunately, that would put the institutions up against the interests of those civilian governments that do not want international evaluation of their quality of democracy. Yet, no Latin American leaders and few scholars point out this discrepancy between justification and policy. If, in fact, illiberal and unconsolidated democracies do promote peace in the region, Latin Americanists have much to contribute to the literature on peace and war and should do so.

Confidence Building and Security Institutions

After the horrors of the bureaucratic-authoritarian governments, Latin American governments and societies developed new conceptions of what security meant. Newly democratic governments created a new set of institutions, and revitalized some old ones, to address those security concerns. These intra-Latin American security institutions have been very active and fairly efficient. They have not been able to turn the region into a zone of positive peace, but the costs governments have paid for those institutions have been minimal. Treaties promoting confidence and security building measures (CSBM) are signed but not ratified, or if ratified, not abided by. If one looks historically, peaceful resolution of conflicts happens when states want conflicts resolved peacefully, just as in the era before this new wave of CSBMs. No study has yet demonstrated through a time series or historical analysis that these institutions have actually had the assumed impact. Had governments wanted something different, they would have designed their CSBM with the same penalties as they endowed the defense of electoral selection of government (as noted in the prior section, it is not actually democracy that matters): violate the rule and you are not allowed to participate in the institution.

Contemporary inter-American security institutions are designed to produce peace and security by promoting and enhancing cooperation among states. Interstate cooperation, in turn, is to be achieved by (1) promoting confidence building and security measures (CSBMs) and the peaceful resolution of conflict; (2) defending democracy; and (3) promoting economic integration. The western hemisphere is pursuing what has been denominated by Johan Galtung as positive peace and security in which states work together to promote common goals such as development and human security. This contrasts with negative peace, which simply means that states are not warring with each other. The creation of a positive peace is a significantly more ambitious goal than the traditional one of simply maintaining peace among neighboring states.

Intra-Latin American CSBMs function across three levels of interstate relationships: unilateral, bilateral, and subregional.[11] Unilateral measures, by the very nature of the security arena, are rare. Chile's decision to produce and make public a Defense White Paper detailing its presumptions about the security environment the country faces, its defense structure, goals and policies, represents an effort to provide confidence-building information to neighbors in a transparent fashion and serves as an example to the rest of Latin America. The subsequent call by the OAS and the Summit process for the development of Defense White Papers as a CSBM illustrates the utility of the Chilean unilateral act. Clearly, analysts who see these documents as important need to develop a common accounting and agreed upon criteria for classification, develop arguments about how different aspects of these documents do or do not function as CSBMs, and then subject these arguments to quantitative or qualitative tests.

Bilateral CSBMs

Bilateral efforts at confidence and security building proliferated in the 1980s in the aftermath of the Malvinas War, the Central American civil wars and the war scares in 1978 among Argentina, Chile, Peru and Bolivia. After its defeat in the Malvinas War, Argentina was involved with its traditional rivals Brazil and Chile in far-reaching bilateral measures covering nuclear policy, border delimitation and military movements. Chile, in turn, embarked on CSBMs with its traditional rivals, Peru and Bolivia, but the territorial dispute with the latter has limited the relationship.

While more activity is occurring with CSBMs at the subregional level, today than ever before, the daily activity of confidence and security building continues to be at the bilateral level. But in the absence of a methodology to distinguish between mere contact and the actual building of confidence, it is difficult to evaluate the impact of activities such as a military ski championship between Chile and Argentina; Peruvian efforts to spur tourism by military personnel with its neighbors; or Brazilian military students taking courses in Mexico. Even the countries that are ostensibly building confidence with the other do not agree on what measures build confidence. Hence Colombia listed five CSBMs of a military nature with Ecuador in 1995, but the latter reported nine such measures between them; Peru did not list Argentina as a country with whom it was engaged in such measures, but the latter listed Peru eleven times in its inventory.[12] OAS efforts to provide guidelines are virtually useless as their experts came up with five single-spaced pages listing measures that could be considered CSBMs.[13] The efficiency of this level of detail (in terms of the manpower used to track and report it) undoubtedly exceeds its benefits since the lower level of reporting by other countries is deemed to have met the requirements. The same needs for definition, hypothesis generation and testing as we saw regarding White Papers are relevant here.

Subregional CSBMs

A consensus exists in the western hemisphere that many security issues or threat characteristics are peculiar to only parts of the region, that priorities may differ across the hemisphere and that neighboring states may find it easier to cooperate on particular security issues than would states at opposite ends of the hemisphere. Consequently, the hemisphere has had a veritable explosion of subregional CSBMs. Among the most important are Mercosur's democracy requirement for membership and Central America's Framework Treaty on Democratic Security in Central America. The latter has explicit sections detailing conflict prevention and early warning measures, creating or strengthening existing Central American peaceful resolution of conflict mechanisms. The Union of South American States (UNASUR) has weighed in on the Colombia-Ecuador-Venezuela fallout after the U.S. military base agreement in 2009.

Not everyone has been happy with the proliferation of subregional groupings and CSBMs specific to them. Questions that arise include whether they are duplicating efforts at the regional level. Do they have overlapping functions? Are they relatively autonomous? What has remained unspoken is perhaps the most pressing question: can CSBMs at the subregional level actually be de-stabilizing for other subregions or the region as a whole?

Economic Integration

Promoting economic integration among members of the American community entails two aspects: creating the economic integration institutions themselves and stimulating the flow of goods, services and investment capital. The goal is to create economic integration agreements that are deeper and wider, that is, cover more goods and services, as well as ancillary aspects that further promote integration, such as international exchanges among businessmen that encourage joint ventures and business relationships. In addition, these agreements will be more than pieces of paper: the flow of goods and services among the parties will increase at rates beyond those that would have been generated simply by the facts of national economic growth and geographical proximity.

The costs associated with promoting economic integration include challenges to sovereignty, not simply the political and economic costs of adjusting policy. Sovereignty costs develop when comparative advantage suggests that the industrialization that nations have seen as advantageous in the international political economy is precluded by one's participation in the integration scheme. Proponents of economic integration may expect long-run economic costs to be low, but they could be extremely high to the economy as a whole, or to particular actors in the short term. The political costs to a government can be extremely high in the short term if those hurt by economic integration decide to protest through demonstrations or by voting the opposition into office.

With respect to institutional approaches to economic integration, it is clear that Mercosur needs rejuvenation, but there is little consensus about whether it has confronted inherent limitations in a region where sovereignty remains a priority. Domestic interests may be a fundamental factor in the creation of Mercosur and its evolution,[14] but theories of international cooperation do not ignore domestic interests. Rather, they postulate that institutional design can create contexts in which pursuing domestic interests produces international cooperation. Specification of those components and the testing of their hypothesized implications will advance both general IPE theorizing as well as our understanding of the prospects for, and limits to, greater economic integration within Latin America. Systematic analyses that compare the Central American (+Dominican Republic), Andean, and Mercosur processes and accomplishments are required, too. The implications of overlapping memberships in distinct trade agreements which have widely varying philosophies and goals (e.g., Bolivia is an Associate Member of Mercosur, a member of ALBA, and a member of the Andean Community) also merits analysis.

Among the most important discussions occurring in the region today is that of energy integration. Multiple projects have been discussed, initiated and developed linking Bolivia with Brazil and Argentina, Colombia with Venezuela and Ecuador, and Guatemala with Mexico; these successes stand out in scholarship and policy discussions. But little analysis has been undertaken regarding the failures of energy integration—why Bolivia can't get past the territorial issue and sell natural gas to energy poor Chile or why Chávez blocks trade (not limited to natural gas) with Colombia. The implications of the inability of Bolivia to meet its gas export contracts with Argentina are also ignored. Perhaps the most important omission in these analyses is the relatively quick fiasco of the deepest energy integration to date: Chile with Argentina. In 2004, despite a 1995 treaty granting the Chilean market equivalency to the Argentine market (national treatment), the Argentine government adopted policies that created severe shortages of natural gas in Chile. Argentine energy policy continues to discourage gas exploration and production, and so Chile has turned to non-regional markets for gas.

Another important issue for analysis is the largely new phenomenon of intra-Latin American investments, by both public and private enterprises. While this phenomenon may signify successful progress on economic integration, in order to know for sure we must evaluate the setbacks that have occurred. Looking at state capital first, Venezuela's national oil company PDVSA has projects in Ecuador and Bolivia, and discussed joint ventures with Brazil's national oil company Petrobras including oil production in the Venezuelan Orinoco, a joint venture refinery in Brazil, and the Gasoducto del Sur pipeline that is supposed to connect Venezuela to Argentina through the Amazon. Petrobras has invested in Argentina and is the most important foreign company in Bolivia's gas fields; Brazil's national development bank, BNDES, invests in infrastructure projects throughout Latin America. With regard to the private sector, Mexican companies are investing in South America; Brazil's giant Odebrecht firm has engineering and construction as well as chemical and petrochemical projects in Latin America and beyond. Smaller scale Chilean capitalists are active in Bolivia and Peru.

These experiences, however, have not yet had much impact on our understanding of economic nationalism in Latin America. Yet, they challenge our understanding about Latin American nationalizations, which emphasized the exploitation of Latin American resources by private U.S. and European companies. We now see nationalization affecting major investment by other Latin American countries. For example, the Mexican Cemex company was nationalized by Venezuela, Ecuador sent troops to take control of a giant hydroelectric and irrigation project built and operated by Odebrecht, and Bolivia dispatched troops to Petrobras facilities when it nationalized them. We should now be thinking about how state capital invested in other Latin American countries affects integration, development, and social welfare. Do these capital flows discriminate against ideological rivals (e.g., is Brazilian investment less than expected in Colombia and Peru, and more than expected in Venezuela and Ecuador)? Where are the studies that parallel those done on U.S. and European foreign direct investment (FDI)? Is intra-Latin American investment more likely to promote broad-based development, be environmentally friendly, and actually promote Latin American integration beyond the specific investments (e.g., if Chileans invest in Peru in order to export to China should we consider this investment promoting Latin American integration)?

Conclusion

The study of intra-Latin American relations has largely been ignored and when studied generally lacks theoretical rigor. For theoretical and empirical reasons, it is an exciting time to study intra-Latin American relations. This chapter has demonstrated the importance of historical context and comparative analysis. I have not been able to address all of the interesting puzzles for scholars interested in intra-Latin American relations, but I have tried to provide provocative examples of areas demanding our attention. What should be clear is that the tension between cooperation and competition is historic and that competition has consistently won out.

Unlike the European case, there is no sense that Latin American states will relinquish a degree of sovereignty to cross-national institutions in order to pursue a greater economic or security good. This is so despite the rhetorical and conceptual nod to the idea that Latin America is inspired to build a Latin American version of either the EU or NATO. The use of military force to coerce behavior or remind rivals that an issue remains unsolved has not been eliminated, contrary to those who call it a zone of peace. If one looks systematically for evidence, one can easily find it. Not only did Colombian forces attack a guerrilla camp in Ecuador in 2008, with Venezuela mobilizing its military as well, in 2009 Paraguay complained at the OAS that Brazilian military maneuvers on the border were meant to coerce it over negotiations on a revised treaty concerning the Itaipú hydroelectric project and Brazilian soybean farmers in Paraguay. Nicaragua's government told Costa Rica in 2010 that its military would defend national sovereignty if the latter's police continued to cross the border without authorization and the Nicaraguans have repeatedly used military rhetoric to warn Colombia about licensing oil and gas exploration in the seas disputed around the San Andres Islands.

The historical variation between cooperation and competition provides rich material for theory building and testing. To return to the opening questions of this chapter, we can conclude that historically Latin Americans have wanted to cooperate with each other to provide peace, security and development. Cooperative endeavors have periodically won out over competition in different subregions and on different issues over time. But progress towards a cooperative region has been neither uniform nor consistent. Contemporary efforts are similar enough to what has been tried in the past that we can think of the Latin American experience as one large data set that can be used to advance political science as a discipline and help Latin America overcome the obstacles to more fruitful collaboration.

Notes

1 Kenneth N. Waltz, *Theory of International Relations* (Reading, MA: Addison-Wesley 1979).

2 Robert O. Keohane, *After Hegemony*. (Princeton: Princeton University Press, 1984); Art Stein, *Why Nations Cooperate* (Ithaca, NY: Cornell University Press 1990).

3 Charles Ameringer, *The Caribbean Legion*. (University Park: Pennsylvania State Press, 1995).

4 Sandra W. Meditz and Dennis M. Hanratty, editors. *Panama: A Country Study*. (Washington, D.C.: U.S. Government Printing Office for the Library of Congress, 1987).

5 The classic history of this period is Robert N. Burr, *By Reason or Force: Chile and the Balance of Power in South America* (Berkeley: University of California Press, 1974).

6 George Phillip, *Oil and Politics in Latin America* (Cambridge: Cambridge University Press, 1982), 194–195.

7 Donald W. Baerresen, Martin Carnoy, and Joseph Grunwald, *Latin American Trade Patterns* (Washington, D.C.: Brookings, 1965), 39–55.

8 Oscar Pinochet de la Barra, "Chile y sus vecinos: problemas y oportunidades" [Chile and its neighbors: Challenges and Opportunities] in Heraldo Munoz, ed., *Chile: Política Exterior para la Democracia* (Santiago: Pehuen, 1989), 166–167.

9 Definition generated by the Correlates of War project, founded in 1963 by J. David Singer, a political scientist at the University of Michigan.

10 Edward Mansfield and Jack Snyder, "Democratization and War" *Foreign Affairs* May/June (1995), pp. 79–97.

11 For efforts at the level of the western hemisphere, see David R. Mares, "Confidence and Security-Building Measures as Inter-American Security Institutions: Relevance and Efficiency" in Gordon Mace, Jean-Phillipe Thérien and Paul Haslam, eds., *Governing the Americas: Regional Institutions at the Crossroads* (Boulder, CO: Lynne Reinner, 2006).

12 Inter-American Defense Board, 1995. "Report of the Inter-American Defense Board on the Draft Inventory of Confidence-building Measures of a Military Nature That are Being Implemented in the Hemisphere" http://www.oas.org/csh/english/csbmreportscosegre10.asp.

13 Committee on Hemispheric Security, Miami Group of Experts, 2003. "Illustrative List of Confidence – And Security-Building Measures for Countries to Consider Adopting on the Bilateral, Sub-Regional and Regional Level" February 3–4, 2003 http://www.oas.org/csh/english/documents/cp10733e04.doc.

14 Cf., Karl Kaltenthaler and Frank O. Mora, "Explaining Latin American Economic Integration: The Case of Mercosur" *Review of International Political Economy*, Vol. 9, No. 1 (March, 2002), pp. 72–97.

24

INTERNATIONAL ECONOMIC RELATIONS/INTERNATIONAL DEVELOPMENT INSTITUTIONS

Grigore Pop-Eleches

Even though most Latin American countries gained independence much earlier than other former colonies, the region's economic development in the last century has been marked decisively by the specter of international economic dependence and by a variety of policy efforts to overcome this dependence. This chapter discusses the evolution and the politics of Latin American trade and capital flows and the relations between Latin American countries and international development institutions in recent decades. This overview suggests that despite some genuine progress in promoting domestic industrial development, many countries in the region continue their traditional reliance on primary commodity exports and foreign financial capital. The cyclical nature of commodity prices and international capital flows, which in the Latin American context is reinforced by the shifting power balance between social actors with different international policy preferences, has contributed to a series of dramatic swings in nature of the region's engagement with international markets as well as the international development institutions. As this chapter illustrates, much of Latin America's international political economy has fluctuated between periods of rapid growth fueled by commodity export booms and often excessive capital inflows and buttressed by generally harmonious relations with foreign investors and international financial institutions, and periods of painful recessions, whose depth and length were exacerbated by capital flight and were often punctuated by acrimonious relations with international creditors.

For obvious reasons, much of the discussion is devoted to identifying broad regional trends and putting them in a global perspective through a number of inter-regional comparisons to other parts of the developing world. Since such broad generalizations run the risk of doing violence to the very real intra-regional diversity of developmental levels and trajectories, this chapter will identify at least some of the more notable differences in how different Latin American countries have managed the political challenges of integrating with international markets.

Trade

The evolution of trade in Latin America is deeply rooted in its colonial past. Until the 19th century the region served primarily as a source of raw materials for the European colonial powers, and the combination of trade openness and a heavy emphasis on agricultural and mineral exports continued after independence. While these policies produced fairly rapid growth in much of the region, trade openness primarily benefitted large agricultural producers, who had pushed out small farmers in most Latin American countries. When the Depression of the 1930s drastically reduced the demand for and profitability of Latin American primary exports, much of the region turned away from free trade and adopted what eventually became known as import-substituting industrialization (ISI).[1] While Latin American countries differed somewhat in the timing and the specifics of their ISI policies, their broad goal was to promote domestic industrial production through a set of economic measures designed to protect the region's nascent industries from their more advanced European and U.S. competitors. During the first *labor-intensive* version of ISI, these measures included high tariff protection and currency devaluations, which raised the prices of imports and thereby shifted domestic consumption towards local producers. While this approach produced very positive results in terms of both growth and poverty reduction (at least for unskilled urban workers), after 1945 it was gradually replaced by a second *capital intensive* version of ISI, which used a combination of tariffs, multiple exchange rates, overvalued currencies, state subsidies and low interest rates to encourage a shift towards more capital intensive industries. This approach, which was promoted at the time by the UN Economic Commission for Latin America and the Caribbean (ECLAC) under the leadership of Raul Prebisch, was intended to help the region overcome its economic backwardness and it produced some impressive periods of growth (especially in Brazil and Mexico). However, it eventually had a number of negative repercussions, which contributed to its downfall in the early 1980s. First, through its greater emphasis on relatively scarce capital and skilled labor, the approach failed to build on the region's relative advantage in unskilled labor, which reduced growth rates and exacerbated economic inequality. Second, for a number of domestic and international political reasons, ISI policies in Latin America failed to promote industrial exports to the same extent as their competitors in East Asia.[2] The modest export performance, combined with the high

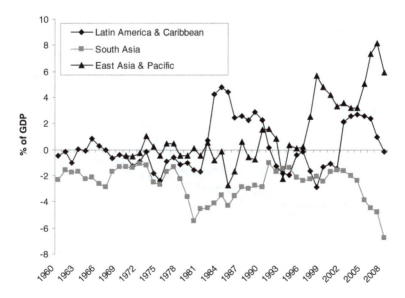

Figure 24.1   Trade Balance — Cross-Regional Trends

imports of capital goods contributed to high trade deficits (see Figure 24.1) and growing foreign debt in much of Latin America in the 1960s and 1970s.

Even though the debt crisis of the 1980s ultimately represented the death knell of ISI in Latin America, the process occurred only gradually and unevenly. Thus, while fiscal austerity measures undermined the elaborate system of subsidies to the industrial sector, the IMF was initially less concerned with reducing tariff rates. Instead, the IMF promoted currency devaluations, which combined with the high tariffs led to a reversal of the high trade deficits of the late 1970s. While Latin American countries did achieve significant trade surpluses in the mid 1980s (see Figure 24.1) and were thereby able to earn at least part of the foreign currency necessary to service their foreign debt, the improving trade balance reflected at least in part the recession-driven lower demand for imports, and thus came at a high economic cost. Moreover, since many domestic producers relied on imported capital goods, the devaluation fueled inflation, which was already high in many Latin American countries. Meanwhile, after an initial rise in 1982–84, regional exports were largely flat for the rest of the decade and—as illustrated in Figure 24.2—the late 1980 and early 1990s were the period when Latin America fell far behind East Asia in terms of international trade integration. Even though Latin American trade growth picked up slightly in the mid-1990s, progress was slower than in both East and South Asia. Moreover, the region's consistent trade deficits from 1992–2001 suggest that this trade expansion was driven by primarily by higher imports. After 2002, driven by a combination of higher commodity prices and the dramatic Argentine devaluation, the Latin American trade balance once again turned positive but its magnitude was lower than in East Asia and it had vanished by 2008.

While the trade volume and trade balance trends discussed above suggest that, especially compared to East Asia, Latin America's insertion into world trade have been less successful during both the ISI period and its neoliberal aftermath, the trends in trade composition suggest a somewhat more positive picture. Even though by 2008 Latin America still relied more heavily on primary exports than Eastern Europe, East Asia and South Asia, the temporal trends illustrated in Figure 24.3 nevertheless a fairly significant shift in trade

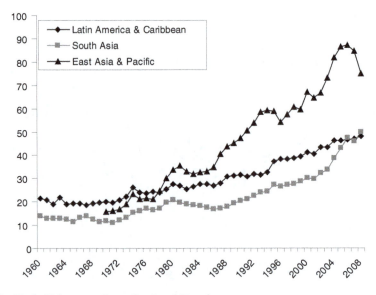

Figure 24.2 Trade Volume — Cross-Regional Trends

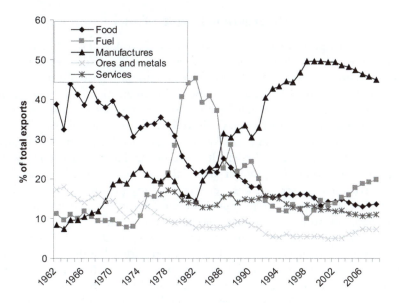

Figure 24.3   Composition of Latin American Trade

composition in the direction that ISI architects had hoped for. Thus, whereas in the early 1960s traditional agricultural exports still represented by far the largest export category, they gradually lost ground to manufactures, which by 2008 accounted for almost half of Latin American exports. Remarkably—and somewhat ironically—the rapid rise of manufacturing exports occurred as the region started to move away from ISI policies in the context of the debt crisis of the 1980s and continued through the heyday of neoliberalism in the early and mid 1990s before plateauing again since the late 1990s. Meanwhile, fuels and ores/minerals continued to represent an important component of Latin American exports, though their relative importance tracked the highly volatile world commodity prices and varied quite dramatically across different countries in the region.

Finally, while so far we have analyzed how overall regional trade patterns have responded to the policy efforts designed to reverse Latin America's traditional commodity dependence, it is worth discussing at least a few of the most important aspects of the great intra-regional diversity in Latin American trade patterns. First, the overall low trade exposure of Latin America was much more pronounced in the regions largest countries (especially Brazil and pre-2002 Argentina), which not only pursued much more aggressive ISI policies until the 1970s but were also slower in opening up their trade since the 1980s. Meanwhile, trade exposure in Mexico and a number of smaller Central American and the Caribbean countries was significantly higher and arguably reflected the strong gravitational pull of the US economy. Second, the export profiles of Latin American countries have also varied quite substantially. Thus, a few countries rely for the bulk of their export earnings on traditional primary commodities such as fuels for Bolivia, Colombia, Ecuador, and particularly Venezuela; ores and minerals in Chile and Peru and agricultural products in Argentina and Uruguay. Meanwhile manufacturing exports predominate in a number of Central American and Caribbean countries (including Mexico) and once again arguably reflect the proximity of U.S. markets, whose influence has been reinforced by the emergence of export processing zones[3] and regional trade agreements (especially CAFTA and NAFTA).

International Capital Flows

The second crucial aspect of Latin America's historical economic dependence has been its heavy reliance on external borrowing, whose cyclical and volatile nature has reinforced the domestic boom-bust cycles of Latin American economic development. Since achieving independence in the early 19th century, most Latin American countries went through a series of booms, characterized by rapid commodity-driven economic growth accompanied by rapidly accumulating foreign debt and followed with remarkable regularity by economic busts, driven by falling demand for Latin American commodity exports and usually accompanied by widespread sovereign debt defaults and prolonged periods of economic stagnation and international isolation.[4] For the purpose of the current discussion, we will primarily focus on the dynamics of the two most recent cycles during the post-World War II period.

The shift from labor-intensive to capital-intensive ISI in the post-war period required significant capital investments, and since Latin American saving rates were not sufficient to finance this expansion, Latin American governments and private sectors increasingly turned to foreign borrowing as an alternative. These trends reinforced in the 1970s by a combination of low investment returns in developed countries and an abundance of petro-dollars following the oil shock of 1974, which gave commercial banks strong incentives to lend to Latin American countries. As a result—as illustrated in Figure 24.4—Latin American debt to commercial banks almost doubled as a share of GDP between 1970–79, and when U.S. interest rates rose significantly after 1980, Latin American debtors suddenly experienced serious difficulties in servicing their ballooning foreign debt.

Following Mexico's announcement in August 1982 that it could no longer service its foreign debt, most observers (including the IMF) initially diagnosed it as a temporary liquidity crisis and predicted a relatively rapid regional economic recovery. However, in a belated effort to reduce their high exposure to Latin American debt, the Western commercial banks practically stopped all new loans to the region and thereby further exacerbated the liquidity problems of many debtor countries.[5] Furthermore, Latin American governments were

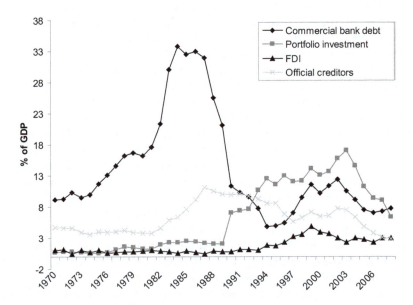

Figure 24.4   Debt Composition in Latin America (1970–2008).

burdened by the rapidly rising interest rates and by the fact that many of them ended up assuming large portions of the private sector debt as part of the initial adjustment packages promoted by the IMF. Several Latin American countries under the leadership of newly democratic Argentina tried to form a debtor cartel to obtain more favorable debt settlements but the so-called "Cartagena Consensus" ultimately failed when some of the region's largest debtors, including Brazil and Mexico, decided to engage instead in case-by-case negotiations with their foreign creditors. Predictably, this collective action failure resulted in worse debt renegotiation terms for most debtor countries; despite adopting painful austerity measures to cope with their rising debt service payments, Latin American countries were actually significantly more indebted to both private and official creditors in 1988 than they had been in 1982 at the start of the debt crisis (see Figure 24.4).

Not surprisingly, the process of external adjustment in the context of the debt crisis raised a number of complicated and contentious dilemmas about the roots of the crisis and, therefore, about the optimal policy solutions.[6] Perhaps the central question was about the relative share of blame between debtors and creditors: on the one hand, Latin American debtor countries clearly used the easily available credit of the 1970s to live beyond their means and racking up unsustainable fiscal and trade deficits. On the other hand, many Latin Americans argued that despite sustaining significant losses[7] and being pressured by the IMF to extend additional involuntary loans to Latin American debtors, the commercial banks were ultimately allowed to get off too easily for their irresponsible lending behavior in the run-up to the crisis. A further complication was the issue of "odious debt," which arose from the fact that many of the region's new democracies (such as Argentina and Bolivia) were forced to pay off the debts incurred by their former military regimes. Given that many of these loans had been used either to line the pockets of the military juntas or on unnecessary military expenditures, democratic politicians repeatedly argued that their countries should not be responsible for such debts, since Western lenders had knowingly engaged in the financially risky and morally questionable practice of lending to the military regimes. A second debate focused on whether the crisis largely reflected temporary liquidity constraints induced by exogenous changes in international financial markets or whether it was indicative of deeper structural problems with ISI in Latin America. Whereas initially even the international financial institutions endorsed the first point of view, as the crisis dragged on into the second part of the decade and successive heterodox adjustment programs achieved only short-lived economic stabilization, proponents of a deeper structural overhaul started to gain the upper hand first in the international community and gradually (and unevenly) in many Latin American countries.

Of course, while the 1980s are generally referred to as Latin America's lost decade, the trajectories of individual Latin American countries varied significantly during the 1980s. At one extreme, poor and externally vulnerable countries like Bolivia, whose foreign debt problems were exacerbated by declining terms of trade and crippling domestic political conflict, suffered staggering economic shocks, characterized by deep recessions and hyperinflationary episodes. At the other extreme, Venezuela and Colombia benefitted from high oil prizes and more manageable debt levels and therefore managed to survive the 1980s largely unscathed. In between these two extremes, much of the rest of Latin America managed to avoid the complete collapse of Bolivia in 1985 and Peru in 1989–90 but nevertheless experienced weak growth, high inflation (and in some cases hyperinflation), rising poverty and declining wages and public services as a result of their efforts to service their increasingly onerous foreign debt burdens.

Despite these efforts and a number of international initiatives designed to restart lending to developing countries (such as the Baker Plan of 1985), there was limited progress until after 1989, when a combination of lower international interest rates and the more flexible design of the Brady plan[8] reduced both the overall debt and the debt service burden of Latin American countries, and thereby paved the way for their return to international capital markets. However, the nature of international lending to Latin America changed dramatically after 1990. As illustrated in Figure 24.4, commercial banks continued to reduce their exposure to Latin America in the early 1990s and even though lending rates picked up again in the mid-1990s commercial bank debt never again came close to the peak levels from the previous two decades. This funding gap was filled by different financial instruments, and particularly by portfolio investment (bonds and equity), which became the single largest source of external finance for Latin America from 1993 until 2008.[9] At the same time, driven by privatization and more investor-friendly business environments, foreign direct investment (FDI) levels quadrupled between the late 1980s and the late 1990s, before declining again in the context of the greater economic and political uncertainty of the last decade.

However, it is important to remember that the international financial boom of the post-1990 period was highly uneven across different Latin American countries. Thus, several poor Central American and Andean countries (including Bolivia, Honduras and Nicaragua) have been largely bypassed by the lending boom of the 1990s and continue to rely on bilateral and multilateral official loans for most of their financing needs. Meanwhile in the region's largest and/or wealthiest countries, particularly Argentina, Brazil, Mexico, Chile and more recently Venezuela, both governments and private companies have successfully tapped international capital markets for their financing needs, which fueled their healthy (though uneven) growth rates in the last two decades. But as the Argentine default of 2002 suggests, even some of the region's more attractive investment targets have not been able to overcome the traditional boom–bust cycles of Latin America's relationship with international financial markets.

The Politics of Trade and Financial Liberalization

With the notable exception of Chile, the process of international opening and structural reforms had its roots in the traumatic experience of the debt crisis of the 1980s. Since that period coincided with an intense involvement of the IMF and the World Bank in the region (see below), and since at least in the second part of the 1980s the two organizations increasingly advocated greater trade and financial liberalization as part of a broader neoliberal reform package to address the shortcomings of ISI, it is not surprising that many Latin Americans have interpreted these reforms as instruments of continued economic and political domination by developed countries (and particularly the United States). While Western economic interests obviously played a role in driving the globalization process, such a perspective ignores the important domestic political dimension of trade and capital account liberalization in Latin America.

First, as discussed above, the region had extensive prior experiences with free trade and capital flows, which benefitted and therefore elicited political support from the traditional commodity sectors (especially agriculture and mining) in which Latin American countries had a comparative advantage. This point was vividly reinforced by the prolonged and massive protests launched by the Argentine agricultural sector in 2008 in response to the Kirchner government's efforts to raise export taxes on agricultural products. Second—and this point goes back to one of the key arguments of dependency school theorists[10]—international financial interests had important domestic political allies among part of the national bourgeoisie in many Latin American countries, and more broadly among individuals involved in the "internationalized" sectors of the economy. Third, according to one of the fundamental models in international trade, the Heckscher-Olin model, trade liberalization tends to benefit the abundant factor of production in any given country, which means that trade liberalization should have been beneficial to Latin America's abundant unskilled labor pool. However, the empirical evidence of this theoretical prediction is mixed,[11] arguably reflecting the important differences between formal and informal sector workers and between sectors with different degrees of international competitiveness in the absence of ISI-type protectionist policies. More broadly, these three points underscore that the politics of trade liberalization were not simply driven by external actors, but reflected the interests of a broad range of social actors who felt that their economic interests had not been properly represented by the urban ISI coalition between the industrial bourgeoisie and organized labor.

Another important distinction, which is often ignored by broad discussions about the impact of globalization on Latin American societies, is that between trade and capital account liberalization. While both types of reforms occurred around the same time and were promoted by some of the same domestic and international actors, a few important differences are worth noting. First, the neoliberal Washington Consensus of the early 1990s emphasized the importance of trade liberalization and foreign direct investment promotion but it did not call for unrestricted capital flows.[12] Second, even though globalization generally increases the economic vulnerability of developing countries to international market fluctuations, the dangers of contagion and speculative attacks are significantly higher in the context of highly mobile financial capital, particularly portfolio investment. Moreover, a number of observers have argued that the constant threat of rapid capital flight and the collective action problems inherent in the large number of portfolio investors (compared to the relatively small number of commercial banks) has significantly narrowed the scope of economic policy making choices by democratic politicians in Latin America and beyond. Third, and related, empirical evidence suggests that in Latin America greater financial liberalization was associated with significantly worse poverty and inequality outcomes, whereas trade liberalization had (albeit modest) positive effects.[13]

Beyond these differences, one of the common concerns with both trade and financial liberalization was that they would further increase the mobility of capital. Since labor has much lower cross-border mobility levels, a number of observers have argued that the easier exit options afforded by globalization strengthened the relative bargaining power of capital and therefore resulted in a race to the bottom, characterized by lower social spending.[14] On the other hand, the risks associated with greater international exposure may increase the demands for higher government spending, and cross-national research confirms the positive correlation between trade and government size.[15] Moreover, certain aspects of international integration may actually benefit organized labor as well, as illustrated by the ability of Mexican labor unions to obtain greater concessions from the government in the months preceding the ratification of NAFTA.[16]

Relations with International Development Institutions

International development institutions (IDIs) have played an important and often controversial role in mediating the relationship between Latin American countries and the global economy. While anti-globalization critics tend to portray most of these organizations as thinly disguised tools for pursuing the economic and political interests of advanced industrial countries (and especially the United States) in the region, a closer look at the historical evidence reveals a great deal of variation across several crucial dimensions: the type of the institution, the time period and the broader international economic environment, and the particular fit (or lack thereof) between the policy prescriptions of IDIs and the political agenda of key domestic political actors.

Different Types of International Development Institutions

The overall tone of the relationship has varied significantly with the type of international development institution. At one end of the spectrum, ECLAC was one of the key architects of ISI policies, which were very popular with large segments of Latin American elites and publics. However, the crisis and eventual collapse of the ISI model in the face of the debt crisis of the 1980s undermined the appeal of structuralist economic ideas and weakened ECLAC's influence on Latin American policy making. While starting in the 1990s ECLAC has tried to articulate a neo-structuralist response to neoliberalism by proposing a "high road to globalization," with the partial exception of post-Pinochet Chile these efforts have failed to restore ECLAC to its previous influence on Latin American economic policy makers. At the same time, however, despite some criticisms that starting in the early 1990s ECLAC's retreat from the key structuralist tenets unwittingly reinforced global capitalism,[17] ECLAC continued to act primarily as a partner of Latin American governments eager to find alternatives to the dominant neoliberal model advanced by other international organizations.

At the other extreme, relations with the International Monetary Fund (IMF) have often been much tenser. These tensions were particularly visible during the debt crisis of the 1980s, when the IMF was widely regarded as an inflexible debt collector, who placed the solvency of Western commercial banks above the welfare of average Latin American citizens. Moreover, starting in the late 1980s and the early 1990s the Fund's growing emphasis on structural economic reforms and international openness made it into one of the most prominent promoters of the Washington Consensus and thus a prominent target of criticisms from Latin American leftists and populists. Following the East Asian Crisis and especially the Argentine crisis of 2001, these critics were increasingly joined by mainstream economists (including from other international organizations),[18] and reflected the Fund's failure to recognize and address some of the significant drawbacks of the neoliberal model it had promoted in the early and mid 1990s. However, at the same time it is important to recognize that in many cases the IMF was used by Latin American politicians as a scapegoat for unpopular policies, which were either largely inevitable for addressing prior economic imbalances (as in the case of the unsustainable fiscal deficits of the late 1970s) or were favored by domestic elites for distributional reasons.[19] Meanwhile, when Latin American governments disagreed with IMF policy prescriptions they could either avoid IMF programs altogether—as many of the region's leftist governments have done in recent years—or they could drag their feet on the implementation front (as suggested by the high proportion of incompletely implemented IMF programs in the 1980s and 1990s). However, as illustrated by the catastrophic repercussions of Alan Garcia's defiant attitude towards the Fund in the late 1980s, such policy deviations could carry a very significant cost especially during periods of global economic crisis.

By comparison, the World Bank's role in Latin America's political economy has received somewhat less political scrutiny, at least in part because its presence has not been as concentrated during periods of extreme crisis as that of the IMF. Moreover, at least in a few select cases, such as Argentina in the late 1980s, the Bank showed somewhat greater flexibility towards the political challenges facing Latin American governments trying to bridge the tension between international economic pressures and democratic politics. Of course, the Bank's activity in Latin America was not immune to criticism. Thus, a series of environmental disasters tied to World Bank programs in Brazil (and elsewhere in the region) in the early 1980s triggered growing criticisms from environmentalists and eventually persuaded large developed countries to pressure the Bank to change its lending practices to take into account environmental concerns.[20] Others criticized the limited effectiveness of World Bank's health and education promotion programs[21] and even internal World Bank studies found that domestic political economy variables played a much greater role in explaining the success of Bank-supported structural adjustment programs than any of the factors under the Bank's control.[22] Despite this ineffectiveness, the World Bank's structural adjustment programs were subject to similar criticisms as IMF lending programs, though the Bank arguably became less of a public enemy during both the 1980s debt crisis and the region's post-2001 leftist turn than its more assertive Bretton Woods sister institution.[23]

Temporal Variation

Another important—and often underappreciated—source of variation in the relationship between Latin American governments and IDIs are the important temporal differences based on the changing nature of the international financial environment. These changes are illustrated most clearly by the evolution of the IMF's role in the region but (as mentioned earlier) other IDIs also went through important changes in their involvement with Latin American countries. Thus, the IMF played a relatively minor role in the immediate post-World War II period, and while a number of countries experimented with IMF programs during the 1960s and 1970s, the Fund's influence in the region was limited by the lending boom of the 1970s, which gave all but the region's poorest members fairly easy access to private capital with few if any economic policy strings attached. The situation changed drastically during the debt crisis of the 1980s, which marked a dramatic increase in the number of Latin American IMF programs. Though slightly less ubiquitous, the Fund's presence in Latin America continued to be significant during the boom of the 1990s (especially following the Mexican Tequila Crisis of 1994/5 and in the run-up to the Argentine default of 2001). However, a combination of rising commodity prices and an explicit—though primarily rhetorical—rejection of IMF-style economic policies has led to the virtual disappearance of IMF adjustment programs in recent years.

The fluctuations were equally dramatic with respect to the nature of IMF interventions and the domestic politics of IMF programs. Thus, whereas in the 1970s the IMF had largely acted as an international lender of last resort for the region's most vulnerable countries, the debt crisis of the 1980s catapulted the Fund into the crucial role as an intermediary between Latin American debtors and the heavily exposed Western commercial banks. While the Fund did pressure the banks to extend additional loans to Latin American debtors, program countries received few tangible benefits in return for the harsh austerity measures they had to adopt to comply with IMF program conditions. The high economic and human costs of this economic adjustment process drew widespread criticisms not only from the Left but even from some other development institutions.[24] As a result, the politics of IMF programs during this period were marked by significant ideological disagreements and by important tensions between IMF-style economic reforms and democratic politics. During the 1990s the nature of its interactions with Latin American countries improved significantly, even though in the 1990s the IMF further broadened the scope of its conditionality to include important structural conditions in addition to its traditional balance-of-payments focus. The main reason for this change-of-heart was that following the resolution of the debt crisis, the IMF's seal of approval became a crucial component for allowing Latin American countries to take advantage of the financial market boom of the 1990s. This change was also reflected in the domestic politics of IMF programs, which in the 1990s were no longer at odds with democratic politics and also no longer exhibited different patterns between left and right governments.[25]

Cross-country Variation

Even after taking into account the significant variations in the nature of IDI missions and the international economic context, there were important differences across Latin American countries in their interactions with international development institutions. These differences can be traced to significant variations in the international and domestic political context in which these relationships were imbedded.[26]

While in theory international development institutions are supposed to treat all their members according to the same technocratic standards, in practice the interactions often bear the imprint of unequal international power relations. One source of inequality, which has been documented extensively across the world, is that developed countries use their influence over IDIs to secure preferential treatment for their allies. While such considerations may have played a role in individual Latin American countries,[27] their salience was arguably lower than in other regions (such as the Middle East and Eastern Europe) where U.S. geopolitical interests were more acute than in the Western Hemisphere.

A second type of preferential treatment, illustrated by the surprising IMF tolerance for Argentine and Brazilian heterodox adjustment programs in the mid-1980s, arises from the simple fact that some countries are "too big to fail" in the sense that their economic collapse could have serious regional and even global spillover effects. The threat of such contagion translated into a much greater bargaining power for the region's largest economies—Brazil, Mexico, and to a lesser extent Argentina—in their interactions with international institutions. While such preferential treatment, which was at times reinforced by direct interventions from top U.S. officials, resulted in greater responsiveness and more generous financial packages in the context of IMF programs, a few caveats should be noted. First, such preferential treatment was largely confined to situations of extreme crises, such as the debt crisis or the Mexican Tequila crisis, whereas in less dire circumstances, such as the Argentine default of 2001, countries eventually found out that they were not too big too fail. Second, preferential treatment for large countries did not apply equally across issue areas: thus, while the IMF showed greater flexibility vis-à-vis the details of domestic adjustment policies in Argentina and Brazil in the 1980s, it was actually less willing to agree to substantial debt reductions for the large debtors than for some of the smaller countries (such as Bolivia), where such reductions were significantly cheaper for Western creditors. Third, as illustrated by the World Bank's special relationship with Argentina in the late 1980s and the IMF's excessively soft response to Argentina's mounting economic woes in the late 1990s, the short-run political and economic benefits of preferential treatment may well be overshadowed by the greater costs of delayed economic adjustment.

The third type of preferential treatment is in many ways the mirror image of the "too big to fail mechanism" and arises from the fact that in order to deal with the frequent criticisms levied against their economic policy prescriptions, IDIs often need to be able to present showcase examples of the successes of their program countries. In return for their rather strict adherence to economic orthodoxy, such countries may get preferential treatment in other areas, such as more favorable financial conditions. Perhaps the best example of such a case is Bolivia in 1985–87, where the IMF let the newly elected Paz government get away with a partial debt moratorium and facilitated generous debt renegotiation terms in return for the country's exemplary adherence to domestic fiscal and monetary discipline.[28] While this "showcase" strategy is one of the more promising options for small developing countries, its replicability is limited by the fact that the "propaganda" value of any given showcase country declines with the number of countries who chose to go along with IDI requirements.

The other major source of variation in the relationship between Latin American countries and international development institutions is rooted in domestic politics. While IDIs generally consider themselves as non-partisan sources of technocratic policy advice and financial support to facilitate the pursuit of the program countries' domestic developmental priorities, in practice the policies required by most IDI programs are closely intertwined with the domestic political debates in program countries. This is the case not only because most economic policies create winners and losers (and therefore trigger distributional conflicts) but because the policy prescriptions of international institutions invariably reflect the ideological preferences of their staff and their principals. Not surprisingly, then, the relations between IDIs and Latin American countries have tended to be closer and more harmonious when IDI staff and Latin American government officials had similar backgrounds and ideological preferences: for example, Chile's engagement with the IMF was particularly intense during the 1980s as the Pinochet government's broad ideological agreements with the Fund's pro-market policy prescriptions reinforced the economic incentives of the debt crisis. By contrast, in the 1990s successive center-left *Concertación* governments cultivated closer ties with ECLAC but did not enter any new IMF programs.[29]

The conflict potential between the global agenda of IDIs and the domestic political priorities of Latin American governments becomes much clearer once we look beyond the cases where elective ideological affinities encouraged greater cooperation between the two sides. Arguably, the best lens for understanding these tensions is to look at the politics of IMF programs, because the IMF has been widely associated with a neoliberal ideological agenda and because countries confronted with severe external economic imbalances often have few alternatives to the IMF for addressing their problems. The dynamics of Latin American IMF programs are particularly telling during the debt crisis of the 1980s, when both cross-country and within-country differences in IMF relations usually reflected the shifting partisan balance in different Latin American countries. Thus, after a series of failed attempts to address its spiraling debt and inflationary crises in the context of an IMF program, the leftist Siles government in Bolivia was eventually replaced by a center-right coalition, which executed a dramatic U-turn and launched an ambitious and successful orthodox stabilization program, which eventually attracted support from the IMF and other IDIs. Around the same time, Peru moved in the opposite direction, as its freshly elected leftist-populist President, Alan Garcia, reversed the country's earlier IMF cooperation and put it on a collision course with the IMF and Western lenders. While in the Peruvian case this conflict was exacerbated by Garcia's inflammatory rhetoric, these clear partisan shifts reflect the deeper underlying political conflicts triggered by the severe distributional consequences of IMF-style adjustment programs in the 1980s.

These conflicts abated somewhat during the 1990s, when the healthy economic growth experienced by most Latin American countries led to broader improvements in living standards (despite the persistence of high inequality), and not surprisingly this relative "harmony" was also reflected in the much weaker politicization of IMF programs, which found such unlikely political champions as the Argentine Peronist President Carlos Menem. However, in retrospect the 1990s represented more of a hiatus than a turning point in the conflictual relationship between the Latin American left and the IDIs: thus, following the Argentine default of 2001 and the rise of the Left in much of Latin America, some of the region experienced a renewed rhetorical and policy turn against both the IMF and the neoliberal policies that the Fund has been associated with. While the global economic crisis of 2008–09 has left much of Latin America unscathed and has therefore produced a much smaller "crop" of new IMF programs, we should expect the political logic of the next wave of IMF-style adjustment politics to have much more in common with the political tensions and partisan polarization of the 1980s than with the comparatively placid period of the 1990s.

Conclusion

This brief overview of Latin America's engagement with international trade and capital markets suggests that even though the economies and societies of many countries in the region have changed in profound ways in the past half century, they are still confronted with many of the same challenges that ISI promoters had hoped to overcome. Thus, despite some significant progress of shifting from food to manufactured exports since the 1960s, many countries—and particularly Venezuela, Bolivia, Ecuador, Chile and Peru—still rely on primary commodities for the bulk of their export earnings and this dependence has actually increased in the last decade (especially in Bolivia and Peru). While the potential pitfalls of this dependence have been masked in recent years by high international commodity prices, in the long run it is likely to exacerbate the region's seeming inability to break out of the boom-bust cycle of its economic development trajectory.

The cyclical nature of Latin American political economy is also apparent in the interactions of many Latin American countries with international financial markets and international development institutions. Thus, even though the nature of international capital flows to the region has changed substantially since the 1980s, Latin American reliance on foreign capital has continued to be a cornerstone of its developmental model and one that is still subject to large and often rapid fluctuations between economic booms fueled by massive and often speculative capital inflows, which are inevitably followed by dramatic economic collapses exacerbated by capital flight, debt crises and often by defaults. Just as predictably, relations with international development institutions—and particularly with the International Monetary Fund—have fluctuated between reasonably cordial cooperation (or benign neglect) during periods of financial booms to serious tensions punctuated by open conflict and recriminations during periods of financial crises.

While these cycles are rooted at least in part in the fluctuations of international trade and capital flows, they have arguably been more extreme in Latin America than in other regions. In addition to the aforementioned high reliance on volatile primary exports, Latin America's vulnerability to international fluctuations has been exacerbated by the widespread failure to enact counter-cyclical fiscal policies that could be used to reduce both the overheating tendencies of the boom periods and the depth of subsequent recessions. In turn, these fiscal imbalances and the accompanying inflationary tendencies are symptomatic of the region's unresolved political conflict between different social classes and sectors,[30] as well as of the weak taxation capacities of most Latin American states.

More broadly, Latin America serves as a vivid reminder of the intimate interconnectedness of domestic and international economic interests and politics. While a comprehensive analysis of the roots and mechanisms of the politics of international economic integration in peripheral countries has been at times undermined by somewhat arbitrary distinctions across different disciplines (e.g., economics vs. political science vs. sociology) or even within disciplines (e.g., between comparative politics and international political economy in political science), Latin America has long been the breeding ground for theoretical efforts to integrate the different disciplinary strands.

Such integrative efforts help counteract two types of temptations: the first, reflected in some of the early dependency school approaches but also in some of the more recent globalization literature, is to see Latin American development as simply a side-product of the imperial project of developed countries.[31] In this respect, a vibrant literature has emphasized the importance of domestic elites in mediating external pressures and shaping the nature of economic adjustment since the debt crisis.[32] However, these debates would benefit from a more direct incorporation of non-elite interests into the political calculus of international trade and financial integration, perhaps through a dialogue with survey-based studies of Latin American public opinion towards political economy issues. Such an approach might help us understand the extent to which political and economic elites can shape public opinion on international economic policy questions or whether average citizens can play a more active role in checking elite interests. The second risk is that of the potential "provincialism" of academic literatures that focus exclusively on a region (and often on a handful of countries within a given region). This does not obviously mean that Latin America cannot be productively be analyzed on its own terms or that it invariably needs to be imbedded in a global sample of countries but that our understanding of the region's insertion into the world economy can benefit from more explicit comparisons to the experiences of other regions. While a number of prominent exceptions—often in the form of edited volumes—exist,[33] they still represent a very small proportion of the analyses of Latin American international political economy. Finally, given the strong cyclical nature of Latin America's interactions with international trade and capital, our understanding of the subject would be well served by more systematic cross-temporal comparisons of the politics of international booms and busts in the region. Such studies would not only help us avoid reinventing the wheel for every "new" historical episode but they may also highlight which aspects of the region's current challenges and opportunities are genuinely new and may require a reevaluation of the conventional wisdom.

Notes

1 For an excellent overview of this historical developments, see James Sheahan "External Trade, Industrialization, and Economic Growth," in *Patterns of Development in Latin America* (Princeton, NJ: Princeton University Press, 1987), pp. 74–98.

2 These reasons included the greater penetration of transnational capital and multinational corporations in Latin America at the outset of the ISI period, the stronger position of the state vis-à-vis the local bourgeoisie in East Asia, and the more favorable trade conditions extended by the United States towards East Asian countries due to geopolitical considerations tied to the Cold War. See Peter Evans, "Class, State, and Dependence in East Asia: Lessons for Latin Americanists," in F. C. Deyo (ed.), *The Political Economy of the New Asian Industrialism* (Ithaca, NY: Cornell University Press, 1987).

3 See Andrew Schrank and Markus Kurtz (2005) "Credit Where Credit is Due: Open Economy Industrial Policy and Export Diversification in Latin America and the Caribbean," *Politics & Society*, 33(4): 671–702.

4   For an extensive review, see Graciela Kaminsky "Two Hundred Years of International Financial Integration: Latin America since Independence" [mimeo] (2010).

5   Edwards, Sebastian, *Crisis and Reform in Latin America: From Despair to Hope* (Washington DC: World Bank Press, 1995).

6   For more on the debt crisis, see Rosemary Thorp and Laurence Whitehead (eds.), *Latin American Debt and the Adjustment Crisis* (University of Pittsburgh Press, 1987), and Robert Kaufman and Barbara Stallings (eds.), *Debt and Democracy in Latin America*, (Boulder, CO: Westview, 1989).

7   These losses were sustained by either outright debt forgiveness as part of successive waves of debt renegotiations or by selling Latin American debt at high discounts in the secondary debt markets (for example, given the low chance of repayment, Bolivian debt sold for about 11 cents to the dollar in 1985).

8   Unlike earlier initiatives, the Brady plan contained a significant debt relief component as lenders generally either accepted a 30–50% discount on the face value of the loans or agreed to significantly below-market interest rates for the Brady bonds they received.

9   While it may be too soon to speculate about yet another tectonic shift in foreign lending to Latin America, the significant decline in portfolio investment after 2003 (driven in part by the drawn-out conflict between Argentina and its bondholders) suggests that the era of equity finance may be coming to an end in Latin America.

10 See Fernando Henrique Cardoso and Enzo Faletto, *Dependency and Development in Latin America* (Berkeley: University of California Press, 1979).

11 Thus, Weyland finds that democratization promoted greater trade openness since it marginalized many of the narrow vested interests who benefitted most under ISI but Baker shows that trade liberalization received stronger support among skilled rather than unskilled workers. See Kurt Weyland, *The Politics of Market Reform in Fragile Democracies: Argentina, Brazil, Peru, and Venezuela* (Princeton, NJ: Princeton University Press, 2002); Andy Baker "Why is trade reform so popular in Latin America? A consumption based theory of trade policy preferences." *World Politics* (2003) 55: 423–465.

12 See John Williamson "What Washington Means by Policy Reform," in John Williamson (ed.), *Latin American Adjustment: How Much has Happened?* (Washington, D.C.: Institute for International Economics, 1990), pp. 7–38.

13 Nancy Birdsall and Miguel Székely, "Bootstraps, Not Band-aids: Poverty, Equity, and Social Policy," in P. P. Kuczynski and J. Williamson (eds.), *After the Washington Consensus: Restarting Growth and Reform in Latin America*, (Washington, D.C.: Institute for International Economics, 2003).

14 Erik Wibbels "Dependency Revisited: International Markets, Business Cycles, and Social Spending in the Developing World." *International Organization* (2006) 60: 433–68.

15 Dani Rodrik. "Why Do More Open Economies Have Larger Governments?" *Journal of Political Economy* (1998) 106(5): 997–1032.

16 Cook, Lorena. "Regional Integration and Transnational Politics: Popular Sector Strategies in the NAFTA Era, in Douglas Chalmers et al. (eds.), *The New Politics of Inequality in Latin America* (Oxford University Press).

17 See Fernando Ignacio Leiva. *Latin American Neostructuralism: The Contradictions of Post-Neoliberal Development* (Minneapolis: University of Minnesota Press, 2008).

18 Joseph Stiglitz. "What I Learned at the World Economic Crisis," *The New Republic* (2000, April 17): 56–60; Martin Feldstein "Argentina's Fall: Lessons from the Latest Financial Crisis," *Foreign Affairs* (2002, March/April).

19 For example, Vreeland argues that governments often enter IMF programs despite their negative growth effects, because such programs raise economic inequality and thereby ultimately leave economic elites better off. See James Vreeland, *The IMF and Economic Development* (Cambridge: Cambridge University Press 2003).

20 See Daniel L. Nielson and Michael J. Tierney, "Delegation to International Organizations: Agency Theory and World Bank Environmental Reform," *International Organization* (2003) 57: 241–276.

21 See David Brown and Wendy Hunter, "World Bank Directives, Domestic Interests and the Politics of Human Capital Investments in Latin America," *Comparative Political Studies* 33 (2000, February): 113–143.

22 David Dollar and Jakob Svensson, "What Explains the Success or Failure of Structural Adjustment Programmes?" *The Economic Journal* (2000) 110: 894–917.

23 In part this was due to the greater accountability triggered by the grassroots campaign against the Bank's earlier environmental failures. See Jonathan Fox, Dana Clark and Kay Treakle (eds.), *Demanding Accountability: Civil Society Claims and the World Bank Inspection Panel* (Lanham, MD: Rowman and Littlefield, 2003).

24 For example, in its 1990 Annual Report, the Inter-American Development Bank noted that the policy pressures of the 1980s had left little space for "adjustment with a human face."

25 For a more detailed comparison of the politics of IMF programs during these two periods see Grigore Pop-Eleches, *From Economic Crisis to Reform: IMF Programs in Latin America and Eastern Europe* (Princeton, NJ: Princeton University Press, 2009).

26 This section draws on the analysis in Pop-Eleches (2009).

27 For example, the generous treatment of Bolivia by both the IMF and the World Bank was arguably tied to its cooperation with the U.S. War on Drugs, while the IMF's close cooperation with the Pinochet regime in Chile was embedded in Cold War concerns about the spread of communism.

28 See Manuel Pastor, *Inflation, Stabilization, and Debt: Macroeconomic Experiments in Peru and Bolivia* (Boulder, CO: Westview Press, 1992).

29 However, it should be noted that Chile maintained good relations with the IMF after 1990.

30 See, for example, Albert Hirschman, "The Social and Political Matrix of Inflation: Elaborations on the Latin American Experience," in A. Hirschman (ed.), *Essays in Trespassing* (Cambridge: Cambridge University Press, 1981).

31 See, for example, Cardoso's critique of some of the early excesses of dependency theory F.H. Cardoso, "The Consumption of Dependency Theory in the United States," *Latin American Research Review* (1977) 12(3): 7–24

32 See, for example, Ben Ross Schneider, "Big Business and the Politics of Economic Reform: Confidence and Concertation in Brazil and Mexico," in Sylvia Maxfield and Ben Ross Schneider (eds.), *Business and the State in Developing Countries* (Ithaca, NY: Cornell University Press, 1997), pp. 191–215.

33 See, for example, Stephan Haggard and Robert R. Kaufman (eds.), *The Politics of Economic Adjustment* (Princeton, NJ: Princeton University Press, 1992).

25

THE POLITICS OF DRUGS AND ILLICIT TRADE IN THE AMERICAS

Peter Andreas and Angelica Duran Martinez

Illicit trade has long been a central feature of the political economy of the Americas. Since colonial times, when smuggling flourished as a way to circumvent the rigidities and restrictions on commerce derived from mercantilist imperial policies, illicit commerce has had a profound impact on public security, the configuration of state power, and cross-border relations.

Yet, partly due to a lack of adequate data as well as insufficient comparative and theoretical analysis, scholarship in this area remains uneven and limited. Some prominent illicit cross-border economic activities (most notably drug trafficking) have been subject to extensive analyses, while others (such as the illicit wildlife trade and antiquities smuggling) remain much more obscure. Much of the existing literature on illicit trade is policy driven, single-issue focused, and devoid of comparative-historical perspective. For the most part, the literature does not deeply engage the major theoretical trends and debates in political science. With some notable exceptions, political scientists have arrived late to the study of illicit trade and its political repercussions. This is unfortunate, given that some of the field's central preoccupations, ranging from democracy to development to violence, are intimately intertwined with illicit trade and the domestic and international politics of policing such trade. And nowhere is this more evident than in the Americas.

In this chapter we first briefly sketch the scope and dimensions of illicit trade in the region, and stress the importance of various types of power asymmetries. Drawing on illustrations primarily from drug trafficking (by far the most studied and documented case), we then outline in a very preliminary fashion some of the contributions to political science in general and to the study of Latin American politics in particular that may be derived from a focus on illicit trade. We concentrate on three themes: (1) the relationship between illicit trade and democratic governance; (2) the relationship between illicit trade and organized violence; and (3) the relationship between illicit trade and neoliberalism. We conclude by encouraging more political science interest and attention but also highlight the considerable obstacles and pitfalls of conducting research in this area.

Scope, Dimensions, and Power Asymmetries

The illicit side of cross-border trade in the Americas includes the smuggling of prohibited commodities (such as cocaine and heroin), the smuggling of legal commodities (such as cigarettes), the black market in stolen commodities (such as intellectual property), and the trafficking in bodies and body parts (migrants, sex workers, babies, endangered species, human organs, animal parts). Some of these illicit trading activities are fairly obscure and minimally policed (the smuggling of rare orchids), some are little more than a law enforcement nuisance (the cross-border trade in stolen vehicles), but others receive intense policy attention and media scrutiny (drug trafficking and migrant smuggling), and still others have clear and direct security implications (most notably arms trafficking). A number of illicit trades also have serious environmental consequences (the smuggling of endangered flora and fauna, the trade in toxic waste, the dumping of chemicals used to process psychoactive substances such as cocaine). Despite their enormous diversity, these illicit trades all share some basic characteristics: they are unauthorized by the sending and/or receiving jurisdiction, and they move across borders via mechanisms designed to evade detection and apprehension.

Illicit trade patterns reflect broader power asymmetries. First and most obviously, illicit trade is an increasingly prominent source of conflict and tension between highly unequal countries—most notably, between the United States and its southern neighbors. Concerns over illicit cross-border economic activities (especially drug trafficking and migrant smuggling) dominate U.S. relations with many Latin American countries, from Mexico to Colombia to Bolivia. In an era of economic liberalization otherwise defined by deregulation and the loosening of controls over cross-border economic exchange, there is a counter move of re-regulation through intensified policing and surveillance of illicit trade.

Some Latin American and Caribbean countries otherwise at the margins of the global economy have a market niche and comparative advantage in illicit trade: black market baby adoptions from Guatemala, migrant workers from Ecuador, and coca/cocaine from Bolivia. Other countries specialize in "transit trade" (Paraguay) and "sex tourism" (Cuba). And still others have a niche in laundering and sheltering illicit financial flows (Cayman Islands, Panama). Many countries in the region are becoming more economically integrated with wealthier countries such as the United States, but it is often the illicit side of the integration process that is most entrepreneurial and responsive to market forces (for example, drugs and migrant workers are two of Mexico's most important exports, but are not formally part of NAFTA). Moreover, remittances from migrant workers (both legal and illegal) have become a leading source of revenue for countries such as the Dominican Republic, El Salvador, and Mexico.

Illicit trade also reflects much broader economic inequalities in the Americas, which are reinforced by borders and their enforcement. For instance, formally excluded from first world labor markets through the front door, workers from Mexico, Central America, and elsewhere attempt to gain clandestine access to the U.S. labor market through the backdoor by hiring professional smugglers. Some peasant farmers cope with growing economic inequalities by either facilitating illicit trade (such as drug crop cultivation) or by actually becoming objects of the illicit trade (a smuggled migrant). Clandestine entrepreneurs produce, transport, sell, or otherwise enable illicit trade as an alternative ladder of upward socioeconomic mobility where opportunities for advancement in the legal economy may be limited or blocked. And still others attempt to challenge power asymmetries through organized violence—partly aided and sustained through illicit trades ranging from drugs to guns. Some of these conflicts prompt various forms of external involvement, including an influx of military aid and training. For instance, through the U.S.-sponsored international "war on drugs" and the merging of counternarcotics and counterinsurgency, Colombia has become a leading recipient of military assistance.

Power asymmetries also influence which illicit trades are at the top of the region's policing and security agendas. Thus, regulating the illicit antiquities trade (which is especially a concern for source countries such as Peru and Guatemala) is relatively anemic, with wealthy collectors in the United States and other advanced industrialized countries the primary source of black market demand. Similarly, illicit toxic waste exports from north to south receive considerably less law enforcement scrutiny than the export of labor from south to north. The United States has successfully exported its anti-drug agenda and enforcement methods across this region and the world while at the same time obstructing and weakening international initiatives to more forcefully police the illicit trade in small arms.

Indeed, it is not too much of an exaggeration to say that the very history of what trading activities are and are not prohibited in the first place is largely a story of the most powerful countries exporting their criminal law preferences and procedures to weaker countries. Thus, not just illicit trade, but the policing of such trade mirrors broader geopolitical power asymmetries. Importantly, there is also an enormous asymmetry between the power to legally prohibit particular trades and the power to effectively enforce such prohibitions—and at the most basic level, it is this asymmetry that creates the clandestine transnational space within which various illicit trade activities flourish. For example, smuggling opportunities, incentives, methods, and routes are powerfully shaped by asymmetries in policing will, capacities, and priorities. These asymmetries prompt both growing tension and cooperation between highly unequal countries, as evident not only in U.S.-Latin American counternarcotics cooperation but also in a range of other law enforcement issues such as efforts to combat money laundering and human trafficking.

Illicit Trade and Democratic Governance

Illicit trade, most notably drug trafficking, has direct and indirect effects on democratic governance.[1] Corruption associated with illicit trade directly affects the quality of political institutions, drug-related violence undermines public security, and these two factors undermine citizens' trust in democracy. In some cases, the perception that democracy does not deal effectively with crime issues[2] may foster citizens' support for iron fist or militarized responses to crime that further undermine civil rights and liberties. This has been prominently the case in a number of Central American countries, and is also illustrated by public support of militarized responses to drug trafficking in Mexico.[3] Furthermore, in countries such as Bolivia, Peru, and Colombia, coca crop eradication has contributed to political instability and social unrest as many peasant populations depend on coca cultivation. But the relationship between democratic governance and illicit trade also works in the opposite direction, as weak democratic institutions further undermine and complicate the possibilities of effectively curbing illicit trade. Consequently, a closer analysis of illicit trade would broaden significantly our current understanding of the variation in democratic outcomes across the region.

Corruption, and its negative repercussions for accountability and transparency, has arguably constituted one of the main obstacles to the consolidation of Latin American democracies. Those engaged in illicit trade attempt to access the state or parts of it in order to secure the non-enforcement of the law. Simply put, they attempt to buy off the state because they cannot entirely bully or bypass it. Prominent cases such as the involvement of Alberto Fujimori's close advisors with drug traffickers in Peru, the connections between politicians and illicit actors in Colombia, the relations between military officers and traffickers in Guatemala, and the pervasive police corruption and protection traditionally provided by PRI officials to traffickers in Mexico, constitute only some of the most well known illustrations. Yet, illicit trade is associated with corruption in more diverse and complex ways than is often understood. Corruption has many different manifestations and dynamics. It does not pervade the state to the same extent in all countries and it is entrenched (to different degrees and in different ways) in different branches of government and political institutions. Drug related corruption in Mexico, for example, has evolved in distinct phases depending on the patterns and organization of drug trafficking activities at particular times.[4] This highlights the dynamic nature of the relation between state and illicit actors, which evolves not only depending on market conditions, but also on institutional and political contexts.

Thus, to fully understand the impact of drug related corruption on Latin American democracies it is necessary to more clearly specify different types and levels of corruption. A crucial question that needs closer scrutiny is how different configurations of state power affect the opportunities and dynamics of corruption. Scholars in Colombia and Mexico suggest that different state structures (a unitary versus a federal state) and patterns of political competition explain variation in relations between state officials and drug traffickers. In their view, political competition in Colombia reduced the capacity of the state to control its relations with drug traffickers, whereas in Mexico due to the PRI hegemony, traffickers were more dependent on politicians.[5] Although the contrasting image of ultra powerful Colombian traffickers and ultra powerful Mexican politicians may be overstated, it highlights that the organizational structure of the state as well as the dynamics of electoral competition shape the relation between traffickers and state officials in different ways in each country and over time. In Mexico, the democratization process is intuitively associated with shifts in drug trafficking and corruption patterns. In Colombia, the institutional and social transformations that made electoral politics more competitive in the 1980s facilitated, and sometimes were even reinforced by, the entrance of a burgeoning criminal class in politics. Yet, political competition also hindered the possibilities of some prominent drug traffickers to become directly involved in electoral politics.[6]

These complex relations raise troubling questions that remain to be answered: Do criminal actors shape political practices or do political practices determine the incentives of illicit actors? Does democratization increase the opportunities for corruption or does it change its dynamics (rather than its scope) by making corruption less predictable and more fragmented?[7] How do democratic checks and balances affect criminal behavior?

Literature on the dynamics of different regime types and the institutional legacies of dictatorships and armed conflict can further illuminate the complex relation between democratic governance and illicit trade. In Guatemala, the legacies of dictatorship and counterinsurgency made the military a central actor in politics at least until the signing of peace accords in 1996. This powerful institutional legacy may explain why the military has been one of the actors more closely associated with drug-related corruption as reflected not only in the accusations against high ranking military officers but also in the alleged role that former Guatemalan military members, known as Kaibiles, have played in training drug traffickers within and across the U.S.-Mexico border.[8] By contrast, in neighboring countries such as Nicaragua, where legacies of armed conflict translated into the party system, drug corruption has been more closely related to electoral politics.[9] Such contrasts require further research.

From a more historical perspective, an interesting but understudied area that relates to the literature on state formation is how interaction with illicit trade has shaped state institutions. Regardless of their effectiveness in combating crime, state institutions have frequently changed and been redesigned in order to carry out their crime-fighting function.

For instance, constant purges and anticorruption campaigns have resulted in the creation and recreation of security and law enforcement agencies in Guatemala and Mexico;[10] and the transformation of militaries in some countries through a greater crime-fighting mission (especially militarized drug enforcement) has profound implications, including for civil-military relations and protection of human rights and civil liberties.

These institutional changes, it should be emphasized, have often been greatly influenced by external pressures and expectations—whether by major powers (most notably the United States),[11] or more broadly by global prohibition regimes and the growing internationalization of law enforcement cooperation.[12] This includes, for instance, the proliferation of mutual legal assistance treaties as well as highly contentious extradition agreements. Indeed, the politics of extradition would be an especially fruitful area to explore the relation between external pressures and domestic processes of policy making. Historically, the country where the most extraditions have been conducted is Colombia (and indeed, extradition was a crucial factor in the escalating violence between drug traffickers and the state in the 1980s). In Mexico, although an extradition treaty dates back to 1980, effective extraditions were not a regular practice until 2006 despite the large influence of the United States on Mexican policy. Thus, further research in this understudied realm would help illuminate the contentious politics of extradition, and the variation in timing, frequency, and domestic sensitivity to external pressure.

Finally, the analysis of the relation between democratic governance and illicit trade would benefit from a more systematic analysis and comparison of the social basis of illicit export crop production. This could include, for example, comparing different degrees and types of political mobilization and organization of peasant coca producers[13]—contrast the coca sector in Bolivia and its relatively high level of mobilization (including the election of a former coca producer union leader, Evo Morales, as president of the country) to the more politically marginalized and less organized coca producers in neighboring Peru. A closer comparative analysis of patterns of mobilization can help explain the variation in anti-narcotic policies as well as different degrees of government responsiveness to demands such as the suspension of aerial fumigation of coca crops.[14]

Illicit Trade and Organized Violence

Violence, like corruption, is often viewed as an inherent attribute of illicit trade.[15] It is safe to assert that, on the whole, illicit trade is more prone to violence than licit trade. The basic reason for this is that illicit trade operates beyond and outside the law. Participants in illicit trade do not have recourse to the law to enforce contracts—and thus business disputes are more likely to be dealt with by shooting rather than suing. But while violence occurs more commonly in connection with illicit than licit trade, careful examination reveals considerable variation in violence across and within illicit trade sectors, as well as across time and place, requiring more nuanced scrutiny. Illicit trade-related violence is typically selective and instrumental rather than random and gratuitous and victims tend to be other market participants rather than state actors or the general public (and some state actors are targeted because they are actually market participants). Yet, criminals can sometimes target the state—police, prosecutors, judges, politicians. Furthermore, violent acts vary in form, intensity, frequency, and focus, even when targets are market participants. Thus, violence itself needs to be systematically "unpacked" to identify variation across these dimensions.

The link between violence and illicit trade is most evident in the case of drug trafficking, and it is no doubt partly for this reason that the drug trade generates so much public concern and media and policy attention. Consider, for instance, the wave of drug related violence in Mexico that according to some estimates claimed more than 40,000 lives since 2006.[16] This wave of violence has been facilitated by the increased availability of sophisticated weaponry, grenades, and bombs for trafficking organizations, underscoring a link between the illicit arms trade (with much of the supply originating in the United States) and more deadly forms of violence (though it should be stressed that the availability of arms is a necessary, but not sufficient, condition for escalating drug violence). Yet, the disproportionate attention to the most violent aspects of the international drug trade obscures and glosses over some important and interesting variation. For example, far more attention is devoted to cocaine and heroin (relatively high violence) than cannabis and MDMA (comparatively low violence). Furthermore, even within the trade in hard drugs there is striking variation, and beyond the clear violent manifestations there is a more complex and ambiguous reality. Contrast Colombia, which has been plagued by high violence, to Bolivia, which has been characterized by much lower violence[17]—yet both are deeply enmeshed in the coca/cocaine trade (Bolivia arguably even more so on a per capita basis). Similarly, consider the variation of violence over time in Mexico, where modern forms of drug trafficking date back to the 1940s, yet until the mid-1990s the market was relatively more peaceful (or more precisely, violence was less visible).[18]

Thus we need more research about the conditions under which illicit trade generates violence. It requires differentiating forms and types of violence and addressing questions such as how do prohibitions and their enforcement shape the nature and level of organized violence across illicit trading activities? What are the mechanisms connecting enforcement and violence? What policing and regulatory methods and strategies are least or most likely to inhibit or exacerbate illicit trade-related violence? This question is crucial considering that high-profile police crackdowns can unintentionally fuel more trade-related violence—as some actors are removed, new ones emerge to fill the void and claim market share through violent competition. Considering that excessive violence can be bad for illicit business (since it is disruptive and invites unwanted police and media scrutiny), another key question that emerges is: does violence follow rational motivations? Ideas about the rationality of violence derived from the analysis of civil wars and ethnic conflicts provide a theoretical lens to advance the study of violence related to illicit trade. They show that seemingly irrational forms of violence can be instrumental to maintain influence or compliance when distributions of power become unstable and thus can better explain why illicit actors become more violent when they face internal disputes and external pressure. Finally, considering the wide variety of actors that engage in illicit practices, it is worth exploring how the internal structure and organization of trafficking actors affect the dynamics of violence. Descriptive evidence and insights derived from the analysis of civil wars and terrorism suggests that the size and organization of groups affects the type of violence used. For example, a large centralized organization may be more capable of engaging in violence, yet at the same time may be more able to control individual violent behavior of their members.[19]

A more careful consideration of the conditions under which violence emerges also requires paying more attention to less studied geographic areas. Perhaps most strikingly, the tri-border area of Paraguay is the epicenter of a variety of flourishing illicit trade activities given its strategic location, yet has remained far less violent than, say, Colombia or Mexico. Perhaps for this reason, it has largely been overlooked as a focus of study.[20]

The relationship between insurgents and drug trafficking is a dimension of drug related violence that has been widely studied in Colombia (mainly in relation to the FARC Revolutionary Armed Forces of Colombia) and to a lesser extent in Peru (with *Sendero Luminoso*).

While the most common association is that the proceeds from drug trafficking can strengthen armed actors by providing them with a lucrative source of funding, the story is considerably more complex and subject to heated debate. According to the "narco-guerrilla" thesis (which has enjoyed considerable influence in policy circles for several decades), drugs and insurgency are inseparably intertwined and thus should be combated simultaneously and with similar methods. But critics have long questioned the underlying assumptions of this argument as overly simplistic, with counterproductive policy implications.[21] Recent studies detail the importance of political capital insurgents generate in rural areas by protecting peasant drug producers from government eradication and interdiction efforts—and thus more intensive anti-drug operations perversely plays into the hands of insurgents.[22]

The narco-guerrilla thesis also ignores that in many cases armed conflict long precedes the emergence of drug trafficking, as in Colombia, and thus it would be erroneous to simply reduce an insurgency to an interest in drug profits. It also ignores that some armed groups have not become heavily involved in drug trafficking even if they have the opportunity to do so, or that some engage primarily in the cultivation stages while others engage in the whole trafficking chain or in its most profitable stages. In this regard, existing knowledge on the relation between drugs and conflict would be strengthened by a deeper analysis of armed groups that lack of a close connection to drug trafficking such as those in Mexico. By asking more systematically under which conditions armed groups engage in illicit trade we can analyze the impact that ideology, capacities, and transnational connections have in shaping relations between armed groups and illicit business.

Besides financial and social connections, armed groups and traffickers may connect in other ways. Several studies in Colombia have analyzed the historical deep connections between paramilitary groups and drug trafficking.[23] As these studies point out, the story of paramilitary groups is complex and involves many actors and motivations, yet it is clear that drug traffickers played a key role in organizing paramilitary groups as their branch of armed protection in the 1980s. As these groups grew and advanced, they eventually became more autonomous and towards the early 2000s became a crucial player in the Colombian drug trade. This story raises three important questions. First, why traffickers decide to create armed structures that can eventually pose a threat to them by attracting excessive law enforcement and media attention, and by transferring crucial power to individuals who can potentially overpower traffickers? Second, what conditions facilitate the creation of such structures, and how do they evolve and reproduce? Third, how do changes in the security apparatus of the state relate to the creation of these armed structures? A useful comparative case in helping to answer these questions is the Zetas, the armed branch of the Gulf Drug Trafficking Organization in Mexico, formed in 1997 with deserted members of a special military and antiguerrilla force known as GAFES (Special Forces of Aerial Groups).

Finally, the connection between drug trafficking and violence can occur through the engagement of youth gangs. As in the case of armed groups, trafficking activities provide gangs more financial clout while at the same time creating incentives for their proliferation. Yet, in some cases such as those of Central American countries, the connection between gangs, drug trafficking, and violence is not, despite widespread perception, as prevalent as in other cases, like Brazil. As of 2007 the United Nations estimated that about 70,000 gang members existed in Central America alone, mostly in Guatemala, El Salvador and Honduras. Yet, as the same UN report points out, the association between youth gangs, crime, and international trafficking is based on shaky assumptions, such as that gang members are responsible for most homicides in Central America, that diasporas are crucial in providing international connections for gangs when in fact few individuals detained in the

United States for drug trafficking are from Central America, or that drug consumption rates have increased due to growing distribution networks.[24] In Brazilian cities, by contrast, the gangs-trafficking-violence connection is clearer as the main drug trafficking actors are youth gangs such as the *Comando Vermelho* in Rio de Janeiro. Yet, even within Brazil, differences between the more concentrated and stable drug markets of Rio de Janeiro and the less organized of Sao Paulo, explain changing gang behaviors and dynamics of violence.[25] Thus, even though the origin, organization and emergence of youth gangs constitutes a separate research area on its own, it is worth asking how the violence generated by youth gangs as they engage in drug trafficking is different from that conducted by drug trafficking organizations, why youth gangs become salient in drug trafficking in some places but not in others,[26] and why forms of violence vary between those gangs associated with trafficking.

Illicit Trade and Neoliberalism

The spread of neoliberal free market reforms—including the liberalization of trade and finance and privatization of state owned enterprises—have been the focus of considerable research in recent decades.[27] Largely overlooked in this political economy literature, however, is how these shifts in the formal economy have interacted with the illicit export economy. For instance, the liberalization of trade and relaxation of trade barriers has had the positive externality of reducing the incentives to smuggle legal commodities. This is quite significant, as evading taxes and other restrictions on legitimate trade has historically been a major motivation to smuggle. At the same time, reducing barriers for licit trade may also have the unintended consequence of facilitating illicit trade. Consider the case of NAFTA. Trade across the U.S.-Mexico border has more than doubled since the mid-1990s, making it increasingly challenging for border authorities to "weed out" illicit goods such as drugs. While simultaneously facilitating legal trade and enforcing laws against illegal trade has always been a frustrating and cumbersome task, it is made all the more difficult by the rapid growth of commercial cargo through already highly congested ports of entry. Further analysis is needed to evaluate both the viability of border interdiction in the context of deepening economic integration, and the impact of tighter border controls on the integration process.

It should be pointed out that trade agreements have also become tangled up in the politics of policing illicit flows. In the campaign for NAFTA, Mexican President Carlos Salinas famously promised that the trade agreement would help Mexico "export tomatoes" instead of "tomato pickers," while he also launched a high-profile anti-drug crackdown to appease and impress Washington critics (even as drug trafficking and related corruption worsened). Likewise, for a number of Andean countries, extensions of trade preferences with the United States have been conditional on the cooperation with anti narcotics efforts, as in the case of the ATPA (Andean Trade Preference Act) in 1991 and the ATPDEA (Andean Trade Preference and Drug Eradication Act) in 2002.[28] Bolivia was excluded from these preferences in 2008 as the Bush administration determined that the country did not meet antinarcotic cooperation agreements. Thus the analysis of the connections between trade liberalization and the politics of policing efforts, and the evolution of these connections over time as trade liberalization schemes shift towards more multilateralism, constitute a promising area of research.[29]

More research is also needed to determine the extent to which the illicit economy has provided an immediate cushion of sorts for those most negatively affected by the shocks of neoliberal market reforms. For example, in the 1990s, clandestine migration and illicit drug crop cultivation became more attractive coping mechanisms for Mexican peasants displaced by sweeping agricultural reforms (such as the lifting of government price supports and protections for the traditional ejido system).[30] Throughout the region, shifts in prices and dynamics of commerce derived from free trade policies may have created incentives and pressures to turn to the illicit economy. In Peru, some analysts have noted that when prices for agricultural products collapsed in the 1990s, local populations in the valleys around the Ene and Apurimac rivers that grew coca for traditional local consumption, entered the cocaine export economy.[31] Similarly, in Bolivia the illicit economy may have acted as a cushion for increasing urban unemployment rates derived from economic liberalization in the mid 1980s.[32]

Although requiring further study, there have also been some indications that privatization and financial liberalization have unintentionally facilitated investing the proceeds of illicit trade. The Mexican experience again provides a useful illustration. According to the U.S. Federal Bureau of Investigation, many of the state-owned companies privatized under the Salinas administration were bought up by drug traffickers.[33] Financial liberalization in the 1990s also apparently enabled narcoinvestment. According to the Economist Financial Intelligence Unit, the liberalization of finance and capital markets in Mexico has facilitated money laundering and narco-investment.[34]

Finally, another interesting channel through which neoliberal market reforms may have influenced illicit trade is by reconfiguring relations between political and criminal actors. As mentioned above, in Colombia, proceeds from illegal activities expanded criminal influence on electoral politics, sometimes providing emerging politicians with an opportunity to compete and others allowing traditional politicians to maintain their control. In Colombia and other countries like Brazil and Mexico, this process may have been exacerbated by market reforms and deregulation, as these curtailed the availability of public resources for clientelistic exchanges—thus increasing the incentives for politicians to turn to other private and illicit funding sources.[35]

Conclusions

For the study of illicit trade to gain more traction in political science, scholarship in this area will need to more explicitly and deeply engage larger debates and questions at the center of the field. In this chapter we have provided a brief sketch of just a few of the possibilities here, ranging from issues of democratic governance to organized violence to neoliberalism. To some extent, this is simply a matter of theoretical framing and asking research questions that are most relevant to the discipline. But it also relates to research design, case selection, and methods.

As a starting point, political scientists interested in this area should become more voracious consumers of works in other disciplines. Reading broadly beyond political science is always a good thing, of course, but is an absolute necessity in this particular research domain. This includes works by anthropologists,[36] economists,[37] sociologists,[38] and historians[39] working on topics related to illicit trade. A handful of interdisciplinary collections and collaborations also stand out.[40] There are also a number of more policy-oriented collections that demonstrate the utility of work that not only crosses disciplines but also the policy-academia divide.[41]

The field of political science has always been good at "smuggling in" insights and methods from other disciplines (with economics, it seems, particularly fashionable in recent years)—and nowhere would this be more appropriate than in the study of smuggling itself.

This is illustrated by a handful of recent books by political scientists. Michael Kenney, for instance, has applied organizational theory from sociology to help explain organizational adaptation by Colombian trafficking groups in response to pressure from law enforcement.[42] Peter Andreas has drawn from theatrical metaphors and analogies inspired by the sociologist Erving Goffman to analyze the politics of high-profile border policing campaigns.[43] Desmond Arias has utilized micro-level ethnographic methods more common to anthropology in understanding everyday drug trafficking dynamics in the *Favelas* of Rio de Janeiro.[44] Mixing economics and political science, Ernesto Dal Bó, Pedro Dal Bó, and Rafael Di Tella, have used game theory and formal modeling to derive predictions about interactions between illicit market actors and the state.[45]

Finally, substantial barriers to research should be recognized, with mutually reinforcing practical, professional, and political factors inhibiting scholarship in this area. The most obvious practical constraint, of course, is that studying illicit trade up close can be considerably more risky and even dangerous than studying licit trade (and it can also become an additional hurdle for U.S.-based scholars seeking approval from their university's Institutional Review Board). Related to this is the basic fact that the object of study is usually trying to avoid being observed, counted, and scrutinized. Bad (or non-existent) data is thus the Achilles heel of research on illicit trade. The "large N" studies that are typical in political science are not as viable given the extremely poor quality of the aggregate data (at the same time it should be noted that the common use of bad data related to illicit trade, including its influence on political debates and the policy process, is itself an interesting subject worthy of greater scrutiny).[46] Professional incentives reinforce these practical concerns. Simply put, the study of illicit trade and efforts to regulate it are by definition considered fringe topics in the field, more the domain of criminologists than of political scientists (despite the fact that "policing" is a core state function and the term has a closely overlapping lineage with "politics"). Last but not least are a number of political obstacles. Not surprisingly, illicit trade is often a politically sensitive topic (as are related concerns such as corruption)—and indeed in the cases of illegal drugs, human trafficking, and migrant smuggling, are considered "hot button" issues. Consequently, the data is not only often bad but highly politicized, and the most relevant state actors may be especially reluctant to talk (or at least talk candidly) and share useful information with researchers. Having said that, the cumulative work to date across many disciplines suggests that the research challenge is far from insurmountable. Moreover, it is these very political obstacles that are an essential part of understanding the politics of illicit trade in the first place and contributes to making this an especially fascinating research area.

Notes

1 For a more general discussion of the democratic governance literature, see Part I of this handbook.
2 According to the 2009 Latinobarometro survey, only 25 percent of Latin American citizens surveyed consider that democracy effectively protects them from crime.
3 At the beginning of President Felipe Calderon's mandate in 2006, 84 percent of the population supported the mobilization of the military in the war against drugs. Three years later, despite opposition in some sectors, surveys show that a significant sector of the population still supports Calderon's militarized strategy. Surveys conducted by Mitofsky and Reforma in August 2009 reported a 50 percent approval of the war on drug trafficking, a support rate far higher than support for economic and social policies.
4 Peter Lupsha, "Drug Lords and Narco-corruption: the Players Change but the Game Continues," *Crime, Law and Social Change*, Vol. 16 (1991): 41–58.

5 See Luis Astorga, *El Siglo de las Drogas* (Plaza & Janes, 2004); Gustavo Duncan, "Narcotraficantes, mafiosos y guerreros, Historia de una subordinación" in *Narcotráfico en Colombia: Economía y Violencia* (Fundación Seguridad y Democracia, 2005); Carlos Flores, *El Estado en Crisis: Crimen Organizado y Política: Desafíos para la Consolidación Democrática* (Universidad Nacional Autónoma de México, 2005); Carlos Resa Nestares, *El Estado como Maximizador de Rentas del Crimen Organizado, El Caso del Tráfico de Drogas en México* (Instituto Internacional de Gobernabilidad, Documento No. 88. October 2001); Monica Serrano, "Narcotráfico y Gobernabilidad en México," *Pensamiento Iberoamericano* 1 (2007): 251–278.

6 On the relation between criminality and politics, see Francisco Gutierrez, ¿Lo que el viento se llevo? Los Partidos Politicos y la Democracia en Colombia 1958–2002 (Norma 2007) especially Chapter 8; on the political aspirations of drug traffickers see, Alvaro Camacho and Andres Lopez, "From Smugglers to Drug Lords, to Traquetos: Changes in the Colombian Illicit Drug Organizations," in Christopher Welna and Gustavo Gallon, *Peace, Democracy and Human Rights in Colombia* (Notre Dame University Press, 2001), 60–89.

7 Snyder and Duran Martinez also demonstrate that this question has implications for patterns of drug-related violence. See Richard Snyder and Angelica Duran Martinez, "Does Illegality Breed Violence? Drug Trafficking and State-Sponsored Protection Rackets," *Crime, Law, and Social Change*, Vol. 52, No. 3 (September 2009): 253–274.

8 For details on cases involving the Guatemalan military: Frank Smyth, "The Untouchable Narco-State: Guatemala's Army defies DEA," *The Texas Observer*, November 18, 2005. On the role of the military see Susanne Jonas, "Democratization through Peace: The Difficult Case of Guatemala," *Journal of Interamerican Studies and World Affairs,* Vol. 42, No. 4 (2000): 9–38; Mark Ruhl, "The Guatemalan Military since the Peace Accords: The Fate of Reform under Arzú and Portillo," *Latin American Politics and Society*, Vol. 47, No. 1 (Spring 2005): 55–85.

9 For a discussion of the relation between different institutional configurations in Central America and the extent of drug related corruption see Julie Bunck and Michael Fowler, *Bribes, Bullets, and Intimidation: Narcotics Trafficking in Central America* (Pennsylvania State University Press, forthcoming).

10 In Guatemala the replacement of the corruption ridden Department of Antinarcotics Operations (DOAN) by the Servicio Nacional de Información Antinarcoticos (SAIA) is crucial but has not been significantly analyzed. In Mexico, the creation and dismantling of the Dirección Federal de Seguridad DFS is key to understanding state-criminal relations.

11 For a more detailed discussion, see Coletta Youngers and Eileen Rosen, eds., *Drugs and Democracy in Latin America: The Impact of U.S. Policy* (Lynne Rienner, 2004).

12 For a broad introduction, see Peter Andreas and Ethan Nadelmann, *Policing the Globe: Criminalization and Crime Control in International Relations* (Oxford University Press, 2006).

13 Such discussion would clearly benefit from the vast literature on social movements, for example, a general discussion of the uneven politicization of indigenous groups in Latin America is particularly illuminating. See Deborah Yashar, "Contesting Citizenship: Indigenous Movements and Democracy in Latin America," *Comparative Politics*, Vol. 31, No.1 (Oct 1998): 23–42.

14 Attempts by coca growers to delay eradication campaigns have succeeded sometimes and failed in others, especially when groups are internally divided. A nice illustration in the Peruvian case is described by Ursula Durand, "Coca o muerte; the radicalization of the cocalero movement," MA dissertation (University of Oxford, 2005) and Luis Pariona Arana, "En el Centro del Conflicto: Cocaleros, Narcotráfico y Sendero Luminoso en el Alto Huallaga," Ideele No. 163 (May 2004); on the mobilization of coca growers in Bolivia, see Benjamin Dangl, *The Price of Fire: Resource Wars and Social Movements in Bolivia* (AK Press, 2007) especially chapter 2 pp. 36–54; on mobilization in Colombia, see Maria Clemencia Ramirez "The Politics of Recognition and Citizenship in Putumayo and in the Baja Bota of Cauca: The Case of the 1996 Cocalero Movement" in Boaventura de Sousa, ed., *Democratizing Democracy* (Verson, 2005), 220–256.

15 For a more detailed analysis across a range of disciplines, see the special issue of *Crime, Law and Social Change* Vol. 52, No. 3, 2009.

16 These statistics mainly capture the so-called "narco-executions." See Secretariado Ejecutivo del Sistema Nacional de Seguridad Publica Base de Datos de Fallecimientos occurridos por presunta rivalidad delincuencial, and also David Shirk, *Drug Violence in Mexico: Data and Analysis from 2001–2009* (Trans-border Institute, Joan B. Kroc School of Peace Studies. University of San Diego, 2009).

17 It is important to note here that in the period 1997–2004 Bolivia faced increased violence associated with militarized responses to coca growers' mobilization in the Chapare region, and also that there have been important variations over time in Colombia.

18 Overall homicide rates were on the decline in Mexico between 1990 and 2007 and high numbers of drug related killings reflected the increase in brutal and visible killings such as beheadings and executions but not necessarily an overall increase in levels of violence. The situation changed drastically in 2008 with a spike of 50% in homicide rates. For an interesting discussion of the evolution of homicide in Mexico see Fernando Escalante, *El Homicidio en Mexico entre 1990 y 2007* (El Colegio de Mexico, 2009).

19 Just to name two examples, Gianluca Fiorentini and Sam Peltzman analyze how monopolies and large organizations can reduce the level of violence in illicit markets in, *The Economics of Organized Crime* (Cambridge University Press, 1995); Wendy Pearlman discusses how internal power dynamics in extremist groups determine the use of violence in the context of peace processes in, "Spoiling Inside and Out: Internal Political Contestation and the Middle East Peace Process," *International Security,* Vol. 33, No. 3 (Winter 2008): 79–109.

20 But see, Daniel K. Lewis, *A South American Frontier: The Tri-border Region* (Chelsea House Publications, 2006).

21 See, for example, Peter Andreas, Eva Bertram, Morris Blachman, and Kenneth Sharpe, "Dead-End Drug Wars," *Foreign Policy,* Issue 85 (Winter 1991).

22 Vanda Felbab-Brown, *Shooting Up: Counterinsurgency and the War on Drugs* (Brookings, 2009).

23 See for example Mauricio Romero, *Paramilitares y Autodefensas: 1982–2003* (IEPRI, 2003).

24 See Crime and Development in Central America: Caught in the Crossfire, (UNODC, May 2007). For an interesting discussion of the evolution of gangs and illicit activities in Managua see Dennis Rodgers, "Living in the Shadow of Death: Gangs, Violence and Social Order in Urban Nicaragua, 1996–2002," *Journal of Latin American Studies,* 38 (2006): 267–292.

25 For a comparative perspective on Brazilian gangs, see Benjamin Lessing, "As facções cariocas em perspectiva comparativa," *Novos estudios — CEBRAP* No. 80 (March 2008); also Guaracy Mingardi, "Money and the International Drug Trade in Sao Paulo" *International Social Science Journal,* Vol. 53, Issue 169 (2001): 379–386. For a focus on the social dimensions of drug trafficking and gangs see Alba Zaluar, "Perverse Integration: Drug Trafficking and Youth in the Favelas of Rio de Janeiro," *Journal of International Affairs,* Vol. 53, No. 2 (2000): 653–671.

26 For example in an interesting argument Geffray traces back the salience of Brazilian urban gangs to transformations in drug trafficking along the Bolivian border in the mid 1980s. See Christian Geffray, "Brasil: Drug trafficking in the Federal State of Rondonia," *International Social Science Journal,* Vol. 53, Issue 169 (2001): 443–450.

27 For a more general discussion, see Corrales in this handbook.

28 See June S. Beittel, "Paraguay: Political and Economic Conditions and U.S. Relations" (Congressional Research Service, 2010). For a more detailed discussion of ATPA, see J.F. Hornbeck, *The Andean Trade Preference Act: Background and Issues for Reauthorization* (Congressional Research Service, 2002).

29 The use of aid conditionalities to advance U.S. drug control policies and also the failure to effectively make drug assistance conditional on respect for human rights and civil liberties have been analyzed extensively. Yet, there is less discussion about the connections between trade liberalization and drug controls.

30 See Drug Enforcement Administration, *The New Agricultural Reform Program and Illicit Cultivation in Mexico,* 14 October 1992, cited in Peter Andreas, "When Policies Collide: Market Reform, Market Prohibition, and the Narcotization of the Mexican Economy," in H. Richard Friman and Peter Andreas, eds., *The Illicit Global Economy and State Power* (Rowman & Littlefield, 1999), 132–133.

31 Isaías Rojas, "Peru: Drug Control Policy, Human Rights and Democracy," in Coletta A. Youngers and Eileen Rosin, eds., *Drugs and Democracy in Latin America* (Lynne Rienner, 2005), 185–230.

32 See Elena Alvarez, "Economic Development, Restructuring and the Illicit Drug Sector in Bolivia and Peru: Current Policies," *Journal of Interamerican Studies and World Affairs,* Vol. 37, No. 3 (1995): 125–149.

33 Cited in Tim Golden, "Mexican Connection Grows as Cocaine Supplier to U.S.," *New York Times,* 30 July, 1995, A1.

34 "Political Outlook: Party Stability," *Economist Intelligence Unit Country Forecast*, 30 May 1995.

35 The decline of public resources and their replacement with illegal money in clientelist exchanges was discussed by Christian Geffray in *Globalisation, Drugs and Criminalisation: Final Research Report on Brazil, China, India and Mexico* (UNESCO-MOST and UN-ODCCP, 2002).

36 See, for example, the contributors to Josiah Heyman, ed., *States and Illegal Practices* (Berg, 1999).

37 See Francisco E. Thoumi, *Illegal Drugs, Economy, and Society in the Andes* (Johns Hopkins University Press, 2003); R.T. Naylor, *Wages of Crime* (Cornell University Press, 2005); Gianluca Fiorentini and Sam Peltzman, eds., *The Economics of Organized Crime* (Cambridge University Press, 1997).

38 See Luis Astorga, *Drogas Sin Fronteras* (Grijalbo, 2003); David Spener, *Clandestine Crossings: Migrants and Coyotes on the Texas-Mexico Border* (Cornell University Press, 2009). It should be noted that while there is a substantial sociological literature on the informal economy in Latin America, this literature typically does not include the more transnational and criminalized dimensions of informal economic activity.

39 See, for instance, Lance Grahn, *The Political Economy of Smuggling: Regional Informal Economies in Early Bourbon New Granada* (Westview, 1997); Steve Gootenberg, *Andean Cocaine: The Making of a Global Drug* (University of North Carolina Press, 2009); David T. Courtwright, *Forces of Habit: Drugs and the Making of the Modern World* (Harvard University Press, 2002).

40 See, for example, David Kyle and Ray Koslowski, eds., *Global Human Smuggling* (Johns Hopkins University Press, 2001); Willem van Schendel and Itty Abraham, eds., *Illicit Flows and Criminal Things: States, Borders, and the Other Side of Globalization* (Indiana University Press, 2005), and Paul Gootenberg, ed., *Cocaine: Global Histories* (Routledge, 1999).

41 In this regard, see, for example, Tom Farer, ed., *Transnational Crime in the Americas* (Routledge, 1999).

42 Michael Kenney, *From Pablo to Osama: Trafficking and Terrorist Networks, Government Bureaucracies, and Competitive Adaptation* (Pennsylvania State University Press, 2007).

43 Peter Andreas, *Border Games: Policing the U.S.-Mexico Divide* (Cornell University Press, 2009, 2nd ed.).

44 Desmond Arias, *Drugs and Democracy in Rio De Janeiro: Trafficking, Social Networks, and Public Security* (University of North Carolina Press, 2006).

45 Ernesto Dal Bó, Pedro Dal Bó and Rafael Di Tella, "Plata o Plomo?: Bribe and Punishment in a Theory of Political Influence," *American Political Science Review*, Vol. 100, No.1 (February 2006): 41–53.

46 See Peter Andreas and Kelly M. Greenhill, eds., *Sex, Drugs, and Body Counts: The Politics of Numbers in Global Crime and Conflict* (Cornell University Press, 2010).

PART V

Theories/Methods

26

INSTITUTIONALISM

Aníbal Pérez-Liñán and Néstor Castañeda Angarita

Institutional analysis has blossomed over the past two decades, becoming one of the preferred perspectives for the study of Latin American politics. The approach is predicated on the idea that institutions shape political behavior and, by extension, policy outcomes. This claim opens three questions: What is a political institution? How are political institutions able to shape policy outcomes? And to what extent is this approach able to illuminate the dynamics of Latin American politics?

Economists and political scientists often rely on a useful metaphor, asserting that institutions are "the rules of the game"—and, by implication, that politicians and economic organizations are players. The insight is circular, however, because rule-bound games are just a particular type of social institution.[1] By *political* institutions we refer to the norms that regulate the formation of binding policy decisions and the selection of the people in charge of such decisions in a polity. In modern societies, such rules are typically codified into law, but some of those norms—as we discuss below—may be informal.

In this chapter we offer an integrated framework to articulate the logic of institutional analysis. We claim that political institutions produce three types of causal effects: they alter the distribution of authority among policymakers, they shape incentives for political actors, and they create long-term, unexpected historical legacies. In the first section of the chapter, we discuss four fundamental principles of the institutional approach in political science. Although we are unable to provide an exhaustive map of the literature, in the second part we show how these principles helped elucidate two classic issues in the study of Latin American politics.[2] Our conclusions underscore the reasons why institutional analysis has become one of the dominant approaches in the study of Latin American politics, describe the main theoretical challenges ahead, and warn our colleagues against illusions of constitutional engineering.

Four Building Blocks of Institutional Analysis

1. Actors and Preferences

The initial assumption of institutional analysis is that political actors, defined either as individuals (voters, presidents, legislators, judges) or by extension, as the organizations they command (parties, agencies, committees, courts), have preferences about what the government should do. We commonly refer to those as "policy preferences" even though actors may pursue specific decisions or complex outcomes. In any case, we assume that such preferences are exogenous: they are determined by the actors' ideology, class, market position, religion, ethnicity, prior socialization, and so on. Note that, in this way, any of these explanatory variables may comfortably enter institutional analysis through the back door.

This initial focus on actors and their preferences gives the institutional perspective two advantages. First, institutional arguments are able to explain aggregate historical outcomes as a result of how actors' preferences interact in a given institutional environment. Institutionalists are thus proud of their ability to pinpoint the "micro-foundations" of macro-political outcomes. Second, actors' policy preferences can sometimes be represented as a position in a policy space (a single dimension, or a two-dimensional plane). Institutional arguments thus have an elective affinity with formal spatial models of policymaking.

In addition to policy preferences, political actors are expected to pursue other important objectives. Alternative goals are relevant for institutional accounts because they occasionally trade off against policy preferences, giving other players the ability to gain leverage over the actors' policy choices. Among these goals, institutional analysis has placed a particular emphasis on career ambitions. Most actors can be assumed to have static ambitions (e.g., legislators want to retain their seats) or progressive ambitions (e.g., judges in lower courts want to become justices in the Supreme Court). Identifying typical career paths, and thus the modal ambitions prevailing in each country, is a critical step to construct sensible institutional interpretations.

2. Powers

Preferences are irrelevant for policy outcomes unless actors can do something to affect the policy-making process. This is the first reason why formal institutions play a crucial role in politics. Legal rules empower some actors to make particular decisions and preclude others from doing so. For example, the constitution may authorize the lower House to create new taxes, and may prevent the creation of taxes by the Executive Branch. Norms about citizenship may empower women to vote but they may disenfranchise some ethnic groups. We refer to these as the first-order effects of institutions: legal norms grant decision-making power to some actors but also impose constraints on them. In this way, norms make the preferences of some actors directly relevant (or irrelevant) for the policy-making process.

We can classify the first-order effects of political institutions according to the content of the rules and to the immediacy of their effects. Depending on the content of the rules, legal norms empower or constrain political actors in seven ways: (1) they authorize them to participate in collective decisions (e.g., voters elect the president); (2) they empower them to block a proposal made by others (presidents may veto a law); (3) they authorize them to initiate exclusive proposals (presidents may nominate members of the Supreme Court); and (4) they empower them to make unilateral decisions (presidents may appoint members of the cabinet without confirmation). The institutional literature has described these four roles as those of voters, veto players, agenda-setters, and decisive players, respectively. Additionally, norms may constrain actors by (5) imposing prohibitions (officers cannot enter private property without a warrant); (6) establishing requirements (only lawyers may become judges); or (7) mandating procedures (legislative seats may be allocated proportionally).

Depending on the immediacy of their effects, norms may empower (or constrain) political actors directly in their capacity to make policy, or indirectly, through their capacity to appoint or remove others who make policy. For example, the constitution may create a Constitutional Tribunal to exercise judicial review, but it may determine that Congress will nominate all members of the Tribunal. The power to appoint officials is critical because political actors may select ideological "clones," or individuals with their same preferences to make decisions about relevant policies; the power to remove them is relevant because actors may dismiss policymakers with incompatible policy preferences. But more important, these powers are essential because they create incentives for career-minded politicians, bureaucrats, and judges.

3. *Incentives*

To the extent that political actors are concerned with their future, they must be sensitive to the preferences of those with power to affect their careers. Occasionally, this means relinquishing some of their programmatic goals for the sake of long-term professional considerations. We call these the second-order effects of political institutions: because formal rules give some actors leverage over the careers of others, they indirectly shape the incentives of the latter. Such incentives may "correct" the initial preferences of political actors when they make decisions about policy.

Democratic institutions, or course, are designed to make the careers of politicians dependent on the preferences of voters. Even if politicians prefer to adopt policies consistent with their own ideology or interests, they are partially constrained by the outcomes desired by voters. Depending on the institutional design, however, voters may enjoy unequal degrees of influence over particular politicians. For a presidential candidate elected in a nation-wide district, the preferences of all citizens may count. For a legislator elected in a local district, only the preferences of a small subset of the national electorate may be truly relevant. For a judge appointed with life tenure, the preferences of voters may be trivial.

Institutional incentives can be generally represented by principal-agent models. Formal institutions grant some actors (the "principals") the power to appoint or remove other officers ("the agents"). Thus, principals will seek to appoint agents who are as close to their policy preferences as possible, subject to the need to secure technical expertise and to the constraints of the nomination process. In turn, agents will seek to maximize their policy goals, subject to the constraints imposed by the principals. For example, if a Supreme Court justice is subject to reappointment every four years, her capacity to contradict the preferences of the senators when ruling on particular cases will be lower than if she enjoys life tenure.

If we define politics as the interaction of competing social forces with different powers and interests, it is tempting to believe that institutionalism provides a comprehensive theory of politics. According to the approach described in the previous pages, political actors pursue their preferences using powers (authorizations minus constraints) granted to them by the legal framework. However, those preferences are weighted against the desires of other powerful actors with capacity to influence their careers. The interaction of those actors in a given institutional environment produces aggregate outcomes of relevant social consequences.

When summarized in this way, the institutional approach unveils two characteristically "bourgeois" assumptions: (1) actors value their careers above other goals, and (2) they are expected to abide by the letter of the law. But, why should they? The first assumption is often justified with a simple claim: political careers involve political power, and power is necessary to achieve diverse goals such as serving society, enjoying the benefits of corruption, or indulging in ideological adventures. However, the second assumption cannot be taken for granted—particularly in the study of Latin American politics. We shall return to the problem of compliance below.

4. Long-Term Consequences

In order to assert that institutions create incentives, we must assume that political actors are strategic, that is, that they anticipate the preferences of other players and adjust their responses accordingly. This assumption is critical to understand not only principal-agent relations but also bargaining interactions among equals. For example, legislators will be more willing to delegate decree authority to the president when the executive shares their policy preferences, but Supreme Court justices will be more willing to strike down presidential decrees when the president lacks power to retaliate against them. The idea of strategic behavior is the cornerstone of "rational choice" institutionalism.

However, political scientists should be careful to assume perfect information when analyzing political institutions. Although this problem may be seen as a mere nuisance when we study the impact of institutions in the short run, it becomes crucial when we analyze the effect of institutions over longer periods.

The issue of unexpected consequences has become a central theme of "historical" institutionalism. Historical institutionalists do not just focus on the implications of constitutional rules for contemporary policy decisions, they also trace the implications of past institutional structures (and the policies framed under them) for the power and the incentives of present-day political actors. For example, the sequence in which different types of decentralization (political, fiscal, and administrative) were progressively adopted produced a lasting impact in the balance of powers among different levels of government in Latin America.[3] We refer to those consequences as the third-order effects of political institutions. Institutions produce historical legacies that, although not anticipated by their designers, may have enduring implications for the operation of the political system.

From this long-term perspective, the distinction between policies and institutions is often blurred, because historical institutionalism emphasizes how complex policy programs evolve over time into dense policy *networks*.[4] Such networks integrate the initial institutions and political actors that gave birth to the policy, new actors nourished by the policy over time (e.g., government agencies, constituencies), and additional rules generated under the program (e.g., technical regulations), all of which interact in a changing historical environment. Thus, reversing a major policy—such as a comprehensive welfare program or an import-substitution strategy—requires in the long run the dismantlement of a complex array of related institutions.

Early studies in this line tended to emphasize the continuity of institutions and their lasting consequences. Commonly used terms like "path dependence" or "punctuated equilibrium" reflect the belief that institutions define historical trajectories from which it is costly (or sometimes impossible) to backtrack, and that they change only at "critical junctures" when the existing equilibrium shifts dramatically. The literature has also discussed extensively the role of "policy ratchets," coalitions that benefit from the status-quo and use their institutional powers to promote the expansion of a policy or prevent its retraction.[5]

More recent studies, however, have emphasized that institutions may be sticky but they are not static. Mahoney and Thelen have argued that "subversive" actors tend to layer new rules on top of the old ones, "parasitic" actors fail to comply with institutional goals, allowing institutions to drift away from their original mission, "opportunists" reinterpret the meaning of the rules, converting institutions to perform new functions, and "insurrectionary" actors progressively displace the existing rules in favor of new ones.[6] This nuanced view of institutional change represents an extension of the classic framework of historical institutionalism, and offers a promising angle to analyze Latin American political development in innovative ways.

Two Classic Themes

In this section we illustrate how the four principles of institutional analysis have contributed to our understanding of Latin American politics. Rather than providing an exhaustive survey of topics, we have chosen two classic issues in order to unpack the logic of institutional analysis.

1. Legislative Politics and Party Discipline

Traditional views of Latin American political parties claimed that many party organizations were undisciplined and dysfunctional, harming effective governance. Thus, several studies of political parties in the region sought to understand party cohesion, emphasizing the relationship between electoral rules and party discipline.

Actors and Preferences. The literature on party discipline has focused on three actors: members of Congress, party leaders, and voters (sometimes on presidents and governors as well). Legislators and party leaders often disagree on their policy preferences, particularly when they belong to "catch-all" parties. As a result, rank-and-file members may deviate from the party line, creating legislative gridlocks and raising transaction costs when the president negotiates with Congress. Differences between legislators and party leaders can be explained by purely exogenous factors, such as the ideological distance between them, factional disputes, or the social cleavages they represent, but more often the literature has claimed that disagreements can be explained by their career incentives, a topic that we discuss below.[7]

Although studies of the U.S. Congress assume that legislators have static ambitions, studies of Latin America have documented that legislators often pursue career paths other than reelection. Some countries just impose term limits; in addition, proportional representation systems create complex patterns of identifiability because multiple candidates compete in the same party list. Therefore, politicians adjust their career ambitions to the local institutional context. For example, they may become national legislators as an intermediate step to reach other positions at the state or local levels.[8]

Powers. Legislators' ability to affect policymaking depends on the rules that regulate the flow of the legislative process—agenda-setting procedures, committee appointments, seniority, procedural rules in the floor, and so on. But in order to explain party discipline, the literature has focused on the rules that empower party leaders to influence their careers.

Because elective positions require candidates to be nominated and non-elective positions require candidates to be appointed, party leaders may have considerable leverage over the careers of legislators. On one end, party officials may control the nomination of candidates or rank the order of candidates in a closed-list electoral system. For example, in Argentina regional party bosses maintain control over nominations and deputies remain loyal to their provincial-level machines, while major party leaders occupy prominent positions in electoral lists to attract voters but play a limited role in Congress.[9] Despite the use of a mixed electoral system and recent electoral reforms, political leaders in Mexico continue recruiting party loyalists as candidates. On the other end, open primaries may determine the selection of candidates and leaders may lack authority to control party labels or the order of open lists. For instance, in Brazil and Colombia party leaders hardly control nominations, and the consequences for future defections from party alignments are minimal. When congressional leaders have control over careers, they can threaten legislators with reprisals if they fail to comply with the party line. The fact that in some countries legislative seats legally belong to parties rather than legislators dissuades party switching and makes those sanctions more effective.[10]

Elective positions also require success at the polls, which adds an additional layer of complexity. The main sources of empowerment come from the electoral formula (the rules determining how legislators are elected) and the magnitude of the districts (how many representatives are elected in each territorial unit). When legislative elections take place under closed-list proportional representation in large districts, voters are unable to recognize most members of the list and simply support the party label. By contrast, if voters can select specific candidates within the lists or if district magnitude is small, candidates are able to cultivate a personal reputation in their constituencies and may develop independence from their parties.[11]

Incentives. As a result of those conditions, legislators in some systems have greater incentives to follow the party line than others. Consider for illustration four different institutional configurations identified in the literature. First, scholars have shown that legislators have strong incentives for party discipline where legislative reelection is allowed, party organizations control the selection and ranking of candidates, electoral districts are large, and closed-lists are used as the ballot system (e.g., Venezuela 1958–1993). Second, studies of the Chilean case indicate that the combination of open lists with small two-member districts, strong party coordination of nominations, and high reelection rates has also encouraged party discipline within coalitions and strengthened the ties of legislators to local constituencies.[12]

Third, researchers have found that party discipline is not always created by *national* party structures. National legislators may respond to regional bosses if reelection is forbidden or unlikely and if local leaders control the distribution of desired sub-national offices. For example, Argentine electoral rules, which empower provincial governors and local party leaders to control the nomination of congressional candidates, limit legislators' ability to develop a long legislative career and reduce their incentives to specialize. "Amateur" legislators build their careers rotating through different offices at the national and sub-national levels. Therefore, party discipline in Argentina is often based on provincial politics.[13]

Finally, legislators are more inclined to build individual political careers in those contexts in which reelection is allowed, political parties have no control over candidate selection and ranking, and districts are large. For instance, the use of open-list proportional representation in Brazil has created a context in which party leaders have no influence on the rank order of candidates, and candidates of the same party compete against each other in large districts. Thus, politicians' best electoral strategy is to cultivate a personal vote, which favors a narrow focus of representation and individualistic behavior in the legislature.[14] The case of Colombia is quite similar, especially after the constitutional reform in 1991.[15]

Long-Term Consequences. The institutional narrative on party discipline assumes that legislators' career preferences are exogenous and that electoral rules are stable. However, in the short term, Latin American legislators may not take institutions as fixed. Because electoral rules affect their careers, they may seek to modify electoral and party regulations in order to achieve their goals.

In the long-run, if those electoral rules become stable, new cohorts of legislators will be socialized into the idea that political success equals a long legislative career, a sequence of lateral moves between national and sub-national governments, or some other career path, depending on the inherited institutional framework. Thus, from a historical perspective career ambitions should be seen as endogenous to the political process. And such goals will in turn reinforce or undermine the framework. Electoral "ratchets" may prevent the elimination of inherited disproportional systems in Chile or in the United States, for example. Scholars have found significant problems in recognizing the endogenous character of political preferences because it complicates the usual direction of causality from institutions to actors. For example, the shift from one electoral system to another can be explained by the effort of well-established parties to retain power or adapt their structures when new parties emerge or social cleavages change.[16]

2. Institutions and Public Spending

The political economy literature has extensively studied how the rules of political interaction have a systematic effect on economic policymaking. One of the most interesting cases is the study of fiscal policymaking, the political definition of the size of government and the composition of public spending.

Actors and Preferences. In general, the literature has studied fiscal policymaking as the interaction between the president and Congress, albeit some studies have also included sub-national governments and interest groups.[17] Scholars have typically assumed that the executive branch is a unitary actor, but some works have challenged this assumption.[18] Only rarely has Congress been treated as a unitary actor, because it is evident that parties, coalitions, and individual legislators play key roles in the budgetary process.[19] Voters are always present in the background of these narratives.

Institutional analyses have often used ideology and partisanship as proxies for exogenous preferences about government expenditures. It is expected that, ceteris paribus, rightist presidents and legislators will be more fiscally conservative while their leftist counterparts will be more prone to increase government spending.[20] In the Latin American context, other scholars have similarly argued that populist leaders are more prone to overspending than non-populist leaders.[21]

Moreover, institutional studies have relied on party identification as the main proxy to determine whether the preferences of the president and Congress are congruent. A president is said to have strong "partisan powers" when he or she controls a large congressional party which is also very cohesive.[22] This condition, which may be taken as exogenous in studies of policymaking, is the focus of studies of party discipline discussed in the previous section.

Powers. Two types of institutional powers are typically invoked to explain fiscal policymaking. The first one refers to the constitutional authority granted to the president and Congress in order to bargain about spending. The second one refers to the influence that electoral rules give voters and interest groups over presidents and legislators. We address the latter below to discuss second-order effects related to the incentives confronted by policymakers.

Executives in presidential regimes are endowed with particular institutional powers that make them predominant actors in the policy-making process. A canonical literature has sought to rank Latin American presidents according to their constitutional powers vis-à-vis

Congress. This literature has identified general proactive (e.g., decrees) and reactive powers (e.g., veto), but it has also described specific authority over the budget in terms of exclusive initiation and execution.[23]

Scholars have also described legislators granted with institutional authority to approve the budget and define the rules of that process. Committees—rather than the floor—are the critical stage for fiscal bargaining. Once budget committees approve or modify the budget proposal, the bill usually sails through the chambers with minimal difficulty. The literature has also noticed that legislative authority to modify budget is significantly constrained by fiscal rules and in many cases legislators are only authorized to cut expenditures or reallocate items, but not to raise spending.[24]

Incentives. Irrespective of their ideological preferences, politicians have career ambitions that are closely related to their choices about fiscal policy. Presidents are elected in nation-wide constituencies. Therefore, they want to spend in broad national programs. At the same time, because their chances of success and reelection (if allowed) are a function of public responses to the economy, presidents also need to secure macroeconomic stability.[25]

By contrast, legislators are typically elected to represent local constituencies, and their careers are less affected by macroeconomic stability. Consequently, every legislator faces different incentives over the allocation of public spending. These incentives are determined by the electoral system and the nature of constituencies, and often lead to the distribution of patronage or pork at the regional or local level.[26]

The literature has shown that presidents often use pork barrel tactics to keep legislative coalitions together. Fiscal policy is negotiated extensively with members of the coalition and with sub-national governments. Thus, the president's fiscal commitments can be included into the budget proposal or into other pieces of legislation. This bargain is inter-temporal; it does not stop when the budget bill is approved, and it extends into the implementation and even the control stages.[27]

Long-Term Consequences. Although government budgets are known to be quite rigid, the institutional literature has not explored systematically *longue durée* patterns of fiscal policy. Studies of market reforms have explored how policy ratchets supporting import-substitution industrialization were deactivated in a context of crisis in the 1990s.[28] But as we have shown above, institutional analysis has usually provided only short-run theories of fiscal policymaking. Long-term conditions that affect the size of government and the composition of spending cross-nationally—for instance, political-business cycles, the openness of the economy, and intergenerational issues—have been ignored by many institutional analyses.[29] One of the best examples of this lack of attention to the long-run effects of political institutions on fiscal policy is the study of the dynamics of taxation. This is unexplored territory not only because tax structures in the region have remained relatively constant over long periods of time, but also because tax revenue is not generally a subject of political negotiations every fiscal year.

Institutionalism and the Limits of Constitutional Engineering

"Institutions matter" was the battle cry of the institutionalist movement of the 1990s. Following Latin American transitions from authoritarianism, this working assumption was intellectually attractive and offered a straightforward research program. When confronted with a pressing problem, analysts wondered: Is the institutional framework giving too much power to actors with the wrong preferences? Is it creating the wrong incentives for policymakers? This approach yielded promising answers and has become one of the dominant perspectives for the study of Latin American politics. Several institutions not discussed in this chapter, such as the judiciary, have received considerable attention, while others, such as the public bureaucracy or the security forces, remain to be explored.[30]

However, solutions for pressing problems based on "constitutional engineering" proved to be elusive. For example, the 1998 Ecuadorian constitution, intended to strengthen the executive branch, was a parchment barrier against the overthrow of two presidents within a few years. The adoption of mixed-member electoral systems in Bolivia and Venezuela, intended to improve political representation, offered but a fancy electoral framework for the demise of those party systems.

This activist approach to the crafting of political institutions assumed that constitutional designers could anticipate which actors would be empowered by institutional change and how others would react to their preferences. Unfortunately, the precise consequences of institutional experiments are hard to predict for five reasons.

First, institutional design by itself cannot alter exogenous policy preferences, and thus institutional incentives may be insufficient to correct entrenched policy-making practices. For example, computer simulations of spatial models suggest that the influence of institutions on policy outcomes is minor when compared to the preexisting location of the players in the policy space.[31] Therefore, institutional adjustments may be an incomplete solution for problems rooted in the distribution of preferences among actors.

Second, the effect of institutions may be mediated by non-institutional variables such as the quality of leadership, levels of competition, or popular mobilization.[32] For instance, Zaremberg found that the extension of voting rights to women had very different policy implications in Argentina and in Mexico in the early 1950s. The Peronist regime was uncertain about its hegemony and mobilized women actively, while the PRI regime was consolidated and felt no need to offer female voters widespread policy benefits. Similarly, the power of Congress to impeach the president may have different consequences in countries where social movements mobilize against the government and in countries where they do not.[33]

Third, institutional design is often endogenous, meaning that it can be shaped by the same processes that it is expected to influence. Consider the effect of presidential elections on the party system. The literature has pointed out that two-round presidential elections allow citizens to vote sincerely in the first round, encouraging the proliferation of political parties. However, it is also plausible that constitutional designers living under fragmented party systems will adopt runoff elections to avoid minority presidents. Thus, the correlation between *ballotage* and multi-party systems does not clarify the direction of the causal effect. More generally, Negretto has shown that key features of constitutional design may result from the institutional powers and incentives of groups dominating the assembly at the time a constitution is adopted.[34]

Fourth, to the extent that political actors can anticipate the effects of institutional design, they can modify their strategies to counter the goals of the designers and mitigate any undesired consequences. The Colombian constitutional reform of 1991 created a nation-wide district for the Senate, hoping that candidates would campaign on national issues. However, under the existing electoral rules established politicians found effective ways to concentrate their votes in few regional strongholds, reproducing traditional politics.[35]

Fifth, compliance with formal rules is never guaranteed, because politicians are often able to re-interpret or ignore some norms. For example, although the Argentine constitution grants Supreme Court justices life tenure, Helmke documented that incoming presidents have reshuffled the Court by legal or illegal means. This type of problem gave birth to a nascent literature on informal institutions—rules that are not in the statutes but nevertheless are enforced by political actors. A useful way to conceptualize this problem is by thinking of political actors as players confronting a probability distribution over a set of feasible rules. Under the so-called "rule of law," the text of the statutes is an accurate guideline for how socially-enforced rules operate. But, in cases of "informal institutionalization," the gap between written and expected rules may be considerable.[36]

Proper conceptualization of these five theoretical challenges, more than the extension of the institutional approach into new realms, constitutes, in our view, the pressing research agenda for the years to come. The fundamental assumption that "institutions matter" must be questioned in order to explore when (and not just how) particular rules become relevant. Perhaps the most important lesson of the institutional approach is that institutions matter most when they matter the least—that is, when they are potentially crucial and yet not respected.

Notes

1 Roger Caillois, *Man, Play, and Games* (Urbana: University of Illinois Press, 2001 [1958]).
2 On institutionalism, see B. Guy Peters, *Institutional Theory in Political Science: The New Institutionalism* (London: Pinter, 1999). For applications to Latin America, Gerardo Munck, "Democratic Politics in Latin America: New Debates and Research Frontiers," *Annual Review of Political Science* 7 (2004); J. Mark Payne et al., *Democracies in Development — Politics and Reform in Latin America* (New York: Inter-American Development Bank and International Institute for Democracy and Electoral Assistance, 2002).
3 Tulia G. Falleti, *Decentralization and Subnational Politics in Latin America* (New York: Cambridge University Press, 2010).
4 For instance, Evelyne Huber, ed. *Models of Capitalism: Lessons for Latin America* (University Park: Pennsylvania State University Press, 2003).
5 David Collier and Ruth Berins Collier, *Shaping the Political Arena* (Princeton: Princeton University Press, 1991); James Mahoney, *The Legacies of Liberalism: Path Dependence and Political Regimes in Central America* (Baltimore: Johns Hopkins University Press, 2001).
6 James Mahoney and Kathleen Thelen, "A Theory of Gradual Institutional Change," in *Explaining Institutional Change: Ambiguity, Agency, and Power*, eds. James Mahoney and Kathleen Thelen (Cambridge: Cambridge University Press, 2010).
7 John M. Carey, *Legislative Voting and Accountability* (New York: Cambridge University Press, 2009).
8 David Samuels, *Ambition, Federalism, and Legislative Politics in Brazil* (Cambridge: Cambridge University Press, 2003).
9 Julio Burdman, "Alfas, ranas y testimoniales: la cultura política de las elecciones legislativas de medio término en Argentina," *PostData: Revista de Reflexión y Análisis Político* 15, no. 1 (2010).
10 Peter Siavelis and Scott Morgenstern, *Pathways to Power: Political Recruitment and Candidate Selection in Latin America* (University Park: Pennsylvania State University Press, 2008). Flavia Freidenberg and Manuel Alcántara Sáez, eds., *Selección de Candidatos, Política Partidista y Rendimiento Democrático* (México: Tribunal Electoral del Distrito Federal 2009).
11 John M. Carey and Matthew Soberg Shugart, "Incentives to Cultivate a Personal Vote: A rank Ordering of Electoral Formulas," *Electoral Studies* 14, no. 4 (1995).
12 Peter Siavelis, *The President and Congress in Postauthoritarian Chile: Institutional Constraints to Democratic Consolidation* (University Park: Pennsylvania State University Press, 2000); Scott Morgenstern and Benito Nacif, eds., *Legislative Politics in Latin America*, Cambridge Studies in Comparative Politics (Cambridge: Cambridge University Press, 2002).
13 Mark P. Jones et al., "Amateur Legislators — Professional Politicians: The Consequences of Party-Centered Electoral Rules in a Federal System," *American Journal of Political Science* 46, no. 3 (2002); Mark P. Jones, Pablo Sanguinetti, and Mariano Tommasi, "Politics, institutions, and

fiscal performance in a federal system: an analysis of the Argentine provinces," *Journal of Development Economics* 61, no. 2 (2000).

14 The literature on Brazil is extensive and debates are intense. See Barry Ames, *The Deadlock of Democracy in Brazil* (Ann Arbor: University of Michigan Press, 2001); Scott P. Mainwaring, *Rethinking Party Systems in the Third Wave of Democratization: The Case of Brazil* (Stanford, CA: Stanford University Press, 1999); Octavio Amorim Neto, Gary W. Cox, and Mathew D. McCubbins, "Agenda Power in Brazil's Câmara Dos Deputados, 1989-98," *World Politics* 55, no. 4 (2003); Argelina Cheibub Figueiredo and Fernando Limongi, "Presidential Power, Legislative Organization, and Party Behavior in Brazil," *Comparative Politics* 32, no. 2 (2000); Timothy J. Power and Nicol C. Rae, *Exporting Congress?: The Influence of the U.S. Congress on World Legislatures* (Pittsburgh PA: University of Pittsburgh Press, 2006). S. W. Desposato, "Parties for rent? Ambition, ideology, and party switching in Brazil's chamber of deputies," *American Journal of Political Science* 50, no. 1 (2006).

15 Scott Mainwaring, Ana María Bejarano, and Eduardo Pizarro Leongómez, *The Crisis of Democratic Representation in the Andes* (Stanford CA: Stanford University Press, 2006); Brian Crisp and Rachael E. Ingall, "Institutional Engineering and the Nature of Representation: Mapping the Effects of Electoral Reform in Colombia," *American Journal of Political Science* 46, no. 4 (2002).

16 Laura Wills-Otero, "Electoral Systems in Latin America: Explaining the Adoption of Proportional Representation Systems During the Twentieth Century," *Latin American Politics and Society* 51, no. 3 (2009).

17 Ernesto Stein, Alejandro Grisanti, and Ernesto Talvi, "Institutional Arrangements and Fiscal Performance: the Latin American Experience," in *Fiscal Institutions and Fiscal Performance*, eds. James M. Poterba and Jürgen von Hagen (Chicago: University of Chicago Press, 1999); E. Alemán, "Policy Gatekeepers in Latin American Legislatures," *Latin American Politics and Society* 48, no. 3 (2006).

18 Ernesto Stein et al., *The Politics of Policies: Economic and Social Progress in Latin America* (Washington, DC: Inter-American Development Bank and David Rockefeller Center for Latin American Studies at Harvard University, 2006); M. Hallerberg and P. Marier, "Executive Authority, the Personal Vote, and Budget Discipline in Latin American and Caribbean Countries," *American Journal of Political Science* 48, no. 3 (2004).

19 Scott Morgenstern, "Patterns of Legislative Politics: Roll Call Voting in Latin America and the United States." (New York: Cambridge University Press, 2004); Scott Morgenstern and Benito Nacif, "Legislative Politics in Latin America." (New York: Cambridge University Press, 2002).

20 Alberto Alesina et al., "Budget Institutions and Fiscal Performance in Latin America," *Journal of Development Economics* 59, no. 2 (1999); Gregg B. Johnson and Brian F. Crisp, "Mandates, Powers, and Policies," *American Journal of Political Science* 47, no. 1 (2003).

21 Rudiger Dornbusch and Sebastian Edwards, eds., *The Macroeconomics of Populism in Latin America* (Chicago IL: University of Chicago Press,1991).

22 Scott Mainwaring and Matthew S. Shugart, eds., *Presidentialism and Democracy in Latin America* (Cambridge: Cambridge University Press,1997).

23 Matthew S. Shugart and John M. Carey, *Presidents and Assemblies. Constitutional Design and Electoral Dynamics.* (Cambridge: Cambridge University Press, 1992).

24 Lisa Baldez and John M. Carey, "Presidential Agenda Control and Spending Policy: Lessons from General Pinochet's Constitution," *American Journal of Political Science* 43, no. 1 (1999); Hallerberg and Marier, "Executive Authority, the Personal Vote, and Budget Discipline in Latin American and Caribbean Countries."

25 Mark Hallerberg, Carlos Scartascini, and Ernesto Stein, *Who Decides the Budget? A Political Economy Analysis of the Budget Process in Latin America* (Washington, DC: Inter-American Development Bank: Harvard University Press, 2009). Alesina et al., "Budget Institutions and Fiscal Performance in Latin America."

26 Michele M Taylor-Robinson and Chris Diaz, "Who Gets Legislation Passed in a Marginal Legislature and is the Label Marginal Legislature Still Appropriate? A Study of the Honduran Congress," *Comparative Political Studies* 32, no. 5 (1999).

27 Pablo Spiller and Mariano Tommasi, *The Institutional Foundations of Public Policy in Argentina* (New York: Cambridge University Press, 2007); Andrés Mejía Acosta, *Informal Coalitions and Policymaking in Latin America: Ecuador in Comparative Perspective* (New York: Routledge, 2009).

28 Kurt Weyland, *The Politics of Market Reform in Fragile Democracies: Argentina, Brazil, Peru, and Venezuela* (Princeton, NJ: Princeton University Press, 2002); Susan C. Stokes, *Mandates and Democracy: Neoliberalism by Surprise in Latin America* (Cambridge: Cambridge University Press, 2001); María Victoria Murillo, *Labor Unions, Partisan Coalitions, and Market Reforms in Latin America* (Cambridge: Cambridge University Press, 2001); Javier Corrales, *Presidents Without Parties — The Politics of Economic Reform in Argentina and Venezuela in the 1990s* (University Park: The Pennsylvania State University Press, 2002).

29 Ernesto Stein, "Fiscal Decentralization and Government Size in Latin America," in *Democracy, decentralisation and deficits in Latin America*, ed. Kiichiro Fukasaku and Ricardo Hausmann (Washington, DC: Inter-American Development Bank, 1998); Stein, Grisanti, and Talvi, "Institutional Arrangements and Fiscal Performance: the Latin American Experience."; Alesina et al., "Budget Institutions and Fiscal Performance in Latin America."

30 Daniel M. Brinks, *The Judicial Response to Police Killings in Latin America* (Cambridge: Cambridge University Press, 2008); Gretchen Helmke and Julio Ríos-Figueroa, eds., *Courts in Latin America* (Cambridge: Cambridge University Press, 2011); Barbara Geddes, *Politician's Dilemma: Building State Capacity in Latin America* (Berkeley: University of California Press, 1994); Kent Eaton, "Paradoxes of Police Reform: Federalism, Parties and Civil Society in Argentina's Public Security Crisis," *Latin American Research Review* 43, no. 3 (2008).

31 Aníbal Pérez-Liñán and Juan Carlos Rodríguez-Raga, "Veto Players in Presidential Regimes: Institutional Variables and Policy Change," *Revista de Ciencia Política* 29, no. 3 (2009).

32 Manuel Alcántara Sáez, ed. *Politicians and Politics in Latin America* (Boulder: Lynne Rienner, 2008); Peter R. Kingstone, "Privatizing Telebrás: Brazilian Political Institutions and Policy Performance," *Comparative Politics* 36, no. 1 (2003); Laurence Whitehead, "Fernando Henrique Cardoso: The *Astuzia Fortunata* of Brazil's Sociologist-President," *Journal of Politics in Latin America* 1, no. 3 (2009): 127.

33 Gisela Zaremberg, *Mujeres, votos y asistencia social en el México priista y la Argentina peronista* (México: Flacso México, 2009); Kathryn Hochstetler, "Rethinking Presidentialism: Challenges and Presidential Falls in South America," *Comparative Politics* 38, no. 4 (2006); Scott Morgenstern, Juan Javier Negri, and Aníbal Pérez-Liñán, "Parliamentary Opposition in Non-Parliamentary Regimes: Latin America," *Journal of Legislative Studies* 14, no. 1 (2008).

34 Adam Przeworski, "Institutions Matter?," *Government and Opposition* 39, no. 2 (2004); Matthew S. Shugart and Rein Taagepera, "Plurality Versus Majority Election of Presidents — a Proposal for a Double Complement Rule," *Comparative Political Studies* 27, no. 3 (1994); Gabriel L. Negretto, "Political Parties and Institutional Design: Explaining Constitutional Choice in Latin America," *British Journal of Political Science* 39, no. 1 (2009); Gabriel L. Negretto, *Making Constitutions. Presidents, Parties, and Institutional Choice in Latin America* (Cambridge University Press, forthcoming).

35 Crisp and Ingall, "Institutional Engineering and the Nature of Representation: Mapping the Effects of Electoral Reform in Colombia"; Eduardo Pizarro Leongómez, "La Atomización Partidista en Colombia: el Fenómeno de las Micro-Empresas Electorales," in *Degradación o Cambio: Evolución del Sistema Político Colombiano*, ed. Francisco Gutiérrez Sanín (Bogotá: Norma, 2002).

36 Gretchen Helmke, *Courts under Constraints: Judges, Generals, and Presidents in Argentina* (Cambridge; New York: Cambridge University Press, 2005); Gretchen Helmke and Steven Levitsky, eds., *Informal Institutions and Democracy: Lessons from Latin America* (Baltimore: Johns Hopkins University Press, 2006). Mahoney and Thelen, "A Theory of Gradual Institutional Change." Mejía Acosta, *Informal Coalitions and Policymaking in Latin America: Ecuador in Comparative Perspective*; Guillermo O'Donnell, "Illusions About Consolidation," *Journal of Democracy* 7, no. 2 (1996).

27

CULTURE AND/OR POSTMODERNISM

Sujatha Fernandes

The cultural and postmodern turn in the study of Latin American politics, and in the social sciences more generally, began in the late 1980s. Cultural studies is a theory and method pioneered in Britain during the 1960s, which seeks to expand the study of culture to enhance our understanding of politics, power, and society. Postmodernism is a constellation of ideas that rejects the meta-narratives (broad explanatory frameworks) of modernism, in favor of multiple realities, fragmentation, and discontinuity. In the North American context, postmodernism and cultural studies tended to meld together. They were mostly centered in the humanities, in disciplines like English and comparative literature. Cultural studies in the United States followed the postmodern tendency to interpret social and political processes through the discursive level. North American cultural studies focused on popular cultures as an expression of resistance, and displaced the primacy of economic class in a postmodern celebration of diverse identities. While the British school of cultural studies also incorporated elements from postmodern theory, in contrast to North American cultural studies the British school spanned the social sciences and humanities, had a strong material, class-based approach, and sought to theorize the constraints posed by the culture industry. Although Latin Americans did not simply adopt this approach from British cultural studies, they likewise generally kept the two fields of postmodernism and cultural studies distinct.

In this chapter I will show how postmodernism and cultural studies approaches have helped to broaden and decenter traditional views of politics. As these theories came to be applied within the field of Latin American studies during the 1990s, they also gave rise to heated controversies and competing schools of thought. This article will assess the impact of culture and postmodern thought for the study of Latin American politics and society and it will suggest future directions for the field.

The Cultural Turn in Latin American Studies

Over the course of the 1970s and 1980s, postmodern and post-structural approaches gradually came to influence academic disciplines in advanced capitalist nations and, to a lesser degree, third world countries, especially in fields such as literature and anthropology. By the end of the 1980s, cultural studies also reached the Americas. Cultural studies as an interdisciplinary field of inquiry originated in Britain at the Center for Contemporary Cultural

Studies (CCCS) at the University of Birmingham. Scholars associated with the Center such as Richard Hoggart, Stuart Hall, Paul Willis, Angela McRobbie, and Dick Hebdige[1] were particularly influenced by the work of the Italian Marxist Antonio Gramsci[2] and his concept of hegemony, as the naturalization of dominant ideologies through both the cultural dissemination of values and a coercive state apparatus. They found this framework particularly valuable to understand the shifting allegiance of the strongly unionized British working classes toward the politically conservative politician Margaret Thatcher.[3] These scholars turned to mass popular culture, the media, and subcultures to explore the ways in which elite dominance through cultural hegemony was created, sustained, and contested.

The trend of globalization that had begun in the 1980s—consisting of free trade agreements, outsourcing of manufacturing from Western capitalist nations to third world countries, and cross-border flows of people and goods—also created a greater role for culture, thereby spurring on the growth of cultural studies. The global culture industries grew in scope and intensity due to the spread of media conglomerates and music corporations. Culture was promoted by global corporations as the grounds for building a consumer base. Technologies such as cable television and the Internet expanded dramatically through corporate sponsorship and promotion, creating new avenues for the dissemination of culture. At the same time, as traditional avenues for political participation such as trade unions and political parties receded, culture was taken up by marginal groups as a site of political struggle.

This confluence of factors gave rise to a critical rethinking of long-held assumptions within traditional disciplines that had an impact on the study of Latin American politics and society. Structural approaches such as Marxism and dependency theory were seen by many scholars as overly focused on economics and inadequate to understanding the role of culture and symbolic orders. Political science was narrowly focused on elections and voting as a means to understand political processes. Even though democratization processes across the region were producing a greater interest in elections and voting as an object for study, high abstention rates and voter apathy were all suggesting that we might look outside the traditional political realm if we want to understand the ways that ordinary people engaged with and talked about politics.

Culture itself was quite narrowly conceived in traditional disciplines. Within political science, culture was viewed as a bounded entity or fixed system of meaning. "Chinese culture" or more broadly "Islamic civilization" were part of a set of analytical categories employed by political scientists such as Samuel Huntington.[4] While in the humanities this static view of culture had been challenged from various quarters, there was still a tendency in disciplines such as literature and art history to see culture as a clearly defined object, as in elite-produced art and literature showcased in museums or literary canons. Yet globalization was revealing culture to be more porous, hybrid, and contested than was previously imagined. Critical theories of postmodernism and cultural studies entered at this juncture and aided scholars in rethinking these long-held assumptions as they devised new paradigms.

Critical Theories of Postmodernism and Cultural Studies

There were several claims that came to predominate in the field of Latin American studies as a result of the influence of postmodernism and cultural studies. The first was the conceptualization of culture as a field of struggle rather than as a bounded entity or fixed object. Gramscian concepts of "hegemony" and "counter-hegemony" had opened up the possibilities of culture as a place where dominant and subordinate groups each tried to construct and popularize their own views of the world. The French sociologist Pierre Bourdieu, also important in the field of cultural studies, developed the concept of the "cultural field," or culture as a somewhat autonomous realm that was guided by its own laws.[5] Bourdieu broadened Marx's concept of capital from the purely economic to the symbolic and cultural realms. He used the concepts of cultural and symbolic capital as tools to be wielded by marginalized groups who had no economic capital.[6] At the same time, culture, and consumption were crucial arenas for the market to renew the dominance of an elite through carving out differentiated spheres for the bourgeoisie and popular classes.[7]

These ideas strongly influenced Latin Americanists who were seeking to understand the place and possibilities for culture within Latin American societies. Jesus Martín Barbero argued that the mass entertainment industry was producing conformity within new global orders—as the scholars of the Frankfurt School had earlier argued—but that it also provided grounds for contesting those orders through creative reception and manipulations of the mass media.[8] These claims were also made by cultural critics Jean Franco and Carlos Monsiváis, who argued respectively that forms such as popular women's literature and American television were not experienced as monolithic by Latin American consumers, but rather contained spaces where viewers could interact and even resist dominant narratives.[9] For Franco, this takes place by means of "plotting" in Mexican popular fiction, as both a literary and a social device. The disjuncture between plots emphasizing contradictory ideals of consumerism, incorporation into the work force, emancipation from the family, and traditional morality produces unexpected, sometimes even feminist responses from women readers. The focus on production and reception in addition to textual analysis was similar to the British cultural studies approach.

Seeking to understand the specificities of Latin American cultures, the Argentine anthropologist Néstor García Canclini developed the idea of "hybrid cultures," as the liminal spaces where multiple temporalities, identities, and social formations overlap. He gives the examples of painters who reelaborated pre-Columbian and colonial images using computers and lasers.[10] García Canclini translates this cultural hybridity to the political realm also, where he shows how modern democracy could be overlaid with authoritarian habits and traditional power relations. Even after Argentina transitioned from a military dictatorship to democracy in the 1980s, religious fundamentalist movements railed against political and sexual liberalism, and the church threatened deputies with excommunication when they sought to discuss divorce or pluralism in education.[11] For García Canclini, Martín Barbero, Franco, and Monsiváis, culture is conceived as a field of struggle. It is through hybridized or mass cultures that subordinate classes can develop an independent and critical view of the world.

Latin Americanists drew on innovations within cultural studies and postmodern theory to inform their own analysis of unfolding events and processes. However, they were also aware of the limitations of European-based theories for Latin American realities. For instance, García Canclini noted that the distinction between elite and popular art that was central to Bourdieu's concept of differentiated spheres of consumption did not necessarily hold in Latin America, where art museums often had mass popular attendance or literary works sold in supermarkets.[12] García Canclini and others recognized the need to learn from metropolitan theories, but then to go beyond those theories in developing their own analyses of local conditions.

The second claim that was developed in conversation with cultural and postmodern approaches was that universal categories such as class or nation should be eschewed in favor of a politics of difference. A politics of difference foregrounds particularity by recognizing multiple sources of oppression, as compared to a universal point of view that actually serves to mask elite interests. Feminist writers, along with others seeking to understand long-entrenched patterns of gender and racial hierarchy in Latin America have productively used these frameworks to understand the multiple levels in which exclusion happens. For instance, Latin American literary critic Ileana Rodríguez has shown how language often conceals gender biases through use of labels such as "the people" or "the nation." Vanguard parties and revolutionary leaders in Latin America adopted a universal positionality that was masculine and authoritative, while women were often demeaned and marginalized.[13] Scholars sought to deconstruct universal categories to reveal the power relations that structured them.

The politics of difference gave voice to marginal languages and subjectivities through strategies of cultural resistance. It is not surprising that this approach was pioneered by feminist cultural critics such as the Chilean Nelly Richard who experienced the violent overthrow of a democratically elected socialist government and the imposition of a military regime that repressed dissent. Richard was an active feminist during the years of the Augusto Pinochet dictatorship (1974–1990), organizing literary events and conferences. Given the difficulties of working under such a repressive regime, she found an avenue for artistic and political expression in the fragmentary and partial postmodern aesthetic of avant-garde art. She highlights the value of local theory and situated knowledge in developing a micro-politics of difference, focusing on the borders, the margins, and her own alterity as a subversive feminist activist.[14] The politics of difference approach is helpful for understanding the rise of alternative and critical movements based on racial, sexual or gender-based identities. In my earlier work on Cuba, I described how filmmakers made critical films about homophobia in Cuban society, rappers identified with blackness as a political identity, and black artists challenged racism through their exhibitions.[15] This kind of identity-based cultural expression provided a forum for politically taboo issues to be raised.

The third claim that influenced Latin American Studies was the postmodern idea that power operated not in a top down manner, but rather through a diffuse and decentered mode known as governmentality. The idea of governmentality as introduced by the French philosopher Michel Foucault referred to the historical devolution of power from that exercised by a sovereign over his people to modes of social control operating from within the social body itself through hospitals, schools, prisons, and other institutions.[16] This theoretical perspective helped to broaden understandings of power in Latin America, which had been overly focused on the populists, *caudillos* (strong leaders), and patriarchs that ruled over Latin American nations. The governmentality perspective encouraged the study of a range of other sites where power was being enabled. Rachel Sieder looked at the proposed incorporation of customary indigenous law into official legality in Guatemala as a form of governmentality, where recognition of indigenous law was also a means of controlling it.[17] Finn Stepputat and Sarah Radcliffe studied the construction of spaces such as rural villages in Guatemala and the territorial organization of the state itself in Ecuador as sites of governance,[18] while Fiona Wilson explored provincial schools in Peru as institutions that relay state power at the local level.[19] The governmentality approach marked a shift from earlier theories of state corporatism, which showed how authoritarian states co-opted social organizations by licensing them. For theorists of governmentality, the state extends its power not by expanding its bureaucratic reach, but by decentralizing its tasks of governance to the local level.

Competing Schools of Thought in the 1990s

Postmodern and cultural studies approaches shaped the new paradigms that were prominent in Latin American studies from the 1980s onwards. During the 1990s, the field split into competing schools of thought that sought to engage in distinct ways with the concepts of culture and power. By the end of the 1990s, these schools had somewhat imploded, although the methodological differences that had emerged continued to shape interactions between scholars in the field in important ways. This section will explore these developments in more detail.

One of the dominant trends to emerge during the early 1990s was the Latin American Subaltern Studies Group. The Latin American group was formed in response to the South Asian Subaltern Studies Group, a collective of intellectuals who drew loosely on Gramsci's concept of the "subaltern" to unearth histories and voices of the subordinated classes. According to the school, history was mostly narrated from the perspective of the dominant classes, and if we wished to understand how subordinated or subaltern classes experienced it, we would have to do an alternative reading of the historical archives. While their South Asian counterparts were mostly interested in new conceptions of historiography, the Latin American group were literary and cultural critics who were concerned with the logic of the present. Moreover, as one of the key figures of the group, John Beverly, put it, they also added a postmodern concern with transnationalization and the deterritorialization of the nation-state. The concept of the nation was openly recognized as a fiction generated by creole elites to obscure the presence of subaltern subjects.[20] One of the key objects of study for the Latin American subalternists were *testimonios*, or testimonial narratives. Adherents of the group were concerned to elevate testimonios within the literary canon as a genre worthy of literary criticism and study. But beyond this, the subalternists sought to challenge what Beverley describes as the "essentially modernist ideology of cultural agency" perpetuated by cultural studies. As compared to the descriptive emphasis of most cultural studies work, Beverley claims for the subalternists a partisan project that recognizes subalterns as agents of transformation.

The most prominent case from the testimonios genre is the controversial *I, Rigoberta Menchú* written by an indigenous Guatemalan woman.[21] The autobiography denounces the military regime in Guatemala for its genocidal actions against the Mayan population. Ten years after the book was published, the anthropologist David Stoll challenged various details of the narrative presented by Menchú. Based on research done in her community, he claimed that some of the facts she presented in the book, such as the death of Menchú's younger brother by starvation, the poverty of her family, and her lack of schooling were false.[22] Stoll argued that Menchú invented her story to advance the political aims of her organization, the Ejercito Guerrillero de los Pobres (Guerrilla Army of the Poor, EGP), and herself as defender of the peasantry. Beverley and other subalternists defended Menchú against these criticisms. In answer to Menchú's critics, Beverley asserts that subalterns should have the ability not only to be witnesses—as in the anthropological tradition—but "the power to create their own narrative authority and negotiate its conditions of truth and representativity."[23] The *testimonio* is more than a literary text, for the subalternists it is also a means to provoke discussion and dramatize the deplorable situation of the subaltern.

A second and competing school of thought that emerged during this same period was the Inter-American Cultural Studies Network. Directed by George Yúdice, and including García Canclini among others, this school attempted to develop connections between North American-based Latin Americanists and those based in Latin America. The school developed the field of transnational cultural studies that was concerned with global networks of NGOs, popular culture, and the media as they impacted questions of democracy and citizenship. As compared to the subalternists who were mainly literary theorists, the Inter-American network was more social science focused in its disciplinary representation and its concerns. Like the subalternists, the Inter-American network scholars also sought to rethink dominant paradigms in the light of critiques of postmodernism and cultural studies. However, their analysis also carried a strong socio-economic component, specifically related to the neoliberal reforms of the 1980s.

The Inter-American network scholars held several critiques of the subalternists. They argued that the division between elite and subordinate classes and the autonomous subaltern culture posited by the subalternists did not take into account the hybrid penetrations between these classes and the operation of hegemony as subordinate classes often participated in and reinforced dominant ideas. The Inter-American network scholars criticized the subalternists for their lack of attention to institutions—the culture industry, consumer markets, state institutions, and the like. They also argued that the category of the subaltern was too broad to cover the diversity of classes that existed in Latin America, particularly as a result of neoliberal restructuring.[24]

Another point of contention between these two schools of thought was methodology. While the Inter-American network tended to be more empirical, the subalternists relied on mostly textual analysis. The subalternists were skeptical about attempts to "know the other" through ethnographic fieldwork as they saw native informants as speaking through colonialist and Eurocentric paradigms. They were suspicious of strategies of representation, since these were formed through dominant media conglomerates and circuits. By contrast, the Inter-American network scholars could not conceive of a subaltern politics where the so-called subaltern was absent. Yúdice has argued that the subalternists emphasized the negativity in the concept of the subaltern. There are no actual "actors" in the subaltern conception, the subaltern exists only as a negation of elite power.[25] The Inter-American scholars questioned how the subalternists could advance a political project when the subaltern technically could not speak because its voice was always mediated by discourses of power.

These debates reached a climax at the Latin American Studies Association (LASA) Congress in Guadalajara, Mexico in 1997, and the schools shortly thereafter imploded. The Latin American Subaltern Studies Group announced that it was disbanding. While the group had been extremely influential and provocative for a time, there were many differences among its members that could not be reconciled. Into the vacuum left by the demise of these competing schools came another trend that involved Inter-American network scholars such as George Yúdice along with anthropologist Arturo Escobar, and political scientists Sonia Alvarez, Veronica Schild, and Evelina Dagnino. In a series of edited volumes, Escobar and Alvarez criticized the lack of attention to culture in conventional social science and sought to develop the links between culture and politics.[26] As compared with the earlier Latin American cultural studies focus on the mass media, culture industries, and consumerism, they proposed the study of cultural politics, as "the process enacted when sets of social actors shaped by, and embodying, different cultural meanings and practices come into conflict with each other."[27] In their conception, cultural politics does not only refer to those groups explicitly deploying cultural protest or cultural forms. It also includes the attempts by social movements to challenge and redefine the meanings and practices of the dominant cultural order.

These cultural politics scholars were critical of standard theories of collective action within sociology and political science, which often failed to address the cultural dimensions of social movements, the discursive struggles in which they engage, and the construction of identity. The cultural politics scholars affirmed the positive contributions of postmodernism and cultural studies—especially the mutual constitution of meanings and practices. But they also criticized the highly textual emphasis of much U.S.-based cultural studies, and sought to return to the more material and political concerns of British cultural studies scholars such as Stuart Hall. They were also concerned that cultural studies was overly focused on consumption and had not paid enough attention to social movements as an important aspect of cultural production.

Cultural politics scholars were strongly concerned with the twin processes of democratization and neoliberalization that had occurred across the region during the 1980s and 1990s. They were especially interested in the ways in which the human rights, feminist, indigenous, and barrio-based movements that flourished during transitions to democracy were being co-opted under new democratic regimes. These scholars, including Sonia Alvarez, Veronica Schild, and Julia Paley, reframed the Foucaultian idea of governmentality as neoliberal governmentality, defined as a mode of power that appropriated discourses of "civil society" and "participation" to create legitimacy for processes of neoliberal economic restructuring. For instance, in her study of social movements in post-dictatorship Chile, Paley argued that civil society organizations functioned as a means for incorporating citizen activity into the state, thereby reducing protest against structural adjustment and also providing services in a context where the welfare state was retreating.[28] As compared to the normative ideal that civil society had become in political science and sociology, cultural politics scholars were concerned to reveal its ideological underpinnings.

One of the goals of the cultural politics group was to bring culture back into a consideration of neoliberal projects. While neoliberal restructuring had only been studied in terms of its economic and institutional effects, political scientists like Schild argued for the need to look at the cultural effects of neoliberalism as well. How were people's consciousness, worldviews, and self-conceptions being reshaped by neoliberalism? In her work on the women's movement in Chile, Schild explores how in the post-dictatorship context women were being repositioned as individual subjects who could develop their individualism through the marketplace.[29] Neoliberalism as a mode of power operates not just through subjecting populations to new economic orders, but also through the process of subject-making, that is, encouraging people to refashion themselves as self-sufficient, self-regulating clients who will bring themselves out of poverty.

One of the offshoots of this theory of neoliberal governmentality was the theory of neoliberal multiculturalism developed by Latin America scholars. Anthropologist Charles Hale argued that in addition to encouraging the formation of civil society and social capital, neoliberalism also enshrined cultural rights. While neoliberal reforms increased social inequalities and negatively impacted marginal groups, these reforms also granted collective rights to disadvantaged groups. But while governments passed legal reforms to recognize the cultural particularity of racial and ethnic groups such as indigenous peoples, at the same time these reforms drove a wedge between the cultural rights of these groups and their control over resources.[30] Like with the concept of civil society, the promotion of cultural rights was a way to demobilize social movements and deter them from their more critical demands.

In the late 1990s and early part of the twenty-first century, Latin America scholars were coming to terms with the apparent dominance of the neoliberal paradigm, as the model was consolidated in uneven ways by governments across the region. In breaking from purely economic and structural approaches, scholars sought to understand the modes of power through which neoliberal orders were sustained and the cultural formations they created. By focusing on questions of subject-making and subjectivity, as well as the legitimating discourses of civil society, participation, and cultural rights, cultural studies and postmodern scholars were able to more fully understand the ways in which hegemony functioned under neoliberal orders and how acquiescence was maintained. But when a new cycle of protests broke out in the new millennium, often putting in place left wing parties and leaders with anti-neoliberal agendas, postmodern theory fell short. In particular, the theory of governmentality tended to focus mainly on the production of consent to regimes of structural adjustment, with little room for explaining how or if they might be contested. The large scale, coalitional movements that emerged in places like Bolivia and Ecuador also presented a challenge to theories of micro-politics that valorized fragmentary and local resistance. Cultural studies and postmodern theories risked becoming peripheral at a time when they could still offer insights into the changes taking place in the region. But scholars would need to find a way to build change into theories that had become static in their understanding of power and would have to account for the rise of broad-based political forces making universal demands for social justice and rights.

New Cycles of Protest in the Americas

Political scientists and anthropologists, mostly those working on indigenous movements, sought to address the shortcomings of cultural studies and postmodern theory by coming up with a new framework for understanding the rise of protest against neoliberal orders in Latin America. Political scientist Deborah Yashar argues that the political openings created by democratization, combined with the decline in corporatist representation as a result of the shrinking state under neoliberalism spurred on the development of independent indigenous movements in places where organizational networks were strong.[31] Other political scientists, Shannon Mattiace and Jose Antonio Lucero, were also concerned with changing structures of representation and citizenship under neoliberalism that made spaces available for indigenous organizing, albeit unintentionally.[32] Anthropologists Nancy Postero, Daniel Goldstein, and Susana Sawyer likewise argued that neoliberal reforms had several unintended and unexpected consequences that produced new forms of protagonism.[33] For instance, in her study of indigenous groups in the oil rich Ecuadorian Amazon, Sawyer claims that the role played by the state in facilitating transnational capital undermined the legitimacy of the state by revealing its lack of accountability and gave rise to transgressive subjects who challenged the neoliberal order. All of this work challenged the view that neoliberalism was a hegemonic form of governance that uniformly produced obedience. By disaggregating neoliberalism into the various policies, rationalities, and structures it produced, these theorists were able to show the disjunctures internal to neoliberalism itself that produced contestation.

Further, while many cultural studies scholars had understood identity as partial, fragmented, and localized—or disconnected from broader struggles over rights and resources—the contemporary wave of social movements in Bolivia, Venezuela, Ecuador, and Brazil were linking cultural identity to claims over public space, access to resources, recognition of land titles, and the right to participate in governance. Cultural studies scholars had made significant contributions in theorizing the importance of cultural identities as corporate identities based on class or party were waning. But they had not foreseen the ways that these movements would appeal to broader universals of social justice. Postero points to the shift that she observes in social movement organizing in Bolivia, which brought together an emerging collectivity of autonomous neighborhood groups and indigenous organizations, as well as more traditional unions. Protestors described themselves as "the Bolivian people" (*el pueblo boliviano*), but rather than masking power relations, the term was referring to multiple levels of exclusion. In contrast to neoliberal multiculturalism, Postero terms this process "post-multicultural citizenship." As indigenous actors in places like Bolivia embraced the language of neoliberal multicultural reforms and contested the exclusions inherent in them, they forged new modes of citizenship and engagement.[34] Social movement coalitions born out of a postmodern politics of difference were now searching for a way to reincorporate a universal politics of social justice and rights.

Cultural studies and postmodern frameworks still had value in understanding this contemporary moment, but they needed to be reworked. Some scholars working in a Foucaultian tradition began to incorporate ideas from Gramsci, mostly his notion of culture as a site of struggle. Up until this point the Foucaultian and Gramscian traditions had been somewhat separate, even competing, perspectives within cultural studies. Foucaultians were less concerned with the worldviews and ideologies that constituted cultural hegemony, and more interested in the rationalities and techniques through which power was produced. But as the upheavals of the 1990s were showing the limitations of Foucault's governmentality theory, scholars sought to bring Foucault's insights about the decentralization of power and dispersed forms of governance together with Gramsci's insistence on practical politics and the negotiation of hegemony from below.[35] This framework has become especially useful for understanding the contemporary phase of politics in Latin America, which involves the consolidation of left wing orders in places like Venezuela, Ecuador, and Bolivia with leaders carrying out anti-neoliberal policies.

To date there has been little empirical work done on this relatively new phase. But for my own work on social movements in Chávez's Venezuela, I have found the Foucaultian-Gramscian framework helpful in exploring what I see as a post-neoliberal hybrid state formation under Chávez, which has mounted challenges to the neoliberal paradigm, but remains subject to the internal and external constraints of global capital. The governmentality framework sheds light on the market-based rationalities that persist in state institutions even under an anti-neoliberal order, while the Gramscian perspective can help us understand how social movements contest these rationalities.[36] While most political scientists working on Venezuela have tended towards state-centric and top-down structuralist analysis, the cultural studies and postmodern approach can help us to get at the dynamics of popular contestation and state-society negotiations.

What is especially needed is a way of understanding the nature of political life at a moment when the traditional sites of politics and representation such as political parties, trade unions, and organized civil society are in decline. Many social scientists see the crisis of these traditional institutions as a crisis of democracy, without paying attention to the emergent institutions of popular politics, such as barrio assemblies, cultural organizations, and low power radio that are reinvigorating political life.[37] In places like Venezuela, categories of "civil society" have been taken over by middle-class and elite groups to define their opposition to the Chávez government, and have tended to exclude poor and marginal sectors as "uncivilized." There is a need for a new set of categories to guide social analysis and describe emerging forms of political life with their basis in cultural identity and place. The framework provided by cultural studies would be valuable here, along with ethnographic thick description, in defining these new categories from within the experiences of everyday life. For instance, in *Who Can Stop the Drums? Urban Social Movements in Chávez's Venezuela*, I describe how barrio residents in Caracas self-excluded from categories of civil society which they felt belonged to the middle classes and political parties that they identified with the state. They rather sought to define themselves as members of popular assemblies based in the barrio, as fiesta organizers belonging to the local cofradía or brotherhood, or as members of community-based organizations with long histories. How might we generate new categories from these self-descriptions given by poorer sectors? I think that there is a need for further studies of poor and working class sectors that are deeply informed by ethnography and thick description.

The schools of subaltern studies, cultural politics, and governmentality produced a rich body of literature informed by cultural studies and postmodernism that continues to produce exciting trends in research today. One important trend in Latin American studies has sought to understand the construction of a new, post-neoliberal narrative as neoliberalism is being dislodged from its quasi-hegemonic position in the socio-political imagination.[38] Scholars working in this area recognize the substantial changes that two decades or more of neoliberal policy have brought in the polities and economies of Latin American nations, and they are interested to explore how this has changed the terrain in which social actors operate. One fruitful area where the changed conditions for social action are being studied is that of law and legal arrangements. James Holston, Rachel Sieder, and Mark Goodale see law as both a way of representing the social order, but also as a means of social action.[39] Given the importance of constitutional reforms, the legalization of rights, and debates over indigenous customary law, it appears that law and the idea of law have become an important site for negotiating power, particularly in post-neoliberal orders. One of the main platforms of social movements has been a call for constituent assemblies to rewrite the constitution, and this has taken place amidst much conflict in Venezuela, Bolivia, and Ecuador. The underside of this interest in the law is a growing concern with disorder, violence, and "misrule of law" which has also produced a growing body of scholarship.

A further promising area of research that builds on the transnationalism concerns of cultural studies scholars is one that takes multiple research sites in an exploration of the new channels of mobility that globalization has produced. This has often meant a questioning of the division between fields like Latin American and Latino studies. Robert Smith's ethnographic research on Mexicans in New York and Puebla shows how this mobility may also give rise to new transnational forms of political organizing.[40] This work ventures beyond traditional studies of immigration to look at the implications of the globalization of labor on local, national, and supra-national scales.

After more than two decades of engagement with postmodern theories and cultural studies, the study of Latin American politics has evolved more towards an understanding of the importance of culture and cultural identity in political organizing, the decentered modes of governance and subject formation through which power is exercised, and the discourses that structure the social order. After a series of competing approaches appeared in the 1990s, Latin Americanists tended to move closer to the materialist concerns of early British cultural studies. But the contemporary period has presented a new set of challenges that go beyond what British cultural studies theorists had imagined possible. Contending with the latest cycle of protests and its recomposition into new social orders will hopefully produce creative frameworks and innovations that will ensure the continuing viability of cultural studies and postmodern theory for our study of the region.

Notes

1 For the works of these authors, see Richard Hoggart, *Contemporary Cultural Studies: An Approach to the Study of Literature and Society* (University of Birmingham, Center for Contemporary Cultural Studies, 1969); Stuart Hall, *The Hard Road to Renewal: Thatcherism and the Crisis of the Left* (London: Verso Books, 1988); Paul Willis, *Learning to Labor: How Working Class Kids Get Working Class Jobs* (New York: Columbia University Press, 1982); Angela McRobbie, *Zoot Suits and Second Hand Dresses* (London: Routledge, 1989); and Dick Hebdige, *Subculture: The Meaning of Style* (London: Routledge, 1981).

2 Antonio Gramsci, *Selections from the Prison Notebooks* (New York: International Publishers, 1971).

3 See in particular, Hall, *The Hard Road to Renewal*.

4 Samuel P. Huntington, "Clash of Civilizations," *Foreign Affairs*, Vol. 72, No. 3, pp. 22–44.

5 Pierre Bourdieu, *The Field of Cultural Production* (New York: Columbia University Press, 1993).

6 Pierre Bourdieu, "The Forms of Capital," in J.G. Richardson (ed.), *Handbook for Theory and Research for the Sociology of Education* (New York: Greenwood press, 1986), pp. 241–258.

7 Pierre Bourdieu, *Distinction: A Social Critique of the Judgment of Taste.* (Cambridge: Harvard University Press, 1984).

8 Jesús Martín-Barbero, *Communication, Culture and Hegemony: From the Media to Mediations* (London: Sage, 1993).

9 Jean Franco, "Plotting Women: Popular Narratives for Women in the United States and in Latin America," in Ana del Sarto et al. (eds.), *The Latin American Cultural Studies Reader* (Durham: Duke University Press, 2004), pp. 183–202; Carlos Monsiváis, "Would So Many Millions of People Not End Up Speaking English? The North American Culture and Mexico," in Ana del Sarto et al. (eds.), *The Latin American Cultural Studies Reader*, pp. 203–232.

10 Néstor García Canclini, *Hybrid Cultures: Strategies for Entering and Leaving Modernity* (Minneapolis: University of Minnesota Press, 1995), pp. 2–3.

11 García Canclini, *Hybrid Cultures*, p. 114.

12 García Canclini, *Hybrid Cultures*, p. 17.

13 Ileana Rodríguez, *Women, Guerillas, and Love: Understanding the War in Central America.* (Minneapolis: University of Minnesota Press, 1996).

14 Nelly Richard, "Margins and Institutions: Art in Chile since 1973." Special Issue of *Art & Text* (Melbourne) 21 (1987).

15 Sujatha Fernandes, *Cuba Represent! Cuban Arts, State Power, and the Making of New Revolutionary Cultures* (Durham: Duke University Press, 2006).

16 Michel Foucault, "Governmentality," in *The Foucault Effect*, Graham Burchell et al. (eds.), (Chicago: University of Chicago Press, 1994), pp. 87–104.

17 Rachel Sieder, "Rethinking Citizenship: Reforming the Law in Postwar Guatemala," in Thomas Blom Hansen and Finn Stepputat (eds.), *States of Imagination: Ethnographic Explorations of the Postcolonial State* (Durham: Duke University Press, 2001), pp. 203–220

18 Finn Stepputat, "Urbanizing the Countryside: Armed Conflict, State Formation, and the Politics of Place in Contemporary Guatemala," and Sarah Radcliffe, "Imagining the State as a Space: Territoriality and the Formation of the State in Ecuador," in Hansen and Stepputat (eds.), *States of Imagination*, pp. 284–312 and 123–145.

19 Fiona Wilson, "In the Name of the State? Schools and Teachers in an Andean Province," in Hansen and Stepputat (eds.), *States of Imagination*, pp. 313–344.

20 John Beverley, "Writing in Reverse: On the Project of the Latin American Subaltern Studies Group," in del Sarto et al. (eds.), *The Latin American Cultural Studies Reader*, pp. 623–641.

21 Rigoberta Menchú, *I, Rigoberta Menchú: An Indian Woman in Guatemala,* (London: Verso, 1984).

22 David Stoll, *Rigoberta Menchú and the Story of All Poor Guatemalans* (Boulder: Westview Press, 1999).

23 Beverley, "Writing in Reverse," pp. 636–638.

24 George Yúdice, "Translators Introduction" to Néstor García Canclini, *Consumers and Citizens: Globalization and Multicultural Conflicts* (Minneapolis: University of Minnesota Press, 2001), pp. ix–xxxviii.

25 Yúdice, "Translators Introduction," p. xxxii.

26 Arturo Escobar and Sonia Alvarez (eds.), *The Making of Social Movements in Latin America: Identity, Strategy, and Democracy* (Boulder: Westview Press, 1992); Sonia Alvarez, Evelina Dagnino,

and Arturo Escobar (eds.), *Cultures of Politics/Politics of Cultures: Re-visioning Latin American Social Movements* (Boulder: Westview Press, 1998).

27 Sonia Alvarez, Evelina Dagnino, and Arturo Escobar, "Introduction: The Cultural and the Political in Latin American Social Movements," in Alvarez et al., *Cultures of Politics/Politics of Cultures*, p. 7.

28 Julia Paley, *Marketing Democracy: Power and Social Movements in Post-Dictatorship Chile* (Berkeley: University of California Press, 2001).

29 Verónica Schild, "New Subjects of Rights? Women's Movements and the Construction of Citizenship in the 'New Democracies'" in Alvarez et al., *Cultures of Politics/Politics of Cultures,* pp. 93–117.

30 Charles Hale, "Neoliberal Multiculturalism: The Remaking of Cultural Rights and Racial Dominance in Central America," *Political and Legal Anthropology Review* 28, No. 1 (2005): 10–28.

31 Deborah Yashar, *Contesting Citizenship in Latin America: The Rise of Indigenous Movements and the Postliberal Challenge* (Cambridge University Press, 2005).

32 Shannon Mattiace, *To see with two eyes: peasant activism & Indian autonomy in Chiapas*, Mexico (Albuquerque: New Mexico Press, 2003), Jose Antonio Lucero, *Struggles of Voices: The Politics of Indigenous Representation in the Andes* (Pittsburgh: University of Pittsburgh Press, 2008).

33 Nancy Postero, *Now We are Citizens: Indigenous Politics in Postmulticultural Bolivia* (Stanford: Stanford University Press, 2007), Daniel Goldstein, *The Spectacular City: Violence and Performance in Urban Bolivia* (Durham: Duke University Press, 2004), Susana Sawyer, *Crude Chronicles: Indigenous Politics, Multinational Oil, and Neoliberalism in Ecuador* (Durham Duke University Press, 2004).

34 Postero, *Now We are Citizens*, p. 221.

35 See especially Hansen and Stepputat (eds.), *States of Imagination*

36 Sujatha Fernandes, *Who Can Stop the Drums? Urban Social Movements in Chávez's Venezuela* (Durham: Duke University Press, 2010).

37 See, for instance, the edited volume by Jennifer McCoy and David Myers, *The Unraveling of Representative Democracy in Venezuela* (Baltimore: The Johns Hopkins University Press, 2004).

38 Alejandro Grimson and Gabriel Kessler, *On Argentina and the Southern Cone: Neoliberalism and National Imaginations* (New York: Routledge, 2005).

39 James Holston, *Insurgent Citizenship: Disjunctions of Democracy and Modernity in Brazil* (Princeton: Princeton University Press, 2008); Rachel Sieder, Line Schjolden and Alan Angell, *The Judicialization of Politics in Latin America*, (New York: Palgrave Macmillan, 2005). Mark Goodale, *Dilemmas of Modernity: Bolivian Encounters with Law and Liberalism* (Palo Alto: Stanford University Press, 2008).

40 Robert Smith, *Mexican New York: Transnational Lives of New Immigrants* (Berkeley: University of California Press, 2005).

28

THE INTEGRATION OF RATIONAL CHOICE INTO THE STUDY OF POLITICS IN LATIN AMERICA

Barbara Geddes

Rational Choice, the brash self-conscious teenage rebel of the 1980s, now goes to the office every day and engages in routine, productive interaction with those who once found him alarming. Although rational choice has a long history in economics and political science, very few students of Latin American politics used it before the redemocratization of most Latin American countries in the 1980s. The return of democratic politics, however, brought in its wake the spread of rational choice theories about politics as analysts sought interesting ways to understand democratic decision making, campaign strategies, and party behavior. These initial efforts to extend theories that had been developed to study politics in the United States and Western Europe to Latin America sometimes met with hostility or mystification from other scholars who found the approach simplistic or misguided. Now, however, the rational choice approach has become so integrated into the standard way analysts think about some topics, that most research that makes use of its basic elements does not mention rational choice or make its standard assumptions explicit because readers understand without being told. Some analysts who depend on the basic assumptions of the rational choice approach to underpin the logic of their arguments may not even be aware that they are doing so, and the edges between rational choice and other approaches have become blurred, as most scholars combine it with empirical research and arguments drawn from other intellectual traditions. Currently, few studies ignore the insights provided by rational choice completely, and fewer still limit themselves to ideas from rational choice alone.

Rational choice has become a part of the standard toolkit for many Latin Americanists, as it is for many other social scientists, because it helps us to understand some aspects of the political world. The approach has been most useful for explaining the behavior of political elites; for figuring out what happens when decisions or actions have to be taken by groups of individuals organized in different ways, for example, in legislatures or military juntas; and for analyzing the behavior of multiple actors whose individual decisions depend on one anothers' choices, as do competing politicians who choose campaign strategies with an eye to what other candidates are doing. Those whose research focuses on the values, attitudes, or individual actions of ordinary citizens often find the rational choice approach

419

less useful, but there are some exceptions. All who study mass behavior now take the logic of collective action into account, for example, and the rational choice approach has proved quite helpful in analyzing the individual behavior that perpetuates political machines and clientelist networks.

In this chapter, I summarize the most important assumptions that underpin the rational choice approach in order to explain why it became more attractive after redemocratization and why it provides more leverage for analyzing some aspects of politics than others. The default unit of analysis for rational choice theories is the individual, but its greatest theoretical contributions have arisen from efforts to understand what happens when multiple people interact. In subsequent sections, I discuss rational choice analyses of how formal political institutions affect those interactions and of the logic underlying informal institutions such as clientelism. In the last section, I parse the rational choice approach to strategic interactions. I note some examples of relevant research in each section, but it would not be possible for a single person to read all the work that has used the rational choice approach, much less to summarize it in a short article.

Basics of the Rational Choice Approach

The central features of the rational choice approach are (1) methodological individualism, meaning that the actors studied are either individual people or other entities that can be plausibly treated as unitary actors; (2) the explicit attribution by the analyst of goals, called preferences in rational choice jargon, to the actors under study; (3) the assumption of means–ends rationality, meaning that actors choose behaviors, policies, institutions, and so on—called strategies in the jargon—based on calculations about how best to attain their goals at the lowest cost; (4) the explicit identification by the analyst of the institutions and other contextual factors that determine the strategy options available to actors and the costs associated with them; and (5) deductive logic that connects the above elements to expected outcomes.

The assumptions about human behavior required by the rational choice approach have implications for the kinds of subjects that the rational choice approach has most success explaining. The assumption of means–ends rationality requires that the actors under study be able to (weakly) rank order how they feel about potential outcomes, meaning they have to prefer one to another (or be indifferent between possibilities). This is an inconsequential requirement as long as actors are individuals, but it eliminates many groups from being analytically treated as actors because typically groups that are not hierarchically organized with well developed means of monitoring and disciplining members cannot rank order their preferences. In most groups, different procedures for reaching decisions or different agenda setters can change the preference orderings expressed by the group from one day to the next. Moreover, in most groups, nothing requires members to abide by decisions made by leaders or any particular decision-making process. For these reasons, the Catholic hierarchy or a disciplined communist party can be treated as the actor in a rational choice analysis, but classes, ethnic groups, and most Latin American parties generally cannot. Of course, the individuals who make up these groups can be, and very interesting rational choice-influenced analyses have explained how rules and leadership structures have shaped decision making within such groups.

If rational choice is to have bite, the analyst must be able to attribute plausible preferences or goals to the actors without reference to the behavior to be explained. If the analyst infers goals from observed behavior, the argument is vacuous. So, for example, the attribution of a preference for democracy to officers who have taken a softline stance renders the analysis unsatisfying because the analyst in effect says: I can tell he prefers democracy because of his softline position, and this preference explains his support for democratization.

Within the rational choice idiom, preferences are the deep underlying goals of actors, such as wanting more wealth or wanting to continue a political career. The word "preference" does not refer to desired policies, institutions, democracy, or other ordinary-language preferences that actors seek in order to achieve something else. These are called strategies. In order to make good use of the rational choice approach, the analyst must be able to say plausibly that most actors in a situation share the same goal, in the limited sense of preferring more to less wealth or preferring election victory to defeat. Not everyone need share the goal; as long as most do, the rational choice argument can explain average behavior. If, however, the individuals being analyzed appear to have different goals with no single preference ordering predominant, the rational choice approach will not explain the behavior of most people in the group. It is up to the analyst to identify groups in which reasonable assumptions about preferences can be made. Rational choice also usually fails to explain individual behavior motivated by unusual goals, such as joining an apparently hopeless revolutionary movement.

The assumption of means–ends rationality requires either that actors know what options exist and be able to calculate how different strategy choices will affect both the likelihood and the cost of achieving their goals, or that they behave *as if* they did. The assumption that actors have the information and abilities needed to make rational strategy choices is more plausible for high stakes decisions than for actions with little impact like voting. Politicians, whose future success depends on understanding how arcane electoral rules affect which strategy for appealing to voters gives them an advantage over competitors, usually invest in acquiring the information and expertise they need in order to make good decisions, including hiring political consultants and campaign managers. Voters, who understand that their single votes have little influence, have no reason for similar investments. This is the reason that rational choice arguments have had considerable success explaining the behavior of politicians, but quite a bit less explaining turnout and other aspects of voting behavior.

In some circumstances, people can behave as if they were making means–ends calculations when they are not. This can result from either learning or evolution. That is, individuals may not find out what candidates stand for and then calculate which policies would be most likely to leave them better off, but instead, they may learn from experience that their wages tend to rise more under one party rather than another, so that they subsequently vote for that party. Learning can occur within individuals or be passed from one to another and across generations, but it always requires that the same choices confront decision makers repeatedly.

People and other creatures can also behave as if they were calculating the odds because those who do not are weeded out by evolutionary pressures. Some legislators, for example, care more about leading the fight for particular policy changes than winning the next election, but if leading the good fight is not a good reelection strategy, then such deputies will tend to be weeded out of the legislature by competition, leaving only those who follow policy and campaign strategies similar to what they would have chosen if they had made calculations before every vote. In situations in which a plausible evolutionary argument can be made, and better yet, shown empirically to be occurring, the rational choice approach can be used even if we know that individuals are not self-interested and/or able to calculate. As with learning, evolutionary arguments can only apply to repeated actions or interactions.

One of the reasons that rational choice arguments have had considerable success explaining the behavior of candidates, elected officials, and parties in Latin America is that no one doubts that the evolutionary pressures created by political competition have a major influence on which politicians have successful careers and which parties survive.

Rational choice has made the largest contribution to the study of Latin American politics through analyses of the effects of political institutions on the behavior of politicians and parties. This may seem paradoxical given the focus of rational choice on individual behavior, but the rational choice approach requires the analyst to identify the institutions and other contextual factors that shape the incentives that determine individual decisions and spell out the precise ways they can be expected to influence behavior. This careful attention to mechanisms has led to the huge body of literature that now explains the effects of most of the rules that affect politicians' campaign strategies, legislative behavior, bargaining between presidents and legislators, the maintenance of political machines, decisions about splitting parties, and efforts to change existing political institutions.[1]

Democratization and Rational Choice

When dictators ruled most Latin American countries, few used the rational choice approach to analyze them.[2] It was hard to see the relevance of rational choice (or other) theorization of party and legislative politics when parties, if legal, faced only rigged competition and legislatures, if they existed, rubber stamped decisions made elsewhere. Because decision making in dictatorships is seldom observable, few analysts were able to get good information about the process, and the widely held belief that dictatorships made policy on behalf of the wealthy reduced the perceived need to investigate the politics of policy making.

As countries democratized, politics became more transparent and also more routinized—both necessary for the development of theories to explain it. Democratization also brought with it new questions to explore, such as how party systems evolve, how legislative institutions affect the quality of governance, what leads to judicial reform, and how political institutions affect decision making in various policy domains. Older ways of thinking about politics did not offer much leverage for answering these kinds of questions, so some analysts investigated the rational choice theories available in mainstream political science. Among these scholars, The State, conceived as an actor, receded in theoretical importance, as analysis focused on the institutionally structured choice processes of politicians whose actions determine what the state does. Most analysts now focus on the effects of particular political institutions on political decision making, trying to explain policies, choice of leadership, and institutional change, rather than treating the state as a black box, unitary actor, or embodiment of elite interests.

Standard theories of democratic politics begin with the assumption that citizens vote, if they do, for candidates they expect to favor the policies and provide the individual benefits and services best for that voter. Politicians are assumed to seek the continuation and enhancement of their political careers. Democracy thus gives those who seek political careers an incentive to respond to the citizen interests that will help to keep them in office. Some aspects of democracy in Latin America, however, have disappointed both observers and citizens. Disappointment helped to motivate efforts to understand why democratic policy making did not routinely lead to the policies citizens said they wanted;[3] why legislatures seemed unable to take on the role of co-equal governors with presidents;[4] why politicians focused so much attention on the delivery of favors and small individual goods to constituents rather than on policy changes that might improve their lot more; and why voters appeared to elect parties and candidates who did not even promise to initiate policies that would improve their welfare.[5]

Within Latin America, despite similar cultures, histories, and recent experiences with dictatorship, some countries have fragmented, unstable party systems while others have had some of the most unchanging two-party systems in the world.[6] Linked to these differences, in some countries citizens identify deeply with parties, while in others many citizens seem to change affiliation at every election. Some countries have had highly disciplined parties much like those in Western Europe, and others have had undisciplined parties among which politicians switch to and fro. Some countries have been well-governed with a record since redemocratization of good economic performance, but in others one crisis has succeeded another, and massive popular protests sometimes accompanied by illegal congressional actions have ousted presidents repeatedly.[7] Some countries responded to the economic crisis of the 1980s with reasonably quick policy changes while others were immobilized for more than a decade.[8] In a few countries inequality has lessened since redemocratization, but in most it has worsened.[9] The indigenous formed successful political parties much more rapidly after democratization in some countries than others.[10] Clientelism pervades politics in some countries and regions of countries but not in all. In short, there are lots of differences to explain in Latin America, and scholars have used the rational choice approach to try to explain many of them.

The Focus on Institutions

The routinization and transparency of politics in democracies increased the salience of formal political institutions for explaining such differences because formal institutions play a larger and more predictable role in shaping politics in democracies than in dictatorships. The greater importance of institutions increased the usefulness of the rational choice approach. The rational choice assumption that people use means-ends calculations to choose their actions (or behave as if they did) shifts the analyst's focus from individual attitudes and values—which the rational choice approach provides no leverage for explaining—to the institutions and other features of context that determine the costs and advantages of different choices for people in different circumstances. Thus the first extensive use of the rational choice approach to understanding politics in Latin American countries involved investigations of the effects of different electoral rules on party fragmentation, campaign strategies, and legislative behavior, which some observers linked to governability and representation problems.

The first flush of studies underpinned by rational choice assumptions focused on the effects of specific institutions, such as the rules for translating votes into legislative representation, the timing of elections relative to each other, the proportion of votes needed to win, the size of electoral districts, and whether each vote cast affected the election chances of candidates, parties, or both.[11] These details seem arcane and uninteresting to many citizens, including quite a few political scientists, but professional politicians put a lot of effort into understanding them because they affect their chances of winning. Some political scientists have also put a lot of effort into understanding their effects. These studies examine the effects of formal rules on the strategic behavior of citizens as they pursue their goal of improving their own welfare and politicians as they pursue their goal of remaining in office.

Studies underpinned by rational choice assumptions have shown that institutions affect which candidates citizens consider voting for, which citizens politicians respond to, what kind of campaign strategies politicians choose, how many parties survive, how disciplined parties become, whether politicians and parties focus on offering policy goods or individual favors and benefits, whether effective legislative institutions arise, whether legislative grid-lock immobilizes the president, and the strength of the status quo bias in policy. Of special salience in Latin America are a number of issues mostly irrelevant in West European democracies and hence not much studied before redemocratization in Latin America: the need to build a theoretical understanding of presidentialism; the search for the reasons for the perpetuation of high levels of clientelism and corruption in open competitive democratic systems; and the effects of institutions and policies imposed by outgoing dictators.

Presidential elections create centrist tendencies in party systems for the same reason that single-member legislative districts do. Most Latin American countries have either proportional or mixed PR and single-member-district legislative electoral rules. The proportional election of legislators pulls the party system simultaneously in the opposite direction, toward more ideologically dispersed multipartism. Research on the Latin American presidential systems has discovered that rules that affect the size of presidential coattails determine which pull dominates. Where presidential and legislative elections occur at the same time, presidential coattails are strong, and parties that cannot compete for the presidency often fade away; two-party systems tend to emerge and persist. Where elections for different offices occur on different schedules, parties that have no hope of winning presidential elections can nevertheless continue to do well in legislative, state, and municipal elections, and thus survive.[12] Contrary to the conventional wisdom developed in the study of Europe, district magnitude has less effect on party fragmentation than presidential run-offs and concurrent election schedules.[13]

Despite the great importance of presidents in Latin American political systems, until about 20 years ago scholars had carried out little theoretical analysis of how the office works in practice. Most earlier literature treated presidents as unilateral decision makers, but recent scholarship, much of it done by analysts who include rational choice in their toolkits, has eroded that view. At a minimum, scholars now see the legislature as having veto power over presidential policy initiatives. Shugart and Carey interpret the substantial presidential powers that do exist as the delegation of powers by members of Congress intent on improving their future electoral chances rather than as usurpation by presidents.[14] The big questions in this area include: How much of what the president wants can he accomplish? And how does he accomplish what he does? Several scholars who use or are influenced by the rational choice approach have taken steps toward understanding why some presidents have more control over policy than others. In the 1990s observers put a lot of emphasis on decree powers,[15] but they have turned out to be less important than more subtle constitutional and legislative rules. More recent theoretical analysis and empirical research based on new collections of data on bill passage, legislative amendments, and previously understudied legislative rules, has demonstrated the importance of differences in the order in which bills and amendments are voted in Latin American legislatures, the amendatory veto (the right of some presidents to add clauses to bills passed by the legislature), and variations in presidential agenda setting powers. Subtle differences in these rules influence how much of presidents' legislative agendas actually pass.[16]

Stereotypes of Latin American parties emphasize clientelism, but some parties function much as those in long established European democracies do: parties base their appeals on ideology; interbranch relations depend on party loyalties and policy compromises, not pork and patronage; and campaigns focus on party programs rather than distribution and favors. In other countries, however, pork rather than shared policy goals hold legislative and inter-branch alliances together, and campaigns focus on the distribution of favors, jobs, and other individual benefits. Explaining these differences continues to rank high on the research agenda for Latin Americanists.

Analysts have made some progress in identifying political institutions that perpetuate candidate-centered, clientelistic systems. These include the open-list (in which citizens vote for candidates, and their votes determine the order of the party list) in PR systems and multiple lists run under the same party label. Such electoral rules create competition among co-partisans, which increases the emphasis on individual favors and goods since candidates cannot distinguish themselves from co-partisans on the basis of programmatic appeals.[17] Other observers have noted the deleterious effects of governors' influence on party discipline and effective governance in federal systems.[18] Still others note the importance of non-institutional factors such as the preferences of the very poor and uneducated for immediate individual goods rather than promises of policy change that may never materialize. The observation that poorer voters have shorter time horizons and greater difficulty monitoring whether politicians keep their policy promises than do richer, better educated voters explains why some citizens might prefer tangible individual goods to policies that, if delivered and successful, would have a greater impact on their lives.[19]

During transitions to democracy, the outgoing authoritarian government often tried to negotiate or impose conditions that would protect its members and allies from future prosecution and unwanted policy changes. Many granted themselves amnesties for human rights violations. A number also changed electoral rules in order to prevent future victories by parties they distrusted. A great deal was written soon after redemocratizations about the long-term anti-democratic consequences expected from these legacies, but most have turned out to have only short-term effects. Analysts using the rational choice approach have done a number of the most insightful explanations of why most did not last and how those that did last really worked. As Guillermo O'Donnell has shown, simply outlawing popular parties is an unsuccessful institutional manipulation almost guaranteed to backfire because of the incentives such laws create for politicians competing for votes to circumvent them.[20] Most of the institutional manipulations initiated by authoritarian governments were similarly unsophisticated and have had little long-term significance because new democratic governments have strong electoral motivations to change them, as Wendy Hunter has shown in an analysis of why Brazilian politicians reduced the budgets and influence of the military after democratization.[21] Her argument focuses on the electoral incentives that led Brazilian legislators to reduce military prerogatives that many had thought would last longer, but it can be generalized to many other issues. Politicians' search for votes gives them good reasons to override dictatorial legacy policies that either limit their ability to use resources to benefit constituents or exclude substantial numbers of voters from participation. Any time laws exclude a large number of voters, some politicians can improve their election chances by including them. This is the reason that outlawing popular leftist parties never works as a long-term strategy, and suffrage restrictions are eventually abandoned.

The effects of a number of electoral rules have been pretty thoroughly worked out in studies that combine rational choice assumptions about politicians' behavior and empirical tests of both rational choice and other theories. These include the effect of presidential run-offs and different election schedules on party fragmentation; the effect of preference voting, term limits, and allowing multiple lists under the same party label on party discipline in the legislature and candidate campaign strategies; and the effect of legislative procedures on the presidents' ability to pass their policy agendas.[22] These are the nuts and bolts of democratic politics, and scholars have made a great deal of progress in figuring them out. The important contribution of the rational choice approach is not the demonstration that institutions explain all politicians' behavior, but rather that using the approach puts a useful structure on empirical investigation so that analysts can figure out how much of which puzzling behaviors are caused by certain institutions and which are caused by other factors such as ideology.

Most of the work noted above focuses on the effects of political institutions, but such analyses always lead back to the prior question: what caused the institutions in the first place? The transitions permitted the careful investigation of this question in many countries that chose new democratic institutions or modified old ones. Scholars analyzing these decisions have shown that those who served in the legislatures and constituent assemblies that picked them chose new political institutions to further their own electoral interests.[23] During and soon after democratization, institutional reforms aimed at increasing judicial independence from the executive were also introduced in a number of countries. Analysts influenced by rational choice have explained these reforms in a number of countries.[24]

Bringing Citizens Back In: Clientelism

Much of the research influenced by the rational choice approach focuses on elite decision making and strategies, as would be expected given the demanding requirements for information and calculating ability assumed by the rational choice approach. The investigation of clientelism is a partial exception. In many parts of Latin America, clientelism and vote-buying influence election outcomes. No one knows how much, but since politicians seem to devote a lot of effort to supplying campaign contributors and constituents with individual favors and goods, most observers see it as important. If the analyst tends to look at the world through the rational choice lens, the prevalence of clientelism raises some questions. Most basic, why would a poor landless laborer trade her vote for a bag of groceries rather than voting for the party that promises land reform that would provide a much larger benefit? And why would a politician spend much of his campaign chest to hire the people who deliver those bags of groceries rather than trying to distribute more through a less costly impersonal delivery system or via provision of public goods?

Clientelism, defined here as the personal delivery, via a somewhat stable political network that extends from the politician to the voter, of divisible, excludable goods in exchange for votes or other kinds of political support, is inefficient in multiple ways. As Gary Cox noted some time ago, there are economies of scale in the delivery of benefits, and once the number of political participants is large, providing public goods would enable more goods to reach more people.[25] Clientelism is also widely believed to be economically inefficient since the resources distributed go to the most politically useful recipients, not to their best economic use. One of the most frequent criticisms of clientelism is that benefits often do not reach the poorest citizens or excluded groups such as the indigenous because they lack political connections. Clientelist distribution also typically requires the employment of many people to staff the networks needed to reach large numbers of voters individually, which means that resources have to be spent to pay them rather than on the goods or services being distributed. Finally, although there is no reason that parties could not provide both clear programmatic leadership and clientelist benefits—as Chilean parties have since the 1930s—most parties seem to emphasize one at the expense of the other in practice.

Since clientelism seems irrational from various points of view, analysts have given a lot of thought to why it persists. The poor may sincerely prefer a bag of groceries today to the promise of land reform because they do not know whether the promise will be kept and whether they will personally get land if it is kept. In rational choice jargon, this is a principal-agent problem. The less educated have great difficulty monitoring whether politicians keep their promises and understandably little faith that they will. Because the poor may be desperate for groceries today, they also may not have the luxury of, in effect, investing in a future policy change. These reasons for some voters' apparent preference for small individual benefits have been suggested by analysts who use the rational choice approach.[26] They are consistent with a lot of evidence showing that that politicians from poorer electoral districts engage in various behaviors thought to go along with clientelism (e.g., party switching, making pork-laden budget amendments) and that the poor often vote for conservative parties that oppose policies aimed at income equalization, but have clientelist reputations.

Arguments about the poor leave unexplained why politicians seem to prefer delivering benefits via clientelist networks rather than in some more impersonal way. To answer that question, analysts have suggested that clientelism allows politicians to monitor whether the voter actually votes for the candidate from whom she received the groceries. Since modern democracies have secret ballots, voters cannot be monitored directly, but a local party worker knows the voters in his area and knows who will support the right politician.[27] Cutting edge research in this area investigates both the small details of how clientelist benefits are distributed and the attitudes and network connections of people living in poor neighborhoods likely to have access to benefits provided via political machines. Most empirical research tends to show that citizens personally linked to political machines receive more help from officials and party workers, but recent investigation of the political effects of means-tested cash transfer programs suggests that voters reward politicians given credit for providing benefits regardless of whether they are linked into a clientelist network.[28]

Strategic Interactions

The main theoretical contribution of the rational choice approach, as noted above, derives from the insights generated from focusing on individual motivations when trying to understand the behavior of groups. Scholars using the rational choice approach were the first to develop systematic explanations for why groups often fail to reflect the interests of the average person in them. It is hard to believe now, but when Mancur Olson first explained the logic of collective action, it was a controversial and revolutionary idea for political scientists. At one time, analysts assumed that groups such as classes, elites, and ethnic groups would behave as though they were unitary actors pursuing the interests of the modal person in the group. Now, however, almost everyone who studies such unorganized or loosely organized groups takes into account the temptation to free ride and the inability of such groups either to make decisions as a single actor would or to monitor members' behavior in order to enforce decisions made by leaders. Scholars now focus on the contextual conditions and organizational features that enable some groups to overcome these problems. To take a non-Latin American example, Susanna Lohmann explains how the small demonstrations against the East German dictatorship escalated into a massive uprising as media coverage persuaded increasing numbers of people that the risk was acceptable.[29] She devised the model to explain why thousands of citizens would suddenly take the apparently irrational risk of publicly opposing a repressive dictatorship. Her argument can be applied in any setting in which latent popular opposition to a dictatorship finally bursts out, for example, demonstrations at the end of the Argentine military regime in 1983.

The logic of collection action and Lohmann's information cascade model share another feature besides the assumption of means-ends rationality and the focus on individuals as the building blocks of group behavior: individuals consider not only their own interests when making decisions but also what they expect others to do and how these actions will affect the final outcome. This is a feature of many applications of rational choice logic.

Several analysts whose intuitions have been influenced by Latin American experience have used strategic interaction models to illuminate regime change. The tipping game proposed by Adam Przeworski explains why politicians rarely defect from stable autocracies, but then jump ship en masse when the regime seems threatened.[30] In stable dictatorships, politicians (and others) who cooperate with the dictator reap many rewards, but if they were to join the opposition, they would lose access to future benefits while facing the risk of jail, exile, or in some places murder. So regardless of their sincere beliefs, the tipping game shows that they have good reasons to remain loyal as long as most others do. If, however, events create the expectation that the regime will collapse, then those same regime insiders can no longer expect future benefits and, in fact, can best protect their futures by returning to the barracks or leading their faction of the ruling party into the opposition.

I have used simple games to highlight general differences in the way different kinds of dictatorship break down. I show that the military's intolerance for internal conflict makes military dictatorships more fragile than those led by civilians, and that larger exogenous changes are needed to push dominant-party regimes to the tipping point.[31] Beatriz Magaloni uses a series of games to explain why the Mexican transition took so long and why it finally happened. She shows how the loss of mass support caused by economic crisis changed the incentives that had prevented PRI politicians from defecting from the regime for so long. Her work thus explains how popular opposition affects when the elite tipping point that causes regime breakdown occurs.[32]

Daron Acemoglu and James Robinson's models focus on economic rather than political incentives. They claim to explain democratization everywhere but fit Latin American experience better than that of the rest of the world.[33] In their models, a united rich political elite offers democracy to the poor when they fear that continuing the unequal and dictatorial status quo will lead to revolution. The rich maintain the status quo as long as they believe that economic conditions prevent the poor from organizing to rebel, but they prefer democratic redistribution to revolution. Consequently, if they believe the poor can rebel, they democratize in order to make their promise to redistribute more credible.[34]

These examples have in common that they begin with self-interested individuals as building blocks, but that the outcomes to be explained arise from the interactions of multiple individuals whose decisions are shaped by what they expect others to do within an economic or institutional context that determines what choices are available and the costs and advantages associated with each choice. The use of strategic models such as these has increased because they are levers and pulleys for the imagination. Just as you can lift more with a lever than with your bare hands, you can sometimes figure out more about a situation if you devise a simplification that captures the most basic features of an interaction than if you had to rely on your untutored intuitions alone.

Conclusion

The idea that much of human behavior is motivated by self-interest and means-ends rationality has been the central building block of economic theory for centuries and also informs commonsense explanations of events. The main contribution of rational choice to political science has come not from this idea, which has always been widely used, but from close attention to the details of how specific institutions and other contextual features systematically affect the costs and benefits associated with different choices and thus affect the behavior of many actors; and from its attention to how the behavior of other individuals affects the costs and benefits associated with each individual's actions. A general model of politicians' behavior as they decide what policy positions to take, for example, would see each politician as simultaneously engaged in a largely cooperative "game" with supporters, in which the politician exchanges policies and other things for support, and a competitive game with other politicians in which each of them makes policy choices based on what his supporters want, what positions he expects other politicians to take, and how those positions will affect the likely voter response to any position he takes. To maximize his vote, the politician needs to consider not only what voters want, but also the location of other politicians in the policy space and how he can locate himself to maximize the number of voters who are closer to him than to other candidates. This basic understanding of politicians' behavior underlies many of the standard findings of the study of the effects of political institutions, for example, the expectation of centrist policy positions in two-party systems. Analogous analyses of how institutions and other contextual factors affect not only individual action but also how each individual's actions affect the costs and benefits associated with the actions taken by others explain many other political phenomena as well.

The basic elements of the rational choice approach have become integrated into most recent studies of politicians' behavior, whether in campaigns, constructing political machines, voting on legislation, or bargaining with each other. Although rational choice ideas have influenced many scholars, they may not self-consciously identify with the approach. Instead, most Latin Americanists who work on these subjects use increasingly sophisticated empirical methods to compare explanations derived from rational choice assumptions with other possible causes of outcomes they want to explain. Scholars interested in why party systems in some countries are more volatile than others, for example, often include in their data analysis indicators for economic performance to test the standard rational choice argument that voters punish the incumbent for poor economic performance, as well as institutional measures expected to affect politicians' behavior, but they also include variables that reflect non-rational causes of volatility, such as the size of the informal sector.[35] Prior research has suggested that people who work in the informal sector, like the indigenous, are less likely to be organized into stable voting blocs, and thus that they contribute to electoral volatility, but no one has argued that lack of political organization is a rational strategy for them.

The rational choice approach has also shaped much of the recent theoretical work on regime transition and institutional change. Latin Americanists who focus on public opinion and voting behavior, like their counterparts in the United States and Europe however, have less often integrated rational choice ideas into their analyses. As noted above, the assumptions the rational choice approach makes about information and calculating ability are more plausible when applied to politicians whose careers depend on quality information than for ordinary citizens who are well-informed about things that matter to them but often not about politics. This difference probably explains why the rational choice approach has generally had less success explaining individual attitudes and voting. Scholars who work on protest movements and the politics of identity have also used rational choice less, despite the applicability of the logic of collective action to protests, the availability of interesting theoretical treatments of how to overcome collective action problems, and the use of rational choice arguments to illuminate ethnic politics in other parts of the world. This choice reflects taste differences, but also reliance on fieldwork-intensive inductive research strategies that tend to lead to a focus on the individuals who participate in protests and indigenous movements. As with other forms of individual political behavior, means-ends calculations based on reasonably accurate information about how particular actions are likely to affect outcomes may not explain much about such participation.

In short, Latin Americanists now use rational choice where they find that it helps to explain interesting outcomes, and they ignore it where they find it unhelpful.

Notes

1 For citations to literature on these topics, see the section on institutions below.
2 Guillermo O'Donnell, "The Impossible Game," in his *Modernization and Bureaucratic-Authoritarianism: Studies in South American Politics* (Berkeley: Institute of International Studies, 1973) is an important exception.
3 For example, Susan Stokes, *Mandates and Democracy: Neoliberalism by Surprise in Latin America* (New York: Cambridge University Press, 2001).
4 Matthew Shugart and John Carey, *Presidents and Assemblies: Constitutional Design and Electoral Dynamics* (New York: Cambridge University Press, 1992); George Tsebelis and Eduardo Alemán, "Presidential Conditional Agenda Setting in Latin America," *World Politics* 57 (2005): 396–420; Eduardo Alemán and Thomas Schwartz, "Presidential Vetoes in Latin American Constitutions," *Journal of Theoretical Politics* 18 (2006): 98–120.
5 For example, Michelle Taylor-Robinson, *Do the Poor Count? Representation and Accountability in the Context of Poverty* (State College: Pennsylvania State University Press, 2010).
6 Kenneth Roberts and Erik Wibbles, "Party Systems and Electoral Volatility in Latin America: A Test of Economic, Institutional, and Structural Explanations," *APSR* 93 (1999): 575–90; Barbara Geddes, *Paradigms and Sand Castles: Theory Building and Research Design in Comparative Politics*, ch. 4 (Ann Arbor, University of Michigan Press, 2003).
7 For descriptions, see Aníbal Pérez-Liñán, *Presidential Impeachment and the New Political Instability in Latin America* (New York: Cambridge University Press, 2007); Kathryn Hochstetler, "Rethinking Presidentialism: Challenges and Presidential Falls in South America," *Comparative Politics* 38 (2006), 401–18.
8 A good entry point for the vast literature on the political impediments to economic reform is Stephan Haggard and Robert Kaufman, *The Political Economy of Democratic Transition* (Princeton: Princeton University Press, 1995).
9 Leonardo Gasparini, "Income Inequality in Latin America and the Caribbean: Evidence from Household Surveys," Working Paper No. 2, Centro de Estudios Distributivos, Laborales y Sociales, Universidad Nacional de La Plata, Argentina (www.depeco.econo.unlp.edu.ar/cedlas.htm).
10 Jóhanna Kristín Birnir, "Stabilizing Party Systems and Excluding Segments of Society? The Effect of Formation Costs on New Party Formation in Latin America," *Studies in Comparative International Development* 39 (2004), 3–27.
11 See John Carey, "Institutional Design and Party Systems," in *Consolidating the Third Wave Democracies*, ed., Larry Diamond, Marc Plattner, Yun-han Chu, and Hung-mao Tien (Baltimore: Johns Hopkins University Press, 1998) for an overview of basic findings.
12 Matthew Shugart, "The Electoral Cycle and Institutional Sources of Divided Government," *AJPS* 89 (1995): 327–43.
13 Mark Jones, *Electoral Laws and the Survival of Presidential Democracies* (South Bend: University of Notre Dame Press,1995).
14 Shugart and Carey, *Presidents and Assemblies.*
15 For example, John Carey and Matthew Shugart, eds., *Executive Decree Authority: Calling out the Tanks or Just Filling out the Forms?* (New York: Cambridge University Press, 1998).
16 Tsebelis and Alemán, "Presidential Conditional Agenda Setting,"; Eduardo Alemán and Ernesto Calvo, "Unified Government, Bill Approval and the Legislative Weight of the President," *Comparative Political Studies* 43 (2010): 511–34; Alemán and Schwartz, "Presidential Vetoes"; Eduardo Alemán, "Policy Gatekeepers in Latin American Legislatures," *Latin American Politics and Society* 48 (2006): 125–55; Sebastián Saiegh, "Political Prowess or Lady Luck? Evaluating Chief Executives' Legislative Success Rates," *Journal of Politics* 71 (2009): 1342–56.
17 For example, John Carey and Matthew Shugart, "Incentives to Cultivate a Personal Vote: Rank Ordering of Electoral Formulas," *Electoral Studies* 14 (1995): 417–39; Barry Ames, "Electoral

Strategy under Open-List Proportional Representation," *AJPS* 39 (1995): 406–33; Scott Morgenstern, "Organized Factions and Disorganized Parties: Electoral Incentives in Uruguay," *Party Politics* 7 (2001): 235–56.

18 David Samuels, *Ambition, Federalism, and Legislative Politics in Brazil* (NY: Cambridge University Press, 2003); Mark Jones et al., "Amateur Legislators-Professional Politicians: The Consequences of Party-Centered Electoral Rules in a Federal System," *AJPS* 46 (2002), 656–69; Sebastiàn Saiegh and Mariano Tommasi, "Why Is Argentina's Fiscal Federalism So Inefficient? Entering the Labyrinth," *Journal of Applied Economics* (Buenos Aires) II (1999).

19 Taylor-Robinson, *Do the Poor Count?*

20 O'Donnell, "The Impossible Game".

21 Wendy Hunter, *Eroding Military Influence in Brazil: Politicians against Soldiers* (Chapel Hill: University of North Carolina Press, 1997).

22 This literature is vast. Besides those listed above, see, for example, Argelina Cheibub Figueiredo and Fernando Limongi, "Presidential Power, Legislative Organization, and Party Behavior in Brazil," *Comparative Politics* 32 (2000): 151–70; John Carey, *Term Limits and Legislative Representation* (New York: Cambridge University Press, 1996); Michelle Taylor, "Formal versus Informal Incentive Structures and Legislative Behavior: Evidence from Costa Rica," *Journal of Politics* 54 (1992): 1055–73; Gary Cox and Matthew Shugart, "In the Absence of Vote Pooling: Nomination and Vote Allocation Errors in Colombia," *Electoral Studies* 14 (1995): 441–60. Carey summarizes many of the basic findings in "Institutional Design and Party Systems".

23 Barbara Geddes, "The Initiation of New Democratic Institutions in Eastern Europe and Latin America" in *Institutional Design in New Democracies*, ed., Arend Lijphart and Carlos Waisman (Boulder: Westview, 1996); Gabriel Negretto, "Choosing How to Choose Presidents: Parties, Military Rulers, and Presidential Elections in Latin America," *Journal of Politics* 68 (2006): 421–33; Negretto, "Political Parties and Institutional Design: Explaining Constitutional Choice in Latin America," *British Journal of Political Science* 39 (2009), 117–39; Alberto Diaz-Cayeros and Beatriz Magaloni, "Party Dominance and the Logic of Electoral Design in Mexico's Transition to Democracy," *Journal of Theoretical Politics* (2001) 13: 271–93.

24 Beatriz Magaloni, *Voting for Autocracy: Hegemonic Party Survival and Its Demise in Mexico* (New York: Cambridge University Press, 2006); Beatriz Magaloni and Guillermo Zepeda, "Democratization, Judicial and Law Enforcement Institutions, and the Rule of Law in Mexico," in *Dilemmas of Political Change in Mexico*, ed., Kevin Middlebrook (La Jolla: Center for US-Mexican Studies, UCSD, and Institute of Latin American Studies, University of London, 2004); Gretchen Helmke, *Courts under Constraints: Judges, Generals and Presidents in Argentina* (New York: Cambridge University Press, 2005); Jodi Finkel, *Judicial Reform as Political Insurance: Argentina, Peru and Mexico in the 1990s* (South Bend: University of Notre Dame Press, 2008).

25 Gary Cox, *The Efficient Secret: The Cabinet and the Development of Political Parties in Victorian England* (Cambridge: Cambridge University Press, 1987).

26 Taylor-Robinson, *Do the Poor Count?*; Barbara Geddes, *Politician's Dilemma: Building State Capacity in Latin America* (Berkeley, University of California Press, 1994); but see Mona Lyne, *The Voter's Dilemma and Democratic Accountability: Latin America and Beyond* (State College: Pennsylvania State University Press, 2008), who notes correctly that richer voters also demand individual benefits and favors from politicians in return for support.

27 Susan Stokes, "Perverse Accountability: A Formal Model of Machine Politics with Evidence from Argentina," *APSR* 99 (2005): 315–25; Valeria Brusco, Marcelo Nazareno, and Susan Stokes, "Vote Buying in Argentina," *Latin American Research Review* 39 (2004): 66–88.

28 Ernesto Calvo and María Victoria Murillo, "Who Delivers? Partisan Clients in the Argentine Electoral Market," *AJPS* 48 (2004), 742–57; Ernesto Calvo and María Victoria Murillo, "Selecting Clients: Partisan Networks and the Electoral Benefits of Targeted Distribution," presented Dept. of Government and Politics, University of Maryland, 2009; Alberto Diaz-Cayeros, Federico Estévez, and Beatriz Magaloni, *Strategies of Vote-Buying: Poverty, Democracy, and Social Transfers in Mexico*, unpublished manuscript, Stanford University, 2010; Cesar Zucco, "The President's 'New' Constituency: Lula and the Pragmatic Vote in Brazil's 2006 Presidential Election," *Journal of Latin American Studies* 40 (2008): 29–49.

29 Susanna Lohmann, "Dynamics of Informational Cascades: The Monday Demonstrations in Leipzig, East Germany, 1989–1991" *World Politics* 47: 42–101.

30 Adam Przeworski, "Some Problems in the Study of the Transition to Democracy," in *Transitions from Authoritarian Rule*, eds., Guillermo O'Donnell, Philippe Schmitter, and Laurence White-head (Baltimore: Johns Hopkins University Press, 1986).

31 Barbara Geddes, *Paradigms and Sand Castles*, ch. 2.

32 Magaloni, *Voting for Autocracy.*

33 Daron Acemoglu and James Robinson, "A Theory of Political Transitions," *American Economic Review* 91 (2001), 938–63; Acemoglu and Robinson, *Economic Origins of Dictatorship and Democracy* (New York: Cambridge University Press, 2006).

34 For a more detailed summary of their argument along with a critique, see Barbara Geddes, "What Causes Democratization?" in *The Oxford Handbook of Political Science*, ed., Robert E. Goodin (Oxford: Oxford University Press, 2009).

35 Roberts and Wibbles, "Party Systems and Electoral Volatility," 1999.

29

THE ENDURING INFLUENCE
OF HISTORICAL-STRUCTURAL
APPROACHES

Jennifer Cyr and James Mahoney

[D]ata have to be interpreted in the historical-structural context.

(Fernando Henrique Cardoso and Enzo Faletto, Dependency and
Development in Latin America, *p. xiii)*

In *Dependency and Development in Latin America*, Cardoso and Faletto formulated a new
approach for studying the political economy of Latin America. They proposed that "the
analysis of social life is fruitful only if it starts from the presupposition that there are relatively stable global structures." At the same time, they insisted that "although enduring,
social structures can be, and in fact are, continuously transformed." Cardoso and Faletto
characterized this approach "as both structural and historical ... our methodology is
historical-structural."[1]

The historical-structural approach proposed by Cardoso and Faletto is distinguished
by three defining features. First, the approach is designed to explain specific outcomes in
particular cases. Rather than examine the average effects of variables within large populations of cases, historical-structuralism is fundamentally "case-oriented" and geared toward
identifying the causes of outcomes in specific cases. Second, historical-structural work is
centrally concerned with the temporal dimensions of political explanation. It is "historical"
in part because it pays attention to the duration, pace, and timing of events when developing
explanations. Such a temporal orientation contrasts with other approaches in political science that rely mainly or exclusively on cross-sectional data or "snapshots" in time to derive
inferences. Finally, historical-structural work is macro-oriented and focuses centrally on
patterned relationships among aggregate groups and societies. The "structural" dimension
of the approach is embodied in its focus on the relations among groups within societies and
the interrelationships among societies themselves. This kind of macro orientation differs
markedly from other approaches in political science that put rationally behaving individuals
at the center of the analysis.

Forty years after the publication of *Dependency and Development*, Cardoso contends
that historical-structural work is "still useful" for analyzing political processes in Latin

America.[2] In this chapter, we assess his conclusion by taking stock of the literature on Latin American politics that has employed the distinctive features of historical-structuralism in recent decades. We find that this approach has indeed had an enduring influence within the field. Many of the leading works on Latin American politics implicitly or explicitly employ a historical-structural framework. Much of what we know about politics in the region can be attributed to work that uses this approach.

We discuss the uses and contributions of the historical-structural framework across two broad areas. First, we examine substantive research about Latin American politics. We find that scholars using the framework have generated major insights and knowledge, both for classic historical-structural themes and for topics that reflect the main political concerns of our times. In addition, the framework seems to hold much promise for the study of emerging topics in the field.

Second, we consider how the approach has evolved over time with respect to theory and method. We look at three topics: the temporal horizon of historical-structural work; the role of agency within the approach; and the incorporation of quantitative methods. Regarding the temporal horizon, we see that, while some historical-structural scholars continue to look back decades and even centuries in time to explain more contemporary outcomes, others take as their starting point more recent periods, such as the transition to democracy in the 1980s or the adoption of market-oriented economic policies in the 1990s. With respect to agency, we find that many authors explore the extent to which visionary leaders, everyday individuals, and social movements can alter structural paths and thus turn historical corners through "a passion for the possible."[3] Finally, although some historical-structural works continue to be purely qualitative, we certainly see a new body of mixed-method research that is partly historical-structural and partly statistical in its methodology.

Contributions to Substantive Knowledge

Scholars of Latin America who employ historical-structural approaches raise questions about macro outcomes in specific cases. Although their goal is often to explain the particular cases under investigation, their studies also yield general knowledge about political processes. To assess the contribution of historical structuralism to this kind of knowledge generation, we examine scholarship across three broad research areas: social revolutions, democratization, and social rights and the environment. These areas include both older and newer themes, and they represent topics for which historical-structural work has had varying levels of prominence.

A Classic Research Area: Social Revolutions

When Cardoso and Faletto were writing, scholars knew very little about the causes and consequences of social revolutions in Latin America, even though the Cuban Revolution was often regarded as an archetype. Since that time, a great deal has been learned, mostly from analysts using historical-structural approaches. Let us explore the knowledge that has been accumulated.

A key strand of scholarship focuses on the question of why some countries, especially Cuba (1959) and Nicaragua (1979), experienced full-blown social revolutions, whereas other seemingly similar countries did not.[4] To explain this divergence, historical-structural explanations highlight the role of political regime type, class, and international structures as causal factors. In terms of regime type, historical-structural scholarship suggests that neopatrimonial regimes, in which a dictator controls the state (including the military) as a personal instrument, are especially vulnerable to social revolutionary overthrow. These regimes tend to generate broad-based opposition, and they tend to foster total state collapse when the dictator is removed. Thus, the governments of Fulgencio Batista in Cuba and Anastasio Somoza in Nicaragua were structurally vulnerable to social revolution in a way that military governments elsewhere in Latin America (e.g., in Guatemala and El Salvador) were not.

In combination with political regime type, certain kinds of class structures and international factors also promote social revolutions.[5] Revolutionary oppositions that bridge class divisions are especially capable of dislodging incumbent regimes. Agricultural structure also matters: regions with sharecropping or squatting are prone to the formation of guerrilla movements, especially when socioeconomic conditions are not improving.[6] Divisions within elite class groups, as existed in Cuba and Nicaragua, in turn facilitate the success of these movements once they have formed. International dependency on a superpower patron fosters successful social revolutions by handcuffing neo-patrimonial dictators when they face a crisis situation. For instance, Batista and Somoza were constrained by the United States at key moments in revolutionary dramas in ways that military regimes confronting revolutionaries elsewhere in the region were not.[7]

Historical-structural works have also yielded important findings about the outcomes and consequences of social revolutions.[8] In line with Skocpol's structural theory,[9] revolutionary consolidation in Bolivia, Cuba, and Nicaragua yielded larger, more bureaucratic, and more mass-mobilizing states. In the years following the revolutions, these new states were more capable of reaching into society than their pre-revolutionary counterparts. Yet in part because the revolutions entailed the overthrow of U.S. patrons, the effort by revolutionaries to remake society invited economic and military intervention from the United States. This intervention, in turn, shaped the whole post-revolutionary process and buffeted the extent to which revolutionaries could actually enact far-reaching reforms without aid from another superpower patron (i.e., the USSR). In the end, revolutionaries in Bolivia and Nicaragua had limited success transforming class structures, whereas the price of economic and social transformation in Cuba was political closure and a new dependence on the Soviet Union.[10]

In short, the study of social revolutions is a classic topic in which scholars using a historical-structural approach have had success in concrete knowledge generation. From this work, we have the following findings: (1) democracies are nearly invulnerable to social-revolutionary overthrow; (2) neo-patrimonial regimes that lack ties to societal groups are especially vulnerable to social revolution; (3) class structures associated with sharecropping are more likely to yield guerrilla movements; (4) historical dependence on the United States makes governments more vulnerable to social revolutionary overthrow; and (5) this same dependence on the United States is likely to check the extent to which social transformation occurs.

A Contemporary Research Area: Democratization

Unlike the study of revolutions, work on democratization has been marked by a wide variety of approaches, only one of which is historical structuralism. Nevertheless, historical-structural studies have made key contributions to our substantive knowledge in this area, including the transition to democracy, the possibility of democratic consolidation, and the quality of democracy. For each topic, an exploration of preexisting conditions and pre-democratic legacies has proven useful in generating causal explanations.

Many non-historical and non-structural approaches to democratization have emphasized the ways in which political elites matter at the time of the transition to democracy. By definition, these elites are the individuals at the negotiating table, arguing over the terms of the new democracy, and their decisions shape the process of transition.[11] Yet, work within the historical-structural tradition suggests that the path that leads political elites to negotiate a democratic transition is influenced by other societal forces, including the lower classes. For example, several scholars have challenged elite-centered works by showing that democracy was sometimes driven "from below."[12] In cases such as Peru (1980), Argentina (1983), and El Salvador (1994), large-scale societal mobilization explicitly aimed at destabilizing authoritarian rule and establishing democracy marked the transition. These protest movements helped create a climate of ungovernability and, once the negotiations were underway, helped the transition move forward.

To be sure, scholars within the historical-structural tradition do not reject the thesis that democratization is often negotiated in a bargaining game among elites. However, they ask questions about who those elites represent, how much leverage they have, and when they become willing to negotiate in certain ways and not others. To answer, factors such as structurally-rooted economic crises, prior authoritarian regime institutions, and historical modes of international influence often figure prominently.[13] For example, economic crises, sparked by past economic decisions or growing mobilization, often provoked the negotiating games that marked the transitions. In fact, other than Chile (1990), it is hard to find Latin American cases where the transition did not unfold in a climate of economic crisis. Likewise, prior regime institutions shape the nature of the players present at the negotiating table and those active in civil society. For example, the authoritarian regime in Uruguay collaborated with the traditional political parties, relying on them for political legitimization. As a result, party leaders were central in the conversations that led to the primary elections of 1982, the Naval Club Pact of 1984, and the elections that brought a democratic government to power in 1985. Finally, factors such as a country's historical relationship with the United States also matter for the timing and content of the transition. We can see this in cases such as Nicaragua (1990) and El Salvador (1994), where the launching of the transition and the nature of the bargaining game were interwoven with United States foreign policy and intervention.

Transitions themselves provide no guarantee that the democratic regime will be stable or effective. Historical-structural works have shed light on the conditions that are likely to lead to greater consolidation and democratic quality. A comparison of prior authoritarian regime types, for example, reveals that authoritarian legacies have varying and lasting effects on the democracies that succeed them.[14] Democratic consolidation is not possible where authoritarian leaders and paramilitary forces control the countryside, as they did in Guatemala.[15] Where democracies do take root, the bequeathments of authoritarian regimes often produce paradoxical results, as with the case of post-transition civil-military relations. At the time of their democratic transitions, the Chilean and Brazilian militaries were quite strong vis-à-vis the entering civil government. While this balance of power relationship made the punishment of past human rights transgressions impossible in the short term, it nonetheless allowed for a relatively peaceful transition and the increasing professionalization of the military under civilian rule. In Argentina, on the other hand, the military's strength was greatly reduced at the time of the transition. Nevertheless, extended efforts by President Raúl Alfonsín to try the armed forces for torture and repression were derailed by a growing guerrilla movement within the military hierarchy. After almost ten years of struggle, the military was eventually granted full amnesty. Paradoxically, then, weaker militaries at the time of the transition can lead to a more painful and protracted establishment of democratic civil-military relations.[16] Without looking at the structural forces in play at the time of the democratic transitions, it is difficult to make sense of such paradoxes.

Historical-structural works have also explored the roots of political competition and representation in Latin America.[17] Scholars have linked different types of contemporary political party systems back to the mode in which labor was incorporated into the political system in the early 20th century. Where labor could feasibly be integrated into the traditional (oligarchic) political parties, as in Colombia and Uruguay, the longstanding two-party system was preserved. By contrast, when both labor and peasants were mobilized and the traditional oligarchy was not as cohesive, as in Venezuela and Mexico, the need to control both sectors led to the implementation of key urban and agrarian reforms. In the short term, these reforms helped to forge a radical populist alliance, but in the long term they led to integrative party systems dominated by one (Mexico) or two (Venezuela) parties.[18]

Although it is a truism to assert that political parties matter for representative democracy, historical-structural scholarship has shown that democracies are most stable, and the rule of law best respected, when partisan representation is both meaningful and diverse. For example, in strongly presidential systems, judicial autonomy comes under attack more often than not when a single party dominates the political arena. Within Argentina, the rule of law is weakly implanted precisely in provinces where the *Partido Justicialista* has historically controlled politics, such as San Luis. By contrast, judicial autonomy is better respected in those provinces where power is more fragmented among two or more political parties, such as Mendoza.[19]

Finally, a historical focus leads us to reconsider the value of key institutions and policies and their impact on democracy.[20] Decentralization, for example, has been increasingly promoted as a potential cure-all for democratic woes.[21] By devolving political, administrative, and fiscal power to subnational governments, which are "closer" to the citizens they represent, decentralization is supposed to increase accountability and responsiveness. This conclusion is based, however, on the assumption that rational individuals *qua* citizens will become more engaged in the democratic process, and more demanding of it, when it is closer to them. Some historical-structural works have found, to the contrary, that the causal arrow can go the other way: decentralization processes may be most developed where democratic initiatives have long been in place. Thus, the United States has much higher levels of decentralization and much more active local civil society organizations than other federal countries, such as Mexico and Brazil.

In all, historical-structural scholarship has drawn some important and often surprising conclusions about the well-studied area of democratization. This is true in terms of when and how transitions occur, why they may (not) consolidate, and to what extent they are effective. These conclusions often emerged by looking beyond the immediate causes emphasized in other scholarship and delving into the historical developments that led to the outcome of interest—a method for which historical-structuralism is eminently qualified.

A Research Frontier: Social Rights and the Environment

Finally, historical structuralism has begun to examine the circumstances under which the struggle for different social and environmental rights can be successful. The pursuit of greater freedoms and the protection of the environment have become important concerns for many citizens in Latin America. While this is a relatively new area for scholarship, historical-structural works have made contributions.

Scholars working in this tradition have found, for example, that the achievement of specific women's rights does not necessarily correlate positively with democratization.[22] Historical-structural works instead emphasize the relationship among aggregate groups in society, such as the church and state, to make sense of cross-national variations. Thus, the legalization of divorce has occurred when historically strong ties between the church and the state are temporarily severed due to conflicts over human rights abuses, economic policy, and authoritarianism more generally. Somewhat surprisingly, divorce became legal in Brazil during the military dictatorship of General Ernesto Geisel. In Argentina, by contrast, legalization occurred after the democratic transition. The Radical government was able to push through the reform by confronting the church over its tacit support of the previous military regime.[23]

Since the early 1990s, indigenous movements have emerged to resist and reform economic and political regimes that they perceive as exclusive and unjust. Yet, success in these pursuits has varied greatly. Historical-structural works suggest reasons why this is the case.[24] For example, indigenous movements in Bolivia were able to successfully integrate into an influential political party, *Movimiento al Socialismo*. In Peru, on the other hand, efforts by indigenous movements to become electorally competitive have failed. Historical-structural factors can explain this difference: Bolivia's *Movimiento al Socialismo* emerged in an environment where permissive electoral laws and a decentralized political system were present at the time that the traditional political party system entered into decline. These conditions were lacking in Peru when the traditional party system declined, posing large obstacles to the formation of an effective indigenous political party.[25] In other words, where the timing of particular institutional and structural factors coincided, indigenous-based social movements were able to translate their demands into a more formal mechanism for change.

Finally, while the fight for environmental protection in Latin America has been driven in large part by international non-governmental organizations, local communities in countries like Brazil and Ecuador have been important actors as well.[26] A basic structural hypothesis would posit a positive relationship between the strength and cohesion of local groups and the success of campaigns against environmentally damaging projects. Thus, whereas efforts to protect the Ecuadorian Amazon from harmful oil drilling practices were successful thanks to strong local organizations, the campaign against the government's *Polonoroeste* development project in Rondônia, Brazil, had less immediate impact. As local grassroots groups in Brazil gained strength, however, they were able to fight more effectively for their own interests and shape the project in ways that were positive both to the community and the environment.[27]

In sum, looking at social rights from a historical-structural perspective suggests that, while the attainment of certain social and environmental rights has been a relatively recent phenomenon in Latin America, the struggle to achieve them is often the result of longer-term processes, including the growing strength of the social movements advocating for such rights and/or the emergence of a fortuitous structural and institutional environment. Today's contemporary successes and failures often cannot be adequately explained without taking into consideration that broader historical trajectory.

Overall, knowledge accumulation in the areas of revolution, democratization, and social rights and the environment has benefited from works that adopt a historical-structural perspective. In all three areas, we have important general findings have been derived from works aimed at identifying the causes of outcomes in specific cases. These findings emphasize historical processes and the structural relationships among different aggregate groups.

Undoubtedly, historical-structuralism has proven itself capable of reaching solid conclusions about the nature of Latin American politics.

Developments in Theory and Method

As an approach to explanation, historical-structuralism places emphasis on temporal processes and structural causes and tends to adopt a qualitative orientation to analysis. Although historical structuralism continues to adopt these emphases, recent years have seen it combine with other theoretical and methodological approaches. In this section, we explore the ways in which historical-structural works have employed: (1) new modes of temporal analysis, (2) frameworks for integrating agency and structure, and (3) mixed method research designs that combine qualitative and quantitative methods.

Modes of Temporal Analysis

One of historical-structuralism's principal claims is that the causes of outcomes often have their roots decades and sometimes even centuries in the past. In recent years, this basic idea has been developed more formally through frameworks designed for temporal analysis. At the same time, as the pace of political change in the region has seemingly accelerated, the timeline between cause and effect in historical-structural works has been shortened.

Important historical-structural findings concern the role of timing and sequencing. For example, the (relative) lack of external warfare in the years following Latin American independence hindered the development of a strong and autonomous state in the twentieth century. When post-independence wars did occur, they tended to take place before an institutional or administrative state core had been developed. Thus, rather than promote additional state development, warfare eroded extant state structures—wars served to *unmake* the Latin American state.[28] The key difference with Europe concerns timing and sequence: wars in Europe happened *after* individual states had attained a certain level of administrative and institutional capacity, enabling them to extend bureaucratization and taxation.[29]

While temporal processes matter as a rule for historical-structuralism, adopters of this approach also identify the effects that specific types of temporal processes have on political development. Take, for example, the use of critical junctures and path dependence. In studies that utilize these concepts,[30] historical-structural scholars call attention to crucial actor choices that establish certain directions of change and foreclose others in a way that shapes long-term trajectories of development.[31] For example, the dominant political regimes of 20th-century Central America have been treated as legacies of different patterns of liberal reform undertaken during the late 19th and early 20th centuries, when political elites made choices about how to modernize the state and agriculture. Harsh military-authoritarian regimes emerged in countries, such as Guatemala and El Salvador, where liberal reformers built up the army and pursued rapid agrarian commercialization. By contrast, where reforms were pursued more gradually, as in Costa Rica, the resulting political dynamics allowed for the inclusion of previously excluded sectors and the eventual establishment of a stable democratic regime.[32]

Historical-structuralism has revealed that the outcomes of temporal processes can also be cumulative in nature. Mexican business groups, for example, grew in political and organizational strength thanks to an extended over-time series of friendly overtures that the single-party regime made to business. The Argentine and Brazilian business sectors were less lucky, however. Long-term state efforts in these two countries to exclude business groups from policymaking resulted in a weakly organized business sector overall.[33] Thus, variations in the organizational strength of Latin American business associations are rooted in part in the cumulative effects of long-term interactions between state and business.

While temporal processes such as path dependence and cumulative causes by their very nature imply the *longue durée*, other historical-structural scholars shorten the timeline of causality and examine the effects of more recent events.[34] These works focus on the short-to medium-term consequences of major economic and political decisions, such as the relatively recent return to democracy in the region or the adoption of neoliberal economic reforms. Historical-structural scholarship emphasizes how the effects of recent market-oriented reforms can vary, even within regions of the same country. The class dynamics of coffee production in the Mexican states of Puebla and Oaxaca, for example, have influenced the kinds of re-regulatory projects that the central state implemented. Whereas the state could exclude the weak and thus politically disengaged small producers in Puebla from their policy framework, they were forced to address and eventually include into their framework Oaxaca's stronger small producers.[35] This is an example of how the historically determined strength of aggregate economic actors shapes contemporary policy-making decisions at the subnational level.

Finally, emerging political dynamics have been put in sharp relief through a historical perspective. For example, the emergence of associational networks as a new basis for expressing interests and influencing politics in contemporary Latin America is best understood against the backdrop of the decline of union-party alliances, which previously were the main vehicles for interest aggregation and articulation. Through the comparison of these two different interest regimes—associational networks and union-party alliances—one can better understand the possibilities and impossibilities for representing popular interests following the era of market-oriented reforms and democratization.[36] If the timing were different, that is, if the changes in interest aggregation occurred *before* the adoption of market-oriented reforms, we would expect the challenges to popular representation, and the very nature of that representation, to be different. Both the fact and the timing of their emergence matter for the theoretical conclusions drawn.

Integrating Agency and Structure

Historical-structural works view structural factors, such as the nature of class relations, as providing certain opportunities and setting certain constraints for purposive and goal-seeking agents. While this structural framework is privileged, scholars have pursued various strategies to allow space for individuals and groups to set, shape, and change political trajectories. In doing so, they offer different and innovative ways of integrating agency into historical-structuralism.

Some historical-structural works combine agency with structure by constructing explanations that systematically move from more structural variables to more agency-centered ones. In effect, the researcher starts with structural factors and works to explain an outcome on the basis of these factors. Once the explanatory power of structural factors has been exhausted, however, the researcher examines factors associated with human agency, such as (un)skilled political leadership. A classic example is Linz and Stepan's edited project on *The Breakdown of Democratic Regimes*.[37] In that work, contributors explore the role of political leadership in explaining regime breakdown without denying the importance of structure. For example, in his explanation of the breakdown of democracy in Brazil in 1964, Stepan concludes that structural factors (e.g., withdrawal of foreign aid) were decisively important, but still left a "small margin of maneuverability" in which leadership could play a role. Stepan focuses especially on the poor choices and behaviors of President João Goulart, arguing that, "Combined with the structural weaknesses in the regime, Goulart's political acts, strategies and styles paved the way for the final breakdown."[38]

The role of actor choice is also often emphasized in critical juncture explanations. These studies are distinctive in that they focus on actor choices during key historical moments. Thus, whereas Linz and Stepan emphasize agency in the moments immediately before an outcome of interest, critical juncture studies may call attention to agency during temporally distant episodes.[39] Likewise, whereas Linz and Stepan view agency as a factor that enters into play only after structure has done its explanatory work, critical juncture studies see agent choices as creating structural conditions that set long-run paths of development and that deeply constrain subsequent agency and choice.

More recently, historical-structural scholarship has focused on the kinds of agents that make up aggregate actors, such as the state and social movements, when explaining outcomes. For example, consider Evan's argument about "embedded autonomy" as a source of economic growth in the developing world.[40] On the one hand, he treats embedded autonomy as a structural relationship between the state and society—i.e., embedded autonomy exists when the state is autonomous from but still connected to key groups in society. But, on the other hand, his account and other works suggest that these structural relationships are often forged by movements and leaders who exhibit political agency.[41] If one applies this framework to the case of Costa Rica, for instance, the ability of governments to deliver social welfare benefits in the rural sector and reduce inequality since the mid-20th century seems linked to the state's relative autonomy from any powerful landlord class. Yet this state autonomy is rooted in the social movements and political leaders that emerged in the periods immediately before and after the Civil War of 1948. The actions of the communist and anti-communist political parties, Presidents Rafael Angel Calderón Guardia and José Figueres Ferrer, and various social movements seem critical to explaining how state autonomy was achieved in the first place and why state actors have taken advantage of increased autonomy to promote broad-based developmental goals.[42]

Agency is also emphasized in broadly historical-structural works on social movements in Latin America. For example, women and historically excluded ethnic groups have participated in contemporary revolutionary movements, such as that of the Zapatistas in Chiapas, at higher rates than earlier ones, as with the 1950s guerrilla movement in Cuba. In turn, their participation has had important effects on the objectives of these movements and the results they have achieved. In Mexico, authorities have been forced to show greater respect for gender and indigenous rights because of the composition of the Chiapas revolutionary movement. On the other hand, the opportunity for these groups to act in Chiapas only became possible as a result of the (structural) social and economic changes that took place in the years following the Cuban Revolution.[43] Thus, we arrive at a vision of structural conditions defining the possibilities for actor choice, and actor choices in turn shaping new structural outcomes. This dialectical interplay between structure and agency seems common in many historical-structural works, both old and new.

Mixed-Methods Research

Historical-structural works have generally been qualitative in nature. Focusing on large-scale outcomes in a small number of cases, the framework typically uses historical narrative and process tracing rather than regression analysis and statistics to evaluate causal arguments.

Yet, as more and more good quantitative data become available, historical-structural scholars are finding creative ways to integrate it into their research on Latin American politics. The result is a new strand of mixed-method research that joins statistical analysis with the historical-structural approach.

Work on the effects of policy decisions for different sectors of the economy and society illustrate this new mixed-method research. Historical-structural analysis has demonstrated, for example, that the stability of free market democracy in Chile was achieved by undercutting democratic participation in the rural sectors. The implementation of market reforms disarticulated the peasantry, making their support easier to corral by conservative elites in elections and keeping rural potentates secure under democracy. While a historical-structural approach is used to explain this process of stabilization via rural disarticulation, new quantitative data on elections, unionization, and political activity provide numerical support for the qualitative argument advanced. Taken together, these findings suggest convincingly that market-oriented reforms both helped sustain formal democracy by giving rural elites electoral security and eroded substantive democracy by undercutting and atomizing the peasantry.[44] The combination of the historical-structural approach and statistical analysis in both examples serves to strengthen the theoretical argument by triangulating the evidence proffered.

Research on social policy has also featured mixed methods, combining regression analysis with case studies that use a historical-structural approach. For example, the extent to which public pension systems have been fully replaced by private ones varies quite a lot, ranging from cases of nearly full privatization (e.g., Chile, Mexico, Bolivia), to the maintenance of mostly or fully public systems (e.g., Brazil, Ecuador, Venezuela), to various hybrid combinations (e.g., Peru, Colombia, Argentina, Uruguay, Costa Rica). Statistical tests account for some of this variation through variables such as the extent of pension spending and the degree to which the ruling party controls the legislature. Historical-structural case studies expand upon these findings by tracing the longer-run causal path leading to pension reform. This more qualitative approach suggests that aggressive pension privatization is rooted in a sequence of serious domestic capital shortages, substantial influence from the World Bank and pro-free market economists, and reforms promoted by a well-disciplined party that controlled the presidency and legislature.[45] These economic, ideational, and political factors have varying levels of prominence at different stages in the reform process, a conclusion that could only be drawn by paying attention to timing and sequence.

Mixed-method scholarship in a more cross-regional vein has compared social-welfare models in Latin America, East Asia, and Eastern Europe. Quantitative data illustrate well the major differences in spending across and within these three regions. The inability of statistical analysis to uncover unambiguous causal results, however, motivates a more historical-structural approach that emphasizes critical realignment periods. Differences in the way in which governments positioned themselves vis-à-vis leftist parties and labor during the first half of the 20th century can go a long way to explaining Latin America's focus on social provisions for formal workers, East Asia's emphasis on education, and Eastern Europe's universal social entitlements.[46]

As these examples demonstrate, historical-structural and statistical analyses have been used in tandem in an effort to triangulate methods and thus increase leverage for valid explanation. Whereas large-N statistics allow authors to find (theoretically-grounded) associations in areas such as social welfare policy, historical-structural analyses allow the authors to delineate the causal processes and mechanisms that underpin these sequences. By integrating quantitative analysis into their historical-structural works, several authors have been able to generalize their argument to a large number of cases, even as they provide detailed information about the mechanisms that connect cause and effect in particular historical cases.

Conclusion

Forty years since the original publication of *Dependencia y desarrollo*, the tradition of historical-structuralism remains alive and well in the study of Latin American politics. The approach continues to animate work and generate major substantive findings on a wide range of topics, including classic themes such as social revolutions as well as contemporary issues such as democratization and social rights. It retains the core features that have distinguished the approach from its inception: a concern with developing explanations of specific outcomes in particular cases, a focus on historical processes and sequences, and an emphasis on the structural relationships among aggregate groups.

Despite the continued relevance of historical-structuralism, the use of the framework has not remained a static enterprise. Its theoretical and methodological emphases have evolved over time. Contemporary scholars have devised new ways of incorporating agency into the historical analysis, as with critical juncture studies that emphasize the long-run importance of key actor choices. Likewise, with the rise of statistical analysis and the increasing availability of quantitative data sets, scholars have been more apt to combine historical structuralism with quantitative data analysis, thus yielding mixed-methods studies that expand the overall number of cases examined while still emphasizing the causal mechanisms at play in particular cases.

In our view, these trends point toward the resilience of historical-structuralism even as the region continues to evolve politically and as the methodological tools at our disposal multiply. The approach continues to offer a powerful basis for addressing both longstanding questions and the most pressing contemporary issues. Cardoso and Faletto could hardly have hoped for more when they first proposed their historical-structural approach to the study of Latin American politics.

Notes

1 Fernando Henrique Cardoso and Enzo Faletto, *Dependency and Development in Latin America*, trans. Marjory Mattingly Urquidi (Berkeley: University of California Press, 1979), pp. ix–x. Originally published as *Dependencia y desarrallo en América Latina* (Mexico: Siglo Veintiuno Editores, 1969).

2 Fernando Henrique Cardoso, "New Paths: Globalization in Historical Perspective," *Studies in Comparative International Development* vol. 44 (2009), p. 315.

3 Albert Hirschman, *A Bias for Hope* (New Haven: Yale University Press, 1971), p. 27. As cited by Cardoso and Faletto, *Dependency and Development*, p. xi.

4 John Foran, *Taking Power: On the Origins of Third World Revolutions* (Cambridge: Cambridge University Press, 2005); Jeff Goodwin, *No Other Way Out: States and Revolutionary Movements, 1945–1991* (Cambridge: Cambridge University Press, 2001); Timothy P. Wickham-Crowley, *Guerrillas and Revolution in Latin America: A Comparative Study of Insurgents and Regimes Since 1956* (Princeton: Princeton University Press, 1992).

5 In addition to the work cited in the previous footnote, see Susan Eckstein, ed., *Power and Popular Protest: Latin American Social Movements* (Berkeley: University of California Press, 2001); Jeffery M. Paige, *Coffee and Power: Revolution and the Rise of Democracy in Central America* (Cambridge, MA: Harvard University Press, 1997).

6 Wickham-Crowley, *Guerrillas and Revolution*, chap. 6.

7 Foran, *Taking Power*.

8 Susan Eckstein, "The Impact of Revolution on Social Welfare in Latin America," *Theory and Society* 11 (1982): 43–94; John Foran and Jeff Goodwin, "Revolutionary Outcomes in Iran and Nicaragua: Coalitional Fragmentation, War, and the Limits of Social Transformation," *Theory and Society* 22 (1993): 209–47.

9 Theda Skocpol, *States and Social Revolutions: A Comparative Analysis of France, Russia, and China* (Cambridge: Cambridge University Press, 1979).

10 Richard R. Fagen, Carmen Diana Deere, and José Luis Coraggio, eds., *Transition and Development: Problems of Third World Socialism* (New York: Monthly Review Press, 1986); Cole Blasier, *The Hovering Giant: U.S. Responses to Revolutionary Change in Latin America, 1910–1985* (Pittsburgh: University of Pittsburgh Press, 1985).

11 Two well-known works centered on Latin America that adopt this perspective are Guillermo O'Donnell and Philippe Schmitter, *Transitions from Authoritarian Rule: Tentative Conclusions about Uncertain Democracies* (Baltimore: Johns Hopkins University Press, 1986); and John Higley and Richard Gunther, eds., *Elites and Democratic Consolidation: Latin America and Southern Europe* (Cambridge: Cambridge University Press, 1993). See also Robert A. Dahl, *Polyarchy: Participation and Opposition* (New Haven: Yale University Press, 1971); and Adam Przeworski, *Democracy and the Market: Political and Economic Reforms in Eastern Europe and Latin America* (Cambridge: Cambridge University Press, 1991).

12 Dietrich Ruechemeyer, Evelyne Huber Stephens, and John D. Stephens, *Capitalist Development and Democracy* (Chicago: University of Chicago Press, 1992); Ruth Berins Collier, *Paths Toward Democracy: The Working Class and Elites in Western Europe and South America* (Cambridge: Cambridge University Press, 1999); and Elisabeth Jean Wood, *Forging Democracy from Below: Insurgent Transitions in South Africa and El Salvador* (Cambridge: Cambridge University Press, 2000).

13 In addition to the works cited in the note above, see Stephan Haggard and Robert R. Kaufman, *The Political Economy of Democratic Transitions* (Princeton: Princeton University Press, 1995); Juan J. Linz and Alfred Stepan, *Problems of Democratic Transition and Consolidation: Southern Europe, South America, and Post-Communist Europe* (Baltimore: Johns Hopkins University Press, 1996); Paige, *Coffee and Power*; and Deborah J. Yashar, *Demanding Democracy: Reform and Reaction in Costa Rica and Guatemala, 1870s–1950s* (Stanford: Stanford University Press, 1997).

14 Alfred Stepan, *Rethinking Military Politics: Brazil and the Southern Cone* (Princeton: Princeton University Press, 1988); Katherine Hite and Paola Cesarini, eds., *Authoritarian Legacies and Democracy in Latin America and Southern Cone* (Notre Dame: University of Notre Dame Press, 2004); Juan J. Linz and Alfred Stepan, *Problems of Democratic Transition and Consolidation*; and Deborah Yashar, *Demanding Democracy*.

15 Yashar, *Demanding Democracy*.

16 Stepan, *Rethinking Military Politics*, chap 6. See also Anthony Pereira, *Political (In)justice: Authoritarianism and the Rule of Law in Brazil, Chile and Argentina* (University of Pittsburgh Press, 2005).

17 Ruth Berins Collier and David Collier, *Shaping the Political Arena: Critical Junctures, the Labor Movement, and Regime Dynamics in Latin America* (Princeton: Princeton University Press, 1991); Edward L. Gibson, *Class and Conservative Parties: Argentina in Comparative Perspectives* (Baltimore: The Johns Hopkins University Press, 1996); Kenneth Roberts, *Deepening Democracy? The Modern Left and Social Movements in Chile and Peru* (Stanford: Stanford University Press, 1998); and Rebecca Bill Chávez, *The Rule of Law in Nascent Democracies: Judicial Politics in Argentina* (Stanford: Stanford University Press, 2004).

18 Collier and Collier, *Shaping the Political Arena*.

19 Bill Chávez, *The Rule of Law in Nascent Democracies*.

20 Aníbal Pérez-Liñán, *Presidential Impeachment and the New Political Instability in Latin America* (Cambridge: Cambridge University Press, 2007); Robert H. Wilson, Peter M. Ward, Peter K. Pink, and Victoria E. Rodríguez, eds., *Governance in the Americas: Decentralization, Democracy, and Subnational Government in Brazil, Mexico, and the USA* (Notre Dame: University of Notre Dame Press, 2008).

21 George E. Peterson, *Decentralization in Latin America: Learning through Experience* (Washington, DC: World Bank Publications, 1997), p. 1.

22 See, especially, Mala Htun, *Sex and the State: Abortion, Divorce, and the Family Under Latin American Dictatorships and Democracies* (New York: Cambridge University Press, 2003). Other works that address feminism more generally include Karen Kampwirth, *Women and Guerrilla Movements: Nicaragua, El Salvador, Chiapas, Cuba* (University Park: The Pennsylvania State University

Press, 2002) and *Karen Kampwirth, Feminism and the Legacy of Revolution: Nicaragua, El Salvador, Chiapas* (Athens: Ohio University Press, 2004).

23 Htun, *Sex and the State,* chap 4.

24 Deborah Yashar, *Contesting Citizenship in Latin America: The Rise of Indigenous Movements and the Post-Liberal Challenge* (New York: Cambridge University Press, 2005); Donna Lee Van Cott, *The Friendly Liquidation of the Past: The Politics of Diversity in Latin America* (Pittsburgh: University of Pittsburgh Press, 2000); Donna Lee Van Cott, *From Movements to Parties in Latin America: The Evolution of the Ethnic Politics* (Cambridge: Cambridge University Press).

25 Van Cott, *From Movements to Parties in Latin America.*

26 Maria Guadalupe Moog Rodrigues, *Global Environmentalism and Local Politics: Transnational Advocacy Networks in Brazil, Ecuador, and India* (Albany: State University of New York Press, 2004); Katherine Hochstetler and Margaret E. Keck, *Greening Brazil: Environmental Activism in State and Society* (Durham: Duke University Press, 2007).

27 Moog Rodrigues, *Global Environmentalism and Local Politics.*

28 Miguel Angel Centeno, *Blood and Debt: War and the Nation-State in Latin America* (University Park: Pennsylvania State University Press, 2002).

29 Charles Tilly, *Coercion, Capital, and European States, AD 990–1992* (Cambridge, MA: Wiley-Blackwell, 1992).

30 The analysis of critical junctures and path dependence often go together. This is because choices and events at key moments in time (i.e., critical junctures) tend to have an (often unintended) impact on the extent to which future choices and events are possible. See Paul Pierson, *Politics in Time: History, Institutions, and Social Analysis* (Princeton: Princeton University Press, 2004).

31 Collier and Collier, *Shaping the Political Arena*; James Mahoney, *The Legacies of Liberalism: Path Dependence and Political Regimes in Central America* (Baltimore: Johns Hopkins University, 2001); Pierson, *Politics in Time.*

32 James Mahoney, *The Legacies of Liberalism.*

33 Ben Ross Schneider, *Business Politics and the State in Twentieth-Century Latin America* (Cambridge: Cambridge University Press, 2004).

34 Kenneth Roberts, *Deepening Democracy? The Modern Left and Social Movements in Chile and Peru* (Stanford: Stanford University Press, 1988); Victoria Maria Murillo, *Labor Unions, Partisan Coalitions, and Market Reforms in Latin America* (Cambridge: Cambridge University Press, 2001); Katrina Burgess, *Parties and Unions in the New Global Economy* (Pittsburgh: University of Pittsburgh Press, 2004); Marcus J. Kurtz, *Free Market Democracy and the Chilean and Mexican Countryside* (Cambridge: Cambridge University Press, 2004); and Sybil Rhodes, *Social Movements and Free-Market Capitalism in Latin America: Telecommunications, Privatization, and the Rise of Consumer Protest* (Albany: State University of New York Press, 2006).

35 Richard Snyder, *Politics after Neoliberalism: Reregulation in Mexico* (Cambridge: Cambridge University Press, 2001).

36 Ruth Berins Collier and Samuel Handlin, eds., *Reorganizing Popular Politics: Participation and the New Interest Regime in Latin America* (University Park: The Pennsylvania State University Press, 2009).

37 Juan J. Linz and Alfred Stepan, eds., *The Breakdown of Democratic Regimes* (Baltimore: Johns Hopkins University Press, 1978).

38 Alfred Stepan, "Political Leadership and Regime Breakdown: Brazil," in Linz and Stepan, eds., *The Breakdown of Democratic Regimes,* p. 133.

39 Collier and Collier, *Shaping the Political Arena*; Mahoney, *The Legacies of Liberalism.*

40 Peter B. Evans, *Embedded Autonomy: States and Industrial Transformation* (Princeton: Princeton University Press, 1995).

41 Atul Kohli, *State-Directed Development: Political Power and Industrialization in the Global Periphery* (Cambridge: Cambridge University Press, 2004).

42 Yashar, *Demanding Democracy.*

43 Kampwirth, *Women and Guerrilla Movements.*

44 Marcus J. Kurtz, *Free Market Democracy and the Chilean and Mexican Countryside* (Cambridge: Cambridge University Press, 2004).

45 Raúl L. Madrid, *Retiring the State: The Politics of Pension Privatization in Latin America and Beyond* (Stanford: Stanford University Press, 2003). See also Sarah M. Brooks, *Social Protection and the*

Market in Latin America: The Transformation of Social Security Institutions (Cambridge: Cambridge University Press, 2009).

46 Stephen Haggard and Robert R. Kaufman, *Development, Democracy, and Welfare States: Latin America, East Asia, and Eastern Europe* (Princeton: Princeton University Press, 2008).

30

NATURAL AND FIELD EXPERIMENTS IN THE STUDY OF LATIN AMERICAN POLITICS

Thad Dunning

Confounding poses pervasive problems in the social sciences. For example, does granting property titles to poor land squatters boost access to credit markets, thereby fostering broad socioeconomic development (De Soto 2000)? To investigate this question, researchers might compare poor squatters who possess land titles to those who do not. However, differences in access to credit markets could in part be due to factors—such as family background—that also make certain poor squatters more likely to acquire titles to their property. Investigators may seek to control for such confounders, by comparing titled and untitled squatters with similar family backgrounds. Yet, even within strata defined by family background, there may be other difficult-to-measure confounders—such as determination—that are associated with obtaining titles and that also influence economic and political behaviors. Conventional quantitative methods for dealing with confounding, such as multivariate regression, require other essentially unverifiable modeling assumptions to be met, which is a further difficulty.

Social scientists have thus sharply increased their use of field and lab experiments and observational studies such as natural experiments, which may provide a way to address confounding while limiting reliance on the assumptions of conventional quantitative methods (Gerber and Green 2008; Morton and Williams 2010; Dunning 2008a, 2010a). Researchers working on Latin American politics are no exception. In fact, some of the most interesting recent exemplars of this style of research arguably come from research in Latin America, where natural and field experiments have increasingly been used to investigate questions of broad substantive import. Moreover, these methods are sometimes combined with extensive qualitative fieldwork and contextual knowledge that—as I shall argue below—are in fact indispensable for their persuasive use. Natural and field experiments may therefore provide ready complements to the traditional strengths of many researchers working on Latin American politics.

Yet, field and natural experiments can also have significant limitations, which are also important to explore. In this chapter, I describe the growing use of these methods in the study of Latin American politics. After introducing an evaluative framework developed in previous research (Dunning 2010a), I ask whether these methods can answer the kinds of "big" causal questions typical of research on Latin American politics—such as the relationship of democratization to redistribution, the causes and consequences of federalist transfers, or the relationship of electoral rules to policy-making. I argue that while these methods may often be insufficient to answer such questions on their own, they can usefully complement other approaches, and they could be employed with greater intellectual profit in a number of substantive domains.

Natural and Field Experiments in Latin America

It is useful to begin by distinguishing natural and field experiments from other research designs, such as lab experiments, quasi-experiments, or conventional controlled comparisons. Though regrettable from the point of view of terminological clarity, only two of these labels—field and lab experiments—in fact refer to true experiments; natural experiments, quasi-experiments, and controlled comparisons instead refer to observational studies, a distinction I discuss further below. Figure 30.1 charts the conceptual relationship between these various research designs.

Direct manipulation of treatment conditions is the first hallmark of true experiments (left side of Figure 30.1). Thus, in an experiment to estimate the effects of land titles, researchers would extend land titles to some poor squatters (the treatment group), while other squatters would only retain their *de facto* claims to plots (the control group).[1] Such experimental manipulation of treatments plays a key role in experimental accounts of causal inference (Holland 1986).

In randomized controlled experiments, the second hallmark is randomization, which also plays a crucial role. To continue the example above, in a hypothetical randomized controlled experiment, assignment of squatters to *de jure* land titles or the status quo property claims would be done through an actual randomizing device, such as a lottery.[2] Randomization implies that more determined squatters are just as likely to be assigned to the control group—and continue with their status quo property claims—as they are to go into

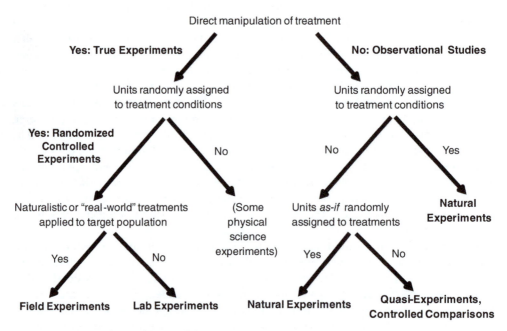

Figure 30.1 A Typology of Research Designs

the treatment group and thereby obtain land titles. Thus, because of randomization, possible confounders such as family background or determination would be balanced across the assigned-to-treatment and assigned-to-control groups, up to random error (Fisher 1935). Large post-titling differences across these groups would then provide reliable evidence for a causal effect of property titles.

Randomized controlled experiments can be further classified as field experiments or lab experiments.[3] Field experiments are randomized controlled experiments in which target populations (or samples thereof) are exposed to naturalistic or "real-world" treatments (bottom-left of Figure 30.1). These are sometimes distinguished from laboratory experiments both by the nature of the experimental stimuli and of the types of units exposed to it; the treatments in lab experiments are sometimes seen as less "naturalistic" and administered to subjects who may not be drawn from a target population of direct interest.[4] However, as Gerber and Green (2008) point out, whether any given study should be thought of as a lab or field experiment depends on the research question being posed. For example, a canonical lab experiment in psychology or behavioral economics might ask college students to play stylized games, as a way to assess attitude formation or decision-making processes. Yet, if one seeks to understand the decision-making of college students in abstract economic settings, such lab experiments in which undergraduates make allocative decisions could be regarded as field experiments. Notwithstanding these conceptual gray spots, I will describe the randomized controlled experiments discussed in this chapter as field experiments, since they largely involve the exposure of Latin American citizens to real-world stimuli—for instance, corruption allegations against politicians involved in actual political campaigns.[5]

Such true experiments can be contrasted with observational studies, in at least two ways. First, with observational studies, there is no experimental intervention or manipulation (right-side of Figure 30.1); this is the definitional criterion. Here, the researcher studies the world as she encounters it. Observational studies remain the dominant form of research in most social-science disciplines; one reason for this is that in many political or economic settings, direct experimental manipulation may be expensive or unethical. Moreover, institutional variables and other treatments of interest to political scientists may not often be amenable to direct experimental manipulation.

Second, many observational studies also lack randomization. Standard controlled comparisons such as "matching" designs, for example, do not involve randomization to treatment conditions (bottom-right of Figure 30.1). In the "quasi-experiments" discussed by Donald Campbell and Stanley (1963), non-random assignment to treatments is also a central feature (Achen 1986: 4).[6] For example, in many observational studies, subjects self-select into treatment or control groups. For instance, some squatters may exert effort that allows them to obtain land titles, while others do not. Politicians may also choose to extend titles to favored constituents. Such selection processes raise standard concerns about confounding, because squatters who obtain land titles (perhaps by cultivating favors from politicians) may be more determined than those who do not, or may differ in other ways that matter for socio-economic outcomes. Thus, post-titling differences between titled and untitled squatters are difficult to attribute to the effects of titles: they could be due to the titles, the confounders, or both.

Natural experiments differ from other observational studies in this second respect, however. While there is no direct manipulation by the researcher of assignment to treatment conditions—and thus, natural experiments are observational studies—with a natural experiment, a researcher can make a credible claim that treatment assignment is random—or as good as random. In some natural experiments, as Figure 30.1 suggests, a lottery or other true randomizing device assigns subjects at random to treatment and control conditions. In this case, the distinction between a randomized controlled experiment and a natural experiment with true randomization simply concerns whether the investigator has planned and manipulated a particular treatment—in the case of a randomized controlled experiment—or instead has simply found that this treatment has been applied at random by policy makers or other actors.[7]

In other natural experiments, by contrast, social and political processes instead are claimed to have assigned units *as-if* at random to a key intervention—even though there is no true randomizing device involved. With such natural experiments, much attention should be focused on evaluating the central assumption and definitional criterion of *as-if* random assignment.

Social scientists increasingly seek to discover and use natural experiments, because of their potential usefulness in overcoming standard problems of confounding; another advantage with natural as well as field experiments is that data analysis can be substantially simpler and can rest on more credible assumptions than conventional quantitative tools such as multivariate regression (Dunning 2008a, 2010a; Sekhon 2009). Yet, there can be substantial limitations as well, which I discuss below.

Natural Experiments in Latin America Politics

Table 30.1 provides a non-exhaustive list of unpublished, forthcoming, or recently published studies of Latin American politics that use natural experiments. The listed studies suggest the breadth of substantive topics that have been investigated using these methods, as well as the range of countries in which such studies have been undertaken. In this section, I survey several recent examples of natural experiments in Latin America, before turning to a discussion of field experiments.

As Table 30.1 suggests, natural experiments include several types—including what I call "standard" natural experiments, as well as specialized types such as regression-discontinuity (RD) designs and instrumental-variables (IV) designs. Standard natural experiments involve random or as-if random assignment to treatment and control conditions but otherwise may encompass a variety of different specific designs; the more specific features of RD and IV designs are discussed below. One may also distinguish natural experiments by whether treatment assignment is truly randomized or is only claimed to be as good as random, as noted in the second column of Table 30.1.

An example of a natural experiment with true randomization is the study by De la O (2010), who compares Mexican villages randomly selected to receive conditional cash transfers, through the government's PROGRESA program, twenty-one months before the 2000 presidential elections to those randomly selected to enter the program only six months before the elections. She finds that early enrollment in PROGRESA caused an increase in electoral turnout of 7 percent and an increase in incumbent vote share of 16 percent, a finding that sheds light on the electoral efficacy of federal transfers in this context.

Similarly, Angrist and colleagues (Angrist et al. 2002; Angrist, Bettinger, and Kremer 2006) provide an example of a natural experiment in which authorities used randomized lotteries to distribute vouchers for private schools in Bogotá, Colombia.[8] These authors compare school completion rates and test scores among lottery winners—who received vouchers at random—with lottery losers, finding that winners were more likely to finish eighth grade as well as secondary school and scored 0.2 standard deviations higher on achievement tests. While the focus here is on the educational impacts of vouchers,

Table 30.1 Natural Experiments in the Study of Latin American Politics

Authors	Standard natural experiment, RD, or IV design★ (random or as-if random assignment)	Substantive focus	Source of field or natural experiment	Country	Simple difference-of-means test (without controls)?
Angrist et al. (2002, 2006)	Standard (random)	Effects of private school vouchers on school completion rates and test performance	Allocation of vouchers by lottery	Colombia	Yes (2002 has cohort dummies)
Boas and Hidalgo (2010)	RD (as-if random)	Effect of incumbency on access to media	Comparison of approval rates for community radio license applications by near-winners and near-losers of elections	Brazil	Yes
Boas, Hidalgo, and Richardson (2010)	RD (as-if random)	Effect of campaign donations on access to government contracts	Compares public works contracts obtained by donors to near-winners and near-losers	Brazil	No
Brollo and Nannicini (2010)	RD (as-if random)	Effect of partisan affiliation of incumbent mayor on federal transfers to municipalities	Compares winners and losers of close elections, stratifying on whether winner is member of federal executive's coalition	Brazil	No
Brollo, Nannicini, Perotti, and Tabellini (2010)	RD (as-if random)	Effect of transfers from federal government to municipalities on municipal corruption and candidate quality	Discontinuities based on population-based revenue-sharing formula	Brazil	No
Chamon, de Mello, and Firpo (2009)	RD (as-if random)	Effects of second-round runoff on political competition and fiscal outcomes	Population-based discontinuity in voting system used in mayoral elections	Brazil	No

(continued)

Table 30.1 Continued

Authors	Standard natural experiment, RD, or IV design* (random or as-if random assignment)	Substantive focus	Source of field or natural experiment	Country	Simple difference-of-means test (without controls)?
De la O (2010)	Standard (random)	Effect of length of time in conditional cash transfer program on voter turnout and support for incumbent	Comparison of early- and late-participating villages based on randomized roll-out of program	Mexico	No★★
Ferraz and Finan (2008)	Standard (as-if random) CHECK	Effect of corruption audits on electoral accountability	Public release of randomized corruption audits in Brazil	Brazil	Yes (but with state fixed effects)
Ferraz and Finan (2010)	RD (as-if random)	Impact of monetary incentives on politician quality and performance	Salary caps for municipal politicians based on municipality size	Brazil	No
Fujiwara (2008)	RD (as-if random)	Effects of second-round runoff on first-round vote shares	Population-based discontinuity in voting system used in mayoral elections	Brazil	No★★★
Fujiwara (2009)	RD (as-if random)	Effects of electronic voting technology on de facto enfranchise-ment and fiscal policy	Discontinuity in use of voting technology at threshold of registered voters	Brazil	No★★★
Galiani and Schargrodsky (2004)	Standard (as-if random)	Effects of land titling for the poor on economic activity and attitudes	Judicial challenges to transfer of property titles to squatters	Argentina	Yes
Hidalgo (2010)	RD (as-if random)	Effects of electronic voting technology on de facto enfranchise-ment, support for programmatic parties, and fraud	Discontinuity in use of voting technology at threshold of registered voters	Brazil	Yes

Authors	Standard natural experiment, RD, or IV design* (random or as-if random assignment)	Substantive focus	Source of field or natural experiment	Country	Simple difference-of-means test (without controls)?
Hidalgo, Naidu, Nichter, and Richardson (2010)	IV (as-if random)	Effects of economic conditions on land invasions in Brazil	Shocks to economic conditions due to rainfall patterns	Brazil	No****
Litschig and Morrison (2009)	RD (as-if random)	Effects of federal transfers to municipalities on incumbent re-election probabilities	Discontinuities based on population-based revenue-sharing formula	Brazil	Yes
Manacorda, Miguel, and Vigorito (2009)	RD (as-if random)	The effect of a cash-transfer program on support for the incumbent government	Discontinuity in program assignment based on a pre-treatment eligibility score	Uruguay	Yes
Titiunik (2009)	RD (as-if random)	Incumbency advantage in mayoral elections	Comparison of municipalities barely won and barely lost by political parties	Brazil	Yes

* See text for the distinction drawn between standard natural experiments, regression-discontinuity (RD) designs and instrumental-variables (IV) designs.

** Some complications are introduced by non-overlapping units of assignment and outcome, which leads to estimation of interaction models.

*** Local linear regression is used, though graphic difference-of-means comparisons are made.

**** The treatment conditions and/or instrumental variables are continuous in these studies, complicating the calculation of differences-of-means. – Full results are pending.

researchers could certainly take advantage of such lotteries to ask political questions: for example, how does exposure to private schooling influence political attitudes towards the proper role of government in the economy?

Other standard natural experiments rely instead, however, on the assumption of *as-if* random assignment. Galiani and Schargrodsky (2004) provide an interesting example on the effects of land titling in Argentina. In 1981, a group of squatters organized by the Catholic church occupied an urban wasteland in the province of Buenos Aires, dividing the land into similar-sized parcels which were allocated to individual families. A 1984 law, adopted after the return to democracy in 1983, expropriated this land, with the intention of transferring title to the squatters. However, some of the original owners then challenged the expropriation in court, leading to long delays in the transfer of titles to property owned by those owners, while other titles were ceded and transferred to squatters immediately.

The legal action therefore created a "treatment" group—squatters to whom titles were ceded immediately—and a control group—squatters to whom titles were not ceded. Galiani and Schargrodsky (2004) find significant differences across the treatment and control groups in average housing investment, household structure, and educational attainment of children—though not in access to credit markets, which contradicts De Soto's theory that the poor will use titled property to collateralize debt.

Yet, was the assignment of squatters to these treatment and control groups really as good as random—as must be true in a valid natural experiment? In 1981, these authors assert, neither squatters nor Catholic church organizers could have successfully predicted which *particular* parcels would eventually have their titles transferred in 1984 and which would not. On the basis of extensive interviews and other qualitative fieldwork, the authors argue convincingly that idiosyncratic factors explain the decision of some owners to challenge expropriation; moreover, the government offered very similar compensation in per-meter terms to the original owners in both the treatment and the control groups, which helps makes the assertion of *as-if* random assignment compelling. Galiani and Schargrodsky (2004) also show that pre-treatment characteristics of squatters, such as age and sex, as well as characteristics of the parcels themselves, such as distance from polluted creeks, are statistically unrelated to the granting of titles—just as they would be, in expectation, if squatters were truly assigned titles at random. Note that the natural experiment therefore plays a key role in making causal inferences persuasive. Without it, confounders could explain ex-post differences between squatters with and without titles.

Regression-Discontinuity (RD) Designs

In regression-discontinuity (RD) designs, assignment to treatment is determined by the value of a covariate, sometimes called a forcing variable; there is a sharp discontinuity in the probability of receiving treatment at a particular threshold value of this covariate (Campbell and Stanley 1963: 61–64; Rubin 1977).[9] For example, Thistlewaite and Campbell (1960) compared students who just scored above the qualifying score on a national merit scholarship program—and thus received public recognition for their scholastic achievement—with those who scored just below the required score and thus did not receive recognition from the scholarship program. Because there is an element of unpredictability and luck in exam performance—and so long as the threshold is not manipulated ex-post to include particular exam-takers—students just above the threshold are likely to be very similar to students just below the threshold. Comparisons of students just above and just below the critical threshold may thus be used to estimate the effect of public recognition of scholastic achievement, among this group of students.

As Table 30.1 suggests, regression-discontinuity designs have found especially wide use in recent work on Latin American politics. Fujiwara (2009) and Hidalgo (2010), for instance, use regression-discontinuity designs to study the impact of electronic voting on de facto enfranchisement, patterns of partisan support, and fiscal policy in Brazil. In the 1998 elections, municipalities with more than 40,500 registered voters used electronic ballots, while municipalities with fewer than 40,500 voters continued to use traditional paper ballots. The electronic voting machines displayed candidates' names, party affiliations, and photographs; this was thought to ease the voting process for illiterate voters, in particular. Municipalities "just above" and "just below" the threshold of 40,500 registered voters should on average be highly similar; indeed, since the threshold was announced in May of 1998 and the number of registered voters was recorded in the municipal elections of 1996, municipalities should not have been able to manipulate their position in relation to the threshold. Nor is there any evidence that the particular threshold was chosen by municipalities to exclude or include particular municipalities. (The threshold was applied uniformly throughout the country with the exception of four states). Thus, comparisons around the threshold can be plausibly used to estimate the impact of the voting technology.

Hidalgo (2010) and Fujiwara (2009) find that introduction of electronic voting increased the effective franchise in legislative elections by about 13–15 percentage points or about 33 percent—a massive effect that appears more pronounced in poorer municipalities with higher illiteracy rates. While Fujiwara (2009) finds that this de facto enfranchisement had a large and positive effect on votes received by the Worker's Party (PT) and presents some evidence that states in which a larger proportion of the electorate voted electronically had more progressive fiscal policies, Hidalgo (2010) finds that expansion of the franchise did not greatly tilt the ideological balance in the national Chamber of Deputies and may have even favored center-right candidates, on average. Yet, voting reforms also elevated the proportion of voters who voted for party lists only—rather than choosing individual candidates, as allowed under Brazil's open list proportional representation electoral rules—and also boosted the vote shares of parties with clear ideological identities. Moreover, the introduction of voting machines led to substantial declines in the vote shares of incumbent "machine" parties in several northeastern states. Hidalgo (2010) suggests that the introduction of voting machines contributed to the strengthening of programmatic politics in Brazil, an outcome noted by many scholars studying the country. Thus, here is an example of a natural-experimental study that contributes decisively to a very "big" question of broad importance in developing democracies, namely, the sources of transitions from more clientelistic to more programmatic forms of politics.

Regression-discontinuity research designs have also been used extensively to study the economic and political impacts of federal transfers in Latin America. Green (2005), for example, calculates the electoral returns of the Mexican conditional cash-transfer program, PROGRESA (the same program studied by De La O 2010), using a regression-discontinuity design based on a municipal poverty ranking. Similarly, Manacorda, Miguel, and Vigorito (2009) use a discontinuity in program assignment based on a pre-treatment eligibility score to study the effects of cash transfers on support for the incumbent Frente Amplio government in Uruguay. They find that program beneficiaries are much more likely than non-beneficiaries to support the incumbent, by around 11 to 14 percentage points. Litschig and Morrison (2009) study the effect of federal transfers on municipal incumbents' vote shares in Brazil, while Brollo, Nannicini, Perotti, and Tabellini (2010) study the effect of such transfers on political corruption and on the qualities of political candidates. Both of these latter studies take advantage of the fact that the size of some federal transfers in Brazil depends on given population thresholds, so they can construct regression-discontinuity designs in which municipalities just on either side of the relevant thresholds are compared.

A different kind of regression-discontinuity design, which has also found growing use in Latin America, takes advantage of the fact that in very close and fair elections, there is an element of luck and unpredictability in the outcome; thus, underlying attributes of near-winners may not differ greatly from near-losers. As Lee (2008) suggested in his study of the U.S. Congress, this may allow for natural-experimental comparisons: since near-winners and near-losers of close elections should be nearly identical, on average, comparisons of these groups after an election can be used to estimate the effects of winning office.

For instance, Titiunik (2009) studies the incumbency advantage of political parties in Brazil's municipal mayor elections, comparing municipalities where a party barely lost the

2000 mayor elections to municipalities where it barely won. Contrary to findings in the United States, she finds evidence of a strong *negative* effect of incumbency on both the vote share and the probability of winning in the following election; the significant estimated effect sizes range from around negative 4 percentage points of the vote share for the Liberal Front Party (PFL) to around negative 19 percentage points for the Party of the Brazilian Democratic Movement (PMDB).

Using a related research design, Boas, Hidalgo, and Richardson (2010) study the effect of campaign contributions on government contracts received by donors. In their working paper, these authors compare the returns to donations to near-winners and near-losers of campaigns, showing that public-works companies that rely on government contracts may receive a substantial monetary return on electoral investments. The effect size is striking: these authors find that public works firms who donate to winners receive about 2,300 times their donation in additional federal contracts.

Next, in a study of the relationship between political incumbency and media access, Boas and Hidalgo (2010) show that near-winners of city council elections are much more likely than near-losers to have their applications for community radio licenses approved by the federal government, a finding that reinforces previous research on the political control of the media in Brazil. Finally, Brollo and Nannicini (2010) use an RD design to study the effect of partisan affiliation on federal transfers to municipalities in Brazil, comparing winners and losers of close elections and stratifying on whether winner is member of the president's coalition.

Regression-discontinuity designs have also been used to study the political and economic impact of electoral rules. For instance, Fujiwara (2008) exploits the fact that the Brazilian Federal Constitution states that municipalities with less than 200,000 registered voters must use a single-ballot plurality rule (a first-past-the-post system where the candidate with the most votes is elected) to elect their mayors, while municipalities with more than 200,000 voters must use the dual-ballot plurality rule (second-round "runoff"), a system where voters may vote twice. He finds that in the neighborhood of this threshold, the change from single-ballot to second-round runoff systems increases voting for third-place finishers and decreases the difference between third-place and first- and second-place finishers, a finding consistent both with strategic voting and with the observation of Duverger (1954) and of Cox (1997) that in elections for *m* seats, *m+1* candidates should command most of the votes. Chamon, de Mello, and Firpo (2009) extend this same idea, finding that the greater political competition induced by the discontinuous change in electoral rules in mayor elections at the threshold of 200,000 voters induces greater investment and reduces current expenditures, particularly personnel expenditures. Finally, Ferraz and Finan (2010) take advantage of a constitutional amendment in Brazil that sets salary caps on the wages of local legislators as a function of the population size of municipalities. Using this rule to construct an RD design, they find that higher wages increase legislative productivity and political entry but also increase reelection rates among incumbent politicians.

Instrumental-variables Designs

A final kind of natural experiment worthy of mention is the instrumental-variables (IV) design. Consider the challenge of inferring the impact of a given independent variable on a particular dependent variable—where this inference is made more difficult, given the strong possibility that reciprocal causation or omitted variable bias may pose a problem for causal inference. The solution offered by the IV design is to find an additional variable—an instrument—that is correlated with the independent variable but could not be influenced by the dependent variable or correlated with its other causes. That is, the instrumental variable is treated as if it "assigns" units to values of the independent variable in a way that is *as-if* random, even though no explicit randomization occurred.

For this IV approach to be valid, several conditions must typically hold. First, and crucially, assignment to the instrument must be random or as-if random. Second, while the instrument must be correlated with the treatment variable of interest, it must not independently affect the dependent variable, above and beyond its effect on the treatment variable. For further discussion of these and other assumptions, see Sovey and Green (2011) or Dunning (2008b).

One example of an IV design in research on Latin America is Hidalgo, Naidu, Nichter, and Richardson (2010), who study the effects of economic growth on land invasions in Brazil. Arguing that reverse causality or omitted variables could be a concern—for instance, land invasions could influence growth, and unmeasured institutions could influence both growth and invasions—these authors use rainfall growth as an instrumental variable for economic growth.[10] The idea is that annual changes in rainfall provide as-if random shocks to economic growth. The authors find that decreases in growth, instrumented by rainfall, indeed encourage land invasions.

This application illuminates characteristic strengths and limitations of IV designs. Rainfall certainly appears to affect growth, as required by the IV approach; yet, it rainfall may or may not influence land invasions only through its effect on growth, which is also required for the approach to be valid. Any direct effect of rainfall—for instance, if floods make it harder to organize invasions—would violate the assumptions of instrumental-variables regression model. Variation in rainfall may also influence growth only in particular sectors, such as agriculture, and growth in distinct economic sectors may have idiosyncratic effects on the likelihood of invasions (Dunning 2008b).

Field Experiments in Latin America

Other studies of Latin American politics have instead deployed field experiments, in which the manipulation is under investigators' control. Recent field experiments on Latin American politics have also addressed a variety of substantive questions. However, as the shorter list in Table 30.2 (compared to Table 30.1) may imply, it is fair to say that this methodological approach is in its infancy in this substantive realm.[11]

For instance, do voters hold politicians accountable when exposed to information about politicians' performance in office? To investigate this question, De Figueiredo, Hidalgo, and Kasahara (2010) sent flyers to voters in randomly selected precincts during the 2008 mayoral elections in São Paulo, describing the corruption convictions of the center-right candidate (first treatment) and the center-left candidate (second treatment). They then compared electoral outcomes in these sets of precincts to those in which flyers were not distributed (the control), finding that information about corruption convictions reduced turnout and the vote-share of the center-left candidate, though not for the center-right candidate.

Similarly, Chong, De La O, Karlan, and Wantchekon (2011) randomly assigned precincts in several Mexican states to receive information about municipalities' overall spending, distribution of resources to the poor, and corruption, or to receive no such information. Like De Figueiredo et al. (2010), they found that corruption information suppressed turnout in municipal elections, while expenditure information increased electoral participation and incumbent parties' vote share.

Table 30.2 Field Experiments in the Study of Latin American Politics

Authors	Substantive focus	Source of field experiment	Country	Simple difference-of-means test (without controls)?	Relevance of Intervention
De Figueiredo, Hidalgo, and Kasahara (2010)	Effect of information about corruption on voter behavior	Randomized distribution of flyers informing voters of corruption allegations against mayoral candidates in São Paulo	Brazil	Yes	
De La O, Chong, Karlan, and Wantchekon (2009)	Effect of information about municipal spending, resource distribution to the poor, and corruption on turnout and vote choice	Randomized distribution of auditors reports about spending, distribution, and corruption in several Mexican states	Mexico	Sort of	
Fried, Lagunes, and Venkataramani (2010)	The effect of citizens' social status on corrupt bribe-seeking by police	Randomization of socioeconomic attributes of drivers committing traffic infractions	Mexico	Yes	
Hyde (2010)	Effect of election monitoring on presence and displacement of electoral fraud	Randomization of electoral observers to voting centers and polling stations	Nicaragua	--	
Lagunes (2009)	Socioeconomic attributes and access to government information	Randomized information about individual political/economic connections in freedom of information act requests	Mexico	Yes	

★ Some complications are introduced by non-overlapping units of assignment and outcome, which leads to estimation of interaction models.
★★ Local linear regression is used, though graphic difference-of-means comparisons are made.
★★★ The treatment conditions and/or instrumental variables are continuous in these studies, complicating the calculation of differences-of-means. – Full results are pending.

Other field experiments in Latin America have investigated how wealth or political connections may affect citizens' access to key services of the state. For example, Fried, Lagunes, and Venkataramani (2010) employed an experiment in Mexico City, in which automobile drivers committed identical traffic infractions but socioeconomic characteristics of the drivers and their cars were varied at random; they found some evidence that officers solicited bribes disproportionately from poorer individuals. Lagunes (2009), on the other hand, found that requests for documents under Freedom of Information laws in Mexico were about equally attended to, regardless of any information provided about the wealth and political connections of applicants.

Finally, Hyde (2010) randomly assigned election monitors to voting centers, as well as polling stations within those centers, in the 2006 Nicaraguan general elections. The experimental design allowed her to detect whether electoral monitoring surpressed fraud (by comparing centers with monitors to those without monitors) or displaced fraud (by comparing polling stations with and without monitors, within voting centers assigned to monitoring). Hyde did not find strong evidence of either supression or displacement in this election.

Beyond these natural and field experiments, other experimental work in Latin America can also be mentioned. Of particular interest is Gonzalez-Ocantos, Kiewiet de Jonge, Meléndez, Osorio, and Nickerson (2010), who estimate the incidence of vote-buying using a list experiment embedded in a survey.[12] This technique provides an innovative way to overcome problems with social desirability bias in studies of vote-buying and suggests that the prevalence of this practice may be much greater than traditional surveys suggest. Dunning (2010b) uses an experiment to compare the effects of candidate race and class on voter preferences in Brazil, while Finan and Schechter (2010) use survey-experimental measures of reciprocity and survey data on vote-buying to argue that individuals with greater internalized norms of reciprocity—who are thus less likely to renege on implicit vote-buying contracts—are disproportionately targeted for clientelist transfers in Paraguay. Finally, Desposato (2007) uses an experiment to study the effects of positive and negative campaigning, comparing responses of survey respondents to videos containing negative, positive, or no campaign message and finding strong effects of vote and turnout intentions.

Strengths and Limitations of Field and Natural Experiments in Latin America

The growing use of field and natural experiments in the study of Latin American politics raises the questions: What are their strengths and limitations? Can these methods make important contributions to answering the broad substantive questions that tend to animate scholars of Latin American politics?

Elsewhere, I have suggested three criteria along which natural experiments (as well as other research designs) may be evaluated: the plausibility of *as-if* random assignment, the credibility of statistical models, and the substantive relevance of the intervention (Dunning 2010a). In Latin America as elsewhere, specific field and natural experiments may vary with respect to these three criteria. Tradeoffs between these dimensions may routinely arise in any particular study, and good research can be understood as the process of managing these tradeoffs astutely.

With respect to the first criterion—the plausibility of *as-if* random assignment—field experiments tend to be very strong, barring some failure of randomization. So do natural experiments with true randomization, such as the Colombia voucher studies. Strong regression-discontinuity designs and some "standard" natural experiments (such as the Argentina land titling study) can be quite compelling on these grounds as well.

However, other studies may leave something to be desired in this respect, which can undercut the claim that a natural experiment is being used (see Dunning 2008a, 2010a). In an alleged natural experiment, this assertion should therefore be supported both by the available empirical evidence—for example, by showing that treatment and control groups are statistically equivalent on measured pre-treatment covariates, just as they would likely be with true randomization—and by *a priori* reasoning and substantive knowledge about the process by which treatment assignment took place.[13] As I discuss further below, this kind of knowledge is often gained only through intensive and close-range fieldwork.

On the second criterion—the credibility of statistical models—field and natural experiments should in principle be strong as well. After all, random or as-if random assignment should ensure that treatment assignment is statistically independent of other factors that influence outcomes. Thus, the need to adjust for confounding variables is minimal, and a simple difference-of-means test—without control variables—suffices to assess the causal effect of treatment assignment.[14]

Unfortunately, this analytic simplicity is not inherent in the experimental or natural experimental approach. Indeed, many studies analyzing experimental or natural experimental data only present the results of fitting large multivariate regression models—the statistical assumptions of which are difficult to explicate and defend, let alone validate, and for which risks of data mining associated with the fitting of multiple statistical specifications can arise. Studies of Latin American politics are no exception. In the final column of Table 30.1, I indicate whether a simple, unadjusted difference-of-means test is used to evaluate the null hypothesis of no effect of treatment. While I use a quite permissive coding here, only a bare majority of the studies in the table report unadjusted differences-of-means tests, in addition to any auxiliary analyses.[15] For further discussion of these points, see Dunning (2010a).

Finally, a third dimension along which research designs may vary involves the theoretical and substantive relevance of the intervention. Roughly speaking, this criterion corresponds to answers to the question: does the intervention assigned by Nature shed light on the effects of a treatment about which we are interested for substantive, policy, or social-scientific purposes? Answers to this question might be more or less affirmative for a number of distinct reasons. For instance, the type of subjects or units exposed to the intervention might be more or less like the populations in which we are most interested (Campbell and Stanley 1963). Next, the particular treatment that has been manipulated by Nature might have idiosyncratic effects that are possibly distinct from the effects of treatments we care about most (Dunning 2008a, 2008b). Finally, natural-experimental interventions (like the interventions in some true experiments) may "bundle" many distinct treatments or components of treatments, limiting the extent to which a natural experiment isolates the effect of a treatment that we care most about for particular substantive or social-scientific purposes. Below, I will comment further on the success of field and natural experiments in Latin America along this dimension.

Underlying all three of these dimensions is a fourth that is crucial for achieving success on the first three dimensions: qualitative methods and substantive knowledge. Indeed, the persuasive use of natural experiments often relies on extensive contextual knowledge—for example, in the Argentina squatters study, on the process by which treatment assignment took place. Case-based knowledge is also often necessary to recognize and validate a potential natural experiment, and the skills of many qualitative researchers are well-suited to the implementation of field experiments. In both field and natural experiments, "causal process observations" (Collier, Brady, and Seawright 2010) can enrich understanding of both mechanisms and outcomes, perhaps through the kind of "experimental ethnography" recommended by Sherman and Strang (2004; see Paluck 2008).[16] Indeed, the act of collecting the original data used in natural and field experiments—rather than using off-the-shelf data, as is often the case in conventional quantitative analysis—virtually requires scholars to do fieldwork in some form, which may make scholars aware of the process of treatment assignment and of details that may be important for interpreting causal effects.[17] Many fieldwork-oriented researchers working in Latin America may thus be well-positioned to exploit natural and field experiments as one methodological tool in an overall research program.

Research on Latin American politics has often raised important substantive questions that often end up stimulating research on other regions as well—such as the sources of democratic breakdown and democratization, the causes and consequences of federalism, or the relationship between political parties and social movements. It is therefore natural for a survey of natural and field experiments in Latin America to ask: can these methods help answer such "big" questions? In this respect, assessing the substantive relevance of intervention—the third dimension of the evaluative framework discussed above—seems particularly relevant for studies of Latin American politics.

A first point to make in this respect is that many of the studies discussed above do not consider apparently trivial topics. For instance, these studies investigate such questions as the relationship of voting technologies to de facto enfranchisement of illiterates (Fujiwara 2009); the impact of electoral rules on policy-making (Fujiwara 2008; Chamon et al. 2009); the effect of federal transfers on support for political incumbents (De La O 2010; Manacorda et al. 2009); and the economic returns to campaign donations (Boas et al. 2010). They also estimate the party-based electoral advantage provided by incumbency (Titiunik 2009) and investigate other topics that may be key for democratic "deepening," such as the ability of voters to hold politicians accountable for corrupt acts (De Figueiredo, Hidalgo, and Kasah 2010, Chong et al. 2011). These are important topics, and investigating them empirically has previously posed considerable challenges: after all, confounding factors are typically associated with electoral rules, federal transfers, or campaign donations, which makes it difficult to infer the causal effects of such variables. Thus, it seems that these field and natural experiments usefully contribute to the study of the topics discussed by other contributors to this volume, such as role of political parties in Latin America (chapter 4), the causes and consequences of decentralization and federalism (chapter 3), and the nature of accountability and representation (chapter 8).

Yet, my survey of the recent rise of natural and field experiments in Latin America also suggests some weaknesses. For example, one apparent limitation is the absence to date of large-scale comparison across the various "micro" studies discussed here. Notice, for instance, that all of the studies listed in Table 30.1 are single-country studies.[18] This is not necessarily bad for all research questions. After all, within-country comparisons have been praised for a number of different reasons (Snyder 2001), and they are increasingly prevalent in comparative politics. Yet, the apparent "one-off" character of some of these experimental and natural experimental studies may limit the extent to which their results are integrated in an explicitly comparative framework.

It is important to point out that this defect is not inherent in these methods. Indeed, the results from some of the separate studies listed in Table 30.1 could allow for interesting comparisons across countries. For instance, Manacorda et al.'s (2009) study of the electoral effects of federal transfers in Uruguay is similar to a host of studies on the political impact of

PROGRESA in Mexico (Green 2005; De La O 2010), as well as conditional cash-transfer programs in other countries. In principle, one could also replicate the field experiments listed in the table across multiple countries. Of course, rigorous causal inferences may not be easy to draw from divergent results across countries, since many factors vary across each context. Yet, interesting insights might nonetheless be obtained from integrating experiments or natural experiments in a more systematically comparative framework.

This chapter's survey also suggests that while analysts increasingly employ several particular kinds of natural experiments—such as regression-discontinuity designs in which near-winners and near-losers of elections are compared—there may also be many ways to extend such designs in interesting and novel directions, as in the RD study by Boas and Hidalgo (2010) on the economic returns to campaign contributions in Brazil. In addition, many distinct kinds of "standard" natural experiments (i.e., those in which a regression-discontinuity or instrumental-variables strategy is not used) may await researchers alert to their possible existence. The list of published, forthcoming, or working papers listed in Table 30.1 may represent only the beginning of efforts to use such methods, together with other approaches, to investigate substantively important topics.

In sum, the increasing use of natural and field experiments does appear promising in many ways. After all, strong research design can play a vital role in bolstering valid causal inference. Random or as-if random assignment to treatment plays a key role in overcoming pervasive issues of confounding. Strong research designs also permit simple and transparent data analysis, at least in principle if not always in practice. Finally, field and natural experiments can sometimes be used to address big, important questions, though the extent to which an intervention is deemed theoretically relevant may depend on the nature of the question and the state of scientific progress in answering it.

Yet, research design alone is also rarely sufficient. Many modes of inquiry seem to be involved in successful causal inference, and field and natural experiments may be most likely to be useful when combined with other methods, as one part of an overall research agenda. For scholars of Latin American politics, particularly those oriented towards intensive fieldwork, incorporating natural or field experiments into a broader project may allow successful multi-method work that leverages traditional strengths in the field while also helping to bolster valid causal inference. In this way, natural and field experiments may usefully inform the broad debates discussed by other contributors to this volume.

Notes

1 In some experiments, what is manipulated is *assignment* to treatment conditions; I do not focus further attention on this subtlety here.

2 Though many experiments are randomized controlled experiments, some are not; for instance, in some physical science experiments, stimuli are under the control of the experimental researcher, but there is no randomization of units to treatment conditions (and there may be no "control" group).

3 There are, of course, other varieties of randomized controlled experiments, such as survey experiments, in which the effects of variation in question order, the content of vignettes posed to respondents, or other treatments in the context of survey questionnaires are studied.

4 Thus, a hypothetical experiment in which squatters are assigned at random to receive *de jure* titles or instead retain only *de facto* property claims can be described as a field experiment, if researchers are interested in the effect of actual land titles on the real-world behavior of poor squatters.

5 A number of recent studies might also be described as "lab-in-the-field" experiments, in which subjects from a target population of interest are recruited—for example, through door-to-door

interviews with a probability sample of residents—but play behavioral games or are exposed to other treatments that are standard in lab experiments.

6 The lack of randomization involved in this research design helped generate Campbell's famous check-list of threats to internal validity in quasi-experiments.

7 In some settings, the distinction may not imply a major difference: if scholars are interested in the effects of lotteries for school vouchers in Colombia (an example discussed below), whether the lotteries are conducted by policy makers or by researchers may be trivial. In other settings, however, the greater degree of researcher control over the nature of the manipulation afforded by randomized controlled experiments may be crucial for testing particular theoretical or substantive claims. It is thus useful to retain the distinction between observational studies—even those that feature true randomization—and randomized controlled experiments.

8 Such natural experiments are like true experiments in that the treatment is randomized, yet the manipulation is not typically introduced by the researcher, making these observational studies.

9 If the treatment has an effect, there may be a sharp discontinuity in the regression lines relating the outcome to the forcing variable on either side of the threshold, which is what gives the method its name. This name does not imply that regression modeling is the best way to analyze data from an RD design.

10 The approach is similar to Miguel, Satyanath, and Sergenti's (2004) use of rainfall growth to instrument for economic growth, in a study of the effect of growth on civil war in Africa.

11 Of course, the studies in Tables 30.1 and 30.2 are not intended as exhaustive censuses of existing natural and field experiments in the study of Latin American politics.

12 In this list experiment, respondents are shown a list of activities that might have happened during the last election; the treatment condition includes a mention of vote-buying, while the control condition omits this item. Respondents are asked to report *how many* of the items on the occurred during the last elections, not which ones. The experiment may thus circumvent social desirability biases that prevent the direct reporting of vote buying in response to direct questions. In fact, Gonzalez-Ocantos et al. (2010) show that using the list experiment can sharply elevate estimates of the incidence of vote-buying.

13 "Pre-treatment covariates" are those whose values are thought to have been determined before the intervention of interest took place. In particular, they are not themselves seen as outcomes of the treatment.

14 The causal and statistical model that justifies such simple comparisons is the Neyman (also called the Neyman-Rubin-Holland) model; see Dunning (2010a) for further discussion.

15 If an analyst reports results from a bivariate regression of the outcome on a constant and a dummy variable for treatment, *without control variables*, this is coded as a simple difference-of-means test—even though estimated standard errors can be misleading (Freedman 2008, Dunning 2010a).

16 Experimental ethnography may refer to the deep or extensive interviewing of selected subjects assigned to treatment and control groups. The focus may be qualitative and interpretive in nature, with the meaning subjects attribute to the treatment (or its absence) being a central topic of concern.

17 This seems true to some extent even when scholars hire survey firms, as they must still interact with a local firm to design the study, train investigators, and so on.

18 For apparently fortuitous reasons, Brazil appears quite over-represented, with fully 13 of 22 or nearly 60 percent of studies in Table 30.1 focused on this country.

Bibliography

Achen, Christopher. 1986. *The Statistical Analysis of Quasi-Experiments*. Berkeley: University of California Press.

Angrist, Joshua, Eric Bettinger, Erik Bloom, Elizabeth King, and Michael Kremer. 2002. "Vouchers for Private Schooling in Colombia: Evidence from a Randomized Natural Experiment." *American Economic Review* 92 (5): 1525–57.

Angrist, Joshua, Eric Bettinger, and Michael Kremer. 2006. "Long-Term Consequences of Secondary School Vouchers: Evidence from Administrative Records in Colombia." *American Economic Review* 96(3): 847–62.

Boas, Taylor, and F. Daniel Hidalgo. 2010. "Controlling the Airwaves: Incumbency Advantage and Community Radio in Brazil." Working paper, Boston University and University of California Berkeley.

Boas, Taylor, F. Daniel Hidalgo, and Neal Richardson. 2010. "The Returns to Political Investment: Campaign Donations and Government Contracts in Brazil." Working paper, Boston University and University of California Berkeley.

Brollo, Fernanda, and Tommaso Nannicini. 2010. "Tying Your Enemy's Hands in Close Races: The Politics of Federal Transfers in Brazil." Working paper, Bocconi University.

Brollo, Fernanda, Tommaso Nannicini, Roberto Perotti, and Guido Tabellini. 2010. "The Political Resource Curse." Working paper, Bocconi University.

Campbell, Donald T. and Julian C. Stanley. 1963. *Experimental and Quasi-Experimental Designs for Research*. Boston, MA: Houghton Mifflin.

Chamon, Marcos, João M. P. de Mello, and Sergio Firpo. 2009. "Electoral Rules, Political Competition, and Fiscal Expenditures: Regression Discontinuity Evidence from Brazilian Municipalities." IZA Discussion Paper No. 4658.

Chong, Alberto, Ana De La O, Dean Karlan, and Leonard Wantchekon. 2011. "Information Dissemination and Local Governments' Electoral Returns: Evidence from a Field Experiment in Mexico." Unpublished manuscript.

Collier, David, Henry E. Brady, and Jason Seawright. 2010. "Sources of Leverage in Causal Inference: Toward an Alternative View of Methodology." Chapter 13 in David Collier and Henry Brady, eds., *Rethinking Social Inquiry: Diverse Tools, Shared Standards*. Lanham, MD: Rowman & Littlefield.

Cox, David R. 1958. *Planning of Experiments*. New York: Wiley.

Cox, Gary W. 1997. *Making Votes Count: Strategic Coordination in the World's Electoral Systems*. Cambridge: Cambridge University Press.

De Figueiredo, Miguel F. P., and F. Daniel Hidalgo. 2010. "When Do Voters Punish Corrupt Politicians? Experimental Evidence from Brazil." Working Paper, University of California Berkeley.

De Figueiredo, Miguel F. P., F. Daniel Hidalgo, Yuri Kasahara. 2010. "When Do Voters Punish Corrupt Politicians? Experimental Evidence from Brazil." Working paper, University of California Berkeley.

Deaton, Angus. 2009. "Instruments of Development: Randomization in the Tropics, and the Search for the Elusive Keys to Economic Development." The Keynes Lecture, British Academy, October 9, 2008.

De la O, Ana. 2010. "Do Conditional Cash Transfers Affect Electoral Behavior? Evidence from a Randomized Experiment in Mexico." Working paper, Yale University.

De Soto, Hernando. 2000. *The Mystery of Capital: Why Capitalism Triumphs in the West and Fails Everywhere Else*. New York: Basic Books.

Desposato, Scott. 2007. "The Impact of Campaign Messages in New Democracies: Results From An Experiment in Brazil." Working paper, University of California San Diego.

Di Tella, Rafael, Sebastian Galiani, and Ernesto Schargrodsky. 2007. The Formation of Beliefs: Evidence from the Allocation of Land Titles to Squatters. *Quarterly Journal of Economics* 122: 209–41.

Druckman, James N., Donald P. Green, James H. Kuklinski, and Arthur Lupia. 2006. "The Growth and Development of Experimental Research in Political Science." *American Political Science Review* 100 (4): 627–35.

Dunning, Thad. 2008a. "Improving Causal Inference: Strengths and Limitations of Natural Experiments." *Political Research Quarterly* 61 (2): 282–93.

Dunning, Thad. 2008b. "Model Specification in Instrumental-Variables Regression." *Political Analysis* 16 (3): 290–302.

Dunning, Thad. 2010a. "Design-Based Inference: Beyond the Pitfalls of Regression Analysis?" In David Collier and Henry Brady, eds., *Rethinking Social Inquiry: Diverse Tools, Shared Standards*. Lanham, MD: Rowman & Littlefield, 2nd edition.

Dunning, Thad. 2010b. "Race, Class, and Voter Preferences in Brazil." Working Paper, Yale University.

Duverger, Maurice. 1954. *Political Parties*. London: Methuen. Ferraz, Claudio, and Frederico Finan. 2008. "Exposing Corrupt Politicians: The Effect of Brazil's Publicly Released Audits on Electoral Outcomes." *Quarterly Journal of Economics* 123 (2): 703–45.

Ferraz, Claudio, and Frederico Finan. 2010. "Motivating Politicians: The Impacts of Monetary Incentives on Quality and Performance." Working paper, University of California Berkeley.

Finan, Frederico, and Laura Schecter. 2010. "Vote-Buying and Reciprocity." Working paper, Departments of Economics, University of California Berkeley and University of Wisconsin-Madison.

Fisher, Sir Ronald A. 1935. "The Design of Experiments." In J. H. Bennett, ed., *Statistical Methods, Experimental Design, and Scientific Inference*. Oxford: Oxford University Press.

Freedman, David A. 2009. *Statistical Models: Theory and Practice*. Cambridge: Cambridge University Press, 2nd edition.

Fried, Brian J., Paul Lagunes, and Atheender Venkataramani. 2010. "Corruption and Inequality at the Crossroad: A Multimethod Study of Bribery and Discrimination in Latin America." *Latin American Research Review* 45 (1): 76–97.

Fujiwara, Thomas. 2008. "A Regression Discontinuity Test of Strategic Voting and Duverger's Law." Working paper, University of British Columbia.

Fujiwara, Thomas. 2009. "Can Voting Technology Empower the Poor? Regression Discontinuity Evidence from Brazil." Working paper, University of British Columbia.

Galiani, Sebastian, and Ernesto Schargrodsky. 2004. "The Health Effects of Land Titling." *Economics and Human Biology* 2: 353–72.

Gerber, Alan S., and Donald P. Green. 2008. "Field Experiments and Natural Experiments." In Janet Box-Steffensmeier, Henry E. Brady, and David Collier, eds., *The Oxford Handbook of Political Methodology*. New York: Oxford University Press, 357–81.

Gonzalez-Ocantos, Kiewiet de Jonge, Meléndez, Osorio, and Nickerson. 2010. "Vote Buying and Social Desirability Bias: Experimental Evidence from Nicaragua." Working paper, Notre Dame University.

Green, Tina. 2005. "Do Social Transfer Programs Affect Voter Behavior? Evidence from Progresa in Mexico." Working Paper, University of California Berkeley.

Green, Donald. 2009. "Regression Adjustments to Experimental Data: Do David Freedman's Concerns Apply to Political Science?" Working paper, Yale University.

Gonzalez-Ocantos, Ezequiel, Chad Kiewiet de Jonge, Carlos Meléndez, Javier Osorio, and David W. Nickerson. 2010. "Vote Buying and Social Desirability Bias: Experimental Evidence from Nicaragua." Working Paper, Notre Dame University.

Heckman, James J. 2000. "Causal Parameters and Policy Analysis in Economics: A Twentieth Century Retrospective." *Quarterly Journal of Economics* 115: 45–97.

Hidalgo, F. Daniel. 2010. "Digital Democratization: Suffrage Expansion and the Decline of Political Machines in Brazil." Manuscript, Department of Political Science, University of California Berkeley.

Hidalgo, F. Daniel, Suresh Naidu, Simeon Nichter, and Neal Richardson. 2010. "Occupational Choices: Economic Determinants of Land Invasions." *Review of Economics and Statistics* 92 (3): 505–23.

Holland, Paul W. 1986. "Statistics and Causal Inference." *Journal of the American Statistical Association* 81 (396): 945–60.

Hyde, Susan D. 2010. "Election Fraud Deterrence, Displacement, or Both? Evidence from a Multi-Level Field Experiment in Nicaragua." Working paper, Yale University.

Imbens, Guido. 2009. "Better LATE Than Nothing: Some Comments on Deaton (2009) and Heckman and Urzua (2009)." Working paper, Harvard University.

Lagunes, Paul. 2009. "Irregular Transparency? An Experiment Involving Mexico's Freedom of Information Law." Social Science Research Netwotk. http://ssrn.com/abstract=1398025.

Lee, David S. 2008. "Randomized Experiments from Non-random Selection in U.S. House Elections." *Journal of Econometrics* 142 (2): 675–97.

Litschig, Stephan, and Kevin Morrison. 2009. "Local Electoral Effects of Intergovernmental Fiscal Transfers: Quasi-Experimental Evidence from Brazil, 1982–1988." Working paper, Universitat Pompeu Fabra and Cornell University.

Manacorda, Marco, Edward Miguel, and Andrea Vigorito. 2009. "Government Transfers and Political Support." Working Paper, Department of Economics, University of California Berkeley.

Miguel, Edward, Shanker Satyanath, and Ernest Sergenti. 2004. "Economic Shocks and Civil Conflict: An Instrumental Variables Approach." *Journal of Political Economy* 112 (4): 725–53.

Morton, Rebecca B., and Kenneth C. Williams. 2010. *Experimental Political Science and the Study of Causality: From Nature to the Lab*. New York: Cambridge University Press.

Paluck, Elizabeth Levy. 2008. "The Promising Integration of Qualitative Methods and Field Experiments." *Qualitative and Multi-Method Research* 6 (2): 23–30.

Richardson, Benjamin Ward. 1887 [1936]. "John Snow, M.D." *The Asclepiad* 4: 274–300, London. Reprinted in *Snow on Cholera*. London: Oxford University Press, 1936.

Rosenzweig, Mark R., and Kenneth I. Wolpin. 2000. "Natural 'Natural Experiments' in Economics." *Journal of Economic Literature* 38 (4): 827–74.

Rubin, Donald B. 1977. "Assignment to Treatment on the Basis of a Covariate." *Journal of Educational Statistics* 2: 1–26.

Sekhon, Jasjeet S. 2009. "Opiates for the Matches: Matching Methods for Causal Inference." *Annual Review of Political Science* 12: 487–508.

Sherman, Lawrence, and Heather Strang. 2004. "Experimental Ethnography: The Marriage of Qualitative and Quantitative Research." *The Annals of the American Academy of Political and Social Sciences* 595, 204–22.

Snow, John. 1855. *On the Mode of Communication of Cholera*. London: John Churchill, 2nd edition. Reprinted in *Snow on Cholera*, London: Oxford University Press, 1936.

Sovey, Allison J., and Donald P. Green. 2011. "Instrumental Variables Estimation in Political Science: A Readers' Guide." *American Journal of Political Science* 55 (1): 188–200.

Thistlethwaite, Donald L., and Donald T. Campbell. 1960. "Regression-discontinuity Analysis: An Alternative to the Ex-post Facto Experiment." *Journal of Educational Psychology* 51 (6): 309–17.

Titiunik, Rocío. 2009. "Incumbency Advantage in Brazil: Evidence from Municipal Mayor Elections." Working paper, University of Michigan.

31

PUBLIC OPINION RESEARCH IN LATIN AMERICA[1]

Elizabeth J. Zechmeister and Mitchell A. Seligson

Understanding and interpreting public opinion in Latin America is central to our ability to understand the arena in which democratic politics is played out. We, of course, recognize that institutions matter a great deal in this process, but institutions operate in the context of citizen values, behaviors and choices. Indeed, many institutional choices grow directly from the political cultures in which they operate, often (but not always) resulting in a degree of congruence between societal norms and institutional structure. The task of researchers studying Latin American public opinion is large and complex; its importance for the study of politics in the region is matched by its potential to illuminate new connections, inspire and accommodate methodological innovations, and spur advances in theoretical perspectives on the origin, nature, and consequences of public opinion.

We begin our review of the field by noting that considered as a whole, the study of public opinion in Latin America is burdened with two paradoxes. First, confidence in the correctness of interpretations of the region's public opinion was highest when social scientists' empirically based knowledge of the field was lowest. Today, in contrast, with a wealth of data on which to make evidence-based interpretations, considerable diversity of opinion characterizes the field. Second, although public opinion polling in Latin America emerged early, long before it had reached other developing regions in the world, it lapsed mostly into inactivity for many years. Happily, the period of dormancy is over, as the field has virtually exploded with data, innovation and energy.

In this chapter we explore the early origins of research on Latin American public opinion, account for its initial stagnation, and then focus on the reasons for its current boom. As we demonstrate, this boom has been spurred on by several factors: an increased quantity of national and comparative survey data; the adoption of increasingly sophisticated methods for the implementation and analysis of survey research; and, a challenging but fertile terrain with respect to the theory and practice of democracy in the region. Looking back over the past half-century of the development of the field, what we find is that the factors that retarded the development of the field after its initial promising start have now all but disappeared. Survey research on Latin America in the 21st century is growing in magnitude and sophistication more rapidly than ever before it its history, and is promising to resolve many important puzzles in the field.

Defining the Task

Scholarship on public opinion in modern Latin America is principally concerned with its relationship to democratic politics. There are, of course, countless components of democratic public opinion since democracy itself is a broadly defined concept. Public opinion orientations can be considered with respect to governmental and non-governmental institutions, policies, and individuals; and, these can be considered at the supra-national, national, sub-national, and individual levels. Further, these orientations can be considered in terms of their cognitive, affective, and evaluative components. For example, if researchers are interested in public opinion toward the legislature, they could focus on the extent to which the individuals possess information about and opinions on it; the sentiments individuals feel with respect to it; or, whether individuals make positive or negative assessments of legislative practices and output. We might also draw a distinction between values and practices when considering public opinion. As past scholarship has shown, it is one thing to profess tolerance in the abstract, and it is another to put the value into practice when considering a particularly disliked group (Prothro and Grigg 1960). Finally, scholars of public opinion must concern themselves not only with measuring all these understandings, beliefs, and attitudes, but also with understanding how they interact with each other and the political system. As a result of this complexity, scholars in this field face numerous challenges and, as we will point out later in this chapter, after some decades of scholarship many puzzles remain unsolved, though the leverage we are able to muster over these questions is increasing rapidly in the face of increased quality and opportunities in the field of comparative public opinion research.

Historical Background: The Evolution of Scholarship on Latin American Public Opinion

Strong claims were made about the political culture of Latin America long before there was appropriate empirical evidence on which to base those claims. A large body of widely cited literature, written at a time when much of Latin America was caught in the grip of repressive regimes, argued persuasively that the culture of the region was deeply authoritarian and anti-democratic (e.g., Paz 1961; Fromm and Maccoby, 1970; Dealy 1974; Morse 1974; Wiarda 1974). Yet, those interpretations were largely based on historical studies of inherited Spanish traditions, often mixed with presumed knowledge of indigenous beliefs and cultures rather than evidence drawn from contemporary populations. Since much of Latin America was poor at the time, classic works (e.g., Lipset 1959) that associated poverty with authoritarianism helped fuel the perspective that history, indigenous values, and poverty had produced an inherently anti-democratic political culture in the region (for an extended discussion and refutation see Krishna 2008 and Booth and Seligson 1984, 2008).

The development of survey-based empirical evidence to test these claims emerged only slowly. Systematic surveys of the mass public in the first half of the 20th century were rare phenomena in Latin America, although exceptions do exist such, as in work by László Radványi in Mexico and by the Brazilian Institute of Public Opinion and Statistics (Moreno and Sánchez Castro 2009; Geer 2004). In the mid-1950s, what was then called the United States Information Agency (USIA) but years later was absorbed as a unit of the U.S. State Department, began carrying out surveys in selected Latin American countries. In an effort to better understand the audience for the "Voice of America," a "radio listenership" survey was carried out in Venezuela in 1955, and in 1961 the USIA conducted a survey in Argentina to measure the "climate of opinion" in that country, with questions focused on images of the United States and other countries— particularly Cuba, the U.S.S.R, and China—as well as attention paid to the media. Many of those surveys, which continued for decades, are archived in the Roper Center Public Opinion Archives and some in the U.S. National Archives. Unfortunately, many of the data bases themselves have been lost, and what survive in the National Archives are printed reports providing the survey questions and distributions of marginals. Other early surveys found in the Roper Archive include an October 1957 study limited to Metropolitan Santiago, Chile, which focused on the implications of the launch of the Russian *Sputnik* satellite. Roper also reports on a 1957 USIA national population survey of Guatemala. Most of these early studies focused on a single country, received scant attention, and had limited influence on broader academic programs.

The comparative study of Latin American public opinion began in earnest with the inclusion of Mexico alongside England, Germany, Italy, and the United States in Gabriel Almond and Sydney Verba's (1963) ambitious first effort to measure, assess, and compare indicators of political culture across political systems. Interestingly, the inclusion of Latin America in *The Civic Culture* occurred almost by happenstance with an eleventh hour substitution of Mexico for Sweden (Almond and Verba 1980; Craig and Cornelius 1980). The Mexico survey was carried out in June 1959, and even though some other surveys were carried out in the region, including a couple of multi-nation survey efforts, prior to and around that date (see Frey 1970), none achieved anywhere near the same level of visibility and impact. We therefore take the publication of The *Civic Culture* as the founding moment for modern, systematic Latin American surveys based on something like national representative samples.

The roots of *The Civic Culture* can be traced back to the 1920s, when a group of scholars led by Charles Merriam at the University of Chicago began to marshal in a new era of political science in which more attention would be paid to micro-level analyses and explanations, systematic theory development, and quantitative empirical tests. The behavioral approach unabashedly drew from other disciplines, and these provided strong underpinnings with which to explore new concepts such as political culture (Pye 2010). For several reasons, the initial stirrings of the Behavioral Revolution within the discipline of Political Science were largely limited to the American subfield (see Munck 2007). The expansion of this school of thought to the subfield of Comparative Politics eventually received an important push from Gabriel Almond, whose experience working for the air force in World War II placed him on a team of researchers collecting survey data measuring German attitudes (Almond 2002; Merritt and Merritt 1980). In 1963, Almond and Verba produced *The Civic Culture*, the first scientifically rigorous cross-national analysis of public opinion indicators measuring and comparing various aspects of political culture. The decision to include Mexico in the five-country study placed the study of public opinion in Latin America squarely in the limelight.

While Almond and Verba's (1963) *Civic Culture* pioneered a new approach to comparative politics through its use of systematic cross-national individual level measures of public opinion, the work was not without significant flaws. Craig and Cornelius (1980), among others, raise questions about comparisons that can be made between the data collected in Mexico and those gathered in other national studies. The survey data for Mexico were drawn from a sample that was limited to medium-to-large urban areas, and therefore excluded a substantial portion of the Mexican population whose political culture in theory ought to vary in significant ways from the better educated and better connected urban dwellers represented in the study. Indeed, many surveys find greater within-nation differences across divides such as urban and rural or rich and poor than they do cross-nationally.

In fact, understanding the mechanisms driving within-nation differences can provide critical insight into questions of democratic political stability. For example, Converse (1969) noted comparatively weak levels of party identification in Mexico within Almond and Verba's dataset, and developed a theoretical framework linking age, experiences, partisanship, and partisan stability. Converse argued that empirical experience with democratic politics strengthens partisanship ties while psychological resistance among older age cohorts stabilizes partisanship patterns. In established democracies, then, age is expected to correlate positively with partisanship. In contrast, partisanship will not only be lower in emerging democracies but *negatively* correlated with age.[2] Another perspective on differences across age cohorts is offered by Seligson's (2007) work on support for populist practices. In this case, age is negatively related to support for populism, a fact that Seligson suggests may stem in part from the fact that older cohorts lived through authoritarianism (and have therefore a more concrete sense of the price to be paid for leaving democracy behind) and in part from different propensities to take cavalier stances with respect to democratic politics. Thus, age matters not for itself, but for the tendencies and experiences it represents. These mechanisms may leave certain younger generations in Latin America more willing to develop partisan attachments but, simultaneously, more fickle in their willingness to abide by the democratic rules of the game.

Returning to Almond and Verba (1963), other critiques lodged by Craig and Cornelius (1980) concern problems with the translation of English instruments into Spanish, noting cases in which questions were translated so that the force of various opinion options differed across the versions. These and other problems with the sample and survey instrument were considered by many to be so egregious that Lijphart (1980) reflected that "Secondary analyses of the data of *The Civic Culture* have tended to omit the Mexican sample" (pp. 44–45). Perhaps so, but a search of "Digital Dissertations" finds literally dozens of doctoral dissertations in which Mexico (and the other countries) were included. Moreover, if imitation is the highest form of flattery, then the *Civic Culture* ought to blush with pride; many later surveys carried out in Latin America copied items directly from the Mexican version of the *Civic Culture* questionnaire, and thus it served as a baseline for numerous subsequent investigations.

On the heels of Almond and Verba's work, the academic study of comparative public opinion, in particular that which focused on Latin America, stalled. While some have attributed this paralysis to widespread discussion of flaws in the *Civic Culture* study, that perception itself is flawed. The academic study of Latin American public opinion went into a deep freeze for several decades as the result of at least three factors: a sea shift in the field of comparative politics that affected the field in general, a political reality consisting of mostly undemocratic systems in Latin America that severely limited survey research on political issues, and, finally, an anti-quantitative bias that took hold among many social scientists in Latin America.

In the same decade that *The Civic Culture* debuted, the field of comparative politics shifted in its focus back to macro-level phenomena, in particular to studies of the state, state-society relations, and political institutions. Along with efforts aimed at "Bringing the State Back In" (Evans, Rueschemeyer, and Skocpol 1985), the field put small N case study research back into a privileged position, and produced graduate students and research in accordance with that model.[3]

Complementing and potentially fueling this turn away from cross-national, statistical studies of public opinion was a paucity of high quality survey data in particular in Latin America and other developing regions. Exceptions existed, of course, but they received little attention from the broader academic community. Many Latin American countries from the 1960s through the early 1980s were in the grip of oppressive authoritarian regimes. This made the collection of national public opinion on political issues a mostly unattainable enterprise, and an extraordinarily dangerous one for those who attempted studies under undemocratic conditions. During this time, then, public opinion surveys in Latin America fell largely to commercial polling firms and, to some extent, government projects.

Disaster struck the field in the 1960s. It is hard to overstate the chilling effect that the infamous "Project Camelot" had on empirically-based survey research in Latin America. Documented in a classic edited volume by Irving Louis Horowitz (1974), a small group of social scientists began research in the early 1960s on the causes and prospects for insurgency in Latin America. When it was revealed, however, that the U.S. Army funded the project, it was shut down in that country and canceled by the Army shortly thereafter. That unfortunate incident tainted many political scientists for years to come, creating situations in which U.S. researchers with perfectly legitimate and open grants from the Social Science Research Council, Fulbright and others, had their motives questioned by their national counterparts.[4] Surveys became symbolic in the minds of many Latin American students and professors of a way to gather intelligence on their countries and suspicions ran high that the data would be used to buttress repressive regimes. The tensions of the Cold War in general, with specific Latin American focus on Cuban communism, fed the flames of those concerns for many years.

An anti-quantitative bias that arose in the region among many social scientists also sharply attenuated interest in surveys. There were three main sources of that bias. First, quantitative data were seen as being generated by governments for government purposes and were therefore to be mistrusted, especially given the authoritarian nature of most of the regimes. Second, the Camelot phenomenon cast a pale over any systematic studies that were designed to use data to test hypotheses. Third, the "price of entry" for doing surveys was high, both in terms of the infrastructure that had to be mounted (sample frames, training and payments to interviewers, data entry, software packages) and the intellectual capital that had to be acquired (programming, sample design, and statistical skills). Emblematic of conditions underlying the anti-quantitative bias is the process that led to the publication of what was to become the classic statement of dependency theory (Cardoso and Faletto 1969). Fernando Henrique Cardoso has many times told the story (personal communication and Kahl 1988) that his first research as a sociologist in Brazil was to carry out a survey of entrepreneurs. Not having learned the value of sampling, nor the virtues of closed-ended questions, he ended up with something like 10,000 lengthy paper questionnaires stored in a university campus office that were simply uncodable. He abandoned the project (as well as Brazil because of the military take-over there), and his next project, written in Chile after fleeing a repressive military in Brazil, was a work that ended up constituting what is now considered to be the classic explanation of dependency theory, critics of which have stressed its empirical unverifiability (Packenham 1992). An unfortunate legacy of the early rejection of quantification has been that, until recently, few political scientists at universities in Latin America have had the advanced statistical skills needed for high quality survey research. The impact has been that all too many surveys have fallen below international standards (Seligson 2005). In the last several years, however, the increasing flow of well-trained new Ph.D.s into departments of political science in Latin America has begun to alter that equation.

In the late 1980s the study of public opinion returned in force within the subfield of comparative government, in particular both the United States and Europe. While the study of political behavior had withered in comparative politics, it had continued to develop in rigor, sophistication, and ideas within the subfield of American government. One consequence is that when comparativists returned to the study of public opinion, they at once could borrow from, but also had to question the ability of concepts developed for the U.S. context to travel to other world areas.

The expansion that took place within the study of public opinion in Latin America can be seen through at least two lenses: an exponential increase in the number of survey projects and a significant increase in the number of published articles focused on the Latin American region that refer to survey data. As an exercise aimed at documenting the increase in survey data measuring public opinion in Latin America, we examined the Roper Latin American Database, and created a count of the number of surveys archived for each year between 1960 and recent times. Leaving aside variation across individual years and the fact that survey data for recent years is sparse in the archives, if we compare the number of surveys that were conducted in the period 1960–69 to 1990–99, we see that the number of databases more than triples in the Roper archive.

In addition to substantial growth in surveys that focus on a single country (many of which are housed outside of Roper's confines, for example, in the ICPSR archive, in universities in Latin America, etc.), the region has witnessed the development and expansion of survey projects that collect comparative survey data. These days there are four principal regional survey projects in the Americas: the AmericasBarometer of the Latin American Public Opinion Project (LAPOP), the Latin Barometer, the CIDE Foreign Affairs survey, and the Barómetro Iberoamericano of the Consorcio Iberoamericano de Investigaciones de Mercados y Aseoramiento (CIMA). Of these, the AmericasBarometer is the largest in geographic scope, collecting national level survey data in 26 countries in the Americas in 2010, with sample sizes of 1,500 (sometimes larger) per country, and with over 43,000 interviews conducted in that year. The Latin Barometer (Latinobarómetro) annually covers 18 countries in Latin America and the Dominican Republic, with samples of 1,000–1,200. The CIDE surveys focus largely on foreign affairs and have a more limited inclusion of countries. The CIMA surveys, which include Spain and the United States, employ sample sizes that are more varied, with some as large as 1,000, but many others in the 300–500 range. In addition to survey data focused on comparisons across countries, there has been a growth in panel studies in recent years. Notable projects in this regard include a set of studies conducted in two cities in Brazil (Baker, Ames, and Renno 2006) and a set of panel studies conducted in Mexico (see, for example, McCann and Lawson 2003; Domínguez and Lawson 2003; Domínguez, Moreno, and Lawson 2009).

Alongside these country- and region-specific projects, global survey efforts have expanded their reach into and across the Latin American region. The World Values Survey expanded from no Latin American countries in its 1981–1984 wave, to four Latin American countries in the 1989–1993 wave (Argentina, Brazil, Chile, and Mexico), to six Latin American countries in the 2005–2008 wave, with the addition of Peru and Uruguay. A similar expansion has taken place with respect to the Pew Global Attitudes Survey and the Comparative Study of Electoral Systems. Gallup has had an influence and presence in Latin America from early days, and this public opinion firm has expanded significantly in Latin America over the years. In addition to the growth in survey data and related projects, the region has seen an increase in meetings of scholars of public opinion, for example Latin America conferences associated with the World Association of Public Opinion Research (WAPOR). The Latin American Studies Association meetings also include many papers and panels that are based on survey data from Latin America and the Caribbean, as do panels at the major political science association meetings. In short, we are now in a period of renaissance with respect to studies of public opinion in Latin America. Researchers working within and entering the field for the first time enjoy a plethora of data, a strong infrastructure within which to collect new data, and a large community of scholars who communicate regularly over issues related to public opinion in Latin America.

Despite the significant growth in quantity of survey data measuring public opinion in Latin America, there is nonetheless still an imbalance with respect to the distribution of these studies across space. Some countries have developed robust local capacity supporting the implementation and analysis of public opinion surveys, while others lag behind. An area that has been scarcely tapped is the Caribbean region.[5] Growth in public opinion surveys in this part of the world would allow a more complete picture of public opinion in the Americas, as well as provide scholars of Latin American public opinion with greater leverage over questions involving the influence of contextual factors on public opinion.

Another way we can measure the growth of studies of public opinion in Latin America is to consider published research. We did a quick count of articles in the *Comparative Political Studies* journal from 1968 to 2010 that both focused on a country or set of countries in Latin America and that referred to survey data. The results revealed an upward trend in the appearance of survey data in the journal over time, in particular in the last decade, where we find that the number of articles that incorporate survey data triples in comparison to the prior decade. We also reviewed work published in *Comparative Politics* from 1970 to recent times and, in this case, our count reveals essentially a doubling of the number of articles referencing survey data across the periods 1970–79 (eight articles) and 1990–99 (15 articles). Of the eight articles published in the early time period, two draw on a large-N national survey of Argentina (a study conducted by Kirkpatrick), and the rest are based on survey data that are more limited (e.g., urban or rural samples alone). Our cursory examination of articles from the later time period reveals some continuity to the degree that a number of survey studies still coming from the 1990s focused on metropolitan, urban areas. We also found some interesting continuity in topics addressed across the time periods. Thus, for example, across both time periods there are manuscripts focused on attitudes and values within Latin America and others that look at voting behavior. At the same time, we see an expansion in the number of surveys referred to within a given article, a growth in the number of national surveys assessed across the set of manuscripts, and, more extensive analyses of survey data. A general assessment of articles in other specialized and general-interest journals as well as in comparative politics monographs suggests to us that this expansion is part of a broader trend.

Improvements in Latin American Public Opinion Research

The study of public opinion in Latin America has benefited not only from an increase in available data, but also from an improvement in the quality of that data and methods for analyzing it. Stratified probability samples, often nationally representative, are increasingly the norm in survey research.[6] In our work with the AmericasBarometer, we have introduced the use of handheld electronic devices in the majority of the countries included in our studies. Handheld electronic devices, or PDAs, decrease errors in data entry by allowing interviewers to record directly into the data base the responses they hear, rather than to circle responses on paper, responses that are later transferred (typically with some error) by coders and data entry clerks into the data base. Another major advantage of handhelds is that they allow for the easy execution of complex experimental modules. Experiments can be designed to have certain modules automatically asked only to those who gave certain specific responses to questions earlier in the survey or who possess certain socio-economic or demographic characteristics. Handhelds also permit interviewers to change languages in mid-stream, a distinct advantage in multilingual countries where respondents code-switch in mid-interview.[7]

In addition to improvements in samples and processes in survey research, public opinion scholars increasingly account for multidimensionality with respect to important sets of attitudes. The clearest example comes with respect to measuring support for democracy itself. No single item can possibly tap all of the many ways in which democracy has been defined by the scholarly community. Notions of political tolerance, support for majority rule, minority rights, equality of opportunity, belief in the rule of law, etc. are all important dimensions of democracy that can only be picked up with multi-item measures. In fact, a concern with the multidimensionality of core concepts in public opinion research has become a hallmark of good scholarship on public opinion in general, and with respect to Latin America in particular. Gibson and Bingham (1982) made a relatively early case for the complexity of the concept of political tolerance. Canache, Mondak, and Seligson (2001) argue that classic measures of democratic satisfaction should be understood as tapping into several dimensions simultaneously. Booth and Seligson (2009) adopt a similar stance in their research on political legitimacy in Latin America, demonstrating that legitimacy in the Latin American context (and more broadly, they would argue) is best understood as a supra-concept comprising multiple dimensions that tap into various aspects of political support.

Another important concern in the comparative study of public opinion concerns the cross-individual and cross-national equivalence of survey items. Scholars of public attitudes toward democracy in Latin America are aware that the term "democracy" holds different meanings for different persons and across different countries. Analysis of public opinion surveys by Camp (2001) and Moreno (2001) shows, for example, that across countries, Latin Americans conceive of democracy in very different terms. One solution that has been proposed for this problem is to measure support for democracy indirectly via questions about processes and values that do not reference the term "democracy". Along similar lines, scholars of Latin American public opinion have also grappled with the fact that concepts developed in the study of political behavior in one country or region do not travel perfectly to the Latin American region nor across countries within it. Two concepts whose traveling capacities have been questioned are party identification and ideological placement. With respect to the latter, studies of both elite and mass opinion in Latin America demonstrate that the terms "left" and "right" can vary in meaning across individuals as well as across and within countries (e.g., Zechmeister 2006, Kitschelt et al. 2010). Concerns with the equivalence of terms have been present from the early days of comparative public opinion research (e.g., Frey 1970), and these concerns persist today alongside new attempts to gain leverage over variations in subjective understandings of critical concepts in comparative politics.

As scholarship on public opinion has transitioned from studies principally aimed at the measurement of attitudes in the mass public, to more ambitious attempts to explain their stability, their causes, and their effects, scholars of public opinion increasingly have had to grapple with the challenge of assessing causality with survey data. Important advances have been made on this issue in three principal ways. First, some scholars have been able to gain leverage over attitudinal stability over time and issues of causality by using panel studies. For example, using the 2000 Mexico Panel Study, McCann and Lawson (2003) address stability in political attitudes over the course of an election by examining the extent to which responses to a selected group of survey questions change from one wave of the survey to the next. A second approach to the investigation of issues involving claims of causality in the study of public opinion research in general, and in Latin America in particular, has been the adoption of highly sophisticated statistical methods. Consider the overall problem of determining if democratic regimes produce different outcomes than non-democratic regimes. In short, a central question has long been the impact of democracy on economic development vs. the impact of economic development on democracy. Whereas in the past this may have been dismissed as a "chicken and egg" question, powerful statistical tools today allow us to disentangle these kinds of causal relationships. Mirroring an evolution taking place within the discipline of political science more generally, there is a greater tendency these days, for example, for scholars analyzing survey data to present non-recursive (simultaneous equations) models when two variables are thought to be endogenous, or influenced by, each other. As an example, Morris and Klesner (2010), drawing on the earlier finding of Seligson (2002) that corruption victimization erodes political legitimacy, adopt such an approach in their study of the relationships between trust and corruption in Mexico. Another option available to scholars seeking greater leverage over issues of causality is to apply matching techniques. With this approach, scholars can sort individuals into groups with roughly similar characteristics, except with respect to an independent variable of interest; to the extent that individuals are "matched" on other relevant characteristics across the two groups, the researcher can have greater confidence that differences in selected outcomes are due to differences across scores on the independent variable.[8]

Third, an increasing number of scholars are applying experimental methods to the study of public opinion in Latin America. These studies take at least three forms: limited convenience samples within lab-type studies, field experiments, and experiments embedded into surveys. For example, Merolla and Zechmeister (2009) present results from an experiment in a controlled setting with a sample of students in Mexico, in order to demonstrate the effects that terrorist and economic threat can have on political attitudes. Katz et al. (2010) report on the results of a field experiment involving the use of alternative voting machines in Argentina. Earlier examples of experimental approaches to the study of public opinion exist, for example the field experiment in Argentina's schools assessed by Chaffe, Morduchowicz, and Galperin (1996, see also Catterberg, Neimi, and Bell 1997). Nonetheless, widespread familiarity with and the growing use of experimental approaches are a distinctive feature of the modern era of public opinion research in Latin America.

Related to the last points, surveys are also just beginning to be widely accepted and used as a tool for determining the impact of both large-scale and small-scale policy changes. With respect to the latter, public opinion research in Latin America has recently expanded to the study of impact evaluation using randomized controlled designs. Such research, such as one that LAPOP is currently carrying out in Central America, can help determine if, for example, violence prevention programs work (see Córdova 2010). More broadly speaking, other studies have compared the impact and effects of various programs such as decentralization (Hiskey and Seligson 2003), while still others have attempted to explain the shift to the left in Latin American voting patterns that occurred in the early 21st century (Baker 2009).

Latin American Public Opinion's Challenging but Fertile Research Terrain

While decades have passed since most Latin American countries transitioned to civilian-ruled, formally democratic systems and despite a proliferation of survey data research in the interim, we would argue there are still more questions than answers within the study of Latin American public opinion. Modern Latin American politics has been characterized by numerous instances in which elected officials have left office prior to the formal completion of their term. Valenzuela (2006) counts 13 "interrupted" presidencies between 1985 and 2004 in Latin America, meaning cases in which the sitting executive was forced out due to impeachment (Pérez-Liñán 2007), pressure, or military action. If we add recent cases in which the executive was forced out (such as Honduras in 2009), cases in which legislatures were interrupted (such as Peru in 1992), and partial disruptions such as the brief coup attempt against Hugo Chávez in Venezuela in 2002 and the September 2010 police uprising in Ecuador in which the president was confronted by members of the police force, then the picture indicates even greater instability. Examples abound suggesting that many of Latin America's democracies may be far from consolidated. For scholars of public opinion in Latin America, this raises obvious questions: what role does public opinion play in democratic consolidation, what degrees of ambivalence toward democracy persist in the mass public and with what consequences, and what factors increase or decrease the tendency for citizens to express support for undemocratic political practices and institutions?

Studies of Latin American public opinion continue to explore foundational issues, including those related to political culture, political support, and citizens' preferences over public policies and the channels by which these are expressed. Scholarship on Latin American public opinion already has offered some important answers to these questions, drawing attention to the multi-faceted nature of political and democratic support as well as to the ways that crime, corruption, and other serious problems in Latin American politics and society can erode such support. And, yet, there is work to be done if we are to develop a more comprehensive understanding of the dynamic relationships among public opinion, performance, and democratic government in Latin America.

What is clear is that Latin American public opinion is characterized by a complicated, and often contradictory, mixture of attitudes. In marked contrast to the "received wisdom" of the early, non-empirically based characterizations of authoritarian political culture in Latin America cited in the first part of this chapter, in our own explorations into the public opinion data we find a more nuanced picture: a public opinion that is largely supportive of democracy in the abstract but also often willing to accept military intervention and other interruptions to normal democratic practices. Simultaneously we find that performance matters significantly to citizens' political evaluations. In and of themselves, the presence of contradictions and the importance of performance to public opinion does not make Latin American public opinion unique. But the nature of those contradictions, combined with the far-reaching effects of performance on satisfaction with and support for democracy, carries potential for explaining political instability as well as instances of democratic backsliding and stagnation in the region.

The importance of assessing and detecting contradictions in public opinion emerged soon after the first systematic survey data were gathered. It is a theme that runs through Almond and Verba's study of civic culture. The civic culture, Almond and Verba argue, is a mix of orientations characterized by both moderation and inconsistencies. Consider civil society participation, which, according to Toqueville, was a forte of American politics. What Almond and Verba discovered by looking at both the American and British cases, is that such participation was far from universal, with many citizens reporting none at all. For example, they found that 57% of those in the United States and 47% in Great Britain (Almond and Verba 1963, p. 246) participated in voluntary associations. On average, however, those two polities exhibited higher levels of participation than did Mexico, in which only 25% of those surveyed reported participation in voluntary associations. Nonetheless, the two quintessential democracies in the Almond and Verba study seemed to be getting along fine even though large proportions of their populations were non-participant. This led them to adjust classic democratic theory, and argue that key contradictions found within the civic culture were not, after all, a bad thing, but acted as stabilizing forces within a democratic system. In the case of participation, Almond and Verba (1963) argue, the tendency for individuals to express high levels of political efficacy but only moderate levels of involvement creates a "reserve" of potential political action that serves as a check on elite behavior. In short, some participation is good, lots of participation could be bad. They then argue that the "imbalances and inconsistencies" in the Mexican case were the most extreme of the five countries in their sample.

What we now know, after decades of research beyond the *Civic Culture,* is that these imbalances and inconsistencies are universal, and the gaps between contemporary Latin America and the advanced industrial society are not nearly as stark as once assumed. We also know, however, that systems do get "out of whack," and when they do, instability can follow. For example, Booth and Seligson (2009) combine attitudes concerning core principles, support for institutions, and approval of performance to create profiles of mass publics in eight Latin American countries. Their index of "triply" dissatisfied citizens is intended to gauge the proportion of individuals who are broadly unsupportive of democratic practices, policies, and output, and they compare this to those whose attitudes align on the opposite (supportive) end of all three dimensions. Their results proved prophetic, as the country that stood out as containing the most troubling proportion of triply dissatisfied individuals in 2008 was Honduras (which experienced an executive "interruption," in Valenzuela's terms, in 2009). While advances have been made, it remains a challenge before researchers of Latin American public opinion to determine under what conditions what mixtures of attitudes are most likely to be stabilizing or destabilizing from the perspective of democratic politics.

Is it possible to point to a single indicator among the vast components of public opinion that seems particularly critical, even on its own, for assessing and predicting high-functioning, stable democratic politics in today's Latin America? Without some reluctance over picking favorites, we might point to attitudes related to political parties as one particularly significant gauge of democratic public opinion in Latin America. Converse (1969) identified support for political parties as critical to democratic stability, arguing that "where these loyalties have not had time to develop, it seems likely that electoral support will have numerous capricious overtones, and that in times of severe distress nontraditional and antidemocratic parties may find ready support" (p. 141). Though written over fifty years ago, Converse's insight is as relevant today as it ever has been to scholarship on Latin American politics. Levels of trust in institutions and, in particular, in political parties are dismally low in many Latin American countries (on low levels of trust in political parties across the Americas see, for example, Mendizábel and Moreno 2010). Again, we would note that this does not in and of itself make Latin America unique.

However, low levels of trust in political parties and partisanship may be more consequential to political stability in the region than it is elsewhere (e.g., the United States, where levels of trust in parties these days is lower than that found in many countries in Latin America). Political parties perform essential functions in modern democratic systems, from aiding the dissemination and processing of information to mobilizing and engaging individuals to structuring political processes and facilitating representation. But, as Dalton and Weldon (2007, p. 180) argue "Partisan loyalties may be even more important in new democracies" because they denote "attachment to a key institution that integrates citizens into the new democratic order." In Latin America (e.g., Mainwaring and Scully 1995), and elsewhere, low levels of partisan attachment have been linked to low levels of party system institutionalization and high levels of political instability, at a minimum in the form of high electoral volatility. Thus, low and even weakening party ties in Latin America are an aspect of public opinion that should cause concern. And, yet, even when present, party identification in Latin America may not always be of the moderate quality touted as ideal by Almond and Verba (1963) but, instead, may be associated with inclinations to protest election results, and to participate in particularistic political relationships (e.g., vote buying practices) (see Vidal et al. 2010). This is indicative of the types of important nuances within Latin American public opinion that we believe merit close attention.

While scholars have been making important headway in understanding the causes and consequences of party attachments in Latin America, an area of scholarship that we see as somewhat less developed concerns the relationship between public opinion and trends toward hyperpresidentialism and reduced horizontal accountability in many Latin American countries. In countries where citizens espouse some of the highest levels of support for democracy in the abstract, presidents simultaneously have been reducing checks and balances and concentrating power in the executive office. Hyperpresidentialism raises concerns about the tendencies of populist personalities to ignore basic democratic principles, such as freedom of press, and to prioritize building a personal reputation over creating strong political institutions. Pervasive weak horizontal accountability at and below the level of the executive has more generally been linked to relatively high levels of corruption, which exact financial, social, and political costs. These conditions lead us to ask: to what extent does the ordinary citizen in Latin America have preferences for and information regarding systems of checks and balances? Under what conditions and for how long is a public willing to acquiesce to, or even support, extraordinarily powerful presidents, and at what cost for democratic politics?

Finally, in considering recent scholarship on public opinion in Latin America, we take note that modern political science research has come to recognize that individuals are nested within social networks, communities, and sub-national and national political-economic systems. Consequently, scholars have asked and will continue to ask: what role do environmental factors, such as institutional design, economic performance, and party system structure play in shaping public opinion in Latin America? With the increased availability of high quality survey data representing numerous units within Latin America and the Caribbean, and beyond, we foresee serious growth in the quantity and rigor of research focused on the intersection of context and public opinion in Latin America in the years to come. The widespread availability of computer software that can correctly account for variation at the level of the individual and at the level of political system greatly facilitates this research and is already leading to a growing number of publications using this methodology. At the other extreme, while Almond and Verba (1963) were critiqued for failing to pay sufficient attention to within country variation, much of the work published since then has successfully focused on recognizing and understanding differences across socio-economic and demographic groups within Latin American publics. The greater availability of national, stratified surveys opens opportunities for quantitative studies of public opinion across significant sub-regions within and across Latin American countries.

Conclusion

Never has there been more interest in, acceptance of, and opportunity for the study of public opinion in Latin America. The last twenty years have seen a proliferation of data, an increased sophistication in methods, and a substantial growth in published research focused on understanding Latin American public opinion. Our assessment of the field reveals interesting continuities in the types of questions being asked, important advances in research design and analysis, and an increasing number of studies that take serious the interrelationships and inconsistencies found among the myriad components of public opinion and, as well, the contexts in which they are found. And, yet, in many ways the project of understanding the attitudes, evaluations, and behaviors of citizens within particular Latin American countries, across systems within the region, and in comparison to individuals residing in other parts of the world has just begun.

In the years to come we expect scholars of public opinion in Latin America to continue to traverse new frontiers, in terms of the questions being asked, the methods being applied, and the theoretical perspectives being shaped. Many will focus on some of the topics we have identified here, such as the origin and significance of inconsistencies in public opinion, partisan attachments, attitudes with respect to hyperpresidentialism, but these admittedly only scratch the surface of what is currently being studied and what is possible. In short, we can only conclude that the next decade of research into public opinion in Latin America holds immense promise, as scholars continue to progress toward deeper understandings of the nature, causes, and effects of the attitudes held and expressed by the mass public in Latin America, as these are nested within the rich and varying contexts that define the region.

Notes

1 We thank Alejandro Díaz-Domínguez for research assistance.
2 Over time, as the democracy ages, this relationship would be expected to change. In a manner consistent with Converse's theoretical framework, Lupu and Stokes (2010) make the argument that, in Argentina, over time and controlling for political interruptions, partisanship in general increases.
3 This shift, as part of a broader discussion of paradigmatic shifts within the field of comparative politics, is discussed in Munck (2007).
4 Co-author Seligson in this piece was conducting his dissertation research in Costa Rica in the early 1970s funded by the Social Science Research Council (SSRC), and hosted by the premier academic university in the country, the Universidad de Costa Rica. Suspicion was so high, however, that the university newspaper published an article raising questions about the survey Seligson was carrying out, and was accompanied by a cartoon showing a sword decapitating a hydra-headed dragon, with one head being the SSRC, another the CIA, and another the Ford Foundation.
5 To some extent this may be shifting. In 2010 the AmericasBarometer conducted national surveys in Belize, the Dominican Republic, Guyana, Haiti, Jamaica, Suriname, and Trinidad & Tobago.
6 Stratified samples are those that subdivide the population into important regions, for example the United States might be divided into the Northeast, the Midwest, the South, the Southwest, and the Pacific. When sample designs are stratified they become far more efficient than non-stratified samples because they guarantee that each region will be represented in the final sample. In the AmericasBarometer, for example, each nation is divided into 3–9 strata, and further sub-stratified into urban and rural areas.
7 In Suriname, for example, the handheld computers allowed interviewers to easily switch between Dutch, Sranan Tongo and English, three languages widely spoken in that country.
8 An application of this technique is found in Carlin, Love, and Zechmeister (2011), in which the authors assess the effects of experience with Chile's 2010 earthquake and tsunami on democratic attitudes.

Bibliography

Almond, Gabriel A. 2002. *Ventures in Political Science: Narratives and Reflections.* New York: Lynne Rienner.

Almond, Gabriel A., and Sidney Verba. 1963. *The Civic Culture: Political Attitudes and Democracy in Five Nations.* Princeton, NJ: Princeton University Press.

Baker, Andy. 2009. *The Market and the Masses in Latin America: Policy Reform and Consumption in Liberalizing Economies.* New York: Cambridge University Press.

Baker, Andy, Barry Ames, and Lucio R. Renno. 2006. "Social Context and Campaign Volatility in New Democracies: Networks and Neighborhoods in Brazil's 2002 Elections." *American Journal of Political Science* 50, no. 2: 382–399.

Booth, John A., and Mitchell A. Seligson. 1984. "The Political Culture of Authoritarianism in Mexico: A Reevaluation." *Latin American Research Review* 19, no. 1: 106–24.

———. 2008. "Inequality and Democracy in Latin America: Individual and Contextual Effects of Wealth on Political Participation." In *Poverty, Participation, and Democracy,* Anirudh Krishna (Ed). Cambridge: Cambridge University Press, 94–124.

———. 2009. *The Legitimacy Puzzle: Democracy and Political Support in Eight Latin American Nations.* New York: Cambridge University Press.

Camp, Roderic Ai. 2001. Democracy through Latin American Lenses: An Appraisal. In Roderic Ai Camp (Ed.), *Citizen Views of Democracy in Latin America.* Pittsburgh, PA: University of Pittsburgh Press, pp. 3–23.

Canache, Damarys, Jeffery J. Mondak, and Mitchell A. Seligson. 2001. Meaning and Measurement in Cross-National Research on Satisfaction with Democracy. *Public Opinion Quarterly* 65(4): 506–528.

Carlin, Ryan E., Gregory J. Love, and Elizabeth J. Zechmeister. 2011. Shaking Democracy: The Public Opinion Impact of Chile's 2010 Natural Disaster. *Working Paper,* Georgia State University, University of Mississippi, and Vanderbilt University.

Cardoso, Fernando Henrique, and Enzo Faletto. 1969. *Dependencia y desarrollo en América Latina: Ensayo de interpretación sociológica* [Dependency and Development in Latin America: Sociological Interpretation Test]. México: Siglo Veintiuno Editores.

Chaffee, Steven, Roxana Morduchowicz, and Hernan Galperin. 1997. Education for Democracy in Argentina: Effects of a Newspaper-in-School Program. *International Journal of Public Opinion Research* 9(4): 313–335.

Converse, Philip E. 1969. Of Time and Partisan Stability. *Comparative Political Studies* 2(2): 139–171.

Córdova, Abby. 2010. The Role of Social Capital on Neighborhood Safety and Citizens' Political Attitudes: A Multi-Site Clustered Randomized Experiment in Central America. Paper preesented at the annual meeting of the Midwest Political Science Association, Chicago, Illinois, April 22–25.

Craig, Ann L., and Wayne A. Cornelius. 1980. Political Culture in Mexico: Continuities and Revisionist Interpretations. In Gabriel Almond and Sidney Verba (Eds.), *The Civic Culture Revisited.* New York: Sage, pp. 325–393.

Dalton, Russell J., and Steven Weldon. 2007. Partisanship and Party System Institutionalization. *Party Politics* 13(2): 179–196.

Dealy, Glen. 1974. The Tradition of Monistic Democracy in Latin America. In Howard J. Wiarda (Ed.), *Politics and Social Change In Latin America: The Distinct Tradition.* Amherst, MA: University of Massachusetts Press.

Domínguez, Jorge I., and Chappell H. Lawson, Eds. 2003. *Mexico's Pivotal Democratic Election: Candidates, Voters, and the Presidential Campaign of 2000.* Stanford, CA: Stanford University Press.

Domínguez, Jorge I., Alejandro Moreno, and Chappell H. Lawson, Eds. 2009. *Consolidating Mexico's Democracy: The 2006 Presidential Campaign in Comparative Perspective.* Baltimore, MD: Johns Hopkins University Press.

Evans, Peter B., Dietrich Rueschemeyer, and Theda Skocpol (Eds.). 1985. *Bringing the State Back In.* New York: Cambridge University Press.

Frey, Frederick W. 1970. Cross-cultural Survey Research in Political Science. In Robert T. Holt and John E. Turner (Eds.), *The Methodology of Comparative Research.* New York: Free Press, pp. 173–294.

Fromm, Erich, and Michael Maccoby. 1970. *Social Character in a Mexican Village: A Sociopsychoanalytic Study.* Englewood Cliffs, NJ: Prentice Hall.

Geer, John. G. 2004. *Public Opinion and Polling around the World: A Historical Encyclopedia.* Volume Two. Santa Barbara, CA: ABC-CLIO.

Gibson, James L., and Richard D. Bingham. 1982. On the Conceptualization and Measurement of Political Tolerance. *American Political Science Review* 76(3): 603–620.

Hiskey, Jon, and Mitchell A. Seligson. 2003. Pitfalls of Power to the People: Decentralization, Local Government Performance, and System Support in Bolivia. *Studies in Comparative International Development* 37(4): 64–88.

Horowitz, Irving Louis (Ed). 1974. *The Rise and Fall of Project Camelot: Studies in the Relationship between Social Science and Practical Politics.* Rev. ed. Cambridge, MA: M.I.T. Press.

Kahl, Joseph Alan. 1988. *Three Latin American Sociologists: Gino Germani, Pablo Gonzales Casanova, Fernando Henrique Cardoso.* New Brunswick, NJ: Transaction Books.

Katz, Gabriel, R. Michael Alvarez, Ernesto Calvo, Marcelo Escolar, and Julia Pomares. 2010. Assessing the Impact of Alternative Voting Technologies on Multi-Party Elections: Design Features, Heuristic Processing, and Voter Choice. *Political Behavior.* doi:10.1007/s11109-010-9132-y.

Kitschelt, Herbert, Kirk A. Hawkins, Juan Pablo Luna, Guillermo Rosas, and Elizabeth J. Zechmeister. 2010. *Latin American Party Systems.* New York: Cambridge University Press.

Krishna, Anirudh. 2008. *Poverty, Participation, and Democracy: A Global Perspective.* New York: Cambridge University Press.

Lijphart, Arend. 1980. The Structure of Inference. In Almond, Gabriel A., and Sidney Verba (Eds.), *The Civic Culture Revisited.* New York: Sage, pp. 37–56.

Lipset, Seymour Martin. 1959. Democracy and Working-Class Authoritarianism. *American Sociological Review* 24: 482–502.

Lupu, Noam, and Susan Stokes. 2010. Democracy Interrupted: Regime Change and Partisanship in Twentieth-Century Argentina. *Electoral Studies* 29: 91–104.

Mainwaring, Scott, and Timothy Scully. 1995. *Building Democratic Institutions: Party Systems in Latin America.* Stanford, CA: Stanford University Press.

McCann, James A., and Chappell H. Lawson. 2003. An Electorate Adrift? Public Opinion and the Quality of Democracy in Mexico. *Latin American Research Review* 38(3): 60–81.

Mendizábal, Yuritzi, and Alejandro Moreno. 2010. La confianza electoral: el IFE y los partidos políticos. In Alejandro Moreno (coordinador), *Confianza en las instituciones* [Confidence in Institutions]. Mexico City: Centro de Estudios Sociales y de Opinión Pública, ITAM, pp. 227–247.

Merritt, Anna J., and Richard L. Merritt. 1980. *Public Opinion in Semisovereign Germany: the HICOG surveys, 1949–1955.* Urbana, IL: University of Illinois Press: Office of International Programs and Studies Office of West European Studies.

Merolla, Jennifer L., and Elizabeth J. Zechmeister. 2009. *Democracy at Risk: How Terrorist Threats Affect the Public.* Chicago, IL: University of Chicago Press.

Moreno, Alejandro. 2001. Democracy and Mass Belief Systems in Latin America. In Roderic Ai Camp (Ed.), *Citizen Views of Democracy in Latin America.* Pittsburgh, PA: University of Pittsburgh Press, pp. 27–50.

Moreno, Alejandro, and Manuel Sánchez-Castro 2009. A Lost Decade? László Radványi and the Origins of Public Opinion Research in Mexico, 1941–1952. *International Journal of Public Opinion Research* 21(1): 3–24.

Morduchowicz, Roxana, Edgardo Catterberg, Richard G. Niemi, and Frank Bell. 1996. Teaching Political Information and Democratic Values in a New Democracy: An Argentine Experiment. *Comparative Politics* 28(4): 465–476.

Morris, Stephen D., and Joseph L. Klesner. 2010. Corruption and Trust: Theoretical Considerations and Evidence from Mexico. Comparative Political Studies 43(10): 1258–1285.

Morse, Richard M. 1974. The Heritage of Latin America. In Howard J. Wiarda (Ed.), *Politics and Social Change in Latin America: The Distinct Tradition,* Amherst, MA: University of Massachusetts Press., pp. 91–128.

Munck, Gerardo L. 2007. The Past and Present of Comparative Politics. In Gerardo L. Munck and Richard Snyder (Eds.), *Passion, Craft, and Method in Comparative Politics.* Baltimore, MD: Johns Hopkins University Press, pp. 32–59.

Pérez-Liñán, Aníbal S. 2007. *Presidential Impeachment and the New Political Instability in Latin America.* New York: Cambridge University Press.

Packenham, Robert A. 1992. *The Dependency Movement: Scholarship and Politics in Development Studies.* Cambridge, MA: Harvard University Press.

Paz, Octavio. 1961. *The Labyrinth of Solitude: Life and Thought in Mexico.* New York: Grove Press.

Prothro, James W., and Charles M. Grigg. 1960. Fundamental Principles of Democracy: Bases of Agreement and Disagreement. *Journal of Politics* 22(2): 276–294.

Pye, Lucian. 2010. The Behavioral Revolution and the Remaking of Comparative Politics. In Goodin, Robert E. and Charles Tilly (Eds.), *The Oxford Handbook of Contextual Political Analysis.* New York: Oxford University Press, pp. 797–805.

Seligson, Mitchell A. 2002. The Impact of Corruption on Regime Legitimacy: A Comparative Study of Four Latin American Countries. *Journal of Politics* 64: 408–433.

Seligson, Mitchell A. 2005. Improving the Quality of Survey Research in Democratizing Countries. *PS, Political Science and Politics* 38(1): 51–56.

481

Seligson, Mitchell A. 2007. The Rise of Populism and the Left in Latin America. *Journal of Democracy* 18(3): 81–95.

Valenzuela, Arturo. 2004. Latin American Presidencies Interrupted. *Journal of Democracy* 15(4): 5–19.

Vidal, D. Xavier Medina, Antonio Ugues Jr., Shaun Bowler, and Jonathan Hiskey. 2010. Partisan Attachment and Democracy in Mexico: Some Cautionary Observations. *Latin American Politics and Society* 52(1): 63–90.

Wiarda, Howard J. 1974. Social Change and Political Development in Latin America: Summary, Implications, Frontiers. In Howard J. Wiarda (Ed.), *Politics and Social Change in Latin America: The Distinct Tradition,* Amherst, MA: University of Massachusetts Press, pp. 267–282.

Zechmeister, Elizabeth J. 2006. What's Left and Who's Right? A Q-method Study of Individual and Contextual Influences on the Meaning of Ideological Labels. *Political Behavior* 28(2): 151–173.

PART VI

Critical Reflections on the State of the Field

WHAT'S NEXT? REFLECTIONS ON THE FUTURE OF LATIN AMERICAN POLITICAL SCIENCE[1]

Barry Ames, Miguel Carreras, and Cassilde Schwartz

From the perspective of one old guy and two young scholars, Latin American political science looks pretty good. Over the last thirty or so years, our understanding of the region's political processes, both institutional and behavioral, has advanced rapidly. Political parties, legislatures, elections, civil society; these areas have all witnessed strong research efforts. Credit for much of this advance, of course, goes to Latin America's latest wave of democratization: political scientists do better in open, competitive environments. But our progress is also due to the rising numbers of well-trained political scientists south of the Rio Grande and to the increasing methodological sophistication of Latin Americanists wherever they are rooted.

Suggestions for future research directions may thus seem both gratuitous and presumptuous. We are emboldened by the certainty that scholarship and fashion are not unrelated: our research choices are inevitably influenced by the reward structure of the discipline as a whole and by the methodological tastes of political science colleagues who are not Latin Americanists. So what follows are some easily ignored observations that could serve, we hope, as themes for debate.

Within the area of contemporary political institutions, we believe that increased research efforts should be devoted to two areas: bureaucracy and interest group lobbying. And although we know a lot about the everyday workings of other institutions, we know less about the *formation* and *transformation* of institutions. For such problems we advocate the use of "analytic narratives."

Lobbying and Bureaucracy

That Latin Americanists have rarely analyzed lobbying and bureaucracy seems beyond dispute. Could neglect simply reflect unimportance? At least in the case of lobbying, a perception of business weakness may have contributed to the paucity of research, but a deeper and more insidious cause of the neglect of both lobbying and bureaucracy lies in the methodological evolution of the Latin American field. This evolution has an ahistorical, noncumulative quality: earlier methodological approaches—approaches intrinsic to the development of later methodologies—are forgotten when the most current research approaches are transferred to Latin America.

Consider the major institutions of modern government: legislative, judicial, and executive-bureaucratic. Twenty years ago, all three were research deserts in Latin America. The first to emerge was scholarship on legislatures. Early work built on the literature of the U.S. Congress, applying to Latin America such concepts as the primacy of reelection, credit claiming, and pork barrel. Latin Americanists gradually relaxed the assumptions of American scholars, modifying them to fit Latin American reality. In cases like Brazil, for example, the seeking of reelection is far from automatic, and the institutional perspectives that follow from careerism differ from those of U.S. congressmen. Reelection-seeking deputies in Brazil may actually prefer a stronger executive branch so as to facilitate the flow of pork-barrel benefits to their constituencies (Cunow et al., 2011).

In hindsight, applying the insights of U.S. congressional scholarship to Latin America was easy. National legislatures are found in single locations, the internet facilitates data collection, and Latin American presidentialism makes the basic structures of government similar across the continent. Still, the easy development of Latin American legislative scholarship obscured something important: the absence of the "soaking and poking" tradition characteristic of early work on the U.S. Congress. The rational-choice literature on the U.S. Congress, the work of such scholars as Shepsle (1978), Fiorina (1977), Cox and McCubbins (1993) and others, all relied on the deep, qualitative, and inductively empirical tradition embodied by Richard Fenno's *Power of the Purse* (1966) and *Home Style* (1978), John Manley's *Politics of Finance: The House Committee on Ways and Means* (1970), David Mayhew's *Congress: The Electoral Connection* (1974), and Aaron Wildavsky's *Politics of the Budgetary Process* (1964). With a few exceptions, including Ames's work on Brazil (2001) and John Carey's study of Costa Rica and Venezuela (1996), Latin Americanists have almost never done that kind of inductive and qualitative work. But why? Could it be that scholars whose careers are rooted in U.S. academic institutions naturally find it difficult to spend long periods of time in Latin America? Might new methodologies—both rational choice and narrowly empirical—tend to crowd out old styles of research? And did the shift in methodologies for studying legislatures parallel the general drift in political science from "sociological" to "economic" styles of thinking? Still, in legislative research the absence of qualitative, "soak and poke" analyses in Latin America probably produced not so much *incorrect* findings as simply *limited* findings, that is, findings constrained by the research interests of the U.S. rational-choice tradition.

To strengthen the argument that the decline in "soaking and poking" has adversely affected Latin American political science, consider the development of judicial politics, a field clearly enjoying a growth spurt. Most of this new judicial work, as Daniel Brinks' chapter in this volume points out, focuses on high-level courts, especially constitutional courts. As Brinks notes, "there is very little research on the operation and politics of lower courts, even though it is clear that politics affects them just as much as it affects high courts, and they are crucial to the construction of the day-to-day experience of democracy." Why so little on lower courts? We suspect that local court systems are understudied because (1) little or no aggregate quantitative data exists about local court decisions, (2) local courts are spread out over entire countries, (3) scholars do not understand how local courts work. Let's postpone asking why young Latin Americanists are not doing the spade work on either in legislative or judicial politics while we turn to the third branch of government, the bureaucracy.

I: Bureaucracy

Do we really need to justify the importance of understanding Latin American bureaucracy? Political science is replete with mentions of "clientelism" and "patronage" (Stokes 2005;

Calvo & Murillo 2004). If these ubiquitous ailments really matter, they matter in bureaucracy. Political science journals with titles like "Governance" link politics and bureaucratic capacity. And international financial organizations, including the World Bank and the Inter-American Development Bank, spend serious money on improving "administrative capacity."

Is the importance of bureaucracy matched by the attention political scientists have paid to it? This handbook has no chapter on the subject. The only major monograph focusing on bureaucracy is Barbara Geddes' classic *Politician's Dilemma: Building State Capacity in Latin America* (1994). Not only was it written seventeen years ago, but it was not intended to analyze bureaucracy as such. Instead, it focused on the conditions under which *legislatures* pursue bureaucratic reform. For evidence of such reform, *Politician's Dilemma* necessarily relied on secondary, mostly historical literature.

During the last ten to fifteen years, the dominant theme in discussions of bureaucracy in Latin America has been the "new public management," the bureaucratic reform movement that began in Australia, New Zealand and the UK but has spread over Europe and now into developing countries (Barzelay 2002a,b). Articles on Latin America in specialized public administration journals are often illuminating, but usually they share three characteristics: they are delinked from mainstream Latin American political science, they rarely show evidence of field research in any existing bureaucratic agency, and they focus on "bureaucratic reform" rather than "bureaucracy" or "public administration."

To illustrate these arguments, this section first considers the treatment of bureaucracy in three edited volumes: Ernesto Stein and Mariano Tommasi's *Policymaking in Latin America: How Politics Shapes Policies* (2008), Luis Carlos Bresser Pereira and Peter Spink's *Reforming the State: Managerial Public Administration in Latin America* (1999), and Eduardo Lora's *The State of State Reform in Latin America* (2007).[2] Stein and Tommasi have two theoretical chapters and eight supposedly parallel country chapters. The main theoretical chapter purports to be a survey of the major actors in policy making. Legislatures, though their role in policy making is often quite weak, merit sixteen pages of treatment. Bureaucracies get one page, and most of the discussion is about delegation by legislatures. The country chapters reflect this same bias: "we know more about legislative institutions, so they must be important." The chapter on Argentina has two pages on the bureaucracy (2008: 103–105). The only empirical evidence to support the claim that Argentina's bureaucracy is inept is the comparison of the "Weberianess" of Argentina's bureaucracy with other countries. The empirical basis of this claim is Evans' and Rauch's "Bureaucracy and Growth: A Cross-National Analysis of the Effects of 'Weberian' State Structures on Economic Growth" (1999). Evans and Rauch make quantitative assessments of the quality of national-level bureaucracies, assessments relying totally on individual country-based expert judgments. The methodology seems blissfully unaware of the endogeneity of perceptions of bureaucratic quality to past economic growth and equally unaware that the experts may not be thinking on the same scale. The twelve years since its publication have witnessed little in terms of follow-up research, but it is often convenient, as in Stein and Tommasi, to treat these opinions as real data. The chapter on Chile notes the historically low levels of corruption in Chile and discusses bureaucratic reform post-Pinochet, but it cites no research on the Chilean bureaucracy at all. The chapter on Colombia has two paragraphs on technocrats but nothing on bureaucracy. Chapters on Mexico and Paraguay, chapters written almost exclusively by political scientists, simply do not mention bureaucracy.

Bresser Pereira and Spink are Latin America's leading normative proponents of the "new public management," or what Bresser Pereira calls "managerial public administration." For Bresser Pereira, managerial public administration means

[1] political decentralization with transfer of resources and responsibilities to regional and local political levels; [2] administrative decentralization, through delegation of authority to public administrators transformed into increasingly more autonomous managers; [3] organizations with few hierarchical levels, no longer structured like a pyramid, [4] assumption of limited trust, but not total mistrust by citizens; [5] a posteriori control of results, instead of rigid, step-by-step control of administrative processes; and [6] administration based upon meeting the needs of the citizenry.

(1999: 119)

Bresser Pereira recognizes that these reforms differ from "bureaucratic public administration," which he labels as a Weberian reform focusing on the principles of professional merit. In his view, Brazil had such reforms beginning in the early twentieth century as a substitute for patrimonial administration, which emphasized nepotism and political patronage. Bureaucratic administration turned out to be not much of an improvement: inefficient, sluggish, expensive, self-serving (Bresser Pereira & Spink, 1999: p. 118). Having tried and failed to improve bureaucracy with Weberian reforms, Brazil is now in the same position as New Zealand, Australia, the United Kingdom, and the United States, that is, among the nations adopting the managerial model.

What is striking about this argument is the complete absence of any evidence regarding the actual implementation of "bureaucratic reform." Bresser Pereira and Spink cite no research that includes any assessment of changes in the behavior or bureaucrats pre- and post-reform. In essence, the debate proceeds with no empirical footing. And it is not splitting hairs to suggest that perhaps Brazil's public administration has never quite reached a high level of "Weberianness."[3]

In Eduardo Lora's *The State of State Reform in Latin America* (2007), Koldo Echebarría and Juan Carlos Cortázar take on the task of putting the Inter-American Development Bank's country-level research findings on public sector reform into a comparative framework.[4] The IADB commissioned studies of bureaucratic quality, with a common framework and quantitative metric, in almost every Latin American country. We learn, reasonably enough, that Brazil's bureaucracy (in spite of constant corruption scandals) is much higher on both "merit" and "functional capacity" than the bureaucracy of Honduras. But it turns out that Argentina ranks fifth on merit and fourth on functional capacity (of eighteen countries), barely below Chile. Now compare these results with those of Spiller and Tommasi, authors of the Argentina chapter in *Policymaking in Latin America: How Politics Shapes Policies* (Stein & Tommasi 2008: 103): "One possible way to enforce intertemporal political agreement is to delegate enforcement to a relatively independent, yet accountable bureaucracy. Argentina, however, does not have such a bureaucracy." Spiller and Tommasi cite Rauch and Evans' to claim that in "Weberianness" Argentina is below all the other Latin American countries in that sample, including Colombia, Brazil, Mexico, Chile, Peru, Ecuador, and Uruguay. Finally, Spiller, Tommasi, and Bambaci (2007) approvingly cite Graham's characterization of Argentine bureaucracy: "one of the clearest instances ... of an institutionalized, non-performance-oriented bureaucracy in a society with ample numbers of skilled human resources in which the primary interest within the state apparatus is survival" (p. 221). That such contradictory conclusions can be reached by serious scholars suggests that the empirical data and/or the methodology of comparison are inherently flawed.

In addition to the absence of deep and cross-nationally comparable research, the bureaucracy subfield has been distorted by its emphasis on reform. The central problem of electoral research is not electoral reform, nor do legislative scholars focus on legislative reform.

Defining development administration as administrative or bureaucratic reform creates a selection bias. The consequence, as Tendler and Freedheim put it, is that scholars fail to provide "the same rich case study material on, or generalizations about, the circumstances under which governments actually do well. Much of the advice about public sector reform is therefore derived from a lopsided understanding of developing country performance" (1994: 1771).

Tendler and Freedheim argue that too much of the conceptual thinking on administrative reform has come from models of rational choice and rent-seeking. Cutting the size of the public sector (via layoffs, contracting out, or privatization) limits the damage public-sector workers can do. Subjecting these workers to market-like pressures and incentives reduces their rent-seeking opportunities. Still, this literature not only ignores the experiences of the Asian tigers, with their greater and successful government intervention, it also ignores the sociological tradition in organization theory, a tradition that emphasizes worker commitment and trust between workers and clients (1994: 1771–1772). Tendler and Freedheim present a case study exploring a program of rural health care in Ceará, a poor state in Brazil's Northeast. Ceará ought to be a place where clientelism and patronage rule, but the state government successfully implemented a merit-based, non-clientelistic rural health program. The government created a sense of "mission" around its program, and it relied on high levels of worker commitment. Rather than rent-seeking, workers actually took on tasks beyond their assignments. This was not a case of success through decentralization or outsourcing; in fact, the state government maintained centralized control over hiring, training and socialization of its health agents.

Of course, the Ceará rural health program is just a single case, but it does suggest that equal time should be devoted to successful as well as unsuccessful government programs. And ignoring the extensive literature on the morale and commitment of public-sector workers may well be a consequence of ideological blinders.[5]

The research traditions of organization theory and bureaucratic politics offer a wider theoretical lens for capturing significant characteristics of bureaucrats and bureaucratic organizations. From the organization theory perspective, consider a classic like Herbert Kaufman's *The Forest Ranger* (1960). Kaufman sought to understand the U.S. Forest Service, an agency that is necessarily decentralized but maintained a strong organizational culture. By intensely studying five rangers, Kaufman delineates the administrative tools, including recruiting, staffing, reporting, training, as well as socialization efforts and control mechanisms that create the forester ethos and enable the central organization to carry out its mission while remaining flexible. Morale in the forest service was very high, with the rangers feeling they were in charge of their own futures while carrying out their assigned missions.

The Forest Ranger is really a special case of Lipsky's *Street-Level Bureaucrats* (1980). For Lipsky, the front lines of state-citizen contacts are the day-to-day interactions of clients with police, teachers, judges, prison guards, and so on. These actors are policy makers because they exercise high degrees of discretion and relative autonomy from organizational authority. The inevitable shortages of resources and the ambiguity of conflicting goals lead to a permanent tension between client-centered goals, organization-centered goals, and social engineering goals. Street-level bureaucrats deal with clients who may be inexperienced or even unwilling, and the external environment is chronically short of money, time, and infrastructure. And though they are hard to measure, managers must set performance goals.

Are street-level bureaucrats relevant to the study of Latin American bureaucracy? Public opinion surveys endlessly ask respondents about their confidence in the police, judiciary, schools, and so on. Imagine how much more useful responses to these questions would be if we actually knew something about the street-level bureaucrats who deliver these services. And imagine the substance in the broad discussions of both administrative reform and the differences between clientelistic and Weberian bureaucracies if we actually knew how patronage employees function in their jobs.[6]

As we move from the behavior of individual bureaucrats to the behavior of an agency as a whole, we confront the issue of communication networks. Organization theorists understand that even centralized formal organizations cannot work without informal or self-organizing systems of communications. Individuals in a bureaucratic organization create informal structures to try to control the conditions that affect their situation, but these informal structures can undermine the formal ones.

A classic example of this kind of analysis is Selznick's *TVA and the Grass Roots* (1966). The U.S. central government established the Tennessee Valley Authority in 1933 as a publicly owned corporation. Ostensibly created to dispose of government-owned factories producing war materials during the First World War, TVA was a quintessential development agency, constructing dams, deepening river channels, and producing and distributing electricity. Because its creation did not result from local demands, TVA had to adjust to the interests of local groups. From the beginning, TVA linked itself to its grass roots, to local organizations, and it used its grass roots theory as a protective ideology (Selznick 1966: 262). TVA became so committed to its local agricultural constituencies that local TVA bureaucrats kept other New Deal programs from operating in their communities, and TVA went far astray from one of its central initial missions, that of conservation.[7]

TVA and the Grass Roots is the paradigmatic study of cooptation, "the process of absorbing new elements into the leadership or policy-determining structure of an organization as a means of averting threats to its stability or existence" (Selznick 1966: 13). Cooptation can take two forms, formal and informal. *Formal* cooptation brings people from outside an organization into participatory positions in decision processes and administration. Organizations engage in formal cooptation to legitimize themselves, but this form of cooptation involves no real sharing of power. At times organizations bring in outsiders simply to facilitate administration. Consultation with labor unions, for example, may reduce absenteeism. Though the purpose of this kind of cooptation is to increase efficiency, the process once again may boost the organization's legitimacy. The second form of cooptation, *informal* cooptation, is not an attempt to establish or increase legitimacy; rather, it occurs when forces outside the organization are so strong that they have to be conceded policy-shaping power.

Cooptation by local power holders means that policy-shaping influences flow from the grass roots to bureaucratic authority, but influence can flow in the other direction as well. Bureaucrats may successfully pursue autonomy from politicians and political parties. The best example of this approach is found in the work of Daniel Carpenter. In *The Forging of Bureaucratic Autonomy* (2001), Carpenter examines a series of agencies during the U.S. Progressive era, including the Post Office, the Forest Service, the Interior Department, and the Chemistry Bureau (part of the Department of Agriculture). Of these agencies, some—but not all—successfully legitimated themselves by establishing links to citizens and to their civil society organizations. By doing so, by creating reputations for their agencies of efficiency, expertise, and moral protection, these agencies built autonomy; that is, they were able to enact policies that the bureaucracies' leaders wanted but that legislators did not.

The concept of bureaucratic autonomy, the idea that bureaucrat-politicians proactively bypass legislators to establish links directly with citizens and their civil society organizations, fits well with traditional arguments in American public administration, but it runs counter to the more recent tradition of "principal-agent" models. In these models, voters or parties control bureaucracies; the former are principals, the latter agents. In the cases Carpenter considers, however, legislators could not control the agencies without incurring unacceptable political and electoral costs, because the agencies were implementing popular policies, policies that the agencies themselves had helped make popular. And since these agencies' policy innovations occurred long after their original creation, their autonomy cannot be explained by the enacting mix of legislators, parties, and interest groups.

These approaches are important for scholars of Latin American bureaucracy, because they are conceptually more open than the dominant principal-agent models. They assume neither that politicians control bureaucracies nor that bureaucracies always create their own policy space. They see the independent influence of bureaucrats as natural rather than anomalous, but they recognize as well that local interests can deflect the policy designs of national-level leaders.

Latin Americanists have analyzed cooptation processes at very abstract levels, most notably in government-labor relations and with reference to the policies Mexico's PRI utilized to maintain power (Erickson 1977; Cockroft & Anderson 1966), but the field is bereft of serious research on the relationships between particular bureaucratic organizations and their environments.

The neglect of bureaucratic policy shaping has two possible roots. One is the historic instability of Latin American institutions. When regimes are themselves unstable, intra-institutional and institution-society relationships may be considered secondary or tertiary issues. Bureaucratic policy autonomy has also been neglected because of the influence of U.S. scholars, who typically assume that bureaucratic organizations are simply creatures of the legislature and the president. In the dominant perspective, the perspective of delegation, voters, parties, legislators, and presidents are "principals"; bureaucracies are "agents." Such models have no room for an initiating, policy-shaping role on the part of already existing bureaucratic agencies.

Whether Latin America's democratic regimes continue to stabilize, and whether Latin America's civil society organizations continue to develop, scholars of bureaucracy must maintain an open, unbiased theoretical framework, one that allows for reciprocal influences between parties, legislators, and bureaucratic organizations. Bureaucratic leaders in Latin America may in fact rarely build policy autonomy, but at least the possibility remains open. Indeed, prime candidates for bureaucratic policy shaping exist: consider the influence of Brazil's agricultural research and extension agency, EMBRAPA. Established by the military regime as a public corporation in 1973, EMBRAPA has played a crucial role in the rapid expansion of the Brazilian agricultural export sector (see, for example, "The Miracle of the Cerrado," 2010). A principal-agent explanation might explain EMBRAPA's inception—its bias toward large-scale agriculture fit the predispositions of the military regime—but EMBRAPA has thrived during every subsequent democratic administration as well, including the administrations of the PT. Its imported strains of grass have transformed unproductive areas of the Northeast into export platforms, and it successfully lobbied for the adoption of genetically modified plant strains over strong opposition from the PT's more radical factions and the environmental left. EMBRAPA's policies have created a class of large-scale farmers who depend on its research programs (but not on state subsidies). The politics of EMBRAPA remain an untold story, but the case for bureaucratic autonomy seems strong, and we suspect that similar cases exist across Latin America.

II: Lobbying

Curiously, the linkage between U.S. and Latin American legislative scholarship has no parallels in the area of lobbying and interest groups. Interest group behavior has received little attention by Latin Americanists despite its obvious importance in policy making. This section begins by reviewing evidence of interest group influence in Latin America. We then provide some guidelines for further research, focusing on both theoretical and methodological avenues for advancement.

Research on lobbying in Latin America has mostly dealt with business and agricultural interests. Karcher and Schneider's chapter in this volume, which provides an excellent review of the literature, concludes that the study of business lobbying has suffered from benign neglect. "Research on business politics is first characterized by how little there is. Beyond scarcity, research on business politics suffers from some biases and blind spots." Neglect, clearly, and, we would agree, perhaps a biased neglect. [8]

In order to help explain the absence of interest group literature, we examine one important case of an interest that has been pushed aside: business interests. Because business associations in Latin America have seemed largely incapable of solving their collective action problems, and because at times state actors have stimulated or initiated organized business behavior, Latin Americanists have mostly downplayed the role of business interests and agricultural interests in policy making. Indeed, some authors actively dismiss their importance, especially pre-liberalization. Bates and Krueger (1993) and Haggard and Kaufman (1995) contend that business associations played very small parts in the ISI-liberalization transition. Bates and Krueger in particular argue that business associations were too fragmented to be powerful. As a result, technocrats and political elites were the primary actors throughout the economic transitions of the eighties and nineties. [9] Durand and Silva (1998), accepting the weakness of business, look for less direct means of influence, such as agenda-setting and demand-raising. Because business associations were initially organized by and became largely dependent on the state, business was sometimes regarded as a basically passive, state-dependent actor, an actor allowing the state and its technocrats to dominate public policy (Schneider 2004).

Perhaps business influence in the policy process really is something new in Latin America. Some scholars argue that the corporatist structure of Latin American states during most of the twentieth century led to a dependent relationship between interest groups and regimes, and it was precisely the transition between ISI and neoliberalism that activated interest groups vis-à-vis the state (Frieden & Stein 2001; Mancuso 2007; Collier & Handlin 2009). The renewed autonomy of business interests left business more empowered vis-à-vis a state inexperienced in dealing with international competition, but it also left business more vulnerable, unable to depend on the state to protect its interests against foreign competitors. Thus business was simultaneously more capable of influencing the state and more motivated to do so. [10]

Whether or not organized business and agricultural interests were really weak in the era of ISI, there is considerable evidence that they are weak no longer. Signs of successful lobbying—mostly by business interests, but some agricultural interests as well—come from a wide variety of countries, a variety suggesting that most Latin American countries probably follow suit.

Chile is important because it has the longest history of uninterrupted neoliberal policies. Benedicte Bull's (2010) interviews with Chilean businessmen revealed that they felt they had played central roles in policy making, particularly in the negotiation of free trade agreements. Chilean businessmen actively negotiated policies typically opposed by business (especially regulations of labor and the environment) in order to gain increased market access.

Interest group research in Central America has also shown substantial business influence. Indeed, small countries sometimes *depend* on the expertise and knowledge of businessmen when forming agreements with powerful countries like the US, countries that would otherwise dominate the negotiation processes (Carrión 2009, 2010). Local business interests pressured for the privatization and deregulation of telecommunication sectors in Costa Rica, Guatemala, and Honduras (Bull 2004). Perez-Aleman's (2010) analysis of the Mexican and Central American coffee industry confirmed the significant influence of small business interests through NGOs and transnational organizations.

Interest group politics in Colombia has long revolved, not surprisingly, around coffee.[11] Jaramillo, Steiner, and Salazar (2001) demonstrated that Colombia's coffee producers have been a strong and vocal interest group throughout the twentieth century. Before the 1990s, the producers focused on maintaining the domestic price of coffee in order to control their incomes directly. Post-1991, their strategy shifted from strictly domestic concerns to a defense against international competition through the exchange rate. Though the goals and methods of coffee producers have changed, they have always had an important voice in politics.

Since the mid-1990s, Francisco Durand has dominated, through research relying on interviews, news monitoring, and secondary sources, the study of Peruvian business interests. In his most recent publication, Durand argues that in the 1990s business "captured" the state and has maintained strong, decisive influence over policy making in both authoritarian and democratic regimes. He argues that this level of power is problematic for all actors involved, including business actors themselves, who suffer from notorious reputations and a confrontational political environment. Though political regimes have changed drastically, the role of business has remained consistently powerful (2010).

Though scholars have portrayed Brazil as a country where business wields little political influence (Bartell 1995; Durand & Silva 1998; Schneider 2004), Brazil has the most developed interest group literature in Latin America. Wagner Pralon Mancuso's *O lobby da indústria no Congresso Nacional: Empresariado e política no Brasil contemporâneo* (The industry lobby in Congress: Entrepreneurs and Politics in Contemporary Brazil, 2007) is surely the most thorough account of interest group influence. Mancuso argues that business began to involve itself heavily and successfully in policy negotiations after Brazil opened its economy. He succeeds in identifying political pressure in both official and informal settings, in part because business interests are unconcerned with hiding their motives and behavior. By using the *Agenda Legislativa da Indústria,* published annually since 1996, and by sending out questionnaires to industries involved in the *RedIndústria,* Mancuso documents the influence of business groups at various points in the policy-making process: proposals, formulations, discussions, and decisions.

Demonstrating that business has political influence is hardly a trivial undertaking, but the study of interest group politics needs to progress. The field should focus more broadly on interests and organized interest groups, not simply on organized business. A wider lens reveals that the precise definition of interest groups varies greatly, and few interest group characteristics are accepted by all scholars (Leech & Baumgartner 1998). A very restrictive definition centers just on groups actively applying pressure on policy makers through lobbying (Crawford 1939). Broader definitions take in both associations and individual firms (Key 1964), and some scholars adopt a sociological definition that includes all groups open to voluntary membership (Knoke 1986). In this perspective, interest groups may include organized social sectors in the population, social movements, institutions like corporations and government agencies, or individual lobbyists.

Latin American research on lobbying seems continually to ask different versions of the same question, i.e., "Do outside interests affect policy content"? If a research question poses a simple dichotomy between influence and no influence, there is little room for comparison, little room, that is, for asking how influence varies between countries or time periods. We need more analytic questions: How do interest groups work together? Under what conditions do they affect the content of policy? At what stage of the policy-making process do they have the greatest access?

Consider the development of the American interest group literature. U.S. interest group research mainly began with the assumption that groups were the most powerful actors in the political process (Bentley 1908; Truman 1951; Schattschneider 1960; Dahl 1961; Lowi 1964). Over time, more nuanced theories placed organized interests within a context of institutional and electoral influences. Americanists now focus on *networks* between and among groups, the biases and normative implications of organized interests in policy, and the ways groups influence legislation.

Of course, Latin Americanists should not blindly imitate U.S. scholars. Americanists focus on interest group influence over the legislature; Latin Americanists are more likely to stress influence over the executive (Oliveira & Onuki 2007; Batista Araujo 2008; dos Santos 2008). Still, American theories provide some hints about useful questions, questions beyond the "yes" or "no" of group influence.

Do Latin American groups intertwine to build professional networks? Analysts of American interest groups established long ago that groups often do not behave as individual actors; instead, they overlap and cooperate (Truman 1951; Rae & Taylor 1970). In *The Hollow Core*, Heinz et al. (1993) implement an extensive series of interviews to identify an intricate web of inter-group networks. Similar groups within particular policy areas work together, but no single lobby connects all the groups. As the name *Hollow Core* suggests, a sphere with a hollow center spatially represents lobby networks. This pattern occurs, the authors suggest, because client groups distrust mediating brokers, brokers who might work with opposing groups.

Lobbyists are political actors who connect with outside interests and politicians. Network methodologies illuminate these connections by analyzing the conditions facilitating network density, creating partisan divisions, and forming cliques.[12] Network effects determine cooperation between interest groups even when controlling for group preferences (Carpenter, Esterling, & Lazer 2004).

Precisely because Latin Americanists know little about the basic structure of interest politics, network analysis could be productive. Do lobbyists work alone or in professional networks. With whom do they network? How do professional networks, when they exist, affect lobbying tactics and policy outcomes?[13]

Since the *Federalist Papers,* American scholars have worried about bias, about the detrimental effects of particular interests on broad policy making. Do particular interests add "a strong upper-class accent" to legislation (Schattschneider 1960: 35)? An empirical response requires extensive knowledge of the groups involved in a policy area, their constituencies, and their membership incentives. In the United States the response has led to a clear conclusion: major sectors of the population are blatantly unrepresented, and the collective-action problem is a real concern for groups producing public goods (Strolovitch 2006; Yackee & Yackee 2006; Schlozman et al. 2008; Schlozman 2010). This conclusion should be tested in

Latin America as well. What are the implications of interest group influence? Which voices have the most sway over policy?

Some groups function more as information conveyers than as policy makers, and this divergence in goals can yield divergences in lobbying strategy. Because most lobbyists spend their time with legislators who already agree with them, persuasion effects may be minimal (Bauer, Pool, & Dexter 1963; Leech & Baumgartner 1998; Hojnacki & Kimball 1998). Measures of interest group pressure should include the roles that groups play as informers, policy monitors, and momentum builders teaming up with like-minded legislators (Ainsworth 1997; Heaney 2006; Baumgartner et al. 2009). When legislators trust an interest group to supply them with policy details and information, the group has more space to shape the policy-making process (Burstein & Hirsh 2007). And, of course, groups influence policy through manipulating public opinion (Danielian & Page 1994; Berry 1999; Smith 2000). Examining the varying roles of interest groups would be particularly fruitful in Latin American countries, where some scholars are hesitant to believe that interest groups directly influence legislative negotiations.

Interest group research requires fieldwork beyond interviews and lists of registered groups. Interest group scholars attend committee hearings, content analyze news articles, and document the progress of bills. They follow prominent issues along with those unnoticed in the policy-making process.[14] Perhaps these techniques seem obvious, but the modal style of Latin Americanists is quite different. Most Latin American interest group research has been retrospective. An outcome occurring as the result of noticeable business influence, ipso facto, becomes evidence of interest group pressure. Not only does this build in selection bias, but what happens *during* the negotiating process is harder to determine retrospectively.

Without question, implementing these research strategies in Latin America is difficult. Perhaps as a result, most Latin American interest group scholarship has been based on secondary sources and small numbers of interviews.[15] Research on American interest groups, by contrast, typically incorporates hundreds of interviews or probability-based surveys of lobbyists and related government officials. With such techniques, scholars can begin to understand the structure of a network of lobbying and the ways in which individuals work together to influence policy.

Of course, the availability of high-quality, credible data facilitates the research process. The U.S. law requiring registration of lobbying activity and campaign contributions led to a huge amount of empirical work. Scholars use these data to test, for example, the consequences of and strategies behind campaign contributions.[16] Latin Americanists, on the other hand, have not been blessed with similarly accessible data. Nonetheless, Brazil, Chile, and Colombia have begun to require most lobbying activity to be made public, even to the point of recording financial contributions. Recent work on Brazil, for example, utilizes archives of lobbyists registered in the Chamber and Senate, campaign contributions recorded in the electoral tribunal, and the lobbying initiatives found in the *Agenda Legislativa da Indústria*.

Treat official lists of registered interest groups with caution. Luis Alberto dos Santos used official lists to compare the regulation of interest groups in Brazil and the United States, but his examination of Brazilian regulation comes with a disclaimer: "The paucity of records, which results from the incapacity to regulate their activities, or the low number of registered groups in the House or the Senate, hides the existence of interest groups and makes it difficult to measure their dimension using these data" (dos Santos 2008: 419). Some newer Brazilian work uses the campaign data base maintained by the Tribunal Superior Eleitoral (dos Santos 2008; Lance 2010), but David Samuels, who organizes these data on his website, estimates that the TSE files contain only about 25% of all contributions;

the other 75% is the famous under-the-table "caixa dois."[17] In sum, official lists do exist, but with limitations.

An alternative research strategy—one requiring no pre-existing data base—involves following a single set of issues over an entire policy cycle. Peter Van Doren's *Politics, Markets, and Congressional Policy Choices* (1991), for example, focuses on energy policy. Van Doren monitored news, conducted numerous interviews, observed legislative proceedings, and analyzed formal documents. Obviously no single issue is "representative": issues should be chosen deliberately, with a most-different or a most-similar strategy.

In sum, interest groups in Latin America are understudied. One source of this neglect comes from the belief—largely unsupported by research findings—that interest groups, especially business groups, have been weak. A second cause has been the framing of research questions. Too often our questions have been dichotomous: "Do interests affect policy?" Fortunately, methodological innovations from the U.S. context, innovations like network analysis, can help Latin Americanists contribute to the study of interest politics in a comparative framework. Still, the biggest constraint on understanding Latin American interest groups remains the paucity of *empirical* research, whether quantitative or "soaking and poking."

III. Analytic Narratives

Would the study of Latin American politics benefit from the use of analytic narratives? This section begins by defining the concept of "analytic narratives" as a branch of rational choice institutionalism, a branch Latin Americanists currently ignore. We then briefly distinguish between this approach and historical institutionalism. Finally, we explore potential avenues for research that would benefit from the use of analytic narratives.

The Concept of the Analytic Narrative

Rational-choice institutionalism (RCI) puts institutions at the center of research methodology. Institutions limit the array of choices available to individuals in the political arena. They serve as a script determining the rules of the game, i.e., which players can participate in a given political game, what strategies are available for the actors involved, in what sequences the players can develop these strategies, and what sorts of information actors possess when they make their choices (Shepsle 2008; Weingast 1996). The development of RCI has led to many fruitful applications contributing to the study of structured (i.e., formal) political institutions.

RCI has often been criticized on the grounds that it presents institutions as a given set of rules affecting outcomes but fails to provide an accurate explanation of the creation of these institutions. This criticism, of course, is a serious one: if institutions simply reflect *preexisting* informal practices, then serious endogeneity problems threaten RCI (Weyland 2002).[18]

"Analytic narratives" provide a new framework to study the creation and evolution of political institutions, a framework that specifically addresses RCI's limitation by analyzing the moment in which the rules are set. In other words, this approach explores the *sources* of institutional arrangements. It is *narrative* because it traces the historical process leading to the outcome of interest. The focus is always on explaining a specific outcome—institutional formation or institutional change—by conducting an in-depth investigation of the context in which the decision process is embedded. Analytic narratives identify the relevant actors participating in the process, the interests and the resources of each actor, and the way in which the actors' choices led to the outcome of interest (Bates et al. 1998). Although analytic narratives provide micro-level explanations, the actors involved in the processes of institutional change are not necessarily individuals; they can be social groups, professional organizations, or political institutions such as political parties.

This approach is also *analytic* through its use of "explicit and formal lines of reasoning" (Bates et al. 1998: 10). Analytic narratives use formal models to explain political outcomes. An outcome, such as the modification of an existing institution, is presented as an equilibrium representing the optimal strategy for all the actors involved in the game, given the preferences of the actors and a series of exogenous constraints. Note that scholars using this framework do not *assume* the preferences of the various actors in the game. Instead, they implement process tracing: reading documents, consulting archives, and interviewing. This methodology diverges sharply from a traditional "rational choice" approach to the study of institutions.

Analytic narratives have been fruitfully implemented in comparative politics to understand the formation and development of formal institutions. The approach is especially useful when applied to *critical junctures* in which political institutions are either created or fundamentally transformed. Gary Cox (1987) develops an analytic narrative to explain the decisive shift in British political institutions that took place in the second half of the nineteenth century. Cox found that three factors: the expansion of the electorate, the introduction of equally sized single-member districts, and particular technological innovations, together produced an alteration in the preferences of individual legislators. Members of Parliament became less independent and began to rely more on established political parties to run their campaigns and channel their legislative activities. As a result, the cabinet and political parties became the central players in British politics, and high levels of discipline in Parliament were institutionalized.

Analytic narratives are more than just devices allowing researchers to explain institutional change. Once the original equilibrium is reached and an institution created, behavior becomes stable and predictable. In the words of Bates et al. (1998: 8), "should exogenous factors remain the same we would expect behavior to remain the same." In other words, by understanding the factors that influenced the preferences of the agents and led to the original equilibrium, it is possible to explain institutional stickiness and then to focus on the impact of institutions on political behavior.

Analytic narratives also contribute to comparative research. Because they are based on strong theoretical foundations, analytic narratives are well-suited for developing hypotheses testable in comparative analysis. An analytic narrative is confirmed if similar exogenous factors affect the preferences of relevant actors in similar ways and lead to a parallel process of institutional transformation. For instance, in accounting for the abolition of "buying one's way out of military service," Levi (1998) presents three separate narratives (United States, France, and Prussia) in which the same theoretic process is at work.

In sum, analytic narratives have the potential to be much more than explanations of specific cases. The causal mechanisms a narrative identifies can be subsequently tested with evidence from other cases.

Analytic Narratives versus Historical Institutionalism

Analytic narratives and historical institutionalism (HI) can each contribute to the study of Latin American political phenomena, but they are distinct research approaches. The first distinction is the type of event or process that the two approaches seek to explain. HI asks questions about macro-historical processes and large-scale outcomes (Mahoney & Rueschemeyer 2003). Scholars within this tradition raise questions about such topics as the causes of social revolution (Skocpol 1979), the link between capitalist development and democracy (Rueschemeyer, Stepens, & Stephens 1992), and the relationship between patterns of colonization and post-colonial development (Mahoney 2010). Analytic narratives, by contrast, are better equipped to study critical junctures, specific moments of institutional transformation. In her critique of the analytic narratives approach, Skocpol (2000: 674) points out that "game-theoretic models are likely to make sense only of certain kinds of historical situations, where there really were sets of actors deliberately maneuvering in relation to one another." In other words, analytic narratives are more valuable when used to explain *specific political decisions* rather than *broad sociopolitical processes*. Analytic narratives can contribute greatly to our understanding of moments of change or evolution in formal political institutions, such as the adoption of new constitutions, reform of electoral laws, and expansion of the suffrage. These changes all result from processes of negotiation that involve a series of key actors maneuvering to obtain their preferred outcome under situations of uncertainty.

The second main distinction between HI and analytic narratives is the former's focus on *continuity* versus the latter's emphasis on *change*. HI tends to emphasize path-dependent choices that become increasingly hard to modify as they become institutionalized (Pierson 2000, 2003). Path dependence implies that "once a country or region has started down a track, the costs of reversal are very high" (Levi 1997: 28). Still, fundamental institutional changes do occur. Countries democratize, party systems break down, constitutions are revised, geographic distributions of power are amended. The analytic narratives approach has much to offer to scholars interested in explaining these institutional transformations. In other words, in spite of their common interest in utilizing historical and qualitative information to explain political phenomena, HI and analytic narratives are distinct traditions serving different purposes. HI has already produced major contributions to the study of Latin American politics (Collier & Collier 1991; Mahoney 2010; Wickham-Crowley 1992); analytic narratives remain largely unexplored.

Analytic Narratives and the Study of Latin American Politics

Over the last thirty years, the most startling reality of Latin American politics has been the acceleration of sociopolitical change. Countries with weak or nonexistent democratic traditions have become relatively consolidated democracies. Everywhere ISI has yielded to some version of neoliberalism. Many countries adopted new constitutions or made wide-ranging reforms to their existing constitutions (Colombia in 1991, Argentina in 1994, Venezuela in 1999, Ecuador in 2008). A significant number of countries decentralized, breaking with a tradition of Jacobinism. Although scholars from the historical-institutionalism tradition often claim that they are raising the "big questions" (Mahoney & Rueschemeyer 2003), the region's sweeping institutional changes continue to pose fundamental but unanswered questions.

Analytic narratives are particularly well-suited to explain these processes of institutional change. The most consequential are certainly the democratic transitions from the late 1970s to the early 1990s. Though these transitions had wide-ranging consequences for the political organization of Latin American countries, we know very little about the actors involved, their preferences, and the institutional equilibria reached.

The study of democratization in Latin America has been dominated by the "transition paradigm" (O'Donnell & Schmitter 1986; Rustow 1970). The democratic transitions are presented as contingent, uncertain processes in which political actors (moderate representatives of both the authoritarian regime and the political opposition) struggle to define the rules and procedures the political game will follow. Without question, this paradigm has contributed greatly to our understanding of the democratization process, but the transitions framework also has some important limitations. First, there is a methodological and theoretical concern. In the last volume of their seminal contribution, O'Donnell and Schmitter point out that they "did not have (…) a 'theory' to test or to apply to the case studies and the thematic essays in these volumes" (1986: 3). They further argue that "'normal science' methodology is inappropriate in rapidly changing situations, where [the] parameters of political action are in flux." In essence, the transitions scholars built a useful general framework for understanding the complex processes of democratic transition in the third wave of democratization, but it is fair to say that they did not have a social science theory as we normally understand it. This framework was then "implicitly or explicitly followed in most other contributions [to the democratization literature]" (Collier 1999: 5).

The transitions framework has also been limited by its focus on certain actors (individual elites) while neglecting others (collective actors). In fact, the transitions paradigm presents the democratic transition as an uncertain game played by strategically defined *state actors,* moderate representatives (soft-liners) of the authoritarian regime and of the opposition. Societal actors, working-class movements, and civil society organizations are conceptualized as exogenous actors playing a secondary role during the negotiation of the transition pact (Collier 1999: 8). This is very problematic. Some studies have shown that societal actors did play an essential role in the democratic transitions in at least some countries (Collier & Mahoney 1997; Collier 1999; Valenzuela 1989).

As the transitions paradigm developed, then, it gradually forgot the advice—from one of the founding fathers of the transitions framework—that "we need not assume that the transition to democracy is a world-wide uniform process, that it always involves the same social classes, the same types of political issues, or even the same methods of solution" (Rustow 1970: 345).

Analytic narratives can be used by scholars interested in the transition processes and their consequences to overcome the limitations of the mainstream paradigm. Analytic narratives can serve precisely to address the methodological weaknesses of the transition paradigm by (1) devising solid theories to be tested in specific transitions in different Latin American countries, and (2) reaffirming the possibility of conducting rigorous social science research even in contexts where the rules of the game are blurred and the outcome uncertain. As for the more substantive concern—the failure to include relevant collective actors in the analysis—analytic narratives are less prone to error. Building a narrative involves a process-tracing effort that should lead to the identification of all actors influencing the process of institutional change. Moreover, existing analytic narratives often include collective actors in the analysis. Bates et al. (1998: 11) point out that one of the essential steps in designing a narrative is to "identify agents; some are individuals, but others are collective actors, such as elites, nations, electorates, or legislatures." In sum, analytic narratives can usefully be applied to the study of democratic transitions in Latin America. A good analytic narrative will identify the different individual and collective actors involved in the transition process, and it will build a rigorous theoretical model explaining how these different agents form their preferences and then reach a negotiated equilibrium. Given the huge consequences of the transition "pacts" for political institutions in Latin America, the development of analytic narratives will be most welcome.

The Sáenz Peña Law and the Utility of the Analytic Narratives Approach

Let us now turn, as an illustration of the analytic narrative approach, to the adoption of the 1912 Sáenz Peña law in Argentina. The Sáenz Peña law had three main components: (1) secret vote, (2) compulsory vote, (3) proportional representation. Together, the three elements of the reform undermined the political power of the landed elite, a landed elite that through electoral fraud, clientelism, and repression had dominated politics between 1880 and 1912. The rare opposition parties stood no chance of winning elections, because the electoral machine functioned such that only the incumbent could win. Incumbent administrations at both the regional and national level controlled the lists of registered voters, lists systematically favoring the parties in power. Clientelistic practices were effective because the vote was not secret (*voto cantado*). The use of a majoritarian electoral system insured that no real opposition group would be present in Congress (Rock 1975). Why, then, did the political elite adopt a reform that had the potential to undermine its political power and influence?

Previous historical accounts have emphasized the structural transformation of Argentinean society in the first decade of the twentieth century, a transformation that "required" an adjustment in the political system. According to the conventional historical account, the massive influx of immigrants in the late nineteenth century led to the strengthening of two social groups threatening the power of the landed elites: the working class and the middle class. The working class began to organize politically at the end of the nineteenth century. Socially mobile immigrant families joined the middle class. As these groups became more powerful and influential, their complete exclusion from politics became more problematic (Gallo 1986). In the words of Rock (1975: 17), "the more the political role of the immigrants developed, the more likely it was that the position of the landed elite would be threatened." Politicization of the urban sectors created political unrest and threatened the oligarchy with rebellion. A new party (the Unión Cívica Radical) symbolized the aspirations of the middle class by advocating free and fair elections. Confronted with the impossibility of an electoral victory, the UCR staged rebellions in 1890, 1893, and 1905. This view of the Sáenz Peña law is also espoused by Acemoglu and Robinson (2006: 28) who argue that the reform was "driven by the social unrest created by the Radical Party and the rapid radicalization of urban workers."

While changes in these "exogenous factors" certainly played a role in the adoption of the Sáenz Peña law, there are many inconsistencies in the conventional historical account. First, it is unclear why elites succumbed to the societal pressure for democratizing reforms in 1912 and not before, given that the first rebellions took place in the late nineteenth century. The oligarchy had not hesitated to repress severely the revolutions of 1890 and 1893. If anything, it appears that the Radical Party was less successful at threatening the stability of the regime in the first decade of the twentieth century than it had been possible in the past. As Rock points out (2002: 193) "the [1905] rebellion fell far short of its predecessors of either 1890 or 1893. The movement commanded virtually no popular support and remained confined to small military mutinies and civilian uprisings in Buenos Aires." The newspaper *La Nación* went so far as to describe the 1905 rebellion as a "parody of a sedition" (cited in Rock 2002: 193). In fact, all sectors of Argentinean society were benefitting from the exceptional economic boom that the country was experiencing in the beginning of the twentieth century. The quality of life was improving for the middle and lower classes in the urban centers (Rocchi 2000). In sum, the prospects for a successful revolution appeared very low in the first decade of the twentieth century. Any radical rebellion could have been easily wiped out. In sum, the prevailing historical account does not give us the key to solving the puzzle of the timing of the reform.

Extant accounts of the adoption of the Sáenz Peña law also present the Radical victory in 1916 as a big surprise to the Conservatives. The party in power believed it could defeat the UCR in democratic elections. This elite group clearly overestimated its own popularity and underestimated the UCR's support in the rising middle class (Díaz 1983). Similarly, Rock (1987: 190) argues that "Sáenz Peña and his supporters had espoused electoral reform in the belief that the old oligarchic factions would adapt to the new conditions and unite into a strong conservative party that would enjoy large popular support." But why, then, did the Sáenz Peña law promote a reform that implemented proportional representation? Offering free and fair elections would probably have been enough to force the UCR to abandon its decision to boycott elections. The Radical Party would have been discredited if it had chosen not to participate in clean elections. If the oligarchic elites were convinced they would beat the Radicals, why didn't they design an electoral reform that maintained a majoritarian electoral system?

The conventional wisdom, then, offers us an incomplete explanation of the adoption of the Sáenz Peña law, an explanation with important inconsistencies. In particular, the adoption of a proportional electoral system and the timing of the reform are poorly explained in most historical accounts. Two questions remain unanswered: (1) Why did the oligarchic regime decide to accept the demands of the Radical Party in the second decade of the twentieth century when the option of repressing potential rebellions was still clearly available? (2) Why did the oligarchic regime design a proportional electoral system instead of a majoritarian regime that appeared more favorable? In a sense, we are asking a question about something that *did not* happen (i.e., continued repression of Radical and other urban rebellions). Avner Greif (1998: 26) lucidly points out that analytic narratives are particularly useful when applied to these kinds of research questions. He argues that "addressing these questions requires an appropriate model for linking what we observe with what we do not observe, namely analyzing expectations regarding off-the-path-of-play behavior and on-the-path-of-play outcomes."

Space constraints and the complexity of the issue do not permit a full-blown analytic narrative, but we can at least sketch a preliminary model, a model based on a more careful reading of the secondary literature.[19] The first essential step of analytic narratives is the identification of the key actors who played roles in the process of institutional transformation. In this case, the key actors were the political organizations negotiating the reform. The conventional historical account of the electoral reform presents a simple game with two actors: the elite (represented by the conservative coalition in power) versus the middle-class/urban sectors (represented by the Radical Party). As we demonstrated above, it is difficult to understand why the elites accepted this reform at a moment where the Radical threat seemed lower than in the past. The key to the puzzle lies in the fact that the elite was divided into two groups: the "intransigents" (opposing all forms of reform) and the "modernists" (in favor of an electoral reform but strongly opposed to the Radical rebellions).

The second step of any analytic narrative involves identifying the resources and preferences of the main actors, given a set of exogenous factors. In the case of the Sáenz Peña law, we rapidly realize that the elite were not a monolithic bloc opposed to the reform. On the contrary, the "modernist" faction was as interested as the Radical Party in obtaining free and fair elections. As we will show, this is central to understanding the *timing* of the reform. The oligarchic regime began in 1880 with the arrival in power of General Roca. Roca was president between 1880 and 1886 and again between 1898 and 1904. He was an astute politician who held the strings of power until the first decade of the twentieth century even when was not formally serving as the nation's president. Although Roca made agreements with *porteño* politicians, his power was based on a broad coalition with the governors of Argentine provinces. Roca represented the positivist philosophy of the oligarchy. He believed that order and progress were more important than the fairness of the elections. As a result, the negotiated choice of the oligarchic elite was always imposed through corrupt and fraudulent elections. This disdain for democratic elections was soon challenged by the Unión Cívica (and later the Unión Cívica Radical). The conventional wisdom holds that the Radical Party represented the aspirations of the people (or at least the "middle class"). On the contrary, Rock (2002: 149) argues that the Radical movement "largely consisted of a front for the propertied classes of the metropolis and the army (…) [retaining] strong conservative orientations." The UCR did not have a clear reformist program. It simply wanted to limit the worst abuses of the oligarchic regime. The main element distinguishing the Radical Party from other elite factions opposed to Roca is that it was willing to use force to obtain free and fair elections. The third—and often neglected—actor in the process of institutional reform is the "modernist" faction of the elites. This faction emerged very rapidly as a reaction to the fraudulent practices of the oligarchic regime. Modernist politicians were also positivists, but they believed that the best policies would come from the emergence of modern parties and the open debate of ideas. Only an electoral reform could achieve this goal. In 1892 (twenty years before the adoption of the Sáenz Peña law), Roque Sáenz Peña was selected as the presidential candidate of the Modernist faction. Roca reacted by counter-proposing the candidacy of Luis Sáenz Peña, Roque's father, as the candidate of the regime. Roque Sáenz Peña dutifully withdrew his candidacy, which represented a serious blow weakening the Modernist faction for years to come (Rock 2002: 151–152). In sum, two political groups (the Radicals and the Modernists), supported the electoral reform. However, both actors were politically weak. The Modernist faction had few political resources against the political and electoral machine of the oligarchic regime headed by Roca. The Radical Party lost momentum after the failed rebellions of the early 1890s and was incapable of threatening the regime militarily. Moreover, an alliance between Modernists and Radicals was impossible, because Modernists disliked the use of force more than they disliked the fraudulent practices of the regime. Of course, the dominant faction of the oligarchic regime would not support any electoral reform threatening their position of power. Since the coalition orchestrated by Roca had more political resources and more military power than the other political groups, an electoral reform was unconceivable until the first years of the twentieth century.

The puzzle, then, is to explain what upset this previous equilibrium, allowing the adoption in 1912 of the Sáenz Peña law. The prevailing historical wisdom presents the reform as a defensive reaction by the elites against the pressures of the rising middle classes (especially in Buenos Aires). Our analytic model allows us to evaluate this historical narrative. Before analyzing the preferences and resources of the three key political actors in the first decade of the twentieth century, it is important to consider some important exogenous factors that were redesigning these preferences and resources. The start of the oligarchic regime in 1880 coincided with the rebellion of the province of Buenos Aires, a rebellion that was harshly repressed by federal forces. Out of a sense of political opportunity, most *porteño* politicians—most notably Mitre and Pellegrini—decided to enter the oligarchic coalition led by Roca. For twenty years, Roca reached agreements with politicians from Buenos Aires and maintained his position of preeminence. However, these agreements could not avoid a distinct provincial bias in the oligarchic regime. According to Rock (2002: 185), "controlling the Senate and the provincial governors, Roca could usually ignore the city of Buenos Aires." In fact, the metropolitan vote was unneeded to maintain the viability of the oligarchic regime. Still, things were changing at the beginning of the twentieth century. The structure of the economy was changing, especially the weight of the industrial sector. In 1890, the industrial sector accounted for only 13.4% of the GDP. By 1916, it represented 27.8 % of the GDP (Rocchi 2000). Most industrial goods were produced in the cities, and the major industrial center was Buenos Aires. This structural transformation of the economy increased the dissatisfaction with the political status quo of politicians from Buenos Aires. In addition, reformist and democratic movements were beginning to form in Buenos Aires. A student riot in July, 1901, made it clear that discontent with the oligarchic regime was growing. Politicians from Buenos Aires realized that "the new currents were about to tilt the balance against the old" (Rock 2002: 181). As a result of these structural transformations, political leaders from Buenos Aires—led by Pellegrini—abandoned Roca and joined the reformist camp. These desertions changed completely the balance of power between the two elite factions. While the Modernist faction gained momentum with the support of *porteño* politicians, the Roca faction lost much of its power. The position of the Radical Party, however, did not evolve so markedly. As we sketched above, the UCR seemed less threatening to the regime in the first decade of the twentieth century than in the 1890s. Still, the unsuccessful rebellion in 1905 was used by the reformist faction of the regime to exaggerate the threat and push for a reform in their own interest.

When Sáenz Peña took power in 1910, the three main political actors remained the same, that is, the modernist and the intransigent factions of the oligarchic regime along with the Radical Party. Their interests also remained the same. The Radical Party and the Modernists wanted free and fair elections, while the most conservative faction of the elites wanted to maintain the status quo. The balance of power, however, had changed. The modernist faction was now in a much stronger position, because it controlled state resources. But Sáenz Peña wanted to take advantage of this window of opportunity. It was uncertain who would be the next president, and the most conservative faction of the regime still had a lot of political resources, especially in the provinces.

The timing of the reform is better explained with this analytic model than with the conventional historical account. Pressure from the middle classes was not overwhelming, and the threat represented by the Radical Party was lower than it had been in the past. The reform was introduced in 1912 because the balance of power was more favorable than ever to the reformist faction of the oligarchic regime. Social unrest is an important exogenous factor that contributed to changing the preferences of the main players in this game of institutional transformation. But the link is not as direct or as evident as previous studies have argued.

Why did the Sáenz Peña law introduce a proportional electoral system rather than a majoritarian system? This question is a puzzle in previous historical accounts, because these accounts also hold that the oligarchy expected a clear victory in the next elections. Once again, our analytic model provides a better answer. The post-reform period was a highly uncertain one in which many parties representing the different political groups we have analyzed would co-exist. Proportional representation assured the main players in this negotiation that at a minimum they would be represented in Congress in proportion to their electoral force. By showing that the oligarchic regime was divided into two clear and irreconcilable factions—at least with respect to electoral reform—we are in a better position to understand the specificities of the Sáenz Peña law.

In sum, by illuminating the preferences of the different political actors involved in the process of institutional transformation, a good analytic narrative would help solve this important puzzle in Argentine politics. True, the politicization of urban sectors in the beginning of the twentieth century may have pressed the regime to move in the direction of free and fair elections, but the timing and the form of the institutional transformation are better understood through a careful analysis of the preferences of the key players involved in this game.

IV: Bureaucracy, Lobbying, Analytic Narratives: Implications for Research Strategy

Research initiatives in these three areas will require a greater investment in what we call "soaking and poking." Bureaucracies (like the equally neglected area of lower courts) are diffuse, with within-country geographical as well as hierarchical spread. Bureaucracies are also heterogeneous, with differences across countries, across levels of government within countries, and across types of programs administered. Put simply, research on one agency in one country cannot be generalized to "Latin American bureaucracy." Similarly, lobbying research will involve tracing group-specific or industry-specific involvement in the legislative process from the introduction (or non-introduction) of bills to their ultimate failure, modification, or passage. An analytic narrative of an event distant in time will involve extensive interviews along with archival research in documents, memoirs, and letters.

In an increasingly quantitative and formal political science, can we ask scholars, especially younger scholars, to engage in what sounds suspiciously like the dreaded "case study"? Is this not a prescription for unemployment? One response is that case studies and theory are not antithetical. The modal dissertation in comparative politics builds a theoretical argument and tests that argument on carefully chosen cases. Still, this response is disingenuous, because it ignores the *sequence* of research development in areas like legislative politics. Shepsle, Fiorina, and McCubbins needed the "soaking and poking" of Fenno, Manley, and Wildavsky. Carpenter's theory of bureaucratic autonomy built on Pendleton Herring.[20]

How can we provide incentives for more intensive field research in areas with diffuse and heterogeneous research sites? One solution is scholarly collaboration. Particularly at the dissertation level, data can be shared even when theoretical arguments are distinct. For example, two scholars can share data on lobbying techniques in different countries even though their theoretical arguments differ, and data on informal networks in varying bureaucratic agencies can be shared among multiple scholarly projects.

Many years ago the American Political Science Association regularly published subfield-specific lists of "dissertations in progress." Graduate students in the early stages of thesis preparation regularly consulted these lists to see what others were doing, to avoid duplication, and to get ideas. For reasons that are unclear to current staff, the APSA stopped publishing these lists in 1989.[21] Such lists today could serve as invitations to data sharing and collaboration.

The rapid development of high-quality research traditions on the part of political scientists based in Latin American universities also provides new opportunities for collaboration. In terms of field research, Latin American scholars face weaker time pressures than those faced by scholars based outside the region, and they are likely to have useful social and professional networks. Collaborations with U.S. scholars would be particularly attractive to Latin American scholars as they move beyond single-country research.

Ultimately, responsibility for encouraging new directions in research and for rewarding risk-taking projects falls to senior scholars, especially those in programs with a major Latin

American component. The vitality of the study of Latin American politics depends on avoiding the trap of "political science as usual," that is, ever-narrower questions answerable only with quantitative data. Doubtless there are other research questions and strategies as compelling as those we have put forward; in the end we simply want to encourage debate on what's next.

Notes

1 We are grateful for comments to Guy Peters, Jennifer Victor, and the editors of this volume.

2 For a thorough treatment of the policy process as it affects the shape and implementation of administrative reform, see Ben Ross Schneider and Blanca Heredia, *Reinventing Leviathan: The Politics of Administrative Reform in Developing Countries* (2003). Schneider and Heredia provide an excellent discussion of models of administrative reform, and various authors contribute chapters on Latin America and other developing countries, but there are no discussions of the actual functioning of any bureaucratic agency. When reform is the objective, it is simply taken for granted that the diagnosis of bureaucratic disfunctionality is correct.

3 Guy Peters argues that Weberian reforms ought to precede NPM: "Most governments in the world face pressures, either psychological or more tangible, to adopt the modern canon of administration in the form of NPM. For Central and Eastern Europe and Latin America, those pressures are likely to do more harm than good. Despite the appeal of ideas such as deregulation and flexibility, governments attempting to build both effective administration and democracy might require much greater emphasis on formality, rules, and strong ethical standards. The values of efficiency and effectiveness are important but in the short run not so crucial as creating probity and responsibility. Once a so-called Weberian administrative system is institutionalized, then it may make sense to consider how best to move from that system towards a more "modern" system of PA. (2001, p. 176; see also p. 164)

4 These data come from the Bank's "Network on Public Policy Management and Transparency" (Lora 2007).

5 Tendler and Freedheim note the growing literature on industrial performance and workplace transformation in political science, a literature that emphasizes worker commitment and client-worker trust. See, for example, Piore and Sabel (1984). Finally, it might be helpful to compare this kind of program with the administrative style of Bolsa Família

6 See Sotiropoulos (2004) for a very abstract comparison of Southern European (and by extension Latin American) bureaucracy with the rest of West European bureaucracy. Tendler and Freedheim's (1994) project on Ceará's rural health program is precisely a study of street-level bureaucrats.

7 TVA linked itself to the land-grant college system and to the American Farm Bureau Federation. Their pressure led TVA to exclude the Farm Security Administration and the Soil Conservation Service from its area of operation (Selznick 1966). It also led to discriminatory policies against Black farmers.

8 This bias sometimes reveals itself all too clearly. Clive Thomas's *Research Guide to U.S. and International Interest Groups* classifies Latin America as a developing society, starkly different from a developed, pluralist society. "In [developing] societies *interests* as opposed to *interest groups* are more significant politically … In developing societies the major type of interest is the primordial group based on kinship, tribe, lineage, neighborhood, religion, and so on" (2004, 325). In describing the tactics that interests use in places like Latin America, Thomas suggests that "Such formalized and institutional channels are minimal or nonexistent in non-pluralist, transition, and developing societies. In these systems informal personal contacts and power plays within and between government entities and related organizations, such as the ruling party or the court circle around a monarch, are the most significant" (2004, p. 325). Not exactly the Latin America we know.

9   Bates and Krueger note that their country studies "fail to attribute a decisive role to the pressure of organized interests" (1993: 457). Perhaps (and of course "decisive" is a murky term), but their three Latin American cases provide lots of evidence to the contrary. Post-Allende Chile was a dictatorship (hello?), and the import-competing sector *favored* the general policy line of the government even though it opposed draconian trade liberalization (Stallings & Brock 1993).

Brazilian industrialists opposed the government's ill-fated stabilization program of 1979–1984. Payne (1994) and Boschi (1978) found that industrialists used "social ties and personal contacts to influence government both within and outside the context of bureaucratic rings" (cited by Lal & Maxfield 1993: 45). In Ecuador, Grindle and Thoumi discovered that presidents introduced but could not sustain policy innovations, *partly as a result of regional and sectoral interest group pressures* (Grindle & Thoumi 1993).

10 The ambivalence of the literature is thoughtfully treated in Peter Kingstone's *Crafting Coalitions for Reform: Business Preferences, Political Institutions, and Neoliberal Reform in Brazil* (1999). Kingstone focuses on establishing the preferences of various industrial sectors and the ways in which market and political factors interact to shape preferences and behavior.

11 See also Eduardo Sáenz Rovner's investigation of Colombian interest groups in the 1940s, *La Ofensiva Empresarial: Industriales, Políticos y Violencia en los Años 40 en Colombia.*

12 On network density, see Lowery and Gray (1995). On the creation of partisan divisions, see Grossmann and Dominguez (2009). On cliques, see Chwe (2000).

13 Ames, for example, found evidence in Brazil in the early 1990s that some deputies—it is unclear how many—run mini-lobbying enterprises directly from their offices, utilizing staff to lobby the ministries in the name of the deputy but for the benefit of fee-paying private firms.

14 Consider Baumgartner et al.'s *Lobbying and Policy Change* (2009). Utilizing a random sample of approximately one hundred issues between 1999 and 2002, the authors interviewed more than three hundred lobbyists and government officials. With these and follow up interviews, plus official reports and monitoring news throughout all four years, they were able to map the progress made on each issue.

15 Some work uses economic proxies of interest group influence, such as weight of the sector's economic influence as a percentage of GDP (e.g., Frieden, Ghezzi and Stein 2001; dos Santos 2008).

16 On the consequences of campaign contributions, see Hall and Wayman (1990), McCarty and Rothenberg (1996), and Wawro (2001). On the strategies behind such contributions, see Apollonio and La Raja (2004), Gordon et al. (2007), and Wright (1985).

17 Lance (2010) used the data while acknowledging Samuels's disclaimer, arguing that the data serve as conservative estimates. He contends that if he can prove that only the 25% most reputable contributions affect legislation, then the relationship should hold for all contributions.

18 Sophisticated reviews of rational-choice institutionalism present two levels of analysis within the tradition. The first takes institutions as exogenous and fixed; the second allows endogenous institutions and observes their formation and survival (Shepsle 1986). But even adherents of RCI recognize that the former is "far more well developed" than the latter (Weingast 1996: 167)

19 Of course, dressing an analytic narrative of this case would require scholars to consult such primary sources as newspapers, archives, and political memoires.

20 Note, once again, Karcher and Schneider's claim that "The study of business in Latin America may also suffer from a bias in political science for quantitative methods." This bias is only part of the problem of Latin American interest group research, but it also affects work on bureaucracy. One cause of the shallowness of the administrative reform literature is its reliance on easily quantifiable indicators. This bias advantages the approach of "bureaucrats as opportunistic rent-seekers." As we saw in our discussion of Daniel Carpenter's work on U.S. bureaucratic development, a more open theoretical lens, one in which bureaucrat-politicians may try to create policy space for themselves, is critical.

21 Communication with senior APSA staff, June, 2011.

References

Acemoglu, Daron, and James A. Robinson. 2006. *Economic Origins of Dictatorship and Democracy*. New York: Cambridge University Press.

Ainsworth, Scott, 1997. "The Role of Legislators in the Determination of Interest Group Influence." *Legislative Studies Quarterly*, 22: 517–533.

Ames, Barry. 2001. *The Deadlock of Democracy in Brazil*. Berkeley: University of California Press.

Apollonio, Dorie, and Raymond La Raja. 2004. "Who Gave Soft Money? The Effect of Interest Group Resources on Political Contributions." *Journal of Politics*, 66(4): 1134–1154.

Bartell, Ernest, C.S.C. 1995. "Perceptions by Business Leaders and the Transition to Democracy in Chile." In Ernest Bartell and Leigh A. Payne (eds.), *Business and Democracy in Latin America*. Pittsburgh, PA: University of Pittsburgh Press.

Barzelay, Michael. 2002a. "The New Public Management: a bibliographical essay for Latin American (and other) scholars." *International Public Management Journal*, 3: 229–265.

Barzelay, Michael. 2002b. "Origins of the NPM: An International View from Public Administration/Political Science." In Kate McLaughlin, Stephen Osborne, and Ewan Ferlie (eds.), *New Public Management: Current trends and Future Prospects*. London: Routledge.

Bates, Robert, Avner Greif, Margaret Levi, Jean-Laurent Rosenthal, and Barry Weingast. 1998. *Analytical Narratives*. Princeton, NJ: Princeton University Press.

Bates, Robert, and Anne Krueger (eds.). 1993. *Political and Economic Interactions in Economic Policy Reform*. Cambridge, MA: Blackwell.

Batista Araújo, Gustavo. 2008. "O Déficit Entre Acordado e Realizado no Mercosul; A Influência dos Grupos de Interesse e o Estudo do Caso Brasileiro" (Master's Dissertation). Retrieved from The Digital Library of Theses and Dissertations of the University of São Paulo.

Bauer, Raymond, Ithiel de Sola Pool, and Lewis Dexter. 1963. *American Business and Public Policy: The Politics of Foreign Trade*. New York: Atherton Press.

Baumgartner, Frank, Jeffrey Berry, Marie Hojnacki, David Kimball and Beth Leech. 2009. *Lobbying and Policy Change: Who Wins, Who Loses, and Why*. Chicago: University of Chicago Press.

Bentley, Arthur. 1908. *The Process of Government*. Chicago: University of Chicago Press.

Berry, Jeffrey. 1999. *The New Liberalism: The Rising Power of Citizen Groups*. Washington, DC: Brookings Institution.

Boschi, Renato Raul. 1978. "National Industrial Elites and the State in Post-1964 Brazil." (Doctoral Dissertation). University of Michigan, Ann Arbor, MI.

Bresser Pereira, Luis Carlos, and Peter Spink, eds. 1999. *Reforming the State: Managerial Public Administration in Latin America*. Boulder, CO: Lynne Rienner.

Bull, Benedicte. 2004. "The Role of Local Economic Groups in Telecommunication Privatization in Central America." *Journal of Developing Societies*, 20(3-4): 227–246.

Bull, Benedicte. 2010. "Free Trade Negotiations, Business Participation and the Impact of Environmental and Labour Regulation: The Case of Chile." In José Carlos Marques and Peter Utting (eds.), *Business, Politics and Public Policy: Implications for Inclusive Development*. New York: Palgrave Macmillan.

Burstein, Paul, and Elizabeth Hirsh. 2007. "Interest Organizations, Information, and Policy Innovation in the U.S. Congress." *Sociological Forum*, 22(2): 174–199.

Calvo, Ernesto and Victoria Murillo. 2004. "Who Delivers? Partisan Clients in the Argentine Electoral Market." *American Journal of Political Science*, 48: 742–57.

Carey, John. 1996. *Term Limits and Legislative Representation*. Cambridge: Cambridge University Press.

Carpenter, Daniel. 2001. *The Forging of Bureaucratic Autonomy: Reputations, Networks, and Policy Innovation in Executive Agencies, 1862–1928*. Princeton, NJ: Princeton University Press.

Carpenter, Daniel, Kevin Esterling, and David Lazer. 2004. "Friends, Brokers, and Transitivity: Who Informs Whom in Washington Politics?" *Journal of Politics*, 66: 224–246.

Carrión, Gloria. 2009. *Trade, Regionalism and the Politics of Policy Making in Nicaragua*. Geneva: United Nations Research Institute for Social Development.

Carrión, Gloria. 2010. "Business, Politics and Free Trade Negotiations in Nicaragua: Who Were the Winners and Losers?" In José Carlos Marques and Peter Utting (eds.). *Business, Politics and Public Policy: Implications for Inclusive Development*. New York: Palgrave Macmillan.

Chwe, Michael Suk-Young. 2000. "Communication and Coordination in Social Networks." *Review of Economic Studies*, 67: 1–16.

Cockroft, James, and Bo Anderson. 1966. "Cooptation and Control in Mexican Politics." *International Journal of Comparative Sociology*, 7:1, 11–28.

Collier, Ruth Berins. 1999. *Paths Toward Democracy: The Working Class and Elites in Western Europe and South America*. New York: Cambridge University Press.

Collier, Ruth Berins, and David Collier. 1991. *Shaping the Political Arena: Critical Junctures, the Labor Movement, and Regime Dynamics in Latin America*. Princeton, NJ: Princeton University Press.

Collier, Ruth Berins, and Samuel Handlin (eds.). 2009. *Reorganizing Popular Politics: Participation and the New Interest Regime in Latin America*. University Park: Pennsylvania State University Press.

Collier, Ruth Berins, and James Mahoney. 1997. "Adding Collective Actors to Collective Outcomes: Labor and Recent Democratization in South America and Southern Europe." *Comparative Politics*, 29(3): 285–303.

Cox, Gary. 1987. *The Efficient Secret: The Cabinet and the Development of Political Parties in Victorian England*. New York: Cambridge University Press.

Cox, Gary, and Mathew McCubbins. 1993. *Legislative Leviathan: Party Government in the House*. Berkeley: University of California Press.

Crawford, Kenneth. 1939. *The Pressure Boys*. New York: Julian Messner.

Cunow, Saul, Barry Ames, Scott Desposato, and Lucio Rennó. 2011. "Reelection and Legislative Power: Surprising Results from Brazil." (Unpublished manuscript).

Dahl, Robert. 1961. *Who Governs?* New Haven, CT: Yale University Press.

Danielian, Lucig, and Benjamin Page. 1994. "The Heavenly Chorus: Interest Group Voices on TV News." *American Journal of Political Science,* 38: 1056–1078.

Díaz, Honorio. 1983. *Ley Sáenz Peña: pro y contra*. Buenos Aires: Centro Editor de América Latina.

Dos Santos, Luiz Alberto. 2008. "Regulamentação das Atividades de lobby e seu impacto sobre as relações entre políticos, burocratas e grupos de interesse e no ciclo de políticas públicas – Análise comparativa dos Estados Unidos e Brasil." (Unpublished Dissertation). Universidade de Brasilia, Brazil.

Durand, Francisco, and Eduardo Silva (eds.). 1998. *Organized Business, Economic Change, and Democracy in Latin America*. Boulder, CO: Lynne Rienner.

Durand, Francisco. 2010. "Corporate Rents and the Capture of the Peruvian State." In José Carlos Marques and Peter Utting (eds.), *Business, Politics and Public Policy: Implications for Inclusive Development*. New York: Palgrave Macmillan.

Echebarría, Koldo, and Juan Carlos Cortázar. 2007. "Public Administration and Public Employment Reform in Latin America." In Eduardo Lora (ed.), *The State of State Reform in Latin America*. Washington, DC: Inter-American Development Bank.

Erickson, Kenneth. 1977. *The Brazilian Corporative State and Working-Class Politics*. Berkeley: University of California Press.

Evans, Peter, and James Rauch. 1999. "Bureaucracy and Growth: A Cross-National Analysis of the Effects of "Weberian" State Structures on Economic Growth." *American Sociological Review,* 64 (October): 748–765.

Fenno, Richard. 1966. *The Power of the Purse*. Boston: Little, Brown.

Fenno, Richard. 1978. *Home Style: House Members in Their Districts*. Boston: Little, Brown.

Fiorina, Morris. 1977. *Congress: Keystone of the Washington Establishment*. New Haven, CT: Yale University Press.

Frieden, Jeffry, and Ernesto Stein (eds.). 2001. *The Currency Game: Exchange Rate Politics in Latin America*. Washington D.C.: Inter-American Development Bank.

Frieden, Jeffry, Piero Ghezzi, and Ernesto Stein. 2001. "Politics and Exchange Rates: A Cross-Country Approach." In Jeffry Frieden and Ernesto Stein (eds.), *The Currency Game: Exchange Rate Politics in Latin America*. Washington, D.C.: Inter-American Development Bank.

Gallo, Ezequiel. 1986. Argentina: Society and Politics, 1880–1916. In Leslie Bethell (ed.), *The Cambridge History of Latin America* (Vol. 5). Cambridge: Cambridge University Press.

Geddes, Barbara. 1994. *Politician's Dilemma: Building State Capacity in Latin America*. Berkeley: University of California Press Series on Social Choice and Political Economy.

Gordon, Sanford, Catherine Hafner, and Dimitri Landa. 2007. "Consumption or Investment? On Motivations for Political Giving." *Journal of Politics,* 69(4): 1057–1072.

Greif, Avner. 1998. "Self-Enforcing Political Systems and Economic Growth: Late Medieval Genoa." In Robert Bates, Avner Greif, Margaret Levi, Jean-Laurent Rosenthal, and Barry Weingast (eds.), *Analytical Narratives*. Princeton, NJ: Princeton University Press.

Grindle, Merilee, and Francisco Thoumi. 1993. "Muddling Toward Adjustment: The Political Economy of Economic Policy Change in Ecuador." In Robert Bates and Anne Krueger (eds.), *Political and Economic Interactions in Economic Policy Reform: Evidence from Eight Countries*. Cambridge: Blackwell.

Grossmann, Matthew, and Casey Dominguez. 2009. "Party Coalitions and Interest Group Networks." *American Politics Research,* 37(5): 767–800.

Haggard, Stephan, and Robert Kaufman. 1995. *The Political Economy of Democratic Transitions*. Princeton, NJ: Princeton University Press.

Hall, Richard, and Frank Wayman. 1990. "Buying Time: Moneyed Interests and the Mobilization of Bias in Congressional Committees." *American Political Science Review,* 84(3): 797–820.

Heaney, Michael. 2006. "Brokering Health Policy" *Journal of Heath Politics, Policy and Law,* 31(5): 887–944.

Heinz, John, Edward Laumann, Robert Nelson, and Robert Salisbury. 1993. *The Hollow Core: Private Interests in National Policy Making.* Cambridge, MA: Harvard University Press.

Hojnacki, Marie, and David Kimball. 1998. "Organized Interests and the Decision of Whom to Lobby in Congress." *American Political Science Review,* 92: 775–790.

Jaramillo, Juan, Roberto Steiner, and Natalia Salazar. 2001. "A Long-lasting Crawling Peg: Political Determinants of Exchange Rate Policy in Colombia." In Jeffry Frieden and Ernesto Stein (eds.), *The Currency Game: Exchange Rate Politics in Latin America.* Washington, D.C.: Inter-American Development Bank.

Kaufman, Herbert. 1960. *The Forest Ranger.* Baltimore: Johns Hopkins University Press for Resources for the Future.

Key, V. O. 1964. *Politics, Parties and Pressure Groups.* New York: Thomas Crowell.

Kingstone, Peter.1999. *Creating Coalitions for Reform: Business Preferences, Political Institutions, and Neo-liberal Reform in Brazil.* College State: Pennsylvania State University Press.

Knoke, David. 1986. "Associations and Interest Groups." *Annual Review of Sociology.* 12: 1–21.

Lal, Deepak, and Sylvia Maxfield. 1993. "The Political Economy of Stabilization in Brazil." In Robert Bates and Anne Krueger (eds.). *Political and Economic Interactions in Economic Policy Reform: Evidence from Eight Countries.* Cambridge: Blackwell.

Lance, Justin. 2010. "An Institutional Approach to Understanding Leftist Party Change in Brazil: Corporate Campaign Contributions, Leadership Moderation, and Societal Interests." (Unpublished Doctoral Dissertation). Graduate Program in Political Science, Ohio State University, Columbus, OH.

Leech, Beth, and Frank Baumgartner. 1998. "Lobbying Friends and Foes in Washington." In Allan J. Cigler and Burdett A. Loomis (eds.), *Interest Group Politics.* 5th edition. Washington, DC: CQ Press.

Levi, Margaret. 1997. A Model, a Method, and a Map: Rational Choice in Comparative and Historical Analysis. In Mark Lichbach and Alan Zuckerman (eds.), *Comparative Politics: Rationality, Culture, and Structure* (Vol. 28). Cambridge: Cambridge University Press.

Levi, Margaret. 1998. "Conscription: the Price of Citizenship." In Robert Bates, Avner Greif, Margaret Levi, Jean-Laurent Rosenthal and Barry Weingast (eds.). *Analytic Narratives.* Princeton, NJ: Princeton University Press.

Lipsky, Michael. 1980. *Street-Level Bureaucracy: Dilemmas of the Individual in Public Services.* New York: Russell Sage Foundation.

Lora, Eduardo, ed. 2007. *The State of State Reform in Latin America.* Washington, DC: Inter-American Development Bank.

Lowery, David, and Virginia Gray. 1995. "The Population Ecology of Gucci Gulch, or the Natural Regulation of Interest Group Numbers." *American Journal of Political Science,* 39: 1–29.

Lowi, Theodore. 1964. "American Business, Public Policy, Case Studies and Political Theory." *World Politics,* 16: 677–715.

Mahoney, James. 2010. *Colonialism and Postcolonial Development: Spanish America in Comparative Perspective.* New York: Cambridge University Press.

Mahoney, James, and Dietrich Rueschemeyer. 2003. "Comparative Historical Analysis: Achievements and Agendas." In James Mahoney and Dietrich Rueschemeyer (eds.), *Comparative Historical Analysis in the Social Sciences.* New York: Cambridge University Press.

Mancuso, Wagner Pralon. 2007. *O Lobby da Indústria no Congresso Nacional: Empresariado e Política no Brasil Contemporâneo* [The industry lobby in Congress: Entrepreneurs and Politics in Contemporary Brazil]. São Paulo: Edusp.

Manley, John. 1970. *The Politics of Finance: The House Committee on Ways and Means.* Boston: Little, Brown.

Mayhew, David. 1974. *Congress: The Electoral Connection.* New Haven, CT: Yale University Press.

McCarty, Nolan, and Lawrence S. Rothenberg. 1996. "Commitment and the Campaign Contribution Contract." *American Journal of Political Science* 40(3): 872–904.

"The Miracle of the Cerrado." 2010. *The Economist.* August 26.

O'Donnell, Guillermo, and Philippe Schmitter. 1986. *Transitions from Authoritarian Rule: Tentative Conclusions about Uncertain Democracies*. Baltimore: Johns Hopkins University Press.

Oliveira, Amâncio, and Janina Onuki. 2007. "Grupos de Interesse e a Política Comercial Brasileira: A Atuação na Arena Legislativa." Papeis Legislativos n°8, OPSA, Dezembro.

Payne, Leigh. 1994. *Brazilian Industrialists and Democratic Change*. Baltimore: John Hopkins University Press.

Perez-Aleman, Paola. 2010. "New Standards and Partnerships in Latin America: Implications for Small Producers and State Policy." In José Carlos Marques and Peter Utting (eds.), *Business, Politics and Public Policy: Implications for Inclusive Development*. New York: Palgrave Macmillan.

Peters, B. Guy. 2001. *The Future of Governing*. 2nd rev. ed. Lawrence: Kansas University Press.

Pierson, Paul. 2000. "Increasing Returns, Path Dependence, and the Study of Politics." *American Political Science Review*, 942: 251–267.

Pierson, Paul. 2003. "Big, Slow-Moving, and ... Invisible: Macrosocial Processes in the Study of Comparative Politics." In James Mahoney and Dietrich Rueschemeyer (eds.), *Comparative Historical Analysis in the Social Sciences*. New York: Cambridge University Press.

Piore, Michael, and Charles Sabel. 1984. *The Second Industrial Divide: Possibilities for Prosperity*. New York: Basic Books.

Rae, Douglas, and Michael Taylor. 1970. *The Analysis of Political Cleavages*. New Haven, CT: Yale University Press.

Rocchi, Fernando. 2000. "El péndulo de la riqueza: La economía argentina en el período 1880–1916." In Marta Z. Lobato (ed.), *Nueva Historia Argentina: El progreso, la modernización y sus límites, 1880–1916*. Buenos Aires: Editorial Sudamericana.

Rock, David. 1975. *Politics in Argentina, 1890–1930: The Rise and Fall of Radicalism*. New York: Cambridge University Press.

Rock, David. 1987. *Argentina, 1516–1987: from Spanish Colonization to Alfonsín*. Berkeley: University of California Press.

Rock, David. 2002. *State Building and Political Movements in Argentina, 1860–1916*. Stanford, CA: Stanford University Press.

Rueschemeyer, Dietrich, Evelyn Stephens, and John Stephens. 1992. *Capitalist Development and Democracy*. Chicago: The University of Chicago Press.

Rustow, Dankwort. 1970. "Transitions to Democracy." *Comparative Politics*, 23: 337–363.

Sáenz Rovner, Eduardo. 1992. *La ofensiva empresarial: industriales, políticos y violencia en los años 40 en Colombia*. Bogotá: Tercer Mundo Editores.

Schattschneider, E. E. 1960. *The Semisovereign People*. New York: Holt, Rinehart, and Winston.

Schlozman, Kay Lehman, Sidney Verba, Henry Brady, Philip Jones, and Traci Burch. 2008. "Who Sings in the Heavenly Chorus? The Shape of the Organized Interest System." Paper prepared for presentation at the Annual Meeting of the American Political Science Association, Boston (Aug. 28–31).

Schlozman, Kay Lehman. 2010. "Who Sings in the Heavenly Chorus? The Shape of the Organized Interest Group System." In L. Sandy Maisel and Jeffrey Berry (eds.), *The Oxford Handbook of American Political Parties and Interest Groups*. Oxford: Oxford University Press.

Schneider, Ben Ross. 2004. *Business Politics and the State in 20th Century Latin America*. New York: Cambridge University Press.

Schneider, Ben Ross, and Blanca Heredia. 2003. *Reinventing Leviathan: The Political of Administrative Reform in Developing Countries*. Miami: North-South Center Press of the University of Miami.

Selznick, Phillip. 1966. *TVA and the Grass Roots: a Study in Formal Organization*. Berkeley: University of California Press.

Shepsle, Kenneth. 1978. *The Giant Jigsaw Puzzle*. Chicago: University of Chicago Press.

Shepsle, Kenneth. 1986. "Institutional Equilibrium and Equilibrium Institutions." In Herbert Weisberg (ed.), *Political Science: The Science of Politics*, pp. 51–81. New York: Agathon.

Shepsle, Kenneth. 2008. "Rational Choice Institutionalism." In R. A. W. Rhodes, Sarah Binder, and Bert Rockman (eds.), *The Oxford Handbook of Political Institutions*. New York: Oxford University Press.

Skocpol, Theda. 1979. *States and Social Revolutions: A Comparative Analysis of France, Russia, and China*. Cambridge: Cambridge University Press.

Skocpol, Theda. 2000. "Commentary: Theory Tackles History." *Social Science History*, (244), 669–676.

Smith, Mark. 2000. *American Business and Political Power: Public Opinion, Elections, and Democracy.* Chicago: University of Chicago Press.

Sotiropoulos, Dimitri. 2004. "Southern European Public Bureaucracies in Comparative Perspective." *West European Politics*, 27 (3): 405–422.

Spiller, Pablo, and Mariano Tommasi. 2007. *The Institutional Foundations of Public Policy in Argentina.* New York: Cambridge University Press.

Spiller, Pablo, Mariano Tommasi, with Juliana Bambaci. 2007. "The Bureaucracy." In Spiller, Pablo and Mariano Tommasi (eds.), *The Institutional Foundations of Public Policy in Argentina.* New York: Cambridge University Press.

Stallings, Barbara, and Philip Brock. 1993. "The Political Economy of Economic Adjustment: Chile, 1973–90." In Robert Bates and Anne Krueger (eds.), *Political and Economic Interactions in Economic Policy Reform: Evidence from Eight Countries.* Cambridge: Blackwell.

Stein, Ernesto, and Mariano Tommasi (eds.). 2008. *Policymaking in Latin America: How Politics Shapes Policies.* Washington, DC and Cambridge, MA: Interamerican Development Bank and David Rockefeller Center for Latin American Studies, Harvard University.

Stokes, Susan. 2005. "Perverse Accountability: A Formal Model of Machine Politics with Evidence from Argentina." *American Political Science Review*, 99(3): 315–325.

Strolovitch, Dara. 2006. "Do Interest Groups Represent the Disadvantaged?" *Journal of Politics*, 68: 893–908.

Tendler, Judith, and Sara Freedheim. 1994. "Trust in a Rent-Seeking World: Health and Government Transformed in Northeast Brazil." *World Development*, 22: 1771–1791.

Thomas, Clive (ed.). 2004. *Research Guide to U.S. and International Interest Groups.* Westport, CT: Praeger.

Truman, David. 1951. *The Governmental Process: Political Interests and Public Opinion.* New York: Alfred A. Knopf.

Valenzuela, J. Samuel. 1989. "Labor Movements in Transitions to Democracy: a Framework for Analysis." *Comparative Politics*, 21(4): 445–472.

Van Doren, Peter. 1991. *Politics, Markets, and Congressional Policy Choices.* Ann Arbor: University of Michigan Press.

Wawro, Gregory. 2001. "A Panel Probit Analysis of Campaign Contributions and Roll-Call Votes." *American Journal of Political Science*, 45(3): 563–579.

Weingast, Barry. 1996. "Political Institutions: Rational Choice Perspectives." In Robert Goodin and Hans-Dieter Klingemann (eds.), *A New Handbook of Political Science.* New York: Oxford University Press.

Weyland, Kurt. 2002. "Limitations of Rational-Choice Institutionalism for the Study of Latin American Politics." *Studies in Comparative International Development*, (371), 57–85.

Wickham-Crowley, Timothy. 1992. *Guerrillas and Revolution in Latin America: A Comparative Study of Insurgents and Regimes Since 1956.* Princeton, NJ: Princeton University Press.

Wildavsky, Aaron. 1964. *The Politics of the Budgetary Process.* Boston: Little, Brown.

Wright, John R. 1985. "PACs, Contributions, and Roll Calls: An Organizational Perspective." *American Political Science Review*, 79(2): 400–414.

Yackee, Jason Webb, and Susan Webb Yackee. 2006. "A Bias Toward Business? Assessing Interest Group Influence on the U.S. Bureaucracy." *Journal of Politics*, 68(1): 128–139.

33

THE BLESSINGS OF TROUBLES

Scholarly Innovation in Response to Latin America's Challenges

Jorge I. Domínguez

Scholars have long responded to the challenges that lived reality poses before their eyes. The outpouring of social science research in response to the collapse of Germany's democratic Weimar Republic and the rise of the Nazis is perhaps the best known example of the past century but so too was the extensive scholarship regarding the Russian revolution and the onset of European decolonization in Africa, Asia, and the Caribbean. Latinamericanist political scientists, too, have addressed an array of challenges that the region experienced over the past half century and, in so doing, contributed to broader scholarly debates in comparative politics.

In this chapter, I identify a number of scholarly insights that served well the study of Latin America and comparative politics more generally. The focus is on the work produced in response to experienced problems since the "take off" in the 1960s of the scholarly study of Latin American politics in the United States and Latin America, which owes much to Ford Foundation funding throughout the hemisphere especially in that decade. I take up four topics in approximate chronological order of their rise onto the scholarly agenda: the political economy of globalization, political regime transitions, presidentialist institutions, and voting behavior. The first two feature a much longer scholarly trajectory whereas the latter two developed with greater vigor since the 1990s. Each topic is intrinsically important. With regard to each, I argue that scholars of Latin America formulated a research agenda in response to the problems they perceived in the countries that they studied and, in so doing, contributed insights of value not just to those focused on Latin America but also more generally to scholars in comparative politics.

The Political Economy of Globalization

One salient question of our time has been the opportunities and constraints that the international economy presents for countries the world over. Europeanists focused on them in the 1980s and, with greater intensity, in more recent times.[1] Scholars sought to understand the structural bases for international economic engagement, the domestic consequences of adjustments to marked setbacks of the international economy, and the competitive strategies of firms and countries, which emphasizes domestic coordination to face the world as small countries engage in international markets. Recent scholarship has examined the impact of international economic globalization on the welfare state and, generally, on the fiscal and budgetary policies of governments to compensate for costs imposed on domestic economies or to enhance the international competitiveness of firms.

Before the late twentieth-century focus on these questions by scholars in the North Atlantic world, a previous body of scholarship on the industrialized economies, rooted in central and eastern Europe and Japan, had emphasized the relatively benign effects of international competition for the development of country strategies: the later developers could learn from the early developers, adopt and adapt technologies discovered elsewhere, and better mobilize international resources.[2]

Latinamericanist scholars were among the first to examine the relationship between the international and the domestic economy much sooner. Much of the work in the late 1940s and 1950s clustered around Raúl Prebisch and his leadership of the United Nations Economic Commission for Latin America. In the 1960s, this scholarly endeavor came to be known collectively as the "dependency" school or approach to the study of the region; it encompassed a variety of different strains. Dependency scholarship was rooted in an argument well summarized by Theotonio Dos Santos. Dependency, he wrote, is "a situation in which the economy of certain countries is conditioned by the development and expansion of another economy, to which the former is subjected."[3] Latin Americanists were much less surprised than Europeanists about the impact of the world economy in domestic markets, and some called the phenomena of the early twenty-first century by the same name as their predecessors had in the 1960s: dependency.[4]

By the 2000s, Latinamericanist scholars responded to the legacy of prior research in the region and the more recent scholarship in North Atlantic countries on the impact of globalization on the welfare state. In most Latin American countries, the notion of the "welfare state" is still an aspiration, not a reality. In the wealthier Latin American countries, the "welfare state" exists principally for those in the economy's formal sector.

In this more constrained context than what prevails in the prosperous North Atlantic countries, scholars of Latin America found that trade integration was most adverse to pensions and that the greater severity of business cycle downswings made countercyclical spending much less feasible at those times. On the other hand, the free play of democratic politics served to protect pensions in the formal sector thanks to the role of labor unions and union-connected political parties. More generally, the relationship between unions and parties was a key factor in explaining the success or failure of market-oriented adjustments and reforms in new international contexts—the closer the alliance between a union and a political party, the more restrained the union turned out to be, whereas inter-partisan competition for the leadership of the unions increased union militancy and reduced the likelihood of market reforms. The interaction between international effects and partisan and union politics contributed to sustained domestic inequality (e.g., pensions for the better off only), even as poverty rates began to decline in Chile, Brazil, and Mexico around the start of the twenty-first century. Democratic governments, however, tended to do a better job than their authoritarian predecessors at protecting spending on health and primary education, both to remedy social ills and to empower citizens and firms to face changing world markets.[5]

In Europe, the political economy of globalization by the end of the twentieth century had led to the growth of the role of the state by means of investing in education to make firms more competitive and also to compensate those adversely affected by globalization. In Latin America, the outcomes encompassed both trends that undermined the state and also trends that provided for new forms of state action especially under democratic regimes. The

Latinamericanist research on the asymmetrical impact of the world economy on domestic politics enriched the wider field of comparative politics, therefore, by demonstrating a wider variation in outcomes than the research on the North Atlantic countries had shown—international asymmetry magnified the impact of exogenous shocks for countries with fewer resources to mitigate them.

In terms of development strategy, Albert Hirschman was an early dissenter from the "happy talk" of scholarship regarding the already industrialized economies.[6] Late-late developers, he argued, adopted technologies without contributing much to applied research or new technological development; they also were less likely to exhibit the entrepreneurial energies that Europeanist scholars had found in comparable firms in historical European contexts. In such situations of technological and entrepreneurial ineffectiveness, breaking out of dependency was difficult. Autonomous efforts to apply science to develop new products, dependency scholars claimed, would likely lead to buyouts by multinational enterprises, leaving little net additional domestic technological development while draining entrepreneurship.[7]

Dependency scholars did not, however, sustain a persistently lugubrious tone. There was also attention to successful strategies. One dependency-management strategy was to ride the international economy. Already in the early 1960s, Dudley Seers argued that Latin America's small open economies in Central America rode the business cycles of the international economy, generally experiencing low inflation and infrequent currency devaluations. Subsequent research showed that Central American economies long remained tethered to the business cycles of the international economy, with cycles of both out-performance and under-performance.[8]

A second successful dependency-management strategy created national champions in the production and export of primary products, ordinarily through state action. Successful cases featured several elements. (1) Multinational enterprises had been under-investing in their companies. (2) Government technocrats had been learning both the technical and business aspects required to run the enterprise. (3) Political parties and elite opinion coalesced to lead to a unanimous or nearly unanimous vote in Congress to expropriate the foreign firm. (4) Market-conforming state enterprises were created, right away or in a short time, that would remain profitable for many years. Multinational enterprises operating in Chile's copper sector were expropriated, yes, under the socialist government of President Salvador Allende but with political support from the entire ideological spectrum in the Chilean Congress. Chile's state-owned copper enterprise remained state-owned and profitable under the subsequent dictatorship of President Augusto Pinochet and since 1990 under democratic rule. Multinational enterprises operating in Venezuela's petroleum sector were expropriated upon a unanimous vote of Congress.[9] The state-owned *Petróleos de Venezuela* would remain a highly profitable market-conforming state enterprise until Hugo Chávez's presidency.

A third successful strategy developed the domestic market capacity to industrialize and to join the industrialized world on one's own terms. Cardoso and Faletto, *gurus* of dependency scholarship, already foreshadowed in the 1970s that Brazil was en route to significant economic growth, which they labeled "associated dependent development" to signal its particular relationship to world markets. The relationship between a strong Brazilian state, capable of intervening effectively in domestic markets, along with multinational enterprises and national private firms, set Brazil on a path to growth.[10] In the decades that followed, medium and small countries—Colombia and Costa Rica—would also wed the state and private firms to enable their economies to compete more effectively in international markets.[11]

The least successful yet frequently-discussed strategy for dependency management in Latin America was regional trade integration or the creation of a common market. Despite moments of apparent success, most recently in the 1990s, attempts at intensifying economic integration in Latin America have had modest results. The southern common market (MERCOSUR/MERCOSUL), the Central American Common Market, or the Andean Community rarely account for more than one-fifth of the international trade of member states. The only significant intensification of economic ties occurred through embracing dependency—the North American Free Trade Agreement (NAFTA) advanced economic integration in North America and accounts for not less than two-fifths of the international trade of its member states.

The dependency literature became best known for what Latin American economies could *not* do—they could not grow, industrialize, integrate, or generate mass prosperity. My reading takes note of some key debilities of Latin America's growth path but it emphasizes the three main strategies that the region undertook, which served it well to address the practical problems that arose during the past half-century: ride international economy commodity booms (of which the most recent unfolded during the first decade of the twenty-first century), develop national champions (by expropriation if necessary) but ensure that they operate by market-conforming principles, and develop the domestic economy with a mix of state action and private markets to compete effectively. Some of Latin America's most successful companies in the new century—CVRD and Embraer, for example—began as state enterprises and the state remains an investor to some extent.

Market-conforming state enterprises are neither an oxymoron nor a legacy of Latin America's Jurassic past (when many of its state enterprises did not at all operate on market principles) but, rather, a normal component of the political economy of market-oriented democracies. In 2003, for example, the asset value of state-owned enterprises as a percentage of gross domestic product ranged between 15 percent and 35 percent in Sweden, Italy, France, South Korea, Turkey, the Czech Republic, New Zealand, and the Netherlands.[12] Brazil, Colombia, and Costa Rica pursued different variants of this strategy but, in each, state and private firms, domestic and international, were crucial. These approaches to dependency management served Latin America well as the twenty-first century opened.

With regard to state enterprises as well, Latinamericanist scholarship contributed more broadly to the study of comparative politics. Consider one example. In the last third of the twentieth century, the premier worldwide scholar on the spread of multinational enterprises was Raymond Vernon, whose professional affiliations spanned the worlds of business school and political science department. Vernon's early work focused on Mexico and more generally on Latin America. He drew from that scholarly experience to write about state enterprises and multinational enterprises in global contexts, anchored in and nurtured by what he learned in Latin America, and he engaged his own students in similar work. At the heart of his research was an endeavor to understand the intertwining between the state and business, the over-time changing asymmetries between multinational private firms and the states, and the rise of state enterprises as one response to the changing world economy.[13]

Political Regime Transitions

Alone among the regions of the world, Latin America has been a participant in the three waves of democratization evident since the nineteenth century and in both counterwaves of authoritarian rule.[14] Latin America's democratization began in Uruguay and Argentina early in the twentieth century. Regime breakdowns repopulated the region with authoritarian regimes in the 1930s. The second wave of democratic regimes appeared or reappeared in the aftermath of World War II, to break down in the 1960s and 1970s as part of the second authoritarian counterwave; by the second half of the 1970s, democratic regimes in the region had become an endangered species. Latin America's third wave of democratization began in the Dominican Republic in 1978 and Ecuador in 1979, thence spreading throughout the region. Early in the twenty-first century, there is an authoritarian counter-ripple: Autocratic tendencies marked President Hugo Chávez's government in Venezuela; in 2008, President Daniel Ortega's government engineered widespread fraud in municipal elections in Nicaragua and, in 2009, a military coup overthrew the constitutionally elected president of Honduras. In contrast, colonial Africa and Asia missed the first wave of democratization and Western Europe missed the second wave back to authoritarian rule. Latin America's public miseries and democratic triumphs are well reflected in a vast scholarly literature, which focused especially on the second wave of authoritarian rule and the third wave of democratization. Here, I attempt to account for the findings.

Structural economic conditions, such as the problems encountered with import substitution industrialization, turned out to matter less as explanations for the rise of the authoritarian regimes of the 1960s and 1970s than it may have appeared at first.[15] Nevertheless, inflation, recession, various dimensions of the business cycle, ideas about the organizations of the economy, and international market shocks played important roles in regime change, sometimes as proximate causes, more often as background causes. For example, Latin America's prolonged and deep economic downturn of the 1980s facilitated exiting from authoritarian regimes that did not govern the economy well.[16] But such conditions were mainly background—political actors had to act.

A key finding regarding the relationship between economics and political regimes is that dictatorship is most common in poor countries while democracies in poor countries are vulnerable to coups.[17] Above some level of economic development, a democratic breakdown is extremely rare. Latin America, alas, has had many democratic attempts in poor countries and, as a result, also many breakdowns of such attempts. Latin America hosts also the only country worldwide whose democratic regime broke down even though it was above the level of development at which no other democratic regime anywhere broke down in the years past 1950: Argentina. In general, therefore, wealth buys many things, among them economic and political liberty but much of Latin America has lacked the "political insurance" of sufficient wealth to secure its democratic regimes.

International political factors—the Cold War—turned out to matter more as explanations for the rise and decline of authoritarian regimes than it may have appeared at first. The scholarship on bureaucratic authoritarian regimes, typically quite aware of international political economy issues, seemed often unaware of the Cold War. A key explanation for the sustained authoritarianism in Central American countries from the 1950s through the 1980s was the policy of the U.S. government in the context of the Cold War.[18] Democratization in Central America in the 1990s had, as a necessary task, the dispelling of the demons that had seized hold of the U.S. government during the preceding decades. Similarly, U.S. Cold War policy is part of the explanation for military coups in Brazil in 1964 and Chile in 1973, just as the change in U.S. policy in the late 1980s also assisted with the end of authoritarian regimes in Paraguay and Chile.[19]

A principal distinction in the two types of political regime change turned out to be simple: the role of military coups. Such coups most often brought about the breakdown of constitutional democratic regimes. While coups sometimes depose dictators and open the path for democratic elections (Colombia in 1957, Venezuela in 1958, Paraguay in 1989), coups are generally much less likely instruments for democratization. The scholarship on political regime change followed by military rule emphasized, first, the shift in the 1960s toward institutional military coups—in contrast to solo dictatorships—and also the greater emphasis in military doctrine on an ideology of "national security" that looked for enemies—most often labeled communists, real or imaginary—among fellow citizens.[20] In the 1960s and 1970s, the military also often expanded their roles to run state enterprises and manage the nation's politics.

As a result, the process of democratization often required ousting the military both from control of the state and also from their roles generally in law enforcement, the leadership of state enterprises, and the making of key budget decisions. The military often sought immunity from prosecution for acts they committed while running the government, including killings and torture of prisoners, and claimed prerogatives to set or to shape significantly policies on budgets, weapons acquisitions, personnel promotion, and other topics. Thus the process of demilitarization under constitutional democracies was often prolonged. The election of a civilian president was often just one step along a longer path toward democratization, which required substantial and sustained contestation. In the end, success was a tribute to inter-party competition in election after election.[21] The actual realization of liberalization and democratization often took a great deal of time even after civilians returned to the presidency because, beyond lingering military claims of immunity and prerogatives, clientelist politics and traditional-politics authoritarian enclaves endured as well.[22]

The interaction of three factors contributed to making military rule harsher in the 1970s than in the 1960s. First, in the 1970s the world economy was marked by slower growth and higher inflation, adversely affecting Latin America's economies. Second, the rising number of military regimes and the wide sharing of the Cold War "national security" ideology intensified and "normalized" the search for domestic enemies. Third, the military coups of the 1970s, and the rulers they buttressed, responded to, and generated, a rising spiral of political violence. Larger numbers of political killings, imprisonment, and torture were the responses of the rulers, to which the courts and other institutions responded poorly and unevenly.[23] More widespread urban insurgency, including terrorist actions in several South American countries and revolution in three Central American countries, were the responses from part of the opposition.

The scholarship on democratization in the 1980s emphasized the role of political elites—hardliners and softliners—in contestation, negotiation, and settlement in the light of political regime transitions. These processes, O'Donnell and Schmitter argued, were marked by "the high degree of indeterminacy embedded in situations where unexpected events (*fortuna*), insufficient information, hurried and audacious choices, confusion about motives and interests, plasticity, and even indefinition of political identities, as well as the talents of specific individuals (*virtù*) are frequently decisive in determining the outcomes."[24] A coup could take place in an instant. Liberalization and democratization would span months, and often years. A coup changed the political regime overnight. Democratization often involved partial, gradual changes, including concessions to the military or conservative elites that would only be reversed years later. An important corrective to this elite-agency approach, which underplayed the role of civil society, was research that showed that labor unions often played crucial roles in opening the gates that would subsequently allow civilian elites to negotiate the transition. The labor movement often placed on the public agenda issues of democratic rights and procedures that negotiating elites dared not forget.[25] Such union action linked the labor movement's voluntary collective action with its structural roots.

The political violence just mentioned was a backdrop to negotiations over democratization in the 1980s. Democratic elites wanted to avoid a hardliner coup either before or following a democratic transition and characteristically opposed a resort to violence. Authoritarian regime softliners held the specter of wider political violence from the opposition in order to induce the hardliners to agree to concessions.

The Latinamericanist scholarship on political regime transitions had a widespread impact. The O'Donnell-Schmitter book, just cited, would be discussed at Harvard Business School executive education programs held in South Africa to help elites prepare for their democratic transition of the early 1990s. One of their key collaborators in the O'Donnell-Schmitter project, Adam Przeworski, went from his work on South America to research on Eastern Europe. His work on both regions employed game-theoretic tools, emphasizing contingency and uncertainty to examine the role of political agency. Schooled in the very Southamericanist scholarship on regime transitions he helped to develop, Przeworski has focused his analysis on political action and criticized purely structuralist arguments that implied that modernization or economic growth led linearly to political democratization.[26] Major producers of the scholarship of regime transitions in Latin America, such as Juan Linz and Alfred Stepan, took their tools to analyze political transitions in former communist Europe, with a focus on institutional choices—how to constitutionalize the armed forces, how to design executive and legislative institutions preferably (see next section) along parliamentary lines, etc.[27]

Political regime transitions, of course, have also strong normative dimensions—how to open up public spaces for citizens to express their views and to associate freely. The normative reasons are also real and pressing—how to avoid killings and torture. The passions that generate political transitions require an optimism whose roots are often difficult to fathom in societies where so many have suffered so grievously for so long. Thus it is worth quoting from a country and a time when optimism seemed a lost cause, just to remember that it is possible to imagine and wish better politics for the human condition. In *The Optimist's Salutation*, the Nicaraguan poet Rubén Darío (1867–1916) wrote as follows: "And thus let Hope be the ever-lasting vision among us."[28]

Presidentialist Institutions

Latin America is the world's only region to feature presidentialist rather than parliamentary systems in democratic regimes. (Europe and the Caribbean host parliamentary democratic regimes; the Middle East features authoritarian regimes; East and Southeast Asia mix presidentialist democratic and authoritarian regimes.) In an essay written in 1984, Juan Linz argued that presidentialist systems are inimical to stable democracy.[29] Empirically, most of the world's stable democracies have parliamentary regimes. In presidentialist systems, president and legislature are elected separately, which reduces the likelihood that the executive would command a legislative majority. Presidents are elected for fixed terms; the legislature may remove them only through impeachment, which often requires a super-majority. Both the president and the legislators claim legitimacy from direct popular election; they can deadlock the government and generate a constitutional crisis. Presidentialism intends to create a strong executive but often sets up the likelihood of confrontation, failure, and, in the extreme case, a coup to resolve the gridlock. In the Latin American cases, moreover, the mix of presidentialism and a multiparty system makes it more difficult to fashion stable governing majorities for democratic rule, creating propitious conditions for a coup.[30]

A giant in the study of comparative politics, Linz was taken seriously by constitutional

Solons. Brazilians actually voted in a plebiscite on whether to adopt parliamentarism; they rejected it. This new Linz-tinted perception of an old problem spawned a new scholarship on the presidency, which for the most part generated a more benign reading of the relationship between presidentialism and democracy.[31]

A critique of anti-presidentialism starts from the claim that there is a spurious correlation. Parliamentary regimes developed in countries that have become wealthy; presidentialist regimes exist more often in poor countries. As already noted, democracy in poor countries is disproportionately vulnerable to breakdown and this—not presidentialism—may explain the breakdown of democratic regimes in much of Latin America. Moreover, there are no parliamentary regimes in Latin America; there are no pure presidentialist regimes in Western Europe. It is thus impossible to say whether, controlling for international, regional, and transocietal *milieu*, presidentialism explains coups in Latin America and parliamentarism explains democratic stability in Western Europe. Breakdowns in one and stability in the other may be associated with factors other than institutional regime in the respective regions.

Moreover, not all presidentialist designs are alike. The associated institutional designs within which a presidency exists matter a great deal. The governability problem is lessened if presidents and legislatures are chosen in concurrent elections, which increase the likelihood that the president would gain stronger legislative support.[32] More generally, concurrent elections along with electing the president by a plurality of votes cast (not through second-round majority run-off elections), and closed party list proportional representation rules for legislative elections, increase the likelihood of voter coordination in executive and legislative elections.[33] Compare Brazil to Mexico, Latin America's two largest countries, both with concurrent elections upon the election of the president. Mexico has closed party lists and plurality presidential election; Brazil has open lists and relies upon a second-round presidential election. Nearly 70 percent of Brazilian voters were ticket-splitters in the 2002 presidential election, whereas only about 9 percent of Mexican voters split their ticket in the 2000 presidential election. Gubernatorial coattails are stronger than presidential coattails in Brazil.[34] Institutional choices matter.

Coordination between president and legislature may also occur past the election. Where presidents must rely on their partisan powers to govern, executive-legislative coordination may follow the path of negotiation; where presidents rely disproportionately on their formal constitutional powers, presidents may use executive-decree powers and veto legislative bills. Presidents who confront or ignore the legislature undermine democratic constitutionalism and may reduce their own prospects to finish their term.[35] Here is a key to Brazil's circumstances notwithstanding the complications created by its electoral institutions: Brazilian presidents have very high constitutional powers but Presidents Cardoso and Lula preferred to use their partisan powers to work through Congress to enact their policies; they promoted changes in the institutional rules of Congress to foster party discipline and coordination, and they successfully employed these among other means to enact laws.[36] The partisan powers of presidents must be continuously constructed and renewed. Presidents are most likely to succeed in the legislature if they work with their fellow party members; presidents are likely to fail if they detach from or neglect their partisan allies.[37]

Finally, since the late 1970s the coerced departures of freely- and directly-elected Latin American civilian presidents resulted in every case in new civilian presidents. In that period, no democratically elected Latin American president, ousted from office, was replaced by a military president. Presidential defenestration has in every case provoked a sort of political bargaining that resembled parliamentarism. This is a form of instability, perhaps more worrisome than Belgium with Acting Prime Ministers for months at a time, but it is no longer the descent into military dictatorship.[38] Moreover, not all interruptions of a presidency are alike—coups bring down democratic regimes, but presidential impeachments are inherently proper procedures in democratic presidentialist regimes. The successful impeachment of the president in Brazil in 1992 or in Paraguay in 1999 sustained rather than derailed a democratic regime. Impeachments are one mechanism whereby presidentialist systems resemble elements of parliamentary systems.[39]

In this subfield, the study of presidentialist systems in Latin America specifically, and comparative politics more generally, greatly overlap. As noted, Latin America is the world's only region to feature presidentialist rather than parliamentary systems in democratic regimes; outside of Latin America, add just a handful of cases. As a result, the generalizations with regard to presidentialist institutions apply well to Latin American cases and were developed first and foremost by Latinamericanist scholars. There would be no comparative politics of executive and legislative institutions in presidentialist systems if it were not for the comparative politics research program that Matthew Shugart and John Carey launched through their work on institutional design in Latin America.[40]

Design matters in presidentialist systems. It accounts for a wide range of variation that the Latin American cases illustrate well, to the benefit of comparative politics scholarship worldwide and the enlightenment of constituent assemblies.

Voting Behavior

The third wave of democratization in Latin America opened a new window of opportunity for practice and research: elections and voting behavior. An ideologically "Right" authoritarian regime in Argentina and an ideologically "Left" authoritarian regime in Peru in the 1970s did away with elections. "Softer" authoritarian regimes, such as those in Brazil and Mexico, held elections either under rigged conditions or, especially in Mexico, infected by fraudulent practices. Today's senior Latin Americanists did not spend much time on elections and voting behavior when they were graduate students. Both the presence of elections and the absence of an older scholarship make this topic rife with opportunity for younger scholars.

Latin Americans vote especially when it is a novelty. "Founding" elections—as political regime transition scholars would expect—exhibit turnout rates considerably higher than in other elections, controlling statistically for other variables thought to be related to turnout. Similarly, the sustained adherence to the protection of political rights and civil liberties increase the likelihood of election turnout. Concurrent elections—following the implications from the previous section—generate higher levels of turnout in both presidential and legislative elections: there is more at stake, there is more media coverage, and more comprehensive partisan and social movement mobilization. Mandatory voting also increases turnout; it is 20 percent higher than turnout in countries with voluntary voting, controlling for other independent variables.[41] In each such instance, the decisions of politicians may have a positive or negative effect on electoral turnout.

Latin American voters have several objectives in mind on election day. In broad terms, sociotropic retrospective national economic voting is an important explanation for voting behavior. This means that Latin American voters support the incumbent president's party when aggregate economic outcomes have been good during this presidency, and punish the incumbent's party when those national economic outcomes have been poor. Nevertheless, the choice of voters is constrained by institutional setting. Restrictive electoral rules sometimes leave voters no choice but to punish an incumbent party by voting for a non-incumbent party that had, during a previous time in office, also been responsible for poor economic governance. Only if the electoral rules permit the rise of third parties, can voters back politicians who had never governed, thus punishing everyone who had ever governed badly, current as well as past incumbent parties.[42]

In some countries, voters had to decide on the incumbent president running for reelection, who prior to his first election may have promised one set of policies but delivered quite another. Around 1990, about half of the successful presidential candidates across Latin America implemented as president policies at odds with the promises they had made during their election campaign. These "switchers" adversely burden democratic accountability. Carlos Menem in Argentina, Alberto Fujimori in Peru, and Carlos Andrés Pérez in Venezuela, elected president within just over a year of each other, are examples of "switchers"—they ran for office as critics of market-oriented policies and went on to implement precisely those policies. In general, at reelection time, voters held their noses, voting to reelect those whose policies had generated economic growth (Menem, Fujimori) and punished Pérez, whose policies had not.[43]

In some instances, more than one issue is salient. Peru started the 1990s suffering from both a severe economic crisis and high levels of political violence. With some hyperbole, Fujimori claimed credit for ending the political violence and reviving the economy. Voters considered his counterinsurgency success a solved problem, which thus had lower impact on the vote; at the time of his reelection, voters rewarded him more for the economic outcomes.[44] This capacity of the voters to discern on questions of importance connects with the previous discussion about ticket-splitting in elections. Voters seek different objectives in their voting for president and legislature, and thus may vote for different parties at different levels of government.

Not all voting is sociotropic. The longest-lasting form of voting responds to individual utility. Politicians and parties have employed clientelistic methods, including individual vote buying, patronage appointments, pork barrel for targeted communities, and the like. By the current century, however, individual vote buying had become less common even in countries, such as Mexico, where it was once widespread.[45] Research on vote buying in Argentina also demonstrates that its aggregate significance is important but modest; it may be focused on increasing turnout from those in communities favorable to a specific party. Moreover, not all parties in the same country are equally effective at using clientelist methods. In Argentina, for example, Peronists trump Radicals and other parties in the efficacy of use of clientelist practices to obtain voting support.[46]

Voting behavior research raises the question of the role of parties in shaping the voting choice. As the twentieth century ended, many long-lived parties had not fared well. In Venezuela, which had had one of Latin America's most institutionalized party systems since its democratic transition in 1958, the two parties that had alternated in governing the country were badly battered. Acción Democrática lost the bulk of its voting support while COPEI (Christian Democrats) disintegrated. In the pivotal 1998 election that brought Hugo Chávez to the presidency, many voters abandoned their previous partisan affiliations, motivated by negative views of parties and dissatisfaction with their past performance. Venezuelans seemed frustrated with the shortcomings of the party system as a whole and its inability to provide citizens with voice and influence.[47]

Some long-fragmented party systems remained so, in part as a result of the fraction of the population that is indigenous. The failure of most parties until the 1990s to represent indigenous peoples adequately led many indigenous voters to support a variety of small populist or leftist parties, which contributed to high and enduring levels of party system fragmentation as well as the relatively low impact of parties on the voting choice. As significant indigenous parties emerged, especially in Ecuador and Bolivia, indigenous voters rallied to support them, albeit to varying extent across time and region.[48]

Where parties had not flourished until the 1980s, partisanship in the current century has proven strong: Brazil and Mexico. In Brazil's presidential election in 2002, the aggregate level of partisanship exceeded levels prevailing in the most recent elections held in Germany, the Netherlands, Korea, and Chile. To be sure, partisanship in Brazil was highly skewed to the benefit of the Workers Party (PT). This is the result of a quarter-century trajectory of party-building efforts as well as the increased frequency of the PT's electoral success. The PT's partisan organization and the involvement of its supporters in politicized social networks account for its success.[49]

Partisanship in Mexico was difficult to discern before the highly contested presidential election held in 1988. The ruling Institutional Revolutionary Party (PRI) was the party of the state, with uncertain "sincere" allegiance from those whom it counted as its voters. A strong party of the left emerged only during and following that election, the Party of the Democratic Revolution (PRD). The long-suffering opposition party, the National Action Party (PAN), was small and, for many years, as concerned about its ideological and partisan purity and integrity as it was about winning elections.

Mexico in the twenty-first century has three strong parties; each commands significant support from a fraction of citizens. The now well-studied Mexican case illustrates some key themes in voting behavior.[50] By the fall of 2005, before the three major parties had chosen their candidates for the July 2006 election, approximately half of all Mexicans had decided for which party to vote for the presidency. Since the mid-1990s, about two-thirds of Mexicans consider themselves committed to one of the top three parties. The principal effect of Mexican campaigns has been to steer voters to support the presidential candidate of the party that has been their ongoing underlying preference.

In every presidential election since 1988, three variables explain much about the distribution of voter preferences: partisanship, assessment of the incumbent president's performance (Mexico prohibits incumbent reelection), and the assessment of the country's economic circumstances. Each has been consistently significant in statistical and other analyses of public opinion and electoral behavior. There were relatively few partisan defectors in each election and, as noted, only limited split-ticket voting. Beginning in 2000 and continuing in 2006, candidate assessments played also a significant role. These were also Mexico's first campaigns that resembled those in other parts of the world. Television debates may have little impact in countries long used to them but in Mexico they are one factor in shaping the election choice. Negative advertising took off as a campaign tactic in the 2000 election and it resurfaced vigorously in the 2006 election. In both elections, negative advertising helped the eventual winner of each election—Vicente Fox and Felipe Calderón. Their party, the PAN, had transitioned from being the party of nice boys and girls to having a nasty edge, hungry for victory.

In many of these respects, Mexican voters turned out to be similar to those in well-established North Atlantic democracies where economic and partisan voting have long mattered. The novelty is that partisanship, so recent in Mexico, has so quickly developed deep roots. In Mexico, as in other recently democratized Latin American countries, research on public opinion and voting behavior has dispelled some stereotypes. Voters in Latin American countries do connect their preferences and interests to their voting behavior. They are capable of sustained loyalty to a specific party. They hold their elected representatives accountable and know how to vote out bad rulers. They discern their electoral choices and behave accordingly.

Perhaps the most interesting contribution of the scholarship on voting behavior in democratic Latin America to the wider scholarship on voting behavior in comparative politics is to demonstrate a wider range of variation than is found in the North Atlantic countries. In Mexico as in Brazil, in El Salvador as in Costa Rica, partisan commitments matter, but from election to election campaigns matter more and thus a larger fraction of voters may change its behavior than has historically been the case in the North Atlantic democracies. Latin American voters, moreover, have adapted to democratic politics far more quickly than some of the agency-based elite-bargaining scholarship on political regime transition had expected—voters are not a tumultuous rabble threatening the consolidation of democracy. Voters in Latin American countries reward good governance and abandon long-supported parties that have performed badly, as good democrats should.

Constrained by international circumstances, long hemmed in by authoritarian regimes, and with their choice shaped by presidentialist contexts, voters in Latin American countries, to paraphrase Karl Marx,[51] may not be able to make their history just as they please but, within circumstances they have not chosen, they try as much as possible to make their own history. They are the greatest source of hope for effective democratic governance in Latin America.

Conclusion

In 1959, with prodding and funding from the Ford Foundation, the Carnegie Corporation, and the Council on Higher Education of the American Republics, the American Council of Learned Societies and the Social Science Research Council established the Joint Committee on Latin American Studies, which still exists. In February 1963, the Joint Committee convened its fourth conference, which was also the first that most foreshadowed the aims and design of this book in its broad assessment of social science research on Latin America. At this event, and for the widely-read book that followed, Kalman Silvert, at the time perhaps the most distinguished U.S. Latinamericanist political scientist, wrote as follows: "Latin America has always been a hearty consumer of European ideas and practices, and the university has long played a vital part in the process of importation, adaptation, and propagation."[52] Silvert was correct, and his accuracy then serves as a benchmark for change.

Latin America's place in the world is unlike Europe's or North America's and its engagement with the international economy has been markedly more subordinate and asymmetric than that of the North Atlantic countries. Latinamericanist scholars had to construct arguments and evidence to assess Latin America's distinct interaction with international markets, specifically the greater burdens from marked asymmetries. The devastating European political experiences with war and genocide during the first half of the twentieth century were mercifully not replicated in Latin America, but this difference demanded of Latinamericanist scholars that they fashion their own frameworks to understand why democratic regimes in this region broke down repeatedly and why authoritarian regimes sprouted again and again. Latin America did not inherit the practice of parliamentarism; Latinamericanists had to figure out why their presidentialist systems varied as much and in what ways they resembled or differed from parliamentary systems. Only with regard to this essay's fourth topic—voting behavior—may Silvert's characterization still apply. Scholars of voting behavior in Latin American countries have for the most part adopted and adapted the theories and techniques first developed in the North Atlantic democracies to describe and explain how citizens in Latin American countries choose their rulers. Yet, even with regard to voting behavior, the scholarship regarding Latin America shows a more diverse range of voter behavior and a more decisive link between the choice on election day and the consolidation of democracy.

The scholarship developed by Latinamericanists regarding the four topics in this essay has shaped how other scholars have thought about the politics of countries outside the North Atlantic world, starting with the relationship between poor countries in other longitudes and the world economy. The Organization of Petroleum Exporting Countries (OPEC) was founded by Venezuela; scholars first studied in Venezuela how a weak state bargained successfully with multinational firms.[53] A century ago, Brazil's State of São Paulo undertook the first successful world market intervention to prop up commodity prices, coffee in this case; scholars who worked on this case have had a broad impact on scholarship worldwide.[54] Latinamericanist scholarship also informed research on patterns of political regime change or endurance in former communist Europe and in East Asia and Africa. Latinamericanist scholarship helped to clarify analytical issues that surround the design and effects of presidentialist institutions worldwide and incorporated reams of new analyses and data regarding voting behavior into the canon of political science. Kal Silvert would have been proud that his historical analysis was not a forecast, and that *change* came to prevail in political science scholarship about Latin America.

Notes

1 Among them, see Peter Gourevitch, *Politics in Hard Times: Comparative Responses to International Economic Crises* (Cornell University Press, 1986); Ronald Rogowski, "Political Cleavages and Changing Exposure to Trade," *American Political Science Review* 81 (December 1987): 1121–1136; Peter Katzenstein, *Small States in World Markets* (Cornell University Press, 1985); Geoffrey Garrett, "Global Markets and National Politics: Collision Course or Virtuous Circle?" *International Organization* 52 (1998): 787–824; Torben Iversen and Thomas R. Cusack, "The Causes of Welfare State Expansion: Deindustrialization or Globalization?" *World Politics* 52 (April 2000): 313–349.

2 Alexander Gerschenkron, *Economic Backwardness in Historical Perspective* (Cambridge: Harvard University Press, 1962); Chalmers Johnson, *MITI and the Japanese Miracle: The Growth of Industrial Policy, 1925–1975* (Stanford: Stanford University Press, 1982).

3 Theotonio Dos Santos, "The Structure of Dependence," *American Economic Review* 60 (1970), 231.

4 For example, Erik Wibbels, "Dependency Revisited: International Markets, Business Cycles, and Social Spending in the Developing World," *International Organization* 60 (2006): 51–75.

5 For example, see Robert Kaufman and Alex Segura-Ubiergo, "Globalization, Domestic Politics, and Social Spending in Latin America," *World Politics* 53 (2001): 553–587; Wibbels, "Dependency Revisited;" George Avelino, David Brown, and Wendy Hunter, "The Effects of Capital Mobility, Trade Openness, and Democracy on Social Spending in Latin America," *American Journal of Political Science* 49 (2005): 625–641; and María Victoria Murillo, *Labor Unions, Partisan Coalitions, and Market Reforms in Latin America* (Cambridge: Cambridge University Press, 2001).

6 Albert O. Hirschman, "The Political Economy of Import-Substituting Industrialization in Latin America, *Quarterly Journal of Economics* 82:1 (1968): 1–32.

7 Gary Gereffi, "Drug Firms and Dependency in Mexico: The Case of the Steroid Hormone Industry," *International Organization* 32 (1978): 237–286.

8 Dudley Seers, "A Theory of Inflation and Growth in Under-Developed Economies Based on the Experience of Latin America," *Oxford Economic Papers* 14 (June 1962): 173–195; Marc Lindenberg, "World Economic Cycles and Central American Political Instability," *World Politics* 42 (1990): 397–421.

9 Theodore H. Moran, *Multinational Corporations and the Politics of Dependence: Copper in Chile* (Princeton: Princeton University Press, 1974); Franklin Tugwell, *The Politics of Oil in Venezuela* (Stanford: Stanford University Press, 1975).

10 Fernando Henrique Cardoso and Enzo Faletto, *Dependency and Development in Latin America*, trans. Marjory Mattingly Urquidi (Berkeley: University of California Press, 1979), Postscript; Peter Evans, "Multinationals, State-Owned Corporations, and the Transformation of Imperialism: A Brazilian Case Study," *Economic Development and Cultural Change* 26 (1977): 43–64.

11 Marcus Kurtz and Sarah Brooks, "Embedding Neoliberal Reform in Latin America," *World Politics* 60 (2008): 231–280.

12 Organization for Economic Cooperation and Development, *Corporate Government of State-Owned Enterprises: A Survey of OECD Countries* (Paris: OECD Publishing, 2005).

13 See, for example, Raymond Vernon, *The Dilemma of Mexico's Development: The Roles of the Private and the Public Sectors* (Cambridge: Harvard University Press, 1963); Raymond Vernon, *Sovereignty at Bay: The Multinational Spread of U.S. Enterprises* (New York: Basic Books, 1971); Raymond Vernon and Yair Aharoni, eds., *State-owned Enterprise in the Western Economies* (London: Croom Helm, 1981); and Raymond Vernon and Ravi Ramamurti, eds., *Privatization and Control of State-owned Enterprises* (Washington: World Bank, 1991).

14 Samuel Huntington coined the "waves" metaphor. See his *The Third Wave: Democratization in the Late Twentieth Century* (Norman: University of Oklahoma Press, 1991).

15 Guillermo O'Donnell, *Modernization and Bureaucratic-Authoritarianism* (Berkeley: Institute of International Studies, University of California, 1973); David Collier, ed., *The New Authoritarianism in Latin America* (Princeton: Princeton University Press, 1979).

16 Among others, see Michael Wallerstein, "The Collapse of Democracy in Brazil: Its Economic Determinants," *Latin American Research Review* 15 (1980): 3–34; Héctor Schamis, "Reconceptualizing Latin American Authoritarianism in the 1970s: From Bureaucratic Authoritarianism to Neoconservatism," *Comparative Politics* 23 (1991): 201–216; Karen Remmer, "Democracy and Economic Crisis: The Latin American Experience," *World Politics* 42 (1990): 315–335; and Stephan Haggard and Robert Kaufman, *The Political Economy of Democratic Transitions* (Princeton: Princeton University Press, 1995).

17 Adam Przeworski and Fernando Limongi, "Modernization: Theories and Facts," *World Politics* 49 (1997): 155–183.

18 For example, see Michael Grow, *U.S. Presidents and Latin American Interventions: Pursuing Regime Change in the Cold War* (Lawrence: University of Kansas Press, 2008); Greg Grandin, *The Last Colonial Massacre: Latin America in the Cold War* (Chicago: University of Chicago Press, 2004).

19 Thomas Carothers, *In the Name of Democracy: U.S. Policy Toward Latin America in the Reagan Years* (Berkeley: University of California Press, 1991).

20 Abraham Lowenthal and J. Samuel Fitch, *Armies and Politics in Latin America* (Revised edition. New York: Holmes and Meier, 1986).

21 Alfred Stepan, *Rethinking Military Politics: Brazil and the Southern Cone* (Princeton: Princeton University Press, 1998); Wendy Hunter, *Eroding Military Influence in Brazil: Politicians against Soldiers* (Chapel Hill: University of North Carolina Press, 1997); Wendy Hunter, "Continuity or Change? Civil-Military Relations in Democratic Argentina, Chile, and Peru," *Political Science Quarterly* 112 (1997): 453–475.

22 Frances Hagopian, *Traditional Politics and Regime Change in Brazil* (Cambridge: Cambridge University Press, 1996).

23 Anthony Pereira, *Political (In)Justice: Authoritarianism and the Rule of Law in Brazil, Chile, and Argentina* (Pittsburgh: University of Pittsburgh Press, 2005).

24 Guillermo O'Donnell and Philippe Schmitter, *Transitions from Authoritarian Rule: Tentative Conclusions about Uncertain Democracies* (Baltimore: The Johns Hopkins University Press, 1986), 5.

25 Ruth Collier and James Mahoney, "Adding Collective Actors to Collective Outcomes: Labor and Recent Democratization in South America and Southern Europe," *Comparative Politics* 29 (1997): 285–303.

26 Adam Przeworski, *Democracy and the Market: Political and Economic Reforms in Eastern Europe and Latin America* (Cambridge: Cambridge University Press, 1991).

27 Juan Linz and Alfred Stepan, *Problems of Democratic Transition and Consolidation: South Europe, South America, and Post-Communist Europe* (Baltimore: The Johns Hopkins University Press, 1996).

28 Rubén Darío, "Salutación del optimista," in *Poesía española contemporánea*, ed. Gerardo Diego (Madrid: Taurus, 1962), 36–38.

29 For the definitive version of this article, see Juan Linz and Arturo Valenzuela, eds., *The Failure of Presidential Democracy: The Case of Latin America* (Baltimore: The Johns Hopkins University Press, 1994).

30 Scott Mainwaring, "Presidentialism, Multipartism, and Democracy: the Difficult Combination," *Comparative Political Studies* 26 (1993): 198–228.

31 Matthew Shugart and John Carey, *Presidents and Assemblies: Constitutional Design and Electoral Dynamics* (Cambridge: Cambridge University Press, 1992).

32 Matthew Shugart, "The Electoral Cycle and the Institutional Sources of Divided Presidential Government," *American Political Science Review* 89 (1995): 327–343; Mark Jones, *Electoral Laws and the Survival of Presidential Democracies* (South Bend: University of Notre Dame Press, 1995).

33 Scott Mainwaring and Matthew Shugart, eds., *Presidentialism and Democracy in Latin America* (Cambridge: Cambridge University Press, 1997), "Conclusion."

34 David Samuels, "Concurrent Elections, Discordant Results: Presidentialism, Federalism, and Governance in Brazil," *Comparative Politics* 33 (2000): 1–20; Barry Ames, Andy Baker, and Lucio Renno, "Split-ticket Voting as the Rule: Voters and Permanent Divided Government in Brazil," *Electoral Studies* 28 (2009): 8–20; Gretchen Helmke, "Ticket Splitting as Electoral Insurance: The Mexico 2000 Elections," *Electoral Studies* 28 (2009): 70–78.

35 Mainwaring and Shugart, *Presidentialism and Democracy in Latin America*, "Conclusion."

36 Argelina Cheibub Figueiredo and Fernando Limongi, "Presidential Power, Legislative Organization, and Party Behavior in Brazil," *Comparative Politics* 32 (2000): 151–170; Carlos Pereira and Bernardo Mueller, "The Cost of Governing: Strategic Behavior of the President and Legislators in Brazil's Budgetary Process," *Comparative Political Studies* 37 (2004): 781–815.

37 Javier Corrales, *Presidents without Parties: The Politics of Economic Reform in Argentina and Venezuela in the 1990s* (University Park: Pennsylvania State University Press, 2002).

38 Kathryn Hochstetler, "Rethinking Presidentialism: Challenges and Presidential Falls in South America," *Comparative Politics* 38 (2006): 401–418.

39 Leiv Marsteintredet and Einar Berntzen, "Reducing the Perils of Presidentialism in Latin America through Presidential Interruptions," *Comparative Politics* 41 (2008): 83–101.

40 Shugart and Carey, *Presidents and Assemblies*.

41 Carolina Fornos, Timothy Power, and James Garand, "Explaining Voter Turnout in Latin America, 1980 to 2000," *Comparative Political Studies* 37 (2004): 909–940.

42 Eduardo Lora and Mauricio Olivera, "The Electoral Consequences of the Washington Consensus," *Economía* 5 (2005): 1–45; Allyson Lucinda Benton, "Dissatisfied Democrats or Retrospective Voters? Economic Hardship, Political Institutions, and Voting Behavior in Latin America," *Comparative Political Studies* 38 (2005): 417–442.

43 Susan Stokes, *Mandates and Democracy: Neoliberalism by Surprise in Latin America* (Cambridge: Cambridge University Press, 2001).

44 Kurt Weyland, "A Paradox of Success? Determinants of Political Support for President Fujimori," *International Studies Quarterly* 44 (2000): 481–502.

45 Wayne Cornelius, "Mobilized Voting in the 2000 Elections: The Changing Efficacy of Vote Buying and Coercion in Mexican Electoral Politics," in *Mexico's Pivotal Democratic Election: Candidates, Voters, and the Presidential Campaign of 2000* (Stanford: Stanford University Press, 2004).

46 Valeria Brusco, Marcelo Nazareno, and Susan Stokes, ""Vote Buying in Argentina," *Latin American Research Review* 39 (2004): 66–88; Simeon Nichter, "Vote Buying or Turnout Buying? Machine Politics and the Secret Ballot," *American Political Science Review* 102 (2008): 19–31; Ernesto Calvo and María Victoria Murillo, "Who Delivers? Partisan Clients in the Argentine Electoral Market," *American Journal of Political Science* 48 (2004): 742–757; Steven Levitsky, *Transforming Labor-Based Parties in Latin America: Argentine Peronism in Comparative Perspective* (Cambridge: Cambridge University Press, 2003).

47 Jana Morgan, "Partisanship during the Collapse of Venezuela's Party System," *Latin American Research Review* 42 (2007): 78–98.

48 Raúl Madrid, "Indigenous Voters and Party System Fragmentation in Latin America," *Electoral Studies* 24 (2005): 689–707; Deborah Yashar, *Contesting Citizenship in Latin America: The Rise of Indigenous Movements and the Postliberal Challenge* (Cambridge: Cambridge University Press, 2005).

49 David Samuels, "Sources of Mass Partisanship in Brazil," *Latin American Politics and Society* 48 (2006): 1–27.

50 Jorge I. Domínguez and James McCann, *Democratizing Mexico: Public Opinion and Electoral Choices* (Baltimore: The Johns Hopkins University Press, 1996); Jorge I. Domínguez and Chappell Lawson, eds., *Mexico's Pivotal Democratic Election: Candidates, Voters, and the Presidential Campaign of 2000* (Stanford: Stanford University Press, 2004); Jorge I. Domínguez, Chappell Lawson, and Alejandro Moreno, eds., *Consolidating Mexico's Democracy: The 2006 Presidential Campaign in Comparative Perspective* (Baltimore: The Johns Hopkins University Press, 2009).

51 Karl Marx, *The 18th. Brumaire of Louis Bonaparte* (New York: International Publishers, 1963), 15.

52 Kalman H. Silvert, "The University Student," in *Continuity and Change in Latin America*, ed. John J. Johnson (Stanford: Stanford University Press, 1964), 220.

53 Tugwell, *The Politics of Oil in Venezuela*; Vernon, *Sovereignty at Bay*.

54 Stephen Krasner, "Manipulating International Commodity Markets: Brazilian Coffee Policy, 1906–1962," *Public Policy* 21 (1973): 493–523.

34

STATE OF THE FIELD

Political Regimes and the Study of Democratic Politics[1]

Robert R. Kaufman

Over the past half century, the countries of Latin America—and of the developing world more generally—have confronted changes far more convulsive than those experienced in the more settled political systems of post-war Western Europe and the United States. The latter, to be sure, have also faced profound changes, not only in their pre-war histories, but in more recent decades as well; the evolution and enlargement of the European Union is but one example. Even so, there is little in the developed countries that can match the tumultuous events and deep social problems that Latin Americans have experienced over the past 50 years: among them, foreign interventions, revolutions, repression, and successive waves of efforts to establish and consolidate democratic regimes.

Research on Latin America has been motivated largely by efforts to describe and analyze these turbulent developments. Much more than in the case of our colleagues who study developed democracies, those of us who have tried to confront this challenge have faced numerous impediments to the construction of a cumulative body of empirically-grounded theory. One has been the paucity of qualitative information and quantitative data about many—if not most—of the countries of the region. In countries like Argentina, Brazil, Chile, and Mexico, some of the descriptive (as well as theoretical) gap came to be filled by monographic studies of history and contemporary politics, often pioneered by scholars from Latin America itself. But, especially in countries with weak academic infrastructures, basic information remained quite limited; and that which was available was often cast in ideographic terms that impeded cross-national comparisons.

Given the often unsettled nature of Latin American political systems, we have also frequently had to aim at moving targets. In this respect, as Barbara Geddes has claimed, it is at least partly true that we have sometimes overreached in our efforts to answer big questions about development and democracy: often publishing before events have run their course, and with insufficient attention to conceptual precision or case selection.[2] Geddes's critique is arguably overstated. As I will suggest below, it underestimates some lasting contributions of debates that flowed from the earlier literature, and it pays too little attention to increasingly sophisticated research strategies that build on the foundations of previous qualitative and historical research.[3] Still, the advice Geddes poses—especially the need to deconstruct large-scale events like revolutions or democratization into more researchable component parts—provides a very important and constructive challenge.

As it happens, some important and relatively recent trends in research have moved in this direction. As more Latin American countries have come to resemble the capitalist democracies of the developed world, the emphasis in the literature has shifted toward more narrowly-focused theoretical concerns and toward quantitative research techniques derived originally from research on the developed-country democracies. In the political realm, these trends are especially notable in work on political behavior and institutions. When attention turns to political economy, we see increasing reliance on theoretical assumptions of utility maximization, and econometric empirical analysis derived from modern economics.

The trend toward "normal science" approaches to the study of Latin American politics should be welcomed. Like earlier research approaches, it reflects real world changes within the region; most notably, the apparent stabilization of at least some democratic systems and the restructuring of Latin American economies in more open and market-oriented directions. Moreover, the growing emphasis on individualistic theoretical orientations and quantitative research approaches have helped to link the study of Latin American politics more closely to the broader fields of American and comparative politics. This in turn has facilitated useful cross-regional comparison between Latin American countries and other parts of the developed and developing world.

The embrace of these theoretical and methodological approaches, however, should be accompanied by a sustained skepticism about whether they can account fully for the continuities and changes we can see in Latin America's complex political landscape. Some of these issues are explored in depth in chapters that focus more directly on specific research questions and methodological approaches. In the pages that follow, however, I will try briefly to signal some substantive questions that seem to call for a continuing engagement with research approaches that deploy qualitative methods and that focus more directly on the social and historical relationships in which political actors are embedded.

Political Regimes and Economic Development: The "Normalization" of Latin American Political-Economies

Before turning directly to these issues, we can get a useful perspective on the state of the field today with a brief review of some earlier research landmarks and debates. I focus on those dealing with the relationship between economic development and political regimes, a theme which has dominated much of the literature since at least the 1960s. Discussion of this relationship has passed through at least three phases, each corresponding with major political developments within the region itself.

The emergence of military dictatorships in the relatively modernized societies of the southern cone and Brazil during the 1960s and 1970s spurred the first phase. At issue was the causal role of social conflicts and the economic constraints allegedly linked to "dependent development." Drawing on the dependency critiques of modernization theory emerging in the 1960s, the most influential accounts of the time emphasized social conflicts arising from pressures to move beyond the easy stages of import-substitution industrialization.[4]

Engagement with this explanatory account led to a series of important challenges. In part, these were empirical. In 1979, a project led by David Collier published essays that questioned several major foundations of the original theory, including both the claims that import-substitution was in fact exhausted, and that the alternative was primarily the "deepening" of industrialization through multinational investment.[5]

In the meantime, a concurrent project on democratic breakdowns offered the foundation for an alternative theoretical perspective, both on the turn toward dictatorship in the 1960s and 1970s and the even more dramatic wave of democratic transitions in the 1980s. It is significant that, rather than returning to a defense of modernization theories, this alternative narrative provided a critique of socioeconomic explanations more generally. Research pioneered by Juan Linz and Alfred Stepan emphasized the importance of political institutions (especially presidential regimes), and the strategies of political actors.[6]

A particularly important contribution to this project was Arturo Valenzuela's analysis of the 1973 coup in Chile. Chile was, in many respects, an easy case for social conflict theories; its long-standing constitutional regime collapsed in the face of economic crisis and deepening class conflict. Yet Valenzuela shows that these socioeconomic pressures were themselves the effects of constitutional stalemates and perverse incentives that discouraged compromise among the competing political parties.[7]

This emphasis on the political realm—like the later literature on democratic transitions—can be criticized for initially failing to reengage with modernization theory, particularly its emphasis on the importance of economic growth and development in the stabilization of democratic regimes. Attention to these economic factors reemerged strongly in the 1990s and 2000s. Nevertheless, the work on democratic breakdowns made at least two enduring and positive contributions.

First, in highlighting the role of constitutional design and electoral rules, the project anticipated much of the more recent "new institutionalist" literature. Debates over the relative stability of parliamentary and presidential democracies flowed directly from this earlier work, as did a variety of efforts to specify other institutional factors that cut across the broad distinctions between parliamentary and presidential systems.[8]

Perhaps even more important, this approach brought the motivations and strategies of political actors back into the analysis—an omission that had been especially glaring in earlier modernization theories. "In modernization theory," as Przeworski and Limongi have noted, "no one does anything to bring democracy about; it is secreted in economic development and social transformation."[9] The Linz and Stepan project on democratic breakdowns provided a major corrective. Specification of these actors has been a central focus of subsequent, and otherwise very different, theories that have attempted to identify the causal links development and democracy.[10]

The withdrawal of military dictatorships in the 1980s helped to generate a second phase of research on political regimes: transitions *from* authoritarianism and (in some cases) toward democracy. The seminal project was led by O'Donnell, Schmitter, and Whitehead.[11] Like the earlier project on the breakdown of democracy, contributors to this project brought political actors "back in." In an analysis intentionally directed at activists as well as scholars, they emphasized the strategic opportunities available to both defenders and opponents of authoritarian regimes.

This approach has been rightly criticized for overemphasizing voluntarism and "fortuna," for focusing too narrowly on negotiations among elite actors, and attaching too much importance to pact making as a foundation for successful democratic transitions. Moreover, despite the crushing constraints of external debt and economic crisis that characterized the "lost decade" of the 1980s, the democratization literature failed to address seriously the ways in which insertion into the international economy might affect the tradeoffs available to domestic political actors. "Ironically," as Barbara Stallings writes, "just as international variables became especially important in the 1980s, they disappeared as the key factor from theories of development."[12]

Again, however, the research agenda developed in this early transitions literature provided a foundation for some enduring contributions and lines of debate. First, and in many respects most important, the distinctions drawn in that project between transitions *away* from authoritarian regimes and movement *toward* democracy provided a conceptual framework for understanding subsequent issues related to the variety of regimes—both democratic and non-democratic—that emerged in the aftermath of authoritarian withdrawals. Although the empirical research was arguably biased toward a focus on successful cases of democratization, these conceptual distinctions established a foundation for work that focuses on backsliding toward less liberal regimes and on the variety of institutional and political forms that these exhibit.[13]

Moreover, the initial intuition of Schmitter and O'Donnell that there was no tight relationship between transitions and socioeconomic or cultural prerequisites has received considerable support in econometric research. Influential work by Przeworski and Limongi shows that transitions to democratic regimes are not endogenous to economic development.[14] Although these findings have not gone unchallenged,[15] experience on the ground also bears out the looseness of the sociological constraints on the initial establishment of democratic regimes. Movement toward democracy during the "third wave" has in fact occurred in a very wide variety of socio-economic circumstances.

As democratization spread from southern Europe and Latin America to other regions of the world, finally, the initial focus on the strategies and behavior of political actors sparked a vigorous and highly useful debate over the role of mass protest and labor pressures, over the effects of authoritarian institutions on the identity and behavior of the actors in the transition, and over the role of economic crisis in undermining military and business support for the incumbent regime.[16]

The "consolidation" of democratic regimes began, predictably, to appear as another phase on the research agenda in the early 1990s, at a time when many countries had held relatively free elections and appeared to reach the end of the transition process itself. Again, landmark studies by Linz and Stepan and by Guillermo O'Donnell led the way.[17]

These and other authors tackled a number of important analytical issues, but two stand out as especially important in light of subsequent developments in the region and elsewhere. The first builds on the distinction between regime and the bureaucratic infrastructure of the state itself. The state bureaucracy is marked in many countries by corruption, problems of coordination, and by the inability to establish a sustainable presence in urban slums and large portions of the interior—"brown areas," as O'Donnell has labeled them.[18] There is, to be sure, considerable cross-national variation in "state capacity"; but in most countries elected governments face severe agency problems with respect to the bureaucratic actors, which in turn make responsiveness to the electorate problematic.

The related issue focuses on the weakness of the institutional checks and balances that are rightly viewed as essential features of liberal democracy. Here again, there are substantial intra-regional differences: in some countries, legislatures have become much more independent than initially expected (Argentina), as well as more able to work cooperatively with presidents in processing a policy agenda (Brazil). But it is also often difficult to establish a workable balance between constitutional stalemates and presidential aggrandizement. Venezuela presents the most obvious example of a slide toward competitive authoritarianism, but the trends are evident as well in other Andean countries and in the even more widespread efforts to remove term limits and expand presidential powers. Judicial checks and rule of law, in turn, is problematic almost everywhere.

Although there has been no lack of concern and discussion of these issues in the literature, however, I do not believe that the focus on consolidation has generated the relatively coherent approaches or engaged debates that characterized work on bureaucratic authoritarianism or democratic transitions. In part, this may be because democracies in Latin America are still works in progress. But it is attributable as well to the vagueness of the concept of consolidation itself. Linz and Stepan's widely cited benchmark ("the only game in town") is evocative, but does not speak clearly to issues of the quality of democracy, accountability, or even institutional stability.[19] Does consolidation refer to absence of back-sliding or to a deepening of democratic practices? What do these terms mean anyway, and how would we know when we see a relatively durable institutional equilibrium?

In the face of these daunting conceptual and empirical problems, much of the research in the field has turned toward more disaggregated studies of sub-components of political processes and institutions, connecting more directly with theoretical approaches and specialized methods first advanced in the American and comparative politics subfields of the political science discipline. There is, for example, a rapidly growing literature on electoral behavior, legislative politics, partisanship and party competition, federalism, and the policy process. Most of this work has moved away from the sociological and political anthropological frames that anchored earlier studies toward a greater emphasis on approaches growing out of rational choice economics and behavioral psychology.

To the extent that regimes *per se* remain the object of study, moreover, much of the direct concern about consolidation has been replaced by (primarily) cross-national quantitative studies that focus on the survival of democratic regimes. Such studies, it should be noted, have also begun to tackle the output side of the question: whether democratic regimes are more capable than authoritarian regimes of delivering public goods. But as I will discuss at greater length below, findings have been mixed, and it is already relatively clear that social and institutional differences among democratic regimes are at least as important as regimes *per se*.

Breaking down questions about the quality, stability, and functioning of democratic regimes into more manageable sub-components is, as already discussed, an entirely appropriate research strategy. Given the emergence of electorally-based (if not entirely democratic) systems, moreover, it is also a significant step forward to turn to theories and quantitative research tools already usefully deployed in the analysis of the democratic politics and economic behavior in the relatively institutionalized democracies of the advanced countries.

However, there are potential drawbacks as well. The emphasis on the formal properties of institutions and on the strategic relationship among political actors risks drawing attention away from the potential effects of historical legacies and informal social networks. Moreover, the highly specialized focus of much of this literature, while useful in some respects, requires a sustained effort to link specific findings back to larger "so-what" questions about the nature and direction of change—especially in a region in which political and economic life remains in considerable flux.

These and other challenges seem to call for broader engagement with modes of research that focus more systematically on social relationships, historical dynamics, case-based knowledge, and small-N comparisons.

In the remaining sections of this chapter, I reflect on these research issues. In doing so, I draw primarily on impressions derived from my own research experience and on a familiarity with other work related at least peripherally to these interests. This necessarily excludes a wide range of pressing challenges facing the region: changing geopolitical connections outside the Western hemisphere, immigration, the flow of drugs, and so forth. I do, however, look specifically at three categories of research that are directly relevant to the survival and quality of democracy in Latin America: (a) work on the demand side of the political process: the mobilization of grievances, political competition, and the linkages between politicians and citizens; (b) the supply side of the political process—especially the institutional effects on the provision of public goods; (c) the broader relationship between economic development, globalization, and democratic politics.

The Demand Side

I turn first to research issues related to the kinds of demands emerging in Latin American societies and the ways they are mobilized politically. These have changed profoundly in the past 20 years, both as a consequence of openings provided by democratization and by social changes associated with the "neoliberal" reforms of the 1980s and 1990s. A clear understanding of the nature of these changes, however, has proved elusive. Reductions in the size of the public sector have partially eroded the base of unions and labor-based parties, but some have adapted to new conditions and remain powerful agents of popular mobilization. At the same time, we have also seen an increasing politicization of divisions based on ethnicity, race, and gender identities, the somewhat surprising survival of clientelistic ties between politicians and voters, and the rapid shifts in partisan alignments as reflected in a region-wide resurgence of "left" parties during the first decade of the twenty-first century. The puzzles raised by these developments have generated a large and growing body of valuable research.

Ethnicity and other forms of identity politics have never been missing entirely from the research agenda, but their political importance appears to have increased considerably in recent decades. In part, as Yashar has argued, this may be attributable to the breakdown of corporatist modes of representation. State corporatist institutions had provided channels through which the rural and urban poor could seek assistance from the state as peasants or workers; and their demise now left a vacuum in which new social movements and interest groups could reassert demands for indigenous, racial, or gender rights.[20]

But how can we account for cross-national and over-time differences in the salience and politicization of such demands? These questions have long been core subjects of study for students of Africa, Asia, the Middle East, and some of the post-socialist countries, but they are still relatively new for most of us working on Latin America.[21] Recent work points to an important role of movement entrepreneurs, and of competing elites in the mobilization of ethnic identities. The rise of ethnopopulism in Bolivia, for example, owed much to Morales's skillful blending of appeals to indigenous identities with broader and more inclusive forms of populism. In Mexico, local Catholic church officials have provided essential support for indigenous mobilization in areas where Protestantism had made substantial inroads.[22]

Analyzing identity politics means entering the long-standing debates over the malleability of ethnic boundaries, the role of social construction, and of political entrepreneurship and institutional change. Although economic grievances are not necessarily irrelevant to this debate, it has long been clear that identities cannot be explained entirely in terms of the socio-economic categories we have conventionally relied on to analyze interest group behavior and political parties. A variety of approaches, including rational choice analysis, may help to explain leadership strategies or the social construction of non-economic identities.[23] But is clear as well an analysis of the emerging importance of racial, ethnic, and gender divisions will require an in-depth understanding of cultural scripts, and repertoires of political protest—the stock in trade of anthropologists and social movement theorists.[24] In this respect, there is much to be learned from comparativists who engage these perspectives in their work on other regions.

A second important item on the demand side research agenda is the persistence of clientelistic linkages between politicians and voters. In a seminal article on programmatic and clientelistic linkages, Herbert Kitschelt hypothesized that the latter might diminish as neoliberal reforms reduced the overall size of the state and the availability of public patronage resources.[25] However, this does not appear to have been the case in Latin America. Indeed, by weakening unions, economic liberalization may actually have increased the incentives for politicians to distribute particularistic benefits as a way of maintaining the electoral support of low-income constituents.[26] Clientelism is facilitated not only by the poverty and inequality that characterizes many Latin American societies, but also by weak mechanisms of accountability that expand politicians' discretion over the distribution of public resources.

Current interest in the subject revives a topic that has long been a major field of study among political anthropologists.[27] The new research differs from this older tradition in its use of surveys and field experiments to document and dissect clientelistic exchanges. But the best of this research also relies on intensive field work and participant observation to describe the nature of the benefits provided and the ways that they enforce the exchange of favors for votes.[28]

Among other things, deep local knowledge is crucial for understanding the *meaning* of the observed linkages, an issue of profound normative as well as analytic importance for democratic politics.[29] In principle, the distribution of particularistic benefits in exchange for votes may reflect a voluntary form of representation, normatively consistent with democratic practices. On the other hand, when politicians exploit the vulnerability of the poor to buy votes and to punish voters for non-compliance, they undermine the fundamental elements of choice on which democracy is based. It is difficult to see how such distinctions can be parsed relying solely on surveys, field experiments, or large-N comparisons alone.

Finally, the wave of left-wing and populist victories across so many countries of the region has produced a surprising reconfiguration of partisan alignments. More than identity politics, these developments can be explained with concepts and tools used to analyze electoral politics in more advanced countries. To an important extent, for example, the shift can be attributable to a normal working of the political market in hard times: incumbent parties were displaced by oppositions that happened to be on the left.[30]

The focus on retrospective voting, however, cannot provide a fully satisfactory account of the shifts without reaching out to other approaches which nest the rise of the left more systematically in a larger social and international context. Insights from the social movement literature, for example, is clearly important for understanding how the Brazilian labor party could thrive in an institutional context biased heavily toward the personal vote and internal party indiscipline. At the same time, the wave phenomenon of recent left victories, also suggests the possibility of transnational diffusion effects (as well as active promotion by Venezuela).

A full explanation of enduring political cleavages, finally, requires systematic comparative historical analysis. In this regard, Ruth and David Collier's groundbreaking work on labor incorporation and partisan alignments remains an essential point of reference for understanding the emerging alignments of the contemporary period, both with respect to substantive background and methodological approach.[31] As Levitsky and Roberts argue, explaining profound differences *among* left governments requires a systematic examination of their divergent historical experiences with respect to authoritarian repression, regime change, and economic liberalization.[32]

In short, notwithstanding the increasing centrality of electoral politics throughout Latin America, we have still not arrived in Kansas. The theoretical and methodological tools imported from electoral studies of advanced countries are essential components of the emerging research agenda. Nevertheless, in situating these in a broader context, it is important to draw more extensively on sociological, anthropological, and historical approaches and to deploy a variety of research methods.

The Supply Side: Institutions and Public Policy

Grappling with the supply side of democratic politics has reinforced a tendency to move away from reified conceptions of "the state" and "state capacity" toward much more disaggregated studies of the actors who occupy roles within the state and how they respond to political and institutional incentives.[33] What *motivates* politicians and/or bureaucrats to address issues of growth, poverty, inequality, or more generally, to provide public goods? What affects their *capabilities* for delivering these goods?[34]

The answers to both questions depend in part on the demands that politicians face. If we accept the widespread assumption that democratic politicians want to be reelected, then they can be expected to be more responsive to constituent preferences as competition increases. I have explored these and other demand-side issues in recent work with Stephan Haggard on cross-regional differences in welfare systems.[35]

But even in democracy, politicians are not simply passive agents of voters or even interest groups; they pursue their own objectives and respond to other, non-electoral incentives as well. Both voter preferences and policy motivations can be reshaped from above by the public policies of leaders like Lula or Chávez who use their control of office to redirect the flow of private and public goods and construct new constituencies.[36] More generally, they are affected by the nature of electoral competition and representative institutions that encourage politicians to privilege some constituencies over others.

"New institutionalist" approaches—both "rational choice" and "historical"—have provided an important perspective on how the design of electoral laws, party organization and competition, and legislatures structure politicians' incentives to respond to or build constituencies. Studies of these institutions began to take off during the 1990s, as concerns about the durability of new democracies began to fade, and we now know a considerable amount about how they work.

The vast majority of such studies build on theoretical and empirical work on the United States and Western Europe, which in turn is relevant to a wide variety of political behaviors and public policies. As in U.S. politics, an understanding of the capacity of presidents to pursue a coherent legislative agenda has also been enhanced by a close examination of congressional norms, committee structure, and legislative leadership. Similarly, the supply of pork and clientelistic exchanges have been persuasively linked to electoral laws, nominating procedures, and other features of party organization that encourage party politicians to cultivate a personal vote.[37] Fiscal federalism has been a major focus of attention as well.[38]

Although institutionalist approaches provide considerable value, it is important to be cautious about the potential for establishing generalized claims about how institutions affect policy choices and outcomes. First, empirical research on these topics is, of necessity, highly labor intensive. Serious studies of legislative politics, for example, require substantial amounts of soaking and poking, as does understanding and mapping party organization and behavior. Showing how such institutions affect policy outputs compounds the practical research challenge.

A related challenge on a more theoretical plane is that the causal claims about the effects of one set of institutions are usually contingent on how they interact with others in the system. The effects of an open list party system, for example, cannot be theorized in isolation from rules governing the relations between federal and state governments, modes of territorial representation in the legislature, and so forth. This can lead to useful, but also highly configurative descriptions that are restricted to specific cases. There have been, to be sure, interesting efforts to facilitate cross-country comparisons by abstracting from more specific to more general sets of institutional properties—for example, Tsebelis's influential theories of veto gates or the "selectorate" theory of Bueno de Mesquita et al.[39] But it is far from easy to connect these broad institutional categories with the more nuanced institutional studies developed on the ground, or with reliable cross-national indicators of public policy.

Most important, institutions in many countries remain subject to major changes. In the past 20 years, entirely new constitutions have been written in Colombia, Venezuela, Bolivia, and Ecuador; and throughout the region, we see almost continuous tweaking of term limits, party organization, and electoral rules. Some of these developments have profound implications not only for public policy, but the future of democracy itself.

Particularly in the face of such changes, studies of the causal effects of institutions face major—perhaps inescapable—problems of endogeneity.[40] We commonly argue that institutions refract and modify the way policy issues are identified and processed. But at some point, this claim needs to be buttressed by a clearer idea about the underlying social and political forces that produce these institutions in the first place.

Here again, interdisciplinary and multi-method approaches may help to sort out some of these issues. Cross-national quantitative studies might provide some help in identifying broad patterns of institutional influences. But additional traction can also come from a variety of approaches that examine the policy effects of institutions on a smaller empirical scale. The analysis of critical junctures and path dependence can shed light, for example, on the "stickiness" of institutions and their capacity to refract political demands. Small-N comparative studies of specific policy issues can also yield important insights into the effects of partisanship, competition, and institutional design at various stages of the policy process.[41] Within-country comparisons of subnational units offer another promising line of research. It allows researchers to control for some important national-level political and institutional factors, while examining the factors that shape the provision and impact of services at the local level.[42]

Such strategies confront problems of their own in terms of the limits to out-of-sample testing and external validity. These disadvantages, however, are at least partially offset by their potential for offering more precise and nuanced insights into the complex causal mechanisms through which democratic institutions do (or don't) supply public goods.

Bringing the Economy Back In

Notwithstanding the waning of debates over dependency and modernization during the 1980s, concern about the effects of economic and social factors never entirely dropped out of the study of Latin American politics—and they have come back with renewed force in the last two decades. Przeworski et al.'s magisterial studies conducted during the decade of the 1990s played an especially important role in advancing long-standing interest in the relationship between economic development and democracy.[43] As discussed above, the primary conclusions spoke directly to some of the earlier debates about the relation between development, democratization, and democratic stability.

During the past decade, the increasing integration of Latin America into the global economy has spurred a second line of research on how globalization has affected growth, distribution, and social protections against risk. These studies have built on quantitative research on developed countries which show that integration has induced states to engage in progressive expansions of social protections. But studies of Latin America and the developing world more generally, have generally reached quite different (if still tentative) conclusions about the propensity of states to expand protection and the distributive effects of the protections that are provided.[44]

More recently still, Carles Boix and Daron Acemoglu and James Robinson have stimulated an important debate about how economic inequality affects democratization and democratic stability. In some respects, their work parallels historical sociological studies that focus on capitalist industrialization and working-class mobilization as the driving force behind the move to democracy.[45] Much differently than this earlier work, however, Boix and Acemoglu and Robinson ground their analysis in rational choice perspective. They start from rationalist assumptions about individual preferences for redistribution and theorize the basic struggle for democracy in terms of a conflict over assets and income between a relatively poor mass of citizens and a richer and more powerful elite.[46]

The research agendas established by these studies are obviously of crucial importance for understanding the course of Latin American politics. Not only do they address questions of democracy and distribution, but they are essential for framing some of the more specific areas of research discussed above on voting and collective action, partisanship and political institutions. With respect to research method, it is difficult to see how the questions they raise can be answered in the absence of cross-national econometric studies that can control for many other causal factors.

Even so, after a decade or more of such research, robust answers to the questions they raise remain elusive. Claims about the relationship between development and democracy rest on the most solid empirical foundations, but the nature of causal connection remains unclear. The results of large-N studies of the *effects* of democracy on development and social welfare are even more mixed, at least so far.

Cross-national statistical findings about the effects of globalization and economic inequality are also highly problematic. The effects of globalization on social outcomes, for example, remain highly unclear. If these effects exist at all, they appear to be heavily mediated by domestic politics and the underlying structure of local economies. We see even greater uncertainty with respect to the effects of inequality on democracy. Some studies have shown that relatively low income inequality enhances the chances for democratization; others show that it reduces those chances; and others show no effect.[47]

Some of this cycling may diminish as new research comes on line. But as valuable (and essential) as these large-N approaches are, they may be reaching a point of diminishing returns, for the time being at least. Data problems remain a formidable impediment to some parts of this quantitative research approach. Although we do have increasingly sophisticated ways to measure democracy,[48] the validity and coverage of other core measures remains highly problematic. Much of the globalization research has focused on the provision of key social policies, such as anti-poverty programs or the provision of health and education. Yet reliable cross-national measures of the type, coverage, and funding of such policies—remain elusive. The validity and comparability of measures of economic inequality are even more problematic. The sampling techniques used to generate the gini index, for example, vary widely in quality and scope, making both cross-country and over time comparisons highly suspect.

Beyond the data problems, however, are problems of specifying models that can adequately tap the complexity of the theory itself. The effects of development on democracy are likely to work through multiple, interacting channels. And, we can expect with considerable confidence, that the political and social effects of both globalization and inequality will be conditioned by the legacy of earlier developments and mediated by various aspects of contemporary political institutions and conflicts. These complex and conditional effects are hard—possibly impossible—to model statistically.

The challenges to cross-national statistical analysis may not be insuperable in the long run. In the meantime, though, it might be possible to push the debate forward with greater emphasis on research programs that trade broad empirical scope for narrower, more intensive ones. The potential utility of in-depth case studies is illustrated by Ziblatt's brilliant study of a non-event: He analyzes the defeat of efforts to reform Germany's multi-tier suffrage laws in 1912 by Prussian legislators from districts with high land concentration.[49]

In this area of research, it may be wise to follow Geddes's advice, cited above, to break the big questions down into more manageable components. Instead of examining the broad effects of globalization or inequality, for example, it may be more useful at this point to examine specific components of the causal chain: as economies become more open, is there an increase in the power of groups that control relatively abundant factors, as Heckscher-Ohlin would predict? Do individuals or groups respond to growing inequality with demands for redistribution? To what extent and under what circumstances do parties or other organized interests facilitate collective action? Some of these questions may be amenable to cross-national measurement, but small-n and case study research can provide considerable leverage as well.

Such suggestions, like those in the preceding section, cannot in themselves provide the basis for broad generalization or a full test of some of the larger claims about the causal effects of social and economic developments. Results, as the methodologists tell us, can be biased by limiting the number of cases selected; and findings about actors or specific policies cannot necessarily be scaled back up to claims about larger outcomes like democratization or globalization. For these reasons, it would be a mistake to abandon efforts to test broader claims through cross-national econometric analysis. It may be time, however, to attach a higher priority to alternative research approaches.

Conclusion

The preceding discussion offers a rather mixed message. On the one hand, the conceptual and methodological tools used to analyze democratic politics in the United States and other developed countries are also essential for mapping and analyzing the emergence of imperfect, but apparently rather durable democratic regimes in many countries of Latin America. In a similar vein, the transition toward more open market economies increases the need to draw on rationalist theoretical assumptions of contemporary political-economy.

On the other hand, I have also tried to suggest limits associated with emphasis on these approaches and the importance of engaging as well with sociology and other disciplines that systematically attempt to situate individuals and institutions in a broader network of social and historical relationships.[50] As I have also suggested above, moreover, such approaches may require us to think smaller and deeper—to focus on critical cases, small-N comparisons, or intensive examinations and comparisons of sub-national regions.

For individuals—especially those at the start of their careers—the mastery of a full range of such research approaches poses an impossible burden. Much more than in the past, the individual researcher would need not only the language skills and field experience relevant to work on Latin America, but also the mathematical skills necessary to deal with formal models and quantitative analysis, a grasp of increasingly sophisticated advances in qualitative method, and a familiarity with allied disciplines. Few if any older scholars possess this range of skills, and it seems beyond the reach of most younger ones as well.

What is impossible for individuals, however, is not necessarily impossible for the field as a whole. Collaborative research which builds on a division of labor among individual scholars can provide a significant part of the way forward. Collaboration, it should be emphasized does not obviate the need for broad academic training, because collaborators have to be able to communicate across the boundaries of their specialties. It does mean that the profession should encourage and reward a diverse range of research options for individual scholars. Teamwork that builds on this diversity is crucial, if the field is to continue to be driven by normative and empirical puzzles about real world problems rather than by the specialized skills available to the researcher.

Notes

1 I am grateful to Jorge Bravo, Stephan Haggard, and Jan Kubik for comments on an earlier draft of this paper, and to Vincent Greco for research assistance.
2 Barbara Geddes, *Paradigms and Sand Castles: Theory Building and Research Design in Comparative Politics* (Ann Arbor: The University of Michigan Press, 2003).
3 For example Henry E. Brady and David Collier, *Rethinking Social Inquiry: Diverse Tools, Shared Standards.* (Lanham, MD: Rowman & Littlefield, 2004). Gary Goertz, *Social Science Concepts: A User's Guide* (Princeton: University Press, 2006).
4 Guillermo O'Donnell, *Modernization and Bureaucratic Authoritarianism: Studies in South American Politics.* Politics of Modernization, no. 9 (Berkeley: Institute of International Studies, 1973).
5 David Collier, ed., *The New Authoritarianism in Latin America* (Princeton: University Press, 1979). See especially, Albert O. Hirschman, "The Turn to Authoritarianism in Latin America and the Search for its Economic Determinants," Jose Serra, "Three Mistaken Theses Regarding the Connection between Industrialization and Authoritarian Regimes," and Robert R. Kaufman, "Industrial Change and Authoritarian Rule in Latin America: A Concrete Review of the Authoritarian Model."
6 Juan Linz and Alfred Stepan, eds., *The Breakdown of Democratic Regimes* (Baltimore: Johns Hopkins University Press, 1978).
7 Arturo Valenzuela, *The Breakdown of Democratic Regimes: Chile* (Baltimore: Johns Hopkins University Press, 1978).
8 For example: Matthew Shugart, *Presidents and Assemblies: Constitutional Design and Electoral Dynamics* (New York: Cambridge University Press, 1992). George Tsebelis. *Veto Players: How Political Institutions Work* (Princeton: University Press and Russell Sage, 2002).
9 Adam Przeworski and Fernando Limongi, "Modernization: Theory and Facts," *World Politics* 49 (1997): 176.
10 See Dietrich Rueschemeyer, Evelyne Huber Stephens, and John Stephens, *Capitalist Development and Democracy* (Chicago: University Press, 1992). Carles Boix, *Democracy and Redistribution* (New York: Cambridge University Press, 2003).
11 Guillemo O'Donnell, Philippe Schmitter, and Laurence Whitehead, eds., *Transitions from Authoritarian Rule* (Baltimore: Johns Hopkins University Press, 1986).
12 Barbara Stallings, "International Influence on Economic Policy: Debt, Stabilization, and Structural Reform," in Stephan Haggard and Robert R. Kaufman (eds.), *The Politics of Economic Adjustment; International Constraints, Distributive Conflict, and the State* (Princeton: University Press, 1992), p. 43.
13 See Steven Levitsky and Lucan A. Way, *Competitive Authoritarianism: Hybrid Regimes after the Cold War* (Cambridge: University Press, 2010).
14 Przeworski and Limongi, "Modernization: Theory and Facts."

15 See Carles Boix and Susan Stokes, "Endogenous Democratization," *World Politics* 55 (2003): 517–549.

16 For example: Ruth Berins Collier, *Paths toward Democracy: Working Class and Elites in Western Europe and South America* (Cambridge: University Press 1999); Stephan Haggard and Robert R. Kaufman, *The Political Economy of Democratic Transitions* (Princeton: University Press 1995).

17 Juan Linz and Alfred Stepan, *Problems of Democratic Transition and Consolidation: Southern Europe, South America, and Post-Communist Europe* (Baltimore: Johns Hopkins University Press 1996). Guillermo O'Donnell, "Illusions about Consolidation," *Journal of Democracy* 7 (1996): 34–51.

18 Guillermo O'Donnell, "Why the Rule of Law Matters," *Journal of Democracy* 15, 4 (October 2004): 40.

19 Linz and Stepan, *Problems of Democratic Transition and Consolidation*, p. 5.

20 Deborah J. Yashar, *Contesting Citizenship in Latin America: The Rise of Indigenous Movements and the Postliberal Challenge* (Cambridge: Cambridge University Press, 2005).

21 The classic work remains Donald L. Horowitz, *Ethnic Groups in Conflict* (Berkeley: University of California Press, 1985).

22 See Raul Madrid, "The Rise of Ethnopopulism in Latin America," *World Politics,* 60 (2008): 475–508; Guillermo Trejo, "Religious Competition and Ethnic Mobilization in Latin America: Why the Catholic Church Promotes Indigenous Mobilization in Mexico," *American Political Science Review* 103 (2009): 323–342.

23 See David D. Laitin, *Identity in Formation: The Russian-speaking Population in the Near Abroad* (Ithaca: Cornell University Press 1998).

24 See Doug McAdam, John D. McCarthy, and Mayer N. Zaid, eds., *Comparative Perspectives on Social Movements: Political Opportunities, Mobilizing Sturctures, and Cultural Framing* (Cambridge: University Press 1996); Doug McAdam, Sydney Tarrow, and Charles Tilly, *Dynamics of Contention* (New York: Cambridge University Press, 2001).

25 Herbert Kitschelt, "Linkages Between Citizens and Politicians in Democratic Polities," *Comparative Political Studies* 33 (2000): 845–879.

26 Steven Levitsky, *Transforming Labor-based Parties in Latin America: Argentine Peronism in Comparative Perspective* (Cambridge: Cambridge University Press, 2003).

27 For example: John Duncan Powell, *The Political Mobilization of the Venezuelan Peasant* (Cambridge, Mass: Harvard University Press. 1971).

28 For example: V. Brusco, M. Nazareno, and S. Stokes, "Vote buying in Argentina," *Latin American Research Review* 39 (2004): 66–88.

29 Ed Schatz, ed. *Political Ethnography: What Immersion Contributes to the Study of Power* (Chicago: University Press, 2009).

30 Maria Victoria Murillo, Virginia Oliveros, and Milan Vaishnav, "Voting for the Left or Governing on the Left," in Steven Levitsky and Kenneth Roberts (eds.), *Latin American Left Turn* (Cambridge University Press, forthcoming).

31 Ruth Collier and David Collier, *Shaping the Political Arena: Critical Junctures, the Labor Movement, and Regime Dynamics in Latin America* (Princeton: University Press, 1991).

32 Steven Levitsky and Kenneth M. Roberts, 2010, "Introduction: Latin America's "Left Turn": A Framework for Analysis," in Levitsky and Roberts (eds.), *Latin American Left Turn*.

33 Barbara Geddes, *Politicians' Dilemma: Building State Capacity in Latin America* (Berkeley: University of California Press, 1994).

34 A related strand of research, which I do not discuss here, focuses on how institutions affect the behavior of economic actors and economic development. See Douglass C. North, *Institutions, Institutional Change, and Economic Performance* (Cambridge: University Press, 1990).

35 Stephan Haggard and Robert R. Kaufman, *Development, Democracy, and Welfare States: Latin America, East Asia, and Eastern Europe* (Princeton: University Press, 2008).

36 Of particular interest in this regard has been the work on conditional cash transfers in Brazil and Mexico, which are based fairly effectively on general entitlements rather than clientelistic exchanges.

37 John M. Carey and Matthew Shugart, "Incentives to Cultivate a Personal Vote: A Rank Ordering of Electoral Formulas," *Electoral Studies* 14: 4 (1995): 417–439.

38 Edward L. Gibson, Ernesto Calvo, and Tulia Faletti, "Reallocative Federalism: Legislative Representation and Public Spending in the Western Hemisphere," in Gibson, Edward L. (ed.), *Fed-

eralism and Democracy in Latin America (Baltimore: The Johns Hopkins University Press, 2004): 173–196.

39 Tsebelis, *Veto Players*; Bruce Bueno de Mesquita, Alastair Smith, Randolph M. Siverson, and James D. Morrow, *The Logic of Political Survival* (Cambridge, Mass.: MIT Press. 2003).

40 Adam Przeworski, "Is the Science of Comparative Politics Possible?" in Carles Boix and Susan C. Stokes (eds.), *Oxford Handbook of Comparative Politics* (New York: Oxford University Press, 2007).

41 Maria Victoria Murillo, *Political Competition, Partisanship, and Policy Making in Latin American Public Utilities* (Cambridge: Cambridge University Press 2009).

42 Alberto Diaz-Cayeros, Federico Estevez, and Beatriz Magaloni, *Strategies of Vote Buying: Poverty, Democracy, and Social Transfers in Mexico* (2007). http://www.stanford.edu/~albertod/buyingvotes/buyingvotes.html.

43 Przeworski and Limongi, "Modernization: Theory and Facts;" Adam Przeworski, Michael Alvarez, Jose Antonio Cheibub, and Fernando Limongi, *Democracy and Development: Political Institutions and Well-Being in the World, 1950–1990* (Cambridge: University Press, 2000).

44 Alex Segura-Ubiergo, *Globalization, Domestic Politics and the Welfare State in the Developing World: Latin America in Comparative Perspective, 1973–2003* (Cambridge: University Press. 2005); Nita Rudra, *Globalization and the Race to the Bottom in Developing Countries: Who Really Gets Hurt?* (Cambridge: University Press, 2008).

45 Rueschemeyer et al., *Capitalist Development and Democracy.*

46 Boix, *Democracy and Redistribution*; Daron Acemoglu and James A. Robinson, *Economic Origins of Dictatorship and Democracy* (New York: Cambridge University Press. 2005). For example of alternative sociological studies, see Rueschemeyer et al., *Capitalist Development and Democracy.*

47 Boix, *Democracy and Redistribution*; Ben Ansell and David Samuels, "Inequality and Democratization" *Comparative Political Studies* 45: 1 (January 2012); Christian Houle, "Inequality and Democracy: Why Inequality Harms Consolidation But Does Not Affect Democratization," *World Politics* 61 (2009): 589–622.

48 For example: Gerardo Munck, *Measuring Democracy: A Bridge Between Scholarship and Politics* (Baltimore, Md.: The Johns Hopkins University Press, 2009).

49 Daniel Ziblatt, "Does Landholding Inequality Block Democratization? A Test of the 'Bread and Democracy' Thesis and the Case of Prussia," *World Politics* 60 (2008): 610–641.

50 Charles Tilly, *Big Structures, Large Processes, Huge Comparisons* (New York: Russell Sage Foundation, 1984).

35

LATIN AMERICAN POLITICAL REGIMES IN COMPARATIVE PERSPECTIVE*

Adam Przeworski

Introduction

I need to begin with a personal disclaimer: I am neither a Latin Americanist nor a Latin American. My interest in Latin America originates from the simple fact that is where the action was during most of the two past centuries. As of 1917, 19 out of 49 independent countries were Latin American; still by 1945, 19 out of 67 were. Between 1789 and 1957, when Ghana became independent, 166 out of 341 constitutions adopted in the entire world were promulgated in Latin America, at least 533 out of 1,821 national legislative elections transpired in Latin America, 260 out of 371 coups, and 117 out of 226 civil wars. Anyone who studies modern political history must consider this vast experience, just because this is where most of it occurred.

My interest, however, is narrower than political history *tout court*. I want to understand the dynamics of political regimes and, even more narrowly, of those we call "democracies." And here the standard historiography is replete with stereotypes. The exotic image of a land gripped by dictatorships is about as accurate as that picturing the United States as the final realization of the Greek ideal of democracy, the new Athens. Latin American countries tried democracy earlier than the rest of the world, except the United States.[1] "Dictatorships," in the current meaning of the term, were rare. Several highly institutionalized regimes, rigorously observing term limits and tolerating at least some opposition,lasted for decades. Moreover, and I know that I am now locking horns with some Latin Americans as well, today several democracies in Latin America—Argentina, Brazil, Chile, Costa Rica, Mexico, Uruguay—have nothing to envy those in the United States, Italy, or France.

My point is that the history of democracy cannot be reduced to the experience of Great Britain, France, and the United States. Since stereotypes are hard to dispel, I take license to be polemical. There are two ethnocentrisms to combat: that of our period in history and that of the "center." Both warp our understanding. To demystify, one has to be careful about labels, and I try to reconstruct some of the language used at different times to characterize political regimes. But I also offer hard evidence, counting the incidence of various institutional forms, political regimes, and political events.[2]

What follows is first a conceptual history of political regimes. Then I introduce some aspects of political history that serves to construct really existing political regimes. Finally, I inquire into their dynamics.

Political Regimes: A Conceptual History

Distinctions among political regimes do not travel easily in history. Both the actual institutions and our labels for them are products of their times. Moreover, reality and language have histories of their own.

The point of departure for any conceptual history of political regimes must be a warning against an anachronistic use of the label of democracy. Due to the work of Dunn (2005), Hansen (2005), Manin (1997), Rosanvallon (1995) and several others, we now know that those who established first modern representative institutions in Great Britain, United States, and France did not think of them as democracies. Indeed, democracy was a negative term, something to be avoided because it presented a danger to the security of property, often coded as anarchy. This much is by now so well known that I refer the reader to the works cited above, as well as to their summary in Przeworski (2010: 3–5). I just want to emphasize that the universal use of the label of democracy to characterize desirable political regimes is very recent: it originated from a deliberate attempt in 1918 by Woodrow Wilson to neutralize the impact of Lenin's self-determination of nations with self-determination of the people (Manela 2007: 39ff; Graubard 2003: 665) and it became an unquestioned norm perhaps only in the 1980s, when Ronald Reagan launched the program of democracy promotion (Munck 2009: 2). It also bears emphasis that the language of democracy emanated from the United States, so it is an import, if not simply an export.

I could not find a similar history of democracy in Latin America.[3] It is clear that the founders of Latin American representative institutions shared the negative view of this system.[4] But it seems that after several Latin American political thinkers spent some years in the Philadelphia in the 1820s, some adopted a positive connotation for this term. The first to use the term representative democracy in a positive sense may have been the Peruvian constitutionalist Manuel Lorenzo de Vidaurre in 1827 (see Aguilar 2011, Chapter 3), but this history remains to be written.

Note that one should not confuse the use of the language of democracy as a label for a political regime with the use of democratic or, in English of the eighteenth century, democratical element of mixed constitutions (Pasquino forthcoming).[5] With an eye on Great Britain, several constitutional theorists proposed systems of representative government in which a democratical or popular element, embodied in the lower house of legislatures, would be counterpoised by an aristocratic one in the form of a Senate and at times also by a monarchy. These were not democracies as we now understand the term.

The history of the concept of dictatorship is no less convoluted. Around 1810, its meaning was precise and clear because the common reference was to the design of this institution in Rome, where dictatorship was a power delegated (normally by the consuls upon a declaration of emergency by the senate) to someone else than those authorizing it, for a strictly defined period (normally six months), not to be used against the delegating body or its members (Nicolet 2004; Pasquino 2010). The duty of the Roman dictatorship, characterized by Schmitt as "commissarial" (McCormick 2004), was to return the polity to the constitutional *status quo ante*. This understanding of dictatorship was prevalent throughout the history of Latin America. Francisco Miranda may have been the first person to bear the title of "dictator" in the modern era but this denomination was still based on the Roman concept of dictatorship.[6] While periods of autocratic rule were not infrequent, they were almost invariably justified by a need to respond to emergencies, crises, or exceptional circumstances. Dictators were saviors whose intervention was to be restricted to restoring the Roman *salus publica*. As Rippy (1965: 93) observed, "Whether sincere or deliberatively deceptive, the documents of the period always employed expressions suggesting a crisis: liberator, restorer, regenerator, vindicator, deliverer, savior of the country, and so on. Somebody was constantly having to 'save' these countries...." The crucial difference from the Roman institution was that, although dictators almost always insisted that they are performing a task authorized by a constitution, claiming the mantle of *gobierno constitucional*, the mission to save the country was unilaterally undertaken, by force and against the existing institutions. Nevertheless, with some exceptions discussed below, dictatorships were seen as something abnormal, something necessitated by exceptional circumstances, and something to self-dissolve when the situation is restored to normal.[7] Dictators assumed power unilaterally but they were also to abdicate unilaterally. To cite Paz (1963: 3–4), "It is significant that the frequency of military coups has never faded (esmaecido) democratic legitimacy from the conscience of our people. For this reason, dictators assuming power almost invariably declared that their government is provisional and that they are ready to restore democratic institutions as soon as circumstances permit."[8]

The exceptions to this general pattern matter because they are a source of an anachronistic use of the term dictatorship in our times. This linguistic transformation is largely due to European difficulties in understanding regimes such as that those of the two Napoleons, Mussolini, Hitler, Stalin, or Franco. "Bonapartism," "Ceasarism," "imperialism," "fascism," "totalitarianism" were all terms groping to identify these regimes. According to Baehr and Richter (2004: 25), the term "dictatorship" in its modern sense was used in Europe only during two periods of the nineteenth century: referring to France between 1789 and 1815 and briefly after 1852 to the Second Empire. The first person to establish a perpetual dictatorship in Latin America was Dr.José Gaspár Rodriguez de Francia who in 1816 proclaimed himself el Dictador Perpetuo of Paraguay and ruled it until 1840 as El Supremo.[9] The idea that dictatorship is necessary when religion fails to sustain order was developed by a Spanish thinker Juan Donoso-Cortés in a speech in 1849. It found echoes in Mexico (Aguillar 2011, Chapter 7) but an explicit argument that dictatorship should be permanent in Latin America was offered only in 1919 by Vallenilla Lanz. The Soviets were the first to use it as a positive self-designation in the "dictatorship of the proletariat" but the term acquired widespread usage only when liberal opponents of the Fascist and Nazi regimes adopted it as the label designating what they were fighting against. As a result, we came to include under the concept of dictatorship regimes that were "foundational," in Schmitt's language "sovereign," based on the rejection of representative institutions, designed to be permanent. Moreover, the ambiguity is not only conceptual: several military governments in Latin America after 1930 were themselves split or confused as to whether their mission was to be only to eradicate the foreign virus of subversion from the body of the nation and to abdicate once this body was sanitized or to establish a new permanent authoritarian order.[10]

If not democracy and dictatorship, as regimes are typically dichotomized in the post World War II era, then what? Following Machiavelli, the most important distinction during the nineteenth century was between monarchies and republics, with the third type distinguished by Montesquieu, despotism, relegated to the exotic and less known Asia. While monarchical sentiments were equent in the years following independence,[11] all Latin American countries ended up establishing republics. This is not to say that republics were all the same: as Gargarella (2000, 2011) amply documents, the weight of the democratic element varied importantly across different forms of republican governments. But the Western Hemisphere became the reserve of republics, as the United States would insist they be, while several European countries continued as monarchies, with a gradual transfer of control over governments from the crown to parliaments (Przeworski, Asadurian, and Bohlken 2010).

None of these terms—"democracy," "dictatorship" in its expanded meaning, "republic" or "monarchy," however, identifies the type of political regimes that were frequent in Latin America and until quite recently in the rest of the world. The traditional Latin American reference was "oligarchic republics" but this term emphasizes political and economic exclusion and this characterization is insufficient. They are recently identified by a plethora of labels: "electoral authoritarianism" (Schedler 2006), "competitive authoritarianism" (Levitsky and Way 2010), "hybrid regimes" (Karl 199; Diamond 2002), "semi-democracies," "authoritarian democracies," and what not. Those who coined these terms tend to think that the phenomenon is new[12] but while authoritarian is a neologism, the phenomenon itself is as old as the institution of elections, beginning with 1797 in France (Crook 2002). Moreover, to label them "authoritarian" is to miss their central feature: this term suggests that someone is seen as naturally or historically endowed with the infallible authority to govern, while in these regimes the right to rule is granted only by "other-authorization" (Dunn forthcoming) in the form of elections. Louis XIV was authoritarian because he believed that his right to rule was due to the grace of God; eighteenth-century aristocracy was authoritarian because it maintained that its political authority was given by nature. "The right to make laws belongs to the most intelligent, to the aristocracy of knowledge, created by nature," the Peruvian constitutionalist Bartolomé Herrera, declared in 1846 (Sobrevilla 2002: 196); the Peruvian José María Pando maintained that a "perpetual aristocracy ... is an imperative necessity"; the Venezuelan Andrés Bello wanted rulers to constitute u*n cuerpo de sabios* (Gargarella 2005: 120): they were authoritarians. But even the repressive Soviet regime, whether or not it was "totalitarian," still felt the need after 1936 to justify itself every few years by gleefully announcing that 99 percent of the people authorize the Communists to rule. That these elections were non-competitive, indeed some were just sham, makes no theoretical difference: to legitimize their rule, the rulers had to rely on the ceremony of elections. Such regimes were recognized at the time simply as "representative government" and for the moment I leave it at that.

Facts and Distinctions

Turmoil and Rule without Elections

Following O'Donnell, Schmitter, and Whitehead (1986), we are accustomed today to think about political history in terms of political regimes and transitions between them. But there are periods when countries do not have regimes of any kind. Regimes, after all, are some stable patterns of relations between the state and the society[13] and there are times when everything is in turmoil.

An election is held, someone wins, someone else contests, several people try to storm the presidential palace, someone drapes himself in a presidential mantle, only to be deposed by someone else, who then gets himself elected and in Latin America often proclaims a new constitution, only to be deposed again, etc.[14] Consider a few schematized sequences of events following elections: (1) In the Dominican Republic a person designated by someone who held office by force, lost an election in 1878, the winner assumed office but was overthrown by the military, which held another election, this time won by the incumbent military ruler, who assumed office but was again overthrown by a different military faction, which in turn was deposed one year later. (2) In Panama the incumbent party lost an election in 1948 but the loser remained in office, was replaced by another member of the party that lost, then by yet another one, who was in turn replaced by the original winner, who resigned in favor of his constitutional successor, who was forced out of office three years later. (3) In Bolivia, the first round of presidential elections of 1979 did not generate a clear result, the winner of election by the Congress was overthrown by the military, a non-partisan person was chosen pro-tempore but was again overthrown by the military, two more military coups followed, until the original winner assumed and served until the next election. Table 35.1 is a count of people who occupied the office of the chief executive after an election until someone held it for at least one full year or a new election occurred, whichever was first.

Most elections resulted in the winner assuming office and serving until the next election. But what kind of a regime is it if three, four, or as many as nine, people try to get into office and no one succeeds to hold it even one year? What regime is there if over a long period the average tenure of chief executives is 6.5 months, as in Honduras between 1820s and 1876? For a lack of a better term, I call such periods simply "turmoil."[15]

Now, turmoil should be distinguished from the periods when some ruler holds power for a long period of time without holding elections. Such periods were surprisingly rare after countries experienced at least one election: the qualification is necessary because I do not have information about periods preceding the establishment of first representative institutions in each country, which means that Saudi Arabia and other Gulf countries that never held national elections are not included here. But it is still startling that there were only ten instances in the entire world during the past 200 years in which someone ruled without elections and coups during at least sixteen years in a country that had previously experienced an election. Libya under Gaddafi holds the palm for not having held elections during thirty-nine years, closely followed by Spain under Franco. Francia's reign in Paraguay is the third longest at twenty-nine years but there are only two other Latin American cases on this list. Pinochet's rule of sixteen years is a major aberration in Latin American history as well as are the first seventeen years following the Cuban revolution of 1959.

Table 35.1 Number of Occupants of Office After Elections

Occupants	Number of Observations	of which Latin America
1	2776 (0)	660 (0)
2	134 (11)	57 (1)
3	63 (2)	27 (1)
4	25 (0)	13 (3)
5	11 (0)	7 (0)
6	10 (2)	3 (0)
7	7 (0)	3 (0)
8	1 (0)	0 (0)
9	2 (0)	0 (0)

Note: If two elections occurred in the same year, I count from the first one until someone holds office for a year after the second one or until the next election, whichever comes first. Numbers in parentheses are for years in which there were two elections.

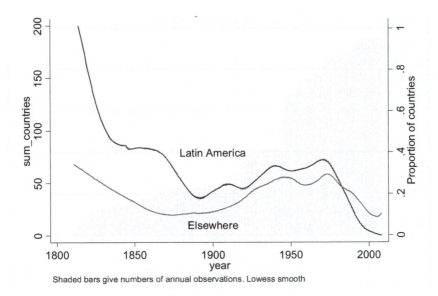

Figure 35.1   Periods of Instability or Rule Without Elections

Figure 35.1 shows by year the proportion of countries, in Latin America and in the rest of the world, in which either elections were not held regularly or they were held but the winners did not complete their term in office.[16]

Periods without regular elections were significantly shorter in Latin America than in the rest of the world. If one considers the instances in which no elections were held or they were held but no one completed a full term in office, there were 226 such periods in Latin America and they lasted on the average 3.83 years, while in the rest of the world there were 315 such instances with an average duration of 5.62 years. The probability that such periods were shorter in Latin America is 1.0.[17] Hence, these data confirm the historians' observation that Latin American dictatorships, while frequent, tended to be short-lived. While power was usurped by the dictators, except for Francia's rule in Paraguay, Pinochet's in Chile, and the early years of communist rule in Cuba, they were rarely foundational, as were Bonapartism, fascism, and communism in Europe.

Periods without elections were shorter in Latin America because elections results were not respected. If we consider again all years in which regular elections were not held or they were held but the winners did not complete a term in office, elections occurred in Latin America with the frequency of 0.20 per year, while in the rest of the world they transpired with the frequency of 0.12, a difference which would occur by chance with probability 0.0000. Moreover, this is not an effect of Africa or other countries that gained independence late: the difference between Latin America and Europe is equally significant ($p = 0.0013$). As I argued elsewhere (Przeworski 2009a), the fact that Latin America experienced frequent breakdowns of constitutional order should not be taken as an indication of anti-democratic tendencies on this continent. Indeed, the contrary is true: Latin Americans tended to experiment with elections earlier and, most importantly, at lower levels of per capita income. And because in poorer countries attempts to select rulers by elections are more likely to end in coups, they often did end in this way, only to be repeated again.

Uncontested Elections

Events called elections in which no one is selected because no opposition is permitted are a puzzling phenomenon. Voting is not the same as electing: it can obviously have other functions (Przeworski 2008). Most scholars interpret such elections as a facade intended to demonstrate that the regime is legitimate but in my view they have more instrumental functions. One is to provide the dictator who comes into power by force some autonomy with regard to the armed forces supporting him: being dependent exclusively on people with arms is risky for the dictator because these people may turn against him. Another is to intimidate the potential opposition by demonstrating that the rulers can force large masses of people to perform this inconsequential ritual. (For the latter interpretation, see Gandhi and Przeworski 2006.) It may well be that rulers who entered power by force did not tolerate opposition but still needed to protect themselves from their allies by having been elected, while stable one-party regimes used elections as an instrument of intimidation. It is striking that uncontested elections were frequent in Latin America during the nineteenth century but became rare exactly when Lenin's invention of one-party systems spread around the world, indicating that uncontested elections in Latin America were not foundational in the sense of establishing a permanent one-party system (see Figure 35.2).

Representative Government

The conceptual difficulties in identifying what these days we call "democracies" arise from the fact that many countries over long periods of time regularly held contested elections which incumbents (persons, parties, or designated successors) always won. Labels aside, the observable features of these regimes were the following:

1. They held regular elections for the president or for the legislature.
2. They were politically pluralistic, in the sense that voters were offered a choice in elections. More precisely elections were pluralistic if, with minor exception of instances

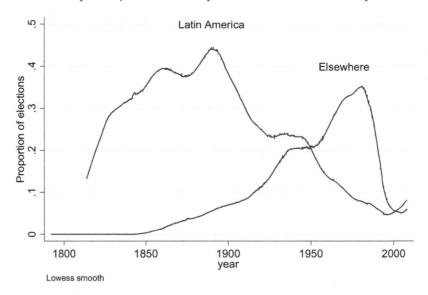

Figure 35.2 Uncontested Elections

where political parties agreed to a unique candidate (as in Chile in 1891), there was more than one candidate for president and voters in at least some districts faced a choice between candidates or lists in legislative elections.[18]

3. The incumbent person or party or the candidate selected by the outgoing government never lost elections.

The mechanism that maintained this non-competitive pluralism was simple. The incumbent government offered candidates, the Ministry of Interior administered the elections, and the newly elected legislature validated the results. This system was universal in the world until 1920 when Austria, Czechoslovakia, and Canada, followed by Chile in 1925, Greece in 1927, as well as Brazil and Uruguay in 1932, transferred the administration or the validation of elections to an independent body.[19] The instruments at the disposal of incumbents included the use of the state apparatus, manipulation of the electoral rules, and often fraud.[20] The idea of an official government list submitted to voters for a plebiscitary approval was present already in France under the Directorate (Crook 2002), used under Restoration, and perfected under Napoleon III (Zeldin 1958). Promoting government candidates was not a transgression but a duty of public officials: the French Prime Minister, de Vilèlle, issued in 1822 a circular instructing "All those who are members of my ministry must, to keep their jobs, contribute within the limits of their right to the election of M.P.s sincerely attached to the government"(quoted in Zeldin 1958: 79). The same was true in Latin America. As Domingo Santa Maria, the President of Chile between 1881 and 1886, unabashedly admitted, "Giving away votes to unworthy people, to the irrational passions of the parties, and even with universal suffrage, is a suicide for a ruler and I will not commit suicide before a chimera."[21]

The stability of such systems—Brazil between 1833 and 1889, Mexico between 1946 and 1999, Chile between 1841 and 1890, Argentina between 1874 and 1915, Paraguay between 1963 and 1988, Uruguay between 1938 and 1966—was remarkable. Table 35.2 offers a list of regimes that continuously held pluralistic elections in which the incumbents never experienced a defeat.

Pluralistic elections continuously won by incumbents were less frequent in Latin America during the nineteenth century because, as we have seen, for a long time winners of elections were often deposed or there was no opposition (see Figure 35.3).

Now, were these democracies as we tend to define such regimes today?

Here is the crux of the difficulty. When one looks at this list in Table 35.2, some of the regimes look like democracies and most observers classify them as such. Almost everyone thinks that post-war Japan and Italy were democracies even during the long periods during which elections did not produce a partisan alternation in office.

Most observers think the same about Botswana, where following independence in 1966 until today the same party won all elections. Przeworski et al. (2000) coped with this difficulty by invoking a retrospective criterion: a regime is a democracy if the period of successive victories of incumbents was followed by an instance of alternation under the same rules. But the results of applying this criterion obviously depend on the date when a country is observed. Hence, Botswana was not a democracy because alternation did not occur until today, even if it may occur some day, while Mexico was not a democracy before 2000 because the transfer of the administration of elections to an independent body (Instituto Federal Electoral [IFE])in 1990 constituted a change of rules. In any case, the alternation criterion will not get us very far with regard to the nineteenth-century Latin America for a simple reason that electoral defeats of incumbents were extremely rare and peaceful

Table 35.2: Long-Lasting Regimes with Regular Pluralistic Elections Always Won by Incumbents

Country	Year ended	Years lasted	Reason ended
Luxembourg	1974	126	Alternation
Norway	1890	74	Alternation
Romania	1939	73	War
Netherlands	1873	59	Alternation
Brazil	1889	55	Monarchy abolished
Mexico	1999	54	Alternation
Denmark	1900	52	Alternation
Germany	1918	51	Monarchy abolished
Italy	1995	50	Alternation
Chile[a]	1890	50	Civil war
Tunisia	2008	49	Continued as of 2008
Japan	1992	47	Alternation
Spain[b]	1922	47	Coup
Taiwan	1999	46	Alternation
Austrian Empire	1910	44	Alternation
Botswana	2008	44	Continued as of 2008
Argentina	1915	42	Alternation
Nepal	2004	42	Autocoup.
Portugal	1973	40	Revolution

[a]The legislature was temporarily closed in 1841, otherwise the continuity would be dated back to 1831, with the duration of 60 years.
[b]Control over government alternated regularly between two parties during this period but alternations always occurred before elections and governments newly chosen by the King never lost.

alternation in office even less so. As Halperin-Donghi (1973: 116)wryly observed, "Among the many ways of overthrowing the government practiced in postrevolutionary Spanish America, defeat at the polls was conspicuously absent."

One may thus conclude that the alternation criterion is too exacting: as long as elections are contested and their results are obeyed, the regime is a democracy. But then all forms of representative government constitute democracy even if no opposition ever wins. Hence, we are in a quandary: either there were almost no democracies in nineteenth-century Latin America or all the regimes in which there was a modicum of electoral opposition were democracies.

Now, incumbents may win elections because they are genuinely popular but also because they exploit their control over the state apparatus, manipulate the rules, or commit fraud. These reasons cannot be isolated empirically so that incumbents always can, and do, claim that their victory is an authentic verdict of the people.[22] It may be that incumbents exert so much political control that the chances of the opposition to win are practically zero but it may also be that the opposition had a fair chance and lost. This is what we would ideally want to know: whether incumbents *could have been* defeated. To put it differently, instead of characterizing regimes *ex post* by the results of elections, we would want to characterize them *ex ante* by the probability that the opposition could win elections and assume office as their result. If we knew which elections were free and fair, to use the current jargon, we could separate those which incumbents won because they were unfair or unfree from those

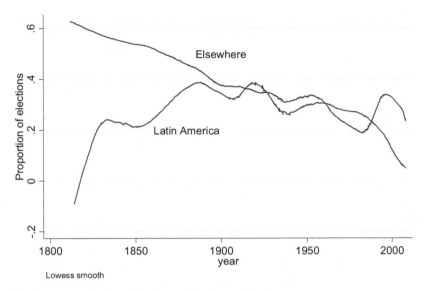

Lowess smooth

Figure 35.3 Contested Elections Continuously Won by Incumbents

which they won because they were popular. Yet even if many researchers, including Smith (2005), are willing to make judgments of his sort, I fear that these assessments are often biased by the knowledge of the actual outcomes.

Consider a procedural approach to this problem. Dahl (1971) lists several conditions, pertaining to rights and freedoms, under which elections should be considered democratic. The procedural approach is to observe if these conditions are satisfied and to classify regimes on these bases, with the hypothesis that if they are satisfied, elections are competitive.[23] As argued by Munck (2009), this approach may be effective today, given the widespread use of election monitoring. But given the paucity of equivalent information, the discriminating power of this approach is weak when applied to earlier elections. We do know whether elections were direct and whether balloting was secret, we know the franchise qualifications, and for a smaller subset we have information about the actual proportion of the population eligible to vote, but we do not know whether elections were clean by modern standards. Statistical analyses show that incumbents were more likely to lose if elections were direct and if voting was secret or if electoral eligibility was higher.[24] But the predictive power of these procedural features is too weak to provide reliable predictions of the instances in which incumbents lost. Moreover, per capita income alone has the same predictive power and in the presence of per capita income none of the institutional matter.[25] Hence, the procedural approach does not take us far with the available data.

Faced with these difficulties, I adopt a different tack. Instead of classifying political regimes, I investigate specific events: terminations of non-competitive pluralistic systems and the occurrence of the first partisan alternation in office as a result of elections.[26]

Regime Dynamics

Terminations of "Representative Governments"

"Representative governments," as defined above, can end their life for a number of different reasons: (1) rule without elections or elections after which the winners do not complete their

Table 35.3 Causes of Termination of Pluralistic Non-Competitive Regimes

Cause	World	LA
Turmoil, no elections	89 (0.33)	39 (0.51)
Repression of opposition	42 (0.16)	22 (0.29)
Alternation	93 (0.35)	14 (0.18)
Continuing	42 (0.16)	2 (0.03)
Total	266 (1.0)	77 (1.0)

terms; (2) repression of all opposition while continuing to hold non-pluralistic elections; (3) partisan alternation in office as a result of an electoral defeat of the incumbent. The frequencies of these reasons for termination are listed in Table 35.3.

Statistical analysis[27] shows that the determinants of these terminations are unsurprising, at least in so far as that higher per capita income makes termination by coups less likely. Turmoil is more likely to ensue if the rate of electoral participation—proportion of voters to the population—is higher: it seems that non-competitive but pluralistic regimes cannot withstand high participation. Yet higher participation does not increase the probability of suppressing the opposition or of partisan alternation. Older pluralistic regimes are less likely to repress opposition while presidential systems are more likely to do so. Representative government in countries which experienced in the past a breakdown of pluralistic regimes—whether or not they were competitive—is more likely to end in partisan alternation.[28] Finally, presidential systems as well as systems with bicameral legislature are less likely to experience alternations.

Latin American representative governments were more often terminated by breakdowns of constitutional order than those outside Latin America, while they were equally likely to end in repression of the opposition or in alternation. Note that while almost all Latin American political institutions were presidential, only about one-half presidential systems were located in Latin America. Hence, the effect of presidentialism—to make alternations less likely and uncontested elections somewhat more likely—is independent of the location in Latin America.

The Origins of Political Competition

When and how do elections become competitive, with their results obeyed by the losers? Considered here are the instances in which either the incumbent rulers did not present themselves or their political allies in an election or did present themselves and lost, in both cases as long as the winner peacefully assumed office and held it at least for one year or until the next election. There are quite a few instances in which the incumbent lost an election but the winner was prevented from assuming office: such instances are not considered as alternations. Hence, the question concerns the origins of electoral competition, as evidenced by constitutionally regulated partisan alternation in office.

Table 35.4 lists first partisan alternations that occurred anywhere in the world as a result of elections. Only seven alternations occurred in Latin America during the nineteenth century, out of 328 presidential elections for which we have this information. Moreover, only in Colombia after 1837 and after 1848, Dominican Republic after 1849, and Argentina after 1878, did the victorious winner survive a full term in office. If one were to apply to the

Table 35.4 Partisan Alternations in Office as a Result of Elections

Country	First	Second	Third
US	1800	1828	1840
UK	1831	1841	1852
Colombia	1837	*1848*	*1930*
Spain	1837	*1851*	*1865*
Belgium	1847	1856	1870
Dom Rep	1849	1853	*1978*
Honduras	1852	*1928*	1932
Portugal	1860	1864	1865
Italy	1867	1876	1892
Argentina	1868	1916	*1989*
Liberia	1869	1871	1877
Netherlands	1874	1877	1888
France	1877	1881	188S
Sweden	1884	1901	1911
Costa Rica	1889	1909	1923

Note: Italic fonts indicate that coups or civil wars occurred between the previous alternation and the date appearing in italics.

nineteenth century the criteria used to classify regimes after 1945, these would have been
the only democracies in Latin America.

Examining over time the proportion of elections that resulted in alternation shows that
(1) alternations have been rare everywhere until quite recently, (2) for a long time they were
less frequent in Latin America than elsewhere (which was basically Europe), (3) they have
become exceptionally frequent in Latin America recently. My hunch is that alternations
were easier to tolerate by the losers in monarchies, where less is at stake in elections, than
in presidential republics.[29] The frequency of alternations in Latin America during the past
three decades is thus even more striking.

To anticipate the conclusions, note that alternations have also become much more
frequent in Europe in the past thirty years, so that this difference between Latin America
and the rest of the world is due largely to non–European countries (see Figure 35.4). Even
so, the rate of alternations in Latin America after 1980 is still slightly higher than in Europe.

The circumstances under which first alternations tend to occur depend on the antecedent
status quo.[30] A direct transition from rule by force to competitive elections is more likely at
higher levels of per capita income. Transitions from uncontested elections are more likely
when the rulers fail to make people participate in the ceremony of elections.[31] Finally, we
already know that alternations are more likely to happen under representative government
in countries which experienced in the past a breakdown of pluralistic regimes and less likely
in presidential systems with bicameral legislatures. Latin America differs from the rest of the
world only in that direct transitions from military rule to competitive elections have been
more frequent than elsewhere. These patterns, however, do not add up to much: transitions
to democracy are notoriously difficult to predict because they occur for a large variety of
reasons (Przeworski et al. 2000).

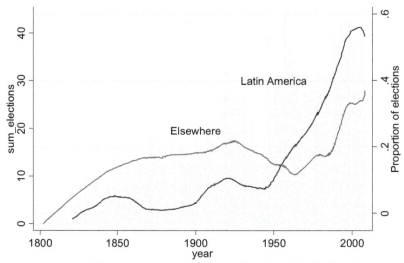

Lowess smooth. Sum of annual number of elections in the entire world on the left scale.

Figure 35.4 Alternations by Year

It merits noting that neither the extent of franchise nor the proportion of the population participating in elections affect the probability of the first alternation occurring under representative government. Because this is a topic that looms large in conceptual debates about democracy, it deserves more detailed attention. Note first that many people, including Dahl (1971) and Vanhanen (1997) but not only scholars, insist that a regime is not democratic unless the right to participate in elections is widespread. Dahl goes as far as to require that at least one half of the adult population have the right to vote, so for him the United States became a democracy (polyarchy in his language) only in 1950. These two dimensions— contestation and participation—are clearly distinct conceptually. Moreover, while political conflicts before World War I focused mainly on suffrage, after 1918 universal suffrage became widespread and the main political issue became the right to contest elections. But the question is whether these conceptually distinct dimensions are historically related: whether contestation is a consequence of extended suffrage (see Table 35.5).

Table 35.5 Proportion of Elections Lost by Incumbents, by Suffrage Qualifications

Qualification	Males	and Females[a]	Total
Property	0.13 (70)	—(0)	0.13 (70)
Income and Literacy	0.07 (91)	0.23 (13)	0.09 (104)
Income alone	0.20 (259)	0.00 (11)	0.19 (270)
Income or Literacy	0.14 (111)	0.15(47)	0.15(158)
"Independent"	0.11 (146)	0.17 (6)	0.11 (152)
Universal	0.14 (400)	0.26 (1520)	0.23 (1920)
Total	0.14 (1077)	0.25 (1597)	0.21 (2674)

Note: The numbers of elections occurring under each type of qualifications are in parentheses.
[a] In 50 cases women faced additional restrictions (higher age, only widows of the military, etc.).

Two aspects of Table 35.5 merit attention. When suffrage was limited to males, the incidence of incumbents losing was not different when it was additionally restricted by property, income, or literacy than when it was universal.[32] Yet incumbents lost more frequently when suffrage was qualified specifically by income (the difference from universal male suffrage is significant, $p = 0.0151$). The reason is that income was the most restrictive criterion in its effect on the proportion of the population qualified to vote, even more restrictive than the property requirements which were very lax in Canada and New Zealand, and more restrictive than the literacy qualification, which continued in place well after most males were literate.

The proportion of elections lost by incumbents became clearly higher when women gained the right to vote. Yet statistical analysis shows that the effect of female suffrage vanishes when controlled by per capita income, as does the effect of universal suffrage. In turn, the effect of income qualifications does survive in the presence of this control ($p = 0.0320$).

These finding add up to the conclusion that suffrage and competition constitute historically independent dimensions. If anything, the oligarchical republics, at least those in which the access to the oligarchy was regulated by income and gender, were more competitive than mass democracies. Hence, there are grounds to believe that elites were more willing to compete when competition was restricted to elites.

Statistical analyses indicate the conditions under which it happened but not how it happened. The circumstances under which first competitive elections occur are highly varied. "Jump starting"—competitive elections following a civil war—occurred after wars destroyed most of what the fighting was about, so hat little was to gain by continuing (Wantchekon 2004). Transitions from uncontested elections often entailed overthrowing the dictator by force, while those from institutionalized one-party systems were highly conditioned by geopolitical factors. Elections became competitive in this context, I believe, when none among the forces opposed to the extant regime could impose itself by force over its allies in overthrowing it.[33] The question I find fascinating is why at some definite moments the incumbent rulers, whether they entered office by force or by non-competitive elections, become willing to risk their hold on power at the polls.

What is crucial in my view is whether the incumbents expect that if they were to hold a competitive election, giving someone else a chance to win, the eventual winner would reciprocate. As the experience of the U.S. elections of 1800 demonstrates (see Weisberger 2000; Dunn 2005), the decision to release the reins of power is extremely difficult: Jefferson may have prevailed only as a consequence of Madison's threat to mobilize the Virginia militia. And it took twenty-eight years, seven electoral periods, before the next alternation occurred in the United States. In New Granada in 1837, General Santander, who believed that the country was not ready for a civilian chief executive, supported General Obando to be his successor. Yet a civilian, Dr.José Ignacio de Márquez won the plurality of electoral votes and the Congress confirmed his victory (Posada Carbó 1999). According to Bushnell (1993: 90), "Santander then delivered his office to someone he had opposed—taking pains to point out, in a proclamation, that he had thus respected the will of the people and the law of the land." Obando did rise against Márquez two years later, but was defeated, and Márquez completed his term.[34] Party lines were fluid until around 1850, but regular elections followed and terms of office were completed until the coup of 1854.

One might expect that partisan alternations would be easier in monarchies because the monarchs can provide the guarantee to the losers that they could return to office. This was generally true, but not without a significant and sometimes long resistance from the kings, who had partisan preferences of their own. In England, the king appointed a Tory prime minister in spite of the Tory electoral defeat in 1834 and only the repeated victory of the opposition forced him to accept Melbourne government. In Belgium, Liberals had to win twice before assuming office in 1847, in Denmark minority right-wing governments stayed in office in spite of repeated defeats between 1872 and 1901, in the Netherlands the same was true between 1856 and 1871.

The expectation that the losers can return to office is crucial because it means that that holding onto power is not a matter of survival, so the stakes are not very high. When incumbents believe that an electoral defeat may mean a loss of life or at least of their fortunes, as in contemporary Russia, the risk is just too high (see Makarenko forthcoming, on tolerable uncertainty). To put it differently, what matters is not *whether* the incumbents would lose but *what* they would lose.[35] Whether this belief is a matter of trust, of relations of physical force, or of the degree to which the interests between the rulers and the opposition happen to converge, is unfortunately not a question that can be resolved by a recourse to observation. The fact that alternations are more likely to transpire at higher income levels indicates that the size of the stakes matter: when incomes are higher, there is less to gain by holding onto power and less to lose by releasing the reins of power. But it is striking that elections that resulted in a peaceful partisan alternation in office tend to be followed by periods during which competitive elections become the norm, coups are less frequent, and elected governments complete their terms.[36] Hence, there is strong evidence of path dependence, specifically that once political leaders see that having lost office is not a disaster, they are willing to put their hold onto power at risk again.

Latin America in a Comparative Context

One cannot attend a Latin American meeting without hearing two canonical phrases: "In my country, as in the rest of Latin America, ..." and "In contrast to advanced countries, in Latin America...." If we are to believe what we hear, Latin America is internally homogenous and different from the rest of the world or at least from advanced countries, established democracies, or something of the sort. The evidence presented here indicates that this claim may have been true in a distant past. But it is true no longer.

To summarize the patterns presented above, consider the annual incidence of rule by force in Latin America compared to Europe. A note of caution with regard to this regionalization is, however, in order first. Regionalizations also have a history, often resulting from geopolitical interests. My native country, Poland, was a part of Christian Europe, Slavic Countries, Middle Europe (Mitteleuropa), Eastern Europe during the Cold War, is now a part of "Post-Communist Countries," and perhaps will be simply in Europe within the near future. The idea of the "Americas" and later "Western Hemisphere" served to separate it from monarchical Europe: as Rojas (2009: 15) observes, for many influential Latin American intellectuals at the time of independence, "lo americano ... no estuviera adjetivado por lo 'latino' o lo 'hispano'" ["the American ... would not be qualified by 'Latin' or 'Hispanic'."] The invention of a Latin race by a Frenchman, Michel Chevalier, was intended to juxtapose it to Anglo-Saxon domination.[37] "Latin America" is a product of the 1850s.

"Europe," in turn, changed meanings several times, extending and contracting to the East and the South (Davies 1998). How arbitrary are these regionalizations is evidenced by a football game between Aktobe Lento, Kazakhstan, and FC Tbilisi, Georgia (Lento won 2:0), which took place within the European Champions League.

With this caveat, I compare the Spanish and Portuguese speaking countries south of the Rio Grande and the Caribbean Islands with countries bordered by the Ural in the East and the Mediterranean in the South. Included under rule of force are instances in which no elections were held regularly or they were held but their results were not obeyed or they were held without opposition. The complement to these cases are thus instances in which pluralistic elections were held regularly, regardless of their results.

As is well known, civil wars and other forms of political violence continued in Latin America long after independence and when order finally prevailed around 1870, it was imposed by force. Europe in the meantime began to hold elections, which were typically pluralistic, even if non-competitive. Pluralistic elections became more frequent in Latin America after 1870 and rule by force reached its lowest level by about 1920. The end of World War I gave birth to several new countries in Europe and some of them quickly succumbed to the rule of force (see Figure 35.5). Most puzzling, and to my best knowledge never analyzed jointly, is the simultaneous eruption of political instability in mid-1920s in Europe and Latin America.[38] The aftermath of World War II saw the rise of several one-party regimes in what became Eastern Europe, while pluralistic electoral regimes became more frequent again in Western Europe and well as in Latin America. The major contrast is that Greece was the only European country where pluralism subsequently collapsed, while not a single democracy that existed in Latin America as of 1946 survived. As I argued elsewhere (Przeworski 2009a, also Cheibub 2007), the different fates of democracy on the two continents must have been due at least in part to the outcome of the war, which resulted in defeat of authoritarian forces in Western Europe, while it left them intact in Latin America. In consequence, just when the last regimes based on force in Western Europe—Greece, Portugal, and Spain—collapsed, the Southern Cone was in the grip of exceptionally brutal military dictatorships.

But all this is a past, now distant by at least a generation.[39] Pluralistic electoral regimes are as entrenched now in most countries of Latin America as they are in most of Europe. The differences do not run across regional lines: Argentina, Brazil, Chile, Costa Rica, Mexico,

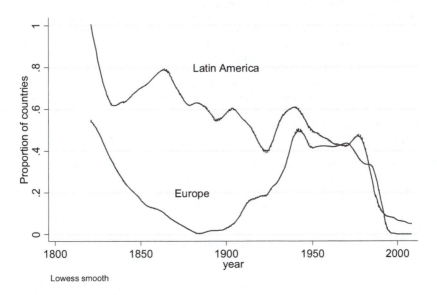

Figure 35.5 Rule by Force in Latin America and in Europe

Uruguay have stable and reasonably well functioning democratic regimes that have nothing to envy the United States, Italy, or France. I know that this assertion will raise objections: Latin Americans will point out to corruption, unscrupulous tactics of politicians, influence of money over the media, in some cases even to electoral irregularities.

But it takes a second to find the same phenomena in several old, developed, long-established democracies. One can quibble whether democracy in Sweden is better than in Chile, in France than in Argentina, in the United States than in Brazil, but these will be quibbles. Lula could not have won an election in the United States and, even if the election of Obama was a miracle, the former was much more effective in implementing his program of reforms than the latter. In turn, significant intra-regional differences remain on both continents: Argentina has more in common with France than with Honduras, Sweden more in common with Chile than with Belarus.

This is a new world, and I do not hesitate to say, a democratic one. True, everyday life of really existing democracies is not an inspiring spectacle. But conflicts, peace, and liberty do not coexist easily: this is why through most of history, civil peace could be maintained only by force. Given the history recounted here we should not lose the sight of how privileged we are to be free from oppression, free to process our conflicts in peace. When Donoso-Cortés could say in the middle of the nineteenth century, "What is good is the correction that disobedient peoples receive from tyrants and tyrants receive from revolutions," we can now say that what is good is that people are free under laws and the lawmakers are chosen by the people.

Notes

* I appreciate comments by José Antonio Aguilar Rivera, Robert Barros, Joanne Fox-Przeworski, Roberto Gargarella, Fernando Limongi, Gerardo Munck, Pasquale Pasquino, Julio Saguir, Juan Carlos Torre, and the editors of this volume.

1 Annino (1998: 10) observed that "el caso latino americano presenta una extraordinaria precoci-dad en el contexto internacional.... Si miramos al espacio euroatlántico en su conjunto es evi-dente que América Latina se encuentra en una situación de vanguardia." Hartlyn and Valenzuela (1994: 99-100) observe that Latin American regimes "were largely comparable to the restricted representative regimes in Europe of the same period." Drake (2009: 2) stresses that "contrary to conventional wisdom, the countries leading the region in making democratic advances did not lag very far behind the United States and Europe."

2 All the data used here are from the PIPE data set.

3 Neither could Posada-Carbó (2008: 16), and he knows better.

4 See McEvoy (2008) on José Ignacio Moreno in Peru, Posada-Carbó (2008) on Eloy Valenzuela in Colombia. Sarmiento (quoted in Zimmerman 2008: 12) referred to "la democracia conseg-rada por la Republica de 1810" but only in 1845.

5 According to Saguir's (2011) account of the Argentine Constitutional Convention of 1816-19, democracy was seen as a danger because it portended anarchy but a democratic element, in the form of the lower house representing the lower classes and checked by the Senate, would be needed to absorb them into the constitutional system.

6 In 1808–9, Miranda wrote an *Esquise de Gouvernement fédéral*, a blueprint where he justified an exceptional dictatorship by invoking the experience of Rome (Aguilar 2000: 169).

7 When Bolivar wanted to resign from his first of three dictatorships, for example, he was asked to keep the office in the following terms: "Remain, your Excellency, as a Dictator, improve your efforts at saving the Fatherland, and once you have done it, then restore full exercise of sovereignty by proposing a Democratic Government.".On Bolivar and dictatorship, see Aguilar (2000: Chapter V).

8 Already Bolivar, in the speech accepting the position of the Dictador Jefe Supremo de la República, announced that "ya respiro devolviéndos esta autoridad."(Discurso de Angostura, in Bolivar 1969: 93).

9 Francia is the protagonist of a richly documented historical novel by Augusto Roa Bastos, *Yo el supremo,* but I could not find there any surprise at the notion of a perpetual dictator, an oxymoron in the language of the time.

10 The 1930 coup in Argentina, for example, was led by General Uriburu, who intended to replace individual by functional representation, while General Justo, who became president in 1931, participated in the coup "solamente como un soldado mas de la revolución," wanting only to depose President Irigoyen. See Ibarguen (1955), Pinedo (1946).

11 In the National Assembly of Tucuman, Argentina (1816), General Belgrano put forward *una monarquia temperada,* a monarchical project having a king native to the Americas, a monarch of Inca descent rather than that of European lineage. General San Martin also favored a monarchical solution (López-Alves 2000: 179). Sentiments for monarchy under an Italian or British prince were present in Uruguay. Yet in the end only Brazil adopted this solution until it became a republic in 1889. In Mexico the first emperor, Agustin de Iturbide lasted two years, with a brief return of monarchy between 1862 and 1867. The reasons monarchical projects failed, according to Rippy (1965: 89) were that "the royalties of Europe and the monarchists of America had difficulty in reaching an agreement, the United States was opposed to American kings, the princes were difficult to find, and the people were not disposed to tolerate them."

12 Levitsky and Way (2010: 14): "We contend that competitive authoritarianism is a new phenomenon...."

13 According to O'Donnell and Schmitter (1986:73) a regime is "the ensemble of patterns, explicit or not, that determines the forms and channels of access to principal government positions, the characteristics of the actors who are admitted and excluded from such access, and the resources and strategies that they can use to gain access.... This necessarily involves institutionalization, i.e., to be relevant the pattern defining a given regime must be habitually known, practiced, and accepted at least by those whom these same patterns defining a given regime must be habitually known, practiced, and accepted at least by those whom these same patterns define as participants in the process."

14 Obviously my favorite nighttime reading is the impressive collection of some Latin American political chronologies, available from http://libraries.ucsd.edu/locations/sshl/resources/featured-collections/latin-american-elections-statistics/

15 Safford's (2008: 349-50) characterization of the post-independence period in Latin America is so clear analytically that it merits being quoted in extenso: "Formal constitutional systems were enacted, most of which provided for the transfer of power through elections and guaranteed individual liberties. But these formal constitutional provisions frequently proved a dead letter. No political group believed that its adversaries would abide by them. Those who held power bent constitutional principles and often harshly repressed those in opposition in order to retain the government. Those out of power believed, generally correctly, that they could not gain possession of the state by means formally pre-scribed by the constitution, because those who held the government controlled the elections. Opposition politicians, both military and civilian, therefore waited for, and took advantage of, moments of government weakness in order to overthrow the ruling group. Governments were unable to resist these rebellions, often because they were too weak financially to maintain dominant military force or to provide sufficient patronage to buy the allegiance of potential rebels.

16 "Lowess smooth," used in all the figures, is just a slowly moving average.

17 All the statements about probabilities of differences occurring by chance are based on t-tests with unpaired cases and unequal variances.

18 I do not consider as pluralistic those situations in which there was one organized party and independent candidates (as in Portugal in 1954), only those in which there was more than one party, faction, or sentiment or in which everyone ran as independent.

19 Based on Lehoucq (2002) According to IDEA's 2006 survey of 214 countries and territories, the system in which the government administers and validates still prevails in 26 percent of countries covered, in 15 percent elections are administered by the executive and an independent judicial body certifies, while electoral management bodies are nominally independent in 55 percent of countries. In a remaining 4 percent, elections are not held.

20 On the difficulties of defining fraud, see Annino (1995: 15-18). On corrupt electoral practices in Latin America, see Posada-Carbó (2000).

21 Collier and Sater (1996: 58) report that "Delivering the vote was a vital aspect of the Intendant's [equivalent of French prefet] work.... Yet Intendants could at times go too far.... When the young Intendant of Colchagua, Domingo Santa Maria [future president], interpreted the president's instructions to win the elections 'at all costs' a trifle too enthusiastically, this was seized by his enemies as the pretext for his dismissal."

22 A Russian proponent of sovereign democracy, Mikhail Leontiev (in an interview with a Polish newspaper, *Dziennik*, of 19 January 2008), exploits this ambiguity: "I do not understand what is undemocratic in that some force enjoying overwhelming social support wins elections."

23 This is, for example, the approach used by the Freedom House, with a well known ideological bias.

24 The "or" is due to colinearity: when secret, direct, and eligibility are introduced in the same specification, only eligibility has a significant coefficient.

25 These results are based on probit regressions with country-clustered standard errors, conditioned on the presence of opposition. The predictive power is measured by the area under receiver operating curves, which ranges from 0 to 1: this is perhaps the best measure of the fit of probit predictions. The respective values are 0.6 for secret and direct, 0.59 for eligibility, and 0.59 for per capita income alone.

26 Throughout the text, I consider only alternations in the partisan control over the office of the chief executive that result from elections, but to avoid repetitions below I refer to them simply as alternations.

27 These results are based on multinomial logit of these reasons for termination, conditioned on the current state being representative government, with country-clustered standard errors.

28 On the effect of past history on regime dynamics, see Przeworski et al. (2000) and Przeworski (2009a).

29 It is interesting that this was the conclusion of Mexican conservatives in 1846. After only two governments completed their terms in twenty-two years, they concluded that solution to the instability is monarchy. See Aguilar (2011).

30 The statistical results summarized here are based on the coefficients of multinomial logits of transition to competitive elections from turmoil, uncontested elections, and representative government.

31 Przeworski (2011) argues that a fall of participation in one-party systems is a signal to the potential opposition that the regime is losing control and that, as a consequence, makes the fall of such regimes more likely. This argument has been confirmed in a statistical analysis by Corvalan (2011).

32 The "independent" category is *sui generis*. See Przeworski(2009b).

33 The prospect of joining Europe was obviously also important in the Eastern European part of the former Soviet bloc.

34 Posada-Carbó (2008: 31) points out the contrast with the events in Venezuela at two years earlier: "Although in Venezuela President Páez's favourite, General Soublette, also lost at the polls and Páez handed in power to the victor, Dr José M. Vargas—a civilian—the latter was ousted seven months later, when Páez returned to the presidency and then practically ruled Venezuela for the next two decades."

35 This is literally what a communist reformer said to me on the streets of Warsaw in 1987.

36 Once the first alternation occurs in a country, about one subsequent election in three (0.35 of 1,355 elections) results in peaceful alternations. Before the first alternation, coups occur with annual frequency of 0.0682, after the first alternation with the frequency of 0.0310. Before the first alternation, years of completed constitutional terms constitute 0.63 of 6,210 years, after the first alternation they make 0.82 of 4,753 years. The effect of first alternation on coups and completed terms survive in probit regressions controlled for per capita income.

37 In the words of José María Torres Caicedo (*Las dos Américas*, 1857),
La raza de la América latina
Al frente tiene la sajona raza
Enemiga mortal que ya amenaza
Su libertad destruir y su pendón.

38 According to Rouquie (1994: 223), "Between February and December of 1930, the military were involved in the overthrow of governments in no fewer than six, widely differing Latin American nations—Argentina, Brazil, the Dominican Republic, Bolivia, Peru, and Guatemala.

The same year also saw four unsuccessful attempts to seize power by force in other Latin American countries. Over the following years, Ecuador and el Salvador in 1931, and Chile in 1932, joined the list of countries in which military-provoked political shifts and unscheduled changes of the executive had taken place."

39 Perhaps the most striking piece of evidence is that one can now participate in large academic conferences on Latin America in which the word "military" is not mentioned once.

References

Aguilar Rivera, José Antonio. 2000. *En pos de la quimera.Reflexiones sobre el experimento constitucional atlántico*. México City: CIDE.

Aguilar Rivera, José Antonio. 2010."Las ideologías políticas en América Latina: de la metamorfosis al ocaso del liberalismo, 1870-1930." Mexico City: CIDE

Aguilar Rivera, José Antonio. 2011. *Ausentes del Universo: Reflexionessobre el Pensamineto Político Hispanoamericano en la Era de la Construcción Nacional: 1821–1850*. Mexico City: CIDE.

Annino, Antonio. 1995. "Introducción." In Antonio Annino (ed.), *Historia de las elecciones en Iberoamérica, siglo XIX*. México City: Fondo de Cultura Económica.

Annino, Antonio 1998. "Vote et décalage de la citoyenneté dans les pays andins et meso-americains."In Ra¤aele Romanelli (ed.), *How Did They Become Voters? The History of Franchise in Modern European Representation*. The Hague: Kluwer, pp 155–182.

Baehr, Peter, and Melvin Richter. Eds. 2004. *Dictatorship in History and Theory: Bonapartism, Ceasarism, and Totalitarianism*. Cambridge: Cambridge University Press.

Bolívar, Simon. 1969. *Escritos politicos*. Edited by Graciela Soriano. Madrid: Alianza Editorial.

Bushnell, David. 1993. *The Making of Modern Colombia*. Berkeley: University of California Press.

Cheibub, José Antonio. 2007. *Presidentialism, Parliamentarism,and Democacy*. New York: Cambridge University Press.

Collier, Simon, and William F. Sater. 1996. *A History of Chile, 1808–1994*. Cambridge: Cambridge University Press.

Corvalan, Alejandro. 2011. "Is Participation Harmful to Democracy?" Working Paper, Department of Economics, New York University.

Crook, Malcom. 2002. *Elections in the French Revolution*. Cambridge: Cambridge University Press.

Dahl, Robert A. 1971. *Polyarchy: Participation and Opposition*. New Haven, CT: Yale University Press.

Diamond, Larry. 2002. "Thinking about Hybrid Regimes." *Journal of Democracy* 13(2): 21–35.

Davies, Norman. 1998. *Europe: A History*. New York: Harper.

Drake, Paul. 2009. *Between Tyranny and Anarchy: A History of Democracy in Latin America,1800–2006*. Stanford, CA: Stanford University Press.

Dunn, John. 2005. *Democracy: A History*. New York: Atlantic Monthly Press.

Dunn, John. 2010. Judging Democracy as Form of Government for Given Territories: Utopia or Apologetics? In Adam Przeworski and others, *Democracy in the Russian Mirror*. Forthcoming.

Dunn, Susan. 2004. *Jefferson's Second Revolution: The Election Crisis of 1800 and the Triumph of Republicanism*. Boston: Houghton Mifflin.

Gandhi, Jennifer, and Adam Przeworski. 2006. "Cooperation, Cooptation, and Rebellion under Dictatorships." *Economics Politics* 18: 1–26.

Gargarella, Roberto. 2000. *Los fundamentos legales de la desigualdad: El constitucionalismo en América (1776–1860)*. Madrid: Siglo XXI.

Gargarella, Roberto. 2010. *200 años de constitucion alismo en América Latina (1810–2010)*. Universidad de Buenos Aires, Buenos Aires.

Graubard, Stephen R. 2003. "Democracy." In *The Dictionary of the History of Ideas*. University of Virginia Library: The Electronic Text Center. http://etext.lib.virginia.edu/cgi-local/DHI/dhi.cgi?id=dv1-78

Halperin-Donghi, Tulio. 1973. *The Aftermath of Revolution in Latin America*. New York: Harper & Row.

Halperin-Donghi, Tulio. 1987. "En el transfondo de la novela de dictadores: la dictadura hispanoamericana como problema histórico." In El *espejo de la Historia: Problemas argentinos perspectivas & latino américanas*. Buenos Aires, pp. 17–39.

Hansen, Mogens Herman. 2005. *The Tradition of Ancient Democracy and Its Importance for Modern Democracy*. Copenhagen: Royal Danish Academy of Arts and Letters.

Hartlyn, Jonathan, and Arturo Valenzuela. 1994. "Democracy in Latin America since 1930." In Leslie Bethell, (ed.), *The Cambridge History of Latin America Vol.VI. Latin America since 1930 Part 2. Politics and Society*. New York: Cambridge University Press, pp. 99–162, 610–622.

Ibarguen, Carlos. 1955. *La historia que he vivido*. Buenos Aires: Ediciones Peuser.

Karl, Terry Lynn. 1995. "The Hybrid Regimes of Central America." *Journal Of Democracy* 6(3): 72–87.

Lehoucq, Fabrice. 2002. "Can Parties Police Themselves? Electoral Governance and Democratization." *International Political Science Review* 23(1): 29–46.

López-Alves, Fernando. 2000. *State Formation and Democracy in Latin America, 1810–1900*.Durham, NC: Duke University Press.

McEvoy, Carmen. 2008. *The Forking Path: Elections and Democracy in Peru, 1912–1872*. Paper presented at the Seminar on the Origins of Democracy in the Americas, Notre Dame University, South Bend, IN, September 18-21.

McCormick, John P. "From Constitutional Techniques to Ceasarist Ploy: Carl Schmitt on Dictatorship, Liberalism, and Emergency Powers." In Peter Baehr and Melvin Richter (eds.), *Dictatorship in History and Theory: Bonapartism, Ceasarism, and Totalitarianism*. Cambridge: Cambridge University Press, pp. 197–220.

Makarenko, Boris. 2011. "The Role of Elections in Democracy." In Adam Przeworski and others, *Democracy in a Russian Mirror*. Forthcoming.

Manin, Bernard. 1997. *The Principles of Representative Government*. Cambridge: Cambridge University Press.

Munck, Gerardo L. 2009. *Measuring Democracy: A Bridge between & Scholarship and Politics*. Baltimore: The John Hopkins University Press.

Nicolet, Claude. 2004. "Dictatorship in Rome." In Peter Baehr and Melvin Richter (eds.), *Dictatorship in History and Theory: Bonapartism, Ceasarism, And Totalitarianism*. Cambridge: Cambridge University Press, pp. 263–278.

O'Donnell, Guillermo, Philippe C. Schmitter, and Laurence Whitehead. 1986. *Transitions from Authoritarian Rule: Tentative Conclusions about Uncertain Democracies*. Baltimore: The Johns Hopkins University Press.

Pasquino, Pasquale. 2010. "Machiavel: dictature et salus & reipublicae." In Brigitte Krulic (ed.), *Raison(s) d'Etat(s)en Europe, Traditions, Usages, et Re-compositions*. pp. 12–34.

Pasquino, Pasquale. 2011. "Democracy: Ancient and Modern, Good and Bad." In Adam Przeworski and others, *Democracy in a Russian Mirror*. Forthcoming.

Paz, Octavio. 1965. "A Democracia e a América Latina." *Caderno de Cultura de Estadode São Paulo*, ano II, numero 128.

Pinedo, Federico. 1946. *En Tiempos de la Republica*. Buenos Aires: Editorial Mundo Forense.

Posada-Carbó, Eduardo. 1999. "Alternancia y república: Elecciones en la Nueva Granada y Venezuela, 1835–37." In Hilda Sábato (ed.), *Ciudadanía políticay formación de las naciones. Perspectivas históricas de América Latina*. México, City: Colegio de México.

Posada-Carbó, Eduardo. 2000. "Electoral Juggling: A Comparative History of the Corruption of Su¤rage in Latin America, 1830–1930." *Journal of Latin American Studies* 32: 611–644.

Posada-Carbó, Eduardo. 2008. *Origins of Democracy in Colombia, 1808–1886*. Paper presented at the Seminar on the Origins of Democracy in the Americas, Notre Dame University, South Bend, IN, September 18-21.

Przeworski, Adam. 2008. "Constraints and Choices: Electoral Participation in Historical Perspective." *Comparative Political Studies* 20: 1–27.

Przeworski, Adam. 2009a. "The Mechanics of Regime Instability in Latin America." *Journal of Politics in Latin America* 1: 5–36.

Przeworski, Adam. 2009b. "Conquered or Granted? A History of Suffrage Extensions." *British Journal of Political Science* 39: 291–321.

Przeworski, Adam. 2010. *Democracy and the Limits of Self-Government*. New York: Cambridge University Press.

Przeworski, Adam. 2011. "Political Institutions and Political Order." In Adam Przeworski and others, Democracy in the Russian Mirror. Forthcoming.

Przeworski, Adam. 2011. PIPE: Political Institutions and Political Events Data Set. Department of Politics, New York University.

Przeworski, Adam, Michael E. Alvarez, José Antonio Cheibub, and Fernando Limongi. 2000. *Democracy and Development*. New York: Cambridge University Press.

Przeworski, Adam, Tamar Asadurian, and Anjali Bohlken. 2010. "The Origins of Parliamentary Responsibility." Revised paper presented at the Conference on Constitutional Design, University of Chicago Law School, October 16–17, 2009. Unpublished manuscript.

Rippy, Fred J. 1965. "Monarchy or Republic?" In Hugh M. Hamill, Jr. (ed.), *Dictatorship in Spanish America*. New York: Alfred. A. Knopf, pp. 86–94.

Rojas, Rafael. 2009. *Las repúblicas de aire. Utopía y desencanto en la Revoluciónde Hispanoamérica*. México City: Taurus.

Rosanvallon, Pierre. 1995. "The History of the Word 'Democracy' in France." *Journal of Democracy* 5(4):140-154.

Rouquie Alain. 1994. "The military in Latin American Politics since 1930." In Leslie Bethell (ed.), *The Cambridge History of Latin America, Volume VI, Part 2:1930 to the Present*. Cambridge: Cambridge University Press, pp. 233–306.

Safford, Frank. 2008 (1985). "Politics, Ideology, and Society in Post-Independence Spanish America." In Leslie Bethell (ed.), *The Cambridge History of Latin America, Vol. III*, available from Cambridge Histories on Line, Cambridge University Press, pp. 347–421.

Saguir, Julio. 2011. El Congreso de 1816–19 y la Constitución de 1819. Ms.

Schedler, Andreas. 2006. *Electoral Authoritarianism: The Dynamics of Unfree Competition*. Boulder, CO: Lynn Rienner.

Smith, Peter H. 2005. *Democracy in Latin America*. New York: Oxford University Press.

Sobrevilla, Natalia. 2002. "The Influence of the European 1848 Revolutions in Peru." In Guy Thomson (ed.), *The European Revolutions of 1848 and the Americas*. London: Institute of Latin American Studies, pp. 191–216.

Vanhanen, Tatu. 1997. *Prospects of Democracy: A Study of 172 Countries*. New York: Routledge.

Vallenilla Lanz, Laureano. 1919. *Cesarismo democratico: estudios sobre las bases & sociólogicas de la constitución efectivade Venezuela*. Caracas.

Wantchekon, Leonard. 2004. "The Paradox of 'Warlord Democracy': A Theoretical Investigation." *American Political Science Review* 98: 17–33.

Weisberger, Bernard A. 2000. *America on Fire: Jefferson, Adams, and the First Contested Election*. New York: HarperCollins.

Zeldin, Theodore. 1958. *The Political System of Napoleon III*. New York: W.W. Norton.

Zimmermann, Eduardo. 2008. "Elecciones y Representación politíca: Los Origines de una Traditición Democratica en la Argentina, 1810-1880." Paper presented at the Seminar on the Origins of Democracy in the Americas, Notre Dame University, South Bend, IN, September 18-21.

36

POPULAR REPRESENTATION IN CONTEMPORARY LATIN AMERICAN POLITICS

An Agenda for Research

Ruth Berins Collier and Christopher Chambers-Ju

The problem of mass politics and popular, or lower-class, political representation has been an abiding issue in Latin America. While Latin American countries exhibit a long history of democratic constitutions, the lower classes have not been well represented, especially relative to their large numbers. Throughout the region, historically the world's economically most unequal, anti-popular political actors have pursued a variety of strategies to reduce lower-class political influence. The military regimes launched by the coups of the 1960s and 1970s are a dramatic example: the resort to authoritarianism was historically the response to a perceived threat stemming from lower-class political pressures. Since the 1980s, when the region established relatively stable democratic regimes, the question of popular representation has become particularly salient, and many studies have explored a great variety of topics related to this issue. It is now time to build on these studies and pose the question of mass politics and popular representation and to undertake macro comparisons across historical periods and across countries.

The issue of popular representation has arisen in the contemporary period in light of the dual transitions of marketization and democratization, with seemingly different implications. On the one hand, changes in the international economy and the debt crisis led to a process of economic reform and a new market-oriented economic model that was often adopted despite political opposition. Its initial consequences included increased inequality, social dislocation, and hardship. It thus seemed adverse to the representation of popular interests. At the same time, the region's seemingly more stable and institutionalized democracies have created space, opportunities, and resources for social mobilization; the proliferation of popular associations has provided a potential organizational infrastructure for popular interest politics; unprecedented initiatives in social policy have been directed toward the traditional "outsiders" in the informal and rural sectors; and the election of left-leaning presidents in the new century seems to usher in a new period of responsiveness to popular interests. These economic and political changes have raised the question of the nature of democracy, accountability, and the political representation of the popular classes—the question with which Latin American countries have struggled for over a century.

Scholars have directed much attention to these issues, focusing on the implementation of economic policies and their social consequences, the nature and functioning of democratic institutions, political parties, and popular associations. However, these studies have generally remained ahistorical and fragmented, usefully focusing on discrete components or aspects of structures of popular representation and frequently limited to a restricted set of comparisons. This more restricted purview in part reflects the difficult empirical and conceptual task of analyzing popular—or lower-class—representation at a macro level. In this chapter, we advocate the importance of a research program that adopts a comparative framework and integrates many of these topics at a higher level of aggregation. We discuss an approach for this research agenda in terms of two complementary analytic perspectives.

The first perspective is historical, as over-time change and temporal comparisons are illuminating, both descriptively and causally. Historically, the question of mass politics and popular representation was first posed in the earlier part of the 20th century with the formation of a new working class, which organized labor unions to advance its interests. In the contemporary period the question of mass politics and lower-class inclusion has been posed again, in part reflecting the decades-long formation of a new segment of the working classes in the informal sector. The informal sector has formed new organizations and made new demands. At the same time, economic conditions have also changed, affecting, differentially, all sectors of the working class as well as their "representational weight" relative to other classes. Thus an analysis of popular representation that takes world historic time and historical change seriously is appropriate.

The second perspective approaches macro comparisons, whether historical or "cross-sectional," through the lens of something akin to Schmitter's (1992) notion of a "partial regime." Specifically, we refer to two partial regimes of popular representation—or more accurately of state-society intermediation—in which communication and influence goes in both directions between state and society. The first is the party system; the second is the "popular interest regime," the set of organizations through which the popular sectors have sought to pursue their interests (Collier and Handlin 2009:4). The concept of "partial regimes" focuses attention on structures, institutions, and organizations as well as the behavior of political actors within these interacting arenas, or sites, of interest intermediation. The analysis in Collier and Collier's *Shaping the Political Arena* (1991) can be interpreted as arguing that these two partial regimes were initially constructed during the critical juncture of labor incorporation, when party systems were substantially restructured and a new popular interest regime was founded. Since those partial regimes have recently undergone significant change, now is an appropriate time to adopt a macro perspective on both historical and cross-sectional comparisons.

Because we urge historical as well as cross-national comparisons, we take as a starting point the analysis in *Shaping the Political Arena* and implicitly have in mind the same comparison set of relatively advanced countries in Latin America: Argentina, Brazil, Chile, Colombia, Mexico, Peru, Uruguay, and Venezuela. This chapter first reviews the way the two partial regimes, the party system and popular interest regime, emerged as durable legacies from the critical juncture of labor incorporation. It then highlights major discontinuities in those legacies in the contemporary period and raises the question of whether a critical juncture analysis is again appropriate for understanding the contemporary period. The last section turns to the question of how new structures of popular representation are being reconfigured. Despite the rise of "post-material" interests and some findings that party systems do not express class cleavages, analysts should consider the way in which the material interests of the popular sector may be not less salient, but rather demobilized. Finally, the chapter begins a discussion for orienting research on popular representation around the analysis of the two partial regimes.

The Critical Juncture of Labor Incorporation

In setting up the basis for a historical comparison, we start with an analysis of the initial partial regimes of popular representation, founded in connection with the process of labor incorporation, when mass politics was first introduced in the region. In the framework of a critical juncture analysis, new institutions or structures for interest intermediation can be analyzed as the outcome of strategic decisions made in response to changing economic and social conditions, which, once founded, are enduring. For present purposes, the causal logic of the critical juncture of labor incorporation can be understood through the following sequence: socio-economic change generates a new political challenge, the resolution of which results in new (or reconfigured) partial regimes. This causal sequence took the following form.

By the first part of the 20th century, economic and social change brought an unprecedented political challenge: the inclusion of the formal working class.[1] The export boom at the end of the 19th century spurred new urban commercial and industrial activities, which transformed the social structure of many Latin American countries from a two-class model, based on lord and peasant in the rural economy, to a four-class model, based in the new urban economy as well as in the export sector. The four-class model included the landed oligarchy and peasants plus two new actors; the middle sectors—a rising, rival elite that would challenge the land-based oligarchy—and a growing proletarian class of wage earners in the new economic activities. These two new classes posed the challenge of their own political inclusion, though in quite different ways. The middle sectors challenged the political dominance of the traditional landed elite; the working class challenged the larger capitalist system through strikes, protest, and revolutionary ideology. The middle sectors were thus engaged in a bi-frontal struggle, against both the old oligarchy and, as capitalists and employers, the working class. Once middle-sector interests captured the presidency, they turned immediately to the "social question"—the response to radical, working-class protest.

This response was the foundational moment of "labor incorporation," in which the working class became a legitimate, legally recognized political actor. It constituted the initial episode in constructing an institutionalized arena of mass politics. The common component in this response was to legalize and regulate unions, creating a formal, legal system for channeling and resolving class conflict through a system of industrial labor relations. In this way, unions became the primary organizations of the urban working class, intermediating state/working-class relations, channeling labor-capital bargaining, and ending the cycles of protest and violent repression that preceded incorporation.

Within this common pattern, differences emerged as a result of distinct coalitional patterns and strategic interactions of elites and the working class—the interaction of strategies from above and below. From above, the strategic choice of the new political leaders was whether or not to mobilize the labor movement as a base of political support, and the decision was influenced by the nature of oligarchic opposition. From below, the choice was whether or not to respond to any such "overture," and the decision was influenced by the strength of the working class and the concessions it wrung in exchange for that support.

These dynamics may be seen most clearly in two polar types. Mexico and Venezuela exemplify the pattern of mobilizing labor support, and Chile and Brazil exemplify the strategy of controlling and demobilizing labor. Two types of class coalitions resulted: a cross-class "populist" coalition of the middle sectors and working class in the former pattern and, in the latter, a cross-sectoral, urban-rural "accommodationist" coalition of the middle sectors and traditional elite, against, in effect, the lower classes. Thus, when mass politics were born, in the first pattern the working class was part of a cross-class coalition, whereas in the second pattern no cross-class coalition with the working class was formed. The type of class-coalitional pattern, which would endure, gave rise to quite different structures of mass politics. In Mexico, for instance, mass politics began in the wake of the 1910–17 Revolution and in Chile with the 1920 election of Alessandri. In Mexico, the subsequent presidents constructed multi-class coalitions, whereas in Chile the subsequent President Carlos Ibáñez did not and left instead a legacy of class-based politics.

In terms of the present discussion, these coalitional strategies led to the founding of the two partial regimes of popular interest intermediation. With respect to the party system, the new class coalitions served as the basis for party formation and party system crystallization. Where political leaders mobilized labor support, as in Mexico, a political party vehicle was necessary to attract and channel worker and union support in the electoral arena. These leaders thus founded a cross-class "populist" party—that is, a union-affiliated or labor-based party (LBP). The transition of labor incorporation was the unique "opportunity," the historical moment, when populist LBPs were founded. The populist LBP became the largest party in the country, anchoring and stabilizing the party system and resulting in a one- or two-party system.[2] The long-ruling dominance of Mexico's PRI is the clearest example of this pattern. Alternatively, where a populist LBP was not founded, the union movement became affiliated to a 20th-century classist LBP—smaller Socialist or Communist parties—and the result was a fractionalized, multi-party system that exhibited increasing polarization and instability. Chile provides the clearest example of this second coalitional pattern; party fractionalization, polarization, and class-based politics culminating in the victory of Marxist parties under Allende, and then the military coup that deposed him.

With respect to the interest regime, labor incorporation established a common structure, albeit with some variations. This popular interest regime has been analyzed as the Union-Party Hub, or the UP-Hub, to highlight the key commonality: the central position of party-affiliated unions as the organizations of lower-class interest intermediation.[3] Unions became the privileged organizations for intermediating lower-class interests in both the interest regime and the party system. In the interest regime, unions were controlled by extensive state regulation enshrined in labor law. This law underlay a state corporatist system that shaped the structure and activities of unions through extensive constraints. At the same time the law also contained a number of "inducements," which bestowed benefits on legally recognized unions. Through legal standing, membership requirements, subsidies, and state access, unions were privileged not only vis-à-vis dissident unions but also vis-à-vis other types of lower-class organizations. This overall outcome characterizes cases in both patterns (those more similar to Mexico—such as Argentina, Peru, and Venezuela—and those more similar to Chile, namely Brazil) even though the latter put greater reliance on constraints in the legal regulation of unions. In both patterns, too, unions were active participants in the party system, as they were affiliated to political parties and delivered electoral support to them, whether they were linked to multi-class LBPs as in Mexico or to more classist parties, as in Chile. Because of these union-party linkages, the two partial regimes of popular interest intermediation were thus significantly integrated or interpenetrated.

From the point of view of popular representation, these structures exhibited two serious flaws. First, unions were controlled by a corporatist labor law, and, in addition, either both types of LBPs, populist and classist, had representational drawbacks. Where unions were affiliated to a populist party, as in Mexico, they were a core constituency of the largest party, which brought unions into the governing coalition, provided the party was not banned by the military, precisely because of its links to unions.[4] However, the working class was a *junior* member of the coalition, and party affiliation served to control workers as well as to represent them. Where instead unions were affiliated to classist parties (or banned populist parties), they were consigned to the opposition coalition for most of the post-WWII period. Yet, as in Chile, these classist LBPs grew in electoral strength over the post-WWII period, as did, accordingly, the political influence and access of the union movement. However, this growing influence was perceived as a threat by elite interests, and politics became increasingly polarized and unstable. The result, ultimately, was a strong backlash and military coup. Thus, in all cases, albeit in different ways, this first historic structuring of mass politics proved to be problematic from the perspective of popular representation.

A second representational flaw was the exclusivity of the UP-Hub. Given the pre-WWII timing of these origins, the UP-Hub as a popular interest regime centered on the formal working class but substantially marginalized the informal working class, whose subsequent growth came to outpace that of formal workers. Other organizations, such as neighborhood associations, existed, but these played a peripheral role compared to unions, which had the advantages of a membership base, organizational and material resources, and access to the state primarily, but not exclusively, through political parties. Thus the scope or "density" of especially the privileged part of the interest regime was restricted under the UP-Hub.

These structures of popular representation, emanating from the politics of labor incorporation, endured through the period of Import-Substitution Industrialization (ISI). This growth model had a demand-side logic to support a domestic market for national production based on increased mass purchasing power. Because workers' wages could be seen not only as a labor cost but also as a source of demand, the model could underwrite a degree of "class compromise"—or at least a cross-class populist coalition. Employment in the state bureaucracy and parastatals likewise expanded aggregate purchasing power. Unionization, if it had any effect on wages and employment levels, had the same demand-side advantage. Thus, ISI was compatible with a kind of "organized capitalism," based on a unionized formal sector. The ISI model supported the reproduction of the UP-Hub as an interest regime that privileged unions as popular organizations and LBPs as potentially viable governing parties.

The period of labor incorporation has thus been analyzed as a critical juncture, a founding moment that signaled a new period of mass politics and established a particular set of enduring political structures. During this period, unions were legalized, and the pattern of their partisan affiliation to either populist or classist LBPs was established. Three components of an enduring legacy were set in this founding moment. First, patterns of class coalitions were constructed in which, most importantly for present discussion, the formal and especially unionized working class either was bound up in a multi-class coalition or remained independent of such coalitions. Second, distinct types of party systems were established: either one- or two- party sytems with unions comprising the core constituency of the largest (populist) party, or fractionalized and polarizing multi-party systems with unions affiliated to classist parties. Third, the first popular or lower-class interest regime was established, the UP-Hub, in which these party-affiliated unions, having official state recognition and greater access, became the privileged lower-class interest organizations, although they were regulated and controlled by the state through labor laws, in a pattern characterized as state corporatism.

The End of the Legacy: A New Critical Juncture?

Although these party systems and interest regimes were enduring legacies of the critical juncture of labor incorporation, the contemporary period has seen substantial discontinuities in both partial regimes. These discontinuities signal the end of this legacy. The critical juncture was analyzed as the response to economic and social structural change and to the political challenge of the new interests and demands thus produced. The end of the legacy and change in the partial regimes in the contemporary period can be analyzed in terms of a parallel causal sequence. Economic and social structural change has produced a new political challenge: a new set of demands, again for policy reform and for the inclusion of new groups. Is it then appropriate to analyze the contemporary transformation in partial regimes as a new critical juncture? While we can observe discontinuity and may also be able to discern the beginnings of divergent trajectories of change, temporal and cross-national variation itself does not justify the use of a critical juncture analysis. We review the economic and social transformations leading to change in the partial regimes. Yet we suggest that, until we can distinguish an outcome, a stable legacy, it may yet be premature to apply the analytics of a critical juncture framework to the contemporary period.

Socioeconomic Change

Since labor incorporation, social and economic change has been profound. It has consisted of both incremental change and more sudden shocks. Incrementally, Latin American economies changed from being primarily agricultural and pre-industrial to substantially industrial and urban. In the process, social structure has also been gradually transformed. If the earlier critical juncture reflected a change from a two-class to a four-class structure, when landlords and peasants were joined by workers and diverse "middle sectors" who constituted a new industrial and commercial elite strata, a more complex structure now adds a middle class and the informal sector, at the same time that all classes are quite highly differentiated, in part because of their different relations to the market (Portes and Hoffman 2003).

If it once made sense to speak of "the middle sectors," it now no longer does. While there is still a sector of relatively small, weak commercial and industrial interests, there is also a stronger and varied modern capitalist class in the industrial, financial, and agri-business sectors. Economic openness, capital mobility, and asset concentration has increased the structural power of segments of the capitalist classes vis-à-vis the working classes. Meanwhile, the landed elite has either integrated into this capitalist class or shrunk considerably. A larger and differentiated middle class composed of white collar workers, managers, and professionals has also emerged from "the middle sectors" and now occupies a space between the capitalist class and working class. There is now also a more differentiated set of working classes: formal workers, like employers, are more differentiated in terms of openness to the international economy, and informal workers have increased in size and importance. Hence, incremental social change that has accumulated since party systems were crystallized has increased both the middle class and an informal sector of lower-class workers.

More abrupt was a change away from the economic model based on ISI. This change was a response partly to internal economic factors and partly to changes in the international economy starting in the 1970s—with the end of the Bretton Woods exchange rate regime and the onset of new patterns of trade openness, global production, and increasing flows of international finance capital. The impact of these changes culminated with the debt crisis of the 1980s and its aftermath. Latin American governments responded by shifting from state-led ISI to a new model of greater market coordination. The new model has a quite different logic. Most importantly, in terms of political implications, it put unions on the defensive in a way that constituted a challenge to both LBPs and the UP-Hub. Wages became primarily a cost rather than also a source of aggregate demand. The model thus produced incentives for flexibilizing the labor market and for reversing the privileged position, political access, and gains of unions. The logic of the ISI model, which provided the economic basis for a "class compromise," has largely been superseded, although countries have varied in their response to these incentives, according to political factors.

Party System Change

Accommodating these social and economic changes put enormous strain on the "traditional" parties of the post-incorporation period.[5] Unions have lost much of their salience and privileged position as the core constituencies of LBPs, both populist and classist, or at least the types of concessions and the linkages parties have vis-à-vis unions have changed. These parties vary in the extent to which they have successfully appealed to the growing middle classes and informal workers as electoral constituencies. The decline of traditional parties as a group can be seen in their vote share in elections to the lower house in the national legislature. For the comparison set of countries in *Shaping the Political Arena*, a dramatic decline of the traditional parties occurred in the six cases without fractionalized party systems (see Figure 36.1). Early in the 1980s the vote share of the two top parties (or the single party in Mexico) was between 70 and 90 percent; by the late 1990s this share had declined dramatically, typically below a majority.[6] In the fractionalized, multi-party systems of Brazil and Chile, the top two parties never achieved a large combined vote share and did not witness similar decline.

With the decline of the traditional parties the region has witnessed a rise of the partisan left and an increasing personalization in the party system. By the late 2000s, Argentina, Uruguay, Peru, and Venezuela all had presidents representing various shades of the left, while in Mexico a leftist presidential candidate mounted a serious challenge (see Weyland, Madrid, and Hunter 2010; Levitsky and Roberts forthcoming). The ascendency of the left is remarkable in light of the prior period when the election of leftist presidents provoked military interventions. Personalistic parties have also tended to move into the void created by the decline of traditional parties, as both ex-presidents and political newcomers have become presidential candidates independent of party organizations and reliant on their own brand (Corrales 2008).

Interest Regime Change

The popular interest regime has also shown a sharp discontinuity; specifically, the popular interest regime has shifted from the UP-Hub to the Associational Network, or A-Net. The change in economic model signaled a political reversal for unions as organizations of popular representation, and they no longer occupy the central, privileged position that they used to. At the same time popular associations have proliferated and potentially provide informal workers with an unprecedented array of organizations to advance diverse popular interests. The popular interest regime is composed of what Evans (2010) has called a "concatenated diversity" of loosely and flatly linked organizational forms, with different capacities, interests and strategies.

The A-Net has a number of traits that set it apart from the UP-Hub. First, then, the

Non-Fractionalized Party Systems

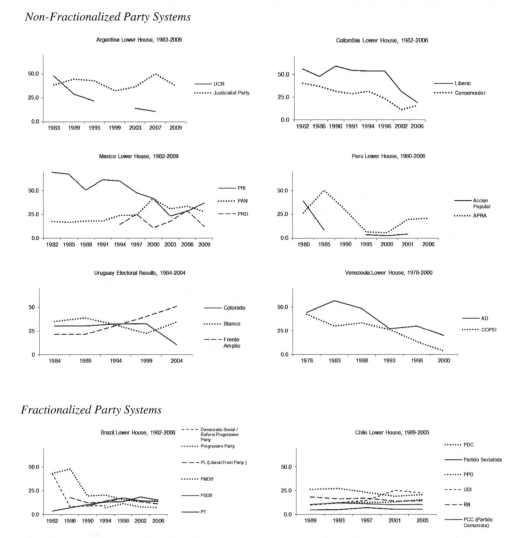

Fractionalized Party Systems

Figure 36.1 Traditional Party Decline. *Source:* Georgetown Electoral Systems for Argentina, Brazil, Colombia, Mexico, and Peru; Luna (2010) citing www.elecciones.gov.cl for Chile; Luna (2007) citing Buquet 2005 for Uruguay Roberts (forthcoming) citing *Consejo Nacional Electoral, Gobierno de Venezuela* for Venezuela.

nature of the "base organization" of the popular interest regime has changed, with a decline in the salience of unions and a rise in a multiplicity of associations organized around consumption-related issues (e.g., neighborhood, food distribution, health, education, housing), as well as associations of peasants and of rural workers. Table 36.1 shows the relative decline in union density. Second, parties are less central and have grown more distant to popular organizations, both to associations, many of which have no partisan links, and often to unions as party strategies and policy orientations have shifted. Third, the A-Net has the horizontal structure of a network rather than the more vertical, hierarchical structure of the UP-Hub, given that union structure tends to culminate in a national, peak-association.

Table 36.1 Union Density Before and After Neoliberal Reform (percent of total labor force unionized)

	Pre Reform (1980)*	Post Reform (1995)	Percentage Point Difference	Percentage Difference
Argentina	44.7	22.3	-22.4	-50.1
Brazil	13.6	23.8	+10.2	+75.0
Chile	35.0	12.7	-22.3	-63.7
Colombia	9.2	5.9	-3.3	-35.9
Mexico	24.1	22.4	-1.7	-7.1
Peru	23.0	5.7	-17.3	-75.2
Uruguay	20.9	12.0	-8.9	-42.6
Venezuela	25.2	13.5	-11.7	-46.4

* Because reform in Chile occurred during the military period before 1980, the pre-reform date is 1973, the year of the military coup. .
Source: Roberts (forthcoming)

This difference in the structure of the A-Net reflects both (1) the decline in union central-ity (the move away from a "hub" in the interest regime in the aggregate) and (2) the fact that the greater variety of active popular organizations scale and coordinate much less than unions and generally have the fluid interactions of a network.

Interpreting the Changes

With the change in party system and interest regime, some analysts have seen the contem-porary period in terms of a new critical juncture. Two approaches to identifying a new critical juncture have explicitly or implicitly received attention. These correspond to the two contemporary macro changes in Latin America—and, indeed, in the world. The first examines the challenge of moving to a new neoliberal economic model and argues that the varying experiences in responding to that challenge had an important impact on the party system and unions. The second emphasizes the effects of the third wave of democratization. It focuses on the challenge of incorporating the burgeoning informal sector at a world his-toric moment of social movement mobilization and civil society activation and under more politically open, democratic institutions. For example, Roberts (2002) and Reygadas and Filgueira (2010) suggest, respectively, that the contemporary period is marked by a "neolib-eral critical juncture" or a "second incorporation crisis." Given these fundamental disconti-nuities, can one say that a new critical juncture has taken place in Latin American politics?

A critical juncture is not an empirical phenomenon—or even a discontinuity—that "objectively exists" in the world. Rather, a critical juncture is an analytic assertion which involves two components. The first, perhaps more obviously, is that the analyst must assert that some important, common transformation has taken place and must identify the varia-tion in the ways that countries experience it. Analytically, this cross-national variation in the character of their transformation amounts to different "scores" on an independent vari-able. Second, the analyst must assert that a consequence of this transformation, and corre-sponding to these scores, is a set of identifiable political structures and organizations that are sticky or that produce a causal sequence or path of change. That is, an analyst must identify systematic variation in a durable outcome in order to posit a critical juncture argument.

On this basis, we argue that it may be premature to employ the analytics of a critical juncture. To be sure, Roberts (2002, forthcoming) has noted a pattern of profound party system change in countries with LBPs; and Collier and Handlin (2009) have noted a change away from the UP-Hub to the A-Net, as well as some cross-national variations in types of A-Nets. Thus, some new trajectories and diversity of outcomes can be detected. However, these analyses are just the initial stages of identifying new patterns in either partial regime. In order to make a critical juncture argument, it is not sufficient to establish a discontinuity, or to argue for the end of a legacy or even a "new beginning." A critical juncture argument is an assertion about a "founding moment," in which the analyst must identify what is founded. In terms of the partial regimes of present interest, the challenge is to assert that clearly defined, stable structures have been founded, or that patterns of change have flowed from variation in responses to a common "critical juncture" challenge—and further, to supply the logic or mechanisms that link these patterns to the variation in response to the challenge.

The Ongoing Problem of Popular Representation: Toward a Research Agenda

In approaching such a research program, two questions arise. First, in the 21st century, does it "makes sense" to study "popular" representation? This question arises in light of analyses suggesting that class may no longer structure the party system or electoral politics. Second, among the many traits for comparison, how might one conceptualize more aggregate dimensions for comparison at a macro-level? This is a difficult question, and we can only suggest some preliminary dimensions of analysis.

The (De)mobilization of Material Interests

During the 20th century, social class was the dominant cleavage in party politics and structures of interest representation. At the end of the 20th century, however, some analysts challenged the salience of class cleavages in electoral and interest politics. For example, in the contemporary period, some scholars of Western European politics have suggested that post-materialist issues are more salient than material interests, as more prosperous and equal social groups mobilize along rights, cultural, identity, and cross-cutting policy issues (e.g., environmentalism, human rights, democracy, indigenous rights, among others) (Inglehart and Rabier 1986). Despite a parallel literature on economic adjustment to globalization and the issue of retrenchment of social protection, many scholars have argued that "class analysis has grown increasingly inadequate" (Clark and Lipset 1991: 397). In Latin America, Torcal and Mainwaring (2003) similarly suggest that in Chile regime cleavages, which aligned voters into pro- and anti-authoritarian blocs, are more salient than class cleavages, and similar arguments have been made about the regime cleavage that brought the right and left together against the PRI in Mexico. In light of these developments, does it still make sense to analyze "popular" representation, conceived largely in terms of "class" categories or social categories along a materialist dimension?

We suggest that it does; the contemporary period is a profoundly materialist moment in Latin America. With respect to Latin America's two macro transitions to democracy and markets, mobilization for democracy has all but ended, and the regime-based cleavage has receded. In contrast, issues of poverty and marketization—the restructuring of capital both internationally and nationally, the political salience of economic reform, and the economic role of the state—is an ongoing, long-term and unfolding materialist issue. The recent rise of the left, substantially as a reaction to neoliberal reforms and the incidence of their negative impacts, indicates that materialist issues have not been superseded. To be sure, Latin American identity-based movements have emerged, particularly movements organized around indigenous and gender rights. However, rather than signaling a shift towards post-material interests, mobilization based on these identities is typically also in part a strategy for advancing material interests. For example, in Bolivia and Ecuador, indigenous mobilization is a means for advancing the interests of the lower-class rural sector and a means for demanding the state's provision of goods and services as much as an expression of cultural identity. The mix of indigenous and materialist strains is also clearly seen in Mexico's Zapatista movement, which dramatically burst into public view on the day that NAFTA went into effect.

Evidence from the *Latinobarómetro* surveys supports the claim that material interests remain salient. When asked "what is the most important problem facing your country?" respondents overwhelmingly identified materialist issues. In the years between 1995 and 2007, "employment" alone was most frequently identified as the most important problem (except in Colombia, where in most years during that period it was surpassed by terrorism). These data are all the more remarkable given that the responses were to an open ended question. Although the indicator shows some volatility and some decline by the mid-2000s, the evidence suggests that public opinion in Latin America places a very high priority on materialist issues (see Table 36.2).

Although material interests remain salient, they may not structure the party system or electoral politics. Rather, the material interests of the popular sector may be strategically demobilized, or they may remain unmobilized by problems of collective action. More systematic comparative analysis remains to be done to explain variation in the priming of materialist or non-materialist cleavages and the incapacity of the lower classes to articulate their interests through the party system and to activate them in the interest regime.

On the one hand, then, material interests of the popular classes may be demobilized actively from above, as part of a political strategy. As Gibson (1996) noted, the core constituency and ideology of parties on the political right provide incentives to prime *non-class* cleavages and to emphasize valence issues in their appeal to voters. For left parties, whether they are in government or opposition is also important. It has been widely noted that the policy constraints on parties, even LBPs, that govern in "neoliberal times" and especially in times of austerity may discourage class mobilization. Quite different may be the incentives of opposition parties and the conditions under which they either radicalize or moderate

Table 36.2 Salience of Material Interests, 1995–2007 (percent of years problem identified as most important in open-ended response)

	Argentina	Brazil	Chile	Colombia	Mexico	Peru	Venezuela
Employment*	91.7	75.0	66.7	27.3	66.7	100.0	41.7
Low Salaries			8.3				
Inflation					8.3		8.3
Education			8.3				33.3
Health		16.7					
Corruption	8.3	8.3			8.3		
Crime			16.7		16.7		16.7
Terrorism				72.7			
Total Number of Year Observations	12	12	12	11	12	12	12

*Includes unemployment and employment instability
Source: Latinobarómetro (1995–1998, 2000–2007)

their appeals in vote-maximizing strategies. Understanding the incentives that political entrepreneurs face regarding the mobilization of lower-class interests, the formation of cross-class alliances, and the framing of policy debates in terms of class appeals in the contemporary period thus remains an important item on the research agenda.

On the other hand, the demobilization of material interests of the popular classes may result from problems of collective action from below. Constructing common interests and identities across fragmented groups, and scaling or networking atomized, local associations are both serious challenges to coordinating collective action. The new economic model, the attendant relative decline of unions, and the often accelerated process of informalization has exacerbated a number of working-class divides—such as wage employees and own-account workers, formal/insider and informal/outsider workers, public and private-sector workers, those in tradables and those in nontradables. Further, as the base unit of organization in the interest regime has shifted from unions to associations, the collective action problem of scaling up across organizations has increased, since associations are diverse, are often territorially based, and lack organic linkages to parties, which could serve as brokers. Future research should consider class (de)mobilization as a process both from above and from below.

Macro Comparative Analysis

This section begins to lay out an agenda for macro-level research on structures of popular interest representation based on the two partial regimes of state-society intermediation, the interest regime and the party system, which may serve as the building blocks of analysis. The analytic challenge is to conceptualize interesting dimensions of popular representation rooted in a cross-national comparison of these partial regimes and their inter-relationship. The additional task is to derive propositions that explain variation in country "scores" and/ or explore outcomes such as the policy process. We cannot here definitively identify the dimensions for such an analysis but begin by identifying, as points of departure, some of the less aggregated themes in the existing literature.

Both individual parties and party systems are central to any macro level study of popular representation, and extant studies focus on a number of traits. The task is to aggregate them conceptually into a macro party-system dimension of variation. The types of linkages parties establish with voters have become a major topic of analysis, and many studies have paid particular attention to those that are clientelistic, programmatic, or personality based (Stokes 2005; Roberts 1995; Kitschelt et al. 2010). Organizational linkages, however, should not be ignored. A variety of types of linkages, exchanges, and perhaps dependencies exist between different types of parties and types of organizations. These linkages may be important for parties despite the trend toward more "capital-intensive" campaigning and catch-all, media-based vote-getting strategies, based on more individual, instrumental, and contingent linkages with citizens (Boas 2010).

At the level of the party system, several traits are relevant for studying popular representation. Linkage types may be variously distributed across parties, and the nature of intermediation and representation of party systems as a whole may vary accordingly. While electoral volatility has received substantial attention, the European literature reminds us that one should analyze volatility both within and across party blocs of the right, left, and center (Bartolini and Mair 1990). This question raises yet another: the degree to which the party system is a vehicle for expressing or subordinating class interests and to which lower-class interests are expressed by a governing coalition. In examining the distribution of class support among the parties and the degree to which party systems as a whole are class-based, analyses traditionally look at the distribution of lower-class support. It would also be interesting to look at the distribution of upper-class voting as an alternate indicator. The analytical task, however, is to conceptualize the ways key dimensions of representation may combine to produce overall types of party systems.

Studies of the interest regime remain incipient and disaggregated, often restricted to a limited number of associations, often in a few neighborhoods, and rarely reaching the macro level of "regime." Broader gauged comparisons, at the municipal, national, and cross-national levels, are necessary for building a macro analysis. With the shift to the A-Net, a large variety of urban and rural associations are now prominent in the popular interest regime, and the empirical task of aggregation may be daunting. Further, to some degree unionism is also more diverse with the formation of dissident labor confederations more oriented toward social movement unionism and with ties to community-based association.

Again, analysis should not only proceed at the associational level but also conceptualize ways to aggregate up to the broader interest regime. Scholars have distinguished types of associations, the most common being between professionalized NGOs and more community-based, participatory associations; however more conceptual and empirical work could lay a better basis for developing typologies, perhaps on dimensions such as participation and the nature of relations to the base or "target" population, material resources, human capital, expertise, and strategies of action. Studies should also explore the collective action problems faced by different types of associations, both to attract and sustain grass-roots participation and to coordinate across associations. Collier and Handlin (2009) have suggested that these collective action problems may be related to two sets of factors: (1) traits of associations and the nature of the demands they make and (2) state policy towards both associations and the substantive areas associations engage. However, much empirical work is needed to pursue these issues. It is important to analyze the distinct problems of collective action faced by different societal interests, because these challenges affect their effectiveness and influence within the larger interest regime. Relations and coordination among organizations across both similar and diverse issues and types are also key, as are demand-making activities, including patterns of participation in state-sponsored policy councils.

The interpenetration of the two partial regimes primarily focuses on party-association linkages. Party ties to popular associations will not replicate the more organic—or cooptive—relations parties traditionally had with unions, given the fluid organization of the A-Net, but it is nevertheless essential to understand the variety of party-association linkages that have emerged among different types of parties and different types of associations. The panoply of ties is the result of interacting incentives on both sides. On the organizational side, questions include: Under what conditions do organizations make demands for discretionary, distributive goods, and under what conditions do they demand rule-based, programmatic benefits? When do organizations pursue these demands through parties, and when do they opt for extra-partisan strategies?

The goal is to aggregate these themes to derive conceptual dimensions that reveal interesting variation in the intermediation and hence representation of popular interests at the macro level. Collier and Handlin (2009) have suggested some dimensions for analysis and some emergent cross-national differences, though others may prove fruitful. The dimension of *autonomy* from the state, well analyzed for unions in the UP-Hub, is as important for the A-Net, though it is more complex given the decentralized and more heterogeneous nature of the A-Net. Another dimension is the level and nature of *coordination* across the two partial regimes, as well as the scaling of more diverse associations through a network, rather than a confederated structure of more similar organizations, as in the UP-Hub. *Access* to the state and to policy making remains important, and in the current period it has come to include access through participatory state institutions. The relations popular organizations have to political parties—and to political leaders—are relevant to all these dimensions, as these ties can either compromise autonomy from the state or bolster demand making, provide access to the state and policy-making venues or divert attention from programmatic aims through clientelistic distributions, and function to broker cross-organizational coordination and scaling or act to compartmentalize types of associations.

Assessing these macro dimensions requires an approach to aggregation that must occur across the wide variety of popular interest organizations, popular constituencies, and interests, as well as across parties. An equally tricky task is to assess the relative weight of diverse popular-sector interests compared with opposing interests. Our concern with structures of interest intermediation focuses on their role in popular representation, but representation may be a relative or relational concept. Perhaps the best approach to this thorny issue may be policy-making studies. A focus on the policy process is one approach for assessing the comparative "weights" and interactions of opposing interests and understanding the mechanisms of representation at different sites and stages of policy formation and implementation.

★★★★★

Since the wave of democratization in Latin America in the 1980s, much of the political science literature has focused attention on many topics pertinent to popular representation. Relevant studies have examined properties of the electoral system, the nature of political parties, the incentives of politicians qua representatives as they also pursue careers, "new" social movements and popular organizing, the politics of economic reform, new social policies, participatory institutions, and the new left. This research, which has been accumulating for about three decades, has generated rich, descriptive analysis and insights that have contributed to theory building. It is now time to push the agenda of popular representation forward by aggregating these topics and adopting a more macro perspective and one that is comparative, both historically and cross-nationally. The party system and interest regime are central structures of interest intermediation and are key foci for advancing this agenda. Aggregation at this level is conceptually and empirically difficult; but it a fascinating challenge.

Notes

1 The following is based on the analysis of Collier and Collier (1991).
2 Sometimes a two-party system also resulted as a holdover, where the union movement became electorally mobilized by the traditional 19th-century liberal party that confronted the traditional conservative party, as in Colombia and Uruguay.
3 In this chapter, the discussion of the popular interest regime is based on the analysis of Collier and Handlin (2009).
4 In Argentina and Peru the military banned populist parties, prohibiting them from occupying the presidency.
5 It may be noted that though the military regimes of the c.1970s often sought to transform the party system, they generally failed in this mission. In most cases, the post-military party systems looked remarkably like those preceding military rule. The identity of the parties changed most in Brazil, though a fractionalized multi-party system remained, despite original military intentions.
6 In Uruguay, only one of the two traditional parties experienced a steep decline. In Argentina, only the historically smaller UCR declined, while the PJ has remained strong.

Bibliography

Bartolini, Stefano, and Peter Mair (1990) *Identity, Competition and Electoral Availability: The Stabilisation of European Electoraates, 1885–1985*. Cambridge, UK: Cambridge University Press.

Boas, Taylor (2010) "Varieties of Electioneering: Success Contagion and Presidential Campaigns in Latin America." *World Politics* 62: 636–675

Clark, Terry Nichol, and Seymour Martin Lipset (1991) "Are Social Classes Dying?" *International Sociology* 6 (4): 397–410.

Collier, Ruth Berins, and David Collier (1991) *Shaping the Political Arena: Critical Junctures, the Labor Movement, and Regime Dynamics in Latin America*. Princeton, NJ: Princeton University Press.

Collier, Ruth Berins, and Samuel Handlin (2009) *Reorganizing Popular Politics: Participation and the New Interest Regime in Latin America*. University Park: Pennsylvania State University Press, Chs. 1–3, 9.

Corrales, Javier (2008) "Latin America's Neocaudillismo: Ex-presidents and Newcomers Running for Office in Latin America." *Latin American Politics and Society* 50:3 (Fall):1–35.

Evans, Peter (2010) "Is it Labor's Turn to Globalize? Twenty-first Century Opportunities and Strategic Responses. *Global Labour Journal* 1:3, http://digitalcommons.mcmaster.ca/globallabour

Gibson, Edward (1996) *Class and Conservative Parties: Argentina in Comparative Perspective*. Baltimore: Johns Hopkins University Press.

Inglehart, Ronald, and Jacques-René Rabier (1986) "Political Realignment in Advanced Industrial Society: From Class-Based Politics to Quality-of-Life Politics." *Government and Opposition* 21:4 (October): 456–479.

Kitschelt, Herbert, Kirk A. Hawkins, Juan Pablo Luna, Guillermo Rosas, and Elizabeth J. Zechmeister (2010) *Latin American Party Systems*. Cambridge, UK: Cambridge University Press.

Levitsky, Steven, and Kenneth Roberts (forthcoming) *Latin America's Left Turn*. Baltimore: Johns Hopkins University Press.

Luna, Juan Pablo (2007) "Frente Amplio and the Crafting of a Social Democratic Alternative in Uruguay." *Latin American Politics & Society* 49:4 (Winter): 1–30

———. (2010) "Segmented Party–Voter Linkages in Latin America: The Case of the UDI." *Journal of Latin American Studies* 42, 325–356.

Portes, Alejandro, and Kelly Hoffman (2003) "Latin American Class Structures: Their Composition and Change during the Neoliberal Era." *Latin American Research Review* 38:1: 41–82.

Reygadas, Luis, and Fernando Filgueira (2010) "Inequality and the Incorporation Crisis: the Left's Social Policy Toolkit." In Maxwell A. Cameron and Eric Hershberg, eds. *Latin America's Left Turns: Politics, Policies, and Trajectories of Change*. Boulder, CO: Lynne Rienner.

Roberts, Kenneth M. (1995) "Neoliberalism and the Transformation of Populism in Latin America: The Peruvian Case." *World Politics* 48:1 (October): 82–116.

———. (2002) "Social Inequalities Without Class Cleavages in Latin America's Neoliberal Era." *Studies in Comparative International Development* 36:4 (Winter): 3–33.

———. (forthcoming) *Changing Course: Party Systems in Latin America's Neoliberal Era*. Cambridge, UK: Cambridge University Press.

Schmitter, Philippe C. (1979) "Modes of Interest Intermediation and Models of Societal Change in Western Europe. In Philippe C. Schmitter and Gerhard Lehmbruch, eds., *Trends toward Corporatist Intermediation*. Beverly Hills: Sage.

———. (1992) "The Consolidation of Democracy and Representation of Social Groups." *American Behavioral Scientist* 35: 422.

Stokes, Susan (2005) "Perverse Accountability: A Formal Model of Machine Politics with Evidence from Argentina." *American Political Science Review* 99: 315–325.

Torcal, Mariano, and Scott Mainwaring (2003) "The Political Recrafting of Social Bases of Party Competition: Chile, 1973–95." *British Journal of Political Science* 33: 55–84.

Weyland, Kurt, Raul Madrid, and Wendy Hunter (2010) *Leftist Governments in Latin America: Successes and Shortcomings.* Cambridge, UK: Cambridge University Press.

INDEX

Page numbers in italics refer to figures or tables.

A

Abortion, 325
Accountability, 101, 105
  courts, 67
  decentralization, 107–108
  defined, 102–103
  democracy, 104
  democratization, 107–108
  electoral system, 105–106
  forms, 101
  future reshaping, 106–109
  neoliberalism, 108–109
Afro-Latin Americans, 302–315
Agenda-setting powers, presidents, 28
Almond, Gabriel, 4, 469–470
Amnesty, 123
Analytic narratives, 496–504
  concept, 496–497
  democratization, 496–497
  historical institutionalization, compared, 497–498
  institutional change, 496–497
  research strategy, 504–505
  Sáenz Peña, 500–504
Andean Community, 355
Andersen, Martin Edwin, 297
Appiah, Kwame Anthony, 303
Armed forces, *see* Military
Asociación Latinoamericana de Sociología del Trabajo, 268
Authoritarianism
  labor, 263–264
  neopluralism, 255
Authoritarian rule
  Catholic Church, 252–253

  civil society, 251–254
  gender, 325–326
  mode of transition, 12–13
  party systems, 53
  rational choice approach, 425
  relationship between economics and political regimes, 516
  women, 325–326
  women's movements, 322–323
Authority
  courts, 63–64, *64*
  defined, 62
  judiciaries, 63–64, *64*
Autonomy
  bureaucracy, 490–491
  courts, 63–64, *64*
  defined, 62, 81
  judiciaries, 63–64, *64*
  military, 81

B

Barbero, Jesus Martin, 409
Bargaining, 136
Belém do Pará Treaty, 329–330
Bicameral systems, 25
Biodiversity, 184
  conservation, 191–192
Black nationalist perspective, 305
Bolsa Escola, Brazil, 214–216
Bolsa Familia, Brazil, 214–216
Brady Plan, 138, 370
Brundtland Commission, 182, 191
Brysk, Alyson, 288
Bureaucracy, 485–492
  autonomy, 490–491
  communication networks, 490
  cooptation, 490

Bureaucracy (*continued*)
importance, 486–487
legislatures, 486–487
new public management, 487–489
policy shaping, 491
reforms, 487–489
research strategy, 504–505
Business politics, 273–281
business groups, 276–277
campaign finance, 278–279
capital mobility, exit threats, 279
impact of families on, 279
interest groups, 485–486, 492–494, 492–496
large business groups, 276
lobbying, 278–279, 485–486, 492–494, 492–496
party finance, 278–279
regulation, 277
research, scarcity, 273
small firms, 277
state capture, 279–280
Business power, 278–280
institutionalized consultation in policy-making, 278
Business preferences, 275–277
Business structure, 274–275
business size, 274
family ownership and management, 274

C
Campaign finance, business politics, 278–279
Candidate selection, informal institutions, 90
Capital investments, import-substitution industrialization, 368, *368*
Capitalist development theories, 9–10
democracy, 9–10
Capital mobility, business politics, exit threats, 279
Cardoso, Fernando Henrique, 4, 433
Catholic Church, 321
authoritarian regimes, 252–253
civil society, 252–253
indigenous politics, 288
Causality, public opinion research, 474–475
Central American countries, economic relations, 355, *356*
China, neoliberalism, 149–150
Citizen participation, *see* Participation
Civic culture thesis, 7–9
survey data, 8
Civilian control
defense, 82–84
military, 80–82
needs, 81–82
security, 82–84
Civilian protesters, 84–85
military, 84–85

Civil-military relations
informal institutions, 95
military, 80–82
Civil society
authoritarian rule, 251–254
autonomous organizational activity, 253–254
Catholic Church, 252–253
definition, 252
liberation theology, 252–253
participation, 254–258
lack of engagement, 255
transitions to democracy, 251–254
Class-based analysis, 237–238
Clean Development Mechanism, climate change, 193
Clientelism, 273, 534
exchanges, 51–52
rational choice approach, 424–425, 426–427
representation, 103, 105–106
Climate change, 191, 192–193
Clean Development Mechanism, 193
Joint Implementation, 193
Closed list systems, 26
Cold War, 516
military rule, 115
Collier, David, 11, 263
Collier, Ruth Berins, 11, 263
Colonialism
constructing identities and politics after, 353
creating national states out of Colonial America, 351–355
trade, 364–365
Commodity-dependence curse, neoliberalism, 151
Communication networks, bureaucracy, 490
Community organizations
decentralization, 39–40
mayors, 39–40
Company opportunism, regulatory policy, 227–228
Comparative politics
classic works, 4
defined, xiii
explanatory theories, 5
variations at macro level, 5
Competition, intra-Latin American relations, 348
history, 351–355
Concurrent elections, 25
Conditional cash transfer programs, 206–207, 214–216
Brazil's Bolsa Familia, 214–216
criticisms, 206–207
Mexico's Progresa, 214–216
Confederation of Indigenous Nationalities of Ecuador, 287–288, 291, 294–295
Confidence building and security measures, intra-Latin American relations, 359–360

bilateral, 359–360
subregional, 360
Confounding, 447
Conservative parties, neoliberal reforms, 56
Constitutional engineering, institutional analysis,
402–404
Constitutional powers
president
legislative powers, 27
non-legislative powers, 27
separation of powers, 61
Contributory social insurance, 200, 210–211
Cooperation
defined, 350
intra-Latin American relations, 348–349
history, 351–355
promotion and defense of democracy,
357–359
sovereignty, relationship, 350
Cooptation, bureaucracy, 490
Core political issues, xxii
Corporatism, labor, 263
Corruption
democratic governance, 382–383
drugs, 382–383
illicit trade, 382–383
Cotler, Julio, 297–298
Courts, *see also* Specific type
accountability, 67
authority, 63–64, *64*
autonomy, 63–64, *64*
changes, 61
constitutional separation of powers, 61
crime, 68
cultural change, 65–66
democracy, 67–68
gender, 329–330
human rights, violations from prior regimes,
66
institutional variables, 65
insurance logic, 65–66
judicial activism, 65–66
not uniformly progressive, 68
political fragmentation, 64–65
political origins of judicial behavior, 66
rule of law, 69
state violence, 68
substantive rights, 67–68
traditionally marginalized communities and
unpopular issues, 68
transitional justice, 66–67
veto player logic, 65–66
women, 329–330
Cox, Gary, 497
Crime, 61, *see also* Drug trade
citizen concern about, *70, 71*
courts, 68

politics, 61
rule of law, 69–72, *70*
Criminal syndicates, 83
Critical juncture models, key features, 10–11
Cultural diversity, intra-Latin American relations,
353
Cultural identity, 414–415
Cultural studies
competing schools of thought in 1990s,
411–414
critical theories, 408–410
defined, 407
democratization, 413
Latin American studies, cultural turn,
407–408
neoliberalization, 413
new cycles of protest, 414–416
Culture
characterized, 408
hybrid cultures, 409

D

Debt crisis, 137
Decentralization
accountability, 107–108
changes due to, 38–42
community organizations, 39–40
consequences, 41–42
cross-national differences, 35
decentralized budgeting, 40
defined, 42
democratization, 36–37
depth of changes, 35
economic liberalization, 36
elections, 37
features, 33–35
federalism, 42–43
forms, 33–35
in-kind contributions, 41
intermediate-level governments, 43
liberalization, 36
mayors, 38–39
neoliberal reformers, 36
neopluralism, 257
new subnational governments, 41–42
pacification, 37–38
participatory budgeting model, 40
political parties, 39–40
subnational elections, 39
reasons for, 35–38
relationships among subnational governments,
44–45
representation, 107–108
sequencing decisions, 35
unitary systems, 43
which level of subnational government to
privilege, 35

Decentralized budgeting, 40
Defense
  civilian control, 82–84
  military, 82–84
  preparedness, 83
Defined benefit public pension system, 204
Deforestation, 189, 190
De-institutionalization, party systems, 54
Delegative democracy, neopluralism, 255–256
Democracy
  accountability, 104
  breakdown, 5
  capitalist development, 9–10
  class origin, 9–10
  consolidation, 5
  courts, 67–68
  dual transitions, 48–49
  durability, 3–15
  indigenous politics, 295–298
  Latin America
    capitalist development theories, 9–10
    civic culture thesis, 7–9
    critical juncture models, 10–11
    debates, 6–13
    economic modernization thesis, 6–7
    explanatory theories, 6–13
    political-institutional theories, 11–13
    regimes, 4–6
    research agenda, 4–6
    research frontiers, 13–14
    social class theories, 9–10
  origins, 3–15
  paradox, 48
    core representative institutions, 48
  presidentialism, 22–23
    electoral democracies, 22–23
  quality, 5, 14
  representation, 104
  third wave, xiii, xxi
  transition, 3, 5
    civil society, 251–254
    labor, 263–264
    mode, 12–13
Democratic governance
  corruption, 382–383
  drugs, 382–384
  illicit trade, 382–384
  informal institutions, 93–96
    benefits, 93–94
    limitations, 93
Democratic peace argument, intra-Latin
    American relations, 357–359
Democratic politics
  demand side research, 533–535
  economic politics, 536–537
  state of the field, 528–539
  supply side research, 535–536

Democratization, 515–520
  accountability, 107–108
  analytic narratives, 496–497
  consolidation of democratic regimes, 531–532
  cultural studies, 413
  decentralization, 36–37
  historical-structural approaches, 435–437
  intra-Latin American relations, 357–359
  New Left, 342–343
  nongovernmental organizations, 241–243
  political elites, 517
  privatization, 231–233
  rational choice approach, 422–423
  representation, 107–108
  social movements, 240–243
    failures, 242–243
    nongovernmental organizations form,
      241–242
    transition from military to civilian rule, 241
  U.S.-Latin American relations, 342
Dependency management, political economy,
    514–515
Dependency theory, 136
  participation, 251
  theorists, 4
Development, 181–196
  environment
    actors, 185–188, *186*
    interests, 185–188, *186*
    politics, 185–188, *186*
    power, 185–188, *186*
  natural resources, 188–191
    livelihood-based conceptualizations, 190–
      191
    market-friendly conceptualizations, 189–190
  relationship of conceptualizations to analytic
      approaches, *184*
Developmental state school, 138
Diamint, Rut, 80
Dictatorship, 544
Direct primaries, 24–25
Double-complement rule, 23–24
Drug trade
  cartels, 71, 83
  corruption, 382–383
  democratic governance, 382–384
  dimensions, 380–382
  neoliberalism, 387–388
  power asymmetries, 380–382
  scope, 380–382
  U.S.-Latin American relations, 344–345
  violence
    forms, 385
    gangs, 386–387
    geographic areas, 385–386
    insurgents, 385–386
    organized violence, 384–387

war on drugs, U.S.-Latin American relations, 338–339
Dulitzky, Ariel E., 307
Durand, Francisco, 493

E
Economic change, representation, 569–570
Economic Commission for Latin American and the Caribbean, United Nations, 365, 372
Economic crisis
  labor movements, 55
  leftist parties, 55
  party systems, 54–55
  peasant movements, 55
  populist parties, 55
Economic development, political regimes, 529–537
Economic integration, intra-Latin American relations, 360–362
Economic liberalization, decentralization, 36
Economic modernization thesis, 6–7
Economic policy
  gender, 326
Economic politics
  democratic politics, 536–537
  political regimes, 536–537
Economic relations
  Central American countries, 355, *356*
  intra-Latin American relations, 354–355
Education
  gender, 320–321
  increasing access, 161–162, *162*
  inequality decline, 161
  market reforms, 208–209
  women, 320–321
    Catholic Church, 321
Education Gap, 161–163, *162*
Elections, 14
  decentralization, 37
  indigenous politics, 288
  party systems
    stability, 51–52
    volatility, 51–52
Electoral competition, party systems, 54–55
Electoral politics, race, 311
Electoral rules
  informal institutions, 90
  rational choice approach, 425–426
Electoral systems, 26
  accountability, 105–106
Electoral trends, neoliberalism, 143–144
Emerging multinational corporations, 274, 275
Empirical testing, 14
Energy, intra-Latin American relations, 361
Environment, 181–196
  approaches, 181
  development

actors, 185–188, *186*
  interests, 185–188, *186*
  politics, 185–188, *186*
  power, 185–188, *186*
government agencies, politics, 187–188
historical-structural approaches to environmental rights, 437–439
institutional development, politics, 187–188
natural resources, 188–191
  livelihood-based conceptualizations, 190–191
  market-friendly conceptualizations, 189–190
relationship of conceptualizations to analytic approaches, *184*
safe water, 209
scale, 181
scope, 181
Equity, neoliberalism, 142–143
Ethnicity, 533
Ethno-nationalism, intra-Latin American relations, 356–357
Europe, Latin America, comparative context, 556–558
Evans, Peter, 276
Executive branch
  gender, 328–329
    election to presidency, 328–329
Executive-legislative relations, presidentialism, 27–29
  party system related factors, 28–29
Experiments
  characterized, 448
  types, *448*
External borrowing, *368,* 368–370
  debt composition, *368*
  liquidity problems, 368–369

F
Faletto, Enzo, 4, 433
Family planning, 209
Federalism
  decentralization, 42–43
  defined, 42
  history, 42
  moves toward, 42–45
Feminism, 322
  institutionalized *vs.* autonomous, 324
  regional level, 323
  transnational, 323
Field experiments, 447–460
  defined, 449
  Latin American politics, 457–459, *458*
  limitations, 459–460
  strengths, 459–460
Financial liberalization, trade, 370–377
Foreign direct investment, 370

Foreign investment, outward, 275
Forests, 189, 190
Formal institutions
    exogenous origin, 95
    informal institutions, relationships, 95–96
    rational choice approach, 423–426
    weakness, 95
Foucault, Michel, 410, 415
Franco, Jean, 409
Free Trade Agreement of the Americas, social
        movements, 244
Free trade agreements, social movements, 244
Free Trade Area of the Americas, 338, 344
    labor, 266
Freidenberg, Flavia, 50
Friedman, Milton, 136

G
Gangs, 71, 83, 386–387, *see also* Drug trade
García Canclini, Néstor, 409
Gays, 325
Geddes, Barbara, 528
Gender, 26, 319–331
    authoritarian rule, 325–326
    changes in status of women, 319
    courts, 329–330
    demographic trends, 320–321
    economic policy, 326
    education, 320–321
        Catholic Church, 321
    executive branch, 328–329
        election to presidency, 328–329
    gender-based movements, 321–324
    human rights, 325
    indigenous politics, 296
    leftist movements, 322
    legislative politics, 326–328
        behavior, 326–328
        gender quotas, 326–328
    multiculturalism, 296–297
    nongovernmental organizations, 323
    public policy, 324–326
    revolutionary movements, 322
    role of men, 330–331
    theories of modernization, 320
    United Nations, 323, 329–330
    violence, 325
    women presidents, 319
Gender quota legislation, 26–27
Generalized System of Preferences, labor, 266
Geopolitical dynamics, military rule, 117
Germani, Gino, 4
Global climate change, 191, 192–193
Globalization, 408
    labor, 264–266
    neoliberalism, 264–266
    political economy, 512–515

relationship between international and
        domestic economy, 513
    welfare state, 513
Global war on terror, U.S.-Latin American
        relations, 339
Governance by surprise, 141
Governmentality, 410
Gramsci, Antonio, 415

H
Hawkins, Kirk A., 52–53
Health care, 208, 211–214
Health insurance, reform, 204–205
Hegemony
    defined, 340
    U.S.-Latin American relations, 340–341
Hemispheric Social Alliance, labor, 266
Heritage Foundation Index of Economic
        Freedoms, neoliberalism, 144–147, *145,
        146, 147*
Hirschman, Albert, 514
Historical institutionalization, analytic narratives,
        compared, 497–498
Historical-structural approaches, 433–443
    contributions to substantive knowledge,
        434–439
    defining features, 433
    democratization, 435–437
    integrating agency and structure, 440–441
    mixed method research, 441–443
    social revolutions, 434–435
    social rights, 437–439
    temporal analysis modes, 439–440
    theory and method developments, 439–443
Homicides, *70,* 70–71
Human rights, 123–126
    gender, 325
    judiciaries, 66
    movement participation, 256
    trials of perpetrators, 124
    violations from prior regimes, 66
    women, 325
Hybrid cultures, 409
Hyperinflation, 138
Hyperpresidentialism, public opinion research,
        478

I
Identity, 414–415
Identity-based representation, 102
Identity politics, 533
Illicit trade, *see also* Specific type
    corruption, 382–383
    democratic governance, 382–384
    dimensions, 380–382
    neoliberalism, 387–388
    power asymmetries, 380–382

scope, 380–382
violence
  forms, 385
  gangs, 386–387
  geographic areas, 385–386
  insurgents, 385–386
  organized violence, 384–387
Impeachment, presidentialism, 23
Import-substitution industrialization
  capital investments, 368, *368*
  characterized, 365
  debt crisis of 1980s, 366
  history, 365
Inclusionary discrimination, 308
Income inequality, *see also* Inequality decline
  effects, 158
  international, 159, *160*
Independence
  constructing identities and politics, 353
  creating national states out of Colonial
    America, 351–355
Indigenismo, intra-Latin American relations,
  356–357
Indigenous politics, 285–299
  Catholic Church, 288
  class-based rural contention, 291
  democracy, 295–298
  elections, 288
  gender, 296
  history, 285–289
  Indian problem, 285–286
  indigenous people as obstacles to modernity,
    285–286
  internal colonialism, 286
  labor, 288
  languages, 286
  movements, 238
    success and failure, 289–292
  multiculturalism, 292–295
  neoliberalism, 292–295
  nongovernmental organizations, 290, 291, 292
  past research approaches, 285–287
  perversity thesis, 292–295
  Protestant Church, 288
  radicalized, 297
  return, 287–289
  rights, intra-Latin American relations, 356–357
  security concerns, 297
  social movements, 287
  transnational networks, 288
  United Nations, 289
  women, 296
  World Bank, 289
Individual retirement accounts, 205
Industrialization
  military rule, 115–117
  party systems, 51

Inequality decline, 158–174, *160*
  change, 158–159, *159*
  economic causes, 159–163
  education, 161
  effects, 158
  key economic indicators by political regime,
    178–180
  leftist regimes, 163–171, *164, 165, 166*
    government effectiveness, 169, *169*
    macroeconomic policies, 165–167, *166*
    permanent or transitory, 169–171, *170*
    social policy changes, *167,* 167–169, *168, 179*
    transparency, 169, *169*
  market-oriented reforms, 159–160
  middle class, 171–173
  political causes, 159–163
  social policies, 161
Inflation, 138
Informal institutions, 88–96
  accommodating, 91, *91*
  benefits, 89
  candidate selection, 90
  civil-military relations, 95
  competing, *91,* 91–92
  complementary, 90–91, *91*
  defined, 89
  democratic governability, 93–96
    benefits, 93–94
    limitations, 93
  dysfunctional effects, 89
  electoral rules, 90
  formal institutions, relationships, 95–96
  importance, 89–90
  judicial politics, 90
  Mexico, 88
  pervasiveness, 88–89
  presidentialism, 93–94
  reasons for, 92–93
  substitutive, *91,* 92
  typology, 90–91, *91*
  varieties, 90–92
Informal rules, pervasiveness, 88–89
In-kind contributions
  decentralization, 41
  mayors, 41
Institutional analysis, 395–404
  actors, 395–396, 399, 401
  building blocks, 395–399
  constitutional engineering, 402–404
  incentives, 397–398, 400, 402
  legislative politics, 399–401
  long-term consequences, 398–399, 400–401,
    402
  party discipline, 399–401
  powers, 396–397, 399–400, 401–402
  preferences, 395–396, 399, 401
  public spending, 401–402

Institutional change, analytic narratives, 496–497
Institutional checks and balances, 531
Institutionalism
  limitations, 88
  resurgence, 88
Institutionalization, party systems, 50–53, 53–54
Institutional reforms, neoliberalism, 142–143
  renewed investment in social programs, 143
Institutions
  rational choice approach, 423–426
  supply side research, 535–536
Institutions of governance, 142
Institution-structure trap, neoliberalism, 152
Instrumental-variables designs, 456–457
Insurance logic
  courts, 65–66
  judiciaries, 65–66
Integrated anti-poverty programs, 208
Inter-American collaboration, 344–345
  U.S.-Latin American relations, 344–345
Inter-American Cultural Studies Network,
  411–412
Inter-American Development Bank, regulatory
  policy, 226
Interest groups
  business interests, 485–486, 492–494, 492–496
  network analysis, 494
Interest regime, representation, 570–572, *572*
Internal colonialism, 286
International capital flows, *368,* 368–370
  debt composition, *368*
  liquidity problems, 368–369
International development institutions, 371–377
  cross-country variation, 374–375
  domestic politics, 375–376
  temporal variation, 373–374
  types, 372–373
International economic relations, 364–377
International Monetary Fund, 371–377
  cross-country variation, 374–375
  domestic politics, 375–376
  Independent Evaluation Office, 141–142
  regulatory policy, 226
  temporal variation, 373–374
  trade, 366
  types, 372–373
Intra-Latin American investments, 361–362
Intra-Latin American relations, 348–363
  competition, 348
    history, 351–355
  confidence building and security measures,
    359–360
    bilateral, 359–360
    subregional, 360
  constructing identities and politics, 353
  contemporary research, 356–362
  cooperation, 348–349

  history, 351–355
    promotion and defense of democracy,
      357–359
  creating national states out of Colonial
    America, 351–352
  cultural diversity, 353
  culture *vs.* ideology, 353
  democratic peace argument, 357–359
  economic integration, 360–362
  economic relations, 354–355
  energy, 361
  ethno-nationalism, 356–357
  indigenismo, 356–357
  indigenous rights, 356–357
  mestizaje, 356–357
  nation state, redefinition, 356–357
  political leaders in exile, 353
  research challenges, 356–362
  security institutions, 359–360
  security relations, 354
  sovereignty, 348
  transition from colony to sovereignty, 351–352
  unresolved interstate disputes, *352*

J
Joint Committee on Latin American Studies, 523
Joint Implementation, climate change, 193
Judicialization
  defined, 62
  regressive effect, 58–59
Judicial politics, 62–69
  informal institutions, 90
  political origins of powerful courts, 62–63
Judicial power, defined, 62
Judiciaries
  authority, 63–64, *64*
  autonomy, 63–64, *64*
  changes, 61
  constitutional separation of powers, 61
  cultural change, 65–66
  dualism, 61–62
  human rights, violations from prior regimes, 66
  institutional variables, 65
  insurance logic, 65–66
  judicial activism, 65–66
    courts, 65–66
    judiciaries, 65–66
  political fragmentation, 64–65
  political origins of judicial behavior, 66
  rule of law, 69
  veto player logic, 65–66

K
Kaufman, Herbert, 489
Keck, Margaret, 243, 266
Kitschelt, Herbert, 52–53, 109
Krueger, Anne, 136

L

Labor, 262–270
  authoritarianism, 263–264
  corporatism, 263
  directions for future research, 269–270
  Free Trade Area of the Americas, 266
  gaps, 269–270
  Generalized System of Preferences, 266
  globalization, 264–266
  Hemispheric Social Alliance, 266
  incorporation, 263
  indigenous politics, 288
  Latin American scholarship, 268–269
  leftist regimes, 266–267
  market reforms, 265
  neoliberalism, 264–266
  North American Free Trade Agreement, 266
  North American scholarship, 267–268
  political parties, party-labor relations, 265
  political science studies, 262–270
    history, 263–266
  populism, 263
  post-authoritarian era, 266–267
  post-neoliberal era, 266–267
  representation, critical juncture of labor
      incorporation, 566–568
  resurgence, 269
  social movements, 264
  trade agreements, 266
  trade policy, 266
  transitions to democracy, 263–264
Laboratory experiments, defined, 449
Labor movements
  decline, 55
  economic crisis, 55
  neoliberal reforms, 56
Landed interests, military rule, 117
Late justice, 124–125
Latin America
  changing position in world order, 346
  democracy
    capitalist development theories, 9–10
    civic culture thesis, 7–9
    critical juncture models, 10–11
    debates, 6–13
    economic modernization thesis, 6–7
    explanatory theories, 6–13
    political-institutional theories, 11–13
    regimes, 4–6
    research agenda, 4–6
    research frontiers, 13–14
    social class theories, 9–10
  Europe, comparative context, 556–558
  regimes
    capitalist development theories, 9–10
    civic culture thesis, 7–9
    critical juncture models, 10–11

debates, 6–13
    economic modernization thesis, 6–7
    explanatory theories, 6–13
    political-institutional theories, 11–13
    research agenda, 4–6
    research frontiers, 13–14
    social class theories, 9–10
  U.S.-Latin American relations, 345–346
Latin American Free Trade Association, 354–355
Latin American Integration Association, 354–355
Latin American studies, cultural turn, 407–408
Latin American Subaltern Studies Group, 411–
    412
Le Foulon, Carmen, 229
Leftist movements
  economic crisis, 55
  resurgence, 57
  women, 322
Leftist regimes
  inequality decline, 163–171, *164, 165, 166*
    government effectiveness, 169, *169*
    macroeconomic policies, 165–167, *166*
    permanent or transitory, 169–171, *170*
    social policy changes, *167,* 167–169, *168,*
      179
    transparency, 169, *169*
  labor, 266–267
  reforms, public utilities, 229–230
Legal issues, 61–73
Legalization
  defined, 62
  regressive effect, 58–59
Legislative decree power, presidents, 28
Legislative elections
  legislature, 25–27
    closed list systems, 26
    electoral systems, 26
    gender, 26
    mixed-member system, 26
    open list systems, 26
    party lists, 26
    preference voting, 26
    proportional representation, 26
    women legislators, 26
  presidentialism, 25–27
Legislative politics
  gender, 326–328
    behavior, 326–328
    gender quotas, 326–328
  institutional analysis, 399–401
  women, 326–328
    behavior, 326–328
    gender quotas, 326–328
Legislatures
  bureaucracy, 486–487
  legislative elections, 25–27
    closed list systems, 26

Legislatures (*continued*)
    electoral systems, 26
    gender, 26
    legislator re-election, 27
    mixed-member system, 26
    open list systems, 26
    party lists, 26
    preference voting, 26
    proportional representation, 26
    women legislators, 26
  political science, 486–487
  presidentialism, 519–520
  veto, 27–28
Lesbians, 325
Levitsky, Steven, 50
Liberalism, neoliberalism, distinguished, 134
Liberalization, decentralization, 36
Liberation theology, civil society, 252–253
Lijphart, Arend, 21
Linz, Juan J., 12, 22, 518–519
Lipset, Seymour, 4, 6
Livelihoods conceptualization of sustainable
    development, 183
Lobbying
  business interests, 485–486, 492–494, 492–496
  business politics, 278–279
  network analysis, 494
  research strategy, 504–505
Local institutions of participatory democracy, 104
Lucero, Jose Antonio, 414
Luna, Juan Pablo, 52–53
Lupu, Noam, 56

M
Mainwaring, Scott, 22
Majority runoff method, 23, 24
Managerial public administration, 487–488
Mandate representation, 102, 104
Mann Doctrine, 116
Marginality theory
  modernization theory, 250–251
  participation, 250
Market liberalism, party systems, 55–56
Market liberalization, 48–49
  party systems, 56
    leftist political alternatives, 56–57
    programmatic realignment, 58
Market-oriented reform, 276
Market reforms
  education, 208–209
  labor, 265
  social insurance, 209
Mattiace, Shannon, 414
Mayors
  community organizations, 39–40
  decentralization, 38–39
  in-kind contributions, 41

Means-ends rationality, rational choice approach,
    420, 421
Mestizaje, 285–286, 303–304
  intra-Latin American relations, 356–357
Metaconstitutional powers, 89–90
Methodological individualism, rational choice
    approach, 420
Methodological pluralism, xxii
Mexico
  informal institutions, 88
  Progresa, 214–216
Mexico City Conference on Women, 243
Microfinance, 205–206
Middle class
  changes, 171–172, *172*
  defined, 171
  inequality decline, 171–173
Middle-income trap, neoliberalism, 151
Military, 76–85, *see also* Civil-military relations
  adaptability, 85
  anti-crime and anti-narcotic missions, 94
  asymmetric power relations, 81–82
  authoritarian legacies, 79
  autonomy, 81
  centrality of military figures, 79
  civilian control, 80–82
    needs, 81–82
  civilian protesters, 84–85
  countervailing reactions, 79
  defense, 82–84
  democratic transition, 79
  guarding its own corporate well-being, 80
  history, 76, 77–78
  institutional arrangements, 79
  legacy effect, 79
  origins, 77–78
  overthrow other governments, 84
  path dependence, 79
  perks and privileges, 80–81
  as political agent, 76
  political culture of militarism, 79
  prerogatives, 81
  representation, 104
  research trends, 76–77
    institutionalists, 76–77
    rationalists, 76–77
  rule of law, 81–82
  security, 82–84
    need for, 83–84
  shirking of responsibilities, 84–85
Military abuses, 114–128
Military coups, regime change, 516–517
Military intervention
  causes, 77–79
  modernization theory, 77
  waves, 77
Military regimes, 114

Cold War, 115
  geopolitical dynamics, 117
  history, 114–118
  industrialization, 115–117
  landed interests, 117
  modes of transition, 123
  national and regional cultures, 117–118
  patterns of regression
    clandestine, 120
    degree of legalization, 120
    international, 121
    inter-service rivalry, 120
    public, 120
    security units, 120–121
  patterns of repression, 118–121, *119*
  political economy, 116–118
  political economy arguments of origins,
    115–118
  pre-emptive coups, 119
  resistance, 121–123
    Church-sponsored organizations, 121–122
    direct, armed resistance, 122
    forms, 121–122
    non-violent resistance, 122
    well-known victims, 122
  roll-back coups, 119
  state violence, 118–121, *119*
  violence, characteristics, 116
Millán, Jaime, 229
Mixed-member system, 26
Modernization theory, 6–7
  gender, 320
  literature, 4
  military intervention, 77
  participation, 250–251
  theory
    alternatives, 4
  theory of marginality, 250–251
Molyneux, Maxine, 321–322
Monopoly, state to private sector transfer, 224–
  225
Monsiváis, Carlos, 409
Morgan, Jana, 55
Multiculturalism
  gender, 296–297
  indigenous politics, 292–295
  women, 296–297
Multidimensionality, public opinion research, 474
Multinational corporations, 275
  efficiency-seeking, 276
  market-seeking, 276
  resource-seeking, 276

N

Nation state, intra-Latin American relations,
  redefinition, 356–357
Natural aristocracy, 102

Natural experiments, 447–460
  characterized, 449–450
  Latin American politics, 450–457, *451–453*
  limitations, 459–460
  standard natural experiments, 450–453
  strengths, 459–460
Natural resources
  development, 188–191
    livelihood-based conceptualizations, 190–
      191
    market-friendly conceptualizations, 189–190
  environment, 188–191
Neoliberal governmentality, 413
Neoliberalism
  accountability, 108–109
  ascendance, 136–142
  asset bubbles, 151–152
  characterized, 133–135
  China, 149–150
  commodity-dependence curse, 151
  criticisms, 135–136
  cultural studies, 413
  distrust of economic intervention, 133–134
  drugs, 387–388
  electoral trends, 143–144
  equity, 142–143
  faith in markets, 133–134
  globalization, 264–266
  Heritage Foundation Index of Economic
    Freedoms, 144–147, *145, 146, 147*
  heyday, late 1980s–early 2000s, 138–142
  history, 136–142
  illicit trade, 387–388
  imposition, 140
  indigenous politics, 292–295
  institutional reforms, 142–143
    renewed investment in social programs, 143
  institution-structure trap, 152
  labor, 264–266
  liberalism, distinguished, 134
  middle-income trap, 151
  moderation of leftist governments, 150–151,
    151
  polarizing, 141
  policy trends, 144–151, *145, 146, 147, 148–*
    149, 151
  political costs, 138
  price mechanisms, 135
  productivity gap, 152
  reforms, 139
    conservative parties, 56
    decentralization, 36
    labor parties, 56
    party systems, 55–56
    populist parties, 56
  representation, 108–109
  slowdown, 149–151

Neoliberalism (*continued*)
  social movements, 239–240
    atomization theorists, 239
    economic mechanisms of demobilization,
      239–240
    mobilization theorists, 239–240
  state *vs.* market failures, 134–135
  United States, 149–150
  victorious globalizers, 137
Neoliberal multiculturalism, 413
Neopluralism
  authoritarianism, 255
  decentralization, 257
  defined, 255
  delegative democracy, 255–256
  economic criteria for social and political
    inclusion, 257
  negative impact, 255–256
  new mode of interest intermediation, 255
  participation, 256, 257
    participatory budgeting, 257–258
Neostructuralism, 137–138
Network analysis
  interest groups, 494
  lobbying, 494
New Left
  democratization, 342–343
  U.S.-Latin American relations, 342–343
New public management, bureaucracy, 487–489
Nongovernmental organizations
  democratization, 241–243
  form, 241–242
  gender, 323
  indigenous politics, 290, 291, 292
  social movements, 241–243, 243–244
  women, 323
Non-violent resistance, women, 122
North American Free Trade Agreement
  labor, 266
  social movements, 244

O

Observational studies, 449
O'Donnell, Guillermo, 5, 254
Omi, Michael, 303
Open list systems, 26
Organization of American States, 354
Organized labor, *see* Labor

P

Pacification, decentralization, 37–38
Pan-Africanist perspective, 305
Paradox, democracy, 48
  core representative institutions, 48
Parliamentary government, 21
Participation
  changing levels and types, 249

civil society, 254–258
  lack of engagement, 255
dependency theory, 251
human rights movements, 256
Latin America's exceptionalism, 250–251
making democracy relevant, 258–259
modernization theory, 250–251
neopluralism, 256, 257
  participatory budgeting, 257–258
theory of marginality, 250
women's movements, 256
Participatory budgeting, 257–258
  decentralization, 40
Participatory democracy, local institutions of, 104
Partisan representation, *see* Party systems
Party systems, 48–58
  authoritarian interludes, 53
  change, 53–57
  continuity, 53–57
  crisis of representation, 48
  cross-national research, 51
  decentralization, 39–40
    subnational elections, 39
  decline of mass party organizations, 54
  de-institutionalization, 54
  discipline, institutional analysis, 399–401
  diverse developmental experiences, 51
  dual transitions, 48–49
  economic crisis, 54–55
  elections
    stability, 51–52
    volatility, 51–52
  electoral competition, 54–55
  exclusionary, 103
  explaining variation, 49–53
  finance, business politics, 278–279
  formal party structures, 50
  industrialization, 51
  informal party structures, 50
  institutionalization, 50–53, 51, 53–54
  market liberalism, 55–56
  market liberalization, 56
    leftist political alternatives, 56–57
    programmatic realignment, 58
  mixed record, 48
  modal patterns or traits, 49
    limitations, 49–50
    under-measured, 49–50
    under-theorized, 49–50
  neoliberal reform, 55–56
  party-labor relations, 265
  party lists, 26
  patron-clientelism, 51–52
  presidentialized, 50
  programmatic competition, 50–53
  programmatic linkages, 55–56
    between parties and voters, 52

programmatic structuring, 52–53
public opinion research, 477–478
rational choice approach, 424–425
reconstituted breakdown, 57–58
regime breakdowns, 53
representation, party system change, 570, *571*
research agenda, 57–58
social movements, 242
stability, 51
unrepresentative, 103
voting behavior, 521–522
widespread variation, 50–51
Patron-clientelism, party systems, 51–52
Peasant movements
    decline, 55
    economic crisis, 55
Peña, Yesilernis, 306
Pensions, 204, 205
Perversity thesis, indigenous politics, 292–295
Policy-making, U.S.-Latin American relations,
    341–342
Policy shaping, bureaucracy, 491
Political activity, race, 309–311
    regional focus, 310–311
Political dynamics, regimes, 12
Political ecology, 190–191
    political economy, distinguished, 190–191
Political economies
    dependency management, 514–515
    globalization, 512–515
    military rule, 116–118
    normalization, 529–537
    political ecology, distinguished, 190–191
Political fragmentation
    courts, 64–65
    judiciaries, 64–65
Political-institutional theories, 11–13
Political opportunism, regulatory policy, 228
Political regimes
    comparative perspective, 542–558
    competition, *554,* 5540555
    conceptual history, 543–545
    demand side research, 533–535
    dynamics, 542, 551–552
    economic development, 529–537
    economic politics, 536–537
    origins of political competition, 552–556, *553,*
        554
    representative government, 548–551, *550, 551*
        termination, 551–552, *552*
    rule without elections, 545–547, *546, 547*
    state of the field, 528–539
    suffrage, *554,* 5540555
    supply side research, 535–536
    turmoil, 545–547, *546, 547*
    types, 543–545
    uncontested elections, 548, *548*

Political representation, research agenda, 57–58
Political science
    future directions, 485–505
    legislatures, 486–487
Politics of difference, 409–410
Popular representation, 564–573
    research agenda, 573–577
Populism, labor, 263
Populist parties
    economic crisis, 55
    neoliberal reforms, 56
    resurgence, 57
Postmodernism
    competing schools of thought in 1990s,
        411–414
    critical theories, 408–410
    defined, 407
    new cycles of protest, 414–416
Poverty, *see also* Inequality decline
    privatization, 232–233
Powell, Bingham, 104
Power
    change, 335–336
    meaning, 336
    of U.S. in Latin America, 335–339
Preference voting, 26
Prerogatives
    defined, 81
    military, 81
Presidentialism, 21–30, 518–520
    democracy, 22–23
        electoral democracies, 22–23
    executive-legislative relations, 27–29
        party system related factors, 28–29
    impeachment, 23
    informal institutions, 93–94
    legislative elections, 25–27
    legislature, 519–520
    level of responsiveness of legislators, 29
    presidential elections, 23–25
        concurrent elections, 25
        directly elected, 23
        direct primaries, 24–25
        double-complement rule, 23–24
        majority runoff method, 23, 24
        re-election, 24
        selection process, 24–25
Presidential-legislative relations, 23
Presidents
    agenda-setting powers, 28
    constitutional powers
        legislative powers, 27
        non-legislative powers, 27
    legislative decree power, 28
    rational choice approach, 424
    veto, 27–28
Primary health care, 211–214

Privatization
  democratization, 231–233
  poverty, 232–233
  public utilities, 224–233
    history, 224
    reform, 228–231
  reform, 228–231
  1990s, 224–232
Productivity gap, neoliberalism, 152
Productivity revolution, reform, 140
Programmatic competition, party systems, 50–53
Programmatic linkages, party systems, 55–56
Programmatic structuring, party systems, 52–53
Progresa, Mexico, 214–216
Progressive women's movements, 322
Proportional representation, 26
Protestant Church, indigenous politics, 288
Public opinion research, 467–479
  causality, 474–475
  challenges, 468
  comparative survey data, 472
  contradictions in public opinion, 476–477
  cross-individual and cross-national equivalence
    of survey items, 474
  expansion, 472–473
  experimental methods, 475
  global survey efforts, 472–473
  hyperpresidentialism, 478
  improvements, 473–475
  multidimensionality, 474
  paradoxes, 467
  political parties, 477–478
  reduced horizontal accountability, 478
  regional survey projects, 472
  research history, 468–473
  research terrain, 475–478
  U.S. State Department, 468–469
Public policy
  supply side research, 535–536
  women, 324–326
Public security, deteriorated, 61
Public spending, institutional analysis, 401–402
Public utilities
  privatization, 224–233
    history, 224
    reform, 228–231
  regulation, 224–233
    access, 231–232
    history, 224
    reform, 228–231

Q
Quotas, representation, 104

R
Race, 302–315
  categories, 303–305
  contested concept, 303
  electoral politics, 311
  ethno-racial government initiatives, legislation
    and public policy, 312–313
  identities, 303–305
  mixture, 303–305
  political activity, 309–311
    regional focus, 310–311
  social construction, 303
  social movements, 309–311
    regional focus, 310–311
Racial democracy, 285–286, 302, 305, 306
  staying power of myth, 305
Racial ideologies, 305–307
Racial inequality, 307–308
Racial mixing, 285–286, 303–305
Racism, 305–307
Radu, Michael, 297
Randomization, 448–449
Randomized controlled experiments, defined,
    448–449
Rational choice approach, 419–430
  assumptions about human behavior, 420, 421
  attributing plausible preferences, 420–421
  authoritarian government, 425
  characterized, 420–422
  clientelism, 424–425, 426–427
  democratization, 422–423
  electoral rules, 425–426
  evolutionary pressures created by political
    competition, 421–422
  formal institutions, 423–426
  institutions, 423–426
  means-ends rationality, 420, 421
  methodological individualism, 420
  political parties, 424–425
  presidents, 424
  strategic interactions, 427–428
  strengths, 419–420
Re-centralization, 44
Re-election, legislators, 27
Reforms, *see also* Specific type
  authoritarian regimes *vs.* democracies, 139–140
  bureaucracy, 487–489
  constituency, 140–141
  leftist regimes, public utilities, 229–230
  neoliberalism, 139
  outcomes, 140
  privatization, 228–231
  productivity revolution, 140
  regulatory policy, 228–231
    causes, 228–231
    political transaction costs, 230
Regime change, 515–520
  military coups, 516–517
  U.S.-Latin American relations, 341–342
  violence, 517–518

Regimes
  breakdowns, party systems, 53
  capitalist development theories, 9–10
  civic culture thesis, 7–9
  critical juncture models, 10–11
  debates, 6–13
  economic modernization thesis, 6–7
  explanatory theories, 6–13
  political dynamics, 12
  political-institutional theories, 11–13
  research agenda, 4–6, 13–14
  social class theories, 9–10
Regional trade integration, 515
Regional welfare model, 202–203
Regression-discontinuity designs, 454–456
Regulatory policy
  best practice approach, 226
  business politics, 277
  company opportunism, 227–228
  government opportunism, 227
  Inter-American Development Bank, 226
  International Monetary Fund, 226
  political economy, 224–232
    academic literature, 225–227
  political opportunism, 228
  public utilities, 224–233
    access, 231–232
    history, 224
    reform, 228–231
  reforms, 228–231
    causes, 228–231
    political transaction costs, 230
  time inconsistency, 227–228
  World Bank, 226
Representation, 101, 564–573
  clientelism, 103, 105–106
  contending perspectives on organization, 109–110
  critical juncture of labor incorporation, 566–568
  decentralization, 107–108
  defined, 102–103
  (de)mobilization of material interests, 573–575, *574*
  democracy, 104
  democratization, 107–108
  forms, 101
  future reshaping, 106–109
  historically underrepresented interests in, 104
  interest regime, 570–572, *572*
  macro comparative analysis, 575–577
  military, 104
  neoliberalism, 108–109
  party system change, 570, *571*
  political regimes, 548–551, *550, 551*
    termination, 551–552, *552*
  quotas, 104

representational crisis, 141
research agenda, 573–577
social change, 569–570
tentative emergence, 103–106
Research designs, typology, *448*
Revista Latinoamericana de Estudios del Trabajo, 268
Revolutionary movements, 238
  women, 322
Richard, Nelly, 410
Rio Conference on Environment Development, 243–244
Rosas, Guillermo, 52–53
Rule of law, 69–72
  courts, 69
  crime, 69–72, *70*
  defined, 69
  dualism, 61–62
  judiciaries, 69
  military, 81–82
  purposes, 69
  shortcomings, 71–72
  violence, 69–72, *70*

S
Sáenz Peña, analytic narratives, 500–504
Salamanca survey, 50
Samuels, David, 50
Sanitation, 209
Sawyer, Mark, 306, 308
Schmitter, Philippe C., 103, 254
Security
  civilian control, 82–84
  intra-Latin American relations, 354
    security institutions, 359–360
  military, 82–84
    need for, 83–84
Selznick, Phillip, 490
Senates, 25–26
Shugart, Matthew, 22, 50
Sidanius, Jim, 306
Sikkink, Kathryn, 243, 266
Slavery, 305
Social assistance, 200
  criticisms, 206–207
Social change, representation, 569–570
Social class theories, 9–10
Social Emergency Funds, 205
Social insurance, 200, 210–211
  history, 202, 203
  market reforms, 209
  public spending, 200–202, *201*
Social Investment Funds, 205
Social movements, 237–245, *see also* Specific type
  democratization, 240–243
    failures, 242–243
      nongovernmental organizations, 241–242
      transition from military to civilian rule, 241

Social movements (*continued*)
  Free Trade Agreement of the Americas, 244
  free trade agreements, 244
  indigenous politics, 287
  labor, 264
  neoliberalism, 239–240
    atomization theorists, 239
    economic mechanisms of demobilization, 239–240
    mobilization theorists, 239–240
  nongovernmental organizations, 241–243, 243–244
  North American Free Trade Agreement, 244
  political parties, 242
  race, 309–311
    regional focus, 310–311
  research
    criticisms, 244–245
    historical and intellectual development, 237–238
    proposals for future research, 244–245
    recent, 239–244
  small-scale movements, 238
  transnational context, 243–244
Social policies, 200–217
  characteristics, 202–209
  consequences, 202–209
  determinants, 210–216
  funding, *201*
  inequality decline, 161
  reform, 204–206
  regional welfare model, 202–203
  types, 200
Social revolutions, historical-structural approaches, 434–435
Social rights, historical-structural approaches, 437–439
Social services
  general revenue-funded basic social services, 200
Soft power
  defined, 340
  U.S.-Latin American relations, 340–342, *341*
Sovereignty
  cooperation, relationship, 350
  defined, 349–350
  intra-Latin American relations, 348
State capture, 136
  business politics, 279–280
State formation, 3
State violence, 61
  courts, 68
  military regimes, 118–121, *119*
Stockholm Conference on the Human Environment, 243
Stokes, Susan, 105
Structuralist theory, 136

Subnational authoritarianism, 102
Substantive rights, courts, 67–68
Supreme Courts, 62–63, *see also* Courts
Survey data research, *see also* Public opinion research
  civic culture thesis, 8
Sustainable development, 182–184
  alternative livelihoods-centered perspective, 183
  compatibility, *185*
  history, 182
  market-friendly type, 182–183
    characteristics, 182–183
  principles, 182
  urban landscapes, 193–195

T
Technopols, 136
Telles, Edward, 308
Tennessee Valley Authority, 490
Terrorism, 83
Testimonios genre, 411
Theorization, 13
Theory of marginality
  modernization theory, 250–251
  participation, 250
Time inconsistency
  defined, 227
  regulatory policy, 227–228
Torres-Saillant, Silvio, 307
Trade
  balance, 366
  colonialism, 364–365
  composition, 366–367, *367*
  financial liberalization, 370–377
  history, 364–367
  International Monetary Fund, 366
  intra-regional diversity, 367
  politics, 370–377
  volume, *366*
Trade agreements, labor, 266
Trade policy, labor, 266
Trade unions, *see* Labor
Transitional justice, 123–126
  courts, 66–67
  defined, 123
  efficacy, 125–126
  forms, 123
  truth commission, 124
Transnational context
  feminism, 323
  social movements, 243–244
Transnational networks, indigenous politics, 288
Truth commission, transitional justice, 124

U
Unconditional cash transfer programs, 207–208

Unemployment insurance, 205
Unicameral systems, 25
Union of South American States, 360
United Nations
    Economic Commission for Latin American
        and the Caribbean, 365, 372
    indigenous politics, 289
    women, 323, 329–330
    World Conferences on Women, 323
Universal categories, 410
Urban landscapes, sustainable development,
        193–195
U.S.-Latin American relations, 335–346
    changing power relationships, 335–339
    chronological perspective, 339
    commercial rearrangements, 336–338, *337*
    democratization, 342
    drug trade, 344–345
    global war on terror, 339
    hegemony, 340–341
    importance, 345
    inter-American collaboration, 344–345
    neoliberalism, 149–150
    New Left, 342–343
    organizations excluding, 343
    policy-making, 341–342
    regime change, 341–342
    soft power, 340–342, *341*
    U.S. domination, *336,* 336–337
    U.S. losing geopolitical leverage, 336–337,
        337
    U.S. neglect of Latin America, 338
    U.S. shares of Latin America's imports, 337,
        337
    war on drugs, 338–339
U.S. State Department, public opinion research,
        468–469

V
Valenzuela, Arturo, 22
Valenzuela, Samuel, 10
Van Cott, Donna Lee, 293
Van Doren, Peter, 496
Verba, Sydney, 469–470
Veto
    legislature, 27–28
    presidents, 27–28
    veto player logic
        courts, 65–66
        judiciaries, 65–66
Violence, *see also* State violence
    drugs
        forms, 385
        gangs, 386–387
        geographic areas, 385–386
        insurgents, 385–386
        organized violence, 384–387

illicit trade
    forms, 385
    gangs, 386–387
    geographic areas, 385–386
    insurgents, 385–386
    organized violence, 384–387
military rule, characteristics, 116
regime change, 517–518
rule of law, 69–72, *70*
women, 325
von der Fehr, Nils, 229
von Hayek, Friedrich, 136
Voting behavior, 520–523
    founding elections, 520
    individual utility, 521
    objectives, 520–521
    political parties, 521–522

W
War on drugs, U.S.-Latin American relations,
        338–339
Washington Consensus, 137–138, 224
Welfare state, globalization, 513
Whitening, 305
Williamson, John, 137
Winant, Howard, 303
Women, 319–331
    authoritarian rule, 325–326
    changes in status of women, 319
    courts, 329–330
    demographic trends, 320–321
    economic policy, 326
    education, 320–321
        Catholic Church, 321
    executive branch, 328–329
        election to presidency, 328–329
    gender-based movements, 321–324
    human rights, 325
    indigenous politics, 296
    leftist movements, 322
    legislative politics, 326–328
        behavior, 326–328
        gender quotas, 326–328
    multiculturalism, 296–297
    nongovernmental organizations, 323
    non-violent resistance, 122
    public policy, 324–326
    revolutionary movements, 322
    theories of modernization, 320
    United Nations, 323, 329–330
    violence, 325
    women legislators, 26
    women presidents, 319
Women's movements, 238
    authoritarian regimes, 322–323
    participation, 256
Working-class movements, 238

World Bank, 189, 371–377
    cross-country variation, 374–375
    domestic politics, 375–376
    indigenous politics, 289
    regulatory policy, 226
    temporal variation, 373–374
    types, 372–373

Y
Yashar, Deborah J., 296, 414

Z
Zack, Naomi, 303
Zapatistas, 287–288
Zechmeister, Elizabeth J., 52–53